IF FOUND, please notify and arrange return to owner. This text is an important study guide for the owner's business law/legal studies classes or continuing professional education.

Name of Business Student
or Practitioner ____

Address ____

City, State, Zip ____

Telephone ( ) ____

Additional copies of *Business Law/Legal Studies Objective Questions and Explanations* are available for $14.95 direct from:

Accounting Publications, Inc.
P.O. Box 12848, University Station
Gainesville, Florida 32604
(904) 375-0772

Other similar study manuals:

Auditing & EDP Objective Questions and Explanations $14.95
Managerial Accounting Objective Questions and Explanations 14.95
Federal Tax Objective Questions and Explanations 14.95
Financial Accounting Objective Questions and Explanations 14.95

Also available are:

CIA Examination Review Volume I Outlines and Study Guides, 3rd ed. $21.95
CIA Examination Review Volume II Problems and Solutions, 3rd ed. 21.95
CIA 1990 Updating Edition 15.95
All three CIA books for $49.90 (save $9.95)

CMA Examination Review Volume I Outlines and Study Guides, 4th ed. 23.95
CMA Examination Review Volume II Problems and Solutions, 4th ed. 23.95

Order forms for these and all of our other publications are provided at the back of this book.

All mail orders must be prepaid and are shipped postpaid, i.e., our prices include postage and handling. Shipping charges will be added to telephone orders, and to library and company orders which may be on account. Florida residents must add 6% sales tax. All payments must be in U.S. funds and payable on a U.S. bank. Please call or write for prices and availability of all foreign country shipments. The book(s) will usually be shipped on the day after your order is received. Allow 10 days for delivery. Please contact us if you do not receive your shipment within 2 weeks.

Accounting Publications, Inc. guarantees an immediate, complete refund on all direct-mail orders if a resalable text is returned within 30 days.

REVIEWERS AND CONTRIBUTORS

Maria Bolanos, B.A.Ed., University of Florida, is our production manager. She coordinated and supervised the production staff and reviewed the entire text.

Jeff Caress, a J.D. candidate at the University of Florida, reviewed Chapters 9, 20, and 24.

Kristen DiGiacomo, a B.S.Acc. candidate at the University of Florida, reviewed Chapters 31 and 35.

Russ Gillis, CPA and J.D. candidate at the University of Florida, drafted questions and answers for Chapters 5, 7, and 8.

Holger D. Gleim, LL.M., CPA, coauthored the first and second editions.

Grady M. Irwin, J.D., University of Florida Holland Law Center, has taught in the University of Florida College of Business. He provided first drafts for many questions and answer explanations as well as extensive editorial assistance for this and previous editions.

Windy Kemp, M.Acc. (Auditing), University of Florida, assisted in the overall production of the book.

Michael Kohl, a J.D. candidate at the University of Florida, reviewed Chapters 11, 13, 16, 18, and 33.

Ted Lieber, an LL.M. candidate at the University of Florida, drafted questions and answers for Chapters 26, 31, 32, and 35 and reviewed Chapters 7, 8, 12, 25, and 28.

Louis Moor, M.Acc. (Auditing), University of Florida, drafted questions and answers for Chapters 13, 15, 19, 20, 22, 23, 24, 27, and 30.

Bruce Nearon, M.Acc. (Auditing), CPA, drafted questions and answers for Chapters 14 and 34.

John F. Rebstock, CIA, is a graduate of the School of Accounting at the University of Florida. He has passed the CPA exam and is a CMA candidate. Mr. Rebstock prepared the page layout and reviewed the entire edition.

Rick Sierra, a J.D. candidate at the University of Florida, reviewed Chapters 19 and 29.

Lori Stephens, an M.Acc. (Auditing) candidate at the University of Florida, drafted questions and answers for Chapters 17, 21, and 26 and reviewed Chapters 4, 6, 15, and 30.

Mary Ann Vorce, M.Acc. (Auditing), University of Florida, drafted questions and answers for Chapters 29 and 33.

Dan White, an LL.M. candidate at the University of Florida, drafted questions and answers for Chapters 10 and 31.

Willis Williams, an LL.M. candidate at the University of Florida, drafted questions and answers for Chapters 4, 5, 6, 9, and 25 and reviewed Chapters 5, 10, 26, 32, 34, and 35.

Chris Yost, an M.Acc. (Auditing) candidate at the University of Florida, reviewed Chapters 14, 17, 21, 22, 23, and 27.

A PERSONAL THANKS

This manual would not have been possible without the extraordinary efforts and dedication of Ann Finnicum and Connie Steen, who typed the entire manuscript, all revisions, and prepared the camera-ready format.

The authors also appreciate the proofreading and reviewing assistance of Angela Austin, Rose Barker, Kirk Collier, Timothy David, Robert Francis, Gillian Hillis, Andy Mason, Ann Preston, Caroline Roche, Tony Roig, and Cris Shaw.

Finally, we appreciate the encouragement, support, and tolerance of our families throughout this project.

Third Edition

BUSINESS LAW/ LEGAL STUDIES

Objective Questions and Explanations

by

Irvin N. Gleim, Ph.D., CPA, CIA, CMA

Jordan B. Ray, J.D.

with the assistance of
Grady M. Irwin, J.D.

ABOUT THE AUTHORS

Irvin N. Gleim is Professor Emeritus in the Fisher School of Accounting at the University of Florida and is a member of the American Accounting Association, American Business Law Association, American Institute of Certified Public Accountants, Association of Government Accountants, Florida Institute of Certified Public Accountants, Institute of Internal Auditors, Institute of Certified Management Accountants, and the National Association of Accountants. He has had articles published in the *Journal of Accountancy, The Accounting Review,* and *The American Business Law Journal* and is author/coauthor of numerous accounting and aviation books and CPE courses.

Jordan B. Ray, Chairman of the Department of Management and Legal Studies at the University of Florida, is a member and past president of the American Business Law Association and the Southeast Regional Business Law Association. He is the author of a number of business law articles and has served as editor of Notes, Comments, and Case Digests for the *American Business Law Journal*. He has taught proprietary and university CPA Review and CLU courses and has served as the legal consultant to the Florida Real Estate Commission.

Accounting Publications, Inc.
P.O. Box 12848
University Station
Gainesville, Florida 32604

Library of Congress Catalog Card No. 89-82539
ISBN 0-917537-37-8

ACKNOWLEDGMENTS

The authors appreciate and thank the American Institute of Certified Public Accountants for permission to use Uniform Certified Public Accountant Examination questions, copyright © 1971, 1972, 1973, 1974, 1975, 1976, 1977, 1978, 1979, 1980, 1981, 1982, 1983, 1984, 1985, 1986, 1987, 1988, and 1989 by the American Institute of Certified Public Accountants.

The authors also appreciate and thank the Institute of Internal Auditors, Inc. for permission to use the Institute's Certified Internal Auditor Examination questions, copyright © 1975, 1976, 1977, 1978, 1979, 1980, 1981, 1982, 1983, 1984, and 1985 by The Institute of Internal Auditors, Inc.

The authors also appreciate and thank the Institute of Certified Management Accountants of the National Association of Accountants for permission to use questions from past CMA examinations, copyright © 1972, 1973, 1974, 1975, 1976, 1977, 1978, 1979, 1980, 1981, 1982, 1983, 1984, 1985, 1986, 1987, 1988, and 1989 by the National Association of Accountants.

The authors also appreciate and thank the National Conference of Bar Examiners for permission to use Multistate Bar Examination questions, copyright © 1972, 1974, 1978, 1980, and 1981 by the National Conference of Bar Examiners/Educational Testing Service.

PREFACE FOR BUSINESS LAW AND LEGAL STUDIES STUDENTS

The purpose of this study manual is to help you understand business law and concepts dealing with the legal environment of business and their applications. In turn, these skills will enable you to perform better on your undergraduate examinations, as well as look ahead to (and prepare for) professional examinations.

One of the major benefits of this study manual is comprehensive coverage of business law and legal environment topics. Accordingly, when you use this book to help prepare for your courses and examinations, you are assured of covering virtually all topics that can reasonably be expected to be studied in typical college or university business law and legal environment courses.

The question-and-answer format is designed and presented to facilitate effective study. Students should be careful not to misuse this text by referring to the answers before independently answering each question.

Many of the questions in this book are from past CIA, CMA, CPA, and Multistate Bar examinations. Although a citation for the source of each question is provided, a substantial number of them have also been modified to accommodate changes in law, to clarify questions, and/or to emphasize a point of law or its application. In addition, hundreds of publisher-written questions are used to provide comprehensive coverage of the material in current textbooks. Finally, we are pleased to be using some questions submitted by business law and legal studies professors.

Note that this study manual should not be relied upon to prepare for the professional examinations. You should use review manuals specifically developed for each such examination. *CIA Examination Review, CMA Examination Review,* and *CPA Examination Review* are up-to-date manuals that comprehensively cover all material necessary for successful completion of each examination. Further description of these and other books is provided on page 771. An order form is provided on page 772.

Thank you for your interest in this book. We deeply appreciate the many letters and suggestions received during the past years from students and educators, as well as CIA, CMA, and CPA candidates. Please send us your suggestions, comments, and corrections concerning this edition. The last page has been designed to help you note corrections and suggestions throughout your study process. Please tear it out and mail it to us with your comments.

Please read the first three chapters carefully. They are very short but nevertheless very important.

Good Luck on Your Exams,

Irvin N. Gleim
Jordan B. Ray

February, 1990

PREFACE FOR PRACTITIONERS

The first purpose of this book is to permit you to assess your technical proficiency concerning business law and related legal environment of business topics such as consumer protection and accountants' legal liability. The second purpose is to facilitate your review and update of business law concepts with our compendium of almost 2,000 objective questions. The third purpose is to provide CPE credit for your self-assessment and review/update study effort.

This new approach to CPE is both interactive and intense. You should be continuously challenged to answer each question correctly. When you answer a question incorrectly or have difficulty, you should pursue a complete understanding by reading the answer explanation and consulting reference sources as necessary.

Most of the questions in *Business Law/Legal Studies Objective Questions and Explanations* were taken from various professional examinations, but many have been revised, adapted, etc. to provide broader and up-to-date coverage of the body of legal knowledge. In addition, hundreds of publisher questions cover material not directly tested on the professional certification examinations.

We ask for any supplemental comments, reactions, suggestions, etc. that you may have as you complete our CPE program. Please attach them to the Course Evaluation Sheet (handwritten notes are fine). The last two pages of this study book have been designed to help you note corrections and suggestions throughout your study process. Just tear them out and return them to us with your comments. Pages 772-775 provide an order form and further descriptions of our CPE programs.

Chapters One through Three of *Business Law/Legal Studies Objective Questions and Explanations* are directed primarily to accounting and business law students. Those practitioners interested in multiple certification, however, may find the discussion of the certification programs in Chapter Three to be useful. If, as you work through this study book and take the open-book CPE final exams, you find you need to refer to a current textbook, Chapter One contains a list of current titles. You should be sure to read carefully the "Introduction: How to Use This CPE Program" in the accompanying CPE book.

Thank you for your interest, and we look forward to hearing from you.

Best Wishes in Your CPE Endeavors,

Irvin N. Gleim
Jordan B. Ray
February, 1990

TABLE OF CONTENTS

CONTRIBUTING PROFESSORS

We are especially grateful to the following professors who submitted questions for the Second and Third Editions. We welcome further submissions of questions, either for the Fourth Edition of *Business Law/Legal Studies Objective Questions and Explanations* or for future editions of our other Objective Question and Explanation books.

Anderson, Wayne .... Southwest Missouri State University
Arnold, E. Elizabeth .... University of San Diego
Cherry, Jr., Robert L. .... Appalachian State University
Costantino, Diane .... Providence College
Elwell, Karen J. .... Bloomsburg University
Fischl, Louis J. .... San Jose State University
Folkenroth, John C. .... Loyola University
Karl III, Peter A. .... State University of New York at Utica-Rome
Levin, Daniel A. .... University of Colorado
Levin, Murray S. .... University of Kansas
MacDonald, Diane B. .... Pacific Lutheran University
Mescon, Debbie L. .... Salisbury State University
Norwood, John M. .... University of Arkansas
O'Connor, Eugene .... Canisius College
Paas, David .... Texas Woman's University
Pittman, Jeffrey .... Arkansas State University
Rahm, Elinor .... Central Missouri State University
Rand, Shirley M. .... St. Vincent College
Rogers, Suzy .... University of Wisconsin, River Falls
Rubert, Ellen B. .... College of Lake County
Schuster, William .... California State University
Schwartz, Ira .... Towson State University
Sibary, Scott .... California State University
Sipes, Daphne .... University of Texas
Welton, Ralph .... Clemson University
Wilburn, Kay .... University of Alabama, Birmingham
Willey, Susan .... University of Wisconsin, La Crosse
Woods, Dexter .... Ohio Northern University

CHAPTER ONE
HOW TO USE THIS BOOK

INTRODUCTION

This chapter explains how and why this study manual was written. More important, it directs you on how to use this book efficiently. The format and content of this book are innovative to the business law and legal studies text market. The first purpose is to provide business law and legal studies students with a well-organized, comprehensive compendium of objective questions covering the topics taught in undergraduate business law and legal environment courses. The second purpose is to provide accounting professionals with a comprehensive presentation of diagnostic objective questions for both self-diagnostic use and/or review of basic level business law standards and procedures.

This study manual consists solely of objective questions and answer explanations, with the exception of the first three chapters:

1. How to Use This Book
2. How to Answer Objective Questions
3. Professional Certification Examinations

The chapter titles and organization of Chapters 4 through 35 are based on the following current business law and legal environment books.

Allison, Prentice, *The Legal Environment of Business,* Third Edition, The Dryden Press, 1988.

Anderson, Fox, Twomey, *Business Law*, Twelfth Edition (UCC Comprehensive Volume), South-Western Publishing Co., 1984.

Ashcroft, Ashcroft, *College Law for Business*, Tenth Edition, South-Western Publishing Co., 1984.

Barnes, Dworkin, Richards, *Law for Business,* Richard D. Irwin, Inc., 1987.

Blackburn, Klayman, Malin, *The Legal Environment of Business,* Third Edition, Richard D. Irwin, Inc., 1988.

Bohlman, Dundas, Jentz, *The Legal Environment of Business,* West Publishing Company, 1989.

Brody, *Business and Its Legal Environment,* D.C. Heath & Co., 1986.

Butler, *The Legal Environment of Business: Government Regulation and Public Policy Analysis,* South-Western Publishing Co., 1987.

Cameron, Scaletta, *Business Law: Legal Environment, Transactions, and Regulations,* Third Edition, Richard D. Irwin, Inc., 1989.

Cheeseman, *The Legal and Regulatory Environment of Business,* Macmillan Publishing Co., 1985.

Clark, Kinder, *Law and Business,* Second Edition, McGraw-Hill, Inc., 1988.

Clarkson, Miller, Jentz, Cross, *West's Business Law,* Fourth Edition, West Publishing Co., 1989.

Conry, Ferrera, Fox, *The Legal Environment of Business,* Second Edition, Allyn & Bacon, Inc., 1990.

Corley, Reed, *The Legal Environment of Business: Briefed Case Edition,* Second Edition, McGraw-Hill, Inc., 1989.

Corley, Reed, Shedd, *The Legal Environment of Business,* Eighth Edition, McGraw-Hill, Inc., 1990.

Corley, Shedd, *Fundamentals of Business Law,* Fifth Edition, Prentice-Hall, Inc., 1990.

Corley, Shedd, *Principles of Business Law,* Fourteenth Edition, Prentice-Hall, Inc., 1989.

Davidson, Knowles, Forsythe, Jespersen, *Business Law: Principles and Cases,* Third Edition, PWS-Kent Publishing Co., 1990.

Dunfee, Bellace, Rosoff, *Business and Its Legal Environment,* Second Edition, Prentice-Hall, Inc., 1987.

Dunfee, Gibson, Blackburn, Whitman, McCarty, Brennan, *Modern Business Law,* Second Edition, McGraw-Hill, Inc., 1989.

Fisher, Jennings, *Law for Business,* West Publishing Co., 1986.

Fisher, Phillips, *The Legal Environment of Business,* Third Edition, West Publishing Co., 1988.

Frascona, et al., *Business Law,* Third Edition, Allyn & Bacon, Inc., 1987. 4th Edition expected by 1991.

Halbert, Ingulli, *Law & Ethics in the Business Environment,* West Publishing Co., 1990.

Harron, *The Legal Environment for Business Managers,* Second Edition, Allyn and Bacon, Inc., 1984.

Howell, Allison, Henley, *Fundamentals of Business Law,* The Dryden Press, 1984.

Howell, Allison, Prentice, *Business Law,* Fourth Edition and Fourth Alternate Edition, The Dryden Press, 1988.

Jennings, *Business and the Legal Environment,* PWS-Kent Publishing Company, 1988.

Jentz, Clarkson, Miller, *West's Business Law,* Second Edition, West Publishing Company, 1984.

Kolasa, *The Legal Environment of Business,* Addison-Wesley Publishing Co., 1984.

Leete, *Business Law,* Second Edition, Macmillan Publishing Co., Inc., 1982.

Leete, Fox, *Business Law and the Legal Environment,* Third Edition, Allyn & Bacon, Inc., 1989.

Lieberman, Siedel, *Business Law and the Legal Environment,* Second Edition, Harcourt Brace Jovanovich, Inc., 1988.

Lyden, Reitzel, Roberts, *Business and the Law,* McGraw-Hill, Inc., 1985.

Maurer, *Business Law,* Second Edition, Harcourt Brace Jovanovich, Inc., 1987.

McAdams, Donnella, Freeman, Newlund, *Law, Business, and Society,* Second Edition, Richard D. Irwin, Inc., 1989.

McCarty, Bagby, *The Legal Environment of Business,* Richard D. Irwin, Inc., 1990.

McGuire, *The Legal Environment of Business: Commerce and Public Policy,* Charles E. Merrill Publishing Co., 1986.

Metzger, Mallor, Barnes, Bowers, Phillips, *Business Law and the Regulatory Environment: Concepts and Cases,* Seventh Edition, Richard D. Irwin, Inc., 1989.

Miller, Jentz, *Business Law Today,* West Publishing Company, 1988.

Moran, *Practical Business Law,* Second Edition, Prentice-Hall, Inc., 1989.

Reiling, Thompson, Brady, Macchiarola, *Business Law: Text and Cases,* Kent Publishing Co., 1981.

Reitzel, Lyden, Roberts, Severance, *Contemporary Business Law: Principles and Cases,* Fourth Edition, McGraw-Hill, Inc., 1990.

Scaletta, Cameron, *Foundations of Business Law,* Second Edition, Richard D. Irwin, Inc., 1990.

Schantz, Jackson, *The American Legal Environment: Individuals, Business Law and Government,* Second Edition, West Publishing Co., 1984.

Schantz, Jackson, *Business Law,* Second Edition, West Publishing Company, 1987.

Shaw, Wolfe, *The Structure of the Legal Environment,* PWS-Kent Publishing Company, 1987.

Smith, Mann, Roberts, *Business Law and the Regulation of Business,* Second Edition, West Publishing Company, 1990.

Smith, Mann, Roberts, *Essentials of Business Law,* Third Edition, West Publishing Company, 1989.

Smith, Roberson, Mann, Roberts, *Smith and Roberson's Business Law,* Seventh Edition, West Publishing Co., 1988.

Spiro, *The Legal Environment of Business,* Prentice-Hall, Inc., 1989.

Story, Ward, *American Business Law and the Regulatory Environment,* South-Western Publishing Co., Inc., 1987.

Whitman, Gergacz, *The Legal Environment of Business,* Second Edition, McGraw-Hill, Inc., 1988.

Some textbooks may inadvertently have been omitted from the above list, for which we apologize. The last section in this chapter (see page 9) contains the tables of contents for each of the above business law textbooks, with cross-references to modules in this study manual.

OUR USE OF "MODULES"

Each chapter of this book is divided into subtopics (i.e., groups of questions) to assist your study program. We call these subtopics "modules." Modules permit us to break down broad and perhaps overwhelming topics into more manageable study components. The number of questions in each module is large enough to allow comprehensive coverage without presenting an insurmountable task. We have defined each module so it is narrow enough to cover a single topic and broad enough so the questions are not overly repetitious.

Page 4 presents a complete consecutive listing of modules as they appear in chapters 4 through 35. Page 5 presents a complete alphabetical listing. The purpose here is to provide a 1-page overview of the coverage of topics in this book in an effort to give you a "feel" for the book in its entirety. In other words, to "unbury" topical coverage. Reference should be made here to page 9 where we discuss how to find questions to study in this book, based upon the chapter(s) you are studying in your textbook.

List of Modules in Consecutive Order

List of Modules in Alphabetical Order

SOURCES OF OBJECTIVE QUESTIONS

Past CIA, CMA, CPA, and Multistate Bar examinations were used as sources of some questions for this study manual. Your authors prepared a substantial number of the questions (coded in this text as "Publisher") based upon the content of the business law and legal environment textbooks listed on pages 1 through 3. These "Publisher" questions were developed to review topics not adequately covered by questions from the other sources. In addition, professors from several schools around the country contributed questions. See page viii for a list of their names and school affiliations.

The source of each question appears in the first line of its answer explanation, in the column to the right of the question. Summary of sources:

CIA	Certified Internal Auditor Examination
CMA	Certified Management Accountant Examination
CPA	Certified Public Accountant Examination
MBE	Multistate Bar Examination
Publisher	Your authors
Professor Name	Professor who contributed question

IDENTIFICATION OF THE SOURCE OF EACH QUESTION

After each source code (except Publisher or a professor), codes for the following are given:

Month and year (e.g., 584)
Part of exam (see below)
Question number (see below)

The month and year are not given for the Multistate Bar Exam (MBE) questions which were released in 1978 and 1980 as they are published in one book made up of Parts I to V, Multistate Bar Examination Questions. The 1972 MBE (the first MBE given) has also been released and questions from that exam are identified as MBE 272. Examples:

(CPA 1185 L-2)	CPA exam, November 1985, Business Law section, question 2
(CIA 586 IV-5)	CIA exam, May 1986, Part IV, question 5
(CMA 686 3-20)	CMA exam, June 1986, Part 3, question 20
(MBE Part II-18)	MBE questions released in 1978 or 1980 published in MBE book, Part II, question 18
(MBE 272 131)	MBE, February 1972, question 131

ORDER OF QUESTIONS IN EACH MODULE

Within each module, the multiple-choice questions are presented in a sequence moving from the general to the specific, elementary to advanced, etc. to provide an effective learning sequence. Duplicate questions and redundant explanations have been kept to a minimum.

UNIQUENESS OF OBJECTIVE QUESTIONS

The major advantage of objective questions is their ability to cover (i.e., to study or to test) a large number of topics with little time and effort when compared with essay questions.

A multiple-choice question is actually a series of four or five statements, of which all but one are incorrect given the facts of the question. The advantage of multiple-choice questions over true-false questions is that they require more analysis and result in a lower score for those with little or no knowledge. Random guessing on a true-false test results in an expected grade of 50%.

Students and practitioners both like multiple-choice questions. Because they present alternative answers and only one alternative needs to be selected, they are relatively easy to answer. Professors like objective questions because they are easy to grade and much more material can be tested in the same period of time.

ANSWER EXPLANATIONS ALONGSIDE THE QUESTIONS

Our efficient format presents objective questions and their answer explanations side by side. The example below was written by your authors.

24. Gudrun owned a 2,000-acre country estate. She signed a written agreement with Johann, selling the house on the property and "a sufficient amount of land surrounding the house to create a park." The price was stated to be $200,000. When Gudrun refused to honor the agreement, Johann brought suit. What will be the result?

a. Gudrun will win because the agreement is not reasonably definite.

b. Johann will win because the quantity of land is implied.

c. Johann will win because the parties intended to make a contract.

d. Gudrun will win because no financing term was included in the agreement.

The correct answer is (a). *(Publisher)*

REQUIRED: The result when a contract for the sale of land does not state the quantity.

DISCUSSION: For an agreement between the parties to be enforceable, it must be reasonably definite and certain (not ambiguous). A court must be able to determine with reasonable accuracy what the parties agreed upon. In this case, it is not reasonably clear from the writing what land Gudrun agreed to sell.

Answers (b) and (c) are incorrect because some objective basis must exist for measuring the implied term. The court would have no means of determining how much land is needed for a park. Answer (d) is incorrect because the quantity term is more significant than the financing term. The price is given and payment in cash (or its equivalent) is implied.

The format in this book (illustrated above) is designed to facilitate your study of objective questions, their answers, and the answer explanations. The intent is to save you time and effort by eliminating the need to turn back and forth from questions to answers when they are presented on different pages.

Be careful, however. You must exercise restraint against misusing this format, i.e., consulting the answers before you have answered the questions. Misuse of the readily available answers will give you a false sense of security and result in your performing poorly on examinations. The best way to use this study manual is to cover up the answer explanations with a sheet of paper as you read and answer each question. As a crucial part of the learning process, you must honestly commit yourself to an answer before looking at the answer explanation. Whether you are right or wrong, your memory of the correct answer will be reinforced by this process.

USING OBJECTIVE QUESTIONS TO STUDY FOR UNDERGRADUATE EXAMS

Testing experts are increasingly favoring multiple-choice questions as a valid means of testing various levels of knowledge. For example, 60% of each part of the current CPA examination consists of objective questions and in 1994 the percentage will increase to 85%. Using objective questions to study for these examinations and your undergraduate examinations is an important tool in obtaining good grades. The following suggestions can be used as a guideline for your study purposes in conjunction with any of our Objective Question and Explanation books described on page i. An order form is provided on page 772.

1. Locate the chapter and module that contain questions on the topic you are currently studying. The end of Chapter 1 has cross-references to the tables of contents of most textbooks.
2. Work through a series of questions, one or more modules at a time.
   a. Cover the answers and explanations as you work the questions.
   b. Circle the answer you think is correct.
   c. Check your answer.
3. DO NOT CONSULT THE ANSWER OR ANSWER EXPLANATIONS ON THE RIGHT SIDE OF EACH PAGE UNTIL AFTER YOU HAVE CHOSEN AND WRITTEN DOWN AN ANSWER.
   a. It is crucial that you cover the answer explanations and intellectually commit yourself to an answer. This method will help you understand the concept much better, even if you answered the question incorrectly.
4. Study the explanations to each question you answered incorrectly. In addition to learning and understanding the concept tested, analyze WHY you missed the question. Did you misread the question? Misread the requirement? Make a computational error? Not know the concept tested? Now you can identify your weaknesses in answering multiple-choice questions and take corrective action (before you take a test).
   a. Studying the important concepts that we provide in our answer explanations will help you understand the principles to the point that you can answer that question (or any other like it) successfully.
5. Prepare a summary analysis of your work on each module (topic). It will show your weaknesses (areas needing more study) and also your strengths (areas of improvement). You can improve your performance on objective questions both by increasing your percentage of correct answers and by decreasing the time spent per question. Here are sample column headings for the summary analysis:

Date	Module	Time to Complete	Number of Questions	Minutes Per Question	Number Correct	Percent Correct

Use of the ***Gleim Series*** of Objective Question and Explanation books really works! You can pretest yourself before class to see if you are strong or weak in the assigned area. You can retest after class to see if you really understand the material. The questions in these books cover all topics in your related courses, so you will encounter few questions on your exams for which you will not be well prepared. Furthermore, each book covers the material generally taught in two or three courses, so your cost per course is nominal.

CHAPTER CROSS-REFERENCES TO BUSINESS LAW TEXTBOOKS

The next 39 pages contain the tables of contents of current business law and legal environment of business textbooks, with cross-references to the related modules in this study manual. The texts are listed in alphabetical order by the (first) author. As you study a particular chapter in your business law text, you can easily determine which module(s) to study in this manual. The numbers given are the module numbers in this study manual. You should review all the questions in the module.

Professors, students, and accounting practitioners should all note that even though new editions of the following texts may be published as you use this book, the new tables of contents will usually be very similar, if not the same. Thus, the Second Edition of *Business Law/Legal Studies Objective Questions and Explanations* will remain current and useful.

Allison, Prentice, *The Legal Environment of Business,* Third Edition, The Dryden Press, 1988.

Anderson, Fox, Twomey, *Business Law,* Twelfth Edition (UCC Comprehensive Volume), South-Western Publishing Co., 1984.

Part 3 - Personal Property and Bailments
Chapter 19 - Personal Property - 19.2
Chapter 20 - Bailments - 19.3
Chapter 21 - Special Bailments and Documents of Title - 13.10, 19.3
Part 4 - Sales
Chapter 22 - Nature and Form of Sales - 12.1-12.3
Chapter 23 - Risk and Property Rights - 12.4
Chapter 24 - Obligations and Performance - 12.5
Chapter 25 - Warranties and Other Product Liabilities - 12.8, 12.9
Chapter 26 - Remedies for Breach of Sales Contract - 12.6, 12.7
Part 5 - Commercial Paper
Chapter 27 - Kinds of Paper, Parties, and Negotiability - 13.1-13.3
Chapter 28 - Transfer of Commercial Paper - 13.4, 13.6
Chapter 29 - Rights of Holders and Defenses - 13.1-13.6
Chapter 30 - Presentment of Paper for Payment and Acceptance - 13.6
Chapter 31 - Discharge of Commercial Paper - 13.6
Chapter 32 - Checks and Customer-Bank Relationship - 13.7
Part 6 - Secured Transactions, Creditors' Rights, and Insurance
Chapter 33 - Secured Transactions Under Article 9 - 17.1-17.5
Chapter 34 - Other Security Devices - 13.9, 18.1-18.3
Chapter 35 - Bankruptcy - 26.1-26.5
Chapter 36 - Insurance - 23.1
Chapter 37 - Kinds of Insurance - 23.2-23.4
Part 7 - Agency and Employment
Chapter 38 - Agency -- Creation and Termination - 14.1, 14.6
Chapter 39 - Principal and Agent - 14.2, 14.3
Chapter 40 - Third Persons in Agency - 14.4, 14.5
Chapter 41 - Employment - 29.4-29.6
Part 8 - Business Organizations
Chapter 42 - Forms of Business Organizations - 15.1, 16.1
Chapter 43 - Creation and Termination of Partnerships - 15.1, 15.4
Chapter 44 - Powers and Duties of Partners - 15.2, 15.3
Chapter 45 - Nature, Creation, and Termination of Corporations - 16.1, 16.2, 16.8
Chapter 46 - Corporate Powers - 16.3
Chapter 47 - Corporate Stock and Shareholders - 16.5-16.7
Chapter 48 - Management of Corporations - 16.4
Part 9 - Real Property
Chapter 49 - Nature and Ownership of Real Property - 20.1-20.3, 21.1
Chapter 50 - Leases - 22.1-22.5
Part 10 - Estates
Chapter 51 - Decedents' Estates - 24.1-24.3
Chapter 52 - Trusts - 24.4

Ashcroft, Ashcroft, *College Law for Business*, Tenth Edition, South-Western Publishing Co., 1984.

Part 1 - The Legal System and the Legal Environment of Business
Chapter 1 - Introduction to Law - 4.1-4.3
Chapter 2 - Courts and Court Procedure - 5.1, 5.2
Chapter 3 - Government Regulation of Business - 27.1-27.6, 29.1-29.6
Part 2 - Contracts
Chapter 4 - Contracts -- Nature and Classes - 11.1
Chapter 5 - Offer and Acceptance - 11.2, 11.3
Chapter 6 - Defective Agreements - 11.5
Chapter 7 - Capacity to Contract - 11.6
Chapter 8 - Consideration - 11.4
Chapter 9 - Illegal Agreements - 11.7
Chapter 10 - Form of Contracts - 11.8, 11.9
Chapter 11 - Third Parties and Contracts - 11.10, 11.11
Chapter 12 - Termination of Contracts - 11.12, 11.13
Part 3 - Sales
Chapter 13 - Sales of Personal Property - 12.1
Chapter 14 - Formalities of a Sale - 12.2, 12.3
Chapter 15 - Transfer of Title and Risk in Sales Contracts - 12.4-12.7
Chapter 16 - Warranties of the Seller - 12.8
Chapter 17 - Consumer Protection - 12.9, 30.1, 30.2
Part 4 - Bailments
Chapter 18 - Principles of Bailments - 19.3
Chapter 19 - Common Carriers - 19.3
Chapter 20 - Hotelkeepers as Bailees - 19.3

Part 5 - Commercial Paper
Chapter 21 - Nature of Commercial Paper - 13.1
Chapter 22 - Essentials of Negotiability - 13.3
Chapter 23 - Promissory Notes and Certificates of Deposit - 13.2
Chapter 24 - Drafts - 13.2
Chapter 25 - Checks - 13.2, 13.7
Chapter 26 - Liabilities of the Parties to Commercial Paper - 13.6
Chapter 27 - Negotiation and Discharge - 13.4, 13.6
Chapter 28 - Holders in Due Course - 13.5
Chapter 29 - Defenses - 13.6
Part 6 - Agency and Employment
Chapter 30 - Creation of an Agency - 14.1
Chapter 31 - Operation and Termination of an Agency - 14.2-14.6
Chapter 32 - Employer and Employee - 29.2-29.6
Chapter 33 - Labor Legislation - 29.1
Part 7 - Partnerships
Chapter 34 - Formation of a Partnership - 15.1
Chapter 35 - Operation of a Partnership - 15.2, 15.3
Chapter 36 - Dissolution of a Partnership - 15.4
Part 8 - Corporations
Chapter 37 - Nature of a Corporation - 6.1-6.3
Chapter 38 - Ownership of a Corporation - 6.5-6.7
Chapter 39 - Management and Dissolution of a Corporation - 6.4, 6.8
Part 9 - Risk-Bearing Devices
Chapter 40 - Nature of Insurance - 23.1
Chapter 41 - Life and Annuity Insurance - 23.2
Chapter 42 - Property Insurance - 23.3
Chapter 43 - Automobile Insurance - 23.4
Chapter 44 - Security Devices - 17.1-17.5, 18.1-18.3
Part 10 - Property
Chapter 45 - Nature of Property - 19.1, 20.1
Chapter 46 - Transfer of Real Property - 20.3
Chapter 47 - Real Estate Mortgages - 21.1
Chapter 48 - Landlord and Tenant - 21.1-22.5
Chapter 49 - Wills and Inheritances - 24.1-24.3
Chapter 50 - Bankruptcy - 26.1-26.5

Barnes, Dworkin, Richards, *Law for Business*, Third Edition, Richard D. Irwin, Inc., 1987.

Part One - Introduction to the Law
Chapter 1 - Law and Its Sources - 4.1-4.3
Chapter 2 - Means of Dispute Settlement - 6.1, 6.2
Chapter 3 - Crimes and Intentional Torts - 9.1-9.4, 10.1-10.5
Chapter 4 - Negligence and Strict Liability - 9.5, 9.6
Part Two - Contracts
Chapter 5 - The Nature and Origins of Contracts - 11.1
Chapter 6 - Creating a Contract: Offers - 11.2
Chapter 7 - Creating a Contract: Acceptances - 11.3
Chapter 8 - Voluntary Consent - 11.5
Chapter 9 - Capacity to Contract - 11.6
Chapter 10 - Consideration - 11.4
Chapter 11 - The Form and Meaning of Contracts - 11.8, 11.9
Chapter 12 - Illegality - 11.7
Chapter 13 - Third Parties' Contract Rights - 11.10, 11.11
Chapter 14 - Performance and Remedies - 11.12, 11.13
Part Three - Sales
Chapter 15 - Introduction to Sales - 12.1
Chapter 16 - Title, Risk of Loss, and the Terms of Sales Contracts - 12.2-12.4
Chapter 17 - Product Liability - 12.8, 12.9
Chapter 18 - Performance of Sales Contracts - 12.5
Chapter 19 - Remedies for Breach of Sales Contracts - 12.6, 12.7
Part Four - Agency and Employment
Chapter 20 - Agency Authority and Termination - 14.1, 14.3, 14.6
Chapter 21 - Liability of Principals and Agents to Third Persons - 14.4, 14.5
Chapter 22 - Duties of Principals and Agents to Each Other - 14.2
Chapter 23 - Employment Laws - 29.1-29.6

Part Five - Business Organizations
Chapter 24 - Which Form of Business Organization? - 15.1, 16.1
Chapter 25 - Formation and Operation of Partnerships - 15.1-15.3
Chapter 26 - Dissolution of Partnerships - 15.4
Chapter 27 - Limited Partnerships and Related Forms - 15.5
Chapter 28 - Formation and Termination of Corporations - 16.1, 16.2, 16.8
Chapter 29 - Management of the Corporate Business - 16.3, 16.4
Chapter 30 - Shareholder Functions, Rights, and Liabilities - 16.5, 16.7
Chapter 31 - Close Corporations - 16.1
Chapter 32 - Securities Regulation - 16.6, 26.1-26.3
Chapter 33 - Legal Liability of Accountants - 33.1-33.5
Chapter 34 - Business Ethics and Corporate Social Responsibility - 35.1-35.3
Part Six - Property
Chapter 35 - Personal Property - 19.2
Chapter 36 - Bailments - 19.3
Chapter 37 - Real Property - 20.1-20.3, 21.1
Chapter 38 - Landlord and Tenant - 22.1-22.5
Chapter 39 - Estates and Trusts - 24.1-24.5
Part Seven - Commercial Paper
Chapter 40 - Negotiable Instruments - 13.1-13.3
Chapter 41 - Negotiation and Holder in Due Course - 13.4, 13.5
Chapter 42 - Liability of Parties - 13.6
Chapter 43 - Checks and Bank Collections - 13.7
Part Eight - Credit Transactions
Chapter 44 - Introduction to Secured Transactions - 17.1
Chapter 45 - Secured Consumer Transactions - 17.2-17.5
Chapter 46 - Secured Commercial Transactions - 17.2-17.5
Chapter 47 - Bankruptcy - 26.1-26.5
Chapter 48 - Insurance - 23.1-23.4
Part Nine - Government Regulation
Chapter 49 - Government Regulation of Business
Chapter 50 - The Antitrust Laws - 27.1-27.5
Chapter 51 - Consumer Protection Laws - 30.1-30.5
Chapter 52 - Computer Law - 34.1-34.7

Blackburn, Klayman, Malin, *The Legal Environment of Business,* Third Edition, Richard D. Irwin, Inc., 1988.

Part I - Introduction to Law and Business
Chapter 1 - Business Ethics - 35.1-35.3
Chapter 2 - Nature of Law and Legal Reasoning - 4.1-4.4
Chapter 3 - Business and the Courts - 5.1, 5.2
Part II - Public Law Basis of Business Regulation
Chapter 4 - Constitutional Law - 7.1-7.8
Chapter 5 - Administrative Law - 8.1-8.6
Chapter 6 - Environmental Law - 31.1-31.5
Part III - Private Law Basis of Business Regulation
Chapter 7 - Contracts - 11.1-11.13
Chapter 8 - Torts - 9.1-9.6
Chapter 9 - Business Organizations - 15.1, 16.1
Part IV - Business and the Financial Markets
Chapter 10 - Securities Regulation - 28.1-28.4
Chapter 11 - Debtor-Creditor Relations - 25.1-25.4, 26.1-26.5
Part V - Business and the Marketplace
Chapter 12 - Consumer Protection: Product Safety and Advertising - 30.1-30.5
Chapter 13 - Restraints of Trade - 27.2
Chapter 14 - Monopolies and Mergers - 27.3
Chapter 15 - Special Topics in Antitrust - 27.4-27.6
Chapter 16 - International Business Transactions - 32.1-32.3
Part VI - Business and Its Employees
Chapter 17 - Labor Management Relations - 29.1
Chapter 18 - Equal Employment Opportunity - 29.3
Chapter 19 - Labor Standards and Employee Safety - 29.2, 29.4

Bohlman, Dundas, Jentz, *The Legal Environment of Business*, First Edition, West Publishing Company, 1989.

Part I - Introduction to Law
Chapter 1 - Introduction to Law and Its Sources - 4.1-4.4
Chapter 2 - The Judicial System and Litigation - 5.1, 5.2, 6.1
Chapter 3 - The Constitution and the Regulation of Business - 7.1-7.8
Chapter 4 - Administrative Agencies and the Regulation of Business - 8.1-8.6
Chapter 5 - Alternative Dispute Resolution Procedures - 6.2
Chapter 6 - Legislative and Executive Process - 4.3
Chapter 7 - Ethics and Corporate Social Responsibily - 35.1-35.3
Chapter 8 - White Collar Criminal Law - 10.3
Part II - Business and Private Law
Chapter 9 - Contracts and Sales Law - 11.1-11.13, 12.1-12.9
Chapter 10 - Commercial Paper and Secured Transactions - 13.1-13.10, 17.1-17.5
Chapter 11 - Rights of Consumers, Debtors, and Creditors - 25.3, 26.3, 26.4, 30.1-30.5
Chapter 12 - Torts and Product Liability - 9.1-9.4, 12.9
Chapter 13 - Consumer Protection - 30.1-30.5
Chapter 14 - Property Law and Computer Law - 19.1, 20.1, 34.1-34.7
Chapter 15 - Agency and Employment Law - 14.1-14.6, 29.1-29.6
Part III - Business Formation
Chapter 16 - Business Enterprises: Sole Proprietorships and Partnerships - 15.1-15.5
Chapter 17 - Corporate Law and Franchising Law - 16.1-16.8
Part IV - Business and Government Regulation
Chapter 18 - Securities Regulation - 28.1-28.4
Chapter 19 - Antitrust Law: Statutes and Exemptions - 27.2-27.6
Chapter 20 - Antitrust Law: Enforcement and Trends - 27.1
Chapter 21 - Legislative Control over Labor and Labor Relations - 29.1-29.6
Chapter 22 - Employment Law and Equal Opportunity - 29.3
Chapter 23 - Environmental Law - 31.1-31.5
Chapter 24 - International Business Law - 32.1-32.3

Brody, *Business and Its Legal Environment*, D.C. Heath & Co., 1986.

Part 1 - Overview of the Legal System
Chapter 1 - Introduction to Business Law, Statutes and Cases - 4.1-4.4
Chapter 2 - The Courts and Jurisdiction - 5.1, 5.2
Chapter 3 - Civil Litigation - 6.1
Part 2 - Basic Fields of Law
Chapter 4 - Constitutional Law and Business - 7.1-7.8
Chapter 5 - Contracts and Business - 11.1-11.13, 12.1-12.8
Chapter 6 - Torts and Business - 9.1-9.6
Chapter 7 - Property Law and Business - 19.1-19.3, 20.1-20.3, 21.1, 22.1-22.5, 24.1-24.3
Part 3 - Administrative Law and Proceedings
Chapter 8 - Introduction to Agency Regulation - 14.1-14.6
Chapter 9 - The Administrative Process - 8.1-8.6
Part 4 - Corporations and Other Business Organizations
Chapter 10 - The Law of Agency - 14.1-14.6
Chapter 11 - Corporations - 16.1-16.8
Chapter 12 - Partnerships and Other Associations - 15.1-15.5
Chapter 13 - Financing and Securities Law - 16.6, 20.1-20.3, 28.1-28.3
Part 5 - Antitrust Law
Chapter 14 - Introduction to Antitrust Matters - 27.1
Chapter 15 - The Sherman Act - 27.2, 27.3
Chapter 16 - The Clayton Act and the Federal Trade Commission Act - 27.4-27.6
Part 6 - Labor Law
Chapter 17 - Labor Standards and Related Matters - 29.2, 29.4, 29.6
Chapter 18 - Civil Rights and Equal Employment Opportunity - 29.3
Chapter 19 - Labor and Management Relations - 29.1, 29.2
Part 7 - Environmental Law
Chapter 20 - Environmental Regulation of Business - 31.1
Chapter 21 - Federal Environmental Laws - 31.2-31.5
Part 8 - Consumer Law
Chapter 22 - Deceptive Trade Practices - 30.4
Chapter 23 - Credit, Purchase, and Debt Collection - 30.3
Chapter 24 - The Uniform Commercial Code - 12.1-12.9, 13.1-13.10, 17.1-17.5
Chapter 25 - Products Liability - 12.8, 12.9, 23.4, 30.5
Part 9 - Criminal Liability of Corporations, Management, and Other Employees
Chapter 26 - Criminal Law and Business - 10.1-10.5
Chapter 27 - Corporate Crimes, Business Ethics, and Social Responsibility - 10.2, 35.1-35.3

Butler, *The Legal Environment of Business: Government Regulation and Public Policy Analysis*, South-Western Publishing Co., 1987.

Cameron, Scaletta, *Business Law: Legal Environment, Transactions, and Regulations*, Third Edition, Richard D. Irwin, Inc., 1989.

Part Six - Property
Chapter 31 - Forms of Co-Ownership; Personal Property - 19.2
Chapter 32 - Bailments and Carriers - 19.3
Chapter 33 - Real Property -- Acquisitions, Transfer, and Financing - 20.1, 20.3, 21.1
Chapter 34 - Real Property -- Landlord and Tenant - 22.1-22.5
Chapter 35 - Real Property -- Land Use and Environmental Regulation - 20.2, 31.1-31.5
Chapter 36 - Trusts and Decedents' Estates - 24.1-24.5
Chapter 37 - Insurance Law - 23.1-23.4
Part Seven - Business Associations
Chapter 38 - Agency -- Creation, Principal's Liabilities, Termination - 14.1, 14.4-14.6
Chapter 39 - Agency -- Other Rights and Duties - 14.2
Chapter 40 - Partnership -- Creation and Termination - 15.1, 15.4
Chapter 41 - Partnership -- Rights, Powers, Duties, and Liabilities - 15.2, 15.3
Chapter 42 - Limited Partnerships - 15.5
Chapter 43 - Corporations -- Nature, Formation, and Powers - 16.1, 16.2
Chapter 44 - Corporations -- Shareholders' Rights and Liabilities - 16.5, 16.6
Chapter 45 - Corporations -- Management Powers and Duties - 16.3, 16.4
Chapter 46 - Foreign Corporations - 32.1-32.3
Chapter 47 - Business Ethics and Corporate Social Responsibility - 35.1-35.3
Part Eight - Government Regulation
Chapter 48 - Securities Law - 28.1-28.4
Chapter 49 - Antitrust Law - 27.1-27.6
Chapter 50 - Unfair Trade Practices and Consumer Protection - 30.1-30.5
Chapter 51 - Labor Relations Law - 21.1, 29.2, 29.4-29.6
Chapter 52 - Employment Discrimination Law - 29.3

Cheeseman, *The Legal and Regulatory Environment of Business*, Macmillan Publishing Co., 1985.

Part I - The Legal Framework of Business
Chapter 1 - The Nature of the Law - 4.1-4.4
Chapter 2 - The Social Responsibility of Business - 35.1-35.3
Chapter 3 - The American Court System - 5.1, 5.2
Chapter 4 - The Litigation Process - 6.1, 6.2
Chapter 5 - Administrative Agencies - 8.1-8.6
Chapter 6 - The Constitution and Business - 7.1-7.8
Chapter 7 - The Bill of Rights and Business - 7.5
Part II - Antitrust Law
Chapter 8 - Monopolization - 27.1, 27.3
Chapter 9 - Restraints of Trade - 27.2
Chapter 10 - Mergers - 27.4
Chapter 11 - Price Discrimination - 27.5
Chapter 12 - Franchising - 19.2
Part III - Securities Regulation
Chapter 13 - Distribution of Securities - 28.1, 28.2
Chapter 14 - Trading in Securities - 28.3
Chapter 15 - Proxy Contests and Tender Offers - 28.3
Chapter 16 - Commodities Regulation
Part IV - The Social Responsibility of Business
Chapter 17 - Environmental Protection - 31.1-31.5
Chapter 18 - Product Safety - 12.8, 12.9, 30.5
Chapter 19 - Debtor-Creditor Relation - 30.3
Chapter 20 - Bankruptcy - 26.1-26.5
Part V - Ethical Considerations and Business
Chapter 21 - Advertising - 30.4
Chapter 22 - Trademarks, Copyrights, and Patents - 9.4
Chapter 23 - Business Torts - 9.4
Chapter 24 - Business Crimes - 10.1-10.5, 28.4
Part VI - The Employer-Employee Relation
Chapter 25 - Labor Unions - 29.1
Chapter 26 - Discrimination in Employment - 29.3
Chapter 27 - Occupational Safety and Security - 29.2, 29.4-29.6

Clark, Kinder, *Law and Business,* Second Edition, McGraw-Hill, Inc., 1988.

Part I - Law and Society
  Chapter 1 - An Introduction to American Law - 4.1-4.4
  Chapter 2 - Dispute Resolution - 6.1, 6.2
  Chapter 3 - Ethics and Torts - 35.1-35.3, 9.1-9.6
  Chapter 4 - Criminal Law - 10.1-10.5
Part II - Contracts
  Chapter 5 - Offer - 11.2
  Chapter 6 - Acceptance - 11.3
  Chapter 7 - Consideration - 11.4
  Chapter 8 - Lack of Consent, Incapacity, and Illegality - 11.5-11.7
  Chapter 9 - Written Contracts and Their Interpretation - 11.8, 11.9
  Chapter 10 - Third Parties - 11.10, 11.11
  Chapter 11 - Performance and Remedies for Nonperformance - 11.12, 11.13
Part III - Agency and Employment
  Chapter 12 - The Relationship between Principal and Agent - 14.2
  Chapter 13 - The Liability of Principals and Agents to Third Parties - 14.4
  Chapter 14 - Employee Rights and Benefits - 14.1
Part IV - Business Organizations
  Chapter 15 - Forming and Managing Partnerships - 15.1, 15.2
  Chapter 16 - Partnerships: Relations with Third Parties and Dissolution - 15.3, 15.4
  Chapter 17 - Forming and Financing Corporations - 16.1, 16.2, 16.7
  Chapter 18 - Operating Corporations - 16.3
  Chapter 19 - Shareholders and Extraordinary Transactions - 16.5
  Chapter 20 - Limited Partnerships, Close Corporations, and Franchises - 15.5, 16.1
  Chapter 21 - Securities and Their Regulations - 16.6
  Chapter 22 - Legal Liabilities of Accountants - 33.1-33.5
Part V - Property
  Chapter 23 - Personal Property and Fixtures - 19.1, 19.2
  Chapter 24 - Bailments - 19.3
  Chapter 25 - Real Property - 20.1-20.3, 21.1
  Chapter 26 - The Relationship between Landlord and Tenant - 22.1-22.5
  Chapter 27 - Wills, Estates, and Trusts - 24.1-24.5
  Chapter 28 - Insurance - 23.1-23.4
Part VI - Sales
  Chapter 29 - Formation of Sales Contracts - 12.2
  Chapter 30 - Risk of Loss and Title - 12.4
  Chapter 31 - Performance - 12.5
  Chapter 32 - Warranties and Product Liability - 12.8, 12.9
  Chapter 33 - Remedies - 12.6, 12.7
Part VII - Commercial Paper, Checks, and Documents of Title
  Chapter 34 - Negotiability - 13.3
  Chapter 35 - Negotiation and Holders in Due Course - 13.4, 13.5
  Chapter 36 - Payment and the Liabilities of the Parties - 13.6
  Chapter 37 - Banking, Documents of Title, and Investment Securities - 13.7, 13.10
Part VIII - Secured Transactions and Bankruptcy
  Chapter 38 - Suretyship - 18.1-18.3
  Chapter 39 - Security Interests in Personal Property - 17.2
  Chapter 40 - Security Interests in Real Property - 17.2
  Chapter 41 - Bankruptcy - 26.1-26.5

Clarkson, Miller, Jentz, Cross, *West's Business Law,* Fourth Edition, West Publishing Co., 1989.

Unit One - The Legal Environment of Business
  Chapter 1 - Introduction to Law and Legal Reasoning - 4.1-4.4
  Chapter 2 - Courts and Civil Dispute Resolution - 5.1, 5.2, 6.1, 6.2
  Chapter 3 - Constitutional Authority to Regulate Business - 7.1-7.8
  Chapter 4 - Torts - 9.1-9.3
  Chapter 5 - Torts Related to Business - 9.4
  Chapter 6 - Criminal Law - 10.1-10.5
Unit Two - Contracts
  Chapter 7 - Nature and Terminology - 11.1
  Chapter 8 - Agreement - 11.2, 11.3
  Chapter 9 - Consideration - 11.4
  Chapter 10 - Capacity and Genuineness of Assent - 11.5, 11.6
  Chapter 11 - Legality - 11.7
  Chapter 12 - Writing and Form - 11.8, 11.9
  Chapter 13 - Third Party Rights - 11.10, 11.11
  Chapter 14 - Performance and Discharge - 11.12
  Chapter 15 - Breach of Contract and Remedies - 11.13

Conry, Ferrera, Fox, *The Legal Environment of Business,* Second Edition, Allyn & Bacon, Inc., 1990.

Section III - The Legal Environment of Employer-Employee Relations
Chapter 15 - The Employment Relationship - 29.2, 29.4-29.6
Chapter 16 - Equal Employment Opportunity - 29.3
Chapter 17 - Business and Labor Unions - 29.1
Section IV - Government Regulation of Business
Chapter 18 - Antitrust I -- Monopolizing and Horizontal Restraints of Trade - 27.2, 27.3
Chapter 19 - Antitrust II -- Vertical Relations - 27.2, 27.3
Chapter 20 - Securities Relations I - 28.2
Chapter 21 - Securities Relations II - 28.3
Chapter 22 - Environmental Law - 31.1-31.5
Chapter 23 - Regulation of Advertising - 30.4
Section V - Business and Consumers
Chapter 24 - Consumer Rights - 30.1-30.5
Chapter 25 - Debtor-Creditor Relations - 25.1-25.4, 26.1-26.5
Chapter 26 - Product Liability - 12.9, 30.5

Corley, Reed, *The Legal Environment of Business: Briefed Case Edition,* Second Edition, McGraw-Hill, Inc., 1989.

Part I - Introduction
Chapter 1 - Introduction to Law - 4.1-4.4
Chapter 2 - The Powers and Functions of Courts - 5.1
Chapter 3 - Court Systems - 5.1, 5.2
Chapter 4 - Litigation and Other Methods for Resolving Disputes - 6.1-6.2
Part II - Constitutional and Administrative Law
Chapter 5 - The Constitution and Business - 7.1-7.8
Chapter 6 - The Bill of Rights and Business - 7.5
Chapter 7 - Administrative Law - 8.1-8.6
Part III - Contracts and Torts
Chapter 8 - Contract Law and Private Enterprise - 11.1-11.13
Chapter 9 - Torts in the Business Environment - 9.4
Chapter 10 - Products and Service Liability - 12.9
Part IV - Conducting Business
Chapter 11 - Forms of Business Organizations: Selected Process - 15.1, 15.2
Chapter 12 - Liability of Business Organizations and Managers
Chapter 13 - International Transactions - 32.1, 32.2
Chapter 14 - Worker Protection - 29.4-29.6
Chapter 15 - Discrimination in Employment - 29.3
Chapter 16 - Unfair Labor Practices - 29.2
Part V - Protecting Parties to Transactions
Chapter 17 - Investor Protection - 28.1-28.4
Chapter 18 - Right to Union Activity - 29.1
Chapter 19 - Consumer Protection - 30.1-30.5
Chapter 20 - Creditor and Debtor Protection - 25.1-25.4, 26.1, 26.4
Part VI - Protecting Society
Chapter 21 - Protecting Competition - 27.1
Chapter 22 - Sherman Act Enforcement - 27.2, 27.3
Chapter 23 - Clayton Act and FTC Act Enforcement - 27.4-27.6

Corley, Reed, Shedd, *The Legal Environment of Business,* Eighth Edition, McGraw-Hill, Inc., 1990.

Part I - Introduction
Chapter 1 - The Law and Lawyers - 4.1-4.4
Chapter 2 - The Powers and Functions of Courts - 5.1
Chapter 3 - Court Systems - 5.2
Chapter 4 - Litigation - 6.1
Chapter 5 - Arbitration - 6.2
Part II - Constitutional and Administrative Law
Chapter 6 - The Constitution and Business - 7.1-7.8
Chapter 7 - The Bill of Rights and Business - 7.5
Chapter 8 - Administrative Law - 8.1-8.6
Part III - Contracts and Torts
Chapter 9 - Contract Law and Private Enterprise - 11.1-11.13
Chapter 10 - Torts in the Business Environment - 9.4
Chapter 11 - Products and Service Liability - 12.9
Part IV - Conducting Business
Chapter 12 - Selecting the Form of Business Organization - 15.1-15.5, 16.1-16.8
Chapter 13 - Liability of Business Organizations and Managers - 15.1-15.5, 16.1-16.8
Chapter 14 - International Business Transactions - 32.1-32.2

Corley, Shedd, *Fundamentals of Business Law,* Fifth Edition, Prentice-Hall, Inc., 1990.

Corley, Shedd, *Principles of Business Law,* Fourteenth Edition, Prentice-Hall, Inc., 1989.

Part I - Introduction to Law and Business
- Chapter 1 - Law - 4.1-4.4
- Chapter 2 - Resolving Controversies and Influencing Conduct - 6.2
- Chapter 3 - Court Systems - 5.1, 5.2
- Chapter 4 - Litigation - 6.1
- Chapter 5 - The Law of Torts and Business - 9.1-9.6
- Chapter 6 - The Criminal Law and Business - 10.1-10.5

Part II - Contracts
- Chapter 7 - Introduction to Contracts and Remedies - 11.1
- Chapter 8 - The Agreement: Offer and Acceptance - 11.2, 11.3
- Chapter 9 - Bargained-for Consideration - 11.4
- Chapter 10 - Contractual Capacity and Genuine Assent - 11.5, 11.6
- Chapter 11 - Illegality and Public Policy - 11.7
- Chapter 12 - Form and Interpretation of Contracts - 11.8, 11.9
- Chapter 13 - Contract Performance - 11.12
- Chapter 14 - Excuses for Nonperformance and Discharge - 11.13
- Chapter 15 - Contract Rights of Third Parties - 11.10, 11.11

Part III - Sales Transactions
- Chapter 16 - Introduction to Sales Contracts - 12.1, 12.2
- Chapter 17 - Breach and Remedies - 12.6, 12.7
- Chapter 18 - Warranties - 12.8
- Chapter 19 - Products Liability - 12.9

Part IV - Commercial Paper
- Chapter 20 - Introduction to Commercial Paper - 13.1
- Chapter 21 - Negotiable Instruments - 13.2
- Chapter 22 - Holders in Due Course and Defenses - 13.5
- Chapter 23 - Liability of Parties to Commercial Paper - 13.6

Part V - Creditors and Debtors
- Chapter 24 - Introduction to Article 9 Transactions - 17.1
- Chapter 25 - Issues in Article 9 Transactions - 17.3-17.5
- Chapter 26 - Real Property as Security - 17.2
- Chapter 27 - Additional Laws Assisting Creditors - 25.1-25.4
- Chapter 28 - Laws Assisting Debtors - 26.4
- Chapter 29 - Bankruptcy - 26.1-26.5

Part VI - Property
- Chapter 30 - Introduction to the Law of Property - 19.1
- Chapter 31 - Acquiring Title to Property - 20.3
- Chapter 32 - Leases and Bailments - 19.3
- Chapter 33 - Wills, Trusts, and Estate Planning - 24.1-24.5

Part VII - Agency
- Chapter 34 - The Principal-Agency Relationship - 14.2
- Chapter 35 - Agency and the Law of Contracts - 14.3, 14.4
- Chapter 36 - Agency and the Law of Torts - 14.5
- Chapter 37 - Termination of the Agency Relationship - 14.6

Part VIII - Business Organizations
- Chapter 38 - Choosing the Form of Business Organization - 15.1, 16.1
- Chapter 39 - Formation of Partnerships - 15.1
- Chapter 40 - Operating Partnerships - 15.2, 15.3
- Chapter 41 - Dissolution of Partnerships - 15.4
- Chapter 42 - Formation of Corporations - 16.1, 16.2
- Chapter 43 - Operating Corporations - 16.3
- Chapter 44 - Corporate Dissolutions, Mergers, and Consolidations - 16.8
- Chapter 45 - Conducting International Business - 32.1-32.3

Part IX - Government Regulation of Business
- Chapter 46 - The Constitution and Business - 7.1-7.8
- Chapter 47 - Administrative Law - 8.1-8.6
- Chapter 48 - Antitrust Law - 27.1-27.6
- Chapter 49 - Labor Law - 29.1-29.6
- Chapter 50 - Securities Regulation - 28.1-28.4

Part X - Professional Responsibility
- Chapter 51 - Accountants' Liability - 33.1-33.5

Davidson, Knowles, Forsythe, Jespersen, *Business Law: Principles and Cases,* Third Edition, PWS-Kent Publishing Co., 1990.

Part 1 - Foundations of American Law
- Chapter 1 - Introduction - 4.1
- Chapter 2 - The American Legal System - 4.1-4.4
- Chapter 3 - Torts - 9.1-9.6
- Chapter 4 - Crimes and Business - 10.1-10.5
- Chapter 5 - Anatomy of a Civil Lawsuit - 6.1-6.2
- Chapter 6 - The Attorney-Client Relationship and the Accountant's Legal Liability - 33.1-33.5
- Chapter 7 - Business Ethics - 35.1-35.3

Part 2 - The Law of Contracts
- Chapter 8 - An Introduction to the Law of Contracts - 11.1
- Chapter 9 - Contractual Agreement: Mutual Assent - 11.2, 11.3, 11.5
- Chapter 10 - Consideration: The Basis of the Bargain - 11.4
- Chapter 11 - Contractual Capacity: The Ability to Agree - 11.6
- Chapter 12 - Legal Agreements - 11.7
- Chapter 13 - Genuineness of the Contractual Assent - 11.5
- Chapter 14 - Interpretation and Proper Form of Contracts - 11.8, 11.9
- Chapter 15 - The Rights of Third Parties - 11.10, 11.11
- Chapter 16 - Methods of Discharging the Contract - 11.11, 11.12
- Chapter 17 - Contractual Remedies - 11.13

Part 3 - The Law of Sales
- Chapter 18 - Formation of the Sales Contract - 12.2
- Chapter 19 - Performance of the Sales Contract - 12.5
- Chapter 20 - Title, Risk of Loss, and Bulk Sales - 12.4
- Chapter 21 - Warranties and Product Liability - 12.8, 12.9
- Chapter 22 - Remedies for Breach of the Sales Contract - 12.6, 12.7

Part 4 - The Law of Commercial Paper
- Chapter 23 - An Introduction to Commercial Paper - 13.1, 13.2
- Chapter 24 - Negotiability - 13.3
- Chapter 25 - Negotiation and Holders in Due Course - 13.4, 13.5
- Chapter 26 - Liability and Discharge - 13.6
- Chapter 27 - Bank -- Customer Relations - 13.7

Part 5 - Debtor-Creditor Relations
- Chapter 28 - Secured Transactions: Security Interests and Perfection - 17.2, 17.3
- Chapter 29 - Secured Transactions: Priorities - 17.4
- Chapter 30 - Secured Transactions: Default - 17.5
- Chapter 31 - Straight Bankruptcy - 26.1-26.5
- Chapter 32 - Alternatives to Straight Bankruptcy - 26.1

Part 6 - The Law of Agency
- Chapter 33 - The Creation and Termination of an Agency - 14.1, 14.6
- Chapter 34 - Agency: Liability for Contracts - 14.4, 14.5
- Chapter 35 - Agency: Liability for Wrongs and Losses - 14.4, 14.5

Part 7 - Business Organizations
- Chapter 36 - Formation of a Partnership - 15.1
- Chapter 37 - Operation of a Partnership - 15.2
- Chapter 38 - Termination of a Partnership - 15.4
- Chapter 39 - Formation of a Corporation - 16.2
- Chapter 40 - Operation of a Corporation - 16.3
- Chapter 41 - Management of a Corporation - 16.4
- Chapter 42 - Dissolution, Merger, Consolidation, and Other Acquisitions - 16.8
- Chapter 43 - Franchising - 16.1
- Chapter 44 - Securities Regulation - 16.6

Part 8 - Government Regulations
- Chapter 45 - An Introduction to Government Regulation - 27.1, 28.1, 29.1, 31.1
- Chapter 46 - Antitrust Legislation - 27.1-27.6
- Chapter 47 - Consumer and Environmental Protection - 30.1-30.5, 31.1-31.5
- Chapter 48 - Labor and Fair Employment Practices - 29.1-29.6

Part 9 - Property Protection
- Chapter 49 - Real Property and Joint Ownership - 20.1-20.3
- Chapter 50 - Personal Property and Bailments - 19.1-19.3
- Chapter 51 - Insurance - 23.1-23.4
- Chapter 52 - Wills and Estates - 24.1-24.3
- Chapter 53 - Trusts and Trust Administration - 24.4, 24.5

Part 10 - The Emerging Business Environment
- Chapter 54 - International Business - 32.1-32.3
- Chapter 55 - Computers and the Law - 34.1-34.7

Dunfee, Bellace, Rosoff, *Business and Its Legal Environment,* Second Edition, Prentice-Hall, Inc., 1987.

Part I - Processes and Structure of the American Legal System
- Chapter 1 - The Role of Law in the United States - 4.1-4.4
- Chapter 2 - Structure and Functions of the Legal System - 5.1
- Chapter 3 - Civil Litigation and Alternatives - 6.1, 6.2
- Chapter 4 - The Constitutional Framework - 7.1-7.8
- Chapter 5 - Administrative Law: The Process of Government Regulation - 8.1-8.6

Part II - The Legal Foundations of Business: Commercial and Property Law
- Chapter 6 - The Law of Contracts - 11.1-11.13
- Chapter 7 - The Law of Commercial Transactions - 13.1-13.10
- Chapter 8 - The Law of Property - 19.1-19.3, 20.1-20.3, 21.1, 22.1-22.5, 23.3

Part III - Ethics, Torts, Business Crimes, and Products Liability
- Chapter 9 - Business Ethics and the Social Responsibility of Business - 35.1-35.3
- Chapter 10 - Tort Law and White Collar Crime - 9.1-9.4, 10.3
- Chapter 11 - Products Liability - 12.9, 30.5

Part IV - Antitrust and Consumer Protection
- Chapter 12 - Antitrust Enforcement and Exemptions - 27.1
- Chapter 13 - Anticompetitive Business Practices - 27.2
- Chapter 14 - Price Discrimination, Monopolizing, and Mergers - 27.3-27.6
- Chapter 15 - Unfair Competition and Consumer Protection - 30.1-30.4

Part V - Corporation and Securities Law
- Chapter 16 - Law of Business Organizations - 15.1, 15.5, 16.1
- Chapter 17 - Securities Law - 28.1-28.4

Part VI - Employment and Environmental Law
- Chapter 18 - Equal Opportunity in Employment - 29.3
- Chapter 19 - Labor Law: Securing Representation Rights - 29.1
- Chapter 20 - Regulating Terms and Conditions of Employment - 29.2, 29.4-29.6
- Chapter 21 - Environmental Law - 31.1-31.5

Dunfee, Gibson, Blackburn, Whitman, McCarty, Brennan, *Modern Business Law,* Second Edition, McGraw-Hill, Inc., 1989.

Part I - Legal Environment of Business
- Chapter 1 - The Functions and Sources of Law - 4.1-4.4
- Chapter 2 - Legal Systems - 5.1, 5.2
- Chapter 3 - Introduction to Criminal Law - 10.1
- Chapter 4 - Business and Ethics - 35.1-35.3
- Chapter 5 - Social Responsibility of Business - 35.2, 35.3
- Chapter 6 - Intentional Torts - 9.2, 9.3
- Chapter 7 - Competitive Torts - 9.4
- Chapter 8 - Negligence and Strict Liability - 9.5, 9.6

Part II - Contracts
- Chapter 9 - Introduction to the Law of Contracts - 11.1
- Chapter 10 - The Offer - 11.2
- Chapter 11 - The Acceptance - 11.3
- Chapter 12 - Consideration - 11.4
- Chapter 13 - Genuine Assent - 11.5
- Chapter 14 - Capacity to Contract - 11.6
- Chapter 15 - Illegality - 11.7
- Chapter 16 - Legal Form - 11.8, 11.9
- Chapter 17 - Rights of Third Parties - 11.10, 11.11
- Chapter 18 - Performance, Discharge, and Remedies - 11.12, 11.13

Part III - Commercial Transactions
- Chapter 19 - Sales Law - 12.1-12.4
- Chapter 20 - Sales Performance - 12.5
- Chapter 21 - Remedies - 12.6, 12.7
- Chapter 22 - Warranties - 12.8
- Chapter 23 - Products Liability - 12.9
- Chapter 24 - Commercial Paper: Introduction and Negotiability - 13.1-13.3
- Chapter 25 - Transfer, Negotiation, and Holder in Due Course - 13.4, 13.5
- Chapter 26 - Liability of Parties and Defenses - 13.6
- Chapter 27 - Checks and Electronic Fund Transfers - 13.7, 13.8
- Chapter 28 - Secured Transactions - 17.1-17.5
- Chapter 29 - Bankruptcy - 26.1-26.5

Part IV - Business Organizations
Chapter 30 - The Agency Relationship - 14.1
Chapter 31 - The Effect of Agency Relations - 14.2-14.5
Chapter 32 - Nature and Formation of Partnerships - 15.1
Chapter 33 - Operation and Dissolution of Partnerships - 15.2-15.4
Chapter 34 - Nature and Formation of Corporations - 16.1, 16.2
Chapter 35 - Financing the Corporation - 16.7
Chapter 36 - Operating the Corporation - 16.3
Chapter 37 - Securities Regulation - 16.6, 28.1-28.4
Part V - Property and Related Topics
Chapter 38 - Personal Property - 19.2
Chapter 39 - Interests in Real Property - 20.1
Chapter 40 - Acquisition, Financing, and Control of Real Property - 20.3, 21.1
Chapter 41 - Wills, Trusts, and Estates - 24.1-24.5
Chapter 42 - Insurance - 23.1, 23,3
Part VI - Government Regulations
Chapter 43 - Government Regulation of Business and the Role of Administrative Agencies - 8.1-8.6
Chapter 44 - Antitrust Laws: Enforcement and Content - 27.1-27.6
Chapter 45 - The Federal Trade Commission and Consumer Protection - 30.1-30.5
Chapter 46 - Fair Employment Practices - 29.1-29.6

Fisher, Jennings, *Law for Business*, West Publishing Co., 1986.

Part One - Introduction to Law
Chapter 1 - Law and Legal Ethics - 4.1
Chapter 2 - Sources of Law: Courts and Legislatures - 4.2, 4.3
Chapter 3 - Ways to Settle Disputes - 6.1, 6.2
Chapter 4 - Business Crimes - 9.4, 10.3
Chapter 5 - Negligence and Strict Liability - 9.5, 9.6
Chapter 6 - Intentional Torts - 9.2, 9.3
Part Two - Business and Government
Chapter 7 - The Constitution and Business - 7.1-7.8
Chapter 8 - Government Regulation: An Overview - 8.1
Chapter 9 - Government Regulation: How Regulations Are Made - 8.2-8.4
Chapter 10 - Government Regulation: Enforcement and Adjudication of a Regulation - 8.5, 8.6
Chapter 11 - Consumer Protection - 27.6, 30.1, 30.2, 30.4
Chapter 12 - Environmental Law: Particular Federal Statutes - 31.1, 31.5
Chapter 13 - Antitrust Law: The Sherman Act - 27.2, 27.3
Chapter 14 - Antitrust Law: The Clayton and Robinson-Patman Acts - 27.4, 27.5
Chapter 15 - The Federal Trade Commission - 27.6, 30.4
Chapter 16 - Securities Regulation - 28.1-28.4
Part Three - Contracts
Chapter 17 - Nature, Definition, and Classification of Contracts - 11.1
Chapter 18 - The Agreement: Offer and Acceptance - 11.2, 11.3
Chapter 19 - Consideration - 11.4
Chapter 20 - Misconduct or Mistake in Formation - 11.5
Chapter 21 - Capacity - 11.6
Chapter 22 - The Writing Requirement - 11.8, 11.9
Chapter 23 - Illegality and Public Policy - 11.7
Chapter 24 - Third Party Rights and Duties - 11.10, 11.11
Chapter 25 - Performance and Discharge - 11.12
Chapter 26 - Remedies for a Breach of Contract - 11.13
Part Four - Sales
Chapter 27 - Introduction to Sales and Formation of Sales Contracts - 12.1-12.3
Chapter 28 - Terms Under Article II - 12.2
Chapter 29 - Terms: Identification, Title, and Risk of Loss - 12.3, 12.5
Chapter 30 - Warranties and Product Liability - 12.8, 12.9
Chapter 31 - Obligations and Performance - 12.5
Chapter 32 - Remedies Under Article II - 12.6, 12.7
Part Five - Agency and Employment
Chapter 33 - Creation of the Agency Relationship - 14.1
Chapter 34 - Rights and Duties Between Employers and Employees - 12.2, 12.6
Chapter 35 - Employer and Employee Liability to Third Parties - 12.3, 12.5
Chapter 36 - Accountants' Legal Liability - 33.1-33.5
Chapter 37 - Employment Law: Some Important Statutes - 29.2-29.6
Chapter 38 - Federal Labor Law: Unionization and Collective Bargaining - 29.1

Part Six - Business Organizations
Chapter 39 - Types of Business Organizations - 15.1, 15.5, 16.1
Chapter 40 - Partnerships: Forming and Ending Them - 15.1, 15.4
Chapter 41 - Partnership Operation - 15.2, 15.3
Chapter 42 - Nature, Formation, and Termination of Corporations - 16.1, 16.2, 16.8
Chapter 43 - Management of Corporations - 16.3, 16.4
Chapter 44 - Rights and Responsibilities of Shareholders - 16.5-16.7
Part Seven - Property
Chapter 45 - Personal Property - 19.1, 19.2
Chapter 46 - Bailments - 19.3
Chapter 47 - Real Property Interests and Regulation - 20.1
Chapter 48 - Real Property Transfers - 20.1, 20.3, 21.1
Chapter 49 - Landlord-Tenant Relationships - 22.1-22.5
Chapter 50 - Wills, Estates, and Trusts - 24.1-24.5
Part Eight - Commercial Paper
Chapter 51 - Commercial Paper: The Basic Concepts - 13.1-13.3
Chapter 52 - Commercial Paper: Transfer and Negotiation - 13.4, 13.5
Chapter 53 - Commercial Paper: Liability of the Parties - 13.6
Chapter 54 - Banks and Commercial Paper - 13.7
Part Nine - Creditor/Debtor Relationships
Chapter 55 - Consumer Protection for Credit Transactions - 30.3
Chapter 56 - Introduction to Secured Credit Transactions - 17.1-17.3
Chapter 57 - Priorities of Creditors in Secured Credit Transactions - 17.4
Chapter 58 - Enforcement and Collection of Credit Transactions - 17.5
Chapter 59 - Bankruptcy - 26.1-26.5
Chapter 60 - Insurance - 23.1-23.4
Part Ten - International Law
Chapter 61 - Law in International Business - 32.1-32.3

Fisher, Phillips, *The Legal Environment of Business,* Third Edition, West Publishing Co., 1988.

Module One - Legal and Business Ethics, Overview, and Finding the Law
Chapter 1 - Law; Legal and Business Ethics - 35.1-35.3
Chapter 2 - Overview and Finding Law - 4.1-4.2
Module Two - Business and Legal Systems: Courts, Legislatures, Administrative Agencies, and Constitutional Law Affecting Regulation
Chapter 3 - Sources of Law: Political and Institutional - 4.3, 4.4, 5.1
Chapter 4 - Settling Legal Disputes: Alternative Dispute Resolution, Civil and Criminal Lawsuits - 6.1, 6.2
Chapter 5 - Business and the Constitution: Power to Regulate - 7.1-7.7
Chapter 6 - Business and the Constitution: Independent Constitutional Checks - 7.8
Chapter 7 - Government Regulation: Overview - 8.1-8.3
Chapter 8 - Government Regulation: Anatomy of a Regulation - 8.4
Chapter 9 - Law in International Business - 32.1-32.3
Module Three - Private Law Affecting Entrepreneurs
Chapter 10 - Torts: Negligence, Strict Liability, and Intentional Torts - 9.1-9.6
Chapter 11 - Nature, Definition, and Classification of Contracts - 11.1
Chapter 12 - Property - 19.1-19.3, 20.1-20.3
Module Four - Law Affecting Business's Personnel Department
Chapter 13 - Employer-Employee Relations: Common Law Rules - 14.1
Chapter 14 - Employer-Employee Relations: Some Important Statutes - 29.2-29.6
Chapter 15 - Employment Discrimination - 29.3
Chapter 16 - Federal Labor Law: Unionization and Collective Bargaining - 29.1
Module Five - Law Affecting Business's Financing
Chapter 17 - Business Organizations - 15.1, 15.5, 16.1
Chapter 18 - Securities Regulation - 28.1-28.4
Module Six - Law Affecting the Marketing Department
Chapter 19 - Antitrust Law: The Sherman Act - 27.2, 27.3
Chapter 20 - Antitrust Law: The Clayton Act - 27.4
Chapter 21 - The Federal Trade Commission - 27.6, 30.4
Chapter 22 - Consumer Protection - 27.6, 30.1, 30.2, 30.4
Module Seven - Law Affecting the Manufacturing Department
Chapter 23 - Product Liability - 12.9, 30.5
Chapter 24 - Environmental Law: Particular Federal Statutes - 31.1-31.5

Frascona, et al., *Business Law,* Third Edition, Allyn & Bacon, Inc., 1987. 4th Edition expected by 1991.

Part 1 - The Foundations of Legal Systems
- Chapter 1 - The Nature of Legal Systems and Law - 4.1
- Chapter 2 - Organization of the United States Legal System - 4.2-4.4, 5.1, 5.2
- Chapter 3 - Criminal Law - 10.1-10.5
- Chapter 4 - The Law of Torts - 9.1-9.6

Part 2 - Contracts
- Chapter 5 - Concept of Contractual Agreement - 11.1
- Chapter 6 - Formation of a Contract - 11.2, 11.3
- Chapter 7 - Relief from Contractual Obligations - 11.5
- Chapter 8 - Consideration/Value Given for a Promise - 11.4
- Chapter 9 - Capacity/Ability to Create a Contract - 11.6
- Chapter 10 - Public Policy and Contractual Purpose - 11.7
- Chapter 11 - Contractual Form -- Requirement of a Writing for Enforceability, Statute of Frauds - 11.8, 11.9
- Chapter 12 - Contractual Duties of Performance, Nonperformance, and Discharge - 11.12
- Chapter 13 - Contractual Rights, Third Parties, and Remedies for Breach of Contract - 11.10, 11.11, 11.13

Part 3 - Agency and Employment
- Chapter 14 - Nature and Creation of Agency - 14.1
- Chapter 15 - Duties of Principal and Agent to Each Other - 14.2
- Chapter 16 - Agency and the Law of Contracts and Torts - 14.3-14.5
- Chapter 17 - Termination of Agency - 14.6
- Chapter 18 - Employment - 29.1-29.6

Part 4 - Personal Property and Bailments
- Chapter 19 - Personal Property - 19.1, 19.2
- Chapter 20 - Bailments - 19.3
- Chapter 21 - Carriers, Documents of Title, and Innkeepers - 13.10, 19.3

Part 5 - Sales and Consumer Law
- Chapter 22 - Introduction to the Uniform Commercial Code - 12.1
- Chapter 23 - Formation and Interpretation of the Sales Contract - 12.2-12.4
- Chapter 24 - Performance of the Sales Contract - 12.5
- Chapter 25 - Breach of the Sales Contract, Courses of Action, and Remedies - 12.6, 12.7
- Chapter 26 - Consumer Law -- Seller's Warranties - 12.7
- Chapter 27 - Consumer Law -- Manufacturer's Liabilities and Recent Consumer Protection Legislation - 12.8, 30.3-30.5

Part 6 - Commercial Paper
- Chapter 28 - Introduction to Commercial Paper and Banking Operations - 13.1-13.3, 13.7
- Chapter 29 - Transfer and Negotiation - 13.4
- Chapter 30 - Holder, Holder in Due Course, and Defenses - 13.5
- Chapter 31 - Banks, Checks, and Customer Relations - 13.7
- Chapter 32 - Deadlines and Discharge - 13.6

Part 7 - Government Regulation of Business
- Chapter 33 - Antitrust Law - 27.1-27.5
- Chapter 34 - Administrative Law - 8.1-8.6
- Chapter 35 - Labor Law - 29.1
- Chapter 36 - Environmental Law - 31.1-31.5

Part 8 - Business Organizations

A. General Partnerships and Special Ventures
- Chapter 37 - Creation and Termination of General Partnerships - 15.1, 15.4
- Chapter 38 - Partnership Management and the Authority of Partners - 15.2, 15.3
- Chapter 39 - Rights, Duties, and Remedies of Partners Among Themselves - 15.2
- Chapter 40 - Special Ventures - 15.5

B. Corporations
- Chapter 41 - Nature and Classes - 16.1
- Chapter 42 - Creation and Termination - 16.2, 16.8
- Chapter 43 - Corporate Powers - 16.3
- Chapter 44 - Corporate Stock and Shareholders - 16.5-16.7
- Chapter 45 - Corporate Management - 16.4

Part 9 - Real Property
- Chapter 46 - Real Property and Its Ownership - 20.1
- Chapter 47 - Transferring Ownership of Realty - 20.1, 20.3, 21.1
- Chapter 48 - Renting Realty - 22.1-22.5

Part 10 - Secured Transactions, Bankruptcy, and Insurance
- Chapter 49 - Creation of Security Interests in Personal Property - 17.1-17.3
- Chapter 50 - Enforcement of Personal Property Security Interests; and Suretyship - 17.4, 17.5, 18.1-18.3
- Chapter 51 - Bankruptcy Under the Bankruptcy Reform Act of 1978 - 26.1-26.5
- Chapter 52 - General Principles of Insurance Law - 23.1
- Chapter 53 - Life, Fire, and Automobile Insurance Law - 23.2-23.4

Part 11 - Wills and Decedents' Estates, and Trusts
    Chapter 54 - Wills and Decedents' Estates - 24.1-24.3
    Chapter 55 - Trusts - 24.4, 24.5
Part 12 - Business Law in the International Marketplace
    Chapter 56 - Business Law in the International Marketplace - 32.1-32.3

Halbert, Ingulli, *Law & Ethics in the Business Environment*, West Publishing Co., 1990.

Chapter One - An Introduction to Law and Ethics: The Duty to Rescue
Chapter Two - The Duty of Loyalty: Whistleblowing - 35.3
Chapter Three - The Right of Privacy: Drugtesting at the Workplace - 9.2
Chapter Four - Secrecy & Disclosure: Insider Trading - 28.3
Chapter Five - Competition: Trade Secrets - 19.2
Chapter Six - Government Regulation of Business: Workplace Safety - 29.4
Chapter Seven - Product & Environmental Safety: Industrial Hazards - 30.5, 31.1-31.5
Chapter Eight - Equal Treatment: Sexual Harassment - 29.3
Chapter Nine - Economic Equity: Affirmative Action - 29.3

Harron, *The Legal Environment for Business Managers*, Second Edition, Allyn and Bacon, Inc., 1984.

Part I - Introduction to the Study of Law
    Chapter 1 - The Definition and Meaning of Law - 4.1-4.4
    Chapter 2 - The Judicial Process - 5.1, 5.2
    Chapter 3 - Constitutional Basis for Business Regulation - 7.1-7.8
    Chapter 4 - The Administrative Process - 8.1-8.6
    Chapter 5 - Agency Procedures - 8.3, 8.4
    Chapter 6 - Reform of Administrative Agencies - 8.6
Part II - Law and Regulations Affecting the Securities Markets
    Chapter 7 - Stockholder Rights and Liabilities - 16.1-16.8
    Chapter 8 - Securities Act of 1933 - 28.1, 28.2
    Chapter 9 - Securities Exchange Act of 1934 - 28.3
Part III - Laws and Regulations Affecting Business Growth and Practices
    Chapter 10 - The Sherman Antitrust Act - 27.2, 27.3
    Chapter 11 - The Clayton Act - 27.4, 27.5
    Chapter 12 - Regulation of Unfair Business Practices - 9.4, 27.6, 30.4
Part IV - Laws and Regulations Affecting Consumers
    Chapter 13 - Product Liability - 12.9, 30.5
    Chapter 14 - Consumer Protections - 30.1, 30.2, 30.5
    Chapter 15 - Consumer Credit Protections - 30.3
Part V - Laws and Regulations Affecting Employment
    Chapter 16 - Laws Regulating Employment - 14.1-14.6, 29.1, 29.6
    Chapter 17 - Laws Regulating Labor Management Relations - 29.1
    Chapter 18 - Legal Protections from Occupational Injuries - 29.4, 29.5
    Chapter 19 - Employment Discrimination - 29.3
Part VI - Laws and Regulations Affecting the Environment
    Chapter 20 - Environmental Protection - 31.1-31.5
Part VII - Business and Society
    Chapter 21 - Social Responsibility of Business - 35.1-35.3

Howell, Allison, Henley, *Fundamentals of Business Law*, The Dryden Press, 1984.

Part I - Introduction to the Legal System
    Chapter 1 - The American Legal System - 4.1-4.4, 5.1, 6.1
    Chapter 2 - Major Bodies of Law - 7.1, 8.1
Part II - Principles of Contract Law
    Chapter 3 - Nature and Classification of Contracts - 11.1
    Chapter 4 - The Agreement - 11.2, 11.3
    Chapter 5 - Consideration - 11.4
    Chapter 6 - Contractual Capacity - 11.6
    Chapter 7 - Illegality - 11.7
    Chapter 8 - Reality of Consent - 11.5
    Chapter 9 - Contracts in Writing - 11.8, 11.9
    Chapter 10 - Rights of Third Parties - 11.10, 11.11
    Chapter 11 - Discharge of Contracts - 11.12, 11.13

Howell, Allison, Prentice, *Business Law,* Fourth Edition and Fourth Alternate Edition, The Dryden Press, 1988.

Part V - Secured Transactions and Bankruptcy
 Chapter 29 - Secured Transaction - 17.1-17.5
 Chapter 30 - Bankruptcy - 26.1-26.5
Part VI - Business Organizations
 Chapter 31 - Forms of Business Organization - 15.1, 15.5, 16.1
 Chapter 32 - Partnerships: Nature, Formation, and Property - 15.1
 Chapter 33 - Partnerships: Operating the Business - 15.2, 15.3
 Chapter 34 - Partnerships: Termination - 15.4
 Chapter 35 - Limited Partnerships - 15.5
 Chapter 36 - Corporations: Nature and Formation - 16.1, 16.2
 Chapter 37 - Corporations: Corporate Powers and Management - 16.3, 16.4
 Chapter 38 - Corporations: Rights and Liabilities of Shareholders and Managers - 16.5-16.7
 Chapter 39 - Corporations: Merger, Consolidation, and Termination - 16.8
 Chapter 40 - Legal Liability of Accountants - 33.1-33.5
Part VII - Property: Ownership, Control, and Protection
 Chapter 41 - Real Property - 20.1
 Chapter 42 - Landlord and Tenant - 22.1-22.5
 Chapter 43 - Personal Property and Bailments - 19.1-19.3
 Chapter 44 - Wills, Trusts, and Estate Planning - 24.1-24.5
 Chapter 45 - Insurance and Risk Management - 23.1-23.4
Part VIII - Government Regulation of Business
 Chapter 46 - Government Regulation: An Overview - 27.1
 Chapter 47 - Antitrust Law: The Sherman Act - 27.2, 27.3
 Chapter 48 - Antitrust Law: The Clayton and Robinson-Patman Acts - 27.4, 27.5
 Chapter 49 - Employment Law - 29.1-29.6
 Chapter 50 - Securities Regulation - 28.1-28.4
 Chapter 51 - Consumer Transactions and the Law - 30.1-30.4
 Chapter 52 - The Legal Aspects of International Business - 32.1-32.3

Jennings, *Business and the Legal Environment*, PWS-Kent Publishing Company, 1988.

Part I - Laws and the Court System
 Chapter 1 - Introduction to Law - 4.1-4.4
 Chapter 2 - The Judicial System - 5.1, 5.2
 Chapter 3 - Lawsuits and Dispute Resolution - 6.1, 6.2
 Chapter 4 - Administrative Law - 8.1-8.6
 Chapter 5 - Business and the Constitution - 7.1-7.8
 Chapter 6 - Business Crime - 9.4, 10.1-10.5
Part II - Business Management -- Employment and Labor Law
 Chapter 7 - Management of Employee Conduct -- Agency - 14.1-14.6
 Chapter 8 - Management of Employee Welfare -- Statutory Protections - 29.2-29.6
 Chapter 9 - Personnel Management Issues - 29.3
 Chapter 10 - Labor Law - 29.1
Part III - Business Forms and Capitalization
 Chapter 11 - Forms of Doing Business - 15.1, 15.5, 16.1
 Chapter 12 - Securities Law - 28.1-28.4
 Chapter 13 - Takeovers, Mergers, and Consolidations - 27.1-27.6
Part IV - Business Production and Sales
 Chapter 14 - Contracts - 11.1-11.13
 Chapter 15 - Credit Regulation - 25.1-25.4, 30.3
 Chapter 16 - Advertising and Deceptive Trade Practices - 30.4
 Chapter 17 - Product Liability - 12.9, 30.5
 Chapter 18 - Environmental Regulation - 31.1-31.5
Part V - Business and Competition
 Chapter 19 - Horizontal Trade Restraints - 27.2
 Chapter 20 - Vertical Trade Restraints - 27.3
 Chapter 21 - Business Interference -- Tort Protection - 9.4
Part VI - Business Interaction with Law and Society
 Chapter 22 - Business Ethics - 35.1-35.3
 Chapter 23 - Legal and Political Strategic Planning

Jentz, Clarkson, Miller, *West's Business Law*, Second Edition, West Publishing Company, 1984.

Unit I - The Legal Environment of Business
- Chapter 1 - Introduction to the Study of Law - 4.1-4.4
- Chapter 2 - Courts and Procedures - 5.1, 5.2
- Chapter 3 - Torts - 9.1-9.3
- Chapter 4 - Torts Related to Business - 9.4
- Chapter 5 - Criminal Law - 10.1-10.5

Unit II - Contracts
- Chapter 6 - Contracts/Nature, Form, and Terminology - 11.1
- Chapter 7 - Contracts/Agreement - 11.2, 11.3
- Chapter 8 - Contracts/Consideration - 11.4
- Chapter 9 - Contracts/Contractual Capacity - 11.6
- Chapter 10 - Contracts/Legality - 11.7
- Chapter 11 - Contracts/Genuineness of Assent - 11.5
- Chapter 12 - Contracts/Writing and Form - 11.8, 11.9
- Chapter 13 - Contracts/Third Party Rights - 11.10, 11.11
- Chapter 14 - Contracts/Performance and Discharge - 11.12
- Chapter 15 - Contracts/Breach of Contract and Remedies - 11.13

Unit III - Personal Property and Bailments
- Chapter 16 - Personal Property - 19.1, 19.2
- Chapter 17 - Bailments - 19.3

Unit IV - Commercial Transactions and the Uniform Commercial Code
- Chapter 18 - Sales/Introduction to Sales Contracts and Their Formation - 12.1, 12.2, 12.3
- Chapter 19 - Sales/Title, Risk, and Insurable Interest - 12.4
- Chapter 20 - Sales/Introduction to Sales Warranties - 12.8
- Chapter 21 - Sales/Products Liability - 12.9
- Chapter 22 - Sales/Performance and Obligation - 12.5
- Chapter 23 - Sales/Remedies of Buyer and Seller for Breach of Sales Contracts - 12.6, 12.7
- Chapter 24 - Commercial Paper/Basic Concepts of Commercial Paper - 13.1
- Chapter 25 - Commercial Paper/The Negotiable Instrument - 13.2
- Chapter 26 - Commercial Paper/Transferability and Negotiation - 13.4
- Chapter 27 - Commercial Paper/Holder in Due Course - 13.5
- Chapter 28 - Commercial Paper/Liability, Defenses, and Discharge - 13.6
- Chapter 29 - Commercial Paper/Checks and the Banking System - 13.7
- Chapter 30 - Secured Transactions/Introduction - 17.1-17.3
- Chapter 31 - Secured Transactions/Liens and Priorities - 17.4, 17.5

Unit V - Creditors' Rights and Bankruptcy
- Chapter 32 - Rights of Debtors and Creditors - 25.3, 26.4
- Chapter 33 - Bankruptcy and Reorganization - 26.1-26.5

Unit VI - Agency and Employment
- Chapter 34 - Agency Creation, and Duties and Rights of Agents and Principals - 14.1, 14.2
- Chapter 35 - Liability of Principals and Agents to Third Parties and Termination of Agency Relationship - 14.3-14.6

Unit VII - Business Organizations
- Chapter 36 - Forms of Business Organization - 15.1, 15.5, 16.1
- Chapter 37 - Partnerships/Creation and Termination - 15.1, 15.4
- Chapter 38 - Partnerships/Operation and Duties - 15.2, 15.3
- Chapter 39 - Partnerships/Limited Partnerships - 15.5
- Chapter 40 - Corporations/Nature and Classifications - 16.1
- Chapter 41 - Corporations/Formation and Corporate Financing - 16.2, 16.7
- Chapter 42 - Corporations/Corporate Powers and Management - 16.3, 16.4
- Chapter 43 - Corporations/Rights and Duties of Directors, Managers and Shareholders - 16.5-16.7
- Chapter 44 - Corporations/Merger, Consolidation and Termination - 16.8
- Chapter 45 - Corporations/Financial Regulation and Investor Protection - 16.6
- Chapter 46 - Corporations/Private Franchises - 16.1

Unit VIII - Government Regulation
- Chapter 47 - Government Regulation/Regulation and Administrative Agencies - 8.1-8.6
- Chapter 48 - Government Regulation/Consumer Protection - 30.1-30.5
- Chapter 49 - Government Regulation/Environmental Protection - 31.1-31.5
- Chapter 50 - Government Regulation/Antitrust: Statutes and Exemptions - 27.2-27.6
- Chapter 51 - Government Regulation/Antitrust: Enforcement and Trends - 27.1
- Chapter 52 - Government Regulation/Employment and Labor Relations Law - 29.1-29.6

Unit IX - Protection of Property and Other Interests
- Chapter 53 - Nature and Ownership of Real Property - 20.1
- Chapter 54 - Future Interests, Nonpossessory Interests, and Land Use Control - 20.2, 20.3, 21.1
- Chapter 55 - Insurance - 23.1-23.4
- Chapter 56 - Wills, Trusts, and Estates - 24.1-24.5

Kolasa, *The Legal Environment of Business*, Addison-Wesley Publishing Co., 1984.

Part I - Introduction to the Legal System and Process
Chapter 1 - Law, Business, and Society - 4.1-4.4
Chapter 2 - The Dynamic Bases of Law - 7.1, 8.1
Chapter 3 - Legal Systems - 5.1, 5.2
Chapter 4 - Legal Process - 6.1, 6.2
Part II - Fundamental Functional Areas of Law
Chapter 5 - Business Organizations - 15.1, 15.5, 16.1
Chapter 6 - Contracts - 11.1-11.3
Chapter 7 - Financial Operations - 13.1-13.10
Chapter 8 - Sales and Secured Transactions - 12.1-12.9, 17.1-17.5
Chapter 9 - Property - 19.1-19.3, 20.1-20.3, 21.1, 22.1-22.5
Chapter 10 - Crimes - 10.1-10.5
Chapter 11 - Torts - 9.1-9.6
Part III - Work and the Disposition of Wealth Attained
Chapter 12 - Taxation
Chapter 13 - Estates and Trusts - 24.1-24.5
Chapter 14 - Labor Law - 29.1-29.6
Part IV - Government Regulation of Business
Chapter 15 - Government Regulation: Trade and Transportation - 27.1
Chapter 16 - Government Regulation: Antitrust - 27.1-27.6
Chapter 17 - Government Regulation: Health and Safety - 12.8, 12.9, 29.4, 30.5
Chapter 18 - Government Regulation: Financial Protection - 26.1-26.5, 28.1-28.3, 29.5, 29.6, 30.3
Part V - Emerging Areas of Legal Concern
Chapter 19 - Computers and the Law - 34.1-34.7
Chapter 20 - Transnational Business Law - 32.1-32.3
Chapter 21 - Ethics and Responsibility - 35.1-35.3

Leete, *Business Law*, Second Edition, Macmillan Publishing Co., Inc., 1982.

Section I - Introduction
Chapter 1 - Nature, History, and Sources of Law - 4.1-4.4
Chapter 2 - Legal Procedure and the Judicial System - 5.1, 5.2
Chapter 3 - An Introduction to Torts and Crimes - 9.1, 10.1
Section II - Contracts
Chapter 4 - Introduction to Contracts - 11.1
Chapter 5 - Agreement: The Offer - 11.2
Chapter 6 - Agreement: The Acceptance - 11.3
Chapter 7 - Agreement: Reality of Consent - 11.5
Chapter 8 - Consideration - 11.4
Chapter 9 - Capacity to Contract - 11.6
Chapter 10 - Illegality - 11.7
Chapter 11 - Writing Requirements - 11.8, 11.9
Chapter 12 - Third-Party Rights - 11.10, 11.11
Chapter 13 - Contractual Performance and Discharge - 11.12
Chapter 14 - Contractual Breach and Remedies - 11.13
Section III - Sales
Chapter 15 - Creation of the Contract for Sale of Goods Under the Uniform Commercial Code - 12.1-12.3
Chapter 16 - Risk of Loss, Delivery Terms, and Transfer of Title - 12.4, 12.5
Chapter 17 - Warranties Under the Uniform Commercial Code, the Magnuson-Moss Warranty Act, and Products Liability - 12.8, 12.9
Chapter 18 - Performance of the Contract - 12.5
Chapter 19 - Rights and Remedies - 12.6, 12.7
Chapter 20 - Financing the Sale: Secured Transactions - 17.1-17.5
Section IV - Commercial Paper
Chapter 21 - Introduction, Nature, Types, Parties - 13.1, 13.2
Chapter 22 - Negotiability - 13.3
Chapter 23 - Transfer and Negotiation - 13.4
Chapter 24 - Holder in Due Course - 13.5
Chapter 25 - Presentment, Dishonor, Notice of Dishonor, and Protest - 13.6
Chapter 26 - Liability of the Parties and Discharge - 13.6
Chapter 27 - Checks and the Relationship of the Bank to Its Customers - 13.7
Section V - Property
Chapter 28 - General Considerations and Personal Property - 19.1, 19.2
Chapter 29 - Bailments - 19.3
Chapter 30 - Real Property - 20.1, 20.3, 21.1
Chapter 31 - Landlord and Tenant - 22.1-22.5
Chapter 32 - Wills, Trusts, and Decedent's Estates - 24.1-24.5

Section VI - Agency
Chapter 33 - Nature, Creation, and Termination of the Agency Relationship - 14.1, 14.6
Chapter 34 - Duties and Liabilities of Agent and Principal - 14.2
Chapter 35 - Rights and Liabilities of Principal and Third Party - 14.3-14.5
Chapter 36 - Rights and Liabilities of Agent and Third Party - 14.3-14.5
Section VII - Partnership
Chapter 37 - Definition, Creation, and Property - 15.1, 15.5
Chapter 38 - Relationships Among Partners and Third Parties - 15.2, 15.3
Chapter 39 - Dissolution and Winding Up - 15.4
Section VIII - Corporations
Chapter 40 - Nature and Formation - 16.1, 16.2
Chapter 41 - Corporate Powers - 16.3
Chapter 42 - The Financial Structure of Corporations - 16.6, 16.7
Chapter 43 - Shareholder Rights and Liabilities - 16.5
Chapter 44 - Management of the Corporation - 16.4
Chapter 45 - Corporate Dissolution - 16.8
Section IX - Government Protection of Business and the Consumer
Chapter 46 - The Antitrust Laws: An Overview - 27.1-27.6
Chapter 47 - Consumer Protection - 30.1-30.5
Chapter 48 - Background of the Bankruptcy Code and Chapter 7 Liquidation - 26.1-26.4
Chapter 49 - Reorganization and Adjustment of Debts Under the Bankruptcy Code - 26.5

Leete, Fox, *Business Law and the Legal Environment,* Third Edition, Allyn & Bacon, Inc., 1989.

Part I - Introduction to Business Law
Chapter 1 - Nature, History, and Sources of Law - 4.1-4.4
Chapter 2 - Legal Procedure and the Judicial System - 5.1, 5.2
Chapter 3 - The Constitutional Basis for Governmental Regulation of Business - 7.1-7.8
Chapter 4 - Torts -- International, Negligence and Strict Liability - 9.5, 9.6, 32.1
Chapter 5 - Business and Criminal Law - 10.1-10.5
Part II - Contracts
Chapter 6 - Introduction to Contracts - 11.1
Chapter 7 - Agreement: The Offer - 11.2
Chapter 8 - Agreement: The Acceptance - 11.3
Chapter 9 - Agreement: Reality of Consent - 11.5
Chapter 10 - Consideration - 11.4
Chapter 11 - Capacity to Contract - 11.6
Chapter 12 - Illegality - 11.7
Chapter 13 - Writing Requirements - 11.8, 11.9
Chapter 14 - Third-Party Rights - 11.10, 11.11
Chapter 15 - Contractual Performance and Discharge - 11.12
Chapter 16 - Contractual Breach and Remedies - 11.13
Part III - Sales
Chapter 17 - Creation of Contracts for Sale of Goods Under the Uniform Commercial Code - 12.1-12.3
Chapter 18 - Risk of Loss, Delivery Terms, and Transfer of Title - 12.4
Chapter 19 - Warranties Under the Uniform Commercial Code and the Magnuson-Moss Act - 12.8
Chapter 20 - Product Liability -- Negligence, Warranty and Strict Liability - 12.9
Chapter 21 - Performance of the Contract - 12.5
Chapter 22 - Rights and Remedies - 12.6, 12.7
Chapter 23 - Financing the Sale: Secured Transactions - 17.1-17.5
Part IV - Commercial Paper
Chapter 24 - Commercial Paper and Negotiability - 13.1-13.3
Chapter 25 - Transfer and Negotiation - 13.4
Chapter 26 - Holder in Due Course - 13.5
Chapter 27 - Liability of Parties - 13.6
Chapter 28 - Checks and the Relationship of the Bank to its Customers - 13.7
Part V - Property
Chapter 29 - General Considerations and Personal Property - 19.1, 19.2
Chapter 30 - Bailments - 19.3
Chapter 31 - Real Property - 20.1, 20.3, 21.1
Chapter 32 - Landlord and Tenant - 22.1-22.5
Chapter 33 - Wills, Trusts, and Decedent's Estates - 24.1-24.5
Part VI - Agency and Partnership
Chapter 34 - Nature, Creation, and Termination of Agency Relationship - 14.1, 14.6
Chapter 35 - Duties and Liabilities of Agent and Principal - 14.2
Chapter 36 - Rights and Liabilities of Principal, Agent, and Third Parties - 14.3-14.5
Chapter 37 - Partnerships: Definition, Creation, and Property - 15.1
Chapter 38 - Relationships Among Partners and Third Parties - 15.2, 15.3
Chapter 39 - Dissolution and Winding Up - 15.4

Part VII - Corporations
- Chapter 40 - Corporations: Nature, Formation, and Dissolution - 16.1, 16.2, 16.8
- Chapter 41 - Corporate Powers - 16.3
- Chapter 42 - The Financial Structure of Corporations - 16.7
- Chapter 43 - Corporations: Shareholder Rights and Liabilities - 16.5-16.7
- Chapter 44 - Management of the Corporation - 16.4

Part VIII - The Legal Environment: Government Regulation of Business and Consumer Protection
- Chapter 45 - Administrative Agencies and the Administrative Process - 8.1-8.6
- Chapter 46 - The Antitrust Laws: An Overview - 27.1-27.6
- Chapter 47 - The Federal Trade Commission and Consumer Protection - 27.6
- Chapter 48 - Securities Regulation - 28.1-28.4
- Chapter 49 - Employment and Labor Relations Law - 29.1-29.6
- Chapter 50 - The Federal Bankruptcy Code - 26.1-26.5
- Chapter 51 - Insurance and Its Regulation - 23.1-23.4

Part IX - The Legal Environment: Ethical and Social Considerations
- Chapter 52 - Liability of Accountants and Other Professionals - 33.1-33.5
- Chapter 53 - Business Ethics - 35.1-35.3
- Chapter 54 - The International Environment of Business - 32.1-32.3

Lieberman, Siedel, *Business Law and the Legal Environment*, Second Edition, Harcourt Brace Jovanovich, Inc., 1988.

Part One - The Legal Environment
- Chapter 1 - Law and the Legal System - 4.1-4.4
- Chapter 2 - Courts and the Legal Process - 5.1, 5.2, 6.1, 6.2
- Chapter 3 - Criminal Law - 10.1-10.5
- Chapter 4 - Torts - 9.1-9.4
- Chapter 5 - Administrative Law - 8.1-8.6
- Chapter 6 - Business Ethics and Social Responsibility - 35.1-35.3

Part Two - Contracts
- Chapter 7 - Introduction to Contract Law - 11.1
- Chapter 8 - The Agreement - 11.2, 11.3
- Chapter 9 - Consideration - 11.4
- Chapter 10 - Legality and Consumer Credit Transactions - 11.7
- Chapter 11 - Free Will, Knowledge, and Capacity - 11.6
- Chapter 12 - Form and Meaning - 11.8, 11.9
- Chapter 13 - Outsiders - 11.10, 11.11
- Chapter 14 - Discharge of Obligations - 11.12
- Chapter 15 - Remedies - 11.13

Part Three - The Sale, Storage, and Shipment of Goods
- Chapter 16 - Introduction to Sales - 12.1-12.3
- Chapter 17 - Title and Risk of Loss - 12.4
- Chapter 18 - Performance and Remedies - 12.5-12.7
- Chapter 19 - Product Liability - 12.9
- Chapter 20 - Bailments and the Storage and Shipment of Goods - 19.3

Part Four - Commercial Paper
- Chapter 21 - Nature and Form of Commercial Paper - 13.1-13.3
- Chapter 22 - Negotiation of Commercial Paper - 13.4
- Chapter 23 - Holder in Due Course and Defenses - 13.5
- Chapter 24 - Liability and Discharge - 13.6
- Chapter 25 - Legal Aspects of Banking - 13.7

Part Five - Debtors and Creditors
- Chapter 26 - Secured Transactions and Suretyship - 17.1-17.5, 18.1-18.3
- Chapter 27 - Mortgages and Nonconsensual Liens - 21.1-21.4
- Chapter 28 - Bankruptcy - 26.1-26.5

Part Six - Property, Estate Planning, and Insurance
- Chapter 29 - Introduction to Property: Personal Property and Fixtures - 19.1, 19.2
- Chapter 30 - Intellectual Property - 19.2
- Chapter 31 - The Nature and Regulation of Real Estate - 20.1
- Chapter 32 - The Transfer of Real Estate by Sale - 20.3, 21.1
- Chapter 33 - Landlord and Tenant Law - 22.1-22.5
- Chapter 34 - Estate Planning: Wills, Estates, and Trusts - 24.1-24.5
- Chapter 35 - Insurance - 23.1-23.4

Part Seven - Agency
- Chapter 36 - Relationships Between Principal and Agent - 14.2
- Chapter 37 - Liability of Principal and Agent; Termination of Agency - 14.3-14.6

Part Eight - Partnership
- Chapter 38 - General Characteristics and Formation - 15.1
- Chapter 39 - Partnership Operation and Termination; Other Forms - 15.2-15.5

Part Nine - Corporations
Chapter 40 - General Characteristics and Formation - 16.1, 16.2
Chapter 41 - Legal Aspects of Corporate Finance - 16.6, 16.7
Chapter 42 - Corporate Powers and Management - 16.3, 16.4
Chapter 43 - Securities Regulation - 16.6
Chapter 44 - Corporate Expansion and Dissolution - 16.8
Part Ten - The Regulatory Environment
Chapter 45 - Antitrust 1: Restraints of Trade - 27.1, 27.2
Chapter 46 - Antitrust 2: Concentrations of Power - 27.3
Chapter 47 - Unfair and Deceptive Trade Practices - 30.4
Chapter 48 - International Aspects of Doing Business - 32.1-32.3
Chapter 49 - Labor and Employment Law - 29.1-29.6
Chapter 50 - Liability and Regulation of Professionals - 33.1-33.5

Lyden, Reitzel, Roberts, *Business and the Law,* McGraw-Hill, Inc., 1985.

Part One - Law and the Legal System
Chapter 1 - The Background and Scope of Business Law - 4.1-4.4
Chapter 2 - The Court System; Civil Procedure; Arbitration - 5.1, 5.2, 6.1, 6.2
Part Two - Tort and Criminal Law
Chapter 3 - The Nature of Torts; Intentional Torts - 9.1-9.3
Chapter 4 - Unintentional Torts and Business Torts - 9.4-9.6
Chapter 5 - Criminal Law; Computer and Other White-Collar Crimes - 10.1-10.5
Part Three - Contracts
Chapter 6 - Introduction to the Law of Contracts - 11.1
Chapter 7 - Offer - 11.2
Chapter 8 - Acceptance - 11.3
Chapter 9 - Consideration - 11.4
Chapter 10 - Contractual Capacity; Avoidance of Contracts - 11.5, 11.6
Chapter 11 - Illegal Agreements - 11.7
Chapter 12 - Form and Interpretation of Contracts; Parol Evidence Rule - 11.8, 11.9
Chapter 13 - Rights and Duties of Third Parties - 11.10, 11.11
Chapter 14 - Performance, Breach, and Discharge; Remedies in Contract Actions - 11.12, 11.13
Part Four - Sales
Chapter 15 - Introduction to the Law of Sales; The Sales Contract - 12.1-12.3
Chapter 16 - Distribution of Goods; Transfer of Title and Risk of Loss - 12.4, 13.10
Chapter 17 - Performance of the Sales Contract - 12.5
Chapter 18 - Product Liability - 12.8, 12.9
Chapter 19 - Remedies for Breach of the Sales Contract - 12.6, 12.7
Part Five - Agency
Chapter 20 - Creation of Agency; Contract Rights and Obligations of Principal and Agent - 14.1, 14.3-14.5
Chapter 21 - Principal's Liability for an Agent's Torts - 14.4, 14.5
Chapter 22 - Obligations of Principals and Agents to Each Other; Termination of Agency - 14.2, 14.6
Part Six - Property and Estates
Chapter 23 - Nature of Property; Personal Property (Including Bailments) - 14.1-14.3
Chapter 24 - Real Property: Nature, Acquisition, and Ownership - 20.1-20.3
Chapter 25 - Interests in Real Property - 20.1, 20.3, 21.1, 22.1-22.5
Chapter 26 - Estates and Wills - 24.1-24.5
Part Seven - Secured Transactions and Insurance
Chapter 27 - Purpose and Types of Secured Transactions; Suretyship - 18.1-18.3
Chapter 28 - Secured Transactions in Personal Property - 17.1-17.5
Chapter 29 - Insurance - 23.1-23.4
Part Eight - Commercial Paper
Chapter 30 - Nature of Commercial Paper; Negotiable Form; Personal and Real Defenses - 13.1-13.3, 13.5
Chapter 31 - Negotiation of Commercial Paper; Holder-in-Due-Course Status - 13.4, 13.5
Chapter 32 - Liability of the Parties; Discharge - 13.6
Chapter 33 - Checks; Relationship Between Bank and Customer - 13.7
Part Nine - Business Organizations
Chapter 34 - Introduction to Business Organizations; Formation of Partnerships - 15.1
Chapter 35 - Termination of Partnerships - 15.4
Chapter 36 - Limited Partnerships - 15.5
Chapter 37 - Formation of Corporations - 16.1, 16.2
Chapter 38 - Financing of Corporations - 16.6, 16.7
Chapter 39 - Management of Corporations - 16.3, 16.4
Chapter 40 - Shareholders' Powers, Rights, and Liabilities - 16.5
Part Ten - Government Regulation of Business
Chapter 41 - Regulating Business Conduct, Scope, and Size - 8.1, 27.1-27.6
Chapter 42 - Consumer Protection - 27.6, 30.1-30.5
Chapter 43 - Employment-Labor Law; Workers' Compensation - 29.1-29.6
Chapter 44 - Bankruptcy - 26.1-26.5

Maurer, *Business Law*, Second Edition, Harcourt Brace Jovanovich, Inc., 1987.

McAdams, Donnella, Freeman, Newlund, *Law, Business, and Society*, Second Edition, Richard D. Irwin, Inc., 1989.

Part I - Business and Society
  Chapter 1 - Capitalism and Collectivism
  Chapter 2 - Ethics - 35.1-35.3
  Chapter 3 - The Corporation in Society: Social Responsibility - 35.2
Part II - Introduction to Law
  Chapter 4 - The American Legal System - 4.1-4.4, 5.1, 6.1
  Chapter 5 - Constitutional Law and the Bill of Rights - 7.1-7.8
Part III - Trade Regulation and Antitrust
  Chapter 6 - Government Regulation of Business: An Introduction - 8.1
  Chapter 7 - Administrative Agencies and the Regulatory Process - 8.1-8.6
  Chapter 8 - Business Organizations and Securities Regulation - 28.1-28.4
  Chapter 9 - Antitrust Law - Monopolies and Mergers - 27.3
  Chapter 10 - Antitrust Law - Restraints of Trade - 27.2
Part IV - Employer-Employee Relations
  Chapter 11 - Labor and General Employment Law - 29.1-29.6
  Chapter 12 - Employment Discrimination - 29.3
Part V - Business and Selected Social Problems
  Chapter 13 - Consumer Protection - 30.1-30.5
  Chapter 14 - Products Liability - 12.9, 30.5
  Chapter 15 - Environmental Protection - 31.1-31.5

McCarty, Bagby, *The Legal Environment of Business*, Richard D. Irwin, Inc., 1990.

Part 1 - The American Legal System
  Chapter 1 - Law and the Legal System - 4.1-4.4
  Chapter 2 - The American Legal System - 5.1, 5.2
  Chapter 3 - Dispute Resolution - 6.1, 6.2
  Chapter 4 - Constitution Law - 7.1-7.8
  Chapter 5 - Administrative Law - 8.1-8.6
Part 2 - Private Law
  Chapter 6 - Property - 19.1-19.3, 20.1-20.3
  Chapter 7 - Contracts - 11.1-11.13
  Chapter 8 - Torts - 9.1-9.6
Part 3 - Consumer Law
  Chapter 9 - Product Liability - 12.9, 30.5
  Chapter 10 - Consumer Financing - 30.3
Part 4 - Business Organizations
  Chapter 11 - Agency - 14.1-14.6
  Chapter 12 - Partnerships and Corporations - 15.1-15.5, 16.1-16.8
  Chapter 13 - Securities Regulations - 28.1-28.4
Part 5 - Antitrust Law
  Chapter 14 - Monopolies and Mergers - 27.3
  Chapter 15 - Antitrust Law: Restraints of Trade, Price, Discrimination and Unfair Trade Practices - 27.2, 27.4-27.6
Part 6 - Labor Law
  Chapter 16 - Labor Relations Management: Regulations of Management - 29.2
  Chapter 17 - Labor Relations Management: Regulation of Unions - 29.1
  Chapter 18 - Employee Standards, Compensation, and Safety - 29.4-29.6
  Chapter 19 - Equal Opportunity - 29.3
Part 7 - Government Regulation and Social Policies
  Chapter 20 - Environmental Law - 31.1-31.5
  Chapter 21 - The Legal Environment for International Business - 32.1-32.3
  Chapter 22 - The Social Responsibility of Business - 35.1-35.3

McGuire, *The Legal Environment of Business: Commerce and Public Policy*, Charles E. Merrill Publishing Co., 1986.

Part I - The Legal Process
  Chapter 1 - The Cornerstones of Law and Government - 4.1-4.4
  Chapter 2 - The American Constitution: Background, the Commerce Clause, and Economic Liberties - 7.1-7.8
  Chapter 3 - The Bill of Rights - 7.5
  Chapter 4 - The American Court System - 5.1, 5.2
  Chapter 5 - Administrative Agencies - 8.1-8.6
Part II - The Common Law Foundations
  Chapter 6 - The Common Law Heritage: Contracts, Torts, and Property - 4.3, 9.1-9.6, 11.1-11.13, 20.1
  Chapter 7 - The Legal Structure of Business: Agency, Partnerships, and Corporations - 14.1-14.6, 15.1-15.5, 16.1-16.8

Part III - Regulation of the Relationship Between Business, Its Competitors, and Its Suppliers
Chapter 8 - Antitrust Law: Background, Structures, and the Sherman Act - 27.1-27.3
Chapter 9 - Antitrust Law: Price Discrimination, Monopolization, and Legal Monopolies - 27.2, 27.3, 27.5
Chapter 10 - Antitrust Law: Regulation of Mergers - 27.4
Part IV - Regulation of the Relationship Between Business and Its Customers
Chapter 11 - Deceptive Advertising and Unfair Competition: The Common Law and the FTC - 27.6, 30.4
Chapter 12 - Consumer Law - 30.1-30.5
Part V - Regulation of the Relationship Between Business and Its Employees
Chapter 13 - Labor Law: Labor-Management Relations - 29.1
Chapter 14 - Labor Law: Regulation of Worker Safety, Wages, and Security - 29.2-29.6
Part VI - Regulation of the Relationship Between Business and Its Investors
Chapter 15 - Regulation of Securities and Corporate Structure - 16.6, 16.7, 28.1-28.4
Part VII - Regulation of the Relationship Between Business and the Public
Chapter 16 - Discrimination - 29.3
Chapter 17 - Regulation of Energy and the Environment - 31.1-31.5
Part VIII - Other Relationships of Business and Government
Chapter 18 - Taxation
Chapter 19 - Economic Regulation and the Concept of "Deregulation"
Part IX - Beyond the Law: The Social and Ethical Responsibilities of Business
Chapter 20 - Ethics and the Law - 35.1-35.3

Metzger, Mallor, Barnes, Bowers, Phillips, *Business Law and the Regulatory Environment: Concepts and Cases*, Seventh Edition, Richard D. Irwin, Inc., 1989.

Part One - The American Legal System
Chapter 1 - The Nature of Law - 4.1-4.4
Chapter 2 - Court Structure, Jurisdiction, and Civil Procedure - 5.1, 5.2, 6.1, 6.2
Part Two - Crimes and Torts
Chapter 3 - Crimes - 10.1-10.5
Chapter 4 - Intentional Torts - 9.2, 9.3
Chapter 5 - Negligence and Strict Liability - 9.5, 9.6
Chapter 6 - The Protection of Creative Endeavor and Competitive Torts - 9.4
Part Three - Contracts
Chapter 7 - Introduction to Contracts - 11.1
Chapter 8 - The Agreement: Offer - 11.2
Chapter 9 - The Agreement: Acceptance - 11.3
Chapter 10 - Reality of Consent - 11.5
Chapter 11 - Consideration - 11.4
Chapter 12 - Capacity of Parties - 11.6
Chapter 13 - Illegality - 11.7
Chapter 14 - Writing - 11.8, 11.9
Chapter 15 - Rights of Third Parties - 11.10, 11.11
Chapter 16 - Performance and Remedies - 11.12, 11.13
Part Four - Sales
Chapter 17 - Formation and Terms of Sales Contracts - 12.1-12.3
Chapter 18 - Product Liability - 12.8, 12.9
Chapter 19 - Performance of Sales Contracts - 12.5
Chapter 20 - Remedies for Breach of Sales Contracts - 12.6, 12.7
Part Five - Property
Chapter 21 - Personal Property and Bailments - 19.1-19.3
Chapter 22 - Real Property - 20.1-20.3, 21.1, 22.1-22.5
Chapter 23 - Estates and Trusts - 24.1-24.5
Part Six - Credit
Chapter 24 - Introduction to Credit and Secured Transactions - 17.1
Chapter 25 - Security Interests in Personal Property - 17.1, 17.3
Chapter 26 - Bankruptcy - 26.1-26.5
Part Seven - Commercial Paper
Chapter 27 - Negotiable Instruments - 13.1-13.3
Chapter 28 - Negotiation and Holder in Due Course - 13.4, 13.5
Chapter 29 - Liability of Parties - 13.6
Chapter 30 - Checks and Documents of Title - 13.7, 13.10
Part Eight - Agency Law
Chapter 31 - The Agency Relationship - 14.1, 14.2, 14.6
Chapter 32 - Third-Party Relations of the Principal and the Agent - 14.3-14.5
Part Nine - Partnership Law
Chapter 33 - Introduction to Sole Proprietorship, Partnership and Related Forms - 15.1
Chapter 34 - Operation of Partnerships and Related Forms - 15.2, 15.3
Chapter 35 - Dissolution, Winding Up and Termination of Partnerships - 15.4
Chapter 36 - Limited Partnerships - 15.5

Part Ten - Corporations
Chapter 37 - History and Nature of Corporations - 16.1
Chapter 38 - Organization, Financial Structure, and Dissolution of Corporations - 16.2, 16.7, 16.8
Chapter 39 - Managing the Corporation - 16.3, 16.4
Chapter 40 - Shareholders' Rights and Liabilities - 16.5
Chapter 41 - Securities Regulation - 28.1-28.4
Chapter 42 - Legal Responsibilities of Accountants - 33.1-33.5
Part Eleven - Regulation of Business
Chapter 43 - Business and the Constitution - 7.1-7.8
Chapter 44 - Administrative Agencies - 8.1-8.6
Chapter 45 - Antitrust: The Sherman Act - 27.1-27.3
Chapter 46 - The Clayton Act, The Robinson-Patman Act, and Antitrust Exemptions and Immunities - 27.4, 27.5
Chapter 47 - The Federal Trade Commission and Consumer Protection Laws - 27.6, 30.1-30.5
Chapter 48 - Employment Law - 29.1-29.6
Chapter 49 - Environmental Regulation - 31.1-31.5
Chapter 50 - The Legal Environment for International Business - 32.1-32.3
Chapter 51 - Computer Law - 34.1-34.7
Chapter 52 - Business Ethics, Corporate Social Responsibility, and the Control and Governance of Corporations - 35.1-35.3

Miller, Jentz, *Business Law Today*, West Publishing Company, 1988.

Unit One - The Legal Environment of Business
Chapter 1 - Law as a Contemporary Social Force - 4.1-4.4
Chapter 2 - Courts and Procedures - 5.1, 5.2, 6.1, 6.2
Chapter 3 - Torts - 9.1-9.6
Chapter 4 - Criminal Law - 10.1-10.5
Unit Two - Contracts
Chapter 5 - Nature and Classification - 11.1
Chapter 6 - Agreement and Consideration - 11.2, 11.3
Chapter 7 - Capacity and Legality - 11.6, 11.7
Chapter 8 - Genuineness of Assent and Form - 11.5, 11.8, 11.9
Chapter 9 - Third-Party Rights and Discharge - 11.10-11.12
Chapter 10 - Breach and Remedies - 11.13
Unit Three - Commercial Transactions, Sales, and the Uniform Commercial Code
Chapter 11 - Introduction to Sales Contracts and Their Formation - 12.1-12.3
Chapter 12 - Title, Risk, and Insurable Interest - 12.4
Chapter 13 - Performance and Breach - 12.5-12.7
Chapter 14 - Warranties and Product Liability - 12.8, 12.9
Chapter 15 - Commercial Paper -- Basic Concepts - 13.1
Chapter 16 - Commercial Paper -- The Negotiable Instrument, Transferability, and Negotiation - 13.2-13.4
Chapter 17 - Commercial Paper -- Holder in Due Course, Liability, and Defenses - 13.5, 13.6
Chapter 18 - Commercial Paper -- Checks and the Banking System - 13.7
Chapter 19 - Secured Transactions - 17.1-17.5
Chapter 20 - Creditors' Rights and Bankruptcy - 25.3, 26.1-26.5
Unit Four - Business Organizations
Chapter 21 - The Entrepreneur's Options - 15.1, 15.5, 16.1
Chapter 22 - Agency - 14.1-14.6
Chapter 23 - Partnerships -- Creation and Termination - 15.1-15.4
Chapter 24 - Partnerships -- Operation and Duties - 15.2, 15.3
Chapter 25 - Corporations -- Formation and Classification - 16.1, 16.2
Chapter 26 - Corporations -- Corporate Powers and Management - 16.3, 16.4
Chapter 27 - Corporations -- Rights and Duties of Directors, Managers, and Shareholders - 16.4, 16.5
Chapter 28 - Corporations -- Merger, Consolidation, and Termination - 16.8
Chapter 29 - Corporations -- Financing, Financial Regulation, and Investor Protection - 16.6, 16.7
Unit Five - Government Regulation
Chapter 30 - Antitrust - 27.1-27.6
Chapter 31 - Consumer and Environmental Law - 30.1-30.5, 31.1-31.5
Chapter 32 - Employee and Labor Law - 29.1-29.6
Unit Six - Property, Its Protection, and the International Legal Environment
Chapter 33 - Personal Property and Bailments - 19.1-19.3
Chapter 34 - Real Property - 20.1-20.3, 21.1, 22.1-22.5
Chapter 35 - Insurance, Wills, and Trusts - 23.1-23.4, 24.1-24.5
Chapter 36 - International Law in a Global Economy - 32.1-32.3
Unit Seven - Ethics and Social Responsibility
Chapter 37 - Ethics and Social Responsibility - 35.1-35.3

Moran, *Practical Business Law*, Second Edition, Prentice-Hall, Inc., 1989.

Part One - Introduction to the Law
- Chapter 1 - The History of Law - 4.1-4.4
- Chapter 2 - The American Legal System - 4.3
- Chapter 3 - Court Practice and Procedure - 5.1, 5.2, 6.1
- Chapter 4 - Criminal Law and Procedure - 10.1-10.5
- Chapter 5 - Torts - 9.1-9.6

Part Two - Contract Law
- Chapter 6 - Contracts: An Introduction - 11.1
- Chapter 7 - Agreement - 11.2, 11.3
- Chapter 8 - Consideration - 11.4
- Chapter 9 - Legal Capacity - 11.6
- Chapter 10 - Lawful Purpose - 11.7
- Chapter 11 - Form and Interpretation - 11.8, 11.9
- Chapter 12 - Rights of Third Parties - 11.10, 11.11
- Chapter 13 - Remedies for Breach of Contract - 11.13
- Chapter 14 - Contractual Defenses - 11.12

Part Three - Commercial Law
- Chapter 15 - Sales: Title and Warranties - 12.1-12.4, 12.8, 13.10
- Chapter 16 - Sales: Performance and Risk of Loss - 12.4, 12.5
- Chapter 17 - Sales: Products Liability - 12.8, 12.9
- Chapter 18 - Sales: Buyer's Remedies - 12.6
- Chapter 19 - Sales: Seller's Remedies - 12.7
- Chapter 20 - Commercial Paper: Form and Negotiation - 13.1-13.4
- Chapter 21 - Commercial Paper: Holder in Due Course - 13.5
- Chapter 22 - Commercial Paper: Liability of the Parties, Bank Deposits, and Collections - 13.6, 13.7
- Chapter 23 - Secured Transactions - 17.1-17.5

Part Four - Property Law
- Chapter 24 - Bankruptcy - 26.1-26.5
- Chapter 25 - Bailments - 19.3
- Chapter 26 - Insurance - 23.1-23.4
- Chapter 27 - Suretyship - 18.1-18.3
- Chapter 28 - Real Estate Transactions - 20.1-20.3
- Chapter 29 - Forms of Ownership and Mortgages - 21.1
- Chapter 30 - Landlord and Tenant - 22.1-22.5
- Chapter 31 - Wills and Trust - 24.1-24.5

Part Five - Business Law
- Chapter 32 - Agency: Creation and Duties - 14.1, 14.2
- Chapter 33 - Agency: Liability and Termination - 14.3, 14.6
- Chapter 34 - Partnerships: Formation and Duties - 15.1, 15.2
- Chapter 35 - Partnerships: Dissolution and Liabilities - 15.3, 15.4
- Chapter 36 - Limited Partnerships - 15.5
- Chapter 37 - Corporate Formation - 16.1, 16.2
- Chapter 38 - Corporate Management - 16.3, 16.4
- Chapter 39 - Corporate Antitrust Legislation - 27.1-27.6

Reiling, Thompson, Brady, Macchiarola, *Business Law: Text and Cases,* Kent Publishing Co., 1981.

Part I - Introduction
Chapter 1 - Objectives and Nature of Law - 4.1-4.4
Chapter 2 - The Judicial Process - 5.1, 5.2, 6.1
Part II - Torts
Chapter 3 - Personal Injuries - 9.1-9.6
Part III - Contracts
Chapter 4 - Introduction to Contracts - 11.1
Chapter 5 - Manifestation of Assent - 11.2, 11.3
Chapter 6 - The Reality of Assent - 11.5
Chapter 7 - Consideration - 11.4
Chapter 8 - Capacity and Illegality - 11.6, 11.7
Chapter 9 - Proper Legal Form - 11.8, 11.9
Chapter 10 - Third Parties - 11.10, 11.11
Chapter 11 - Interpretation and Conditions - 11.12
Chapter 12 - Discharge, Breach, and Remedies - 11.12, 11.13
Part IV - Agency
Chapter 13 - Definition and Creation of Agency - 14.1
Chapter 14 - Principal's Relationship with Agent and Third Parties - 14.2-14.5
Chapter 15 - Agents, Third Parties, and Termination of Relationships - 14.3-14.6
Part V - Sale of Goods
Chapter 16 - Introduction to Sales - 12.1-12.3
Chapter 17 - Warranties of Quality - 12.8
Chapter 18 - Attempts to Limit Warranties - 12.8
Chapter 19 - Negligence and Strict Liability: Alternative Theories Protecting Against Defective Goods - 12.9
Chapter 20 - Risk of Loss - 12.4
Chapter 21 - Buyer's Rights and Remedies - 12.5-12.7
Chapter 22 - Seller's Rights and Remedies - 12.5-12.7
Chapter 23 - Good Faith Purchasers - 12.4
Part VI - Commercial Paper
Chapter 24 - Introduction to Commercial Paper - 13.1-13.4
Chapter 25 - The Holder in Due Course - 13.5, 13.6
Chapter 26 - Checks and Notes - 13.7
Part VII - Partnerships
Chapter 27 - Introduction to Partnerships - 15.1, 15.5
Chapter 28 - Partners, Partnership Property, and Third Parties - 15.2, 15.3
Chapter 29 - Dissolution and Winding Up - 15.4
Part VIII - Corporations
Chapter 30 - Introduction to Corporations - 16.1-16.3
Chapter 31 - Directors and Officers - 16.4
Chapter 32 - Stockholders' Rights - 16.5-16.8
Chapter 33 - Federal Security Regulations - 28.1-28.4
Part IX - Government Regulation of Employment and Competition
Chapter 34 - Government Regulation: In General and of Employment - 8.1, 29.1-29.6
Chapter 35 - Antitrust - 27.1-27.6
Part X - Control and Transfer of Property
Chapter 36 - Introduction to Property - 19.1
Chapter 37 - Personal Property - 19.2
Chapter 38 - Real Property - 20.1-20.3, 21.1, 22.1-22.5
Chapter 39 - Bailments - 19.3
Part XI - Secured Transactions and Suretyship
Chapter 40 - Secured Transactions - 17.1-17.5
Chapter 41 - Suretyship - 18.1-18.3
Part XII - Bankruptcy, Insurance, and Wills and Estates
Chapter 42 - Bankruptcy - 26.1-26.5
Chapter 43 - Basic Insurance Law - 23.1-23.4
Chapter 44 - Wills and Estates - 24.1-24.5

Reitzel, Lyden, Roberts, Severance, *Contemporary Business Law: Principles and Cases*, Fourth Edition, McGraw-Hill, Inc., 1990.

Part I - Law, Ethics, and the Legal System
- Chapter 1 - Nature and Development of Law in the United States - 4.1-4.4
- Chapter 2 - Law and Business Ethics - 35.1-35.3
- Chapter 3 - The Court System; Civil Procedure Arbitration - 5.1, 5.2, 6.1, 6.2

Part II - Tort and Criminal Law
- Chapter 4 - Nature of Torts; Intentional Torts - 9.1-9.3
- Chapter 5 - Unintentional Torts: Negligence and Liability without Fault - 9.5, 9.6
- Chapter 6 - Business Torts: Interference with Business Rights - 9.4
- Chapter 7 - Criminal Law; Computer and other White-Collar Crimes - 10.1-10.5

Part III - Contracts
- Chapter 8 - Introduction to the Law of Contracts - 11.1
- Chapter 9 - Mutual Assent: Offer and Acceptance - 11.2, 11.3
- Chapter 10 - Consideration - 11.4
- Chapter 11 - Avoidance of Agreement - 11.5
- Chapter 12 - Illegal Agreement - 11.7
- Chapter 13 - A Writing as a Requirement; the Parol Evidence Rule - 11.8, 11.9
- Chapter 14 - Rights and Duties of Third Persons - 11.10, 11.11
- Chapter 15 - Performance, Breach, and Discharge of Contracts; Remedies for Breach of Contract - 11.12, 11.13

Part IV - Sales
- Chapter 16 - Introduction to the Law of Sales; the Sales Contract - 12.1-12.3
- Chapter 17 - Part One: Delivery and Storage of Goods; Documents of Title - 12.4, 13.10
  Part Two: Transfer of Title and Risk of Loss; Title of Good Faith Purchasers - 12.3
- Chapter 18 - Product Liability - 12.8, 12.9
- Chapter 19 - Performance of the Sales Contract; Remedies for Breach of Contract - 12.5-12.7

Part V - Property and Estates -
- Chapter 20 - Nature and Importance of Property; Personal Property - 19.1, 19.2
- Chapter 21 - Real Property; Nature, Acquisition, and Ownership - 20.1-20.3, 21.1
- Chapter 22 - Interests in Real Property - 20.1
- Chapter 23 - Estates, Wills, and Trusts - 24.1-24.5

Part VI - Debtor-Creditor Relations
- Chapter 24 - Purpose and Types of Secured Transactions; Suretyship - 18.1-18.3
- Chapter 25 - Secured Transactions in Personal Property - 17.1-17.5
- Chapter 26 - Bankruptcy - 26.1-26.5

Part VII - Insurance
- Chapter 27 - Insurance - 23.1-23.4

Part VIII - Commercial Paper
- Chapter 28 - Nature of Commercial Paper; Negotiable Form - 13.1-13.3
- Chapter 29 - Personal and Real Defenses; Negotiation of Commercial Paper - 13.4
- Chapter 30 - Holder-in-Due-Course Status; FTC Limits - 13.5
- Chapter 31 - Liability of the Parties; Discharge - 13.6
- Chapter 32 - Checks; Relationship Between Bank and Customer; Electronic Funds Transfer - 13.7, 13.8

Part IX - Agency
- Chapter 33 - Creation of Agency; Contract Rights and Obligations of Principal and Agent - 14.1, 14.2
- Chapter 34 - Principals' Liability for Agents' Torts - 14.3-14.5
- Chapter 35 - Obligations of Principals and Agents to Each Other; Termination of Agency - 14.2, 14.6

Part X - Business Organizations
- Chapter 36 - Introduction to Business Organizations; Formation of Partnerships; Rights and Duties of Partners - 15.1-15.3
- Chapter 37 - Termination of Partnerships - 15.4
- Chapter 38 - Limited Partnerships - 15.5
- Chapter 39 - Nature and Formation of Corporations - 16.1, 16.2
- Chapter 40 - Financing Corporations - 16.6, 16.7
- Chapter 41 - Management of Corporations - 16.4
- Chapter 42 - Shareholders' Powers, Rights, and Liabilities - 16.5-16.8
- Chapter 43 - Securities Regulation and Accountants' Liability - 28.1-28.4, 33.1-33.5

Part XI - Government Regulation
- Chapter 44 - Role of Administrative Law in the Regulatory Process - 8.1-8.6
- Chapter 45 - Introduction to Antitrust Law; The Sherman Act - 27.1-27.3
- Chapter 46 - The Clayton, Robinson-Patman, and Federal Trade Commission Acts - 27.4-27.6
- Chapter 47 - Law of Labor and Employment - 29.1-29.6

Part XII - International Business Law
- Chapter 48 - Legal Aspects of International Business Transactions - 32.1-32.3

Scaletta, Cameron, *Foundations of Business Law,* Second Edition, Richard D. Irwin, Inc., 1990.

Part One - Legal Process and Legal Environment
- Chapter 1 - Legal Systems and Legal Sources - 4.1-4.4
- Chapter 2 - Courts and Civil Procedure - 5.1, 5.2, 6.1, 6.2
- Chapter 3 - Constitutional Law and Administrative Regulation - 7.1-7.8, 8.1-8.6
- Chapter 4 - International Law - 32.1-32.3
- Chapter 5 - Antitrust Law and Trade Practices Regulation - 27.1-27.6
- Chapter 6 - Criminal Law - 10.1-10.5
- Chapter 7 - Tort Law - 9.1-9.6
- Chapter 8 - Liability of Accountants and Other Professionals - 33.1-33.5

Part Two - Contract Law
- Chapter 9 - Introduction to Contract Law - 11.1
- Chapter 10 - Formation of the Agreement - 11.2, 11.3
- Chapter 11 - Consideration - 11.4
- Chapter 12 - Statute of Frauds and Parol Evidence Rule - 11.8, 11.9
- Chapter 13 - Defenses -- Lack of Capacity - 11.6
- Chapter 14 - Defenses -- Lack of Real Consent - 11.5
- Chapter 15 - Defenses -- Illegality and "Public Policy" - 11.7
- Chapter 16 - Assignment and Third Party Beneficiary Contracts - 11.10, 11.11
- Chapter 17 - Excuses for Nonperformance - 11.12
- Chapter 18 - Remedies for Breach - 11.13

Part Three - Sales of Goods
- Chapter 19 - Sales: Title, Risk of Loss, and Other Interests - 12.4
- Chapter 20 - Warranties and Products Liability - 12.8, 12.9
- Chapter 21 - Special Performance and Breach Rules - 12.5
- Chapter 22 - Special "Entrusting" and Bulk Sales Rules - 25.4

Part Four - Creditors and Debtors
- Chapter 23 - Bankruptcy - 26.1-26.5
- Chapter 24 - Surety and Secured Transactions - 17.1-17.5, 18.1-18.3
- Chapter 25 - Secured Transactions: Priorities and Remedies on Default - 17.4, 17.5
- Chapter 26 - Consumer Protection in Credit Transactions - 30.3

Part Five - Commercial Paper
- Chapter 27 - Types of Instruments; Requirements of Negotiability - 13.1-13.3
- Chapter 28 - Negotiation and Holders in Due Course - 13.4, 13.5
- Chapter 29 - Liabilities of Parties - 13.6
- Chapter 30 - Defenses and Discharge - 13.5, 13.6
- Chapter 31 - Bank Deposits and Collections - 13.7

Part Six - Property
- Chapter 32 - Forms of Co-Ownership; Personal Property - 19.1, 19.2
- Chapter 33 - Bailments - 19.3
- Chapter 34 - Real Property; Acquisition and Transfer of Ownership; Financing of Real Property Transactions - 20.1-20.3, 21.1
- Chapter 35 - Real Property; Landlord and Tenant - 22.1-22.5
- Chapter 36 - Real Property; Zoning, Environmental Regulation, and Eminent Domain - 20.2
- Chapter 37 - Trusts, Estate Planning, and Administration of Decedent's Estates - 24.1-24.5
- Chapter 38 - Insurance: Nature, Types; Special Legal Problems - 23.1-23.4

Part Seven - Business Associations
- Chapter 39 - Agency -- Creation, Principal's Liabilities, and Termination - 14.1, 14.3-14.6
- Chapter 40 - Agency -- Other Legal Relationships - 14.2
- Chapter 41 - Government Regulation of Employment Relationships - 29.1-29.6
- Chapter 42 - Partnerships -- Nature, Creation, and Termination - 15.1, 15.4
- Chapter 43 - Partnerships -- Operation, Powers, Duties and Liabilities - 15.2, 15.3
- Chapter 44 - Limited Partnerships and Other Forms of Business Organizations - 15.5
- Chapter 45 - Corporations -- Nature, Formation, and Powers - 16.1-16.3
- Chapter 46 - Corporations -- Stocks; Shareholders' Rights - 16.5-16.7
- Chapter 47 - Corporations -- Management Duties - 16.4
- Chapter 48 - Securities Law - 28.1-28.4
- Chapter 49 - Foreign Corporations - 32.1-32.3
- Chapter 50 - Business Ethics, Corporate Social Responsibility, and the Law - 35.1-35.3

Schantz, Jackson, *The American Legal Environment: Individuals, Business Law and Government,* Second Edition, West Publishing Co., 1984.

Chapter 1 - The Meaning, Function, and Making of Law - 4.1-4.4
Chapter 2 - Government, Courts, and Individual Rights - 5.1, 5.2
Chapter 3 - Civil, Equitable, Criminal, and Other Procedure - 6.1, 6.2
Chapter 4 - Business and Other Torts, Crimes, and Family Law - 9.1-9.6, 10.1-10.5
Chapter 5 - Administrative Law and Government Agencies - 8.1-8.6
Chapter 6 - Partnerships, Corporations, and the Regulation of Securities - 15.1-15.5, 16.1-16.8, 28.1-28.4
Chapter 7 - Employee, Antitrust, and Labor Law - 27.1-27.6, 29.1-29.6
Chapter 8 - The Ownership of Property - 19.1, 20.1
Chapter 9 - Contracts - 11.1-11.3
Chapter 10 - Insurance, Negotiable Instruments, and Agency - 13.1-13.10, 14.1-14.6, 23.1-23.4
Chapter 11 - Bailments, Sales, and Consumer Protection - 12.1-12.9, 19.3, 30.1-30.5
Chapter 12 - Bankruptcy, Secured Creditors, and Accountants' Responsibilities - 17.1-17.5, 18.1-18.3, 26.1-26.5, 33.1-33.5
Chapter 13 - Trusts, Estates, Taxes, and Environmental Law - 24.1-24.5, 31.1-31.5

Schantz, Jackson, *Business Law,* Second Edition, West Publishing Company, 1987.

Part I - The Legal Environment of Business
 Chapter 1 - The Basics of American Law - 4.1-4.4, 5.1, 6.1
Part II - Contracts
 Chapter 2 - Mutual Assent - 11.2, 11.3, 11.5
 Chapter 3 - Mistake, Undue Influence, Duress, Fraud, Unconscionability - 11.6
 Chapter 4 - Consideration, Capacity, Legality - 11.4, 11.6, 11.7
 Chapter 5 - Conditions, Statute of Frauds, Discharge, Breach, Damages, Third-Party Beneficiary Contracts - 11.8-11.13
Part III - Negotiable Checks, Notes, and Drafts
 Chapter 6 - Assignment versus Negotiation - 13.1-13.3
 Chapter 7 - Negotiation and the Holder in Due Course - 13.4, 13.5
 Chapter 8 - Liabilities on Negotiable Instruments - 13.6
 Chapter 9 - Negotiable Instruments and Bank Customers - 13.7
Part IV - Insurance
 Chapter 10 - The Law of Insurance - 23.1-23.4
Part V - Sales
 Chapter 11 - Bailments, Carriers, Warehousepersons, Documents of Title - 13.1, 19.3
 Chapter 12 - Identification and Risk of Loss - 12.4
 Chapter 13 - Rights of Buyer and Seller - 12.6, 12.7
 Chapter 14 - Product Liability, Sales by Nonowners, Letters of Credit - 12.8, 12.9, 13.9
Part VI - Doing Business
 Chapter 15 - Employers, Employees, Independent Contractors
 Chapter 16 - Agency - 14.1-14.5
 Chapter 17 - Partnerships - 15.1-15.5
 Chapter 18 - Corporations - 16.1-16.8
 Chapter 19 - Securities - 28.1-28.4
 Chapter 20 - Antitrust and Labor Law - 27.1-27.6, 29.1-29.6
Part VII - Property
 Chapter 21 - Meshing Real and Personal Property (Minerals, Trees, Crops, Fixtures, Rentals)
 Chapter 22 - Personal Property Law - 19.2
 Chapter 23 - Real Property Law - 20.1
 Chapter 24 - Concurrent Ownership and Incidental Rights - 21.4
 Chapter 25 - Deeds, Adverse Possession, Easements - 21.1
Part VIII - Creditors' Rights
 Chapter 26 - Debtor-Creditor Law and Bankruptcy - 25.1-25.4, 26.1-26.5
 Chapter 27 - Security Interests, Mortgages, Suretyship, and Bulk Sales - 17.1-17.5, 18.1-18.3, 21.1, 25.4
Part IX - Management Through Trusts and Transferring at Death
 Chapter 28 - Trusts - 24.4, 24.5
 Chapter 29 - Wills - 24.3
Part X - Business and Professional Responsibility
 Chapter 30 - Business Torts, Business Crime, Accountants' Professional Responsibility - 9.4, 10.3, 33.1-33.5

Shaw, Wolfe, *The Structure of the Legal Environment,* PWS-Kent Publishing Company, 1987.

Part I - Introduction to the Study of the American Legal Environment
- Chapter 1 - Introduction to the Study of the Legal Environment of Business - 4.1-4.4
- Chapter 2 - Foundations of the American Legal System - 5.1, 6.1
- Chapter 3 - Constitutional Law: Basic Concepts - 7.1-7.8
- Chapter 4 - Constitutional Law: Issues in Business and Society - 7.1-7.8

Part II - Commercial Law
- Chapter 5 - Contract Law - 11.1-11.13
- Chapter 6 - Agency Law - 14.1-14.6
- Chapter 7 - Corporations, Partnerships, and Other Forms of American Business Organizations - 15.1-15.5, 16.1-16.8

Part III - Consumers and the Legal Environment of Business
- Chapter 8 - Manufacturers' Liability for Defective Products - 12.9, 30.5
- Chapter 9 - Government Regulation of Product Safety - 30.5
- Chapter 10 - Regulation of Deceptive Trade Practices and Credit - 27.6, 30.4

Part IV - Administrative Law and Practice
- Chapter 11 - Government Regulation and Administrative Law - 8.1-8.6
- Chapter 12 - Administrative Searches and Control of the Administrative Process - 8.3

Part V - Competitive Markets and the Legal Environment of Business
- Chapter 13 - Antitrust Law: Basic Concepts - 27.1
- Chapter 14 - Merger - 27.4
- Chapter 15 - Monopolization and Industrial Structure - 27.3
- Chapter 16 - Selected Trade Practices - 27.2
- Chapter 17 - Federal Securities Regulation: Introduction and Explanation of the Securities Act of 1933 - 28.1, 28.2
- Chapter 18 - The Securities Exchange Act of 1934 and the Law of Continuing Corporate Disclosure - 28.3

Part VI - Emerging Issues in the Legal Environment of Business
- Chapter 19 - Labor Law - 29.2
- Chapter 20 - Employment Law - 29.1-29.6
- Chapter 21 - Environmental Law - 31.1-31.5
- Chapter 22 - International Law and Business Transactions - 32.1-32.3
- Chapter 23 - Emerging Issues in Computers, Robotics, and Artificial Intelligence - 34.1-34.7

Part VII - Law, Morality, and the Structure of American Business
- Chapter 24 - The Study of Ethics and Corporate Social Responsibility - 35.1-35.3
- Chapter 25 - Selected Legal and Moral Issues: Tensions Between Individual/Minority Rights and Group Objectives - 7.7, 29.3
- Chapter 26 - International Business and the Clash in Cultural Beliefs - 32.1-32.3

Smith, Mann, Roberts, *Business Law and the Regulation of Business*, Second Edition, West Publishing Company, 1990.

Smith, Mann, Roberts, *Essentials of Business Law,* Third Edition, West Publishing Company, 1989.

Part One - The Legal Environment of Business
- Chapter 1 - Introduction to Law - 4.1-4.4
- Chapter 2 - The Judicial System - 5.1, 5.2, 6.1
- Chapter 3 - Constitutional and Administrative Law - 7.1-7.8, 8.1-8.6
- Chapter 4 - Criminal Law - 10.1-10.5
- Chapter 5 - Intentional Torts - 9.1-9.4
- Chapter 6 - Negligence and Strict Liability - 9.5, 9.6

Part Two - Contracts
- Chapter 7 - Introduction to Contracts - 11.1
- Chapter 8 - Mutual Assent - 11.2, 11.3
- Chapter 9 - Conduct Invalidating Assent - 11.5
- Chapter 10 - Consideration - 11.4
- Chapter 11 - Illegal Bargains - 11.7
- Chapter 12 - Contractual Capacity - 11.6
- Chapter 13 - Contracts in Writing - 11.8, 11.9
- Chapter 14 - Third Parties to Contracts - 11.10, 11.11
- Chapter 15 - Performance, Breach and Discharge - 11.12
- Chapter 16 - Remedies - 11.13

Part Three - Sales
- Chapter 17 - Introduction to Sales - 12.1-12.3
- Chapter 18 - Transfer of Title and Risk of Loss - 12.4
- Chapter 19 - Products Liability: Warranties and Strict Liability - 12.8, 12.9
- Chapter 20 - Performance - 12.5
- Chapter 21 - Remedies - 12.6, 12.7

Part Four - Commercial Paper
- Chapter 22 - Form and Content - 13.1-13.3
- Chapter 23 - Transfer - 13.4
- Chapter 24 - Holder in Due Course - 13.5
- Chapter 25 - Liability of Parties - 13.6
- Chapter 26 - Bank Deposits and Collections - 13.7

Part Five - Agency
- Chapter 27 - Relationship of Principal and Agent - 14.1, 14.2, 14.6
- Chapter 28 - Relationship With Third Parties - 14.3-14.5

Part Six - Partnerships
- Chapter 29 - Nature and Formation - 15.1
- Chapter 30 - Rights and Duties - 15.2, 15.3
- Chapter 31 - Dissolution, Winding Up, and Termination - 15.4
- Chapter 32 - Limited Partnerships - 15.5

Part Seven - Corporations
- Chapter 33 - Nature and Formation - 16.1, 16.2
- Chapter 34 - Financial Structure - 16.7
- Chapter 35 - Management Structure - 16.3, 16.4
- Chapter 36 - Fundamental Changes - 16.8

Part Eight - Debtor and Creditor Relations
- Chapter 37 - Secured Transactions and Suretyship - 17.1-17.5, 18.1-18.3
- Chapter 38 - Bankruptcy - 26.1-26.5

Part Nine - Regulation of Business
- Chapter 39 - Trade Regulation - 27.1-27.6
- Chapter 40 - Securities Regulation - 28.1-28.4
- Chapter 41 - Consumer Protection - 30.1-30.5
- Chapter 42 - Employment Law - 29.1-29.6
- Chapter 43 - International Business Law - 32.1-32.3

Part Ten - Property
- Chapter 44 - Introduction to Real and Personal Property - 19.1, 20.1
- Chapter 45 - Bailments and Documents of Title - 19.3, 21.1
- Chapter 46 - Interests in Real Property - 20.1
- Chapter 47 - Transfer and Control of Real Property - 20.3
- Chapter 48 - Trusts and Wills - 24.1-24.5
- Chapter 49 - Insurance - 23.1-23.4

Smith, Roberson, Mann, Roberts, *Smith and Roberson's Business Law*, Seventh Edition, West Publishing Co., 1988.

Part One - The Legal Environment of Business
- Chapter 1 - Introduction to Law - 4.1-4.4
- Chapter 2 - The Legal Process - 5.1, 5.2, 6.1
- Chapter 3 - Constitutional and Administrative Law - 7.1-7.8, 8.1-8.6
- Chapter 4 - Criminal Law - 10.1-10.5
- Chapter 5 - Intentional Torts - 9.1-9.4
- Chapter 6 - Negligence and Strict Liability - 9.5, 9.6

Part Two - Contracts
- Chapter 7 - Introduction to Contracts - 11.1
- Chapter 8 - Mutual Assent - 11.2, 11.3
- Chapter 9 - Conduct Invalidating Assent - 11.5
- Chapter 10 - Consideration - 11.4
- Chapter 11 - Illegal Bargains - 11.7
- Chapter 12 - Contractual Capacity - 11.6
- Chapter 13 - Contracts in Writing - 11.8, 11.9
- Chapter 14 - Rights of Third Parties - 11.10, 11.11
- Chapter 15 - Performance, Breach, and Discharge - 11.12
- Chapter 16 - Remedies - 11.13

Part Three - Agency
- Chapter 17 - Relationship of Principal and Agent - 14.1, 14.2, 14.6
- Chapter 18 - Relationship with Third Parties - 14.3-14.5

Part Four - Sales
- Chapter 19 - Introduction to Sales - 12.1-12.3
- Chapter 20 - Transfer of Title and Risk of Loss - 12.4
- Chapter 21 - Products Liability: Warranties and Strict Liability in Tort - 12.8, 12.9
- Chapter 22 - Performance - 12.5
- Chapter 23 - Remedies - 12.6, 12.7

Part Five - Commercial Paper
- Chapter 24 - Form and Content - 13.1-13.3
- Chapter 25 - Transfer - 13.4
- Chapter 26 - Holder in Due Course - 13.5
- Chapter 27 - Liabilities of Parties - 13.6
- Chapter 28 - Bank Deposits and Collections - 13.7

Part Six - Partnerships
- Chapter 29 - Nature and Formation - 16.1
- Chapter 30 - Duties, Rights, and Liabilities - 15.2, 15.3
- Chapter 31 - Dissolution, Winding Up, and Termination - 15.4
- Chapter 32 - Limited Partnership - 15.5

Part Seven - Corporations
- Chapter 33 - Nature, Formation, and Power - 16.1-16.3
- Chapter 34 - Financial Structure - 16.7
- Chapter 35 - Management Structure - 16.4
- Chapter 36 - Fundamental Changes - 16.8

Part Eight - Debtor and Creditor Relationships
- Chapter 37 - Secured Transactions in Personal Property - 17.1-17.5
- Chapter 38 - Suretyship - 18.1-18.3
- Chapter 39 - Bankruptcy and Relief of Debtors - 26.1-26.5

Part Nine - Regulation of Business
- Chapter 40 - Unfair Competition and Business Torts - 9.4, 27.1
- Chapter 41 - Antitrust - 27.1-27.6
- Chapter 42 - Consumer Protection - 30.1-30.5
- Chapter 43 - Employment Law - 29.1-29.6
- Chapter 44 - Securities Regulation - 28.1-28.4
- Chapter 45 - Accountants' Legal Liability - 33.1-33.5

Part Ten - Property
- Chapter 46 - Introduction to Real and Personal Property - 19.1, 20.1
- Chapter 47 - Bailments and Documents of Title - 19.3, 21.1
- Chapter 48 - Interests in Real Property - 20.1
- Chapter 49 - Transfer and Control of Real Property - 20.3
- Chapter 50 - Trusts and Wills - 24.1-24.5
- Chapter 51 - Insurance - 23.1-23.4

Spiro, *The Legal Environment of Business*, Prentice-Hall, Inc., 1989.

Part 1 - The Nature of Law and the U.S. Legal System
Chapter 1 - What is Law? - 4.1-4.4
Chapter 2 - Ethics and Social Responsibility - 35.1-35.3
Chapter 3 - The Constitution and Business - 7.1-7.8
Chapter 4 - The Court System - 5.1, 5.2
Chapter 5 - Litigation and Other Types of Dispute Resolution - 6.1, 6.2
Chapter 6 - Administrative Agencies - 8.1-8.6
Part 2 - Organizing to Do Business
Chapter 7 - Forms of Business Organization - 15.1, 15.5, 16.1
Chapter 8 - Securities Regulation - 28.1-28.4
Part 3 - Regulating Private Business Conduct and Crime
Chapter 9 - Contracts - 11.1-11.13
Chapter 10 - Torts - 9.1-9.6
Chapter 11 - Product Liability - 12.9, 30.5
Chapter 12 - Business Crime and Criminal Procedure - 10.1-10.5
Part 4 - Employment and the Law
Chapter 13 - Labor Relations - 29.1
Chapter 14 - Labor Standards - 29.2, 29.4-29.6
Chapter 15 - Employment Discrimination - 29.3
Part 5 - The Legal Environment of the Marketplace
Chapter 16 - Antitrust and the Sherman Act - 27.1-27.3
Chapter 17 - The Clayton and Robinson-Patman Acts - 27.4, 27.5
Chapter 18 - Trade Practices and Intellectual Property - 19.2, 30.4
Chapter 19 - Debtor-Creditor Relations - 25.1-25.4, 26.1-26.5
Chapter 20 - Property and Land Use - 20.1, 20.2
Chapter 21 - International Business Law - 32.1-32.3

Story, Ward, *American Business Law and the Regulatory Environment*, South-Western Publishing Co., Inc., 1987.

PROLOGUE
Chapter 1 - Law as Process: An Introduction to Civil Procedure - 4.1-4.4, 5.1, 6.1
Chapter 2 - Constitutional Law I: The Powers of Government and Substantive Due Process - 7.1-7.8
Chapter 3 - Constitutional Law II: Limiting the Manner of Regulation - 7.1-7.8
BOOK ONE - Civil Obligation
Part One - Tort Law
Chapter 4 - Introduction to the Law of Torts - 9.1
Chapter 5 - Intentional Torts - 9.2-9.4
Chapter 6 - The Rise of the Negligence Principle - 9.5, 9.6
Part Two - Common Law Contracts
Chapter 7 - An Introduction to the Law of Contracts - 11.1
Chapter 8 - The Origin of Binding Promise: Mutual Assent in the Common Law - 11.2, 11.3
Chapter 9 - Form and Meaning in Promises - 11.6-11.9
Chapter 10 - Selective Enforcement of Promises: The Doctrines of Consideration, Promissory Estoppel and Beneficial Obligation - 11.4
Chapter 11 - Voluntariness I: Reality of Consent - 11.5
Chapter 12 - Voluntariness II: Abuse of Superior Bargaining Power - 11.5
Chapter 13 - The End of Promise: Performance and Breach Under the Common Law - 11.12
Chapter 14 - Remedies for Breach of Contract: Closing the Gap Between Promise and Performance - 11.13
Chapter 15 - Third Parties and the Obligations of Contract - 11.10, 11.11
Part Three - Sales Contracts
Chapter 16 - Contract Formation and Remedies Under the Uniform Commercial Code - 12.1-12.3, 12.6, 12.7
Chapter 17 - The End of Promise: Performance and Breach Under the Uniform Commercial Code - 12.5-12.7
Chapter 18 - Product Liability: The Illicit Intercourse of Tort and Contract - 12.8, 12.9
Part Four - Quasi-Contract or Contorts
Chapter 19 - Quasi-Contract or Contorts - 11.1
BOOK TWO - Property
Part One - Acquiring and Transferring Property
Chapter 20 - Acquiring and Transferring Property - 19.1, 19.2, 20.3, 21.1
Part Two - Real Property
Chapter 21 - Real Property I: From the Right to Exclude - 20.1, 22.1-22.5
Chapter 22 - Real Property II: To the Right to be Included - 20.1, 22.1-22.5

Part Three - Commercial Law
- Chapter 23 - The Risk Buyers: An Overview of the Law of Commercial Paper - 13.1-13.6
- Chapter 24 - The Note - 13.2
- Chapter 25 - The Check, Check-Like Instruments, and New Payment Systems - 13.2, 13.7
- Chapter 26 - Bailments and Documents of Title - 13.10, 19.3
- Chapter 27 - Secured Transactions - 17.1-17.5
- Chapter 28 - Bankruptcy and Reorganization - 26.1-26.5

BOOK THREE - Enterprise Organization and Control
- Chapter 29 - Organizing the Business Enterprise - 15.1, 15.5, 16.1
- Chapter 30 - Agency: The Common Thread - 14.1-14.6
- Chapter 31 - Partnership Law: Experiments in Concurrent Ownership - 15.1-15.5
- Chapter 32 - Corporate Governance: Inside the Black Box - 16.1-16.8
- Chapter 33 - Employment Law: Toward the Job as Property Right - 29.1-29.6
- Chapter 34 - Disclosure: Regulating the Market for Investment Securities - 28.1-28.3
- Chapter 35 - Regulating Competitive Markets: Federal Antitrust Law - 27.1-27.6
- Chapter 36 - Intellectual and Literary Property Rights - 19.2
- Chapter 37 - Regulation by Administrative Agency: A Lesson from Broadcast Licensing - 8.1-8.6

Whitman, Gergacz, *The Legal Environment of Business,* Second Edition, McGraw-Hill, Inc., 1988.

Part I - Introduction to Law and Business
- Chapter 1 - Introduction to the Law and the Legal Environment of Business - 4.1-4.4

Part II - The American Legal System
- Chapter 2 - Introduction to Courts - 5.1, 5.2
- Chapter 3 - Civil Litigation and Alternative Dispute Resolution - 6.1, 6.2
- Chapter 4 - Judicial Reasoning and Decision Making - 4.4
- Chapter 5 - The Legislature, Legislation, and the Executive Branch - 8.1-8.6
- Chapter 6 - The Constitution and Business - 7.1-7.8
- Chapter 7 - The Administrative Agency - 8.1-8.6

Part III - The Legal Foundations of American Business: Common Law and Its Development
- Chapter 8 - Contracts - 11.1-11.13
- Chapter 9 - Torts - 9.1-9.4
- Chapter 10 - Property Rights and Land Use Regulation - 20.1-20.3

Part IV - Legal Aspects of the Firm and the Regulation of Its Power
- Chapter 11 - Corporations, Agency, and Other Forms of Business Organization - 14.1-14.6, 15.1-15.5, 16.1-16.8
- Chapter 12 - Federal Securities Regulation - 28.1-28.4
- Chapter 13 - Introduction to Antitrust - 27.1
- Chapter 14 - Antitrust Law - 27.2-27.6
- Chapter 15 - The Clayton Act: Mergers and Price Discrimination - 27.4
- Chapter 16 - White-Collar and Business Crime: Regulation of Business through the Criminal Process - 10.1-10.5
- Chapter 17 - Ethics and Business: Extra-Legal Controls on Business and Business Decision Making - 35.1-35.3

Part V - Regulation of Business Activity
- Chapter 18 - Products Liability - 12.9, 30.5
- Chapter 19 - Consumer Law - 30.1-30.5
- Chapter 20 - Labor-Management Relations: The Regulation of Management - 29.2, 29.4-29.6
- Chapter 21 - Labor-Management Relations: The Regulation of Union Activity - 29.1
- Chapter 22 - Employment Discrimination - 29.3
- Chapter 23 - Environmental Law - 31.1-31.5

Part VI - International Regulation of Business Activity
- Chapter 24 - The International Legal Environment of Business - 32.1-32.3

CHAPTER TWO
HOW TO ANSWER OBJECTIVE QUESTIONS

You need a control system for answering objective questions on examinations. The objective is to obtain the highest score given your knowledge of the material tested. The following suggested procedures are based on extensive analysis of examination experience by both university students and those taking professional certification examinations.

The following series of steps is suggested for multiple-choice questions. The important point is that you need to devote attention to and develop YOUR OWN APPROACH to objective questions. This is also true for computational problems and essay questions which are beyond the scope of this book.

Practice your objective question answering technique on groups of questions in this book (see also page 8 in Chapter 1).

1. Work individual questions in order.
   a. If a question appears too long or difficult, skip it until you can determine that extra time is available. Put a "?" or an "X" in the margin beside the question as a reminder to return to questions you have skipped or need to review.
2. Cover the answer choices before reading each question.
   a. The answers are frequently ambiguous, and one may even be deliberate nonsense, which may cause you to misread or misinterpret the question.
   b. Also, the answers may distract you from reading the question/fact situation correctly.
3. Read each question carefully.
   a. Study the requirements first so you know what data are important.
   b. Be especially careful to note when the requirement is an <u>exception</u>, e.g., "Which of the following is <u>not</u> valid acceptance of an offer?"
   c. When one fact situation or set of data is the basis for two or more questions, read the requirements of each of the questions <u>before</u> beginning to work the first question (sometimes it is more efficient to work the questions out of order or simultaneously).
4. Anticipate the answer <u>before</u> looking at the alternative answers.
5. Read <u>all</u> the answers and select the <u>best</u> alternative.
   a. Even if answer (a) or (b) appears to be the correct choice, do <u>not</u> be tempted to skip the rest of the choices. "All of the above" or "a and c above" may be a better choice under answer "d".
   b. Treat each answer as a true-false question. Consider marking a "T" or "F" next to each alternative as you analyze it.
6. Mark the correct (or best guess) answer on the examination itself.
   a. Note that most examinations do not penalize guessing because the score is determined by the number of correct responses.
   b. If a subtraction is made for incorrectly answered questions (in contrast to unanswered questions), guessing is penalized.
   c. When guessing is not penalized, you should answer every question.

7. Budget your time carefully.
   a. Before beginning a series of multiple-choice questions, write the time you start on the exam booklet near the first multiple-choice question.
   b. Compute the minutes allowed for each multiple-choice question after you have allocated exam time to all of the overall questions on the exam; e.g., if the first overall question consists of 20 individual multiple-choice questions and is allocated 30 minutes on the exam, you would want to spend a little over 1 minute per individual multiple-choice question (always budget some extra time for transferring answers to answer sheets, interruptions, etc.).
   c. As you work the individual multiple-choice questions, check your time, e.g., assuming the above allocation of 30 minutes for 20 questions, if you have worked 5 multiple-choice questions in 5 or 6 minutes, you are fine; but if you spent 10 minutes on 5 questions, you need to speed up.
8. After completing all of the individual questions in an overall question, transfer the answers to a separate answer sheet (if one exists) with extreme care.
   a. Be very careful not to fall out of sequence with the answer sheet, which may result in many questions being answered incorrectly.
   b. Review to check that you have transferred the answers correctly.
   c. Do not postpone this step until the end of the examination as you may find yourself with too little time to transfer your answers to the answer sheet with the necessary care.

CHAPTER THREE
PROFESSIONAL CERTIFICATION EXAMINATIONS

INTRODUCTION

The purpose of this chapter is to describe the three primary accounting certification examinations and other professional business examinations which test business law and legal studies topics. This discussion is not intended to be all inclusive due to space constraints; however, it does provide you with an overview of professional examination coverage of business law and legal studies topics, and demonstrates part of the relevance of business law and legal studies to the undergraduate curriculum. If you are a practitioner, you should consider these examinations as professional development opportunities rather than as examinations.

OVERVIEW OF ACCOUNTING CERTIFICATION PROGRAMS

The CPA exam is the grandfather of all the professional accounting examinations. Its origin was in the 1896 public accounting legislation of New York. In 1916, the American Institute of CPAs (AICPA) began to prepare and grade a uniform CPA exam. This exam is currently used to measure the technical competence of those applying to be licensed as CPAs in all 50 states, Guam, Puerto Rico, the Virgin Islands, and Washington, D.C. Over 140,000 candidates sit for the two CPA exams administered each year.

The CIA (Certified Internal Auditor) and CMA (Certified Management Accountant) examinations are neophytes compared to the CPA exam. The CMA exam was first administered in 1972, and the CIA exam was first administered in 1974.

The CPA examination has very heavy coverage of business law: 3½ hours out of 19½ total exam hours. The CMA examination is more "user oriented." It tests governmental regulations (e.g., SEC, antitrust, OSHA, etc.) in Parts 1 and 2. These same types of topics are tested lightly throughout the CIA examination, which primarily focuses on auditing topics.

CHARTERED PROPERTY CASUALTY UNDERWRITER (CPCU)

The CPCU designation is granted by the American Institute for Property and Liability Underwriters, located in Malvern, Pennsylvania (outside of Philadelphia). The CPCU designation is granted after successful completion of ten 3-hour essay examinations in addition to fulfilling certain ethics and experience requirements. (Note: This is one of the very few certification examinations that does not rely heavily on multiple-choice questions.) The ten topics tested are

1. Principles of Risk Management and Insurance
2. Personal Risk Management and Insurance
3. Commercial Property Risk Management and Insurance
4. Commercial Liability Risk Management and Insurance
5. Insurance Company Operations
6. The Legal Environment of Insurance
7. Management
8. Accounting and Finance
9. Economics
10. Insurance Issues and Professional Ethics

Part 6, "The Legal Environment of Insurance," is based on the typical business law course, but emphasizes tort, contract, and agency law with application to insurance situations. Those interested in the program should write

American Institute for Property and Liability Underwriters
720 Providence Road
Malvern, PA 19355-0770
(215) 644-2100

CERTIFIED LIFE UNDERWRITER (CLU)

The CLU designation is granted by The American College in Bryn Mawr, Pennsylvania. There are over 60,000 CLUs, and another 40,000 candidates are actively pursuing the designation.

The CLU program consists of a series of 10 examinations, each 2 hours long, given by computer at Controlled Data Centers, on demand. Of the 11 topics shown below, the first 6 plus 4 of the last 5 are required.

1. Individual Insurance
2. Life Insurance Law
3. Introduction to Financial Planning
4. Group Benefits
5. Income Taxation
6. Investments
7. The Financial System in the Economy
8. Planning for Retirement Needs
9. Fundamentals of Estate Planning I
10. Fundamentals of Estate Planning II
11. Planning for Business Owners and Professionals

The business law section of the second exam emphasizes contract formation, policy provisions, etc. of insurance policies. CLUs need to understand the rights and obligations of both insureds and insurers.

More information about the CLU may be obtained from

The American College
270 Bryn Mawr Avenue
Bryn Mawr, PA 19010
(215) 526-1000

STATE REAL ESTATE LICENSURE EXAMINATIONS

All states have real estate licensing examinations, usually a salesperson exam and a broker exam. The sales examination generally tests the laws, rules, etc. of the particular state, including real estate law (which makes up to 50% of the exam). The broker examination tests more advanced topics, but also has up to 50% coverage of real estate law. These tests are usually multiple-choice and consist of 30 to 100 questions, depending on the state. The broker exams are usually the longer of the two exams.

Real estate law includes contracts, agency, property, leases, mortgages, etc.

LAW SCHOOL ADMISSION TEST (LSAT)

The LSAT is a standard admission test developed and administered by Law School Admission Services in Newtown, Pennsylvania. This one-half-day test is given worldwide four times a year: February, June, September, and December. Law schools generally require that you take the test by December to be considered for admission the following Fall (with a similar lead time for admission other times of the year). There is a Law Services Information Booklet (includes a sample LSAT exam) and an LSAT registration form which can be acquired from a nearby law school or by writing:

Law Services
Box 2000
Newtown, PA 18940
(215) 968-1001

The LSAT consists of four 45-minute sections of about 30 multiple-choice questions, of which only three sections (you do not know which three) are "official." The other section is used to validate and test both new and old questions. The LSAT tests:

1. Reading comprehension
2. Logical reasoning
3. Analytical reasoning

Remember that you are required to complete four sections and are not told which three are official, i.e, which will determine your grade. Note that the LSAT does NOT test business law or other legal topics. The LSAT tests reading and reasoning skills.

The final part of the LSAT is a 30-minute writing exercise. You are asked to write a short essay on a defined topic. Rather than grade the writing exercise, the administrators make a copy available to law schools to which you apply, along with your scores on the multiple-choice sections of the exam.

There are numerous LSAT preparation books, courses, etc. We recommend that you use some form of assistance to become better acquainted with the examination. Since the LSAT does test basic aptitudes and skills that are developed over a long period of time, we do not believe you can cram for it. However, any review (familiarity) is better than going in "cold." Carefully planned programs to increase reading comprehension and reasoning (e.g., logic courses) may be most helpful.

MULTISTATE BAR EXAMINATION

The Multistate Bar Examination has been developed by the National Conference on Bar Examiners for those state bars which choose to use it. Forty-six states now participate in the program.

The examination is 6 hours long and consists of 200 multiple-choice questions on the following topics: Contracts (40 questions); Torts (40); Constitutional Law (30); Criminal Law (30); Evidence (30); and Real Property (30). More information is available from

National Conference of Bar Examiners
333 North Michigan Avenue
Suite 1025
Chicago, Illinois 60601
(312) 641-0963

CHAPTER FOUR
THE LEGAL SYSTEM AND LEGAL ENVIRONMENT

4.1 Nature of Law

1. Law has proven to be difficult to define. Many attempts have been made but none has gained universal acceptance. Nevertheless, certain definitions are more relevant to the modern American experience than others. The definition least likely to be acceptable in the context of that experience is that law is a

a. Group of moral precepts backed by the power of the state.

b. Set of principles, standards, and rules applied by courts to controversies.

c. Limit on personal liberty.

d. Means of promoting the interests of society through the use of sanctions.

The correct answer is (a). *(Publisher)*

REQUIRED: The definition of law that is least likely to be acceptable in the U.S.

DISCUSSION: Moral precepts certainly affect the law, but law and morals clearly are not the same in American society. For example, the law may impose civil liability on a manufacturer of a defective product even though all due care was taken by the defendant. This liability results from considerations of social policy, not because the manufacturer's act was immoral. Conversely, much conduct that the community brands as immoral is not subject to either civil or criminal sanctions. For example, many people believe they have a moral duty to come to the aid of an injured person, yet the duty to rescue is not a legal one.

Answer (b) is incorrect because the American Law Institute defines law as "the body of principles, standards, and rules that the courts of a particular state apply in the decision of controversies brought before them." Answers (c) and (d) are incorrect because H.E. Willis in "Introduction to American Law" defines law as "a scheme of social control which, by means of legal capacities backed and sanctioned by legal redress, delimits personal liberty for the protection of social interests."

2. The word "law" has many definitions. Some of these definitions are broader than others. Which of the following is a definition of law?

a. The enterprise of subjecting human conduct to the governance of rules.

b. Constitutions, treaties, statutes, regulations, and case law.

c. The Ten Commandments.

d. All of the above.

The correct answer is (d). *(Publisher)*

REQUIRED: The definition(s) of law.

DISCUSSION: "Law" has a variety of meanings. Professor Lon Fuller, a famous 20th century legal scholar, defined law as "the enterprise of subjecting human conduct to the governance of rules." Other scholars have found law in the Ten Commandments. These scholars believe the law is based on higher principles. Still other scholars define law in terms of its manifestations: constitutions, treaties between nations, statutes, administrative regulations issued by the executive branch, and case (judge-made) law.

Answers (a), (b), and (c) are incorrect because each is a possible definition of law.

3. According to an old legal maxim, ignorance of the law is

a. A good excuse for corporations because they are artificial entities.

b. A good excuse for nonresident aliens.

c. Almost always a good excuse.

d. Never a good excuse.

The correct answer is (d). *(D. Woods)*

REQUIRED: The correct statement of the maxim about ignorance of the law.

DISCUSSION: Ignorance of the law is no excuse. People have a duty to find out what the law is and to obey it. But ignorance of the law may be a mitigating factor in certain cases, especially if another is taking advantage of that ignorance.

Answers (a), (b), and (c) are incorrect because people are charged with constructive knowledge of the law.

4. Jurisprudence is the science or philosophy of law. What school of jurisprudence adheres to the belief that law is based on ultimate principles that transcend society and its customs?

a. Legal realism.

b. Natural law.

c. Legal positivism.

d. Historical.

The correct answer is (b). *(Publisher)*

REQUIRED: The jurisprudential theory that bases law on ultimate principles.

DISCUSSION: The natural law philosophy is based on the belief that ideal concepts of law exist outside of human culture and are knowable through the proper application of human reason. Some find the source of natural law in divine revelation. Others discover it in the inherent nature of humanity or the natural order of the universe.

Answer (a) is incorrect because legal realism is a sociological approach that pragmatically views law as a process. It is concerned with which law is really in force. Answer (c) is incorrect because it views law as the command of a sovereign authority. Answer (d) is incorrect because the historical philosophy treats law as custom evolved over a long period.

5. The legal environment of business

a. Concerns all the ways in which the law affects business.

b. Only includes persons or organizations whose primary purpose is the making of a profit.

c. Includes statutory regulation of business, but does not include the impact of the common law on business.

d. Is merely the body of environmental law that regulates the relationship between business and the public.

The correct answer is (a). *(Publisher)*

REQUIRED: The correct statement about the legal environment of business.

DISCUSSION: The legal environment of business includes traditional legal topics such as business associations, contracts, and agency. In addition, the legal environment includes all laws, regulations, and rules that are promulgated by any governmental body or agency and affect the business firm.

Answer (b) is incorrect because the legal environment includes all business organizations regardless of their purposes. Thus, labor unions, political parties, and public service entities are included. Answer (c) is incorrect because the legal environment includes both statutory and common law regulation of business. Answer (d) is incorrect because the legal environment of business includes all laws that affect business. The body of law that is commonly referred to as environmental law is included as are areas of contract law, criminal law, and all others that affect the business organization.

6. The legal environment of business is composed of relationships between business and various groups of persons or entities. These groups include the public, competitors, suppliers, creditors, customers, employees, investors, and government. Which of the following is probably the most significant? The relationship of business to

a. The public.

b. Investors.

c. Customers.

d. Government.

The correct answer is (d). *(Publisher)*

REQUIRED: The most significant relationship within the legal environment of business.

DISCUSSION: The relationship of business and government is the most significant because it has the greatest effect on the other relationships. That relationship includes the laws that regulate the other relationships.

Answers (a), (b), and (c) are incorrect because the relationship of business and government encompasses the limitations and controls (executive, legislative, and judicial) that guide the other relationships.

7. Which of the following is the least desirable characteristic of law?

a. The law should be certain.

b. The law should be flexible.

c. The law should have retroactive effect.

d. The law should be known by those required to obey it.

The correct answer is (c). *(Publisher)*

REQUIRED: The least desirable characteristic of the law.

DISCUSSION: Retroactive effect sometimes cannot be avoided. But retroactive application often conflicts with the principles of certainty and knowledgeability. The clearest example is in the criminal law. If a penal statute is given retroactive effect, action known to be rightful at the time it was taken is subsequently punished. Thus, one could not be certain what conduct is lawful. For this reason, the Constitution prohibits ex post facto criminal laws.

Answers (a) and (b) are incorrect because a paradox of the law is that it should be reasonably certain and reliable but also able to change to meet new conditions. Modern commercial practices, for instance, are based upon the assurance that contracts will be enforceable in the future according to the same principles applied today. Answer (d) is incorrect because knowledge of the law is highly desirable. In practice, no one knows all the law. Access to it is available either directly or through experts (lawyers) who can research the law. But an educated citizenry should at least know the general principles underlying a society's legal system.

8. Remedies available in a civil proceeding include all but which of the following?

a. Compensatory damages.

b. Temporary restraining orders.

c. Declaratory relief.

d. Imprisonment.

The correct answer is (d). *(Publisher)*

REQUIRED: The remedy not available in a civil proceeding.

DISCUSSION: One distinction between the civil and criminal law is the differing remedies available. The sanctions available to punish a criminal include capital punishment (death), imprisonment, and fines. Criminal law is designed to punish wrongdoing. Civil law is designed to compensate for injury. Imprisonment is therefore a criminal remedy and not available in a civil proceeding.

Answer (a) is incorrect because compensatory damages are usually available in civil proceedings. Answer (b) is incorrect because temporary restraining orders (short term injunctions which restrain or command an action until a hearing can be convened) are available in civil proceedings. Answer (c) is incorrect because declaratory relief is a civil remedy in which a statement of the rights and duties of the parties is made but no coercive relief is granted.

9. Remedies available in criminal actions include

a. Fines.

b. Punitive damages.

c. Declaratory judgments.

d. Injunctions.

The correct answer is (a). *(Publisher)*

REQUIRED: The remedy available in a criminal action.

DISCUSSION: The remedies available in a criminal action range from capital punishment (death) to imprisonment and fines of varying magnitude. They are imposed for breaches of duties imposed upon all persons which are regarded as wrongs to society and are enforced by the appropriate governmental entity.

Answer (b) is incorrect because punitive damages is a civil remedy available as a penalty for extreme or aggravated behavior. Answer (c) is incorrect because a declaratory judgment (a noncoercive form of relief which states the rights and duties of the parties) is a civil remedy. Answer (d) is incorrect because an injunction is a civil remedy, whether temporary or permanent, which commands a person to do or refrain from doing some action. Criminal actions are already forbidden by law.

10. During World War II, rents were controlled throughout the country. Defendant Landlord refused to comply with the law. Instead, he financed a suit in federal court by Plaintiff, one of his tenants, for violation of the statute, intending to defend on the basis of its unconstitutionality. Plaintiff took no part in the litigation other than lending his name to the complaint. Should the suit be heard?

a. Yes, because defendant violated the statute.

b. Yes, because the statute was unconstitutional.

c. No, because the issues are not ripe.

d. No, because the suit was collusive.

The correct answer is (d). *(Publisher)*

REQUIRED: The correct decision as to whether to dismiss a friendly suit.

DISCUSSION: The conduct of litigation requires a genuine adversity between parties. In theory, the most effective exposition of the opposing points of view will be achieved only if the parties have genuinely conflicting interests. Accordingly, a collusive suit does not meet the case or controversy requirement.

Answers (a) and (b) are incorrect because the merits of the case are irrelevant if no genuine controversy is presented. Answer (c) is incorrect because the issues were suitably ripe (when the subject of the controversy has a direct adverse effect on the complaining party).

11. The power of judicial review

a. Is limited to review of actions of the executive branch.

b. Enables courts to review laws enacted by legislative bodies and to declare them unconstitutional.

c. Is expressly conferred by the U.S. Constitution.

d. Refers to liberal interpretation of remedial statutes.

The correct answer is (b). *(Publisher)*

REQUIRED: The correct statement concerning the doctrine of judicial review.

DISCUSSION: Both state and federal courts have the power to judicially review actions of the legislative and executive branches of the government. The judicial branch is given the authority to determine whether actions of the other branches are in accordance with the Constitution and, if not, to declare such actions void.

Answer (a) is incorrect because the power of judicial review extends to actions of the legislative branch as well as those of the executive branch. Answer (c) is incorrect because judicial review is not expressly conferred by the U.S. Constitution; it is an implicit judicial function. Answer (d) is incorrect because judicial review involves the evaluation of the constitutionality of governmental actions, not statutory construction.

12. The principle that gives past judicial decisions binding authority in similar cases is known as

a. The rule of dictum.

b. Stare decisis.

c. Judicial review.

d. Civil law system.

The correct answer is (b). *(Publisher)*

REQUIRED: The principle that gives past cases binding authority.

DISCUSSION: A distinguishing feature of a common law legal system is that past judicial decisions are binding in present cases with similar fact patterns. This principle is known as stare decisis.

Answer (a) is incorrect because dictum is a statement in a judicial opinion which is unnecessary for the decision of the case. Answer (c) is incorrect because judicial review is the power of courts to review the constitutionality of acts of government and the power to review decisions of lower courts. Answer (d) is incorrect because a civil law system is based on legislative laws only. There is no common law; i.e., past judicial decisions are not binding. In the United States, only Louisiana uses a civil law system.

4.2 Classifications of Law

13. Law can be classified variously. Examples are civil and criminal, substantive and procedural, and public and private. Which of the following is public rather than private law?

a. Contract law.

b. Constitutional law.

c. Property law.

d. Tort law.

The correct answer is (b). *(Publisher)*

REQUIRED: The branch of law that is classified as public rather than private.

DISCUSSION: Public law concerns the structure and powers of governing bodies and their relationship with the population. It includes administrative and criminal law as well as constitutional law. In the American system, constitutional law concerns the rights of the people and the allocation of authority between the federal and state systems and among the legislative, executive, and judicial branches at both levels. Private law concerns the relations among private individuals or entities.

Answers (a), (c), and (d) are incorrect because the law of contracts, torts, property, agency, and business organizations fall within the scope of private law.

14. The classification of law also requires a distinction between substance and procedure. Which of the following is incorrect?

a. Substantive law is that body of law which creates rights and imposes duties.

b. Procedural law is the body of rules which govern the manner in which rights are asserted or duties are imposed.

c. A court will always apply the substantive law of the forum but may apply procedural rules of another jurisdiction.

d. A court always applies the procedural rules of its own jurisdiction.

The correct answer is (c). *(Publisher)*

REQUIRED: The false statement concerning the distinction between substantive and procedural law.

DISCUSSION: The distinction between substance and procedure is that substantive law concerns the definition of rights, while procedural law is concerned with measures to implement those rights. An example of a substantive right is that which permits one to recover when injured by the negligence of another. An example of a procedural rule is the requirement limiting when and where a suit for negligence may be brought. One reason the distinction is significant is that if a law is deemed substantive, the forum court may feel compelled to apply the law of another jurisdiction (e.g., if the case arose out of a transaction in another jurisdiction), while if it is considered procedural, the forum court will generally apply its own law.

Answers (a), (b), and (d) are incorrect because they are correct statements regarding substantive or procedural law.

15. The distinction between civil and criminal law is important in any legal system. The distinction is vital because it determines the nature of the remedies as well as the parties and procedure in a legal proceeding. Which is the correct statement concerning this distinction?

a. A civil action involves a suit brought by the civil authorities for the breach of a duty imposed by law.

b. A criminal action involves a prosecution by the appropriate governmental entity of a person who has committed a tort.

c. A civil action normally involves a dispute between private persons with regard to duties imposed by law or created by contract.

d. Criminal law governs felonies, misdemeanors, and torts.

The correct answer is (c). *(Publisher)*

REQUIRED: The correct statement concerning the distinction between civil and criminal law.

DISCUSSION: A criminal prosecution is brought by governmental authorities for an injury to society as a result of a breach of duty imposed upon all persons by the law. A civil action may also involve a breach of a duty imposed by the law upon all persons, but the injury is deemed to be private and is enforced by a private person rather than a governmental entity. Moreover, a civil action may also involve the breach of a duty created by agreement between the parties.

Answer (a) is incorrect because civil actions are generally brought by private persons. Answers (b) and (d) are incorrect because a tort is generally considered a breach of a private duty imposed by the law on all persons. It is not a crime but rather gives rise to a remedy in a civil action. Crimes include capital crimes, felonies, and misdemeanors.

16. Civil law makes a distinction between torts and contracts. Which of the following is a correct statement of the distinction between tort and contract law?

a. A tort is a crime because it is a violation of a duty imposed by law upon all individuals within the society.

b. Tort and contract law are similar in that each is concerned with the imposition of civil duties.

c. Liability in contract is enforced by private persons whereas liability in tort is enforced by the appropriate governmental entity.

d. Contract law exclusively involves the enforcement of duties voluntarily assumed with respect to property arrangements.

The correct answer is (b). *(Publisher)*

REQUIRED: The correct statement regarding the distinction between tort and contract law.

DISCUSSION: A tort is a breach of a civil duty imposed by the law upon all persons. A breach of contract involves the breach of a duty imposed by agreement between the specific parties. Torts and contracts are two aspects of the law concerning private liability. Both are designed to compensate a party who has been injured by the defendant's wrong.

Answer (a) is incorrect because torts give rise to private liability while crimes give rise to public liability. The injury caused by a crime is deemed to be done to all individuals in the society, while the harm caused by a tort is essentially private in nature. Answer (c) is incorrect because liability in both tort and contract is enforced by private persons. Answer (d) is incorrect because contract law also extends to virtually any matter on which two persons may enter into an agreement, e.g., the rendition of services.

17. The distinction between law and equity has both historical and practical significance for today's legal system. Which of the following is the incorrect statement concerning the distinction?

a. Equity provides different remedies from those available at law.

b. Suits in equity are not tried before juries.

c. Separate courts of law and equity are not found in the American legal system.

d. An action for damages is equitable in nature.

The correct answer is (d). *(Publisher)*

REQUIRED: The false statement concerning the distinction between law and equity.

DISCUSSION: The historical distinction between law and equity arose because the English common law courts could not furnish sufficiently flexible remedies for the legal needs of the population. The answer was the evolution of courts of equity with power to give remedies when laws were not sufficient. The action for damages was and is essentially a legal (as opposed to an equitable) remedy.

Answer (a) is incorrect because equity and law do give different remedies. Injunctions, declaratory actions, and specific performance are examples of equitable remedies. Answer (b) is incorrect because suits in equity are not tried before juries, while suits in law are tried before juries if the parties so choose. This is one reason modern courts continue to make the distinction between legal and equitable action. Answer (c) is incorrect because it is true that American courts have no administrative distinction between law and equity. The same court may exercise both legal and equitable powers.

4.3 Sources of American Law

18. A fundamental characteristic of the American legal system is that it is adversarial. The best description of such a system is that

a. Truth is best served by an independent investigation of the facts by the judicial decision-maker.

b. Justice is best served if the respective sides to a dispute are represented by interested parties whose interests are in conflict and who have a full opportunity to be heard by an impartial tribunal.

c. The court appoints attorneys to represent the respective sides.

d. A person with a stake in the outcome is a poor advocate of his/her position in a legal dispute.

The correct answer is (b). *(Publisher)*

REQUIRED: The best description of an adversarial legal system.

DISCUSSION: An adversarial legal system operates on the assumption that the truth may best be determined through the clash of opposing viewpoints. It attempts to harness the energy of partisanship to ensure that each side of a dispute is as well represented as possible.

Answers (a) and (d) are incorrect because in an adversarial system, an assumption is made that the interested parties are best able to investigate and present the facts and legal arguments related to a dispute. Answer (c) is incorrect because courts rarely appoint attorneys except to protect the rights of defendants in criminal cases.

19. A complex legal system has many classifications of law. In the American legal system such classifications of binding legal authority include

a. Constitutions, statutes, and regulations.

b. Attorney general opinions, executive orders, and treaties.

c. Authoritative pronouncements by designated legal authorities such as the National Conference of Commissioners on Uniform State Laws.

d. Advisory opinions of the U.S. Supreme Court.

The correct answer is (a). *(Publisher)*

REQUIRED: The sources of law that provide binding legal authority.

DISCUSSION: The federal and state constitutions, statutes enacted by Congress and state legislatures, and regulations issued by administrative agencies are all forms of binding legal authority. A constitution is the highest form of legal authority and must be followed if applicable. Statutes are also binding upon courts, and regulations will be followed if in conformity with the related statute.

Answer (b) is incorrect because while executive orders and treaties have the status of binding legal authority, attorney general opinions provide only advisory authority. Answer (c) is incorrect because while pronouncements by respected legal scholars may be highly persuasive, they do not compel compliance by any court. Answer (d) is incorrect because the Supreme Court does not issue advisory opinions.

20. While it is true that courts have a law-making function which has emerged through the evolution of case law, the principal law-making function is carried out by legislative bodies in the American legal system. The legislative law-making power is subject to judicial interpretation. This judicial function is known as

a. Statutory construction.

b. Adjudication.

c. Judicial review.

d. Judicial legislation.

The correct answer is (a). *(Publisher)*

REQUIRED: The term descriptive of the judicial function of interpretation.

DISCUSSION: Statutory construction is the judicial function in which courts determine the meaning of statutes. The purpose is not to create law but to resolve ambiguities in the statutes as written.

Answer (b) is incorrect because adjudication is the judicial function of resolving disputes. Answer (c) is incorrect because judicial review is the power of courts to review the constitutionality of acts by the other branches of government. The term is also used to describe the power of appellate courts to review the decisions of lower courts and administrative agencies. Answer (d) is incorrect because the process of interpreting statutes is not a law-making function of the courts; it is simply a determination of the meaning of the statute.

21. The United States is a complex society with an equally complex legal system. Understanding that system requires an awareness of the hierarchy of laws. Which of the following has the greatest authority?

a. Constitution of the U.S.

b. Treaties of the U.S.

c. Statutes of the U.S.

d. Regulations of the U.S.

The correct answer is (a). *(Publisher)*

REQUIRED: The most authoritative U.S. law.

DISCUSSION: The U.S. Constitution is the supreme law in the United States. All other federal laws are made pursuant to the authority granted in the Constitution.

Answers (b) and (c) are incorrect because federal statutes and treaties are second in hierarchy to the Constitution. Federal statutes and treaties have equal authority. Answer (d) is incorrect because administrative agencies write regulations pursuant to a statutory grant of authority.

22. Allocation of power has been referred to as a fundamental purpose of a constitutional arrangement. Which of the following is a correct statement about the ways in which the U.S. Constitution allocates power?

a. The federal government cannot exercise powers not specifically enumerated.

b. Powers not specifically delegated to the federal government or to the states are reserved to the federal government.

c. State statutes control whenever not in direct conflict with federal statutes.

d. Federal law prevails if federal and state statutes conflict.

The correct answer is (d). *(Publisher)*

REQUIRED: The allocation of powers between the federal government and the states.

DISCUSSION: The federal Constitution is the supreme law. Next come the federal statutes and treaties provided they are properly enacted. When state and federal law conflict, federal law controls if a federal issue is involved.

Answer (a) is incorrect because the federal government also has implied powers that are necessary and proper for exercising the enumerated powers. Answer (b) is incorrect because the powers not specifically delegated or implied to the federal government are reserved to the states or to the people. Answer (c) is incorrect because even if state statutes do not directly conflict with federal statutes, state law is invalid if material uniform regulation is required, the federal government has preempted the field, or the state statute otherwise violates the U.S. Constitution.

23. Which of the following is a correct statement about the ranking of federal and state laws?

a. If the federal statute relates to a power delegated to the federal government by the Constitution and the state statute is validly enacted under the state constitution, the state statute prevails.

b. Federal and state statutes may often regulate the same subject matter without either being invalid.

c. When federal statutes regulate a given subject, state law is preempted.

d. When no federal law has been enacted on a subject, the state law is necessarily valid.

The correct answer is (b). *(Publisher)*

REQUIRED: The true statement about ranking federal and state law.

DISCUSSION: If the subject matter of a federal law is within the constitutional powers of the federal government, a conflicting state law will be invalid under the supremacy clause of the U.S. Constitution. But the exercise of federal authority does not necessarily preclude state regulation of many matters also subject to federal law, e.g., securities regulation. But state regulation must not be unreasonably burdensome to the federal interest.

Answer (a) is incorrect because a conflicting state statute would be invalid. If the laws do not conflict, both are generally valid. Answer (c) is incorrect because although federal legislation on a federal matter may expressly or impliedly preempt state legislation, nonconflicting federal and state laws often coexist. Answer (d) is incorrect because a state law may concern a subject that requires uniform national regulation or be in violation of the Constitution.

24. Which classification of state law has the least authority?

a. The state's constitution.

b. Statutes.

c. Common law.

d. Regulations.

The correct answer is (c). *(Publisher)*

REQUIRED: The state law that has the least authority.

DISCUSSION: The constitution of a state is the ultimate source of legal authority for that state. Validly enacted statutes and regulations are next in the hierarchy. Cases decided by courts (common law) must defer to a constitutional statute or regulation.

Answers (a), (b), and (d) are incorrect because each has greater authority than case (common) law.

4.4 Common Law

25. The American legal system is based on common law. The essence of the common law is that cases decided by courts become binding precedent under the doctrine of stare decisis for later decisions in similar cases by the same court or by lower courts within the same system. Just what rule of law a given case stands for is often a difficult question. To discover this rule (the holding of a case), one must

a. Read the transcript of the trial.

b. Determine the precise issues which had to be decided in order to obtain the result in the case.

c. Pay attention to dicta in the opinion.

d. Read the dissenting opinion.

The correct answer is (b). *(Publisher)*

REQUIRED: The principle followed to discover the rule of law for which a given case stands.

DISCUSSION: How to determine the holding of a case (the principle of law which may have binding authority in future cases) is not a matter agreed upon by lawyers, judges, and legal authorities. Most agree, however, that only statements of law contained in the opinion which relate to issues which had to be decided to resolve the dispute have binding legal authority.

Answer (a) is incorrect because only opinions of reported cases are used as precedent. Reported cases have a written opinion by the judge(s) which summarizes the case and the legal decision. Answer (c) is incorrect because dicta are statements which relate to issues which were not technically required to be resolved to decide the case. Answer (d) is incorrect because the statement of law made by the majority of the court provides the rule of the case. Statements in dissenting opinions may be highly persuasive and representative of future trends, but they are not binding rules.

26. Plaintiff brought a suit in equity to dissolve a corporation of which she was a major shareholder. The petition alleged that corporate assets were being wasted through certain improper actions of management and the other shareholders. Plaintiff conceded that she had also engaged in certain wrongful conduct regarding use of corporate assets. Which of the following is correct?

a. A court applying equitable rules should dismiss the suit.

b. The court may issue an injunction to prohibit future criminal conduct of the kind alleged.

c. The plaintiff's rights should be vindicated on the merits of the case regardless of her wrongful actions.

d. The court should only apply rules of law to the case.

The correct answer is (a). *(Publisher)*

REQUIRED: The correct approach to a suit brought in equity.

DISCUSSION: A suit brought in equity is subject to prevailing notions of what is just as well as existing legal rules. An equity court applies equitable maxims such as clean hands doctrine ("He who comes into equity must do so with clean hands"). Thus, a plaintiff complaining about waste of corporate assets lacks the necessary clean hands to seek equitable relief from such misconduct by others when she has also engaged in improper conduct.

Answer (b) is incorrect because generally future criminal conduct cannot be enjoined since it is already barred by existing criminal statutes. Also the accused may be wrongly deprived of a jury trial. Answer (c) is incorrect because the plaintiff in equity must have clean hands. Answer (d) is incorrect because a suit in equity is brought when legal rules are inadequate to do justice.

27. The landmark Supreme Court decision in "Erie Railroad v. Tompkins" (1938) had a great impact on the allocation of judicial power between the state and federal courts because it

a. Permitted the development of a federal general common law.

b. Permitted federal courts to apply state statutory law in diversity cases.

c. Permitted state courts to decide federal questions.

d. Required federal courts to apply unwritten state law in diversity cases.

The correct answer is (d). *(Publisher)*

REQUIRED: The effect of the "Erie" decision on the allocation of judicial power.

DISCUSSION: The Judiciary Act of 1789 provided for federal courts to apply the appropriate state law in diversity cases. An early decision of the Supreme Court, "Swift v. Tyson," held that federal courts were not bound to apply state common law in such cases. As a consequence, a federal general common law began to develop. Since the states did not follow this law, uniform administration of state law was prevented. Reasoning that the Constitution did not give to federal courts the power to declare state law, the "Erie" court held that they must apply the whole substantive law of the state in a diversity case. There is thus no federal common law with respect to state issues.

Answer (a) is incorrect because "Erie" abolished federal general common law. Answer (b) is incorrect because federal courts must now apply state common law as well as statutory law in diversity cases. Answer (c) is incorrect because state courts previously had concurrent jurisdiction over some federal questions.

28. The law has many purposes and performs a wide variety of functions. Which of the following is not an accepted function of law in modern American society?

a. Protecting the public order by shaping society so that it complies with the moral values of the elected officials.

b. Ensuring public safety by punishing persons who deviate from accepted norms.

c. Resolving disputes between groups and individuals in a systematic way.

d. Maintaining a system of social control while facilitating social life.

The correct answer is (a). *(Publisher)*

REQUIRED: The incorrect statement of a function of law.

DISCUSSION: As noted below, the functions of the law include maintaining the social order, resolving disputes, and ensuring public safety. The law also serves to protect the status quo while at the same time permitting necessary change to occur in a rational and systematic manner. However, enforcement of the values of public officials is emphatically not a function of law. Elected and other officials have a duty to uphold the law irrespective of their personal views. The law of a society with institutions of representative government should reflect the will of all the people.

Answer (b) is incorrect because the law has a significant part in ensuring public order, that is, public health, welfare, and safety. It provides a means for punishing those who injure others. Answer (c) is incorrect because the courts interpret and apply the law to resolve the disputes brought before them. Society would be in chaos without a peaceful and systematic method of disposing of conflicts. Answer (d) is incorrect because maintaining social control is possibly the most vital role played by the legal system. The law introduces stability and predictability into all aspects (political, economic, social) of society by prohibiting conduct harmful to the social order and providing sanctions for violations of those prohibitions. The law thus promotes acceptable norms of behavior and permits all members of society to have a reasonable expectation of such conduct by others.

CHAPTER FIVE
THE U.S. COURT SYSTEM

5.1 Structure and Function of Federal and State Court Systems

1. The court system in the United States consists of

a. A federal system and a second state court system that provides for uniformity among the 50 states regarding nonfederal issues.

b. State and federal courts.

c. Courts that apply substantive law and others that apply procedural law.

d. A federal judicial system that may decide any kind of dispute.

The correct answer is (b). *(Publisher)*

REQUIRED: The correct statement describing the U.S. court system.

DISCUSSION: The United States has a dual court system. The federal government has its own court system as does each of the 50 states and the District of Columbia. This dual system is necessary because of federalism, which entails an allocation of powers between the federal and state governments.

Answer (a) is incorrect because although the U.S. has a dual system, there is no uniformity among the court systems of the 50 states. Each state is sovereign regarding state law matters. Answer (c) is incorrect because courts are impartial tribunals established by government to settle disputes. For this purpose, all courts use two types of law. Substantive law defines the litigants' various rights and duties, and procedural law provides the means of enforcing the substantive law. Answer (d) is incorrect because unless a federal statutory or constitutional question is involved or the parties are from different states (and $50,000 or more is in dispute), the case cannot be litigated in a federal court.

2. The court system in the U.S. consists essentially of two functional types of courts: trial and appellate courts.

a. The principal function of trial courts is to resolve disputes through determination of factual issues and application of the law to the facts thus found.

b. Juries are exclusively responsible for determination of the facts at trial.

c. The function of the trial court judge is to preside over all proceedings and to determine issues of law but not of fact.

d. The trial court judge determines all issues of law and fact in civil cases.

The correct answer is (a). *(Publisher)*

REQUIRED: The true statement concerning the functions of trial and appellate courts.

DISCUSSION: The main service performed by the trial court is to act as a trier of fact. Trial court procedure is primarily involved with defining and resolving factual issues. A trial is never conducted unless a factual issue remains in the case. Appellate courts almost exclusively decide questions of law.

Answers (b) and (c) are incorrect because whereas the jury is largely a fact-finding body, the court (judge) must act as a trier of both law and fact in the many cases tried without juries. Answer (d) is incorrect because if the case is tried by a jury, the jurors will determine the facts.

3. The functions of an appeals court include

a. The rendering of decisions with precedential value only if made by the highest court in the system.

b. Reviewing errors committed by lower courts within the same system.

c. Reviewing errors of law but not of fact made by lower courts within the same system.

d. The exercise of exclusive jurisdiction over suits in equity.

The correct answer is (b). *(Publisher)*

REQUIRED: The true statement of a function of an appeals court.

DISCUSSION: An appeals court is chiefly concerned with reviewing decisions made by lower courts within the same system. Due process requires that in almost all cases litigants have access to at least one appeal.

Answer (a) is incorrect because the highest court in the system has the greatest authority, but cases decided by lower-level appellate courts also have precedential effect unless overruled by a higher court. Moreover, reported trial court opinions may have some value as precedent. Answer (c) is incorrect because in practice appeals courts also review the legal sufficiency of findings of fact. An appellate court will reverse if the findings of fact were "clearly erroneous." Answer (d) is incorrect because our legal system observes no administrative distinction between suits in law and suits in equity.

4. The American legal system is a federal system and therefore allocation of power between the respective state court systems and the federal courts is crucial. Under the U.S. Constitution,

a. Federal courts have unlimited jurisdiction.

b. The court of last resort of the state is the final authority in resolving issues regarding that state's law.

c. The federal courts must apply federal case law in diversity cases pursuant to the decision in Erie Railroad v. Tompkins.

d. The U.S. Supreme Court is the final authority on all questions of state and federal law.

The correct answer is (b). *(Publisher)*

REQUIRED: The correct statement concerning the allocation of judicial power.

DISCUSSION: The theory of federalism is that the federal government and its courts have broad but limited powers. The U.S. Supreme Court is the final authority on all federal matters. With regard to matters left to the province of the states (those not involving any federal question), the federal courts must defer to the authoritative determinations of the courts of last resort in the respective states. For example, private law (e.g., contracts and torts) rarely involves a federal question, although public law (such as criminal or constitutional law) tends to generate federal questions.

Answer (a) is incorrect because federal courts have broad but specifically limited jurisdiction. Answer (c) is incorrect because the landmark Erie decision required the application of both state statutory and common law by federal courts in cases heard under diversity jurisdiction. Answer (d) is incorrect because the U.S. Supreme Court must defer to the highest court of the state with regard to questions concerning state law.

5. One night, Paula Plaintiff was walking along a path adjacent to railroad tracks. As a train passed, something protruding from it struck and injured Plaintiff, causing her personal injuries resulting in $75,000 of medical expenses. Plaintiff, a resident of State Y where the incident occurred, wished to sue the railroad company, which had its principal place of business and was incorporated in State X. The applicable laws of States X and Y differ. Which of the following is true?

a. Plaintiff must sue in State X for jurisdictional reasons.

b. Plaintiff may sue in federal court if she wishes to have the case tried under the federal common law of torts.

c. Plaintiff must sue in State X if she wishes to have that state's law applied.

d. Plaintiff may sue in State X, State Y, or in federal court, but the same law will probably be applied by any of the possible forums.

The correct answer is (d). *(Publisher)*

REQUIRED: The true statement about jurisdiction and choice of law.

DISCUSSION: This question is based on the facts of Erie Railroad v. Tompkins, a Supreme Court decision significant for the allocation of power between the federal and state systems. The injury occurred in State Y,, and the defendant is subject to suit there. The defendant corporation had a principal place of business and was incorporated in State X, so it is subject to suit there as well. Because the parties had diverse citizenship, the action could have been brought in federal court because the jurisdictional amount was sufficient (the amount in controversy must exceed $50,000).

Each state has a set of conflict of laws rules to determine which state's substantive law to apply. A federal court will follow the conflict of law rules of the state in which it is located. In a tort case, the traditional rule is to apply the substantive law of the place of injury regardless of where the suit is actually tried. Most states use an interest analysis to determine the state having the most significant relationship to the case. Under either method, the law of State Y would probably be applied.

Answer (a) is incorrect because Plaintiff can also sue in State Y or federal court. Answer (b) is incorrect because federal courts apply state law in diversity cases. No federal common law exists regarding state law matters, such as torts. Answer (c) is incorrect because State X's conflict of law rules would probably apply State Y's substantive law.

6. The federal judicial power is articulated in the Constitution. Under the Constitution,

a. The U.S. District Courts, the U.S. Courts of Appeals, and the Supreme Court are expressly created as the principal courts in the federal system.

b. Congress has power to limit the jurisdiction of the federal courts.

c. Federal judges hold office for the specific terms of years established in the Constitution.

d. Federal courts have unlimited subject-matter jurisdiction.

The correct answer is (b). *(Publisher)*

REQUIRED: The correct statement concerning the federal judicial power.

DISCUSSION: Article III, Section I of the U.S. Constitution provides, "The judicial power of the United States shall be vested in one Supreme Court, and in such inferior courts as the Congress may from time to time ordain and establish." Because Congress has the power to create the lower federal courts, the Supreme Court has held that it also has the power to limit their jurisdiction. Article III also specifically gives Congress the power to make exceptions and to establish regulations for the exercise of the Supreme Court's appellate jurisdiction.

Answer (a) is incorrect because Article III of the Constitution expressly creates only the U.S. Supreme Court. Answer (c) is incorrect because Article III does not establish specific terms of years. It provides that federal judges shall hold their offices during good behavior. Answer (d) is incorrect because federal courts have limited subject-matter jurisdiction. The judicial power of the United States as defined in Article III is itself limited. The powers not enumerated in the Constitution as belonging to the federal government belong to the states and to the people under the 10th Amendment.

7. Which of the following is a true statement about the organization of the federal court system?

a. It has three levels of courts.

b. The United States District Courts have greater authority than any federal court except the U.S. Supreme Court.

c. United States District Courts are primarily appellate courts.

d. Any of the 13 United States Courts of Appeals may review the decisions of any of the District Courts.

The correct answer is (a). *(Publisher)*

REQUIRED: The true statement about the organization of the federal court system.

DISCUSSION: The federal court system consists of three levels. The 97 District Courts are trial courts at the lowest level in the system. The 13 Courts of Appeals constitute the middle level. They are courts of review. At the top level of the federal court system is the Supreme Court. The Supreme Court principally reviews decisions of the Courts of Appeals, but does have original jurisdiction in a very few cases.

Answer (b) is incorrect because the Courts of Appeals have power to review decisions of the District Courts. Answer (c) is incorrect because the District Courts are trial courts, not appellate courts. Answer (d) is incorrect because each Court of Appeals except that for the Federal Circuit reviews the decisions of the District Courts in its circuit. The Court of Appeals for the Federal Circuit hears various specialized appeals, e.g., those from Claims Court, and patent, trademark, and copyright cases.

8. The U.S. Supreme Court derives its powers from the Constitution. The Constitution establishes

a. The grant of certiorari jurisdiction to the U.S. Supreme Court.

b. That the Supreme Court has extensive original jurisdiction that it shares concurrently with the lower federal courts.

c. That the Supreme Court shall have nine Justices.

d. No express provision for judicial review.

The correct answer is (d). *(Publisher)*

REQUIRED: The true statement concerning the U.S. Supreme Court.

DISCUSSION: The doctrine of judicial review arose from the Supreme Court's decisions interpreting the Constitution and is not expressly granted. According to the doctrine, the judiciary possesses the power to review actions of the other branches of government to determine their constitutionality. If the courts declare such an action to be unconstitutional, it is null and void.

Answer (a) is incorrect because the Constitution does not mention certiorari (discretionary) jurisdiction. This appelate jurisdiction is conferred by statute. Under the Supreme Court's rules, the agreement of four Justices is sufficient to invoke this jurisdiction by issuing a writ of certiorari. The writ is, in effect, a demand that a specific case be brought before the Court for review. Answer (b) is incorrect because the Supreme Court's original jurisdiction is narrow and rarely exercised. Answer (c) is incorrect because the Constitution does not establish the number of Justices that sit on the Supreme Court. The number is determined by federal statute.

9. The U.S. Supreme Court, a court that is "infallible because final," is the ultimate arbiter of law within the federal system. The Supreme Court

a. May function as a trial court in some cases.

b. Has no discretionary appellate jurisdiction.

c. Exercises mandatory appellate jurisdiction in several important classes of cases.

d. Has no original jurisdiction.

The correct answer is (a). *(Publisher)*

REQUIRED: The true statement concerning the U.S. Supreme Court.

DISCUSSION: The Constitution gives the Supreme Court original or trial jurisdiction in certain cases, e.g., in cases involving foreign ministers and ambassadors. In practice, the Supreme Court's original jurisdiction is held concurrently with the lower federal courts (except for controversies between two or more states), and the Supreme Court refuses to exercise it.

Answers (b) and (c) are incorrect because virtually all Supreme Court cases are heard at the discretion of the Justices. Certain appeals formerly required to be heard, e.g., an appeal from a decision by the highest court of a state invalidating a federal statute as unconstitutional, are now within the Court's discretionary jurisdiction. Congress eliminated the Supreme Court's mandatory appellate jurisdiction in 1988. Answer (d) is incorrect because Article III establishes original jurisdiction in two classes of cases: those affecting ambassadors and similar persons and those in which a state is a party.

10. The United States Circuit Courts of Appeals

a. Have been established pursuant to congressional enactment.

b. Were expressly created in the Constitution.

c. Hear only cases appealed from U.S. District Courts.

d. Hear cases only if more than $10,000 is in controversy.

The correct answer is (a). *(Publisher)*

REQUIRED: The correct statement concerning the United States Circuit Courts of Appeals.

DISCUSSION: The Constitution gives Congress the right to establish inferior federal courts in both Article I and Article III. If Congress desired, it could dispense with the lower federal courts altogether.

Answer (b) is incorrect because there is no express mention of the Circuit Courts of Appeals in the Constitution. Answer (c) is incorrect because although the Circuit Courts must hear most cases heard by appeal from the District Courts, they also have original jurisdiction, e.g., over the actions of certain administrative agencies, such as the NLRB. Answer (d) is incorrect because federal courts have jurisdiction over federal question cases, which have no amount-in-controversy requirement, and certain cases with a requirement that differs from the amount (more than $50,000) required for diversity cases.

11. The Tax Court of the United States

a. Has removal jurisdiction with regard to tax cases originally filed in U.S. District Court.

b. Has appellate jurisdiction of tax cases originating in the Claims Court.

c. Hears tax cases without juries.

d. Is not a true court but an administrative body within the Treasury Department.

The correct answer is (c). *(Publisher)*

REQUIRED: The true statement concerning the Tax Court.

DISCUSSION: The Tax Court of the United States is established by Section 7441 of the Internal Revenue Code as a court of record under Article I of the U.S. Constitution. It hears exclusively federal tax cases without juries. To obtain a jury trial in a federal tax case, the action must be brought before a federal District Court.

Answer (a) is incorrect because removal jurisdiction applies to the removal of certain cases from state courts to federal District Courts. Answer (b) is incorrect because monetary claims brought against the United States in the Claims Court are appealed to the Court of Appeals for the Federal Circuit. Answer (d) is incorrect because the Tax Court is a court of record under Article I.

12. The federal court system is a complex structure that includes numerous specialized courts. Which of the following is a national trial court?

a. U.S. District Court.

b. Court of Appeals for the Federal Circuit.

c. U.S. Claims Court.

d. U.S. Bankruptcy Court.

The correct answer is (c). *(Publisher)*

REQUIRED: The specialized federal court that functions as a national trial court.

DISCUSSION: The U.S. Claims Court is a trial level court with nationwide jurisdiction. It hears cases involving monetary claims against the United States, including certain tax cases.

Answer (a) is incorrect because the jurisdiction of the District Courts is usually limited to defendants subject to the jurisdiction of the courts in the state where the District Court is located. Also, venue would not be proper in every district. Answer (b) is incorrect because it is an intermediate-level appellate court that hears appeals in certain specialized cases, e.g., from the Claims Court and the Court of International Trade. Answer (d) is incorrect because the Bankruptcy Courts are adjuncts to the District Courts.

13. Which of the following statements regarding state courts is correct?

a. Under the supremacy clause of the Constitution, state courts must uphold a federal law that conflicts with state law.

b. The U.S. Supreme Court has no authority to overrule the decisions of state supreme courts.

c. State courts cannot hear cases that involve questions of federal law.

d. A case begun in a state court cannot be transferred to a federal court.

The correct answer is (a). *(Publisher)*

REQUIRED: The correct statement regarding state courts.

DISCUSSION: Under the supremacy clause, a state statute is invalid if it is in direct conflict with a federal law. Hence, a state court must uphold a federal law if that law is in direct conflict with a state statute.

Answer (b) is incorrect because under the doctrine of judicial review, the U.S. Supreme Court has the authority to overrule a state supreme court if the case involves a question of federal law. Answer (c) is incorrect because many claims arising under federal law may be tried in state courts. Answer (d) is incorrect because if certain conditions are met, a case can be transferred (removed) from state to federal court.

14. A typical state court system includes all but which of the following?

a. A court of last resort.

b. Intermediate-level appeals courts.

c. Small claims courts.

d. Bankruptcy courts.

The correct answer is (d). *(Publisher)*

REQUIRED: The court not found in a typical state court system.

DISCUSSION: Proceedings in bankruptcy are within the exclusive jurisdiction of the federal courts. Article I of the Constitution gives Congress the power to enact uniform laws on the subject of bankruptcy throughout the U.S.

Answer (a) is incorrect because each state has a supreme court or court of last resort that is the final authority within that state on matters of state law. Answer (b) is incorrect because most states have an intermediate level of appeals courts. Such courts typically handle the bulk of mandatory appeals from the trial courts within the system. Answer (c) is incorrect because the typical state court system includes small claims courts that hear minor claims in an informal and relatively inexpensive manner.

15. Most state court systems include small claims courts for the resolution of minor disputes. In small claims court,

a. Appeals cannot be taken.

b. Jurisdictional amounts are not established.

c. The ordinary rules of civil procedure are often not followed.

d. Lawyers are never permitted.

The correct answer is (c). *(Publisher)*

REQUIRED: The true statement about practices in a small claims court.

DISCUSSION: Small claims litigation varies from state to state, but the essential purpose of these courts is to assure affordability by expediting the resolution of minor legal disputes through a more informal civil procedure than that available under the customary rules. Formal pleadings, discovery, and evidentiary rules are dispensed with, and the judge often assumes the role of mediator between parties who represent themselves.

Answer (a) is incorrect because some states permit appeals from small claims decisions. Answer (b) is incorrect because a low jurisdictional amount (e.g., $1,500) is established. Larger claims are litigated in regular courts. Answer (d) is incorrect because some states permit representation by attorneys.

5.2 Jurisdiction of Courts

16. Subject-matter jurisdiction is the court's

a. Power over the person of the defendant.

b. Power over a thing that allows it to seize and hold the object for some legal purpose.

c. Jurisdiction based on a person's interest in property.

d. Competence to hear a particular category of cases.

The correct answer is (d). *(Publisher)*

REQUIRED: The correct definition of subject-matter jurisdiction.

DISCUSSION: Subject-matter jurisdiction is the court's power to hear a particular type of case. Subject-matter jurisdiction is defined by constitutions and statutes.

Answer (a) is incorrect because power over the person of the defendant is in personam jurisdiction. Answer (b) is incorrect because power over a thing is referred to as in rem jurisdiction. Answer (c) is incorrect because jurisdiction based on a person's interest in property is quasi in rem jurisdiction.

17. The subject-matter jurisdiction of state courts

a. Does not extend to cases arising under the U.S. Constitution.

b. Does not extend to cases involving persons residing in different states.

c. Extends to all cases except those over which the federal courts have exclusive jurisdiction.

d. Extends to all cases having "minimum contacts" with the particular state.

The correct answer is (c). *(Publisher)*

REQUIRED: The correct statement concerning subject-matter jurisdiction of state courts.

DISCUSSION: The federal government has limited power. It may not exercise powers not granted to it in the Constitution. The states may exercise any powers not exclusively exercised by the federal government. Thus, the state courts may hear any case except one over which the federal courts have exclusive jurisdiction, e.g., bankruptcy, federal taxation, customs, and patent cases.

Answer (a) is incorrect because the jurisdiction of state and federal courts over cases arising under the U.S. Constitution is concurrent. Either system may hear most such cases. Answer (b) is incorrect because both state and federal courts have jurisdiction over diversity cases. Federal courts may hear such cases provided the amount in controversy exceeds $50,000. Otherwise, the state courts have exclusive jurisdiction. Answer (d) is incorrect because whether a case has "minimum contacts" with a state is relevant to the determination of personal, not subject-matter, jurisdiction.

18. Curt Smith, a citizen of Florida, is injured in an auto accident in Miami. The driver of the other vehicle is a citizen of New York. Smith wishes to recover the $6,000 he incurred for medical expenses and repairs to his car. Can Smith bring an action in federal court based on diversity of citizenship?

a. No, because a citizen of one state cannot sue a citizen of another state in federal court.

b. No, because the suit would not involve a federal statute.

c. No, because diversity suits in federal court must involve more than $50,000.

d. Yes, because he and the driver of the other car are citizens of different states.

The correct answer is (c). *(Publisher)*

REQUIRED: The requirements for bringing a diversity action in federal court.

DISCUSSION: A person can bring an action in federal court based on diversity of citizenship if 1) the plaintiff and the defendant are citizens of different states, and 2) the amount involved exceeds $50,000. In this case, Smith's action would fail because it does not involve the required minimum amount.

Answer (a) is incorrect because a citizen of one state can sue a citizen of another state in federal court if the requirements are met. Answer (b) is incorrect because violation of a federal statute is not required in a diversity action. Answer (d) is incorrect because diversity of citizenship alone is not sufficient. The amount in controversy must still exceed $50,000.

19. Federal courts have broad but limited jurisdiction. In which instance would the federal courts not always have jurisdiction?

a. Cases arising under the U.S. Constitution.

b. Admiralty cases.

c. Cases in which the controversy is between two states.

d. Controversies between citizens of different states.

The correct answer is (d). *(Publisher)*

REQUIRED: The cases in which the federal courts have partial jurisdiction and the states have full jurisdiction.

DISCUSSION: A controversy between citizens of different states may always be brought in one of the state courts. These are called diversity cases. The judicial power of the United States also extends to diversity cases but only those in which the amount in controversy exceeds $50,000.

Answers (a), (b), and (c) are incorrect because federal courts always have jurisdiction in these types of cases.

20. The federal judiciary currently includes 97 United States District Courts. They

a. Are the exclusive trial courts in the federal court system.

b. Hear appeals from the Claims Court and the Tax Court.

c. Have removal jurisdiction in appropriate cases.

d. Have exclusive jurisdiction of claims against the U.S. government.

The correct answer is (c). *(Publisher)*

REQUIRED: The correct statement concerning the U.S. District Courts.

DISCUSSION: If a civil action could originally have been brought in a District Court and if the case has not yet gone to trial, a nonresident defendant in a state court may have the case automatically removed to the appropriate U.S. District Court.

Answer (a) is incorrect because the Claims Court, the Tax Court, and the Bankruptcy Courts are also trial courts within the federal system. Answer (b) is incorrect because appeals from the Claims Court are heard by the Court of Appeals for the Federal Circuit. Appeals from the Tax Court are heard by the Circuit Courts of Appeals. Answer (d) is incorrect because nontort claims against the U.S. government are heard by the Claims Court.

CHAPTER SIX
THE LITIGATION PROCESS

6.1 Civil Litigation

1. Acme Corporation's latest annual report states that Acme is a party to a lawsuit entitled "Algonquin Products v. Samna, Inc."

a. Acme's potential liability must be minimal because it is not a named party.

b. The case is a criminal or a civil proceeding.

c. The case is a civil proceeding.

d. Algonquin Products is the plaintiff.

The correct answer is (c). *(M. Levin)*

REQUIRED: The information conveyed by a case name.

DISCUSSION: A case name can reveal some information about the case, for example, whether it is a criminal or civil matter. A suit brought by a private party will be a civil suit. There is much, however, that one cannot conclude from a simple reference to the case name. Some parties may not be named, and the ordering of the names will not necessarily reflect the status of plaintiff and defendant.

Answer (a) is incorrect because exclusion from the case name has no bearing on that party's role or potential for liability. The case name will not necessarily identify all parties. Given multiple plaintiffs and defendants, a case is ordinarily identified by an abbreviated reference to just two parties. Answer (b) is incorrect because criminal actions are always prosecuted by the government. This suit has been brought by a private party. Answer (d) is incorrect because this conclusion cannot be reached with certainty. If this case is on appeal, the first-named party is the appellant (the party who is appealing), and the second-named party is the appellee (the party defending the appeal). Either a plaintiff or a defendant may have grounds for appeal.

2. The first question a court must resolve in a civil proceeding is whether it has jurisdiction of the subject matter and of the parties, whether it has power to resolve the particular kind of dispute and to give a remedy which will affect the rights and duties of the parties before the court.

a. A court may exercise jurisdiction over both property and persons.

b. A state court may not exercise jurisdiction over persons not resident within the forum state.

c. Long-arm statutes have been invalidated under the U.S. Constitution.

d. The "International Shoe" decision established a "minimum contacts" test to be observed by courts in determining whether they have jurisdiction in federal question cases.

The correct answer is (a). *(Publisher)*

REQUIRED: The correct statement concerning a court's jurisdiction.

DISCUSSION: Courts may exercise jurisdiction over both property (in rem) and persons (in personam). Some lawsuits affect only a particular piece of property. Some lawsuits affect the rights and duties of persons, and as a result extend to any property they own.

Answer (b) is incorrect because modern concepts of long-arm jurisdiction permit a state court to exercise power over nonresidents. Answer (c) is incorrect because a long-arm statute is valid as long as it meets the "minimum contacts" test announced by the Supreme Court. Answer (d) is incorrect because the landmark "International Shoe" decision established a "minimum contacts" test to be observed by state courts in determining whether they have personal jurisdiction over defendants. The defendant must have such minimum contacts with the state as to render it fair for him/her to be called upon to defend in the forum.

3. A statute of limitations compels a plaintiff to bring an action within a reasonable time. It prevents unfairness to defendants, avoids state claims, and encourages litigation while witnesses and evidence are still available. The typical statute

a. Begins to run when the last element constituting the cause of action occurs.

b. Requires that litigation be completed before it expires.

c. Begins to run when the first element constituting the cause of action occurs.

d. Permits tolling only for the plaintiff's incapacity.

The correct answer is (a). *(Publisher)*

REQUIRED: The correct statement about the application of a statute of limitations.

DISCUSSION: A statute of limitations is in force for most civil and criminal actions. It codifies the common law principle of laches: undue delay in bringing a suit, with consequent prejudice to the other party, results in forfeiture of the right. The statutory period begins to run when the plaintiff's right to bring suit arises, that is, when the last element constituting the cause of action occurs.

Answer (b) is incorrect because filing the complaint tolls the statute. Answer (c) is incorrect because it begins to run when the last element occurs. Answer (d) is incorrect because the running of the statute may be stopped (tolled) for various reasons, e.g., insanity, absence of the defendant from the jurisdiction, court order, or minority of the plaintiff.

4. A state court is least likely to have jurisdiction over the person of the defendant when (s)he

a. Has no contacts with the forum state but is personally served with process in another state.

b. Has a residence in the forum state and process is served at the residence.

c. Consents even though no other basis for jurisdiction exists.

d. Cannot be located and the plaintiff in a divorce action advertises in a local newspaper.

The correct answer is (a). *(Publisher)*

REQUIRED: The method of acquiring personal jurisdiction least likely to be effective.

DISCUSSION: Service of process (a copy of the summons and of the complaint) is effective to gain jurisdiction over a person within the forum state barring some impropriety. Personal service outside the state is ineffective unless the defendant has minimum contacts with the jurisdiction. The constitutional principle is that personal jurisdiction must be based upon at least minimum contacts with the forum state.

Answer (b) is incorrect because when a defendant has a domicile in the forum state, leaving the summons and complaint at that place with a person of mature years is usually sufficient. Answer (c) is incorrect because a defendant may always consent to personal jurisdiction. Answer (d) is incorrect because a mailing process to the defendant's last known address and advertising periodically in a publication of general circulation (constructive service) may meet the requirement of providing adequate notice when the person cannot be located.

5. Herr was a resident of New York who had never lived in Florida. Frau was a resident of Florida. They maintained a romantic relationship for many years although they were married to others. Through various misleading statements, Frau induced Herr to fly to Miami. When he disembarked, a deputy sheriff served him with a summons. Herr immediately flew back to New York. Based on the personal jurisdiction thus obtained, Frau won a Florida judgment for seduction under promise of marriage in an action in which Herr made no appearance. When Frau attempted to enforce the judgment in New York, the court's ruling regarding personal jurisdiction was that service of process

a. On a person physically within the state was sufficient.

b. Was insufficient for lack of minimum contacts.

c. Was unnecessary because defendant was within the reach of Florida's long-arm statute.

d. Was insufficient because defendant was fraudulently induced to enter Florida.

The correct answer is (d). *(Publisher)*

REQUIRED: The ruling on personal jurisdiction when service of process is procured by trickery.

DISCUSSION: Ordinarily, the "minimum contacts" test is met by physically serving process on a party while (s)he is voluntarily within the geographic jurisdiction of the forum court. A defendant impliedly consents to personal jurisdiction by his/her presence, assuming proper service of process. But a plaintiff may not resort to deception to obtain the defendant's presence for this purpose.

Answer (a) is incorrect because presence of a party may not be obtained by deception. Answer (b) is incorrect because voluntary presence is a sufficient contact to justify actual service. Answer (c) is incorrect because a long-arm statute cannot operate in the absence of a minimum contact.

6. Lu Walker lived in Georgia. Returning by automobile from Texas, Walker struck a vehicle driven by Harley Kell, a Florida resident on his way to Alabama, while traveling on a Florida highway. After stopping for repairs, Walker left Florida, never to return. Walker had no other contacts with the state. If Kell wishes to sue Walker for negligence, he

a. Must bring the action in a Georgia state court.

b. Must bring the action in federal court.

c. May bring the suit in a state court in Georgia or Florida or in a federal court, but Georgia law will apply.

d. May bring the action in Florida under Florida law.

The correct answer is (d). *(Publisher)*

REQUIRED: The court where suit might be filed when a tort is committed by an out-of-state defendant.

DISCUSSION: Long-arm statutes solve the problem of personal jurisdiction over nonresidents who commit torts while temporarily in the state. Although the defendant's contact with the state may have consisted solely of an automobile accident, the typical long-arm statute allows extension of jurisdiction provided that the suit arose out of the contact. Kell's action in Florida would probably be tried under Florida law since that is where the injury occurred and the minimum contacts exist.

Answers (a) and (b) are incorrect because the lawsuit could be brought in Florida or Georgia (where the defendant resides) or even in federal court if the damages exceed $10,000. Answer (c) is incorrect because Florida law will probably apply since that is the state with minimum contacts where the injury occurred, and it has the greatest interest in having its law applied.

7. An essential preliminary step before a court may take up a dispute is to determine whether that court is the proper venue for adjudication of the case.

a. The concept of the inconvenient forum (forum non conveniens) permits a court with jurisdiction to decline to exercise it.

b. A defect in venue is assertible at any time before the conclusion of litigation.

c. Venue is proper only in the location that is the most convenient for the parties, the witnesses, and the court.

d. Venue is a concern only in federal courts.

The correct answer is (a). *(Publisher)*

REQUIRED: The correct statement concerning venue.

DISCUSSION: When a court has jurisdiction over the subject matter and the parties, the court will customarily exercise it. The doctrine of the inconvenient forum is an exception to a court's duty to exercise its jurisdiction. If bringing suit in the forum state would seriously inconvenience the courts, parties, or witnesses, and if a more convenient forum is available elsewhere, the forum court may dismiss without prejudice to the plaintiff's rights to bring the action in another court.

Answer (b) is incorrect because judicial systems are divided into territories, and venue rules assign the particular territory within the judicial system in which an action must be brought. A defect in venue must be objected to at an early stage in litigation for it not to be waived. Answer (c) is incorrect because the venue rules do not attempt to locate the action in the best forum, only a reasonably convenient one. Answer (d) is incorrect because every state has rules concerning the appropriate venue for an action.

8. Before a party may seek judicial relief, (s)he must not only establish that the particular court has subject matter and personal jurisdiction, but also that the case is appropriate for judicial resolution. Which is the false statement concerning justiciability of controversies?

a. In the federal system a court may not hear a case unless it presents a "case or controversy" within the meaning of the U.S. Constitution.

b. Courts refuse to entertain collusive suits because the adversary system is best served if the opposing parties have a genuine dispute with substantial consequences for each side.

c. In order to bring an action a party must have standing.

d. Whether the issues are moot is irrelevant to justiciability.

The correct answer is (d). *(Publisher)*

REQUIRED: The false statement concerning justiciability of controversies.

DISCUSSION: The adversary system is based on the theory that courts function best when the parties before it have a genuine dispute the resolution of which has actual consequences for each. If the issues of a case have become moot with the passage of time, a court will normally not regard the case as fit for decision on the merits.

Answer (a) is incorrect because Article III of the Constitution does provide that the judicial power may only be exercised when a "case or controversy" exists, i.e., a genuine dispute with legal consequences. Answer (b) is incorrect because the court will not hear the case if the presence of one party has been procured by the adverse party solely to obtain a forum. The requisite clash of conflicting viewpoints would be absent. Answer (c) is incorrect because a party must have standing to bring a cause of action; i.e., the party must claim a direct and immediate injury.

9. A fundamental problem in adjudicating disputes is the choice of the law to be applied by the court. The problem is especially acute when a court in one state must decide a case involving either a party domiciled in another state or a cause of action that arose in another state. Which statement is true concerning state choice of law rules?

a. They generally follow the law of the place of the injury in tort actions.

b. Most states have adopted a variation of interest analysis with respect to some part of their conflict of law rules.

c. The law of the forum state always applies in a state court.

d. The UCC forbids parties to choose the applicable law in transactions governed by the UCC.

The correct answer is (b). *(Publisher)*

REQUIRED: The correct statement concerning state choice of law rules.

DISCUSSION: In a lawsuit involving parties from more than one jurisdiction, a problem may arise as to which substantive law should be applied to determine the outcome of the case. Courts have evolved conflict of law (choice of law) rules to determine which law to apply. The majority of states follow the interest analysis approach, which emphasizes a logical scrutiny of the problem rather than the blind application of a rule. An interest analysis requires an application of the minimum contacts doctrine and a determination of which jurisdiction has the greatest relationship to the facts and parties. The substantive law of that jurisdiction is then used.

Answer (a) is incorrect because although the traditional rule in tort actions was to follow the law of the place of the injury, today the trend is to use some form of interest analysis. Answer (c) is incorrect because the court will always apply its own procedural law, but not necessarily its own substantive law. Answer (d) is incorrect because UCC 1-105 permits parties to choose the applicable law subject to a reasonable relationship test.

10. An essential guarantee in the American legal system is that a litigant must have timely notice and a reasonable opportunity to be heard before a court may affect his/her rights.

a. The U.S. Supreme Court has held that a defendant in a civil suit must in every case receive either personal notice or notice by mail of a pending action.

b. The U.S. Supreme Court has held that the proper form of notice is that which is reasonable in the circumstances.

c. Most state statutes do not provide for notice by substituted service or by publication in appropriate circumstances.

d. The principal constitutional underpinning for the right to notice lies in the equal protection clause.

The correct answer is (b). *(Publisher)*

REQUIRED: The correct statement concerning the requirement of notice.

DISCUSSION: Before a court may exert personal jurisdiction over a defendant, due process requires that (s)he be served with appropriate notice. The Supreme Court has held that the requirements of due process are met if notice is given which is reasonable in the circumstances. The circumstances might dictate that actual notice be given. In other cases, when the whereabouts or identity of the parties is unknown, notice by publication may suffice.

Answer (a) is incorrect because the U.S. Supreme Court has adopted only a reasonableness standard with respect to notice. Answer (c) is incorrect because most state statutes do provide for substituted service and notice by publication. Substituted service of process involves leaving a copy of the complaint and a summons with a person of mature years at the residence of the defendant. Notice by publication involves a legal notice in a paper of general circulation when the location of the defendant is unknown. Answer (d) is incorrect because the due process clause is the constitutional basis for the notice requirement.

11. The initial stage of a civil lawsuit involves the filing of pleadings by the respective parties. The purpose of pleadings is to give notice to the parties and to the court of the assertions of each side and to assist in the determination of the issues. The complaint is the first pleading filed and has the effect of initiating the lawsuit. The complaint should include all except which of the following?

a. A short statement of the jurisdictional facts.

b. A request for relief.

c. An exact listing of what the plaintiff must prove that is couched in precise legal terminology.

d. A short and plain statement of the basis for the plaintiff's claim.

The correct answer is (c). *(Publisher)*

REQUIRED: The item not required to appear in a complaint.

DISCUSSION: Modern pleading rules have considerably simplified the task of the parties to a lawsuit. The complaint does not need to include any detailed listing of proof nor be couched in legal terminology.

Answer (a) is incorrect because the complaint should indicate facts sufficient to establish both the subject-matter jurisdiction and personal jurisdiction of the court. Answer (b) is incorrect because the complaint should indicate the nature of the relief sought by the claimant. Answer (d) is incorrect because the complaint should include sufficient facts to enable the court and the opposing party to understand the basis for the plaintiff's claim.

12. The complaint is one form of claim for relief. Which of the following is not a proper claim for relief?

a. A counterclaim by a defendant against a plaintiff.

b. A crossclaim.

c. A third-party claim filed against a nonparty.

d. A crossclaim by a defendant against a plaintiff.

The correct answer is (d). *(Publisher)*

REQUIRED: The response that is not a proper claim for relief.

DISCUSSION: A crossclaim is a claim by a party against a co-party (e.g., defendant against a co-defendant) which is based on the same transaction or occurrence as the main claim. A crossclaim is not asserted by a defendant against a plaintiff.

Answer (a) is incorrect because a claim by a defendant against a plaintiff is a counterclaim. It usually need not relate to the plaintiff's original claim. Answer (b) is incorrect because a crossclaim, as noted above, is a permissible form of claim. Answer (c) is incorrect because a defendant may file a third-party claim against a nonparty who may be liable for all or any part of a judgment obtained by the original claimant against the defendant.

13. The rules of civil procedure provide numerous occasions for the parties to make motions to the court. A motion is essentially an application to the court for an order. Motions appropriate at the pleading stage include a motion

a. For a directed verdict.

b. To dismiss for failure to state a claim upon which relief could be granted.

c. To strike evidence.

d. For a new trial.

The correct answer is (b). *(Publisher)*

REQUIRED: The motion appropriate at the pleading stage.

DISCUSSION: A motion to dismiss for failure to state a claim is appropriate at the pleading stage because it tests the legal sufficiency of the opponent's claim for relief. It will be granted if the claim does not state an injury for which the law will give a remedy. Some older cases use the term demurrer rather than motion to dismiss.

Answer (a) is incorrect because a motion for a directed verdict is appropriate only after the defendant's evidence is presented. Answer (c) is incorrect because a motion to strike evidence is appropriate only at trial. Answer (d) is incorrect because a motion for a new trial would only be appropriate during or after trial.

14. The rules of civil procedure permit a case to be disposed of in appropriate circumstances during or at the conclusion of the pleading stage. One such vehicle for early resolution of the case is the summary judgment. A summary judgment

a. Will be granted if a genuine issue of material fact remains.

b. Is the same as a judgment on the pleadings.

c. Is a decision on the merits.

d. May not be granted as to a part of a case.

The correct answer is (c). *(Publisher)*

REQUIRED: The correct statement concerning a summary judgment.

DISCUSSION: At any time before the beginning of the trial, the court may grant a motion for summary judgment. The early disposition of the case in this manner would be based upon the absence of any genuine dispute of material fact between the parties. Pleadings, affidavits, and testimony would be taken into account. The judgment rendered is on the merits of the case, not on a procedural or technical ground.

Answer (a) is incorrect because summary disposition of the case is not permissible when a genuine issue of material fact remains to be determined by the trier of fact. Answer (b) is incorrect because a judgment on the pleadings is rendered solely on the basis of what appears on the face of the pleadings. Answer (d) is incorrect because a summary judgment may be partial; e.g., it may be rendered with regard to the issue of liability, with trial going forward solely on the issue of damages.

15. If a case has survived the pleading stage, the next procedural step is discovery. The purposes of discovery include all except which of the following?

a. Providing an opportunity to preserve relevant information.

b. Eliminating issues between the parties by agreement.

c. Compelling a party to disclose relevant information in his/her possession.

d. Permitting a party to develop his/her own case to the fullest while preserving the element of surprise.

The correct answer is (d). *(Publisher)*

REQUIRED: The purpose not served by discovery.

DISCUSSION: A principal purpose of discovery is to avoid surprise. In theory, each side is entitled to notice of the content of the other side's case to provide an opportunity to prepare to meet it. Surprise undermines the basis of the adversarial system which emphasizes permitting each side to present the best possible case. A secondary purpose of discovery is to facilitate settlements and reduce court workloads.

Answer (a) is incorrect because discovery does permit the preservation of relevant information; e.g., a deposition would preserve the testimony of a witness which might be lost if the witness became unavailable. Answer (b) is incorrect because discovery can help refine the issues so that only those in genuine dispute are dealt with at the trial. Answer (c) is incorrect because an adversary can be compelled to disclose relevant information in his/her possession.

16. The methods of discovery under the federal rules of civil procedure do not include

a. Depositions.

b. Physical or mental examinations without a court order.

c. Written requests for admissions.

d. Interrogatories addressed to parties.

The correct answer is (b). *(Publisher)*

REQUIRED: The impermissible method of discovery.

DISCUSSION: Physical and mental examinations are a permissible method of discovery only if made pursuant to a court order. Since such an examination involves a substantial invasion of the person, it must be sanctioned by the court.

Answer (a) is incorrect because a deposition is a proper method of discovering and preserving information by the examination of a person in the presence of an impartial third party who certifies the proceedings. A court order is not required. Answer (c) is incorrect because one may make a formal written request for an admission by the opposing party. A bad faith refusal to admit may result in an imposition of sanctions by the judge. Answer (d) is incorrect because one may submit written questions (called interrogatories) to the opposing party to solicit relevant information. This is often the first step in the discovery phase.

17. The scope of discovery is not unlimited. To be discoverable, information

a. Must appear to be relevant to the subject matter of the pending action.

b. May be privileged but not admissible as evidence at trial.

c. May be the work product of an attorney.

d. Must be admissible as evidence at trial.

The correct answer is (a). *(Publisher)*

REQUIRED: The correct statement concerning the scope of discovery.

DISCUSSION: The scope of discovery is not totally unlimited, but the parties have substantial freedom to make a wide-ranging investigation. Accordingly, a party may discover matter which relates to the overall context of the action.

Answer (b) is incorrect because matter that is subject to a privilege may not be discovered, e.g., confidential communications between attorney and client. Answer (c) is incorrect because as a general rule, the work product of an attorney is not subject to discovery. Answer (d) is incorrect because evidence may be discoverable even though it is not admissible at trial. Such information may present a fruitful line of inquiry even though it is too prejudicial to be presented to the trier of fact.

18. The pre-trial conference is a valuable aid to the efficient administration of the trial phase. At the pre-trial conference the trial judge and the attorneys consider a variety of matters not including

a. Sharpening and simplifying the issues.

b. Limiting the number of witnesses and testimony.

c. The possibility of an out-of-court settlement.

d. The extension of the suit to embrace other claims.

The correct answer is (d). *(Publisher)*

REQUIRED: The matter not properly considered at the pre-trial conference.

DISCUSSION: The pre-trial conference is an informal affair in which the attorneys and the judge endeavor to dispose of the case without trial or to simplify the issues and in general provide guidelines for the most efficient presentation of the respective cases at trial. The result of the conference is a pre-trial order which governs the subsequent conduct of litigation. The presentation of other claims would not be appropriate at the conference.

Answers (a), (b), and (c) are incorrect because each represents a proper function of the pre-trial conference.

19. Trial by jury in a civil case

a. In a federal court would not be available in most suits at common law.

b. Would be available in a civil case in a federal court if the suit were filed in equity.

c. Would be guaranteed by the typical state constitution whether the suit was legal or equitable.

d. Is guaranteed in federal courts for suits at common law.

The correct answer is (d). *(Publisher)*

REQUIRED: The correct statement concerning trial by jury in a civil case.

DISCUSSION: The 7th Amendment, which applies directly to the federal government, provides for trial by jury in suits at common law if "the value in controversy shall exceed $20."

Answer (a) is incorrect because a jury trial is usually available. Answers (b) and (c) are incorrect because suits filed in equity are not tried before juries in either the federal or the state courts. The right to a jury trial in a civil case is not guaranteed.

20. A jury trial will involve both questions of law and questions of fact. A question of law is

a. An issue involving the resolution of a factual dispute.

b. An issue involving the application or interpretation of a law.

c. Determined by the jury.

d. Determined by the counsel for the defendant.

The correct answer is (b). *(Publisher)*

REQUIRED: The correct definition of a question of law.

DISCUSSION: Jury trials involve both questions of law and questions of fact. A question of law is an issue involving the application or interpretation of a statute, case precedent, or constitutional provision. Questions of law are determined by the court, or more specifically, the judge. Questions of fact are determined by the trier of fact, either a jury or the trial judge in a nonjury case.

Answer (a) is incorrect because an issue involving the resolution of a factual dispute is a question of fact. Answer (c) is incorrect because the jury determines questions of fact, not questions of law. Answer (d) is incorrect because questions of law are determined by the court, not by the defendant's counsel.

21. If a case is tried before a jury, a jury must be selected prior to the making of opening statements. During jury selection,

a. The attorneys will conduct the venire examination in order to determine the acceptability of the jurors.

b. Each side has an unlimited number of peremptory challenges.

c. Each side has a limited number of challenges for cause.

d. The attorneys will conduct a voir dire examination of prospective jurors.

The correct answer is (d). *(Publisher)*

REQUIRED: The correct statement concerning jury selection.

DISCUSSION: Before the jury may be selected, the respective attorneys will customarily engage in an examination of the prospective jurors to discover possible prejudices. This is known as the voir dire examination.

Answer (a) is incorrect because the venire is the panel of prospective jurors. Answer (b) is incorrect because peremptory challenges are limited in each jurisdiction by statute. A peremptory challenge permits a party to dismiss a prospective juror without cause. Answer (c) is incorrect because if one side can establish a legally recognized basis for challenging a juror, that juror must be dismissed for cause. The number of challenges for cause is unlimited.

22. The opening statements introduce the evidential phase of the trial. Which statement is correct?

a. The opening statements are evidence in the case.

b. The plaintiff's attorney customarily makes the first opening statement.

c. The defendant's attorney ordinarily makes the first opening statement.

d. The trial judge customarily makes the opening statement.

The correct answer is (b). *(Publisher)*

REQUIRED: The correct statement regarding the opening statements.

DISCUSSION: As a matter of custom, the plaintiff's attorney makes the first opening statement.

Answer (a) is incorrect because the purpose of an opening statement is to provide a summary of that side's case. It is not considered evidence. Answers (c) and (d) are incorrect because the attorneys for the parties to the suit make the opening statements, the plaintiff's attorney customarily making his/hers first.

23. Following the opening statements the trial enters its evidentiary phase. Each side has an opportunity to present evidence to support its assertions or rebut those of the opponent. The presentation of evidence will be made in accordance with the rules of evidence in effect in the forum jurisdiction.

a. Each side has the right to examine and cross-examine its own witnesses.

b. One may not ask leading questions of one's own witnesses in any situation.

c. The scope of the cross-examination is limited to the scope of the direct examination.

d. One may not call an adverse party as a witness in a civil action.

The correct answer is (c). *(Publisher)*

REQUIRED: The correct statement concerning the presentation of evidence at trial.

DISCUSSION: After one side has directly examined a witness, the other side has a right to cross-examine. Cross-examination is limited to the scope of the direct examination for purposes of judicial economy. Matters beyond the scope of the direct examination may be brought out in the cross-examiner's own case.

Answer (a) is incorrect because one is not permitted to cross-examine one's own witnesses. Answer (b) is incorrect because one may ask leading questions (those which are highly suggestive of the answer) of one's own witnesses if the witnesses turn out to be hostile or adverse. Answer (d) is incorrect because in a civil action, an adverse party may be called to testify since there is no civil law privilege not to be a witness against oneself.

24. If evidence is offered and objected to at trial, an appeals court may not reverse

a. On the ground that the evidence was wrongly excluded.

b. On the ground that the evidence was wrongly admitted.

c. If the record contained no statement of what evidence was excluded or what specific objection was made to evidence which was admitted.

d. On the ground of wrongful exclusion of evidence if the case is tried without a jury.

The correct answer is (c). *(Publisher)*

REQUIRED: When an appeals court may not reverse a decision on the admissibility of evidence.

DISCUSSION: An appeals court must make its decisions based upon the record made in the lower court, the briefs filed by the parties in the appeal, and the oral arguments presented. Accordingly, a party who objects to the admission or exclusion of evidence at trial must make a specific objection for insertion in the record if (s)he wishes to appeal the lower court's ruling on the objection at a later time.

Answers (a), (b), and (d) are incorrect because each is a proper basis for reversal on appeal provided the objection was properly taken and the error was harmful.

25. Several requirements are necessary for evidence to be admissible in court. One requirement is that it have a logical tendency to prove or disprove a proposition in the case. The term for this is

a. Material.

b. Probative.

c. Relevant.

d. Competent.

The correct answer is (b). *(Publisher)*

REQUIRED: The term describing evidence that has a logical tendency to prove or disprove a proposition.

DISCUSSION: Admissible evidence must be probative; i.e., it must have a logical tendency to prove or disprove a material proposition in the case. This and other terms used to determine when evidence is admissible have a tendency to overlap.

Answer (a) is incorrect because materiality refers to the importance of evidence and its relationship to the case. Answer (c) is incorrect because relevancy embraces both probativeness and materiality; evidence must relate to a substantive legal issue in the case. Answer (d) is incorrect because competent evidence is not in violation of an exclusionary rule. A confidential communication between an attorney and client might not be admissible because it is subject to an exclusionary rule, i.e., not competent.

26. Hearsay

a. Could not consist of evidence of statements made in a court.

b. Is evidence of statements made verbally or nonverbally.

c. Is admissible but not discoverable.

d. Is discoverable but not admissible.

The correct answer is (b). *(Publisher)*

REQUIRED: The correct statement concerning hearsay.

DISCUSSION: The Federal Rules of Evidence define hearsay as "a statement other than one made by the declarant while testifying at the trial or hearing, offered in evidence to prove the truth of the matter asserted." The statement alluded to may be a verbal or a nonverbal statement. It might include body language or written statements.

Answer (a) is incorrect because hearsay might involve a statement made in a courtroom at an unrelated trial or hearing. Answer (c) is incorrect because anything which is admissible is also discoverable under the rules of discovery. Answer (d) is incorrect because hearsay is discoverable only if it relates to the subject matter of the pending litigation and is not privileged. Hearsay may be admissible if one of the numerous exceptions to the hearsay rule is applicable.

27. While driving to an aerobics class after work, Degas hit Paine as Paine was walking across a street with a green walk signal. A passerby who did not see the accident testified that afterward Degas jumped from the car, ran to Paine's prostrate body, and said, "I was in a hurry because I was late for class. I'm so sorry." This testimony should be

a. Excluded as hearsay.

b. Admitted under the spontaneous exclamation exception to the hearsay rule.

c. Admitted since it is not hearsay.

d. Excluded since it is not material.

The correct answer is (b). *(Publisher)*

REQUIRED: The admissibility of a statement made by defendant immediately after an accident.

DISCUSSION: Hearsay is admissible if one of the numerous exceptions to the rule applies. The element common to the exceptions is reliability. If the out-of-court statement was made in a situation in which the speaker was unlikely to lie, it will usually be admissible. The spontaneous exclamation permits admission of statements uttered concurrently with an event in circumstances not affording the opportunity to make a self-serving statement.

Answer (a) is incorrect because the testimony is admissible as an exception. Answer (c) is incorrect because the testimony is hearsay; it repeated an out-of-court statement made by another person and was offered to prove the truth of the matter asserted. Answer (d) is incorrect because the testimony is material since it relates to an issue on which plaintiff must present evidence.

28. Testimonial privileges protect confidential communications between certain persons. In appropriate circumstances, confidential communications between which persons are protected?

a. Directors and a corporation.

b. Attorney and client.

c. Partners and a partnership.

d. Trustees and a trust.

The correct answer is (b). *(Publisher)*

REQUIRED: The persons who are entitled to a testimonial privilege.

DISCUSSION: Statements made in certain confidential relationships may be neither discovered nor admitted at trial. State and federal laws vary as to the privileges, but they protect certain confidential relationships. The privilege is often established between attorney-client, husband-wife, clergy-penitent, and physician-patient.

Answers (a), (c), and (d) are incorrect because no testimonial privilege exists for these relationships.

29. Which is the correct statement concerning directed verdicts?

a. A verdict may not be directed when the case is tried with a jury since the right to a jury trial includes the right to a jury verdict.

b. A party who seeks and fails to obtain a directed verdict loses his/her case.

c. A party who has successfully sought a directed verdict will have the benefit of a final decision on the merits.

d. A judge may not direct a verdict upon the motion of the plaintiff.

The correct answer is (c). *(Publisher)*

REQUIRED: The correct statement concerning directed verdicts.

DISCUSSION: A directed verdict is a decision by a judge that, in light of the evidence presented, no reasonable person could decide the case in any other way. A directed verdict is a decision on the merits, and when appeals are exhausted the decision will be final.

Answer (a) is incorrect because the right to a jury trial does not include the right to a jury verdict. A verdict may be directed when the case is tried to a jury if the judge determines that no genuine issue of fact remains to be decided by the jury. Answer (b) is incorrect because if the motion for a directed verdict is denied, the case proceeds in its normal course. Answer (d) is incorrect because either side may move for a directed verdict.

30. In his/her instructions to the jury, the judge is required to do all except which of the following?

a. Specify the type of verdict to be rendered.

b. Explain the law to be applied.

c. Define the issues to be determined.

d. Limit the time of deliberation.

The correct answer is (d). *(Publisher)*

REQUIRED: The purpose not served by the judge's instructions to the jury.

DISCUSSION: A judge may not specify an exact time limit for the jury's deliberations. The jury instructions are limited essentially to explaining the law to be applied, defining the issues to be decided, and specifying the type of verdict to be rendered. There are general verdicts (who wins) and special verdicts (answers to specific factual questions).

Answers (a), (b), and (c) are incorrect because each is required in jury instructions.

31. The jury does not have unlimited power in rendering a verdict in a civil case. The judge may do all except which of the following?

a. Enter a judgment notwithstanding the verdict.

b. Prohibit appeal of a reasonable award of damages.

c. Require a plaintiff who has received an excessive damage award to accept a reduction in damages unless the plaintiff is willing to accept a new trial.

d. Grant a motion for a new trial.

The correct answer is (b). *(Publisher)*

REQUIRED: The action a judge in a civil case may not take.

DISCUSSION: With rare exceptions, actions of a trial judge are appealable under due process. A trial judge has no authority to prohibit appeals.

Answer (a) is incorrect because a judge may enter a judgment notwithstanding the verdict (essentially a directed verdict rendered after a verdict). The decision would reflect the judge's belief that the jury acted unreasonably. Answer (c) is incorrect because judges in most jurisdictions have the power to grant a defendant's motion for a new trial to influence a plaintiff to accept a reduced damage award. Answer (d) is incorrect because a judge may elect to grant a motion for a new trial instead of directing a verdict.

32. After the trier of fact enters a verdict, and assuming that motions for directed verdicts or for new trials have been denied, the judge will enter a judgment.

a. A final judgment of a court of competent jurisdiction is effective only within the state in which rendered.

b. The privileges and immunities clause of the 14th Amendment protects nonresidents of a state from enforcement of judgments rendered by the courts of the state.

c. The full faith and credit clause of the Constitution provides that the judicial proceedings of one state must be respected by other states.

d. The full faith and credit clause applies in practice most often to state statutes, not to judgments.

The correct answer is (c). *(Publisher)*

REQUIRED: The correct statement concerning the effect of final judgments.

DISCUSSION: Article IV of the U.S. Constitution states that "full faith and credit shall be given in each state to the public acts, records and judicial proceedings of every other state." The clause has been interpreted most often to apply to final judgments rendered in courts of competent jurisdiction. The full faith and credit clause is a necessary protection in a federal system because it facilitates the enforcement of judgments without relitigation when a defendant or his/her property is not in the state in which the judgment was rendered.

Answer (a) is incorrect because the final judgment of a court of competent jurisdiction is effective in every state. Answer (b) is incorrect because the privileges and immunities clause of the 14th Amendment essentially guarantees federal rights of citizens against abridgment by the states. Answer (d) is incorrect because the full faith and credit clause is seldom applied to state statutes. It is almost always applied to enforcement of final judgments.

33. Judgments for monetary damages

a. Have an indefinite duration.

b. May be enforced by execution.

c. Cannot be discharged in bankruptcy.

d. Expire after 20 years and may not be renewed.

The correct answer is (b). *(Publisher)*

REQUIRED: The correct statement concerning judgments for monetary damages.

DISCUSSION: A party who has recovered a civil judgment for damages may, if the defendant fails to pay, have recourse to judicial process to seize, sell, and receive the proceeds from property of the defendant, i.e., execute the judgment. Discovery process may be used if desired.

Answer (a) is incorrect because judgments normally have an initial statutory duration (e.g., 20 years) although they are usually renewable. Answer (c) is incorrect because most civil judgments may be discharged in bankruptcy. Answer (d) is incorrect because judgments are customarily renewable.

34. The principle of res judicata

a. Prevents relitigation of issues which have been fully, fairly, and finally decided on the merits by a court of competent jurisdiction.

b. Is synonymous with comity.

c. Is the basis for requiring that the subject matter of a suit (the res) be located within the forum state in order for the court to have in rem jurisdiction.

d. Permits a court to adjudicate disputes.

The correct answer is (a). *(Publisher)*

REQUIRED: The correct statement concerning the principle of res judicata.

DISCUSSION: Res judicata is the principle by which a reasonable end is mandated for litigation. It provides that a litigant may have his/her day in court but that this right is limited by concern for the efficient use of judicial resources and fairness to the other parties.

Answer (b) is incorrect because comity is the respect which one sovereign gives to the legislative, executive, or judicial actions of another. Answer (c) is incorrect because res judicata is a bar to excessive litigation, not a limit on the court's jurisdiction over property. Answer (d) is incorrect because res judicata does not provide a court with the authority to adjudicate; it limits the power of parties to relitigate a case.

35. The border of State X with State Y is a river. Plaintiff, an X corporation, owned land on the X side and defendant, a Y corporation, owned the opposite property on the Y side. Over the years the river changed course, thereby enlarging defendant's holdings and decreasing plaintiff's. Accordingly, plaintiff sued in a State Y court to obtain title to the property that had changed hands as a result of the shift. All issues, including jurisdiction, were fully, fairly, and finally litigated in the courts of State Y. Plaintiff lost after a determination that the disputed land was in State Y. Plaintiff then brought suit in the courts of State X, from which the case was removed to federal court. Which of the following is correct?

a. Plaintiff should prevail if it disputes removal.

b. Defendant should prevail on the grounds of res judicata.

c. Plaintiff should prevail if it can show that State Y had no jurisdiction because the land was in State X.

d. Defendant should win because collateral attack of judgments is never allowed.

The correct answer is (b). *(Publisher)*

REQUIRED: The correct outcome of a collateral attack on a final judgment.

DISCUSSION: Once an issue has been finally decided by a court of competent jurisdiction, the matter is res judicata; i.e., the dispute is settled by judgment and may not be litigated further (although it may be appealed). The full faith and credit clause is the constitutional embodiment of this principle. The courts should give full faith and credit to a final judgment of another state's court. If the court in State Y lacked jurisdiction (e.g., because the disputed realty was not located in State Y), res judicata would be inapplicable. But State Y courts are competent to rule on the question of their own jurisdiction, and defendant was therefore not required to relitigate the merits of the case.

Answer (a) is incorrect because removal to a federal court is appropriate in a diversity case. Answer (c) is incorrect because the State Y courts have jurisdiction to determine their boundaries and the issue of jurisdiction was litigated. Answer (d) is incorrect because if jurisdiction had not been litigated in State Y and if the federal court had determined that the State Y court had no jurisdiction, its final judgment would not have been entitled to full faith and credit.

36. The class action suit permits numerous persons with individually insignificant claims to vindicate their rights. Which of the following is ordinarily a requirement for class action suits?

a. Members of the class who do not actively participate in the lawsuit are not bound by the judgment.

b. Questions of law but not of fact must be common to all members of the class.

c. All members of the class must be named as parties.

d. The class must be represented by parties whose claims are typical.

The correct answer is (d). *(Publisher)*

REQUIRED: The class action requirement ordinarily applicable.

DISCUSSION: Questions of law and fact must ordinarily be common to everyone in the class, the class must be too large for all members to be named as parties, the claims of class representatives must be typical, and the representatives must fairly and adequately represent the class. The Supreme Court has also said that notice must be given to all members of the class when they can be "identified through reasonable efforts."

Answer (a) is incorrect because members of the class who are notified of the class action are bound by the judgment unless they ask to be excluded when first notified. Answer (b) is incorrect because questions of both law and fact must be common. Answer (c) is incorrect because all plaintiffs are not named since there are so many. This is the reason for a class action.

6.2 Arbitration and Other Dispute Resolution Methods

37. Arbitration is a non-judicial dispute resolution mechanism. Arbitration is

a. Synonymous with mediation.

b. A method whereby the parties to a controversy may resolve their dispute by agreeing to be bound by the decision of an impartial third party.

c. Confined chiefly to labor management issues.

d. Normally conducted under governmental auspices.

The correct answer is (b). *(Publisher)*

REQUIRED: The correct statement concerning arbitration.

DISCUSSION: Arbitration is used as an alternative to a traditional trial in court. It provides speedy, less expensive, and often more expert resolution of conflicts. Settlement of disputes by arbitration arises from an agreement between the parties to be bound by the decision of an impartial third person who is often a professional arbitrator and expert in the particular field.

Answer (a) is incorrect because arbitration is binding under the parties' agreement, whereas mediation is merely advisory. Mediation is most frequently employed in labor-management conflicts. Answer (c) is incorrect because arbitration is not confined to labor-management issues but can extend to any matter upon which the parties may reach a binding agreement. Answer (d) is incorrect because arbitration is normally conducted privately rather than under governmental auspices.

38. Arbitrators render decisions

a. In accordance with precedent.

b. After hearings conducted with fewer formalities than in judicial proceedings.

c. Which are not binding upon the parties.

d. After hearings which are required to be open to the public.

The correct answer is (b). *(Publisher)*

REQUIRED: The correct statement concerning decision making by arbitrators.

DISCUSSION: One of the advantages of arbitration is that it may be conducted without the complex rules of procedure and evidence required in litigation. Many arbitration proceedings follow the adversarial model, but not with the same strictness as court proceedings.

Answer (a) is incorrect because an arbitrator, unlike a judge, is not bound by decisions in past cases. Answer (c) is incorrect because an arbitration decision is binding upon the parties based upon their agreement, subject to judicial review. Answer (d) is incorrect because arbitration hearings may be conducted privately.

39. Churchill was a wealthy customer of a brokerage firm that was a member of the New York Stock Exchange (NYSE). He asserted that an agent of the firm had fraudulently induced him to make a large stock purchase. Accordingly, he sought arbitration under NYSE rules. Churchill signed a submission to arbitration to determine damages after sale of the stock. He claimed $50,000 in damages. Without explanation, the arbitrator awarded him $50. Churchill may

a. Not challenge the award in court.

b. Challenge the arbitrator's award because no reasons were given.

c. Challenge the arbitrator's award because no opinion was written.

d. Challenge the arbitrator's award because arbitration is nonbinding.

The correct answer is (a). *(Publisher)*

REQUIRED: The effect of declaring an arbitration award without providing an explanation.

DISCUSSION: Churchill's agreement bound him to accept the result even though the arbitrator did not write a formal opinion or provide an explanation. Unless specifically required by the agreement, the arbitrator may render a decision without providing reasons. Arbitration is an alternative to the regular court system. Therefore, courts should not review decisions of arbitrators except in cases of alleged corruption.

40. Numerous states and the U.S. Congress have enacted arbitration legislation. Which of the following statements is not usually true concerning such legislation?

a. Such statutes make arbitration agreements between the parties irrevocable.

b. Such statutes make arbitration agreements between the parties revocable.

c. Such statutes regulate the standards of conduct of arbitrators.

d. Such statutes limit judicial review of arbitration awards.

The correct answer is (b). *(Publisher)*

REQUIRED: The statement not usually true concerning arbitration legislation.

DISCUSSION: The effect of arbitration legislation has been to make arbitration agreements irrevocable between the parties. Such legislation is important because in the absence of a statute, courts usually hold that the arbitration agreement is revocable any time before the final award is made by the arbitrator.

Answers (a), (c), and (d) are incorrect because each is a correct statement concerning arbitration legislation.

41. Which of the following is not a function of a conciliator?

a. Rendering binding decisions.

b. Explaining issues to the disputants.

c. Serving as an intermediary.

d. Improving communications between the disputants.

The correct answer is (a). *(Publisher)*

REQUIRED: The activity that is not a function of a conciliator.

DISCUSSION: A conciliator is the third party selected by disputants to aid in the resolution of a dispute by using conciliation techniques. Conciliation, unlike arbitration, does not result in a binding decision.

Answers (b), (c), and (d) are incorrect because explaining issues, acting as an intermediary, and improving communications are all functions of a conciliator.

42. Which of the following alternative dispute resolution methods is nonbinding and involves a third party that proposes possible solutions for the disputants' consideration?

a. Consensual arbitration.

b. Conciliation.

c. Mediation.

d. Compulsory arbitration.

The correct answer is (c). *(Publisher)*

REQUIRED: The nonbinding dispute resolution method involving a third party who offers solutions.

DISCUSSION: Mediation is a nonbinding method of dispute resolution. Mediation involves the use of a third party, the mediator, who is selected by the disputants. The disputants attempt to reach an agreement with the help of the mediator. The mediator employs the techniques used in conciliation but also proposes potential solutions to the problem.

Answer (a) is incorrect because consensual arbitration is binding even though the parties voluntarily submit the dispute to arbitration. Answer (b) is incorrect because conciliation does not include a third party who suggests solutions to problems. The conciliator improves communications, coordinates meetings, explains issues, and discusses differing opinions with the parties. Answer (d) is incorrect because compulsory arbitration is required by statute and is binding.

CHAPTER SEVEN
CONSTITUTIONAL LAW

7.1 Nature and Overview of the American Constitution

1. The U.S. Constitution

a. Like the British Constitution consists of well-established tradition rather than a written document.

b. Consists of seven articles and 26 amendments.

c. Consists of three articles and the Bill of Rights.

d. Is generally considered to include the Bill of Rights although that is an Act of Congress and not an amendment.

The correct answer is (b). *(Publisher)*

REQUIRED: The true statement about the nature of the U.S. Constitution.

DISCUSSION: The U.S. Constitution consists of seven articles and 26 amendments. Articles I, II, and III establish the powers and organization of the legislative, executive, and judicial branches, respectively, of the federal government. Article IV is the states' relations article. Article V provides an amendment procedure. Article VI contains the supremacy clause. Article VII pertains to ratification. The amendments cover matters ranging from personal rights to the right of 18-year-olds to vote.

Answer (a) is incorrect because the U.S. Constitution has been formally enacted. Answers (c) and (d) are incorrect because the first 10 of the 26 amendments are commonly referred to as the Bill of Rights.

2. The U.S. Constitution defines the powers of the federal government. Which of the following is an incorrect statement concerning the scope of those powers?

a. Congress has the power to make all laws that are necessary and proper for carrying into effect the enumerated powers conferred by the Constitution upon the U.S. government.

b. Powers not delegated to the states by the Constitution or prohibited by it are reserved to the United States exclusively.

c. The states have an implicit police power to provide for the general health, safety, welfare, and morals.

d. The powers not delegated to the United States by the Constitution, or prohibited by it to the states, are reserved to the states respectively, or to the people.

The correct answer is (b). *(Publisher)*

REQUIRED: The false statement concerning the powers of the federal government.

DISCUSSION: The federal government has express powers and implied powers that are derived from the Constitution. Article I, Section 8 expressly gives Congress the power to legislate in areas that affect business. Examples are the right to collect taxes, to regulate interstate commerce, and to enact a bankruptcy law. Implied powers are not specified in the Constitution but are "necessary and proper" for carrying out the express powers. Examples of the federal government's implied powers are the right to establish a central bank (the Federal Reserve system) and to prohibit racial discrimination in public accommodations. If the Constitution does not expressly delegate powers to the federal government or prohibit states from exercising them, they are reserved to the states or to the people, not to the federal government. An example is a state's police power to limit the personal freedom and property rights of persons for the protection of the public safety, health, welfare, and morals, and for the promotion of the public convenience and general prosperity.

Answers (a), (c), and (d) are incorrect because each is a true statement about the federal government's powers defined in the U.S. Constitution.

3. Assume that a state on the Eastern seaboard prohibits commercial fishing in its coastal waters by nonresidents. A federal statute licenses commercial fishing vessels for operations in coastal waters. The state statute is

a. Invalid under the commerce clause.

b. Valid as a legitimate exercise of the state police power.

c. Invalid under the supremacy clause of the U.S. Constitution.

d. Valid under "the new federalism."

The correct answer is (c). *(Publisher)*

REQUIRED: Whether a state statute that conflicts with a federal statute is valid.

DISCUSSION: The U.S. Constitution provides that the Constitution and laws made in pursuance thereof are the supreme law of the land. When state and federal statutes are in direct conflict, the federal statute will prevail.

Answer (a) is incorrect because while the Constitution gives the federal government the power to regulate commerce between the states, it does not prohibit regulation of commerce by the states. However, state regulation may not directly conflict with federal law and may not place an undue burden on interstate commerce. Answer (b) is incorrect because the conflict with federal law invalidates the state statute. Answer (d) is incorrect because under the concept of federalism, a supremacy clause is vital to avoid conflict.

4. Which of the following reflects the constitutional doctrine of separation of powers?

a. Issuance of regulations by an executive agency.

b. The decision after an administrative hearing to deny a license renewal.

c. The decision by a court to adopt comparative negligence as the law of a state.

d. The Supreme Court's exercise of judicial review.

The correct answer is (d). *(Publisher)*

REQUIRED: The item reflecting the application of the separation of powers doctrine.

DISCUSSION: The theory of the separation of powers provides for each of the three branches of government (legislative, executive, judicial) to perform special functions (making law, administering the law, interpreting and applying the law to resolve disputes). But the separation of powers is not absolute. For example, Congress has the power to make law, but the judiciary creates common law when it decides cases. In the U.S. legal system, decisions by courts, especially appellate courts, are binding in future cases having similar facts. Inherent in the American constitutional scheme is that the separation of powers is reinforced and safeguarded by a system of checks and balances. Examples of the enforcement of the checks and balances system are the judiciary's power to invalidate legislation and executive branch actions as unconstitutional (judicial review), and the power of Congress to impeach the president, vice-president, and federal civil officers (including members of the judiciary) for committing high crimes and misdemeanors.

Answers (a) and (b) are incorrect because each is an exception to the separation of powers. Officers of administrative agencies are entitled to hold hearings to decide controversies, and are in fact carrying out a quasi-judicial function. Administrative agencies also have rule-making (legislative) power. Answer (c) is incorrect because a court's function of creating common law is an exception to the separation of powers doctrine.

5. A city enacted a fair-housing law to prohibit racial discrimination in the sale or rental of real property. The constitutionality of the law was questioned in a suit brought by an owner of property in the city. The city should

a. Lose because the law violates the constitutional prohibition against impairing the obligation of contracts.

b. Win because the law is a valid exercise of the police power.

c. Lose because the law deprives constitutionally protected property rights.

d. Win because the contract clause of the Constitution applies only to the federal government.

The correct answer is (b). *(Publisher)*

REQUIRED: The outcome of a suit attacking the constitutionality of a law banning racial discrimination in realty transactions.

DISCUSSION: State and local entities have an inherent police power to enact laws regulating the public health and safety and promoting the public welfare. Property and contract rights are subject to the reasonable exercise of this power, for instance, to promote racial equality.

Answers (a) and (d) are incorrect because the contract clause of the Constitution prohibits states (but not the federal government) from impairing the obligations of contracts, but this clause is not literally interpreted so as to supersede the reasonable exercise of police power. Answer (c) is incorrect because property rights as well as contract rights are subject to reasonable exercise of the police power.

6. A group of citizens from Rochester, New York bring a lawsuit against Penfield, an unincorporated municipality adjacent to Rochester. The citizens allege that Penfield's zoning regulations effectively prevent persons of low and moderate income from living in Penfield in violation of the 14th Amendment. Applying the doctrine of standing, the Supreme Court would most likely

a. Dismiss the suit unless the plaintiffs can show that the Penfield zoning regulation caused them some personal injury.

b. Permit the suit to continue because it involves a constitutional issue.

c. Dismiss the suit because the plaintiffs are not residents of Penfield and therefore lack standing to challenge Penfield's zoning regulation.

d. Permit the suit to continue because it involves a civil rights issue.

The correct answer is (a). *(Publisher)*

REQUIRED: The correct application of the doctrine of standing in constitutional litigation.

DISCUSSION: Under the doctrine of standing, which is derived from the case or controversy requirement for federal jurisdiction (see Article III of the Constitution), an individual or group seeking to bring a lawsuit based on a perceived constitutional violation must show that the violation has caused an injury in fact to them. In addition, the plaintiff(s) must show that the injury would be redressed by a favorable decision. Simply disagreeing with a law is not enough to create a "case" or "controversy."

Answer (b) is incorrect because the existence of a constitutional issue is insufficient. Those persons bringing the suit must still demonstrate that they have standing. Answer (c) is incorrect because the litigants need not be citizens of the municipality to bring a suit based on a constitutional issue. Answer (d) is incorrect because the nature of the controversy does not confer standing to bring a lawsuit. The litigants must still meet the requirements of standing.

7.2 Regulation of Commerce

7. The commerce clause of the U.S. Constitution provides that "Congress shall have power to regulate commerce with foreign nations and among the several states and with the Indian tribes." This federal power

a. Has been liberally interpreted to give Congress very extensive authority to regulate economic activity.

b. Has the effect of preempting all state authority over commercial activity.

c. Applies only to interstate or international commerce and not to intrastate commerce.

d. Does not apply to intrastate commerce even though it has a substantial effect on interstate commerce.

The correct answer is (a). *(Publisher)*

REQUIRED: The correct statement concerning the commerce clause.

DISCUSSION: The commerce clause has been the basis for a gigantic expansion of federal power over economic activity. If an "activity" has a "national economic effect," Congress has power to regulate. Congress also has power over the channels of interstate commerce and substantial power even after the interstate commerce comes to an end.

Answer (b) is incorrect because federal power to regulate commerce is held concurrently with the states. The states may regulate commerce provided such regulation is not in conflict with federal law and does not unduly burden interstate commerce. Answers (c) and (d) are incorrect because the commerce clause applies even to intrastate activity if such activity has a "national economic effect."

8. A local restaurant located on an interstate highway refuses to serve people of the Catholic faith. The Civil Rights Act of 1964 specifically prohibits discrimination in restaurants on the basis of race, color, religion, national origin, or sex. If a Catholic patron sues, (s)he will win because

a. The 14th Amendment guarantees equal protection.

b. The commerce clause gives Congress the power to regulate purely local businesses.

c. State action is present because of serving food to the residents of the state.

d. The commerce clause gives Congress the power to regulate interstate commerce; and discrimination impedes interstate commerce.

The correct answer is (d). *(D.L. Mescon)*

REQUIRED: The basis for prohibiting religious discrimination in public accommodations.

DISCUSSION: Article I, Section 8 of the Constitution gives Congress the power to regulate interstate commerce. Congress has determined that discrimination in a place of public accommodation impedes interstate commerce. When Congress has made this determination, it then has the power to regulate the discrimination under the interstate commerce clause. This determination and regulation have been upheld by the Supreme Court.

Answer (a) is incorrect because even though the 14th Amendment does guarantee equal protection, it only applies to action by a government. No "state action" is involved. Answer (b) is incorrect because Article I, Section 8 gives Congress the power to regulate interstate, not intrastate, commerce. Intrastate commerce is the realm of the individual state. Answer (c) is incorrect because "state action" requires some governmental involvement.

9. The Shady Oaks Motel is located near the intersection of two interstate highways and derives approximately 75% of its business from interstate travelers. The motel advertises in national travel magazines and in newspapers in several large cities. The motel's owner refuses to rent rooms to African-Americans. As a basis for the federal government's prohibition of this discrimination, the commerce clause,

a. Cannot be used because it applies to commerce, not people.

b. Cannot be used because the case involves civil rights issues.

c. Cannot be used because this local business has only a minimal impact upon interstate commerce.

d. Can be used because discriminatory practices by motels discourage interstate travel by African-Americans and therefore negatively affect interstate commerce.

The correct answer is (d). *(Publisher)*

REQUIRED: The correct statement regarding the commerce clause's ability to reach local businesses that engage in discriminatory practices.

DISCUSSION: The commerce clause can reach local businesses even though they may have only a minimal impact on interstate commerce. In regulating local businesses, the Court will usually consider the aggregate effect of all such businesses on interstate commerce. Although one motel that discriminates against African-Americans may have only a negligible impact, the combined effect of such discrimination by many motels would be substantial. The Court has held that racial discrimination by motels discourages interstate travel by a substantial proportion of African-Americans, and thus comes under the regulatory authority of the commerce clause. The Court has further stated that it is irrelevant that regulation of discriminatory practices accomplishes a principally moral and social objective rather than a purely economic one.

Answer (a) is incorrect because the commerce clause gives Congress the authority to regulate all aspects of interstate commerce, including the movement of people. Answer (b) is incorrect because the commerce clause can reach cases that involve civil rights if interstate commerce is affected. Answer (c) is incorrect because local businesses can be regulated if their aggregate impact on interstate commerce would be substantial, even though their individual impact may be minimal.

10. The Arizona legislature enacts a statute making it illegal to operate a train of more than 14 passenger cars or 70 freight cars within the state. Almost every other state permits the operation of longer trains. The Arizona legislature states that its purpose in passing the law is to reduce the number of railroad accidents within the state. A California railroad company brings a suit against Arizona on the grounds that the statute violates the commerce clause. In ruling on the case, the Supreme Court would be most likely to

a. Defer to the Arizona legislature and allow the statute to stand because it is a safety measure.

b. Declare the statute to be unconstitutional because only the federal government has the authority to enact laws to regulate interstate commerce.

c. Conduct its own fact-finding to determine if the statute does have a rational relation to the objective stated by the legislature.

d. Balance the benefit to the state against the burden placed on interstate commerce and strike down the statute if its contribution to safety is less than its detrimental effect on interstate commerce.

The correct answer is (d). *(Publisher)*

REQUIRED: The true statement about a state's power to regulate activities affecting interstate commerce.

DISCUSSION: The Supreme Court will ordinarily give a greater degree of deference to a state statute that affects interstate commerce if that statute rationally protects a legitimate state objective, such as the safety of the state's citizens. However, even a statute enacted to protect the state's citizens will usually be subject to a balancing test. The Court will weigh the benefit to the state against the burden imposed on interstate commerce. This balancing is ordinarily deferential to state policies, but if the statute is determined to have only a marginal impact on safety, it will usually be invalidated.

Answer (a) is incorrect because even a statute enacted to protect public safety will be subject to a balancing test and will be invalidated if the benefit to the public does not outweigh the burden placed on interstate commerce. Answer (b) is incorrect because a state does have limited authority under its police power to enact statutes that will have an incidental impact on interstate commerce, although a state cannot directly regulate interstate commerce. Answer (c) is incorrect because the Supreme Court will not conduct its own inquiry into the facts of a case. It will customarily defer to the finding of facts by the state legislature.

11. Arizona is a major producer of grapefruit. The Arizona legislature passes a law restricting the importation of grapefruit from California. In ruling on the constitutionality of this law, the Supreme Court would most likely

a. Defer to the state legislature and allow the law to stand under the doctrine of state sovereignty.

b. Declare the law to be unconstitutional per se because of its discriminatory nature.

c. Declare the law to be unconstitutional unless Arizona can show a compelling state interest that outweighs the burden on interstate commerce.

d. Allow California to pass a law restricting the importation of grapefruit from Arizona as a retaliatory measure.

The correct answer is (c). *(Publisher)*

REQUIRED: The true statement about the constitutionality of a state restricting the importation of a product from another state.

DISCUSSION: The Supreme Court will strictly scrutinize state laws that discriminate against commerce from other states. A law that is intended to promote a state's economy by shutting out competition from other states will usually be declared unconstitutional. Even if the state shows a compelling state interest (such as protecting the safety of the state's citizens), the Court will usually balance the benefit to the state against the burden to interstate commerce. Unless the state can show that the benefit it derives from the law outweighs the burden placed on interstate commerce, the Supreme Court will strike down the law.

Answer (a) is incorrect because the Supreme Court has the power to invalidate state laws if it finds them to be in violation of the Constitution. Answer (b) is incorrect because the Supreme Court has not ruled that state laws restricting the importation of products from competing states are unconstitutional per se. Instead, the Court will apply the balancing test described above. However, at least two Justices currently sitting take the position that "protectionist" legislation is per se unconstitutional, regardless of the benefit to the state or the burden on interstate commerce. Answer (d) is incorrect because the Court will not uphold retaliatory protectionist legislation. As Justice Cardozo stated, "... the Constitution was framed upon the theory that the peoples of the several states must sink or swim together..."

12. Congress enacted a statute regulating the design, size, and movement of oil tankers. A state also enacted a statute governing those matters with regard to oil tankers operating in its waters, but the state requirements were stricter. Various oil companies brought an action against the state, asserting that its regulation was unconstitutional. Which of the following is the best basis for the court's decision?

a. The commerce clause.

b. Separation of powers.

c. The preemption doctrine.

d. State police power.

The correct answer is (c). *(Publisher)*

REQUIRED: The best basis for deciding a case involving state and federal regulation of the same matter.

DISCUSSION: Laws made in pursuance of the Constitution are the supreme law of the land. State statutes that conflict with such laws are invalid if the conflict is direct and substantial or if the federal government has expressly or impliedly preempted the field. Preemption will apply when the scheme of federal regulation is so pervasive as to leave no room for state supplementation or when the federal interest is so completely dominant as to preclude enforcement of the state law. Also, the objectives of the federal law and the nature of obligations imposed may be evidence of such a purpose. In the case of oil tanker design, Congress plainly intended to set a uniform national standard. That intent would be frustrated by enforcing the state law.

Answer (a) is incorrect because the commerce clause permits state regulation of interstate commerce that is not unduly burdensome. Answer (b) is incorrect because it refers to the balance between the legislative, executive, and judicial branches of government. The present case involves a supremacy question. Answer (d) is incorrect because the power of the state to regulate on behalf of the public safety, health, welfare, and morals is preempted by the overriding federal interest.

13. Sam's Barbecue is a small, family-owned and operated restaurant in southern Alabama. Sam's is located in a rural area, away from interstate highways, and caters exclusively to local residents. Sam's purchases about half of its meat from suppliers in Georgia. Sam's Barbecue

a. Cannot be regulated under the commerce clause because it is a local business and has no significant impact on interstate commerce.

b. Can be regulated under the commerce clause because the meat that it purchases from out-of-state suppliers moves through interstate commerce.

c. Can be regulated under the commerce clause because the states have authority under it to regulate businesses that can have an effect on the health, safety, and welfare of their citizens.

d. Cannot be regulated under the commerce clause because it does not cater to interstate travelers.

The correct answer is (b). *(Publisher)*

REQUIRED: The applicability of the commerce clause to local businesses.

DISCUSSION: That a business may be purely local does not exempt it from regulation under the commerce clause. The Supreme Court has used the "cumulative effects principle" to extend the commerce clause's reach to local businesses. Under this principle, the local business's impact on interstate commerce is considered in light of the combined impact of similar businesses. For example, the meat purchased by Sam's Barbecue through interstate channels may have only a trivial impact on interstate commerce. But the aggregate impact of all locally-owned barbecue restaurants on interstate commerce might be significant. It is the aggregate impact of all the individual restaurants that is the basis for regulation.

Answer (a) is incorrect because although Sam's Barbecue may have only a trivial impact on interstate commerce, the combined impact of all individual barbecue restaurants may be significant. Answer (c) is incorrect because the commerce clause does not give states the authority to regulate businesses that affect the health, safety, or welfare of their citizens. Answer (d) is incorrect because a business may still have an impact on interstate commerce even though it does not sell its finished product through interstate channels. If it purchases its raw materials or components through interstate commerce, it may have an impact on interstate commerce.

7.3 Taxing and Spending Powers

14. Congress believes that it must do something to halt drunk driving on the nation's highways. Congress therefore enacts a statute denying federal highway funds to any state with a minimum drinking age less than 21. Georgia challenges the statute on the grounds that it is an unconstitutional interference with its police power. In reviewing the statute, the Supreme Court will probably hold that it is

a. Constitutional, even if a direct congressional establishment of a national minimum drinking age would be unconstitutional.

b. Unconstitutional, because it is an attempt to indirectly accomplish an objective that cannot be accomplished directly.

c. Unconstitutional, because it induces the states to pass laws that violate the constitutional rights of their citizens.

d. Constitutional, because Congress has the authority to set a minimum national drinking age.

The correct answer is (a). *(Publisher)*

REQUIRED: The Supreme Court's probable holding regarding a statute that indirectly accomplishes Congress's goals through the use of the federal spending power.

DISCUSSION: Congress derives its spending power from Article I, Section 8, which is the same article that authorizes Congress to tax. Congress can use its spending power indirectly to achieve its objectives even if a direct regulation would violate the Constitution. The Supreme Court has held that Congress can deny federal highway funds to any state that allows persons below a certain age to purchase alcoholic beverages, even though a statute establishing a minimum national drinking age would be unconstitutional. As long as it does not violate the constitutional rights of the state's citizens, Congress may use its conditional spending power to induce a state to take some action that Congress desires.

Answer (b) is incorrect because Congress can constitutionally use its spending power to achieve objectives that it cannot attain directly. Answer (c) is incorrect because setting a minimum drinking age is not a violation of the constitutional rights of the state's citizens. Answer (d) is incorrect because Congress does not have the authority under the Constitution to set a minimum national drinking age.

15. The federal taxing power is the means by which the federal government obtains revenue to pay its expenses. Which of the following is a correct statement about this essential power?

a. Taxpayers generally have standing to sue the government based on the amount of taxes paid.

b. The taxation of interstate commerce by state and local governments is permitted under the commerce clause.

c. Taxation is an inappropriate means of implementing social policy.

d. Taxation is an insignificant regulatory tool.

The correct answer is (b). *(Publisher)*

REQUIRED: The correct statement about the taxing power.

DISCUSSION: Interstate commerce is not the exclusive domain of the federal taxing authorities. State and local governments may levy property, income, sales, or other taxes in the appropriate circumstances. The Supreme Court has announced a four-part test regarding when such taxation is valid: the nexus between the tax and the activity taxed is sufficient, the tax is fairly apportioned, the tax does not discriminate against interstate commerce, and the tax is fairly related to services provided by the taxing authority.

Answer (a) is incorrect because payment of taxes seldom gives the taxpayer standing to challenge the use of governmental funds. Answer (c) is incorrect because taxes have often been imposed to further social policies. The estate tax is a direct example. Answer (d) is incorrect because taxation is a principal means of regulating business. Tax credits and depreciation allowances are obvious examples.

16. Congress derives its basic power to tax from Article I, Section 8 of the Constitution. The purpose of taxes is to raise revenue for the government. In some instances, however, Congress has enacted tax statutes that serve more to regulate some aspect of society than to raise revenue. The Supreme Court has sometimes declared such statutes to be unconstitutional because they serve as penalties. In determining whether such a statute is constitutional, the Court will ordinarily

a. Strictly scrutinize Congress's intent in enacting the tax statute.

b. Look to the amount of revenue produced by the tax.

c. Look to the regulatory impact of the tax statute.

d. Hold that a penalty disguised as a tax is unconstitutional per se because it denies due process.

The correct answer is (b). *(Publisher)*

REQUIRED: The Supreme Court's method of determining whether a regulatory tax is constitutional.

DISCUSSION: In determining whether a tax statute that also serves to regulate and/or penalize some aspect of society is constitutional, the Court will look to the amount of revenue raised by the tax. Almost all taxes have at least some regulatory impact. Some taxes, such as excise taxes on cigarettes, serve a dual purpose: raising revenues while discouraging a practice Congress believes is detrimental to society. In recent cases, the Court has placed great emphasis on the amount of revenue raised by the tax in question, and has not probed to discover hidden regulatory motives.

Answer (a) is incorrect because the Court will usually not scrutinize Congress's purpose for enacting the statute as long as the tax is revenue-producing on its face. Answer (c) is incorrect because the key element considered by the Court is the amount of revenue produced. Answer (d) is incorrect because the Court does not hold that a tax that also serves as a penalty is unconstitutional per se.

7.4 Import-Export Clause, State Relations, and Contract Clauses

17. Under the Constitution, state governments have the power to protect the health, safety, or general welfare of state residents. This power is known as

a. State sovereignty.

b. State police power.

c. Eminent domain.

d. State supremacy.

The correct answer is (b). *(Publisher)*

REQUIRED: The term for a state's power to safeguard the health, safety, or welfare of its citizens.

DISCUSSION: The term applied to the power granted to states to protect the health, safety, or welfare of state citizens is "state police power." An action by a state under its police power is ordinarily valid under federal law unless it violates some specific limitation imposed by the U.S. Constitution. For example, a state law that interferes with the flow of interstate commerce may be held unconstitutional even if it was intended as a safety measure.

Answer (a) is incorrect because state sovereignty is the right of states to enact their own laws to the extent that they do not conflict with federal law. Answer (c) is incorrect because eminent domain is the power of both federal and state governments to take private property for public use. Answer (d) is incorrect because the term supremacy ordinarily refers to the supremacy of federal law over conflicting state law.

18. The Indiana Supreme Court decides a case based on an Indiana statute. The case does not involve federal issues and the decision does not conflict with the U.S. Constitution. What action may the U.S. Supreme Court take regarding the Indiana Supreme Court's decision?

a. The U.S. Supreme Court has the authority to review the decisions of state courts under the doctrine of judicial review and can overturn the ruling if it finds that the decision conflicts with the state's constitution.

b. The U.S. Supreme Court may not review state court decisions that merely rule on questions of state law; therefore, the U.S. Supreme Court can take no action on the case.

c. Under the supremacy clause, the U.S. Supreme Court can review the case even if no federal or constitutional issues are involved.

d. The U.S. Supreme Court can issue an advisory opinion if requested to do so by the state court.

The correct answer is (b). *(Publisher)*

REQUIRED: The Supreme Court's authority to review the decisions of the state courts.

DISCUSSION: The U.S. Supreme Court has the authority to review the judgment of a state court, and to overrule that judgment if it conflicts with the U.S. Constitution. However, the Court has no authority to review state court decisions that concern state law only. The Supreme Court's review of state court judgments is limited to questions of federal law. The case decided by the Indiana Supreme Court does not involve questions of federal law; thus, the U.S. Supreme Court has no authority to review or overturn its decision.

Answer (a) is incorrect because the U.S. Supreme Court can review state court decisions only if those decisions conflict with federal law. Answer (c) is incorrect because the supremacy clause provides that federal law preempts directly conflicting state law. In this case, no federal issues were involved. Answer (d) is incorrect because the U.S. Supreme Court does not issue advisory opinions. It decides "cases" and "controversies."

19. Minnesota enacted a statute requiring employers who closed down their operations in the state to pay pension benefits to any employee who had worked for the company for more than 10 years. This statute applied to any pension plan the company might have, and was intended to apply retroactively. The Supreme Court would most likely declare this statute to be a violation of the

a. Commerce clause.

b. Contract clause.

c. Supremacy clause.

d. Due process clause of the 14th Amendment.

The correct answer is (b). *(Publisher)*

REQUIRED: The constitutional basis for invalidating the state statute described.

DISCUSSION: The contract clause is found in Article I, Section 10. It prohibits states from passing any laws impairing the obligation of contracts. Under their police power, states are allowed to make minor modifications to contracts. However, the Court has held that states cannot make substantial modifications to contracts unless 1) there is an emergency; 2) the statute is enacted to protect a basic societal interest, not a favored group; 3) the relief is appropriately tailored to the emergency; 4) the modification is reasonable in scope; and 5) the statute is limited to the duration of the emergency. Hence, the Court would probably hold that the Minnesota statute is a substantial modification of employer-employee contracts, and that it will be declared unconstitutional unless the state can show that the requirements for substantial modification are met.

Answer (a) is incorrect because the commerce clause gives Congress the authority to regulate interstate commerce. Unless the Minnesota statute has some impact on interstate commerce, the commerce clause will not apply. Answer (c) is incorrect because the supremacy clause provides that a state law that is in direct conflict with a federal law must yield to the federal statute. Unless the Minnesota statute directly conflicted with a federal statute, the supremacy clause would not apply. Answer (d) is incorrect because the due process clause of the 14th Amendment incorporates most of the rights guaranteed by the Bill of Rights and makes them applicable to the states. Unless the statute is found to violate such a right, the due process clause will not apply.

7.5 The Bill of Rights and Business

20. The Bill of Rights consists of the first ten amendments to the U.S. Constitution. These amendments state a variety of fundamental rights which

a. Apply directly and expressly both to the federal and state governments.

b. Apply directly and expressly to the federal government only.

c. Apply directly and expressly to the federal government and are fully incorporated within the 14th Amendment due process clause which is directly applicable to the states.

d. Do not apply expressly or directly to state governments. Citizens of the several states must look to their respective state constitutions for guarantees of rights which are enumerated in the Bill of Rights.

The correct answer is (b). *(Publisher)*

REQUIRED: The correct statement concerning the Bill of Rights.

DISCUSSION: The U.S. Supreme Court has held that the Bill of Rights applies expressly and directly only to the federal government. However, most of the guarantees in the Bill of Rights are indirectly applicable to the states through incorporation in the guarantee of due process stated by the 14th Amendment.

Answer (a) is incorrect because the Bill of Rights applies only indirectly to state governments. Answer (c) is incorrect because a majority of the Supreme Court has never held that all the guarantees stated in the Bill of Rights are embraced within the single guarantee of due process that the states must respect under the 14th Amendment. Answer (d) is incorrect because whereas the "total incorporation" theory has never prevailed, the overwhelming majority of individual guarantees specified in the Bill of Rights have been held (on a piecemeal basis) to be embraced within the due process clause of the 14th Amendment, and thus are applicable to the states.

21. Freedom of the press is guaranteed in the U.S. Constitution. This fundamental right is interpreted

a. To provide a constitutional shield for communications between members of the news media and their informants.

b. To impose a different standard of liability in defamation cases brought against the news media.

c. To permit the existence of prior restraints on publication if a showing of probable cause is made.

d. To protect publications which are considered not to be obscene under the "redeeming social value" standard.

The correct answer is (b). *(Publisher)*

REQUIRED: The correct statement concerning the interpretation of freedom of the press.

DISCUSSION: Because of the essential role played by a free press in safeguarding liberty within a democratic society, the news media are allowed greater leeway under the law of defamation than private persons. If the plaintiff is a public figure or a public person with respect to the subject of the alleged defamation, the plaintiff must prove not only the usual elements of the tort of defamation, but also that the defendant acted with "actual malice."

Answer (a) is incorrect because some states have enacted "shield" laws, but no 1st Amendment requirement safeguards members of the news media from the duty to answer questions during legal proceedings. Answer (c) is incorrect because the 1st Amendment usually prohibits the imposition of any system of censorship or prior restraints. Answer (d) is incorrect because the currently prevailing obscenity standard relies upon the application of "contemporary community standards." "Redeeming social value" is no longer the test.

22. Dixie was the sole owner of a small proprietorship. She transferred daily accounting records of the business to a lawyer for the preparation of a tax return. The IRS attempted to subpoena the records. What will be the result?

a. Dixie will prevail if she pleads an unreasonable search and seizure.

b. Dixie will prevail if she pleads a reasonable expectation of privacy.

c. The IRS will prevail even if the items are personal diaries in the possession of the defendant.

d. The IRS will prevail against a self-incrimination defense.

The correct answer is (d). *(Publisher)*

REQUIRED: The correct result of a government attempt to obtain business records.

DISCUSSION: The 4th Amendment prohibition against unreasonable searches and seizures is related to the 5th Amendment protection against self-incrimination: the use of a person's private papers as evidence against him/her is a form of self-incrimination. But private papers are defined narrowly to include only those in which the accused had a reasonable expectation of privacy. Business papers created in the ordinary course of business receive no constitutional protection since they are regarded as transactional rather than personal documents.

Answer (a) is incorrect because the attempt to obtain business records material to a lawsuit is not unreasonable under the 4th Amendment. Answer (b) is incorrect because daily accounting records are transactional, not personal. Answer (c) is incorrect because personal diaries and letters are constitutionally protected.

23. A newly enacted state criminal statute provides, in its entirety, "No person shall utter to another person in a public place any annoying, disturbing, or unwelcome language." Smith followed an elderly woman for three blocks down a public street, yelling offensive four-letter words in her ear. The woman repeatedly asked Smith to leave her alone, but he refused. In the subsequent prosecution of Smith, the first under this statute, Smith

a. Can be convicted.

b. Cannot be convicted, because speech of the sort described here may not be punished by the state because of the 1st and 14th Amendments.

c. Cannot be convicted, because, though his speech here may be punished by the state, the state may not do so under this statute.

d. Cannot be convicted, because the average user of a public street would think his speech/action here was amusing and ridiculous rather than "annoying," etc.

The correct answer is (c). *(MBE Part 3-5)*

REQUIRED: Whether the defendant may be convicted under the statute.

DISCUSSION: The 1st Amendment guarantee of free speech is not absolute. Speech may be subject to appropriate time, place, and manner requirements. But free speech is a fundamental right, and any restrictions will be carefully scrutinized and narrowly interpreted. The statute is probably unconstitutional on the grounds of vagueness and overbreadth. A reasonable person would not be able to determine what conduct was prohibited. Moreover, the statute is so broadly drawn that it prohibits constitutionally protected conduct.

Answer (a) is incorrect because Smith could not be convicted under a statute which is void both for vagueness and overbreadth. Answer (b) is incorrect because freedom of speech may be subject to reasonable restrictions. Answer (d) is incorrect because although a reasonable person would regard such conduct as at least annoying, the statute is still unconstitutional.

24. A state statute declared the advertising of the prices of prescription drugs by a licensed pharmacist to be unprofessional conduct. The statute was

a. Upheld because commercial speech is unprotected by the 1st Amendment.

b. Struck down because commercial speech is protected to the same extent as noncommercial speech.

c. Upheld as a reasonable exercise of the police power.

d. Struck down because commercial speech is protected if it concerns a lawful activity and is not misleading.

The correct answer is (d). *(Publisher)*

REQUIRED: The constitutionality of banning advertising by pharmacists of prices of prescription drugs.

DISCUSSION: In recent years, the Supreme Court has extended 1st Amendment protection to commercial as well as noncommercial speech. In the case on which this question is based, the court concluded that both consumers and society in general would benefit from a free flow of purely commercial information consisting of truthful data about a lawful activity. Commercial speech, however, is afforded less protection than the noncommercial variety: a narrowly drawn restriction has been held valid if it directly advances a substantial governmental interest. For example, placing restraints on the erection of commercial billboards has been upheld but a general ban on noncommercial billboards in the same ordinance was deemed to be unconstitutional.

Answer (a) is incorrect because commercial speech is protected. Answer (b) is incorrect because commercial speech is less protected. Answer (c) is incorrect because the vital interests protected by the 1st Amendment were held to outweigh the state's interest in regulating the professional conduct of pharmacists.

25. If Congress in response to the concern of the majority of voters about overpopulation has passed a statute imposing a substantial monetary fine on couples who have more than two children, a plaintiff who wishes to have more than two children should most likely

a. Seek to elect new representatives to Congress.

b. Bring suit to declare the law unconstitutional.

c. Move to a state whose constitution conflicts with the federal law.

d. Persuade the appropriate administrative agency to overturn the law.

The correct answer is (b). *(D. Woods)*

REQUIRED: The most appropriate action to challenge the statute described.

DISCUSSION: The constitutional right of privacy protects the rights of persons (including those in the minority) with respect to matters of private concern, such as matters relating to reproduction. That right would likely protect persons against the law described.

Answer (a) is incorrect because electing a majority of representatives who oppose the law may be difficult if public opinion favors it. Answer (c) is incorrect because under the federal supremacy clause, federal statutes and constitutional provisions are superior to state statutes and constitutions. Answer (d) is incorrect because the duty of an administrative agency is to implement the laws that Congress passes. Administrative agencies can only act pursuant to congressional enabling statutes.

7.6 Privileges and Immunities

26. The privileges and immunities clause of Article IV, Section 2

a. Applies to all constitutional rights, both fundamental and otherwise.

b. Prevents states from discriminating against citizens of other states.

c. Does not apply if the state is a participant in a market.

d. Applies to corporations as well as to natural citizens.

The correct answer is (b). *(Publisher)*

REQUIRED: The correct statement regarding the privileges and immunities clause.

DISCUSSION: The privileges and immunities clause of Article IV, Section 2 (as distinguished from the privileges and immunities clause of the 14th Amendment) was designed to prevent states from discriminating against residents of other states. As the Supreme Court stated in Toomer v. Witsell, the clause "was designed to insure to a citizen of State A who ventures into State B the same privileges which the citizens of State B enjoy."

Answer (a) is incorrect because the Supreme Court has held that the privileges and immunities clause applies only to fundamental rights. Answer (c) is incorrect because the privileges and immunities clause does apply even though the state participates in the markets it is attempting to regulate. Answer (d) is incorrect because the privileges and immunities clause does not protect corporations.

27. The state of Texacka has enacted a statute giving employment preferences in the oil industry to its residents, asserting that the law will reduce unemployment in the state. If the law is challenged, what is the probable outcome?

a. The statute will be upheld.

b. The statute will be invalidated because only the federal government can regulate interstate commerce.

c. The statute will be invalidated as a violation of the privileges and immunities clause.

d. The statute will be invalidated as an intrusion on the federal government's right to regulate employment.

The correct answer is (c). *(Publisher)*

REQUIRED: The result of a challenge to a law giving employment preference to state residents.

DISCUSSION: The privileges and immunities clause of the U.S. Constitution prohibits discrimination in favor of state residents, but it has not been literally interpreted to prevent all distinctions between residents and nonresidents of a state. For example, residency requirements for voting, holding office, and payment of resident tuition at state schools have been upheld. However, restrictions on property ownership and the erection of state tariffs have been struck down. In the case on which this question is based, the Supreme Court held that the discrimination was unconstitutional because, even though a substantial reason for the discrimination existed, the statute was not closely tailored to remedy the situation in the least discriminatory way and, in any event, nonresidents were not the "peculiar source of evil" attempted to be corrected.

Answer (a) is incorrect because the statute should be struck down. Answer (b) is incorrect because states may regulate intrastate commerce. They may also regulate interstate commerce if the regulation is not unduly burdensome. Answer (d) is incorrect because the federal government has no exclusive right to regulate employment relations.

7.7 Fourteenth Amendment: Due Process and Equal Protection

Questions 28 and 29 are based on Barnes, who was hired as an assistant professor of mathematics at Reardon State College and is now in his third consecutive one-year contract. Under state law he cannot acquire tenure until after five consecutive annual contracts. In his third year, Barnes was notified that he was not being rehired for the following year. Applicable state law and college rules did not require either a statement of reasons or a hearing, and in fact neither was offered to Barnes.

28. Which of the following, if established, sets forth the strongest constitutional argument Barnes could make to compel the college to furnish him a statement of reasons for the failure to rehire him and an opportunity for a hearing?

a. There is no evidence that tenured teachers are any more qualified than he is.

b. He leased a home in reliance on an oral promise of reemployment by the college president.

c. He was the only teacher at the college whose contract was not renewed that year.

d. In the expectation of remaining at the college, he had just moved his elderly parents to the town in which the college is located.

The correct answer is (b). *(MBE Part I-91)*

REQUIRED: The strongest constitutional argument for procedural due process.

DISCUSSION: A statement of reasons and an opportunity for a hearing are a necessary part of minimal compliance with the dictates of the 14th Amendment due process clause. To be entitled to due process protection, Barnes must show that he was deprived of a "life, liberty, or property" interest. "Property" has been broadly interpreted to include various entitlements to benefits. Thus, if Barnes detrimentally changed his position in reliance upon an oral promise of reemployment, he could argue that state action had deprived him of a "property" right without due process.

Answer (a) is incorrect because colleges are given wide discretion in choosing their faculty and qualification creates no "property right." Answer (c) is incorrect because being the only teacher whose contract was not renewed does not establish a property interest. Answer (d) is incorrect because unilateral action without some basis for claiming an entitlement does not establish that a protected interest was deprived without due process.

29. Which of the following, if established, most strongly supports the college in refusing to give Barnes a statement of reasons or an opportunity for a hearing?

a. Barnes's academic performance had been substandard.

b. A speech he made that was critical of administration policies violated a college regulation concerning teacher behavior.

c. Barnes worked at the college for less than five years.

d. Barnes could be replaced with a more competent teacher.

The correct answer is (c). *(MBE Part I-92)*

REQUIRED: The strongest argument for the college not to comply with due process.

DISCUSSION: Since Barnes could not have acquired tenure (a form of "property" right) until after 5 years, the college should argue that Barnes's termination after the third year did not involve the deprivation of an interest protected by due process. Under this theory, the college would not be required to follow due process.

Answer (a) is incorrect because the quality of Barnes's academic performance would only be relevant if he had a "property" right to protect. Answer (b) is incorrect because a refusal to give a statement of reasons and an opportunity for a hearing due to a speech would suggest that a "liberty" interest had been deprived without due process. Answer (d) is incorrect because the availability of a more competent replacement is irrelevant to the constitutional question of due process.

30. The constitutional guarantee of due process

a. As stated in the 5th Amendment prohibits any state from depriving any person of life, liberty, or property without due process of law.

b. As stated in the 14th Amendment prohibits the federal government from depriving any citizen of the United States of life, liberty, or property without due process of law.

c. As stated in the 14th Amendment prohibits any state from depriving any person of life, liberty, or property without due process of law.

d. As stated in the 5th Amendment prohibits the federal government from depriving states of their rights without due process of law.

The correct answer is (c). *(Publisher)*

REQUIRED: The correct statement concerning due process.

DISCUSSION: The 14th Amendment provides that a state may not deprive a person of his/her rights (life, liberty, or property) in an unfair and unjust manner (denial of due process). This Amendment applies specifically to the states, not the federal government. It also extends its protection to all persons, not just to individuals or citizens.

Answer (a) is incorrect because the due process guarantee found in the 5th Amendment applies only against the federal government. Answer (b) is incorrect because the due process clause in the 14th Amendment applies specifically against the states and protects any persons (not only citizens) who may have rights deprived by state actions. Answer (d) is incorrect because the 5th Amendment protects any person (not states) from deprivation of life, liberty, or property by the federal government without due process.

31. In which of the following instances has the court adopted a substantive due process approach?

a. The court invalidates a statute limiting the dollar amount of government liability because the limitation bears little or no relationship to losses that may be incurred.

b. The court decides that the firing of a teacher by a school board without a hearing at year-end did not involve the deprivation of a protected interest because (s)he did not have tenure.

c. The court finds that the suspension of a student without any form of hearing was unjustified.

d. The court holds that the firing of a football coach at the whim of the alumni of a private university did not involve state action.

The correct answer is (a). *(Publisher)*

REQUIRED: The situation in which a substantive due process approach was taken.

DISCUSSION: Under the 5th Amendment, no person may be deprived of life, liberty, or property without due process. The 14th Amendment extends the prohibition to action by a state. Procedural due process essentially requires that the proceedings be fair, whereas substantive due process requires that the substantive part of the law itself be fair. If a liability limitation in a statute has no rational relationship to the harm, substantive due process may be violated.

Answers (b), (c) and (d) are incorrect because each involves a question as to whether a procedural due process issue has been raised.

32. The State of Wilshire passes a law providing that a police officer may 1) stop a person who is driving in such a way that (s)he appears to be drunk; 2) administer a breath test to that person; and 3) if the test shows that the person has a blood alcohol content of 0.15% or more, immediately revoke that person's driver's license for 1 year. The law says nothing about a hearing. If a court holds this law to be unconstitutional, the reason will probably be that the law violates the

a. Due process clause of the 14th Amendment.

b. First Amendment.

c. Equal protection clause of the 14th Amendment.

d. Administrative Procedure Act of the state.

The correct answer is (a). *(D. Levin)*

REQUIRED: The provision of the U.S. Constitution that is violated by a state statute authorizing revocation of a driver's license without provision for a hearing.

DISCUSSION: The right to drive is a form of liberty that is protected from state deprivation by the due process clause of the 14th Amendment. Although a person's driver's license may be revoked for driving with excessive alcohol in his/her blood, such revocation cannot constitutionally be accomplished without affording the driver notice and an opportunity to be heard.

Answer (b) is incorrect because the right to drive is not considered a protected form of conduct under the 1st Amendment. Answer (c) is incorrect because the statute does not treat similarly situated persons in a dissimilar way. Answer (d) is incorrect because a state legislature has the power to pass a statute regulating drivers' licenses issued by that state. The purpose of the legislature need not be accomplished by means of an administrative regulation, the enactment of which must comply with the state's Administrative Procedure Act.

33. The constitutional guarantee of equal protection

a. As stated in the 14th Amendment prohibits any state from denying any person the equal protection of the laws.

b. As stated in the 5th Amendment prohibits the federal government from denying to any person the equal protection of the laws.

c. As stated in the 5th Amendment prohibits any state from denying any person the equal protection of the laws.

d. As stated in the 14th Amendment prohibits the federal government from denying to any person the equal protection of the laws.

The correct answer is (a). *(Publisher)*

REQUIRED: The correct statement concerning equal protection.

DISCUSSION: The equal protection clause of the 14th Amendment, like the due process clause, prohibits state action that denies any person (not just a citizen) certain rights. The right of equal protection does not require identical treatment for all persons; it requires that similarly situated persons be treated the same unless sufficiently strong reasons justify dissimilar treatment.

Answer (b) is incorrect because the 5th Amendment contains no express equal protection clause. It has been interpreted, however, to contain an implicit equal protection guarantee applicable against the federal government. Answer (c) is incorrect because the 5th Amendment applies against the federal government, not the states. Answer (d) is incorrect because the 14th Amendment applies against the states.

34. The constitutional guarantee of equal protection

a. Requires that all citizens of the United States be treated in the same manner.

b. Is enforced with regard to sex-based classifications by means of a strict scrutiny test.

c. Is enforced by means of a strict scrutiny test when the basis for classification is race or national origin.

d. Permits the establishment of any classification of persons so long as it meets the rational basis test.

The correct answer is (c). *(Publisher)*

REQUIRED: The correct statement concerning equal protection.

DISCUSSION: If state action has resulted in different treatment of classes of persons and the basis for classification is inherently "suspect," the courts will apply a "strict scrutiny" test which can only be passed if the state can show that a "compelling" state interest was involved. Classifications based upon race or national origin are regarded as "suspect."

Answer (a) is incorrect because equal protection does not require identical treatment of all persons. It prohibits discriminations which have an inadequate basis in public policy. Answer (b) is incorrect because sex-based classifications are subject to an intermediate level of scrutiny which involves no presumptions either for or against validity. Answer (d) is incorrect because while many classifications only require a rational basis, certain classifications are subject to more stringent examination, e.g., those based on race, national origin, alienage, sex, age, poverty, etc.

35. The Constitution does not explicitly empower the federal government to take private property for public use. The federal government's authority to do so is derived from the

a. Fifth Amendment clause stating that private property shall not be taken for public use without just compensation.

b. Fourteenth Amendment clause stating that no state may deprive any person of life, liberty, or property without due process of law.

c. Doctrine of preemption.

d. Supremacy clause.

The correct answer is (a). *(Publisher)*

REQUIRED: The source of the federal government's authority to take private property for public use.

DISCUSSION: The Constitution does not explicitly authorize the federal government to take private property for public use if just compensation is given. However, the courts have interpreted the 5th Amendment as the source of an implied power of eminent domain.

Answer (b) is incorrect because the 14th Amendment applies to the states, not to the federal government. The due process clause of the 14th Amendment is usually held to be the source of state authority to take private property. Answer (c) is incorrect because the doctrine of preemption holds that if the federal government legislates in an area previously regulated by the states, the federal regulation will preempt the existing state regulation under the supremacy clause. Answer (d) is incorrect because the supremacy clause of Article IV applies to conflicts between state and federal regulation. Under the supremacy clause, if a state regulation directly conflicts with a federal regulation, the state law must yield to the federal law.

36. Both state and federal governments have the authority to take private property for public use. Which of the following would most likely be considered a "taking"?

a. A zoning regulation that impairs an owner's use of his/her property.

b. A landmark preservation scheme that prevents an owner from altering a building considered to be historically significant.

c. A regulation enacted to protect the environment that causes a diminution of the value of property.

d. A permanent physical occupation of the property by a government that causes only a minor interference with the owner's use.

The correct answer is (d). *(Publisher)*

REQUIRED: The item that constitutes a "taking."

DISCUSSION: The Supreme Court has held that a permanent physical occupation of private property is a taking, no matter how minor the interference with the owner's use. The Court has stated that the occupation of private property is "qualitatively more intrusive than perhaps any other category of property regulation" and therefore constitutes a taking even if its economic impact on the property's owner is minimal.

Answer (a) is incorrect because a zoning regulation will usually not be considered a taking unless it is "clearly arbitrary and unreasonable." Answer (b) is incorrect because the Court has held that as long as landmark preservation is carried out as part of a comprehensive preservation scheme, the owner of an individual building can be prevented from altering the building in a way that would destroy its historical significance. Answer (c) is incorrect because the Court will usually not strike down a regulation enacted to protect the public welfare, even if the value of an owner's property is diminished.

37. The equal protection clause of the U.S. Constitution

a. Requires that a law treat all persons in the same way.

b. Prohibits a law from treating persons of different races differently.

c. Prohibits a law from treating women differently from men.

d. Prohibits a law from treating persons of different economic status differently.

The correct answer is (b). *(D. Woods)*

REQUIRED: The effect of the equal protection clause.

DISCUSSION: The equal protection clause does not permit the law to treat persons of different races differently. Race is a suspect classification, and there is never a good reason for distinctive treatment based on race.

Answer (a) is incorrect because the equal protection clause does not require that a law treat all persons in the same way. Treatment must be "equal" but need not be identical. Answer (c) is incorrect because a law can treat men and women differently as long as there is a compelling reason to do so. For example, men can be required to fight in a war, but women cannot. Answer (d) is incorrect because the law can treat persons of different economic status differently if a rational basis exists. For example, persons in high tax brackets have higher tax rates than those in lower tax brackets.

7.8 Judicial Review

38. Judicial review

a. Allows the courts to determine the constitutionality of actions of both the executive and legislative branches.

b. Allows the Supreme Court to declare a law unconstitutional of its own volition.

c. Is expressly provided for in the U.S. Constitution.

d. Has little importance to the business community today.

The correct answer is (a). *(Publisher)*

REQUIRED: The correct statement about judicial review.

DISCUSSION: Judicial review is the power of the courts to determine whether actions of the other branches (executive and legislative) are in accordance with the Constitution and, if not, to declare such actions void.

Answer (b) is incorrect because judicial review is appropriate for any court only when a case or controversy is brought before it through the normal judicial process. Answer (c) is incorrect because judicial review is an implied power, not one expressly conferred by the Constitution. Answer (d) is incorrect because statutes are frequently found unconstitutional by courts and many of these substantially affect businesses.

39. Under the doctrine of judicial review, the Supreme Court has the power to decide whether a statute enacted by Congress is unconstitutional. The Supreme Court derives this power from

a. The necessary and proper clause of Article I.

b. The privileges and immunities clause of Section 1 of the 14th Amendment.

c. Chief Justice John Marshall's interpretation of the Constitution in Marbury v. Madison.

d. Common law.

The correct answer is (c). *(Publisher)*

REQUIRED: The source of the Supreme Court's power of judicial review.

DISCUSSION: The Constitution does not expressly state that the Supreme Court shall have the power to interpret the Constitution and decide whether acts of the other branches of the federal government are in conflict with the Constitution. The Court's power in this regard was established in the opinion given by Chief Justice John Marshall in deciding the case of Marbury v. Madison. In that case, Justice Marshall declared that a statute expanding the Supreme Court's original jurisdiction was unconstitutional. He asserted, "It is emphatically the province and duty of the judicial department to say what the law is."

Answer (a) is incorrect because the necessary and proper clause gives Congress the power to make the laws "necessary and proper" to carry out the powers given to it by the Constitution. Answer (b) is incorrect because the privileges and immunities clause of the 14th Amendment was intended to act as a restraint on state government action against individuals. Answer (d) is incorrect because the Supreme Court does not derive the power of judicial review from common law.

40. Maryland enacts a statute making it illegal to publish statements critical of elected state officials. A Baltimore newspaper brings a lawsuit against the state on the grounds that the law violates the 1st Amendment's guarantee of free speech. The Maryland Supreme Court holds that the law is constitutional, and the newspaper appeals the decision through the federal court system. What action can the U.S. Supreme Court take?

a. None. The U.S. Supreme Court does not have the authority to review the decisions of state courts.

b. None. Under the doctrine of state sovereignty, states can pass laws to govern the conduct of their citizens.

c. The U.S. Supreme Court can review the decision of the state court, but has no power to overrule the decision.

d. The U.S. Supreme Court can review the decision of the state court and overrule it if the decision violates federal law.

The correct answer is (d). *(Publisher)*

REQUIRED: The Supreme Court's authority over state courts.

DISCUSSION: The U.S. Supreme Court has the power to review the decisions of state courts and overturn those decisions if they conflict with federal law. This power is derived from the doctrine of judicial review. Thus, the Supreme Court exercises the power of judicial review not only with regard to the actions of the executive and legislative branches of the federal government, but also the decisions of state courts that involve questions of federal law. In this case, the issue is free speech, a federal issue. Thus, the U.S. Supreme Court may exercise its power of judicial review over the state court's decision.

Answer (a) is incorrect because the U.S. Supreme Court does have the authority to review the decisions of state courts if those judgments involve questions of federal law. The Supreme Court does not have the power to review state court decisions that involve only questions of state law. Answer (b) is incorrect because states cannot enact laws that conflict with federal law. Under the doctrine of state sovereignty, states can pass laws that do not conflict with existing federal law. Answer (c) is incorrect because the U.S. Supreme Court does have such power if the decision involves a question of federal law.

CHAPTER EIGHT
ADMINISTRATIVE LAW

8.1 Origin and Purpose of Administrative Agencies

1. The best description of an administrative agency is that it is a governmental board, commission, officer, bureau, or department

a. Independent of the executive, legislative, or judicial branches of government.

b. With the power to make rules and adjudicate disputes affecting private rights.

c. Within only the executive branch of the federal or a state government.

d. With the power primarily to enforce the law.

The correct answer is (b). *(Publisher)*

REQUIRED: The best description of an administrative agency.

DISCUSSION: An administrative agency is a public board, commission, officer, etc. (other than a judicial or legislative body) with limited power to enforce the law, make rules, and adjudicate disputes involving private rights and duties. It may be independent (the SEC, FTC, FCC) or executive (OMB, cabinet departments). These agencies affect almost all aspects of the nation's social, economic, commercial, and political life.

Answers (a) and (c) are incorrect because some agencies are within the executive branch and some are independent. Answer (d) is incorrect because while agencies do have some enforcement power, it is limited, and ultimate enforcement rests with the courts.

2. Administrative law is

a. The substantive law produced by an administrative agency.

b. Found only in statutes.

c. Any law regarding the powers and procedures of an administrative agency.

d. Produced only by an independent administrative agency.

The correct answer is (c). *(Publisher)*

REQUIRED: The true statement about administrative law.

DISCUSSION: Broadly defined, administrative law is any law regarding the powers and procedures of administrative agencies. For example, the federal Administrative Procedure Act (APA) establishes the procedures that govern the carrying out of the various functions (rulemaking, adjudication) of a federal agency.

Answer (a) is incorrect because the substantive law produced by the agency is best categorized according to the body of law to which it relates, such as tax or antitrust. Answer (b) is incorrect because administrative law is also found in constitutions, agency rules and decisions, and the opinions of courts. Answer (d) is incorrect because executive agencies also produce administrative law.

3. In general, federal administrative agencies may exercise

a. Judicial power only.

b. Executive power only.

c. Both judicial and executive power, but not legislative power.

d. Executive, judicial, and legislative power.

The correct answer is (d). *(CPA 1183 L-32)*

REQUIRED: The power(s) exercisable by an administrative agency.

DISCUSSION: The activity of an administrative agency is an exception to the separation of powers doctrine because the agency has the power to enforce the law (executive power), make rules and regulations (legislative power), and decide disputes (judicial power). Because an agency is not a formally separate branch of government, it exercises only that power delegated to it, and any act outside the scope of the delegation is unconstitutional. Today, courts ordinarily uphold extremely broad delegations of power to administrative agencies, although they do require that standards be set by the delegating authority to guide the rulemaking and adjudicatory activities of the agency.

Answers (a), (b), and (c) are incorrect because administrative agencies have executive, judicial, and legislative functions.

4. Certain operations of administrative agencies are apparent exceptions to the doctrine of separation of powers. This follows from the exercise by administrative agencies of all but which of the following powers?

a. The hearing of appeals from certain federal courts.

b. Rulemaking.

c. Adjudication.

d. Investigation and enforcement.

The correct answer is (a). *(Publisher)*

REQUIRED: The power that may not be exercised by an administrative agency.

DISCUSSION: Although regulatory agencies are part of the executive branch of government, their activities embrace more than the traditional investigative and enforcement powers. They exercise a lawmaking function under which they promulgate rules. They also engage in a quasi-judicial function by resolving (adjudicating) a large number of controversies, e.g., the licensing disputes decided by the FCC. Administrative agencies, however, do not hear appeals from federal courts. Instead, courts may review agency action.

Answers (b), (c), and (d) are incorrect because each is a power exercised by regulatory agencies.

5. Which of the following statements best describes how regulatory agencies of the U.S. government are restricted in the adoption of specific regulations?

a. Regulations must be consistent with standards established in the legislation that created the agency.

b. The agencies must first conduct a study showing that the benefits of a proposed regulation exceed its costs.

c. Businesses subject to the regulation must be given notice 1 year before the regulation will be put into effect.

d. The President of the United States must sign the regulation before it becomes effective.

The correct answer is (a). *(CMA 680 1-12)*

REQUIRED: The statement best describing a restriction on the adoption of regulations by regulatory agencies.

DISCUSSION: Regulatory agencies are given the authority to prescribe regulations for implementing statutes. These regulations must be consistent with the standards established by the statute which created the regulatory authority.

Answer (b) is incorrect because cost-benefit analysis is not a requirement for the promulgation of a regulation. Answer (c) is incorrect because the Administrative Procedure Act requires publication of the rule at least 30 days before its effective date. Answer (d) is incorrect because the President may approve a statute by signing it, but (s)he is not required to sign regulations for them to become effective.

6. Congress creates administrative agencies to regulate various industries and businesses. Which of the following is not a valid reason for the creation of an agency?

a. To regulate technologically complex industries.

b. To improve efficiency and provide greater flexibility.

c. To increase the power of the legislative branch at the expense of the executive branch.

d. To provide specialized expertise in regulating large industries.

The correct answer is (c). *(Publisher)*

REQUIRED: The invalid reason for creation of an administrative agency.

DISCUSSION: Congress has neither the time nor the expertise to regulate all aspects of business. Congress therefore creates administrative agencies and delegates the authority to make rules and to regulate the activities of businesses and industries. Agency experts can devote all their efforts to investigation, rulemaking, and adjudication in one problem area, which provides greater efficiency and flexibility. Agencies are not created to draw power away from the executive branch.

Answers (a), (b), and (d) are incorrect because they are valid reasons for the creation of an administrative agency.

7. Administrative agencies are of two types: executive or independent.

a. Independent agencies tend to be less subject to political control.

b. Executive agencies include the Internal Revenue Service (IRS) and the Securities and Exchange Commission (SEC).

c. Independent agencies include the Food and Drug Administration (FDA) and the Occupational Safety and Health Administration (OSHA).

d. The heads of executive agencies usually serve for fixed terms and can be removed only for cause.

The correct answer is (a). *(Publisher)*

REQUIRED: The true statement about executive and independent agencies.

DISCUSSION: Executive agencies are those within the departments of the president's cabinet or the Executive Office of the President. Heads of these agencies are appointed by and serve at the pleasure of the president. Consequently, they tend to be more responsive to political influences than the heads of independent agencies. The latter often consist of boards or commissions whose members 1) are appointed by the president with the advice and consent of the Senate, 2) serve for a fixed term, and 3) are removable only for cause.

Answer (b) is incorrect because the SEC is an independent agency. Answer (c) is incorrect because the FDA (Department of Health and Human Services) and OSHA (Department of Labor) are executive agencies. Some well-known independent agencies are the Federal Trade Commission, the Federal Communications Commission, the National Labor Relations Board, and the U.S. Postal Service. Answer (d) is incorrect because it states a characteristic of independent, not executive, agencies.

8.2 The Administrative Procedure and Federal Register Acts

8. Rulemaking by an administrative body

a. At the federal level is not governed by the Administrative Procedure Act because the Act is concerned only with adjudicatory matters.

b. Is required to meet the same rigid procedural standards as adjudication.

c. At the federal level is subject to the Administrative Procedure Act.

d. Unlike that of a legislative body, does not involve public proceedings.

The correct answer is (c). *(Publisher)*

REQUIRED: The correct statement concerning rulemaking by an administrative body.

DISCUSSION: The Administrative Procedure Act (APA) governs both rulemaking and adjudicatory action by administrative agencies. In general, it provides that rulemaking must proceed in an orderly manner allowing those affected by the regulatory process to have notice of and an opportunity to contribute to the enactment of regulations. When an agency proposes a regulation, general notice must be published in the Federal Register.

Answer (a) is incorrect because the APA is concerned with adjudication and rulemaking. Answer (b) is incorrect because the procedural standards for rulemaking are not as stringent as those for adjudication. Specific rights are not involved. Answer (d) is incorrect because notice of proposed rulemaking must be given and the public must be allowed to participate if the rules are legislative, that is, if they fill the gaps in a statute.

9. The Administrative Procedure Act (APA) was enacted in 1946 as a response to criticism of the discretion and power that Congress had granted to administrative agencies. Its main function is to

a. Provide the authority for administrative agencies to make laws.

b. Provide for congressional review of the laws created by administrative agencies.

c. Provide a legislative veto power to Congress so that Congress can overrule laws created by administrative agencies.

d. Specify the procedures agencies must follow in making rules and establish standards for judicial review of agency action.

The correct answer is (d). *(Publisher)*

REQUIRED: The function of the Administrative Procedure Act.

DISCUSSION: The Administrative Procedure Act applies to all federal agencies and serves to standardize the procedures by which those agencies make laws. It supplements but does not supersede stricter procedural requirements imposed on an agency by Congress in the agency's enabling legislation. The APA applies in cases in which the agency's enabling legislation is silent as to the procedures to be followed in creating laws. The APA also establishes standards for judicial review of agency action.

Answer (a) is incorrect because the authority for agencies to make rules is typically determined by the statute establishing the agency. The APA provides for the procedures to be followed in making rules. Answer (b) is incorrect because the APA does not provide for congressional review of laws created by agencies. The authorizing committees for each house of Congress directly oversee each agency. Answer (c) is incorrect because the APA does not provide a legislative veto. Legislative vetoes of agency actions have been ruled unconstitutional by the Supreme Court. Congress can veto agency rules only by passing legislation subject to the president's veto power.

10. There are three types of administrative rules: procedural, interpretive, and legislative. Which, if any, of these rules are subject to the rulemaking requirements of the Administrative Procedure Act (APA)?

a. Procedural rules.

b. Interpretive rules.

c. Legislative rules.

d. All three types of rules are subject to the APA's rulemaking procedures.

The correct answer is (c). *(Publisher)*

REQUIRED: The administrative rules to which the APA applies.

DISCUSSION: Legislative rules are those created by an administrative agency under the authority delegated to it by Congress. These rules have the force of law and are binding on the agency, the courts, and the public. Such rules are subject to the rulemaking requirements of the APA. For example, the rule requiring warning labels on cigarette packages is a legislative rule.

Answer (a) is incorrect because the APA's requirements do not apply to procedural rules. Procedural rules govern the administrative agency's own conduct. An example is a set of requirements for giving notice of proposed rulemaking. Answer (b) is incorrect because interpretive rules are statements by an agency that express the agency's understanding and interpretations of the statutes it administers. Thus, the Income Tax Regulations are the Treasury Department's interpretations of the Internal Revenue Code. Answer (d) is incorrect because only legislative rules are governed by the APA.

11. The authority of an agency to make law is typically determined by

a. The Administrative Procedure Act (APA).

b. The executive branch.

c. The statute that created the agency.

d. The agency itself.

The correct answer is (c). *(Publisher)*

REQUIRED: The source of an agency's authority to legislate.

DISCUSSION: The authority of an agency to make law is typically determined by the statute that creates the agency. The legislative branch, in writing the statute, provides standards and guidelines that limit and direct the authority to be exercised by the agency.

Answer (a) is incorrect because the APA governs the procedures to be followed by the agency when engaged in rulemaking. It does not provide the authority for the agency to make rules, but outlines the procedures to be followed. Answer (b) is incorrect because the executive branch of government does not determine an agency's authority to make rules. Answer (d) is incorrect because agencies do not have inherent authority to make law. Their authority is delegated by Congress and is determined by the legislative statute establishing the agency.

12. In accordance with the Federal Register Act of 1935,

a. The Federal Register prints the names and addresses of all governmental agencies.

b. The Government Manual contains all federal regulations currently in force.

c. The Code of Federal Regulations (CFR) is published daily to provide notice of proposed regulations.

d. A three-part Federal Register system was created.

The correct answer is (d). *(Publisher)*

REQUIRED: The true statement about the Federal Register Act.

DISCUSSION: The Federal Register, Government Manual, and the Code of Federal Regulations are the parts of the system. They provide current information about federal agencies and regulations.

Answer (a) is incorrect because the Federal Register is published every business day. It gives information about such matters as notices of agency hearings, presidential proclamations, and proposed and promulgated regulations. Answer (b) is incorrect because the Government Manual is published annually to provide the names and addresses of and other pertinent data about federal agencies. Answer (c) is incorrect because the CFR includes all current regulations arranged by agency.

8.3 Control of Administrative Agencies

13. Federal regulatory agencies do not have power to

a. Impose criminal sanctions on violators.

b. Issue rules and regulations.

c. Investigate and prosecute violations of statutes and rules.

d. Conduct hearings and decide whether violations have occurred.

The correct answer is (a). *(CMA 679 1-38)*

REQUIRED: The power not possessed by federal regulatory agencies.

DISCUSSION: Federal regulatory agencies do not have the power to impose criminal sanctions on violators. Criminal sanctions determined by statute are imposed by the U.S. Justice Department.

Answers (b), (c), and (d) are incorrect because each is a power of federal regulatory agencies.

14. In the exercise of their investigatory functions, administrative agencies may conduct inspections and searches. Which of the following warrantless searches by an agency would be considered unreasonable under the Constitution?

a. A safety inspector arrives to search a business that has been substantially damaged by a still-smoldering fire. The owner of the business refuses to allow the inspector on the premises.

b. An inspector arrives to search the records of a store that sells rifles and other firearms. The owner denies the inspector access to the records of gun sales.

c. An inspector arrives to search a clothing store for workplace dangers. The store manager refuses to admit the inspector.

d. An inspector arrives to search a shoe factory for workplace hazards. The factory superintendent consents to the search.

The correct answer is (c). *(S. Willey)*

REQUIRED: The warrantless administrative agency search not in compliance with the 4th Amendment.

DISCUSSION: The 4th Amendment prohibits unreasonable searches and seizures of information by administrative agencies. Warrantless searches are ordinarily considered reasonable if the party voluntarily consents to the search; the search is conducted in an emergency; the business is in a special industry in which warrantless searches are considered automatically valid, such as liquor and firearms; or the business is hazardous (e.g., a coal mine), and a statute expressly provides for warrantless searches. Because a clothing store is not in a hazardous industry or one in which warrantless searches are automatically valid, the inspector must have a warrant in this nonemergency situation if the store manager does not voluntarily agree to the search.

Answer (a) is incorrect because the emergency justifies the search. Answer (b) is incorrect because warrantless searches are automatically valid in the firearms industry. Answer (d) is incorrect because consent validates a search.

8.4 Rulemaking

15. Many agencies promulgate regulations that have the force and effect of law. This process is known as

a. Rulemaking.

b. Enforcement.

c. Adjudication.

d. Delegation.

The correct answer is (a). *(Publisher)*

REQUIRED: The correct term for the creation of regulations by agencies.

DISCUSSION: The process by which agencies promulgate regulations that have the force and effect of law is known as rulemaking. The Administrative Procedure Act (APA) defines a rule as "an agency statement of general or particular applicability and future effect designed to interpret, complement, or prescribe law or policy." Agencies may create regulations, but must follow the procedures provided in their enabling legislation and in the APA.

Answer (b) is incorrect because enforcement is the execution of existing laws, not the creation of new laws. Answer (c) is incorrect because adjudication is an administrative proceeding conducted by an agency to determine if a statute or regulation has been violated. Answer (d) is incorrect because delegation is the transfer of power by a branch of government that vests authority in an agency.

16. Which of the following is a correct statement about legislative and interpretive rules issued by an administrative agency?

a. Interpretive rules are not subject to judicial review.

b. The making of interpretive rules is subject to the notice and public participation requirements.

c. Legislative rules are not subject to judicial review.

d. The making of legislative rules is subject to the notice and public participation requirements.

The correct answer is (d). *(Publisher)*

REQUIRED: The correct statement about legislative and interpretive rules.

DISCUSSION: Legislative rules issued by an administrative agency are substantive in that they are intended to fill the gaps in a statute passed by the legislative branch. The power to issue such regulations may be express or implied. Rulemaking of this kind is subject to a notice requirement. At the federal level, notice of the time, place, and nature of the proceedings and of the substance of the proposed rule must be published in the Federal Register. Also, the agency must permit the public to participate in the process through submission of written or oral arguments and data. Legislative rules are not judicially reviewable under a "correctness" standard. Such rules are presumed to be valid and will be struck down only if the agency has made an error of law.

Answers (a) and (c) are incorrect because both legislative and interpretive rules are judicially reviewable. Interpretive rules interpret a statute or another regulation. Because interpretation is a matter of law, a court may substitute its judgment for the agency's. Answer (b) is incorrect because adoption of interpretive rules, general statements of policy, or the agency's own organization and procedures is not subject to the notice and public participation requirements.

17. The Administrative Procedure Act sets forth two methods of rulemaking by administrative agencies: formal and informal. The major difference between these two methods is that

a. Formal rulemaking requires that the agency creating the rule publish a notice of proposed rulemaking in the Federal Register.

b. Formal rulemaking requires that the agency conduct formal hearings at which all its evidence justifying its proposed regulation is presented.

c. Informal rulemaking requires that the agency hold public hearings.

d. The formal method is more efficient because it allows any objection to the rule to be taken into consideration prior to the rule's final adoption.

The correct answer is (b). *(Publisher)*

REQUIRED: The difference between formal and informal rulemaking.

DISCUSSION: Formal and informal rulemaking are similar in most respects. Both require publication of the proposed rulemaking in the Federal Register so that the public can participate in the proceedings. The major difference is that formal rulemaking requires that the agency hold formal trial-type hearings. Informal rulemaking permits but does not require the agency to hold public hearings.

Answer (a) is incorrect because both formal and informal rulemaking require that the agency publish notice. Answer (c) is incorrect because an agency conducting informal rulemaking may hold public hearings, but it is not required to do so. Answer (d) is incorrect because the informal method is the more efficient because the lack of required hearings minimizes the opportunities for delay.

8.5 Adjudication

18. Under its adjudicatory powers, an administrative agency has the authority to perform judicial functions. Which of the following statements regarding adjudication is false?

a. Agency adjudication is intended to settle factual disputes among a relatively small group of parties.

b. An administrative agency's adjudications are concerned with general policy to a greater extent that a court's.

c. A party required to appear before an agency investigative hearing is entitled to be represented by an attorney.

d. A defendant in an agency adjudicatory action has the right to a jury trial.

The correct answer is (d). *(Publisher)*

REQUIRED: The false statement regarding adjudication.

DISCUSSION: Under their adjudicatory powers, administrative agencies perform many of the same functions as courts. However, the Supreme Court has ruled that a defendant in an adjudicatory action does not have a right to a jury trial.

Answer (a) is incorrect because agency adjudication is not intended to settle general controversies involving the public at large. Answer (b) is incorrect because an agency hearing is more likely to be concerned with general conditions, and the administrative law judge is more likely to consider the effect of a decision on the public. Answer (c) is incorrect because parties have rights to notice, to be represented by attorneys, to present evidence, and to cross-examine opposing witnesses.

19. In the exercise of its adjudicatory power, an administrative agency

a. Unlike a court, need not observe procedural due process.

b. Is required to observe procedural due process.

c. Is represented at a hearing by an administrative law judge whose functions within the agency include both investigation and adjudication of disputes.

d. Must afford parties who come before it in adjudicatory hearings the full panoply of procedural rights available in a judicial proceeding.

The correct answer is (b). *(Publisher)*

REQUIRED: The correct statement concerning the adjudicatory power of an administrative agency.

DISCUSSION: The due process clauses of the 5th and 14th Amendments apply to the deprivation of rights by federal or state action regardless of whether the deprivation occurs through a judicial or a quasi-judicial process. Procedural due process requires that an administrative agency may not adjudicate unless it observes certain fair and reasonable formalities.

Answer (a) is incorrect because an administrative agency is bound by the due process clause. Answer (c) is incorrect because under the Administrative Procedure Act an administrative law judge would be prohibited from investigating disputes to insure his/her impartiality. Answer (d) is incorrect because the enormous number of cases heard by administrative agencies limits the procedural rights available to parties. The circumstances normally dictate the extent of rights granted.

20. Adjudication is a quasi-judicial function performed by administrative agencies. Adjudicatory hearings resemble a trial and are conducted by an administrative law judge (ALJ). Regarding adjudicatory hearings, which of the following statements is true?

a. Adjudicatory hearings follow much less restrictive rules of evidence than trials in other courts.

b. The ALJ can impose a criminal penalty.

c. The decision of the ALJ in the adjudicatory hearing is final and cannot be appealed.

d. The Administrative Procedure Act (APA) does not apply to adjudicatory hearings.

The correct answer is (a). *(Publisher)*

REQUIRED: The true statement regarding adjudicatory hearings.

DISCUSSION: One of the major differences between adjudicatory hearings and court trials is that the former follow much less restrictive rules of evidence. Agencies need not follow common-law rules that tend to restrict the types of evidence a court may consider. For example, the hearsay rule need not be observed. However, the legal residuum rule requires that a finding of fact be based upon at least some evidence that would be admissible in a court.

Answer (b) is incorrect because administrative agencies do not have the power to impose criminal penalties on violators. Answer (c) is incorrect because the decision handed down by an ALJ can be appealed to a higher level of the agency. Moreover, final agency action can be judicially reviewed. Answer (d) is incorrect because the APA does provide rules governing adjudicatory hearings.

8.6 Judicial Review

21. In reviewing agency action, courts practice considerable self-restraint for all except which of the following reasons?

a. The complexity of the substantive questions presented and the recognition of the special competence of the agencies in handling them.

b. The impracticability of reviewing more than a small fraction of agency decisions.

c. Respect for the concept of separation of powers.

d. Lack of jurisdiction.

The correct answer is (d). *(Publisher)*

REQUIRED: The reason a court would not exercise self-restraint in reviewing agency action.

DISCUSSION: The judicial branch of government has the power of judicial review to inquire into the constitutional propriety of actions of the executive branch. Lack of jurisdiction is ordinarily not a basis for the courts' exercise of self-restraint in reviewing agency action.

Answer (a) is incorrect because judicial self-restraint is necessary given the highly technical expertise often required to deal with the subject matter of agency action. Answer (b) is incorrect because court dockets are already overloaded, and courts can review only a few agency actions. Answer (c) is incorrect because too much activity by the court would infringe upon the proper exercise of executive authority and thus violate the constitutional separation of powers.

22. As part of the administrative law process, which of the following is a major function of judicial review?

a. Providing political oversight, control, and in general shaping and influencing entire regulatory programs and their basic policies.

b. Assuring that the agency is acting in accordance with the enabling legislation.

c. Correcting the deficiencies contained in the relevant legislation.

d. Providing a re-examination of the findings of fact contained in the agency determinations.

The correct answer is (b). *(CPA 584 L-26)*

REQUIRED: The major function of judicial review in administrative law.

DISCUSSION: An administrative agency operates within the guidelines established by the enabling legislation. The rulemaking power of the agency is dependent upon the statute creating it or the statute it is directed to enforce. Rules made pursuant to the appropriate procedures that lie within the guidelines established by the statute will have the force and effect of law. Whether the agency has acted within these limitations is a question of law that a court may decide. A second major judicial review function is to determine that due process has been observed.

Answers (a) and (c) are incorrect because each states a function of the legislative rather than the judicial branch of government. Answer (d) is incorrect because judicial review of an agency's findings of fact is ordinarily limited to whether the findings were supported by substantial evidence (i.e., not insignificant) in the record.

23. Judicial review of administrative action

a. Is not available when that action was adjudicatory in nature under the theory of res judicata.

b. Is permitted regardless of whether administrative remedies are exhausted.

c. Is subject to the ripeness doctrine.

d. Extends more often to review of questions of fact than of law since the administrative agency is deemed to have great expertise in the enforcement of the enabling legislation.

The correct answer is (c). *(Publisher)*

REQUIRED: The correct statement concerning judicial review of administrative action.

DISCUSSION: A court will not review agency action unless the issues are ripe for judicial determination. The agency must have issued a final determination and administrative remedies must have been exhausted.

Answer (a) is incorrect because agency action is not subject to the res judicata doctrine. The agency is not a court. Also, judicial review is an appellate process. Answer (b) is incorrect because judicial review is not permitted when the litigant can still pursue a remedy within the administrative structure. Answer (d) is incorrect because judicial review of administrative action extends to questions of law rather than fact. The agency is better equipped for factual determination than the court.

24. Able Corporation was charged with a violation of the Federal Trade Commission Act. Harp, an FTC examiner, concluded that Able had violated the Act and made adverse determinations on several issues. Able believes Harp has been arbitrary in several of the determinations and clearly incorrect in others. Able

a. Must accept the determination unless it was denied due process.

b. Should immediately proceed in the local state court to obtain injunctive relief ordering Harp to reopen the case and redetermine his conclusions.

c. Should appeal immediately to the local federal District Court to overturn the determination.

d. Must exhaust the available administrative remedies before relief in court can be sought.

The correct answer is (d). *(CPA 1183 L-31)*

REQUIRED: The appropriate action by a person who wishes to overturn a decision by an administrative agency.

DISCUSSION: Exhaustion of administrative remedies is necessary prior to judicial review. In part, this principle is based on the need for efficiency: interruption of the administrative process may be wasteful of time and resources. The deference of courts to the superior expertise of the agency also plays a role. Moreover, the exhaustion of remedies requirement reflects the separation of powers concept: executive branch autonomy is respected until the agency has completed its action or clearly exceeded its authority.

Answer (a) is incorrect because plaintiff may seek judicial review on many grounds other than violation of due process. Answers (b) and (c) are incorrect because judicial review of an FTC action would be appropriate in a federal court but only when administrative remedies are exhausted.

25. In reviewing an adjudicatory decision by an administrative agency, a court will invalidate the agency action

a. If the circumstances required a formal hearing and no jury was provided to act as a trier of fact.

b. If the agency's determination of facts was incorrect.

c. Unless the agency's determination was supported by substantial evidence in the record.

d. Only if the agency exceeded the authority conferred upon it by the enabling statute.

The correct answer is (c). *(Publisher)*

REQUIRED: When a court will invalidate agency action.

DISCUSSION: The reviewing court is not as well-equipped as the agency to make findings of fact, and it will not substitute its judgment for that of the agency on factual questions. Instead, it will inquire whether as a matter of law the agency's findings of fact are supported by substantial evidence in the record. Substantial evidence is evidence from which a reasonable person might reach the same conclusion as the agency. It need not be a preponderance of or greater weight of the evidence.

Answer (a) is incorrect because juries never serve as triers of fact in agency proceedings. Answer (b) is incorrect because the reviewing court does not properly ask whether the agency's finding was incorrect, only whether the finding was supported by substantial evidence. Answer (d) is incorrect because whereas a court may strike down an agency action as exceeding its authority, other grounds exist for reviewing agency action, e.g, compliance with procedural due process.

26. In reviewing an administrative agency's decision, a court will usually

a. Accept jurisdiction whether or not all administrative appeals have been exhausted.

b. Make its own independent determinations of fact.

c. Make a redetermination as to the credibility of witnesses who testified before the agency.

d. Affirm the decision of the agency if it is both reasonable and rational.

The correct answer is (d). *(CPA 1184 L-36)*

REQUIRED: The true statement about judicial review of agency action.

DISCUSSION: When reviewing adjudication by an agency, a court will not substitute its judgment for that of the agency on questions of fact. The standard of review is not "correctness" but whether the record contains substantial evidence that a reasonable and rational person might accept as adequate.

Answer (a) is incorrect because administrative remedies must usually be exhausted (the agency action must be final) before the court may take jurisdiction. Answer (b) is incorrect because the reviewing court is essentially an appeals court and will not make independent findings of fact. Answer (c) is incorrect because the reviewing court has not seen and heard the witnesses and tried the case and is thus in no position to make a factual determination regarding the credibility of witnesses.

27. Sam Roberts receives an unfavorable ruling in an administrative agency's adjudicatory hearing. He decides to appeal the action to the U.S. Circuit Court of Appeals. That court, in reviewing the agency's holding, will usually

a. Reweigh the facts of the action as determined by the agency.

b. Not question the agency's interpretation of the statute in question unless it is patently inconsistent with the statute.

c. Substitute its judgment for that of the agency.

d. Re-try the case.

The correct answer is (b). *(Publisher)*

REQUIRED: The correct statement regarding the appeals court's action in reviewing an agency's decision.

DISCUSSION: A federal court reviewing the decision made by an administrative agency has the authority to determine issues of statutory or constitutional interpretation and other issues of law. However, the court usually will not question an administrative agency's statutory interpretation unless it is clearly inconsistent with a reasonable reading of the statute. The courts ordinarily consider the agency to have the greater expertise in determining the correct interpretation of the statute, and therefore defer to the agency's interpretation.

Answers (a) and (c) are incorrect because the courts ordinarily are not disposed to question an agency's findings unless a violation of procedural due process occurred, the record of the proceedings indicated a lack of substantial evidence to support the finding, or the agency exceeded its authority. Answer (d) is incorrect because appeals courts are not trial courts. However, if the case is appealed to a federal district court, the case is in effect re-tried.

CHAPTER NINE
TORT LAW

9.1 Introduction to Torts

1. Which of the following is tortious conduct?

a. Beth agrees to sell 10 wickets to May for $100 each. On the day of delivery, Beth tenders 10 widgets.

b. Andre intentionally fails to report a substantial amount of income, thereby reducing his apparent federal tax liability.

c. Pops promises David a car for his birthday but reneges.

d. Myra abducts Reginald at gunpoint and holds him for ransom.

The correct answer is (d). *(Publisher)*

REQUIRED: The action that constitutes a tort.

DISCUSSION: In "Handbook of the Law of Torts," Prosser defines a tort as "a civil wrong other than breach of contract for which the court will provide a remedy in the form of an action for damages." A tort entails the imposition of civil rather than criminal liability for conduct affecting another person that society (through its judges and legislatures) views as wrongful. Because tort law must reflect changing circumstances, this branch of law is constantly evolving. New torts are recognized, old ones are modified, and some are no longer actionable. Enforcement is customarily by way of a lawsuit brought by the person whose injury was caused by the wrongful conduct. When Myra committed the crime of kidnapping, she also became civilly liable for the tort of false imprisonment: intentional confinement of another without legal justification. But she should be tried separately for her criminal conduct.

Answer (a) is incorrect because Beth breached a contract. Answer (b) is incorrect because Andre committed a federal crime. Answer (c) is incorrect because a breach of a promise to make a gift is ordinarily not actionable.

2. A tort is

a. Based on socially unreasonable conduct.

b. An offense against the state.

c. The civil equivalent of a crime.

d. A breach of contract.

The correct answer is (a). *(Publisher)*

REQUIRED: The true statement about the nature of a tort.

DISCUSSION: A tort is based on socially unreasonable conduct. It is a balancing of competing interests. In principle, when the social utility of one person's freedom of action is outweighed by the harm caused by interference with the personal or property rights of another, courts and legislatures will provide a remedy for the injury. For instance, free speech becomes unreasonable when damage is done to the reputation of an innocent party.

Answer (b) is incorrect because a crime is an offense against the state. A tort is a breach of a duty owed by one person to another which is the proximate (direct) cause of damage to the person or property of the victim. Answer (c) is incorrect because torts and crimes are not coextensive although many actions are the basis for both a criminal prosecution and a civil action for damages. Answer (d) is incorrect because a tort is generally defined as a civil wrong other than a breach of contract. Nevertheless, there is some conduct which may be both a tort and a breach of contract, e.g., fraud.

3. In what way is the law of torts similar to criminal law?

a. Enforcement is by the state, not the individual.

b. A tort is a breach of a duty imposed by the state.

c. The primary purpose is to compensate injured persons.

d. The defendant must have acted with a wrongful intent.

The correct answer is (b). *(Publisher)*

REQUIRED: The similarity between torts and crimes.

DISCUSSION: A tort is the breach of a duty owed by one person to another. Unlike contractual duties, which are voluntarily assumed, tort law is imposed by the state on all its citizens. Tort law is mainly state law. In this respect, a tort is like a crime, and many torts arise from the same circumstances that produce criminal liability.

Answer (a) is incorrect because the party injured by a tort must sue for damages, while in a criminal case, the state prosecutes the wrongdoer. Answer (c) is incorrect because the primary purpose of criminal law is to protect the public by punishing the wrongdoer; the purpose of tort law is to compensate the injured party. Answer (d) is incorrect because tort liability is often imposed even when the defendant had wholly innocent motives, for example, in negligence or strict liability cases.

9.2 Intentional Torts to the Person

4. Which of the following is an essential element of the tort of assault?

a. A harmful or offensive bodily contact.

b. Actual danger of bodily harm.

c. The plaintiff's awareness of the defendant's conduct.

d. The defendant's intent to cause a battery.

The correct answer is (c). *(Publisher)*

REQUIRED: The essential element of the tort of assault.

DISCUSSION: An assault is an unprivileged intentional act by the defendant to create an apprehension by the plaintiff of an immediate harmful or offensive bodily contact. The plaintiff must have been aware of the act and felt threatened by it. Moreover, the plaintiff's apprehension must have been reasonable in the circumstances.

Answer (a) is incorrect because an assault does not require physical contact (a battery). Answer (b) is incorrect because the defendant's threat must be accompanied only by an apparent present ability to execute it. A threat to shoot the plaintiff is an assault as long as the plaintiff does not know that the gun is actually unloaded. Answer (d) is incorrect because the intent required in the tort of assault is to cause an apprehension of contact. The defendant need not have intended to carry out the threat.

5. Which of the following is an essential element of the tort of battery?

a. A harmful or offensive bodily contact.

b. Actual danger of bodily harm.

c. The plaintiff's awareness of the defendant's conduct.

d. The defendant's intent to cause the particular battery.

The correct answer is (a). *(Publisher)*

REQUIRED: The essential element of the tort of battery.

DISCUSSION: A battery is an intentional unprivileged bodily contact that would be harmful or offensive to a reasonable person. It includes a touching by some instrumentality set in motion by the defendant.

Answer (b) is incorrect because the touching may cause no harm at all and yet constitute a battery. Answer (c) is incorrect because a battery may be committed on an unconscious plaintiff. Answer (d) is incorrect because the element of intent in the tort of battery can be satisfied by an intent to cause a battery to another person or an intent to cause an assault.

Questions 6 and 7 are based on the following information. Husband and Wife, walking on a country road, were frightened by a bull running loose on the road. They climbed over a fence to get onto the adjacent property, owned by Grower. The fence was posted with a large sign, "No Trespassing." Grower saw Husband and Wife and came toward them with his large watchdog on a long leash. The dog rushed at Wife. Grower had intended only to frighten Husband and Wife, but the leash broke, and before Grower could restrain the dog, the dog bit Wife.

6. If Husband asserts a claim based on assault against Grower, will Husband prevail?

a. Yes, because the landowner did not have a privilege to use excessive force.

b. Yes, if Husband reasonably believed that the dog might bite him.

c. No, if the dog did not come in contact with him.

d. No, if Grower was trying to protect his property.

The correct answer is (b). *(MBE Part I-118)*

REQUIRED: Whether Husband will prevail on a claim of assault.

DISCUSSION: An assault is an act by a defendant intended to, and which does, create a reasonable apprehension of a harmful or offensive contact to the plaintiff. The apprehension of an unlawful touching is only required to be reasonable; i.e., it need not actually occur or even be possible.

Answer (a) is incorrect because Husband will prevail on an assault theory regardless of the degree of force. Answer (c) is incorrect because assault does not require an actual touching (only the apprehension of a touching). Answer (d) is incorrect because while Grower is entitled to use reasonable force to protect his property, he is also under a duty to request the trespassers to desist before using force of any kind.

7. If Wife asserts a claim based on battery against Grower, will Wife prevail?

a. Yes, because Grower intended that the dog frighten Wife.

b. Yes, because the breaking of the leash establishes liability under res ipsa loquitur.

c. No, because Wife made an unauthorized entry on Grower's land.

d. No, because Grower did not intend to cause any harmful contact with Wife.

The correct answer is (a). *(MBE Part I-117)*

REQUIRED: Whether Wife will prevail in a claim based on battery and why.

DISCUSSION: The intent to commit the assault (causing a reasonable apprehension of contact by the dog) is transferred to the battery (the actual harmful or offensive touching by the dog). Therefore, Grower is liable for battery.

Answer (b) is incorrect because res ipsa loquitur ("the thing speaks for itself") is a legal doctrine that permits the finding of a tort from circumstantial evidence. It is inapplicable here because direct evidence is available. Answer (c) is incorrect because an owner of land has a duty to avoid intentional torts even to trespassers. Answer (d) is incorrect because Grower's intent to commit the assault is transferred to the battery.

8. Jim is very short and small for his age, and Jack is very large and muscular. One day Jim accidentally bumped into Jack while Jack was carrying a tray filled with food. The collision caused Jack to spill the contents of his tray. Angry over the mishap, Jack hit Jim with the tray. Jim did not see the tray coming before it struck him.

a. Jack committed an assault and battery when he hit Jim with the tray.

b. Jim committed an assault and battery when he bumped into Jack causing him to spill his food.

c. Jack committed an assault on Jim.

d. Jack committed a battery on Jim.

The correct answer is (d). *(W. Anderson)*

REQUIRED: The differences between an assault and battery.

DISCUSSION: The tort of assault requires an intentional action by the defendant that causes a reasonable apprehension by the plaintiff of harmful or offensive contact. A battery is an intentional harmful or offensive contact. Jack intentionally hit Jim with a tray, which certainly could be classified as a harmful or offensive contact. The discrepancy in size between Jim and Jack might bear on whether the plaintiff had a reasonable apprehension of an assault. Moreover, it may be relevant as to whether the contact was harmful or offensive.

Answers (a) and (c) are incorrect because Jim had no apprehension of contact with the tray. Hence, no assault occurred. Answer (b) is incorrect because the action was unintentional. Assault and battery are intentional torts.

9. Defendant is charged with battery. The plaintiff was struck in the face by Defendant's fist. In which situation is Defendant most likely to be not liable for battery?

a. Defendant had been hypnotized at a party and ordered by the hypnotist to strike the person he disliked the most.

b. Defendant was suffering from an epileptic seizure and had no control over his motions.

c. Defendant was heavily intoxicated and was shadow boxing without realizing that the plaintiff was near him.

d. Defendant, who had just awakened from a deep sleep, was not fully aware of what was happening and mistakenly thought the plaintiff was attacking him.

The correct answer is (b). *(MBE Part I-75)*

REQUIRED: The situation in which Defendant is most likely to be not liable for battery.

DISCUSSION: To be liable for the tort of battery, the defendant must have willfully done an act bringing about a harmful or offensive contact with the plaintiff. A person who commits the touching of another during an epileptic seizure is not liable for battery because it was not willful.

Answer (a) is incorrect because an act done under hypnosis is considered a voluntary act. Answer (c) is incorrect because intoxication is not an excuse since Defendant is chargeable with having voluntarily put himself in a state of intoxication. Answer (d) is incorrect because the act of striking was intentional and the mistaken thought is not a defense.

10. Lender demanded that Borrower pay a debt owed to him, and threatened to punch Borrower in the nose. A fight ensued between them. Mann came upon the scene just as Lender was about to kick Borrower in the head. Noting that Lender was getting the better of the fight, Mann pointed a gun at Lender and said, "Stop, or I'll shoot." If Lender asserts a claim against Mann based on assault, will Lender prevail?

a. Yes, because Mann threatened to use deadly force.

b. Yes, unless Mann was related to Borrower.

c. No, if it was apparent that Lender was about to inflict serious bodily harm upon Borrower.

d. No, because Lender was the original aggressor by threatening Borrower with battery.

The correct answer is (c). *(MBE Part I-3)*

REQUIRED: The result of an assault by a defendant acting in defense of another.

DISCUSSION: Self-defense (or defense of another) is a defense to assault. The defense will only be effective if Mann's threat of deadly force was justified by the apparent level of harm with which Borrower was threatened. Generally, apprehension of serious bodily harm is justification for using deadly force as a defense.

Answer (a) is incorrect because Mann's threat to use deadly force could be justified if Borrower could legally have used deadly force in self-defense. Answer (b) is incorrect because the relation of the parties is irrelevant. Answer (d) is incorrect because Lender's status as the original aggressor in the altercation did not by itself justify Mann's action.

11. Soldier, who had been drinking heavily in a bar, began arguing with Bartender, an employee of Owner, who had refused to serve Soldier any more drinks. Soldier said, "If you weren't the bartender here, I would break your skull," and while saying this, Soldier leaned over and tapped Bartender on the hand. At Bartender's instruction, two bouncers took Soldier into the men's room, doused his face with cold water, and threatened him with physical harm if he did not remain there until he sobered up. If Soldier sues Owner, a claim for relief that would likely succeed would be for

a. False imprisonment in that Owner, through her agents, confined Soldier in the men's room.

b. Negligence for refusing to serve him as a guest.

c. Strict liability for her failure to serve persons in public accommodations.

d. Trespass for denying Soldier continued access to the premises after having been invited as a public guest.

The correct answer is (a). *(MBE 272 53)*

REQUIRED: The claim that would most likely succeed in an action by a patron against an innkeeper.

DISCUSSION: Soldier's best chance for legal relief would be to assert a claim of false imprisonment against Owner. False imprisonment is the intentional confining or restraining of the plaintiff within some area, e.g., putting Soldier in the men's room and using threats to keep him there. The confinement need not be by an actual physical restraint. Owner would be liable for the torts of her employees acting within their employment.

Answer (b) is incorrect because Owner might have been liable and negligent for continuing to serve an obviously intoxicated person. Answer (c) is incorrect because an innkeeper has no duty to serve every person who appears on his/her premises. Answer (d) is incorrect because Owner cannot be a trespasser on her own premises.

12. Dime Store's private security guard reasonably believed he saw Fran put a lipstick into her purse and leave the store without paying for it. The guard ran after Fran into the parking lot screaming, "Stop, thief!" When he caught Fran, the guard threw her to the ground and sat on her until the police came. Fran had shoplifted the lipstick, but she sued Dime Store for false imprisonment. Will she likely win?

a. No, because the guard acted on reasonable belief.

b. No, because Fran had shoplifted the lipstick.

c. Yes, because a private security guard has no right to detain a person in the parking lot.

d. Yes, because the guard used unreasonable force and an unreasonable means of detention.

The correct answer is (d). *(E. Arnold)*

REQUIRED: The correct statement regarding a shopkeeper who abused a qualified privilege.

DISCUSSION: Merchants have a qualified privilege to detain suspected shoplifters. If merchants or their agents abuse the privilege by using unreasonable means of detention, however, they lose the privilege and incur liability for false imprisonment. In this case, the guard used excessive force in detaining Fran.

Answer (a) is incorrect because a reasonable basis for asserting the privilege fails in light of the unreasonable detention. Answer (b) is incorrect because the act of shoplifting does not provide a basis for an unreasonable detention. Answer (c) is incorrect because the guard, as the merchant's agent, did have a qualified privilege to detain Fran.

13. Lowe Ricard posed as a trick-shot artist with the Great Wild West Show. He asked Jane Witt to try out as his partner. Ricard requested Witt to stand 75 feet away and hold a lighted cigarette between her lips. Ricard three times shot a cigarette out of her mouth. He was enthusiastic about her performance and told her to report to the Wild West Show's headquarters. Witt reported but was informed that Ricard was not connected with the show. He had been a trick-shot artist with the show for many years but had been discharged because of failing eyesight and mental instability. At this point, Witt became hysterical, requiring sedation and hospitalization for a severe nervous reaction. Witt's best chance of recovering from Ricard for emotional distress is

a. As added damages in an assault action.

b. As added damages in a battery action.

c. On the basis that perpetrators of "sick" jokes should have to pay for the damages caused by their jokes.

d. On the basis of the tort of intentional infliction of severe emotional distress.

The correct answer is (d). *(MBE 272 142)*

REQUIRED: The plaintiff's best chance of recovering for her emotional distress.

DISCUSSION: The tort of intentional infliction of emotional distress involves intentional conduct by the defendant that is so outrageous and so far beyond the bounds of civilized behavior as to cause the plaintiff extreme emotional suffering. Ricard's intentional actions could meet the outrageous conduct requirement, and Witt's hospitalization was indicative of severe emotional distress.

Answer (a) is incorrect because there is no indication that Witt had any apprehension of bodily contact at the time of the shooting. Answer (b) is incorrect because there is no indication of contact to which Witt did not consent. Answer (c) is incorrect because it does not state a legal basis for recovery.

14. Which of the following is an essential element of the tort of defamation?

a. A writing.

b. Publication to a third party.

c. Intentional communication of a false statement.

d. In most states, special damages must be proven for slander per se but not libel per se.

The correct answer is (b). *(Publisher)*

REQUIRED: The essential element of the tort of defamation.

DISCUSSION: Defamation is the unjustifiable communication (publication) to a third party of a false statement that injures the plaintiff's reputation and holds him/her up to hatred, contempt, or ridicule. Oral defamation is slander. Defamation published in more permanent form (newspaper, letter, film) is libel.

Answer (a) is incorrect because defamation may be oral. Answer (c) is incorrect because the publication may be careless or negligent. It need not be intentional. Answer (d) is incorrect because slander per se or libel per se are defamatory statements alleging criminal acts, professional incompetence, serious sexual misconduct, etc. Proof of special damages is not required for either; damages are presumed.

15. In a tort action based on defamation, a defendant may plead

a. An absolute privilege if (s)he is a former employer asked by a prospective employer for information about plaintiff's character.

b. A conditional privilege if (s)he is a witness called to testify about the plaintiff in a suit to which plaintiff was not party.

c. A constitutional privilege if (s)he is a public figure.

d. The truth of the defamatory statement even though it was uttered with malicious intent.

The correct answer is (d). *(Publisher)*

REQUIRED: The defense that a defendant may plead in a defamation suit.

DISCUSSION: In most jurisdictions, truth is an absolute defense to defamation regardless of the defendant's intent. A few require truth plus good motive. In some cases, however, plaintiff may be able to avoid this defense by pleading and proving invasion of privacy.

Answer (a) is incorrect because in these circumstances, the privilege is only qualified or conditional. The limited privilege is lost if the defendant acts maliciously or abusively. A limited privilege is often given to protect an interest of the defendant or to permit free communication among persons with a valid interest in a subject. Answer (b) is incorrect because an absolute (not conditional) privilege is given to participants in judicial proceedings. Answer (c) is incorrect because the constitutional privilege is extended to statements about (not by) public figures uttered without malice (knowledge of falsity or reckless disregard for the truth).

Questions 16 and 17 are based on the following information. Photo, a free-lance photographer, took a picture of Player in front of Shoe Store. Player was a nationally known amateur basketball star who had received much publicity in the press. At the time, the window display in Shoe Store featured "Jumpers," a well-known make of basketball shoes. Photo sold the picture, greatly enlarged, to Shoe Store and told Shoe Store that Photo had Player's approval to do so and that Player consented to Shoe Store's showing the enlarged picture in the window. Shoe Store made no effort to ascertain whether Player had given his consent to Photo. In fact, Player did not even know that Photo had taken the picture. Shoe Store put the enlarged picture in the window with the display of "Jumpers" shoes. The college that Player attended believed that Player had intentionally endorsed Shoe Store and "Jumpers" shoes, and the college canceled his athletic scholarship.

---

16. If Player asserts a claim based on defamation against Shoe Store, will Player prevail?

a. Yes, if Shoe Store was reckless in accepting Photo's statement that Photo had Player's approval.

b. Yes, because the defamatory material was in printed form.

c. No, if Shoe Store believed Photo's statement that Photo had Player's approval.

d. No, because the picture of Player was not defamatory per se.

The correct answer is (a). *(MBE Part I-150)*

REQUIRED: Whether Player will prevail in a defamation action against Shoe Store and why.

DISCUSSION: Defamation requires proof of defamatory language (material), concerning the plaintiff, published to the injury of the plaintiff's reputation. For public figures, proof of malice is also required and can be met by proving a reckless disregard for the truth. Player may be a public figure due to his basketball reputation, and Shoe Store did disregard the truth. The other elements are met because a photograph can be defamatory material, it concerned Player, was published in the display window, and caused injury to Player's reputation as an amateur basketball player by implying that Player had violated NCAA rules by endorsing the store and the shoes.

Answer (b) is incorrect because defamatory material in printed form would not be sufficient in this case without recklessness (malice). Answer (c) is incorrect because Shoe Store's subjective belief is insufficient if its conduct was in reckless disregard of the truth. Answer (d) is incorrect because even if the picture was not defamatory per se (on its face), Player might prevail by proving damages and facts which establish the defamatory content of the photograph.

17. If Player asserts a claim based on invasion of privacy against Shoe Store, will Player prevail?

a. Yes, because Photo had no right to take Player's picture.

b. Yes, because Shoe Store, without Player's permission, used Player's picture for profit.

c. No, because Player was already a basketball star who had received much publicity in the press.

d. No, because Shoe Store believed it had permission.

The correct answer is (b). *(MBE Part I-151)*

REQUIRED: Whether Player will prevail on a claim based on invasion of privacy and why.

DISCUSSION: The tort of invasion of privacy includes appropriation of the plaintiff's name or picture for the commercial advantage of the defendant. This occurred since Shoe Store used Player's picture to promote its products.

Answer (a) is incorrect because the taking of the photograph in public was not improper. Answer (c) is incorrect because Player's public reputation only increases the amount of damages. Answer (d) is incorrect because a mistaken good faith belief that Shoe Store had permission is no defense to the tort of invasion of privacy.

18. The tort of invasion of privacy may take a number of forms. In which case will the defendant most likely prevail?

a. Defendant published a newspaper article reporting that plaintiff, a local political candidate, had many years before been convicted of burglary in another state.

b. Defendant landlord installed a two-way mirror in the plaintiff's bedroom through which he secretly viewed plaintiff's activities.

c. Defendant caused a newspaper advertisement opposing abortion to be published with a list of names of those purportedly supporting her views. Plaintiff's name was among those listed. She is president of a pro-choice group.

d. Defendant published a newspaper article revealing that plaintiff had served time in prison 20 years ago but had ever since been both respectable and a valuable member of the community while shunning notoriety.

The correct answer is (a). *(Publisher)*

REQUIRED: The action for invasion of privacy in which defendant will most likely prevail.

DISCUSSION: Invasion of privacy consists of four separate torts: appropriation, intrusion, public disclosure of private facts, and false light in the public eye. Appropriation involves using the plaintiff's name or likeness for commercial gain. Intrusion is an unreasonable interference with a person's solitude or seclusion. Public disclosure of private facts results in liability when offensive publicity is given to private information. False light in the public eye is unreasonable and offensive publicity attributing to the plaintiff views (s)he does not hold or traits (s)he does not have. In the case of a political candidate's criminal record, liability would not be imposed because the matter is of legitimate public interest, and public figures in general receive less protection than private citizens in both defamation and invasion of privacy actions.

Answer (b) is incorrect because it states a classic instance of intrusion. Answer (c) is incorrect because it is an example of false light in the public eye. Answer (d) is incorrect because it is an example of public disclosure of private facts (not newsworthy or lack legitimate public interest).

19. Edmond was a butler in the home of Ville, the local district attorney. On September 17, Ville's wife, Mercedes, questioned Edmond about the loss of certain jewelry. The next day Ville and the police accused Edmond and asked to search his belongings. Edmond consented and nothing was found. Ville decided to charge Edmond with grand theft since Edmond was the only nonfamily member living in the house. Edmond was arrested, tried, and found not guilty. Who will prevail if Edmond brings a civil action against Ville?

a. Edmond will succeed on a theory of malicious prosecution.

b. Edmond will win on a theory of intentional infliction of emotional distress.

c. Ville will prevail if the claim is based on malicious prosecution.

d. Edmond will win on a theory of false imprisonment.

The correct answer is (c). *(Publisher)*

REQUIRED: Who will prevail in an action for malicious prosecution of a criminal action and upon what theory.

DISCUSSION: To prevail on the tort theory of malicious prosecution, the plaintiff must show that the defendant initiated criminal proceedings against him, the case ended favorably for plaintiff, there was no probable cause for prosecution, and defendant acted with malice. However, a prosecutor, such as Ville, is generally privileged and may not be sued for malicious prosecution.

Answer (a) is incorrect because Ville is privileged as a district attorney. Answer (b) is incorrect because to prevail, the plaintiff would have to show that the defendant's conduct was intended to cause severe emotional distress and was so outrageous that it exceeded all civilized limits. Answer (d) is incorrect because a legal arrest cannot be the basis for false imprisonment even if the individual is not guilty.

20. One who has wrongfully initiated legal proceedings may be liable in tort under various theories. Which of the following intentional torts does not require proof of lack of probable cause?

a. Malicious prosecution of a criminal proceeding.

b. Abuse of process.

c. Malicious prosecution of a civil proceeding.

d. Malicious prosecution of a criminal or civil proceeding.

The correct answer is (b). *(Publisher)*

REQUIRED: The tort not requiring the plaintiff to prove lack of probable cause.

DISCUSSION: The tort of malicious prosecution of a criminal or civil action involves proof of three elements: the prosecution complained of was without probable cause; the proceedings ended favorably for the person bringing the malicious prosecution suit; and the initiator of the proceedings acted with malice (for an improper purpose). In a suit for malicious prosecution of a civil action, a fourth element must be shown: that plaintiff suffered actual harm.

Abuse of process, however, is somewhat different. This tort entails the use of legal proceedings for a primary purpose other than that for which they are intended, for example, bringing a suit complaining of a nuisance on a neighbor's property as a means of compelling him/her to sell the land. An abuse of process suit may be successful even though probable cause existed and the legal proceedings did not end favorably for the person suing for abuse of process.

9.3 Intentional Torts to Property Rights

21. Defendant (D) will most likely prevail in a suit brought for trespass to real property in which situation?

a. The limbs of a tree on D's land extend over the boundary line into the air above Bonita's property.

b. While walking on his own wooded land, D became lost and walked onto Neighbor's land.

c. Mike shoved D over a fence and into Irv's yard.

d. D dug a tunnel from his house, under Larry's land to Curly's property.

The correct answer is (c). *(Publisher)*

REQUIRED: The case in which D is not guilty of trespass to real property.

DISCUSSION: Trespass to real property is an intentional and unjustifiable entry onto land possessed by someone else, causing an object or a third person to do so, remaining on the land, or failing to remove from the land an object that one is under a duty to remove. Since D did not enter Irv's yard of his own volition, he is not liable for trespass. Mike is liable, however, because he caused a third person to enter the land.

Answer (a) is incorrect because the land includes the airspace above it (to a limited height) and the ground below it. D has either caused an object to enter Bonita's property or failed to remove it. Answer (b) is incorrect because D intentionally stepped on the land that turned out to be Neighbor's even though he did not know it was Neighbor's. Answer (d) is incorrect because a trespass may also be committed beneath the land.

22. Without permission, Olivia borrowed Portia's new car for a trip to the beach. While returning the vehicle later the same day, Olivia had an accident that caused minor damage to the fender and headlights. Olivia will be liable to Portia on the theory of

a. Conversion for the actual damages.

b. Conversion for the full value of the property.

c. Trespass to personal property for the full value of the property.

d. Trespass to personal property for actual damages.

The correct answer is (d). *(Publisher)*

REQUIRED: The basis for and nature of recovery for temporarily dispossessing plaintiff of personal property.

DISCUSSION: The tort of trespass to personal property is the intentional and unjustifiable taking or damaging of personal property possessed by someone else. Recovery is for the actual harm done to the property or the loss of possession. The tort of conversion is an intentional interference with the plaintiff's right to possess his/her property. The interference must be so serious that it would be appropriate for the defendant to pay the full value of the property to plaintiff in damages. Theft, destruction, or wrongful detention of property are acts of conversion. Since the car was returned with minor damage on the same day, plaintiff is only entitled to the lesser recovery allowed for the tort of trespass to personal property.

Questions 23 and 24 are based on the following information. In 1950, Cattle Company paid $30,000 for a 150-acre tract of agricultural land well suited for a cattle feed lot. The tract was ten miles from the city of Metropolis, then a community of 50,000 people, and five miles from the nearest home. By 1989, the city limits extended to Cattle Company's feed lot, and the city had a population of 350,000. About 10,000 people lived within three miles of the cattle feeding operation. The Cattle Company land is outside the city limits and no zoning ordinance applies. The Cattle Company land is now worth $300,000, and $25,000 has been invested in buildings and pens. Cattle Company, conscious of its obligations to its neighbors, uses the best and most sanitary feed lot procedures, including chemical sprays, to keep down flies and odors, and frequently removes manure. Despite these measures, residents of Metropolis complain of flies and odors. An action has been filed by five individual homeowners who live within half a mile of the Cattle Company feed lot. The plaintiffs' homes are valued currently at $40,000 to $110,000 each. Flies in the area are five to ten times more numerous than in other parts of Metropolis, and extremely obnoxious odors are frequently carried by the wind to the plaintiffs' homes. The flies and odors are a substantial health hazard.

23. If plaintiffs assert a claim based on public nuisance, plaintiffs will

a. Prevail if plaintiffs sustained harm different from that suffered by the public at large.

b. Prevail if Cattle Company's acts interfered with any person's enjoyment of his/her property.

c. Not prevail, because only the state may bring an action based on public nuisance.

d. Not prevail, because plaintiffs came to the nuisance.

The correct answer is (a). *(MBE Part I-179)*

REQUIRED: Whether neighbors will recover on a claim based on public nuisance.

DISCUSSION: A public nuisance is an act which unreasonably interferes with the health, safety, or property rights of the community at large. A private party may recover only if (s)he has sustained a unique form of harm not suffered by the public at large, e.g., if the smell was a nuisance to the public but the flies were a health hazard only to the neighbors who are suing.

Answer (b) is incorrect because interference with enjoyment of property is not sufficient to sustain a claim based on public nuisance. Answer (c) is incorrect because private parties may bring actions based on public nuisance if they have suffered a unique harm. Answer (d) is incorrect because coming to the nuisance is not a defense if plaintiffs purchased in good faith and without the intent to acquire a lawsuit. Nuisance is a form of trespass against the plaintiff that is not affected by which property was developed first.

24. If the plaintiffs assert a claim based on private nuisance, plaintiffs will

a. Prevail, because Cattle Company's activity unreasonably interfered with plaintiffs' use and enjoyment of their property.

b. Prevail, because Cattle Company's activity constitutes an inverse condemnation of their property.

c. Not prevail, because Cattle Company had operated the feed lot for more than 25 years.

d. Not prevail, because Cattle Company uses the most reasonable procedures to keep down flies and odors.

The correct answer is (a). *(MBE Part I-180)*

REQUIRED: Whether neighbors can prevail on a claim based on private nuisance.

DISCUSSION: Private nuisance involves a substantial and unreasonable interference with the use and enjoyment of the land of another. Flies, extremely obnoxious odors, and a substantial health hazard constitute a substantial interference with an ordinary person's use and enjoyment of his/her own property.

Answer (b) is incorrect because condemnation is the taking of property for public purposes by the government. Answer (c) is incorrect because Cattle Company will lose even though it has been in operation for a long time if its operations substantially and unreasonably interfere with the use and enjoyment of the neighboring properties. Answer (d) is incorrect because the Cattle Company may be liable without fault or any intent to do harm.

25. Thief steals goods from Owner. Thief then stores the goods with Bailee who is unaware of the theft. Owner learns of the location of the goods and gives notice to Bailee.

a. If Owner demands the goods from Bailee and Bailee refuses to surrender them, Owner may seek the remedy of replevin.

b. If Bailee had no notice of the theft and returned the goods to Thief, Owner could bring an action for conversion against Bailee.

c. Owner should bring an action for trespass to chattels against Thief rather than an action for conversion.

d. If the goods are destroyed while in the possession of Bailee after (s)he has received notice from Owner, Bailee will be liable for conversion.

The correct answer is (a). *(Publisher)*

REQUIRED: The legal consequence of storing stolen goods with an innocent bailee.

DISCUSSION: The tort of conversion is an intentional interference with the plaintiff's right to possess his/her property. The interference must be so serious that it would be appropriate for the defendant to pay the full value of the property to plaintiff in damages. Theft, destruction, or wrongful detention of property are acts of conversion. Bailee's refusal to return the goods to the rightful owner is also an act of conversion. Plaintiff may seek the actual damages or to reacquire the property by means of replevin (a civil action brought to regain possession of wrongfully detained property).

Answer (b) is incorrect because if Bailee acted in good faith and without notice that Thief had no right to the goods, Bailee will not be liable. Answer (c) is incorrect because the action for trespass to chattels is proper for a lesser interference with the plaintiff's right to possess; e.g., minor damage to the plaintiff's car. Answer (d) is incorrect because Bailee will not be liable for conversion if (s)he has not refused a request to return the goods to Owner.

26. The intent or scienter element necessary to establish a cause of action for fraud will be satisfied if the plaintiff can establish that the

a. Plaintiff actually relied on the defendant's misrepresentation.

b. Plaintiff justifiably relied on the defendant's misrepresentation.

c. Defendant made a false representation of fact.

d. Defendant made a misrepresentation with a reckless disregard for the truth.

The correct answer is (d). *(CPA 1188 L-15)*

REQUIRED: The element needed to establish fraud.

DISCUSSION: The following are the elements of the tort of fraud (deceit, intentional misrepresentation): 1) a misrepresentation (a misstatement or an omission when defendant had a duty of disclosure), 2) of a material fact, 3) made with scienter, 4) intended to induce reliance, 5) that was reasonably relied upon, and 6) that proximately caused the plaintiff's injury. Scienter exists when the defendant makes a false representation with knowledge of its falsity or with reckless disregard as to its truth.

Answer (a) is incorrect because the plaintiff's reliance is an element of fraud in addition to the scienter element. Answer (b) is incorrect because the plaintiff's justifiable (reasonable) reliance on the misrepresentation is also an additional element of fraud, but it does not establish scienter. Answer (c) is incorrect because an innocent misrepresentation of fact does not constitute fraud.

27. The tort of intentional misrepresentation (fraud) consists of the following elements: a material misrepresentation with scienter and an intent to induce reliance that proximately causes damages to a defendant who reasonably relied upon the misrepresentation. Which is the correct statement concerning this tort?

a. When one party to a transaction knows that the other has no knowledge of a material fact, it is intentional misrepresentation not to disclose it.

b. Scienter exists only when defendant made a false representation with actual knowledge of its falsity.

c. Plaintiff may not prove justifiable reliance if the false representation was one of opinion rather than of fact.

d. Plaintiff may show that (s)he justifiably relied upon the false representation even though (s)he has undertaken no investigation of the factual statement.

The correct answer is (d). *(Publisher)*

REQUIRED: The correct statement concerning the tort of intentional misrepresentation.

DISCUSSION: To recover for the tort of intentional misrepresentation (fraud, deceit), plaintiff must prove justifiable reliance upon the false representation. This is normally accomplished when plaintiff shows that defendant has made a false representation of a material fact (that it was a substantial factor influencing his/her decision). Plaintiff may rely on the representations without investigation unless the falsity of the representations could be discovered without an unreasonable (costly, difficult, etc.) investigation.

Answer (a) is incorrect because failure to disclose a material fact is not intentional misrepresentation as long as it was not done to induce reliance and the fact was obvious or could have been discovered by reasonable inspection. Answer (b) is incorrect because scienter also exists when defendant made a false representation with reckless regard as to its truth. Answer (c) is incorrect because in certain instances a plaintiff may justifiably rely upon an opinion, e.g., that of an expert.

28. Sly offered Merry Lamb a watch for $100 and falsely represented that it was studded with diamonds, which would make its retail value $650. In reliance on Sly's statement, Merry paid $100 for the watch. She later learned that its stones were fake and its retail value was only $100. In a tort action based on fraud, what would be the measure of Merry's damages in the majority of states?

a. $0.

b. $100.

c. $550.

d. $650.

The correct answer is (c). *(Publisher)*

REQUIRED: The measure of fraud damages under the majority rule.

DISCUSSION: The majority of states adhere to the "loss-of-bargain" theory under which the measure of damages is the difference between the value received and the value as represented. Since the watch was stated to be worth $650 and was actually worth only $100, damages would equal $550. The minority view is that damages should be based on plaintiff's "out-of-pocket" loss. Since Merry paid $100 for a watch worth $100, applying the minority rule would result in no damages.

Note that the misrepresentation was of a fact, i.e., whether the stones on the watch were diamonds. Usually a misrepresentation as to only value is considered an opinion and not a misrepresentation of fact.

9.4 Business Torts

Also see Chapter 27, "Antitrust," Chapter 30, "Consumer Protection," and Chapter 33, "Accountants' Legal Responsibilities."

29. Supplier has a contract with Factory to provide its needs for gidgets. Fabriken, a major competitor of Factory, hoping to disrupt Factory's production schedule, induces one of Supplier's subcontractors to delay delivery of materials necessary for the production of gidgets. As a result, Factory sustains millions of dollars in losses when the gidgets are not promptly delivered. On what theory could Factory prevail in an action against Fabriken?

a. Interference with contractual relations.

b. Fraud.

c. Breach of contract.

d. Factory has no action against Fabriken.

The correct answer is (a). *(Publisher)*

REQUIRED: The theory upon which Factory could prevail in an action against Fabriken.

DISCUSSION: Factory appears to have an action based on intentional interference with contractual relations. Factory must show that it had a valid and enforceable contract with Supplier, Fabriken intentionally caused a material interference with the contract relationship, and such interference proximately caused plaintiff's damages. The contract between Supplier and Factory created rights which the law will protect.

Answer (b) is incorrect because there is no evidence that a false representation was made by defendant or was relied upon by plaintiff. Answer (c) is incorrect because Fabriken did not contract with Factory and could not have breached a contract. Answer (d) is incorrect because Fabriken has intentionally interfered with contractual relations.

30. Competitor runs an ad in the newspaper in which it states that Seller's product has a serious design defect. As a result, Seller's sales slide.

a. Competitor has committed the tort of disparagement or trade libel if the statement is false regardless of whether Competitor had knowledge of the falsehood.

b. Competitor has committed the tort of disparagement or trade libel only if it knew of the falsehood of the statement or acted with reckless disregard for the truth.

c. Competitor has committed the tort of interference with contractual relations.

d. Seller may sue Competitor for the tort of deceit.

The correct answer is (b). *(Publisher)*

REQUIRED: The liability for publicly degrading a competitor's product.

DISCUSSION: The law of torts provides several means to protect persons from interference with their economic interests. An action for disparagement (called trade libel) may be based upon an intentional false or reckless statement made concerning the quality of another's product. (A few states base the tort on negligent misrepresentation.) The intent of the defendant is usually crucial. If Competitor's statement was honestly made, even though mistaken, an action for disparagement would not be available.

Answer (a) is incorrect because disparagement usually requires an intentional or reckless falsehood. Answer (c) is incorrect because an action for interference with contractual relations would exist only if the defendant had hindered performance of a valid and enforceable contract. Answer (d) is incorrect because an action for deceit (fraud) can only be brought by one who justifiably relied upon the false representation.

31. Dont Products sells Notions door to door. Tiff Co. is its primary competitor. In order to increase its own sales and to reduce Dont's sales, Tiff initiated a successful campaign to recruit most of Dont's sales people, who are not under contract for a specified time. In a suit brought by Dont, Tiff will

a. Lose because it acted with malice when inducing Dont's employees to terminate their employment.

b. Lose because the contractual relation interfered with was current rather than prospective.

c. Win because the employees' contracts were terminable at Dont's will.

d. Win because it is not a tort to offer someone a better job.

The correct answer is (a). *(Publisher)*

REQUIRED: The outcome of a suit against a firm that recruited a competitor's employees.

DISCUSSION: Malicious interference with the contractual relationship between an employer and an employee is a tort. Malice in this context means that the conduct was intentional. When there is no contractual obligation between the employee and employer (terminated at will), the malice must also include an intent to injure the plaintiff. Since Tiff's recruitment of Dont's personnel was obviously to gain a competitive advantage at the expense of Dont and to damage Dont's economic condition, Tiff will lose.

Answer (b) is incorrect because Tiff should lose because it acted maliciously, not because the contractual relation was current. Answer (c) is incorrect because Tiff should lose since the motive of the conduct complained of was clearly to injure Dont. Answer (d) is incorrect because enticing an employee away is a tort if it interferes with a contract or if the purpose is to injure the competitor.

32. Bippo is a highly successful mass marketer of a ball-point pen whose form and design are highly distinctive and well-known to the general public. Bippo's patent for its pen has expired, and a pen very similar in form and design has appeared on the market. The imitator, however, has stamped its own trade name and the country of manufacture on the product. What will be the outcome if Bippo sues in tort?

a. Bippo will win because the product has acquired a secondary meaning.

b. Bippo will lose because the public is not likely to be confused by the imitator.

c. Bippo will lose because courts do not recognize palming off as a tort.

d. Bippo will win because no one has a privilege to imitate the physical appearance of a highly advertised product.

The correct answer is (b). *(Publisher)*

REQUIRED: The outcome of a suit by a manufacturer against an imitator of its product.

DISCUSSION: Palming off has two elements: the original product has a secondary meaning, and the imitation and the original are so similar that the public may confuse the two. Secondary meaning is the association by the public of a manufacturer with its product. But if the imitator does not fraudulently market the product, and if the public is not likely to confuse the imitation with the original, tort liability will not be imposed.

Answer (a) is incorrect because a secondary meaning alone is insufficient to protect the form and design of the original if the public is not likely to confuse it with the copy. Answer (c) is incorrect because palming off is one of several torts in the category of unfair trade practices. Answer (d) is incorrect because one may imitate the form and design of a product not under patent or trademark protection if the public is not likely to confuse the two.

33. In which case is the defendant (D) most likely to prevail in a suit by plaintiff (P) for infringement of a trademark or trade name?

a. D sells a soft drink called Coke.

b. D uses a trademark which P registered with the U.S. Patent Office. P did not affix the trademark to the goods identified but merely placed it on a tag attached to the goods.

c. D sells a beer it describes as "light" beer.

d. D sells a cough syrup called Smith's with a picture of two bearded men on the container.

The correct answer is (c). *(Publisher)*

REQUIRED: The instance which is probably not an infringement of a trademark or trade name.

DISCUSSION: A trademark is a distinctive design, word, symbol, mark, picture, etc. affixed to a product and adopted by its seller or manufacturer to identify it. A trade name is generally regarded as referring to a business and the goodwill it has generated, for example, Exxon. In general, trademark protection is not given to a term that is generic or commonly descriptive. "Light" has been used in the beer industry for years to describe a certain set of characteristics and thus it is not protected.

Answer (a) is incorrect because "Coke" is a nickname associated in the public mind with the products of a particular company, and it has thereby acquired a secondary meaning that is protected from infringement. Answer (b) is incorrect because placement on a tag, label, container, or associated display suffices. Answer (d) is incorrect because even common personal names or place names can be trademarked if accompanied by a distinctive design or logo.

34. A copyright is one means of protecting intellectual property consisting of "original works of authorship in any tangible medium of expression, now known or later developed" (Copyright Act). Which of the following is true?

a. A book written in 1986 may be copyrighted only until 2036 even though the author is still alive at that date.

b. Protection does not begin until the copyright is registered in the appropriate state office.

c. Conveyance of a copyright may be oral or in writing. A copyright may also pass by will or intestate succession.

d. A college professor who copies a few pages from a copyrighted book and distributes them to the five members of a graduate seminar has not committed infringement.

The correct answer is (d). *(Publisher)*

REQUIRED: The true statement about the protection afforded by the Copyright Act.

DISCUSSION: The Copyright Act permits fair use of the copyrighted material "for purposes such as criticism, comment, news reporting, teaching (including multiple copies for classroom use), scholarship, or research." Whether a use is fair depends upon factors such as the effect on the market for the work, the substantiality of the portion used in relation to the whole work, the nature of the copyrighted work, and the purpose and character of the use, including whether the use is commercial or for a nonprofit educational purpose. The professor's use therefore appears to be fair.

Answer (a) is incorrect because for works created after 1977, the duration of the copyright is the life of the author plus 50 years. Answer (b) is incorrect because copyrights need not be registered to give protection. A copyright is established by placing on all publicly distributed copies a notice of copyright, including the name of the owner and year of first publication. At this time, the work is copyrighted and no one may legally copy it except as allowed by law. Registration with the federal (not state) Copyright Office merely must be done before a copyright owner can sue in federal court for infringement. Answer (c) is incorrect because conveyance must be in writing and signed by the owner of the rights or his/her agent.

35. Trade secrets receive a substantial measure of protection under the tort law. In which case will defendant (D) prevail against plaintiff (P), assuming no patent protection?

a. D offers a lucrative job to Albert, who is employed by P, a competitor in the electronics industry. Albert has specialized knowledge of certain components developed by P and highly useful to D but has no contract with P.

b. D's R&D department discovers an old article in an obscure technical journal written by a researcher who helped formulate P's product. The article enables D to produce an identical product at a lower price.

c. P required a unique machine for its process. Accordingly, it asked Judy to manufacture the equipment according to P's design but to keep the specifications confidential. D paid Judy for the machine's plans.

d. D conducted aerial surveillance of P's plant site during its construction phase. The site was surrounded by a fence and the grounds were patrolled by security people. The only gate was guarded 24 hours a day. The reconnaissance revealed details about a new process.

The correct answer is (b). *(Publisher)*

REQUIRED: The means of discovering a trade secret not resulting in liability.

DISCUSSION: A trade secret is information of economic value to a business that it wishes to keep confidential. The courts protect this interest even though the trade secret cannot be copyrighted or patented. A competitor is not prevented, however, from obtaining the knowledge by lawful means such as independent research, purchase of the product in the open market, or the plaintiff's voluntary disclosure or failure to take reasonable precautions.

Answer (a) is incorrect because Albert may work for D but can be enjoined on the grounds of unfair competition from revealing P's trade secrets. Answers (c) and (d) are incorrect because industrial espionage is tortious. In each case, the plaintiff took reasonable precautions to protect its secrets.

36. Under the Patent Act, "Whoever invents or discovers any new and useful process, machine, manufacture, or composition of matter, or any new and useful improvement thereof, may obtain a patent therefor."

a. The duration of a patent is 17 years. It may not be renewed.

b. A computer program may be patented but not copyrighted.

c. Since naturally occurring substances are not patentable, a genetically engineered bacterium is not protected.

d. The only requirement for a process, machine, manufacture, or composition of matter to be patentable is novelty (not in conflict with an existing patent or a prior pending application).

The correct answer is (a). *(Publisher)*

REQUIRED: The true statement about federal patent law.

DISCUSSION: The Constitution permits Congress to enact legislation to secure for a limited time to inventors the exclusive right to their respective discoveries. Under current law, the right to a patent lasts for a nonrenewable term of 17 years. Upon expiration, the invention enters the public domain.

Answer (b) is incorrect because a single computer program can be copyrighted but not patented. Methods of calculation, fundamental truths, principles, laws of nature, ideas, and the like are not patentable. Answer (c) is incorrect because such a bacterium is human-produced and therefore patentable. Answer (d) is incorrect because the process, etc. must have utility and be nonobvious as well as novel.

37. M.A. Genius invented and is manufacturing and distributing a flashlight needing no batteries if used in direct sunlight. Genius did not apply for a patent. Noveltyco bought one at a retail store, analyzed and copied it, and is now selling an identical product under its own name. Which of the following is true?

a. Genius can enjoin Noveltyco's activities on the basis of a trade secret violation.

b. Genius can enjoin Noveltyco's activities even though the solar flashlight was not patented because it clearly meets the novelty, utility, and nonobviousness criteria.

c. Noveltyco can continue to make and sell the solar flashlights, but will have to pay Genius a royalty.

d. Noveltyco has not violated any legal duty owed to Genius and therefore may continue selling its solar flashlight without liability.

The correct answer is (d). *(M. Levin)*

REQUIRED: The protection afforded to ideas and their representation in new products.

DISCUSSION: Society's interest in free competition is so strong that copying a competitor's product is lawful unless a trademark, trade secret, patent, or copyright is infringed. If a product is not protected by a patent, competitors can use information gained through "reverse engineering."

Answer (a) is incorrect because trade secrets receive only limited protection. If a competitor can discover a secret through independent means not involving a misappropriation, the owner has no protection against duplication. Furthermore, the question does not offer sufficient information on which to conclude that there was a trade secret. Answer (b) is incorrect because patentability affords no protection unless a patent is obtained. Answer (c) is incorrect because Genius cannot claim a royalty if he has no exclusive right to his product.

9.5 Negligence in Torts

38. In which case will defendant (D) be liable for the tort of negligence?

a. D throws a baseball intending to hit her brother and strikes a passerby.

b. While playing golf, D swings a club on the fairway. Because of a design defect, the head of the club flies off and strikes a fellow golfer standing 20 yards away.

c. D takes medication that she knows causes drowsiness at the maximum dosage. D takes this dose prior to flying her aircraft. Her lack of alertness causes a crash in which a passenger is injured.

d. While driving her car, D, without warning, has a sudden, stabbing chest pain that causes her to lose control and crash into another vehicle.

The correct answer is (c). *(Publisher)*

REQUIRED: The instance that meets the definition of negligence.

DISCUSSION: The Restatement (Second) of Torts defines negligence as "conduct that falls below the standard established by law for the protection of others against unreasonable risk of harm." This standard is that of a reasonable person acting with the care due in the circumstances. A person who knowingly pilots an aircraft after taking medication she knows will impair her capacities has behaved negligently.

Answer (a) is incorrect because D has committed the intentional tort of battery. The intent to strike one person is transferred to the individual actually hit. Answer (b) is incorrect because unless D had reason to know that the club was defective, she has no liability since she could not have prevented the harm by the exercise of reasonable care. Answer (d) is incorrect because assuming the attack was unforeseeable, D will not be liable in tort.

39. Traditionally, a plaintiff in an action for the tort of negligence must prove that

a. Defendant acted with the intent to cause harm.

b. The instrumentality used was abnormally dangerous.

c. Defendant's action breached a duty but not that the breach caused actual damages.

d. Defendant's action proximately caused injury to plaintiff.

The correct answer is (d). *(Publisher)*

REQUIRED: The element traditionally included in the tort of negligence.

DISCUSSION: The following are the four traditional elements of negligence: a duty owed by defendant to plaintiff; breach of the duty; actual injury; and legal or proximate causation of the injury by the breach.

Answer (a) is incorrect because negligence is not an intentional tort. Only lack of due or reasonable care must be proven. Answer (b) is incorrect because the relative amount of danger that an activity presents is an important factor in determining the care required. When the instrumentality that causes harm is abnormally dangerous, strict liability may be imposed. Liability for negligence may be imposed for failure to exercise due care in an ordinary activity. Answer (c) is incorrect because plaintiff must prove actual damages.

40. Bystander was walking on the streets of Big Town when he turned a corner and found Victim lying on the sidewalk having what appeared to be a heart attack. Bystander loosened Victim's tie but then, deciding not to get involved, left the scene without calling for help. Victim survived but suffered a permanent disability as a consequence of not receiving immediate aid. If Victim asserts a claim against Bystander, will he prevail?

a. Yes, because a reasonably prudent person would have aided Victim.

b. Yes, because by beginning the rescue, Bystander assumed a duty to aid.

c. Yes, because Victim is a foreseeable plaintiff.

d. No, because Bystander did not make Victim's situation any worse.

The correct answer is (d). *(Publisher)*

REQUIRED: Whether a failure to render assistance to an endangered person is a basis for liability.

DISCUSSION: The general rule is that a person has no legal duty or obligation to rescue or aid another person in distress (it is of course a moral responsibility). One may even begin to assist another and then abandon the effort. However, liability will result if a rescuer's actions leave the victim in a worse situation.

Answer (a) is incorrect because the law imposes no affirmative duty to act for the benefit of another person. The law only directs that one should not harm another. Answer (b) is incorrect because one does not assume a duty to aid another unless by beginning a rescue one has prevented or deterred another from giving assistance. Answer (c) is incorrect because Bystander owed no legal duty to plaintiff, and his act did not cause the injury to Victim.

41. The duty of care owed by an owner or occupier of land may vary with the legal status of persons who enter the land. Which is the correct statement concerning the duty owed by the possessor of land to those who enter it?

a. The possessor owes no duty to undiscovered trespassers and to anticipated trespassers.

b. The owner or occupier of the property owes to a social guest the duty owed to an invitee.

c. The duty extended to a licensee includes warning of concealed and dangerous conditions known to the possessor of the property, the use of ordinary care in active operations upon the property, and the making of reasonable inspections to discover dangerous conditions and to make them safe.

d. The owner or occupier of land owes the highest duty to invitees.

The correct answer is (d). *(Publisher)*

REQUIRED: The correct statement concerning the duty of care owed by a possessor of land to those who enter upon it.

DISCUSSION: Under the law of negligence, the duty owed by a possessor of land varies with the legal status of parties who enter the land. Invitees (persons expressly or impliedly invited onto the property for the possessor's business interest or members of the public if the property is held open to the public) receive the greatest protection. Answer (c) states the duty owed to an invitee.

Answer (a) is incorrect because while a possessor owes no duty to an undiscovered trespasser, (s)he does owe a duty to not intentionally harm anticipated trespassers (e.g., not set traps, etc.). Answer (b) is incorrect because a social guest is a licensee who is owed a duty of reasonable care (in active operations and warning of dangers of which the possessor should know), but not the duty to inspect for defective conditions. Answer (c) is incorrect because it describes the duty owed to an invitee, not a licensee.

42. In a negligence case, the finder of fact (either the judge or a jury) must determine whether defendant's conduct breached the duty to exercise the care required in the circumstances. The standard to which defendant's behavior is compared is that of the hypothetical ordinary reasonable person. The application of the standard is subject to the particular circumstances of the case, but the same criterion is applied regardless of the defendant's

a. Superior skill or knowledge.

b. Mental deficiency.

c. Infancy (under age of majority).

d. Physical disability.

The correct answer is (b). *(Publisher)*

REQUIRED: The factor that does not alter the standard used to determine negligence.

DISCUSSION: A person who is insane or otherwise mentally deficient is nevertheless expected to conduct him/herself as would an ordinary reasonable person in the circumstances who is not mentally deficient. Justifications include the difficulty of distinguishing mental deficiency from the ordinary variations of emotions and intellect; the difficulty of proving and the ease of feigning mental deficiency; and the belief that liability will be an incentive to guardians to look after the mentally deficient.

Answer (a) is incorrect because one who has or claims superior knowledge or skill is held to a higher standard. Answers (c) and (d) are incorrect because the ordinary reasonable person criterion is modified to allow for the person's infancy or physical disability. Children are not expected to have the same maturity of judgment as an adult, and a handicapped person is expected to act as would a reasonable person with the same impairment.

43. While shopping with his mother at the Supermarket, fourteen-year-old Ronald dropped a banana peel on the floor in the produce department. Three hours later, Mr. Customer slipped on the peel and broke his leg.

a. Customer can probably recover from Supermarket if it has failed to frequently inspect and clear the floor of foreign objects.

b. Customer could not recover from Ronald because he is a minor.

c. If Supermarket did not have actual knowledge of the condition, it cannot be held liable.

d. If Supermarket cleans and waxes its floor each night, it cannot be held liable.

The correct answer is (a). *(M. Levin)*

REQUIRED: The standard of care that a business owes to an invitee.

DISCUSSION: A high degree of care is owed to a business visitor (an invitee). The possessor of the property has a duty to exercise reasonable care to protect the invitee against dangerous conditions. A licensee such as a social guest would only be owed a duty to warn of known dangerous conditions that the licensee was unlikely to discover. Since slips and falls of this kind often occur in a grocery store setting, reasonable prudence requires that the floor be frequently inspected and that such hazards be promptly eliminated (three hours is much too slow). If the store's employee had caused the dangerous condition or allowed it to continue after discovery, the store would be immediately liable for injuries without consideration of the elapsed time.

Answer (b) is incorrect because infancy is not a tort defense although it may be a mitigating factor. Answer (c) is incorrect because defendant has an affirmative duty to make the premises safe for an invitee. Lack of actual knowledge would only be a defense against a trespasser or licensee. Answer (d) is incorrect because reasonable care requires more than a once-a-day cleaning in such circumstances.

44. Defendant is a store owner who keeps his place of business open in spite of a local ordinance requiring Sunday closing. Plaintiff was a customer of Defendant's who appeared in the store one Sunday and suffered an injury in a fall. Plaintiff sues Defendant for damages.

a. Plaintiff will recover because Defendant's violation of the statute was negligence per se.

b. Defendant will prevail if Plaintiff could not show that the statute was intended to prevent the kind of harm incurred by plaintiff.

c. The violation of a criminal statute in a negligence case always establishes a presumption of the existence of a duty and breach of that duty.

d. Compliance with an applicable criminal statute conclusively establishes that the duty of due care has not been breached.

The correct answer is (b). *(Publisher)*

REQUIRED: The effect of a violation of a statute upon defendant's liability.

DISCUSSION: To recover for Defendant's negligence, Plaintiff must show that Defendant breached a duty of care owed to him. If a statute providing a criminal penalty is applicable, it may be used to establish the required duty of care and establish that the duty has been breached. Plaintiff must show that he is both a member of the class intended to be protected by the statute and that the statute was intended to prevent the kind of injury that he sustained. Since the kind of harm intended by a Sunday closing law does not embrace the physical injuries from a fall, Plaintiff could not use the violation of the law as evidence of Defendant's negligence.

Answer (a) is incorrect because the harm proscribed by the statute was not that suffered by the plaintiff. Answer (c) is incorrect because although some courts do hold that the violation of an applicable criminal statute creates a conclusive presumption, others hold it to be only rebuttable evidence of negligence. Answer (d) is incorrect because mere compliance with an applicable criminal statute does not necessarily establish that due care has been exercised.

45. In which case is M liable?

a. M was filling a sinkhole in a highway but had not erected a barrier. Motorist saw the danger but plunged into the sinkhole at 60 mph when her brakes failed. A barrier could not have stopped the vehicle.

b. M negligently failed to install a fire escape. While sleeping, M's guest died of smoke inhalation in a fire set by an arsonist.

c. M, B, and C became separated while hunting. Thinking they were firing at a deer, M and C negligently discharged their firearms in B's direction. Each shot gave B a fatal wound.

d. Motorist was driving 50 mph in a 55 mph zone after having her brakes repaired by M. When a child darted in front of the car, the brakes failed and the child was killed. Motorist would not have been able to stop in time if the brakes had worked.

The correct answer is (c). *(Publisher)*

REQUIRED: The case in which M's conduct is a cause in fact of plaintiff's injury.

DISCUSSION: An element of the tort of negligence is causation. The act of the defendant must have actually caused the injury of the plaintiff (cause in fact). The act is an actual cause of the injury if one can say that "but for" the defendant's negligence no injury would have occurred. The "but for" test must be supplemented, however, when concurring causes inflicted plaintiff's injury. For example, M could argue that B's death would have occurred without M's action. Under the "substantial factor" test, however, both M and C will nevertheless be liable since both contributed substantially to B's death.

Answers (a), (b), and (d) are incorrect because in each case, M's conduct was not a cause in fact since one cannot say the injury would not have occurred but for M's negligence.

46. To establish a prima facie case of negligence, the plaintiff must show that defendant's act proximately caused the injury complained of. Which of the following is true?

a. The purpose of the proximate cause doctrine is to extend defendant's liability.

b. Proximate cause is synonymous with actual cause.

c. If plaintiff's injury is inflicted by an intervening force, a defendant will usually be liable if his/her conduct was a direct cause in fact of the injury even though both the nature of the harm and of the force were unforeseeable and a third party will also be liable.

d. According to the Restatement (Second) of Torts, a court may find for defendant if it appears highly extraordinary after the event and looking back from the harm to his/her conduct that it should have caused the plaintiff's injury.

The correct answer is (d). *(Publisher)*

REQUIRED: The true statement about the proximate cause doctrine.

DISCUSSION: In addition to actual cause, the defendant's negligence must also be the proximate cause of the plaintiff's injury. The proximate cause doctrine is a means of limiting the defendant's liability. Defendants are not liable for all the actual consequences of their conduct, but agreement as to what constitutes proximate cause has eluded the courts. One factor to be considered in measuring the limits of liability is foreseeability. That the defendant neither foresaw nor should have foreseen the extent of the harm or the manner in which it occurred does not necessarily prevent him/her from being liable, but it may not be a legal cause when after the event and looking back it appears to the court highly extraordinary that the defendant's action should have brought about the harm. In a famous case, for example, defendant drove a car into another car. Explosives in the second car detonated, blowing out windows in a far-away building. Defendant's act was held to be a cause in fact but not a proximate cause of the injury caused by the flying glass.

Answer (a) is incorrect because proximate cause limits liability. Answer (b) is incorrect because every proximate cause is an actual cause but not vice versa. Answer (c) is incorrect because an intervening force occurring after defendant's act may have a significant effect on plaintiff's injury and relieve defendant of liability.

47. Roofer entered into a written contract with Orissa to repair the roof of Orissa's home, the repairs to be done "in a workmanlike manner." Roofer completed the repairs and took all of his equipment away, with the exception of a 20 foot extension ladder which was left against the side of the house. He intended to come back and get the ladder the next morning. At that time, Orissa and her family were away on a trip. During the night, a thief, using the ladder to gain access to an upstairs window, entered the house and stole some valuable jewels. Orissa has asserted a claim against Roofer for damages for the loss of the jewels. In her claim against Roofer, Orissa will

a. Prevail, because by leaving the ladder Roofer became a trespasser on Orissa's property.

b. Prevail, because by leaving the ladder Roofer created the risk that a person might unlawfully enter the house.

c. Not prevail, because the act of the thief was a superseding cause.

d. Not prevail, because Orissa's claim is limited to damages for breach of contract.

The correct answer is (b). *(MBE Part I-22)*

REQUIRED: The liability of a roofer for leaving a ladder which was used for burglary.

DISCUSSION: Liability for negligence requires a foreseeable risk of harm that could have been avoided. It was foreseeable by a reasonable person that someone might use the ladder to enter the house. Therefore, Roofer owed a duty to Orissa to exercise due care to avoid the risk.

Answer (a) is incorrect because leaving his ladder on the premises overnight after completing the contract probably did not make Roofer a trespasser (he was probably a licensee). Also, trespass is not an appropriate basis to recover damages for loss of the jewels. Answer (c) is incorrect because the act of the thief was reasonably foreseeable; therefore it is not an intervening (superseding) cause. Answer (d) is incorrect because a duty of reasonable care to avoid actions which proximately cause injury to another exists regardless of contractual relations.

48. K owns a large department store. In the rear is a freight elevator used by the employees of the shipping and receiving departments. A state statute for the protection of employees requires that all such elevators have a specified safety device. Employee B and supplier C are injured as a result of a failure to install the device. Which of the following is true?

a. As a result of the statute, K is negligent per se with regard to B but not C.

b. As a result of the statute, K is negligent per se with regard to C but not B.

c. The rule of res ipsa loquitur applies.

d. The rule of res ipsa loquitur applies only to C.

The correct answer is (a). *(Publisher)*

REQUIRED: The consequence of a defendant's failure to adhere to a statute.

DISCUSSION: One means of establishing breach is to prove that defendant committed an unexcused violation of a statute intended to protect the class of persons to which plaintiff belongs. The statute defines the standard of conduct of the ordinary reasonable person. In the majority of states, K would therefore be irrebuttably presumed, in the absence of a sufficient excuse, to have been negligent toward its employee B, a member of the class for whom the statute was specifically enacted.

Answer (b) is incorrect because C did not belong to the class the legislature named and could not rely on the statute to prove negligence. Had the statute been more general it would probably be interpreted to apply to all users, and C could use it rather than the regular requirements of negligence. Answers (c) and (d) are incorrect because res ipsa loquitur ("the thing speaks for itself") is a rule that allows the trier of fact to infer both negligent conduct and causation from the mere occurrence when the event is of a kind that ordinarily does not occur in the absence of negligence; other causes are eliminated; and the indicated negligence is within the scope of the defendant's duty to the plaintiff. For instance, plaintiff goes into surgery to repair a broken arm and emerges with a broken leg. When no testimony can be elicited regarding events in the operating room, the rule of res ipsa loquitur applies.

49. Mort Morpheus parked his car on the railroad tracks in a contributory negligence state thinking that this stretch of track was abandoned. Casey Jones, the engineer on the Highball Express, was operating the train at a safe speed when he saw Morpheus's car parked on the tracks ahead. Because Casey was eating, by the time he could put his foot down and apply the brakes it was too late. A collision between train and car resulted. In an action brought by Morpheus against Jones and the railroad,

a. Contributory negligence will be a complete defense.

b. Morpheus might prevail under the last clear chance doctrine.

c. Contributory negligence of the plaintiff will reduce his award proportionate to his negligence.

d. The railroad will have no liability since the engineer had the last clear chance to avoid the accident.

The correct answer is (b). *(Publisher)*

REQUIRED: Contributory negligence and the last clear chance doctrine.

DISCUSSION: In those states that continue to recognize the defense of contributory negligence, if the negligence of the plaintiff contributed to his/her damages, plaintiff will be absolutely barred from recovery. Morpheus was negligent and contributed to his own damages by parking on the tracks. The last clear chance doctrine (evolved to soften the effect of this rule) is applicable here. It applies when, despite plaintiff's prior negligence, injury could have been avoided if defendant had acted with reasonable care. Because Jones arguably had the "last clear chance" to avoid the accident, Morpheus may prevail against the engineer and the railroad. This decision is for the trier of fact.

Answer (a) is incorrect because the last clear chance doctrine removes the bar of contributory negligence. Answer (c) is incorrect because reduction of a damage award proportionate to the plaintiff's negligence occurs under the theory of comparative (not contributory) negligence. Answer (d) is incorrect because if Jones is liable, the railroad will also be liable as his employer.

50. Construction Company sued Toni Trucker for her alleged negligence in colliding with a major support beam on a building under construction. Damages were $50,000. Trucker responded that the accident occurred because of Construction Company's negligence in failing to adequately mark the driveway to the construction site. In a contributory negligence state, which of the following is the most correct statement?

a. If Trucker is negligent, she will be liable for $50,000 regardless of Construction Company's negligence.

b. If Construction Company is negligent, Trucker will not be liable.

c. If Trucker and Construction Company are both negligent, each will be liable for $25,000.

d. If Trucker and Construction Company are both negligent, but Trucker is determined to be 40% at fault and Construction Company 60% at fault, Trucker will be liable for $20,000.

The correct answer is (b). *(M. Levin)*

REQUIRED: The correct statement about contributory negligence.

DISCUSSION: Contributory negligence is an absolute bar to recovery by the plaintiff. If the rule of contributory negligence applies, the degree of defendant's negligence is immaterial. Contributory negligence should not be confused with comparative negligence.

Answer (a) is incorrect because Trucker will not be liable if Construction Company is found to be contributorily negligent. Answers (c) and (d) are incorrect because under the rule of contributory negligence, liability is not apportioned. In comparative negligence states, however, damages are allocated. But the majority of such states do not permit plaintiff to recover any damages if (s)he is 50% or more at fault.

51. Hemlock Holmes lives in a contributory negligence state. Holmes drank four ounces of straight gin in thirty minutes and became quite intoxicated. Then on an unlighted street, he walked without looking from between two parked cars in front of a speeding car. Because she was so close, the driver was unable to stop before hitting Holmes, who suffered serious personal injuries and has sued the driver to recover for all of his damages. Will he win?

a. Yes, to the extent the driver's speeding contributed to Holmes's injuries.

b. Yes, because the driver had the last clear chance to prevent the injury.

c. No, because Holmes contributed to his own injury.

d. No, because Holmes had the last clear chance to prevent the injury.

The correct answer is (c). *(E. Arnold)*

REQUIRED: The correct statement about the implications of contributory negligence.

DISCUSSION: Contributory negligence is an absolute bar to recovery by a plaintiff. It is conduct on plaintiff's part that is below the standard required for his/her own protection and that legally contributes to the harm. Holmes's self-induced intoxication rendered him unable to properly attend to his own safety on the streets.

Answer (a) is incorrect because liability is not apportioned in contributory negligence states. Answer (b) is incorrect because the facts show the driver had no last clear chance to avoid the impact. Answer (d) is incorrect because the last clear chance doctrine does not apply to plaintiffs (it applies to defendants).

52. Assume the same facts as those set forth in the previous question except Holmes lives in a comparative negligence state. Will he prevail?

a. Yes, to the extent the driver's speeding contributed to Holmes's injuries.

b. Yes, because the driver had the last clear chance to prevent the injury.

c. No, because Holmes contributed to his own injury.

d. No, because Holmes had the last clear chance to prevent the injury.

The correct answer is (a). *(E. Arnold)*

REQUIRED: The correct statement about the implications of comparative negligence.

DISCUSSION: The comparative negligence doctrine offers a compromise solution to the "either/or" solution of contributory negligence with its accompanying harsh results for plaintiffs who were not diligent in securing their own safety. States that recognize the doctrine apportion damages based on the plaintiff's and defendant's respective degrees of fault. The majority of such states, however, do not allow a plaintiff to recover if his/her negligence contributed to 50% or more of the injury.

Answer (b) is incorrect because the driver had no chance to stop before striking Holmes. Answer (c) is incorrect because Holmes's contribution to his own injuries does not prevent recovery from the driver for her contribution to his injuries. Answer (d) is incorrect because even with a last chance to prevent the accident, Holmes can use comparative negligence to recover for the driver's contribution to his injuries.

53. Polly Plaintiff and Dennis Defendant went on a social outing to Defendant's fish camp. At the fish camp was a partially completed pier supported by pilings. The deck of the pier consisted of planking set close together except at the far end. Plaintiff walked onto the pier. Defendant warned her not to go onto the unfinished pier and that the boards at the end were not closely spaced. Plaintiff heard the warning but continued on without replying. After reaching the end of the pier, she started back, choosing her steps carefully. A loose board then gave way and she fell, tearing ligaments in her knee. The best argument by Defendant is

a. Express assumption of the risk.

b. Implied assumption of the risk.

c. Contributory negligence.

d. Lack of proximate cause.

The correct answer is (b). *(Publisher)*

REQUIRED: The best defense assertible by a defendant who has expressly warned plaintiff of a dangerous condition.

DISCUSSION: Assumption of the risk is a complete defense to negligence. Only a few of the comparative negligence jurisdictions have abolished it. The elements of this defense are a risk of harm caused by the defendant's conduct, actual knowledge of the risk, and a voluntary choice to remain within the area of risk. Defendant's pier was in an unsafe condition, Plaintiff actually knew of the risk, and Plaintiff voluntarily chose to continue walking on the pier. Since she impliedly assumed the risk, she will not be entitled to any damages.

Answer (a) is incorrect because express assumption of risk entails an agreement in advance, by contract or otherwise, whereby the plaintiff expressly agrees to accept a risk arising from the defendant's negligence. Answer (c) is incorrect because Plaintiff voluntarily consented to be exposed to the risk, but having ventured onto the pier, she thereafter exercised due care, so the defense of contributory negligence is not available. Answer (d) is incorrect because the defective condition of the pier was evidently a legal (proximate) as well as a direct cause of the injury.

54. Proof of damages is an essential element of the prima facie case of the tort of negligence. The purpose of tort damages is to make the plaintiff whole, to place him/her in the position in which (s)he would have been if there had been no injury. Plaintiff may therefore recover for all damages including

a. Reasonable attorney's fees.

b. Health care costs, except for those which have been mitigated by receipt of benefits from collateral sources; e.g., health insurance payments.

c. Punitive damages.

d. An award for impaired earning capacity discounted to present value.

The correct answer is (d). *(Publisher)*

REQUIRED: The correct statement concerning the award of damages in a negligence case.

DISCUSSION: If the defendant's actions have resulted in injury to the plaintiff such that future earning capacity is impaired, a lump sum award compensating for this reduced earning capacity would be a proper element of damages. To avoid an excess award, the lump sum would represent the present value of the stream of lost future income discounted at an appropriate interest rate.

Answer (a) is incorrect because the fees of attorneys are not considered properly recoverable in negligence unless provided by statute. Answer (b) is incorrect because damages are awarded regardless of payment of benefits from collateral sources. Answer (c) is incorrect because punitive damages may be awarded only when a defendant was grossly negligent or acted in a willful and wanton manner.

Questions 55 and 56 are based on the following information. Passer was driving his pickup truck along a lonely road on a very cold night. Passer saw Tom, who was a stranger, lying in a field by the side of the road and apparently injured. Passer stopped his truck, alighted, and discovered that Tom was intoxicated and in danger of suffering from exposure to the cold. However, Passer returned to his truck and drove away without making any effort to help Tom. Tom remained lying at the same place and was later injured when struck by a car driven by Ms. Traveler. Traveler, who was drowsy and inattentive, had veered off the road into the field and hit Tom. Traveler did not see Tom prior to hitting him.

55. If Tom asserts a claim against Passer for damages for his injuries, will Tom prevail?

a. Yes, because by stopping and examining Tom, Passer assumed a duty to aid him.

b. Yes, if a reasonably prudent person under the circumstances would have aided Tom.

c. No, if Passer did not, in any way, make Tom's situation worse.

d. No, because Tom himself created the risk of harm by becoming intoxicated.

The correct answer is (c). *(MBE Part I-20)*

REQUIRED: Whether a failure to render assistance to an endangered person is a basis for liability.

DISCUSSION: The general rule is that a person has no legal duty or obligation to rescue or aid another. One may even begin to aid another and then abandon the aid. However, liability will result if a rescuer leaves the victim in a worse situation.

Answer (a) is incorrect because one does not assume a duty to aid another unless beginning to aid has caused another to not provide aid. Answer (b) is incorrect because the law imposes no affirmative duty to act for the benefit of another person. Answer (d) is incorrect because intoxicated or not, a pedestrian should not bear the risk of cars driving off the road.

56. If Tom asserts a claim against Traveler, will Tom prevail?

a. Yes, because Traveler was negligent in going off the road.

b. Yes, because Tom was in a helpless condition.

c. No, because Traveler did not see Tom before Tom was struck.

d. No, because Tom's intoxication was the cause in fact of his harm.

The correct answer is (a). *(MBE Part I-21)*

REQUIRED: The liability of a driver for injuring an unseen plaintiff.

DISCUSSION: Traveler's inattention clearly was a cause in fact of Tom's injury. Moreover, under the test established by the Restatement (Second) of Torts, Traveler's inattention proximately caused Tom's injury. After the fact and looking back from the harm to Traveler's conduct, a court would probably not find the harm to be a highly extraordinary result of such conduct. It is reasonable to expect that when a driver loses control of his/her vehicle someone nearby will be hurt. The exact damage does not have to be foreseeable. Traveler owed a duty of reasonable care toward Tom, and Traveler breached this duty by being inattentive.

Answer (b) is incorrect because Tom will prevail as a result of Traveler's breach of duty of care, not due to his helpless condition. Answer (c) is incorrect because Traveler will be liable even though she had no actual knowledge of Tom's presence. It is the foreseeability that "someone" could be injured by going off the road that creates a duty of care. Answer (d) is incorrect because intoxicated or not, a pedestrian should not bear the risk of cars driving off the road.

57. Ohner owns the Acme Hotel. When the International Order of Badgers came to town for its convention, its members rented 400 of the 500 rooms, and the hotel opened its convention facilities to them. Badgers are a rowdy group, and during their convention they littered both the inside and the outside of the hotel with debris and bottles. The hotel manager knew that objects were being thrown out of the hotel windows. At his direction, hotel employees patrolled the hallways telling the guests to refrain from such conduct. Ohner was out of town and was not aware of the problems which were occurring. During the convention, as Smith walked past the Acme Hotel on the sidewalk, he was hit and injured by an ashtray thrown out of a window in the hotel. Smith sued Ohner for damages for his injuries. Will Smith prevail in his claim against Ohner?

a. Yes, because a property owner is strictly liable for acts on his premises if such acts cause harm to persons using the adjacent public sidewalks.

b. Yes, if the person who threw the ashtray cannot be identified.

c. No, because Ohner had no personal knowledge of the conduct of the hotel guests.

d. No, if the trier of fact determines that the hotel employees had taken reasonable precautions to prevent such an injury.

The correct answer is (d). *(MBE Part I-63)*

REQUIRED: The liability of a hotel owner for injuries caused by hotel employees or guests.

DISCUSSION: The owner of land has a duty to undertake reasonable precautions to prevent injury to persons off the land as a result of activities of the land owner or his/her guests. If the trier of fact determines that Ohner's employees had exercised due care to prevent the injury, then Smith will not prevail.

Answer (a) is incorrect because a property owner is not strictly liable for acts on his/her premises which cause harm to persons off the premises. The owner is only required to exercise reasonable care. Answer (b) is incorrect because whether the person who threw the ashtray can be identified will not affect Ohner's liability. Answer (c) is incorrect because Ohner needs no personal knowledge to be held liable if his employees had the knowledge.

58. Agnes and Buford went camping to celebrate their 50th wedding anniversary. While eating under the moonlit sky, Agnes and Buford conversed about days gone by. Suddenly the mood was spoiled when Buford discovered a rat's ear in the bottom of his can of Best-of-the-Rest baked beans. Buford wants to sue Best-of-the-Rest. Buford's best theory of liability is

a. Respondeat superior.

b. Strict liability for design defects.

c. Res ipsa loquitur.

d. Assumption of the risk.

The correct answer is (c). *(K. Wilburn)*

REQUIRED: The best theory of liability for discovery of a foreign object in a sealed container.

DISCUSSION: Res ipsa loquitur ("the thing speaks for itself") permits an inference or presumption that the defendant was negligent. It is useful when the circumstances make proof difficult because the defendant is the only party with knowledge of how the harm was caused. According to the Restatement (Second) of Torts, three elements must be shown to invoke the doctrine to establish that the plaintiff's harm was caused by the defendant's negligence: "the event is of a kind that ordinarily does not occur in the absence of negligence; other responsible causes, including the conduct of the plaintiff and third persons, are sufficiently eliminated by the evidence; and the indicated negligence is within the scope of the defendant's duty to the plaintiff." When res ipsa loquitur is established, the burden of proof shifts, and the defendant must prove (s)he was not negligent.

Answer (a) is incorrect because respondeat superior is a doctrine of vicarious liability used to hold an employer liable for the acts of an employee committed within the course and scope of employment. Answer (b) is incorrect because strict liability for design defects applies when the product is in the condition intended by the manufacturer, but was designed in a way that makes it unreasonably dangerous in normal use. Answer (d) is incorrect because assumption of the risk is a defense to a plaintiff's tort action for negligence.

59. Owner employed Earl to deliver pizzas in Collegetown. Earl was a conscientious and reliable employee. One day as Earl rushed across Collegetown with a pizza, he lost control of his car. The car careened into the front window of Drinknow Liquors, smashing several thousand dollars of liquor inventory. Drinknow intends to sue Owner for damages that resulted from the wreck. What legal theory can Drinknow assert in an action against Owner for damages resulting from Earl's accident?

a. Respondeat superior.

b. Last clear chance.

c. Assumption of the risk.

d. Res ipsa loquitur.

The correct answer is (a). *(Publisher)*

REQUIRED: The legal theory supporting the liability of an employer for an employee's act.

DISCUSSION: The doctrine of respondeat superior imputes the negligence of an employee to the employer. The employee's tortious act must occur within the course and scope of his/her employment.

Answer (b) is incorrect because the last clear chance doctrine is an exception to the contributory negligence rule and allows a plaintiff to recover even though his/her own negligence would otherwise bar recovery. It applies when plaintiff's negligence preceded defendant's, and the latter had the "last clear chance" to avoid the injury by using due care. Answer (c) is incorrect because assumption of the risk is an affirmative defense that, if successfully asserted, bars the plaintiff from recovery if (s)he voluntarily and knowingly encountered a danger. Answer (d) is incorrect because res ipsa loquitur may be asserted when certain events strongly imply negligence by the defendant and other possible causes are virtually eliminated by the evidence.

9.6 Strict Liability in Tort

Also see "Product Liability" in Chapter 12, "Sales of Goods."

60. Early tort law was often based on the theory of strict liability. In the nineteenth century, the concepts of negligence law emerged to limit the liability of defendants. The twentieth century has seen a return to strict liability. Which of the following best states the basis of this current tort theory?

a. Products liability.

b. Liability based on fault regardless of intent.

c. Liability without fault.

d. Liability based on intentional wrongdoing.

The correct answer is (c). *(Publisher)*

REQUIRED: The correct basis of strict liability in tort.

DISCUSSION: Strict liability in tort is imposed without regard to the defendant's fault, i.e., even if there is no negligence and no intentional misconduct. The courts and legislatures have decided in certain circumstances that an involved party, although without fault, is better able to bear a loss than the injured party. Generally, full recovery for personal injuries and property damages are allowed without application of contributory or comparative negligence, waivers, or disclaimers. Assumption of risk is a valid defense only when the plaintiff has willfully incurred the risk.

Answer (a) is incorrect because strict liability is imposed in other ways besides products liability cases, e.g., workers' compensation and abnormally dangerous activities. Answer (b) is incorrect because strict liability is not based on fault. Answer (d) is incorrect because strict liability may involve no wrongful intent nor any wrongful conduct.

61. Gerald, an 18-year-old high school student, stole a tiger cub from a zoo and took it home. Although Gerald built a large, apparently secure cage for the cub in his bedroom and otherwise took excellent care of it, the cub escaped from the cage and bit Edward, Gerald's neighbor. Edward sued Gerald to recover damages. If Edward wins the lawsuit, the court will probably rely on the doctrine of

a. Negligence.

b. Quasi-contract.

c. Express contract.

d. Strict liability.

The correct answer is (d). *(D. Levin)*

REQUIRED: The appropriate theory of liability for damages caused by a wild animal.

DISCUSSION: Courts impose strict liability (liability without fault) on a defendant after considering such factors as whether 1) the activity is likely to injure others even though the defendant uses reasonable or even great care, 2) the gravity of the harm is likely to be great, 3) the activity is uncommon or not appropriate to the area, and 4) the value of the activity to the community. One basis for strict liability is the keeping of wild animals, such as tigers. If one keeps a wild animal and the animal injures someone, the keeper is strictly liable, regardless of the care exercised or whether the animal trespassed on another's land.

Answer (a) is incorrect because Gerald exercised reasonable care for the safety of others by keeping the tiger cub in an apparently secure cage. Answer (b) is incorrect because the circumstances do not justify the remedy of quasi-contract; Gerald has not been unjustly enriched at the expense of Edward. Answer (c) is incorrect because Gerald and Edward have not entered into a contract.

62. Strict liability in tort is imposed for abnormally dangerous activities. In which case will defendant Q who is not at fault most likely prevail?

a. Q stores a large quantity of flammable liquid in the heart of a city. The liquid explodes and destroys a city block.

b. Q uses dynamite to blast away rock during construction of a building, breaking glass a mile away.

c. Q drills for oil in a residential area, causing pollution of a neighbor's well.

d. Q stores dynamite in the middle of a city. There is no explosion, but the wall of the building where the dynamite is stored crumbles and falls on a pedestrian.

The correct answer is (d). *(Publisher)*

REQUIRED: The situation in which strict liability is least likely to be imposed.

DISCUSSION: Whether activity is abnormally dangerous depends on the probability of harm to the person, land, or property of others; the gravity of the harm is great; the risk cannot be eliminated by the exercise of reasonable care; the activity is uncommon; the activity is inappropriate to the place where it is carried on; and the value of the activity to the community. Strict liability is imposed if the possibility of the kind of injury suffered was what made the activity abnormally dangerous in the first place. Since the crumbling of the wall without an explosion was not why storing dynamite in the city was abnormally dangerous, there is no strict liability for the injury to the pedestrian.

Answers (a), (b), and (c) are incorrect because each is an example of an abnormally dangerous activity.

63. Liability without fault is most likely to be imposed when the plaintiff was

a. Injured during the course and within the scope of her employment as a lathe operator in the defendant's machine shop.

b. Bitten by a horse on defendant's property. The animal had been raised as a pet and had previously been perfectly docile.

c. Intentionally injured by himself during employment.

d. Injured in the crash of defendant's private plane.

The correct answer is (a). *(Publisher)*

REQUIRED: The case in which strict liability is most likely to be imposed.

DISCUSSION: Workers' compensation laws in all states provide compensation to injured employees without regard to the fault of the employer or employee. The employee must only show that (s)he was injured during the course and scope of employment. The recovery is fixed by statute. The employee may not sue the employer in regular court but is not barred from legal action against third parties.

Answer (b) is incorrect because strict liability is not generally imposed for the actions of domesticated animals that are not trespassers and have not previously shown dangerous propensities. Answer (c) is incorrect because intentional self-infliction of injury is a bar to recovery even under workers' compensation laws. Answer (d) is incorrect because flying an aircraft is not considered abnormally dangerous.

64. Some states have enacted no-fault automobile insurance statutes. The typical statute

a. Removes all claims for automobile accident injuries from the courts to an administrative agency.

b. Provides that if the law applies the injured party will collect from his/her insurer if the amount of damages is less than a specified amount.

c. Allows for recovery in amounts comparable to average damage awards by courts in similar cases.

d. Excludes from coverage personal injury to individuals not traveling in a vehicle involved in the accident.

The correct answer is (b). *(Publisher)*

REQUIRED: The effect of no-fault automobile insurance statutes.

DISCUSSION: A no-fault automobile insurance statute essentially tries to do for damages arising from automobile accidents what workers' compensation laws do for work-related injuries. If the claim is within the statute, the injured party need not prove fault but may automatically receive a small but certain amount that is potentially less than that recoverable in court. If the claim is below the statutory maximum, the injured person receives payment from his insurer.

Answer (a) is incorrect because claims for damages above a certain threshold amount may still be litigated in court. Answer (c) is incorrect because no-fault awards are limited by statute and will generally be lower than those by courts. Answer (d) is incorrect because persons not traveling in a vehicle are covered by the vehicle's insurance.

65. Tina Tint is suing the manufacturer, the wholesaler, and the retailer for bodily injuries caused by a snowblower Tint purchased. Under the theory of strict liability,

a. Contributory negligence on Tint's part will always be a bar to recovery.

b. Privity will be a bar insofar as the wholesaler is concerned if the wholesaler did not have a reasonable opportunity to inspect.

c. Tint may recover from all the defendants despite her inability to prove negligence.

d. The manufacturer will avoid liability if it can show it followed the custom of the industry.

The correct answer is (c). *(CPA 586 L-33)*

REQUIRED: The correct statement concerning strict liability.

DISCUSSION: Under the theory of strict liability, a seller engaged in the business of selling a particular product is liable for injuries caused by the product if it was sold in a defective and unreasonably dangerous condition. A seller is therefore liable regardless of whether it was negligent. Such a seller is defined to include the buyer's immediate seller and also the prior sellers in the distribution chain, including the wholesaler and manufacturer.

Answers (a), (b), and (d) are incorrect because contributory negligence, lack of privity, adherence to industry custom, and lack of an opportunity to inspect are not defenses to an action based on strict liability. Possible defenses are use of the product for a purpose other than that intended and assumption of the risk. Plaintiff is deemed to have assumed the risk of injury and cannot recover if (s)he made voluntary use of the product despite knowledge that it was defective and unreasonably dangerous as a result.

CHAPTER TEN
CRIMINAL LAW AND PROCEDURE

10.1 Introduction to Criminal Law

1. In what way is criminal law most distinguishable from tort law?

a. The criminal defendant is presumed innocent until proven guilty.

b. Guilt must be proven by a preponderance of the evidence.

c. A crime is a violation of public law and is prosecuted in the name of the state.

d. Punishment of a crime may be by imposition of a fine.

The correct answer is (c). *(Publisher)*

REQUIRED: The way in which criminal law most differs from tort law.

DISCUSSION: A crime is a breach of a duty imposed by the state upon all persons. It is a violation of a public rather than private law and is accordingly prosecuted by and on behalf of the state. Tort law is private law. A violation must be prosecuted by the victim in his/her own name. The criminal law protects society. Tort law safeguards individual rights.

Answer (a) is incorrect because in a civil case, the liability of the defendant is also not presumed. That liability must be established through proof or admission. Answer (b) is incorrect because it states the burden of proof in a civil case. The prosecution must prove a criminal defendant's guilt beyond a reasonable doubt, which is a greater burden of proof. Answer (d) is incorrect because a fine in a criminal case is similar to the imposition of punitive damages in a tort action. The purpose is to inflict a monetary penalty.

2. Which of the following statements is false regarding the thinking that underlies the modern body of criminal law?

a. One justification commonly given for maintaining a body of criminal law is to deter future wrongs from being committed against society.

b. General objectives of criminal law include retribution and the restraint and rehabilitation of perpetrators of more serious antisocial acts.

c. If a person is found guilty of committing a crime, (s)he is adjudicated criminally liable to the victim for any damages that the victim may have personally sustained.

d. If a person is found guilty of committing a crime, (s)he may be required to atone for the action by paying a fine, or being incarcerated, or both.

The correct answer is (c). *(Publisher)*

REQUIRED: The false statement about the underlying theoretical basis of criminal law.

DISCUSSION: In theory, crimes are wrongs committed against society as a whole. Accordingly, one who is found guilty in a criminal proceeding is liable to society. Thus, a criminal proceeding does not seek to compensate the specific victims of crimes. On the contrary, the victim's remedy rests in the form of a separate civil action against the criminal wrongdoer.

Answers (a) and (b) are incorrect because they state the four general objectives of the criminal law system: deterrence, retribution, restraint, and rehabilitation. Answer (d) is incorrect because monetary damages and incarceration are obvious manifestations of three of the objectives stated above: Deterrence, retribution, and restraint.

3. Which of the following statements does not correctly state the relationship between the criminal and civil bodies of law?

a. If a person is found guilty of committing a crime, the constitutional doctrine of double jeopardy requires that the culprit not be held civilly liable to the victims for the same actions.

b. The Sherman Act, a federal antitrust law, is an example of a law that provides for civil and criminal liability for the same act or course of action.

c. An individual who hits and physically injures another person after excessive alcohol consumption may be criminally liable to the state under its drunk driving laws as well as civilly liable to the victim under the state's tort law.

d. The constitutional theory of double jeopardy deals only with criminal charges and has nothing to do with civil liability.

The correct answer is (a). *(Publisher)*

REQUIRED: The false statement about the relationship of civil and criminal law.

DISCUSSION: The same act or course of action may give rise to both criminal and civil liability. The constitutional doctrine of double jeopardy operates only on the criminal law level. It prohibits the state from retrying a defendant on a criminal charge after (s)he has been convicted or acquitted of the specific offense.

Answers (b) and (c) are incorrect because they state prime examples of circumstances in which civil and criminal liability may arise from the same act or course of action. The Sherman Act explicitly defines certain acts as criminal and also allows private parties to sue for treble (triple) civil damages. The drunk driver will be criminally prosecuted under the state's drunk driving laws. Unlike the Sherman Act, however, these laws do not usually provide a statutory civil remedy to the victim. The victim instead will sue the wrongdoer for civil damages under the state's general body of tort law. Answer (d) is incorrect because it states the correct application of the constitutional doctrine of double jeopardy.

4. In a criminal action, the state prosecutes the defendant for violation of a duty to society the breach of which requires punishment. Which of the following is a true statement about the elements of a crime?

a. The defendant has the burden of disproving at least one element of the crime charged.

b. The elements of a crime generally do not include the state of mind of the accused.

c. The prosecution must generally prove both an actus reus (wrongful action) and a mens rea (criminal intent).

d. The prosecution must generally prove only that a specific act was committed by the defendant.

The correct answer is (c). *(Publisher)*

REQUIRED: The true statement about the elements of criminal law.

DISCUSSION: Most crimes are defined in terms of two elements: a wrongful action or failure to act (actus reus) and a mental state or criminal intent (mens rea). For example, first-degree murder requires proof of premeditation as well as the act of homicide. Some crimes, however, may be defined without regard to the mental state of the accused.

Answer (a) is incorrect because the burden of proof in a criminal action is on the state. The defendant is always presumed innocent. When the defense by reliable proof (either direct evidence or by cross-examination) raises a reasonable doubt as to the prosecution's charges, the verdict must be for the defendant. Answers (b) and (d) are incorrect because both an actus reus and a mens rea must usually be proven.

5. A substantive criminal offense and the conspiracy to commit that offense are separate crimes. Which of the following is a true statement?

a. Without more, a conspiracy is found when two or more persons have agreed to commit a crime.

b. The same person cannot be convicted of both the substantive offense and conspiracy.

c. Oral or written statements are necessary to a conspiracy.

d. A conspirator who took no action may be convicted.

The correct answer is (d). *(Publisher)*

REQUIRED: The true statement about the crime of conspiracy.

DISCUSSION: To constitute a conspiracy, an agreement between two or more persons to commit a crime must be furthered by some action on the part of at least one conspirator. Even though the substantive crime is not committed or the attempt is not completed, such action will be sufficient to impose criminal liability on all parties to the conspiratorial agreement.

Answer (a) is incorrect because overt action in support of the agreement must be undertaken, e.g., setting money aside in a bank account for a bribe. Answer (b) is incorrect because the crimes do not merge. Conviction for both is possible. Answer (c) is incorrect because nonverbal communication (e.g., handshake) may suffice for an agreement, or the facts of the case may support an inference of conspiracy.

6. The attempt to commit a crime is an inchoate crime. Which of the following is true?

a. Attempt is similar to conspiracy in that some action in furtherance of the substantive crime is necessary.

b. The mere intent to commit a crime constitutes an attempt.

c. A person may be separately charged and convicted of both attempt and the substantive crime committed.

d. Impossibility is a defense to the crime of attempt.

The correct answer is (a). *(Publisher)*

REQUIRED: The true statement about the crime of attempt.

DISCUSSION: A person may be charged with a crime even though (s)he has only begun but not committed the intended offense. One who plans or attempts to commit a crime may be tried for such inchoate crimes as conspiracy, attempt, or aiding and abetting. Aiding and abetting is the giving of assistance in the commission or concealment of a crime. The elements of the crime of attempt are an intent to commit a crime and some action in furtherance thereof. A person who fails to consummate a crime may nevertheless be charged with the attempt. Unlike conspiracy, one person may commit the crime of attempt.

Answer (b) is incorrect because some action in furtherance of the crime is needed. Answer (c) is incorrect because unlike conspiracy, the two crimes merge. Answer (d) is incorrect because impossibility, e.g., breaking into a building to steal something that was not there, is not a defense to the crime of attempt.

10.2 Criminal Liability of Corporations

7. A corporation is a separate legal entity that may sue and be sued, own property, and engage in many of the same activities as individuals. A corporation

a. Can have no criminal liability because it cannot form the necessary intent.

b. May be criminally liable for the acts of its agents.

c. Can have no criminal liability because it acts only through agents.

d. Is criminally punishable in the same manner as an individual.

The correct answer is (b). *(Publisher)*

REQUIRED: The true statement about the criminal liability of a corporation.

DISCUSSION: Corporations are held criminally liable for the acts of their agents within the scope of their employment, for example, for violations of regulatory statutes (antitrust, tax, and security laws). For a corporation to possess the requisite mens rea and actus reus for criminal liability, the mental intentions and physical acts of the corporation's agents (including employees) must be imputed to it because the corporation is an artificial person.

Answers (a) and (c) are incorrect because a corporation obviously cannot form the intent to commit a crime. However, deterrence of certain activity is believed to be enhanced if the corporation can be punished. Thus, criminal liability is imposed on the basis of the acts and intent of its officers. Answer (d) is incorrect because a corporation cannot be imprisoned.

8. Paul Place was the chief executive of Nadir Company, a large retail food chain. An FDA inspection pursuant to the federal Food, Drug, and Cosmetic Act revealed unsanitary conditions in a warehouse. When notified by the FDA, Place consulted with Nadir's vice-president for legal affairs, who gave assurances that the divisional vice-president with responsibility for the warehouse would take corrective action. A subsequent inspection disclosed that the problem had not been corrected. Nadir and Place were subsequently indicted under the Act for introducing adulterated articles into interstate commerce. Place is

a. Not liable in the absence of any "awareness of some wrongdoing."

b. Not liable because only corporate liability can be imposed for corporate crime.

c. Strictly liable because he has a responsible relation to the situation and the authority to deal with it.

d. Liable solely by reason of occupying the chief executive's position.

The correct answer is (c). *(Publisher)*

REQUIRED: The true statement about an individual's liability for corporate action.

DISCUSSION: The Food, Drug, and Cosmetic Act imposes strict liability for the introduction of misbranded and adulterated articles into interstate commerce. The defendant need not have had a "consciousness of wrongdoing" or criminal intent to be found guilty. Normally, when the criminal prosecution is not based on strict liability, the corporate officer is criminally liable only if (s)he knew of the wrongdoing (had the requisite intent). In the case on which this question is based, liability attached to a corporate official who had a "responsible relation to the situation" and "by virtue of his/her position had authority and responsibility to deal with the situation." Place's guilt was thus not predicated solely on occupying a certain position in the corporation.

Answer (a) is incorrect because the applicable statute imposes strict liability regardless of intent. Answer (b) is incorrect because individuals are also liable. "The only way in which a corporation can act is through the individuals who act on its behalf." Answer (d) is incorrect because "a responsible share in the transaction that the statute outlaws" is also required.

10.3 White Collar Crime

9. Embezzlement is a white-collar crime that was not recognized by common law. In a prosecution for embezzlement,

a. The intent of the defendant to return the property is generally a complete defense.

b. The state must only show that a fiduciary has converted or appropriated the property regardless of intent.

c. The state must prove the same elements as the crime of larceny.

d. Entrustment is a crucial element of the prima facie case.

The correct answer is (d). *(Publisher)*

REQUIRED: The correct statement about the elements of the crime of embezzlement.

DISCUSSION: The term "white collar" crimes encompasses those types of crimes committed in a commercial setting by persons holding a position of authority within a business organization. These crimes typically are not associated with the use of force or violence. Embezzlement is the fraudulent conversion or appropriation of the property of another by a fiduciary to whom it was lawfully entrusted. The fiduciary (a bailee, employee, trustee, etc.) must usually be shown to have had a fraudulent intent to deprive the rightful owner of his/her property.

Answer (a) is incorrect because it states a minority rule. Answer (b) is incorrect because proof of fraudulent intent is normally needed. Answer (c) is incorrect because common larceny does not include the element of entrustment.

10. The crime of bribery

a. Applies only to attempts to influence public officials.

b. Is committed both by the offeror and the recipient of the bribe.

c. Is similar to extortion.

d. Must involve an immediate transfer of money or property.

The correct answer is (b). *(Publisher)*

REQUIRED: The true statement about the scope of the crime of bribery.

DISCUSSION: The crime of bribery entails the giving of something of value to influence unlawfully either a public official or a private person. The essence of the crime is the intent to affect the unlawful actions of the offeree. The crime is committed by the offeror and by an offeree if (s)he accepts the bribe.

Answer (a) is incorrect because bribery applies to public and private persons. Answer (c) is incorrect because extortion involves coercion as opposed to inducement. Answer (d) is incorrect because the transfer may be prospective and consist of anything of value.

11. Computer Shop sold a used computer knowingly and intentionally misrepresenting that it was new. Which of the following statements is most correct?

a. Computer Shop has committed an act of criminal fraud.

b. The buyer would have to elect between bringing criminal charges and filing a civil suit, because Computer Shop cannot be charged twice with the same offense.

c. In a criminal suit against Computer Shop, the buyer can be awarded a remedy of actual and punitive damages.

d. In the interests of judicial economy, criminal and civil suits based on this activity can be consolidated into one case.

The correct answer is (a). *(M. Levin)*

REQUIRED: The true statement about an intentional misrepresentation by a seller.

DISCUSSION: Criminal fraud, which consists essentially of any word or deed by which one party deceives another causing a loss to the deceived person, can take a variety of forms. It is similar in its elements to the tort of deceit. The deceived victim can initiate criminal proceedings and bring a separate civil suit for money damages.

Answer (b) is incorrect because the constitutional protection (5th Amendment) regarding double jeopardy prohibits trying a defendant on a criminal charge of which (s)he has previously been convicted or acquitted. It does not affect a civil suit based on the same events. Answer (c) is incorrect because actual and punitive damages are civil awards, not criminal sanctions. Answer (d) is incorrect because the two suits cannot be consolidated; they involve different wrongs and are subject to different standards of proof.

12. In what way is the crime of deceit distinguishable from both larceny and embezzlement?

a. The accused obtains possession of the victim's property.

b. The accused obtains possession of the victim's property with his/her consent.

c. The accused is entrusted with the victim's property.

d. The accused obtains title to the victim's property.

The correct answer is (d). *(Publisher)*

REQUIRED: The characteristic distinguishing criminal deceit from larceny and embezzlement.

DISCUSSION: The crime of deceit or false pretenses is similar to the tort of fraud. It consists of a misrepresentation of a material past or existing fact that the defendant knew to be false but uttered with an intent to deceive. The victim must surrender money or property in reliance on the misrepresentation. Deceit results in obtaining title to as well as possession of money or property.

Answer (a) is incorrect because possession is obtained in all three crimes. Answer (b) is incorrect because the victim gives consent in embezzlement and deceit but not larceny. Answer (c) is incorrect because no entrustment occurs in larceny or deceit.

13. R. Leslie induced people to invest their savings in a business venture that he represented to be risky. Because the planned venture never became operational, Leslie never applied the investors' funds in the way he promised. Instead, he used the funds to pay for his personal expenses. The investors wanted the state to charge Leslie with fraud but state prosecutors declined. What was the most probable reason for that decision?

a. The investors were not justified in relying on Leslie's statements about the proposed business venture.

b. Leslie did not induce the people to invest since each made his/her independent decision.

c. No proof is available to show that Leslie had fraudulent intent when he talked with the investors.

d. Leslie's statements to investors about the proposed business venture did not include facts.

The correct answer is (c). *(E. Arnold)*

REQUIRED: The first element necessary to prove fraud.

DISCUSSION: Fraud is often claimed and rarely proved because of the requirement of wrongful intent at the time the defendant acted. These facts show no fraudulent intent at the time Leslie accepted the investors' funds. The usual risky business venture holds, at the beginning, high hopes, a bit of greed, and bad business judgment, but no criminal intent. A tort action may be appropriate, however.

Answer (a) is incorrect because the facts show neither basis nor lack of basis for justifiable reliance. Answer (b) is incorrect because the facts state Leslie did induce the investors to invest. Answer (d) is incorrect because Leslie gave the investors facts about risk.

14. Damiano borrowed money for currency speculation from several lenders and issued promissory notes in return. She promised to pay the notes in 90 days at 150% of the amount lent. She paid some notes in full after 45 days by using funds borrowed from other lenders. She collected millions but made no investments and continued to pay old notes with funds obtained from new lenders. What is the best characterization of Damiano's activities?

a. A pyramid scheme.

b. Embezzlement.

c. A legal Ponzi investment.

d. A tort but not a crime.

The correct answer is (a). *(Publisher)*

REQUIRED: The best term for the activities described.

DISCUSSION: A pyramid scheme is a form of criminal deceit. It entails using the funds obtained from subsequent investors to pay off the initial investors who were promised a large return in a short time. The resources obtained from additional investors are then used to pay the prior investors. The scheme fails when no new investors can be found, that is, when the base of the pyramid can no longer be expanded.

Answer (b) is incorrect because embezzlement involves lawful entrustment to a fiduciary. Answer (c) is incorrect because pyramid schemes are generally unlawful. The facts of this question are similar to a famous case, "Cunningham, Trustee of Ponzi v. Brown." Thus, it is also called a Ponzi scheme. Answer (d) is incorrect because both a tort and a crime were committed.

15. Which of the following constitutes forgery?

a. A student signs his/her name to a scholarly paper that (s)he did not write.

b. One spouse signs the name of the other to a check without permission.

c. An artist orally makes a false representation that (s)he created a specific work.

d. An agent signs the name of his/her principal to a deed with permission.

The correct answer is (b). *(Publisher)*

REQUIRED: The activity constituting the crime of forgery.

DISCUSSION: The crime of forgery entails making or altering a writing with fraudulent intent so that the legal rights and obligations of another person are apparently affected. Signing another's name to a check without permission evidences a fraudulent intent. Marriage to the other person is not a defense to forgery.

Answer (a) is incorrect because the falsification must be one with apparent legal significance such as a check, promissory note, or deed. Answer (c) is incorrect because forgery cannot be oral. Answer (d) is incorrect because when the signing was with permission, fraudulent intent cannot be proven.

16. Which of the following is a true statement about the crime of receiving stolen property?

a. The property may consist of money or tangible property but not stock certificates or credit cards.

b. In most states, the person who stole the property is also guilty of receiving it.

c. The elements of knowledge and intent must be proven.

d. In most states, the person who stole the property may be convicted of larceny or receiving stolen property.

The correct answer is (c). *(Publisher)*

REQUIRED: The true statement about the crime of receiving stolen property.

DISCUSSION: To be convicted, the defendant must have received property knowing it to be stolen and with a fraudulent intent to deprive the lawful owner of the property. In some cases, the belief that the property was stolen has been found sufficient to convict even though the property had not in fact been stolen.

Answer (a) is incorrect because any form of property may be involved. Answers (b) and (d) are incorrect because, in most states, the person who stole the property cannot be convicted of receiving stolen property. In a minority of states, one may be convicted of either larceny or receiving stolen property but not both.

17. The Racketeer Influenced and Corrupt Organizations Act (RICO) concerns, among other things, the connections between organized crime and business. The Act

a. Is invoked only in prosecutions of organized crime figures.

b. Applies only to illegitimate business activities.

c. Permits the confiscation of legitimate businesses.

d. Creates accounting requirements for businesses that report to the SEC.

The correct answer is (c). *(Publisher)*

REQUIRED: The effect of the RICO Act on the relation between organized crime and business.

DISCUSSION: Under RICO, profits from "racketeering" activities may be forfeited. The statute not only makes racketeering a federal offense, it also permits tracing of the proceeds to legitimate enterprises. These businesses can now be seized, thus reducing the effect of organized crime on legal business activities.

Answer (a) is incorrect because the civil provisions of the Act have been applied to activities of persons not related to organized crime. Answer (b) is incorrect because RICO allows the seizure of legal businesses purchased with funds obtained through illegal activities. Answer (d) is incorrect because the Foreign Corrupt Practices Act created these requirements.

18. Under the Racketeer Influenced and Corrupt Organizations Act (RICO), an injured party who is not a governmental entity

a. Cannot bring suit.

b. May bring suit for treble damages.

c. May bring suit for punitive damages.

d. May bring suit to recover only the amount of the actual injury plus any court costs.

The correct answer is (b). *(R. Welton)*

REQUIRED: The correct statement about RICO actions by private parties.

DISCUSSION: An injured party who is not a governmental entity may bring suit under the civil provisions of RICO for treble damages (three times the actual loss). In addition, the party may also recover court costs and reasonable attorney's fees.

Answer (a) is incorrect because RICO permits a civil remedy. Answer (c) is incorrect because the plaintiff may not recover punitive in addition to treble damages, which are themselves intended as a penalty. Answer (d) is incorrect because the plaintiff may recover attorney's fees, court costs, and treble damages.

19. In general, the provisions of RICO prohibit

a. Specific acts of racketeering, such as murder or trafficking in stolen property.

b. Organized crime from operating legitimate businesses.

c. Organized crime from operating illegitimate businesses.

d. Operation of any business with funds obtained through a pattern of racketeering acts.

The correct answer is (d). *(R. Welton)*

REQUIRED: The true statement about the scope of RICO.

DISCUSSION: RICO prohibits 1) direct or indirect investment of funds obtained through a pattern of racketeering acts in a business, 2) the acquisition or control of a business through a pattern of racketeering acts, 3) participation in an enterprise through a pattern of racketeering acts, or 4) a conspiracy to do (1), (2), or (3).

Answer (a) is incorrect because RICO does not prohibit acts of racketeering per se. Answers (b) and (c) are incorrect because RICO does not prohibit the mere ownership or operation of a business by organized crime.

10.4 Computer Crime

For more about computer law, see Chapter 34.

20. As computer applications have proliferated, so too have computer crimes. Which of the following does not reflect a problem that society is facing, or has faced, in prosecuting these types of crimes?

a. The judicial system has been slow and at times even reluctant to apply existing law to new applications involving computers.

b. The business community has virtually banned from employment any person even remotely connected to computer crime.

c. The complexity of modern computer systems and the growing sophistication of users and operators makes improprieties extremely difficult to detect.

d. Victimized companies have been reluctant to pursue perpetrators of computer crimes for fear of adverse publicity.

The correct answer is (b). *(Publisher)*

REQUIRED: The problem not facing society in prosecuting computer crimes.

DISCUSSION: Many companies compete to hire convicted computer "hackers" to assist them in providing security for their own computer systems. This practice has, in effect, condoned the perpetration of certain computer crimes, if not in fact glorified them.

Answer (a) is incorrect because the law has tended to lag behind rapid changes in technology. Answer (c) is incorrect because wrongdoing is difficult and expensive to detect and prevent. Answer (d) is incorrect because companies are concerned about their customers' perception of and confidence in the company.

21. Computer crimes ordinarily are not new crimes per se, but involve old crimes that involve a computer. Which of the following traditional crimes generally will not arise with the assistance or use of a computer?

a. Larceny.

b. Criminal fraud.

c. Embezzlement.

d. Burglary.

The correct answer is (d). *(Publisher)*

REQUIRED: Understanding and distinguishing types of traditional crimes.

DISCUSSION: Burglary is the breaking and entering into the dwelling of another at night with the intent to commit a felony. Because physical entry is required, a computer is not normally associated with burglary.

Answers (a), (b), and (c) are incorrect because larceny, fraud, and embezzlement involve the wrongful taking, obtaining, and conversion of another's property and are easily committed with a computer.

22. Jim is employed by First Bank in its operations department. Jim's job entails writing computer programs for different banking applications. While working on a program that calculates the interest earned by customers and allocates it to their individual accounts, Jim realizes that rounding differences involve substantial amounts. Jim writes a program to credit all rounding differences to his personal account. If Jim is caught and tried in a criminal action, he will be convicted of

a. Embezzlement.

b. Robbery.

c. Larceny.

d. Burglary.

The correct answer is (c). *(Publisher)*

REQUIRED: The correct type of crime committed.

DISCUSSION: Larceny is the wrongful or fraudulent taking and carrying away of the personal property of another. Interest earned by the customers is personal property. The wrongful allocation of interest is the taking and carrying away necessary to larceny.

Answer (a) is incorrect because embezzlement occurs when property is entrusted to a person who subsequently converts the property to his/her own use. Answer (b) is incorrect because robbery involves the use of force or fear to unlawfully take property from another. Answer (d) is incorrect because burglary requires breaking and entering the dwelling of another at night with intent to commit a felony.

23. Without the authorization or knowledge of their employer, Robb and Conn used the company computer to develop a set of programs to be marketed commercially for their personal gain. In furtherance of this scheme, they mailed promotional letters to potential clients. A state computer crime statute was enacted 6 months after these events. Robb and Conn are

a. Liable under the computer crime statute.

b. Liable under the federal mail fraud statute.

c. Not liable unless they appropriated property or money of the employer.

d. Not liable even if they appropriated computer programs and electronically stored information.

The correct answer is (b). *(Publisher)*

REQUIRED: The liability of persons making unauthorized use of computer facilities.

DISCUSSION: The federal government and the states have begun to enact specific statutes directed toward computer crime, but in many cases courts have had to extend existing law to punish wrongdoing involving computers. In this case, the court applied the federal mail fraud statute to impose criminal liability on Robb and Conn. The court held that they executed a scheme using the U.S. mails to defraud their employer for illicit personal gain. Solicitation by means of the mails for a fraudulent purpose is a federal offense. An activity otherwise fraudulent under state law becomes a federal crime when the mails are used to convey a writing furthering a scheme to solicit money under false pretenses.

Answer (a) is incorrect because imposition of criminal sanctions retroactively (on actions before the statute existed) is unconstitutional. Answers (c) and (d) are incorrect because various kinds of computer usage are illegal. For example, computers have been used to assist the direct theft of money and embezzlement, to maintain false records, or to steal intangibles such as computer programs and electronically stored data. Unauthorized access to a computer is by itself a crime under the federal Comprehensive Crime Control Act of 1984.

10.5 Criminal Procedure and Constitutional Safeguards

24. Criminal law is a separate branch of American law. It follows procedural rules that may differ from those of the civil law. In the trial of a criminal case,

a. The prosecution can obtain a conviction on appeal.

b. Guilt must be proven by a preponderance of the evidence.

c. The accused is presumed to be innocent.

d. The prosecution may call the defendant as a witness.

The correct answer is (c). *(Publisher)*

REQUIRED: The true statement about criminal procedure in American courts.

DISCUSSION: American concepts of due process provide many protections for the accused. One very important protection is that the defendant is presumed to be innocent.

Answer (a) is incorrect because the defendant can successfully appeal a guilty verdict, but the state cannot obtain an appellate reversal of a not guilty verdict. Once acquitted, an accused cannot be placed in jeopardy (charged) again for the same offense. Answer (b) is incorrect because the state must prove the guilt of the accused beyond a reasonable doubt. This rule minimizes the possibility of convicting an innocent person. Answer (d) is incorrect because the 5th Amendment states that no person "shall be compelled in any criminal case to be a witness against himself."

25. In criminal cases, the U.S. Constitution has been interpreted to

a. Prohibit capital punishment.

b. Require court appointment of an attorney for a defendant in certain instances.

c. Permit questioning of the accused by the police without prior warning of his/her right to remain silent.

d. Prohibit questioning of the accused by the police when (s)he has not consulted with an attorney.

The correct answer is (b). *(Publisher)*

REQUIRED: The correct interpretation of the Constitution regarding the rights of the accused.

DISCUSSION: In Gideon v. Wainwright, the U.S. Supreme Court held that a criminal defendant who could not afford counsel had a right to a court-appointed attorney in a case involving a possible prison sentence. This right has been narrowed in more recent decisions, for example, by a ruling that indigents are not entitled to counsel for discretionary appeals.

Answer (a) is incorrect because capital punishment has been held not to be inherently cruel and unusual under the 8th Amendment. Answer (c) is incorrect because the police must still warn the accused that (s)he has the right to remain silent and the right to consult with an attorney (Miranda warnings). Answer (d) is incorrect because the accused may waive his/her right to consult with an attorney.

26. Which of the following protections is provided to defendants in criminal cases in federal but not necessarily in state courts?

a. The right against self-incrimination.

b. Double jeopardy safeguard.

c. Due process.

d. Grand jury indictment.

The correct answer is (d). *(Publisher)*

REQUIRED: The protection given a criminal defendant in federal but not necessarily in state court.

DISCUSSION: All states do not generally require a grand jury indictment in criminal cases, but the 5th Amendment requires it in federal courts. A grand jury is a panel of jurors who do not determine guilt but merely whether probable cause of guilt is sufficient to issue charges against a person. In many state cases, criminal charges result from an "information" (charges) filed by a prosecuting officer.

Answers (a), (b), and (c) are incorrect because each is a required constitutional safeguard in both federal and state criminal cases.

27. Unreasonable searches and seizures are prohibited by the 4th Amendment of the U.S. Constitution. Which of the following is the true statement about its implications for the criminal law?

a. The 4th Amendment is the basis for the exclusionary rule.

b. A valid search and seizure requires a warrant.

c. Search warrants shall be issued only upon reasonable suspicion.

d. The manner in which evidence is obtained does not affect its admissibility.

The correct answer is (a). *(Publisher)*

REQUIRED: The true statement about the 4th Amendment.

DISCUSSION: The 4th Amendment states, "The right of the people to be secure in their persons, houses, papers, and effects, against unreasonable searches and seizures, shall not be violated." If a search and seizure violates the 4th Amendment, the exclusionary rule (a rule of court) prohibits introduction of the evidence thus obtained in a criminal case brought against the party whose rights were infringed. The Supreme Court, however, has created numerous exceptions to the rule.

Answer (b) is incorrect because a search and seizure may be made with consent of an accused or in the course of a lawful arrest. Answer (c) is incorrect because a search warrant requires probable cause, supported by a sworn statement particularly describing the place to be searched and the persons or things to be seized. Answer (d) is incorrect because the exclusionary rule is still in force although subject to many exceptions.

28. Defendant was charged with criminal trespass. The trial by a six-member jury ended in a mistrial. The case was subsequently postponed for two terms of court. After Defendant moved to determine when he would be brought to trial, the state moved to release him from custody while retaining the right to prosecute at its discretion. This motion was granted. On appeal, Defendant should win because

a. His right to a speedy trial was denied.

b. His right to a trial by a 12-person jury was denied.

c. Once released from custody, he cannot be tried.

d. He cannot be tried twice for the same offense.

The correct answer is (a). *(Publisher)*

REQUIRED: The constitutional basis for a criminal defendant's successful appeal.

DISCUSSION: In the actual case, the Supreme Court held that indefinite postponement of the trial without stated justification and over the objection of the defendant violated his right to a speedy trial. The 6th Amendment states, "In all criminal prosecutions, the accused shall enjoy the right to a speedy and public trial." This protection has been incorporated in the 14th Amendment's due process clause ("nor shall any state deprive any person of life, liberty, or property, without due process of law") and thus applies to the states.

Answer (b) is incorrect because no specified number of jurors is constitutionally required. Answer (c) is incorrect because release from custody while awaiting trial is a common action, e.g., out on bail. Answer (d) is incorrect because a mistrial declared by necessity is an exception to the double jeopardy safeguard.

29. The 5th Amendment to the U.S. Constitution protects a person accused of a crime by providing a privilege to avoid self-incrimination (compelled testimony against him/herself). This privilege is the basis for the "Miranda warnings" required to be given to criminal suspects prior to custodial interrogation. The landmark Supreme Court case of Miranda v. Arizona is the origin of the requirement. Which of the following is not a Miranda warning?

a. The individual has the right to counsel before answering any question.

b. The individual has the right to counsel even if (s)he cannot afford an attorney.

c. The individual has the right to remain silent.

d. The individual has the right to represent him/herself in a criminal trial.

The correct answer is (d). *(Publisher)*

REQUIRED: The element not included among the Miranda warnings.

DISCUSSION: Although an individual has the right to represent him/herself in a criminal trial, the decision in Miranda v. Arizona does not require law enforcement officers to advise the individual of this right prior to questioning. The Miranda warnings relate to rights of the individual that are pertinent to the decision to answer or not answer questions by law enforcement officers.

Answers (a), (b), and (c) are incorrect because the suspect also has the right to have counsel present during questioning and to know that any statement the individual makes can be used against him/her.

30. After being arrested, an individual must be charged with a specific crime before being brought to trial. A charge issued by a grand jury is

a. An indictment.

b. An information.

c. An arraignment.

d. A complaint.

The correct answer is (a). *(Publisher)*

REQUIRED: The correct name for a criminal charge issued by a grand jury.

DISCUSSION: After an individual is arrested, a grand jury or a magistrate determines if the evidence is sufficient to justify a trial. If the evidence is deemed to be sufficient, a formal charge is issued against the individual. A charge made by a grand jury is an indictment. An indictment may only be handed down for a felony.

Answer (b) is incorrect because an information is issued by a magistrate in most misdemeanor cases. Occasionally, an information is issued in a felony case. Answer (c) is incorrect because an arraignment is the proceeding in which the individual is formally charged with a specific crime. Answer (d) is incorrect because a complaint is the document filed by a plaintiff to initiate a civil lawsuit.

CHAPTER ELEVEN
CONTRACTS

The explanations for the answers in this chapter are based almost entirely on common law. The answers have few references to authority because there are no uniform acts on contracts. The Restatement of Contracts is intended to embody the common law, but, because it is not used extensively in undergraduate texts, it is omitted here.

A few questions concern sales of goods because that area is closely related to general contract law. The explanations should be sufficiently complete so you will not have trouble with these questions even if you are not familiar with contracts for the sale of goods (covered in Chapter 12, "Sales of Goods").

11.1 Nature and Classification of Contracts

1. Over the last century, contract law has undergone considerable change in response to social, economic, and political shifts. Which of the following is a true statement about current contract law?

a. Contract formation is more difficult than formerly.

b. Greater freedom of contract is permitted.

c. Once a contract is formed, the parties are less likely to be excused from performance.

d. The principles of caveat emptor and laissez-faire are less influential.

The correct answer is (d). *(Publisher)*

REQUIRED: The current status of contract law after a century of change.

DISCUSSION: In the nineteenth century, contract theory was dominated by the notions of caveat emptor ("let the buyer beware") and laissez-faire (the idea that economic activity should be unregulated or "left alone" by government). In today's complex society, contract law has changed to reflect the disparity of bargaining power between buyers and sellers, governmental influence in commercial matters, economic effects, and social reality.

Answers (a), (b), and (c) are incorrect because nineteenth-century contract law made both contract formation and excuse from performance more difficult because complete autonomy in contracting was the ideal. Today, freedom to drive a hard bargain has been curtailed, the means of escaping liability are more numerous, and contracts are more readily found to exist.

2. The principal legal authority governing contractual activity is state common law. Article 2 of the Uniform Commercial Code (UCC), however, also applies to many sales transactions. The UCC applies to contracts involving sales of

a. Tangible personal property.

b. Real property.

c. Services.

d. Patents and copyrights.

The correct answer is (a). *(Publisher)*

REQUIRED: The applicability of Article 2 of the Uniform Commercial Code (UCC).

DISCUSSION: The UCC has been adopted in various forms in all states (Louisiana has not adopted Art. 2). Article 2 applies to sales of goods, which are all things movable at the time of identification to the contract. Article 2 therefore concerns transactions in tangible personal property. Tangible property is that having some physical existence (e.g., equipment, furniture, food). Intangible property has no physical existence but may be represented by a document (e.g., shares of stock, bonds, contract rights, patents, copyrights). Personal property is that which is not classifiable as real property (land, buildings, and fixtures).

Answers (b), (c), and (d) are incorrect because each is excluded from coverage by Article 2.

3. Which of the following is not a required element of a contract?

a. Legality.

b. Consideration.

c. Legal capacity.

d. A writing.

The correct answer is (d). *(Publisher).*

REQUIRED: The item that is not a required element of a contract.

DISCUSSION: There are four essential elements of a contract: an agreement (offer and acceptance), consideration, legal capacity of the parties to contract, and a legal objective or purpose. A writing is not required in order to enter into a contract. However, some contracts are not enforceable unless there is a writing evidencing the contract.

Answers (a), (b), and (c) are incorrect because each is a required element of a contract.

4. The Estate of Buck Sonn was liquidated at auction. Among the items sold was an old safe purchased for a small sum by Ann Little. Both the auctioneer and Little were aware that the safe had a locked inner compartment. When the compartment was opened, a large sum of money was found. The Sonn Estate sued to recover the money. The Estate should

a. Win because the parties did not intend to contract regarding the money.

b. Lose because the parties objectively manifested an intent to contract regarding the safe and its contents.

c. Win because of a mutual mistake.

d. Lose because it had a subjective intent to sell the safe.

The correct answer is (b). *(Publisher)*

REQUIRED: The outcome and the reason therefor when the parties lacked specific knowledge of the subject matter of the contract.

DISCUSSION: Mutual assent is a necessary element of a contract. The parties must intend to be contractually bound. Intent is determined according to an objective standard rather than the subjective or actual intent of the parties. The subject matter of the contract is ascertained according to an objective standard: What would an ordinary reasonable third person have concluded from the external manifestations of the parties? In this case, an objective third person could reasonably decide from the circumstances that the parties intended to contract regarding a safe and its unknown contents. Thus, the Estate should lose.

Answer (a) is incorrect because the circumstances suggested an intent to sell whatever the safe contained. Answer (c) is incorrect because no mistake occurred. Both parties knew that the safe contained a locked compartment. Answer (d) is incorrect because subjective intent is legally irrelevant.

5. The objective manifestation rule is used to argue the enforceability of a promise that

a. Is not supported by consideration.

b. Requires the performance of an illegal act.

c. Is made by a person who lacks contractual capacity.

d. May be interpreted as a serious proposal.

The correct answer is (d). *(E. Rahm)*

REQUIRED: The purpose of the objective manifestation rule.

DISCUSSION: The objective manifestation rule is used to determine whether the parties intended a contract. If a reasonable person would have thought that the other party made a serious proposal, the person making the proposal will be bound to the contract even though (s)he secretly may not have intended to make a contract.

Answer (a) is incorrect because consideration is relevant to the decision of whether the parties "intended" an agreement. Answer (b) is incorrect because the objective manifestation rule has no relationship to the performance of an illegal act. Answer (c) is incorrect because contractual capacity is not related to the decision that a serious proposal was made.

6. Spring agreed to buy Summer's car. Because the actual purchase was not to take place for several months, they drew up a lengthy agreement that specified all of the rights and obligations of each of the parties that they could think of. They took this two-page, single-spaced document to an attorney for review. The attorney suggested a few changes. They had the document retyped and they signed it. The contract is referred to as

a. A formal contract.

b. An executed contract.

c. A simple contract.

d. An implied contract.

The correct answer is (c). *(Publisher)*

REQUIRED: The type of contract into which Spring and Summer entered.

DISCUSSION: Formal contracts are those the law has historically treated specially, based on the form used to create the contract. In early law these included contracts for which a personal seal was required. They also include negotiable instruments and contracts of record (those entered into the records of a court). All other contracts are simple contracts, even if they are in writing and evidenced by a document.

Answer (a) is incorrect because typing a lengthy document does not make a contract formal. Answer (b) is incorrect because an executed contract is one in which both parties have completed their performance, e.g., after the car is exchanged for money. Answer (d) is incorrect because this is an express contract. The terms of an implied contract are inferred from surrounding circumstances.

7. Which of the following represents the basic distinction between a bilateral contract and a unilateral contract?

a. Specific performance is available if the contract is unilateral whereas it is not if the contract is bilateral.

b. Only one promise is involved if the contract is unilateral but two promises if the contract is bilateral.

c. The Statute of Frauds applies to a bilateral contract but not to a unilateral contract.

d. The rights under a bilateral contract are assignable, whereas rights under a unilateral contract are not assignable.

The correct answer is (b). *(CPA 1179 L-5)*

REQUIRED: The basic distinction between a unilateral and a bilateral contract.

DISCUSSION: In a bilateral contract, the promise of one party to perform is consideration for the promise of the other. In a unilateral contract, one party makes a promise in exchange for the other party's act, instead of in exchange for a promise from the other party (as in a bilateral contract). Therefore, a unilateral contract only involves one promise, while a bilateral contract involves two promises.

Answers (a), (c), and (d) are incorrect because the availability of specific performance, the applicability of the Statute of Frauds, and the assignability of rights are not affected by the distinction between unilateral and bilateral contracts. Each of these may be available in either a unilateral or bilateral contract.

8. Ina Turner owned a parcel of real property that she wished to sell. She signed a written agreement with Ali Bike, a real estate broker, stating that if he found a purchaser willing and able to pay a stated price, she would pay Bike a commission. Bike located a buyer who signed a written offer to purchase and tendered a down payment. When Turner refused the offer, Bike brought suit to obtain his commission. Which of the following is true?

a. The buyer has a cause of action against Turner.

b. Bike has a cause of action against Turner on a unilateral contract.

c. Bike has a cause of action against Turner on a bilateral contract.

d. No contract was formed.

The correct answer is (b). *(Publisher)*

REQUIRED: The contract liability, if any, of one who listed realty with a broker.

DISCUSSION: In effect, Turner made an offer when she promised to pay a commission to Bike if he produced a purchaser able and willing to buy the property at stated terms. Bike made no return promise. Instead, a unilateral contract (a promise in return for the actual rendition of the desired performance) was created when Bike accepted the offer by finding a buyer who met the given conditions. Bike was therefore entitled to his commission even though no sale occurred.

Answer (a) is incorrect because Turner's refusal to sell was a rejection of the buyer's offer, which is not actionable by the buyer. Answer (c) is incorrect because a bilateral contract requires mutual promises. Answer (d) is incorrect because a unilateral contract was formed.

9. Certain contracts have absolutely no effect and are not recognized under law. If two or more parties enter into such an agreement, it is

a. Valid.

b. Void.

c. Voidable.

d. Unenforceable.

The correct answer is (b). *(Publisher)*

REQUIRED: The correct term for contracts that are not effective or recognized under law.

DISCUSSION: Contracts that are of no effect and not recognized under law are void. Neither party has a legal obligation to the other based on the contract. The parties may go through with their performance, but there is no means of providing remedies in the event of breach.

Answer (a) is incorrect because a valid contract can be enforced and remedies are available to both parties in the event of breach. Answer (c) is incorrect because a voidable contract is valid, but only enforceable by one party. For example, a contract entered into by fraud may be enforced by the innocent party but not by the fraudulent party. Answer (d) is incorrect because an unenforceable contract has been validly formed but cannot be enforced because of a flaw. An example is a contract required to be written by the Statute of Frauds but entered into orally by the parties.

10. On the first day of the month, Thomas and Moore orally agreed that Thomas was to deliver to Moore's place of business a case of wickets on each Monday of the current month. Moore was to pay the $300 price on the first of the following month. On the 15th of the month, the agreement should be classified as

a. Executed.

b. Executory.

c. Unexecuted because the agreement was oral.

d. Cancelable at any time with respect to future deliveries.

The correct answer is (b). *(Publisher)*

REQUIRED: The classification of a partially performed oral contract.

DISCUSSION: An executed contract is one in which the parties have completed their performance. A contract is executory to the extent it has not been fully performed. As of the 15th, Thomas had partially performed but Moore had not performed at all. The contract was thus executory.

Answer (a) is incorrect because both parties had not completed performance. Answer (c) is incorrect because in the context of contract classification, the terms executory and executed refer to the performance of the contract, not to its form. Although the word executed in ordinary usage may mean signed, an oral contract can never be executed or unexecuted in this sense because there is no written document. Answer (d) is incorrect because the entire contract is enforceable and there are no provisions allowing it to be canceled.

11. When a client accepts the services of an accountant without an agreement concerning payment, the result is

a. An implied-in-fact contract.

b. An implied-in-law contract.

c. An express contract.

d. No contract.

The correct answer is (a). *(CPA 1181 L-11)*

REQUIRED: The type of contract formed when a client accepts an accountant's services.

DISCUSSION: Enforceable contracts may be created without an express agreement of terms if the facts of the situation indicate (imply) an objective intent of both parties to contract. Objective intent means the apparent intent of an ordinary, reasonable person and not the actual (subjective) intent. When a client accepts the services of an accountant, there is an implied agreement to pay for them. Because the facts indicate a contract was formed, it is an implied-in-fact contract.

Answer (b) is incorrect because a contract implied in law (quasi-contract) prevents unjust enrichment of one party when the facts do not indicate both parties intended to form a contract. Answer (c) is incorrect because an express contract is one in which the terms (such as payment) are specifically agreed upon. Answer (d) is incorrect because a contract implied in fact was formed.

12. A quasi-contract is imposed by law to prevent unjust enrichment of one party at the other party's expense. Such a contract is also referred to as

a. A contract implied in law.

b. A contract implied in fact.

c. An unenforceable contract.

d. A bilateral contract.

The correct answer is (a). *(Publisher)*

REQUIRED: The alternative term for a quasi-contract.

DISCUSSION: Quasi-contracts are not actual contracts because the parties did not agree on their rights and duties. Such contracts are created by courts to prevent unjust enrichment at another's expense. These are sometimes called contracts implied in law because they are created by law and not by mutual consent or reference to the parties' intent.

Answer (b) is incorrect because a contract implied in fact is inferred from the conduct of the parties or from surrounding circumstances when there is no express agreement. Answer (c) is incorrect because a quasi-contract is enforceable when it is recognized in law. Answer (d) is incorrect because a bilateral contract is one in which two parties exchange promises. There is no exchange of promises in a quasi-contract.

13. Cara offered to pay Peter to paint a house located at 103 Canton Street, and he accepted. However, Peter incorrectly wrote down the address as 108 Canton Street. As a result, he painted the wrong house. Fred Fibs, the owner of 108 Canton Street, saw Peter painting his house but said nothing. When the job was completed, Peter tried to collect the contract price. He will be able to recover from

a. Cara under the theory of unjust enrichment.

b. Fibs under the theory of quasi-contract.

c. Neither Cara nor Fibs because of his unilateral mistake.

d. Neither Cara nor Fibs because of lack of consideration.

The correct answer is (b). *(D. Costantino)*

REQUIRED: The legal effect of accepting the benefits of a contract to which one is not a party.

DISCUSSION: Quasi-contracts are not actual contracts because the parties did not agree on their rights and duties. Such contracts are created by courts to prevent unjust enrichment at another's expense. These are sometimes called contracts implied in law because they are created by law and not by mutual consent or reference to the parties' intent. Fibs had knowledge of the benefit conferred on him by Peter and accepted it although no contract was formed between them. To ensure an equitable result, the law will therefore impose an obligation on Fibs and prevent his unjust enrichment at the expense of Peter.

Answer (a) is incorrect because Cara received no benefit and thus could not have been unjustly enriched. Answer (c) is incorrect because Peter can recover in quasi-contract from Fibs. He has no basis for recovery from Cara because he did not perform. Answer (d) is incorrect because Peter will be able to recover the reasonable value of his services from Fibs based on a quasi-contract.

14. Sam Student was hit by a car crossing the street and knocked unconscious. Fast Ambulance Service took him to the hospital while he was still unconscious. What is Sam's liability for Fast Ambulance's fee?

a. Not liable because no contract was formed.

b. Liable under an implied-in-fact contract theory.

c. Liable under the UCC.

d. Liable under quasi-contract (implied-in-law contract) theory.

The correct answer is (d). *(R. Cherry, Jr.)*

REQUIRED: The liability of the recipient of emergency services.

DISCUSSION: Fast Ambulance should recover the reasonable value of its services (not the potential contract price) under the theory of quasi-contract. Liability is imposed to prevent unjust enrichment and because no other basis of recovery is available.

Answer (a) is incorrect because the fee is recoverable under quasi-contract theory. Answer (b) is incorrect because an implied-in-fact contract is inferred from the actions of the parties. An unconscious person cannot manifest contractual intent. Answer (c) is incorrect because the UCC does not apply.

15. A contract contains several promises made by each of the parties, but one party must complete performance of all his/her promises before the other is to perform. This contract is

a. Divisible.

b. Entire.

c. Executed.

d. Formal.

The correct answer is (b). *(Publisher)*

REQUIRED: The correct term for a contract that must be performed wholly on one side before the other is to perform.

DISCUSSION: The terms entire or whole refer to a contract that is not divisible. This means that a party is required to perform all of his/her promises to hold the other party liable. For example, a contract provides for three deliveries, but unless all three are received, the purchaser is not liable to pay for any of them.

Answer (a) is incorrect because a divisible contract is one in which partial performance by one party is intended to be matched with a partial performance by the other; e.g., a contract for three weekly deliveries is divisible if proportionate payment is to be made at the time of each delivery. Answer (c) is incorrect because an executed contract is one that has already been performed by both parties. Answer (d) is incorrect because a formal contract is a contract under seal, a negotiable instrument, or a contract of record (judgments and recognizances entered in court records).

16. Adhesion contracts are sometimes held to be unconscionable, but their use is often justified. An adhesion contract is most appropriate if a seller

a. Has few transactions.

b. Drafts a standard contract containing extremely favorable terms and refuses to negotiate with buyers who wish to alter its terms.

c. Thereby realizes efficiencies that reduce transaction costs.

d. Has substantially greater bargaining power than the buyer.

The correct answer is (c). *(Publisher)*

REQUIRED: The statement that justifies the use of adhesion contracts.

DISCUSSION: Many businesses could function only on a small scale if all adhesion contracts were prohibited. Their use permits large businesses to avoid the costs associated with negotiating the terms of individual transactions. Consequently, the transaction costs of inexpensive goods and services are reduced.

Answer (a) is incorrect because adhesion contracts are most appropriate when a company has many similar transactions. Answers (b) and (d) are incorrect because courts often hold adhesion contracts to be unconscionable when buyers have little or no meaningful choice with regard to the terms.

11.2 Offer

17. For an offer to confer the power to form a contract by acceptance, it must have all of the following elements except

a. Be communicated to the offeree in a communication made or authorized by the offeror.

b. Be sufficiently definite and certain.

c. Be communicated by words to the offeree by the offeror.

d. Manifest an intent to enter into a contract.

The correct answer is (c). *(CPA 588 L-16)*

REQUIRED: The element not needed for an offer to confer the power to form a contract by acceptance.

DISCUSSION: Offers may be made orally, in writing, or through any means of nonverbal communication. The manner of communication of offers is not important as long as they are communicated as intended by the offeror.

Answers (a), (b), and (d) are incorrect because each is a necessary element of an offer.

18. Defendant was a seller of new, improved wibbets. Her company sold millions of dollars worth of wibbets annually. She publicly stated before a state regulatory board that she would pay $100,000 to anyone who found a defective wibbet. This statement elicited laughter from those present. Plaintiff learned of the statement and notified Defendant that he had a defective wibbet. Defendant assured Plaintiff that the offer had been made seriously and that the money was in escrow. Plaintiff subsequently presented the faulty wibbet. Defendant refused to pay on the grounds that her remark was made in jest. In the subsequent lawsuit for the $100,000, Plaintiff will

a. Lose if Defendant shows that she actually intended the statement as a joke.

b. Lose regardless of Defendant's subjective intent.

c. Win because Defendant's statement was an offer that could be accepted.

d. Win because he reasonably relied on Defendant's statement.

The correct answer is (c). *(Publisher)*

REQUIRED: The outcome of an action based on acceptance of an extravagant offer.

DISCUSSION: A statement made in jest, under the stress of highly unusual circumstances, or as a bluff will not be construed as an offer capable of acceptance unless a reasonable person would believe that such an offer had been made. The actual intent of the speaker is not relevant. The courts consider only the inferences that an objective observer could reasonably draw from the external manifestations of the parties. In consequence, a speaker may find him/herself contractually bound despite a lack of subjective intent. That Defendant's public statement was a serious proposition is supported not only by her subsequent conversation with Plaintiff but also by the dollar amount in question in relationship to the annual sales of the firm. Such an amount is a reasonable sum to be paid for promotion. Accordingly, Plaintiff will win because Defendant's statement was a valid offer for a unilateral contract.

Answers (a) and (b) are incorrect because only objective intent is relevant. Answer (d) is incorrect because the facts do not suggest detrimental reliance. Plaintiff can recover on the basis that a valid contract was formed.

19. The following conversation took place between Mary and Ed: "Ed, if you wanted to sell your table, what would you ask for it?" Ed: "I suppose $400 would be a fair price." Mary: "I'll take it, if you will have it refinished." Ed: "Sold." Thus,

a. Ed's statement: "I suppose $400 would be a fair price" constituted an offer.

b. Mary's reply: "I'll take it, if you will have it refinished" was a conditional acceptance, terminating Ed's offer.

c. No contract resulted because Ed never stated he would actually sell the table for $400.

d. A contract was formed when Ed said: "Sold."

The correct answer is (d). *(CPA 1184 L-18)*

REQUIRED: The correct contractual implication of the statements.

DISCUSSION: An offer usually makes a promise and requests a return promise or act. Mary's first question was merely a request for information. It contained no promissory language and evidenced no intention to be bound, so it could not have been construed as an offer. Ed's first reply was at best a negotiatory statement and likewise contained no language construable as an offer. Mary's second statement effectively contained a promise to pay $400 for the table if Ed had it refinished. Mary thereby manifested an intention to be bound if Ed made a return promise or performed a certain act. Ed's response of "sold" was an acceptance and formed a contract.

Answer (a) is incorrect because Ed's first reply lacked the necessary elements of an offer. Answer (b) is incorrect because Mary's second statement was an offer. Answer (c) is incorrect because Ed impliedly acquiesced to a sale at the price he quoted and upon the condition stated in Mary's offer.

20. On May 1, Wendy posted the following notice on a campus bulletin board:

> NEEDED: Tutor for Business Law I. I don't know a tort from a torte. $10.00 an hour. Call Wendy, 555-3335, evenings.

On May 4, Sarah saw the sign and left a message with Wendy's roommate that Sarah accepted Wendy's offer. On May 5, Wendy wrote in red ink across the sign, "Forget it! Dropped the class." Later that evening Wendy received Sarah's message.

a. A contract was formed because Sarah accepted the offer before it was revoked.

b. A contract was formed because Wendy's offer was not properly revoked.

c. No contract was formed because Sarah did not give her acceptance directly to Wendy.

d. No contract was formed because no offer was made.

The correct answer is (d). *(S. Rogers)*

REQUIRED: The effect of posting a notice seeking performance of services, an attempted acceptance, and a cancellation of the notice.

DISCUSSION: Wendy's sign is merely an invitation to the public to negotiate. This invitation is not an offer because it contains no words of promise, is addressed to more people than could possibly fill the position, and manifests no clear intent to make an offer. Also, the notice concerns personal services. Thus, the party who published the notice is more likely to desire further negotiation before being bound than if a sale of property were contemplated.

Answers (a) and (b) are incorrect because there was no offer to accept or revoke. Answer (c) is incorrect because Sarah's message was an offer.

21. Mildred saw a vase in an antique shop. A tag on the vase said "Genuine Chinese Vase, $125." Mildred said to the owner of the shop, "I'll buy this vase for $125." Milford, the owner of the shop, refused to sell the vase. In a lawsuit brought by Mildred against Milford,

a. Mildred will win because a contract was formed when Mildred said she would buy the vase.

b. Mildred will win because the vase was a unique chattel.

c. Milford will win because he rejected Mildred's offer.

d. Milford will win because the contract was not written.

The correct answer is (c). *(E. Rahm)*

REQUIRED: The effect of a customer's attempt to purchase at an advertised price.

DISCUSSION: Advertisements or price quotations made to the public are not offers. Advertisements (in any format) are usually only invitations to negotiate. They are not considered offers because they contain no words of promise, they are addressed to the public (the quantity accepted could exceed the supply), and they are usually indefinite.

Answer (a) is incorrect because the tag was not the offer. The offer was made when Mildred said she would purchase the vase for $125. Answer (b) is incorrect because the uniqueness of the item is irrelevant to contract formation. Answer (d) is incorrect because no contract was formed.

22. To announce the grand opening of a new retail business, Hudson placed an advertisement in a local newspaper quoting sales prices on certain items in stock. The grand opening was so successful that Hudson was unable to totally satisfy customer demands. Which of the following statements is correct?

a. Hudson made an invitation seeking offers.

b. Hudson made an offer to the people who read the advertisement.

c. Anyone who tendered money for the items advertised was entitled to buy them.

d. The offer by Hudson was partially revocable as to an item once it was sold out.

The correct answer is (a). *(CPA 589 L-25)*

REQUIRED: The legal effect of a newspaper advertisement quoting sales prices.

DISCUSSION: Newspaper ads that merely cite prices on items in stock are invitations to negotiate, not offers. Only in rare instances when an ad is definite and manifests clear intent will it constitute an offer and not a solicitation of offers; e.g., a promise to give one mink stole for $1 to the first person requesting it on April 5 is an offer.

Answer (b) is incorrect because the advertisement was only an invitation seeking offers. Answer (c) is incorrect because one who responds to an ad does not create a contract by acceptance, but instead makes an offer. In rare instances, an ad may be so definite and manifest such clear intent that it constitutes an offer and not a solicitation of offers. Answer (d) is incorrect because no offer was made by the ad. The existence of a limited quantity and a potentially unlimited demand is one reason for finding that the advertisement does not manifest an intent to make an offer.

23. To be effective, an offer must be definite and complete. Which of the following is correct?

a. All terms in the offer must be expressed.

b. Absolute definiteness is required.

c. The acceptance cannot be used to meet the definiteness requirement.

d. Only reasonable definiteness is necessary.

The correct answer is (d). *(Publisher)*

REQUIRED: The true statement about the need for a definite offer.

DISCUSSION: The terms of a contract must be reasonably definite and complete. The agreement will not be enforced if an essential term has been omitted. The parties, the subject matter, the price, and the place and time of performance are terms usually regarded as vital to the agreement.

Answer (a) is incorrect because terms may be implied if the parties clearly wished to contract and a basis exists for an objective determination of the missing terms. Answer (b) is incorrect because reasonable definiteness is acceptable. For example, an agreement by one party to purchase "all" of the other party's output is reasonably definite. Answer (c) is incorrect because an indefinite offer requiring definite terms in the acceptance may, taken together with an appropriate acceptance, constitute a reasonably definite agreement.

24. Gudrun owned a 2,000-acre country estate. She signed a written agreement with Johann, selling the house on the property and "a sufficient amount of land surrounding the house to create a park." The price was stated to be $200,000. When Gudrun refused to honor the agreement, Johann sued.

a. Gudrun will win because the agreement is not reasonably definite.

b. Johann will win because the quantity of land is implied.

c. Johann will win because the parties intended to make a contract.

d. Gudrun will win because no financing term was included in the agreement.

The correct answer is (a). *(Publisher)*

REQUIRED: The result when a contract for the sale of land does not state the quantity.

DISCUSSION: For an agreement between the parties to be enforceable, it must be reasonably definite and certain (not ambiguous). A court must be able to determine with reasonable accuracy what the parties agreed upon. In this case, it is not reasonably clear from the writing what amount of land Gudrun agreed to sell.

Answers (b) and (c) are incorrect because some objective basis must exist for measuring the implied term. The court would have no means of determining how much land is needed for a park. Answer (d) is incorrect because the quantity term is more significant than the financing term. The price is given and payment in cash (or its equivalent) is implied.

25. Western Sugar Company and Skarda Trucking Company entered into an agreement for Skarda to transport "such tonnage of sugar beets as may be loaded by the sugar company at its beet receiving stations" between October 1 and February 15. Skarda was obligated to furnish insurance, suitable trucks and equipment, labor, maintenance, fuel, and all necessary licenses. Its compensation was dependent upon haulage at a rate per ton, varying with the length of the haul. Skarda transported sugar beets for Western until mid-November when Western notified it that its services were no longer needed. Skarda then sued for lost profits and the forced sale of its trucks at a loss.

a. Skarda will win. Western breached an enforceable contract.

b. Skarda will win. The court will imply a contract from the course of conduct between the parties.

c. Skarda will win. The court will estop Western from asserting lack of consideration for the canceled shipments.

d. Western will win. The agreement is unenforceable for lack of mutuality of assent.

The correct answer is (d). *(S. Willey)*

REQUIRED: The enforceability of an agreement to provide an indeterminate amount of transportation services.

DISCUSSION: Contracts require mutuality of assent and reasonably definite terms to be enforceable. A bilateral contract must contain genuine promises that are definite enough to obligate the parties to perform. An agreement to "haul such tonnage as may be loaded" does not contain a definite promise to haul a specific or reasonably determinable quantity and is thus an illusory promise. Western had no obligation under the agreement to let Skarda haul any particular amount of tonnage. Consequently, it could terminate the agreement at any time. This agreement should be contrasted with requirements and output contracts (see the next question).

Answer (a) is incorrect because without a specified quantity, the agreement is so indefinite that no contract exists because the parties never really agreed on anything. Answer (b) is incorrect because no court would imply a contract for the transport of more beets from the shipments between October 1 and November 15. Answer (c) is incorrect because Western has promised to pay only for beets that are actually transported. Skarda's change of position in reliance upon this promise is unreasonable and would not provide a basis for promissory estoppel.

26. Which of the following agreements is unenforceable because of indefiniteness?

a. The seller agrees to supply all of the buyer's requirements for machine parts for the next year.

b. The buyer agrees to purchase all of the seller's output of cotton in the next season.

c. The buyer agrees to purchase all of the seller's output of pork bellies and to deal exclusively in the seller's goods.

d. The seller agrees to supply a quantity of orange juice concentrate dependent upon the will of the buyer.

The correct answer is (d). *(Publisher)*

REQUIRED: The contract unenforceable for indefiniteness.

DISCUSSION: Historically, requirements and output contracts were unenforceable because they were too indefinite; i.e., the quantity was not determined. A requirements contract is one in which the seller agrees to supply all the buyer needs. An output contract is one in which the buyer agrees to purchase all the seller produces. Under current common law and UCC 2-306, requirements and output contracts are valid and enforceable. Both parties are required to act in good faith and not vary substantially from the estimated or normal quantity. The definiteness criterion is met because the output or requirements term is defined by the reasonable needs of the seller's or buyer's business, not by the whim or will of any party.

Answers (a), (b), and (c) are incorrect because under the modern approach, requirements and output contracts do not fail for indefiniteness. Agreements for exclusive dealing that are lawful under federal antitrust statutes are also recognized by UCC 2-306.

27. Water Works had a long-standing policy of offering employees $100 for suggestions actually used. Because of inflation and a decline in the level and quality of suggestions received, Water Works decided to increase the award to $500. Several suggestions were under consideration at that time. Two days prior to the public announcement of the increase to $500, a suggestion by Farber was accepted and put into use. Farber is entitled to

a. $500 because Water Works had decided to pay that amount.

b. $500 because the suggestion submitted will be used during the period that Water Works indicated it would pay $500.

c. $100 in accordance with the original offer.

d. Nothing if Water Works chooses not to pay because the offer was gratuitous.

The correct answer is (c). *(CPA 1181 L-7)*

REQUIRED: The amount to which the offeree is entitled.

DISCUSSION: To be effective, an offer must be communicated to the offeree. The new offer of $500 had not been communicated to Farber at the time Farber made the suggestion. The contract was formed when Farber made the suggestion in acceptance of the $100 offer. It was subject to the condition that Water Works use the suggestion.

Answer (a) is incorrect because the subjective intent of Water Works to pay $500 in the future does not affect existing offers or contracts. Answer (b) is incorrect because no term in the new offer stated that it was effective for all suggestions used during the period. Answer (d) is incorrect because Farber's suggestion was consideration for Water Works' promise to pay; i.e., it is what Water Works bargained for.

28. Carol used her dictating machine to record the text of an offer she intended to make to Deanna. John, her secretary, transcribed the tape. During lunch and before the offer had been mailed, John saw Deanna and told her about it. Deanna promptly mailed an acceptance to Carol. Which of the following is true?

a. No contract was formed because the offer was not communicated to the offeree.

b. No contract was formed because the offer was not communicated to the offeree by the means chosen by the offeror.

c. A contract was formed because John was Carol's agent.

d. A contract was formed because Carol intended to make an offer and Deanna learned of the offer in time to make a valid acceptance.

The correct answer is (b). *(Publisher)*

REQUIRED: The effect of communication of an offer by a means not intended by the offeror.

DISCUSSION: An offer is not effective until it is communicated to the offeree. The communication, however, must be by a means chosen by the offeror. Carol evidently intended to communicate the offer by mail. When the offeree learned of the offer in an unauthorized manner, she could only make an offer, not a valid acceptance.

Answer (a) is incorrect because the offer was actually communicated, but not as intended by the offeror. Answer (c) is incorrect because the facts do not indicate that John was an agent for purposes of communicating offers. Answer (d) is incorrect because the offer must be communicated as intended by the offeree.

29. Quick Corp. mailed a letter to Blue Co. on May 1, offering a 3-year franchise dealership. The offer stated the terms in detail and at the bottom stated that the offer would not be withdrawn prior to June 5. Which of the following is correct?

a. The offer cannot be assigned to another party by Blue if Blue chooses not to accept.

b. A letter of acceptance from Blue to Quick sent on June 5 and received by Quick on June 6 does not create a valid contract.

c. The offer is an irrevocable option that cannot be withdrawn prior to June 5.

d. The Statute of Frauds does not apply to the proposed contract.

The correct answer is (a). *(CPA 1186 L-24)*

REQUIRED: The true statement about an offer of a franchise dealership.

DISCUSSION: Offers are never assignable except by express approval of the offeror. An attempted acceptance by an assignee would operate as an offer that Quick could accept or reject. In contrast, a contract is assignable unless prohibited by express agreement or implication because of its personal nature.

Answer (b) is incorrect because the acceptance was effective when mailed on June 5. Unless the offer has lapsed or states other requirements, an acceptance forms a contract when dispatched by any reasonable means, not when received. Answer (c) is incorrect because no option can be created by an offer alone. An option is itself a contract requiring consideration, offer and acceptance, etc. Answer (d) is incorrect because the Statute of Frauds applies because the contract cannot be performed within 1 year of its making.

30. Dustin received a telephone call on Monday from his oil supplier. The supplier offered him 1,000 barrels of heating oil at $48 a barrel, the current price in a rapidly changing market. Dustin said he would take the offer under advisement. The next day, the market price rose to $50 a barrel and Dustin sent the supplier a letter late that afternoon accepting the offer at $48 a barrel. The letter arrived in the usual course on Thursday morning, by which time the market price had moved to $56 a barrel. The supplier called Dustin and said it would not accept his order. Dustin insisted that he had a contract. Which of the following is correct?

a. Acceptance took place on dispatch of Dustin's letter.

b. Acceptance did not take place upon dispatch as the offer had already expired.

c. Acceptance did not take place because the only means of acceptance Dustin could use was the phone.

d. Acceptance could only be made by a signed writing.

The correct answer is (b). *(CPA 1181 L-1)*

REQUIRED: The effectiveness of an acceptance of the supplier's offer.

DISCUSSION: When an offer designates no time limit for acceptance, it will lapse within a time reasonable under the circumstances. An oral offer is usually considered to lapse at the end of the conversation (if not accepted) unless the offeror indicates otherwise. Here, the parties indicated the offer would continue but did not agree on an actual duration. In a volatile market, the letter was too slow (from Monday to Thursday).

Answer (a) is incorrect because the offer had expired before dispatch of the letter. Answer (c) is incorrect because Dustin could have used any reasonable means to accept the offer. A contract for the sale of goods is governed by the Uniform Commercial Code. According to UCC 2-206, acceptance may be by any means reasonable in the circumstances if the offer does not specify a mode of acceptance. Answer (d) is incorrect because even though the Statute of Frauds applies to a contract for the sale of goods for $500 or more, an oral acceptance may still be effective unless the offer specifies that it must be written. The Statute of Frauds affects enforceability, not validity.

31. Marcia sent John a telegram offering to sell a certain parcel of land. The undated offer was complete and definite and stated that it was to be held open for 14 days from the date of receipt. The telegram was delayed by the telegraph company for 10 days. Assuming John did not know of the delay, he has

a. 4 days in which to accept.

b. 10 days in which to accept.

c. 14 days in which to accept.

d. A reasonable time to accept.

The correct answer is (c). *(Publisher)*

REQUIRED: The effect of delay in transmission of an offer.

DISCUSSION: The offer did not state a specified time for its termination but instead allowed the offeree 14 days from the date of receipt in which to accept. Given that John did not know of the delay and assuming that he had no reason to know, the life of the offer was extended to 14 days after the date of its actual receipt. If a specified termination date had been given or if John knew or should have known of the delay, the life of the offer would not have been extended even if the delay had been the fault of the offeror.

32. The president of Deal Corp. wrote to Boyd, offering to sell the Deal factory for $300,000. The offer was sent by Deal on June 5 and was received by Boyd on June 9. The offer stated that it would remain open until December 20. The offer

a. Constitutes an enforceable option.

b. May be revoked by Deal any time prior to Boyd's acceptance.

c. Is a firm offer under the UCC but will be irrevocable for only 3 months.

d. Is a firm offer under the UCC because it is in writing.

The correct answer is (b). *(CPA 1188 L-10)*

REQUIRED: The proper interpretation of an offer stating it will be held open for a specified time.

DISCUSSION: Revocation of an offer may be by any method sufficient to give reasonable notice to the offeree. The statement that the offer would be held open was not binding because it was not supported by consideration. Under the UCC, however, a firm offer by a merchant for the sale of goods can be irrevocable.

Answer (a) is incorrect because Boyd gave no consideration to support the promise to keep the offer open. Answers (c) and (d) are incorrect because the UCC's firm offer rule does not apply to a sale of realty.

33. An outstanding offer to sell a tract of real property is terminated at the time the

a. Buyer learns of the seller's death.

b. Seller mails his/her revocation if the original offer was made by mail.

c. Buyer mails a rejection of the offer if the original offer was received by mail.

d. Buyer learns of the sale of the property to a third party.

The correct answer is (d). *(CPA 1174 L-17)*

REQUIRED: The moment an offer to sell property is terminated.

DISCUSSION: An offer to sell property terminates when the offeree learns that the property has been sold to someone else.

Answer (a) is incorrect because the offer is terminated by the offeror's death, not by communication of that fact to the offeree. Answers (b) and (c) are incorrect because revocations and rejections must be received to be effective. Only an acceptance can be effective when mailed or otherwise dispatched.

34. Last year, a series of arsons occurred in the City of Swelter. Early this year, Swelter's City Council adopted this resolution:

> The City will pay $10,000 for the arrest and conviction of anyone guilty of any of the arsons committed here last year.

The resolution was telecast by the city's sole television station once daily for one week. Immediately thereafter the local television station ceased operations. The city's offer will terminate

a. If the City Council by resolution repeals its reward offer.

b. If the City Council by resolution repeals its reward offer and causes this resolution to be broadcast once daily for a week over two local radio stations.

c. Only after the lapse of a reasonable time.

d. Only after the statute of limitations has run.

The correct answer is (b). *(MBE Part I-112)*

REQUIRED: The moment a public offer will terminate.

DISCUSSION: In the absence of a stated period of effectiveness, an offer will terminate after the lapse of a reasonable time or upon effective revocation. Public offers are not different from private offers. The general rule regarding revocation is that offers may be revoked only by actual notice to the offeree. When an offer is transmitted to the public, however, actual notice to every potential offeree is a practical impossibility. Accordingly, the requirement is that revocation be accomplished in the same manner as or in a manner comparable to the publication of the offer.

Answer (a) is incorrect because the revocation must be communicated to the public. Answers (c) and (d) are incorrect because either lapse of time or effective revocation may terminate even a public offer. The duration of the statute of limitations might in some circumstances be deemed a reasonable time.

35. John Love granted Bill Nelson a written option to buy a tract of land in an industrial park. The option stated that it was irrevocable for 11 days and that it was given for $20 and other valuable consideration. The $20 was not paid, and there was no other valuable consideration. Which of the following is a correct statement regarding the option in question?

a. Because real property is involved, Nelson's acceptance must be contained in a signed writing if Nelson is to enforce it against Love.

b. It is an option contract enforceable for the 11-day period.

c. Acceptance must be received at Love's place of business before expiration of the 11 days.

d. It is unenforceable because it lacks consideration.

The correct answer is (d). *(CPA 1183 L-28)*

REQUIRED: The effect on an option of failing to pay the consideration.

DISCUSSION: An option is itself a contract if the necessary elements, including consideration, are present. Revocation before the end of the option period would be a breach of contract permitting the offeree to seek an appropriate remedy. Because the consideration was not paid, however, the offeree cannot enforce the option contract against the offeror.

Answer (a) is incorrect because the written option is sufficient under the Statute of Frauds against Love if he signed it. Only if Nelson is the party sought to be bound would a writing signed by him be required. Answer (b) is incorrect because the consideration was not paid, so the option is not enforceable. Answer (c) is incorrect because if the option had been enforceable, an acceptance by any reasonable means within the stated time would have been effective.

36. Dye sent Hill a written offer to sell a tract of land located in Newtown for $60,000. The parties were engaged in a separate dispute. The offer stated that it would be irrevocable for 60 days if Hill would promise to refrain from suing Dye during this time. Hill promptly delivered a promise not to sue during the term of the offer and to forgo suit if Hill accepted the offer. Dye subsequently decided that the possible suit by Hill was groundless and therefore phoned Hill and revoked the offer 15 days after making it. Hill mailed an acceptance on the 20th day. Dye did not reply. Under the circumstances,

a. Dye's offer was supported by consideration and was not revocable when accepted.

b. Dye's written offer would be irrevocable even without consideration.

c. Dye's silence was an acceptance of Hill's promise.

d. Dye's revocation, not being in writing, was invalid.

The correct answer is (a). *(CPA 589 L-24)*

REQUIRED: The effect of a promise to keep an offer open if the offeree promised to forgo a lawsuit.

DISCUSSION: Hill's prompt promise not to sue during the term of the offer created an option contract. That is, Hill's forbearance of a legal right was consideration for Dye's promise not to revoke the offer for 60 days. Consequently, Dye's attempted revocation was ineffective, and Hill's acceptance within the 60-day period resulted in a contract.

Answer (b) is incorrect because an offer to sell realty is not irrevocable solely because it is in writing. Answer (c) is incorrect because Dye's silence was legally irrelevant because Hill's actions were sufficient to establish a contract. Answer (d) is incorrect because a written revocation would likewise have been invalid.

37. Ann Mayer wrote Tom Jackson and offered to sell Jackson a building for $50,000. The offer stated it would expire 30 days from July 1. Mayer changed her mind and does not wish to be bound by the offer. If a legal dispute arises between the parties regarding whether there has been a valid acceptance of the offer, which of the following is correct?

a. The offer cannot be legally withdrawn for the stated period of time.

b. The offer will not expire prior to the 30 days even if Mayer sells the property to a third person and notifies Jackson.

c. If Jackson phoned Mayer on August 1 and unequivocally accepted the offer, a contract would be formed, provided Jackson had no notice of withdrawal of the offer.

d. If Jackson categorically rejects the offer on July 10th, Jackson cannot validly accept within the remaining stated period of time.

The correct answer is (d). *(CPA 1178 L-29)*

REQUIRED: The correct statement as to termination of an offer.

DISCUSSION: A rejection of an offer terminates the offer. An offeree cannot accept an offer after rejecting it. An attempted acceptance after rejection is a new offer.

Answer (a) is incorrect because the offer may be legally withdrawn at any time prior to acceptance even though it states it will be held open for a specified period. It is not a "firm offer" under the UCC because it is not for a sale of goods. Answer (b) is incorrect because notice to the offeree of sale of the property to a third person has the effect of terminating the offer. Answer (c) is incorrect because an acceptance on August 1st would be ineffective. The time limit for acceptance expires on July 31.

38. Which of the following statements concerning the effectiveness of an offeree's rejection and an offeror's revocation of an offer is ordinarily correct?

	An Offeree's Rejection is Effective When	An Offeror's Revocation is Effective When
a.	Received by offeror	Sent by offeror
b.	Sent by offeree	Received by offeree
c.	Sent by offeree	Sent by offeror
d.	Received by offeror	Received by offeree

The correct answer is (d). *(CPA 589 L-22)*

REQUIRED: The true statements about the effectiveness of an offeree's rejection and an offeror's revocation of an offer.

DISCUSSION: The rule in most jurisdictions is that a revocation of an offer is effective when received by the offeree. Receipt occurs when the revocation comes into possession of the offeree or his/her agent, or when it is delivered to his/her office. Similarly, a rejection must actually be received to be effective. Only an acceptance can be effective upon dispatch.

39. On January 1, Lemon wrote Gina Martin offering to sell Martin a ranch for $80,000 cash. Lemon's letter indicated that the offer would remain open until February 15 if Martin mailed $100 by January 10. On January 5, Martin mailed $100 to Lemon. On January 30, Martin telephoned Lemon stating that she would be willing to pay $60,000 for the ranch. Lemon refused to sell at that price and immediately placed the ranch on the open market. On February 6, Martin mailed Lemon a letter accepting the original offer to buy the ranch at $80,000. The following day, Lemon received Martin's acceptance. At that time the ranch was on the market for $100,000. Which of the following is correct?

a. Martin's mailing of $100 to Lemon on January 5 failed to create an option.

b. Martin's communication on January 30 automatically terminated Lemon's offer of January 1.

c. The placing of the ranch on the market by Lemon constituted an effective revocation of the offer of January 1.

d. Martin's letter of February 6 formed a binding contract based on the original terms of Lemon's January 1 letter.

The correct answer is (d). *(CPA 1184 L-19)*

REQUIRED: The effect of a counteroffer when an option contract exists.

DISCUSSION: Martin's telephone call was a counteroffer because it varied the price term of the offer. Although a counteroffer normally is a rejection of the offer, the option contract was not affected. Martin could still accept under the terms of the option. Furthermore, even an outright rejection would not terminate the option unless the principle of estoppel applies.

Answer (a) is incorrect because mailing the $100 by January 10 furnished the consideration necessary to enforce the promise to hold the option open. Answer (b) is incorrect because the telephone call did not affect Lemon's contractual obligation to hold the offer open. Answer (c) is incorrect because Lemon had no power to rescind the contract unilaterally.

40. Baker Corporation sent a letter to Sampson Company in which Baker offered to purchase 10 acres of certain real estate from Sampson for $4,000. Sampson responded that it would sell 8 of these acres for that price. Baker and Sampson have created

a. A contract for sale of 8 acres for $4,000.

b. A contract for sale of 10 acres for $4,000.

c. A contract to sell 8 acres for $3,200.

d. No contract in this connection.

The correct answer is (d). *(CPA 576 L-6)*

REQUIRED: The effect of the differing statements about the quantity term.

DISCUSSION: The response to the offer contained a different term, thus constituting a counteroffer rather than an acceptance. There is no contract unless Baker accepts Sampson's counteroffer. Under common law, any variation of an offer by the offeree would prevent an acceptance, especially if the variation is material. Differences in quantity and price are material.

Answers (a), (b), and (c) are incorrect because no contract exists.

41. Beal offered in writing to sell Crane a parcel of land for $150,000. If Beal dies, the offer will

a. Automatically terminate prior to Crane's acceptance.

b. Automatically terminate despite Crane's prior acceptance.

c. Terminate prior to Crane's acceptance only if Crane received notice of Beal's death.

d. Remain open for a reasonable period of time after Beal's death.

The correct answer is (a). *(CPA 587 L-12)*

REQUIRED: The legal effect of the offeror's death.

DISCUSSION: The offeror's death or insanity terminates the offer and deprives the offeree of the power to accept even if (s)he has no reason to know of the event. The offeree's death or insanity also terminates the offer.

Answer (b) is incorrect because the decedent's estate continues to be liable on any nonpersonal contracts. A personal contract is terminated because performance would be impossible. Hence, Crane's prior acceptance of the offer to sell land would bind Beal's estate. Answers (c) and (d) are incorrect because the offer is terminated by the offeror's death, not by the receipt of notice by the offeree.

42. An offer is not terminated by operation of law solely because the

a. Offeror dies.

b. Offeree is adjudicated insane.

c. Subject matter is destroyed.

d. Subject matter is sold to a third party.

The correct answer is (d). *(CPA 589 L-23)*

REQUIRED: The event that does not terminate an offer by operation of law.

DISCUSSION: Certain events automatically terminate an offer prior to acceptance: the incapacity (death or adjudicated insanity) of either party, destruction of the subject matter, and supervening illegality. But sale of the subject does not automatically terminate the offer. The offeree must receive actual notice of the sale before it can be effective as a revocation. Thus, an offeree who has not received such notice may nevertheless bind an offeror by a valid acceptance made after the sale of the subject matter to a third party.

43. Barnes was holding an annual auction at his farm to sell tools, animals, and leftover crops. Adams showed up at the auction and saw a plow among the merchandise which she wanted to buy very much. Adams bid $50 for the plow, but no one bid against her. The auctioneer did not accept Adams' bid and stated that the plow would not be sold for such a low price.

a. Adams' bid constituted an acceptance which formed a valid contract.

b. Adams' bid was only an offer.

c. The plow could not be withdrawn from the auction.

d. There must be two bids before property can no longer be withdrawn from an auction.

The correct answer is (b). *(Publisher)*

REQUIRED: The correct statement concerning the sale of goods at an auction.

DISCUSSION: Putting property up for auction is an invitation to negotiate. The purchasers make offers by bidding. The auctioneer accepts an offer by the falling of the hammer or an announcement that the property is sold. Adams' bid was only an offer, so no contract was formed.

Answer (a) is incorrect because the bid is only an offer which need not be accepted by the auctioneer. Answer (c) is incorrect because property subject to an auction can be withdrawn at any time prior to acceptance of a bid unless the auction was "without reserve." If an auction is "without reserve," property may not be withdrawn and the highest bid must be accepted after the auction has begun. Answer (d) is incorrect because whether there is one bid or many is irrelevant.

11.3 Acceptance

44. An agreement is an essential element of a contract. Ordinarily, the required mutual assent is achieved by means of an offer and an acceptance. Acceptance

a. Requires a subjective intent to accept.

b. Is never accomplished by silence.

c. Requires manifestation of an intent to accept.

d. May ordinarily be made by anyone with knowledge of the offer.

The correct answer is (c). *(Publisher)*

REQUIRED: The correct statement about accomplishing an acceptance.

DISCUSSION: Mutual assent requires that a valid offer be accepted by the intended offeree in a manner stipulated by the offeror. The overt manifestation of the offeree's assent should signify an intent to accept. For example, performance of an act requested by an offer does not result in a contract if the offeree had not yet learned of the offer.

Answer (a) is incorrect because acceptance requires an objective intent to accept, not subjective. Answer (b) is incorrect because silence may be an effective method of acceptance in cases in which both parties understand it as such. Answer (d) is incorrect because only the intended offeree may accept. There is no mutual assent unless both parties agree to contract.

45. Flaxx, a sales representative of Dome Home Sites, Inc., escorted Mr. and Mrs. Grand through several acres of Dome's proposed subdivision and showed the Grands various one-acre lots for sale at $27,000 each. Upon conclusion of the tour, the Grands expressed interest in purchasing a lot in the near future. Flaxx urged them to show their good faith and sign a letter of intent, which stated, "We, the undersigned, having decided to purchase a lot from Dome Home Sites in the future, deliver to the corporation's agent one hundred dollars ($100) earnest money." This was signed by the Grands at the bottom of the form and the $100 was delivered to Flaxx by the Grands. Under the circumstances,

a. The Grands have made an offer to buy a lot from Dome.

b. If all the lots are sold by Dome, the Grands have a cause of action for breach of contract.

c. If no deal is consummated, the Grands have the right to the return of $100.

d. The $100 constitutes liquidated damages and will be forfeited in the event the Grands do not purchase a lot.

The correct answer is (c). *(CPA 1183 L-27)*

REQUIRED: The contractual implications of giving earnest money.

DISCUSSION: Earnest money is a deposit paid by a buyer to show good faith and to bind a seller to his/her obligation. Often, earnest money is treated as liquidated damages if the buyer breaches the agreement. The Grands, however, did not have a contract with Dome. Their undertaking to purchase a lot in the future did not constitute an offer that could have been accepted because it was not reasonably definite and complete. For instance, it did not specify such vital terms as the lot to be purchased or the financing terms. In the absence of a contract, therefore, no breach could have occurred, and Dome could not have been entitled to damages. The Grands have a right to the $100.

Answer (a) is incorrect because the undertaking by the Grands was not an offer. It was not reasonably definite and complete. Answer (b) is incorrect because in the absence of a valid offer, no contract was formed and Dome could not be held liable. Answer (d) is incorrect because no contract was formed and the Grands could not be held liable.

46. Able made a public offer of a reward for information leading to the arrest of a murderer. Without knowledge of the reward, Baker furnished information to the police that resulted in solving the crime. Which is true?

a. Baker accepted the unilateral offer by performing the required action and should collect.

b. Baker cannot collect because acceptance of an offer requires knowledge of its existence.

c. Baker should collect because Able was benefited by Baker's action.

d. Baker should collect because all citizens have constructive knowledge of a public offer.

The correct answer is (b). *(Publisher)*

REQUIRED: The outcome when a reward is claimed by one who unknowingly met its terms.

DISCUSSION: Able's obligation to pay was based on the offer. For the offer to be binding, however, it had to be accepted. Because acceptance required knowledge of the offer, Baker's performance of the required action was not a proper acceptance, and Baker thus has no right to recover.

Answers (a) and (c) are incorrect because to recover, Baker would have had to perform the desired action with the intent to accept. Answer (d) is incorrect because actual knowledge of the offer is required. Constructive knowledge is imputed by operation of law when actual communication is impracticable. For example, everyone is presumed to have knowledge of the law and of documents filed in public records.

47. An offer may be accepted

a. By an assignee of the designated offeree.

b. Only by a specific individual named in the offer.

c. By anyone who learns of its existence prior to acceptance by the designated offeree.

d. Only by the designated offeree.

The correct answer is (d). *(Publisher)*

REQUIRED: The person(s) who may accept an offer.

DISCUSSION: The offeror has the right to specify who may accept the offer. When an offer designates a specific offeree, only that person may accept. When an offer designates a specific group of offerees, only members of that group may accept. Some offers, however, may be extended to the general public.

Answers (a) and (c) are incorrect because an offer can be accepted only by a person who is designated as an offeree by the offeror. It may not be assigned. Answer (b) is incorrect because offers may be made to the members of a group, to the general public, or to persons that are not individuals, such as corporations.

48. Justin made an offer to pay Benson $1,000 if Benson would perform as a magician at his son's birthday party. Acceptance of Justin's offer occurs when Benson

a. Promises to perform.

b. Prepares to perform.

c. Promises to perform and begins preliminary performance.

d. Completes the performance.

The correct answer is (d). *(CPA 583 L-8)*

REQUIRED: The moment that an offer for a unilateral contract is accepted.

DISCUSSION: Justin's offer requested an act (performance) rather than a promise and was thus unilateral. Completing or at least substantially performing the required act is the only means of acceptance.

Answer (a) is incorrect because an act is requested, not a promise. Answers (b) and (c) are incorrect because either completion or substantial performance of the act is needed for acceptance.

49. On December 3, Joncie posted a letter to Stumos offering to buy her stereo for $1,000 upon her delivering it to Joncie's home on or before December 24. Stumos immediately sent a letter to Joncie accepting the offer and promising to make delivery. What is the significance of the letter sent by Stumos?

a. Joncie could revoke the offer after receiving the letter.

b. The parties formed a bilateral contract upon receipt.

c. The parties formed a unilateral contract upon dispatch.

d. The letter was effective as a notice of performance by the offeree.

The correct answer is (a). *(Publisher)*

REQUIRED: The effect of responding with a letter of acceptance to an offer to purchase upon receipt of the goods.

DISCUSSION: The offer by Joncie was to enter into a unilateral contract (a promise to pay for the act of delivery to a specified place by a given time). Because the letter of acceptance did not conform to the offer (a unilateral offer cannot be accepted by a promise), it was not effective and would not prevent revocation. It was effective only as a counteroffer.

Answers (b) and (c) are incorrect because an offer to enter into a unilateral contract can be accepted only by performing the requested act. Answer (d) is incorrect because in general, notice of completed performance is not required unless stipulated in the offer. However, an offeree may need to give notice if the performance is not likely to come to the offeror's attention within a reasonable time. In any event, the letter contained only a promise to perform, not notice of completed performance.

50. Under common law, an acceptance of an offer for a bilateral contract is effective

a. Even though it adds to or subtracts from the terms of the offer.

b. Only if it is the mirror image of the offer.

c. Only if it is expressed in words.

d. Even though it alters or qualifies a term of the offer.

The correct answer is (b). *(Publisher)*

REQUIRED: The true statement about effectiveness of an acceptance of a bilateral offer.

DISCUSSION: The common law rules regarding acceptance apply to all transactions except those governed by the UCC provisions related to sales of goods. Under common law, the acceptance of a bilateral offer may not add to, subtract from, alter, or qualify any term in the acceptance. An acceptance that departs from the offer is conditional or a "counteroffer" and creates no contract. UCC 2-207 permits an acceptance that contains additional or different terms for a contract for the sale of goods.

51. Jackson paid Brady $100 for a 90-day option to purchase Brady's 160-acre farm for $32,000. The option agreement was in writing and signed by both parties. The agreement referred only to the option, its period, a legal description of the farm, and the purchase price. Jackson wrote Brady 30 days later: "I hereby exercise my option to purchase your farm for $32,000 subject to closing details to be worked out by you and my attorney." Jackson's letter

a. Rejects Brady's offer and terminates the option agreement.

b. Accepts Brady's offer leaving customary details to be worked out during formalization of the contract.

c. Accepts Brady's offer leaving a matter to be negotiated during formalization of the contract.

d. Has no effect on the option agreement.

The correct answer is (b). *(CPA 1173 L-4)*

REQUIRED: The effect of an acceptance of an offer to sell real property subject to working out details of closing.

DISCUSSION: Jackson's letter exercising the option effectively accepts the offer. The letter does not state additional or different terms from those contemplated by the offer so it is not a counteroffer. The details of closing can be left to be worked out later without affecting the validity of the contract.

Answer (a) is incorrect because the letter operates as an effective acceptance. Even if it operated as a rejection, the letter would not terminate the option because consideration had been given to hold it open for 90 days. Answer (c) is incorrect because acceptance was made and no additional matters are to be negotiated, only a few closing details to be worked out. Answer (d) is incorrect because the acceptance represents an exercise of the option and therefore terminates it.

52. Foster offered to sell Fred Lebow a garage for $27,000. The offer was in writing and signed by Foster. Foster gave Lebow 5 days to decide. On the fourth day Foster accepted a better offer from Dilby, who was unaware of the offer to Lebow. Foster subsequently conveyed the property to Dilby. Unaware of the sale to Dilby, Lebow telephoned Foster on the fifth day and unconditionally accepted the offer. Under the circumstances, Lebow

a. Is entitled to specific performance by Foster.

b. Has no rights against Foster.

c. Is entitled to damages.

d. Can obtain specific performance by Dilby upon depositing in court the $27,000 he agreed to pay.

The correct answer is (c). *(CPA 582 L-13)*

REQUIRED: The rights of an offeree after the offeror sells the property to another person.

DISCUSSION: Lebow validly accepted the written offer by phone before it lapsed and before it was revoked. Foster's sale of the garage to Dilby on the fourth day would have revoked the offer if it had been actually communicated to Lebow prior to acceptance. Because Lebow did not know of the revocation by sale, however, he retained the ability to form a contract. A valid contract was formed, and Lebow is entitled to damages for Foster's breach (nonperformance).

Answer (a) is incorrect because Foster no longer has the property and cannot perform. Answer (b) is incorrect because Lebow does have rights against Foster under the contract. Answer (d) is incorrect because Dilby was an innocent purchaser for value and thus would take the property free of any claim by Lebow.

53. The mailbox rule ordinarily makes acceptance of an offer effective at the time the acceptance is dispatched. The mailbox rule does not apply if

a. Both the offeror and offeree are merchants.

b. The offer proposes a sale of real estate.

c. The offer provides that an acceptance shall not be effective until actually received.

d. The duration of the offer is not excess of 3 months.

The correct answer is (c). *(CPA 1189 L-9)*

REQUIRED: The circumstance in which the mailbox rule is inapplicable.

DISCUSSION: Acceptance is effective upon dispatch by the offeree by the same mode of communication used for transmittal of the offer. This mode of transmission is impliedly authorized by the offeror. If the contract is for the sale of goods, the UCC provides that acceptance may be by any means reasonable under the circumstances and will be effective upon dispatch. The UCC rule is also gaining acceptance under the common law. However, the effects of the mailbox rule can be avoided if the offeror stipulates the moment when acceptance will be effective.

Answer (a) is incorrect because whether the parties are merchants often affects their rights and duties regarding sales of goods, but neither the common law nor the UCC exempts merchants from the mailbox rule. Answer (b) is incorrect because the rule applies whether the subject matter is personalty or realty. Answer (d) is incorrect because whether an acceptance is effective on dispatch or receipt is a function of what method is authorized, not the duration of the offer.

54. On April 2, Bonn & Co., CPAs mailed Marble Corp. a signed proposal to perform certain accounting services for Marble provided Marble accepts the proposal by April 30. Under the circumstances,

a. If Marble accepts by telephone on April 30, no contract will be formed between the parties.

b. Marble must accept the Bonn proposal in writing in order to form a contract.

c. A contract will be formed between the parties if Marble mails an acceptance to Bonn on April 29, even if it is not received by Bonn until May 3.

d. Bonn may not withdraw its proposal prior to May 1.

The correct answer is (c). *(CPA 587 L-11)*

REQUIRED: The legal effect of mailing an offer stating a definite period for acceptance.

DISCUSSION: Unless the offer specifies otherwise, acceptance is effective upon dispatch by the offeree by the same mode of communication used for transmittal of the offer. This mode of transmission is impliedly authorized by the offeror. If a contract is for the sale of goods, not the rendition of services, the UCC provides that acceptance may be by any means reasonable under the circumstances and will be effective upon dispatch. The UCC rule is also gaining acceptance under the common law and thus is applicable in some states even though the UCC does not govern the contract. Accordingly, in those states, acceptance by telegram or another reasonable method other than the mail may also be effective upon dispatch.

Answer (a) is incorrect because unless the offer specified another means of acceptance, a telephone call within the stated period is effective to create a contract. An acceptance by a means other than that impliedly (as opposed to explicitly) authorized is effective on receipt according to traditional common law principles. Answer (b) is incorrect because absent an explicitly designated means of acceptance, Marble's acceptance by any reasonable method will be effective on dispatch in jurisdictions adhering to the UCC rule. Otherwise, an acceptance by an unauthorized method will be effective upon receipt. Thus, although Bonn has impliedly authorized acceptance by mail, Marble may accept in other ways. Answer (d) is incorrect because Bonn's offer to permit acceptance by April 30 is unsupported by consideration and does not constitute a firm offer, so it may be revoked at any time.

55. Able Sofa, Inc. sent Noll a letter offering to sell Noll a custom-made sofa for $5,000. Noll immediately sent a telegram to Able purporting to accept the offer. However, the telegraph company erroneously delivered the telegram to Abel Soda, Inc. Three days later, Able mailed a letter of revocation to Noll that was received by Noll. Able refused to sell Noll the sofa. Noll sued Able for breach of contract. Able

a. Would have been liable under the deposited acceptance rule only if Noll had accepted by mail.

b. Will avoid liability because it revoked its offer prior to receiving Noll's acceptance.

c. Will be liable for breach of contract.

d. Will avoid liability because of the telegraph company's error.

The correct answer is (c). *(CPA 586 L-2)*

REQUIRED: The effect of an acceptance lost by the transmitting agency.

DISCUSSION: Assuming the offer did not specify a means of acceptance, the contract was formed when Noll sent the acceptance by telegraph. If the contract is for the sale of goods (a sofa), acceptance may be by any means reasonable under the circumstances and will be effective upon dispatch (UCC 2-206). This rule is gaining acceptance under common law also. A properly dispatched acceptance is effective upon dispatch and the risk of its loss or delay is on the offeror. Hence, the negligence of the telegraph company does not excuse the offeror's failure to perform.

Answer (a) is incorrect because the UCC's deposited acceptance rule permitted Noll to accept by any reasonable means. Able Sofa did not specify the means of acceptance. Answer (b) is incorrect because the attempted revocation came after the acceptance was effective. Answer (d) is incorrect because the offeror bears the risk that the transmitting agency may lose or delay the acceptance.

Questions 56 and 57 are based on the following information. On April 2, Jet Co. wrote to Ard, offering to buy Ard's building for $350,000. The offer contained all of the essential terms to form a binding contract and was duly signed by Jet's president. It further provided that the offer would remain open until May 30 and an acceptance would not be effective until received by Jet. On April 10, Ard accepted Jet's offer by mail. The acceptance was received by Jet on April 14.

56. For this item only, assume that on April 11 Jet sent a telegram to Ard revoking its offer and that Ard received the telegram on April 12. Under the circumstances,

a. A contract was formed on April 10.

b. A contract was formed on April 14.

c. Jet's revocation effectively terminated its offer on April 12.

d. Jet's revocation effectively terminated its offer on April 11.

The correct answer is (c). *(CPA 1188 L-11)*

REQUIRED: The outcome when an acceptance and a revocation are attempted.

DISCUSSION: The offer expressly stated that an acceptance would be effective only upon receipt. The acceptance was received on April 14. However, Jet's revocation was effective when received by the offeree on April 12. Thus, the offer had been terminated before the acceptance could have formed a contract.

Answer (a) is incorrect because the offer stated that receipt was necessary for an acceptance to be effective, and the offer was terminated prior to receipt on April 14. Answer (b) is incorrect because the offer was terminated on April 12. Answer (d) is incorrect because revocation occurred on April 12, the time of receipt.

57. For this item only, assume that on April 13 Ard sent a telegram to Jet withdrawing the acceptance and rejecting Jet's offer and that Jet received the telegram on April 15. Under the circumstances,

a. A contract was formed on April 14.

b. A contract was formed on April 10.

c. Ard's rejection effectively terminated Jet's offer on April 13.

d. Ard's rejection effectively terminated Jet's offer on April 15.

The correct answer is (a). *(CPA 1188 L-12)*

REQUIRED: The legal effect of sending a rejection and an acceptance.

DISCUSSION: The offer stipulated that an acceptance would be effective only upon receipt, an event that occurred on April 14. A rejection is also effective only upon receipt. But because the acceptance formed a contract on April 14, the receipt of the rejection on April 15 had no effect.

Answer (b) is incorrect because the offer specified that acceptance would be effective on receipt, not dispatched. Answer (c) is incorrect because a rejection is effective, if at all, on the date of receipt. Answer (d) is incorrect because the rejection had no effect because a contract had already been formed.

58. On July 1, Silk, Inc., sent Blue a telegram offering to sell Blue a building for $80,000. In the telegram, Silk stated that it would give Blue 30 days to accept the offer. On July 15, Blue sent Silk a telegram that included the following statement: "The price for your building seems too high. Would you consider taking $75,000?" This telegram was received by Silk on July 16. On July 19, Tint made an offer to Silk to purchase the building for $82,000. Upon learning of Tint's offer, Blue, on July 27, sent Silk a signed letter agreeing to purchase the building for $80,000. This letter was received by Silk on July 29. However, Silk now refuses to sell Blue the building. If Blue commences an action against Silk for breach of contract, Blue will

a. Win, because Blue effectively accepted Silk's offer of July 1.

b. Win, because Silk was obligated to keep the offer open for the 30-day period.

c. Lose, because Blue sent the July 15 telegram.

d. Lose, because Blue used an unauthorized means of communication.

The correct answer is (a). *(CPA 588 L-17)*

REQUIRED: The outcome when the offeree has made both an inquiry about terms and an acceptance.

DISCUSSION: An attempt by the offeree to add terms to or change the offer serves as a rejection (and counteroffer) that terminates the offer. But if Blue's telegram is construed as a mere inquiry about terms, the offer would not have terminated on July 16. Thus, it would still have been effective when the acceptance was received by the offeror on July 29, a date within the 30-day acceptance period. This interpretation is reasonable because the telegram is tentative and does not indicate a definite intent to reject the offer. In other words, Blue was still considering the offer. Also, Blue's knowledge of Tint's offer did not revoke the offer. Only a sale to Tint communicated to Blue prior to acceptance would have revoked the offer. Hence, Blue should prevail because it validly accepted an offer that had not terminated by lapse of time, rejection, or revocation.

Answer (b) is incorrect because Silk received no consideration to keep the offer open. Answer (c) is incorrect because if the telegram was an inquiry rather than a counteroffer, it did not terminate the offer. Answer (d) is incorrect because the mail is a reasonable means of acceptance if no method was stipulated by the offeror.

59. In which of the following instances will silence by the offeree constitute acceptance?

a. The offeror stated that silence would constitute an acceptance and the offeree intended to reject the offer but forgot.

b. During the course of prior business dealing, the offeree has always sent a rejection if the items were not wanted. The offeror always shipped the items if such a rejection was not received.

c. An offeree receives unordered goods in the mail along with a letter from the sender that the offeree must return them if they are not wanted.

d. The offeree tells the offeror that (s)he will accept or reject the next morning. (S)he intends to reject but fails to respond to the offeror.

The correct answer is (b). *(Publisher)*

REQUIRED: The instance in which silence will constitute an acceptance.

DISCUSSION: There are few times when silence will constitute an acceptance of an offer. Some surrounding facts or circumstances must indicate that the offeree intended silence as an acceptance. A prior course of business dealing might furnish the required inference that silence was intended as acceptance.

Answer (a) is incorrect because the offeror cannot require the offeree to respond to avoid a contract. Answer (c) is incorrect because unordered goods received in the mail may be retained by the recipient without any obligation to pay. Answer (d) is incorrect because silence will only constitute an acceptance if it was so intended by the offeree. If the offeree retains goods and uses them for his/her benefit, however, silence plus the use of goods can constitute an acceptance.

60. In August, the Rayville City Commission voted to renew Jay B. Jordan's contract as City Manager for 1 year. Jordan was present at the meeting and thanked the Commission members for their support as he had done the preceding year. In September, the motion was rescinded before a contract had been drafted and signed. Jordan, who had not sought other employment in the interim between the two motions, brought suit.

a. Rayville will win because no writing was signed.

b. Rayville will win because Jordan failed to manifest an unequivocal acceptance.

c. Jordan will win because the parties evidently intended to be bound before a writing was signed.

d. Jordan will win because the preparation and signature of a writing have no bearing on the existence of the agreement.

The correct answer is (c). *(Publisher)*

REQUIRED: The outcome of an action on an oral agreement repudiated by one of the parties.

DISCUSSION: The parties to an oral agreement may contemplate the preparation and signing of a written contract. The question is whether a contract comes into being when the oral agreement is reached or when the writing is signed. The answer depends upon the intent of the parties as inferred from all the circumstances. The facts suggest that the parties intended to be bound prior to the drafting of a memorial of the agreement.

Answer (a) is incorrect because an employment contract need not be written. Answer (b) is incorrect because acceptance of a bilateral offer is not dependent on particular words or actions. Jordan's words and actions support an inference that he intended to accept. Answer (d) is incorrect because the preparation and signature of a writing indicate an agreement, but a signed document is not necessary to the formation of an employment contract that can be performed within 1 year.

61. Tom Payne has a terrible toothache one day and stops by Quick Fix Dentist during Payne's lunch hour. Although Payne has never been to Quick Fix before, Fix accepts Payne as a patient and pulls a tooth. On Payne's way out, the receptionist hands him a bill for $500. Payne is outraged and claims that a contract was never formed.

a. Payne is not liable because he never made an offer for Quick Fix to accept.

b. Payne is not liable because he never accepted any offer that may have been made by Quick Fix.

c. Payne is liable for the $500 because he accepted Quick Fix's services.

d. Payne is only liable for a reasonable amount determined by what other dentists in the area charge.

The correct answer is (d). *(Publisher)*

REQUIRED: The correct statement concerning liability for accepting services without an express agreement about the cost.

DISCUSSION: A person who accepts the services of another known to be in the business of providing services for a fee is liable for the reasonable value of such services. This is an implied contract; i.e., the intent of the parties is inferred from the circumstances. The reasonable value is measured by what others in the locality charge, i.e., the market price.

Answers (a) and (b) are incorrect because although it is not clear who is implied to have made the offer and the acceptance, either Payne or Quick Fix has made an offer and the other an acceptance. Answer (c) is incorrect because Payne is liable for $500 only if it is a reasonable amount based on charges by other dentists in the area.

11.4 Consideration

62. In deciding whether consideration necessary to form a contract exists, a court must determine whether

a. The consideration given by each party is of roughly equal value.

b. There is mutuality of consideration.

c. The consideration has sufficient monetary value.

d. The consideration conforms to the subjective intent of the parties.

The correct answer is (b). *(CPA 588 L-18)*

REQUIRED: The correct statement regarding consideration.

DISCUSSION: An essential aspect of consideration is that it be bargained for and given in exchange for the consideration provided by the other party. This means that the consideration is mutual because each party is bargaining for something.

Answers (a) and (c) are incorrect because consideration may be unreasonable, disproportionate, inadequate, or unfair as long as it is mutual and properly bargained for. Only unequal exchanges of money or fungible goods or other unconscionable agreements will be found inadequate to support a contract if no other consideration exists. Also, a promise supported by mere nominal consideration (e.g., "$1 and other valuable consideration") may be treated as a gift unless it was truly bargained for. Answer (d) is incorrect because courts do not look to the subjective intent of the parties when determining whether the elements of a contract are present. Instead, they are concerned only with the external or objective manifestations of the parties' intent.

63. In order to be valid, consideration must

a. Be stated in the contract.

b. Be based upon a legal obligation as opposed to a moral obligation.

c. Be performed simultaneously by the parties.

d. Have a monetary value.

The correct answer is (b). *(CPA 1176 L-36)*

REQUIRED: The correct statement regarding valid consideration.

DISCUSSION: Legal and moral obligations are not synonymous. Moral obligations are insufficient as legal consideration; e.g., one ought to keep a promise, but the law will not enforce it absent some consideration beyond an ethical duty. A legal obligation, however, is sufficient legal consideration because the obligor is bound by law to carry out the obligation.

Answer (a) is incorrect because consideration may be implied and not expressed in the contract. Answer (c) is incorrect because simultaneous rendering or receipt of consideration is unnecessary; e.g., an offer frequently contains a promise conditioned on the acceptance of the contract by the offeree. Answer (d) is incorrect because only a legal benefit to the promisee or a legal detriment incurred by the promisor is required, not monetary value.

64. Lydia promised to pay Lavinia $10,000 if she refrained from smoking for 1 year. Lavinia refrained and brought suit when Lydia failed to pay. Who will win?

a. Lydia will win because she received no actual benefit.

b. Lydia will win because Lavinia incurred no actual detriment.

c. Lydia will win because Lavinia incurred no legal detriment.

d. Lavinia will win because Lydia received a legal benefit.

The correct answer is (d). *(Publisher)*

REQUIRED: The outcome of a suit turning upon whether forbearance from an act is consideration.

DISCUSSION: A unilateral contract was formed when the promisee refrained from performing an act that she had a legal right to perform, i.e., smoking for 1 year. The promise to pay thus became enforceable because it was supported by consideration that constituted a legal detriment to the promisee (forbearing to smoke). The consideration also may be viewed as a legal benefit to the promisor because she obtained a forbearance to which she had no previous legal right.

Answers (a) and (b) are incorrect because consideration is legally sufficient if the promisor receives a legal rather than actual benefit or if the promisee incurs a legal rather than actual detriment. Answer (c) is incorrect because Lavinia gave up a legal right.

65. For there to be consideration for a contract, there must be

a. A bargained-for detriment to the promisor(ee) or a benefit to the promisee(or).

b. A manifestation of mutual assent.

c. Genuineness of assent.

d. Substantially equal economic benefits to both parties.

The correct answer is (a). *(CPA 1189 L-10)*

REQUIRED: The element necessary for consideration to exist.

DISCUSSION: The consideration provided by one party (the promisee) to support the enforceability of the other party's (the promisor's) promise may consist of a bargained-for legal detriment to the promisee or legal benefit to the promisor. For example, if A promises to run a marathon if B promises to donate a certain sum to a specified charity and B agrees, each is both a promisor and promisee. Each can also be viewed as incurring a legal detriment and being entitled to a legal benefit.

Answers (b) and (c) are incorrect because mutual genuine assent is an element of a contract distinct from consideration. Answer (d) is incorrect because courts seldom inquire into the adequacy or equality of consideration unless the bargain is clearly unconscionable.

66. Harry promised to sell his bubblegum card collection to Harriet who promised to pay $1,000. After Harriet tendered payment, Harry reneged on his promise, so Harriet filed suit. Which of the following is correct?

a. The consideration for Harry's promise is both a legal detriment to Harriet and a legal benefit to him.

b. This is a unilateral contract so only Harry is bound.

c. Harriet cannot enforce Harry's promise because she neither incurred a legal detriment nor received a legal benefit.

d. In a bilateral contract, each party is bound only if each both receives a legal benefit and incurs a legal detriment.

The correct answer is (a). *(Publisher)*

REQUIRED: The true statement about the consideration requirement in a contract involving mutual promises.

DISCUSSION: The contract is bilateral because each party has made a promise. Each is therefore both a promisor and a promisee. The consideration necessary to support the enforceability of a promise may consist either of a legal detriment to the promisee or a legal benefit to the promisor. Both will usually be found but either is legally sufficient. For example, Harriet's promise to pay is a legal detriment to her because she had no prior obligation to pay $1,000. It is also a legal benefit to Harry because he had no prior legal right to the money.

Answer (b) is incorrect because this is a bilateral contract and both parties are bound. Answer (c) is incorrect because Harriet incurred a detriment by becoming obligated to pay $1,000. She received a benefit because she obtained a right to the collection. Answer (d) is incorrect because the promisor is bound when either the promisee incurs a legal detriment or the promisor receives a legal benefit. Both are not needed.

67. Theodore agreed to pay Hal Hays, the owner of a grocery store, $50 if Hays would send a $100 gift certificate, identifying Theodore as the donor, to a recipient chosen randomly from a phone book. Hays mailed the gift certificate. Which of the following is correct?

a. The gift recipient is liable to Theodore for $50.

b. Theodore is liable to Hays for $100, the value of the gift certificate.

c. Theodore is not required to pay Hays because Theodore received no value.

d. Theodore's promise to pay is supported by consideration.

The correct answer is (d). *(J. Pittman)*

REQUIRED: The proper application of common law mutual assent and consideration rules.

DISCUSSION: A bilateral exchange of promises will be enforceable if each promise is supported by consideration. Each party must incur a bargained-for detriment. Here, Theodore and Hays each incurred a detriment in promising to do something he was not otherwise obligated to do. The contract is enforceable under its express terms.

Answer (a) is incorrect because a gift recipient is not legally obligated to the gift donor. Answer (b) is incorrect because the express provisions of the contract called for payment of $50. Answer (c) is incorrect because the law does not require the consideration to flow directly to the contract parties.

68. Gus Parker owned a race horse that had not made a good showing in the last 10 races. Disgusted with the horse, Parker stated that he would sell the horse for $1.00. Sam Hood was in the group to whom Parker was speaking and immediately said that he would accept the horse for $1.00. Parker agreed to accept $1.00 after the afternoon's race in which Parker was obligated to participate. In the afternoon's race, the horse won and Parker decided that he did not really want to sell the horse for $1.00.

a. The contract is unenforceable because the consideration is not adequate.

b. The courts will review whether the consideration is good consideration.

c. One dollar constitutes sufficient consideration.

d. The sufficiency of the consideration depends on whether Parker was serious.

The correct answer is (c). *(Publisher)*

REQUIRED: The correct statement concerning the consideration of $1.00.

DISCUSSION: Courts will usually not look into the value or the adequacy of consideration. One dollar is adequate consideration as long as that is the amount bargained for, whether or not it is a fair value.

Answer (a) is incorrect because $1.00 was bargained for and is adequate consideration. Answer (b) is incorrect because courts will usually not review whether consideration is adequate. The term "good consideration" has historically referred to a promise founded on love or affection. Answer (d) is incorrect because the sufficiency or adequacy of consideration does not depend on the seriousness of the offer. Whether the offer was in jest would bear on whether a meeting of the minds had occurred.

69. Tim Carlton was swimming at the beach and happened to see Fay Hudson drowning. Carlton saved Hudson's life. Hudson was so grateful that she promised Carlton a job for the rest of his life if he would come to work for her. Carlton did go to work for Hudson, but a few months later Hudson found that she did not get along with Carlton and demanded Carlton's resignation. The contract is

a. Unenforceable because it was not definite enough.

b. Unenforceable because Carlton did not give consideration.

c. Enforceable because Hudson gave consideration in the form of job security.

d. Enforceable because there was mutuality of assent.

The correct answer is (b). *(Publisher)*

REQUIRED: The enforceability of a contract for life employment.

DISCUSSION: A contract for life employment is ordinarily terminable at the option of the employee, but the employer has no such option. The reason for this rule is that one cannot be required to perform personal services. The employer can be bound not to terminate the contract without good cause if the employee has given consideration. The saving of Hudson's life was not consideration, however, because it was "past consideration." Past consideration, that is, an act performed before the making of the agreement, does not satisfy the consideration requirement for the formation of a contract.

Answer (a) is incorrect because a contract for life employment states a definite enough period of time. Answer (c) is incorrect because the unenforceability of the contract is based on the lack of consideration given by Carlton. Answer (d) is incorrect because although there is mutuality of consent, the contract is not enforceable. Carlton gave no consideration.

70. Which of the following creates a valid contract between the parties?

a. A reward was posted for the capture of Tom Jones. Maypole Burden, the county sheriff, captured Jones and claimed the reward.

b. Slim Polestone promised to give Mabel Abbot a wedding present.

c. Anxious Father promised to pay Albert Niceguy $4,000 to take his daughter to the annual Mulestone Dance. Albert agreed.

d. Festival Fanny was drowning in her hot tub. Her boyfriend pulled her out. After the rescue, Festival's husband promised to pay her boyfriend $4 for rescuing his wife.

The correct answer is (c). *(E. Rahm)*

REQUIRED: The situation in which a valid contract is formed.

DISCUSSION: To form a valid contract the parties' promises must be supported by consideration. Consideration may consist, for example, of a promise to give up a legal right. Anxious Father gave consideration when he promised to give $4,000 to Niceguy. Niceguy's consideration is his promise to take the daughter to the dance.

Answer (a) is incorrect because the sheriff's performance of a pre-existing duty to capture the criminal was not consideration. Answer (b) is incorrect because Mabel forfeited no legal rights in exchange for Slim's promise to make the gift. Answer (d) is incorrect because the promise to pay was made after the rescue was performed. Past consideration is not valid consideration.

71. Culler Construction Company agreed with the City of Orange Key to build a road in a coastal section of Florida. The project was to begin on December 1. One week after work began, a hurricane struck the site, washing away so much land that the construction would be twice as expensive. As a result, Culler refused to continue the job unless Orange Key paid a large sum in addition to the initial contract price. A promise by Orange Key to pay more than the original price is

a. Unenforceable because Orange Key received no additional legal benefit.

b. Unenforceable because Culler incurred no additional legal detriment.

c. Unenforceable because of the pre-existing contractual obligation.

d. Enforceable because Culler encountered unforeseeable difficulties.

The correct answer is (d). *(Publisher)*

REQUIRED: The enforceability of a promise to pay more than the contract price.

DISCUSSION: If Culler had simply made a bad bargain or had met foreseeable difficulties, such as labor problems, equipment malfunctions, or materials price increases, Orange Key's additional promise would have been unenforceable for lack of consideration. Culler was already contractually obligated to perform the promised act. Unforeseen difficulties, however, create an exception to this principle. Because Culler could not reasonably have anticipated a hurricane in December, even in Florida, the promise to pay additional compensation would probably be enforceable.

Answers (a) and (b) are incorrect because Orange Key received an additional legal benefit and Culler incurred an additional legal detriment in that the former received the right to and the latter assumed the obligation to provide a post-hurricane performance, one that the parties could not reasonably have anticipated when they concluded their original bargain. Answer (c) is incorrect because unforeseen difficulties create an exception to the rule.

72. Ron Williams purchased a heating system from Radiant Heating for his factory. Williams insisted that a clause be included in the contract calling for service within 1 day to be rendered 1) free of charge during the first year of the contract and 2) for a flat fee of $200 per year for the next 2 years. During the winter of the second year, the heating system broke down. Williams phoned Radiant and was told that the $200 per year service charge was uneconomical and that Radiant could not do the work for several days. Williams in desperation promised to pay an additional $100 if Radiant would send someone that day. Radiant did so and sent a bill for $100 to Williams. Is Williams legally required to pay this bill and why?

a. No, the pre-existing legal duty rule applies to this situation.

b. No, the Statute of Frauds will defeat Radiant's claim.

c. Yes, Williams made the offer to pay the additional amount.

d. Yes, that it was uneconomical for Radiant to perform constitutes economic duress that freed Radiant from its obligation to provide the agreed-upon service.

The correct answer is (a). *(CPA 579 L-9)*

REQUIRED: The enforceability of a promise to pay more than the contract price.

DISCUSSION: The promise was unenforceable because it was supported only by Radiant's performance of a pre-existing duty and not by any new consideration. Radiant was already obligated to perform 1-day service under the contract. That the contract was uneconomical did not affect Radiant's duty unless it was unconscionable or impracticable.

Answer (b) is incorrect because service contracts are not within the Statute of Frauds unless they are not capable of being performed within 1 year. The promise of $100 for service the same day does not indicate that it is for more than a year's service. Answer (c) is incorrect because a promise not supported by legally acceptable consideration is not enforceable. Answer (d) is incorrect because making a bad bargain does not excuse one from performing. Furthermore, Radiant made its profit on the sale of the heating system that was part of the consideration for the service agreement.

73. Adele borrowed $1,000 from Beatrice and signed a promissory note due on January 1. On December 1, Beatrice agreed to accept immediate payment of $800 in full satisfaction of the debt. In January, Beatrice sought to receive the $200 unpaid balance. What will be the result?

a. Adele will win because she provided consideration for Beatrice's new promise.

b. Adele will win because the debt was unliquidated.

c. Beatrice will win because of the pre-existing contractual obligation rule.

d. Beatrice will win because the debt was liquidated.

The correct answer is (a). *(Publisher)*

REQUIRED: The result when a creditor accepts partial payment prior to the due date.

DISCUSSION: The debt was liquidated (undisputed in amount). Because a debtor has a pre-existing contractual obligation to pay the full amount, a creditor's promise to accept partial payment in full satisfaction is unenforceable for lack of consideration unless the debtor furnishes new or different consideration, such as payment before the due date. Beatrice had no right to early payment, so she received a new legal benefit. Adele was under no obligation to make early payment, so she incurred a new legal detriment. Adele can therefore enforce Beatrice's promise to accept a lesser amount in full satisfaction of the debt.

Answer (b) is incorrect because the debt was liquidated (not subject to honest dispute). Answers (c) and (d) are incorrect because Adele provided new consideration.

74. Denise Smolen hired David Vause to construct an exercise center in her home. After completing the job, he sent her a bill for $3,000. Based on the cost of similar work done for several of her neighbors, Smolen stated that $2,000 was a fair price. Vause said that the market rate for quality work was $3,000, but that he would accept $2,500. Smolen agreed and remitted a $2,500 check in full payment of the debt. The parties have

a. Compromised a liquidated debt.

b. Concluded a composition with a creditor.

c. Reached an accord and satisfaction.

d. Reached an accord without satisfaction.

The correct answer is (c). *(Publisher)*

REQUIRED: The correct description of an agreement to settle a disputed debt and the subsequent payment.

DISCUSSION: The parties had an honest dispute as to the amount of the debt. The agreement to compromise was an accord. The payment of the agreed amount was a satisfaction. The accord and satisfaction is enforceable because of mutuality of consideration: Vause's acceptance of a lesser amount is consideration for Smolen's payment of a greater amount and vice versa.

Answer (a) is incorrect because the debt was unliquidated or honestly disputed. Answer (b) is incorrect because a composition is an agreement among a debtor and two or more creditors to accept lesser sums from the debtor in full satisfaction of their claims. Answer (d) is incorrect because the remittance of the check was the satisfaction.

75. Adolf Anderssen performed accounting services for Carla Jung and sent her a bill for $500. She responded in good faith that the value of the services was $300 but that she was willing to pay $375 to avoid litigation. Accordingly, she sent Anderssen a check for that amount marked "payment in full." Anderssen received the check, crossed out the notation "payment in full," cashed it, and filed suit in small claims court for $125 and costs. If he desired to recover the full $500, Anderssen's best course of action was

a. To keep the check instead of cashing it.

b. To cash the check without crossing out the satisfaction recital.

c. The one he actually chose.

d. To return the check.

The correct answer is (d). *(Publisher)*

REQUIRED: The creditor's best course of action upon receipt of a check marked "payment in full."

DISCUSSION: A debt is deemed to be unliquidated if a genuine controversy exists as to its amount. Tender of the check by Jung was an offer of settlement that Anderssen effectively accepted by cashing it. Returning the check would have been an unequivocal rejection of the offer. If the debt had not been disputed, cashing a check for a lesser sum (even if marked "payment in full") would not have been an acceptance of an offer to settle for the lesser amount.

Answer (a) is incorrect because holding the check beyond a reasonable time for returning it would also have been an acceptance of Jung's offer. Answer (b) is incorrect because whether the recital is crossed out does not affect the legal significance of cashing the check. Answer (c) is incorrect because the actual course chosen is deemed an acceptance of a lesser sum than that claimed.

76. Which of the following requires consideration in order to be binding on the parties?

a. A written promise signed by a merchant to keep an offer to sell goods open for ten days.

b. Material modification of a sale of goods contract under the UCC.

c. Ratification of a contract by a person after reaching the age of majority.

d. Material modification of a contract involving the sale of real estate.

The correct answer is (d). *(CPA 1186 L-11)*

REQUIRED: The act that requires consideration to bind the parties.

DISCUSSION: Under the common law of contracts, a promise to modify the contractual duty of one party to a contract must be supported by consideration to be enforceable. If the buyer of realty agreed to pay an additional sum when the seller refused to perform under the original agreement, the promise would be unenforceable if the seller agreed to do no more than perform his/her pre-existing contractual duty. Some additional consideration would be necessary.

Answer (a) is incorrect because a merchant's firm offer needs no consideration to be binding (UCC 2-205). Answer (b) is incorrect because modification of a contract for the sale of goods needs no consideration (UCC 2-209). Answer (c) is incorrect because ratification is confirmation of the intent to be bound by an agreement reached during the person's minority. No consideration is required beyond that involved in the original agreement.

77. Which of the following does not require consideration to be effective and binding?

a. Waiver of a breach.

b. Mutual rescission.

c. Modification of a contract.

d. Composition with creditors.

The correct answer is (a). *(Publisher)*

REQUIRED: The contractual action that does not require consideration to be effective.

DISCUSSION: Most contractual actions require consideration because they involve either the formation or modification of a contract. Once a breach has been committed, however, one can waive his/her remedies without any consideration. Waiver of remedies prior to breach is a modification of a contract and needs consideration unless the agreement is within the UCC.

Answer (b) is incorrect because the cancellation of a contract by mutual rescission is a modification needing consideration. The mutual promises to rescind usually constitute the required consideration. Answer (c) is incorrect because modification of a contract is itself a contract and thus needs consideration. Answer (d) is incorrect because a composition with creditors is a contract for which the consideration is the creditors' mutual promises.

78. Which of the following will be legally binding on all the parties despite the lack of consideration?

a. A promise to donate money to a charity that was relied upon by the charity in incurring large expenditures.

b. An oral employment agreement for a term of 9 months from the date the agreement was formed.

c. An irrevocable oral promise by a merchant to keep its offer open for 60 days.

d. A material modification signed by the parties to a contract to purchase and sell a parcel of land.

The correct answer is (a). *(CPA 587 L-14)*

REQUIRED: The basis for binding all parties despite the lack of consideration.

DISCUSSION: The charity should prevail on the theory of promissory estoppel despite lack of consideration for the promise. It must show 1) that a promise was made that the promisor should reasonably have expected to induce action or forbearance by the promisee, 2) that the promise actually induced such action or forbearance, and 3) that enforcement is the only way to avoid injustice. Promissory estoppel is a means of enforcing a promise in the absence of consideration when a promisee has justifiably and detrimentally relied upon the promise.

Answer (b) is incorrect because an employment agreement that can be performed within 1 year from its making is not within the Statute of Frauds and need not be written, but the promise it contains must be supported by consideration. Answer (c) is incorrect because a firm offer is not binding unless contained in a writing signed by the merchant-offeror. Answer (d) is incorrect because a material modification of a contract not for the sale of goods requires consideration.

79. Which of the following promises is enforceable in most states?

a. Creditor promises to accept a lesser sum than due.

b. A written promise to pay a debt barred by the statute of limitations.

c. A promise to perform an illegal act.

d. A promise to pay a debt after the discharge of the debt in bankruptcy was granted.

The correct answer is (b). *(Publisher)*

REQUIRED: The promise that is enforceable in most states.

DISCUSSION: A new promise to pay a debt barred by the statute of limitations requires no consideration to be enforceable because it is only the waiver of a defense. Some courts, however, take the view that consideration is supplied by the old debt. Nevertheless, most states require the new promise to be in writing.

Answer (a) is incorrect because a promise to accept a lesser sum must be supported by additional consideration. Answer (c) is incorrect because legality is an essential element of a contract. Answer (d) is incorrect because the Bankruptcy Reform Act of 1978 requires that the new promise (a reaffirmation agreement) be made before the discharge is granted. Moreover, the debtor has 30 days to revoke the agreement after it becomes enforceable.

80. Lucy agreed to construct a gazebo in Larry's garden. While the contract was still wholly executory, the parties mutually and voluntarily agreed to abandon the project. Some weeks later, Lucy proposed to build the gazebo to the same specifications if Larry would pay her an additional $1,000. Larry accepted and the work was done. When Larry refused to pay more than the original price, Lucy brought suit. Who will win?

a. Lucy, because the original agreement had been mutually rescinded.

b. Larry, because of the pre-existing contractual duty rule.

c. Lucy, because of the unforeseen difficulties exception.

d. Larry, because of lack of consideration.

The correct answer is (a). *(Publisher)*

REQUIRED: The outcome of an action to recover additional consideration for the performance called for in the original contract.

DISCUSSION: If a party is already under a contractual duty, there is no consideration for a new promise to carry out that duty. Because the original contract between Lucy and Larry had been mutually rescinded, Lucy was not under a contractual duty to Larry when she promised to build the gazebo in return for a $1,000 increase in the price. Lucy should prevail because Larry's promise was enforceable.

Answer (b) is incorrect because the original contractual duty no longer existed after mutual rescission of the contract. Answer (c) is incorrect because the facts do not suggest the existence of unforeseen difficulties. Answer (d) is incorrect because in the absence of a pre-existing duty, Lucy's promise was consideration for Larry's promise.

11.5 Reality of Assent

81. In order for a purchaser of land to avoid a contract with the seller based on duress, it must be shown that the seller's improper threats

a. Constituted a crime or tort.

b. Actually induced the purchaser to assent to the contract.

c. Would have induced a reasonably prudent person to assent to the contract.

d. Were made with the intent that the purchaser be influenced by them.

The correct answer is (b). *(CPA 587 L-20)*

REQUIRED: The element that must be shown to prove duress.

DISCUSSION: Duress is an improper act or threat that induces fear in another person so that his/her will is overcome. The threat or act is often of physical violence but can also be a threat or act that causes fear of anything else that will overcome one's will or leave one without a reasonable alternative. Contracts entered into under duress are voidable at the option of the victim. Accordingly, plaintiff must prove that the defendant's wrongful actions coerced him/her into agreeing to the contract.

Answer (a) is incorrect because a threat may be improper even though it does not constitute a crime or a tort. For example, the threat to bring a criminal prosecution is ordinarily improper, and economic duress may be found in a threat to breach a contract. Even a threat to bring a well-founded civil action may be improper if made in bad faith and for an ulterior motive. Answer (c) is incorrect because the traditional common law rule required that the threats be sufficient to coerce a person of ordinary courage. The modern rule emphasizes the alternatives available; that is, if the threats gave the victim no reasonable alternative, coercion will be found. Answer (d) is incorrect because plaintiff need not establish the defendant's intent. Duress has two essential elements: an improper threat and an actual coercive effort sufficient to overcome the victim's will.

82. King had several outstanding unsecured loans with National Bank. In addition, King had a separate loan with National that was secured by a mortgage on a farm owned by King. King was delinquent on the mortgage loan but not on the unsecured loans. National asked King to sign renewal notes for the unsecured loans at substantially higher interest rates. When King refused, National informed King that it would foreclose on the farm's mortgage if King did not sign. King signed but later disaffirmed the new unsecured notes and National sued. King's best defense is

a. Undue influence.

b. Unconscionability.

c. Duress.

d. Fraud in the inducement.

The correct answer is (c). *(CPA 589 L-28)*

REQUIRED: The best defense on a contract entered into under a threat to foreclose a mortgage.

DISCUSSION: Duress has two elements: an improper threat and sufficient coercive effect. The threat need not be of violence, an illegal act, a tort, or a breach of contract. In some circumstances, a threat may be improper even though based on a legal right. Such a threat may be wrongful if made in bad faith and with an ulterior motive. Thus, although National had a right to foreclose the mortgage, a court might find economic duress, that is, pressure on King going beyond mere hard bargaining.

Answer (a) is incorrect because the facts suggest coercion by threats, not improper persuasion by a dominant person or by one enjoying a confidential relationship with the victim. Answer (b) is incorrect because there is no indication that the agreement was so oppressive as to shock the conscience of the court. Answer (d) is incorrect because no misrepresentation of a material fact affecting the consideration is alleged.

83. Sisk contracted to sell Bleu a building for $470,000. If Sisk wishes to avoid the contract based on undue influence, one element that Sisk must prove is that Bleu

a. Induced Sisk to sell the building by unfair persuasion.

b. Was in a fiduciary relationship with Sisk.

c. Misrepresented material facts to Sisk.

d. Made improper threats to Sisk.

The correct answer is (a). *(CPA 1187 L-4)*

REQUIRED: The element that must be shown to prove undue influence.

DISCUSSION: The essence of undue influence is wrongful persuasion rather than coercion by means of threats. The plaintiff in an undue influence case has contractual capacity but is in a vulnerable position in relation to the other party, possibly because of a physical or psychological dependence that is exploited by the dominant individual. These cases often involve unfair bargains made by an ill or infirm person with a caregiver, close relative, trusted adviser, or attorney. The law provides that a person may avoid the contracts entered into when subject to undue influence because the capacity to bargain freely has been impaired.

Answer (b) is incorrect because the relationship need not be fiduciary, such as that with a trustee or attorney. Indeed, no particular confidential relationship is needed if one party is in a position to exert overmastering psychological influence over the other. Answer (c) is incorrect because it states an element of fraud. Answer (d) is incorrect because threats constitute an element of duress.

84. Don Bradford sold a parcel of land to Jones who promptly recorded the deed. Bradford then resold the land to Wallace. In a suit against Bradford by Wallace, recovery will be based on the theory of

a. Bilateral mistake.

b. Ignorance of the facts.

c. Unilateral mistake.

d. Fraud.

The correct answer is (d). *(CPA 1189 L-14)*

REQUIRED: The theory of recovery after defendant has sold the same property to different buyers.

DISCUSSION: In a contract action for fraud, the plaintiff must prove that the defendant made a false representation of fact, that the representation was known to be false or was made with reckless disregard for its truth or falsity, that the intent was to induce reliance on the representation, and that such reliance was justifiable. In a tort case, plaintiff must also prove damages. Wallace will therefore prevail on a fraud theory because Bradford must have made a false representation of fact he knew to be false and intended to be relied upon.

Answers (a) and (c) are incorrect because a mistake is distinguished from a misrepresentation (innocent or fraudulent) in that it does not follow from another party's false statements. Wallace's presumed erroneous belief about the ownership of the property resulted from Bradford's dishonesty. Answer (b) is incorrect because ignorance cannot be pleaded. Jones's recording of the deed gave constructive notice of the sale.

85. Sardy, a famous football player, was asked to autograph a pad of paper held by Maple. Unknown to Sardy, Maple had carefully concealed a contract for the sale of Sardy's home to Maple in the pad that Sardy signed. If Maple seeks to enforce the contract, Sardy's best defense to have the contract declared void would be

a. Fraud in the inducement.

b. Fraud in the execution.

c. Mistake.

d. Duress.

The correct answer is (b). *(CPA 586 L-8)*

REQUIRED: The term for misleading someone as to the contents of a document.

DISCUSSION: When the content of an agreement or the nature of a document is purposely misrepresented to a party to the contract, fraud in the execution has occurred. Such an agreement is void. It is fraudulent if based on a false representation, made with knowledge that it was false, intended to induce another to act, and the person does act in justifiable reliance thereon.

Answer (a) is incorrect because fraud in the inducement occurs when the underlying consideration is misrepresented, i.e., the nature or quality of the goods or services. Such an agreement is voidable. Answer (c) is incorrect because this case involved not a mistake of fact but an intentional deceit. Answer (d) is incorrect because duress entails a wrongful threat that induces fear sufficient to overcome one's free will.

86. To establish a cause of action based on fraud in the inducement, one of the elements the plaintiff must usually prove is that

a. It is impossible for the plaintiff to perform the terms of the contract.

b. The contract is unconscionable.

c. The defendant made a false representation of a material fact.

d. There has been a mutual mistake of a material fact by the plaintiff and defendant.

The correct answer is (c). *(CPA 588 L-25)*

REQUIRED: The element of a prima facie case of fraud in the inducement.

DISCUSSION: The classic elements of fraud are a false representation of a material fact, scienter (the defendant's knowledge of the falsehood or reckless disregard for the statement's truth or falsity), an intent to deceive, and reliance on the false representation that is both justifiable and detrimental. Fraud in the inducement occurs when the underlying consideration is misrepresented, i.e., the nature or quality of the goods or services. Such an agreement is voidable.

Answers (a), (b), and (d) are incorrect because none is an element of fraud.

87. Park entered into a contract to sell Reed a parcel of land. Park was aware that Reed was purchasing the land with the intention of building a high-rise office building. Park was also aware of the fact that a subsurface soil condition would prevent such construction. The condition was extremely unusual and not readily discoverable in the course of normal inspections or soil evaluations. Park did not disclose the existence of the condition to Reed, nor did Reed make any inquiry of Park as to the suitability of the land for the intended development. Park's silence as to the soil condition

a. Renders the contract voidable at Reed's option.

b. Entitles Reed only to money damages.

c. Renders the contract void.

d. Does not affect the validity of the contract.

The correct answer is (a). *(CPA 1187 L-5)*

REQUIRED: The legal result of a seller's silence regarding an unusual condition of the land sold.

DISCUSSION: An element of fraud is a false representation of fact. A false representation may consist of a failure to disclose a material fact when the law imposes a duty to speak. When a seller of land knows of a condition affecting it that is not obvious or discoverable by a reasonable inspection, the modern trend is to require the disclosure. As a result of Park's silence, Reed may void (rescind) the contract within a reasonable time after discovery of the fraud.

Answers (b), (c), and (d) are incorrect because the party fraudulently induced to enter into the contract may void or enforce it at his/her option. The contract is voidable, not void. (S)he may also sue for damages or simply assert fraud as a defense in an action brought to enforce the contract.

88. Which of the following parties will be bound by the "puffing" that (s)he used to induce another to enter into a contract?

a. An expert in the area of the contract whose "puffing" is relied upon.

b. A public official who "puffed" in connection with a construction contract.

c. The sales manager of a publicly held corporation subject to the jurisdiction of the Securities and Exchange Commission.

d. The seller of medical equipment.

The correct answer is (a). *(Publisher)*

REQUIRED: The party who will be bound by "puffing" that induces another to enter into a contract.

DISCUSSION: "Puffing" is sales talk or opinions, not statements of fact, about the quality of a product made by a salesperson. As long as it constitutes ordinary sales talk, "puffing" does not become part of the contract. However, if an expert "puffs" and is relied upon, the other party can hold the expert to the "puffing" or rescind the contract.

Answer (b) is incorrect because the "puffing" of a public official is not different from that of any other person, except an expert. Answer (c) is incorrect because being subject to the jurisdiction of the SEC has no effect on contractual obligations. Answer (d) is incorrect because the seller of medical equipment is as entitled to "puff" as anyone else unless (s)he is considered an expert and the purchaser is relying on this expertise.

89. A party to a contract who seeks to rescind the contract because of that party's reliance on the unintentional but materially false statements of the other party will assert

a. Reformation.

b. Actual fraud.

c. Misrepresentation.

d. Constructive fraud.

The correct answer is (c). *(CPA 1189 L-15)*

REQUIRED: The legal theory justifying rescission because of reliance on unintentional but materially false statements.

DISCUSSION: Innocent misrepresentation is a false representation of a material fact that was intended to induce reliance and justifiably relied upon. The only remedy customarily available for innocent misrepresentation is rescission, which is the cancellation of the agreement and the restoration of the parties to their position prior to contracting.

Answer (a) is incorrect because reformation of the contract is a remedy, not a basis for giving a remedy. Answers (b) and (d) are incorrect because proof of fraud requires a showing that the defendant knowingly or recklessly made a false representation of a material fact with the intent that it be relied upon. Constructive fraud is a willful and reckless disregard for the truth or falsity of a representation (gross negligence). It has the same legal effect as actual knowledge of falsity (actual fraud).

90. Blume owns three motorcycles: a 1986 Kawasaki, a 1989 Honda, and a 1985 Honda. Rich is interested in purchasing a motorcycle. If Blume makes a written offer to sell and Rich accepts, in which case is the agreement enforceable?

a. Blume, meaning to offer the 1985 Honda, inadvertently wrote Kawasaki instead. Rich accepted in good faith.

b. Blume, meaning the 1985 model, offered to sell the Honda. Rich, meaning the 1989 model, accepted in good faith.

c. Blume, meaning to offer the Kawasaki, inadvertently wrote Honda instead. Rich, realizing from the price offered that an error had been made, accepted in hopes of getting a bargain.

d. Blume, meaning the 1985 Honda, offered to sell "the motorcycle." Rich, knowing only that Blume owned a 1986 Kawasaki, accepted in good faith.

The correct answer is (a). *(Publisher)*

REQUIRED: The contract offer that could be validly accepted with a mistake in the language.

DISCUSSION: A contract is voidable 1) when it is based upon a mutual mistake regarding a material fact that induced the making of the contract; 2) when it arises from different, good faith interpretations of a material ambiguity in the contractual language; or 3) when one party makes a material mistake about which the other knew or should have known. In these cases, the requisite meeting of the minds is deemed not to have occurred. If Blume offered to sell the Kawasaki and neither the price nor anything else in the transaction alerted Rich to the error, the acceptance was binding despite the unilateral mistake in the description of the subject matter.

Answers (b) and (d) are incorrect because there are mutual mistakes regarding a material fact. Answer (c) is incorrect because no contract is formed when one party knows or has reason to know of the other's unilateral mistake.

91. On April 6, Apple entered into a signed contract with Bean, by which Apple was to sell Bean an antique automobile having a fair market value of $150,000, for $75,000. Apple believed the auto was worth only $75,000. Unknown to either party the auto had been destroyed by fire on April 4. If Bean sues Apple for breach of contract, Apple's best defense is

a. Unconscionability.

b. Risk of loss had passed to Bean.

c. Lack of adequate consideration.

d. Mutual mistake.

The correct answer is (d). *(CPA 1188 L-16)*

REQUIRED: The result when the parties do not know that the subject matter has been destroyed.

DISCUSSION: The existence of the subject matter of the contract is a material fact. A mistake made by both parties regarding a past or current material fact is grounds for rescission or a sufficient defense in an action on the contract. Because the parties are usually assumed to accept the risks concerning future events, a mistake about future facts is ordinarily not a basis for relief.

Answer (a) is incorrect because an agreement is unconscionable if it is so unfair as to be oppressive, but the facts do not suggest that Bean took unfair advantage of Apple. Answer (b) is incorrect because the seller initially has the risk of loss. No event occurred that transferred the risk to Bean. Answer (c) is incorrect because courts seldom inquire into the adequacy or value of consideration.

92. On September 22, Michael offered to sell his 1962 Bolanos automobile to Alicia for $25,000. Unbeknownst to either party, Maria Bolanos, the originator and designer of the aforementioned car, had died shortly before the offer was made. Her death caused the fair market value of the Bolanos to jump from $25,000 to $100,000. Alicia duly and unconditionally accepted the offer on September 23. Upon learning of this price increase, Michael

a. May rescind the contract if he can prove that Alicia knew or should have known of the price change.

b. May rescind the contract based on mutual mistake of a material fact.

c. Will be unable to receive more than the contract price.

d. Will have to sell the car under the terms of the contract but will receive damages in the amount of $75,000.

The correct answer is (c). *(D. Costantino)*

REQUIRED: The effect of the parties' mistake as to the value of the subject matter.

DISCUSSION: Proving that Alicia had knowledge of the mistake would not be sufficient to rescind the contract based on unilateral mistake. Another condition for rescinding based on unilateral mistake is that the mistake concerned some material past or current fact, not a matter of judgment or valuation. Thus, Michael assumed the risk of his own ignorance or bad judgment about valuation.

To avoid a contract based on mutual mistake of a material fact, the mistake must concern the subject matter of the contract. Here, the mistake is only as to the value of that subject matter. Mutual ignorance as to the value of a contract does not prevent the formation of a valid contract. A valid offer and acceptance occurred. At the time of contracting, there was no mistake as to what was being sold; both parties agreed on the sale of the Bolanos and on the price of $25,000. Thus, no mutual mistake occurred as to the subject matter of the contract. Given a valid and enforceable agreement, Michael must sell for $25,000.

Answers (a) and (b) are incorrect because as explained above, neither unilateral nor mutual mistake is a basis for voiding the contract. Answer (d) is incorrect because Michael has no grounds for receiving damages.

93. Sting Corp., a general contractor, obtained bids from several plumbers to install piping. Joe Lite, a licensed plumber, submitted a bid for $60,000 that was $20,000 less than the next lowest bid. Lite made an obvious and substantial arithmetic error in his bid. Sting did not have actual knowledge of Lite's mistake. If Sting accepts Lite's bid, Lite

a. Must perform the contract for $60,000 because Sting did not have actual knowledge of the error.

b. Must perform the contract for $60,000 unless he can show that Sting caused the error.

c. Can avoid liability for refusing to install the piping for $60,000 because Sting should have known of Lite's error.

d. Can avoid liability for refusing to install the piping for $60,000 only if the error was not caused by his negligence.

The correct answer is (c). *(CPA 587 L-22)*

REQUIRED: The effect of a unilateral computational mistake.

DISCUSSION: Lite's offer contained a unilateral mistake of fact. Because the offeree should have been aware of an obvious mistake, no contract was formed. If the offeree had not known or had no reason to know of the mistake, the offeror would have been bound by the acceptance. The offeror would likewise have been bound if the error had been one of judgment or opinion rather than fact, e.g., the valuation of a purchased item.

Answer (a) is incorrect because constructive knowledge is imputed to Sting Corp. if it should have known of the error. Actual knowledge is not required. Answers (b) and (d) are incorrect because Lite's liability is determined by whether Sting knew or had reason to know of the mistake of fact.

94. Which of the following types of mistakes ordinarily will not allow a contract to be rescinded?

a. Mutual mistake of fact.

b. Unilateral mistake of fact known to the other party.

c. Mistake of law.

d. Mistake as to the existence of the object of the contract.

The correct answer is (c). *(Publisher)*

REQUIRED: The type of mistake that will not allow a contract to be rescinded.

DISCUSSION: A mistake of law is based on either a lack of knowledge of the law or an incorrect interpretation of the law. A contract may not ordinarily be rescinded on such a basis because everyone is deemed to have constructive knowledge of the law. However, a few decisions have allowed it as a defense on the same basis as mistake of fact and granted relief.

Answer (a) is incorrect because a mutual mistake of fact occurs when both parties to a contract make a mistake as to a material fact. They can rescind the contract on this basis. Answer (b) is incorrect because a unilateral mistake of fact occurs when only one party to a contract makes the mistake. The contract can be rescinded if the mistake is material and the other party either knew of the mistake or should have known given the surrounding facts. Answer (d) is incorrect because a mistake as to the existence of the object of the contract totally defeats its purpose and permits it to be rescinded.

95. A contract will be enforceable even if the party seeking to avoid performance alleges and proves

a. Innocent misrepresentation.

b. Fraud.

c. Mutual mistake of material fact.

d. Extreme hardship.

The correct answer is (d). *(CPA 1176 L-37)*

REQUIRED: The circumstances in which a contract will be enforceable.

DISCUSSION: Mere hardship does not excuse performance for it does not negate reality of consent. A contracting party assumes the risk that subsequent events may render performance unduly burdensome.

Answers (a), (b), and (c) are incorrect because each provides a valid basis for avoiding performance of a contractual obligation if alleged and proven.

11.6 Capacity

96. Kent, a 16-year-old, purchased a used car from Mint Motors, Inc. Ten months later, the car was stolen and never recovered. Which of the following statements is correct?

a. The car's theft is a de facto ratification of the purchase because it is impossible to return the car.

b. Kent may disaffirm the purchase because Kent is a minor.

c. Kent effectively ratified the purchase because Kent used the car for an unreasonable period of time.

d. Kent may disaffirm the purchase because Mint, a merchant, is subject to the UCC.

The correct answer is (b). *(CPA 1189 L-11)*

REQUIRED: The contractual effect of a minor's purchase of goods.

DISCUSSION: In general, the law protects minors by permitting them to avoid or disaffirm contracts made with adults. The rationale is that minors lack contractual capacity because of their immaturity and inexperience. Contracts of minors are valid but voidable, not void. Disaffirmance may occur during minority or a reasonable time thereafter.

Answers (a) and (c) are incorrect because in the majority of states, a minor may disaffirm even though (s)he cannot return the consideration. Moreover, ratification cannot occur until the minor reaches his/her majority. Use of the car for an unreasonable period after the age of majority would be a ratification, however. Answer (d) is incorrect because the minor's power to disaffirm is not dependent on the UCC. Indeed, the UCC adopts by reference the common law relative to capacity to contract as a supplement to its provisions (UCC 1-103).

97. When Elvira was 13, she signed a promissory note to pay for a funeral service. When she was 14, a judgment was entered against her on the note (but unknown to Elvira). At the age of 20, 2 years after attaining her majority, Elvira learned of the judgment when she inquired about her credit status. She brought an action 2 months later to reopen the judgment and avoid the contract on which it was based. Elvira should

a. Win because she disaffirmed within a reasonable time.

b. Lose because she waited more than 2 years after reaching her majority.

c. Lose because she did not repudiate the contract while she was a minor.

d. Win because all contracts of a minor are void.

The correct answer is (a). *(Publisher)*

REQUIRED: The effect of a minor's entering into a contract and disaffirming after reaching majority.

DISCUSSION: Most contracts entered into by a minor may be disaffirmed if (s)he acts during minority or within a reasonable time thereafter. Because Elvira filed suit to disaffirm 2 months after learning of the existence of the judgment, she acted within a reasonable time.

Answer (b) is incorrect because the circumstances determine what is a reasonable time in which to act. Answer (c) is incorrect because disaffirmance may be made after attaining majority. Answer (d) is incorrect because most contracts of minors are voidable by the minor (not void).

98. Toni Minor purchased an automobile from Majority Motors on September 17. She attained the age of majority on October 5. In the early morning of October 6, she was involved in an accident that destroyed the vehicle, which was not insured. On November 1, she informed Majority Motors that she would make no further payments. In the majority of states, if Majority Motors sues, it would

a. Lose even if defendant had misrepresented her age.

b. Lose because disaffirmance is permitted even though the property has been destroyed.

c. Win because defendant attempted to avoid the contract only after reaching her majority.

d. Win because an effective disaffirmance would have required defendant to return the property or its equivalent.

The correct answer is (b). *(Publisher)*

REQUIRED: The outcome of an action to enforce a minor's contract after the property has been destroyed.

DISCUSSION: An effective disaffirmance of a voidable contract usually requires a tender of the goods or property received. One usually cannot accept the benefits and avoid the burdens of a contract. However, a minor may disaffirm even though (s)he cannot return the property or can return it only in damaged condition.

Answer (a) is incorrect because the majority view is that a minor is liable for fraud. Although Toni could still avoid the contract, she could be liable in tort. Answer (c) is incorrect because she could avoid the contract a reasonable time after reaching her maturity. Answer (d) is incorrect because the majority of states permit disaffirmance by a minor even if the consideration cannot be returned.

99. Joe Minorca purchased a motorcycle from Big Rig Company on May 1. Joe's birthday is June 17, at which time he will have attained his majority. Which of the following actions is ineffective as a ratification of the contract of purchase?

a. On June 21, Joe sold the property to his sister.

b. On June 20, Joe made an oral promise to honor the contract.

c. On June 16, Joe remitted an installment payment.

d. As of November 17, Joe was still using the vehicle.

The correct answer is (c). (Publisher)

REQUIRED: The action ineffective to constitute ratification of a minor's contract.

DISCUSSION: Contracts of minors are usually voidable at the option of the minor. Upon attainment of the age of majority, however, the minor can ratify the contract. After ratification, (s)he will be bound from the inception of the contract. An attempt to ratify while still a minor is not effective. One who lacks contractual capacity clearly lacks the capacity to ratify. Performance of the contract by making installment payments is a ratification but only if done after the minor comes of age.

Answer (a) is incorrect because sale of the property is an implied ratification. It is inconsistent with an intention to disaffirm. Answer (b) is incorrect because an express promise, whether oral or written, is sufficient to bind an adult to a contract formed during his/her minority. Answer (d) is incorrect because failure to disaffirm within a reasonable time after reaching one's majority is ratification.

100. The age of majority in the State of Gibraldi is 21. At the age of 20, Carol decided to leave school to seek employment sufficient to support herself. She therefore concluded an agreement with The Employment Agency (TEA) to pay a fee if it located a job for her. TEA did find a job but Carol refused to pay. At the time of her refusal, Carol was still 20. In an action against Carol, TEA will most likely

a. Lose because Carol was a minor when she contracted.

b. Lose because Carol disaffirmed while still a minor.

c. Win because Carol is liable as an emancipated minor.

d. Win because Carol is liable for necessaries.

The correct answer is (d). *(Publisher)*

REQUIRED: The outcome of an action against a minor for an employment agency's fee.

DISCUSSION: Minors are liable under contracts for necessaries such as food, clothing, shelter, medicine, and tools of a trade. Other items may be considered necessaries depending upon the circumstances. This rule protects the minor: a person may be unwilling to contract to supply necessaries to a minor who is not liable on the agreement. Nevertheless, a minor may still disaffirm a contract for necessaries. In that event, the minor will be liable in quasi-contract for the reasonable value of the necessaries, not for the contract price.

Answer (a) is incorrect because minors are liable for the reasonable value of necessaries. Answer (b) is incorrect because Carol could disaffirm the contract but not avoid liability in quasi-contract. Answer (c) is incorrect because the facts do not indicate that Carol was legally emancipated. Minors who are emancipated in the sense of being free of parental constraint still lack contractual capacity.

101. Contractual capacity of the parties is a prerequisite to the formation of a binding agreement, but the consequences of different forms of incapacity vary. The contracts of a person are void if (s)he is

a. A minor.

b. Under guardianship of a court.

c. Lacks the capacity to understand but has not been declared incompetent by a court.

d. Intoxicated.

The correct answer is (b). *(Publisher)*

REQUIRED: The incapacity that will render contracts void.

DISCUSSION: If a person has been adjudicated an incompetent by a court, a guardian will be appointed to conserve his/her property. The adjudication has the effect of depriving the incompetent of all capacity to contract. The contractual efforts of such an individual are thus of no legal effect. They are void.

Answer (a) is incorrect because a minor's contracts are voidable by the minor. Answer (c) is incorrect because the contracts of a person who lacks the capacity to understand the nature and consequences of a transaction but who has not been adjudicated incompetent are voidable. Answer (d) is incorrect because intoxication ordinarily has the same effect as mental incompetence. The intoxicated person's contracts are voidable provided the impairment is sufficient to prevent an understanding of the nature and consequences of the act.

102. Meed entered into a written agreement to sell a parcel of land to Beel for $80,000. At the time the agreement was executed, Meed had consumed a large amount of alcoholic beverages that significantly impaired Meed's ability to understand the nature and terms of the contract. Beel knew Meed was very intoxicated and that the land had been appraised at $125,000. Meed wishes to avoid the contract. The contract is

a. Void.

b. Legally binding on both parties in the absence of fraud or undue influence.

c. Voidable at Meed's option.

d. Voidable at Meed's option only if the intoxication was involuntary.

The correct answer is (c). *(CPA 1186 L-13)*

REQUIRED: The effect of intoxication on contractual liability.

DISCUSSION: In general, an intoxicated person receives the same legal protection as an incompetent, but the courts usually require a person to be very drunk. (S)he may ratify or disaffirm a contract entered into with a party who was aware that the intoxicated person was unable to understand the nature and consequences of his/her actions or was unable to act reasonably. The contract is therefore voidable at Meed's option.

Answers (a) and (b) are incorrect because the contract is voidable. Answer (d) is incorrect because the rule is the same for voluntary intoxication. In either case, however, the courts will strictly enforce the requirement of restitution. The intoxicated person will also be liable in quasi-contract for the reasonable value of necessities.

11.7 Illegality

103. Mix entered into a contract with Dan Small that provided for Small to receive $10,000 if he stole trade secrets from Mix's competition. Small performed his part of the contract by delivering the trade secrets to Mix. Mix refuses to pay Small for his services. Under what theory may Small recover?

a. Quasi-contract, in order to prevent the unjust enrichment of Mix.

b. Promissory estoppel, because Small has changed his position to his detriment.

c. None, because of the illegal nature of the contract.

d. Express contract, because both parties bargained for and exchanged promises in forming the contract.

The correct answer is (c). *(CPA 584 L-11)*

REQUIRED: The basis of recovery by a party who performed a bargain to steal trade secrets.

DISCUSSION: The requirements of a contract are offer and acceptance, consideration, capacity, and legality. An agreement involving the commission of a crime or tort, the violation of a statute, or activity contrary to public policy fails to meet the legality requirement. The illegality may be in the formation of the agreement, the performance promised, or the consideration for the promise. Because a theft of trade secrets is a crime, the bargain was illegal. The general rule is that neither party may enforce an illegal agreement.

Answers (a) and (b) are incorrect because it is improper to use the judicial process to enforce an illegal bargain. In some cases, the result may therefore be the unjust enrichment of one party or the incurrence of an uncompensated detriment by the other. Answer (d) is incorrect because no contract was formed.

104. Parr is the vice-president of research of Lynx, Inc. When hired, Parr signed an employment contract prohibiting Parr from competing with Lynx during and after employment. While employed, Parr acquired knowledge of many of Lynx's trade secrets. If Parr wishes to compete with Lynx and Lynx refuses to give Parr permission, which of the following statements is correct?

a. Parr has the right to compete with Lynx upon resigning from Lynx.

b. Parr has the right to compete with Lynx only if fired from Lynx.

c. In determining whether Parr may compete with Lynx, the court should not consider Parr's ability to obtain other employment.

d. In determining whether Parr may compete with Lynx, the court should consider, among other factors, whether the agreement is necessary to protect Lynx's legitimate business interests.

The correct answer is (d). *(CPA 1188 L-13)*

REQUIRED: The true statement about the enforceability of a covenant not to compete.

DISCUSSION: A covenant not to compete may be in violation of the common law public policy to preserve and promote competition. Thus, such an agreement must be narrowly drawn to serve the legitimate business interests of the parties and to interfere as little as possible with competition. It should be ancillary to an otherwise enforceable agreement and not the sole object of the contract. It should also state reasonable time, geographic area, and scope restrictions on the prohibition against competition. Moreover, the covenant should not unduly burden the public interest or the party who is prevented from competing. The hardship factor is especially important if the covenant is part of an employment contract. Hence, restrictions on future employment tend to be more strictly scrutinized than covenants found in agreements to sell a business. If the restraint is unreasonable, a court may void the provision or reformulate it in an acceptable form.

Answers (a) and (b) are incorrect because whether Parr resigns or is fired is irrelevant to the enforceability of the covenant. Answer (c) is incorrect because the ability to find other employment is a factor in determining how heavily the covenant will weigh upon the employee.

105. A state statute establishes a maximum interest rate of 10% for loans or forbearance of money when the debtor is not a corporation. Arrears and Buck, a large retailer, charges consumers an annual rate of 18% on the unpaid balances of their credit card purchases.

a. Arrears and Buck is guilty of usury.

b. The time-price doctrine may apply.

c. Arrears and Buck's rates are in violation of public policy.

d. Arrears and Buck's rates are unconscionable.

The correct answer is (b). *(Publisher)*

REQUIRED: The effect on consumer interest rates of a usury statute.

DISCUSSION: Because of the need for more consumer credit, courts developed the time-price differential theory to exempt consumer credit sales from the effect of usury statutes, which limit the interest that may be charged for a loan of money. The cash price is in theory the lowest price at which the seller will make the sale. The time-price is the higher price charged for a credit sale, the difference being attributable to the greater risk borne by the seller. Under the time-price theory, the difference is not interest, the transaction is not a loan, and the usury statute is not violated.

Answer (a) is incorrect because consumer credit sales may be exempt under the time-price doctrine. Answers (c) and (d) are incorrect because Arrears and Buck's rates reflect modern consumer credit reality.

106. Bill Cratchett leased an apartment from Grendel. Cratchett was a person of limited means in a locality where low-income housing was scarce. Shortly after signing the agreement, he fell in an unlit stairwell when a step unexpectedly gave way. At the trial of the suit for damages, Grendel relied on a clause in the lease stating, "Tenant agrees to hold Owner harmless from any claims for damages no matter how caused." Cratchett should

a. Win because the exculpatory clause was unenforceable as a violation of public policy.

b. Win because the lease was a contract of adhesion.

c. Lose because nothing indicates that the lease was unconscionable as a whole.

d. Lose because exculpatory clauses are usually upheld in the interest of freedom of contract.

The correct answer is (a). *(Publisher)*

REQUIRED: The outcome of a lessee's suit when the lease contained an exculpatory clause.

DISCUSSION: A bargain may fail to meet the legality requirement for enforceability if it constitutes a violation of public policy even though no crime, tort, or violation of a statute is contemplated. An exculpatory clause is viewed with disfavor by the courts because it may enable a person to escape paying damages for wrongful conduct. Whereas not all such clauses are held to be against public policy, the clause in question is most likely invalid when the parties have unequal bargaining power and the terms have been imposed upon one party by the other.

Answer (b) is incorrect because most standard-form contracts (contracts of adhesion) are enforceable. Answer (c) is incorrect because an outrageously unfair (unconscionable) clause may be invalidated even though the agreement as a whole is fair. Answer (d) is incorrect because the need for freedom and stability of contract may be outweighed by the public interest in compensating injured parties.

107. Tell, an Ohio real estate broker, misrepresented to Allen that Tell was licensed in Michigan under Michigan's statute regulating real estate brokers. Allen signed a standard form listing contract agreeing to pay Tell a 6% commission for selling Allen's home in Michigan. Tell sold Allen's home. Under the circumstances, Allen is

a. Not liable to Tell for any amount because Allen signed a standard form contract.

b. Not liable to Tell for any amount because Tell violated the Michigan licensing requirements.

c. Liable to Tell only for the value of services rendered under a quasi-contract theory.

d. Liable to Tell for the full commission under a promissory estoppel theory.

The correct answer is (b). *(CPA 589 L-26)*

REQUIRED: The recovery for services rendered by a party in violation of a regulatory statute.

DISCUSSION: A person who performs services without obtaining a statutorily required license may recover only if the statute is solely a revenue measure rather than a regulatory device. If the legislative intent was to protect the public from incompetent work by unqualified persons, the statute is regulatory and the contract is unenforceable even though the defendant was benefited and the work performed was satisfactory. Because the court will not give any remedy to a party who violates a regulatory statute, such as the one licensing real estate brokers, Tell will not be able to recover even in quasi-contract although Allen was unjustly enriched.

Answer (a) is incorrect because standard form contracts are not inherently unenforceable. Answers (c) and (d) are incorrect because a violator of a regulatory statute is not permitted any recovery.

108. Phil Fairbanks, an author, was approached by Nickle Corporation to ghostwrite the history of Nickle for $15,000. The president of Nickle told Fairbanks the job was his if he would agree to cleverly defame its leading competitor, Mogul Corporation, using sly innuendo and clever distortion of the facts. Fairbanks wrote the history. It turned out that the Mogul passages were neither sly nor clever, although they were defamatory, and Mogul obtained a judgment against Nickle. Fairbanks is seeking to collect the final $5,000 installment of the contract. Nickle refuses to pay and seeks to recover the $10,000 it has paid. In the event of a lawsuit

a. Fairbanks will recover $5,000.

b. The court will deny relief to either Fairbanks or Nickle.

c. Nickle will recover $10,000.

d. Fairbanks will recover in quantum meruit for the value of his services.

The correct answer is (b). *(CPA 583 L-10)*

REQUIRED: The outcome of a suit based on an agreement to commit defamation.

DISCUSSION: A promise to commit a tort or to induce a tort is unenforceable on public policy grounds. The general principle is that neither party to an illegal bargain can use the judicial process to compel performance, obtain damages, or recover performance or its value.

109. Bertha was in serious financial difficulty. An attorney convinced her to surrender certain property to him by misrepresenting that the transfer was a legal means of defrauding her creditors. He promised to return the property when litigation was concluded but failed to do so. If Bertha brings an action to recover her property, she will

a. Lose because neither party to an illegal bargain can enforce it.

b. Lose because the attorney's promise was unsupported by consideration.

c. Win because the parties were not equally at fault.

d. Win because the agreement was legal.

The correct answer is (c). *(Publisher)*

REQUIRED: The outcome of a suit on an illegal transfer of property.

DISCUSSION: Because the transfer was illegal, the agreement would ordinarily be unenforceable even though one party might be unjustly enriched. An exception to the general rule allows enforcement by a party who was less at fault than the other, for example, by one who was induced to enter into the agreement through the undue influence of the other. The attorney was clearly more at fault because he was able to exert undue influence based on a position of trust.

Answer (a) is incorrect because the party who is less at fault and has been induced by the other to enter the agreement may enforce the bargain. Answer (b) is incorrect because regardless of whether consideration was present, Bertha did not intend for the attorney to keep the property. Answer (d) is incorrect because the agreement was a fraud on the creditors.

110. In general, none of the parties to an illegal contract can obtain judicial relief, but courts permit certain exceptions. Which of the following will be denied a remedy?

a. Ada and Bea form a wagering agreement and give money to Cay to hold. Ada loses the bet but demands return of her money before Cay pays Bea.

b. Dot purchased fire insurance from an unlicensed insurer. After her home was destroyed by fire, she seeks recovery on the policy.

c. Eva is a nurse who signed a 1-year employment contract with a physician. Unknown to her, the man was an impostor and was arrested shortly after. Eva sues on the contract.

d. Frank leased and operated a restaurant-bar, including illegal slot machines in a back room, for a monthly lump-sum payment. When a dispute arose several months later with the lessor causing him to be evicted, Frank sued to enforce the legal portion of the contract.

The correct answer is (d). *(Publisher)*

REQUIRED: The party who will be denied a remedy when suing upon an illegal contract.

DISCUSSION: Courts will ordinarily not enforce a partially illegal bargain on the theory that the illegality affects the whole. If a contract is divisible, however, so that the legal and illegal elements are severable without violating the intent of the parties, a court will enforce the legal portion. Because the slot machine operation was not separate from the restaurant-bar and the agreement called for a single consideration to be given for both, the bargain was indivisible, void, and unenforceable.

Answer (a) is incorrect because when the illegal part of an agreement (payment of the wager) has not been performed, either party may withdraw and recover the performance already rendered. Answer (b) is incorrect because Dot belongs to the class of persons protected by the licensing statute and will be permitted a remedy. Answer (c) is incorrect because Eva will win assuming she was justifiably ignorant of the facts rendering the bargain illegal.

111. Gala leases her B-25 to pilots who enjoy flying vintage aircraft. One Saturday morning in the fall, Hanna called and offered to rent the B-25 for the day. Gala agreed. Unknown to her, Hanna had been hired by Lana to use the aircraft to fly at an extremely low altitude over a crowded football stadium that afternoon. The flight would be in violation of state and federal law. Who may enforce the agreement?

a. Only Gala.

b. Only Hanna.

c. Only Lana.

d. None of the parties.

The correct answer is (a). *(Publisher)*

REQUIRED: The person who can enforce an agreement when one has no knowledge of an intended illegal use.

DISCUSSION: When one party to an agreement has no knowledge that what (s)he is to supply is intended for an illegal use, (s)he may enforce the agreement. The party intending the illegal use may not. The latter result is based on the argument that the bargain would facilitate accomplishment of an illegal objective. Rental of an aircraft, for example, is in itself lawful. In the circumstances, however, it would facilitate achievement of an illegal objective.

112. The Acme Corporation is having a "T.V. giveaway." To win, a person must guess the number of marbles in a large jar. No purchase is necessary. This is probably not an illegal lottery because what element is lacking?

a. A prize.

b. Consideration.

c. Chance.

d. The lottery is illegal in most states.

The correct answer is (b). *(J. Norwood)*

REQUIRED: The characteristics of an illegal lottery.

DISCUSSION: An illegal lottery has the three characteristics of a wager: a prize, consideration, and determination of the outcome by chance. If all three are present, the lottery is illegal and the contract is unenforceable. Because the participants in Acme's promotion were not required to give up anything of value to participate, the element of consideration is lacking. Today, however, many states have enacted statutes to permit state-operated lotteries.

Answer (a) is incorrect because there was a prize to be won. Answer (c) is incorrect because the possibility of success depends upon chance. Answer (d) is incorrect because the described lottery would be considered legal in most states.

11.8 Statute of Frauds

113. Whether a contract must be in writing to be enforceable is a frequently raised issue. Which of the following is the best statement of the law?

a. All contracts must be written to be enforceable.

b. Most contracts need not be written unless the Statute of Frauds applies.

c. All contracts that cannot be fully performed at the time of contracting (i.e., can only be performed in the future) must be written.

d. Executory promises must be written.

The correct answer is (b). *(Publisher)*

REQUIRED: The correct statement of the law about the need for a writing.

DISCUSSION: Despite popular belief to the contrary, most contracts would be enforceable if not in writing. However, the Statute of Frauds requires a signed writing for such classes of contracts as sales of an interest in land, promises to answer for the debt of another, and contracts not performable within one year. The UCC also has two provisions (UCC 1-206 and 2-201) that require a writing. Because a contract within these statutes is unenforceable without a writing but is not void, a party must plead noncompliance as a defense or be bound by the oral agreement.

Answer (a) is incorrect because most oral contracts are enforceable. Answers (c) and (d) are incorrect because the subject matter of the contract, not the extent to which it has been performed, determines whether it must be evidenced by a writing.

114. The Statute of Frauds

a. Prevents the use of oral evidence to contradict the terms of a written contract.

b. Applies to all contracts having consideration valued at $500 or more.

c. Requires the independent promise to pay the debt of another to be in writing.

d. Applies to all real estate leases.

The correct answer is (c). *(CPA 1189 L-12)*

REQUIRED: The effect of the Statute of Frauds.

DISCUSSION: A primary promise is a promise to pay or perform one's own obligation. It is not covered by the Statute of Frauds. A secondary promise is one in which the promisor agrees to answer for the debt or default of another. This promise must be in writing under the Statute of Frauds. However, a promise for one's own benefit, even if in the form of a secondary promise, is an exception to the rule requiring secondary promises to be in writing. Also, a joint promise with another person is a primary promise (even though there may be a right of contribution).

Answer (a) is incorrect because it states the purpose of the parol evidence rule. Answer (b) is incorrect because the Statute of Frauds does not have a dollar minimum. But see the various relevant provisions of the UCC. Answer (d) is incorrect because leases for 1 year or less are usually not required to be in writing.

115. Jay makes the following oral promise to N: "Go ahead and sell these materials to my friend X. I will pay for them." This is a

a. Primary promise enforceable even though oral.

b. Primary promise not enforceable because oral.

c. Secondary promise enforceable even though oral.

d. Secondary promise not enforceable because oral.

The correct answer is (a). *(J. Norwood)*

REQUIRED: The nature and enforceability of an oral promise to pay.

DISCUSSION: Under the Statute of Frauds, a promise to answer for the debt of another (a secondary promise) must be written to be enforceable. A primary promise, however, does not have to be in written form. Jay made a direct and primary promise to pay his own debt.

Answer (b) is incorrect because a writing is not required in the case of a direct or primary promise to pay. Answers (c) and (d) are incorrect because Jay made a primary promise to pay. An example of a secondary promise is a suretyship arrangement: "I will pay upon the default of N."

116. Certain contracts to answer for the debt or default of another must be evidenced by a writing. Which of the following oral promises is within this provision of the Statute of Frauds?

a. Iona promises Jonna to pay her rent if Jonna does not receive her paycheck by the end of the month.

b. Ken is to build houses for Luana. When Ken fails to pay for certain added materials, Luana promises the supplier to pay Ken's current and future debts if Ken does not. Luana has a contract to sell the houses by a certain date to Mara.

c. Nona tells Jackson, "Sell Phoebe $200 worth of supplies for school and send me the bill."

d. Queenie tells Rhoda, "Sell Sue $400 worth of lumber. If she doesn't pay, send me the bill."

The correct answer is (d). *(Publisher)*

REQUIRED: The promise not enforceable without a writing.

DISCUSSION: The suretyship section of the Statute of Frauds provides that a secondary promise to answer for the debt or default of another must be written. Queenie's promise to Rhoda is secondary. She will be liable only if Sue, the primary obligor, fails to pay.

Answer (a) is incorrect because the promise must be made to the creditor, not the debtor. Answer (b) is incorrect because the "leading-object" or "main-purpose" rule is an exception. A promise primarily for one's own benefit is not required to be written even though the debtor is also benefited. Luana has apparently guaranteed Ken's debts to avoid defaulting on her own contract with Mara. Answer (c) is incorrect because the promisor has incurred a direct obligation, not a secondary one.

117. On May 1, Dix and Wilk entered into an oral agreement by which Dix agreed to purchase a small parcel of land from Wilk for $450. Dix paid Wilk $100 as a deposit. The following day, Wilk received another offer to purchase the land for $650, the fair market value. Wilk immediately notified Dix that Wilk would not sell the land for $450. If Dix sues Wilk for specific performance, Dix will

a. Prevail, because the amount of the contract was less than $500.

b. Prevail, because there was part performance.

c. Lose, because the fair market value of the land is over $500.

d. Lose, because the agreement was not in writing and signed by Wilk.

The correct answer is (d). *(CPA 588 L-20)*

REQUIRED: The outcome of a suit on an oral agreement to sell land.

DISCUSSION: A contract for the sale of an interest in real property must be in writing and signed by the party sought to be bound. The writing need only state the essential terms of the transaction; it need not contain all details. Accordingly, Dix cannot enforce the oral agreement.

Answers (a) and (c) are incorrect because the Statute of Frauds sets no dollar minimum regarding sales of realty. Answer (b) is incorrect because payment of a deposit is not part performance sufficient to make the oral agreement enforceable. The part performance exception is intended to prevent injustice when the buyer has substantially changed his/her position, e.g., by taking possession or making improvements.

118. Under the Statute of Frauds, a contract for the sale of an interest in land must be in writing to be enforceable. This rule applies to

a. A 1-year lease.

b. A real estate mortgage.

c. Minerals to be severed by the seller.

d. Growing crops.

The correct answer is (b). *(Publisher)*

REQUIRED: The sale to which the Statute of Frauds applies.

DISCUSSION: Interests in land include real estate and contracts that affect ownership in real estate. Contracts to sell real estate, long-term leases, real estate mortgages, and easements are interests in land.

Answer (a) is incorrect because most states require a lease to be in writing only if it is for more than 1 year. Answer (c) is incorrect because if the seller is to sever the minerals, the contract is for the sale of goods, not an interest in land (UCC 2-107). Answer (d) is incorrect because the sale of growing crops apart from the land and capable of severance without material harm to the land is a sale of goods.

119. On April 2, Streb entered into an oral employment contract with Xeon, Inc. for a term of 3 years at a salary of $2,000 per week. On June 10, Streb was terminated by Xeon. On July 10, Streb commenced an action for breach of the employment contract. Xeon has asserted the Statute of Frauds as a defense. On July 30, Streb died. Under the circumstances, the employment contract is

a. Unenforceable because the value of the consideration given exceeds $500.

b. Unenforceable because it was not in writing and signed by Xeon.

c. Enforceable because it was possible that the contract could have been performed within 1 year from the making of the contract.

d. Enforceable because Streb's death occurred within 1 year from the making of the contract.

The correct answer is (b). *(CPA 587 L-13)*

REQUIRED: The enforceability of an oral employment contract.

DISCUSSION: The Statute of Frauds requires an agreement that cannot be performed within 1 year from the time it was formed to be in writing to be enforceable. This contract cannot be performed within 1 year because it is for a term of 3 years. Thus, it is unenforceable for lack of a writing.

Answer (a) is incorrect because the Statute of Frauds sets no minimum consideration for employment contracts. Answer (c) is incorrect because a contract to provide services for 3 years obviously cannot be performed in 1 year. Answer (d) is incorrect because if the contract had been in writing and signed by Xeon, Streb's estate could recover whatever performance was due from Xeon prior to or as a result of Streb's death.

120. Under the Statute of Frauds, an agreement not able to be performed within 1 year of its making is unenforceable unless in writing and signed by the party to be charged. Assuming the other elements of a contract are present, which of the following oral promises is not enforceable?

a. Tanya promises Ultima to support her for the rest of her life.

b. On January 1, Vance promises to act as Wally's agent for 1 year ending on the following January 1.

c. Xenia promises to serve as legal counsel for Yvonne's company for 2 years.

d. Zoe agrees to serve as Ava Company's vice-president for 1 year if Bee will sit on the board of directors for 18 months. Zoe has completed her performance.

The correct answer is (c). *(Publisher)*

REQUIRED: The oral promise unenforceable under the Statute of Frauds.

DISCUSSION: An oral contract that cannot be performed within 1 year (beginning the day after the contract is entered into) is unenforceable. An oral promise to serve for 2 years is within the Statute and thus unenforceable.

Answer (a) is incorrect because Ultima's life may end at any time and thus the contract could be performed within a year. Courts usually construe the provision so that a possibility of performance within 1 year takes a contract outside the Statute. Answer (b) is incorrect because the contract is to be performed within the year running from January 2 (the day after the contract was formed) to the following January 1. Answer (d) is incorrect because the majority view is that complete performance by one party renders the contract enforceable against the other party.

121. Jones, as seller, and Williams, as buyer, orally agreed for the purchase and sale of a dwelling. The spouse of Williams moved into the dwelling and spent substantial sums for repairs. Jones refused to convey title. Williams sued Jones and Jones pleaded the Statute of Frauds. The decision will be controlled by

a. The doctrine of part performance.

b. The fact that Williams, personally, has not performed.

c. The spouse's knowledge of the contract.

d. Whether Jones had knowledge of the spouse's acts.

The correct answer is (a). *(MBE 272 153)*

REQUIRED: The decisive factor in whether an oral agreement to sell realty will be enforced.

DISCUSSION: The Statute of Frauds ordinarily requires that such agreements be evidenced by a writing signed by the party sought to be bound. However, if the buyer has been permitted to take possession of the premises and has spent substantial sums on improvements or has paid a substantial amount of the purchase price, the seller will be prevented on equitable grounds from asserting the Statute of Frauds.

Answer (b) is incorrect because personal performance by the buyer is not necessary as long as someone tracing his/her rights through the buyer has substantially and detrimentally altered his/her position in reliance on the contract. Answers (c) and (d) are incorrect because what the spouse or Jones knew is irrelevant.

122. Rob Baker, the seller, authorized Smith in writing to sign a contract for the sale and purchase of land for him. Cal Arthur, the buyer, orally authorized Thomas to sign the contract for him. Smith and Thomas signed the contract: "Baker by Smith, his agent" and "Arthur by Thomas, his agent." Arthur refuses to complete the purchase. Baker sues Arthur who pleads the Statute of Frauds. Baker will

a. Win, because the sales contract was in writing.

b. Win, because his agency contract was in writing.

c. Lose, because he himself did not sign the contract.

d. Lose, because Arthur's agency contract was not in writing.

The correct answer is (d). *(MBE 272 60)*

REQUIRED: The result of a suit on a contract for the sale of land against a buyer whose agent signed the contract.

DISCUSSION: The Statute of Frauds requires that a contract to sell or purchase an interest in real property be in writing and signed by the party to be charged. Most states also require that the authority of an agent who signs such an agreement be in writing. The reasoning is that the appointment of an agent to perform a task within the Statute of Frauds should be of "equal dignity" or formality. Because Arthur's agency agreement was oral, Thomas's signature did not bind him. This principle should not be confused with general agency law, which does not require the agency contract to be in writing.

Answer (a) is incorrect because the sales contract was not signed by an agent whose authority was in writing. Answer (b) is incorrect because the Statute of Frauds requires only that the contract be signed by the party to be charged. Whether Baker's agent signed is irrelevant. Answer (c) is incorrect because Baker himself was not required to sign the contract. An agent may sign on behalf of the principal.

123. With regard to an agreement for the sale of real estate, the Statute of Frauds

a. Requires that the entire agreement be in a single writing.

b. Requires that the purchase price be fair and adequate in relation to the value of the real estate.

c. Does not require that the agreement be signed by all parties.

d. Does not apply if the value of the real estate is less than $500.

The correct answer is (c). *(CPA 1187 L-3)*

REQUIRED: The true statement regarding the Statute of Frauds.

DISCUSSION: The Statute of Frauds does not require a completely detailed, formal document. A written memorandum or note suffices, which need be signed only by the party sought to be held to the agreement.

Answer (a) is incorrect because the writing may be composed of more than one memorandum or document. Answer (b) is incorrect because the Statute defines the proof required to establish a contract, not its elements. Moreover, the adequacy of the consideration is not ordinarily a concern of the courts. Answer (d) is incorrect because the Statute sets no minimum value.

124. Vetter and Prue each signed a memorandum stating that Vetter agreed to sell and Prue agreed to purchase a tract of land. The memorandum contains all of the elements deemed necessary to satisfy the Statute of Frauds except for the purchase price. Vetter refused to perform, and Vetter relies upon the Statute of Frauds as a defense. If Prue offers evidence, in addition to the written memorandum, that the parties discussed and agreed upon a purchase price of $35,000 just prior to signing, Prue should

a. Succeed, because Vetter is estopped to deny that such agreed price is a fair one, which will be implied by law as a term of the written memorandum.

b. Succeed, because the law implies that the parties contracted for the reasonable market value of the land, although the price to be paid may not necessarily be that orally agreed upon.

c. Fail, because the price agreed upon is an essential element of the contract and must be in writing.

d. Fail, because the evidence does not show that the price agreed upon is in fact the reasonable market value of the land.

The correct answer is (c). *(MBE Part III-21)*

REQUIRED: The effect of the omission of the price term from the writing.

DISCUSSION: The Statute of Frauds requires that a contract to sell or purchase an interest in real property be in writing, be signed by the party to be charged, and contain a recitation of the material terms of the agreement. Prue should fail because the consideration for the sale of the realty is not stated in the writing evidencing the agreement. The statement of consideration is a material term of the contract.

Answers (a) and (b) are incorrect because a court will not infer the price term of a contract for the sale of real property. This rule contrasts with the UCC provision regarding a contract for the sale of goods. Under the UCC, a reasonable price may often be substituted for an omitted price term if there is sufficient evidence that the parties intended to contract. Answer (d) is incorrect because Prue will fail as a result of the insufficiency of the writing, not because the agreed price is not the reasonable market value. A court will seldom inquire into the reasonableness of consideration.

125. Which of the following will most likely not constitute a signature to satisfy the Statute of Frauds?

a. The printed name in a letterhead.

b. A signature at the top of a memorandum agreement.

c. A form with a pre-printed name of the company on a signature line.

d. Initials of the party.

The correct answer is (a). *(Publisher)*

REQUIRED: The item most likely insufficient as a signature under the Statute of Frauds.

DISCUSSION: A signature may be made in almost any fashion as long as the person making it intends it to authenticate his/her agreement to the document. The printed name in a letterhead could constitute a signature if so intended, but it is ordinarily used as mere identification.

Answer (b) is incorrect because a signature may appear anywhere on an agreement. Answer (c) is incorrect because a pre-printed name, even if not in handwriting, is a signature if so intended. Answer (d) is incorrect because the use of initials is a valid method of signing one's name.

11.9 Parol Evidence Rule

126. A written agreement signed by the two parties was intended to be their entire agreement. The parol evidence rule will prevent the admission of evidence that is offered to

a. Prove the existence of a contemporaneous oral agreement that modifies the contract.

b. Prove the existence of a subsequent oral agreement that modifies the contract.

c. Explain the meaning of an ambiguity in the written contract.

d. Establish that fraud had been committed in the formation of the contract.

The correct answer is (a). *(CPA 589 L-31)*

REQUIRED: The applicability of the parol evidence rule.

DISCUSSION: The parol evidence rule excludes all prior or contemporaneous oral or written agreements that would tend to add to, vary, or contradict the terms of a written agreement intended to be complete. The purpose of the rule is to determine the limits of the contract. If the parties meant their written agreement to be entire, only terms incorporated directly or by reference are part of the contract as it existed at the time it was set forth in writing and signed.

Answer (b) is incorrect because evidence of a later agreement does not modify the contract as it existed at the time it was made. Parties may subsequently change or rescind the contract. Answers (c) and (d) are incorrect because evidence to clarify an ambiguity or to prove fraud, duress, undue influence, mutual mistake, illegality, innocent misrepresentation, or another invalidating condition is admissible.

127. A ship came into port to receive a shipment of goods. The insurance policy provided that the policy would not be enforceable or effective while the ship was in port loading. The ship was fully loaded during the day and remained in port during the night while waiting for a storm to blow over. During the night the storm worsened and the ship was totally destroyed. A question has arisen whether the insurance policy covers the damage because the ship was not actually in the loading process, but was in port for the purpose of loading. Evidence of oral conversations at the time the contract was formed concerning this issue

a. Is prohibited by the parol evidence rule.

b. Is prohibited because all terms in insurance contracts are required to be in writing.

c. May be used only if all parties agree.

d. May be used to explain the meaning of a contractual provision as an exception to the parol evidence rule.

The correct answer is (d). *(Publisher)*

REQUIRED: The ability to use oral evidence to interpret a provision in a contract.

DISCUSSION: The parol evidence rule excludes evidence of prior or contemporaneous oral or written agreements that would add to, vary, or contradict the terms of a written agreement meant to be entire. However, there is an exception for oral evidence to explain ambiguous terms in the agreement.

Answer (a) is incorrect because the oral evidence will be admissible as an exception to the rule. Answer (b) is incorrect because there is no common law requirement that all terms in insurance contracts be in writing, but certain statutes may so provide. Answer (c) is incorrect because the oral evidence may be used to explain an ambiguous term regardless of whether all parties agree.

128. Ward is attempting to introduce oral evidence in an action relating to a written contract between Ward and Weaver. Weaver has pleaded the parol evidence rule. Ward will be prohibited from introducing parol evidence if it relates to

a. A modification made several days after the contract was executed.

b. A change in the meaning of an unambiguous provision in the contract.

c. Fraud in the inducement.

d. An obvious error in drafting.

The correct answer is (b). *(CPA 1189 L-16)*

REQUIRED: The circumstance in which oral evidence will be excluded.

DISCUSSION: The parol evidence rule applies to all prior or contemporaneous oral or written agreements that would tend to modify the terms of a written agreement intended to be complete. The purpose of the rule is to determine the limits of the contract. If the parties meant their written agreement to be entire, only terms incorporated directly or by reference are part of the contract as it existed at the time it was set forth in writing and signed. Thus, unless the parol evidence concerns a later modification or an ambiguity, mistake, or lack of reality of assent (fraud, duress, etc.), it will be excluded.

Answer (a) is incorrect because evidence of a subsequent modification is not excluded. The rule is intended only to protect the contract as it existed when it was made. Answers (c) and (d) are incorrect because evidence of ambiguities, fraud, duress, obvious errors, etc. may be admitted.

129. A clause in a contract stating that it represents all the agreements between the parties and that any changes or modifications must be in writing and signed is a(n)

a. Entirety clause.

b. Merger clause.

c. Parol clause.

d. Performance clause.

The correct answer is (a). *(Publisher)*

REQUIRED: The correct term for a clause representing that the agreement is complete.

DISCUSSION: A complete written contract may not be modified by evidence of prior or contemporaneous oral or written agreements. "Entirety" clauses in contracts indicate that the contracts are meant to be complete and that the parol evidence rule will apply. These clauses often require modifications to be in a signed writing to prevent variance of the contract by subsequent oral agreements.

Answer (b) is incorrect because a merger clause means that prior agreements have been consolidated into the last agreement and only the terms therein can be enforced. Answer (c) is incorrect because a "parol clause" is a nonsense term. Answer (d) is incorrect because a performance clause simply states the obligations of the parties.

130. Twinco agreed to purchase 5,000 square feet of office space from Susan Park. Slightly more than half the space was already occupied. Because Twinco needed the entire space by the closing date (August 31), Park agreed to obtain the tenant's early departure from the premises. If Park were unable to do so, she would construct an additional 2,750 square feet of office space for Twinco. Park obtained the tenant's release, but for October 31 rather than August 31. When Twinco and Park met for the closing on September 7, Twinco insisted that Park build the additional office space under the terms of their agreement. Park refused to close if the deed contained any language requiring her to build more office space. After consulting with its attorney, Twinco signed the closing documents "under protest" because of its need to take possession of the building before its current lease expired on September 30. Must Park construct more office space for Twinco?

a. No. The contract to purchase merged with the deed, thus negating any obligation Park may have had to build under the original agreement.

b. No. The delay in closing invalidated any obligations Park may have had under the contract to purchase.

c. Yes. Even though the deed did not include a provision requiring new construction, this term in the purchase agreement is sufficient to obligate Park to build the new space.

d. Yes. Park's wrongful conduct in refusing to execute a deed with a construction provision forced Twinco to sign the deed against its will and to its economic detriment. Thus, Twinco can assert an "economic duress" defense to the merger doctrine.

The correct answer is (a). *(S. Willey)*

REQUIRED: The effect of a later agreement after one party has refused to perform under a prior one concerning the same subject matter.

DISCUSSION: Under the merger doctrine, a new agreement between the parties supersedes their prior obligations. A deed is presumed to be the final agreement between the parties. By accepting the deed, Twinco waived any rights it may have had under a prior contract. Here, the provision requiring Park to construct new office space if the tenant did not vacate the premises prior to closing was superseded by the deed that contained no such language.

Answer (b) is incorrect because merger is unaffected by the delay. Answer (c) is incorrect because the prior agreement was superseded. Answer (d) is incorrect because although the distinction between Park bargaining and economic duress is a fine one, Twinco cannot plead the latter even though it executed the deed "under protest." The wrongful conduct must create the pressure of a business necessity or economic hardship that compels a party to execute an agreement against its will and to its economic detriment. No threats were used to obtain Twinco's signature, and the facts do not indicate that Twinco was faced with economic ruin if it did not sign. Twinco could have elected to sue for breach of the old agreement instead of signing the closing documents. After consulting with its attorney, Twinco willingly executed the deed, which extinguished Park's obligation to build new office space.

11.10 Third-Party Beneficiaries

131. Jones owned an insurance policy on her life, on which she paid all the premiums. Smith was named the beneficiary. Jones died and the insurance company refused to pay the insurance proceeds to Smith. An action by Smith against the insurance company for the insurance proceeds will be

a. Successful because Smith is a third-party donee beneficiary.

b. Successful because Smith is a proper assignee of Jones' rights under the insurance policy.

c. Unsuccessful because Smith was not the owner of the policy.

d. Unsuccessful because Smith did not pay any of the premiums.

The correct answer is (a). *(CPA 1189 L-17)*

REQUIRED: The outcome of a suit by a beneficiary against an insurer and the reason.

DISCUSSION: A contractual agreement entered into by two or more primary parties that is intended to directly benefit a third person is a third-party beneficiary contract. If the intent is to make a gift of the promised performance, the third party is a donee beneficiary. The beneficiary of a life insurance policy is such a donee if the insured paid the premiums. The obvious intent of the policy is to provide benefits to a named party at the death of the insured. Smith's rights vested at the death of Jones if not before, and Smith has standing to sue on the contract. If Jones did not retain the power to change the beneficiary, Smith's rights would have vested earlier.

Answer (b) is incorrect because no rights held by Jones were transferred (assigned) to Smith, such as the right to borrow against the cash surrender value or change the beneficiary. Answers (c) and (d) are incorrect because Smith prevails as the party intended to be benefited by the contract.

132. Krieg was the owner of an office building encumbered by a mortgage securing Krieg's promissory note to Muni Bank. Park purchased the building subject to Muni's mortgage. As a result of the sale to Park,

a. Muni is not a third-party creditor beneficiary.

b. Krieg is a third-party creditor beneficiary.

c. Park is liable for any deficiency resulting from a default on the note.

d. Krieg was automatically released from any liability on the note.

The correct answer is (a). *(CPA 587 L-23)*

REQUIRED: The result of the sale of property to a buyer who took subject to the mortgage.

DISCUSSION: Muni does not qualify as a third-party creditor beneficiary of the Krieg-Park contract because Park did not assume the mortgage, that is, agree to be personally liable to Muni under its terms. Hence, Krieg's legal duty to pay Muni was not delegated, and Muni received no benefit under the contract because it did not acquire rights against Park.

Answer (b) is incorrect because Krieg is a party to the sale, not a third-party beneficiary. Answer (c) is incorrect because only Krieg is personally liable upon default. Park merely took subject to the mortgage. Answer (d) is incorrect because only an agreement with Muni or performance of the contract could release Krieg from liability.

133. Pete Fenwar purchased a new car from Zippy Auto Sales. Zippy provided a financing package that was to include liability insurance. Several days later Fenwar, while driving the car, ran a red light and injured Myrtle. If Zippy failed to obtain the liability insurance, from whom can Myrtle recover?

a. Only Fenwar.

b. Only Zippy Auto Sales.

c. Only the finance company with which Zippy made the financing arrangements.

d. Both Fenwar and Zippy.

The correct answer is (d). *(Publisher)*

REQUIRED: The person(s) liable when a third party contracted to provide liability insurance for defendant.

DISCUSSION: Myrtle is an intended third-party beneficiary of the contract between Fenwar and Zippy. Although Myrtle was not specifically named or identified in the contract, she is a member of the class of persons who were to benefit from the liability insurance that Zippy promised. Thus, she can recover from Zippy for breach of contract. She can recover from Fenwar on the tort of negligence.

Answers (a) and (b) are incorrect because both Fenwar and Zippy are liable. Fenwar is liable for his own negligent act. Answer (c) is incorrect because the finance company made no contractual promises to obtain the insurance.

134. In January, Insurer and Insured enter into a life insurance contract. Insured retained the right to change the beneficiary. In June, Beneficiary learned of the existence of the agreement. In September, Insured died without naming another beneficiary. When, if ever, did Beneficiary's rights vest?

a. September.

b. June.

c. January.

d. Plaintiff has no rights under the contract.

The correct answer is (a). *(Publisher)*

REQUIRED: The time when a life insurance beneficiary's rights vested.

DISCUSSION: If the primary parties (promisor and promisee) agree to a discharge or modification of their contract before the third-party beneficiary's rights have vested (fixed), (s)he may not be able to enforce the original agreement. The time of vesting varies among the jurisdictions. Some courts hold that vesting occurs at the formation of the contract. Others require detrimental reliance by the beneficiary. A third position is that rights vest when the beneficiary learns of the agreement. In a life insurance contract, however, a beneficiary of an insured who retained the right to change the beneficiary has a mere expectancy until the insured's death.

135. Barr entered into a contract with Gray that required Gray to construct a warehouse on land owned by Barr. The contract specifically provided for Gray to use Apex Corp. pipe fittings for all the plumbing. Gray failed to use Apex pipe fittings. Apex had learned of the contract between Barr and Gray and, in anticipation of receiving an order from Gray, manufactured additional pipe fittings. Apex is

a. Entitled to money damages because of Gray's breach of contract.

b. Entitled to money damages because it changed its position to its detriment by relying on the contract.

c. Not entitled to money damages because it is merely a donee beneficiary.

d. Not entitled to money damages because it is merely an incidental beneficiary.

The correct answer is (d). *(CPA 586 L-13)*

REQUIRED: The status of a manufacturer regarding a construction contract stipulating the use of its product.

DISCUSSION: A person who is neither a primary contracting party nor an intended third-party beneficiary has no standing to sue on a contract. Apex is a mere incidental beneficiary, a person who may have been indirectly affected by the agreement but was not intended to be directly benefited.

Answers (a) and (b) are incorrect because Apex was not an intended beneficiary and has no standing to sue. Answer (c) is incorrect because a person is a donee beneficiary if the promisor's performance was intended as a gift to that person.

136. The Ballet Center entered into a contract with the Merry Toes Troupe to present the Nutcracker Suite a week before Christmas. On December 10, the Merry Toes Troupe canceled its appearance. Earl Eager owns an ice cream shop near the Ballet Center and planned on large profits from the 3-day presentation of the ballet. If Eager sues the Merry Toes, he will

a. Win as a donee beneficiary.

b. Win as a creditor beneficiary.

c. Win because he is in privity.

d. Lose as an incidental beneficiary.

The correct answer is (d). *(S. Rand)*

REQUIRED: The outcome of a suit by a merchant affected economically by the breach of a contract to which he was not a party.

DISCUSSION: Eager was not a party to the contract between the Ballet Center and the Merry Toes Troupe, and he was not contemplated by the parties as a beneficiary of their agreement. Thus, Eager cannot recover from the breaching party. Eager is an incidental beneficiary who possesses no rights under the law.

Answer (a) is incorrect because the parties did not intend to make a gift to Eager. Answer (b) is incorrect because Eager was not a creditor and certainly not intended to receive a contractual benefit. Answer (c) is incorrect because Eager was neither a party to the agreement nor a plaintiff with standing to sue thereon.

11.11 Assignment and Delegation

137. Seller delivers goods to Buyer who agrees to pay the $5,000 price in 60 days. Seller transfers its right to receive the price to Bank at a 10% discount. Which of the following is false?

a. Upon receipt of notice of the assignment, Buyer (the obligor) must pay Bank to discharge its obligations.

b. Seller (the assignor) has no right to make further assignments or collect payments for its own benefit.

c. Seller is obligated to pay the assignee in the event the obligor fails to pay, unless the assignment was specifically without recourse.

d. After notice of the assignment, Bank (the assignee) can sue Buyer directly if Buyer does not pay.

The correct answer is (c). *(Publisher)*

REQUIRED: The false statement about the transfer of a contract right for consideration.

DISCUSSION: Most rights acquired by contract may be transferred by the owner (the assignor) to another person (the assignee). The assignee receives all the rights assigned but is subject to the defenses the obligor has against the assignor. An assignor who receives consideration impliedly warrants that the claim is genuine, that the assignor has not impaired and will not impair the value of the assignment, but not that the claim will be paid. Thus, if the obligor does not pay the assignee, there is no recourse against the assignor unless the assignment is agreed to be with recourse.

Answer (a) is incorrect because after notice and a reasonable opportunity to verify the assignment, the obligor must honor the assignment (by paying the assignee) or risk having to pay twice. Answer (b) is incorrect because an assignor who receives consideration impliedly warrants that (s)he will not impair the value of the assignment. Also, an assignor who receives payment after the assignment must account to the assignee. Answer (d) is incorrect because the assignee may enforce his/her rights against the debtor (the obligor) by direct action.

138. Ecks sells goods to Wei on credit. Ecks then transfers the contract right to receive payment to See for cash. Meanwhile, Wei renders services to Aye, who agrees to pay the debt Wei originally owed to Ecks. All parties have notice of these transactions. Which of the following is true?

a. The Ecks-Wei transaction is an assignment.

b. The Ecks-See transaction is a delegation.

c. The Wei-Aye transaction is a delegation.

d. The Wei-Aye transaction is an assignment.

The correct answer is (c). *(Publisher)*

REQUIRED: The statement correctly describing one of the transactions.

DISCUSSION: Ecks transferred a right to collect a debt to See. This transaction was an assignment: Ecks intended to make a voluntary, present transfer of a right. Wei transferred to Aye a duty to pay a debt. This transaction was a delegation: Wei intended to authorize Aye to perform the obligation owed to Ecks. An assignment extinguishes the transferor's right to receive a performance, but a delegation obligates the transferee without extinguishing the transferor's duty.

Answer (a) is incorrect because Ecks and Wei are the original contracting parties. Answer (b) is incorrect because Ecks assigned a right to See. Answer (d) is incorrect because Wei delegated a duty to Aye.

139. Heather bought a french horn from Patrick on credit. Patrick then sold the receivable to Carol for cash. Heather had notice of the transfer. Which of the following is true?

a. Heather was a delegator, obligor, promisor, and debtor.

b. Carol was an assignor, obligee, promisee, and debtor.

c. Carol was a delegatee and Patrick is a delegator.

d. Patrick was an assignor, obligee, promisee, and creditor.

The correct answer is (d). *(Publisher)*

REQUIRED: The correct description of the parties to the transfer of a receivable.

DISCUSSION: Patrick's transfer to Carol of Heather's promise to pay was an assignment. In the course of these transactions, Patrick was an assignor, a promisee (recipient of a promise), an obligee (the person to whom an obligation is owed), and a creditor of the debtor.

Answers (a) and (c) are incorrect because no delegation of a duty occurred. Answer (b) is incorrect because Carol was an assignee, an obligee, and a creditor, but was never Heather's promisee.

140. Patty sells her bassoon to Karl on credit. Karl then exchanges the bassoon for Ann's tuba. Ann also agrees to pay the debt Karl originally owed to Patty. Which of the following is true?

a. Karl is a delegator, Ann is a delegatee, and Patty is an obligee.

b. Karl is an assignor and Ann is an assignee.

c. Patty is a delegator, obligor, and promisor.

d. Ann is a promisor, debtor, and a delegator.

The correct answer is (a). *(Publisher)*

REQUIRED: The correct description of the parties to a transfer of a duty.

DISCUSSION: Karl authorized Ann to pay the debt owed to Patty. This delegation created a new obligor but did not extinguish the delegator's obligation to perform his promise. Accordingly, Karl is a delegator, obligor, promisor, and debtor. Ann is a delegatee, obligor, promisor (to Karl), and debtor. Patty is a promisee, obligee, and creditor.

Answer (b) is incorrect because a delegation rather than an assignment took place. Answer (c) is incorrect because Patty owes no obligation and was not a party to the delegation. Answer (d) is incorrect because Ann is a delegatee.

141. Alice sells Monica a mink coat for $1,000 due on July 4. Alice assigns the debt to Lola as a gift. On July 4, Monica tells Lola that because of financial reversals she cannot pay. Moreover, the fur has been lost in a fire. In this case, Lola has a legal right to collect $1,000 from

a. Monica.

b. Alice.

c. Either Monica or Alice.

d. Neither party.

The correct answer is (a). *(J. Norwood)*

REQUIRED: The rights of the assignee against the debtor and the assignor.

DISCUSSION: If the debtor fails to pay the assignee, the assignee has rights against the debtor but no recourse against the assignor, unless the assignor guaranteed that the debt would be paid. Even though no consideration was given, Lola is the assignee and has a right to collect on the debt from Monica.

Answers (b) and (c) are incorrect because Lola has no rights against the assignor (Alice) in the absence of consideration and a guarantee that the debt would be paid. Answer (d) is incorrect because Lola does have rights against the debtor.

142. Which of the following is a true statement about the requirements of an assignment?

a. A writing is required that mentions assignment.

b. Consideration is not required.

c. The assignment must be authorized by statute.

d. Only a gratuitous assignment must be in writing.

The correct answer is (b). *(Publisher)*

REQUIRED: The true statement about the requirements of an assignment.

DISCUSSION: Unless a statute provides otherwise, an assignment requires only a manifestation of the assignor's intent to make a present transfer such that the assignor's right to receive the obligor's performance is wholly or partly extinguished in favor of the assignee. The assignment may be oral, gratuitous, and in any form or language.

Answer (a) is incorrect because no writing is required unless the Statute of Frauds or other statute happens to apply, and no particular words need be used. Answer (c) is incorrect because whereas early common law strictly enforced the privity requirement to prevent transfer of contract rights, the needs of a complex commercial society led to the general recognition of assignments. Answer (d) is incorrect because gratuitous (gift) assignments may be oral. However, they are revocable until an effective delivery has been made.

143. Stevens sells personal property to Baurer for $1,700 due in 30 days from the date of delivery. Stevens assigns the account to Adams without consideration. Which action precludes revocation by Stevens?

a. Death or bankruptcy of Stevens.

b. Subsequent assignment of the same rights by Stevens to George.

c. Notice to Adams by Stevens of revocation.

d. Assignment by Adams to Ansel for consideration.

The correct answer is (d). *(Publisher)*

REQUIRED: The act precluding revocation of an assignment made without consideration.

DISCUSSION: Assignments need not be supported by consideration, but as in other situations involving gratuitous promises or executory gifts, revocation is possible. An assignment without consideration is revoked by operation of law upon the death, insanity, or bankruptcy of the assignor; by the subsequent assignment of the same rights by the assignor; or by notice of revocation given by the assignor to the assignee. If the assignee has collected from the obligor or made a further assignment for consideration, the revocation is not effective.

Answers (a), (b) and (c) are incorrect because each states a method of revoking a gratuitous assignment.

144. Abe Walton owed $10,000 to Ted Grant. Grant assigned his claim against Walton to the Line Finance Company for value on October 15. On October 25, Al Hayes assigned his matured claim for $2,000 against Grant to Walton for value. On October 30, Line notified Walton of the assignment of the $10,000 debt owed by Walton to Grant. Line has demanded payment in full. Insofar as the rights of the various parties are concerned,

a. Walton has the right of a $2,000 set-off against the debt that he owed Grant.

b. Walton must pay Line in full, but has the right to obtain a $2,000 reimbursement from Grant.

c. Line is a creditor beneficiary of the debt owed by Walton.

d. The claimed set-off of the Hayes claim for $2,000 is invalid because it is for an amount less than the principal debt.

The correct answer is (a). *(CPA 1182 L-13)*

REQUIRED: The rights of the parties when an assignor-creditor becomes a debtor of the original obligor.

DISCUSSION: Grant was the original creditor (obligee) of Walton. By assignment from Hayes, Walton became a creditor of Grant after Grant had assigned his claim against Walton to Line but before Walton was notified of the transfer. In the absence of the assignment to Line, Walton could have pleaded a $2,000 right of set-off against Grant as a result of the Hayes assignment. An assignee (Line) receives the assignor's (Grant's) rights subject to any defenses, rights of set-off, or counterclaims assertible by the obligor (Walton) against the assignor that arise prior to the receipt of notice of the assignment. Hence, Walton has a right of set-off against Line.

Answer (b) is incorrect because Walton only owes $8,000 to Line after the set-off. Answer (c) is incorrect because Walton and Grant presumably did not intend to benefit Line when they contracted. Line is only an assignee, not a beneficiary. Answer (d) is incorrect because a set-off is possible against all or part of the claim.

145. On May 2, Kurtz Co. assigned to City Bank for $65,000 its entire interest in a $70,000 account receivable due in 60 days from Long. On May 4, City notified Long of the assignment. On May 7, Long informed City that Kurtz had committed fraud in the transaction out of which the account receivable arose and that payment would not be made to City. If City commences an action against Long and Long is able to prove Kurtz acted fraudulently

a. Long will be able to successfully assert fraud as a defense.

b. City will be entitled to collect $65,000, the amount paid for the assignment.

c. City will be entitled to collect $70,000 because fraud in the inducement is a personal defense that was lost on May 2.

d. City will be entitled to collect $70,000 because Long's allegation of fraud arose after notice of the assignment.

The correct answer is (a). *(CPA 587 L-21)*

REQUIRED: The outcome if the debtor asserts a defense against the assignee that is effective against the assignor.

DISCUSSION: The assignee (City) has the same rights but is subject to the same defenses as the assignor (Kurtz) in an action against the debtor (Long). Accordingly, if the defense of fraud would be effective against Kurtz, it will also succeed against City.

Answers (b), (c), and (d) are incorrect because Long's defense against Kurtz is also good against City. Moreover, fraud in the inducement has the status of a personal defense only under the law of negotiable instruments. A personal defense is one that can be asserted between the original parties but not against a holder in due course of the instrument. The facts do not indicate that a negotiable instrument was transferred or that City was a holder in due course.

146. Quick Corp. has $270,000 of outstanding accounts receivable. On March 10, 1988, Quick assigned a $30,000 account receivable due from Pine, one of Quick's customers, to Taft Bank for value. On March 30, Pine paid Quick the $30,000. On April 5, Taft notified Pine of the March 10 assignment from Quick to Taft. Taft is entitled to collect $30,000 from

a. Either Quick or Pine.

b. Neither Quick nor Pine.

c. Pine only.

d. Quick only.

The correct answer is (d). *(CPA 588 L-23)*

REQUIRED: The party liable on an assigned receivable paid prior to the assignee's notice to the debtor.

DISCUSSION: This contract was an assignment of the account receivable. The assignee (Taft) became the owner of the receivable (rather than a holder for security purposes) and was the only party entitled to payment. The debtor (Pine), however, was entitled to notice of the assignment so it would know whom to pay. Until given this notice, it was entitled to pay Quick and be relieved of the debt. Quick, the assignor, must account to the assignee, so Quick but not Pine is liable to Taft. Quick holds the amount paid as trustee for Taft.

147. McDonald was entitled to insurance proceeds from an insurance company. While waiting for payment, McDonald assigned the contract right to Mohawk on July 1. In need of additional funds, McDonald also assigned this contract right to Niagra on July 15 and to Shapiro on August 1. Mohawk neglected to notify the insurance company, but Niagra sent a written notice of the assignment to the insurance company. Shapiro also sent a written notice to the insurance company that was lost after its receipt by the general manager. Which of the following has priority in the contract right if each is present when the insurance company is ready to discharge its obligation?

a. Mohawk.

b. Niagra.

c. Shapiro.

d. McDonald.

The correct answer is (a). *(Publisher)*

REQUIRED: The assignee with priority in a contract right that was the subject of successive assignments.

DISCUSSION: When contract rights are successively assigned to different assignees, the first assignee has priority (unless the assignment was made without consideration). Once the assignment has been made, the assignor has nothing left to assign. A minority rule provides that the first to give notice to the obligor (insurance company) has priority, but this is not the general rule (the minority rule is followed under certain sections of the UCC, e.g., Article 9).

Answers (b) and (c) are incorrect because Niagra and Shapiro were assignees subsequent to Mohawk. Whether notice is given does not affect priority in most states. Answer (d) is incorrect because the assignor has absolutely no rights to the insurance proceeds. An assignor who receives the assigned proceeds is treated as a trustee and must hold them for the assignee.

148. Which of the following warranties by an assignor is not implied in an assignment for value of a contract right?

a. The debtor is solvent and will pay the debt under the contract.

b. The contract right is a valid claim.

c. The assignor will not interfere with collection by the assignee.

d. The parties have the capacity to enter into the original contract.

The correct answer is (a). *(Publisher)*

REQUIRED: The warranty not implied in an assignment for value of a contract right.

DISCUSSION: There is no implied warranty in an assignment of a contract right that the debtor is solvent or will pay. This risk is assumed by the assignee. Thus, many assignments of contract rights are discounted. Express warranties (of solvency, payments, etc.) supported by consideration may be bargained for.

Answer (b) is incorrect because a warranty is implied that the contract right is a valid claim. Otherwise, the assignee for value would be taking a substantial risk that (s)he will receive nothing. Answer (c) is incorrect because the assignor does impliedly warrant not to interfere with collection by the assignee. Answer (d) is incorrect because the capacity to enter into the original contract is a necessary element for the contract right to be a valid claim. Consequently, capacity must also be implied in the assignment.

149. Which of the following is not subject to assignment?

a. Salary not yet earned.

b. A contract to sell specially manufactured goods.

c. Compensation from contracts not yet entered into.

d. A construction contract.

The correct answer is (c). *(Publisher)*

REQUIRED: The improper subject matter for an assignment.

DISCUSSION: Although compensation is usually assignable, compensation from contracts that have not yet been entered into is not assignable. It is considered a mere expectancy; the assignor has no property right to assign until the contract is actually formed.

Answer (a) is incorrect because wages and salary can be assigned even if not yet earned as long as the person is currently in a position to earn them. Many statutes restrict this kind of assignment. Answer (b) is incorrect because contracts to sell goods are assignable whether or not the goods are specially manufactured. Answer (d) is incorrect because construction contracts are commonly assignable; e.g., a general contractor usually assigns part of the contract to subcontractors.

150. A manufacturer contracted with a supplier to obtain a raw material. The agreement included a covenant not to assign the contract. However, the supplier made an "assignment of the contract" as security for a loan. Which of the following accurately states the legal effect of the covenant not to assign the contract?

a. The covenant made the assignment ineffective.

b. The covenant had no legal effect.

c. The assignment was a breach of contract but was nevertheless effective to transfer rights against the obligor.

d. By normal interpretation, a covenant against assignment in a sale-of-goods agreement applies only to the buyer, not the seller.

The correct answer is (c). *(MBE Part I-188)*

REQUIRED: The legal effect of the covenant not to assign the contract.

DISCUSSION: A prohibition against assignment of a contract is construed, with respect to the contract rights, as only a promise not to assign (not an absolute prohibition). Therefore, the assignment is effective, although also a breach of the contract. If the agreement contains plain words making any attempted assignment void, the courts will enforce the restriction except if it is an attempt to prohibit or restrict the assignment of an account or the money to be earned. Under the UCC, such a restriction is ineffective.

Answer (a) is incorrect because the assignment of rights was effective. The covenant is only construed as a promise. Answer (b) is incorrect because the covenant probably is effective to prohibit the delegation of the supplier's duty to perform and to give the manufacturer a possible right to damages (if any). Answer (d) is incorrect because the covenant would apply to both the buyer and the seller.

151. Ordinarily, which one of the following transfers will be valid without the consent of the other parties?

a. The assignment by the lessee of a lease contract if rent is a percentage of sales.

b. The assignment by a purchaser of goods of the right to buy on credit without giving security.

c. The assignment by an architect of a contract to design a building.

d. The assignment by a patent holder of the right to receive royalties.

The correct answer is (d). *(CPA 589 L-33)*

REQUIRED: The transfer valid without the consent of the other parties.

DISCUSSION: Unless agreed otherwise, most rights acquired by contract can be assigned, but when the exercise of contract rights calls for personal skill or judgment, they may not be assigned. Also, an assignment is not effective when it materially changes the duty of the obligor, increases the burden or risk imposed, or impairs the chance of obtaining a repeat performance. Moreover, some assignments may be against public policy, such as those prohibited or regulated by state statutes governing assignment of future wages. The assignment of a right to receive money or goods, however, is usually valid because the burden on the debtor is not materially changed. The right to receive royalties is therefore assignable.

Answer (a) is incorrect because this assignment is invalid without the lessor's consent. The lessor's risk is materially changed because the assignee's sales may be substantially less than those of the assignor. Answer (b) is incorrect because the assignee may not be as creditworthy as the assignor, and the seller's bad debt risk could increase. Answer (c) is incorrect because personal service contracts cannot be assigned.

152. A common law duty is delegable even though the

a. Contract provides that the duty is nondelegable.

b. Duty delegated is the payment of money and the delegatee is not as creditworthy as the delegator.

c. Delegation will result in a material variance in performance by the delegatee.

d. Duty to be performed involves personal services.

The correct answer is (b). *(CPA 1182 L-11)*

REQUIRED: The circumstance in which a common law duty is delegable.

DISCUSSION: Contract rights may be assigned; contract duties may be delegated. Delegation of a contract duty is usually allowed when the delegatee's performance would be substantially the same as that of the delegator. Accordingly, the delegation of a duty to pay money or to perform standardized services is permitted. An important reason for this rule is that a delegated duty is assumed by the delegatee, which results in a third-party beneficiary contract. Thus, in the event of breach, the obligee can hold both delegator and delegatee responsible.

Answer (a) is incorrect because courts protect obligees by enforcing contractual prohibitions against delegation. Answers (c) and (d) are incorrect because a duty is not delegable when the performance would vary materially from that contracted for.

153. A CPA was engaged by Jackson & Wilcox, a small retail partnership, to audit its financial statements. The CPA discovered that, because of other commitments, the engagement could not be completed on time. The CPA therefore unilaterally delegated the duty to Vincent, an equally competent CPA. Under these circumstances, which of the following is true?

a. The duty to perform the audit engagement is delegable in that it is determined by an objective standard.

b. If Jackson & Wilcox refuses to accept Vincent because one of the partners personally dislikes Vincent, Jackson & Wilcox will be liable for breach of contract.

c. Jackson & Wilcox must accept the delegation if Vincent is equally competent.

d. The duty to perform the audit engagement is nondelegable, and Jackson & Wilcox need not accept Vincent as a substitute.

The correct answer is (d). *(CPA 1177 L-3)*

REQUIRED: The effect of the unilateral delegation by a CPA of the duty to audit financial statements.

DISCUSSION: Personal service contracts, or those involving confidential relationships, are not assignable or delegable. Performance by different auditors will not necessarily be substantially the same because of the delicate nature of the relationship and the professional judgments involved. Hence, Jackson & Wilcox need not accept Vincent as a substitute.

Answer (a) is incorrect because the duty to perform the audit engagement is nondelegable. An objective standard is difficult to establish for audits because professional judgment and confidentiality are very significant factors. Answer (b) is incorrect because Jackson & Wilcox has no duty to accept another CPA. The motives of the partners are irrelevant. Answer (c) is incorrect because the competence of the delegates is also irrelevant.

154. Fennell and Mac McLeod entered into a binding contract whereby McLeod was to perform routine construction services according to Fennell's blueprints. McLeod assigned the contract to Conerly. After the assignment

a. Fennell can bring suit under the doctrine of anticipatory breach.

b. McLeod extinguishes all his rights and duties under the contract.

c. McLeod extinguishes all his rights but is not relieved of his duties under the contract.

d. McLeod still has all his rights but is relieved of his duties under the contract.

The correct answer is (c). *(CPA 1181 L-5)*

REQUIRED: The effect of assigning a contract to perform routine construction services.

DISCUSSION: Assignment of rights and delegation of duties under a contract are both permissible when the work is so routine that the hiring party only desires the results and not the personal services of the delegator. After the transfer, McLeod has no more rights under the original contract (because he assigned them to Conerly), but he is still liable for his duties if Conerly does not perform them.

Answer (a) is incorrect because it is not a breach to assign a nonpersonal contract. Conerly should be able to perform the services just as well as McLeod. Answer (b) is incorrect because McLeod is still liable to Fennell if Conerly does not perform. Answer (d) is incorrect because McLeod assigned his rights but is still liable under the original contract to Fennell until Conerly completes construction.

155. Bonnie Brook Wholesalers ordered 10,000 5-pound bags of standard granulated household sugar from Crane Sugar Plantations, Inc. for delivery within 2 months. Because Crane underestimated its existing backlog of orders and overestimated its inventory, it found that it would be either unable or extremely hard-pressed to fill the order on time. Consequently, Crane assigned the contract to Devon Sugars, Inc., a smaller local producer and jobber, and paid Devon $200. Midway through the performance Devon defaulted because one of its suppliers' warehouses was destroyed by fire. Bonnie seeks to recover damages for breach of contract from both Crane and Devon. In the event of litigation, which of the following statements is correct?

a. The unforeseen fire that destroyed the supplier's warehouse negates any liability on Devon's part.

b. Devon will prevail because Devon has no contractual duty to Bonnie.

c. Bonnie will not prevail against either Crane or Devon unless Bonnie first exhausts its rights against the supplier whose warehouse was destroyed.

d. Bonnie will prevail against either Crane or Devon but will be entitled to only one recovery.

The correct answer is (d). *(CPA 578 L-44)*

REQUIRED: The obligee's rights against the original obligor and its assignee.

DISCUSSION: As an assignee of the contract, Devon both acquired the rights and assumed the liabilities of Crane on this contract. However, Crane remained liable if Devon did not perform. As the person to whom the contracted duties were owed (obligee), Bonnie may hold either Crane or Devon liable, but will be entitled to only one recovery of damages.

Answer (a) is incorrect because Devon contracted to supply the goods and could obtain them elsewhere to fulfill its obligation. Answer (b) is incorrect because Devon agreed to accept the contractual obligation to Bonnie. Answer (c) is incorrect because the supplier was a party neither to the assignment nor the contract with Bonnie.

156. Charles Lands offered to sell his business to Donald Bright. The assets consisted of real property, merchandise, office equipment, and the rights under certain contracts to purchase goods at an agreed price. In consideration for receipt of the aforementioned assets, Bright was to pay $125,000 and assume all business liabilities owed by Lands. Bright accepted the offer and a written contract was signed by both parties. Under the circumstances, the contract

a. Represents an assignment of all the business assets and rights Lands owned and a delegation of whatever duties Lands was obligated to perform.

b. Must be agreed to by all Lands' creditors and the parties who had agreed to deliver goods to Lands.

c. Frees Lands from all liability to his creditors once the purchase is consummated.

d. Is too indefinite and uncertain to be enforced.

The correct answer is (a). *(CPA 1174 L-23)*

REQUIRED: The legal effect of a contract to sell a business.

DISCUSSION: The sale of an entire business necessarily involves the assignment of certain rights and the delegation of various duties. Bright will own the physical assets, be able to assert Lands' rights under the purchase contracts, and be responsible for liabilities and performance.

Answer (b) is incorrect because this assignment of rights and delegation of duties need not be agreed to by the creditors or suppliers. A debtor may delegate the simple duty to pay money and other nonpersonal duties, especially because (s)he remains liable unless a novation is made. Answer (c) is incorrect because Lands remains liable to the creditors if Bright does not pay. Answer (d) is incorrect because the contract is sufficiently definite. The rights and liabilities can be precisely ascertained.

Questions 157 and 158 are based on the following information. On February 1, Barron Explosives received an order from Super Construction, Inc. for 200 cases of dynamite at $25 per case with terms of 2/10, net/30, for delivery within 2 months, FOB seller's warehouse. The order was duly accepted in writing by Barron. Super soon discovered that it was already overstocked with dynamite. Thus, it contacted Chubb Construction Company about taking over the contract. Chubb accepted and signed the following agreement on February 10:

> Super Construction, Inc. hereby assigns its contract for the purchase of 200 cases of dynamite at $25 per case ordered from Barron Explosives on February 1 to Chubb Construction Company. Chubb Construction hereby accepts.
>
> (Signed) Super, President
> Super Construction, Inc.
>
> (Signed) Chubb, President
> Chubb Construction Company

Since February 1, the price of dynamite has increased substantially, and as a result, Super now wishes to avoid the assignment and obtain the dynamite for itself. Barron wishes to avoid having to deliver to either party.

---

157. Which of the following statements best describes the legal status of the parties to the contract?

a. Barron can avoid its obligation on the contract if it has reasonable grounds for insecurity because Chubb's credit rating is inferior to Super's.

b. The assignment in question transfers to Chubb both the rights and the duties under the contract.

c. Super can avoid the assignment to Chubb for lack of consideration on Chubb's part.

d. The contract is not assignable because it would materially vary Barron's duty to perform.

The correct answer is (b). *(CPA 575 L-36)*

REQUIRED: The legal status of the parties to a contract for the sale of assigned goods.

DISCUSSION: Rights may be assigned and duties delegated under contracts for the sale of goods unless otherwise agreed or unless the other party's duty to perform or risk incurred would be materially altered (UCC 2-210). All the elements necessary for a valid contract are present to make the Super-Chubb assignment binding.

Answer (a) is incorrect because if Barron has reasonable grounds for insecurity, it may demand adequate assurance of performance. Also, Super is still liable if Chubb breaches. Answer (c) is incorrect because Chubb gave consideration by agreeing to perform Super's duties under the initial contract. An executed assignment requires no consideration, although a promise to assign does. Answer (d) is incorrect because Barron's duty to perform is not materially varied on these facts. Barron will simply collect the payment from Chubb instead of Super.

158. Assume that Super did not assign the contract, but that Barron Explosives found that it could not perform and therefore assigned the contract to a nearby competitor, Demerest Explosives. Demerest promised Barron it would perform on the Super contract and expressly released Barron from any responsibility. Demerest subsequently defaulted and has refused to deliver. Under these circumstances

a. Barron's delegation of its duty to perform to Demerest constitutes an anticipatory breach of contract.

b. Super need not perform because the assignment of the contract materially alters its burden of performing.

c. Super can immediately proceed against Barron upon default by Demerest.

d. Super has recourse only against Barron.

The correct answer is (c). *(CPA 575 L-37)*

REQUIRED: The legal effect of a default by the assignee of a supplier.

DISCUSSION: The assignment, in the absence of a release by Super, did not relieve Barron of its duty to perform. The release by Demerest had no effect except to make it clear that Demerest was assuming liability on the contract. The default by Demerest permits Super to proceed immediately against Barron.

Answer (a) is incorrect because an assignment is not an anticipatory breach of a contract as long as the contract is delegable. Answer (b) is incorrect because Super's burden to perform consists essentially of paying money and taking delivery. A change in the supplier does not affect this duty. Answer (d) is incorrect because Super may elect to recover from either Demerest or Barron.

11.12 Performance

159. A condition in a contract for the purchase of real property that makes the purchaser's obligation dependent upon obtaining a given dollar amount of conventional mortgage financing

a. Can be satisfied by the seller if the seller offers the buyer a demand loan for the amount.

b. Is a condition subsequent.

c. Is implied as a matter of law.

d. Requires the purchaser to use reasonable efforts to obtain the financing.

The correct answer is (d). *(CPA 582 L-51)*

REQUIRED: The legal effect of a condition in a contract.

DISCUSSION: When the obligation of a contracting party is conditioned upon the occurrence of an event and (s)he has some power over the occurrence, the party is required to act in good faith to fulfill the condition. Acting in good faith would include using reasonable efforts to obtain the financing.

Answer (a) is incorrect because the condition calls for conventional mortgage financing, which involves repayment of the loan in installments over a substantial number of years. A demand loan is payable in full upon the creditor's demand and does not satisfy the condition. Answer (b) is incorrect because the condition is precedent. It must occur before the purchaser becomes bound. Answer (c) is incorrect because the condition must be expressed.

160. Bill Nolan agreed to purchase from Damion 1,000 shares of Excelsior Photo, Inc. stock at $100 per share. Nolan was interested in obtaining control of Excelsior, whose stock was closely held. The stock purchase agreement contained the following clause: "This contract is subject to my (Nolan's) obtaining more than 50% of the shares outstanding of Excelsior Photo stock." In this situation

a. The contract is not binding on Damion because it lacks consideration on Nolan's part; i.e., unless he obtains more than 50%, he is not liable.

b. The contract is subject to an express condition precedent.

c. Specific performance would not be available to Nolan if Damion refuses to perform.

d. While the contract is executory, Damion cannot transfer good title to a third party who takes in good faith.

The correct answer is (b). *(CPA 575 L-10)*

REQUIRED: The correct statement concerning a stock purchase agreement subject to a condition.

DISCUSSION: Nolan's duty to perform is expressly contingent upon the prior occurrence of an event; hence, it is subject to a condition precedent. The use of conditions to modify, limit, or suspend contractual obligations is common. Conditions may be concurrent or subsequent as well as precedent.

Answer (a) is incorrect because Damion will be bound if and when Nolan is bound. Nolan's consideration is his promise to pay if the condition is satisfied. Answer (c) is incorrect because specific performance is available if the subject matter is unique. Stock of a closely held corporation is unique because ownership of another corporation would not provide the same benefits and detriments, especially control. Answer (d) is incorrect because a good faith purchaser for value could acquire good title from Damion, although Damion would be liable to Nolan for damages.

161. Mary agrees to sell her home to Marisol for $100,000. The contract is silent regarding the time of payment and the time of delivery of the deed. Thus, payment or tender of the price is a condition of tender or delivery of the deed and vice versa. The conditions involved are

a. Implied in fact.

b. Implied in law.

c. Subsequent.

d. Express.

The correct answer is (b). *(Publisher)*

REQUIRED: The correct classification of the conditions.

DISCUSSION: In these circumstances, the law will impose mutually dependent and concurrent conditions to reach an equitable result even though the actual language of the contract neither implies conditions nor states them expressly. A condition may thus be implied in law although the parties have not understood it to be part of their agreement and it is not contained directly or indirectly in the language of the contract.

Answer (a) is incorrect because a condition implied in fact is part of the basis of the parties' bargain but not stated expressly. Such a condition is implied by the language of the contract. Answer (c) is incorrect because a condition subsequent is an event that terminates an existing contractual duty. Answer (d) is incorrect because an express condition is stated in language customarily regarded as conditional, such as "on condition" or "provided."

162. Alpha promised to convey an apartment house to Beta in return for Beta's promise (1) to convey a farm to Alpha and (2) to pay Alpha $1,000 in cash 6 months after the exchange. The contract contained the following provision: "Beta's obligation to pay the $1,000 6 months after the exchange of the apartment house and the farm shall be voided if Alpha has not, within 3 months after the exchange, removed the existing shed in the parking area in the rear of the apartment house." Alpha's removal of the shed is

a. A condition subsequent in form but precedent in substance to Beta's duty to pay the $1,000.

b. A condition precedent in form but subsequent in substance to Beta's duty to pay $1,000.

c. A condition subsequent to Beta's duty to pay the $1,000.

d. Not a condition, either precedent or subsequent, to Beta's duty to pay.

The correct answer is (a). *(MBE Part IV-39)*

REQUIRED: The proper description of the requirement of removal of the shed.

DISCUSSION: A condition subsequent is a condition the occurrence of which would discharge a pre-existing duty to perform. Beta's duty to pay the $1,000 was created when the contract was made. Accordingly, it is only the occurrence of a condition subsequent (the nonremoval of the shed) that discharges the duty. Practically, however, Alpha's removal of the shed precedes the time when Beta has a duty to pay the $1,000. The classification of the condition as subsequent is largely a matter of form.

Answer (b) is incorrect because the removal is in substance a condition precedent since failure of the condition would discharge Beta's duty. Answer (c) is incorrect because occurrence of a condition subsequent would discharge a duty to perform, not create a duty. Answer (d) is incorrect because removal is a condition since its occurrence or nonoccurrence affects Beta's duty to pay.

163. The mortgage on Orr's home is held by Friendly S&L, a federally chartered savings and loan association. The mortgage agreement provides that the unpaid principal and interest will be due on the sale of the property unless Friendly approves the transaction. Sale without approval

a. Is permissible because a due-on-sale clause is unenforceable.

b. Is a breach of a condition but not of the contract.

c. Is a breach of a condition and of the contract.

d. Is a breach of the contract but not of a condition.

The correct answer is (c). *(Publisher)*

REQUIRED: The legal implication of selling mortgaged property without approval given a due-on-sale clause.

DISCUSSION: Part of the mortgagee's duty is to accept the periodic principal and interest payments in lieu of full and immediate payment. A condition is an event the occurrence or nonoccurrence of which affects a contractual duty to perform. If Orr sells the property without approval, Friendly is released from its duty. Thus, the sale would breach a condition. Because the sale would be contrary to Orr's contractual promise, the sale would also operate as a breach of contract subjecting Orr to immediate liability.

Due-on-sale clauses are controversial. Some states have declared them to be against public policy or an unreasonable restraint on alienation. The U.S. Supreme Court has ruled, however, that federally chartered savings and loan associations may enforce them.

164. The XYZ Construction Company has contracted to build a duplex for Smith for a total price of $100,000. During the course of construction, the contractor inadvertently installed the wrong type of fireplace. The specifications, misread by the contractor, called for a slightly more expensive variety. To remove the old fireplaces and install new ones would cost $25,000. The duplexes are worth $2,000 less as a result of the error. In this case, Smith owes XYZ

a. $100,000.

b. $98,000.

c. $75,000.

d. $25,000.

The correct answer is (b). *(J. Norwood)*

REQUIRED: The rights of the creditor under the doctrine of substantial performance.

DISCUSSION: If the performance is only marginally deficient and the obligor acts in good faith, (s)he has substantially performed and is entitled to receive the contract price minus the cost of correction. If the cost of correction is excessive, the obligor is entitled to receive the contract price minus the diminished value. Because the cost of correcting the defect is unreasonable, XYZ is entitled to receive the contract price ($100,000) minus the diminished value ($2,000).

165. Kent Construction Co. contracted to construct four garages for Magnum, Inc. according to specifications provided by Magnum. Kent deliberately substituted 2 x 4s for the more expensive 2 x 6s called for in the contract in all places where the 2 x 4s would not be readily detected. Magnum's inspection revealed the variance and Magnum is now withholding the final payment on the contract. The contract was for $100,000, and the final payment would be $25,000. Damages were estimated to be $15,000. In a lawsuit for the balance due, Kent will

a. Prevail on the contract, minus damages of $15,000, because it has substantially performed.

b. Prevail because the damages in question were not substantial in relation to the contract amount.

c. Lose because the law unqualifiedly requires literal performance of such contracts.

d. Lose all rights under the contract because it has intentionally breached.

The correct answer is (d). *(CPA 583 L-19)*

REQUIRED: The outcome of a suit by a contractor that deliberately failed to meet specifications.

DISCUSSION: When circumstances make a perfect performance difficult or impossible, the substantial performance standard will permit the breaching party to recover the other party's performance minus any damages if the breach is not material. The doctrine does not apply, however, when the substantially performing party has not acted in good faith. Hence, Kent will lose under the traditional rule because it intended to breach the contract. Many courts have modified the rule and allow defaulting contractors to use quasi contract or quantum meruit to recover the value of work and materials that substantially contributed value to the other contracting party's property.

Answer (a) is incorrect because the substantial performance doctrine does not apply to a willful breach. Answer (b) is incorrect because 15% is usually regarded as substantial. Answer (c) is incorrect because a strict standard is more often applied to contracts able to be performed exactly, such as promises to pay money.

166. A party to a contract who fails to perform according to its terms is in breach of the contract. Which of the following is the best statement of the law?

a. Any breach discharges the other party.

b. A nonmaterial breach discharges the other party if it is not cured within a reasonable time.

c. A material uncorrected breach discharges the other party.

d. A nonmaterial breach does not give rise to an action for damages.

The correct answer is (c). *(Publisher)*

REQUIRED: The best statement respecting the effect of breach.

DISCUSSION: If not cured, a material breach of a contract excuses the innocent party from a duty to perform. Thus, if the breach is characterized as material, the breaching party will be deprived of the benefit of his/her bargain in addition to being subject to an action for money damages. The breaching party is allowed by many courts to recover the amount necessary to avoid unjust enrichment of the nonbreaching party.

Answers (a) and (b) are incorrect because a nonmaterial breach gives rise to a right of action for damages but does not relieve the nonbreaching party of the obligation to perform, regardless of cure. Answer (d) is incorrect because any breach is the basis for an action in damages.

167. With respect to performance, the concept of the divisible contract means

a. Each division of the contract must be performed before there is substantial performance.

b. A material breach of any division will cause the entire contract to be unenforceable.

c. It is treated the same as an entire contract.

d. Breach of one division does not discharge the other party as to any other division.

The correct answer is (d). *(Publisher)*

REQUIRED: The correct statement concerning a divisible contract.

DISCUSSION: A divisible contract can be separated into several parts; each part is independent of the others. Accordingly, breach of one division does not necessarily discharge the nonbreaching party as to any other division. Entire contracts are treated differently. A material breach of any part defeats the essential purpose of the whole and completely discharges the nonbreaching party.

Answer (a) is incorrect because one may substantially perform a division of such a contract regardless of performance of other divisions. Answer (b) is incorrect because a material breach in one division may not affect enforceability. The purposes of the balance of the contract may be achievable. Answer (c) is incorrect because an entire contract is treated in a different manner as discussed above.

168. Whether a breach is material is vital for determining the rights and duties of the parties to a contract. A breach is usually deemed not to be material and will not discharge the nonbreacher when

a. The injured party receives substantially all of the benefits reasonably anticipated.

b. The contract specifies that time is of the essence and performance is delayed.

c. The breach is intentional but minor.

d. The cost to correct the breach is substantial in relation to the contract price.

The correct answer is (a). *(Publisher)*

REQUIRED: The instance in which breach is nonmaterial.

DISCUSSION: The materiality of a breach is determined by the facts of the individual case. Courts may consider numerous factors in reaching a decision: whether the nonbreaching party has received substantially all the benefits bargained for, whether money damages will adequately compensate for the breach, the quantitative measure of the breach, its timing, what the contract states to be material, whether the failure of performance was intentional, whether the breaching party acted in good faith, and the degree of unjust enrichment if the injured party is not required to perform.

Answer (b) is incorrect because within limits, the parties may specify what is material. Failure to perform promptly when time is of the essence will often deprive the other party of the contractual benefits bargained for. Answer (c) is incorrect because a failure of good faith usually results in a holding of materiality. Answer (d) is incorrect because one indication of a material breach is that the cost to correct is substantial in relation to the contract price.

169. Oscar Orange owes Blue $1,000. Under the terms of their agreement, $1,000 is due at noon on January 27 at Blue's place of business. If Orange tenders $1,000 in cash at the agreed place

a. On January 28, he will be discharged if Blue refuses to accept.

b. And time, he will be discharged if Blue refuses to accept.

c. And time and Blue refuses to accept, Orange remains liable for $1,000 but not for interest subsequently accrued.

d. And time, Blue must accept the payment and apply it to the $1,000 debt even though Orange is indebted to Blue on another account.

The correct answer is (c). *(Publisher)*

REQUIRED: The true statement about the consequences of tender.

DISCUSSION: Tender is an offer by a party to a contract to perform according to its terms. The party tendering must be ready, willing, and able to perform. If the other party refuses to accept the tender, the debt is not discharged, but any lien is extinguished, no more interest will accrue, and the tendering party will be relieved of court costs if sued on the debt.

Answer (a) is incorrect because rejection of tender of late payment will not discharge the debt but will prevent the further accrual of interest and deprive the creditor of court costs and damages in a later suit if the debtor keeps the tender good. Answer (b) is incorrect because the debt is not discharged. Answer (d) is incorrect if the debtor has two or more accounts with the creditor and does not specify the application of the tendered payment, the creditor may apply it as (s)he wishes.

170. Anna Park owed Bill Collins $1,000 and $2,000, respectively, on two separate unsecured obligations. Smythe Co. had become a surety on the $2,000 debt at the request of Park when Park became indebted to Collins. Both debts matured on June 1. Park was able to pay only $600 at that time, and she forwarded that amount to Collins without instructions. Under these circumstances

a. Collins must apply the funds pro rata in proportion to the two debts.

b. Collins must apply the $600 to the $2,000 debt because there is a surety on it.

c. Smythe will be discharged to the extent of $400 if Collins on request of Smythe fails to apply $400 to the $2,000 debt.

d. Collins is free to apply the $600 to the debts as he sees fit.

The correct answer is (d). *(CPA 574 L-13)*

REQUIRED: The manner in which a creditor may apply a partial payment to separate, unsecured obligations.

DISCUSSION: If a debtor gives instructions as to the application of partial payment, the creditor must comply. Without instructions, the creditor may apply the payment as (s)he chooses. In this case, Collins may apply the $600 wholly to either obligation or proportionately as he sees fit.

Answer (a) is incorrect because Collins may apply the funds however he chooses. Park gave no instructions. Answer (b) is incorrect because the presence of a surety for the $2,000 debt has no effect on the required application of the partial payment. Answer (c) is incorrect because Smythe has no authority to require application of any part of the partial payment to the debt on which it is a surety.

171. On July 25 Archer, the president of Post Corp., with the approval of the board of directors, engaged Biggs, a CPA, to audit Post's July 31 financial statements and to issue a report in time for the annual stockholders' meeting to be held on September 5. Notwithstanding Biggs' reasonable efforts, the report was not ready until September 7 because of delays by Post's staff. Archer, acting on behalf of Post, refused to accept or to pay for the report because it no longer served its intended purpose. In the event Biggs sues Post, what is the probable outcome?

a. The case would be dismissed because it is unethical for a CPA to sue for a fee.

b. Biggs will be entitled to recover only in quasi-contract for the value of the services to the client.

c. Biggs will not recover. The completion by September 5th was a condition precedent to recovery.

d. Biggs will recover because the delay by Post's staff prevented Biggs from performing on time and thereby eliminated the timely performance condition.

The correct answer is (d). *(CPA 1178 L-32)*

REQUIRED: The probable outcome of a suit by a CPA for payment for services rendered.

DISCUSSION: Completion by September 5 was a condition precedent to Post's performance. Thus, Post was not required to perform (pay Biggs) unless the September 5 date was met. However, a contracting party is under an obligation not to prevent the other from performing. Post kept Biggs from meeting the September 5 date, and Post is liable to Biggs.

Answer (a) is incorrect because it is not unethical for a CPA to sue for a fee. Answer (b) is incorrect because Biggs is entitled to recover on the contract, not merely for the reasonable value of services rendered under a quasi-contractual theory. Answer (c) is incorrect because Biggs will recover. Post's employees prevented performance by September 5.

172. Jones, CPA entered into a signed contract with Foster Corp. to perform accounting and review services. If Jones repudiates the contract prior to the date performance is due to begin, which of the following is not correct?

a. Foster could successfully maintain an action for breach of contract after the date performance was due to begin.

b. Foster can obtain a judgment ordering Jones to perform.

c. Foster could successfully maintain an action for breach of contract prior to the date performance is due to begin.

d. Foster can obtain a judgment for the monetary damages it incurred as a result of the repudiation.

The correct answer is (b). *(CPA 589 L-35)*

REQUIRED: The legal recourse not available to the nonbreaching party after anticipatory repudiation.

DISCUSSION: Express or implied repudiation before the time of performance is an anticipatory breach. An anticipatory breach occurs when a party indicates either expressly or by implication that (s)he will not perform. This indication may be given in many ways, e.g., by an express statement, selling property, going out of business, or not meeting an installment due. The injured party may treat the contract as broken and immediately file suit, or (s)he may elect to treat the contract as continuing and hold the breaching party accountable for nonperformance when the time of performance arrives. However, a contract for personal services cannot be specifically enforced. This remedy is available when damages are not adequate because the subject matter is unique. Personal services may be unique, but requiring performance by an unwilling individual may not be satisfactory for either party, and the remedy could be construed as involuntary servitude.

Answers (a) and (c) are incorrect because anticipatory repudiation gives ground for immediate suit. Answer (d) is incorrect because Foster can recover compensatory damages.

173. Keats Publishing Company shipped textbooks and other books for sale at retail to Campus Bookstore. An honest dispute arose over Campus's right to return certain books. Keats maintained that the books in question could not be returned and demanded payment of the full amount. Campus relied upon trade custom, which indicated that many publishers accepted the return of such books. Campus returned the books in question and paid for the balance with a check marked "Account Paid in Full to Date." Keats cashed the check. Which of the following is a correct statement?

a. Keats is entitled to recover damages.

b. The cashing of the check constituted an accord and satisfaction.

c. The pre-existing legal duty rule applies, and Keats is entitled to full payment for all the books.

d. The custom of the industry argument would have no merit in a court of law.

The correct answer is (b). *(CPA 579 L-13)*

REQUIRED: The correct statement regarding a genuine dispute over the amount of a debt.

DISCUSSION: The cashing of the check marked "Account Paid in Full to Date" operated as an acceptance of an agreement to settle a genuine controversy. Each party's implied promise not to sue on its interpretation of the claim supplies the consideration needed to enforce the agreement. This substitution of performance is called an accord and satisfaction. If the amount of the debt is undisputed, however, any attempt to perform the duty of payment by the tender and acceptance of a lesser sum is invalid for lack of consideration.

Answer (a) is incorrect because Keats accepted the substituted performance by cashing the check. Answer (c) is incorrect because the amount of the debt (duty) was genuinely disputed. Hence, Campus had no pre-existing legal duty. Answer (d) is incorrect because trade custom would bear upon whether the dispute was genuine.

174. On June 1, 1990, Nord Corp. engaged Milo & Co., CPAs to perform certain management advisory services for 9 months for a $45,000 fee. The terms of their oral agreement required Milo to commence performance any time before October 1, 1990. On June 30, 1991, after Milo completed the work to Nord's satisfaction, Nord paid Milo $30,000 by check. Nord conspicuously marked on the check that it constituted payment in full for all services rendered. Nord has refused to pay the remaining $15,000 arguing that, although it believes the $45,000 fee is reasonable, it had received bids of $30,000 and $38,000 from other firms to perform the same services as Milo. Milo endorsed and deposited the check. If Milo commences an action against Nord for the remaining $15,000, Milo will be entitled to recover

a. $0 because there has been an enforceable accord and satisfaction.

b. $0 because the Statute of Frauds has not been satisfied.

c. $8,000 because $38,000 was the highest other bid.

d. $15,000 because it is the balance due under the agreement.

The correct answer is (d). *(CPA 1187 L-1)*

REQUIRED: The effect of cashing a check marked payment in full.

DISCUSSION: The contract called for a fee of $45,000, the work was done to Nord's satisfaction, and Nord conceded that $45,000 was a reasonable amount. Accordingly, the amount of the debt was liquidated, that is, not subject to an honest difference of interpretation. Despite the endorsement by Nord, cashing the check did not constitute an acceptance of an offer to settle for the lesser sum. Nord did not provide new consideration for Milo's acceptance of an amount less than that owed and therefore is still liable for the balance.

Answer (a) is incorrect because no accord was reached. The debt was not in dispute, and no new consideration was given to support the implied promise to accept the smaller sum. Answer (b) is incorrect because the year-clause of the Statute of Frauds does not apply. The contract could have been performed within 1 year. Answer (c) is incorrect because the parties clearly agreed to a $45,000 fee.

175. Dell owed Stark $9,000. As the result of an unrelated transaction, Stark owed Ball that same amount. The three parties signed an agreement that Dell would pay Ball instead of Stark, and Stark would be discharged from all liability. The agreement among the parties is

a. A novation.

b. An executed accord and satisfaction.

c. Voidable at Ball's option.

d. Unenforceable for lack of consideration.

The correct answer is (a). *(CPA 588 L-24)*

REQUIRED: The true statement about an agreement to discharge a debtor from liability.

DISCUSSION: A novation is a mutual agreement between concerned parties for the discharge of an existing agreement by substituting a new contract or new debtor. Here the three-way agreement among the parties substitutes for the old agreement. The novation is the substitution of a new promisor (Dell) for the old (Stark).

Answer (b) is incorrect because an accord is an agreement by the promisee to accept a substituted performance by the promisor. Performance of the accord is the satisfaction. Answer (c) is incorrect because no basis for treating the agreement as voidable is apparent. Answer (d) is incorrect because the promise by Dell to pay Stark's debt is consideration for Ball's discharge of Stark.

176. Mort owes $10,000 to O, $20,000 to P, $20,000 to Q, and $50,000 to R. He is insolvent and has net assets of $50,000. O, P, Q, and R have agreed with Mort and each other to accept proportionate distributions in full satisfaction of the claims. Which of the following is true?

a. The agreement is invalid for lack of consideration.

b. Once the creditors began negotiations, none could attach the debtor's assets.

c. If O were not a party to the agreement, (s)he would nevertheless be bound.

d. The agreement is a valid composition with creditors.

The correct answer is (d). *(Publisher)*

REQUIRED: The true statement about an agreement among creditors to accept lesser sums.

DISCUSSION: A composition with creditors is a common law contractual undertaking between the debtor and the creditors. The participating creditors agree to extend time for payment, take lesser sums in satisfaction of the debts owed, or some other plan of financial adjustment. Under general contract law, the original debts will not be discharged until the debtor has performed the new obligations.

Answer (a) is incorrect because the consideration for the promise of one creditor to accept less than the amount due is found in the similar promises of the other creditors. Answer (b) is incorrect because a disadvantage of a composition is that, prior to agreeing to the contract, the creditors may still seek to seize (attach) the debtor's property. Answer (c) is incorrect because a creditor who does not participate in the composition is not bound by it.

177. A and B are jointly obligated to C. If C accepts consideration

a. To give A a written release, B will also be released.

b. Not to sue A, C cannot then sue B.

c. To give A a written release, only A will be released.

d. Not to sue A or B but not both, the obligation is discharged.

The correct answer is (a). *(Publisher)*

REQUIRED: The legal effect of a release or covenant not to sue.

DISCUSSION: In some states, a release in the form of a sealed writing unsupported by consideration operates to discharge the obligation. Other states require consideration for the release to be effective. A covenant not to sue, if supported by consideration, does not discharge the obligation. Instead it serves as a bar to a suit by the promisor. A release of one joint obligor releases all, but a covenant not to sue one joint obligor does not affect the other joint obligor(s).

Answer (b) is incorrect because a covenant not to sue one obligor allows the creditor to retain rights against other joint obligors on the same debt. Answer (c) is incorrect because a release of one obligor releases the other joint obligors. Answer (d) is incorrect because a covenant not to sue bars the creditor's remedy against parties to the covenant but does not discharge the obligation.

178. If the parties to a contract wish to cancel their contract and be in the same position as they were prior to forming the contract, they should seek to obtain a(n)

a. Rescission.

b. Novation.

c. Accord and satisfaction.

d. Revocation.

The correct answer is (a). *(CPA 586 L-15)*

REQUIRED: The term for a mutual agreement not to perform a contract.

DISCUSSION: When the parties agree to discharge their respective obligations under an existing contract, they have effected a mutual rescission. This agreement itself must meet the requirements of a contract. When the original contract is wholly executory, the surrender of rights under the contract by one party is consideration for the surrender of rights by the other party. If one party has partially performed, however, a mere mutual agreement to terminate the contract may not be effective.

Answer (b) is incorrect because a novation is a new substituted agreement that often involves a new party who replaces an original party. Answer (c) is incorrect because in an accord, the promisee agrees to accept a substituted performance in satisfaction of the promisor's obligation. The completion of the substituted performance is the satisfaction. Answer (d) is incorrect because a revocation is the voiding of a prior action, e.g., an offer.

179. Axel rented from Lester a room overlooking the main thoroughfare of Coastal City. The purpose of the transaction, known to Lester, was to provide Axel with a view of a large parade that was an annual highlight of the holiday season. Unexpectedly, a late-season hurricane struck Coastal City, causing cancellation of the event. Axel refuses to pay the agreed rental. If Lester sues, who should prevail?

a. Lester, because the subject matter of the contract was not destroyed.

b. Lester, because the lease was commercially practicable.

c. Axel, because of frustration of purpose.

d. Axel, because the contract was impossible to perform.

The correct answer is (c). *(Publisher)*

REQUIRED: The outcome of a suit on a contract when a supervening event prevented fulfillment of its purpose.

DISCUSSION: The frustration of purpose doctrine applies. Axel's principal purpose was substantially frustrated without his fault by the occurrence of an event the nonoccurrence of which was a basic assumption on which the contract was made. Because he did not assume the risk of cancellation, Axel is discharged.

Answer (a) is incorrect because fulfillment of the purpose that both parties contemplated was impossible. Answer (b) is incorrect because nothing indicates that Axel had a commercial interest in the rental. Answer (d) is incorrect because renting the room was still possible.

180. Art Sharp, CPA was engaged by Peters & Sons to audit the financial statements that were to be submitted to several prospective partners as part of a planned expansion of the firm. Sharp's fee was fixed on a per diem basis. Sharp completed about half of the necessary field work, then abandoned it because of unanticipated demands upon his time. The planned expansion of the firm failed because the prospective partners lost interest when the audit report was not available. Sharp's offer to complete the task at a later date was refused. Peters & Sons suffered damages of $4,000 as a result. What is the probable outcome of a lawsuit between Sharp and Peters & Sons?

a. Sharp will be compensated for the reasonable value of the services actually performed.

b. Peters & Sons will recover damages for breach of contract.

c. Peters & Sons will recover both punitive damages and damages for breach of contract.

d. Neither Sharp nor Peters & Sons will recover against the other.

The correct answer is (b). *(CPA 1177 L-5)*

REQUIRED: The probable outcome of a lawsuit by a client against an accountant for delay.

DISCUSSION: Sharp's nonperformance is not excused by the press of other obligations. The demands of other clients represent a typical business risk that Sharp assumed when entering into the contract. Hence, Sharp breached the contract without any legal justification, and Peters & Sons can recover damages.

Answer (a) is incorrect because Sharp will not be compensated for the reasonable value of services actually rendered. Peters received no benefit from those services; i.e., there was no unjust enrichment. Answer (c) is incorrect because punitive damages are usually not available for breach of contract. Answer (d) is incorrect because Peters should recover against Sharp.

181. Billy, a peanut grower, entered into an agreement to provide 1,000 pounds of peanuts to Pan, a peanut processor. However, severe flooding ruined the peanut crop in the entire area where Billy farms, so Billy could not provide the peanuts promised.

a. Billy's performance is discharged by an act of God.

b. Billy is liable to Pan for damages because substitute peanuts could be purchased elsewhere.

c. Billy will be allowed to provide the agreed amount of peanuts the next year.

d. Billy is not liable because a farmer's poor season is a risk assumed by a crop purchaser.

The correct answer is (b). *(Publisher)*

REQUIRED: The liability or discharge of a party who could not perform because of destruction of the subject matter of the contract.

DISCUSSION: Although the crop was destroyed, peanuts could have been obtained elsewhere. As long as there was a reasonable opportunity to provide a substitute product, destruction of the crop will not discharge Billy.

Answer (a) is incorrect because Billy's performance would only be discharged by "an act of God" if the area Billy farmed was the only place in which peanuts were grown and no others could be obtained. Answer (c) is incorrect because providing the peanuts in a subsequent year is not an adequate substitution for performance in the current year. Answer (d) is incorrect because the poor season is a risk assumed by a farmer, not a crop purchaser.

182. On Monday, Harry Lime entered into a contract to sell some real estate to Holly, borrowed $10,000 from Welles, agreed to teach a weekend seminar at the Vienna School of Business Ethics, and agreed to ship 100 textbooks to Alida College. Lime died the next day before he could perform under any of these agreements. Lime's estate has not satisfied any of these obligations. The estate will prevail in an action brought by

a. Welles.

b. Vienna.

c. Holly.

d. Alida.

The correct answer is (b). *(Publisher)*

REQUIRED: The party that will lose in an action against a promisor's estate for nonperformance.

DISCUSSION: Lime promised to teach a seminar for Vienna. Nonperformance of this contract is excused by impossibility because it called for the personal services of the promisor. The failure to perform duties that are delegable to others is not excused. The estate is able to convey the real estate to Holly, pay the money owed to Welles, and ship goods to Alida.

183. Simon has been sued by Major for breach of a real estate contract. Simon has raised the statute of limitations as a defense to Major's lawsuit. Under the circumstances, the statute of limitations

a. Runs continuously under all circumstances commencing at the time the contract is breached.

b. Does not apply to the contract between Simon and Major because it involves real estate.

c. Will prevent recovery if the time set forth in the statute has expired.

d. Is 4 years in all states.

The correct answer is (c). *(CPA 586 L-7)*

REQUIRED: The true statement about the statute of limitations.

DISCUSSION: The statute of limitations may be pleaded as a complete defense to a claim if the period for bringing an action has expired. The statute operates to defeat the claim irrespective of the merits of the case.

Answer (a) is incorrect because various events toll (stop the running of) the statute, for example, the infancy of a creditor or the absence of a defendant from the jurisdiction. However, the statute begins to run when a cause of action arises, which is usually the time at which suit may be brought. For contracts, that moment is usually the date of breach. Answer (b) is incorrect because real estate contracts are subject to the statute of limitations. Answer (d) is incorrect because the length of the period varies from state to state and with the kind of claim asserted.

184. On May 1, 1973, Mix, CPA entered into an oral contract with Dell to provide certain accounting services to Dell. The contract was fully performed by both parties on March 31, 1974. On April 25, 1988, Dell commenced a breach of contract action against Mix claiming that Mix had improperly performed the accounting services. Mix's best defense to the action would likely be the

a. Parol evidence rule.

b. Statute of limitations.

c. Statute of Frauds.

d. Lack of consideration.

The correct answer is (b). *(CPA 588 L-22)*

REQUIRED: The best defense to a contract action that was not timely filed.

DISCUSSION: A statute of limitations is enacted to encourage plaintiffs to pursue their remedies promptly. The principle is that justice delayed may be justice denied. After the lapse of a reasonable period, physical evidence may be lost, witnesses may die or otherwise be unavailable, and memories may have dimmed. For these reasons and because it is unfair to defendants for litigation on stale claims to be continuously threatened, statutes stipulate a reasonable but limited time within which an action can be brought. The statute of limitations may be pleaded as a complete defense to a claim if the period for bringing an action has expired. The statute operates to defeat the claim irrespective of the merits of the case.

Answer (a) is incorrect because the parol evidence rule is inapplicable to oral contracts. Answer (c) is incorrect because no reason for requiring the contract to be written is apparent. For example, the contract was performed within 1 year. Answer (d) is incorrect because the facts do not suggest lack of consideration provided by Dell.

11.13 Remedies

185. The contract remedy of compensatory or general damages attempts to protect the injured party's expectation interest. The calculation of these damages usually excludes

a. Reliance damages.

b. Consequential (special) damages.

c. Incidental damages.

d. Loss of value.

The correct answer is (a). *(Publisher)*

REQUIRED: The element excluded from the calculation of compensatory damages.

DISCUSSION: The remedy of compensatory damages attempts to put the plaintiff in as good a position as if the other party had not breached the contract. The remedy of reliance damages puts the injured party in the position (s)he would have occupied if no contract had been entered into. Reliance damages are the costs of performing, preparing to perform, or forgoing other contractual possibilities.

Answers (b), (c), and (d) are incorrect because each is an element of the compensatory damages computation. Special (or consequential) damages flow from some unique circumstances of the contractual situation. Incidental damages are the reasonable costs incurred by the plaintiff to avoid further loss. Loss of value is the difference between the value of the promised performance and the value of the performance actually rendered.

186. The Johnson Corporation sent its only pump to the manufacturer to be repaired. It engaged Travis, a local trucking company, both to deliver the equipment to the manufacturer and to redeliver it to Johnson promptly upon completion of the repair. Johnson's entire plant was inoperative without this pump, but the trucking company did not know this. The trucking company delayed several days in its return of the repaired pump to Johnson. During the time it expected to be without the pump, Johnson incurred $5,000 in lost profits. At the end of that time, Johnson rented a replacement pump at a cost of $200 per day. As a result of these facts, what is Johnson entitled to recover from Travis?

a. The $200 a day cost incurred in renting the pump.

b. The $200 a day cost incurred in renting the pump plus the lost profits.

c. Actual damages plus punitive damages.

d. Nothing because Travis is not liable for damages.

The correct answer is (a). *(CPA 578 L-22)*

REQUIRED: The damages the plaintiff is entitled to recover because of the trucking company's late delivery.

DISCUSSION: The failure of Travis to perform with reasonable promptness was a breach of contract for which Johnson could recover monetary damages. Johnson may recover its general damages, which were those likely and foreseeable as a result of the breach (the pump rental costs).

Answer (b) is incorrect because special damages, those flowing from some unique aspect of the case, are recoverable only if the defendant knew or should have known at the time of contracting of the possibility of their incurrence. By not informing Travis that the plant would be inoperative without the pump, Johnson was precluded from recovering lost profits. Answer (c) is incorrect because punitive damages are normally not granted in contracts cases. Answer (d) is incorrect because Travis is liable for general damages as a result of breaching the contract.

187. Denny rebuilds used motorcycles and sells them to the public. Paine purchased a motorcycle from Denny. The day after the transaction Paine was operating the motorcycle at a safe speed and otherwise observing the traffic laws when the engine unexpectedly blew up causing great personal injury to Paine. Analysis of the wreckage proved that Denny's negligence proximately caused Paine's injury. Which of the following is true?

a. If a contract theory of damages is applied, the court will usually attempt to restore the plaintiff to the position existing before the transaction.

b. If a tort theory of damages is applied, the court will put the plaintiff in the position that would have existed if the goods had been as warranted.

c. Paine can recover as general damages for loss of earnings and earning power, pain and suffering, and medical expenses.

d. Paine cannot recover for personal injury if a contract theory is asserted.

The correct answer is (c). *(Publisher)*

REQUIRED: The true statement about damages recoverable by a buyer of defective goods.

DISCUSSION: Paine can assert a tort theory of recovery because Denny's negligence was the legal cause of the injury. Denny may also assert a contract theory because the injury resulted from a breach of warranty made by the seller to the buyer. Paine's recovery of general damages in tort for personal injuries may embrace medical expenses, loss of earnings and earning power, loss of time, pain and suffering, permanent disability and disfigurement. These damages are the natural and foreseeable results of the serious bodily injury that a reasonable person would expect to occur when a defective motorcycle engine explodes during operation.

Answer (a) is incorrect because the usual contract theory is to give plaintiff the benefit of the bargain (of the contract breached by the other party). Answer (b) is incorrect because the usual tort theory of damages is to restore the plaintiff to the position (s)he would have been in if the tort had not occurred. Answer (d) is incorrect because the personal injury is compensable if the damages flow directly from the breach of the contract. However, general damages for pain and suffering would not be available under contract theory.

188. The Hathaways contracted with Stan Smith to build a house. Part way through the project, before even putting up the roof, Smith decided the contract was uneconomical and quit. Because Smith had spent a considerable amount of time on the job, he demanded payment.

a. The breach is immaterial, so Smith is entitled to a proportionate part of the contract price.

b. If the breach is material, the Hathaways are discharged from any obligation under the contract.

c. If the contract is substantially performed, the Hathaways are liable for the full contract price.

d. Because he partly performed, Smith is entitled to the reasonable value of his services.

The correct answer is (d). *(Publisher)*

REQUIRED: The true statement about liability and rights under an incomplete contract.

DISCUSSION: A party who breaches prior to substantial performance is usually not entitled to any remedies under the contract. This result assumes the other parties receive no benefit from the part performance. However, the courts tend to provide for the reasonable value of a person's services if (s)he has received nothing and the other party has benefited. This equitable remedy, called quantum meruit, does not relieve the breaching party from liability for damages for breach of contract.

Answer (a) is incorrect because the breach is material. It defeats the essential purposes of the contract. Answer (b) is incorrect because the Hathaways are not discharged from liability to Smith for the reasonable value of his services. Answer (c) is incorrect because if the contract is substantially performed, the Hathaways are liable for a proportionate amount of the contract, not the full contract price.

189. Crockett hired Del Drifter to make widgets. They agreed that Drifter would make 10,000 and would be entitled to keep one-fourth of those made as compensation. After Drifter had made 2,000 widgets, he discovered that the price of the widgets had dropped by half and therefore quit. Drifter now sues Crockett for the reasonable value of his services.

a. Drifter is entitled to the reasonable value of his services under the theory of quantum meruit.

b. Drifter is not entitled to anything because the job was less than one-half done.

c. Drifter is liable for returning the widgets already received because there was a material breach of the contract.

d. Drifter can receive no more payment because he had already received compensation under the agreement.

The correct answer is (d). *(Publisher)*

REQUIRED: The recovery to which a person who breaches a service contract is entitled for his/her services.

DISCUSSION: Although the breach by Drifter occurred prior to substantial completion of the contract, Drifter provided services that resulted in a benefit to Crockett. Because the contract specified a remedy (retention of one-fourth of the goods), Drifter will be limited to that even if he made a bad bargain.

Answer (a) is incorrect because quantum meruit is applied only when the person has not benefited at all from the contract. Answer (b) is incorrect because Drifter is allowed one-fourth of the widgets he has produced. Answer (c) is incorrect because Drifter is entitled to compensation in accordance with the agreement to the extent that it was performed. The performance is readily separable.

190. Bill Gator owns a professional football team in North Florida. He enters into a $60,000,000 contract with Jarbay Construction Company to build an air-conditioned, domed stadium in Alachua County. As part of their bargain, Jarbay agreed to pay $2,000 for each day of construction beyond the stated date of completion. This daily payment requirement constitutes

a. Punitive damages.

b. Liquidated damages.

c. An unforceable provision because contracting parties may not determine their own remedies.

d. Actual damages.

The correct answer is (b). *(Publisher)*

REQUIRED: The correct characterization of a clause requiring payments for delayed performance.

DISCUSSION: Liquidated damages are those provided for in the contract. A reasonable liquidated damages clause may save much trouble and expense, but the amount must have a reasonable relationship to the loss expected to result from breach. In relation to a $60,000,000 contract, $2,000 per day seems reasonable.

Answer (a) is incorrect because $2,000 per day seems reasonable for a $60,000,000 building, so it would probably not be considered a penalty (punitive). Answer (c) is incorrect because contracting parties are encouraged to fashion their own reasonable remedies. Answer (d) is incorrect because a liquidated damages clause is merely an estimate of the potential damages. Actual damages may be very difficult to determine in these circumstances.

191. Mac Parlaine is a movie actor and ballet dancer who contracted with Mogul Studios to play the lead in a musical film in which he would sing as well as dance. The film was to be made in his hometown of Hogtown, Florida. Mogul decided not to make the movie but instead offered Mac a less prestigious straight dramatic role in an adventure epic to be shot in the Arctic. His compensation was to be the same as that for the abandoned project. Mac declined the offer and filed suit for the agreed compensation. What will be the result?

a. Mogul will win because it offered suitable substitute employment.

b. Mogul will win because Mac suffered no damages.

c. Mac will win because the employment offered was inferior to that contracted for.

d. Mac will win because he was under no obligation to mitigate damages.

The correct answer is (c). *(Publisher)*

REQUIRED: The outcome of a suit by an employee who has rejected substitute employment.

DISCUSSION: Any party injured by a breach of contract is under a duty to mitigate the damages. Damages are not recoverable if they could have been avoided without undue risk, burden, or humiliation. A wrongfully discharged employee is entitled to recover wages for the remainder of the employment period but must make a reasonable effort to find similar employment. The substitute employment offered to Mac was both different and inferior, and he was not under an obligation to accept it to mitigate damages.

Answer (a) is incorrect because the employment actually offered was quite different from that contracted for. Answer (b) is incorrect because Mac had a contract right to the promised performance. That expectation is the basis for an award of damages. Answer (d) is incorrect because the injured party has a duty to mitigate. An employee has a duty to seek other work of the same general nature in the same vicinity.

192. The remedy of specific performance

a. Is a type of injunction.

b. Is available only if the subject matter of the contract is unique.

c. Is available to a buyer of land if the seller refuses to transfer the land after the sales contract has been entered into.

d. All of the above.

The correct answer is (d). *(D. Levin)*

REQUIRED: The characteristics of the remedy of specific performance.

DISCUSSION: Specific performance is an equitable remedy. Like all equitable remedies, it is only available when money damages will not adequately compensate the plaintiff for the injury (s)he has sustained. Specific performance is an injunction that orders the defendant to perform the contract. It is available when the subject matter of the contract is unique, such as unique goods or land.

Answers (a), (b), and (c) are incorrect because each states one characteristic of the remedy of specific performance.

193. Foster Co. and Rice executed a contract by which Foster was to sell a warehouse to Rice for $270,000. The contract required Rice to pay the entire $270,000 at the closing. Foster has refused to close the sale of the warehouse to Rice. If Rice commences a lawsuit against Foster, what relief would Rice likely be entitled to?

a. Specific performance or compensatory damages.

b. Specific performance and compensatory damages.

c. Compensatory damages or punitive damages.

d. Compensatory damages and punitive damages.

The correct answer is (a). *(CPA 1188 L-19)*

REQUIRED: The relief available for breach of a contract to sell realty.

DISCUSSION: The equitable remedy of specific performance is available only when damages are inadequate to remedy a breach of contract. When the subject matter is unique, the remedy may be given. Individual parcels of land are usually not considered interchangeable, so specific performance of real estate contracts is frequently permitted. But a plaintiff willing to accept compensatory damages may recover them in lieu of specific performance.

Answer (b) is incorrect because Rice is not entitled to a double recovery. The common law election of remedies doctrine requires the plaintiff to choose one remedy in cases not involving sales of goods. However, remedies are cumulative (may be combined) under Article 2 of the UCC. Answers (c) and (d) are incorrect because punitive damages are seldom awarded in contracts cases.

194. Which of the following is not a traditional remedy for breach of a contract?

a. Rescission and restitution.

b. Injunction.

c. Reformation.

d. Punitive damages.

The correct answer is (d). *(Publisher)*

REQUIRED: The remedy not available for breach of a contract.

DISCUSSION: Punitive (penalty) damages are not usually available for breach of a contract because they are against public policy. The purpose of damages and other contractual remedies is to place the parties in the same position as if the contract had been performed, not to punish a breaching party. Punitive damages are intended to punish especially wrongful conduct and deter future wrongs. Thus, they may be awarded in tort actions. When they are permitted in contracts cases, the facts often involve tortious behavior.

Answer (a) is incorrect because rescission (the return of the parties to their position before entering into the contract) is a standard remedy for breach. Restitution is an equitable remedy whereby a court requires a benefited party to indemnify one who has rendered a performance even though no contract exists between them. Answer (b) is incorrect because an injunction (a court's order to do or not do some act) is a contract remedy. Answer (c) is incorrect because reformation is an equitable remedy whereby a written agreement is rewritten by a court to reflect the actual agreement of the parties.

195. Which of the following remedies is available to a party who has entered into a contract in reliance upon the other contracting party's innocent misrepresentations as to material facts?

	Compensatory Damages	Punitive Damages	Rescission
a.	No	No	No
b.	Yes	No	Yes
c.	No	No	Yes
d.	Yes	Yes	No

The correct answer is (c). *(CPA 589 L-30)*

REQUIRED: The relief available in an action for innocent misrepresentation.

DISCUSSION: Innocent misrepresentation involves a false representation of a material fact that was intended to induce reliance and was justifiably and detrimentally relied upon. It differs from fraud in that scienter is not present. Scienter is knowledge of the falsity of the statement or reckless disregard for its truth or falsity. The only remedy customarily available in the absence of scienter is rescission, or cancellation of the agreement and restoration of the parties to their positions prior to contracting.

Answers (a) and (d) are incorrect because rescission is a potential contract remedy. Answers (b) and (d) are incorrect because to recover compensatory damages in a misrepresentation case, plaintiff must prove scienter. Answer (d) is incorrect because punitive damages are seldom allowed in contracts cases, and it is difficult to imagine circumstances in which innocent misrepresentation would justify such an award.

196. Which of the following is a true statement about the award of attorney's fees in a contracts case as an element of damages?

a. Attorney's fees are routinely awarded as court costs.

b. Attorney's fees provided for in the contract are treated as punitive damages and disallowed.

c. Attorney's fees are only awarded pursuant to express statutory authorization.

d. The general rule is that each party pays his/her own attorney's fees.

The correct answer is (d). *(Publisher)*

REQUIRED: The true statement about payment of attorney's fees.

DISCUSSION: The parties to litigation are normally required to pay their own attorney's fees. Specific statutes sometimes provide an incentive for a private party to vindicate a right or enforce a duty by providing for an award of attorney's fees. Also, the parties to a contract, as a form of liquidated damages, may provide for payment of attorney's fees by the losing party. Finally, the powers of a court of equity include the ability to make such an award in appropriate circumstances.

Answer (a) is incorrect because attorney's fees are not routinely treated the same as court costs. Answer (b) is incorrect because attorney's fees may be provided for in a contract, but they are not treated as punitive. Answer (c) is incorrect because attorney's fees may be authorized by contract or by court order.

197. The remedy of quasi-contract is available

a. Although no contract was ever formed.

b. In addition to any contractual remedies.

c. Only when the specific benefit given can be recovered.

d. Regardless of whether unjust enrichment has occurred.

The correct answer is (a). *(Publisher)*

REQUIRED: The true statement about the remedy of quasi-contract.

DISCUSSION: When one person has bestowed a benefit on another in circumstances such that failure to give a remedy would constitute unjust enrichment, a court may allow a recovery in quasi-contract although no contract was formed or attempted to be formed.

Answer (b) is incorrect because a remedy in quasi-contract is given instead of a contractual remedy. Answer (c) is incorrect because if the particular benefit provided can be specifically restored, it is recoverable in quasi-contract. Otherwise, the reasonable value of the benefit is the measure of the remedy. Answer (d) is incorrect because unjust enrichment is the essence of the remedy.

198. X Company is a manufacturer of a product sold in large amounts only at one time of the year. Y Company supplies a critical raw material used in the product. X enters into a contract for the raw material and informs Y that it will be needed promptly for the peak of the selling season. Y failed to deliver the raw material on time. X therefore had to decline orders from regular customers, some of which will be permanently lost. X was able to fill some orders by purchasing a small quantity of the raw material from another supplier at a higher price. What damages should X recover?

a. Compensatory damages only.

b. Compensatory and consequential damages only.

c. Compensatory, consequential, and punitive damages.

d. Only nominal damages.

The correct answer is (b). *(Publisher)*

REQUIRED: The damages recoverable from a breaching party with notice of the consequences of breach.

DISCUSSION: Compensatory damages are intended to compensate for the loss of the bargain. They are the damages normally, directly, and foreseeably flowing from the breach, for instance, the difference between the contract price of goods and the market price. Consequential (special) damages are those arising from the unique facts of the case. The breaching party must know or have reason to know of these circumstances in order for the plaintiff to recover them. The difference between the contract and market price of the raw materials is the measure of X Company's compensatory damages. Because Y Company knew of X's special needs, X can also obtain consequential damages for lost current and future profits.

Answer (a) is incorrect because X Company can also recover consequential damages. Answer (c) is incorrect because punitive damages are seldom allowed in contracts cases. Answer (d) is incorrect because actual damages are available. Nominal damages are given only when a technical breach has occurred but no actual damages can be shown.

199. Edgar owns a parcel of real property. He enters into a written contract to sell it to Charlie. If Edgar refuses to sell

a. The election of remedies doctrine provides that Charlie's remedies will be cumulative.

b. Charlie may only rescind the contract or obtain damages.

c. Charlie may obtain either damages or specific performance, but not both.

d. Charlie may obtain both damages and specific performance.

The correct answer is (c). *(Publisher)*

REQUIRED: The true statement about remedies for a breach of a contract to sell realty.

DISCUSSION: The election of remedies doctrine prevents plaintiff from seeking inconsistent remedies. The purpose of the rule is to avoid injustice by denying a double recovery. By awarding damages and compelling specific performance, the court would allow Charlie to obtain two recoveries from one breach.

Answer (a) is incorrect because the doctrine provides that remedies will be in the alternative. With regard to sales of goods, however, the doctrine has been rejected (UCC 2-703 and UCC 2-711). Under Article 2 of the UCC, remedies are cumulative. Answer (b) is incorrect because specific performance is often granted when the contract is for the sale of real property. The equitable remedy is permitted when the legal remedy would be inadequate because of the uniqueness of the subject matter. Answer (d) is incorrect because the plaintiff must elect one remedy.

200. Nora was a tenant in a low-income apartment building. She had signed a lease that included an exculpatory clause absolving the lessor from any liability for injury to the lessee. One night, Nora fell down an unlighted flight of stairs leading from her apartment and suffered physical injuries. The stairway lights were not operating because of the lessor's negligence. The most likely result is that the lessor's exculpatory clause will

a. Be enforced because the parties have the freedom to contract as long as the basis of their bargain is not illegal.

b. Be enforced because defendant's conduct did not constitute an intentional tort.

c. Not be enforced because contractual limitations of liability are contrary to public policy.

d. Not be enforced because it permits the plaintiff no remedy.

The correct answer is (d). *(Publisher)*

REQUIRED: The likely effect of an exculpatory clause in a lease.

DISCUSSION: Contracting parties are normally free to establish limitations on their liability, including tort liability. Exculpatory clauses, however, are not favored because they completely exclude the plaintiff's remedies. Such a clause might be upheld if the parties are of equal bargaining power and the setting is commercial. Because the lease in question was noncommercial and the likelihood was small that the clause was truly the result of bargaining between equal parties, plaintiff should prevail.

Answer (a) is incorrect because modern contract law disfavors unconscionable bargains. Answer (b) is incorrect because the exclusion of every remedy (even for negligence) is likely to be found contrary to public policy when the parties do not have equal bargaining power. Answer (c) is incorrect because a limitation is acceptable if it does not amount to an exclusion of all remedies and is not unconscionable.

201. Which of the following is a measure of compensatory damages likely to be applied in a majority of jurisdictions?

a. The seller of land unintentionally breaches a contract. The buyer recovers the difference between the market price and the contract price.

b. The seller of textbooks contracts to deliver 100 books at $20 each. When the seller fails to deliver, buyer pays $25 each to another seller. Damages are $2,500.

c. A company agrees to construct a pool. Before work begins, the owner breaches. Damages equal the contract price.

d. A company agrees to construct a tennis court but abandons work when the project is one-third complete. The damages are the value of completed tennis courts.

The correct answer is (a). *(Publisher)*

REQUIRED: The measure of compensatory damages recognized in a majority of states.

DISCUSSION: Compensatory damages for breach of a contract to sell land are usually measured as market price minus contract price regardless of whether the breaching party is the buyer or seller. This gives the injured party "the benefit of the bargain" by placing him/her in the position (s)he would have been in had the contract been performed.

Answer (b) is incorrect because market price ($2,500) minus contract price ($2,000) is the usual measure of damages ($500) when the contract is for the sale of goods. Answer (c) is incorrect because when a construction contract is breached by the owner prior to the start of work, the measure of damages is usually the profit expected to be earned by the builder (contract price minus cost of construction). Answer (d) is incorrect because when the builder abandons the work before substantial completion, damages equal the cost to complete.

202. Johnson and Harris entered into an agreement in which Johnson was to build a drainage canal for Harris. The contract contained a clause providing that either party's sole remedy under the contract was arbitration. If either Johnson or Harris does breach the contract, which statement is correct concerning the arbitration clause?

a. Required arbitration is not enforceable because everyone is entitled to use the court system.

b. The clause is enforceable as the parties' sole remedy.

c. Any decision of an arbitrator must be reviewed by a court before the decision can be specifically enforced.

d. The clause is void as against public policy.

The correct answer is (b). *(Publisher)*

REQUIRED: The correct statement concerning an arbitration clause in a contract.

DISCUSSION: A clause providing that arbitration is the parties' sole remedy in the event of breach is enforceable. The parties may agree to limit their remedies under contract if reasonable. Arbitration has become quite common, and the arbitrator's decision in a case is enforceable. The decision may in limited circumstances be judicially reviewed subject to the state arbitration statute.

Answer (a) is incorrect because although everyone is entitled to use the court system, this right can be waived. Answer (c) is incorrect because the decision of the arbitrator is final although it is subject to review by a court. Answer (d) is incorrect because arbitration clauses are encouraged to reduce the caseload of courts.

CHAPTER TWELVE
SALES OF GOODS

The explanations of the answers in this chapter are based almost solely on Article 2 of the Uniform Commercial Code (UCC). References to the relevant UCC sections are provided for those interested in the source of the law. However, only the major UCC sections supporting the answer are given so as not to inundate the explanation with UCC citations.

12.1 Sales: Fundamental Principles

1. The distinction between contracts that are covered by the UCC and those that are not is

a. Basically dependent upon whether the subject matter of the contract involves the purchase or sale of goods.

b. Based upon the dollar amount of the contract.

c. Dependent upon whether the Statute of Frauds is involved.

d. Of relatively little or no importance because the laws are invariably the same.

The correct answer is (a). *(CPA 1176 L-35)*

REQUIRED: The distinction between contracts covered by the UCC and those that are not.

DISCUSSION: The UCC covers contracts for the purchase or sale of goods (UCC 2-102), and Article 2 of the UCC governs most of these transactions. If a contract is not for the sale or purchase of goods, it is rarely covered by the UCC.

Answers (b) and (c) are incorrect because the application of the UCC is a function of the subject matter of the contract, not its dollar amount or whether the Statute of Frauds is involved. Answer (d) is incorrect because the distinction is of great importance. The UCC made substantial changes in prior legislation and the common law. Furthermore, the UCC allows buyers and sellers substantial, but not unlimited, freedom of contract to modify the UCC's general rules (UCC 1-102).

2. Which of the following is excluded from the UCC's definition of goods?

a. Minerals (including oil and gas) to be severed by the seller.

b. The money in which the price is to be paid, investment securities, and things in action.

c. Growing crops and timber.

d. The unborn young of animals.

The correct answer is (b). *(Publisher)*

REQUIRED: The items excluded from the definition of goods.

DISCUSSION: UCC 2-105 defines goods as all things (including specially manufactured goods) that are movable at the time of identification to the contract for sale other than the money in which the price is to be paid, investment securities (Article 8), and things in action.

Answer (a) is incorrect because minerals are considered goods if they are to be severed by the seller. Answers (c) and (d) are incorrect because goods include growing crops, timber, and the unborn young of animals.

3. The UCC Sales Article applies to the sale of

a. Goods only if the seller is a merchant and the buyer is not.

b. Goods only if the seller and buyer are both merchants.

c. Consumer goods by a nonmerchant.

d. Real estate by a merchant for $500 or more.

The correct answer is (c). *(CPA 1188 L-43)*

REQUIRED: The sales transactions covered by Article 2 of the UCC.

DISCUSSION: Article 2 applies to transactions in goods except for those intended to operate only as security arrangements (UCC 2-102). UCC 2-105 defines goods as all things (including specially manufactured goods) that are movable at the time of identification to the contract for sale other than the money in which the price is to be paid, investment securities (Article 8), and things in action. Goods are classified as consumer goods, equipment, farm products, and inventory. Goods are consumer goods if they are used or bought for use primarily for personal, family, or household purposes (UCC 9-109). Because Article 2 is not limited to transactions by merchants, it follows that sales of consumer goods by nonmerchants are covered.

Answers (a) and (b) are incorrect because Article 2 applies to both merchants and nonmerchants, but special rules are provided for certain aspects of transactions between or with merchants. Answer (d) is incorrect because the UCC does not apply to any sales of realty.

4. Regarding the scope of Article 2 of the UCC, when a contract involves a mixed transaction, such as a sale of goods combined with the rendition of services, which of the following statements is correct?

a. The courts ordinarily will apply Article 2 to any contract that involves goods.

b. The courts ordinarily will apply Article 2 when the contract's focus or predominant feature is the sale of goods.

c. The courts ordinarily will not apply Article 2 to any contract that involves the rendition of services.

d. Applicability of Article 2 depends on the dollar amount of the contract.

The correct answer is (b). *(J. Pittman)*

REQUIRED: The coverage of a mixed goods and services contract by UCC Article 2.

DISCUSSION: Article 2 of the UCC applies to transactions in (sales of) goods (UCC 2-101). Sales of services are not covered. When the contract involves a mixed transaction, the courts ordinarily will apply Article 2 if the predominant feature of the contract as a whole is the sale of goods, with services incidentally involved. The issue arises, for example, when a hospital gives a blood transfusion or a beautician dyes the hair of a customer. Whether these activities are within Article 2 has not been clearly decided by the courts.

Answer (a) is incorrect because unless the context otherwise requires, Article 2 applies to sales of goods but not to transactions intended to operate only as security transactions, bailments, or gifts. Answer (c) is incorrect because if a sale of goods is the major part of the contract, courts will apply Article 2 even though the contract also involves services. Answer (d) is incorrect because the applicability of Article 2 does not depend on the dollar amount of the contract.

5. With regard to a contract governed by the UCC Sales Article, which one of the following statements is correct?

a. Merchants and nonmerchants are treated alike.

b. The contract may involve the sale of any type of personal property.

c. The obligations of the parties to the contract must be performed in good faith.

d. The contract must involve the sale of goods for a price of more than $500.

The correct answer is (c). *(CPA 589 L-54)*

REQUIRED: The true statement about contracts governed by UCC Article 2.

DISCUSSION: Good faith means honesty in fact. UCC 1-203 states, "Every contract or duty within this Act imposes an obligation of good faith in its performance or enforcement."

Answer (a) is incorrect because Article 2 applies to both merchants and nonmerchants, but special rules are provided for certain aspects of transactions between or with merchants. Answer (b) is incorrect because Article 2 concerns sales of goods. Goods do not include such items of personal property as accounts, documents of title, instruments, money, investment securities, copyrights, and patents. Answer (d) is incorrect because no dollar amount is required to bring a sale of goods within Article 2.

6. I. M. Cruck sold refrigerators door to door. Cruck called on Ms. Kalik, a welfare recipient with four small children. Convinced by the sales talk, Kalik signed a form contract that clearly stated the terms of the agreement. After adding credit charges, insurance, and tax, the total price came to over $1,200. The retail value of the appliance was $300. After paying $600, Ms. Kalik defaulted. Ms. Kalik then sued and prevailed on the theory of

a. Duress.

b. Unconscionability.

c. Fraud.

d. Misrepresentation.

The correct answer is (b). *(Publisher)*

REQUIRED: The legal theory allowing a buyer to prevail when the price and value of a good are greatly disparate.

DISCUSSION: UCC 2-302 provides that a court may refuse to enforce an unconscionable contract, it may enforce the remainder without the offending clause, or it may limit the application of any such clause so as to avoid any unconscionable result. The term unconscionable is not defined, but the purpose of the section is to prevent oppression and unfair surprise and to avoid results shocking to the conscience. In a case with similar facts, the court reformed the agreement to set the price term equal to the amount already paid.

Answers (a), (c), and (d) are incorrect because the facts give no indication that threats or intentional or innocent misrepresentations were made.

7. The UCC provides rules of construction that allow unclear contracts to be read in the context of commercial practices and other surrounding circumstances. When the application of these rules results in a conflict, what hierarchy does the UCC establish with regard to the following?

1 Course of performance
2 Course of dealing
3 Usage of trade
4 Express terms

a. 3, 4, 2, 1.

b. 4, 2, 3, 1.

c. 4, 1, 2, 3.

d. 2, 4, 1, 3.

The correct answer is (c). *(Publisher)*

REQUIRED: The order of priority among rules of construction.

DISCUSSION: Course of performance refers to the repeated prior occasions for performance of the same contract. Course of dealing is a sequence of previous conduct between the parties. Usage of trade is any practice or method of dealing having such regularity of observance in a place, vocation, or trade as to justify an expectation that it will be observed with respect to the transaction in question (UCC 1-205).

Express terms control the contract. But when not clear, course of performance or dealing and usage of trade may be used to explain the terms of an agreement and will be interpreted as consistent with each other whenever possible. If not consistent with each other, the hierarchy of answer (c) controls.

8. Mayker, Inc. and Oylco contracted for Oylco to be the exclusive provider of Mayker's fuel oil for 3 months. The stated price was subject to increases of up to a total of 10% if the market price increased. The market price rose 25% and Mayker tripled its normal order. Oylco seeks to avoid performance. Oylco's best argument in support of its position is that

a. There was no meeting of the minds.

b. The contract was unconscionable.

c. The quantity was not definite and certain enough.

d. Mayker ordered amounts of oil unreasonably greater than its normal requirements.

The correct answer is (d). *(CPA 1189 L-51)*

REQUIRED: The best argument for avoiding performance on a requirements contract.

DISCUSSION: Requirements and output contracts were often unenforceable under common law because they were too indefinite. They are permitted under UCC 2-306 provided that the parties act in good faith and demand or tender reasonable quantities. Absent stated estimates, normal or otherwise comparable prior requirements or output will provide the standard of reasonableness. No estimates were made, so if Mayker orders excessive amounts, it will have violated its duties, and Oylco may be able to avoid performance.

Answer (a) is incorrect because under the Code, an agreement that one party will supply the other's requirements for a specified period within a given price range suggests a meeting of the minds (formation of a contract). Hence, Oylco's best argument is breach, not failure to reach an agreement. Answer (b) is incorrect because the difference between 10% and 25% above contract price is not so oppressive and unfair as to render the contract unconscionable. Answer (c) is incorrect because the contract does not fail for indefiniteness given that the parties must act in good faith and demand or tender reasonable quantities.

9. Plaintiff is a large corporation engaged in purchasing and reselling grain crops. In January, it reached an oral agreement with Defendant, a merchant engaged in farming, to purchase 10,000 bushels of soybeans at $6.00 per bushel. In February, Plaintiff signed and sent to Defendant a written confirmation. Defendant made no response until April, when it repudiated the agreement. Plaintiff will prevail because

a. The UCC's Statute of Frauds provision does not apply to the agreement.

b. Growing crops are not goods.

c. It signed the confirmation.

d. Defendant is a merchant.

The correct answer is (d). *(Publisher)*

REQUIRED: The reason plaintiff will win after defendant fails to respond to a written confirmation of an oral contract.

DISCUSSION: A merchant is a person who deals in goods of the kind involved, by occupation holds itself out as having particular knowledge or skill with respect to the goods involved, or employs an agent or broker who holds itself out as having such knowledge or skill (UCC 2-104). Numerous sections of the UCC contain special rules relating to merchants. These provisions may facilitate contract formation and performance between merchants or hold them to a higher standard than nonmerchants because of their superior commercial sophistication. For example, a contract to sell goods for $500 or more is required to be in writing. An oral contract between merchants will be enforceable, however, if, within a reasonable time, a written confirmation is received, the recipient-merchant has reason to know its contents, and written notice of objection is not made within 10 days of receipt (UCC 2-201).

Answers (a) and (b) are incorrect because soybeans, whether growing or harvested, are goods, and the contract was for more than $500. Answer (c) is incorrect because whether the plaintiff signs a writing is irrelevant. The party against whom enforcement is sought must sign except as described above.

10. Sklar, CPA purchased two computers from Wiz Corp. Sklar discovered material defects in the computers 10 months after taking delivery. Sklar commenced an action for breach of warranty against Wiz 3 years later. Wiz has raised the statute of limitations as a defense. The original contract between Wiz and Sklar contained a conspicuous clause providing that the statute of limitations for breach of warranty actions would be limited to 18 months. Under the circumstances, Sklar will

a. Win because the action was commenced within the 4-year period as measured from the date of delivery.

b. Win because the action was commenced within the 4-year period as measured from the time Sklar discovered the breach or should have discovered the breach.

c. Lose because the clause providing that the statute of limitations would be limited to 18 months is enforceable.

d. Lose because the statute of limitations is 3 years from the date of delivery with respect to written contracts.

The correct answer is (c). *(CPA 1186 L-17)*

REQUIRED: The effect of a contractual modification of the statute of limitations.

DISCUSSION: Under UCC 2-725, a 4-year statute of limitations applies to cases involving sales of goods. The parties, however, may reduce (but not extend) the period for suit but not to less than 1 year. An action for breach of warranty accrues (the statute begins to run) when tender of delivery is made. But if the warranty explicitly extends to future performance and discovery of breach must await such performance, the action accrues when the breach is or should have been discovered. Because suit was brought within 4 years of but more than 18 months after both delivery of the goods and discovery of the defects, the issue is not when the action accrued but whether the contractual modification of the statute of limitations is effective. The contract provision for an 18-month limitation on suit is permitted by UCC 2-725 and Sklar will therefore lose.

Answers (a) and (b) are incorrect because when breach occurred is unclear on these facts. The question does not state whether the seller explicitly extended the warranty to future performance. Thus, whether the statute of limitations began to run at delivery or upon discovery of the defects cannot be determined. Nevertheless, the 4-year period provided by UCC 2-725 is inapplicable. Answer (d) is incorrect because UCC 2-725 states that the limitation period is 4 years from the date of accrual. It applies to oral as well as written contracts for the sale of goods.

12.2 Formation of Sales Contracts

11. Anna agreed in writing to sell Bella 1,000 bales of Zots at $1 per pound. The terms were 2/10, net 30, FOB Anna's dock on January 31. Because the price of Zots fell to $.80 per pound prior to delivery, Bella notified Anna that she would not accept delivery. Anna sued for damages, offering evidence that according to local usage a bale weighed 10 pounds.

a. Anna should win because she has a reasonably certain basis for a remedy.

b. Bella should win because evidence of trade usage is inadmissible.

c. Bella should win because the contract is too indefinite.

d. Anna should win because Bella signed a writing evidencing her intention to contract.

The correct answer is (a). *(Publisher)*

REQUIRED: The outcome of a suit on a contract with an indefinite quantity term.

DISCUSSION: Common law requires that to form a contract the parties must reach a clear and complete agreement on all important terms. Failure to do so results in no contract even though the parties believed one existed. However, UCC 2-204 states, "Even though one or more terms are left open, a contract for sale does not fail for indefiniteness if the parties have intended to make a contract and there is a reasonably certain basis for giving an appropriate remedy." Here, the reasonably certain basis for a remedy is supplied by the evidence regarding usage of trade. A damages award may be calculated because usage of trade determines the quantity in pounds.

Answer (b) is incorrect because such evidence is permissible to explain a term of the contract (UCC 1-205). Answer (c) is incorrect because the contract is not too indefinite if the missing or ambiguous terms can be supplied or construed. Answer (d) is incorrect because an intent to contract does not suffice if a reasonably certain basis for a remedy is absent.

12. Al Martin, a wholesale distributor, made a contract for the purchase of 10,000 gallons of gasoline from the Wilberforce Oil Company. The price was to be determined in accordance with the refinery price as of the close of business on the delivery date. Credit terms were net/30 after delivery. Under these circumstances which of the following statements is true?

a. If Martin pays upon delivery, he is entitled to a 2% discount.

b. The contract being silent on the place of delivery, Martin has the right to expect delivery at his place of business.

c. Although the price has some degree of uncertainty, the contract is enforceable.

d. Because the goods involved are tangible, specific performance is a remedy available to Martin.

The correct answer is (c). *(CPA 1176 L-12)*

REQUIRED: The true statement regarding a contract with an open price term.

DISCUSSION: UCC 2-305 permits the parties to conclude a contract even though the price term is left open if they intended to do so (but if objective intent to be bound is missing, there is no contract). The price of the oil is to be set objectively in the future in accordance with the refinery price on the date of delivery. If the price is not settled in accordance with the agreement, the price will be a reasonable price at the time of delivery. A reasonable price is largely determined by market price absent an applicable course of dealing, usage of trade, or course of performance.

Answer (a) is incorrect because nothing in the agreement entitles Martin to a 2% discount for payment upon delivery. Answer (b) is incorrect because if the contract does not specify a place for delivery, UCC 2-308 provides that delivery will be at the seller's, not buyer's, place of business. Answer (d) is incorrect because specific performance will not be available. The subject matter is not unique and money damages would be adequate.

13. Casassa, a merchant in San Francisco, under the terms of a nonshipment contract, agrees to sell 50 cases of packaged macaroni to Paoli, a restaurant owner whose business is in San Jose. At the time of contracting for the sale, both parties are aware that these identified goods are in a warehouse in Fresno. The place for delivery is not specified in the agreement. On the basis of these facts, the place for delivery is

a. San Francisco.

b. San Jose.

c. Fresno.

d. Indefinite, and the contract is unenforceable.

The correct answer is (c). *(L. Fischl)*

REQUIRED: The place of delivery if the delivery term is omitted in a contract for the sale of goods.

DISCUSSION: If a contract for the sale of goods does not expressly designate a place of delivery and none is provided by course of dealing, usage of trade, or course of performance, UCC 2-308 provides that the seller's place of business (if none, his/her residence) will be the place of delivery. However, if the goods are known to be located elsewhere (Fresno) than the seller's place of business, the other location is the place of delivery.

Answers (a) and (b) are incorrect because the seller's place of business is the proper place for delivery in the absence of a designation or unless the goods are known to be elsewhere. Answer (d) is incorrect because if the parties intended to contract and the basis for a remedy exists, the contract will not fail for indefiniteness even if some terms are left open (UCC 2-204).

14. Suggs Company agreed to sell certain goods to Barr Corporation pursuant to a written contract. No shipment or delivery date was specified in the contract. Based on these facts,

a. The time for shipment is within a reasonable time.

b. The time for shipment must be agreed upon.

c. The time for shipment is within 3 months.

d. The contract fails for indefiniteness.

The correct answer is (a). *(CPA 1175 L-6)*

REQUIRED: The effect of failing to state a shipment or delivery date.

DISCUSSION: Under UCC 2-309, the time for shipment or delivery will be a reasonable time if the parties have not specified. Relatedly, UCC 2-307 provides for a single shipment of the goods if the contract does not specify otherwise. These sections reflect the UCC's policy to find a valid contract if the parties so intended and a reasonable basis for a remedy exists.

Answer (b) is incorrect because the time for shipment may be left open. Answer (c) is incorrect because the time for shipment will be a reasonable time. Answer (d) is incorrect because the contract does not fail for indefiniteness even though one or more terms are left open (UCC 2-204).

15. Under the UCC Sales Article, a firm offer will be created only if the

a. Offeree is a merchant.

b. Offeree gives some form of consideration.

c. Offer states the time period during which it will remain open.

d. Offer is made by a merchant in a signed writing.

The correct answer is (d). *(CPA 1188 L-44)*

REQUIRED: The UCC requirement for a firm offer.

DISCUSSION: An offer by a merchant to buy or sell goods in a signed writing that by its terms gives assurance that it will be held open is not revocable for lack of consideration during the time stated. If no time is stated, the time is a reasonable time. But in no event may the period of irrevocability exceed 3 months. Any such term of assurance on a form supplied by the offeree must be separately signed by the offeror (UCC 2-205). A statement specifying when an offer will expire is not a firm offer. A firm offer is a written assurance by a merchant that the offer will remain open.

Answer (a) is incorrect because the firm offer rule also applies to offers made to nonmerchants. Answer (b) is incorrect because if the other requirements of a firm offer are met, no consideration is necessary to support the offeror's promise. Answer (c) is incorrect because if not stated, the time of irrevocability is deemed to be a reasonable time not exceeding 3 months.

16. Doral, Inc. wished to obtain an adequate supply of lumber for its factory extension to be constructed in the spring. It contacted Ace Lumber Company and obtained a 75-day written option (firm offer) to buy its estimated needs for the building. Doral supplied a form contract that included the option. Ace Lumber signed at the physical end of the contract but did not sign elsewhere. The price of lumber has risen drastically and Ace wishes to avoid its obligation. Which of the following is Ace's best defense against Doral's assertion that Ace is legally bound by the option?

a. Such an option is invalid if its duration is for more than 2 months.

b. The option is not supported by any consideration on Doral's part.

c. Doral is not a merchant.

d. The promise of irrevocability was contained in a form supplied by Doral and was not separately signed by Ace.

The correct answer is (d). *(CPA 581 L-18)*

REQUIRED: The best defense of a merchant to avoid being legally bound under a firm offer.

DISCUSSION: Under the firm offer rule of UCC 2-205, if a merchant in a signed writing states that an offer will be held open, the offer may not be revoked during the time stated even if no consideration was given to hold it open. If the offeree supplies the form, however, the firm offer must be separately signed. Ace's best defense is to assert that the firm offer rule does not apply because Ace did not separately sign the promise to hold the offer open. The purpose of this rule is to protect an offeror who is unaware that the offeree's form contains the firm offer term.

Answer (a) is incorrect because such an option is valid for the time stated or, if no time is stated, for a reasonable time, but in no event for more than 3 months. Answer (b) is incorrect because a firm offer made by a merchant need not be supported by consideration. Answer (c) is incorrect because the firm offer rule only requires that the offeror (Ace) be a merchant.

17. Almovar Electronics sent a letter on March 8 to Conduit Sales & Service Company offering an entire lot of electronic parts at a substantial reduction in price. The offer indicated that it was for "immediate acceptance." The terms were "cash, pick up by your carrier at our loading dock and not later than March 15." It also indicated that the terms of the offer were not subject to variance. The letter did not arrive until March 10, and Conduit's letter accepting the offer was not mailed until March 12. The letter of acceptance indicated that Conduit would take the entire lot, would pay in accordance with the usual terms (2/10, net/30), and would pick up the goods on March 16. Which of the following best describes the legal relationship of the parties?

a. The acceptance was not timely, hence no contract was formed.

b. The different terms of the acceptance are to be construed as proposals for changes in the contract.

c. The different terms of the acceptance constituted a rejection of the offer.

d. Because both parties were merchants and the changes in the acceptance were not material, there is a valid contract based on the different terms.

The correct answer is (b). *(CPA 579 L-35)*

REQUIRED: The legal effect of an acceptance by a merchant that varies the terms of an offer made by another merchant.

DISCUSSION: Conduit's letter was a definite, seasonable, and unconditional acceptance and thus formed a contract. Ordinarily, additional or different terms are considered proposals for addition to or changes in the contract. However, between merchants the additional or different terms become part of the contract unless the offer expressly limited acceptance to its terms (which it did), the additional or different terms materially alter the offer, or the offeror objects within a reasonable time (UCC 2-207). Because the offer expressly limited acceptance to its terms, Conduit's letter was an acceptance of the original offer with proposals for changes.

Answer (a) is incorrect because the attempted acceptance was timely. It was effective March 12 (when sent), and the goods did not have to be picked up until March 15. Answer (c) is incorrect because the additional or different terms are construed as proposals to modify the contract. Answer (d) is incorrect because the offer expressly limited acceptance to the terms of the offer.

18. On October 1, Baker, a wholesaler, sent Clark, a retailer, a written, signed offer to sell 200 pinking shears at $9 each. The terms were FOB Baker's warehouse, net 30, late payment subject to a 15% per annum interest charge. The offer indicated that it must be accepted no later than October 10, that acceptance would be effective upon receipt, and that the terms were not to be varied by the offeree. Clark sent a telegram, which arrived on October 6, and accepted the offer expressly subject to a change of the payment terms to 2/10, net/30. Baker phoned Clark on October 7 to reject the change of payment terms. On the phone, Clark then indicated it would accept the October 1 offer in all respects, and expected delivery within 10 days. Baker did not accept Clark's oral acceptance of the original offer. Which of the following is correct?

a. Baker's original offer is a firm offer, hence irrevocable.

b. There is no contract. Clark's modifications effectively rejected the October 1 offer, and Baker never accepted either of Clark's proposals.

c. Clark actually created a contract on October 6. The modifications were merely proposals and did not preclude acceptance.

d. The Statute of Frauds would preclude the formation of a contract in any event.

The correct answer is (b). *(CPA 1183 L-53)*

REQUIRED: The correct statement about the effect of conditioning an acceptance upon assent to a different term.

DISCUSSION: Because the purported acceptance by telegram was expressly conditional upon assent to the different payment terms, it was not effective as an acceptance (UCC 2-207). It operated as a rejection of the offer and a counteroffer. The effect of the counteroffer was to terminate the original offer. Thus, Clark's subsequent unconditional acceptance on October 7 of the original offer was ineffective. The rejection and counteroffer had previously been communicated to the offeror.

Answer (a) is incorrect because even though made by a merchant in writing, the offer did not state that it was irrevocable. Answer (c) is incorrect because an additional or different term is usually deemed a proposal for addition to the contract, but between merchants it becomes an addition to the contract unless the offer expressly limits acceptance to its terms, the additional term materially alters the offer, or notice of objection has already been given or is given within a reasonable time. Clark's payment term failed all three tests. Moreover, the expression of acceptance was conditional and thus not effective as an acceptance. Answer (d) is incorrect because Baker's offer was written and signed. An effective oral acceptance by Clark would have permitted enforcement against Baker.

19. Cookie Co. offered to sell Distrib Markets 20,000 pounds of cookies at $1.00 per pound, subject to certain specified terms for delivery. Distrib replied in writing as follows:

"We accept your offer for 20,000 pounds of cookies at $1.00 per pound, weighing scale to have valid city certificate."

Under the UCC,

a. A contract was formed between the parties.

b. A contract will be formed only if Cookie agrees to the weighing scale requirement.

c. No contract was formed because Distrib included the weighing scale requirement in its reply.

d. No contract was formed because Distrib's reply was a counteroffer.

The correct answer is (a). *(CPA 1189 L-46)*

REQUIRED: The effect of a merchant's adding a term in an unconditional acceptance.

DISCUSSION: Additional or different terms in an unconditional, definite, and seasonable acceptance of an offer for a sale of goods are construed as proposals for addition to the contract. But between merchants such terms become part of the contract unless the offer expressly limits acceptance to its terms, the additional or different terms materially alter the offer, or the offeree objects within a reasonable time (UCC 2-207). Cookie and Distrib are most likely merchants, the acceptance was unconditional, and no exception applies. Hence, the weighing scale term becomes part of the agreement unless objected to in a reasonable time. However, a contract is formed without the additional term if the parties are not merchants.

Answers (b), (c), and (d) are incorrect because an additional term in an unconditional acceptance of an offer for a sale of goods does not constitute a rejection and counteroffer. Thus, a contract was formed regardless of whether either of the parties is a merchant, and the additional term was a proposal for addition to the contract.

20. Rockin Rhonda sent a written order to T-Shirt Inc. for two "Soft Rock Bistro" Tee-shirts for her and her twin sister, Rollin Rhoda. T-Shirt Inc. sent a written acceptance of Rhonda's order, but the acceptance form added a clause disclaiming all warranties relating to the shirts. Rhonda does nothing. A contract was

a. Not formed, but T-Shirt Inc.'s response constitutes a counteroffer under the "Mirror Image" rule.

b. Formed, but the warranty disclaimer does not become part of the contract.

c. Formed, but the warranty disclaimer does not become part of the contract until the twins wear their new shirts.

d. Formed, and the warranty disclaimer becomes part of the contract because it does not materially alter the contract and Rhonda did not object.

The correct answer is (b). *(K. Wilburn)*

REQUIRED: The effect of an additional term in an acceptance sent by a merchant to a nonmerchant.

DISCUSSION: The offeree's response constitutes an acceptance under UCC 2-207 despite the additional term. However, Rhonda is not a merchant, and the additional term in the acceptance form did not become a part of the contract because Rhonda did not accept it.

Answer (a) is incorrect because the common law "Mirror Image" rule does not apply to this sale of goods transaction. The UCC discarded the view that an acceptance must exactly "mirror" the offer to be effective. Answer (c) is incorrect because the disclaimer clause does not become part of the contract even if the purchasers use the merchandise. Answer (d) is incorrect because Rhonda is not a merchant. Accordingly, the term would not become part of the contract unless Rhonda had accepted it.

21. Which of the following is a true statement about acceptance of an offer to buy or sell goods?

a. If the offer does not designate the medium of acceptance, acceptance may be by any reasonable medium.

b. If the offer designates a medium of acceptance, acceptance may be by any medium that is as fast as or faster than the one designated.

c. Acceptance by beginning the requested performance is binding without notice to the offeror if such a mode of acceptance is reasonable in the circumstances.

d. If the offer does not designate the time when acceptance is effective, the contract is usually formed upon receipt of the acceptance.

The correct answer is (a). *(Publisher)*

REQUIRED: The true statement about the UCC's acceptance rules.

DISCUSSION: "Unless otherwise unambiguously indicated by the language or circumstances, an offer to make a contract shall be construed as inviting acceptance in any manner and by any medium reasonable in the circumstances" (UCC 2-206). Some courts hold that the medium is reasonable only if it is as fast as or faster than the medium chosen to transmit the offer. Other courts consider all the circumstances. The UCC takes the latter position.

Answer (b) is incorrect because if the offer specifies a method of acceptance, that method must be used to be effective. Answer (c) is incorrect because an offeror not notified within a reasonable time may treat the offer as having lapsed before acceptance. Answer (d) is incorrect because the acceptance is usually effective upon dispatch (the "mailbox" rule).

22. Taylor signed and mailed a letter to Peel that stated: "Ship promptly 600 dozen grade A eggs." Taylor's offer

a. May be accepted by Peel only by a prompt shipment.

b. May be accepted by Peel either by a prompt promise to ship or prompt shipment with notice.

c. Is invalid because the price term was omitted.

d. Is invalid because the shipping term was omitted.

The correct answer is (b). *(CPA 585 L-41)*

REQUIRED: The true statement about the validity or acceptance of an offer to buy goods for prompt shipment.

DISCUSSION: Unless otherwise unambiguously indicated by the language or circumstances, an order to buy goods for prompt or current shipment invites acceptance either by a prompt promise to ship or by prompt shipment (UCC 2-206). Notice should be given when acceptance is made by prompt shipment because, if the offeror is not notified of acceptance within a reasonable time, (s)he may treat the offer as lapsed. But if the offer clearly requires shipment as the method of acceptance, a promise to ship is not a valid acceptance.

Answer (a) is incorrect because acceptance may also be by a prompt promise to ship. Answers (c) and (d) are incorrect because "even though one or more terms are left open, a contract for sale does not fail for indefiniteness if the parties have intended to make a contract and there is a reasonably certain basis for giving an appropriate remedy" (UCC 2-204).

23. Argot Manufacturing wrote Palm offering to sell specified merchandise with the offer to remain open 30 days. Ten days later, Argot and Palm orally agreed on the terms of the sale, and Argot prepared a letter that it sent to Palm stating, "This incorporates our agreement." The letter specified the goods but failed to include the agreed price. Later, prior to the date specified for delivery, Argot agreed in writing to modify the terms of the contract as requested by Palm, but Argot gave no consideration for the modification. Based on these facts

a. Argot's offer was revocable until accepted by Palm.

b. If Palm seeks to enforce the agreement, Argot may assert the Statute of Frauds as a defense because neither letter specified any price for the goods.

c. Lack of consideration for the modification of the agreement would not prevent its enforceability.

d. Neither Argot nor Palm could enforce the agreement because Palm had not signed any writing.

The correct answer is (c). *(CPA 574 L-25)*

REQUIRED: The legal status of an agreement evidenced by a letter that did not include the price term and was later modified without consideration.

DISCUSSION: Modification of an agreement needs no consideration to be binding (UCC 2-209). Consequently, the agreement is enforceable as modified.

Answer (a) is incorrect because the offer was irrevocable as a firm offer for 30 days under UCC 2-205, assuming Argot is a merchant. Answer (b) is incorrect because the Statute of Frauds only requires that a writing be sufficient to indicate the existence of a contract, and the absence of the price does not prevent formation of a contract. The parties are presumed to have agreed to a reasonable price. Answer (d) is incorrect because the Statute of Frauds requires only that the writing be signed by the party against whom enforcement is sought. Argot signed the letter so Palm can enforce it. Furthermore, if both parties are merchants, a written confirmation binds the recipient if not disputed within 10 days of receipt.

24. Which of the following statements is correct with regard to an auction of goods?

a. The auctioneer may withdraw the goods at any time prior to completion of the sale unless the goods are put up without reserve.

b. A bidder may retract a bid before the completion of the sale only if the auction is without reserve.

c. A bidder's retraction of a bid will revive the prior bid if the sale is with reserve.

d. In a sale with reserve, a bid made while the hammer is falling automatically reopens the bidding.

The correct answer is (a). *(CPA 584 L-50)*

REQUIRED: The true statement about an auction of goods.

DISCUSSION: An auction is with reserve unless the goods are explicitly offered without reserve. When goods are auctioned with reserve, the auctioneer may withdraw them at any time before (s)he announces completion of the sale. In an auction without reserve, the goods may not be withdrawn after the auctioneer calls for bids unless no bid is made (UCC 2-328).

Answers (b) and (c) are incorrect because whether the sale is with or without reserve, a bid is an offer and may be retracted until the auctioneer announces acceptance and completion of the sale. However, a retraction does not revive any previous bid. The bidding would start over. Answer (d) is incorrect because when a bid is made while the hammer is falling (the act of acceptance), the auctioneer may reopen the bidding or declare the goods sold under the bid on which the hammer was falling.

12.3 Statute of Frauds

25. Del Morgan wanted to buy a new super deluxe riding lawnmower for his yard, but he first had to sell his old lawnmower. Morgan's neighbor Sam agreed to buy the old lawnmower for $500 when Morgan's new lawnmower was delivered (expected in 2 months). To be enforceable, this agreement must be in writing because

a. It is a firm offer.

b. It is a contract for the sale of goods for $500 or more.

c. It is a contract for a sale of goods to take place in the future.

d. It is a bilateral contract.

The correct answer is (b). *(Publisher)*

REQUIRED: The reason the contract for the sale of goods must be in writing.

DISCUSSION: UCC 2-201 requires that a contract for the sale of goods for $500 or more be evidenced by a writing and signed by the party sought to be bound.

Answer (a) is incorrect because it is a contract, not an offer. Also, the firm offer rule applies only to merchants, and Morgan does not appear to be a merchant with respect to lawnmowers. Answer (c) is incorrect because the prospective nature of the sale does not require the contract to be in writing. Answer (d) is incorrect because whether a contract is bilateral is not determinative of the need for a writing.

26. Bill Hendrickson, a well-known author, found himself hard-pressed for cash and decided to assign one of his copyrights to Eureka Enterprises. After protracted and often heated negotiations, Hendrickson and Eureka arrived at an oral agreement whereby Hendrickson would transfer to Eureka the copyright for $5,800. Prior to the actual transfer, one of Hendrickson's investments paid off spectacularly, and he refused to transfer the copyright to Eureka, alleging the contract to be null and void or at least voidable for several reasons. Which of the following is correct?

a. If Hendrickson had received a memorandum of the agreement that would bind Eureka and has not objected to it, he is bound.

b. Unless Eureka gave Hendrickson earnest money at the time of the oral understanding, the contract is invalid.

c. The contract is voidable by Hendrickson if he pleads the Statute of Frauds.

d. The contract is null and void in that Hendrickson was under extreme mental stress and financial hardship at the time he made the agreement.

The correct answer is (c). *(CPA 578 L-42)*

REQUIRED: The correct statement concerning the oral agreement to transfer the copyright.

DISCUSSION: A contract for the sale of intangible personal property (except an investment security) for more than $5,000 must be in writing and signed by the party sought to be bound (UCC 1-206). A copyright is an intangible covered by this rule. Accordingly, Hendrickson cannot be bound to the sale because he did not sign a writing.

Answer (a) is incorrect because Hendrickson must sign the memorandum to be bound. The exception in UCC 2-201 for a confirmation between merchants does not apply. Answer (b) is incorrect because earnest money is not required as a general matter of contract law. Answer (d) is incorrect because mental stress and financial hardship alone are not grounds for avoidance of contractual obligations. If a party has freely consented to the contract, (s)he is bound.

27. Which of the following requirements must be met for modification of a sales contract under the Uniform Commercial Code?

a. The modification must satisfy the Statute of Frauds if the contract as modified is within its provisions.

b. There must be consideration present if the contract is between merchants.

c. The parol evidence rule applies and thus a writing is required.

d. There must be a writing if the original sales contract is in writing.

The correct answer is (a). *(CPA 1183 L-50)*

REQUIRED: The requirement for modification of a sales contract under the UCC.

DISCUSSION: Under UCC 2-209, if the modification of a contract brings it within the Statute of Frauds, both the contract and the modification must meet the Statute's requirements even though not originally required. For example, if the original price was $400 and the modification raises it to $500, then the contract as modified falls within the Statute of Frauds and must be written.

Answer (b) is incorrect because good faith modification of a contract requires no consideration whether or not the parties are merchants. Answer (c) is incorrect because the parol evidence rule does not apply to modifications made subsequent to the creation of an agreement. Answer (d) is incorrect because the modification of the contract need not be in writing if the contract as modified is not within the Statute of Frauds.

28. An oral agreement concerning the sale of goods entered into without consideration is binding if the agreement

a. Is a firm offer made by a merchant who promises to hold the offer open for 30 days.

b. Is a waiver of the non-breaching party's rights arising out of a breach of the contract.

c. Contradicts the terms of a subsequent written contract that is intended as the complete and exclusive agreement of the parties.

d. Modifies the price in an existing, enforceable contract from $525 to $475.

The correct answer is (d). *(CPA 1187 L-40)*

REQUIRED: The circumstance in which an oral modification is binding.

DISCUSSION: An oral modification of a contract for the sale of goods does not require consideration to be binding, but the UCC's Statute of Frauds section (UCC 2-201) must be satisfied if the contract "as modified" is within its provisions (UCC 2-209). Because the contract as modified is for less than $500, UCC 2-201 is inapplicable, no writing is required, and the oral agreement is enforceable.

Answer (a) is incorrect because a firm offer must be contained in a signed writing (UCC 2-205). Answer (b) is incorrect because a waiver may be retracted by reasonable notice received by the other party unless such retraction would be unjust in view of a material change in position in reliance on the waiver (UCC 2-209). Answer (c) is incorrect because the parol evidence rule would exclude proof of a prior oral agreement that would modify the terms of a written agreement meant to be entire.

29. To satisfy the UCC Statute of Frauds, a written agreement for the sale of goods must

a. Contain payment terms.

b. Be signed by both buyer and seller.

c. Indicate that a contract for sale has been made.

d. Refer to the time and place of delivery.

The correct answer is (c). *(CPA 589 L-29)*

REQUIRED: The element necessary for a writing to satisfy the UCC Statute of Frauds.

DISCUSSION: A writing must be sufficient to indicate that a contract for sale has been made between the parties and signed by the party sought to be bound or his/her authorized agent or broker. A writing is not insufficient because it omits or misstates a term agreed upon, but it will not be enforceable beyond the quantity of goods shown (UCC 2-201).

Answers (a) and (d) are incorrect because a writing will satisfy the Statute of Frauds even if some terms are omitted. If a contract is intended and a reasonable basis for establishing a remedy exists, the UCC supplies most missing terms. Answer (b) is incorrect because the writing need only be signed by the party against whom enforcement is sought.

30. Under what conditions will the Statute of Frauds be a defense under the Uniform Commercial Code if there is a contract for the sale of goods for $500 or more?

a. The seller has completed goods specially manufactured for the buyer that are not salable in the ordinary course of the seller's business.

b. The written memorandum omits several important terms but states the quantity, and it is signed by the party to be charged.

c. The party asserting the Statute of Frauds admits under oath to having made the contract.

d. The goods in question are fungible and actively traded by merchants in the business community.

The correct answer is (d). *(CPA 1176 L-5)*

REQUIRED: The conditions under which the Statute of Frauds will be a defense.

DISCUSSION: The Statute of Frauds provision (UCC 2-201) applies to contracts for the sale of goods for $500 or more. All goods are subject to this rule including fungible goods actively traded by merchants. Answer (d) is the only choice that is not an exception to the Statute of Frauds.

Answer (a) is incorrect because a contract for specially manufactured goods not salable in the ordinary course of the seller's business, under which a substantial beginning on their manufacture or commitments for their procurement have been made, is an exception to the Statute of Frauds. Answer (b) is incorrect because the Statute of Frauds only requires a signed written memorandum indicating that a contract has been made. Answer (c) is incorrect because a court-related admission (e.g., in a pleading, the discovery process, or testimony) by the party asserting the defense operates as a substitution for the required writing.

31. Which of the following terms usually must be included in a writing that would otherwise satisfy the UCC Statute of Frauds regarding the sale of goods?

a. The warranties to be granted.

b. The price of the goods.

c. The designation of the parties as buyer and seller.

d. The quantity of the goods.

The correct answer is (d). *(CPA 1185 L-46)*

REQUIRED: The term that usually must be included in a writing sufficient under the UCC.

DISCUSSION: Under UCC 2-201, a writing is usually sufficient if it indicates that a contract for sale was made between the parties and signed by the party sought to be bound or by his/her authorized agent or broker. A writing is also usually sufficient even if it omits or misstates a term, but it is not enforceable beyond the quantity shown. Therefore, the quantity term is required.

Answers (a), (b), and (c) are incorrect because each may be omitted from a writing sufficient under UCC 2-201.

32. Greed Co. telephoned Stieb Co. and ordered 30 tables at $100 each. Greed agreed to pay 15% immediately and the balance within 30 days after receipt of the entire shipment. Greed forwarded a check for $450 and Stieb shipped 15 tables the next day, intending to ship the balance by the end of the week. Greed decided that the contract was a bad bargain and repudiated it, asserting the Statute of Frauds. Stieb sued Greed. Which of the following will allow Stieb to enforce the contract in its entirety despite the Statute of Frauds?

a. Stieb shipped 15 tables.

b. Greed paid 15% down.

c. The contract is not within the requirements of the Statute of Frauds.

d. Greed admitted in court that it made the contract in question.

The correct answer is (d). *(CPA 1186 L-47)*

REQUIRED: The circumstance allowing the seller to enforce an oral contract despite the Statute of Frauds.

DISCUSSION: UCC 2-201 permits enforcement of an oral, but otherwise valid, contract for the sale of goods for $500 or more if the party against whom enforcement is sought admits in court to having made the oral contract. The contract will not be enforceable beyond the quantity admitted.

Answer (a) is incorrect because in addition to Stieb's shipment, Greed must receive and accept the tables for that part of the contract to be enforceable. Furthermore, part performance (either of delivery or payment) does not make a contract enforceable beyond the quantity delivered or paid for. Answer (b) is incorrect because Greed's down payment furnishes sufficient basis for Stieb to enforce the contract only to the extent of the partial payment. Answer (c) is incorrect because the contract is within the Statute of Frauds. It is for the sale of goods for $500 or more.

33. Pam wrote Matz setting forth specifications for a printing press of a unique nature to be constructed to order and asked for a firm price offer if Matz were interested. Matz telegraphed Pam 1 week later, "Offer to construct as per your letter for twenty thousand seven hundred dollars cash on November delivery. Offer terminates 2 days. Matz." The telegram omitted the words "seven hundred" when delivered to Pam. Pam immediately phoned Matz and stated, "I accept as stated in your telegram." Matz said, "Done." Based on the above facts and assuming no further writing

a. No contract resulted because Matz did not intend to sell the press for $20,000.

b. Neither party is bound because of mutual mistake.

c. If Matz completed the contract and delivered the press to Pam, Matz would be deemed to have made an implied warranty against infringement of any patent held by others.

d. Pam probably cannot assert the Statute of Frauds as a defense to a suit by Matz if she notifies Matz that she will not take the goods after Matz has completed about 40% of the work.

The correct answer is (d). *(CPA 574 L-26)*

REQUIRED: The correct statement regarding the legal effect of the above facts.

DISCUSSION: A contract for the sale of specially manufactured goods, which are not suitable for sale in the ordinary course of the seller's business and upon which a substantial beginning has been made, is enforceable even if not in writing (UCC 2-201). Thus, the Statute of Frauds would not be a defense for Pam.

Answer (a) is incorrect because Matz, the offeror, was responsible for the accurate communication of the offer and should bear the consequences of the mistake in transmission. Answer (b) is incorrect because the mistake was unilateral; it was made by Matz's chosen method of communication. Also, the mistake was not of sufficient magnitude to place Pam on notice that the price term was erroneous. Answer (c) is incorrect because if the seller constructs the goods according to the buyer's specifications, it is the buyer who must protect the seller against claims of infringement.

34. Filmore purchased a Miracle color television set from Allison Appliances, an authorized dealer, for $499. The written contract contained the usual 1-year warranty as to parts and labor as long as the set was returned to the manufacturer or one of its authorized dealers. The contract also contained an effective disclaimer of any express warranty protection, other than that included in the contract. It further provided that the contract represented the entire agreement and understanding of the parties. Filmore claims that during the bargaining process Surry, Allison's agent, orally promised to service the set at Filmore's residence if anything went wrong within the year. Allison has offered to repair the set if it is brought to the service department, but denies any liability under the alleged oral express agreement. Which of the following would be the best defense for Allison to rely upon in the event Filmore sues?

a. The Statute of Frauds.

b. The parol evidence rule.

c. That all warranty protection was disclaimed other than the express warranty contained in the contract.

d. That Surry, Allison's agent, did not have express authority to make such a promise.

The correct answer is (b). *(CPA 1182 L-49)*

REQUIRED: The best defense by a party seeking to avoid liability on an oral agreement made during contractual negotiations.

DISCUSSION: The writing stated that it was the entire agreement of the parties (an integration). "A writing intended by the parties as the final expression of their agreement with respect to such terms as are included therein may not be contradicted by evidence of any prior agreement or of a contemporaneous oral agreement" (UCC 2-202). This rule does not exclude course of dealing or performance, usage of trade, or subsequent modifications by the parties. Here, the contemporaneous oral agreement contradicted the term providing for servicing of the set upon return to the manufacturer or authorized dealer. Hence, the parol evidence rule is the seller's best defense.

Answer (a) is incorrect because the price is less than $500, so the contract is not within the Statute of Frauds. Answer (c) is incorrect because under UCC 2-316, words or conduct creating an express warranty and words or conduct negating the warranty are construed whenever reasonable as consistent with each other, but negation is inoperative to the extent such construction is unreasonable. Surry's words creating an express warranty were in conflict with the words of the written contract, and the effect of UCC 2-316 would be to negate the disclaimer. However, UCC 2-316 is subject to the parol evidence rule. Answer (d) is incorrect because Surry presumably had at least apparent authority.

12.4 Title and Risk of Loss

35. Assume that the parties have entered into a contract for the sale of goods. Which of the following is an incorrect statement under the UCC?

a. Any retention by the seller of title to the goods delivered to the buyer is limited in effect to a reservation of a security interest.

b. Title to goods may pass under a contract for sale prior to their identification to the contract.

c. Title passes to the buyer at the time and place at which the seller completes the physical delivery of the goods even though a document of title is to be delivered at a different time or place.

d. The identification of the goods to the contract gives the buyer a special property interest in the goods even before delivery.

The correct answer is (b). *(Publisher)*

REQUIRED: The false statement under the UCC.

DISCUSSION: Many provisions of the UCC regarding the rights, duties, and remedies of the parties apply irrespective of title to the goods. Most important are the rules allocating risk between buyers and sellers. Traditionally, risk is assigned to the party holding title (still true in non-UCC situations), but the UCC separates title and risk of loss. Under the UCC, risk of loss is never assigned on the basis of title. The UCC does contain some provisions with respect to passage of title. Under UCC 2-401, the earliest time title may pass is when the goods have been identified to the contract. Subject to this limitation, title passes when the contracting parties intend, but if not expressed, then in accordance with UCC rules.

Answer (a) is incorrect because the seller is treated essentially as a secured party if a sale of goods has taken place and the title has been reserved by the seller. Answer (c) is incorrect because it correctly describes when title passes if the goods must be physically moved. Answer (d) is incorrect because identification does give the buyer a special property interest that also results in an insurable interest. If the seller becomes insolvent and the buyer has paid all the price, the buyer may be able to recover the goods.

36. Assume that in a contract for the sale of goods the seller has reserved a security interest but that there is no other provision concerning the passage of title. Which of the following is a correct statement?

a. If delivery is to be made without moving the goods and the seller is to deliver a document of title, title passes at the time and the place the parties entered into their contract.

b. If delivery is to be made without moving goods that are already identified to the contract and no documents are to be delivered, title will pass when the buyer takes physical possession.

c. The reservation of a security interest by the seller is a retention of title.

d. If the contract requires the seller to deliver the goods at a named destination, title will pass to the buyer on tender there.

The correct answer is (d). *(Publisher)*

REQUIRED: The correct statement concerning passage of title under the UCC.

DISCUSSION: Most provisions of the UCC apply regardless of title. For some purposes, however, it is still necessary to determine who has title, e.g., the probate of an estate, assessment of taxes, or for certain accounting purposes. Passage of title rules depend upon whether the goods are to be moved, where delivery is to be made, and whether documents of title are to be exchanged. If the contract requires the seller to ship the goods to a given destination, title is considered to pass upon tender to the buyer at that point (UCC 2-401).

Answer (a) is incorrect because if the goods are not to be moved and the seller is to deliver a document of title, title passes upon delivery of the document. Answer (b) is incorrect because if the goods are not to be moved, they are already identified to the contract, and no documents are to be delivered, then title passes at the time and place of contracting. Answer (c) is incorrect because the UCC treats even an express retention of title as being no more than a reservation of a security interest if the goods have been delivered to the buyer.

37. Sylvester Swindler pick-pocketed a variety of items in downtown Chicago during the holidays as shoppers bustled by laden with packages. Sylvester then stood on a street corner to sell his wares. A passerby, Gus Goodeal, bought a 14K gold pocket watch, visibly antique, for $25. Should the true owner, Charles, bring an action against Gus to regain the watch,

a. Gus will win under the law of entrustment.

b. Gus will win because he is a bona fide purchaser.

c. Charles will win because Goodeal has voidable title.

d. Charles will win because he has title and Gus has a void title.

The correct answer is (d). *(S. Rand)*

REQUIRED: The outcome of a suit to recover goods sold by a thief.

DISCUSSION: A purchaser of goods acquires all title that his/her transferor had or had power to transfer. The seller who obtained goods from someone under guardianship, by theft or physical duress, or by finding them has a void title (no title at all) and cannot pass title even to a good faith purchaser for value.

Answer (a) is incorrect because entrustment occurs when the true owner provides a merchant with the possession of personal property for some service to be performed. The merchant must deal in the kind of goods with which he is entrusted. Should the merchant sell the personal property to a bona fide purchaser, the title is transferred from the true owner to the bona fide purchaser. Answer (b) is incorrect because title remained with Charles at all times. Also, the circumstances under which the watch was purchased would invalidate a claim that Goodeal was a bona fide purchaser. It is unlikely he took in good faith and without notice of defect. Answer (c) is incorrect because Goodeal has void title.

38. On Monday, Gullible George is induced to sell a computer to Fraudulent Freddy on the basis of Freddy's misrepresentation that he is Wealthy Walter. That same day Freddy resells the computer to Innocent Ivan, a good faith purchaser for value. On Tuesday, Gullible George sells an electronic typewriter to Dishonest David who pays for the goods with a check that is later dishonored by the payor (drawee) bank. Before the check is dishonored, David sells the typewriter to Innocent Irene, a good faith purchaser for value. On the basis of these facts,

a. George's best remedy is to recover the value of the goods from Freddy and David in a tort action for deceit.

b. George is entitled to recover the computer from Ivan, but he is not entitled to recover the typewriter from Irene.

c. George is entitled to recover the typewriter from Irene, but he is not entitled to recover the computer from Ivan.

d. George is entitled to recover the computer from Ivan and the typewriter from Irene.

The correct answer is (a). *(L. Fischl)*

REQUIRED: The effect of a transfer by a person with voidable title to a good faith purchaser for value.

DISCUSSION: In general, a purchaser of goods acquires only the title that his/her transferor had or had power to transfer. Under UCC 2-403, a purchaser who deceived the transferor as to his/her identity or procured delivery of the goods in exchange for a check that is later dishonored has a voidable rather than a void title. The transferor can recover the goods (or damages) from the wrongdoer. However, a person with voidable title may transfer good title to a good faith purchaser for value. Hence, George cannot recover from Ivan or Irene, each of whom has good title.

Answers (b) and (d) are incorrect because Ivan, a good faith purchaser for value, acquired good title from Freddy, whose title was voidable, not void, despite the fraud he perpetrated to induce the purchase from George. Answers (c) and (d) are incorrect because Irene, a good faith purchaser for value, acquired good title from David, whose title was voidable, not void, despite his receipt of delivery of the typewriter in exchange for a check that was later dishonored.

39. Writer takes her typewriter to Merchant, who repairs and sells used typewriters. Merchant repairs the machine and then mistakenly sells it to Student, who pays cash and is unaware that the typewriter belonged to Writer.

a. Merchant could transfer all rights of Writer to Student who was a buyer in the ordinary course of business.

b. If Merchant had sold the typewriter with knowledge that it belonged to Writer, Writer could reclaim it from Student.

c. If a thief had stolen the typewriter from Writer and had left it with Merchant for repair, Writer could not recover it from Student.

d. If Merchant's procurement of the entrustment of the typewriter was larcenous under the criminal law, Merchant could not pass good title to Student.

The correct answer is (a). *(Publisher)*

REQUIRED: The power of a merchant entrusted with goods to transfer good title.

DISCUSSION: The delivery of goods to a repair person is a classic instance of entrustment. If the entrustee is a merchant dealing in goods of that kind, (s)he has power to transfer all rights of the entrustor to a buyer in the ordinary course of business (UCC 2-403). Entrusting does not give the merchant the legal right to transfer (only power), and the merchant is liable to the entrustor for damages. A buyer in the ordinary course of business is a person who, in good faith and without knowledge of any impropriety, buys in the ordinary course from a person in the business of selling goods of that kind, exclusive of pawnbrokers (UCC 1-201).

Answer (b) is incorrect because Merchant's state of mind is irrelevant to whether Writer can reclaim the goods. Answer (c) is incorrect because the entrustee can only transfer to a buyer in the ordinary course of business the rights of the entrustor. If the entrustor is a thief, no rights can be transferred. Answer (d) is incorrect because whether the procurement of the entrustment is larcenous under criminal law is irrelevant if there was a delivery and acquiescence of possession by the entrustee.

40. Sparkle bought a porcelain doll from Doll World. Sparkle asked that the store wrap and keep it for her until Christmas Eve. If creditors of Doll World try to seize the doll,

a. The creditors will win because Doll World has title.

b. Sparkle will win because she has title.

c. Creditors will win because Doll World has the risk of loss.

d. Sparkle will win because she has the risk of loss.

The correct answer is (b). *(S. Rand)*

REQUIRED: The rights of the owner of an entrusted good and the creditors of the entrustee.

DISCUSSION: When a buyer purchases a good from a merchant seller without a document of title, the seller transfers title to the buyer at the time of contracting. Thus, Sparkle had title, and the creditors of Doll World were unable to obtain the doll even though it was still in Doll World's possession. Sparkle entrusted the doll to Doll World, but an entrustee can transfer the rights of the entrustor only to a buyer in the ordinary course of business (UCC 2-403).

Answer (a) is incorrect because title passed from Doll World to Sparkle at the time of contracting. Answers (c) and (d) are incorrect because whether the creditors can seize the doll is a title problem and not a question of risk of loss. The risk of loss issue arises when goods are lost, missing, or damaged, and the concern is which party must sustain that loss. Title problems occur when the goods exist and are not defective but different interests compete for ownership.

41. Which of the following factors is most important in deciding who bears the risk of loss between merchants when goods are destroyed during shipment?

a. The agreement of the parties.

b. Whether the goods are perishable.

c. Who has title at the time of the loss.

d. The terms of applicable insurance policies.

The correct answer is (a). *(CPA 1189 L-48)*

REQUIRED: The most important factor in deciding risk of loss on goods destroyed in transit.

DISCUSSION: The parties to a contract for the sale of goods ordinarily may determine who will have the risk of loss, or they can divide the risk of loss (UCC 2-509 and 2-303). The agreement as to risk may be express or implied from trade usage, course of dealing, or course of performance. Moreover, although the intent of the parties controls the shipping terms, in the absence of contrary agreement, the intent with respect to risk is often determined by shipping and delivery terms. Whether the parties are merchants usually does not affect risk of loss (for discussion of an exception, see Q. 50 on p. 238).

Answer (b) is incorrect because nature of the goods is irrelevant if they have been destroyed in transit. However, a merchant buyer who has rightfully rejected perishables may have a duty to resell (UCC 2-603). Answer (c) is incorrect because under the UCC, risk of loss is never based on title. Answer (d) is incorrect because insurance coverage is a consideration but not as significant as the parties' intent or whether a breach has occurred.

42. Lazur Corp. entered into a contract with Baker Suppliers, Inc. to purchase a used word processor from Baker. Lazur is engaged in the business of selling new and used word processors to the general public. The contract required Baker to ship the goods to Lazur by common carrier pursuant to the following provision: "FOB -- Baker Suppliers, Inc. loading dock." During shipment to Lazur, the word processor was seriously damaged when the carrier's truck was involved in an accident. When the carrier attempted to deliver the word processor, Lazur rejected it and has refused to pay Baker the purchase price. Under the UCC Sales Article,

a. Lazur rightfully rejected the damaged computer.

b. The risk of loss for the computer was on Lazur during shipment.

c. At the time of the accident, risk of loss for the computer was on Baker because title to the computer had not yet passed to Lazur.

d. Lazur will not be liable to Baker for the purchase price of the computer because of the FOB provision in the contract.

The correct answer is (b). *(CPA 589 L-56)*

REQUIRED: The parties' rights under a shipment contract if goods are damaged in transit.

DISCUSSION: FOB means the seller bears both the risk and the expense of getting the goods to the point named. If the shipping term is FOB "place of shipment," the seller has the risk and expense of getting the goods to the carrier. Expenses and risk after delivery to the carrier are borne by the buyer in a shipment contract. Accordingly, absent a contrary agreement, Lazur (the buyer) bears the risk of loss, but it may be able to recover from the carrier or a third party.

Answer (a) is incorrect because the buyer cannot rightfully reject on the grounds of damage incurred after risk of loss passed from the seller. Answer (c) is incorrect because under the UCC, the location of title does not determine risk of loss. Answer (d) is incorrect because the seller may recover the price (and any incidental damages) of conforming goods lost or damaged within a commercially reasonable time after risk of loss has passed to the buyer (UCC 2-709).

43. Parsifal was the president of Grail Enterprises, Inc. He wished to ship an antique drinking cup to his best customer, Arthur. They entered into a shipment contract whereby the goods were to be delivered to a swift cargo carrier, the Avalon, in Calais harbor. The seller was to bear the risk and expense of delivery of the goods to the Avalon. The best term to describe this shipping agreement is

a. COD.

b. FOB destination.

c. FAS vessel.

d. FOB shipping point.

The correct answer is (c). *(Publisher)*

REQUIRED: The best term to describe the shipping agreement.

DISCUSSION: The shipping term "FAS vessel" (which means "free along side") describes the seller's duty to deliver goods at his/her own risk and expense alongside a vessel in a specified port. The seller would also be under a duty to tender a receipt for the goods in exchange for the carrier's duty to issue a bill of lading (UCC 2-319).

Answer (a) is incorrect because COD means "collect on delivery." Answer (b) is incorrect because FOB destination requires the seller, at his/her own risk and expense, to transport the goods to the specified place and there tender delivery. Answer (d) is incorrect because FOB shipping point requires the seller to ship goods from a specified place and bear the risk and expense of putting them in the possession of a carrier.

44. If the contract for a sale of goods requires a seller to properly ship conforming goods and to tender them if they arrive, but creates no obligation upon the seller that the goods will arrive unless the seller has caused the nonarrival, the contract probably contains which term?

a. "Sale on approval."

b. "Sale or return."

c. "No arrival, no sale."

d. "Consignment sale."

The correct answer is (c). *(Publisher)*

REQUIRED: The term indicating that the seller assumes no obligation for nondelivery.

DISCUSSION: The effect of a "no arrival, no sale" term is to leave the risk of loss on the seller until arrival of the goods at the destination, but to provide the seller an exemption from liability in the event of nondelivery (UCC 2-324). The seller must act in good faith and not be the cause of nondelivery to qualify for the exemption. The term is customarily used when the seller is reselling goods that are to be delivered to him/her by a party over whom (s)he has no control.

Answer (a) is incorrect because a "sale on approval" permits the buyer to return conforming goods when the goods are delivered primarily for use. Answer (b) is incorrect because a "sale or return" permits a buyer to return conforming goods that have been delivered primarily for resale. Answer (d) is incorrect because under a "consignment" agreement, the owner of goods places them in the hands of another for purposes of resale without surrender of title.

45. If a contract for the sale of goods includes a C&F shipping term and the seller has fulfilled all of its obligations, the

a. Title to the goods will pass to the buyer when the goods are received by the buyer at the place of destination.

b. Risk of loss will pass to the buyer upon delivery of the goods to the carrier.

c. Buyer retains the right to inspect the goods prior to making payment.

d. Seller must obtain an insurance policy at its own expense for the buyer's benefit.

The correct answer is (b). *(CPA 587 L-54)*

REQUIRED: The effect of a C&F shipping term if the seller has fully performed.

DISCUSSION: The term CIF means that the price includes (in a lump sum) the cost of the goods, insurance, and freight to the indicated destination (UCC 2-320). Unless otherwise agreed by the parties, the use of the term CIF also requires the seller to load the goods, pay the freight, obtain the insurance, etc. It also determines that risk of loss passes to the buyer upon shipment unless the parties have agreed otherwise. The term C&F has the same effect except with regard to insurance.

Answer (a) is incorrect because unless otherwise agreed, title passes under a C&F term at the time and place of shipment. Answer (c) is incorrect because the buyer most likely will have no right to inspect before payment. Under a CIF or C&F term, the buyer ordinarily must make payment against tender of the required documents, and these will commonly arrive and be tendered while the goods are in transit and before inspection (UCC 2-320). Answer (d) is incorrect because a C&F term imposes no obligation on the seller regarding insurance.

46. Sand Corp. sold and delivered a photocopier to Barr for use in Barr's business. According to their agreement, Barr may return the copier within 30 days. During the 30-day period, if Barr has not returned the copier or indicated acceptance of it, which of the following statements is correct with respect to risk of loss and title?

a. Risk of loss and title passed to Barr.

b. Risk of loss and title remain with Sand.

c. Risk of loss passed to Barr but title remains with Sand.

d. Risk of loss remains with Sand but title passed to Barr.

The correct answer is (b). *(CPA 1187 L-39)*

REQUIRED: The effect of delivery on risk of loss and title in a sale on approval.

DISCUSSION: In a sale on approval, title and risk of loss do not pass to the buyer until acceptance (UCC 2-327). Acceptance may be express or implied, i.e., by acts or inaction. A sale is on approval if the goods are delivered to the buyer with an understanding that (s)he may test them for the purpose of determining if (s)he wishes to purchase them and may be returned by the buyer without breaching the contract even though they conform to the contract. Normally, the goods are primarily for the use of the buyer. If the goods are delivered primarily for resale, the transaction is a sale or return, and risk of loss and title pass to the buyer in accordance with the particular delivery situation.

Answers (a), (c) and (d) are incorrect because neither risk of loss nor title passes to the buyer.

47. If goods have been delivered to a buyer pursuant to a sale or return contract, the

a. Buyer may use the goods but not resell them.

b. Seller is liable for the expenses incurred by the buyer in returning the goods to the seller.

c. Title to the goods remains with the seller.

d. Risk of loss for the goods passed to the buyer.

The correct answer is (d). *(CPA 1188 L-46)*

REQUIRED: The effect of delivery to a buyer under a sale or return contract.

DISCUSSION: If goods are delivered to a person for sale and that person keeps a place of business at which (s)he deals in goods of that kind, the goods will be deemed to be on "sale or return." Risk of loss in a sale or return passes at the same time and place as in any other sale of goods, e.g., in accordance with the shipping terms. In cases except a sale on approval, delivery and receipt of the goods will customarily signify that risk of loss has passed to the buyer.

Answer (a) is incorrect because under a sale or return arrangement, delivery is for resale. Answer (b) is incorrect because the return is at the buyer's risk and expense (UCC 2-327). Answer (c) is incorrect because barring a contrary agreement, title passes when the seller completes performance regarding the physical delivery of the goods (UCC 2-401).

48. Amy Artiste designs, manufactures and sells baubles, bangles, and beads in a small shop located in the artists' quarter of a major city. She sells exclusively her own creations. As a special favor, Artiste agreed to sell several baubles made by Bob Friend. They have a written contract concerning the resale of the goods that uses the words "on consignment." Will the friend's baubles be subject to the claims of Artiste's creditors?

a. The creditors could not reach the baubles because the transaction is a "sale on approval."

b. The use of the words "on consignment" will protect Friend's baubles from attachment by Artiste's creditors.

c. The creditors will prevail if the transaction is deemed to be a "sale or return" and Friend has posted no sign evidencing his interest or has failed to file under Article 9.

d. The creditors will prevail if they can show that Artiste was a merchant who deals in goods of the kind involved.

The correct answer is (c). *(Publisher)*

REQUIRED: The rights of the consignee's creditors to a consignor's goods.

DISCUSSION: If goods are delivered to a person for sale and that person keeps a place of business at which (s)he deals in goods of that kind, the goods will be deemed to be on "sale or return." The effect is to render such goods subject to the claims of the consignee's creditors while in the consignee's possession. The consignor is protected only if (s)he complied with applicable law providing for his/her interest to be evidenced by a sign, or filed a financing statement under Article 9 of the UCC (UCC 2-326).

Answer (a) is incorrect because the transaction is a "sale or return." Answer (b) is incorrect because the UCC expressly states that the words "on consignment" do not affect the nature of the transaction. Answer (d) is incorrect because it is not enough for the creditors to show that Artiste was a merchant with respect to goods of the kind involved. If Friend could show that Artiste regularly engaged in selling the goods of others and that this practice was known by the creditors, he could prevail.

49. Which of the following statements is correct regarding risk of loss in a contract for the sale of goods?

a. If the contract does not require delivery at a particular destination, risk of loss passes to the buyer when the goods are delivered to the carrier, unless the shipment is under reservation.

b. If the contract requires delivery at a particular destination, the risk of loss passes to the buyer when the goods are actually received and accepted.

c. If the goods are held by a bailee and are to be delivered without being moved, risk of loss passes to the buyer upon receipt of a negotiable document of title covering the goods.

d. If the contract requires neither shipment by carrier nor delivery of the goods held by a bailee without being moved, the risk of loss passes to the buyer on tender of delivery of the goods if the seller is a merchant.

The correct answer is (c). *(Publisher)*

REQUIRED: The correct statement concerning when risk of loss passes to the buyer.

DISCUSSION: Under UCC 2-509, if goods are in the hands of a bailee and are to be delivered without being moved, risk of loss passes to the buyer upon receipt of a negotiable document of title that covers the goods. If a nonnegotiable document is delivered, risk passes to the buyer when the bailee acknowledges the buyer's rights or the buyer has had a reasonable time to seek the bailee's acknowledgement and has failed to do so. If the bailee refuses to honor the document, the tender of the goods is not proper, and the risk of loss remains with the seller.

Answer (a) is incorrect because if the contract merely requires the seller to deliver to a carrier, the risk of loss passes even though the shipment is under reservation. Answer (b) is incorrect because when the contract requires delivery at a particular destination, risk of loss passes when the goods are tendered to enable the buyer to take delivery. Answer (d) is incorrect because in such cases, when risk of loss passes depends upon whether the seller is a merchant. A merchant-seller retains the risk of loss until the buyer has taken receipt of the goods, but if the seller is not a merchant, risk will pass to the buyer on tender of delivery.

50. Sutter purchased a computer from Harp. Harp is not in the business of selling computers. Harp tendered delivery of the computer after receiving payment in full from Sutter. Sutter informed Harp that Sutter was unable to take possession of the computer at that time, but would return later that day. Before Sutter returned, the computer was destroyed by a fire. The risk of loss

a. Remained with Harp because title had not yet passed to Sutter.

b. Passed to Sutter upon Harp's tender of delivery.

c. Remained with Harp because Sutter had not yet received the computer.

d. Passed to Sutter at the time the contract was formed and payment was made.

The correct answer is (b). *(CPA 1188 L-49)*

REQUIRED: The true statement about risk of loss given that the seller was not a merchant.

DISCUSSION: If the parties have no agreement as to risk of loss, no carrier is involved, and the goods are not in the possession of a bailee, "the risk of loss passes to the buyer on his/her receipt of the goods if the seller is a merchant; otherwise, the risk passes to the buyer on tender of delivery" (UCC 2-509). Because Harp is not a merchant (a person engaged in selling goods of the kind), risk passed to Sutter on tender of delivery.

Answer (a) is incorrect because the UCC never assigns risk of loss to goods on the basis of title. Answer (c) is incorrect because risk would have remained with Harp until receipt only if Harp were a merchant. Answer (d) is incorrect because under the UCC, risk of loss usually is placed upon the party who is in the best position to prevent loss. Contract formation and payment are not significant events for determining when risk of loss passes.

51. Buyer ordered goods from Sue Seller. The contract required Seller to deliver them FOB Buyer's place of business. Buyer inspected the goods, discovered they failed to conform to the contract, and rightfully rejected them. In the event of loss of the goods, which of the following is a correct statement?

a. Seller initially had the risk of loss, and it remains with her after delivery.

b. Risk of loss passes to Buyer upon tender of the goods FOB Buyer's place of business.

c. Buyer initially had the risk of loss, but it is shifted to Seller upon rightful rejection.

d. If Seller used a public carrier to transport the goods to Buyer, risk of loss is on Buyer during transit.

The correct answer is (a). *(CPA 580 L-33)*

REQUIRED: The true statement about risk of loss in the event goods rightfully rejected by the buyer are lost.

DISCUSSION: The shipping term in the contract required the seller to deliver the goods at Buyer's place of business. The effect of this term is that risk of loss would normally pass to the buyer upon tender (UCC 2-509). However, the nonconformity was a breach, and Buyer's rightful rejection caused the risk to remain with Seller (UCC 2-510).

Answer (b) is incorrect because the risk of loss for nonconforming goods never passes to the buyer if the buyer rightfully rejects them. Answer (c) is incorrect because Seller had the risk of loss at all times. Answer (d) is incorrect because use of a carrier is irrelevant. By choice of shipping terms (FOB destination in this case), the parties expressly agreed when risk of loss would pass to the buyer.

52. Bell, by telegram to Major Corp., ordered 10,000 yards of fabric, first quality, 50% wool and 50% cotton. Major accepted the order and packed the fabric for shipment. In the process it discovered that one-half of the fabric packed had been commingled with fabric that was 30% wool and 70% cotton. Because Major did not have any additional 50% wool fabric, it decided to send the shipment to Bell as an accommodation. The goods were shipped, and later the same day Major wired Bell its apology informing Bell of the facts and indicating that the 5,000 yards of 30% wool would be priced at $2 a yard less. The carrier delivering the goods was destroyed on the way to Akron. Who bears the risk of loss?

a. Bell, because Bell has title to the goods.

b. Major, because the order was not a signed writing.

c. Bell, if the shipping terms were FOB Bell's place of business.

d. Major, because it shipped goods that failed to conform to the contract.

The correct answer is (d). *(CPA 584 L-49)*

REQUIRED: The party bearing the risk of loss and the reason if nonconforming goods are destroyed while in transit.

DISCUSSION: If the contract does not cover risk, the most significant factor in determining who has the risk of loss is whether a breach has occurred. If a tender or delivery of goods is so nonconforming as to give a right of rejection, the risk of loss remains on the seller until cure or acceptance (UCC 2-510). The breaching party therefore has the risk of loss. The seller's shipment of nonconforming goods as an accommodation was a breach, so Major has the risk of loss. The result is the same for either a shipment contract or a destination contract.

Answer (a) is incorrect because risk of loss does not follow title when the subject of the contract is goods. Answer (b) is incorrect because the telegram meets the criteria of the UCC's Statute of Frauds provisions. Answer (c) is incorrect because Bell would have had the risk of loss only in a shipment contract (FOB Major's place of business) under which conforming goods had been delivered to the carrier.

12.5 Performance

53. Which of the following is a true statement about the general obligations of the parties to a sale of goods?

a. Tender of delivery is a condition of the buyer's duty to accept the goods.

b. Tender does not entitle the seller to payment.

c. Tender does not entitle the seller to acceptance of the goods.

d. The UCC requires tender as a prerequisite to the buyer's performance, and the parties may not agree otherwise.

The correct answer is (a). *(Publisher)*

REQUIRED: The true statement about the general obligations of parties to a sale.

DISCUSSION: The general obligation of a seller is to transfer and deliver. That of the buyer is to accept and pay in accordance with the contract (UCC 2-301). Tender of delivery is a condition to the buyer's duty to accept the goods. Tender entitles the seller to demand buyer's acceptance of the goods and to payment according to the contract (UCC 2-507).

Answer (b) is incorrect because a proper tender does entitle the seller to payment according to the terms of the agreement. Answer (c) is incorrect because the buyer has a duty to accept a proper tender of conforming goods. Answer (d) is incorrect because the parties are free to alter the obligations established by the UCC.

54. A proper tender of delivery requires that the seller

a. Put and hold conforming goods, or nonconforming goods that the seller reasonably believes will be acceptable, at the buyer's disposition.

b. Furnish facilities reasonably suited to the receipt of the goods.

c. Deliver the goods at the buyer's place of business and keep them available for the time reasonably necessary for the buyer to take possession.

d. Put and hold conforming goods at the buyer's disposition and give any necessary notice.

The correct answer is (d). *(Publisher)*

REQUIRED: The correct statement about a proper tender by the seller.

DISCUSSION: UCC 2-503 states, "Tender of delivery requires that the seller put and hold conforming goods at the buyer's disposition and give the buyer any notification reasonably necessary to enable him/her to take delivery." The manner, time, and place for tender must be reasonable.

Answer (a) is incorrect because under the perfect tender rule (UCC 2-601), the goods must conform precisely to the contract. Otherwise, the buyer may rightfully reject them. Answer (b) is incorrect because the buyer must furnish the facilities for receipt, unless otherwise agreed. Answer (c) is incorrect because unless the parties agree otherwise, the place for delivery is the seller's place of business.

55. Bean ordered 40 beige refrigerators at a list price from Tish Co. Immediately upon receipt of Bean's order, Tish sent Bean an acceptance that was received by Bean. The acceptance indicated that shipment would be made within 10 days. On the tenth day Tish discovered that all of its supply of beige refrigerators had been sold. Instead it shipped 40 white refrigerators, stating clearly on the invoice that the shipment was sent only as an accommodation. Which of the following is correct?

a. Bean's order is a unilateral offer, and can only be accepted by Tish's shipment of the goods ordered.

b. Tish's shipment of white refrigerators is a counteroffer, thus no contract exists between Bean and Tish.

c. Tish's note of accommodation cancels the contract between Tish and Bean.

d. Tish's shipment of white refrigerators constitutes a breach of contract.

The correct answer is (d). *(CPA 1188 L-50)*

REQUIRED: The true statement about the shipment of goods solely as an accommodation.

DISCUSSION: Shipment of a brand different from that stipulated in the contract was a breach of the contract (UCC 2-601). Bean may accept the goods despite their nonconformity, rightfully reject them, or resort to any of the buyer's other remedies under the UCC. UCC 2-206 and 2-508, allowing accommodation shipments and the ability to cure, are not applicable because notice of acceptance was sent, and a cure must be made within the time for performance in most cases.

Answer (a) is incorrect because Bean's order constituted an offer to enter into either a bilateral or unilateral contract. It could be accepted either by a prompt promise to ship or by a prompt shipment, respectively. Answer (b) is incorrect because the shipment was not a counteroffer. The acceptance had already created a contract. Answer (c) is incorrect because the breaching party cannot cancel the contract. Only a mutual rescission or the promised performance will discharge the seller's obligation unless the nonconforming goods are accepted.

56. The requirements of a proper tender of delivery of goods vary according to the place for tender. Which of the following is a proper delivery?

a. In a shipment contract, no delivery is necessary because the buyer is responsible for picking up the goods.

b. In a destination contract, the seller need only deliver the goods to a carrier because the buyer is responsible for obtaining them from the carrier.

c. If the goods are held by a bailee, the seller has no delivery obligation.

d. If the goods are not to be moved and are held by a bailee, the seller can merely deliver a negotiable document of title to the buyer.

The correct answer is (d). *(Publisher)*

REQUIRED: The correct statement about a seller's duty to deliver goods.

DISCUSSION: The seller has the duty to make a proper tender of delivery in accordance with the contract. If the goods are not to be moved and are held by a bailee, the seller can complete performance by delivering a negotiable document of title (UCC 2-503).

Answer (a) is incorrect because in a shipment contract, the seller must deliver the goods to the carrier and provide any necessary documents. Answer (b) is incorrect because in a destination contract, the seller (normally through the carrier) must tender delivery of the goods at the destination named (usually the buyer's place of business) in a reasonable manner, time, etc. with any necessary documents. Answer (c) is incorrect because the contract determines whether there is an obligation to deliver goods. Also, some document of title must usually be delivered when the goods are held by a bailee.

57. Kirk Corp. sold Nix an Ajax freezer, Model 24, for $490. The contract required delivery to be made by June 23. On June 12, Kirk delivered an Ajax freezer, Model 52, to Nix. Nix immediately notified Kirk that the wrong freezer had been delivered and indicated that the delivery of a correct freezer would not be acceptable. Kirk wishes to deliver an Ajax freezer, Model 24, on June 23. Which of the following statements is true?

a. Kirk may deliver the freezer on June 23 without further notice to Nix.

b. Kirk may deliver the freezer on June 23 if it first reasonably notifies Nix of its intent to do so.

c. Nix must accept the nonconforming freezer but may recover damages.

d. Nix always may reject the nonconforming freezer and refuse delivery of a conforming freezer on June 23.

The correct answer is (b). *(CPA 1185 L-48)*

REQUIRED: The true statement about options after a nonconforming tender of goods.

DISCUSSION: When a buyer rejects delivery for nonconformity and the time for performance has not expired, the seller can notify the buyer of his/her intent to cure and then deliver within the contract period (UCC 2-508). Accordingly, Kirk can promptly notify Nix and make a conforming delivery by June 23.

Answer (a) is incorrect because cure is ineffective without reasonable notification. Answer (c) is incorrect because the buyer may rightfully reject a tender that fails in any way to conform to the contract. Answer (d) is incorrect because after receiving notice, Nix must accept conforming goods tendered by the contract date.

58. The buyer's general obligation under a contract for the sale of goods is to accept and pay according to the contract. Unless the parties have agreed otherwise, the UCC states that

a. The buyer must pay before the seller has an obligation to deliver.

b. Payment is due at the time and place at which the goods are to be shipped.

c. When the seller is to ship the goods on credit, the credit period runs from the time of receipt.

d. If the seller demands payment in cash, (s)he must give any reasonably necessary extension of time.

The correct answer is (d). *(Publisher)*

REQUIRED: The UCC requirement concerning payment as performance.

DISCUSSION: "Tender of payment is sufficient when made by any means or in any manner current in the ordinary course of business unless the seller demands payment in legal tender (cash) and gives any extension of time reasonably necessary to procure it" (UCC 2-511). The buyer is thus protected from an unexpected demand for cash. A seller who accepts a check is also protected by UCC 2-511: "Payment by check is conditional and is defeated as between the parties by dishonor of the check on due presentment."

Answer (a) is incorrect because theoretically, tender of delivery and tender of payment are concurrent conditions. As a practical matter, however, delivery and receipt of goods are normally preconditions of the buyer's duty to pay. Answer (b) is incorrect because payment is due at the time and place buyer is to receive the goods (UCC 2-310). Answer (c) is incorrect because the credit period runs from the time of shipment unless the invoice is post-dated or delayed.

59. Unless otherwise agreed in a contract for the sale of goods, the buyer is obligated to pay at the time and place at which the buyer receives the goods. The duty of the buyer, however, is subject to a right of inspection. If the sale is a "documentary sale,"

a. The buyer has no right of inspection if the seller ships under reservation.

b. The buyer has no right of inspection prior to payment.

c. The buyer is under an obligation to pay only when the goods are delivered even if the documents of title representing the goods are tendered previously.

d. The parties have entered into a CIF contract.

The correct answer is (b). *(Publisher)*

REQUIRED: The correct statement concerning documentary sales.

DISCUSSION: A contract for the sale of goods involves a documentary sale if it calls for the buyer to pay for the goods when documents of title are tendered regardless of the time or place of the receipt of the goods. The shipping terms COD and CIF require payment against a tender of documents; FAS and FOB do not. The buyer in a documentary sale would thus not be entitled to inspect the goods before payment unless otherwise agreed (UCC 2-310 and 2-513).

Answer (a) is incorrect because a shipment under reservation specifically allows a buyer a right of inspection even though the sale is a documentary sale, unless the inspection would be inconsistent with the terms of the contract, e.g., if the contract includes a COD term. Answer (c) is incorrect because a documentary sale creates a duty to pay upon tender of documents rather than the goods. Answer (d) is incorrect because whereas a CIF contract is a documentary sale, not every documentary sale is made pursuant to a CIF contract. CIF means that the price includes in a lump sum the cost of the goods, insurance, and freight to the named destination. For risk of loss purposes, it is a shipment contract.

60. Lazur Corp. entered into a contract with Baker Suppliers, Inc. to purchase a used word processor from Baker. Lazur is engaged in the business of selling new and used word processors to the general public. The contract required Baker to ship the goods to Lazur by common carrier pursuant to the following provision in the contract: "FOB -- Baker Suppliers, Inc. loading dock." Assume that the contract between Lazur and Baker is otherwise silent. Under the UCC Sales Article,

a. Lazur must pay Baker the purchase price before Baker is required to ship the word processor to Lazur.

b. Baker does not warrant that it owns the word processor.

c. Lazur will be entitled to inspect the word processor before it accepts or pays for it.

d. Title to the word processor passes to Lazur when it takes physical possession.

The correct answer is (c). *(CPA 589 L-57)*

REQUIRED: The true statement about the rights of a buyer in a sale of goods under Article 2.

DISCUSSION: Unless otherwise agreed, the buyer has a right to inspect the goods before payment or acceptance. Inspection may be at any reasonable time and place and in any reasonable manner. When the seller is to send the goods to the buyer, the inspection may be after their arrival (UCC 2-513). But the buyer has no right to inspect before payment in some cases, for example, when payment is against documents of title.

Answer (a) is incorrect because absent a contrary agreement, payment is due at the time and place of receipt even if the place of shipment is the place of delivery (as in this shipment contract) (UCC 2-310). Answer (b) is incorrect because a contract for the sale of goods includes a warranty of title unless excluded or modified by specific language or by the circumstances (UCC 2-312). Answer (d) is incorrect because in a shipment contract, title passes upon delivery to the carrier (UCC 2-401).

61. Mix Clothing shipped 300 custom suits to Tara Retailers. The suits arrived on Thursday, earlier than Tara had anticipated and on an exceptionally busy day for its receiving department. They were perfunctorily examined and sent to a nearby warehouse for storage until needed. On the following day, upon closer examination, it was discovered that the quality of the linings of the suits was inferior to that specified in the sales contract. Which of the following is correct insofar as Tara's rights are concerned?

a. Tara must retain the suits because it accepted them and had an opportunity to inspect them upon delivery.

b. Tara had no rights if the linings were of merchantable quality.

c. Tara can reject the suits upon subsequent discovery of the defects.

d. Tara's only course of action is rescission.

The correct answer is (c). *(CPA 1184 L-56)*

REQUIRED: The correct statement regarding the rights of a buyer of nonconforming goods.

DISCUSSION: A buyer has the right to inspect the goods at any reasonable place and time and in any reasonable manner (UCC 2-513). Tara did not have a reasonable opportunity to inspect on the day of the delivery. A buyer may reject nonconforming goods within a reasonable time if the seller is properly notified (UCC 2-602). Even if a buyer is deemed to have accepted the goods, it may revoke acceptance within a reasonable time if the acceptance was reasonably induced by the difficulty of discovery (UCC 2-608).

Answer (a) is incorrect because Tara apparently did not have a reasonable opportunity to inspect, and may reject the goods within a reasonable time after acceptance or revoke acceptance. Answer (b) is incorrect because if the linings were not as described in the contract, Mix breached the express warranty regardless of merchantability. Answer (d) is incorrect because Tara may also seek any of the other buyer's remedies under the UCC.

62. Sussex Co. makes cricket wickets in two models, A and T. Retailer ordered 50 dozen of the wickets in January. Sussex delivered the Model A wickets in April although the parties had agreed on the Model T. The goods were not paid for although a timely demand for payment was made. Retailer advised Sussex of the nonconformity 5 months later. Retailer also did not make a timely inspection but still has the goods. Sussex brought an action for the price in December. Who should win?

a. Sussex, because Retailer accepted the goods.

b. Sussex, because Retailer was required to accept nonconforming goods that were reasonably fit for the intended use.

c. Retailer, because it made an effective revocation of acceptance.

d. Retailer, because it made an effective subsequent rejection.

The correct answer is (a). *(Publisher)*

REQUIRED: The outcome of a suit by a seller based on acceptance by the buyer.

DISCUSSION: Under UCC 2-606, acceptance may occur when the buyer after a reasonable opportunity to inspect signifies to the seller that the goods are conforming or that (s)he takes them despite their nonconformity, does an act inconsistent with the seller's ownership, or fails to make an effective rejection or a timely revocation of acceptance. Acceptance can be by words, action, or even silence when there is time to make a rejection but the buyer did not do so. Silence for 5 months therefore constituted acceptance.

Answer (b) is incorrect because a buyer has no duty to accept goods that are nonconforming in any way (perfect tender rule). Answer (c) is incorrect because a revocation of acceptance is effective only within a reasonable time after the buyer discovers or should discover the grounds for it (UCC 2-608). Answer (d) is incorrect because effective acceptance precludes subsequent rejection (but not a rightful revocation) (UCC 2-607).

63. Which of the following is a true statement about the buyer's remedy of rejection of goods?

a. The rejection must be within a reasonable time after delivery.

b. The buyer has no further obligations with regard to goods rightfully rejected.

c. The buyer must seasonably notify the seller of rejection but has no obligations regarding the form or content of the notice.

d. The buyer may rely on a curable defect to establish breach even though (s)he has not seasonably notified the seller of the defect.

The correct answer is (a). *(Publisher)*

REQUIRED: The true statement about the buyer's right of rejection.

DISCUSSION: An effective rejection of goods must be within a reasonable time after their delivery or tender, and the buyer must seasonably notify the seller (UCC 2-602). Acceptance occurs when the buyer fails to make an effective rejection (UCC 2-606).

Answer (b) is incorrect because the buyer may not exercise ownership of the rejected goods and has various duties as discussed in the answer to Q. 66. Answers (c) and (d) are incorrect because the notice must state a particular defect ascertainable by reasonable inspection. Failure to meet this obligation precludes reliance on the defect to justify rejection or establish breach when the seller could have cured (UCC 2-605).

64. Dara bought an automobile needing repairs from Chevalier Motors, Inc. (CMI). CMI promised to repair it, but 1 month later had not yet completed the repairs. Dara was using the car anyway (1 month after purchase) when a fire in the dashboard rendered the vehicle inoperable. Dara returned the automobile immediately and orally informed a representative of CMI that she was demanding the purchase price. Dara sent a written notice of rescission 3 months later and filed suit 3 months after that. Who will most likely prevail, and what is the legal theory that best supports the result?

a. CMI, because Dara accepted goods she knew to be nonconforming.

b. CMI, because Dara did not revoke her acceptance within a reasonable time.

c. Dara, because she made a justifiable revocation of acceptance.

d. Dara, because she made a rightful rejection.

The correct answer is (c). *(Publisher)*

REQUIRED: The likely result of a suit to recover the purchase price of returned goods.

DISCUSSION: Dara decided to take the goods despite their nonconformity and thus accepted them (UCC 2-606). A buyer may revoke acceptance, however, if the following conditions are met: the goods are nonconforming; the nonconformity substantially impairs their value; if the buyer knew of the nonconformity, (s)he acted on the reasonable assumption it would be cured, but it was not seasonably cured; if (s)he did not know, acceptance was reasonably induced either by the difficulty of discovery or by the seller's assurances; and revocation is made within a reasonable time (UCC 2-608). The facts support justifiable revocation of acceptance because Dara purchased the car expecting the repairs to be made, and the value of the car is substantially impaired.

Answer (a) is incorrect because the revocation is effective. Acceptance was predicated upon the reasonable assumption that nonconformity would be cured, and it was not seasonably cured. Answer (b) is incorrect because a reasonable time for revocation normally is longer than that for rejection after tender, notification of breach, or discovery of nonconformity because the remedy will, in most cases, be resorted to only after attempts at adjustment have failed. Answer (d) is incorrect because acceptance precludes rejection (UCC 2-607).

65. In general, if the goods fail in any respect to conform to the contract, the buyer

a. May not accept the whole despite its nonconformity.

b. May not reject the whole because of the nonconformity of part.

c. May accept any commercial unit or units and reject the rest.

d. May accept any nonconforming articles and reject the rest.

The correct answer is (c). *(Publisher)*

REQUIRED: The buyer's options when delivery is improper.

DISCUSSION: In general, a buyer may accept or reject nonconforming goods. (S)he may accept the whole, reject the whole, or accept any commercial unit or units and reject the rest (UCC 2-601). A commercial unit is a unit of goods that in commercial usage is a single whole for purpose of sale, and division of which materially impairs its character or value.

Answers (a) and (b) are incorrect because a buyer may accept the whole delivery or reject it on account of any nonconformity. Answer (d) is incorrect because a buyer cannot accept "any" nonconforming articles and reject the rest unless those accepted constitute a commercial unit.

66. After rightfully rejecting goods,

a. Except for holding them at the seller's disposition for a reasonable time, a buyer has no further obligations.

b. A merchant-buyer may have an obligation to follow reasonable instructions from the seller with respect to the goods.

c. A merchant-buyer who resells nonperishable goods in the absence of instructions from the seller has accepted the goods.

d. A merchant-buyer who resells the goods is entitled to expenses but not to a selling commission.

The correct answer is (b). *(Publisher)*

REQUIRED: The true statement about the duties of a buyer after rejection.

DISCUSSION: A merchant-buyer has more extensive duties after rejection than a nonmerchant. When the seller has no agent or place of business at the place of rejection, a merchant-buyer must follow any reasonable instructions received from the seller with respect to goods in his/her possession or control. In the absence of such instructions, the buyer must make reasonable efforts to sell them for the seller if they are perishable or threaten to decline in value speedily. The seller is entitled to the proceeds, but must indemnify the buyer for expenses (UCC 2-603).

Answer (a) is incorrect because a merchant buyer also has other duties discussed above. Answer (c) is incorrect because a buyer who resells perishable goods for the seller is not treated as having accepted them (UCC 2-604). Answer (d) is incorrect because (s)he is entitled to the commission usual in the trade or, if none is usual, to a reasonable sum not in excess of 10% of the gross proceeds (UCC 2-603).

67. A contract for sale imposes an obligation on each party that the other's expectation of receiving due performance will not be impaired. Accordingly, a party who has grounds for insecurity with respect to the performance of the other party may demand an assurance of due performance.

a. An acceptance of an improper delivery or payment prejudices the aggrieved party's right to demand adequate assurance of future performance.

b. A party who receives a justified demand for assurance repudiates the contract if (s)he does not give it within 30 days.

c. After an oral or written demand for assurance has been made, the party making the demand may, if commercially reasonable, suspend any performance for which (s)he has not already received the agreed return.

d. A party who receives a demand for adequate assurance must within 30 days provide a written assurance of due performance that is in accordance with commercial standards.

The correct answer is (b). *(Publisher)*

REQUIRED: The correct statement concerning the right to adequate assurance of performance.

DISCUSSION: The UCC recognizes that a party may have commercially sound reasons for needing assurance of performance before performance is due. If one party has reasonable grounds for insecurity and makes a demand in writing for adequate assurance of performance, the other party must, within a reasonable time not exceeding 30 days, provide assurance that is adequate in the circumstances. Failure to do so is a repudiation of the contract (UCC 2-609).

Answer (a) is incorrect because UCC 2-609 expressly states that such an acceptance does not prejudice the aggrieved party's right to future assurance. Answer (c) is incorrect because the demand for adequate assurance must be in writing. Answer (d) is incorrect because an adequate assurance of due performance need not be in writing. The circumstances of the particular case are controlling; e.g., undertaking the promised performance would satisfy the requirement.

68. A provision in a contract for the sale of goods providing that the seller may accelerate payment at will when (s)he deems him/herself insecure

a. Is void as against public policy and ignored in determining contract rights.

b. Makes the agreement illusory and prevents contract formation.

c. Gives the seller a preferred creditor's status.

d. Is enforceable subject to the good faith belief of the seller.

The correct answer is (d). *(CPA 574 L-30)*

REQUIRED: The legal effect of accelerating payment because of the seller's insecurity.

DISCUSSION: A clause providing that a seller may accelerate payment or performance "at will" when (s)he deems him/herself insecure is construed to mean it will only be exercised if the seller, in good faith, believes payment or performance is impaired (UCC 1-208).

Answer (a) is incorrect because such clauses are valid subject to good faith belief. Answer (b) is incorrect because an acceleration clause does not make the agreement illusory if it can only be exercised in good faith. Answer (c) is incorrect because acceleration gives no priority among creditors.

69. On March 7, Wax Corp. contracted with Noll Wholesalers to supply Noll with specific electrical parts. Delivery was called for on June 3. On May 2, Wax notified Noll that it would not perform and that Noll should look elsewhere. Wax had received a larger and more lucrative contract on April 21, and its capacity was such that it could not fill both orders. The facts

a. Will prevent Wax from retracting its repudiation of the Noll contract.

b. Are not sufficient to clearly establish an anticipatory repudiation.

c. Will permit Noll to sue only after June 3, the latest performance date.

d. Will permit Noll to sue immediately after May 2, even though the performance called for was not due until June 3.

The correct answer is (d). *(CPA 1188 L-51)*

REQUIRED: The effect of a seller's advance notice to the buyer of an intent to breach.

DISCUSSION: Under UCC 2-610, when either party repudiates a future performance the loss of which will substantially impair the value of the contract to the other party, the possibilities are to 1) await performance for a commercially reasonable time, 2) resort to any remedies for breach available to a buyer (UCC 2-711) or a seller (UCC 2-703), and 3) suspend performance. Hence, an aggrieved buyer may sue immediately for nondelivery (UCC 2-711 and 2-713).

Answer (a) is incorrect because UCC 2-611 permits retraction unless the aggrieved party has indicated that it considers the retraction final, e.g., by canceling. Answer (b) is incorrect because Wax's notice constituted an effective repudiation. Answer (c) is incorrect because Noll may immediately seek any of the remedies provided by the UCC under UCC 2-711.

70. Devold Manufacturing, Inc. contracted to sell to Hillary Company 2,000 CB radios at $27.50 each. After delivery of the first 500 radios, a minor defect was discovered, which Hillary incurred costs to correct. Hillary sent Devold a signed memorandum indicating that it would relinquish its right to recover the costs to correct the defect, provided that the remaining radios were in conformity with the terms of the contract and the delivery dates were strictly adhered to. Devold met these conditions. Shortly before the last shipment of radios arrived, a dispute between the parties arose over an unrelated matter. Hillary notified Devold that it was not bound by the prior generous agreement and would sue Devold for damages unless Devold promptly reimbursed Hillary. In the event of litigation, what will be the result and on what basis?

a. Devold will lose in that Hillary's relinquishment of its rights was not supported by a consideration.

b. Devold will win in that the defect was minor and the substantial performance doctrine applies.

c. Hillary will lose in that the memorandum constituted a waiver of Hillary's rights.

d. Hillary will win in that there was a failure to perform the contract, and Hillary suffered damages as a result.

The correct answer is (c). *(CPA 578 L-41)*

REQUIRED: The result and the basis upon which litigation over a defect and its waiver would be decided.

DISCUSSION: Hillary has effectively waived its rights under the contract. Under UCC 1-107, any claim or right arising out of a breach may be discharged without consideration by means of a written waiver signed and delivered by the aggrieved party. The waiver cannot be retracted because it affected an executed (completed) part of the contract. UCC 2-209 permits retraction of a waiver only if it affects an executory portion of a contract.

Answer (a) is incorrect because the waiver by Hillary was effective without consideration as long as it was contained in a writing signed and delivered by the aggrieved party. Answer (b) is incorrect because the doctrine of substantial performance would not preclude recovery for damages if no waiver had been made. If a breach occurs, damages are recoverable in the absence of a waiver. Substantial performance merely requires the nonbreaching party to go forward with performance. Answer (d) is incorrect because Hillary has waived its right to damages.

71. An airline and an oil company entered into a contract for the sale of jet fuel during a period of rising oil prices. The agreement indexed the price to the government-regulated price of domestically produced oil (although Congress was discussing deregulation). After the contract was concluded, some domestic oil was deregulated and its price increased. The price of imported oil also increased dramatically. Because the oil company used oil from both sources, the price charged for the jet fuel proved to be quite inadequate. The oil company stated that it could not honor the contract unless the airline agreed to a price increase. Nevertheless, the oil company continued to be very profitable. The airline sued. What will be the most likely result, and what is the best legal theory to justify it?

a. The oil company will win because of commercial impracticability.

b. The oil company will win because of the occurrence of a contingency the nonoccurrence of which was a basic assumption of the contract.

c. The airline will win because a change in government regulation does not excuse nonperformance.

d. The airline will win because increased costs alone do not excuse nonperformance.

The correct answer is (d). *(Publisher)*

REQUIRED: The outcome of a suit against a seller who has breached on the basis of a sharp price increase.

DISCUSSION: The UCC states the commercial impracticability doctrine as follows: "Delay in delivery or nondelivery by a seller is not a breach of his/her duty under a contract for sale if performance as agreed has been made impracticable by the occurrence of a contingency the nonoccurrence of which was a basic assumption on which the contract was made" (UCC 2-615). The price increase for imported oil and decontrol of domestic prices, however, were reasonably foreseeable events, not contingencies the nonoccurrence of which were basic assumptions underlying the contract. The common law approach therefore controls. A mere increase in the seller's costs or change in the market price, even a substantial one, does not excuse nonperformance.

Answers (a) and (b) are incorrect because commercial impracticability does not apply as explained above. Answer (c) is incorrect because a change in government regulation may render performance impracticable or impossible (if it was not foreseeable) and thus excusable.

72. In September 1988, Cobb Company contracted with Thrifty Oil Company for the delivery of 100,000 gallons of heating oil at the price of $.75 per gallon at regular specified intervals during the forthcoming winter. Because of an unseasonably warm winter, Cobb took delivery of only 70,000 gallons. In a suit against Cobb for breach of contract, Thrifty will

a. Lose, because Cobb acted in good faith.

b. Lose, because both parties are merchants and the UCC recognizes commercial impracticability.

c. Win, because this is requirements contract.

d. Win, because the change of circumstances could have been contemplated by the parties.

The correct answer is (d). *(CPA 589 L-34)*

REQUIRED: The result and its basis if a seller sues a buyer for nonacceptance of the agreed quantity.

DISCUSSION: The possibility that the buyer might actually need less than the agreed quantity was a risk that was readily foreseeable at the time of contracting. Unseasonably warm weather was not a contingency the nonoccurrence of which was a basic assumption of the contract. Nor was the buyer prevented from receiving the benefit of its bargain. Thus, warm weather was an ordinary business risk of the kind ordinarily assumed by a contracting party and accordingly did not excuse Cobb's breach.

Answer (a) is incorrect because good faith is not an excuse for nonperformance. Answer (b) is incorrect because commercial impracticability is an excuse for nonperformance only if the promisor acted in good faith and the contingency was one "the nonoccurrence of which was a basic assumption on which the contract was made" (UCC 2-615). Absent a specific contractual reference, reasonable commercial understanding would not regard the contract as conditioned upon an assumption about the weather. Answer (c) is incorrect because the contract was for a stipulated quantity, not for the buyer's requirements.

12.6 Sellers' Remedies

73. Under the UCC Sales Article, if a buyer wrongfully rejects goods, the aggrieved seller may

	Resell the Goods and Sue for Damages	Cancel the Agreement
a.	Yes	Yes
b.	Yes	No
c.	No	Yes
d.	No	No

The correct answer is (a). *(CPA 1189 L-52)*

REQUIRED: The seller's remedy(ies) available under the UCC.

DISCUSSION: If a buyer wrongfully rejects or revokes acceptance of goods, fails to make a payment due on or before delivery, or repudiates with respect to a part or the whole, the following general remedies are available to a seller: withholding delivery; stopping delivery by a bailee; identifying goods to the contract as described in UCC 2-704; resale and recovery of damages; recovery of damages for nonacceptance or, in a proper case, the price; and cancellation (UCC 2-703).

74. One of the underlying purposes of the UCC is to permit the parties to exercise considerable contractual freedom. With regard to contractual modification or limitation of remedy, however, this freedom is circumscribed. Which is the true statement about the parties' ability to agree about remedies for breach of their contract for the sale of goods?

a. If the parties have limited the remedies available for breach of their contract, and unforeseen circumstances cause the limited remedy to fail of its essential purpose, the injured party will nevertheless be compelled to adhere to his/her bargain.

b. The limitation of consequential damages for injury to the person in the case of consumer goods and for commercial loss is prima facie unconscionable.

c. The parties may limit the remedies afforded by the UCC but may not create remedies in addition to those provided.

d. The damages for breach by either party may be liquidated in the agreement.

The correct answer is (d). *(Publisher)*

REQUIRED: The correct statement concerning the ability of parties to a contract for the sale of goods to shape their own remedies.

DISCUSSION: The UCC recognizes that it is efficient for parties to agree on remedies for breach and avoid the trouble, expense, and uncertainty of litigation. Under UCC 2-718, damages may be liquidated or specified in the agreement as long as such damages are reasonable in the circumstances.

Answer (a) is incorrect because if an otherwise reasonable remedy agreed to by the parties should fail, the general remedy provisions of the UCC will be available. Answer (b) is incorrect because the limitation of consequential damages for commercial loss is not prima facie unconscionable under UCC 2-719 as it is for injury to a person in the case of consumer goods. Answer (c) is incorrect because the parties are permitted to fashion remedies in addition to those provided in the UCC.

75. The Balboa Custom Furniture Company sells fine custom furniture. It has been encountering difficulties lately with some customers who have breached their contracts after the furniture they have selected has been customized to their order. The company therefore wishes to resort to a liquidated damages clause in its sales contract to encourage performance or provide an acceptable amount of damages. Regarding Balboa's contemplated resort to a liquidated damages clause,

a. Balboa may not use a liquidated damages clause because it is a merchant and is the preparer of the contract.

b. Balboa can simply take a very large deposit that will be forfeited if performance by a customer is not made for any reason.

c. The amount of the liquidated damages stipulated in the contract must be reasonable in light of the anticipated or actual harm caused by the breach.

d. Even if Balboa uses a liquidated damages clause in its sales contract, it will nevertheless have to establish that the liquidated damages claimed did not exceed actual damages by more than 10%.

The correct answer is (c). *(CPA 1180 L-13)*

REQUIRED: The correct statement concerning the seller's use of a liquidated damages clause.

DISCUSSION: A liquidated damages clause is a contractual clause specifying the damages to be paid in the event of breach. UCC 2-718 permits such a clause provided it is reasonable in light of anticipated (at the time the contract is formed) or actual harm, the difficulties of proof of loss, and the inconvenience of otherwise obtaining a remedy. If excessive, it is a penalty and is unenforceable. If a seller has properly withheld delivery of goods, the buyer may receive a refund of monies paid minus any liquidated damages agreed on. If no liquidated damages have been provided for, the seller may retain 20% of the value of the total contract price or $500, whichever is less (UCC 2-718).

Answer (a) is incorrect because a merchant who prepares a contract is not prohibited from using a liquidated damages clause. Answer (b) is incorrect because a very large deposit might be void as a penalty (UCC 2-718) or unenforceable if found unconscionable (UCC 2-302). Answer (d) is incorrect because a liquidated damages clause must be reasonable in light of anticipated damages, not in terms of an arbitrary percentage of actual damages.

76. Lazur Corp. entered into a contract with Baker Suppliers, Inc. to purchase a used word processor from Baker. Lazur is engaged in the business of selling new and used word processors to the general public. The contract required Baker to ship the goods to Lazur by common carrier pursuant to the following provision in the contract: "FOB -- Baker Suppliers, Inc. loading dock." Assume that Lazur refused to accept the word processor even though it was in all respects conforming to the contract and that the contract is otherwise silent. Under the UCC Sales Article,

a. Baker can successfully sue for specific performance and make Lazur accept and pay for the word processor.

b. Baker may resell the word processor to another buyer.

c. Baker must sue for the difference between the market value of the word processor and the contract price plus its incidental damages.

d. Baker cannot successfully sue for consequential damages unless it attempts to resell the word processor.

The correct answer is (b). *(CPA 589 L-58)*

REQUIRED: The true statement about a seller's remedies after wrongful rejection.

DISCUSSION: Resale of the goods and recovery of damages is a seller's remedy provided by UCC 2-703. After the buyer's breach, the resale in good faith and in a commercially reasonable manner permits the seller to recover the difference between the resale price and the contract price, plus any incidental damages allowed under UCC 2-710, minus expenses saved (UCC 2-706).

Answer (a) is incorrect because specific performance is a remedy that may be available to a buyer (UCC 2-716) but not a seller of goods. Answer (c) is incorrect because an aggrieved seller has a variety of possible remedies, including but not limited to a suit for damages for nonacceptance or repudiation. In such an action, the measure of damages is the difference between the market price and the unpaid contract price, plus incidental damages, minus expenses saved. If this measure of damages is inadequate, the seller may recover the profit it would have made from full performance by the buyer, plus incidental damages, with due allowance for costs reasonably incurred and payments or proceeds of resale. Answer (d) is incorrect because the UCC expressly provides for an aggrieved buyer, not a seller, to recover consequential (special) damages (UCC 2-715). But the UCC does not prevent the seller from seeking this common law remedy. Consequential damages are the losses resulting from the unique facts of the case, assuming the breaching party knew or had reason to know of these circumstances. Resale is not a prerequisite to their recovery.

77. When a buyer is in breach of a contract for the sale of goods, the seller's remedies include withholding delivery. Which of the following is true?

a. When the breach regarding one installment substantially impairs the value of the whole contract, all undelivered goods may be withheld.

b. The seller who withholds delivery may not proceed with other remedies.

c. The breach justifying withholding delivery of all undelivered goods need not go to the whole contract.

d. Withholding delivery is no longer available once goods are in the hands of a carrier even though the shipping term is FOB destination.

The correct answer is (a). *(Publisher)*

REQUIRED: The true statement about a seller's remedy of withholding delivery.

DISCUSSION: A seller may withhold delivery of all the undelivered goods if the buyer breaches the contract as a whole. A breach of the whole contract occurs if default on any installment substantially impairs the value of the whole contract (UCC 2-612). The breach may be by wrongful rejection of an installment, revoking acceptance, not paying when due, repudiating, etc. (UCC 2-703).

Answer (b) is incorrect because remedies are cumulative. Answer (c) is incorrect because UCC 2-703 requires a breach of the whole contract. Answer (d) is incorrect because stoppage in transit of any goods is possible when the buyer is found to be insolvent. Carloads, planeloads, truckloads, etc. may be stopped in transit in other circumstances (UCC 2-705).

78. Once goods have been shipped, the seller

a. May stop carloads, truckloads, planeloads, or larger quantities only if the buyer has become insolvent.

b. May not stop delivery when any bailee except a carrier acknowledges to the buyer that the goods are held for the buyer.

c. May stop any delivery when (s)he has for any reason the right to reclaim or withhold the goods.

d. Has no right of stoppage once the buyer has received a negotiable or nonnegotiable document of title to the goods.

The correct answer is (b). *(Publisher)*

REQUIRED: The true statement about a seller's right to stop goods in transit.

DISCUSSION: The seller may stop delivery of goods in the possession of a carrier or other bailee when (s)he discovers the buyer to be insolvent, if the buyer repudiates or fails to make a payment due, or if for any other reason the seller has a right to withhold or reclaim the goods. The seller may stop delivery until the buyer receives the goods or a negotiable document of title, or until a bailee (except a carrier) acknowledges that the bailee holds the goods for the buyer.

Answer (a) is incorrect because the seller may stop carloads, etc. when the seller has a right to withhold or reclaim the goods (see UCC 2-703). Answer (c) is incorrect because the seller may stop any size of delivery when the buyer is insolvent, but only carloads, truckloads, or larger shipments otherwise. Answer (d) is incorrect because receipt by the buyer of a nonnegotiable document of title does not preclude stoppage.

79. When a buyer of goods has wrongfully rejected or revoked acceptance, or failed to make a payment due on or before delivery, or repudiated the contract, the seller may resell the goods and collect damages. Which of the following is true?

a. The resale must be public and the buyer must be given reasonable notice.

b. The goods must have been in existence at the time of breach although not yet completed and identified to the contract.

c. A purchaser in good faith will not take free of any rights of the original buyer if the sale is not conducted in a commercially reasonable manner.

d. The seller is not accountable to the buyer for any profits made.

The correct answer is (d). *(Publisher)*

REQUIRED: The true statement about the seller's resale remedy.

DISCUSSION: Under UCC 2-706, a seller is not accountable for any profits made when exercising his/her right to resell the goods. But a person in the position of a seller, such as someone who holds a security interest or other right in the goods similar to that of a seller, must account to the buyer for any excess over the amount of his/her security interest.

Answer (a) is incorrect because the resale may be private if the buyer is given reasonable notice of the intent to resell. Answer (b) is incorrect because it is not necessary that the goods be in existence or that any or all of them have been identified to the contract before the breach (UCC 2-706). Answer (c) is incorrect because a purchaser who buys in good faith at a resale takes the goods free of any rights of the original buyer even though the seller fails to comply with its obligations (which include conducting the sale in a commercially reasonable manner).

80. Sara contracted to sell goods to Bea for a price of $10,000. Bea repudiated the contract. Sara then resold the goods in accordance with UCC requirements for $7,500. Sales commissions equaled $400. Freight costs saved were $300. Additional costs of storage were $200. The amount of damages receivable is

a. $2,200.

b. $2,500.

c. $2,800.

d. $3,100.

The correct answer is (c). *(Publisher)*

REQUIRED: The amount of damages recoverable by the seller after resale.

DISCUSSION: After the buyer's breach, the resale in good faith and in a commercially reasonable manner permits the seller to recover the difference between the resale price and the contract price, plus any incidental damages allowed under UCC 2-710, minus expenses saved (UCC 2-706). Incidental damages from a buyer's breach include reasonable costs incurred in stopping delivery, transporting the goods after breach, returning or reselling the goods, etc.

Contract price	$10,000
Minus resale	(7,500)
Minus savings	(300)
Plus commissions	400
Plus storage	200
Damages	$ 2,800

81. Cain and Zen Corp. orally agreed that Zen would specially manufacture a machine for Cain at a price of $40,000. After Zen completed the work at a cost of $30,000, Cain notified Zen that it no longer needed the machine. Zen is holding the machine for Cain and has requested payment from Cain. Despite making reasonable efforts, Zen has been unable to resell the machine for any price. Zen has incurred warehouse fees of $500 for storing the machine. If Cain refuses to pay Zen and Zen sues Cain, the most Zen will be entitled to recover is

a. $0.

b. $30,500.

c. $40,000.

d. $40,500.

The correct answer is (d). *(CPA 1188 L-48)*

REQUIRED: The seller's recovery after a buyer's refusal to pay for specially made goods.

DISCUSSION: A seller may recover the contract price ($40,000) and any incidental damages ($500) if circumstances reasonably indicate that an effort at resale would be unsuccessful (UCC 2-709). Because the machine was made-to-order and not adaptable to others' use, Zen should be successful in recovering the price. After recovery of the price, seller would be holding the machine for buyer.

82. Badger Corporation sold goods to Watson. Watson has arbitrarily refused to pay the purchase price. Under what circumstances will Badger not be able to recover the price if it seeks this remedy instead of other possible remedies?

a. If Watson refused to accept delivery and the goods were resold in the ordinary course of business.

b. If Watson accepted the goods but seeks to return them.

c. If the goods sold were destroyed shortly after the risk of loss passed to the buyer.

d. If the goods were identified to the contract and Badger made a reasonable effort to resell them at a reasonable price but was unable to do so.

The correct answer is (a). *(CPA 578 L-39)*

REQUIRED: The circumstances under which the seller will not be able to recover the price.

DISCUSSION: The seller cannot recover the price if the goods have been resold. In that event, Badger's damages would be measured by the difference between the contract price and the resale price, plus any incidental damages, minus expenses saved (UCC 2-706).

Answers (b), (c), and (d) are all incorrect because they present factual settings in which a seller probably could recover the contract price (UCC 2-709).

Questions 83 and 84 are based on Anker, Inc., which on April 5 furnished Bold Corp. with Anker's financial statements dated March 31. The financial statements contained misrepresentations indicating that Anker was solvent when in fact it was insolvent. Based on Anker's financial statements, Bold agreed to sell Anker 90 computers, "FOB -- Bold's loading dock." On April 14, Anker received 60 of the computers. The remaining 30 computers are in the possession of the common carrier and in transit to Anker.

83. If on April 28 Bold discovered that Anker was insolvent, then with respect to the computers delivered to Anker on April 14, Bold may

a. Reclaim the computers upon making a demand.

b. Reclaim the computers irrespective of the rights of any subsequent third party.

c. Not reclaim the computers because 10 days have elapsed from their delivery.

d. Not reclaim the computers because it is entitled to recover the price of the computers.

The correct answer is (a). *(CPA 587 L-52)*

REQUIRED: The right of a seller if the buyer has misrepresented its solvency.

DISCUSSION: When the seller discovers that the buyer has received goods on credit while insolvent, (s)he may reclaim the goods upon demand made within 10 days after the receipt. But if misrepresentation of solvency has been made to the seller in writing within 3 months before delivery, the 10-day limitation does not apply (UCC 2-702). No other remedies are permitted with respect to goods successfully reclaimed.

Answer (b) is incorrect because goods in the possession of a good faith purchaser cannot be reclaimed. Answer (c) is incorrect because the misrepresentation may have been made within 3 months before delivery. In that case, the 10-day limitation is inapplicable. Answer (d) is incorrect because the facts do not indicate that Bold has become entitled to bring an action for the price. Anker has not yet breached. Moreover, Bold is entitled to a reclamation remedy because of Anker's misrepresentation.

84. With respect to the remaining 30 computers in transit, which of the following statements is correct if Anker refuses to pay Bold in cash and Anker is not in possession of a negotiable document of title covering the computers?

a. Bold may stop delivery of the computers to Anker. Their contract is void because Anker furnished false financial statements.

b. Bold may stop delivery of the computers to Anker despite the passage of title to Anker.

c. Bold must deliver the computers to Anker on credit because Anker has not breached the contract.

d. Bold must deliver the computers to Anker because the risk of loss passed to Anker.

The correct answer is (b). *(CPA 587 L-53)*

REQUIRED: The right (duty) of an unpaid seller to stop goods in transit after learning of the buyer's insolvency.

DISCUSSION: When an unpaid seller discovers the buyer is insolvent, it may stop any goods in transit (UCC 2-705). This right may be exercised even when the shipping terms are FOB shipping point and title and risk of loss have passed to the buyer. Once the goods are stopped, Bold may refuse to deliver except for cash (UCC 2-702). If Anker pays cash, including payment for all goods previously delivered, Bold will have no reason to withhold delivery. If the buyer breaches before delivery (e.g., fails to pay an installment or commits fraud), any stoppage in transit must be by carload, truckload, or planeload.

Answer (a) is incorrect because if Bold pays cash, it may enforce the contract against Anker. Answers (c) and (d) are incorrect because the buyer's insolvency justifies nondelivery despite the lack of a breach or the passage of title and risk of loss.

12.7 Buyers' Remedies

85. Johnston contracted to buy 100 bolts of No. 1 quality wool from McHugh. The contract provided that Johnston would make payment prior to inspection. The 100 bolts were shipped and Johnston paid McHugh. Upon inspection, however, Johnston discovered that the wool was No. 2 quality. Johnston thereupon tendered back the wool to McHugh and demanded return of the payment. McHugh refused on the ground that there is no difference between No. 1 quality wool and No. 2 quality wool. What is Johnston's remedy because the wool was nonconforming?

a. Specific performance.

b. Damages measured by the difference between the value of the goods delivered and the value of conforming goods.

c. Damages measured by the price paid plus the difference between the contract price and the cost of buying substitute goods.

d. None. Johnston waived any remedies by agreeing to pay before inspection.

The correct answer is (c). *(MBE Part II-19)*

REQUIRED: The buyer's remedy for nonconformity of goods.

DISCUSSION: Under UCC 2-711 and 2-712, a buyer who has rightfully rejected goods after having prepaid the purchase price may recover as much of the price as has been paid and also use the cover remedy. To cover is to make a timely, good faith purchase of substitute goods, and have as damages the difference between the contract price and the cost of the substitutes.

Answer (a) is incorrect because specific performance is only available for unique goods, e.g., specially manufactured goods. Answer (b) is incorrect because Johnston is entitled to recover the price prepaid as well as the damages accruing from the cover remedy. Instead of tendering the goods back to McHugh, (s)he could have elected to keep the goods and recovered the difference between the value of the goods delivered and the value they would have had if they had been as warranted. Answer (d) is incorrect because the agreement to prepay is not a waiver of the right to inspect or any of the buyer's remedies.

86. If a seller repudiates a contract for the sale of 100 radios with a buyer, the buyer

a. Can "cover," i.e., procure the goods elsewhere and recover the difference.

b. Can obtain specific performance by the seller.

c. Can recover punitive damages.

d. Must await the seller's performance for a commercially reasonable time after repudiation.

The correct answer is (a). *(CPA 1176 L-7)*

REQUIRED: The buyer's recourse if a seller repudiates a contract for the sale of goods.

DISCUSSION: If a seller repudiates (anticipatory breach), the buyer can "cover" by making a good faith purchase of substitute goods within a reasonable time. Damages would equal the difference between the contract price and the cost of cover, plus incidental or consequential damages, minus expenses saved (UCC 2-712).

Answer (b) is incorrect because specific performance is not usually available for ordinary goods. Answer (c) is incorrect because punitive damages are not normally available for breach of contract. Answer (d) is incorrect because upon notice of repudiation, the buyer may immediately seek any reasonable remedy under the UCC even if the time of performance has not been reached.

87. On May 1, Frost entered into a signed contract for the sale of 5,000 pounds of sugar to Kemp Co. at $.30 per pound. Delivery was to be made on June 10. Because of a sudden rise in sugar prices, Frost sent Kemp a letter stating that it would not sell the sugar to Kemp. Kemp received the letter on May 15 at which time the market price of sugar was $.40 per pound. Although Kemp could have reasonably purchased sugar elsewhere in the market, it chose not to do so. On June 10, the market price of sugar was $.50 per pound. In addition to incidental damages, Kemp is entitled to damages of

a. $500.

b. $500 plus consequential damages.

c. $1,000.

d. $1,000 plus consequential damages.

The correct answer is (a). *(CPA 586 L-36)*

REQUIRED: The buyer's damages after an anticipatory breach by the seller.

DISCUSSION: If a buyer does not elect to cover, his/her damages for nondelivery are measured by the difference between the market price at the time (s)he learned of the breach and the contract price, plus any incidental or consequential damages, minus expenses saved (UCC 2-713). Market price at the time of learning of the breach is used because the buyer could have covered at that time. On May 15, when Kemp learned of the breach, the market price was $.40. The difference between $.40 and the $.30 contract price for 5,000 pounds is $500.

Answers (b) and (d) are incorrect because consequential damages may be awarded only if they could not reasonably have been prevented by cover (UCC 2-715). Kemp could reasonably have purchased sugar elsewhere and is thus not entitled to consequential damages. Answers (c) and (d) are incorrect because the measure of damages for repudiation is based on the market price at the date of notice of breach ($.40), not the price at the date of performance ($.50).

88. A buyer who has accepted nonconforming goods

a. Is barred from any remedy.

b. May recover for breach of warranty only the difference between the value of the goods and the value they would have had if they had been as warranted.

c. May not recover consequential damages.

d. May recover damages for nonconformity if (s)he gives notice.

The correct answer is (d). *(Publisher)*

REQUIRED: The true statement about a buyer's remedies after acceptance.

DISCUSSION: A buyer who accepts nonconforming goods still has remedies. The buyer must give notice to the seller. Then (s)he may use any reasonable method under the UCC to determine his/her loss (UCC 2-714).

Answer (a) is incorrect because the buyer may still recover damages. Answers (b) and (c) are incorrect because under UCC 2-714, allowance is made for circumstances that show damages of a different amount. Also, the buyer may recover incidental and consequential damages in a proper case.

89. Pam wrote Tom Matz setting forth specifications for a printing press of a unique nature to be constructed to order and asked for a firm price offer if Matz were interested. Matz telegraphed Pam 1 week later, "Offer to construct as per your letter for twenty thousand seven hundred dollars cash on November delivery. Offer terminates 2 days. Matz." The telegram omitted the words "seven hundred" when delivered to Pam. Pam immediately phoned Matz and stated, "I accept as stated in your telegram." Matz said, "Done." If subsequent writings had been exchanged and Pam and Matz had a definite agreement,

a. Matz warrants by delivery that the goods will perform the printing job Pam had in mind in specifying the unique construction.

b. If Matz completes the press but wrongfully refuses to deliver, Pam may require him to specifically perform.

c. Pam would not have an insurable interest in the press until risk of loss or title passes from Matz.

d. If Matz notifies Pam that he will not complete the contract, Pam gives up the right to damages if she cancels instead of pursuing other remedies.

The correct answer is (b). *(CPA 574 L-27)*

REQUIRED: The correct statement regarding the buyer's rights with respect to specially manufactured goods.

DISCUSSION: UCC 2-716 provides for the remedy of specific performance when goods are unique. A specially manufactured machine made to the buyer's specifications fits that criterion. However, specific performance will be awarded only when monetary damages would be inadequate.

Answer (a) is incorrect because Matz did not warrant the performance. It was Pam who provided the specifications. Matz only warrants that he has met Pam's specifications. Answer (c) is incorrect because Pam has an insurable interest in the press when it is identified to the contract (UCC 2-501). Identification may occur when the press is sufficiently complete so as to clearly meet Pam's specifications and no one else's. Answer (d) is incorrect because if Matz makes an anticipatory repudiation, Pam may seek damages in addition to canceling the contract (UCC 2-711).

90. Leah Reed purchased 50 dozen pen sets from Wok Corp. Reed made substantial prepayments of the purchase price. Wok is insolvent and the goods have not been delivered as promised. Reed wants the pens. Under the circumstances, Reed will not be able to obtain the pens if

a. The goods have not been identified to the contract.

b. Reed was not aware of Wok's insolvency at the time of purchase.

c. Reed can obtain a judgment for damages.

d. Reed did not pay the full price at the time of the purchase even though a tender of the balance was made and held available to Wok upon delivery.

The correct answer is (a). *(CPA 584 L-47)*

REQUIRED: The circumstances that will prevent the buyer from recovering goods from an insolvent seller.

DISCUSSION: A buyer may recover goods from an insolvent seller if the goods have been identified to the contract, the seller became insolvent within 10 days of receipt of the first installment of the price, and tender of any unpaid portion of the price is made and kept open (UCC 2-502). If the pen sets have not been identified to the contract, Reed cannot obtain them.

Answer (b) is incorrect because the buyer's right to reach the goods is not dependent upon knowledge of the insolvency of the seller. Answer (c) is incorrect because the UCC provides for recovery of the goods regardless of the availability of damages. Answer (d) is incorrect because failure to pay the full price will not prevent Reed from obtaining the goods if she makes and keeps open a tender of the unpaid balance of the price.

91. Pippin received and accepted a shipment of goods from Magwich. Pippin subsequently made a justifiable revocation of acceptance, but only after incurring expenses for inspection, transportation, and storage. Pippin

a. Must return the goods and bring an action for damages.

b. Has a security interest in the goods.

c. May cancel the contract but will then be precluded from bringing an action for damages.

d. May cover but not cancel.

The correct answer is (b). *(Publisher)*

REQUIRED: The remedy available when a buyer justifiably revoked acceptance.

DISCUSSION: "On rightful rejection or justifiable revocation of acceptance, a buyer has a security interest in goods in his/her possession or control for any payments made on their price and any expenses reasonably incurred in their inspection, receipt, transportation, care, and custody, and may hold such goods and resell them in like manner as an aggrieved seller" (UCC 2-711).

Answer (a) is incorrect because the buyer may retain the goods as explained above. Answers (c) and (d) are incorrect because a buyer may cancel, but whether (s)he has done so does not affect the right to cover and receive damages.

12.8 Warranties

92. A warranty imposes upon the seller of goods a duty that the goods conform to the promise in the warranty. If they do not, the buyer has an action for breach of warranty. Under the UCC,

a. The warranty of title is an implied warranty.

b. Only express warranties are recognized.

c. Express and implied warranties are treated separately from the warranty of title.

d. Implied warranties are those created by the affirmations of fact or other promises made by the seller.

The correct answer is (c). *(Publisher)*

REQUIRED: The true statement about the types of warranties under the UCC.

DISCUSSION: A warranty is a promise that something is true. In the sale of a product (goods) it is an express or implied promise establishing the characteristics of ownership and level of quality. Under UCC 2-313, express warranties are created by the seller's explicit affirmations of fact or promises. The implied warranties of merchantability (UCC 2-314) and fitness for a particular purpose (UCC 2-315) are created by operation of law and thus arise without intent. The warranty of title is treated separately by the UCC even though it is inherent in the sales transaction.

Answer (a) is incorrect because the UCC treats it as neither an express nor an implied warranty. Answer (b) is incorrect because the UCC also recognizes a warranty of title and implied warranties. Answer (d) is incorrect because it defines express warranties.

93. DaGama bought a used boat from Magellan Marina, which disclaimed "any and all warranties" in connection with the sale. Magellan was unaware that the boat had been stolen from Colon. DaGama surrendered it to Colon when confronted with proof of the theft. DaGama sued Magellan. Who is likely to prevail and why?

a. Magellan, because of the general disclaimer.

b. Magellan, because it was unaware of the theft.

c. DaGama, because the warranty of title has been breached.

d. DaGama, because Magellan is a merchant.

The correct answer is (c). *(CPA 1189 L-47)*

REQUIRED: The party who will prevail and why if neither knew that the subject matter consisted of stolen goods.

DISCUSSION: UCC 2-312 creates a warranty of title by any seller that can only be excluded or modified by specific language or by the buyer's knowledge of circumstances relating to the title. A general disclaimer of warranty, such as a disclaimer of "any and all warranties," is ineffective regarding the warranty of title. Magellan therefore warranted the title by selling the boat to DaGama and will bear the loss. The loss is the fair market value of the property at the time it was taken from DaGama plus consequential damages.

Answer (a) is incorrect because the language must be specific to disclaim the warranty of title. Answer (b) is incorrect because that the seller did not intentionally breach the warranty is not a bar to liability. The loss is placed on the party (the seller) who is better able to avoid the loss. Answer (d) is incorrect because a nonmerchant seller also warrants the title unless (s)he makes a specific disclaimer.

94. Parks furnished specifications and ordered 1,000 specially constructed folding tables from Metal Manufacturing Company, Inc. The tables were unique in design and had not appeared in the local market. Metal completed the job and delivered the order to Parks. Parks sold about 600 of the tables when Unusual Tables, Inc. sued both Parks and Metal for patent infringement. If Unusual wins, what is the status of Parks and Metal?

a. Metal is liable to Parks for breach of the warranty against infringement.

b. Parks is liable to Metal for breach of the warranty against infringement.

c. The warranty against infringement is not available to either Parks or Metal.

d. Parks and Metal are jointly and severally liable and, as such, must pay the judgment in equal amounts.

The correct answer is (b). *(CPA 1178 L-36)*

REQUIRED: The legal status of a buyer and manufacturer of specially made goods if both are successfully sued for patent infringement.

DISCUSSION: A buyer of goods who furnishes specifications to the seller breaches the warranty against infringement if compliance with the specifications results in liability for the seller (UCC 2-312). Parks provided the specifications to Metal and would be liable for breach of this warranty.

Answer (a) is incorrect because the manufacturer is not liable for breach of the warranty against infringement when the buyer furnishes specifications for specially made goods. Answer (c) is incorrect because the warranty against infringement is available to Metal. Answer (d) is incorrect because Parks is liable for the full amount of the judgment and must reimburse any amount Metal is required to pay.

95. With respect to the sale of goods, the warranty of title

a. Provides that the seller deliver the goods free from any lien of which the buyer lacked knowledge at the time of contracting.

b. Provides that the seller cannot disclaim the warranty if the sale is made to a bona fide purchaser for value.

c. Applies only if the seller is a merchant.

d. Applies only if it is in writing and signed by the seller.

The correct answer is (a). *(CPA 1187 L-37)*

REQUIRED: The true statement about the warranty of title.

DISCUSSION: Every contract for the sale of goods warrants that the title is good, its transfer is rightful, and the goods are free of encumbrances not known to the buyer. The warranty of title can be excluded or modified only by specific language or by circumstances giving the buyer reason to know that the transferor has no title or a limited title (UCC 2-312).

Answer (b) is incorrect because the seller may disclaim by specific language to any buyer. Answer (c) is incorrect because a warranty of title can be made by a nonmerchant. Answer (d) is incorrect because a warranty of title can be made orally.

96. Which of the following factors will be most important in determining whether an express warranty has been created concerning goods sold?

a. The seller gave a description of the goods that is part of the basis of the bargain.

b. The buyer or seller is a merchant with respect to the goods being sold.

c. Whether the seller intended to create the express warranty.

d. Whether the buyer relied on the seller's statements.

The correct answer is (a). *(CPA 1188 L-45)*

REQUIRED: The most important factor in creating an express warranty.

DISCUSSION: An express warranty is created if it becomes part of the basis of the bargain by any affirmation of fact or promise made by the seller to the buyer that relates to the goods; by any description of the goods; or by any sample or model (UCC 2-313). The warranty can arise from language or photos contained in catalogs, brochures, sales materials, advertisements, or on or in packaging. It may arise before or after the sale.

Answer (b) is incorrect because nonmerchants are also bound by their express warranties. Answer (c) is incorrect because the intent of the seller is irrelevant. How a reasonable buyer would perceive the seller's statements or acts is important. Answer (d) is incorrect because no reliance by the buyer need be shown as a requirement for including an express warranty in the agreement (Official Comment to UCC 2-313).

97. Lazur Corp. entered into a contract with Baker Suppliers, Inc. to purchase a used word processor from Baker. Lazur is engaged in the business of selling new and used word processors to the general public. Baker also represented in the contract that the word processor had been used for only 10 hours by its previous owner. The contract included the provision that the word processor was being sold "as is" and this provision was in a larger and different type style than the remainder of the contract. With regard to the contract between Lazur and Baker

a. An implied warranty of merchantability does not arise unless both Lazur and Baker are merchants.

b. The "as is" provision effectively disclaims the implied warranty of title.

c. No express warranties are created by the contract.

d. The "as is" provision would not prevent Baker from being liable for a breach of any express warranties created by the contract.

The correct answer is (d). *(CPA 589 L-55)*

REQUIRED: The true statement about the warranties made in the contract.

DISCUSSION: The "as is" provision excludes only implied warranties (UCC 2-316). Furthermore, an express warranty and a disclaimer are to be construed as consistent with each other whenever reasonable. If such an interpretation is unreasonable, however, the disclaimer is ineffective and the express warranty prevails. An express warranty is rarely effectively disclaimed, although it may be modified.

Answer (a) is incorrect because only the seller need be a merchant. Answer (b) is incorrect because the warranty of title is not an implied warranty. Specific language or circumstances known by the buyer are necessary to disclaim the warranty of title. Answer (c) is incorrect because the contract expressly warrants the amount of use of the word processor by the previous owner.

98. Olsen purchased a used van from Super Sales Co. for $350. A clause in the written contract in boldface type provided that the van was being sold "as is." Another clause provided that the contract was intended as the final expression of the parties' agreement. After driving the van for 1 week, Olsen realized that the engine was burning oil. Olsen telephoned Super and requested a refund. Super refused but orally gave Olsen a warranty on the engine for 6 months. The engine exploded 3 weeks later. Super's oral warranty

a. Is invalid because the modification of the existing contract required additional consideration.

b. Is invalid because of the Statute of Frauds.

c. Is valid and enforceable.

d. Although valid, proof of its existence will be inadmissible because it contradicts the final written agreement of the parties.

The correct answer is (c). *(CPA 584 L-53)*

REQUIRED: The true statement about an oral warranty made subsequent to a contract for sale.

DISCUSSION: The promise made by the seller to the buyer related to the goods and became part of the basis of the bargain and thus constituted a valid and enforceable express warranty (UCC 2-313). The basis of the bargain in this case included a subsequent oral modification, which needs no consideration to be binding (UCC 2-209). It need not be written if the agreement as modified is not within the Statute of Frauds and the parties have no written agreement excluding an oral modification or rescission (if they do, it is ineffective against a nonmerchant if the merchant's form exclusion is not separately signed). The contract was not within the Statute of Frauds because the price of $350 and the partial performance (delivery of car and payment) are exceptions (UCC 2-201).

Answer (a) is incorrect because additional consideration is not required for modification. Answer (b) is incorrect because the UCC Statute of Frauds applies to sales of goods for at least $500. Answer (d) is incorrect because the parol evidence rule excludes evidence of prior or contemporaneous oral agreements, not of subsequent oral modifications.

99. The Uniform Commercial Code implies a warranty of merchantability to protect buyers of goods. To be subject to this warranty the goods need not be

a. Fit for all the purposes for which the buyer intends to use the goods.

b. Adequately packaged and labeled.

c. Sold by a merchant.

d. In conformity with any promises or affirmations of fact made on the container or label.

The correct answer is (a). *(CPA 1183 L-54)*

REQUIRED: The characteristic that goods need not have under the warranty of merchantability.

DISCUSSION: The implied warranty of merchantability (UCC 2-314) requires that the goods be of a fair quality that would usually be accepted without objection by buyers, be fit for the ordinary purposes for which they are normally used, and be adequately packaged and labeled. There is no implied warranty that goods be fit for all purposes for which the buyer might intend to use them.

Answers (b), (c), and (d) are incorrect because to be merchantable, goods must meet these and other requirements given in UCC 2-314.

100. Under the UCC, an action for breach of the implied warranty of merchantability by a party who sustained personal injuries may be successful against the seller of the product only when

a. The injured party is in privity of contract with the seller.

b. The seller is a merchant with respect to the product involved.

c. An action based on strict liability in tort can also be successfully maintained.

d. An action based on negligence can also be successfully maintained.

The correct answer is (b). *(CPA 587 L-50)*

REQUIRED: The condition for recovery from the seller for personal injuries resulting from breach of the implied warranty of merchantability.

DISCUSSION: Unless excluded or modified, a warranty of merchantability is implied in a contract for the sale of goods if the seller is a merchant with respect to goods of that kind (UCC 2-314). Thus, an action against a nonmerchant seller could not be maintained for breach of this warranty.

Answer (a) is incorrect because privity of contract is not necessary in an action for breach of warranty (UCC 2-318). Answers (c) and (d) are incorrect because the ability to bring a tort action is not a prerequisite to a breach of warranty suit.

101. Under UCC 2-314, an implied warranty of merchantability arises only if the seller is a merchant. For purposes of this section, the term "merchant" means

a. A person who holds him/herself out as having knowledge or skill peculiar to the goods involved in the transaction, or a person who deals in goods of the kind involved in the transaction.

b. A person who regularly uses the kind of goods involved.

c. Any commercial enterprise regularly engaged in selling goods.

d. Any enterprise whether or not for profit regularly engaged in selling goods.

The correct answer is (a). *(Publisher)*

REQUIRED: The definition of merchant for purposes of the warranty of merchantability.

DISCUSSION: "Unless excluded or modified, a warranty that the goods shall be merchantable is implied in a contract for their sale if the seller is a merchant with respect to goods of that kind. Under this section, the serving for value of food or drink to be consumed either on the premises or elsewhere is a sale" (UCC 2-314). Answer (a) states the definition of a merchant in UCC 2-104.

Answer (b) is incorrect because the person must do more than use the goods; e.g., a saw mill operator may not be a merchant with respect to saws. Answers (c) and (d) are incorrect because the person must deal in goods of the kind involved.

102. Wally, a CPA and Rita's neighbor, offered to sell Rita his power chain saw for $400. Rita stated that she knew nothing about chain saws but would buy the saw if it were capable of cutting down the trees in her backyard, which had an average diameter of 3 feet. Wally assured Rita that the saw "would do the job." Relying on Wally's assurance, Rita purchased the saw. Wally has created a warranty that

a. The saw is of an average fair quality.

b. The saw is fit for the ordinary purposes for which it is used.

c. The saw is capable of cutting the trees in Rita's backyard.

d. Is unenforceable because it is not in writing.

The correct answer is (c). *(CPA 1184 L-54)*

REQUIRED: The warranty created by the seller's assurance that the goods "would do the job."

DISCUSSION: Under UCC 2-315, an implied warranty of fitness for a particular purpose is created (unless excluded or modified) when the seller has reason to know the buyer's particular purpose for the goods and the buyer is relying on the seller's skill or judgment to choose the goods. Wally knew the purpose for which the chain saw would be used and that Rita was relying on his judgment. He did not disclaim any warranty, and an implied warranty of fitness to cut the specific trees was created.

Answers (a) and (b) are incorrect because no implied warranty of merchantability arose since Wally was not a merchant with respect to the goods. Answer (d) is incorrect because no writing is needed to create an implied warranty.

103. Target Company, Inc. ordered a generator from Maximum Voltage Corporation. A dispute has arisen over the effect of a provision in the specifications that the generator have a 5,000 kilowatt capacity. The specifications were attached to the contract and were incorporated by reference in the main body of the contract. The generator did not have this capacity but instead had a maximum capacity of 4,800 kilowatts. The contract had a disclaimer clause that effectively negated both of the implied warranties of quality. Target is seeking to avoid the contract based upon breach of warranty and Maximum is relying on its disclaimer. Which of the following is a correct statement?

a. The 5,000 kilowatt term contained in the specifications does not constitute a warranty.

b. The disclaimer effectively negated any and all warranty protection claimed by Target.

c. The descriptive language (5,000 kilowatt) contained in the specifications is an express warranty and has not been effectively disclaimed.

d. The parol evidence rule will prevent Target from asserting the 5,000 kilowatt term as a warranty.

The correct answer is (c). *(CPA 580 L-32)*

REQUIRED: The correct statement regarding a dispute over an alleged breach of warranty.

DISCUSSION: A description of the goods that is made part of the basis of the bargain between the parties creates an express warranty that the goods shall be conforming (UCC 2-313). A disclaimer of the implied warranties of merchantability and fitness for a particular purpose does not negate an express warranty created by a description of the goods.

Furthermore, an express warranty and a disclaimer are to be construed as consistent with each other whenever reasonable. If such an interpretation is unreasonable, however, the disclaimer is ineffective and the express warranty prevails. An express warranty is rarely effectively disclaimed, although it may be modified.

Answer (a) is incorrect because the 5,000 kilowatt term contained in the specifications constitutes an express warranty by description. Answer (b) is incorrect because the disclaimer failed to negate the warranty protection provided by the express warranty by description. Answer (d) is incorrect because the 5,000 kilowatt term was part of the written contract, so the parol evidence rule is irrelevant.

104. In general, disclaimers of implied warranty protection are

a. Permitted if they are explicit and understandable and the buyer is aware of their existence.

b. Not binding on remote purchasers with notice thereof.

c. Void because they are against public policy.

d. Invalid unless in writing and signed by the buyer.

The correct answer is (a). *(CPA 583 L-39)*

REQUIRED: The correct generalization about disclaimers of implied warranties.

DISCUSSION: With certain exceptions, "to exclude or modify the implied warranty of merchantability or any part of it, the language must mention merchantability and in case of a writing must be conspicuous, and to exclude or modify any implied warranty of fitness, the exclusion must be by a writing and conspicuous" (UCC 2-316).

Answer (b) is incorrect because a disclaimer binding on the buyer also is effective against third parties. Answer (c) is incorrect because the UCC permits such disclaimers. However, under the Magnuson-Moss Warranty Act, a seller of consumer products who makes a written warranty cannot disclaim any implied warranty. Answer (d) is incorrect because a disclaimer of the implied warranty of merchantability may be oral. Moreover, the UCC does not require a buyer to sign a disclaimer.

105. Webster purchased a drill press for $475 from Martinson Hardware, Inc. The press has proved to be defective, and Webster wishes to rescind the purchase based upon a breach of implied warranty. Which of the following will preclude Webster's recovery from Martinson?

a. The press sold to Webster was a demonstration model and sold at a substantial discount; hence, Webster received no implied warranties.

b. Webster examined the press carefully, but the defects were hidden such that a reasonable examination would not have revealed them.

c. Martinson informed Webster that the model was being closed out at a loss because of certain deficiencies and that it was sold "with all faults."

d. The negligence of the manufacturer caused the trouble and the defect could not have been discovered by Martinson without actually taking the press apart.

The correct answer is (c). *(CPA 1182 L-47)*

REQUIRED: The basis for precluding recovery by the buyer for breach of an implied warranty.

DISCUSSION: UCC 2-316 states, "Unless the circumstances indicate otherwise, all implied warranties are excluded by expressions like 'as is,' 'with all faults,' or other language that in common understanding calls the buyer's attention to the exclusion of warranties and makes plain that there is no implied warranty."

Answer (a) is incorrect because in general, language that excludes implied warranties must be clear and specific. Offering a discount is neither a clear nor a specific means of alerting the buyer that implied warranties are being disclaimed. Answer (b) is incorrect because Webster's recovery would be precluded by an inspection only if the defects should have been revealed by the inspection. Answer (d) is incorrect because the retailer may be held strictly liable but would then be able to assert a claim against the manufacturer.

106. The warranty rules of the UCC must be read in light of the federal Magnuson-Moss Warranty Act, which

a. Creates implied warranties in addition to those provided by the UCC.

b. Requires that the seller of consumer goods give a "full warranty" in writing.

c. Requires that the seller of consumer goods give either a "full warranty" or a "limited warranty" in writing.

d. Limits the ability of sellers to disclaim implied warranties.

The correct answer is (d). *(Publisher)*

REQUIRED: The correct statement concerning the Magnuson-Moss Warranty Act.

DISCUSSION: The Magnuson-Moss Act supplements and modifies rather than displaces the UCC's warranty rules. When a seller has given a written warranty in a sales contract (or in a sales contract combined with a contract for service that is entered into within 90 days of the original agreement), the seller may not modify or disclaim the implied warranties of fitness for a particular purpose or merchantability.

Answer (a) is incorrect because the Act creates no implied warranties. Answers (b) and (c) are incorrect because the Act does not require a seller of consumer goods to give any warranty. If the seller does give a written warranty, however, it must be either a "full" or "limited" warranty. A "full" warranty must meet the federal minimum standards (refund, repair, or replace without cost in a reasonable time). A "limited" warranty is one that fails to meet "full" warranty criteria and fairly puts the buyer on notice that the warranty is not full and may not meet certain standards. Whether a warranty is "full" or "limited" must be conspicuously designated in writing, and its duration must be stated.

107. The Uniform Commercial Code's position on privity of warranty as to personal injuries

a. Allows the buyer's family the right to sue only the party from whom the buyer purchased the product.

b. Resulted in a single uniform rule being adopted throughout most of the United States.

c. Prohibits the exclusion on privity grounds of third parties from the warranty protection it has granted.

d. Applies exclusively to manufacturers.

The correct answer is (c). *(CPA 585 L-42)*

REQUIRED: The UCC's position on privity of warranty as to personal injuries.

DISCUSSION: UCC 2-318 provides alternate provisions with respect to the warranty protection extended to third parties that a seller may not exclude or limit. At a minimum, household members and guests of the purchaser are covered. This UCC section was not intended to limit the class of potential plaintiffs, however, but rather to establish a minimum that might be expanded by case law. In general, case law has greatly expanded the rights of plaintiffs in product liability cases.

Answer (a) is incorrect because the courts of most states would permit suit against other parties in the chain of distribution. Answer (b) is incorrect because UCC 2-318 presents three alternatives from which states may select. Answer (d) is incorrect because sellers include other parties such as retailers and wholesalers.

108. Pure Food Company packed and sold quality food products to wholesalers and fancy food retailers. One of its most popular items was "southern style" baked beans. Charles purchased a large can of the beans from the Superior Quality Grocery. Joan, who is the mother of Charles, bit into a heaping spoonful of the beans at a family outing and fractured her jaw. The evidence revealed that the beans contained a brown stone, the size of a marble. In a subsequent lawsuit by Joan, which of the following is correct?

a. Joan can collect against Superior Quality for negligence.

b. Privity will not be a bar in a lawsuit against either Pure Food or Superior Quality.

c. The various sellers involved could have effectively excluded or limited the rights of third parties to sue them.

d. Privity is a bar to recovery by Joan, although Charles may sue Superior Quality.

The correct answer is (b). *(CPA 580 L-37)*

REQUIRED: The correct statement regarding a lawsuit by an injured party who was not the purchaser of the defective goods.

DISCUSSION: Under UCC 2-318, a seller's warranty extends, at a minimum, to household members and guests if it is reasonable to expect they may be affected by the goods. In this case, the sellers (both Pure Food and Superior Quality) made an implied warranty that the food was fit for eating and contained no foreign objects. Joan can sue on this warranty even though she did not purchase the beans. Under strict liability, privity contract is unnecessary.

An object, even if natural (e.g., a fishbone in chowder or a cherry pit in cherry ice cream) is considered foreign when it is not reasonably expected by the consumer. Wire, rocks, glass, needles, and insects are clearly breaches of warranty.

Answer (a) is incorrect because the facts do not suggest that Superior was negligent. A retailer of a closed container would have no reasonable way of knowing the contents were defective. Answer (c) is incorrect because this liability cannot be excluded. It is imposed as a matter of public policy. Answer (d) is incorrect because Joan may sue either Superior or Pure Food even though she was not in privity with either one. Her son can sue only for the price of the product.

109. Which of the following contract clauses is not enforceable under the UCC?

a. "Purchaser only may sue for breach of warranty."

b. "Seller does not warrant title."

c. "Notice of defects must be in writing and received by seller within 30 days of delivery."

d. "Buyer hereby grants to seller a security interest in all currently owned and after-acquired equipment."

The correct answer is (a). *(E. Rubert)*

REQUIRED: The contract clause not enforceable under the UCC.

DISCUSSION: UCC 2-318 concerns third-party beneficiaries of express or implied warranties. It makes a clause limiting the availability of warranties ineffective. Each of the three options provided in UCC 2-318 states that a seller may not exclude or modify the operation of this section.

Answer (b) is incorrect because the UCC allows sellers to disclaim the warranty of title (UCC 2-312). Answer (c) is incorrect because the UCC permits such a clause. Answer (d) is incorrect because Article 9 permits security interests in after-acquired property.

12.9 Product Liability

110. Manufacturer produced a defective product and sold it to Wholesaler who in turn sold it to Retailer. Consumer then purchased the product and used it without alteration for the ordinary purposes for which it was intended. During such use, Consumer's Spouse and Innocent Bystander received personal injuries. In an action based on

a. Negligence, Spouse and Innocent Bystander cannot recover because of lack of privity.

b. Strict liability, Innocent Bystander can recover despite lack of privity.

c. Warranty, Spouse can recover against Retailer but not Wholesaler because of the horizontal privity rule.

d. Tort, vertical privity protects Manufacturer from liability to Spouse but not Consumer.

The correct answer is (b). *(Publisher)*

REQUIRED: The consequence of privity in a product liability action.

DISCUSSION: In actions based on tort (negligence) and strict liability, privity of contract need not be established. In other words, an injured party is deemed to be in vertical privity even with a remote seller in the chain of distribution. Also, horizontal privity is deemed to extend to consumers, users, and innocent bystanders; that is, privity with the seller is in effect extended horizontally from the buyer to other parties. Thus, Manufacturer is potentially liable to a party outside the chain of distribution with whom Wholesaler and Retailer have not dealt.

Answers (a) and (d) are incorrect because plaintiff need not establish privity in a negligence (tort) action. Answer (c) is incorrect because under Alternative A of UCC 2-318, a member of the family or household or a guest in the home of the buyer may recover against the seller.

111. A manufacturer who fails to exercise due care in the manufacture or handling of a product may be held liable for negligence. A defendant manufacturer will prevail, however, when the

a. Negligence was in the design of the product.

b. Product was assembled improperly.

c. Product was designed to be safe for proper use but not for an unforeseeable improper use.

d. Conduct complained of was merely a failure to warn.

The correct answer is (c). *(Publisher)*

REQUIRED: The manufacturer's defense to a negligence action.

DISCUSSION: A manufacturer is negligent if its breach of a legal duty to exercise reasonable care proximately caused injury to the plaintiff. A manufacturer may be liable when the product is unsafe as a result of negligence in its manufacture. Liability will also be found when the design of the product makes it unreasonably dangerous for the uses for which it is manufactured even though all reasonable care is taken in manufacture, assembly, testing, and inspection. The manufacturer also has a duty to use reasonable care to warn when the product is known to be dangerous for the use for which it is supplied and there is no reason to believe that users will be aware of the danger. However, no liability arises when a product is designed to be reasonably safe for proper and foreseeable improper uses but not for unforeseeable improper uses.

Answers (a), (b), and (d) are incorrect because each constitutes a breach of the duty to use reasonable care.

112. A retailer of a defective product that causes injury to the plaintiff will most likely prevail in an action based on negligence when the

a. Defect was in the product's manufacture although the defendant represented the product as its own.

b. Retailer merely failed to inspect because inspection is the duty of the manufacturer.

c. Retailer merely failed to warn of the danger.

d. Fault was in the design or construction of the product.

The correct answer is (d). *(Publisher)*

REQUIRED: The circumstance in which a retailer is most likely to prevail in a negligence action.

DISCUSSION: Negligence is usually a poor theory on which to base recovery from a retailer. The design and manufacture of the product are seldom under the retailer's control, and the retailer may have no more knowledge of the product than the buyer, especially when it is packaged in a sealed container.

Answer (a) is incorrect because the retailer is subject to the same standards as a manufacturer when it holds the product out as its own. Answers (b) and (c) are incorrect because whereas a retailer usually has no duty to inspect or warn, circumstances may arise that alert the retailer to a possible defect and create a duty to inspect and/or warn. For example, a failure of refrigeration may create a duty on the part of a grocer to inspect and warn about its perishables.

113. To establish a cause of action based upon strict liability in tort for personal injuries resulting from the use of a defective product, one of the elements the plaintiff must prove is that the seller (defendant)

a. Was engaged in the business of selling the product.

b. Failed to exercise due care.

c. Defectively designed the product.

d. Was in privity of contract with the plaintiff.

The correct answer is (a). *(CPA 1187 L-38)*

REQUIRED: The element a plaintiff must prove in a strict liability case.

DISCUSSION: In a strict liability suit against a seller of a product, a plaintiff who has suffered physical harm or property damage must prove that the product was defective, the defect rendered it unreasonably dangerous, the unreasonably dangerous condition of the product caused the harm or damage, the seller was engaged in the business of selling the particular product, and the product reached the user or consumer without substantial change from the condition in which it was sold (Restatement of Torts, Second).

Answers (b) and (c) are incorrect because in an action based on strict liability, plaintiff need not prove any defendant was at fault. Answer (d) is incorrect because an ultimate user or consumer may bring an action based on strict liability even though (s)he was not in privity with the defendant seller.

114. Which of the following factors is least important in determining whether a manufacturer is strictly liable in tort for a defective product?

a. The negligence of the manufacturer.

b. The contributory negligence of the plaintiff.

c. Modifications to the product by the wholesaler.

d. Whether the product caused injuries.

The correct answer is (a). *(CPA 1189 L-45)*

REQUIRED: The least important factor in determining whether a manufacturer is strictly liable in tort.

DISCUSSION: The advantage of an action based on strict liability in tort is that the plaintiff need not show that the manufacturer was negligent. Thus, no proof is required that a breach of a legal duty to exercise reasonable care proximately caused the plaintiff's injury. Rather, in a strict liability suit against a seller of a product, a plaintiff who has suffered physical harm or property damage must prove that the product was defective, the defect rendered it unreasonably dangerous, the unreasonably dangerous condition of the product caused the harm or damage, the seller was engaged in the business of selling the particular product, and the product reached the user or consumer without substantial change from the condition in which it was sold.

Answer (b) is incorrect because whether the plaintiff acted reasonably to protect him/herself may be a factor in the outcome of the suit. Thus, contributory negligence has been accepted as an absolute defense in at least a few states, and many states have adopted comparative fault or comparative negligence rules. Answer (c) is incorrect because substantial alteration of the product after its sale by the manufacturer may be a defense if the change caused the plaintiff's injury. Answer (d) is incorrect because plaintiff must prove that physical harm was caused to the ultimate user or consumer or to his/her property as a result of a defective condition of the product that made it unreasonably dangerous.

115. Storekeeper sells new power saws and often rebuilds and sells old power saws. Purchaser informed Storekeeper that she wanted to buy a reconditioned circular saw for use in her business. The reconditioned saw had been manufactured by Power Saw Company. The week after the saw was purchased, Employee, who works for Purchaser, was injured while cutting plywood when the shaft holding the saw blade came loose after a bearing gave way. If Employee asserts a claim based on strict liability in tort against Power Saw, Employee will probably

a. Recover if the shaft that came loose was a part of the saw when it was new.

b. Recover because Power Saw was in the business of manufacturing dangerous machines.

c. Not recover because Employee was not the buyer of the power saw.

d. Not recover because the saw had been rebuilt by Storekeeper.

The correct answer is (d). *(MBE Part I-124)*

REQUIRED: The outcome of a suit by an injured employee whose employer purchased defective reconditioned goods.

DISCUSSION: If Employee asserts a claim based on strict liability in tort, he will probably not recover because the saw did not reach the user in substantially the same condition as when it was manufactured. Power Saw Company should not be held strictly liable for selling a product containing a defect that made it unreasonably dangerous if the defect may have occurred later.

Answer (a) is incorrect because the substantial change in the saw (reconditioning or rebuilding) eliminates a necessary condition for strict liability. Answer (b) is incorrect because strict liability is based on the existence of a defect that makes a product unreasonably dangerous. Power Saw will not be held absolutely liable for every injury caused by its machines. Answer (c) is incorrect because strict liability may be asserted by a plaintiff who is a user, consumer, or foreseeable bystander.

116. Julia rented a new automobile from Mack's Auto Leasing Service. While operating the vehicle in a lawful manner and wearing her shoulder harness, Julia was injured when a defective steering mechanism caused her to lose control. In a strict liability in tort suit, Julia

a. Must show that the automobile was inherently dangerous.

b. May be able to recover in some states even though no sale was made.

c. Need not establish causation.

d. May not sue the manufacturer.

The correct answer is (b). *(Publisher)*

REQUIRED: The true statement about the elements of the plaintiff's case in a product liability action.

DISCUSSION: Ordinarily, a product liability case involves a suit by an injured plaintiff against some seller in the chain of distribution, most often the manufacturer. Some courts, however, have extended the doctrine to lessors and bailors of defective goods. They reason that the danger to the public from defectively maintained motor vehicles placed on the highways by lessors is substantially the same as the danger from defective manufacture by a seller or manufacturer.

Answer (a) is incorrect because Julia must show that the product was unreasonably (not inherently) dangerous. Answer (c) is incorrect because the plaintiff must establish a causal connection between her injuries and the defect. Answer (d) is incorrect because Julia may sue the manufacturer even though no privity of contract is present. The manufacturer will have a defense, however, if the product had been substantially changed by the time it reached the consumer's hands or if it had been misused or abused.

CHAPTER THIRTEEN
COMMERCIAL PAPER AND DOCUMENTS

The first six modules of this chapter deal with negotiable instruments. The answer explanations are based almost entirely on Article 3 of the Uniform Commercial Code (UCC). However, the distinction between negotiable instruments and "Bank Transactions" (which are based on Article 4 of the UCC) is not always clear, so there are also citations to Article 4 in the first six modules and some citations to Article 3 in "Bank Transactions." The answer explanations to "Letters of Credit" are based on Article 5 of the UCC. Article 7 of the UCC is the source of the explanations in "Documents of Title." The answer explanations to Electronic Fund Transfers are based on the Electronic Funds Transfer Act of 1978 (EFTA).

13.1 Nature of Negotiable Instruments

1. Business people routinely use many kinds of commercial documents daily. Which of the following statements is incorrect?

a. Warehouse receipts, bills of lading, certificates of title, corporate stock certificates, and similar documents perform the important business function of providing evidence of ownership or indebtedness.

b. Notes, drafts, checks, and certificates of deposit are a class of commercial documents called commercial paper or negotiable instruments. They are used primarily as a substitute for money or as a means of extending credit.

c. Centuries ago, the law merchant, the medieval body of law governing business dealings, established rules regulating the issuance of negotiable instruments or commercial paper. Today, these rules are codified without substantial change as Article 3 of the UCC.

d. The main benefit that a purchaser of commercial paper receives is the same right to payment held by the transferor.

The correct answer is (d). *(Publisher)*

REQUIRED: The false statement about commercial documents routinely used in the course of business.

DISCUSSION: Commercial paper has evolved as a substitute for money, and includes such documents as checks, drafts, promissory notes, and certificates of deposit. Under ordinary contract law, the negotiation of such a document results in the purchaser's receipt of the same rights in the instrument as the transferor. A third person who accepts commercial paper in negotiable form and qualifies as a holder in due course, however, can obtain rights superior to those of the transferor. A holder in due course is subject only to real defenses of the obligor (fraud in the execution, forgeries and unauthorized signatures, defenses rendering a contract void, bankruptcy discharges, other discharges of which the holder knew or should have known, statutes of limitations, and material alterations). Other holders may be subject to personal defenses as well (lack or failure of consideration, fraud in the inducement, ordinary contract defenses, defenses rendering a contract voidable, violation of a restrictive endorsement, nonbankruptcy discharges of which the holder has received no notice, acquisition of lost or stolen bearer paper, unauthorized completions, and some real defenses despite the negligence of the party attempting defense).

Answers (a), (b), and (c) are incorrect because they are true statements about commercial documents.

2. Commercial paper is payable in money and negotiable. The best description of commercial paper is that it is

a. Both a contract and a kind of property.

b. A simple contract.

c. A security.

d. An assignment.

The correct answer is (a). *(Publisher)*

REQUIRED: The best description of commercial paper.

DISCUSSION: Commercial paper creates rights and duties that could not be created by a simple contract. Because transferees have rights against their immediate transferors and the original issuers that reduce the risk of noncollection, their position is more favorable than assignees of ordinary contract rights. Thus, commercial paper serves both as a superior means of obtaining credit (e.g., promissory notes) and as a relatively safe substitute for currency (e.g., checks). Accordingly, property law as well as most contract principles apply to commercial paper.

Answer (b) is incorrect because commercial paper is a type of formal contract since the form of the document is vital. Answer (c) is incorrect because a security is generally considered a document of an ownership interest in a business venture, while commercial paper is a substitute for money. Answer (d) is incorrect because an assignment is a transfer of a right from one person to another. The term is too broad to be an adequate description of commercial paper.

3. Which of the following negotiable instruments is subject to the provisions of the UCC Article on Commercial Paper?

a. Bearer bond containing a maturity date of December 1, 1987.

b. Bill of lading payable to order.

c. Installment note payable on the first day of each month.

d. Warehouse receipt.

The correct answer is (c). *(CPA 1187 L-45)*

REQUIRED: The negotiable instrument subject to the UCC provisions on commercial paper.

DISCUSSION: Article 3 of the UCC regulates commercial paper. This article specifically lists four kinds of commercial paper: checks, drafts, promissory notes, and certificates of deposit. An installment note falls within Article 3 and is subject to its provisions.

Answers (a), (b), and (d) are incorrect because while they may be negotiable, they do not meet the statutory definition of commercial paper.

4. There are several legally significant differences between a negotiable instrument and a contract right, and the transfer of each. Which of the following statements is correct?

a. A negotiable instrument is deemed prima facie to have been issued for consideration whereas a contract is not.

b. The transferee of a negotiable instrument and the assignee of a contract right take free of most defenses.

c. Neither can be transferred without a signed writing or by a delivery.

d. The Statute of Frauds rules apply to both.

The correct answer is (a). *(CPA 1178 L-49)*

REQUIRED: The correct statement comparing negotiable instruments and contract rights.

DISCUSSION: A negotiable instrument is presumed to have been issued for consideration, but no such assumption is made regarding a contract. One must prove consideration to enforce a contract right, but not a negotiable instrument.

Answer (b) is incorrect because the transferee of a negotiable instrument (who is not a holder in due course) and the assignee of a contract right both take subject to all defenses the third party has against the assignor. Answer (c) is incorrect because a contract right can be transferred orally and without delivery. A negotiable instrument requires an endorsement and delivery if it is order paper or delivery alone if it is bearer paper in order to remain negotiable. Answer (d) is incorrect because the Statute of Frauds applies only to certain contracts, not to all. Negotiable instruments do need to be in writing to be negotiable.

5. Anton promised to pay Beta $10,000 in return for an automobile. Accordingly, Anton executed a contract and delivered it to Beta. Beta then transferred the contract to Carl for value. When Beta failed to perform, Anton refused to pay. If Carl sues Anton,

a. Carl will win because Carl steps into the shoes of the assignor.

b. Anton will win because the contract is not transferable.

c. Anton will win even if the contract is instead a negotiable instrument.

d. Carl will win if the contract is instead a negotiable instrument and the requirements of Article 3 of the UCC are complied with.

The correct answer is (d). *(Publisher)*

REQUIRED: The difference in effect between a contract right and a negotiable instrument.

DISCUSSION: Most contract rights are assignable, and an assignee takes subject to all defenses assertible against his/her assignor. But the taker of a negotiable instrument who conforms to the holder in due course rules of Article 3 of the UCC is not subject to such personal defenses as failure of consideration. Thus, certain good faith transferees for value of negotiable instruments are protected from the effects of disputes between the original contracting parties.

Answer (a) is incorrect because although Carl does step into the shoes of the assignor, Anton may assert the same defenses against both the assignor (Beta) and the assignee (Carl) of a contract. Answer (b) is incorrect because although Anton may win, a right to receive money is transferable. Answer (c) is incorrect because Carl may win if the contract is a negotiable instrument.

6. Although the scope of the Uniform Commercial Code is broad with respect to inclusion of instruments within the definition of commercial paper, it excludes certain instruments from its coverage. Which of the following is not covered by Article 3?

a. A promissory note payable 30 days after presentment for payment.

b. A draft that is an order to pay.

c. A negotiable certificate of deposit issued by a bank.

d. An investment security payable to bearer.

The correct answer is (d). *(CPA 582 L-37)*

REQUIRED: The instrument that is not commercial paper under Article 3 of the UCC.

DISCUSSION: Article 3 of the UCC on Commercial Paper does not apply to money, documents of title, or investment securities (UCC 3-103). Article 8 of the UCC governs investment securities.

Answers (a), (b), and (c) are incorrect because each is a form of negotiable instrument governed by Article 3 of the UCC. A promissory note is a promise by one party to pay another. A draft (e.g., a check) is an order by one person directing another to pay a third person. A certificate of deposit is a written acknowledgment by a bank of receipt of money with an engagement to repay.

7. If an instrument does not meet one of the requirements of negotiability,

a. It will usually be transferable.

b. It will be worthless.

c. It will not be assignable.

d. An innocent transferee will nevertheless take free of the issuer's personal defenses.

The correct answer is (a). *(Publisher)*

REQUIRED: The effect of nonnegotiability of an instrument.

DISCUSSION: If one of the elements of negotiability is not present, innocent transferees will not receive the special protections of the law of commercial paper but will be subject to the general law of assignment of contracts. Nevertheless, the contract right embodied in the nonnegotiable instrument will usually be transferable because most contract rights, especially the right to receive money, are assignable. But the assignee will take no better right than that held by his/her assignor.

Answer (b) is incorrect because a contract right may be quite valuable even though not evidenced by a negotiable instrument. Answer (c) is incorrect because contract rights are generally assignable. Answer (d) is incorrect because a transferee of a nonnegotiable instrument takes subject to all defenses of the obligor.

13.2 Types of Negotiable Instruments and Parties

Questions 8 and 9 relate to the following instrument:

> January 25, 1990
>
> I promise to pay to the order of John Green $2,000 plus 11% interest from the above date.
>
> *Walt Johnson*
> Walt Johnson

8. The instrument is a

a. Promissory note.

b. Draft.

c. Certificate of deposit.

d. Check.

The correct answer is (a). *(Publisher)*

REQUIRED: The term identifying the instrument in the example instrument.

DISCUSSION: The instrument is a promissory note because it is a two-party instrument in which the maker (Walt Johnson) promises to pay a sum certain in money to the payee (John Green).

Answer (b) is incorrect because a draft is a three-party instrument in which one person orders a second person to pay a third person. Answer (c) is incorrect because a certificate of deposit is a written acknowledgment by a bank of receipt of money with a promise to repay. Answer (d) is incorrect because a check is a type of draft payable on demand in which a bank is ordered to make the payment.

9. Walt Johnson is the

a. Acceptor.

b. Maker.

c. Drawer.

d. Holder.

The correct answer is (b). *(Publisher)*

REQUIRED: The term identifying the person who makes the promise to pay a note.

DISCUSSION: The instrument in the above facts is a note. The person who promises to pay a note is called a maker.

Answer (a) is incorrect because an acceptor is the person who accepts and agrees to pay a draft (usually the drawee). Answer (c) is incorrect because a drawer is the person who orders the payment on a draft. Answer (d) is incorrect because a holder is a person who has taken an instrument by negotiation. (Negotiation is a transfer by proper means; see Module 13.4.) In this case, John Green is probably the holder of the note unless he has transferred it.

10. An instrument complies with the requirements for negotiability contained in the UCC Article on Commercial Paper. The instrument contains language expressly acknowledging the receipt of $40,000 by Mint Bank and an agreement to repay principal with interest at 11% six months from date. The instrument is

a. A banker's acceptance.

b. A banker's draft.

c. A negotiable certificate of deposit.

d. Nonnegotiable because of the additional language.

The correct answer is (c). *(CPA 1185 L-36)*

REQUIRED: The term for a bank's acknowledgment of receipt of money with an agreement to repay.

DISCUSSION: A certificate of deposit (CD) is an acknowledgment by a bank of receipt of money with an engagement to repay it. The bank is the maker and the payee is the depositor. Although a CD is essentially a note, it is separately classified because certain laws apply to CDs but not to other notes.

Answer (a) is incorrect because an acceptance is an undertaking to pay a draft. Answer (b) is incorrect because a bank draft is a check drawn by one bank on another bank in which it has deposited money. Answer (d) is incorrect because the additional language is consistent with negotiability. A sum certain in money is to be paid at a definite time.

Questions 11 and 12 are based on the following instrument:

To: Sussex National Bank
Suffolk, N.Y.

October 15, 1990

Pay to the order of Tom Gold $2,000.00
Two Thousand and xx/100 Dollars
on November 1, 1990

Lester Davis
Lester Davis

11. The instrument is

a. A check.

b. A promissory note.

c. A draft.

d. Payable on demand.

The correct answer is (c). *(Publisher)*

REQUIRED: The term that identifies the example instrument.

DISCUSSION: A draft is a three-party instrument in which one person (the drawer) orders a second person (the drawee) to pay a third person (the payee). With this instrument, Lester Davis is ordering Sussex National Bank to pay Tom Gold.

Answer (a) is incorrect because a check is a type of draft in which a bank is ordered to make the payment. Answer (b) is incorrect because a promissory note is a two-party instrument in which one person promises to pay another person. Answer (d) is incorrect because the draft is payable on November 1, 1990, not on demand. Payable on demand gives the holder of the instrument the right to demand payment at any time.

12. If the instrument did not direct Sussex National Bank to pay, but was payable on demand at a bank in another state, it would be

a. A check.

b. A foreign draft.

c. A collateral note.

d. Illegal.

The correct answer is (a). *(Publisher)*

REQUIRED: The term that identifies an instrument payable at a bank in another state.

DISCUSSION: A three-party instrument in which one person directs a bank to pay a third person on demand is a type of draft called a check. The location of the bank is irrelevant.

Answer (b) is incorrect because even though the check is a type of draft, it is not foreign since it is payable at a bank in the United States. Answer (c) is incorrect because a collateral note is a promissory note which is secured by collateral; i.e., the holder has a security interest in some property of the maker. Answer (d) is incorrect because an instrument payable on demand at a bank (a check) located in another state is legal.

13. A company has in its possession the following instrument:

> $500.00 Dayton, Ohio October 2, 1990
>
> Sixty days after date I promise to pay to the order of Cash
>
> Five hundred Dollars
>
> at Miami, Florida
>
> Value received with interest at the rate of nine percent per annum.
> This instrument is secured by a conditional sales contract.
>
> No. 11 Due December 1, 1990 *Craig Burke*
> Craig Burke

This instrument is

a. Not negotiable until December 1, 1990.

b. A negotiable bearer note.

c. A negotiable time draft.

d. A nonnegotiable note because it states that it is secured by a conditional sales contract.

The correct answer is (b). *(CPA 1187 L-48)*

REQUIRED: The type of instrument evidenced by the specified commercial document.

DISCUSSION: The instrument is a signed writing unconditionally promising to pay a sum certain in money at a certain time to the bearer. It thus meets all of the requirements of negotiability. It is a two-party instrument with a maker and a payee, so it is a promissory note. It is a bearer note because it is payable to the order of cash.

Answer (a) is incorrect because negotiability is not altered by an instrument's not being payable until some future date. Answer (c) is incorrect because a draft is a three-party instrument involving a drawer, drawee, and payee. Answer (d) is incorrect because the existence of security does not condition the obligation to pay or affect the note's negotiability.

14.

> October 5, 1990
>
> To: Henry Futterman Suppliers
> 281 Cascade Boulevard
> Spokane, WA 99208
>
> $950.00
>
> Pay to the order of Alex & Co.
> Nine hundred fifty and 00/100 dollars
> one month after acceptance.
>
> Alex & Co.
>
> By *Charles Alex*
> Managing Partner
>
> Alex & Co.
> 264 Liberty Avenue
> Philadelphia, PA 19117
>
> Accepted by: *Laura Futterman, Treasurer*
> Henry Futterman Suppliers
>
> Date: October 15, 1990

The above instrument is

a. Nonnegotiable because the payee is also the drawer.

b. A time promissory note.

c. A trade acceptance imposing primary liability upon Henry Futterman Suppliers after acceptance.

d. A negotiable investment security under the Uniform Commercial Code.

The correct answer is (c). *(CPA 1182 L-37)*

REQUIRED: The true statement about the instrument.

DISCUSSION: A trade acceptance is a type of draft in which the seller directs the buyer (the drawee) to pay the seller. Thus, the seller is both drawer and payee. The buyer accepts by writing the word "accepted", the date, and his/her signature on the face of the instrument. The buyer then has primary liability to pay the amount indicated on the draft to the seller.

Answer (a) is incorrect because negotiability does not require the drawer and payee to be different. The instrument is still treated as a draft even though two of the parties are the same. Answer (b) is incorrect because a draft is a three-party instrument containing an order. A note is a two-party instrument containing a promise. Answer (d) is incorrect because a security is commonly recognized as a medium for investment, and evidence of some share, participation, or other interest in property or an enterprise or evidence an obligation of the issuer (UCC 8-102). It does not include individual drafts.

15. A trade acceptance usually

a. Is an order to deliver goods to a named person.

b. Provides that the drawer is also the payee.

c. Is not regarded as commercial paper under the UCC.

d. Must be made payable "to the order of" a named person.

The correct answer is (b). *(CPA 589 L-59)*

REQUIRED: The correct statement about a trade acceptance.

DISCUSSION: A trade acceptance is a special form of commercial paper known as a time draft used by sellers as a way to extend credit to buyers of their goods. The seller draws a draft ordering the buyer to pay the seller at some time in the future. The seller is thus both drawer and payee of a trade acceptance.

Answer (a) is incorrect because a trade acceptance is a form of commercial paper and must be payable in money. Answer (c) is incorrect because trade acceptances are a type of draft, and as such are recognized as commercial paper under the UCC. Answer (d) is incorrect because a trade acceptance may be payable to order or to bearer.

16. For which of the following negotiable instruments is a bank not an acceptor?

a. Cashier's check.

b. Certified check.

c. Certificate of deposit.

d. Bank acceptance.

The correct answer is (c). *(CPA 1189 L-41)*

REQUIRED: The negotiable instrument for which a bank is not an acceptor.

DISCUSSION: A certificate of deposit is a type of note in which a bank acknowledges receipt of money and promises to repay the money with interest in the future. As a note, a certificate of deposit is only a two-party instrument and does not require acceptance by a drawee.

Answers (a), (b), and (d) are incorrect because each is a three-party instrument (a draft) on which a drawee bank must act as acceptor.

17. Mary issued an instrument in which she directed the Doe State Bank to pay to the order of Rhonda a certain sum of money thirty days after sight. The instrument was presented and Doe gave its signed undertaking to pay on the due date. Doe State Bank is

a. The drawer.

b. The payee and the maker.

c. Both the drawee and the acceptor.

d. Both the drawer and the acceptor.

The correct answer is (c). *(Publisher)*

REQUIRED: The term(s) for the bank on which a draft is drawn.

DISCUSSION: The instrument is a draft because it contains an order by the drawer (Mary) to a drawee (Doe) to pay money to a payee (Rhonda). A person, usually a drawee, who agrees to pay the draft is an acceptor. Generally, this agreement is signified by writing "accepted" on the instrument along with the date and a signature. Doe is therefore a drawee and an acceptor.

Answers (a) and (d) are incorrect because Mary is the drawer. Answer (b) is incorrect because the maker is the person who issues a note. The payee is the person who is to be paid.

18. Harriet issued a promissory note in which she promised to pay a sum certain in money to Bee. Elly signed her name to the instrument for the purpose of lending her name to Harriet. Poe also signed the instrument and added words indicating that, if it were not paid when due, she would pay it without resort by the holder to any other party. Which of the following is true?

a. Bee is a guarantor.

b. Harriet is an endorser.

c. Poe is an acceptor.

d. Elly is an accommodation party.

The correct answer is (d). *(Publisher)*

REQUIRED: The correct identification of a party to an instrument.

DISCUSSION: An accommodation party is one who signs the instrument for the purpose of lending his/her name to another party to it (UCC 3-415). When, as here, the party has signed in the capacity of a maker, the liability will be that of a maker (primary liability).

Answer (a) is incorrect because Bee is a payee. Answer (b) is incorrect because Harriet is a maker. Answer (c) is incorrect because Poe is a guarantor.

13.3 Negotiability

19.

$700.00	Provo, Utah	June 1, 1990
Thirty days after date I promise to pay to the order of		
	Cash	
	Seven hundred	Dollars
at	Boise, Idaho	
Value received with interest at the rate of 10% per annum.		
This instrument is secured by a conditional sales contract.		
No. 20	Due July 1, 1990	Len Blanc

This instrument is

a. A negotiable time draft.

b. A nonnegotiable note since it states that it is secured by a conditional sales contract.

c. Not negotiable until July 1, 1990.

d. A negotiable bearer note.

The correct answer is (d). *(CPA 584 L-39)*

REQUIRED: The nature and negotiability of the instrument.

DISCUSSION: The instrument is a note because it contains a promise by its issuer to pay another person. It is negotiable because it is written and signed by the maker, contains an unconditional promise to pay a sum certain in money, is payable at a definite time, and is payable to the order of bearer (UCC 3-104). The instrument is a bearer note because it is payable to the order of cash (UCC 3-111).

Answer (a) is incorrect because a draft is a three-party (drawer, drawee, payee) instrument containing an order. Answer (b) is incorrect because an instrument is not conditional just because it states that it is secured. This is merely extra information. Answer (c) is incorrect because payment is due at a definite time in the future, so the note is negotiable.

20.

July 2, 1990

McHugh Wholesaler, Inc.
Pullman, Washington

Pay to the order of Luft Manufacturing, Inc., one thousand seven hundred dollars ($1,700) three months after acceptance.

Peter Crandall, President
Peter Crandall, President
Luft Manufacturing, Inc.

Accepted July 12, 1990
McHugh Wholesalers, Inc.

By Charles Towne, President

This instrument

a. Would be treated as a promissory note because the drawee is not a bank.

b. Is a negotiable draft.

c. Is not negotiable under Article 3 (commercial paper) of the Uniform Commercial Code, although it may be negotiable under another Article.

d. Is not negotiable because the drawer and the payee are the same person.

The correct answer is (b). *(CPA 1181 L-35)*

REQUIRED: The correct statement describing the example instrument.

DISCUSSION: The instrument is a draft because it is an order by one person (Luft) directing another (McHugh) to pay a third person (Luft). That the third party is the same as the first party is irrelevant. It is negotiable because all of the requirements of negotiability are met. The instrument is written, is signed by the drawer, contains an unconditional order to pay a definite amount of money at a definite time, is payable to order, and contains no other promises or obligations (UCC 3-104).

Answer (a) is incorrect because a note is a two-party instrument in which one person promises to pay another. Answer (c) is incorrect because the draft is negotiable under Article 3 of the UCC, the sole authority concerning negotiability of instruments. Answer (d) is incorrect because the drawer and the payee may be the same person. This is a means of documenting a third person's (McHugh's) promise to pay a debt.

21. The requirements for an instrument to qualify as negotiable commercial paper

a. May be waived by a separate agreement signed by the original parties to the instrument as long as the variations are fair and voluntarily agreed upon.

b. Prohibit substitutions or variances from the exact language of the UCC.

c. May be satisfied by the insertion of a clause in the instrument indicating that the instrument is negotiable.

d. Must be satisfied at least in principle, although the exact language set forth in the UCC may be varied.

The correct answer is (d). *(CPA 1185 L-38)*

REQUIRED: The true statement about the requirements of negotiability.

DISCUSSION: Under the UCC, the language needed to satisfy the negotiability requirements may vary considerably. For example, a promise or order to pay must be stated, but the instrument may be negotiable even though neither the word "promise" nor the word "order" appears on its face. An instrument must also be payable on demand or at a stated time, but an instrument is payable on demand when no time for payment is stated (UCC 3-108). Still another requirement is that the instrument be payable to order or to bearer, yet this exact language may be omitted. For instance, an instrument payable to cash is deemed to be payable to bearer (UCC 3-111).

Answer (a) is incorrect because whether an instrument is negotiable usually has little significance for the original parties because they are in privity of contract. The original parties have no power to waive requirements intended to protect transferees. Answer (b) is incorrect because exact language is not required. Answer (c) is incorrect because a statement that an instrument is negotiable has no effect. The requirements must be met.

22. Regarding the requirements for a given instrument to qualify as negotiable under the UCC,

a. It is impossible to make an instrument negotiable unless the requirements for negotiability under Article 3 (Commercial Paper) are met.

b. The requirements for qualifying as negotiable commercial paper may be satisfied by a statement of the maker or drawer that clearly manifests an intent that the instrument be treated as a negotiable instrument.

c. The maker is prevented from indicating the transaction out of which the instrument arose or the account to be charged without rendering the instrument nonnegotiable.

d. The requirements do not preclude an instrument from qualifying as negotiable commercial paper despite doubt as to whether it is a draft or a note.

The correct answer is (d). *(CPA 586 L-27)*

REQUIRED: The correct statement concerning the UCC requirements for negotiability.

DISCUSSION: When ambiguities result in doubt as to whether an instrument is a draft or a note, the holder of the instrument may treat it as either. Such ambiguities would not defeat the instrument's negotiability as commercial paper.

Answer (a) is incorrect because even though an instrument may not be negotiable as commercial paper, it may be negotiable as an investment security or as a document of title, which are covered in separate articles of the UCC. Answer (b) is incorrect because although a statement that the maker or drawer intends an instrument to become negotiable can be used to satisfy the requirements regarding an incomplete instrument, a statement of intent cannot be used to make a clearly nonnegotiable instrument negotiable. Answer (c) is incorrect because a negotiable instrument may include extraneous information on its face, provided that such information does not restrict or place conditions on the payment of the instrument. Reference to an account to be charged does not restrict the promise to pay.

23. Which of the following provisions will make an otherwise negotiable note nonnegotiable?

a. Time for payment is a date certain but can be extended by the maker for an unstated period of time.

b. The interest rate is variable.

c. The note is payable in cash or crops.

d. All of the above.

The correct answer is (d). *(E. Rubert)*

REQUIRED: The provision that defeats the negotiability of commercial paper.

DISCUSSION: The UCC provides that a negotiable instrument must be signed by the maker or drawer, contain an unconditional promise or order to pay a sum certain in money on demand or at a definite time, and be payable to order or to bearer. A payment date subject to unlimited extension at the option of the maker is essentially indefinite, and renders an instrument nonnegotiable. Variable interest rates have recently been held by the courts to violate the "sum certain" requirement for negotiability. Notes payable in cash or crops do not satisfy the negotiability requirement for instruments to be payable in money, which is defined as the currency of a domestic or foreign government.

Answer (a) is incorrect because an extension at the maker's option defeats negotiability unless it is to a further definite time (UCC 3-109). Answer (b) is incorrect because courts have recently held that variable rate notes are not negotiable. Answer (c) is incorrect because to be negotiable an instrument must be payable in money only.

24. To be negotiable, an instrument must be written and signed. Which of the following is correct?

a. A drawee's signature is required for the negotiability of a draft.

b. A signature may be any symbol intended by a party to authenticate a writing.

c. A signature must be handwritten.

d. A signature must be placed at the end of the instrument.

The correct answer is (b). *(Publisher)*

REQUIRED: The true statement about the signature requirement.

DISCUSSION: Under UCC 1-201, "signed includes any symbol executed or adopted by a party with present intention to authenticate a writing." Under UCC 3-401, "A signature is made by use of any name, including any trade or assumed name, upon an instrument, or by any word or mark used in lieu of a written signature."

Answer (a) is incorrect because only the drawer's signature is required. Answer (c) is incorrect because a signature may be stamped, printed, typed, or produced by some other mechanical method. Answer (d) is incorrect because the signature may appear almost anywhere, but placement at the end is usual and makes it clear who issued the instrument.

25. Abe Booth is president of ABC Company. He has signed a promissory note on behalf of the corporation. On which signature below will Abe Booth not be personally liable?

a. Abe Booth.

b. ABC Company
Abe Booth.

c. ABC Company
By Abe Booth
Its President.

d. ABC Company, Abe Booth.

The correct answer is (c). *(Publisher)*

REQUIRED: The signature of an agent that does not result in personal liability on a negotiable instrument.

DISCUSSION: An agent who signs his/her own name to a negotiable instrument is personally liable unless both the identity of the principal and the representative capacity are indicated on the face of the instrument (UCC 3-403). By naming the company, stating his title, and using the word "by," Booth avoids personal liability.

Answer (a) is incorrect because Booth has signed as the maker as far as third parties are concerned. There is no indication that he signed for ABC Company. Answers (b) and (d) are incorrect because, again, Booth has not indicated that he has signed in a representative capacity. Each signature makes it appear that both ABC Company and Abe Booth are makers.

26. An instrument will be negotiable only if it contains a promise or order to pay. Accordingly, an instrument is negotiable if it

a. Authorizes payment to a named person.

b. Acknowledges an obligation.

c. Omits the word "promise" but states an undertaking to pay.

d. Omits the word "order" but states a request to pay.

The correct answer is (c). *(Publisher)*

REQUIRED: The language satisfying the promise or order to pay requirement.

DISCUSSION: Under UCC 3-102, "A promise is an undertaking to pay and must be more than an acknowledgment of an obligation." The word "promise" need not be used, however.

Answers (a) and (d) are incorrect because under UCC 3-102, an order is a direction to pay and must be more than an authorization or request. Answer (b) is incorrect because an acknowledgment (IOU $100) is not a promise to pay.

27. A secured promissory note would be nonnegotiable if it provided that

a. Additional collateral must be tendered if there is a decline in market value of the original collateral.

b. Upon default, the maker waives a trial by jury.

c. The maker is entitled to a 5% discount if the note is prepaid.

d. It is subject to the terms of the mortgage given by the maker to the payee.

The correct answer is (d). *(CPA 1188 L-38)*

REQUIRED: The condition defeating the negotiability of a secured promissory note.

DISCUSSION: A negotiable instrument must include an unconditional promise or order to pay. When a promise or order is subject to the provisions of another agreement, it is conditional. A conditional instrument is nonnegotiable because the rights of a holder cannot be ascertained with reasonable certainty from the face of it (UCC 3-105). A note that is subject to the terms of a mortgage given by the maker to the payee violates this requirement and is rendered nonnegotiable.

Answer (a) is incorrect because negotiable instruments are allowed to include a promise to maintain or protect the collateral. Answer (b) is incorrect because the waiver of a benefit for the advantage or protection of the obligor does not affect negotiability. Answer (c) is incorrect because the requirement of a sum certain in money does not preclude a provision for specified prepayment discounts.

28. Anderson agreed to purchase Parker's real property. Anderson's purchase was dependent upon his being able to sell certain real property that he owned. Anderson gave Parker an instrument for the purchase price. Assuming the instrument is otherwise negotiable, which of the statements below, written on the face of the instrument, will render it nonnegotiable?

a. A statement that Parker's cashing or endorsing the instrument is full satisfaction of Anderson's obligation.

b. A statement that payment of the instrument is contingent upon Anderson's sale of his real property.

c. A statement that the instrument is secured by a first mortgage on Parker's property and that, upon default, the entire amount of the instrument is due.

d. A statement that the instrument is subject to the usual implied and constructive conditions applicable to such transactions.

The correct answer is (b). *(CPA 1180 L-46)*

REQUIRED: The statement rendering an instrument nonnegotiable.

DISCUSSION: A statement that payment is contingent upon sale of Anderson's real property imposes a condition which renders the instrument nonnegotiable because it no longer contains an unconditional promise to pay (UCC 3-105).

Answer (a) is incorrect because a statement acknowledging full satisfaction neither imposes a condition on the instrument nor contains any other promises or obligations which might render the instrument nonnegotiable. Answer (c) is incorrect because a statement that the instrument is secured by a mortgage does not make the instrument conditional or impose any other obligations. Nor does acceleration upon default affect the requirement to pay as provided in the note. Answer (d) is incorrect because all instruments are subject to the usual implied and constructive conditions applicable to the transactions from which they arose. These conditions would not affect a holder in due course.

29. Filbert Corporation has in its possession an instrument which Groves, the maker, assured Filbert was negotiable. The instrument contains several clauses which are not typically contained in such an instrument and Filbert is not familiar with their legal effect. Which of the following will adversely affect the negotiability of the instrument?

a. A promise to maintain collateral and to provide additional collateral if the value of existing collateral decreases.

b. A term authorizing the confession of judgment on the instrument if not paid when due.

c. A statement to the effect that the instrument arises out of the November 1st sale of goods by Filbert to Groves.

d. A statement that it is payable only out of the proceeds from the resale of the goods sold by Filbert to Groves on November 1.

The correct answer is (d). *(CPA 579 L-26)*

REQUIRED: The statement rendering the instrument nonnegotiable.

DISCUSSION: One of the requirements of negotiability is that the instrument contain an unconditional promise or order to pay (UCC 3-104). A statement that the instrument is payable only from a particular source, such as the proceeds of resale of certain goods, renders it conditional because no source of payment would be available if the goods were not sold (UCC 3-105). The full credit of the maker must be pledged. But a statement of the account to be charged does not render the instrument conditional, unless the requirement is that the instrument be paid solely out of that account (the funds may be insufficient).

Answer (a) is incorrect because promises to provide collateral do not affect the unconditional promise to pay; they simply add security. Answer (b) is incorrect because a term authorizing a confession of judgment if payment is not made when due does not affect the unconditional promise to pay; it merely states remedies if the instrument is not paid. However, a term authorizing confession of judgment may not be valid in many states. Answer (c) is incorrect because an informational statement, or mere reference, to the source or purpose of the instrument has no effect on negotiability.

30. Which of the following provisions contained in an otherwise negotiable instrument will cause it to be nonnegotiable?

a. It is payable in Mexican pesos.

b. It contains an unrestricted acceleration clause.

c. It grants to the holder an option to purchase land.

d. It is limited to payment out of the entire assets of a partnership.

The correct answer is (c). *(CPA 582 L-43)*

REQUIRED: The provision causing an instrument to be nonnegotiable.

DISCUSSION: Negotiability requires that the instrument contain an unconditional promise or order to pay a sum certain in money (UCC 3-104). An option is a promise to hold an offer to sell open for a specified period. An option does not meet the requirement of a sum certain in money.

Answer (a) is incorrect because a promise to pay in foreign currency is a promise to pay in money. Answer (b) is incorrect because an instrument may be subject to acceleration. Unrestricted acceleration is equivalent to demand. Answer (d) is incorrect because the promise or order to pay from the entire assets of a partnership is not considered to be conditional (UCC 3-105).

31. Which of the following is required to make an instrument negotiable?

a. Stated date of issue.

b. An endorsement by the payee.

c. Stated location for payment.

d. Payment only in legal tender.

The correct answer is (d). *(CPA 1189 L-42)*

REQUIRED: The requirement for negotiability.

DISCUSSION: A negotiable instrument must provide for payment of a sum certain in money. The UCC states that an instrument is payable in money when it is payable in currency or current funds, which are legal tender. Instruments whose terms provide for payment by means other than legal tender are nonnegotiable.

Answer (a) is incorrect because negotiability only requires that an instrument be payable at a certain time or on demand. A specific issue date is not required. Answer (b) is incorrect because whereas the face of the instrument must be signed by the maker or drawer, an endorsement by the payee is not required for negotiability. Such an endorsement may be required in the course of negotiation of the instrument, however. Answer (c) is incorrect because negotiable instruments need not specify the location for payment.

32. Which of the following would cause a promissory note to be nonnegotiable?

a. The maker has the right to prepay the note, subject to a prepayment penalty of 10% of the amount prepaid.

b. An extension clause that allows the maker to elect to extend the time for payment to a date specified in the note.

c. A clause that allows the maker to satisfy the note by the performance of services or the payment of money.

d. A due date is not specified in the note.

The correct answer is (c). *(CPA 1188 L-37)*

REQUIRED: The condition resulting in a nonnegotiable promissory note.

DISCUSSION: A promissory note is a written document requiring the maker of the note to pay a specified amount of money to a payee at some definite time or on demand. A negotiable promissory note may not be satisfied by the performance of services or delivery of goods. Any clause to that effect would render the note nonnegotiable.

Answer (a) is incorrect because the requirement of a sum certain in money does not preclude specific monetary prepayment provisions or default penalties. Answer (b) is incorrect because the negotiable instrument must be payable on demand or at a definite time. A clause allowing the time for payment to be extended to a specified date at the option of the maker does not violate this requirement. Answer (d) is incorrect because an incomplete instrument, such as a note missing a due date, can be made negotiable by showing that such was the maker's intent and by completing the instrument before negotiating.

33.

December 17, 1989

I promise to pay to the order of Johnny Wiley
$1,500 plus 11% interest from the above date.

Wallace Kilgore
Wallace Kilgore

The instrument is payable

a. Immediately.

b. On sight.

c. Thirty days after issue.

d. On demand.

The correct answer is (d). *(Publisher)*

REQUIRED: The correct statement indicating when the given instrument is payable.

DISCUSSION: The instrument does not contain a date for payment. Under UCC 3-108, the instrument is therefore deemed to be payable on demand. An instrument payable on demand includes those payable on sight, on presentation, and those in which no time for payment is stated.

Answer (a) is incorrect because a demand instrument is payable immediately only if the demand happens to be made immediately. Answer (b) is incorrect because an instrument is payable on sight only when it so states, e.g., "pay on sight." Payable on sight means to pay when the payee is personally seen the next time. Answer (c) is incorrect because the instrument is payable 30 days after issue only if it so states.

34. Which of the following prevents an instrument from being negotiable?

a. An endorsement on the back of the instrument reads: "Pay Smith only."

b. An instrument is payable after completion of a contractual obligation that is certain to happen but uncertain as to the time of occurrence.

c. Whether the instrument is intended to be a note or a draft is unclear.

d. The capacity in which the party signed was unclear.

The correct answer is (b). *(CPA 1186 L-43)*

REQUIRED: The condition that defeats the negotiability of an instrument.

DISCUSSION: A negotiable instrument must meet a requirement that the instrument be payable on demand or at a definite time. "Payable at a definite time" means payable at 1) a stated date or a fixed period after such a date; 2) a fixed period after sight; 3) a definite time subject to any acceleration; or 4) a definite time subject to extension by the holder, or to extension to a further definite time by the maker or acceptor or automatically upon or after a specified act or event (UCC 3-109). Hence, no definite time is stated if payment is conditioned upon contractual performance the time of which is uncertain.

Answer (a) is incorrect because a special endorsement does not defeat negotiation. It merely restricts further negotiation until the specially named party has also signed the instrument. Answer (c) is incorrect because uncertainty about whether an instrument is a note or a draft allows the holder to treat it as either. It does not affect the instrument's negotiability. Answer (d) is incorrect because when it is unclear in which capacity a party signs an instrument, the party is assumed to be an endorser, and the instrument remains negotiable.

35. Which of the following on the face of an otherwise negotiable instrument will affect the instrument's negotiability?

a. The instrument is postdated.

b. The instrument is payable 6 months after the death of the maker.

c. The instrument contains a promise to provide additional collateral if there is a decrease in value of the existing collateral.

d. The instrument provides for stated different rates of interest before and after default.

The correct answer is (b). *(CPA 587 L-46)*

REQUIRED: The condition that adversely affects negotiability.

DISCUSSION: The UCC requires that negotiable instruments be payable on demand or at a definite time. An instrument payable after an event with an uncertain date, such as the death of the maker, violates this requirement.

Answer (a) is incorrect because the dating of an instrument has no effect on the negotiability of an instrument. Answer (c) is incorrect because negotiability is not affected by promises included in the instrument whose purpose is to ensure payment of the sum due. Answer (d) is incorrect because a provision for different rates of interest before and after default does not violate the requirement that the promise or order be payable in a sum certain because the amount due at a given time can always be ascertained (UCC 3-106). Hence, such a provision does not affect the instrument's negotiability.

36. An otherwise negotiable instrument "payable on or before December 1, 1990" is

a. Negotiable.

b. Not negotiable because it is not payable at a definite time.

c. Negotiable but the obligor cannot make payment before December 1, 1990.

d. Not negotiable because payment is conditional.

The correct answer is (a). *(J.C. Folkenroth)*

REQUIRED: The negotiability of an instrument payable on or before a specific date.

DISCUSSION: The UCC requires that an instrument be payable on demand or at a definite time to be negotiable. But "definite time" is not limited to one particular date. (See Question 31 for a fuller discussion.)

Answer (b) is incorrect because the instrument is considered payable at a definite time. Answer (c) is incorrect because the obligor is given the option of paying early, but is not required to pay before the stated date. Answer (d) is incorrect because payment is not conditional. The obligor is required to pay no later than December 1, 1990.

37. A client has an instrument that contains certain ambiguities or deficiencies. In construing the instrument, which of the following is incorrect?

a. If there is doubt whether the instrument is a draft or a note, the holder may treat it as either.

b. Handwritten terms control typewritten and printed terms, and typewritten terms control printed terms.

c. An instrument payable only upon the happening of an event that is uncertain as to the time of its occurrence is payable at a definite time if the event has occurred.

d. That the instrument is antedated will not affect the instrument's negotiability.

The correct answer is (c). *(CPA 1180 L-4)*

REQUIRED: The false statement about construing an ambiguous or deficient instrument.

DISCUSSION: An instrument payable only upon the happening of an event that is uncertain as to the time of occurrence is not payable at a definite time because one cannot determine the payment date with certainty. That the event has occurred does not change this result (UCC 3-109).

Answer (a) is incorrect because the holder of an ambiguous instrument may treat it as either a draft or a note if there is doubt (UCC 3-118). Answer (b) is incorrect because handwritten terms control typewritten and printed (typeset) terms, and typewritten terms control printed terms. Answer (d) is incorrect because an instrument may be either antedated or postdated without affecting the instrument's negotiability.

38. Ard is holding the following instrument:

> I, Rosemary Larkin, hereby promise to pay to the bearer twenty thousand dollars ($20,000). This document is given by me as payment of the balance due on my purchase of a 1984 Winnebago mobile home from Ed Dill and is payable when I am able to obtain a bank loan.
>
> Rosemary Larkin
> Rosemary Larkin

This instrument is not negotiable because it

a. Refers to the contract out of which it arose.

b. Is payable to bearer rather than to a named payee.

c. Is not dated on the face of the instrument.

d. Is not payable at a definite time.

The correct answer is (d). *(CPA 588 L-46)*

REQUIRED: The condition rendering an instrument nonnegotiable.

DISCUSSION: To be negotiable, an instrument must be payable at a definite time or on demand. An instrument payable on the contingent event of obtaining a bank loan is not payable at a definite time and is not negotiable.

Answer (a) is incorrect because the mere mention of a prior contract that gave rise to the instrument does not affect negotiability, provided that payment is not governed by that other contract. Answer (b) is incorrect because negotiable instruments may be payable to order or to bearer. Answer (c) is incorrect because the issue date is not required to appear on the face of the instrument.

39. The following instrument is in the possession of Bill North.

> On May 30, 1990, I promise to pay Bill North, the bearer of this document, $1,800.
>
> Joseph Peppers
> Joseph Peppers
>
> Re: Auto Purchase Contract

This instrument is

a. Nonnegotiable because it is undated.

b. Nonnegotiable because it is not payable to order or bearer.

c. Negotiable even though it refers to the contract out of which it arose.

d. Negotiable because it is payable at a definite time.

The correct answer is (b). *(CPA 589 L-48)*

REQUIRED: The negotiability of the instrument given in the facts.

DISCUSSION: The instrument is a nonnegotiable note because it is not payable to order or bearer (UCC 3-104). It is only payable to Bill North, and refers to him specifically as bearer on its face.

Answer (a) is incorrect because an issue date is not necessary for negotiability. Answer (c) is incorrect because the instrument is nonnegotiable because it is not payable to order or to bearer. Reference to a separate agreement would impair negotiability only if the obligation were made subject to the other agreement. Answer (d) is incorrect because payability at a definite time or on demand does not suffice for negotiability.

40. Jane Lane, a sole proprietor, has in her possession several checks that she received from her customers. Lane is concerned about the safety of the checks since she believes that many of them are bearer paper that may be cashed without endorsement. The checks in Lane's possession will be considered order paper rather than bearer paper if they were made payable (in the drawer's handwriting) to the order of

a. Cash.

b. Ted Tint, and endorsed by Ted Tint in blank.

c. Bearer, and endorsed by Ken Kent making them payable to Jane Lane.

d. Bearer, and endorsed by Sam Sole in blank.

The correct answer is (c). *(CPA 1185 L-37)*

REQUIRED: The basis for considering checks to be order paper.

DISCUSSION: An instrument is payable to order when by its terms it is payable to the order of any specified person (UCC 3-110). An instrument payable to order of bearer is bearer paper. But bearer paper can be converted to order paper by a special endorsement. Thus, Ken Kent's endorsement to Jane Lane converted bearer paper back to order paper and Jane's endorsement is required for further negotiation. Although the endorsement by Kent contained no words of negotiability, such as "pay to the order of," the instrument remains negotiable as long as the face of the instrument contains such words.

Answer (a) is incorrect because an instrument is bearer paper when it is payable to the order of cash (UCC 3-111). Answers (b) and (d) are incorrect because an instrument endorsed in blank is bearer paper.

41. Your client has in his/her possession the following instrument:

> No. 1625
> FAIR FOOD WHOLESALERS, INC.
> 22 Woodrow Wilson Hayes Lane
> Columbus, Ohio
> Jan. 10, 1990
> On demand the undersigned promises to pay to
> Bearer $1,200.00
> Twelve hundred & ten/100's Dollars
> Fair Food Wholesalers, Inc.
> By James Duff
> James Duff, President
> For: ________

The instrument is

a. A nonnegotiable promissory note.

b. Nonnegotiable because the instrument is incomplete.

c. A negotiable time draft.

d. Negotiable despite the inconsistency between the amounts in words and in numbers.

The correct answer is (d). *(CPA 1186 L-44)*

REQUIRED: The negotiability of the instrument given in the facts.

DISCUSSION: Negotiability is not defeated by a discrepancy between the words and numbers on a document. In this situation, the words control the figures, unless the words are ambiguous (UCC 3-118). Because this instrument meets the other requirements of negotiability, it is a negotiable note in the amount of $1,200.10.

Answers (a) and (b) are incorrect because the note is a signed writing containing an unconditional promise to pay a sum certain in money to bearer on demand. Thus, it meets all the requirements of negotiability. Answer (c) is incorrect because a draft is a three-party instrument, whereas this document is a two-party promissory note.

42. An instrument reads as follows:

> April 1, 1990
> Pay to the order of
> Donald Kent, Fifteen days after date, $100.00
> One hundred and no/100 Dollars
> Union Corp.
> Ridgefield, Connecticut Dale Cox
> re: down payment on auto purchase

The instrument is

a. Nonnegotiable because it incorporates the auto purchase transaction by reference.

b. A negotiable time draft.

c. A negotiable sight draft.

d. A nonnegotiable trade acceptance.

The correct answer is (b). *(CPA 586 L-26)*

REQUIRED: The nature and negotiability of the document given in the facts.

DISCUSSION: The document meets the requirements of negotiability. It is a draft because by its terms a drawer (Dale Cox) orders a drawee (Union Corp.) to pay money to a payee (Donald Kent). It is a time draft because it is not payable until 15 days after April 1.

Answer (a) is incorrect because a reference to another contract on the face of a negotiable instrument does not defeat negotiability if payment is not conditioned upon or subject to the other contract. Answer (c) is incorrect because a sight draft is payable on demand. Answer (d) is incorrect because a trade acceptance usually has the same party as both drawer and payee, and requires the signature of the drawee acknowledging its obligation.

13.4 Negotiation and Endorsements

43. James Theodore Jason owed a debt to Baker, so he made a promissory note payable to Baker, signed it, "Jason," and mailed it to Baker. Baker refused to accept the note claiming Jason did not properly sign or deliver it for effective negotiation. The note was

a. Properly signed and delivered.

b. Properly signed but not properly delivered.

c. Properly delivered but not properly signed.

d. Neither properly signed nor delivered.

The correct answer is (a). *(Publisher)*

REQUIRED: The correct statement concerning the proper signature and delivery of a note.

DISCUSSION: Under UCC 3-401, no one may be liable on an instrument unless his/her signature appears on it. But the signature may be made by use of any name, including a trade or assumed name, or by any word or mark used in lieu of a written signature. Hence, Jason's signature was proper. Delivery is defined by UCC 1-201 as the voluntary transfer of possession. If Jason intended Baker to have the note and Baker received it, delivery was proper. Delivery is crucial to the validity of a negotiable instrument, although constructive delivery can be effective.

Answer (b) is incorrect because the note was properly delivered. Answer (c) is incorrect because the note was properly signed. Answer (d) is incorrect because the note was properly signed and delivered.

44. Commercial paper must be issued to be legally effective, and it must be delivered before it is deemed to be issued. In which case has a delivery occurred?

a. The drawer of a check placed it in a drawer of her desk. She died of a heart attack before it could be given to the payee.

b. The maker of a note gave it to the agent of the payee but asked for its return before the payee gained possession.

c. The payee of a note found it on the maker's desk and took it without consent.

d. The drawer of a check lost it before mailing it. The finder gave it to the payee.

The correct answer is (b). *(Publisher)*

REQUIRED: The case in which a negotiable instrument is deemed to be delivered.

DISCUSSION: Commercial paper is issued when it is transferred by the maker or drawer to a holder. Because commercial paper is a form of property, its issuance requires a proper delivery. In this context, UCC 1-201 defines delivery as a "voluntary transfer of possession." Delivery takes place, for example, when the maker or drawer voluntarily gives the instrument to an agent of the payee. Even if the note is returned, delivery did occur when given to the payee's agent.

Answers (a), (c) and (d) are incorrect because no voluntary transfer of possession was made by the maker or drawer.

45. To negotiate bearer paper, one must

a. Deliver and endorse the paper.

b. Deliver the paper.

c. Endorse the paper.

d. Endorse and deliver the paper with consideration.

The correct answer is (b). *(CPA 1187 L-47)*

REQUIRED: The proper means of negotiating bearer paper.

DISCUSSION: Under UCC 3-202, "Negotiation is the transfer of an instrument in such form that the transferee becomes a holder. If the instrument is payable to order, it is negotiated by delivery with any necessary endorsement; if payable to bearer, it is negotiated by delivery."

Answer (a) is incorrect because it states the method of negotiating order paper. Answer (c) is incorrect because negotiation of commercial paper requires delivery. Answer (d) is incorrect because consideration is not required for negotiation of commercial paper.

46. Herbert is a holder of a check originally payable to the order of Byron or bearer. These endorsements appear on the back:

Byron
Pay to the order of House
Daugherty
House
Humble

Which of the following is correct?

a. The check was originally order paper.

b. The check was order paper in Humble's hands.

c. The check is bearer paper in Herbert's hands.

d. Byron's signature was necessary for negotiation.

The correct answer is (c). *(Publisher)*

REQUIRED: The true statement about the effect of the endorsements.

DISCUSSION: An instrument payable to order or bearer is order paper unless the bearer words are handwritten or typewritten. Checks do not commonly have "or bearer" printed on them, so the bearer words must have been written or typed. Because the instrument was originally bearer paper, Byron's signature was not necessary for negotiation. Daugherty converted the check to order paper with the special endorsement to House, who negotiated it to Humble with a blank endorsement. By failing to name a payee, House converted the check back to bearer paper. Humble's blank endorsement did not affect the status of the check. Consequently, Herbert holds bearer paper.

Answer (a) is incorrect because the check was originally bearer paper, assuming the bearer language was hand- or typewritten. Answer (b) is incorrect because House converted the check back to bearer paper. Answer (d) is incorrect because Byron held the check when it was bearer paper and thus negotiable by delivery alone.

47. The following endorsements appear on the back of a negotiable promissory note made payable "to bearer." The note is in the possession of James Mix.

Pay to John Jacobs
Mary Nash
John Jacobs
(without recourse)

Which one of the following statements is correct?

a. Mix is not a holder because Jacobs' qualified endorsement makes the note non-negotiable.

b. Mix can negotiate the note by delivery alone.

c. The unqualified endorsement of Mix is required to further negotiate the note.

d. In order for Mix to negotiate the note, Mix must have given value for it.

The correct answer is (b). *(CPA 589 L-50)*

REQUIRED: The true statement regarding the endorsements on a negotiable note given in the facts of the question.

DISCUSSION: The last endorsement on the note specifies no particular endorsee, making it payable to bearer. As holder of bearer paper, Mix can negotiate the document simply by delivery.

Answer (a) is incorrect because the qualified endorsement by John Jacobs only relieves Jacobs of liability if the note is dishonored; it does not invalidate the negotiability of the note. Answer (c) is incorrect because a holder of bearer paper need not endorse the instrument to negotiate it. Answer (d) is incorrect because value is not required for negotiation of commercial paper.

48. Hand executed and delivered to Rex Roy a $1,000 negotiable note payable to Rex or bearer. Rex then negotiated it to Ford and endorsed it on the back by merely signing his name. Which of the following is a correct statement?

a. Rex's endorsement was a special endorsement.

b. Rex's endorsement was necessary to Ford's qualification as a holder.

c. The instrument was initially bearer paper and cannot be converted to order paper.

d. The instrument is bearer paper and Ford can convert it to order paper by writing "pay to the order of Ford" above Rex's signature.

The correct answer is (d). *(CPA 1186 L-41)*

REQUIRED: The true statement about the endorsement of a negotiable note payable to order or bearer.

DISCUSSION: A negotiable note payable to Rex or bearer and endorsed in blank on the back is bearer paper. The paper can be transformed to order paper, however, by making the endorsement a special endorsement through writing "pay to the order of Ford" above the endorsement. The holder of the instrument is allowed to do so.

Answer (a) is incorrect because a special endorsement specifies to whom or to whose order the instrument will be payable. Answer (b) is incorrect because the original note was payable to Rex or bearer, and Rex's signature was not necessary to negotiate the note. Answer (c) is incorrect because bearer paper can be converted to order paper through special endorsement.

49. Teff entered Archer's office and stole from Archer some radios and Archer's wallet containing identification. Subsequently, representing himself as Archer, Teff induced Bane to purchase one of the stolen radios for a fair price. Bane gave Teff his check made out to Archer. Teff indorsed the check "Pay to the order of Crown, Archer" and transferred it to Crown for cash in the amount of the check. Crown endorsed the check "Pay to the order of Fox, Crown" and transferred the check to Fox to be applied to his account. Bane's check was

a. Void from the beginning.

b. Bearer paper when Crown took it.

c. Order paper initially and negotiated by Teff to Crown.

d. Nonnegotiable absent a valid endorsement by the real Archer.

The correct answer is (c). *(CPA 574 L-7)*

REQUIRED: The correct statement regarding the type of check described in the facts.

DISCUSSION: The check was initially order paper because it was payable to the order of Archer, as opposed to bearer or cash (UCC 3-110). It was negotiated by Teff to Crown when Teff fraudulently endorsed it with Archer's name and delivered it to Fox (UCC 3-202).

Answer (a) is incorrect because the check was not initially void since Bane gave it for consideration of the purchase of the radios. Answer (b) is incorrect because it was order paper (payable to the order of Crown) when Crown took it. Answer (d) is incorrect because the forged endorsement does not make the check nonnegotiable. An impostor can effectively endorse the name of the payee when the impostor induced the drawer (Bane) to make the check payable as such (UCC 3-405). This is because the drawer intended to give the check to the impostor (Teff), so the impostor should be able to endorse it even with someone else's name.

50. John Daly received a check originally made payable to the order of one of his customers, Al Pine. The following endorsement was written on the back of the check:

Al Pine, without recourse, for collection only

The endorsement on this check would be classified as

a. Blank, unqualified, and nonrestrictive.

b. Blank, qualified, and restrictive.

c. Special, unqualified, and restrictive.

d. Special, qualified, and nonrestrictive.

The correct answer is (b). *(CPA 1185 L-39)*

REQUIRED: The classification of an endorsement without recourse, for collection only.

DISCUSSION: A blank endorsement specifies no particular endorsee. A special endorsement would have specified the person to whom or to whose order the instrument was payable (UCC 3-204). An endorsement is restrictive if it is "conditional; purports to prohibit further transfer of the instrument; includes the words "for collection," "for deposit," "pay any bank," or like terms signifying a purpose of deposit or collection; or otherwise states that it is for the benefit or use of the endorser or of another person" (UCC 3-205). The endorsement "without recourse" is qualified. It disclaims contract liability but does not eliminate warranty liability.

Answers (a), (c), and (d) are incorrect because the endorsement is blank, restrictive, and qualified.

51. Price has in his possession an otherwise negotiable instrument which reads:

"I, Waldo, hereby promise to pay to the order of Mark or bearer...."

Which of the following is true with respect to the above instrument?

a. Mark's signature is required to negotiate the instrument.

b. The instrument is nonnegotiable.

c. If Mark endorses the instrument, he assumes potentially greater liability to subsequent transferees than if he transfers it by mere delivery.

d. Since the instrument is payable to Mark's order, it is a draft.

The correct answer is (c). *(CPA 577 L-25)*

REQUIRED: The correct statement regarding negotiation of the given instrument.

DISCUSSION: A person who transfers without endorsement only makes warranties to his/her transferee and the payor (maker or drawee) but not to subsequent holders. On the other hand, an endorser makes warranties to all subsequent holders of an instrument. Therefore, Mark would assume greater potential liability by endorsing the instrument (UCC 3-417).

Answer (a) is incorrect because the instrument states that it is payable to "the order of Mark or bearer." It is therefore bearer paper. Only delivery is needed to negotiate it. Answer (b) is incorrect because the instrument is negotiable since it is stated to be otherwise negotiable and contains a promise to pay to "the order of Mark or bearer." Answer (d) is incorrect because the instrument is a note since it is a two-party instrument payable by the maker to the payee.

52. A person who endorses a check "without recourse"

a. Has the same liability as an accommodation endorser.

b. Only negates his liability insofar as prior parties are concerned.

c. Gives the same warranty protection to his transferee as does a special or blank endorser.

d. Does not promise or guarantee payment of the instrument upon dishonor even if there has been a proper presentment and proper notice has been given.

The correct answer is (d). *(CPA 585 L-39)*

REQUIRED: The effect of a "without recourse" endorsement.

DISCUSSION: Under UCC 3-414, unless otherwise specified (such as by words like "without recourse"), every endorser engages that upon dishonor and any necessary notice of dishonor (s)he will pay the instrument to the holder or to any subsequent endorser who takes it up. An endorsement of "without recourse" is a qualified endorsement that disclaims this contract liability. But it does not eliminate warranty liability.

Answer (a) is incorrect because an accommodation endorser incurs the liability of an endorser who does not use a qualified endorsement. Answer (b) is incorrect because the words negate contract liability to subsequent parties as well. Answer (c) is incorrect because a qualified endorsement modifies one of the warranties in UCC 3-417: The endorser warrants only that (s)he has no knowledge of any defenses good against him/her, not that no such defenses exist.

53. Which of the following is a characteristic of a restrictive endorsement?

a. It cannot preclude further transfer or negotiation although it purports to do so.

b. It cannot be conditional at the same time.

c. It prevents the party taking the instrument via such an endorsement from becoming a holder in due course.

d. It releases the endorser from liability on the instrument in the event of nonpayment by the party obligated to pay it.

The correct answer is (a). *(CPA 577 L-21)*

REQUIRED: The characteristic of a restrictive endorsement.

DISCUSSION: A restrictive endorsement cannot preclude further transfer or negotiation, even if it purports to do so. No endorsement can restrict transfer or negotiation because such an attempt will be of no effect (UCC 3-206).

Answer (b) is incorrect because a restrictive endorsement could be conditional, e.g., "Pay Jones only if he has performed under my contract." Answer (c) is incorrect because a party taking an instrument with a restrictive endorsement may become a holder in due course if (s)he either complies with the restrictive endorsement or makes sure that it has been complied with. Answer (d) is incorrect because all endorsers remain liable for warranties made on negotiation of an instrument.

54. Ed Johnson lost a check that he had received for professional services rendered. The instrument on its face was payable to Johnson's order. He had endorsed it on the back by signing his name and printing "for deposit only" above his name. Assuming the check is found by Al Alcatraz, a dishonest person who attempts to cash it, which of the following is correct?

a. Any transferee of the instrument must pay or apply any value given by him/her for the instrument consistent with the endorsement.

b. The endorsement is a blank endorsement and a holder in due course who cashed it for Alcatraz would prevail.

c. The endorsement prevents further transfer or negotiation by anyone.

d. If Alcatraz simply signs his name beneath Johnson's endorsement, he can convert it into bearer paper and a holder in due course would take free of the restriction.

The correct answer is (a). *(CPA 579 L-28)*

REQUIRED: The correct statement regarding the effect of an endorsement "for deposit only."

DISCUSSION: A restrictive endorsement of "for deposit only" puts the burden on subsequent transferees to comply with the endorsement or to be sure that the endorsement has already been complied with (UCC 3-206). Hence, any transferee of Johnson's check is required to act consistently with the endorsement; i.e., (s)he must deposit the check only in Johnson's bank account.

Answer (b) is incorrect because the "for deposit only" statement is called a restrictive endorsement (not a blank endorsement) and subsequent transferees must comply with it. Answer (c) is incorrect because the endorsement merely restricts payment; it does not prevent transfer or negotiation (an endorsement attempting to do so is not effective). Answer (d) is incorrect because the instrument cannot be converted directly into bearer paper because of the restrictive endorsement. Furthermore, a subsequent transferee could not qualify as a holder in due course if the restriction had not been complied with.

55. Anna Karr transferred a negotiable instrument payable to her order for value to Watson. Karr did not endorse the instrument. As a result of the transfer, Watson

a. Obtains such rights as the transferor had in all cases.

b. Can become a holder only if the instrument is endorsed and delivered at the same time.

c. Is presumed to be the owner of the instrument because she gave value.

d. Is entitled to an unqualified endorsement by Karr.

The correct answer is (d). *(CPA 586 L-30)*

REQUIRED: The correct statement concerning the transfer of a negotiable instrument for value.

DISCUSSION: Because Watson received the instrument from Karr for value, Watson has a specifically enforceable right to Karr's cooperation in negotiating that instrument in the absence of an agreement to the contrary (UCC 3-201). Thus, Watson has a right to Karr's unqualified endorsement of the instrument.

Answer (a) is incorrect because Watson, as transferee, may qualify as a holder in due course, and therefore may have rights superior to those of the transferor. Answer (b) is incorrect because it is not necessary for endorsement and delivery to coincide. Watson will not become a holder, however, until the instrument has been negotiated to him through proper endorsement. Answer (c) is incorrect because endorsement and delivery of an instrument define its ownership.

13.5 Holder in Due Course

56. Your client, Robert Rose, has the following instrument in his possession:

> March 1, 1990
>
> One month from date, I, Charles Wallace, do hereby promise to pay Edward Carlson seven hundred and fifty dollars ($750.00).
>
> *Charles Wallace*

Edward Carlson wrote "pay to the order of Robert Rose" on the back and delivered it to Rose.

a. Robert Rose is a holder in due course.

b. The instrument is a negotiable promissory note.

c. Edward Carlson is a holder in due course.

d. All defenses, real and personal, are assertible by Wallace against Rose.

The correct answer is (d). *(CPA 576 L-39)*

REQUIRED: The correct statement regarding the promissory note described.

DISCUSSION: All defenses are assertible by the maker of a promissory note against all parties except a holder in due course. One can only qualify for the special status of holder in due course if the instrument is negotiable. This instrument is not negotiable because it is not payable to order or to bearer (UCC 3-805). Wallace can therefore assert all defenses against Rose.

Answers (a) and (c) are incorrect because neither Rose nor Carlson is a holder in due course. The instrument is not negotiable. Answer (b) is incorrect because the instrument is a nonnegotiable note.

57. Fitz received from Gayle a negotiable instrument payable to the order of Gayle. Fitz received the instrument for value, but Gayle inadvertently did not endorse the instrument.

a. Fitz will be treated as the holder of a bearer negotiable instrument.

b. If Fitz later obtains Gayle's unqualified endorsement, Fitz's rights as a holder in due course are determined as of the time of endorsement.

c. Fitz has a right to require Gayle to endorse, but Gayle may satisfy the right by a qualified endorsement.

d. Fitz has no right after accepting the transferred instrument to require Gayle to endorse since he made no such request at the time of the transfer.

The correct answer is (b). *(CPA 574 L-16)*

REQUIRED: The transferee's rights to endorsement by the transferor and the consequences of a subsequent endorsement.

DISCUSSION: To qualify as a holder in due course, a person must have taken the instrument by proper negotiation (i.e., be a holder). Because the instrument was payable to the order of Gayle, Gayle's endorsement was necessary to properly negotiate it. Thus, Fitz will qualify as a holder in due course only when Gayle endorses the instrument (UCC 3-202). A transferee for value is entitled to his/her transferor's endorsement.

Answer (a) is incorrect because the instrument is order paper. It is payable to the order of Gayle and would only become a bearer instrument if Gayle endorsed it in blank. Answers (c) and (d) are incorrect because unless otherwise agreed, the transfer of order paper for value gives the transferee the right to an unqualified endorsement (UCC 3-201).

58. The status of a holder in due course as opposed to a mere holder of a negotiable instrument

a. Is of little consequence as a practical matter.

b. Eliminates the necessity of making due presentment or giving notice of dishonor.

c. Allows the holder in due course to overcome certain defenses that cannot be overcome by a mere holder.

d. Allows the further negotiation of the instrument.

The correct answer is (c). *(CPA 586 L-31)*

REQUIRED: The correct statement concerning the difference between a holder and a holder in due course.

DISCUSSION: A holder is a person to whom an instrument is negotiated, whereas a holder in due course is a special type of holder who takes an instrument for value, in good faith, and without notice that it is overdue or has been dishonored or of any defense or claim to it. Real defenses are good against both holders and holders in due course; personal defenses are good against holders, but are ineffective against holders in due course.

Answer (a) is incorrect because the ability of the holder in due course to hold the instrument free of personal defenses of previous holders is a significant advantage. Answer (b) is incorrect because due presentment and notice of dishonor are required any time a secondary party is to be held liable on commercial paper. A holder in due course is not excused from this requirement. Answer (d) is incorrect because previous negotiation of an instrument by either a holder or a holder in due course will not defeat the negotiability of that instrument.

59. A holder in due course of an instrument does not have to meet which of the following requirements?

a. Be a maker, payee, drawer, drawee, or endorser.

b. Take for value.

c. Take in good faith.

d. Take without notice of any defense.

The correct answer is (a). *(Publisher)*

REQUIRED: The requirement that need not be met by a holder in due course.

DISCUSSION: Under UCC 3-302, "A holder in due course is a holder who takes the instrument for value; in good faith; and without notice that it is overdue or has been dishonored or of any defense against or claim to it on the part of any person." (S)he may but is not required to be a payee, etc.

Answers (b), (c), and (d) are incorrect because each is a requirement of a holder in due course.

60. Which of the following will not constitute value in determining whether a person is a holder in due course?

a. The taking of a negotiable instrument for a future consideration.

b. The taking of a negotiable instrument as security for a loan.

c. The giving of one's own negotiable instrument in connection with the purchase of another negotiable instrument.

d. The performance of services for the payee of a negotiable instrument who endorses it in payment for the services.

The correct answer is (a). *(CPA 584 L-43)*

REQUIRED: The consideration not constituting value.

DISCUSSION: Under UCC 3-303, the value requirement is met 1) to the extent agreed consideration has been performed, 2) if the holder acquires a security interest in or a lien on the instrument, 3) if the holder takes in payment of or as security for an antecedent claim, or 4) if the holder gives another negotiable instrument or makes an irrevocable commitment to a third person. Future consideration, such as a contractual promise, does not constitute value to qualify as a holder in due course.

Answers (b), (c), and (d) are incorrect because each constitutes a taking for value.

61. Alfredo promises to rebuild the engine in Ernesto's Maserati in exchange for Ernesto's negotiation to him of a promissory note in the amount of $8,000.00. If Alfredo never rebuilds the engine,

a. He cannot qualify as a holder in due course. His promise constitutes consideration, not value.

b. The maker of the note will sue Alfredo for lack of consideration.

c. The maker of the note will sue Ernesto for lack of consideration.

d. He still qualifies as a holder in due course.

The correct answer is (a). *(I. Schwartz)*

REQUIRED: The effect of failure to perform a promise given for the negotiation of a promissory note.

DISCUSSION: To be a holder in due course, the holder of a negotiable instrument must give value in exchange for the instrument. Although Alfredo's promise to perform services in the future may constitute consideration sufficient to support a contract, it does not constitute value until (and to the extent) the promised act is actually performed. If he never rebuilds the engine, Alfredo will not have given value and cannot qualify as a holder in due course.

Answers (b) and (c) are incorrect because the maker of the note presumably received consideration from the payee, and the facts given do not indicate otherwise. Hence, the maker cannot sue Alfredo or Ernesto on this basis. The maker could assert the personal defense of lack of consideration, however, if he were sued on the note by Alfredo; Alfredo is not a holder in due course. Answer (d) is incorrect because Alfredo has not performed by rebuilding the Maserati's engine, and therefore cannot qualify as a holder in due course since he did not take the note for value.

62. To the extent that a holder of a negotiable promissory note is a holder in due course, (s)he takes the note free from which of the following defenses?

a. Minority of the maker if it is a defense to enforcement of a contract.

b. Forgery of the maker's signature.

c. Nonperformance of a condition precedent.

d. Discharge of the maker in bankruptcy.

The correct answer is (c). *(CPA 1186 L-42)*

REQUIRED: The defense not valid against a holder in due course.

DISCUSSION: A holder in due course ordinarily takes an instrument free of all personal defenses. The holder in due course is still subject to real defenses, however. Traditional contract defenses, such as nonperformance of a condition precedent, are usually personal defenses and thus not valid against a holder in due course.

Answers (a), (b), and (d) are incorrect because each states a real defense and may be asserted against a holder in due course.

63. Industrial Factors discounted a $4,000 promissory note, payable in two years, for $3,000. It paid $1,000 initially and promised to pay the balance ($2,000) within 30 days. Industrial paid the balance within the 30 days, but before doing so learned that the note had been obtained originally by fraudulent misrepresentation in connection with the sale of land which induced the maker to issue the note. For what amount will Industrial qualify as a holder in due course?

a. None because the 25% discount is presumptive or prima facie evidence that Industrial is not a holder in due course.

b. $1,000.

c. $3,000.

d. $4,000.

The correct answer is (b). *(CPA 582 L-36)*

REQUIRED: The extent of qualification as a holder in due course after receiving notice of a defense prior to full payment.

DISCUSSION: To be a holder in due course, a holder must take for value, in good faith, and without notice that the instrument is overdue, dishonored, or subject to any defense or claim (UCC 3-302). An unsecured promise to pay is not considered giving value for a negotiable instrument (giving another promissory note or draft would be value). Accordingly, prior to receiving notice of a defense against the instrument, Industrial has given value only to the extent of $1,000 and is a holder in due course only to that extent.

Answer (a) is incorrect because the size of the discount is not so great that Industrial would be considered to have had notice of a defense against or claim to the instrument. Answers (c) and (d) are incorrect because Industrial is a holder in due course only with respect to the $1,000 value given prior to notice of a defense against the instrument.

64. Ajax, Inc. sold a refrigerator to Broadway Bill's Restaurant and accepted Broadway's negotiable promissory note for $600 as payment. The note was payable to Ajax's order one year after the date of issue. Thirty days after receiving the note, Ajax endorsed the note with a blank endorsement and sold it to National Bank for $550. National credited Ajax's checking account with $550, which brought Ajax's balance to $725. Ajax drew checks for a total of $675 which National honored. National then learned that the refrigerator had not been delivered by Ajax. The note is now due and unpaid. When National brings suit, Broadway pleads lack of consideration on the note. Which of the following is a valid statement with respect to the above facts?

a. The discount on the note is so great as to impugn National's taking in good faith.

b. In ascertaining the extent to which value had been given by National, the FIFO rule will apply to checks or notes deposited and the proceeds withdrawn.

c. Broadway has no liability on the note since it never received the refrigerator.

d. Broadway has only secondary liability on the note in question.

The correct answer is (b). *(CPA 1177 L-37)*

REQUIRED: The correct statement regarding liability on a promissory note to a holder in due course.

DISCUSSION: A holder in due course can only assert its rights to the extent that it has given value (UCC 3-302). A bank is only considered to give value on a customer's account to the extent that the funds have been withdrawn from the bank. The FIFO rule (first funds in are the first funds out) applies for this purpose (UCC 4-208 and 4-209). This means that National gave value only to the extent of $500 because $50 of the deposit still remained in Ajax's account.

Answer (a) is incorrect because a $50 discount on a $600 promissory note is not extraordinary in the financial community. Answer (c) is incorrect because Broadway is liable to National as a holder in due course to the extent of $500 (the value given). Answer (d) is incorrect because Broadway is primarily liable as the maker of a promissory note.

65. Barber has in his possession a negotiable instrument which he purchased in good faith and for value. The drawer of the instrument stopped payment on it and has asserted that Barber does not qualify as a holder in due course since the instrument is overdue. In determining whether the instrument is overdue, which of the following is incorrect?

a. A reasonable time for a check drawn and payable in the United States is presumed to be 30 days after issue.

b. A reasonable time for a check drawn and payable in the United States is presumed to be 20 days after the last negotiation.

c. All demand instruments, other than checks, are not overdue until a reasonable time after their issue has elapsed.

d. The instrument will be deemed to be overdue if a demand for payment had been made and Barber knew this.

The correct answer is (b). *(CPA 580 L-22)*

REQUIRED: The false statement regarding when an instrument is overdue.

DISCUSSION: A holder cannot qualify as a holder in due course if (s)he has notice that the instrument is overdue. The holder of a demand instrument (such as a check) has such notice if (s)he takes it more than a reasonable time after issue or after demand has been made. A reasonable time for a check drawn and payable in the United States is 30 days after issue (UCC 3-304).

Answers (a), (c), and (d) are incorrect because each is true as discussed above.

66. Silver Corp. sold 20 tons of steel to River Corp. with payment to be by River's check. The price of steel was fluctuating daily. Silver requested that the amount of River's check be left blank so that Silver could fill in the current market price. River complied with Silver's request. Within 2 days, Silver received River's check. Although the market price of 20 tons of steel at the time Silver received River's check was $80,000, Silver filled in the check for $100,000 and negotiated it to Hatch Corp. Hatch took the check in good faith, without notice of Silver's act or any other defense, and in payment of an antecedent debt. River will

a. Not be liable to Hatch, because the check was materially altered by Silver.

b. Not be liable to Hatch, because Hatch failed to give value when it acquired the check from Silver.

c. Be liable to Hatch for $100,000.

d. Be liable to Hatch, but only for $80,000.

The correct answer is (c). *(CPA 1189 L-44)*

REQUIRED: The effect of an unauthorized completion of a check on the drawer's liability to a holder in due course.

DISCUSSION: Hatch took after proper negotiation, in good faith, without notice of the unauthorized completion, and for value (payment of an antecedent debt). UCC 3-304 expressly provides that mere knowledge that an incomplete instrument has been completed is not notice of a defense. Accordingly, Hatch is a holder in due course, and River is liable for the amount of the check as completed.

Answers (a) and (d) are incorrect because when an incomplete instrument has been improperly completed, a subsequent holder in due course may enforce it as completed (UCC 3-407). Answer (b) is incorrect because a holder takes for value when (s)he takes in payment of an antecedent claim (UCC 3-303).

67. Herb Hunt has in his possession a negotiable instrument originally payable to the order of Carr. It was transferred to Hunt by a mere delivery by Dan Drake, who took it from Carr in good faith in satisfaction of an antecedent debt. The back of the instrument read as follows: "Pay to the order of Drake in satisfaction of my prior purchase of a new video calculator, signed Carr." Which of the following is correct?

a. Hunt has the right to assert Drake's rights, including his standing as a holder in due course, and also has the right to obtain Drake's signature.

b. Drake's taking the instrument for an antecedent debt prevents him from qualifying as a holder in due course.

c. Carr's endorsement was a special endorsement; thus, Drake's signature was not required to negotiate it.

d. Hunt is a holder in due course.

The correct answer is (a). *(CPA 1185 L-41)*

REQUIRED: The correct statement regarding the negotiation of the instrument and the status of a party as a holder in due course.

DISCUSSION: Drake was a holder in due course because the instrument was properly negotiated to him by endorsement, he gave value, took in good faith, and had no notice of any defense (UCC 3-302). As a person taking through a holder in due course, Hunt can assert Drake's rights. As a transferee, Hunt has the right to obtain Drake's signature because endorsement and delivery is the proper method for negotiation of order paper (UCC 3-201).

Answer (b) is incorrect because a holder takes for value when (s)he takes the instrument in payment of an antecedent debt. Answer (c) is incorrect because Drake's signature was required to negotiate an instrument with a special endorsement. Answer (d) is incorrect because the instrument was not endorsed by Drake. A transferee of order paper cannot become a holder (much less one in due course) without proper negotiation (endorsement).

68. Dart induces Shorr by fraud to make a promissory note payable to Dart. Dart negotiates the note for value to Best, who was aware of the fraud. Best negotiates the note to Case, a holder in due course. Subsequently, Best repurchases the note from Case. Which of the following statements is correct?

a. Best does not succeed to Case's rights as a holder in due course.

b. Best becomes a holder in due course upon taking the note from Dart.

c. Because of the fraud by Dart, the note is nonnegotiable.

d. Best's knowledge of Dart's fraud is immaterial in determining Best's status as a holder in due course.

The correct answer is (a). *(CPA 1186 L-40)*

REQUIRED: The effect of a prior holder's knowledge of fraud when (s)he has taken from a holder in due course.

DISCUSSION: A person who takes through a holder in due course acquires the rights of a holder in due course unless the transferee was a prior holder with notice of a claim or defense against the instrument, or was a party to any fraud or illegality affecting the instrument (UCC 3-201). Best was a prior holder with notice of a defense and therefore cannot assert the rights of Case, the holder in due course.

Answers (b) and (d) are incorrect because Best knew of the fraud and thus cannot be a holder in due course. Answer (c) is incorrect because Dart's fraud does not affect the elements of negotiability, but it does create a personal defense effective against anyone except a holder with the rights of a holder in due course.

69. Harrison obtained from Bristow his $11,500 check drawn on the Union National Bank in payment for bogus uranium stock. He immediately negotiated it by a blank endorsement to Dunlop in return for $1,000 in cash and her check for $10,400. Dunlop qualified as a holder in due course. She deposited the check in her checking account in the Oceanside Bank. Upon discovering that the stock was bogus, Bristow notified Union National to stop payment on his check, which it did. The check was returned to Oceanside Bank, which in turn debited Dunlop's account and returned the check to her. Which of the following statements is correct?

a. Dunlop can collect from Union National Bank because Bristow's stop payment order was invalid in that the defense was only a personal defense.

b. Oceanside's debiting of Dunlop's account was improper because she qualified as a holder in due course.

c. Dunlop can recover $11,500 from Bristow despite the stop order, because she qualified as a holder in due course.

d. Dunlop will be entitled to collect only $1,000.

The correct answer is (c). *(CPA 1180 L-8)*

REQUIRED: The rights of a holder in due course to collect on a check that was initially issued under fraudulent circumstances.

DISCUSSION: Bristow's defense of fraud is a personal defense based on the inducement to enter into the purchase. It is not a real defense, so Dunlop is not subject to it as a holder in due course (UCC 3-305). Dunlop can recover the entire $11,500 dollars from Bristow.

Answer (a) is incorrect because Dunlop has no rights against Union National Bank. It is only a drawee and properly acted on Bristow's stop order. Answer (b) is incorrect because Oceanside also acted properly in debiting Dunlop's account when the check was not honored by Union National Bank. Answer (d) is incorrect because Dunlop is entitled to the full $11,500. She paid full value with $1,000 in cash and a check for $10,400 (the $100 discount does not detract from the concept of paying full value).

70. Weber had a negotiable instrument in his possession which he had received in payment of certain equipment he had sold to Roth Merchandising. The instrument was originally payable to the order of Martin Burns or bearer. It was endorsed specially by Burns to Roth who in turn negotiated it to Weber via a blank endorsement. The instrument in question, along with some cash and other negotiable instruments, was stolen from Weber on October 1. Which of the following is correct?

a. The theft constitutes a common law conversion that prevents anyone from obtaining a better title to the instrument than the owner.

b. A holder in due course will prevail against Weber's claim to the instrument.

c. Once an instrument is bearer paper it is always bearer paper.

d. Weber's signature was necessary in order to further negotiate the instrument.

The correct answer is (b). *(CPA 1183 L-49)*

REQUIRED: The correct statement regarding a stolen negotiable instrument.

DISCUSSION: A holder in due course takes free of claims and personal defenses on an instrument except those of the person from whom (s)he took and real defenses such as forgery, material alteration, and certain kinds of fraud (UCC 3-305). Theft of an instrument is a type of claim of which a holder in due course takes free, so Weber's claim will not prevail.

Answer (a) is incorrect because a holder in due course is subject only to the defenses discussed above and takes free of all other adverse claims to the instrument, including those based on theft. Answer (c) is incorrect because bearer paper can become order paper by a special endorsement. Answer (d) is incorrect because Roth negotiated the instrument to Weber with a blank endorsement, which made it bearer paper. Bearer paper is negotiated by mere delivery.

71. A holder in due course will take an instrument free from which of the following defenses?

a. Discharge in insolvency proceedings.

b. Infancy of the maker or drawer.

c. Claims of ownership on the part of other persons.

d. The forged signature of the maker or drawer.

The correct answer is (c). *(CPA 589 L-51)*

REQUIRED: The defense to which a holder in due course will not be subject.

DISCUSSION: A holder in due course takes free of all claims to an instrument on the part of other persons (UCC 3-305). Such claims are usually based on theft of the instrument.

Answers (a), (b), and (d) are incorrect because each is a defense to which a holder in due course is subject (UCC 3-305). These are called real defenses.

72. Which of the following defenses may be successfully asserted by the maker against a holder in due course?

a. Wrongful completion of an incomplete instrument by a prior holder.

b. Total failure to perform the contractual undertaking for which the instrument was given.

c. Fraudulent misrepresentations as to the consideration given by a prior holder in exchange for the negotiable instrument.

d. Discharge of the maker of the instrument in bankruptcy proceedings.

The correct answer is (d). *(CPA 584 L-44)*

REQUIRED: The defense effective against a holder in due course.

DISCUSSION: Under UCC 3-305, a holder in due course takes an instrument free from all claims to it on the part of any person and all defenses of any party with whom the holder has not dealt except real defenses. Real defenses include infancy to the extent that it is a defense to a simple contract; incapacity, duress, or illegality that makes the obligation void; fraud in the execution; and discharge in insolvency proceedings. Material alteration (UCC 3-407) and unauthorized signature (UCC 3-404) may also be real defenses.

Answers (a), (b), and (c) are incorrect because wrongful completion, failure of consideration, and fraud in the inducement are personal defenses.

73. Jack drew a check, payable to the order of Ellen, for $100.00. The check was endorsed in blank by Ellen to John, who skillfully altered the amount of the check to $1,000.00. John then cashed it at his club, which gave value, took in good faith, and had no knowledge or notice of the alteration. The alteration was not detected until Jack received his bank statement. After the fraud was discovered, Jack insisted that his bank recredit his account. Which of the following is true?

a. Jack's bank must recredit the entire amount of $1,000.00 because of the holder in due course doctrine.

b. Jack's bank must recredit only the amount of $900.00 if the drawer did not negligently contribute to the alteration.

c. John is not liable to anyone for any breach of warranty on transfer or presentment because he did not endorse the check.

d. The original tenor rule precludes Jack's bank from debiting his account for $100.00.

The correct answer is (b). *(D. Sipes)*

REQUIRED: The effect of a fraudulent and material alteration of a check on its negotiation.

DISCUSSION: The material alteration of an instrument is a real defense that can be asserted even against a holder in due course (UCC 3-407). The holder in due course may enforce the instrument's original terms, but is not entitled to the altered terms of the document, provided the drawer was not negligent in contributing to the alteration (UCC 3-406). Jack's bank most likely qualifies as a holder in due course, and as such can only debit Jack's account for the $100 original amount of the check (its "original tenor"). The bank must recredit Jack's account for the $900 charged as a result of the alteration. Under UCC 4-401, the bank may charge the indicated account of its customer only according to the original tenor of the altered item.

Answer (a) is incorrect because the bank need only recredit the excess debited to Jack's account because of the alteration. Answer (c) is incorrect because John warranted on transfer and presentment that the check had no fraudulent and material alterations (UCC 3-417). John is liable for the breach of those warranties. Answer (d) is incorrect because the original tenor rule allows holders in due course to enforce the original terms of an instrument.

74. Drummond broke into the Apex Drug Store and took all of the cash and checks that were in the cash register. The checks reflect payments made to Apex for goods sold. Drummond disposed of the checks and has disappeared. Apex is worried about its ability to recover the checks from those now in possession of them. Which of the following is correct?

a. Apex will prevail as long as its signature was necessary to negotiate the checks in question.

b. Since there was no valid transfer by Apex to Drummond, subsequent parties have no better rights than the thief had.

c. Apex will prevail only if the checks were payable to cash.

d. Apex will not prevail on any of the checks since it was the only party that could have prevented the theft.

The correct answer is (a). *(CPA 1182 L-60)*

REQUIRED: The ability of a payee to recover stolen checks.

DISCUSSION: If Apex's signature is needed to negotiate the checks, the thief will have to forge the endorsement. Under UCC 3-404, however, "Any unauthorized signature is wholly inoperative as that of the person whose name is signed unless (s)he ratifies it or is precluded from denying it; but it operates as the signature of the unauthorized signer in favor of any person who in good faith pays the instrument or takes it for value." Forgery is therefore a real defense assertible against a holder in due course.

Answer (b) is incorrect because a thief can negotiate bearer paper by delivery alone and thus give a subsequent party who qualifies as a holder in due course better rights than the thief had. Answer (c) is incorrect because checks payable to cash are bearer paper and negotiable by delivery alone. Answer (d) is incorrect because only if Apex was negligent in its control of the checks will it be precluded from asserting the lack of authority of a forger of any necessary endorsement.

75. Johnson bought a television for $450 on credit from Farin Corporation. As evidence of the debt, Johnson gave a promissory note to Farin, which then discounted the note with Easy Finance Company. Easy Finance Company

a. Will not qualify as a holder in due course if the television was purchased for home use.

b. Will qualify as a holder in due course since the sale was for less than $1,000.

c. Could have qualified as a holder in due course if it had directly financed the purchase pursuant to arrangements by Farin Corporation.

d. Could not qualify as a holder in due course if Johnson had given a check instead of a note.

The correct answer is (a). *(Publisher)*

REQUIRED: Whether a purchaser of commercial paper can qualify as a holder in due course.

DISCUSSION: The Federal Trade Commission has adopted a regulation denying holder in due course status to anyone purchasing a negotiable instrument issued by a consumer for the purchase of goods. The purpose is to protect the consumer's right to stop payment on a negotiable instrument so that (s)he does not have to bring a separate lawsuit against the seller. In order for a person to be a consumer, the goods must have been purchased for personal, family, or household use. The subsequent holders of such an instrument are given notice by a statement required to be printed on the commercial paper.

Answer (b) is incorrect because this anti-holder in due course rule applies to most consumer purchases of goods up to $25,000. Answer (c) is incorrect because the rule also applies when the financing is done directly by the finance company if the customer was referred by the seller or there is a business connection between the seller and the finance company. Answer (d) is incorrect because checks are exempted from the rule so that banking transactions will not be affected.

76. Cynthia purchased a VCR from Video Appliance Sales Enterprises (VASE) for use in her home. She gave a small down payment and executed a promissory note for the balance. VASE then properly negotiated the note to the Finley Company, which gave value, acted in good faith, and had no notice of any defense against or claim to the note. Subsequently, Cynthia was able to assert a defense of failure of consideration against VASE. If the note did not contain the notice required by the FTC,

a. Finley is not treated as a holder in due course.

b. Finley cannot recover from VASE.

c. Finley will prevail against Cynthia.

d. VASE will prevail against Cynthia.

The correct answer is (c). *(Publisher)*

REQUIRED: The effect of omitting the notice required by the anti-holder in due course rule.

DISCUSSION: The FTC has adopted a regulation denying holder in due course status to anyone purchasing a negotiable instrument issued by a consumer for the purchase of goods. For a person to be a consumer, the goods must have been purchased for personal, family, or household use. The subsequent holders are given notice by a statement required to be printed on all commercial paper to which this rule applies. The failure to include the notice is illegal as an unfair trade practice but has the effect of freeing a holder in due course from personal defenses. Accordingly, the omission would allow Finley to prevail against Cynthia in the absence of any real defense.

Answer (a) is incorrect because the notice would have precluded Finley from being treated as a holder in due course. Answer (b) is incorrect because a holder may recover from an endorser if the maker dishonors the note. Answer (d) is incorrect because the facts state that Cynthia has a defense against VASE.

13.6 Liability of Parties

77. Frank Supply Co. held the following instrument:

> Clark Novelties, Inc. April 12, 1990
> 29 State Street
> Spokane, Washington
>
> Pay to the order of Frank Supply Co. on April 30, 1990 ten thousand and 00/100 dollars ($10,000.00).
>
> Smith Industries, Inc.
>
> J. C. Kahn
> J.C. Kahn, President
>
> ACCEPTED: Clark Novelties, Inc.
>
> BY: Mitchell Clark
> Mitchell Clark, President
>
> Date: April 20, 1990

As a result of an audit of this instrument, which was properly endorsed by Frank Supply Co. to your client, the correct conclusion is that

a. Smith Industries was primarily liable on the instrument prior to acceptance.

b. The instrument is nonnegotiable and thus no one has rights under it.

c. No one was primarily liable on the instrument at the time of issue, April 12, 1990.

d. Upon acceptance, Clark Novelties, Inc. became primarily liable and Smith Industries was released from all liability.

The correct answer is (c). *(CPA 586 L-28)*

REQUIRED: The liability associated with the specified instrument.

DISCUSSION: This instrument is a negotiable draft payable on April 12, 1990, with a drawer (Smith), a drawee (Clark), and a payee (Frank). Primary liability results when the terms of an instrument require a party to pay. A draft has no primarily liable party until acceptance by the drawee, which occurred on April 20, 1990. Smith as drawer and Frank as endorser would both have secondary liability, meaning they must pay if and when the primary party does not pay (UCC 3-413 and 3-414).

Answer (a) is incorrect because Smith as drawer has only secondary liability. Answer (b) is incorrect because the instrument is negotiable. Answer (d) is incorrect because Smith retains secondary liability even after acceptance by Clark.

78. Jim Bass is in possession of a negotiable promissory note made payable "to bearer." Bass acquired the note from Mary Frank for value. The maker of the note was Fred Jackson. The following endorsements appear on the back of the note:

> Sam Peters
> Pay Jim Bass
> Mary Frank
> Jim Bass
> (without recourse)

Bass presented the note to Jackson, who refused to pay it because he was financially unable to do so. Which of the following statements is correct?

a. Peters is not secondarily liable on the note because his endorsement was unnecessary for negotiation.

b. Peters is not secondarily liable to Bass.

c. Frank will probably not be liable to Bass unless Bass gives notice to Frank of Jackson's refusal to pay within a reasonable time.

d. Bass would have a secondary liability to Peters and Frank if he had not qualified his endorsement.

The correct answer is (c). *(CPA 589 L-52)*

REQUIRED: The correct statement about the liability of endorsers of a negotiable instrument.

DISCUSSION: Unqualified endorsers of an instrument are secondarily liable on the instrument and are obligated to pay if the primarily liable party fails to do so. But this liability is contingent on the holder's timely notice of dishonor. Bass must give Frank notice of Jackson's dishonor to hold Frank to her secondary liability as endorser of the instrument.

Answer (a) is incorrect because all unqualified endorsers, whether or not their endorsements were necessary for negotiation, are secondarily liable on an instrument. Answer (b) is incorrect because unqualified endorsers are liable to all subsequent endorsers, even if the instrument has multiple endorsers. Answer (d) is incorrect because a subsequent endorser is not secondarily liable to previous endorsers.

79. Libby has primary liability on a negotiable instrument. Carl has secondary liability on the negotiable instrument. Consequently,

a. Libby is liable only after the instrument is dishonored.

b. If Carl is a drawer, he will have no liability after acceptance.

c. Libby cannot be the maker of a certificate of deposit.

d. Carl's liability ordinarily arises only after presentment, dishonor, and notice.

The correct answer is (d). *(Publisher)*

REQUIRED: The true statement about primary and secondary liability.

DISCUSSION: Makers and acceptors have primary liability. Their liability arises when the instrument comes due. Secondary liability, however, is conditional. The drawer of a draft or an endorser of any negotiable instrument will ordinarily be liable only after a proper demand for acceptance or payment (presentment), a refusal to pay or accept (dishonor), and prompt notice of dishonor. These requirements may be waived.

Answer (a) is incorrect because the only condition precedent to primary liability is maturity of the instrument. Answer (b) is incorrect because the drawer of a draft remains secondarily liable after the drawee's acceptance. Answer (c) is incorrect because the maker of a note or CD is primarily liable.

80. Wilson drew a sight draft on Jimmy Foxx (a customer who owed Wilson money on an open account), payable to the order of Burton, one of Wilson's creditors. Burton presented it to Foxx. After examining the draft as to its authenticity and after checking the amount against outstanding debts to Wilson, Foxx wrote on its face "Accepted--payable in 10 days" and signed it. When Burton returned at the end of 10 days, Foxx told him he could not pay and was hard-pressed for cash. Burton did not notify Wilson of these facts. Two days later when Burton again presented the instrument for payment, Burton was told that Foxx's creditors had filed a petition in bankruptcy that morning. Which of the following statements is correct?

a. The instrument in question is a type of demand promissory note.

b. Wilson had primary liability on the draft at its inception.

c. Foxx was secondarily liable on the draft at its inception.

d. Foxx assumed primary liability at the time of acceptance.

The correct answer is (d). *(CPA 1177 L-34)*

REQUIRED: The correct statement regarding a sight draft that has been accepted and then dishonored by the drawee.

DISCUSSION: A sight draft is essentially a demand draft payable on locating the drawee. As drawee, Foxx had no liability until he accepted the draft and, upon acceptance, he assumed primary liability (UCC 3-410 and 3-413). However, the claim must be filed in the bankruptcy proceeding.

Answer (a) is incorrect because the instrument is a type of draft (i.e., a three-party instrument), not a type of note. Answer (b) is incorrect because Wilson only had secondary liability as drawer. Answer (c) is incorrect because Foxx had no liability on the instrument until he accepted it.

81. Blare bought a house and provided the required funds in the form of a certified check from a bank. Which of the following statements correctly describes the legal liability of Blare and the bank?

a. The bank has accepted; therefore, Blare is without liability.

b. The bank has not accepted; therefore, Blare has primary liability.

c. The bank has accepted; therefore, Blare has secondary liability.

d. The bank has not accepted; therefore, Blare is without liability.

The correct answer is (c). *(CPA 1189 L-43)*

REQUIRED: The correct statement about the liabilities involved in payment by certified check.

DISCUSSION: A certified check is one that a bank has accepted (UCC 3-411). Acceptance is the drawee's signed engagement to honor the draft as presented (UCC 3-410). As acceptor, the bank bears primary liability for payment. As drawer, Blare is secondarily liable on the check, and must pay the payee if the bank dishonors the certified check (UCC 3-413).

Answer (a) is incorrect because Blare is secondarily liable. Answers (b) and (d) are incorrect because Blare is secondarily liable, and the bank is primarily liable as an acceptor.

82. Mike Wixstad asked Mel Montrose, his father-in-law, to sign a note as an accommodation co-maker. Montrose did this for Wixstad as a personal favor to his daughter. Both endorsed the note for value to Carlton who had knowledge that Montrose had signed the note for Wixstad's accommodation only. With respect to Montrose's rights and liabilities, which of the following is correct?

a. Carlton has the right to treat either or both parties as primarily liable on the note.

b. Carlton's best basis for recovery is to sue Montrose as an endorser.

c. Montrose has no liability beyond one-half of the face value of the note plus interest.

d. In the event Wixstad defaults on the note, notice must be promptly given to Montrose in order to hold him liable.

The correct answer is (a). *(CPA 1177 L-39)*

REQUIRED: The correct statement regarding the liability of an accommodation co-maker.

DISCUSSION: An accommodation party is one who signs an instrument in the capacity of a surety. As such, that person has liability in the capacity in which (s)he has signed (UCC 3-415), e.g., maker or endorser. Since Wixstad signed as maker and Montrose signed as accommodation co-maker, Carlton can treat either or both parties as primarily liable on the note.

Answer (b) is incorrect because Montrose would be only secondarily liable if he signed as an accommodation endorser, whereas he is primarily liable as an accommodation co-maker. Answer (c) is incorrect because an accommodation co-maker has liability for the full amount of the note. Answer (d) is incorrect because Montrose is automatically liable on Wixstad's default and no notice need be given him since he is primarily liable as an accommodation co-maker.

83. One who signs as an accommodation party to a negotiable instrument

a. Has the same liability on the instrument whether (s)he signs as an accommodation maker or as an accommodation endorser.

b. Has a right of recourse against the party accommodated.

c. Cannot be held liable against a subsequent holder in due course if the party accommodated has a contract (personal) defense against the party to whom the instrument was originally issued.

d. Has no liability to any subsequent taker who knew of the accommodation.

The correct answer is (b). *(CPA 576 L-34)*

REQUIRED: The rights and liabilities of an accommodation party.

DISCUSSION: An accommodation party is very much like a surety. (S)he in effect gives security by assuming liability for the person accommodated. Therefore, if (s)he must pay on an instrument because of the accommodated party's default, (s)he has the rights of a surety against his/her principal for reimbursement (UCC 3-415).

Answers (a) and (d) are incorrect because an accommodation party is liable in the capacity in which (s)he signs. This is the purpose of obtaining the accommodation signature. An accommodation maker is primarily liable and an accommodation endorser is secondarily liable. Answer (c) is incorrect because a holder in due course takes free of personal (contractual) defenses. The accommodation party cannot assert these defenses since the accommodated party could not.

84. If an instrument contains no agreement about a delayed presentment, which of the following is the proper time for presentment?

a. On the same date all other negotiable instruments are presented.

b. Ten days after the due date if it is a promissory note.

c. Within 30 days after issue for the usual uncertified check.

d. A reasonable time after issuance of the instrument regardless of its type.

The correct answer is (c). *(CPA 1177 L-33)*

REQUIRED: The proper time for presentment of a negotiable instrument.

DISCUSSION: The time for presentment varies according to several factors, e.g., whether presentment is for acceptance or payment, whether the instrument is payable on a fixed date, etc. For many instruments (such as checks payable on demand), presentment is due within a reasonable time. With regard to the usual uncertified check, 30 days after issue is deemed to be a reasonable time for purposes of holding the drawer liable (UCC 3-503).

Answer (a) is incorrect because the time for presentment varies by the type of negotiable instrument; e.g., instruments payable on a certain date must be presented for payment on that date, whereas demand instruments must be presented within a reasonable time. Answer (b) is incorrect because a promissory note with a due date must be presented for payment on that date. Answer (d) is incorrect because UCC 3-503 provides that some but not all instruments must be presented within a reasonable time.

85. An instrument which was endorsed by several subsequent holders reads as follows:

PAY	No. 452
	April 1, 1990
One month after date to Richard Williams or bearer	
One Hundred and no/100	Dollars
Fireman's Bank Chicago, Illinois	
	Roberta Peterson

Which of the following statements about this instrument is correct?

a. The instrument is nonnegotiable.

b. Richard Williams' signature is necessary to negotiate the instrument.

c. The instrument in question is a check.

d. Presentment for payment must be made on the due date or next business day to hold the subsequent endorsers liable.

The correct answer is (d). *(CPA 1178 L-45)*

REQUIRED: The correct statement regarding the example instrument.

DISCUSSION: To hold parties liable on a negotiable instrument with a specific payment date, presentment for payment must be made on the due date to hold the secondary parties liable (UCC 3-501 and 3-503). In the event that the due date falls on a nonbusiness day (weekend or holiday), presentment must be made on the next business day.

Answer (a) is incorrect because the instrument meets all the requirements for negotiability. Answer (b) is incorrect because the instrument is bearer paper which needs no signature to negotiate. Answer (c) is incorrect because the instrument is not a check since it is not payable on demand. The instrument is simply a draft.

86. Hoover is a holder in due course of a check that was originally payable to the order of Nelson or bearer and has the following endorsements on its back:

Nelson
Pay to order of Maxwell
Duffy
Without Recourse
Maxwell
Howard

Which of the following statements about the check is correct?

a. It was originally order paper.

b. It was order paper in Howard's hands.

c. Maxwell's signature was not necessary for it to be negotiated.

d. Presentment for payment must be made within 7 days after endorsement to hold an endorser liable.

The correct answer is (d). *(CPA 582 L-40)*

REQUIRED: The correct statement concerning the example check.

DISCUSSION: Under UCC 3-501, presentment is necessary to hold an endorser liable. Under UCC 3-503, this presentment must be within 7 days after an endorsement to hold the endorser liable on an ordinary check.

Answer (a) is incorrect because an instrument payable to order or bearer is order paper unless written. Checks do not commonly have "to bearer" printed on them, so the bearer words would have had to be written or typed in making the instrument originally bearer paper. Answer (b) is incorrect because the instrument was bearer paper in Howard's hands. Maxwell converted the instrument to bearer paper by endorsing in blank; i.e., Maxwell did not sign "Pay to the order of Howard." Answer (c) is incorrect because the instrument in Maxwell's hands was order paper due to Duffy's special endorsement. Order paper cannot be properly negotiated without both endorsement and delivery.

87. A formal protest of dishonor must be made to hold the drawer or endorsers liable for all of the following foreign instruments except

a. Drafts.

b. Promissory notes.

c. Trade acceptances.

d. Checks.

The correct answer is (b). *(CPA 580 L-23)*

REQUIRED: The foreign instrument for which a formal protest of dishonor is not required.

DISCUSSION: A formal protest of dishonor (usually made by a U.S. consul) is required to hold the drawer and endorsers liable on foreign drafts (UCC 3-501). The requirement does not apply to promissory notes, which are two-party instruments.

Answer (a) is incorrect because formal protest specifically applies to foreign drafts. Answers (c) and (d) are incorrect because trade acceptances and checks are forms of drafts and subject to the protest requirement.

88. Presentment of a promissory note for payment is necessary to hold liable

a. The maker.

b. An unqualified endorser.

c. An acceptor.

d. An accommodation maker.

The correct answer is (b). *(J.C. Folkenroth)*

REQUIRED: The party whose liability on a note is dependent upon previous presentment.

DISCUSSION: Presentment is a demand for payment made upon the maker, drawee, acceptor, or other payor on behalf of the holder (UCC 3-504). Presentment of a negotiable instrument for payment is necessary to charge any endorser (UCC 3-501). An unqualified endorser undertakes that upon proper presentment to the primary party, dishonor, and proper notice of dishonor to the endorser, (s)he will pay the instrument. Thus, an endorser is secondarily liable. Presentment is not necessary to charge a primary party.

Answer (a) is incorrect because makers of notes are primarily liable. Answer (c) is incorrect because only drafts can be accepted. Also, acceptors are primarily liable. Answer (d) is incorrect because accommodation parties are liable in the capacity in which they sign, hence accommodation makers are primarily liable.

89. Horace received a check made out by Oliver to Laurel. Laurel, Jones, and Smith had endorsed the back. Horace deposited the check in his bank. Several days later the bank notified Horace that the check had been returned NSF. Horace immediately sent a letter to Oliver informing him of the dishonor of the check. Horace has not heard from Oliver and wants to know whom he can hold liable.

a. Oliver.

b. Laurel.

c. Jones.

d. Smith.

The correct answer is (a). *(Publisher)*

REQUIRED: The party liable to the holder of a dishonored check who has given notice to the drawer.

DISCUSSION: The drawer and endorsers are not liable until an instrument has been presented, dishonored, and they have received notice of the dishonor (UCC 3-501). These requirements can be waived by express agreement. Presentment is a demand for acceptance or payment and can be done by mail, in person, or through a clearing house (UCC 3-504). Horace made presentment through a clearing house after the check entered the banking system. Dishonor occurred when the check was returned NSF (not sufficient funds). Horace gave notice of dishonor by sending the letter to Oliver. Notice of dishonor must be given before midnight of the third business day after receipt of notice of the NSF check (UCC 3-508). Written notice is deemed given when sent, even though not received. Hence, Horace gave timely notice to Oliver and Oliver is liable.

Answers (b), (c), and (d) are incorrect because Horace did not give notice to Laurel, Jones, or Smith. As endorsers, they were discharged for lack of notice of dishonor.

90. A proper presentment, dishonor, and a prompt notice of dishonor are usually required to establish the liability of a secondary party. In some instances, these requirements may be waived or excused. Which of the following is a true statement?

a. A holder is not excused because (s)he is unaware that the instrument is due.

b. If the drawer of a check has countermanded payment, (s)he and subsequent endorsers are not entitled to presentment and notice.

c. Both presentment and notice of dishonor may be waived.

d. Notice of dishonor, but not presentment, may be waived.

The correct answer is (c). *(Publisher)*

REQUIRED: The true statement about waiver or excuse of conditions for secondary liability.

DISCUSSION: Under UCC 3-511, presentment or notice of dishonor may be entirely excused when the party to be charged has waived them expressly or by implication either before or after the instrument is due.

Answer (a) is incorrect because delay in presentment or notice of dishonor is excused when the party does not have notice that it is due or when the delay is caused by circumstances beyond his/her control and (s)he exercises reasonable diligence afterwards. Answer (b) is incorrect because presentment and notice of dishonor is still required for endorsers unless the endorser has dishonored the instrument or has countermanded payment. Answer (d) is incorrect because both presentment and notice of dishonor may be waived.

91. Gomer obtained checks payable to the order of certain repairmen who serviced various large corporations. He observed the delivery trucks of repairmen who did business with the corporations, and then submitted bills on the bogus letterhead of the repairmen to the selected large corporations. The return envelope for payment indicated a local post office box. When the checks arrived, Gomer would forge the payees' signatures and cash the checks. The parties cashing the checks are holders in due course. Who will bear the loss assuming the amount cannot be recovered from Gomer?

a. The defraudedcorporations.

b. The drawee banks.

c. Intermediate parties who endorsed the instruments for collection.

d. The ultimate recipients of the proceeds of the checks even though they are holders in due course.

The correct answer is (a). *(CPA 580 L-19)*

REQUIRED: The party who will bear the loss on checks delivered to an impostor.

DISCUSSION: When an impostor causes a drawer to issue a check to him/her and endorses it in the name of the payee, the endorsement is effective against the drawer (UCC 3-405). The drawer is thereby deprived of the real defense of forgery against holders in due course and others. Thus, the defrauded corporations (drawers) will ultimately have to bear the loss.

Answer (b) is incorrect because drawee banks are never liable until they accept an instrument, and even then, they have recourse against the drawer. Answers (c) and (d) are incorrect because, as discussed above, the drawer will be deprived of the real defense of forgery against holders in due course and others since an impostor caused it to issue the checks.

92. Which of the following parties make warranties upon transferring commercial paper?

a. Transferors for consideration.

b. All endorsers.

c. Only unqualified endorsers.

d. All secondary parties.

The correct answer is (a). *(E. Rubert)*

REQUIRED: The parties subject to warranty liability after transferring commercial paper.

DISCUSSION: Any person who receives consideration for transferring (as opposed to obtaining payment or acceptance of) an instrument makes specific warranties regarding that instrument, and may be held liable for any breach of those warranties (UCC 3-417).

Answers (b) and (d) are incorrect because secondary parties (endorsers and drawers) may transfer an instrument without consideration, for example, as a gift. Answer (c) is incorrect because qualified endorsers also make warranties about the transferred instrument. An endorsement without recourse (a qualified endorsement) simply disclaims contract liability to subsequent holders if a maker or drawee defaults (UCC 3-414). The qualification modifies but does not eliminate warranty liability. Its only effect on the transfer warranties is to change the warranty that no defense of any party is good against the transferor to a warranty of no knowledge of such a defense (UCC 3-417).

93. For consideration, Tom transferred a negotiable instrument to Emma by a blank endorsement and delivery. Emma later transferred the instrument to Felix, who took in good faith. Tom does not warrant to Felix that

a. All signatures are genuine or authorized.

b. The instrument has not been materially altered.

c. The transfer is rightful.

d. The maker, drawer, or acceptor is solvent.

The correct answer is (d). *(Publisher)*

REQUIRED: The warranty not made by one who endorses and transfers an instrument for consideration.

DISCUSSION: Under UCC 3-417, any person who transfers an instrument and receives consideration warrants to his/her transferee that (s)he has a good title to the instrument or is authorized to obtain payment or acceptance on behalf of one who has a good title and the transfer is otherwise rightful; all signatures are genuine or authorized; the instrument has not been materially altered; no defense of any party is good against him/her; and (s)he has no knowledge of any insolvency proceeding instituted with respect to the maker or acceptor or the drawer of an unaccepted instrument.

If the transfer is by endorsement, these warranties are also made to any subsequent holder who takes in good faith. However, the transferor does not warrant that any party is solvent, just that (s)he has no knowledge of any insolvency.

94. An otherwise valid negotiable bearer note is signed with the forged signature of Darby. Art Archer, who believed he knew Darby's signature, bought the note in good faith from Hal Harding, the forger. Archer transferred the note without endorsement to Barker, in partial payment of a debt. Barker then sold the note to Charles Chase for 80% of its face amount and delivered it without endorsement. When Chase presented the note for payment at maturity, Darby refused to honor it, pleading forgery. Chase gave proper notice of dishonor to Barker and to Archer. Which of the following statements best describes the situation from Chase's standpoint?

a. Chase cannot qualify as a holder in due course because he did not pay face value for the note.

b. Chase can hold Barker liable on the ground that Barker warranted to Chase that neither Darby nor Archer had any defense valid against Barker.

c. Chase can hold Archer liable on the ground that Archer warranted to Chase that Darby's signature was genuine.

d. Chase cannot hold Harding, the forger, liable on the note because his signature does not appear on it and thus he made no warranties to Chase.

The correct answer is (b). *(CPA 1180 L-9)*

REQUIRED: The party, if any, who is liable and why.

DISCUSSION: The parties to this note are Harding (the forger of Darby's signature), Archer, Barker, and Chase. The only signature on the note was Darby's forged by Harding. Every transferor of a negotiable instrument for consideration warrants to his/her transferee that no defense of any party is good against him/her (UCC 3-417). Thus, Barker warranted to Chase that neither Darby nor Archer had any defense against Barker. But Darby had a defense of forgery effective even against a holder in due course, and Chase could therefore hold Barker liable.

Answer (a) is incorrect because Chase can qualify as a holder in due course. The purchase of a promissory note at a discount does not mean that value was not paid or that the purchaser had notice of a claim or defense. Answer (c) is incorrect because Archer did not endorse the note. Accordingly, he warranted only to his/her immediate transferee (Barker) that Darby's signature was genuine. Answer (d) is incorrect because Darby's forged signature operates as Harding's own signature, and Harding can be held liable in the capacity of maker of the note (UCC 3-404).

95. When the holder of a negotiable instrument transfers it for consideration by endorsing "without recourse," (s)he

a. Makes no warranty as to title to any subsequent holder.

b. Prevents further negotiability.

c. Makes the same warranties as an unqualified endorser except that (s)he warrants that (s)he does not have knowledge of a defense of any party good against him/her rather than that there is no such defense.

d. Becomes immune from recourse to him/her by a subsequent holder.

The correct answer is (c). *(CPA 574 L-4)*

REQUIRED: The effect of transferring a negotiable instrument by endorsing it "without recourse."

DISCUSSION: The endorsement "without recourse" is a qualified endorsement that modifies the endorser's warranty liability. The warranty against defenses is limited to a warranty that the endorser has no knowledge of defenses good against him/her (UCC 3-417).

Answer (a) is incorrect because the qualified endorsement does not eliminate the warranty of title to subsequent holders. Answer (b) is incorrect because neither the qualified endorsement nor any other endorsement can prevent further negotiability. Answer (d) is incorrect because the qualified endorser is still subject to liability for warranties to subsequent holders.

96. The transferor of a bearer negotiable instrument who transfers without endorsing but for full consideration

a. Is liable to all subsequent holders if there exists a personal defense to the instrument maintainable by the primary party and the transferor was aware of the defense.

b. Warrants to his/her immediate transferee that (s)he has good title.

c. Makes no warranty that prior signatures are genuine or authorized.

d. Engages that (s)he will pay the instrument if his/her immediate transferee is unable to obtain payment upon due presentment and dishonor because of insufficient funds and if due notice is given the transferor.

The correct answer is (b). *(CPA 574 L-3)*

REQUIRED: The liability of a transferor who does not endorse a bearer instrument.

DISCUSSION: A transferor of a negotiable instrument makes several warranties, one of which is good title. However, a transferor who does not endorse the instrument only makes these warranties to his/her immediate transferee, not to subsequent holders (UCC 3-417).

Answer (a) is incorrect because a transferor who does not endorse does not make any warranties to subsequent holders other than the immediate transferee. Answer (c) is incorrect because a transferor for consideration does warrant that prior signatures are genuine or authorized. Answer (d) is incorrect because a transferor does not warrant that the maker, acceptor, or drawer of a negotiable instrument has sufficient funds with which to pay the instrument; but does warrant that (s)he has no knowledge of insolvency proceedings against such persons.

97. Mask stole one of Bloom's checks. The check was already signed by Bloom and made payable to Duval. The check was drawn on United Trust Company. Mask forged Duval's signature on the back of the check and cashed the check at the Corner Check Cashing Company which in turn deposited it with its bank, Town National Bank of Toka. Town National proceeded to collect on the check from United. None of the parties was negligent. Who will bear the loss assuming the amount cannot be recovered from Mask?

a. Bloom.

b. Duval.

c. United Trust Company.

d. Corner Check Cashing Company.

The correct answer is (d). *(CPA 580 L-15)*

REQUIRED: The party who will bear the loss when the payee's signature is forged.

DISCUSSION: As the person obtaining payment on the check, Corner warranted that it had good title (UCC 3-417). However, it did not have good title because the check had been stolen. Corner is therefore liable for breach of warranty to any person (not merely to its transferee) who in good faith paid on the check.

Answers (a) and (b) are incorrect because Bloom and Duval have the defense that Duval's signature was forged. This is a real defense and is good against even a holder in due course. Furthermore, Bloom cannot be held liable since (s)he made the check payable to Duval (as opposed to bearer) and cannot be expected to protect further against forgeries. Answer (c) is incorrect because United was merely a drawee and had no liability until it accepted the check. Even then United had recourse against Corner on the warranty of good title.

98. Which of the following will not discharge a party liable on an instrument?

a. Tender of payment.

b. Cancellation.

c. Reacquisition by a prior holder.

d. Transfer without endorsement.

The correct answer is (d). *(Publisher)*

REQUIRED: The event which will not discharge a party liable on an instrument.

DISCUSSION: Discharge occurs when a person is no longer liable on an instrument (see UCC 3-601 through 3-606). Transfer without endorsement does not discharge anyone's liability. It merely limits the warranties made to a subsequent holder.

Answer (a) is incorrect because tender of payment (the ability and readiness to pay the instrument when or after it is due) does discharge the party's liability for interest, costs, and attorney's fees. Answer (b) is incorrect because cancellation is the removal of a person's signature from an instrument (such as striking it out) by the holder, which discharges that person's liability. Answer (c) is incorrect because reacquisition by a prior holder discharges the intermediary parties as to that holder. However, the intermediary parties will be liable to subsequent holders unless their signatures are canceled.

99. Armando is the maker of a negotiable promissory note and Betty is the payee. Betty specially endorsed the note to Charles who in turn specially endorsed it to Deb, the current holder. The note has not yet become due. Which of the following is true?

a. If Deb accidentally destroys the note, all parties are discharged.

b. If Deb intentionally destroys the note, all parties are discharged.

c. If Deb intentionally strikes out Charles's endorsement, both Betty and Charles are discharged.

d. Deb may discharge any party but only if she gives consideration.

The correct answer is (b). *(Publisher)*

REQUIRED: The true statement about discharge by cancellation.

DISCUSSION: Under UCC 3-605, the holder of an instrument may without consideration discharge any party. It may be done in any manner apparent on the face of the instrument or the endorsement, such as by intentionally canceling the instrument or the party's signature by destruction or mutilation, or by striking out the party's signature. It may also be done by renouncing his/her rights by a writing signed and delivered or by surrender of the instrument to the party to be discharged.

Answer (a) is incorrect because accidental destruction discharges no one. Answer (c) is incorrect because only Charles is discharged when Charles's endorsement is canceled. Answer (d) is incorrect because discharge requires no consideration.

13.7 Bank Transactions

100. Blue is a holder of a check originally drawn by Rush and made payable to Silk. Silk properly endorsed the check to Field. Field had the check certified by the drawee bank and then endorsed the check to Blue. As a result,

a. Field is discharged from liability.

b. Rush alone is discharged from liability.

c. The drawee bank becomes primarily liable and both Silk and Rush are discharged.

d. Rush is secondarily liable.

The correct answer is (c). *(CPA 1185 L-43)*

REQUIRED: The effect of certification of a check.

DISCUSSION: Certification is an unconditional promise to pay or acceptance of primary liability. Prior to certification or acceptance, a drawee is not liable on a check. But once the drawee certifies a check, the drawer and all prior endorsers are discharged if certification is procured by the holder (UCC 3-411). However, certification procured by the drawer would not discharge the drawer.

Answer (a) is incorrect because Field endorsed subsequent to certification and is thus not discharged. He is secondarily liable. Answer (b) is incorrect because all prior endorsers are also discharged. Answer (d) is incorrect because Rush, the drawer, is completely discharged by the certification procured by a holder.

101. A cashier's check is a

a. Check drawn by a bank on another bank.

b. Check drawn by a bank on itself.

c. Check which has been accepted by the drawee bank.

d. Check on which the name of the owner is already signed and which must be countersigned when negotiated.

The correct answer is (b). *(Publisher)*

REQUIRED: The definition of a cashier's check.

DISCUSSION: A check is a draft drawn on a bank and payable on demand. When the drawer is also the drawee, the instrument is a cashier's check.

Answer (a) is incorrect because it describes a bank draft. Answer (c) is incorrect because it describes a certified check. Answer (d) is incorrect because it describes a traveler's check.

102. Drawer writes a check on Drawee Bank. Drawer has sufficient funds in her account and the check is in proper form. When Payee presents the check for payment, Drawee refuses to pay. Drawee is liable to

a. Both Drawer and Payee.

b. Neither Drawer nor Payee.

c. Payee but not Drawer.

d. Drawer but not Payee.

The correct answer is (d). *(Publisher)*

REQUIRED: The liability of a drawee bank for not paying on a check.

DISCUSSION: A bank has no liability to anyone other than its drawer for refusing to pay on a check. Hence, the bank has no liability whatsoever to Payee. Only if the bank accepted (or certified) the check would it be liable to the holder (UCC 3-413.)

Answers (a), (b), and (c) are incorrect because Drawee is liable to Drawer but not Payee.

103. The Mechanics Bank refused to pay a check drawn upon it by Clyde, one of its depositors. Which of the reasons listed below is not a proper defense for the bank to assert when it refused to pay?

a. The bank believed the check to be an overdraft as a result of its misdirecting a deposit made by Clyde.

b. The required endorsement of an intermediary transferee was missing.

c. Clyde had orally stopped payment on the check.

d. The party attempting to cash the check did not have proper identification.

The correct answer is (a). *(CPA 1181 L-2)*

REQUIRED: The statement not a proper defense for a bank to assert when it refused to pay.

DISCUSSION: A bank may refuse payment if the check would be an overdraft. However, if the bank misdirected a deposit made by the drawer, the bank is in error in believing the check to be an overdraft and therefore cannot assert this as a proper defense (UCC 4-402).

Answer (b) is incorrect because the drawee is entitled to have all endorsements on a check prior to payment. Answer (c) is incorrect because an oral stop payment is good for 14 days. Answer (d) is incorrect because a drawee bank is entitled to evidence of identity of the party presenting the check for the purpose of being able to enforce its warranty and contract rights against him/her.

104. Drawer writes a $1,000 check on her account at Drawee Bank. Drawer has only $950 in the account. If Drawer and Drawee have no agreement concerning overdrafts,

a. Drawee may honor the check and charge Drawer's account for $1,000.

b. Drawee may honor the check and charge Drawer's account for no more than $950.

c. Drawee must pay the full amount of the check.

d. Drawee must pay $950.

The correct answer is (a). *(Publisher)*

REQUIRED: The true statement about a bank's rights regarding overdrafts.

DISCUSSION: In the absence of an agreement to permit overdrafts, the bank has no obligation to honor an overdraft. If it chooses to pay the check, the customer has an enforceable implied obligation to reimburse the bank (i.e., effectively a loan). The bank will also have the right to impose a service charge. If the bank and the customer have an agreement permitting overdrafts, the bank will probably charge interest.

Answers (b), (c), and (d) are incorrect because the bank may dishonor the check and return it or pay the check and charge the customer's account even though an overdraft results.

105. Rusty received a check drawn on PDQ Bank by Wallace. It was dated January 1. On August 1, Rusty brought it to PDQ Bank to cash it. If PDQ refuses on the basis that the check was stale,

a. PDQ is liable to Rusty.

b. PDQ is not liable to anyone.

c. PDQ is liable to Wallace.

d. Rusty will lose since the check is stale.

The correct answer is (b). *(Publisher)*

REQUIRED: The correct statement regarding liability on a check that is 7 months old.

DISCUSSION: A drawee is not liable on a check until it accepts the check. Thus, PDQ cannot be liable to anyone except the drawer for dishonoring a check. Under UCC 4-404, a bank is not obligated to pay a stale check, one presented for payment more than 6 months after the date of the check.

Answer (a) is incorrect because as the drawee, PDQ has no liability to Rusty or any other holder until it accepts the check. Answer (c) is incorrect because more than 6 months have passed since the check was issued, so PDQ is not liable for dishonoring it. Answer (d) is incorrect because a drawer remains liable if (s)he receives notice of dishonor. Although the normal time period for presentment of an ordinary check is 30 days in the case of the drawer, the drawer will not be discharged for Rusty's failure to make such presentment unless the check is payable at a bank which becomes insolvent and as a result thereof the drawer is deprived of funds to pay the instrument (UCC 3-501 and 3-502).

106. In general, which of the following statements is correct concerning the priority among checks drawn on a particular account and presented to the drawee bank on a particular day?

a. The checks may be charged to the account in any order convenient to the bank.

b. The checks may be charged to the account in any order provided no charge creates an overdraft.

c. The checks must be charged to the account in the order in which the checks were dated.

d. The checks must be charged to the account in the order of lowest amount to highest amount to minimize the number of dishonored checks.

The correct answer is (a). *(CPA 1188 L-39)*

REQUIRED: The correct statement about the priority among checks presented to a bank for payment.

DISCUSSION: In general, the UCC provides that items may be accepted, paid, certified, or charged to the indicated account of its customer in any order convenient to the bank (UCC 4-303).

Answers (b), (c), and (d) are incorrect because a drawee bank has no obligation to pay the checks in any special order, even to minimize overdrafts.

107. Smith buys a TV set from the ABC Appliance Store and pays for the set with a check. Later in the day Smith finds a better model for the same price at another store. Smith immediately calls ABC trying to cancel the sale. ABC tells Smith that they are holding him to the sale and have negotiated the check to their wholesaler, Glenn Company, as a partial payment on inventory purchases. Smith telephones his bank, the Union Trust Bank, and orders the bank to stop payment on the check. Which of the following statements is correct?

a. If Glenn can prove it is a holder in due course, the drawee bank, Union Trust, must honor Smith's check.

b. Union Trust is not bound or liable for Smith's stop payment order unless the order is placed in writing.

c. If Union Trust mistakenly pays Smith's check 2 days after receiving the stop order, the bank will not be liable.

d. Glenn cannot hold Smith liable on the check.

The correct answer is (c). *(CPA 1181 L-5)*

REQUIRED: The correct statement regarding an oral order to stop payment on a check.

DISCUSSION: An oral order to stop payment is good for 14 days. The drawee bank, however, must be given reasonable time to act on the stop order (UCC 4-403). Because 2 days is probably reasonable time to act on an order to stop payment, the reason the bank will not be liable is that Smith has no defense on the check and will be liable on it. A bank that pays in violation of a stop order succeeds to the rights of the payee (ABC) against the drawer (UCC 4-407).

Answer (a) is incorrect because a drawee bank must honor the order to stop payment and is not liable to any party other than the drawer. Answer (b) is incorrect because an oral order to stop payment is good for 14 days. Answer (d) is incorrect because Smith has no defense on the check and any holder can enforce it.

108. Robb stole one of Markum's blank checks, made it payable to himself, and forged Markum's signature to it. The check was drawn on the Unity Trust Company. Robb cashed the check at the Friendly Check Cashing Company which in turn deposited it with its bank, Farmer's National. Farmer's National proceeded to collect on the check from Unity Trust. The theft and forgery were quickly discovered by Markum who promptly notified Unity. None of the parties were negligent. Who will bear the loss, assuming the amount cannot be recovered from Robb?

a. Markum.

b. Unity Trust Company.

c. Friendly Check Cashing Company.

d. Farmer's National.

The correct answer is (b). *(CPA 580 L-30)*

REQUIRED: The party who will bear the loss when the drawer's signature is forged.

DISCUSSION: Unity must ultimately bear the loss because a drawee bank that pays a check issued over a forged drawer's signature may not charge the customer's account if the customer was not negligent. Unity also may hold neither Friendly nor Farmer's National (the collecting bank) liable on breach of a presentment warranty. On presentment one only warrants that (s)he has no knowledge a drawer's signature is forged (UCC 3-417).

Answers (a), (c), and (d) are incorrect for the reasons discussed above.

109. Path stole a check made out to the order of Marks. Path forged the name of Marks on the back and made the instrument payable to himself. He then negotiated the check to Harrison for cash by signing his own name on the back of the instrument in Harrison's presence. Harrison was unaware of any of the facts surrounding the theft or forged endorsement and presented the check for payment. Central County Bank, the drawee bank, paid it. Disregarding Path, which of the following will bear the loss?

a. The drawer of the check payable to Marks.

b. Central County Bank.

c. Marks.

d. Harrison.

The correct answer is (d). *(CPA 579 L-30)*

REQUIRED: The person bearing the loss when a bank pays over a forged endorsement.

DISCUSSION: This differs from the previous question, which involved the forgery of the drawer's signature. This question involves the forgery of an endorser's signature. Harrison did not qualify as a holder, much less a holder in due course, because the theft and forged endorsement precluded a proper negotiation of the check by the payee. Because Harrison did not acquire title, (s)he breached the presentment warranty of title (UCC 3-417) and is liable to Central County Bank. Harrison's only recourse is against the thief.

Answer (a) is incorrect because the drawer of the check can assert Path's forgery as a defense. Answer (b) is incorrect because Central County Bank can rely on Harrison's warranty of good title. Answer (c) is incorrect because Marks has his own defense of forgery.

110. Which party has the ultimate duty to examine a check for forgeries?

a. Drawer.

b. Drawee.

c. Presenter.

d. Bank of deposit.

The correct answer is (a). *(Publisher)*

REQUIRED: The party who has the ultimate duty to examine checks for forgeries.

DISCUSSION: A drawee bank is expected to know the signature of its drawer and is liable for paying on a forged signature as a general rule. However, the drawer has the ultimate responsibility to discover the forgeries in order to obtain recourse from the drawee bank or any other party (UCC 4-406). A drawer must report any forgeries of his/her signature within one year and has three years to report a forged endorsement.

Answer (b) is incorrect because the UCC puts the ultimate liability on the drawer rather than the drawee. Answer (c) is incorrect because the presenter only makes a warranty that (s)he has no knowledge that the signature of the maker or drawer is unauthorized. Answer (d) is incorrect because the bank of deposit has no responsibility for forgeries unless it happens also to be the drawee bank.

13.8 Electronic Funds Transfers

111. The Electronic Funds Transfer Act (EFTA) is consumer legislation that would not apply to transactions originated through

a. Point-of-sale terminals (POS).

b. Automated tellers (ATM).

c. Machine-generated checks.

d. A transfer by telephone (or pay-by-phone).

The correct answer is (c). *(Publisher)*

REQUIRED: The item to which the EFTA is not applicable.

DISCUSSION: An electronic funds transfer is a "transfer of funds, other than a transaction originated by check, draft, or similar paper instrument, initiated through an electronic terminal, telephonic instrument, or computer or magnetic tape so as to order, instruct, or authorize a financial institution to debit or credit an account." The Act does not apply to machine-generated checks. These checks are negotiable instruments and regulated by UCC Articles 3 and 4.

Answers (a), (b), and (d) are incorrect because point-of-sale devices, automated tellers, direct deposits or withdrawals, and transfers by telephone are within the Act.

112. Acorn Bank received a telexed payment order from Smith directing Acorn to transfer a sum of money from Smith's account to one of Smith's creditors. By midnight of the business day following receipt of the order, however, Acorn had still not made the transfer. Nor did the bank communicate this failure to either Smith or the creditor. Which of the following is true?

a. Acorn Bank is in violation of the midnight notification deadline of UCC Article 4 and is liable for damages.

b. Acorn Bank is in violation of the Commercial Paper Article of the UCC and is therefore liable for damages.

c. Acorn Bank is not in violation of either Article 3 or 4 of the UCC because this is an electronic funds transaction, which is not subject to the UCC. Acorn is not liable for damages under the UCC.

d. Acorn Bank is not in violation of the UCC because the telexed payment order is a negotiable instrument and thus not subject to the midnight notification deadline or liable for damages.

The correct answer is (c). *(Publisher)*

REQUIRED: The true statement about the liability of a bank that fails to carry out a telexed payment order.

DISCUSSION: An unsigned telex is not considered by the courts to be the equivalent of a negotiable instrument. Thus, it cannot be governed by Articles 3 and 4 of the UCC, which concern negotiable instruments, and the transaction is therefore not subject to the midnight notification deadline specified by the UCC.

Answers (a), (b), and (d) are incorrect because the UCC is inapplicable.

113. The average merchant would probably prefer that customers use which of the following types of payment?

a. Point-of-sale transfers.

b. Credit cards.

c. Automated teller machines.

d. Checks.

The correct answer is (a). *(Publisher)*

REQUIRED: The form of payment most likely preferred by most merchants.

DISCUSSION: A point-of-sale (POS) transfer allows a customer to use a debit card to automatically debit his/her account and credit the account of the transferee. The merchant is paid immediately and faces less risk of nonpayment. Hence, most merchants obviously favor POS transfers over more traditional payment methods that involve both more time and more risk.

Answers (b) and (d) are incorrect because each involves more credit risk to the merchant than a POS transfer. Answer (c) is incorrect because ATMs are used to dispense cash, not purchase goods.

114. Under the EFTA, a financial institution holding a customer's account that may be accessed by electronic means must furnish the customer with periodic statements. If the customer discovers an error, the financial institution must comply with certain procedures prescribed by the Act. Which of the following is true?

a. A customer will collect treble damages if the institution is in error.

b. The institution may not require written notice of the error.

c. The institution must recredit the customer's account pending an investigation.

d. After proper notice, the institution is obligated to investigate.

The correct answer is (d). *(Publisher)*

REQUIRED: The true statement about the error resolution procedure under the EFTA.

DISCUSSION: The customer has 60 days to give an oral or written notice of errors in its account, but the institution may require written confirmation within 10 business days of receiving an oral notice. The notice obligates the institution to investigate and report within 10 business days. Any error must be corrected within 1 business day after its discovery. Instead, the institution may temporarily recredit the account within 10 business days of receipt of notice. If it chooses this alternative, it has 45 business days from receipt of notice to complete the investigation. If it finds no error, the institution has 3 business days to mail an explanation to the customer. Failure to adhere to the prescribed procedures or a knowing and willful conclusion (despite the evidence) that the account was not erroneous permits the customer to recover treble damages.

Answer (a) is incorrect because treble damages are available only for failure to follow the rules to resolve an error. Answer (b) is incorrect because written notice can be required. Answer (c) is incorrect because the institution can investigate first if it finishes within 10 days.

115. The EFTA requires financial institutions to provide their customers with written documentation of electronic funds transfers at various times. These times include all of the following except

a. A periodic statement, usually monthly.

b. At the time of each use of an automated teller.

c. At the time of each preauthorized credit to an account.

d. At the time of contracting for EFT services.

The correct answer is (c). *(Publisher)*

REQUIRED: The occasion not requiring the generation of written documentation of an electronic funds transfer.

DISCUSSION: An individual may arrange with a financial institution to have transfers made to his/her account on a prearranged basis. The financial institution and consumer may agree that written notification will only be given when a scheduled credit is not actually made.

Answers (a), (b), and (d) are incorrect because each is written documentation required by the EFTA.

116. Commercial electronic funds transfers, also known as wire transfers, are primarily governed by the

a. Federal Reserve System.

b. Common law of contracts and torts.

c. EFTA.

d. Uniform Commercial Code.

The correct answer is (b). *(Publisher)*

REQUIRED: The source of current law governing commercial electronic fund transfers.

DISCUSSION: Consumer electronic funds transfers are governed by the EFTA. Commercial EFTs, however, are excluded from coverage by the EFTA, the UCC, and most state electronic funds transfer law. Currently, the common law of contracts and torts is used to resolve disputes involving commercial EFTs, or wire transfers.

Answer (a) is incorrect because the Federal Reserve System operates a major wire transfer system, but does not govern all commercial EFTs. Answers (c) and (d) are incorrect because the EFTA and the UCC do not cover commercial EFTs.

117. Hannah Palindrome became aware of the loss of her automated teller card on Monday evening, March 17. The financial statements mailed to Hannah on April 1, May 1, and June 1 showed a $60 withdrawal on March 18 and a $600 withdrawal on March 24 but no other activity in the account. Assuming that the main provisions of the EFTA apply, Hannah is liable for

a. $660 if she reports the loss on June 15.

b. $50 if she reports the loss on May 15.

c. $500 if she reports the loss on March 21.

d. $60 if she reports the loss on March 19.

The correct answer is (a). *(Publisher)*

REQUIRED: The liability of a customer for an unauthorized electronic fund transfer.

DISCUSSION: The consumer's liability is limited to the lesser of $50 or the amount transferred without authorization prior to notifying the financial institution. If the consumer fails to notify the institution within 2 business days after learning of the loss of the means of access, his/her liability is the lesser of $500 or the amount transferred without authorization after 2 business days following discovery of the loss but prior to notification of the institution. If the consumer does not report an unauthorized transfer or error within 60 days of the transmission of a financial statement containing such a transaction or error, the consumer bears the loss. Consequently, if Hannah does not report the loss until June 15, her liability is $660.

Answer (b) is incorrect because Hannah's liability would be $500. Answer (c) is incorrect because Hannah's liability would be $60 (the lesser of $500 or the amount obtained before the report). Answer (d) is incorrect because Hannah's liability would be $50 if she reported the loss within 2 business days.

118. Under the EFTA, a financial institution will avoid liability to its customer for failure to

a. Make a transfer in the proper amount.

b. Make a timely transfer if the terminal does not have sufficient funds.

c. Credit a deposit of funds.

d. Stop payment on a preauthorized transfer when the customer has given sufficient notice.

The correct answer is (b). *(Publisher)*

REQUIRED: The instance in which a financial institution avoids liability under the EFTA.

DISCUSSION: The institution will not be liable when the terminal lacked the cash to complete the transaction or the customer's account had insufficient funds. Except in the case of stop payment orders, the institution may also defend by proving that an act of God or a technical malfunction known to the customer at the time (s)he attempted the transaction caused the failure.

Answers (a), (c), and (d) are incorrect because in general, the financial institution is liable in damages when it fails to make a timely transfer, within the terms of the agreement with the customer, in the correct amount; when it fails to credit a deposit; or when it does not stop payment of a preauthorized transfer (a transfer authorized in advance to be repeated at specified intervals).

13.9 Letters of Credit

119. A letter of credit is

a. A letter documenting a line of credit on which a customer may draw at its bank.

b. An engagement by a financial institution to pay drafts or other demands for payment for its customer.

c. A letter by a buyer or seller of goods that credit is due the other party for defective or returned goods.

d. A credit reference given by a bank.

The correct answer is (b). *(Publisher)*

REQUIRED: The statement that correctly identifies a letter of credit.

DISCUSSION: Letters of credit are governed by Article 5 of the UCC. A letter of credit is an engagement by a bank or other person made at the request of a customer to honor drafts or other demands for payment upon compliance with the conditions specified (UCC 5-103). The holder of a letter of credit merely needs to present the required drafts or other documents (usually documenting a sale of goods to the bank's customer) and will immediately receive payment from the bank up to the limit specified.

Answer (a) is incorrect because it describes a credit on which a customer itself may borrow from a bank. Answer (c) is incorrect because it describes a credit memorandum. At the end of some agreed period such memoranda are netted with invoices to determine what is due from one or the other party. Answer (d) is incorrect because a credit reference is a statement concerning the creditworthiness of a person.

120. Which of the following is required for a valid letter of credit?

a. That consideration is given.

b. That it is written and signed.

c. That it is irrevocable.

d. That consent by the customer is given to modify it.

The correct answer is (b). *(Publisher)*

REQUIRED: The characteristic of a valid letter of credit.

DISCUSSION: Under UCC 5-104, a letter of credit must be in writing and signed by the issuer. Furthermore, any modification of the terms must also be written and signed by the issuer.

Answer (a) is incorrect because consideration is not necessary to establish a letter of credit under UCC 5-105. Answer (c) is incorrect because a letter of credit may be revocable or irrevocable pursuant to the definition in UCC 5-103. Answer (d) is incorrect because a revocable letter of credit may be modified or revoked by the issuer without notice to or consent by the customer or beneficiary, unless otherwise agreed (UCC 5-106).

121. Seattle Seller entered into a sales agreement with Bonn Buyer (in Germany) which required Bonn to issue a letter of credit. Bonn obtained a letter of credit from the Bank of Germany which in turn cabled it to the Bank of New York for Seattle Seller. The letter of credit required a bill of lading to be presented for payment. Seattle Seller shipped the goods and obtained a bill of lading from the carrier. How and when can Seattle Seller receive payment for the goods?

a. From the Bank of Germany after Bonn receives the goods.

b. From the Bank of Germany as soon as the bill of lading can be sent to Germany.

c. From the Bank of Germany upon the Bank of New York's notification of receipt of the bill of lading.

d. From the Bank of New York upon presentment of the bill of lading.

The correct answer is (d). *(Publisher)*

REQUIRED: By whom and when a beneficiary can be paid on a letter of credit issued on a foreign bank.

DISCUSSION: A letter of credit is an engagement by the issuing bank to pay on behalf of its customer when the requirements of the letter of credit are complied with (UCC 5-103). When the beneficiary (in this case Seattle Seller) is in a foreign country, the letter of credit is often sent to a confirming bank that will pay the beneficiary directly and then be paid by the issuing bank. In this case, the Bank of New York is the confirming bank that will pay Seattle Seller upon compliance with the terms so that Seattle Seller need not present the necessary documents and seek payment from the Bank of Germany. The Bank of New York in turn will be repaid by the Bank of Germany through their international credit and monetary exchanges.

Answers (a), (b), and (c) are incorrect for the reasons discussed above.

122. Samantha Clothiers of Denver, Colorado wants to buy men's suits from Altskool & Sons in Frankfurt, Germany. Samantha will send a buyer to Frankfurt carrying an irrevocable letter of credit issued by Big National Bank of Denver and naming Altskool as beneficiary. The letter of credit states that it is governed by UCC Article 5. It permits Altskool to draw a draft of up to $200,000 payable to Altskool through Big National. The bank will honor the draft if it is accompanied by 1) a negotiable bill of lading issued by a carrier to which Altskool has delivered the suits for shipment to Samantha and 2) a certificate of insurance covering the suits. In which of the following circumstances may Big National refuse to honor a draft drawn by Altskool?

a. The documents accompanying the draft do not on their face conform to the requirements of the letter of credit.

b. The suits as shipped contain hidden defects that constitute a breach of warranty.

c. Samantha has become insolvent and is unable to reimburse Big National for amounts Big National pays to Altskool.

d. All of the above.

The correct answer is (a). *(D. Paas)*

REQUIRED: The circumstance allowing dishonor of a letter of credit.

DISCUSSION: UCC 5-114 provides that an issuer (Big National) must honor a draft or demand for payment under a letter of credit regardless of whether the goods or documents conform to the underlying contract of sale (between Samantha and Altskool), but only if the documents conform on their face to the terms of the letter of credit.

Answer (b) is incorrect because the goods need not be conforming. Answer (c) is incorrect because under UCC 5-106, an issuer must honor a letter of credit that is irrevocable once it is received by a party claiming rights under it. Because Altskool has received the letter of credit, Big National must honor its drafts if the documents conform on their face to the terms of the letter of credit. Answer (d) is incorrect because Big National may not dishonor a draft in the circumstances described in (b) and (c).

123. Assume in the preceding question that Samantha and Altskool contract for $200,000 of suits to be shipped to Denver. Altskool delivers the suits to a carrier and obtains a bill of lading that complies with the letter of credit. But it cannot obtain insurance. Altskool forges a blank certificate of insurance so skillfully that the certificate appears to be genuine and complies with the letter of credit. Altskool then draws a draft for $200,000 payable to itself and attaches the bill of lading and the forged certificate.

a. If Altskool presents the draft to Big National, the bank must not pay it.

b. If Altskool presents the draft to Big National, the bank cannot pay if it knows of the forgery; but if it does not know, it may pay.

c. If Altskool negotiates the draft and other documents to a Frankfurt bank for value so that the bank becomes a holder in due course, Big National still has an option either to pay or not pay the Frankfurt bank upon presentment of the draft.

d. If Altskool negotiates the draft and documents to a Frankfurt bank for value so that the bank becomes a holder in due course, Big National must pay the Frankfurt bank.

The correct answer is (d). *(D. Paas)*

REQUIRED: The true statement about the negotiation of letters of credit when defects exist.

DISCUSSION: Under UCC 5-114, a distinction is drawn between holders in due course (HDC) and those who are not. An issuer (Big National) can refuse to honor a beneficiary's draft (such as that drawn by Altskool, a party not a holder in due course) if required documents are forged or fraudulent. But even with respect to a party not a holder in due course, the Code allows an issuer acting in good faith to honor a draft accompanied by forged documents as long as the forgery is not apparent from the face of the documents. However, a court may enjoin such honor.

Answers (a) and (b) are incorrect because the forged insurance certificate is regular on its face and the bank can choose either to honor or dishonor Altskool's presentment. But under UCC 5-114, a holder in due course always must be paid if documents appear on their face to comply with the terms of the letter of credit. Answer (c) is incorrect because the documents are regular and Big National has no choice but to pay.

13.10 Documents of Title

124. Which of the following is not a document of title covered by Article 7 of the UCC?

a. Destination bill.

b. Warehouse receipt.

c. Bill of lading.

d. Chattel mortgage.

The correct answer is (d). *(Publisher)*

REQUIRED: The item not a document of title.

DISCUSSION: A document of title is issued by a bailee covering goods in the bailee's possession or care (UCC 1-201). It represents ownership of the goods and is ordinarily needed to obtain the goods from the bailee. The two major types of documents of title are bills of lading (issued by carriers) and warehouse receipts (issued by warehousemen). A chattel mortgage is a document providing for a security interest in personal property. Chattel mortgages are governed by Article 9 (under the catch-all term "security interests").

Answer (a) is incorrect because a destination bill is a bill of lading which is issued by a carrier at the place of destination to the sender's agent. Answer (b) is incorrect because a warehouse receipt is a document of title issued by a person in the business of storing goods for hire. Answer (c) is incorrect because a bill of lading is a document of title which evidences receipt of goods by the carrier for shipment.

125. Documents of title do not perform which of the following functions?

a. Obligation of repayment.

b. Receipt for a bailment.

c. Contract for storage or shipment.

d. Symbol evidencing ownership of goods.

The correct answer is (a). *(Publisher)*

REQUIRED: The function that documents of title do not perform.

DISCUSSION: Documents of title function as receipts for bailments, contracts for storage or shipment, and symbols evidencing ownership of goods. However, a document of title does not encompass an obligation of repayment. An obligation of repayment is generally represented by a note, draft, certificate of deposit, etc.

Answers (b), (c), and (d) are incorrect because each is a function of a document of title.

126. Under the UCC, a warehouse receipt

a. Will not be negotiable if it contains a contractual limitation on the warehouseman's liability.

b. May qualify as both a negotiable warehouse receipt and negotiable commercial paper if the instrument is payable either in cash or by the delivery of goods.

c. May be issued only by a bonded and licensed warehouseman.

d. Is negotiable if by its terms the goods are to be delivered to bearer or the order of a named person.

The correct answer is (d). *(CPA 589 L-53)*

REQUIRED: The correct statement about a warehouse receipt.

DISCUSSION: Article 7 of the UCC controls documents of title. A document of title known as a warehouse receipt is issued by a person storing goods for hire as a receipt for goods and to represent these goods. A document of title may be negotiable if by its terms the goods are to be delivered to the order of a named person or to bearer (UCC 7-104).

Answer (a) is incorrect because limits on a warehouseman's liability do not affect the negotiability of a warehouse receipt. Answer (b) is incorrect because negotiable commercial paper must be payable only in money. Answer (c) is incorrect because the UCC does not require warehousemen be bonded and licensed before they can issue warehouse receipts.

127. Which of the following is not a warranty made by the seller of a negotiable warehouse receipt to the purchaser of the document?

a. The document transfer is fully effective with respect to the goods it represents.

b. The warehouseman will honor the document.

c. The seller has no knowledge of any facts that would impair the document's validity.

d. The document is genuine.

The correct answer is (b). *(CPA 1188 L-42)*

REQUIRED: The warranty not made by the seller of a negotiable warehouse receipt.

DISCUSSION: The seller of a negotiable warehouse receipt does not guarantee that the warehouseman will honor the document.

Answers (a), (c), and (d) are incorrect because UCC 7-507 provides that a transferor for value makes these specific warranties to his/her immediate purchaser.

128. A negotiable bill of lading

a. Is one type of commercial paper as defined by the UCC.

b. Can give certain good faith purchasers greater rights to the bill of lading or the goods than the transferor had.

c. Cannot result in a loss to the owner if lost or stolen, provided prompt notice is given to the carrier in possession of the goods.

d. Does not give the rightful possessor the ownership of the goods.

The correct answer is (b). *(CPA 583 L-45)*

REQUIRED: The true statement about a negotiable bill of lading.

DISCUSSION: A bill of lading is a document of title evidencing receipt of goods by the carrier for shipment. It is negotiable if by its terms the goods are to be delivered to bearer or to the order of a named person (UCC 7-104). When it is duly negotiated, the transferee will take free of many defenses good against the transferor or even the original bailor. For example, a thief can negotiate by delivery alone a bearer instrument or an order instrument endorsed in blank. A subsequent holder could have taken by due negotiation and acquired rights paramount to the thief's or the original bailor's.

Answer (a) is incorrect because a bill of lading is a document of title. UCC Article 3 is entitled "Commercial Paper" and applies only to drafts, checks, notes, and certificates of deposit. Answer (c) is incorrect because a bearer instrument or one endorsed in blank could be duly negotiated to a good faith purchaser by one who found or stole it. The holder would then have rights paramount to the owner's. Answer (d) is incorrect because a document of title evidences ownership.

129. A carrier who has issued a bill of lading may release the goods to

a. The bailor without surrender of a nonnegotiable document of title.

b. The bailor without surrender of a negotiable document of title.

c. The holder of a document of title as against the previous holder whose endorsement was forged.

d. The bailor as against a holder who took by due negotiation from a thief.

The correct answer is (a). *(Publisher)*

REQUIRED: The party to whom a carrier may release goods subject to a bill of lading.

DISCUSSION: In the case of a nonnegotiable document of title, the document itself is not required in order to obtain the goods so long as the person requesting release can prove (s)he is either the bailor or an assignee of the rights of the bailor.

Answer (b) is incorrect because goods subject to a negotiable document of title can only be released upon presentment of that document since a holder by due negotiation can obtain better rights than the original bailor. The principle is the same as for a holder in due course of a negotiable instrument. Answer (c) is incorrect because a holder claiming under a forged endorsement cannot acquire rights paramount to the previous owner's since the forged endorsement precludes a due negotiation. Answer (d) is incorrect because a thief can negotiate a bearer instrument or an order instrument which was endorsed in blank. A subsequent holder could have taken by due negotiation and acquired rights paramount to the original bailor's.

130. Bond Corp. issued a negotiable warehouse receipt to Grey for goods stored in Bond's warehouse. Grey's goods were lost because of Bond's failure to exercise such care as a reasonably careful person would under like circumstances. The state in which this transaction occurred follows the UCC rule with respect to a warehouseman's liability for lost goods. The warehouse receipt is silent on this point. Under the circumstances, Bond is

a. Liable because it was negligent.

b. Liable because it is strictly liable for any loss.

c. Not liable unless Grey can establish that Bond was grossly negligent.

d. Not liable because the warehouse receipt was negotiable.

The correct answer is (a). *(CPA 1187 L-36)*

REQUIRED: The liability of a warehouseman that failed to exercise reasonable care.

DISCUSSION: A warehouseman is liable for damages for loss of or injury to goods caused by its failure to exercise reasonable care (UCC 7-204). Bond's negligence in failing to exercise the care of a reasonable person makes Bond liable for the lost goods.

Answer (b) is incorrect because warehousemen are not liable for losses caused by events beyond their control, provided that due care was exercised. Answer (c) is incorrect because Grey need not prove gross negligence, only simple negligence. Answer (d) is incorrect because the negotiability of the warehouse receipt is irrelevant to the warehouseman's liability.

131. Thieves broke into the warehouse of Monogram Airways and stole a shipment of computer parts belonging to Valley Instruments. Valley had in its possession a negotiable bill of lading covering the shipment. The thieves transported the stolen parts to another state and placed the parts in a bonded warehouse. The thieves received a negotiable warehouse receipt that they used to secure a loan of $20,000 from Reliable Finance. These facts were revealed upon apprehension of the thieves. Regarding the rights of the parties,

a. Reliable is entitled to a $20,000 payment before relinquishment of the parts.

b. Monogram will be the ultimate loser of the $20,000.

c. Valley is entitled to recover the parts free of Reliable's $20,000 claim.

d. Valley is not entitled to the parts but may obtain damages from Monogram.

The correct answer is (c). *(CPA 1183 L-47)*

REQUIRED: The rights of the parties when goods covered by a document of title are stolen.

DISCUSSION: Under UCC 7-503, "A document of title confers no right in goods against a person who before issuance had a legal right in them and who neither delivered or entrusted them or any document covering them to the bailor with actual or apparent authority to ship, store, or sell or with power to obtain delivery or with power of disposition." Because Valley had a legal right in the goods and did not deliver or entrust them or a document covering them to the bailor (the thieves), the warehouse receipt gave no right to Reliable or anyone else against Valley. It did not represent title to the goods.

Answers (a) and (d) are incorrect because Valley may recover the parts from Reliable. Answers (b) and (d) are incorrect because the carrier (Monogram) will have no liability if it exercised the degree of care in relation to the goods that a reasonably careful person would have exercised in like circumstances (UCC 7-309).

132. Safekeeping, Inc., a public warehouse operator, issued negotiable warehouse receipts to the owner of whiskey stored in the warehouse. As required by law each receipt set forth the storage and other charges for which Safekeeping claimed liens on the whiskey. Safekeeping then became bankrupt and the warehouse was sold to another warehouse operator at a judicial foreclosure sale. The foreclosure sale was for the benefit of all creditors who held claims against Safekeeping. Which of the following is a correct legal conclusion?

a. The judicial foreclosure sale extinguished the legal and equitable interests of the holder of the warehouse receipts in the whiskey held for storage by Safekeeping.

b. The trustee in bankruptcy appointed for Safekeeping was immediately vested with legal title to the whiskey upon the filing of the bankruptcy petition.

c. The negotiable warehouse receipts represent legal ownership of the whiskey, and the owner of the receipts is entitled to the property.

d. The successor warehouse operator is not entitled to the whiskey and cannot collect the storage and other charges against the owner.

The correct answer is (c). *(CPA 1177 L-25)*

REQUIRED: The correct legal conclusion when the issuer of a negotiable warehouse receipt becomes bankrupt and the warehouse is sold.

DISCUSSION: Negotiable warehouse receipts represent complete legal ownership and the right to recover goods put in possession of the bailee. The owner of the receipts is entitled to the property because these goods do not become part of the bankrupt's estate.

Answer (a) is incorrect because the goods are the property of the holder of the negotiable receipts and are merely subject to the warehouseman's lien for storage and other charges. Answer (b) is incorrect because the bailee had no title to the goods (just a lien for charges) covered by the warehouse receipts, and the trustee in bankruptcy could not obtain title to them. Answer (d) is incorrect because although the successor warehouse operator is not entitled to the whiskey, it can collect for storage and other charges which are due under the storage agreement for which the negotiable warehouse receipts were issued.

133. The procedure necessary to negotiate a document of title depends principally on whether the document is

a. An order document or a bearer document.

b. Issued by a bailee or a consignee.

c. A receipt for goods stored or goods already shipped.

d. A bill of lading or a warehouse receipt.

The correct answer is (a). *(CPA 588 L-49)*

REQUIRED: The factor most affecting the negotiation of a document of title.

DISCUSSION: The negotiation of a document of title principally depends on whether the document is an order document or a bearer document. An order document must be endorsed and delivered to be properly negotiated. But delivery suffices to complete the negotiation of a bearer document.

Answers (b) and (c) are incorrect because they are irrelevant to the negotiation of a document of title. Answer (d) is incorrect because bills of lading and warehouse receipts are both documents of title, and negotiation requires the same procedures for both.

134. Manny Klep burglarized the premises of Apple Sales Co. He stole several negotiable warehouse receipts that were deliverable to the order of Apple. Klep endorsed Apple's name on the instruments and transferred them to Margo Wholesalers, a bona fide purchaser for value. As between Apple and Margo,

a. Apple will prevail because the warehouseman must be notified before any negotiation is effective.

b. Apple will prevail because the thief's endorsement prevents a due negotiation.

c. Margo will prevail because it has taken a negotiable warehouse receipt as a bona fide purchaser for value.

d. Margo will prevail because the warehouse receipt was converted to a bearer instrument by Klep's endorsement.

The correct answer is (b). *(CPA 1186 L-48)*

REQUIRED: The effect of a forged endorsement on a document of title.

DISCUSSION: A holder to whom a negotiable document of title has been "duly negotiated" acquires title to the document (UCC 7-502). However, "due negotiation" requires an endorsement as well as delivery if the document runs to the order of a named person (UCC 7-501). In addition, the holder must have purchased in good faith, for value, and in the ordinary course of business. Klep's forgery of Apple's endorsement does not constitute due negotiation, and provides Apple a real defense against Margo, even though Margo was a bona fide purchaser for value.

Answer (a) is incorrect because negotiation does not require notification of the warehouseman. Answer (c) is incorrect because the warehouse receipt was not duly negotiated. Answer (d) is incorrect because a forged endorsement does not convert a warehouse receipt into a bearer instrument.

135. Woody Pyle, a public warehouseman, issued Merlin a negotiable warehouse receipt for fungible goods stored. Pyle

a. May not limit the amount of his liability for his own negligence.

b. Will be absolutely liable for any damages in the absence of a statute or a provision on the warehouse receipt to the contrary.

c. May commingle Merlin's goods with similar fungible goods of other bailors.

d. Is obligated to deliver the goods to Merlin despite Merlin's improper refusal to pay the storage charges due.

The correct answer is (c). *(CPA 584 L-46)*

REQUIRED: The true statement about a warehouseman's rights and duties.

DISCUSSION: Unless otherwise provided by the receipt, "A warehouseman must keep separate the goods covered by each receipt so as to permit at all times identification and delivery of those goods except that different lots of fungible goods may be commingled" (UCC 7-207).

Answer (a) is incorrect because damages may be limited by the warehouse receipt or storage agreement (UCC 7-204). Answer (b) is incorrect because, unless otherwise agreed, Pyle is not liable for damages that could not have been avoided by the exercise of such care as a reasonably careful person would have exercised in the circumstances (UCC 7-204). Answer (d) is incorrect because a warehouseman has a lien on the goods that may be enforced by a public or private sale (UCC 7-209 and 7-210).

CHAPTER FOURTEEN
AGENCY

14.1 Nature and Creation of Agency and Related Matters

1. Lime is the chief executive officer of Alternative Publications, Inc. Jonstock manages the corporate office, and his duties include hiring, sales, and purchasing. Marcar performs clerical duties and acts as an inside salesperson. Rick performs solely a word processing function. Darsey renders clerical and editorial services but has no contact with customers or suppliers. Merwin writes books published by the firm pursuant to instructions received from Lime. Key occasionally provides manuscript material for a fee but is not subject to control by the company. Which of the following is true?

a. Alternative Publications is a principal.

b. Jonstock is a principal.

c. Merwin is an independent contractor.

d. Darsey is an agent.

The correct answer is (a). *(Publisher)*

REQUIRED: The statement accurately describing the parties in the corporate structure.

DISCUSSION: In an agency, one person (the agent) agrees with a second person (the principal) to act for or on behalf of the second person and subject to his/her control or direction. The parties must be competent to act as agent and principal, and the relationship entered into is a fiduciary one. A corporation is clearly a principal since it is a legal person with contractual capacity and can only act through others (its agents).

Answer (b) is incorrect because Jonstock is an agent of a corporate principal since he acts in the place of the corporation and derives his authority therefrom. He may perform legal acts that bind the corporation. Answers (c) and (d) are incorrect because Merwin and Darsey are only employees since their work is completely controlled by the employer and they have no authority to legally bind anyone. Key is an independent contractor, i.e., not controlled by the "employer" as to the means of completing a job.

2. Using the facts in the previous question, which of the following is an agent?

a. Key.

b. Marcar.

c. Rick.

d. Alternative Publications.

The correct answer is (b). *(Publisher)*

REQUIRED: The person correctly described as an agent.

DISCUSSION: An agent is a person competent to act by mutual agreement for or on behalf of another person and subject to that person's direction or control. As a seller of the corporate principal's products, Marcar qualifies as an agent since she has authority to enter legally binding agreements on behalf of the corporation.

Answer (a) is incorrect because Key is an independent contractor but not an agent. Answer (c) is incorrect because Rick is an employee but not an agent. Answer (d) is incorrect because Alternative is a principal.

3. Which of the following is a correct statement about agents, employees, and independent contractors?

a. Income tax and FICA withholding, workers' compensation, and unemployment compensation statutes apply to both independent contractors and employees.

b. Independent contractors are employees but cannot be agents.

c. Independent contractors are not employees but can be agents.

d. An employee cannot be an agent but may be an independent contractor.

The correct answer is (c). *(Publisher)*

REQUIRED: The correct statement about agents, employees, and independent contractors.

DISCUSSION: An independent contractor is a person who contracts with another to perform a task but is neither controlled nor subject to a right of control in the performance of the task. (S)he may or may not be an agent. An example of an independent contractor who is also an agent is a real estate broker. The broker is hired by an owner of real estate to negotiate a sale and is thus an agent by reason of the capacity to act for another. Since a broker is not subject to control but is hired solely to achieve a result, (s)he is an independent contractor. An independent contractor is not an employee (a person subject to control by the employer).

Answer (a) is incorrect because such statutes apply only to employees and employers. Answer (b) is incorrect because independent contractors can be agents but are usually not. Answer (d) is incorrect because an employee can be an agent but not an independent contractor since the employee is subject to the employer's control.

4. The key characteristic of a servant (employee) is that

a. His physical conduct is controlled or subject to the right of control by the employer.

b. He is paid at an hourly rate as contrasted with the payment of a salary.

c. He is precluded from making contracts for and on behalf of his employer.

d. He lacks apparent authority to bind his employer.

The correct answer is (a). *(CPA 1181 L-15)*

REQUIRED: The key characteristic of an employee.

DISCUSSION: Master-servant is old terminology (which you may still run across) for employer-employee. A servant is a type of employee whose actions are entirely subject to control by the employer during the relationship. The servant/employee is employed to do physical acts and perform services for the employer, rather than act as a business representative. Other employees may qualify as agents and be subject to lesser physical control.

Answer (b) is incorrect because servants may be paid at either an hourly rate or by salary. Answer (c) is incorrect because a servant may make contracts for and on behalf of his/her employer as long as the servant has authority. Answer (d) is incorrect because a servant may have apparent authority to bind his/her employer, depending on what the servant is doing.

5. Jay White, an engineer, entered into a contract with Sky, Inc. agreeing to provide Sky with certain specified consulting services. After performing the services, White was paid pursuant to the contract but Social Security taxes were not withheld from his check since Sky considered White an independent contractor. The IRS has asserted that White was an employee and claims that a deficiency exists because of Sky's failure to withhold and pay Social Security taxes. Which of the following factors is most likely to support the IRS's position that White is an employee?

a. White was paid in one lump sum after all the services were performed.

b. White provided his own office and supplies.

c. Sky supervised and controlled the manner in which White performed the services.

d. Sky reserved the right to inspect White's work.

The correct answer is (c). *(CPA 1185 L-22)*

REQUIRED: The factor supporting the view that a person is an employee.

DISCUSSION: An employee's actions are entirely subject to control by the employer during the relationship. An independent contractor is generally hired to achieve certain results without much control over his/her performance. Other factors to be considered are the mode of payment, whether the contracting parties are in distinct businesses or occupations, whether the work is supervised and performed with the employer's tools and supplies, the length of the employment, and the degree of skill involved.

Answers (a) and (b) are incorrect because each states a fact typical of independent contractor status. Answer (d) is incorrect because actual control is the strongest argument in favor of employee status.

6. A principal and agent relationship requires a

a. Meeting of the minds and consent to act.

b. Specified consideration.

c. Written agreement.

d. Power of attorney.

The correct answer is (a). *(CPA 1189 L-1)*

REQUIRED: The requirement of a principal and agent relationship.

DISCUSSION: The requirements to create an agency relationship are an agreement between principal and agent on the relationship and subject matter, legality of the subject matter, and capacity of the principal.

Answer (b) is incorrect because the creation of the agency relationship does not require consideration. Answer (c) is incorrect because most agency relationships do not require a written agreement. Answer (d) is incorrect because power of attorney is a specific type of agency.

7. An agency relationship

a. Must be in writing if it is to be legally enforceable.

b. Creates a fiduciary duty on the principal's part.

c. Can be created by estoppel, i.e., implied as a matter of law.

d. Is normally delegable as a matter of law.

The correct answer is (c). *(CPA 575 L-28)*

REQUIRED: The correct statement regarding an agency relationship.

DISCUSSION: An agency relationship may arise by estoppel when a person represents him/herself as an agent, the alleged principal knows of the representation and does not deny it, and a third person reasonably but detrimentally relies on the existence of an agency. The "principal" is then prevented (estopped) from asserting the nonexistence of the agency relationship.

Answer (a) is incorrect because an agency relationship may usually be oral or implied. Answer (b) is incorrect because the agent has a fiduciary duty, not the principal. Answer (d) is incorrect because an agent may not normally delegate his/her duties unless the principal consents or it is normal under the circumstances.

8. Anker wishes to give Mix power of attorney. In general, the power of attorney

a. May limit Mix's authority to specific transactions.

b. Must be signed by both Anker and Mix.

c. Will be valid only if Mix is a licensed attorney at law.

d. May continue in existence after Anker's death.

The correct answer is (a). *(CPA 1188 L-1)*

REQUIRED: The correct statement concerning a power of attorney.

DISCUSSION: A power of attorney is a written authorization for the agent to act on behalf of the principal. A power of attorney can be general or it can grant the agent restricted authority.

Answer (b) is incorrect because a power of attorney is a delegation of authority and need only be signed by the principal. Answer (c) is incorrect because any person can have power of attorney. One need not be an attorney at law. Answer (d) is incorrect because the death of a principal terminates an agency relationship, but some states have enacted statutes in recent years to allow powers of attorney to continue after death in some situations.

9. Jim entered into an oral agency agreement with Sally whereby he authorized Sally to sell his interest in a parcel of real estate, Blueacre. Within 7 days, Sally sold Blueacre to Dan, signing the real estate contract on behalf of Jim. Dan failed to record the real estate contract within a reasonable time. Which of the following is correct?

a. Dan may enforce the real estate contract against Jim since it satisfied the Statute of Frauds.

b. Dan may enforce the real estate contract against Jim since Sally signed the contract as Jim's agent.

c. The real estate contract is unenforceable against Jim since Sally's authority to sell Blueacre was oral.

d. The real estate contract is unenforceable against Jim since Dan failed to record the contract within a reasonable time.

The correct answer is (c). *(CPA 1184 L-22)*

REQUIRED: The true statement about an oral agency to sell realty.

DISCUSSION: Under the equal dignity rule, if the contract must be in writing, the agent's authority must be in writing if the principal is to be bound. The contract is therefore voidable at Jim's option since it was required by the Statute of Frauds to be written and Sally's agency was oral. In most other situations, the agent's authority may be oral.

Answers (a) and (b) are incorrect because the contract operates only as an offer since the agency was oral. Answer (d) is incorrect because if Jim and Dan had entered into a binding agreement, it would be effective without recordation. Compliance with the recording statute is necessary to protect against parties not privy to the contract.

10. Wok Corp. has decided to expand the scope of its business. In this connection, it contemplates engaging several agents. Which of the following agency relationships is within the Statute of Frauds and thus should be contained in a signed writing?

a. A sales agency.

b. An irrevocable agency.

c. An agency of indefinite duration but terminable upon 1 month's notice.

d. An agency for the forthcoming calendar year entered into in mid-December of the prior year.

The correct answer is (d). *(CPA 585 L-1)*

REQUIRED: The agency relationship that must be contained in a signed writing.

DISCUSSION: The Statute of Frauds requires a contract that cannot be completed within 1 year from its making to be in writing. An agency relationship for the forthcoming calendar year entered into in mid-December cannot be completed for approximately 1 year and ½ month from the time the contract was formed.

Answer (a) is incorrect because a sales agency is not required to be in writing unless the terms of the agency fall within the Statute of Frauds, e.g., to continue for more than 1 year. Answer (b) is incorrect because an irrevocable agency can be created without a writing. Answer (c) is incorrect because an agency terminable upon 1 month's notice does not require more than 1 year to be completed, and is thus not subject to the Statute of Frauds.

11. Hill is an agent for Newman. On behalf of Newman, Hill contracts to purchase furniture from A&M Wholesalers. Hill has previously purchased furniture on behalf of Newman from A&M Wholesalers. This contract is voidable by Newman if

a. It was not in writing.

b. Newman is a minor.

c. A&M Wholesalers is owned 50% by Newman.

d. Hill is a minor.

The correct answer is (b). *(Publisher)*

REQUIRED: The statement which would allow the principal to void a contract entered into by the agent.

DISCUSSION: Any person may act through an agent to the same extent the person may act on his/her own, but a principal cannot gain greater contractual capacity through an agent. Therefore, if Newman is a minor, a contract made by his/her agent is voidable to the same extent it would be if made by Newman.

Answer (a) is incorrect because generally an agency relationship is not required to be written. Answer (c) is incorrect because a contract is valid between a shareholder and a substantially owned corporation. An agent of the shareholder would have the capacity to contract with such a corporation. Answer (d) is incorrect because an agent does not need the capacity to contract as long as the principal has that capacity.

12. Auctioneers are generally considered professional agents. Which statement is correct concerning auctioneers?

a. They are general agents.

b. They are agents of the purchaser.

c. They are servants.

d. They are agents of the seller.

The correct answer is (d). *(Publisher)*

REQUIRED: The correct statement concerning the status of auctioneers.

DISCUSSION: Auctioneers are generally considered agents of the seller. The seller hires the auctioneer to conduct the sale for him/her. After the acceptance of a bid, the auctioneer becomes a dual agent for the purpose of signing the memorandum of sale as agent for the purchaser.

Answer (a) is incorrect because an auctioneer is a special agent engaged to perform a single transaction, i.e., the sale or auction of certain goods. Answer (b) is incorrect because the auctioneer is attempting to obtain the best price for the seller and act on the seller's behalf (except for signing the memorandum of sale for the purchaser). Answer (c) is incorrect because an auctioneer is not subject to the physical control of the seller (principal), and is thus really an independent contractor.

13. Paul employed Terry as his agent to purchase a tract of real property, to sell some bonds owned by Paul, and to investigate a potential investment in a city 1,000 miles away. Terry is a

a. Universal agent.

b. Servant.

c. General agent.

d. Special agent.

The correct answer is (d). *(Publisher)*

REQUIRED: The type of agent when the agent has several broad duties.

DISCUSSION: A special agent is one authorized to conduct a certain transaction. A person may be a special agent with regard to several specific transactions. As long as the authorization is not to perform all transactions, it is still a special agency.

Answer (a) is incorrect because a universal agent is one authorized to perform all acts and transactions which a principal may delegate. Answer (b) is incorrect because a servant is not authorized to contract on behalf of the principal. Answer (c) is incorrect because a general agent is one authorized to perform all transactions in a certain area. A general agent's authority is broader than a special agent's but narrower than a universal agent's.

14. Which of the following acts can a principal employ an agent to perform?

a. Sell real property.

b. Vote for a political candidate with a power of attorney.

c. Commit a crime.

d. Sign a will with a power of attorney.

The correct answer is (a). *(Publisher)*

REQUIRED: The act which a principal can employ an agent to perform.

DISCUSSION: An agency can be created to perform most acts the principal could lawfully perform. The selling of real property is an ordinary business transaction which can be performed by an agent. However, many states require that such an agency be in writing.

Answers (b) and (d) are incorrect because voting and signing a will are each a personal act which cannot be delegated to an agent even with a power of attorney. Answer (c) is incorrect because an act must be lawful to be delegable to an agent.

15. A subagent

a. Is an agent appointed by an agent to serve as an agent of the principal but not of the appointing agent.

b. Has no fiduciary duty to the original principal although the principal knows of the subagency.

c. Does not have the power to subject the original principal to liability.

d. Is an agent of an agent.

The correct answer is (d). *(Publisher)*

REQUIRED: The true statement about a subagent.

DISCUSSION: An agent who has the authority to do so may appoint an agent to transact the original principal's business. Accordingly, the agent effectively becomes a principal. Unless specifically authorized, however, the tasks delegable to the subagent may only be clerical or ministerial, not those requiring the exercise of discretion. The subagent is an agent of both the appointing agent and the original principal.

Answer (a) is incorrect because a subagent is distinguished from an agent appointed by an agent to be an agent only of the principal. For example, a salesperson hired by a sales manager of a company is an agent of the company, not of the sales manager. Answer (b) is incorrect because the subagent owes the original principal the usual duties owed by an agent except those based on a contract. Answer (c) is incorrect because the subagent is an agent of the original principal and has the power of an agent to bind the principal, provided the appointment was expressly or impliedly authorized.

16. An agency coupled with an interest will be created by a written agreement providing that

a. A borrower shall pledge securities to a lender and authorize the lender to sell the securities and apply the proceeds to the loan in the event of default.

b. An employee is hired for a period of two years at $40,000 per annum plus 2% of net sales.

c. A broker is to receive a 5% sales commission out of the proceeds of the sale of a parcel of land.

d. An attorney is to receive 25% of a plaintiff's recovery for personal injuries.

The correct answer is (a). *(CPA 585 L-3)*

REQUIRED: The agreement creating an agency coupled with an interest.

DISCUSSION: The lender is an agent with an interest in the subject matter of the agency separate from the principal's and not existing for the principal's benefit. The agent's power to sell the securities is to the agent's but not the principal's advantage because it secures a loan.

Answers (b), (c), and (d) are incorrect because each is a case in which the agent has no distinct interest in the property of the agency that is not exercised for the benefit of the principal. In each, the power of the agent is exercised to benefit the principal.

14.2 Rights and Duties Between Principal and Agent

17. Which of the following is not an essential element of an agency relationship?

a. It must be created by contract.

b. The agent must be subject to the principal's control.

c. The agent is a fiduciary in respect to the principal.

d. The agent acts on behalf of another and not him/herself.

The correct answer is (a). *(CPA 1181 L-12)*

REQUIRED: The item not an essential element of an agency relationship.

DISCUSSION: The agency relationship may be implied based on duties assigned to the "agent," or may arise by the principal's conduct with third parties (such as remaining silent when another purports to be his/her agent or representing to third parties that another is his/her agent). The agency relationship may also arise in an emergency.

Answer (b) is incorrect because an agent is subject to the principal's control by the very nature of the relationship. Answers (c) and (d) are incorrect because each is an essential element of the agency relationship.

18. What fiduciary duty, if any, exists in an agency relationship?

a. The agent owes a fiduciary duty to third parties he deals for and on behalf of the principal.

b. The principal owes a fiduciary duty to the agent.

c. The agent owes a fiduciary duty to the principal.

d. There is no fiduciary duty in an agency relationship.

The correct answer is (c). *(CPA 579 L-45)*

REQUIRED: The fiduciary duty which exists in an agency relationship.

DISCUSSION: The agent owes a fiduciary duty to the principal. An agent may not profit at the expense of or compete with the principal, and must also disclose material facts and obey reasonable instructions.

Answer (a) is incorrect because the agent owes no duty to third parties. The agent should seek the utmost benefit for the principal in his/her relations with third parties. Answer (b) is incorrect because the principal owes only a contractual duty to the agent to comply with their arrangement, to compensate and indemnify the agent, and not to put the agent in unreasonable danger of harm. Answer (d) is incorrect because the agent is a fiduciary of the principal.

19. Jackson engaged Taylor to purchase 1,000 shares of XYZ stock on his behalf. Unknown to Jackson, Taylor owned 1,000 shares of XYZ stock which he wished to sell. Taylor sold these 1,000 shares of XYZ stock to Jackson at the current market price. Taylor's purchase of his stock on behalf of Jackson was

a. Wrong only if Taylor made a profit.

b. Wrong.

c. Not wrong unless Taylor could have found a better deal elsewhere.

d. An act which terminated the agency relationship.

The correct answer is (b). *(Publisher)*

REQUIRED: Whether an agent may buy from him/herself without the principal's knowledge.

DISCUSSION: An agent is a fiduciary to the principal and owes the duty of utmost loyalty. An agent may not sell his/her own property to the principal without the knowledge and consent of the principal, whether or not the agent makes a profit or the principal benefits.

Answer (a) is incorrect because self-dealing is a violation of the agent's duty whether or not profit is made. Answer (c) is incorrect because self-dealing is a violation of the agent's duty even if the deal was the best available. Answer (d) is incorrect because an agent's violation of his/her duty does not terminate the agency automatically. However, it would give the principal the right to terminate.

20. Kent Corp. hired Blue as a sales representative for 9 months at a salary of $2,000 per month plus 2% of sales. Under the circumstances

a. Kent does not have the power to dismiss Blue during the 9-month period without cause.

b. The agreement between Kent and Blue is not enforceable unless it is in writing and signed by Blue.

c. The agreement between Kent and Blue formed an agency coupled with an interest.

d. Blue is obligated to act solely in Kent's interest in matters concerning Kent's business.

The correct answer is (d). *(CPA 1188 L-3)*

REQUIRED: The correct statement about an employment relationship.

DISCUSSION: As a sales representative, Blue is an agent for Kent Corp. As an agent, Blue owes a fiduciary duty to the principal. An agent must act solely in the interest of the principal, and not in his/her own interest or the interest of a third party.

Answer (a) is incorrect because Kent can dismiss Blue for any reason, but may be liable for damages if the termination is wrongful. Answer (b) is incorrect because employment and agency contracts may be oral unless they cannot be performed within 1 year of their making. Answer (c) is incorrect because the agent must have a beneficial interest in an agency coupled with an interest.

21. Big Bucks hires Agent to manage his apartment building. Subsequently, Agent also becomes the manager of the apartment building across the street. Agent has

a. Breached her duty to Big Bucks.

b. Not breached the agency relationship if managing Big Bucks' apartment was not a full-time job.

c. Not breached the agency relationship unless the agreement with Big Bucks excluded working elsewhere.

d. Breached her duty to Big Bucks because she was earning secret profits.

The correct answer is (a). *(Publisher)*

REQUIRED: Whether an agent has the right to work for more than one principal.

DISCUSSION: An agent is not required to work exclusively for one principal, but may not compete with his/her principal without the principal's knowledge and consent. In this case, Agent is competing with Big Bucks in the second apartment building since both will need tenants and Agent may have to choose which building to interest the tenants in. This type of arrangement would only be permissible with both principals' knowledge and consent.

Answer (b) is incorrect because an agent may not compete with his/her principal even if the agency relationship is not full-time. Answer (c) is incorrect because the duty not to compete with the principal is implied in every agency. Answer (d) is incorrect because Agent has breached a duty by competing, not by earning secret profits.

22. Gladstone has been engaged as sales agent for the Doremus Corporation. Under which of the following circumstances may Gladstone delegate his duties to another?

a. When an emergency arises and the delegation is necessary to meet the emergency.

b. When it is convenient for Gladstone to do so.

c. Only with the express consent of Doremus.

d. If Doremus sells its business to another.

The correct answer is (a). *(CPA 578 L-5)*

REQUIRED: When an agent may delegate his/her duties to another.

DISCUSSION: As a general rule, an agent may not delegate his/her duties without the consent of the principal. However, an agent may delegate his/her duties when an emergency arises and the delegation is necessary to meet the emergency. This emergency exception is applicable to most contractual duties.

Answer (b) is incorrect because Gladstone may not delegate merely when convenient. Answer (c) is incorrect because, although Gladstone may delegate his duties with the consent of Doremus, the delegation may also be allowed in other situations such as an emergency. Answer (d) is incorrect because the sale of the business does not give Gladstone the right to delegate his duties. Depending on the agency agreement, the sale may terminate the agency or Gladstone will continue as agent for the purchaser.

23. An agent owes a fiduciary duty of loyalty to the principal. One aspect of this duty is that the agent is precluded from appropriating the principal's confidential information. Accordingly, an agent

a. May not use such information even after the agency is terminated.

b. May not do business with customers of a former employer.

c. Is bound not to appropriate such information but only if the employment contract explicitly created the obligation.

d. Who uses the principal's facilities and materials to develop an invention will have no right to it although (s)he was not hired to do research.

The correct answer is (a). *(Publisher)*

REQUIRED: The agent's duty not to appropriate the principal's confidential information.

DISCUSSION: The agent's fiduciary duty extends to the use of the principal's trade secrets, customer lists, and other intellectual property knowledge of which was obtained during the agency. Unauthorized use results in liability even after the termination of the agency and even though the restriction was not stated in the employment contract. Generally, the duty applies to information that the principal has taken reasonable precautions to safeguard.

Answer (b) is incorrect because the duty is applicable to confidential customer lists but not to customers discoverable through means available to anyone. Answer (c) is incorrect because the duty is imposed by law upon all agency relationships but is often stated expressly in the contract. Answer (d) is incorrect because a person employed specifically to do research does not own the intellectual property (s)he produces with the employer's resources, but a person not hired to perform such a function will have an ownership right in his/her inventions. In the latter case, the employer will have a shop-right interest, that is, a right to use the inventions without liability for royalties.

24. The principal has a variety of available remedies when the agent breaches his/her duties. Which of the following best states a remedy for the given breach?

a. Representation of parties on both sides of a transaction without full disclosure and consent. Remedy is damages but not rescission.

b. Misappropriation of trade secrets. Remedy is recovery of profits made by the agent or by knowing third-party users.

c. Taking advantage of a business opportunity that should have been offered to the principal. Remedy is an injunction, recovery of profits, and punitive damages.

d. Failure to maintain accounts and render an accounting. No remedy because only a principal has a duty to account.

The correct answer is (b). *(Publisher)*

REQUIRED: The principal's remedies for an agent's breach.

DISCUSSION: The principal may terminate the agency; withhold the agent's compensation; recover secret profits; impose a constructive trust on resources in the agent's possession; seek an injunction against breach; obtain damages for breach of the agency contract; seek reimbursement for liability to third persons caused by the agent's misconduct; and rescind certain contracts. When an agent has misappropriated confidential information, the principal may also recover profits made by the agent or by third parties aware of the misappropriation. An injunction against use of the information may also be obtained.

Answer (a) is incorrect because the contract may also be rescinded. Answer (c) is incorrect because punitive damages are seldom allowed in contract cases. Answer (d) is incorrect because the duty to account may be imposed on both principals and agents with regard to monies held by one for the other.

25. The duty of an agent to a principal

a. Includes communicating notice given to the agent, but a principal has no liability to a third party if the duty is breached.

b. Does not include communicating pertinent information if the parties have no agreement to do so.

c. May sometimes involve refusing to obey reasonable instructions.

d. To use of due care and skill does not apply to an uncompensated agency.

The correct answer is (c). *(Publisher)*

REQUIRED: The true statement about an agent's duty to the principal.

DISCUSSION: An agent is under the control of the principal and must therefore obey reasonable instructions and refrain from unauthorized actions. An exception to the rule is that the agent may deviate from the reasonable instructions in an emergency. For example, an agent reasonably instructed not to make expenditures above a certain amount might in good faith breach the instruction so as to protect the principal from loss in an emergency.

Answers (a) and (b) are incorrect because an agent is impliedly expected to communicate information relevant to the agency to the principal. A principal may incur liability when an agent fails to communicate since the law assumes that notice given to the agent is also given to the principal. Answer (d) is incorrect because all agents undertake to use the care and skill required for the agency.

26. Daniels was an agent for Marvel Signs, which was in the billboard business. The day after obtaining city approval for 10 new billboards, Daniels was at the store purchasing some coffee and supplies for the office. Daniels told the cashier how she had obtained the city approval. She also remarked, "Give me the Green Stamps. I need to take them home to fill up a book, but have these goods delivered to my office." Upon returning to the office, Daniels reimbursed herself from a petty cash fund which was there for office supplies, but without asking permission of Marvel. What duty owed to a principal has Daniels violated?

a. The duty not to divulge confidential information.

b. The duty not to receive secret compensation.

c. The duty to perform services personally.

d. The duty not to act without permission.

The correct answer is (b). *(Publisher)*

REQUIRED: The duty owed by an agent to a principal which has been violated.

DISCUSSION: Unless otherwise agreed, an agent has a duty to account to the principal for all property, money, etc. received or paid out on behalf of the principal. Daniels has violated this duty by not returning the Green Stamps to Marvel Signs since Marvel purchased the goods.

Answer (a) is incorrect because no confidential information was divulged since the 10 new billboards were approved at a public meeting. Answer (c) is incorrect because the duty to perform personally does not extend to insignificant services such as delivering coffee and office supplies. Answer (d) is incorrect because Daniels has not acted without permission unless she was required to ask permission for reimbursement from the petty cash fund, and it appears that a standard procedure was followed.

27. Winter is a sales agent for Magnum Enterprises. Winter has assumed an obligation to indemnify Magnum if any of Winter's customers fail to pay. Under these circumstances, which of the following is correct?

a. Winter's engagement must be in writing regardless of its duration.

b. Upon default, Magnum must first proceed against the delinquent purchaser-debtor.

c. The above facts describe a del credere agency relationship and Winter will be liable in the event his customers fail to pay Magnum.

d. There is no fiduciary relationship on either Winter's or Magnum's part.

The correct answer is (c). *(CPA 578 L-4)*

REQUIRED: The correct statement when a sales agent assumes his/her customers' obligations to pay.

DISCUSSION: A del credere agent is a sales agent who is required to guarantee his/her customers' obligations. In the event the customers fail to pay the principal, the sales agent is liable to the principal for their obligations.

Answer (a) is incorrect because a del credere agency is not subject to the Statute of Frauds because in law the debt is still the agent's and is therefore primary. Answer (b) is incorrect because Magnum, the principal, may proceed directly against Winter upon default by Winter's customers. Winter is a surety and thus has primary liability. Answer (d) is incorrect because Winter is an agent of Magnum and is thus a fiduciary.

28. Farber, a principal, engaged Waters for 6 months as his exclusive agent to sell specific antiques.

a. The creation of such an agency must be in writing.

b. If the principal sells the antiques through another agent, he will be liable to Waters for damages.

c. The principal does not have the legal power to terminate the agency since it is an agency coupled with an interest.

d. Waters has impliedly guaranteed that he will sell the antiques within the 6-month period.

The correct answer is (b). *(CPA 1176 L-25)*

REQUIRED: The correct statement regarding an exclusive sales agency.

DISCUSSION: Normally, a principal may engage more than one agent to perform any duty. However, when the agreement calls for an exclusive sales agency, that agent has the exclusive right to sell the goods and earn the agreed compensation. If the principal sells through another agent or him/herself, (s)he will be liable to the original agent for damages.

Answer (a) is incorrect because most agencies, including an exclusive sales agency, may be created orally. Answer (c) is incorrect because Farber, as principal, may terminate the agency since it is not coupled with an interest. An agency coupled with an interest is one in which the agent has a legal right in the property, such as an ownership interest or a security interest. Answer (d) is incorrect because Waters has impliedly warranted only a good faith attempt to sell the antiques, not their actual sale.

29. On March 15, 1986, Ken Karmel received an oral offer to work as an account executive for Wonder Stock Brokerage Company. Ken orally accepted the offer on April 1, 1986, and agreed to begin work on May 1, 1986. The duration of the contract was one year from May 1, 1986, and provided a $20,000 salary plus a bonus based on commissions earned. Under these circumstances, which of the following is true?

a. Ken has an agency coupled with an interest.

b. The contract in question is not subject to the Statute of Frauds.

c. Ken is permitted to delegate his performance to another equally competent person.

d. Although Ken's contract is silent on the point, Ken has an implied right to reimbursement for the reasonable and necessary expenses incurred on behalf of Wonder.

The correct answer is (d). *(CPA 577 L-28)*

REQUIRED: The correct statement regarding an agency relationship.

DISCUSSION: All agents have a right to reimbursement for reasonable and necessary expenses incurred on behalf of their principal. This is implicit in the agency relationship even if not provided for in the agreement.

Answer (a) is incorrect because there is no property which Ken has legal rights to protect through the agency. Answer (b) is incorrect because the contract was to last for more than one year from when entered into (April 1, 1986 to April 30, 1987), and is therefore within the Statute of Frauds. Answer (c) is incorrect because Ken contracted to provide his personal services, which are not delegable.

30. Smith has been engaged as a general sales agent for the Victory Medical Supply Company. Victory, as Smith's principal, owes Smith several duties which are implied as a matter of law. Which of the following duties is owed by Victory to Smith?

a. Not to compete.

b. To reimburse Smith for all expenditures as long as they are remotely related to Smith's employment and not specifically prohibited.

c. Not to dismiss Smith without cause for one year from the making of the contract if the duration of the contract is indefinite.

d. To indemnify Smith for liability for acts done in good faith upon Victory's orders.

The correct answer is (d). *(CPA 578 L-3)*

REQUIRED: The duty owed by a principal to an agent.

DISCUSSION: A principal is under a duty to indemnify his/her agent for liabilities and to reimburse him/her for expenses incurred while acting in good faith upon the principal's orders. An agent should not suffer loss through his/her actions for the principal. The principal is also under a duty to compensate the agent.

Answer (a) is incorrect because it is the agent (Smith) who owes a duty not to compete with the principal (Victory). Answer (b) is incorrect because Victory has the duty to reimburse Smith only for those expenditures which are directly related to Smith's employment and are authorized. Answer (c) is incorrect because the agency relationship may be terminated at will by either party if the duration of the relationship is not stated.

31. A principal may have a duty to compensate an agent for personal injuries sustained during the course of the agency. Under a state's workers' compensation law, the principal must supply benefits to all employees

a. But not if an injury is caused by a fellow worker.

b. But not if the worker had assumed the risks of the place of employment.

c. Including nonservant agents.

d. Without regard to fault.

The correct answer is (d). *(Publisher)*

REQUIRED: The principal's duty to compensate an agent for injury.

DISCUSSION: All states have enacted workers' compensation laws that allow for reimbursement of covered employees for injuries and disease that are related to their employment. Payment of benefits is not contingent upon the intentional or negligent fault of any party. The cost of workers' compensation is paid by employers who usually purchase insurance from private companies.

Answers (a) and (b) are incorrect because the fellow-servant and assumption-of-the-risk defenses do not apply in workers' compensation cases. Answer (c) is incorrect because a principal has no duty to compensate a nonservant agent (one whose physical activities are not subject to control by the principal), e.g., an independent contractor.

14.3 Authority of Agent and Ratification by Principal

32. An agent has the contractual power to bind the principal within the limits of his/her authority. Which of the following is the best term for the authority of an agent to exercise certain unstated powers reasonably necessary to achieve the purposes of the agency?

a. Implied authority.

b. Apparent authority.

c. Express authority.

d. Authority by ratification.

The correct answer is (a). *(Publisher)*

REQUIRED: The best term for an agent's powers reasonably necessary to carry on his/her work.

DISCUSSION: The agent's actual authority is communicated to him/her by the principal. Because of the impracticability of explicitly stating every power required to carry out an agent's work, the law recognizes that an agent has implied as well as express actual authority. The agent thus possesses those powers that are reasonably necessary to carry out the express authority. Both express and implied authority are considered actual authority.

Answer (b) is incorrect because apparent authority arises from statements or actions of the principal that mislead third parties into the reasonable but erroneous belief that the agent has power to act for the principal. Answer (c) is incorrect because express authority is that explicitly stated. Answer (d) is incorrect because ratification is the principal's subsequent approval of an act of the agent that was neither actually nor apparently authorized.

33. Bo Borg is the vice-president of purchasing for Crater Corp. He has authority to enter into purchase contracts on behalf of Crater provided that the price under a contract does not exceed $2 million. Dent, who is the president of Crater, is required to approve any contract that exceeds $2 million. Borg entered into a $2.5 million purchase contract with Shady Corp. without Dent's approval. Shady was unaware that Borg exceeded his authority. Neither party substantially changed its position in reliance on the contract. What is the most likely result of this transaction?

a. Crater will be bound because of Borg's apparent authority.

b. Crater will not be bound because Borg exceeded his authority.

c. Crater will only be bound up to $2 million, the amount of Borg's authority.

d. Crater may avoid the contract because Shady has not relied on the contract to its detriment.

The correct answer is (a). *(CPA 586 L-59)*

REQUIRED: The most likely result when an agent exceeds his/her authority.

DISCUSSION: Apparent authority exists when a third party has reason to believe that an agent has the authority to enter into contracts of the nature involved, based upon a principal's representations. Secret limitations placed on the agent's normal authority create apparent authority. In this case, it was reasonable for Shady to believe that Borg had the authority to enter into the contract, given Borg's position in the company as vice-president of purchasing. That Dent secretly limited Borg's authority has no effect, and Crater Corp. can be held liable under the contract.

Answer (b) is incorrect because an agent with apparent authority has the power to bind a principal even if the agent exceeds his express authority. Answer (c) is incorrect because a principal is liable to the extent of an agent's apparent authority, not an agent's express authority. Answer (d) is incorrect because reliance is irrelevant once the parties are bound to the contract.

34. Alice Able, on behalf of Pix Corp., entered into a contract with Sky Corp. by which Sky agreed to sell computer equipment to Pix. Able disclosed to Sky that she was acting on behalf of Pix. However, Able had exceeded her actual authority by entering into the contract with Sky. If Pix does not want to honor the contract, it will nonetheless be held liable if Sky can prove that

a. Able had apparent authority to bind Pix.

b. Able believed she was acting within the scope of her authority.

c. Able was an employee of Pix and not an independent contractor.

d. The agency relationship between Pix and Able was formalized in a signed writing.

The correct answer is (a). *(CPA 588 L-4)*

REQUIRED: The important factor in determining if a principal is liable for unauthorized acts of an agent.

DISCUSSION: Apparent authority is what third parties believe an agent possesses because of the actions of the principal or the outward appearances of the agency relationship. It is a form of estoppel. Express limitations do limit an agent's actual authority, but if they are not known by third parties, they do not affect apparent authority.

Answer (b) is incorrect because what is important is what Sky, not Able, believed. Answer (c) is incorrect because employees and independent contractors can both be agents. The type of relationship that created the agency is not important. Answer (d) is incorrect because a signed writing does not affect apparent authority with respect to third parties. The signed writing only has an effect with respect to the parties involved.

35. Rogers gave Mitchell a power of attorney containing the following provision:

"My attorney, Mitchell, is specifically authorized to sell and convey any part or all of my real property."

Mitchell conveyed part of Rogers's land to Stone by deed in the customary form containing covenants of title. Stone sues Rogers for breach of a covenant. The outcome of Stone's suit will be governed by whether

a. Deeds without covenants are effective to convey realty.

b. The jurisdiction views the covenants as personal or running with the land.

c. Stone is a bona fide purchaser.

d. The power to "sell and convey" is construed to include the power to execute the usual form of deed used to convey realty.

The correct answer is (d). *(MBE Part V-27)*

REQUIRED: The correct statement concerning a suit for breach of a covenant of title against a seller who acted through an agent.

DISCUSSION: If Rogers had the capacity to sell and convey real property, she could sell and convey real property through her agent, Mitchell. If the power to "sell and convey" is construed to include the power to execute the usual deed (which contains covenants of title), then Rogers will be liable on these covenants given by Mitchell.

Answer (a) is incorrect because Mitchell gave a deed with covenants of title. It is irrelevant whether another form could have been used. Answer (b) is incorrect because whether the covenants are personal or run with the land is also irrelevant since Rogers is being sued on a covenant actually given in the deed. Answer (c) is incorrect because whether Stone is a bona fide purchaser is relevant only with respect to third parties, not the grantor.

36. Baker Corp. dismissed Abel as its general sales agent. Baker notified all of Abel's known customers by letter. Fam Corp., a retail outlet located outside of Abel's previously assigned sales territory, had never dealt with Abel. However, Fam knew of Abel as a result of various business contacts. After his dismissal, Abel sold Fam goods, to be delivered by Baker, and received from Fam a cash deposit for 25% of the purchase price. It was not unusual for an agent in Abel's previous position to receive cash deposits. In an action by Fam against Baker on the sales contract, Fam will

a. Win, because a principal is an insurer of an agent's acts.

b. Win, because Baker's notice was inadequate to terminate Abel's apparent authority.

c. Lose, because Abel's conduct constituted a fraud for which Baker is not liable.

d. Lose, because Abel lacked any express or implied authority to make the contract.

The correct answer is (b). *(CPA 585 L-4)*

REQUIRED: The outcome of a suit on a contract by a third party against a principal whose agent had no actual authority.

DISCUSSION: When a principal discharges an agent, (s)he must give actual notice to those with whom the agent had previously dealt and constructive notice to others who might have known of the agency. Baker's failure to give constructive notice by publication in a newspaper of general circulation in the place where the agency activities were carried out left Abel with apparent authority. Publication in trade journals of the termination would provide such notice and effectively terminate Abel's apparent authority.

Answer (a) is incorrect because a principal is not an insurer of an agent's acts. A principal is only liable when an agent acts with authority (actual or apparent). Answer (c) is incorrect because Baker is liable on the contract although not for fraud. Abel is liable for fraud. Answer (d) is incorrect because Fam will win since Abel had apparent although not actual authority.

37. Michaels appointed Fairfax as his agent. The appointment was in writing and clearly indicated the scope of Fairfax's authority and also that Fairfax was not to disclose that he was acting as an agent for Michaels. Under the circumstances,

a. Fairfax is an agent coupled with an interest.

b. Michaels must ratify any contracts made by Fairfax on behalf of Michaels.

c. Fairfax's appointment had to be in writing to be enforceable.

d. Fairfax has the implied and apparent authority of an agent.

The correct answer is (d). *(CPA 1180 L-30)*

REQUIRED: The correct statement about a written agency with an undisclosed principal.

DISCUSSION: When an agent has express authority, (s)he also has implied authority to carry out those duties encompassed by the express authority. Furthermore, Fairfax will have apparent authority based on his position and performance of duties for Michaels.

Answer (a) is incorrect because an agent coupled with an interest has a legal interest in the property of the agency, and Fairfax has no such interest. Answer (b) is incorrect because Fairfax has been given actual authority by the appointment, so no ratification is necessary. Answer (c) is incorrect because a writing is not necessary to create an agency relationship as long as the agreement does not require it to last more than 1 year.

38. Jones was a clerk in a lumber yard. Since there were no customers around, Jones decided to take a lunch break. While he was gone, Smith came in to buy some nails. Not seeing anyone around, Smith sat down on the counter to wait. Next in came Proctor to buy some lumber for a house she was building. Thinking Smith worked there, Proctor asked Smith if the lumber could be delivered that afternoon. Smith assured Proctor that it would be done so Proctor paid Smith and left. Smith kept the money and also left. Which statement is incorrect?

a. Smith did not have apparent authority to sell the lumber or agree to deliver it.

b. Jones was in violation of his fiduciary duty to the principal for neglecting his duty.

c. The lumber company can be held liable for not delivering the lumber to Proctor.

d. Proctor can hold either Smith or the lumber company liable.

The correct answer is (a). *(Publisher)*

REQUIRED: The false statement concerning a principal's liability for an impostor acting as an agent.

DISCUSSION: Since Smith was not the lumber yard's agent, he did not have express or implied authority to sell the lumber. Smith did have apparent authority since he was negligently given the opportunity to hold himself out as the lumber yard's agent. This establishes an apparent agency or agency by estoppel. Since Proctor was led to believe that Smith had apparent authority, the lumber yard will be held to Smith's agreement.

Answer (b) is incorrect because Jones was in violation of his fiduciary duty by leaving the lumber yard unattended and allowing this to happen. Answer (c) is incorrect because the lumber company can be held liable for not delivering the lumber as promised. Answer (d) is incorrect because Proctor can hold the lumber company liable based on estoppel, and can hold Smith liable directly for his promise.

39. Ted Simmons, an agent for Jensen, has the express authority to sell Jensen's goods. Simmons also has the express authority to grant discounts of up to 5% of list price. Simmons sold Hemple goods with a list price of $1,000 and granted Hemple a 10% discount. Hemple had not previously dealt with either Simmons or Jensen. Which of the following courses of action may Jensen properly take?

a. Seek to void the sale to Hemple only.

b. Seek recovery of $50 from Hemple only.

c. Seek recovery of $50 from Simmons only.

d. Seek recovery of $50 from either Hemple or Simmons.

The correct answer is (c). *(CPA 589 L-13)*

REQUIRED: Whether the principal can collect from an agent after the agent gave an unauthorized discount.

DISCUSSION: Simmons had the apparent authority to grant a $100 (10% x $1,000) discount to Hemple. Simmons, however, had actual authority to grant only a $50 (5% x $1,000) discount. Simmons has violated his actual authority and is liable to the principal for any loss ($100 - $50 = $50) sustained as a result of his actions.

Answer (a) is incorrect because Simmons had apparent authority, and the principal therefore cannot void the contract by denying the existence of actual authority. Answers (b) and (d) are incorrect because Hemple is not liable to Jensen.

40. Able exceeded her actual authority when she concluded an agreement with Pix Corp. on behalf of Sky Corp. If Pix wishes to ratify the contract with Sky, which of the following statements is correct?

a. Pix must notify Sky that Pix intends to ratify the contract.

b. Able must have acted reasonably and in Pix's best interest.

c. Able must be a general agent of Pix.

d. Pix must have knowledge of all material facts relating to the contract at the time it is ratified.

The correct answer is (d). *(CPA 588 L-5)*

REQUIRED: The correct statement concerning ratification of an authorized act.

DISCUSSION: Ratification is the act of becoming legally bound on a contract that was entered into by an unauthorized person purporting to act as the principal's agent. To ratify a contract, the principal must have full knowledge of the facts regarding the ratification.

Answer (a) is incorrect because a principal does not need to notify a third party to make a ratification effective. Answer (b) is incorrect because whether the agent acted reasonably and in the principal's best interest is irrelevant if the principal has all the facts related to the ratification and the power to ratify. Answer (c) is incorrect because whether a general agency existed has no effect on the principal's power to ratify.

41. Wallace, an agent for Lux, made a contract with Doolittle that exceeded Wallace's authority. If Lux wishes to hold Doolittle to the contract, Lux must prove that

a. Lux ratified the contract before withdrawal from the contract by Doolittle.

b. Wallace was acting in the capacity of an agent for an undisclosed principal.

c. Wallace believed he was acting within the scope of his authority.

d. Wallace was Lux's general agent even though Wallace exceeded his authority.

The correct answer is (a). *(CPA 583 L-1)*

REQUIRED: The requirement for a principal to hold a third party to a contract that exceeded the agent's authority.

DISCUSSION: If the agent had no authority, no contract existed between the third party and the principal. Ratification would validate a contract assuming that the third party did not withdraw prior to ratification or that the situation did not change so markedly that holding the third party to the bargain would be inequitable.

Answer (b) is incorrect because most states do not permit ratification of unauthorized acts by an undisclosed principal. Answer (c) is incorrect because the agent's intent is irrelevant to whether the principal can ratify. Answer (d) is incorrect because actions of special agents may also be ratified.

42. The ratification doctrine

a. Is not applicable to situations in which the party claiming to act as the agent for another has no express or implied authority to do so.

b. Is designed to apply to situations in which the principal was originally incompetent to have made the contract himself, but who, upon becoming competent, ratifies.

c. Requires the principal to ratify the entire act of the agent, and the ratification is retroactive.

d. Applies only if the principal expressly ratifies the contract made on his behalf within a reasonable time in writing.

The correct answer is (c). *(CPA 575 L-30)*

REQUIRED: The correct statement regarding the ratification doctrine.

DISCUSSION: For a principal to ratify an unauthorized act of an "agent," the entire act must be ratified. Otherwise, a principal could pick and choose from unauthorized acts by "agents," which would be unfair to the third parties with whom the "agent" is dealing. Ratification is also retroactive (relates back) to the time the "agent" entered into the contract.

Answer (a) is incorrect because the ratification doctrine specifically applies to situations in which a purported agent has no authority to act. If the agent did have express or implied authority, the ratification doctrine would not be necessary. Answer (b) is incorrect because the principal must be competent when the purported agent entered into the contract since the ratification relates back. Answer (d) is incorrect because ratification may be oral or implied by conduct, and may occur at any time before the third party withdraws from the contract.

43. Starr is an agent of a disclosed principal, Maple. On May 1, Starr entered into an agreement with King Corp. on behalf of Maple that exceeded Starr's authority as Maple's agent. On May 5, King learned of Starr's lack of authority and immediately notified Maple and Starr that it was withdrawing from the May 1 agreement. On May 7, Maple ratified the May 1 agreement in its entirety. If King refuses to honor the agreement and Maple brings an action for breach of contract, Maple will

a. Prevail. The agreement of May 1 was ratified in its entirety.

b. Prevail. Maple's capacity as a principal was known to Starr.

c. Lose. The May 1 agreement is void due to Starr's lack of authority.

d. Lose. King notified Starr and Maple of its withdrawal prior to Maple's ratification.

The correct answer is (d). *(CPA 587 L-6)*

REQUIRED: The outcome of an action by a principal against a third party for breach of contract.

DISCUSSION: When an agent exceeds his/her express, implied, or apparent authority, a principal is not bound until (s)he ratifies. Moreover, certain conditions will terminate the power of ratification, such as the third-party's withdrawal, death, or loss of capacity; changed circumstances; or failure to ratify within a reasonable time. Because King withdrew prior to ratification by Maple, there was no agreement for Maple to ratify and no contract to breach.

Answer (a) is incorrect because even though the agreement must be ratified in its entirety to bind the parties, King's withdrawal prior to Maple's ratification meant there was no agreement. Maple will not prevail since there was no contract for King to breach. Answer (b) is incorrect because knowledge of the principal is irrelevant if the third party withdraws prior to ratification. Answer (c) is incorrect because the agreement is not void due to Starr's lack of authority. The agreement is void because the third party withdrew prior to ratification.

14.4 Liability of Principal and Agent to Third Parties

44. A principal will not be liable to a third party for a tort committed by an agent

a. Unless the principal instructed the agent to commit the tort.

b. Unless the tort was committed within the scope of the agency relationship.

c. If the agency agreement limits the principal's liability for the agent's tort.

d. If the tort is also regarded as a criminal act.

The correct answer is (b). *(CPA 1189 L-2)*

REQUIRED: The liability of a principal to a third party for a tort committed by an agent.

DISCUSSION: A principal is liable for the torts of an agent committed within the course and scope of the agency agreement provided the agent's actions are subject to the control of the principal.

Answer (a) is incorrect because a principal is liable for the torts of his/her agent even if the agent acted without the principal's instruction. Answer (c) is incorrect because an exculpatory clause (a clause relieving a party of a duty or liability) has no effect on a third party not privy to the agreement between the principal and agent. Answer (d) is incorrect because a principal is liable for crimes of his/her agent if the agent acted within the course and scope of his/her employment.

45. Dolby was employed as an agent for the Ace Used Car Company to purchase newer model used cars. His authority was limited by a $3,000 maximum price for any car. A wholesaler showed him a 1938 classic car which was selling for $5,000. The wholesaler knew that Ace only dealt in newer model cars and that Dolby had never paid more than $3,000 for any car. Dolby bought the car for Ace, convinced that it was worth at least $7,000. When he reported this to Williams, Ace's owner, Williams was furious but he nevertheless authorized processing of the automobile for resale. Williams also began pricing the car with antique car dealers who indicated that the current value of the car was $4,800. Williams called the wholesaler, told him that Dolby had exceeded his authority, that he was returning the car, and that he was demanding repayment of the purchase price. What is the wholesaler's best defense in the event of a lawsuit?

a. Dolby had apparent authority to purchase the car.

b. Dolby's purchase was effectively ratified by Ace.

c. Dolby had express authority to purchase the car.

d. Dolby had implied authority to purchase the car.

The correct answer is (b). *(CPA 579 L-40)*

REQUIRED: The best defense for a third party who relied on a contract entered into by an unauthorized agent.

DISCUSSION: Dolby's authority was expressly limited by Ace. The wholesaler knew that Dolby had never paid more than $3,000 for a car, so Dolby did not have apparent authority with regard to the wholesaler. Since Dolby did not have any authority, the wholesaler can only rely on ratification by the principal to retain the benefits of the contract. Ace's owner, Williams, ratified the contract by authorizing processing of the automobile for resale. To avoid liability on the contract, Williams should have returned the car to the wholesaler and demanded the return of the purchase price.

Answer (a) is incorrect because the wholesaler was aware that Dolby had never paid more than $3,000 for any car, and was not led to believe that Dolby had authority. Answer (c) is incorrect because Dolby was expressly limited to a $3,000 maximum price. Answer (d) is incorrect because implied authority is that which is necessary to carry out express authority. An expressly forbidden act could not be performed under implied authority.

46. Futterman operated a cotton factory and employed Marra as a general purchasing agent to travel through the southern states to purchase cotton. Futterman telegraphed Marra instructions from day to day as to the price to be paid for cotton. Marra entered a cotton district in which she had not previously done business and represented that she was purchasing cotton for Futterman. Although directed by Futterman to pay no more than 25 cents a pound, Marra bought cotton from Anderson at 30 cents a pound, which was the prevailing offering price at that time. Futterman refused to take the cotton. Under these circumstances, which of the following is correct?

a. The negation of actual authority to make the purchase effectively eliminates any liability for Futterman.

b. Futterman is not liable on the contract.

c. Marra has no potential liability.

d. Futterman is liable on the contract.

The correct answer is (d). *(CPA 578 L-10)*

REQUIRED: The liability when an agent contracts in excess of express authority.

DISCUSSION: Futterman is liable on the contract because Marra had apparent authority to enter into the contract. Although Marra was instructed to pay no more than 25 cents a pound, this was not known to the cotton sellers. By allowing Marra to enter into contracts for the purchase of cotton, Futterman clothed her with apparent authority (estoppel) to pay any reasonable price.

Answer (a) is incorrect because a principal is liable for contracts entered into by an agent who has apparent authority. Answer (b) is incorrect because Futterman is liable on the contract since Marra had apparent authority. Answer (c) is incorrect because Marra is potentially liable to Futterman for exceeding her authority since an agent has a duty to obey lawful instructions. If the principal is damaged by the breach of this duty, the agent will be liable.

47. Farley Farms, Inc. shipped 100 bales of hops to Burton Brewing Corporation. The agreement specified that the hops were to be of a certain grade. Upon examining the hops, Burton claimed that they were not of that grade. Farley's general sales agent who made the sale to Burton agreed to relieve Burton of liability and to have the hops shipped elsewhere. This was done, and the hops were sold at a price less than Burton was to have paid. Farley refused to accede to the agent's acts and sued Burton for the amount of its loss. Under these circumstances,

a. Farley will prevail only if the action by its agent was expressly authorized.

b. Even if Farley's agent had authority to make such an adjustment, it would not be enforceable against Farley unless ratified in writing by Farley.

c. Because the hops were sold at a loss in respect to the price Burton had agreed to pay, Burton would be liable for the loss involved.

d. Farley is bound because its agent expressly, impliedly, or apparently had the authority to make such an adjustment.

The correct answer is (d). *(CPA 1175 L-15)*

REQUIRED: The party liable on a contract when an agent releases a third party.

DISCUSSION: A principal is bound when its agent releases a third party from a contract as long as the agent has authority. At a minimum, the general sales agent had apparent authority because it is reasonable to expect a general sales agent to be able to enter into and release parties from such contracts.

Answer (a) is incorrect because Farley could win only if the agent lacked any authority to give a release and if Burton's rejection of the goods was wrongful. Answer (b) is incorrect because an adjustment in a contract by a sales agent need not be ratified in writing by the principal. Under UCC 2-209, a modification or waiver of a contractual obligation need not be in writing. Answer (c) is incorrect because Burton would be liable if the release was ineffective and its rejection of the goods was wrongful.

48. Normally a principal will not be liable to a third party

a. On a contract signed on his behalf by an agent who was expressly forbidden by the principal to make it and where the third party was unaware of the agent's limitation.

b. On a contract made by his agent and the principal is not disclosed, unless the principal ratifies it.

c. For torts committed by an independent contractor in an ultrahazardous activity.

d. On a negotiable instrument signed by the agent in his own name without revealing he signed in his agency capacity.

The correct answer is (d). *(CPA 575 L-31)*

REQUIRED: When a principal will not be liable to a third party.

DISCUSSION: A principal is not liable to third parties on negotiable instruments signed by an agent in the agent's own name without revealing the agency relationship. This is a special rule for negotiable instruments.

Answer (a) is incorrect because an express limitation not communicated to the third party would not negate the agent's apparent authority. Answer (b) is incorrect because an undisclosed principal can be held liable by third parties as long as the agent had authority to enter into the contract. Answer (c) is incorrect because although principals generally are not liable for torts committed by independent contractors (due to a lack of control), there is an exception when the independent contractor is engaged to participate in ultrahazardous activities, e.g., dynamite blasting.

49. The liability of a principal to a third party for the torts of his agent

a. Can be effectively limited by agreement with the agent.

b. Cannot extend to the inclusion of a criminal act committed by the agent.

c. Is less onerous if the agent is acting for an undisclosed principal.

d. Is an example of the imposition of liability without fault upon the principal.

The correct answer is (d). *(CPA 582 L-5)*

REQUIRED: The correct statement concerning a principal's liability for its agents' torts.

DISCUSSION: Under the rule of respondeat superior, a principal is held strictly liable for the torts committed by its agent within the course and scope of the agency. The liability is imposed without regard to negligence or other actual fault of the principal.

Answer (a) is incorrect because the principal cannot limit its liability to third parties by agreement with the agent. Such limitation could only be achieved by agreement with the third party. Answer (b) is incorrect because the liability of a principal to a third party for the actions of its agent may extend to the commission of a crime by the agent, e.g., fraud. Answer (c) is incorrect because whether the principal is undisclosed does not affect the principal's liability for torts of its agent.

50. Kent works as a welder for Mighty Manufacturing, Inc. He was specially trained by Mighty in the procedures and safety precautions applicable to installing replacement mufflers on automobiles. One rule of which he was aware involved a prohibition against installing a muffler on any auto which had heavily congealed oil or grease or which had any leaks. Kent disregarded this rule, and as a result a customer's auto caught fire causing extensive property damage and injury to Kent. Which of the following is correct?

a. Mighty is not liable to Kent under the worker's compensation laws.

b. Mighty is not liable to the customer because Mighty's rule prohibited Kent from installing the muffler in question.

c. Kent has no personal liability to the customer for the loss because he was acting for and on behalf of his employer.

d. Mighty is liable to the customer irrespective of its efforts to prevent such an occurrence and its exercise of reasonable care.

The correct answer is (d). *(CPA 1181 L-14)*

REQUIRED: The liability when an employee disregards an employer's instructions and damage results.

DISCUSSION: A principal is liable to third parties for all acts of its agents and employees committed within the course and scope of their employment. Mighty is therefore liable to the customer for the damage caused by Kent, even though Mighty made reasonable efforts to prevent such an occurrence and was not negligent.

Answer (a) is incorrect because the workers' compensation laws provide that a worker injured on the job is entitled to compensation regardless of fault or negligence. Answer (b) is incorrect because a principal is liable to a third party for an agent's act even though the agent was instructed not to perform the act. Answer (c) is incorrect because an agent is always liable for his/her wrongful acts, even when committed in the course of employment. The fact that Kent was acting for and on behalf of Mighty merely makes Mighty liable in addition to Kent.

51. Bing was employed as a taxi driver by Speedy, Inc. While acting in the scope and course of his employment with Speedy, Bing collided with a van driven by Hart. Hart was an independent contractor making a delivery for Troy Corp. The collision was caused solely by Bing's negligence. As a result of the collision, both Bing and Hart suffered permanent injuries. Speedy and Troy were both in compliance with the state's workers' compensation statute. If Hart commences an action against Bing and Speedy for negligence, which of the following statements is correct?

a. Hart is entitled to recover damages from Bing or Speedy.

b. Bing will either be denied workers' compensation benefits or have his benefits reduced because of his negligence.

c. Hart's action for negligence will be dismissed because Hart is an independent contractor.

d. Hart is entitled to recover damages from Speedy's workers' compensation carrier to the extent no duplicate payment has been received by Hart.

The correct answer is (a). *(CPA 588 L-44)*

REQUIRED: The liability of a principal and agent for the negligent acts of the agent.

DISCUSSION: A person is always responsible for his/her negligent acts. Thus, Bing is liable. An employer is liable in tort for acts of employees or agents in the course and scope of employment. Accordingly, Speedy is also liable.

Answer (b) is incorrect because workers' compensation benefits do not depend on lack of fault. Answer (c) is incorrect because whether Hart is an independent contractor is irrelevant. Answer (d) is incorrect because Hart cannot receive workers' compensation benefits from Speedy because Hart is not employed by Speedy.

52. Oliver and Hardy were proprietors of neighboring retail shops. Oliver's errand boy was not in one day, so Oliver asked and received permission to borrow Hardy's errand boy for the afternoon. While running an errand, the boy negligently injured Bertha, who was riding a bicycle down the street. Who is liable for Bertha's injuries?

a. Only Oliver and the errand boy.

b. Only Hardy and the errand boy.

c. Only the errand boy since he acted negligently.

d. Oliver, Hardy, and the errand boy.

The correct answer is (b). *(Publisher)*

REQUIRED: The liability for the negligence of a borrowed employee.

DISCUSSION: A person is always responsible for his/her negligent actions. Therefore, the errand boy is liable. The liability of Oliver and Hardy depends on which employer had the right to control the employee at the time of the accident. The courts generally hold the employer with dominant control liable. In this case, the errand boy was Hardy's and Hardy could expect remuneration from Oliver, so Hardy is the dominant employer. Even though the boy was working on behalf of Oliver, Oliver is probably not liable.

Answer (a) is incorrect because Oliver will probably not be liable as the employer. Answer (c) is incorrect because the employer is liable for the torts of his/her employees including negligence. Answer (d) is incorrect because in the absence of forming partnership or joint venture, both employers probably will not be held liable.

53. For which of the following is a principal liable for damages caused by an independent contractor acting on behalf of the principal?

a. An automobile accident.

b. A dynamite explosion.

c. Fraud.

d. Injury to an independent contractor's workmen when a large beam fell on them.

The correct answer is (b). *(Publisher)*

REQUIRED: The activity in which a principal is liable for damages caused by an independent contractor.

DISCUSSION: A principal is generally not liable for the acts of an independent contractor because an independent contractor is not subject to the control of the employer. However, liability will result in an ultrahazardous activity. The use of dynamite has traditionally been considered an ultrahazardous activity for which a principal can be held liable for damages caused by an independent contractor.

Answer (a) is incorrect because automobile use is generally not considered an ultrahazardous activity. Answer (c) is incorrect because a principal is not liable for the torts committed by an independent contractor since the activity is not under the control of the principal. Answer (d) is incorrect because a principal does not control an independent contractor's workers and is not liable for damages to them.

54. Joe Walters was employed by the Metropolitan Department Store as a driver of one of its delivery trucks. Under the terms of his employment he made deliveries daily along a designated route and brought the truck back to the store's garage for overnight storage. One day instead of returning to the garage as required, he drove the truck twenty miles north of the area he covered expecting to attend a social function unrelated to his employment or to his employer's affairs. Through his negligence in operating the truck while enroute, Walters seriously injured Richard Bunt. Walters caused the accident and was solely at fault. Bunt entered suit in tort against the store for damages for personal injuries, alleging that the store, as principal, was responsible for the tortious acts of its agent. Under these circumstances

a. Metropolitan is not liable because Walters was an independent contractor.

b. Metropolitan is not liable because Walters had abandoned his employment and was engaged in an independent activity of his own.

c. Metropolitan is liable based upon the doctrine of respondeat superior.

d. Bunt can recover damages from both Walters and Metropolitan.

The correct answer is (b). *(CPA 1174 L-14)*

REQUIRED: The liability when an employee deviates from employment and causes injury.

DISCUSSION: An employer (principal) is responsible for personal injuries caused by its employees (agents) within the course and scope of employment. When an employee leaves the course of employment, however, the employer is no longer liable for damages caused by the employee. Walters had clearly left his employment when the accident occurred.

Answer (a) is incorrect because Walters is not an independent contractor since he is subject to the control of Metropolitan in performing his job. Answer (c) is incorrect because Metropolitan is not liable due to the deviation from the course of employment by Walters. If Walters had been in the course of employment when the accident occurred, Metropolitan would be liable based on the doctrine of respondeat superior. Answer (d) is incorrect because Bunt can only recover damages from Walters since Metropolitan is not liable.

55. Brian purchased an automobile from Robinson Auto Sales under a written contract by which Robinson obtained a security interest to secure payment of the purchase price. Robinson reserved the right to repossess the automobile if Brian failed to make any of the required ten payments. Ambrose, an employee of Robinson, was instructed to repossess the automobile on the ground that Brian had defaulted in making the third payment. Ambrose took possession of the automobile and delivered it to Robinson. It was then discovered that Brian was not in default. Which of the following is incorrect?

a. Brian has the right to regain possession of the automobile and to collect damages.

b. Brian may sue and collect from either Robinson or Ambrose.

c. If Ambrose must pay in damages, he will be entitled to indemnification from Robinson.

d. Ambrose is not liable for the wrongful repossession of the automobile since he was obeying the direct order of Robinson.

The correct answer is (d). *(CPA 1181 L-16)*

REQUIRED: The incorrect statement regarding liability when an agent commits a wrongful act under instructions from the principal.

DISCUSSION: Both agent and principal are responsible to third parties for wrongful acts of the agent committed within the course and scope of his/her employment. Principals are liable because they are generally responsible for the acts of their agents. Agents are also liable because they are responsible for their own actions. Therefore, Ambrose is liable for the wrongful repossession of the automobile.

Answer (a) is incorrect because Brian does have the right to regain possession of the automobile and collect damages since the repossession was wrongful. Answer (b) is incorrect because Brian may sue and collect from either Robinson (principal) or Ambrose (agent). They are both liable for damages. Answer (c) is incorrect because it is a fundamental duty of a principal to indemnify his/her agent for liability incurred while acting under the instructions of the principal.

56. Delta sent its agent, Bismark, to purchase some equipment. Bismark was instructed to charge the purchase to Delta's account. However, Bismark charged it to a personal account and did not indicate it was for Delta. Upon returning to Delta, Bismark showed Delta the personal charge and Delta reimbursed Bismark. Later Bismark disappeared and the store seeks to hold Delta liable.

a. Delta is not liable because Bismark charged the goods to his personal account.

b. Delta is not liable because it already paid the price to Bismark.

c. Delta is liable as a partially disclosed principal.

d. Delta is liable because Bismark was instructed to make the purchase.

The correct answer is (d). *(Publisher)*

REQUIRED: The liability of a principal for purchases by an agent using his/her own credit.

DISCUSSION: Bismark had express authority to make the purchase and did so on behalf of Delta. Therefore, Delta is liable for the purchase price. This is similar to the situation in which an undisclosed principal is held liable for contracts entered into by its agent. A few cases take the view that since the agent's credit was originally trusted, the principal should not be required to pay twice. In jurisdictions following this view, the store could not recover from Delta.

Answer (a) is incorrect because the fact that Bismark charged the goods to his personal account does not affect the liability of the principal. Answer (b) is incorrect because the third party has not been paid. In most jurisdictions, this liability of the principal is not discharged by payment to an agent. Answer (c) is incorrect because Delta is an undisclosed principal, not a partially disclosed principal.

57. Agents sometimes have liability to third parties for their actions taken for and on behalf of the principal. An agent will not be personally liable in which of the following circumstances?

a. If he makes a contract which he had no authority to make but which the principal ratifies.

b. If he commits a tort while engaged in the principal's business.

c. If he acts for a principal which he knows is nonexistent and the third party is unaware of this.

d. If he acts for an undisclosed principal as long as the principal is subsequently disclosed.

The correct answer is (a). *(CPA 1180 L-27)*

REQUIRED: The circumstances in which an agent will not be personally liable.

DISCUSSION: An agent will generally not be liable if (s)he discloses that (s)he is acting for another and has authority to make the particular contract. If (s)he had no such authority, (s)he will still escape liability if the principal ratifies.

Answer (b) is incorrect because both principal and agent are liable for the agent's torts committed while engaged in the principal's business. Answer (c) is incorrect because an agent is personally liable when acting for a nonexistent principal. The agent warrants (s)he is an agent for a principal and (s)he has authority to do the act. Answer (d) is incorrect because a third party can hold both agent and principal liable when the principal was originally undisclosed.

58. Wanamaker, Inc. engaged Anderson as its agent to purchase original oil paintings for resale by Wanamaker. Anderson's express authority was specifically limited to a maximum purchase price of $25,000 for any collection provided it contained a minimum of five oil paintings. Anderson purchased a seven-picture collection on Wanamaker's behalf for $30,000. Based upon these facts, which of the following is a correct legal conclusion?

a. The express limitation on Anderson's authority negates any apparent authority.

b. Wanamaker cannot ratify the contract since Anderson's actions were clearly in violation of his contract.

c. If Wanamaker rightfully disaffirms the unauthorized contract, Anderson is personally liable to the seller.

d. Neither Wanamaker nor Anderson is liable on the contract since the seller was obligated to ascertain Anderson's authority.

The correct answer is (c). *(CPA 1179 L-33)*

REQUIRED: The correct legal conclusion when an agent exceeds his/her authority.

DISCUSSION: An agent who enters into a contract without authority can be held personally liable by the third party on the theory of breach of warranty of authority. If Wanamaker does not disaffirm the contract, however, Anderson's act will be ratified and Anderson will not be liable.

Answer (a) is incorrect because apparent authority arises from conduct of the principal which leads third parties to believe the agent has authority in excess of that actually given. If a third party is not aware of a limitation, apparent authority can still exist. Answer (b) is incorrect because the purpose of ratification is to validate a contract when a purported agent did not have authority. Answer (d) is incorrect because the seller is not obligated to ascertain Anderson's authority, and should be able to rely on the agent's representation and apparent authority.

59. Under which of the following circumstances will an agent acting on behalf of a disclosed principal not be liable to a third party for his actions?

a. He signs a negotiable instrument in his own name and does not indicate his agency capacity.

b. He commits a tort in the course of discharging his duties.

c. He is acting for a nonexistent principal which subsequently comes into existence after the time of the agent's actions on the principal's behalf.

d. He lacks specific express authority but is acting within the scope of his implied authority.

The correct answer is (d). *(CPA 1176 L-29)*

REQUIRED: When an agent of a disclosed principal will not be liable to third parties.

DISCUSSION: An agent of a disclosed principal who signs any written agreements in a representative capacity is not liable to third parties when (s)he has actual authority. Implied authority is a type of actual authority which is inferred from the circumstances or is needed to carry out express authority.

Answer (a) is incorrect because an agent who signs negotiable instruments in his/her own name without indicating the agency capacity is personally liable. However, the agent can seek indemnification from the principal if the action was proper. Answer (b) is incorrect because an agent is always personally liable for torts which (s)he commits. Answer (c) is incorrect because an agent is personally liable if there is no principal, e.g., a corporation yet to be formed.

60. Leadfoot was a chauffeur for the Vanderbilts. One day on Leadfoot's way back to the Vanderbilts' from having the car repaired, Leadfoot went a mile out of his way to stop at a favorite tavern for several drinks with some friends. Immediately upon leaving the tavern, Leadfoot rear-ended a car driven by Whiplash. Whiplash now seeks recovery for his neck injuries due to the accident. Which statement is correct?

a. The Vanderbilts are liable.

b. Leadfoot is liable only if the accident was intentional.

c. Leadfoot is liable if he was at fault.

d. If held liable, Leadfoot must be indemnified by the Vanderbilts.

The correct answer is (c). *(Publisher)*

REQUIRED: The liability when a servant deviates from the course of employment.

DISCUSSION: An employee (servant) or agent is liable for his/her actions regardless of potential liability by the employer or principal. Therefore, Leadfoot would be liable if he was at fault.

Answer (a) is incorrect because although an employer is liable for the torts of its employees which occur during the course and scope of employment, when the employee has clearly left the course of employment, the employer is no longer liable. The extent of the deviation determines whether the agent is outside the "course and scope." There is no certain test as to when employment has been reentered, but it has been the trend for the courts to expand the definition of "course and scope." Answer (b) is incorrect because a person is also liable for damage caused by his/her negligent actions. Answer (d) is incorrect because an employer is not responsible for indemnifying an employee for losses which were not incurred during the course of employment, or which were caused by "fault" of the employee.

61. Jackson was a purchasing agent for Retail World, Inc. Unknown to Jackson, Retail World went through a voluntary dissolution. Jackson entered into an agreement to purchase goods signing "Retail World, Inc. by Jackson, its purchasing agent." Who is liable?

a. Retail World, Inc.

b. Both Retail World, Inc. and Jackson.

c. Only Jackson.

d. No one is liable because Retail World, Inc. has been dissolved.

The correct answer is (c). *(Publisher)*

REQUIRED: The party liable under a contract entered into by an agent when the principal no longer exists.

DISCUSSION: An agency relationship terminates immediately when the principal ceases to exist, such as on death or dissolution of a corporation, and the agent can not bind a nonexistent principal. An agent who purports to have authority and does not is personally liable on the contract. An agent is entitled to notification of termination, however, and may have a cause of action against the legal representatives of the principal.

Answers (a) and (b) are incorrect because the agency relationship terminated and Retail World, Inc. cannot be held liable for contracts entered into by an "agent" when the corporation no longer exists. Answer (d) is incorrect because an agent who purports to act on behalf of a nonexistent principal is personally liable.

62. Faithful Agents, Inc., an agent for a sports star, Joe Jones, promised to deliver Jones as a guest at the ABC Basketball Camp July 15 at Siwash College. A contract was signed by Joe Jones and ABC for this appearance, but Faithful Agents did not execute the agreement. Jones failed to appear on July 15 and filed bankruptcy because of the dishonesty of his agent. ABC sued Faithful Agents, Inc. for damages because of the failure of Jones to appear, alleging breach of contract. Which of the following statements is true?

a. A disclosed principal who executes a contract negotiated by its agent with a third party cannot be sued by the third party.

b. Unless an agent adds to or guarantees the performance of the principal by his/her promises, an agent is never liable in contract for the principal's breach.

c. Agents are always personally responsible for contracts entered into between a disclosed principal and a third party.

d. Agents are liable to third parties for all the contract breaches of their principals.

The correct answer is (b). *(E. O'Connor)*

REQUIRED: The agent's liability when the principal goes bankrupt but the agent did not execute the agreement.

DISCUSSION: A person can only be liable for breach of a contract to which (s)he was a party. Because Faithful Agents did not execute the contract between Jones and ABC, Faithful cannot be liable for the breach, regardless of the principal's bankruptcy.

Answer (a) is incorrect because a disclosed principal is liable for contracts negotiated by its agent. Answer (c) is incorrect because agents of disclosed principals are not liable for contracts with third parties unless the agent executes the contract after the principal dies, is incapacitated, or becomes bankrupt. Answer (d) is incorrect because agents are not liable for contract breaches of their principal.

14.5 Liability When Principal Is Undisclosed

63. Steel has been engaged by Lux to act as the agent for Lux, an undisclosed principal. As a result of this relationship

a. Steel has the same implied powers as an agent engaged by a disclosed principal.

b. Lux can not be held liable for any torts committed by Steel in the course of carrying out the engagement.

c. Steel will be free from personal liability on authorized contracts for Lux when it is revealed that Steel was acting as an agent.

d. Lux must file the appropriate form in the proper state office under the fictitious business name statute.

The correct answer is (a). *(CPA 1183 L-14)*

REQUIRED: The legal effect of not revealing the principal's existence.

DISCUSSION: Implied authority is the agent's actual authority that is not specifically conferred by the principal but is reasonably necessary to carry on the work authorized. Whether the principal is disclosed does not affect the agent's implied authority.

Answer (b) is incorrect because any principal who controls the conduct of the agent may be vicariously liable for the agent's torts committed in the course and scope of the agency. Answer (c) is incorrect because the third party may elect to sue the principal, the agent, or both after disclosure of the agency arrangement. Answer (d) is incorrect because no such requirement exists for an undisclosed principal.

64. Fred Frey contracted with Cara Corp. on behalf of Lux, Inc., an undisclosed principal. If Cara repudiates the contract, which of the following statements concerning liability on the contract is not correct?

a. Frey may hold Cara liable and obtain money damages.

b. Frey may hold Cara liable and obtain specific performance.

c. Lux may hold Cara liable upon disclosing the agency relationship with Frey.

d. Cara will be free from liability to Lux if Frey fraudulently stated that he was acting on his own behalf.

The correct answer is (b). *(CPA 1187 L-24)*

REQUIRED: The incorrect statement regarding third party liability to an agent and an undisclosed principal.

DISCUSSION: The agent and the third party are liable to each other prior to disclosure of the principal. The agent may therefore hold the third party liable on the contract, but the remedy is money damages, not specific performance.

Answer (a) is incorrect because the third party may be held liable by the agent for money damages. Answer (c) is incorrect because the principal may hold the third party liable after disclosure of the agency relationship. Answer (d) is incorrect because Frey's fraudulent statement would relieve the third party of liability to the principal.

65. Harper Company appointed Doe as its agent. It was essential that Harper's identity be kept secret. Therefore, Doe was to act in the capacity of an agent for an undisclosed principal. The duration of the agency was for exactly one month commencing Wednesday of the following week. As a result of this agreement between Harper and Doe, Harper

a. Is not liable on the agency contract unless it is in writing.

b. Cannot ratify the unauthorized acts of Doe.

c. Can rely upon the parol evidence rule to avoid liability to third parties if the contract is in writing.

d. Cannot be held liable for torts committed by Doe while acting as an agent.

The correct answer is (b). *(CPA 582 L-6)*

REQUIRED: The status of an undisclosed principal.

DISCUSSION: In most jurisdictions, an undisclosed principal cannot ratify the unauthorized acts of its agent. For an act to be ratifiable, the agent must have purported to act in his/her capacity as an agent. This rule operates to prevent one person from acquiring the contract rights of another.

Answer (a) is incorrect because appointment of an agent usually does not require a writing. All that is required is manifestation of consent. However, some statutes require the appointment of the agent to be in writing if the contract which the agent enters into (on behalf of the principal) is required to be in writing, and the year clause of the Statute of Frauds is applicable to agency agreements. Answer (c) is incorrect because the parol evidence rule has little impact on the undisclosed principal situation. It prevents the introduction of evidence of prior or contemporaneous agreements which would tend to vary the terms of a written agreement intended to be entire. Answer (d) is incorrect because even an undisclosed principal is liable for the torts committed by its agent acting within the course and scope of the agency.

66. Jason Manufacturing Company wished to acquire a site for a warehouse. Knowing that if it negotiated directly for the purchase of the property the price would be substantially increased, it employed Kent, an agent, to secure lots without disclosing that he was acting for Jason. Kent's authority was evidenced by a writing signed by the proper officers of Jason. Kent entered into a contract in his own name to purchase Peter's lot, giving Peter a negotiable note for $1,000 signed by Kent as first payment. Jason wrote Kent acknowledging the purchase. Jason also disclosed its identity as Kent's principal to Peter. In respect to the rights and liabilities of the parties, which of the following is a correct statement?

a. Peter is not bound on the contract since Kent's failure to disclose he was Jason's agent was fraudulent.

b. Jason, Kent, and Peter are potentially liable on the contract.

c. Unless Peter formally ratifies the substitution of Jason for Kent, he is not liable.

d. Kent has no liability since he was acting for and on behalf of an existing principal.

The correct answer is (b). *(CPA 581 L-34)*

REQUIRED: The liability when an agent enters into a contract on behalf of an undisclosed principal.

DISCUSSION: When an agent enters into a contract with a third party for an undisclosed principal, the agent, the principal, and the third party are bound by the contract. The principal is not bound by the contract until the third party discovers the arrangement and elects to hold the principal liable. Hence, Jason, Kent, and Peter are potentially liable on the contract.

Answer (a) is incorrect because concealment of the true party in interest is not fraudulent. Answer (c) is incorrect because Peter is liable and does not need to substitute Jason for Kent. Answer (d) is incorrect because an agent is liable to a third party when (s)he enters into a contract for an undisclosed principal. Kent would have no liability only if both the principal and the agency relationship had been disclosed at the time the contract was formed.

67. Magnus Real Estate Developers, Inc. wanted to acquire certain tracts of land in Marshall Township in order to build a shopping center complex. To accomplish this goal, Magnus engaged Dexter, a sophisticated real estate dealer, to represent them in the purchase of the necessary land without revealing the existence of the agency. Dexter began to slowly but steadily acquire the requisite land. However, Dexter made the mistake of purchasing one tract outside the description of the land needed. Which of the following is correct under these circumstances?

a. The use of an agent by Magnus, an undisclosed principal, is manifestly illegal.

b. Either Magnus or Dexter may be held liable on the contracts for the land, including the land that was not within the scope of the proposed shopping center.

c. An undisclosed principal such as Magnus can have no liability under the contract since the third party believed he was dealing with Dexter as a principal.

d. An agent for an undisclosed principal assumes no liability as long as he registers his relationship to the principal with the clerk of the proper county having jurisdiction.

The correct answer is (b). *(CPA 1179 L-31)*

REQUIRED: The liability when an agent exceeds his/her authority in contracting for an undisclosed principal.

DISCUSSION: A third party can hold either the agent or the undisclosed principal liable on a contract entered into with the agent. Although Dexter exceeded his/her authority in purchasing the land outside the description of the proposed shopping center, Dexter had apparent authority to make the purchase. The test for the apparent authority of an agent for an undisclosed principal is made in the same manner as in disclosed principal situations. However, if Magnus is held liable on the land outside the description of the proposed shopping center, Dexter may be liable to Magnus for the error.

Answer (a) is incorrect because the use of an agency with an undisclosed principal is a common practice and not per se illegal. Answer (c) is incorrect because an undisclosed principal may become liable to a third party who discovers the arrangement and elects to hold the principal liable. Answer (d) is incorrect because an agent is liable on contracts entered into on behalf of an undisclosed principal and there is no common means of registering the relationship with any official.

14.6 Termination of Agency

68. Dent is an agent for Wein pursuant to a written agreement with a 3-year term. After 2 years of the term, Wein decides that he would like to terminate the relationship with Dent. Wein may terminate the relationship

a. Without cause, but may be held liable for breach of contract.

b. Even if Dent is an agent coupled with an interest.

c. Without cause, but may be held liable for the intentional interference with an existing contract.

d. Only if Dent breaches the fiduciary duties owed to Wein.

The correct answer is (a). *(CPA 1184 L-14)*

REQUIRED: The true statement about termination of an agency prior to the end of its contracted-for duration.

DISCUSSION: Either the principal or the agent has a power of termination that (s)he may exercise at will (without cause). Since the termination would occur prior to the end of the contracted-for term, however, the principal has no right to terminate and would be liable in damages for breach of contract.

Answer (b) is incorrect because an agency coupled with an interest cannot be terminated at will since the agent generally has a legal right in the property of the agency. Answer (c) is incorrect because the principal is a party to the agreement and may be held liable for breach. Only a third party could be liable for the tort of intentional interference with the contract. Answer (d) is incorrect because an agency not coupled with an interest may be terminated by the parties at any time for any reason.

69. Which of the following is a true statement about termination of an agency?

a. A hires B to sell land without specifying the duration of the agency. When B sells the land 8 years later, the transaction is binding on A.

b. C hires D to lease or sell C's real estate. D leases the land to E. At the end of the lease, D may sell the realty to F.

c. G authorizes H to act as her agent but is then declared insane. I appoints J as an agent but dies soon afterward. H and J have the power to bind the estate of their respective principals prior to notice of insanity or death.

d. K is a sales agent for L, M, and N. L has filed for a Chapter 7 bankruptcy liquidation. The products sold by M have been declared illegal, and N's business was destroyed in a flood. Each agency has been terminated by operation of law.

The correct answer is (d). *(Publisher)*

REQUIRED: The true statement about termination of an agency.

DISCUSSION: An agency may terminate by operation of law for several reasons. For example, the principal's bankruptcy will terminate agency relationships when the entity is to be liquidated. Reorganization would not have this effect. Illegality and impossibility of performance also automatically terminate the agency. Likewise, a change in circumstances or business conditions such that the agent could reasonably infer that the principal would no longer wish the agency to be carried out terminates the agent's authority.

Answer (a) is incorrect because an agency is terminated when it is for a specified duration, the accomplishment of a stated purpose, or the happening of a certain event and the given time elapses, the purpose is accomplished, or the event occurs. Moreover, an agency for an indefinite time will expire after a reasonable time. Most likely B's sale of land will be ineffective because more than a reasonable time has passed. Answer (b) is incorrect because the purpose of the agency was achieved when the land was leased, so D's agency was terminated before the sale to F. Answer (c) is incorrect because death and insanity terminate an agency immediately.

70. Terrence has been Pauline's agent in the liquor business for 10 years and has made numerous contracts on Pauline's behalf. Under which of the following situations could Terrence continue to have power to bind Pauline?

a. The passage of a federal constitutional amendment making the sale or purchase of alcoholic beverages illegal.

b. The death of Pauline without Terrence's knowledge.

c. The bankruptcy of Pauline with Terrence's knowledge.

d. The firing of Terrence by Pauline.

The correct answer is (d). *(CPA 583 L-2)*

REQUIRED: The event that would not terminate an agent's power to bind a principal.

DISCUSSION: An agent has continuing apparent authority (authority by estoppel) to deal with the principal's customers. When the agency is terminated, the principal has the responsibility to give actual notice to those customers who have dealt with the discharged agent and constructive notice to others. Until such notification, the customer can rely upon the apparent authority of the discharged agent.

Answer (a) is incorrect because the illegality of the subject matter of the agency terminates the agency with respect to all persons. Answer (b) is incorrect because an agency, and with it the agent's power to bind the principal, terminates instantly upon the death of the principal. Answer (c) is incorrect because generally the principal's bankruptcy terminates the agent's authority except as to an agency coupled with an interest.

71. A general agent's apparent authority to bind her principal to contracts with third parties will cease without notice to those third parties when the

a. Agent has fulfilled the purpose for which the agency relationship was created.

b. Time set forth in the agreement creating the agency relationship has expired.

c. Principal and agent have mutually agreed to end their relationship.

d. Principal has received a discharge in bankruptcy under the liquidation provisions of the Bankruptcy Code.

The correct answer is (d). *(CPA 587 L-4)*

REQUIRED: The condition that terminates the apparent authority of an agent without notice to third parties.

DISCUSSION: No notification of third parties is necessary to terminate apparent authority if the principal no longer has capacity (is declared insane or incompetent), dies, or becomes bankrupt.

Answers (a), (b), and (c) are incorrect because fulfillment of purpose, expiration of time, or agreement between principal and agent terminates the agent's apparent authority only upon actual notice to existing customers and constructive notice to others.

72. The apparent authority of a general agent for a disclosed principal will terminate without notice to third parties when the

a. Principal dismisses the agent.

b. Principal or agent dies.

c. Purpose of the agency relationship has been fulfilled.

d. Time period set forth in the agency agreement has expired.

The correct answer is (b). *(CPA 588 L-6)*

REQUIRED: The instance in which an agent's apparent authority is automatically terminated.

DISCUSSION: An agency, and with it the agent's power to bind the principal, terminates instantly upon the death of the principal because the principal must exist at the time the agent acts. In a few states, however, the hardship of this rule is mitigated by allowing the third party to proceed against the principal's estate.

Answer (a) is incorrect because when an agent is dismissed, existing customers must be given actual notice. Other persons must be given constructive notice to terminate apparent authority. Answers (c) and (d) are incorrect because neither fulfillment of the purpose of the agency nor expiration of the agreed period terminates apparent authority.

73. King engages Davis to purchase goods from a seller on King's credit account with the seller. The seller informs Davis that King's account is closed so Davis uses her own check to purchase the goods. Upon returning to King with the goods, King refuses to reimburse Davis and discharges Davis. Which of the following is correct?

a. The agency cannot be terminated because Davis is an agent coupled with an interest.

b. The agency is terminated and King owes Davis nothing.

c. The agency will terminate automatically when King pays Davis.

d. The agency is terminated and King is liable to Davis for the amount of the check.

The correct answer is (d). *(Publisher)*

REQUIRED: The correct statement regarding the termination of an agency.

DISCUSSION: Even though a principal owes a duty to an agent not to terminate the agency wrongfully, the principal does have the power to do so even if liability will result. A principal (King) also has a duty to reimburse an agent (Davis) for expenses incurred in performing duties on behalf of the principal.

Answer (a) is incorrect because Davis was not an agent coupled with an interest since she had no legal interest in the subject of the agency and no property to protect by continuing the agency. Answer (b) is incorrect because, although King may terminate the agency at will, he will be liable to Davis for reimbursement and possibly for compensation for services. Answer (c) is incorrect because the agency relationship was terminated by King and does not continue even though King is still liable to Davis.

74. Pell is the principal and Astor is the agent in an agency coupled with an interest. In the absence of a contractual provision relating to the duration of the agency, who has the right to terminate the agency before the interest has expired?

	Pell	Astor
a.	Yes	Yes
b.	No	Yes
c.	No	No
d.	Yes	No

The correct answer is (b). *(CPA 589 L-11)*

REQUIRED: The person with the right to terminate an agency coupled with an interest.

DISCUSSION: A principal does not have the right or power to terminate an agency coupled with an interest. In any agency relationship, the agent may terminate at any time without liability if no specific period for the agency has been established.

Answer (a) is incorrect because in an agency coupled with an interest, the agent has the right to terminate the agency but the principal does not. Answer (c) is incorrect because the agent does have the right to terminate an agency coupled with an interest. Answer (d) is incorrect because the principal does not have the right to terminate.

75. Park Manufacturing hired Stone as a traveling salesman to sell goods manufactured by Park. Stone also sold a line of products manufactured by a friend. He did not disclose this to Park. The relationship was unsatisfactory and Park finally fired Stone after learning of Stone's sales of the other manufacturer's goods. Stone, enraged at Park for firing him, continued to make contracts on Park's behalf with both new and old customers that were almost uniformly disadvantageous to Park. Park, upon learning of this, gave written notice of Stone's discharge to all parties with whom Stone had dealt. Which of the following statements is incorrect?

a. Park can bring an action against Stone to have him account for any secret profits.

b. Prior to notification, Stone retained some continued authority to bind Park despite termination of the agency relationship.

c. New customers who contracted with Stone for the first time could enforce the contracts against Park if they knew that Stone had been Park's salesman but were unaware that Stone was fired.

d. If Park had promptly published a notification of termination of Stone's employment in the local newspapers and in the trade publications, he would not be liable for any of Stone's contracts.

The correct answer is (d). *(CPA 1180 L-29)*

REQUIRED: The false statement regarding a dismissed agent's continued activities on behalf of the principal.

DISCUSSION: When a principal discharges an agent, (s)he must give actual notice to those with whom the agent had previously dealt to terminate the apparent authority of the agent with those parties. Constructive notice by publication is sufficient to prevent apparent authority only with parties who have not previously dealt with the agent. The appropriate notice must be given before the apparent authority is exercised.

Answer (a) is incorrect because Park can bring an action against Stone (the discharged agent) to have him account for secret profits earned in the unauthorized sales. Answer (b) is incorrect because Stone did retain apparent authority to bind Park (even though there was no express authority) with those who previously dealt with him. Answer (c) is incorrect because even new customers who knew of the agency but were unaware of the firing could rely on Stone's apparent authority.

CHAPTER FIFTEEN
PARTNERSHIPS

Because the Uniform Partnership Act of 1914 has been adopted in almost all states, the answer explanations in this chapter are based on its provisions. The Uniform Partnership Act is reprinted at the back of, or as an appendix to, most business law books. When no provision of the Uniform Partnership Act is applicable, common law is the source of the answer explanation. We have used the abbreviation UPA for the Uniform Partnership Act. In addition, the law of agency forms a basis for many of the answer explanations because each general partner is an agent of the partnership.

Except for the last module, "Limited Partnerships," all answers assume the discussion is of general partners and general partnerships. However, the answer explanations in the last module are based on the Uniform Limited Partnership Act to the extent it is applicable. The Uniform Limited Partnership Act is also reprinted at the back of, or as an appendix to, most business law books. We have used the abbreviation ULPA for the Uniform Limited Partnership Act. It has been amended several times and some texts refer to the latest version as the "revised" ULPA or RULPA. Because most states have adopted the latest version (1976), this is the one reflected herein. The UPA applies to limited partnerships in the absence of an applicable provision in the RULPA or ULPA.

15.1 Partnerships: Nature and Formation

1. The nature of a partnership is unclear. In some respects, it is treated as a separate legal entity, but in others it is regarded as merely an aggregate of its partners. A partnership is regarded solely as an aggregate of its partners when

a. It pays no federal tax on its income and is required to file an informational return.

b. It is dissolved by the death of a partner and the business is allowed to continue as a going concern.

c. The partners are liable for partnership debts but partnership creditors have priority in the firm's assets over creditors of the partners.

d. Each partner has management rights and is regarded as an agent of the other partners.

The correct answer is (d). *(Publisher)*

REQUIRED: The partnership characteristics typical of an aggregate of individuals.

DISCUSSION: A partner is an owner-manager unless (s)he consents to be excluded from management. A partner is also an agent of the other partners with authority to hire other agents who in turn can bind the partners by contract and subject them to liability by their torts. These are characteristics of an aggregate of individuals. Other ways in which a partnership is regarded as an aggregate are creation without legal formalities; a partner cannot sue the partnership; and lack of free transferability of a partner's interest.

Answers (a), (b), and (c) are incorrect because filing a partnership tax return, continuing in business after dissolution, and priority of partnership creditors in partnership assets are all separate entity characteristics. A partnership has entity status in other ways: a partner is an agent of the partnership; many states and the federal courts allow a partnership to sue and be sued; a partnership may go into bankruptcy; and realty may be held and conveyed in the partnership name.

2. For which of the following purposes is a general partnership recognized as an entity by the Uniform Partnership Act?

a. Recognition of the partnership as the employer of its partners.

b. Insulation of the partners from personal liability.

c. Taking of title and ownership of property.

d. Continuity of existence.

The correct answer is (c). *(CPA 583 L-3)*

REQUIRED: The purpose for which a general partnership is treated as an entity.

DISCUSSION: Under the UPA, property acquired on account of the partnership is partnership property. The UPA states, "Any estate in real property may be acquired in the partnership name. Title so acquired can be conveyed only in the partnership name." This is an entity concept.

Answer (a) is incorrect because partners are not treated as employees of a partnership; e.g., they are not entitled to compensation unless agreed otherwise. Answer (b) is incorrect because general partners have unlimited liability. Answer (d) is incorrect because a partnership does not survive a partner's death or withdrawal of a partner. It is dissolved, but the business may be continued as a new partnership.

3. For which of the following is a partnership recognized as a separate legal entity?

a. The liability for and payment of taxes on partnership gains from the sale of capital assets.

b. In respect to contributions and advances made by partners to the partnership.

c. The recognition of net operating losses.

d. The status of the partnership as an employer for workers' compensation purposes.

The correct answer is (d). *(CPA 1181 L-20)*

REQUIRED: When a partnership is recognized as a separate legal entity.

DISCUSSION: Under common law, a partnership (in contrast to the corporation) is not recognized as a separate legal entity. In other words, a partnership is not regarded as being separate from its owners. The UPA recognizes a partnership as an entity for a few purposes, none of which is listed here. Another statutory exception is that a partnership qualifies as an employer under workers' compensation statutes.

Answers (a) and (c) are incorrect because a partnership is not a separate legal entity for the payment of taxes. A partnership is a reporting entity in the sense that a partnership must file tax returns, but otherwise it is a conduit for gains and losses flowing through to the partners. Answer (b) is incorrect because contributions and advances made by partners to the partnership are regarded as the property of the partners.

4. Three independent sole proprietors decided to pool their resources and form a partnership. The business assets and liabilities of each were transferred to the partnership. The partnership commenced business on September 1, but the parties did not execute a formal partnership agreement until October 15. Which of the following is correct?

a. The existing creditors must consent to the transfer of the individual business assets to the partnership.

b. The partnership began its existence on September 1.

c. If the partnership's duration is indefinite, the partnership agreement must be in writing and signed.

d. In the absence of a partnership agreement specifically covering division of losses among the partners, they will be deemed to share them in accordance with their capital contributions.

The correct answer is (b). *(CPA 582 L-1)*

REQUIRED: The correct statement concerning the formation of a partnership.

DISCUSSION: A general partnership comes into being whenever a business entity meets the criteria of a functioning partnership. This occurs when two or more persons associate and carry on a business as co-owners, for profit. No formalities need to be observed, and the partnership may even exist though the persons involved have not so intended. This partnership came into existence upon the commencement of business (or acts in preparation for business), rather than the execution of a formal agreement.

Answer (a) is incorrect because the existing creditors of the individual partners have no say in the transfer of individual assets to the partnership. Answer (c) is incorrect because a general partnership may be formed without a written and signed agreement. Answer (d) is incorrect because in the absence of an agreement specifically covering losses, the UPA provides that losses are to be shared the same as profits, which is equally.

5. B approached L and proposed they form a partnership to exploit a profitable idea of B's. L declined, citing the risk of unlimited liability. B then proposed that L lend B $50,000 and that B go into the business as a sole proprietor. L would receive half the profits and the right to veto any of B's decisions. The debt would have a long-term maturity date to facilitate operation of the business during its development stage. If L accepts the above proposition, the likely result is that

a. A debtor-creditor relationship exists between B and L.

b. B and L are not partners as to each other, or third parties.

c. B and L have formed a partnership even if they did not intend to.

d. If L promises orally to become a partner of B and to transfer real property to the business, the Statute of Frauds would prohibit enforcement of the promise.

The correct answer is (c). *(Publisher)*

REQUIRED: The relationship of a sole proprietor with a lender who receives a share of the profits and has a veto over business decisions.

DISCUSSION: A partnership can be formed without actual intent if there is an association of two or more persons to carry on a business as co-owners for profit. In addition to sharing in profits, L funded the venture and has the right to participate in management. Hence, B and L's arrangement constitutes co-ownership, and a partnership was thereby formed.

Answer (a) is incorrect because a debtor-creditor relationship does not exist. B and L have formed a partnership. The "loan" is really a capital contribution. Possibly B has contracted with L to absorb any losses of capital, but such an agreement would have no effect on their liability as partners. Answer (b) is incorrect because B and L are partners as to each other; however, even if they were not partners as to each other, they could be held liable as partners by estoppel to third parties. Answer (d) is incorrect because even though the Statute of Frauds denies enforcement of an oral agreement for the sale or transfer of real property, most courts do not appear to apply it to an oral agreement concerning contribution of land to a partnership.

6. James Fine is doing business as Fine's Apparels, a sole proprietorship. In the past year Fine had regularly joined with Charles Walters in the marketing of bathing suits and beach accessories. Which of the following factors is the most important in ascertaining whether Fine and Walters have created a partnership relationship?

a. A partnership agreement is not in existence.

b. Each has a separate business of his own which he operates independently.

c. Fine and Walters divide the net profits equally on a quarterly basis.

d. Fine and Walters did not intend to be partners.

The correct answer is (c). *(CPA 1180 L-23)*

REQUIRED: The most important factor in ascertaining whether a partnership exists.

DISCUSSION: Section 7 of the UPA creates a presumption that a person who receives a share of the profits of a business is a co-owner and therefore a partner in the business. However, this presumption does not exist if the profits are received in payment of a debt, as wages or rent, as interest on a loan, as payment for sale, or as an annuity to a deceased partner's representative.

Answer (a) is incorrect because the existence of a partnership may be implied from the facts of the situation even though no agreement, either oral or written, is in existence. Answer (b) is incorrect because nothing prevents an individual from becoming a partner even though (s)he operates another business. Answer (d) is incorrect because a partnership may be implied from the objective facts of the case even though the individuals had no subjective intent to be partners.

7. Which of the following is a characteristic of an unincorporated association?

a. It is generally used in profit-oriented ventures.

b. Members who actively manage the association may be held personally liable for contracts they enter into on behalf of the association.

c. Certificates representing ownership in the association must be distributed to the members.

d. Its duration must be for a limited period of time not to exceed 12 months.

The correct answer is (b). *(CPA 1185 L-1)*

REQUIRED: The characteristic of an unincorporated association.

DISCUSSION: A person who enters into a contract on behalf of an unincorporated association is in a position similar to that of a promoter of a corporation not yet in existence. (S)he will be liable as an agent of a nonexistent principal since the association is not usually regarded as a separate legal person. The individual member of the association who authorized the contract may and should be liable.

Answer (a) is incorrect because an unincorporated association is generally used for nonprofit purposes. When the profit motive exists, such an organization would meet the criteria for a partnership. Answer (c) is incorrect because such an entity has no owners. The relations of the members are controlled by ordinary contract principles, and no specific form of organization is necessary. Answer (d) is incorrect because duration is governed by the intent of the parties to associate for a common purpose.

8. Rivers and Lee want to form a partnership. For the partnership agreement to be enforceable, it must be in writing if

a. Rivers and Lee reside in different states.

b. The agreement cannot be completed within 1 year from the date of its formation.

c. Either Rivers or Lee is to contribute more than $500 in capital.

d. The partnership intends to buy and sell real estate.

The correct answer is (b). *(CPA 589 L-14)*

REQUIRED: The condition requiring a written partnership agreement.

DISCUSSION: Most oral agreements to enter into a partnership are valid. If the partnership agreement is for a definite period in excess of 1 year, however, the majority of states require that the partnership agreement be in writing to be enforceable. This is consistent with the "year clause" of the Statute of Frauds. If the Statute of Frauds is not complied with, a partnership at will results.

Answer (a) is incorrect because the residence of the partners has no relevance to whether the agreement must be in writing. Answer (c) is incorrect because there is no limit on capital contributions that requires a written agreement. The $500 requirement applies to contracts for the sale of goods. Answer (d) is incorrect because although a contract to transfer an interest in real estate must be in writing, a partnership agreement to enter into the real estate business does not involve the transfer of real estate and therefore does not need to be in writing.

9. Sally Rhee worked with Pat Price in operating a beauty salon. When she threatened to quit unless she was paid more, they made a written agreement stating that they were forming a partnership. They agreed as follows: The name of the partnership was to be Pat & Sally's Beauty Salon; Pat was to furnish all capital, be liable for all losses, and have the absolute right to manage the enterprise; Sally was to work full-time and do whatever was necessary to successfully carry on the business; Sally was to receive $200 per week on a drawing account; profits were to be shared 80-20 by Pat and Sally, respectively; and each had the right to inspect the books. Which of the following is correct?

a. Pat and Sally formed a partnership.

b. Pat is Sally's employer.

c. The important element in the formation of a partnership is capital contribution.

d. That Pat and Sally called themselves partners leaves the court no choice but to conclude that they are partners.

The correct answer is (b). *(Publisher)*

REQUIRED: The correct statement regarding the formation of a partnership.

DISCUSSION: A partnership is defined as an association of two or more persons to carry on a business as co-owners for profit. No partnership was formed because the parties were not co-owners. That Pat retained all management rights is crucial to determining co-ownership. The lack of capital contributions by Sally is significant but not controlling. The sharing of profits is important (as creating a presumption of a partnership) but not controlling because enough other factors are missing. The sharing of profits in this case is simply a means of compensation to an employee.

Answer (a) is incorrect because Pat and Sally did not form a partnership as discussed above. Answer (c) is incorrect because capital contribution is not an extremely important element in the formation of a partnership. However, it does have a bearing on whether co-ownership exists. Answer (d) is incorrect because calling oneself a partner has no effect on whether a partnership actually exists. It would, however, give a third party the right to rely on such a declaration.

10. Foote leased space in Jacque's Department Store to operate a shoe department. During the year Foote and Jacque operated in the same store and shoe sales were advertised under the name of Jacque's. Major Shoe Co. has sold shoes on credit to Foote many times under the name Jacque's Department Store. Foote is insolvent and owes Major $5,971.80. If Major Shoe seeks to recover from Jacque's Department Store, the likely result is

a. That Jacque's Department Store is in partnership with Foote Shoes.

b. Jacque's and Foote are partners by estoppel.

c. Foote is entitled to examine the books of account of Jacque's Department Store upon reasonable notice and at a reasonable time.

d. Jacque's personal creditors have priority over Major Shoe.

The correct answer is (b). *(Publisher)*

REQUIRED: The ability of a vendor to collect from a vendee's lessor if the vendee and lessor acted as partners.

DISCUSSION: A partnership by estoppel is a term used to describe the situation when creditors are able to hold parties liable as partners after they have held themselves out to the public as partners. In this case, Jacque's became liable as a partner to Major Shoe Company since Foote operated out of Jacque's store, they advertised together, and Foote purchased shoes under the name of Jacque's store. Third-party creditors are allowed to rely on this type of representation. Two other theories of liability are to treat Foote as Jacque's agent or to hold Foote and Jacque as joint principals on the contract.

Answer (a) is incorrect because Jacque's Department Store is not in partnership with Foote Shoes; they have a landlord-tenant relationship. Answer (c) is incorrect because Foote is not entitled to examine the books of Jacque's Department Store since Foote is not a partner with Jacque. Answer (d) is incorrect because Jacque will be held liable as a partner with Foote and, therefore, Major Shoe will have first priority to the "partnership" assets and will share with personal creditors in the personal assets.

11. Bonnie was a very bright and mature 16 year old who invented a new wangle. She got the following persons together one afternoon: her rich aunt (on furlough from a mental hospital) to contribute money; her uncle who was a very good salesman when sober; and the president of Ultra Corporation which had the capability to manufacture the wangles. These four met and decided to form a partnership to manufacture and sell the wangles. They all signed a partnership agreement, although the uncle was extremely intoxicated at the time and the president signed on behalf of Ultra Corporation. Which of the following could become a partner?

a. Bonnie, only with the consent of her legal guardian.

b. The aunt.

c. The uncle.

d. Ultra Corporation.

The correct answer is (d). *(Publisher)*

REQUIRED: The person with the capacity to become a partner.

DISCUSSION: The general rule is that anyone who has the capacity to contract can become a partner. It is a test of contract law rather than partnership law. Ultra has the capacity to become a partner. A corporation has this power unless its articles of incorporation (or by-laws) provide otherwise.

Answer (a) is incorrect because Bonnie does not need the consent of her legal guardian to enter into a valid partnership agreement. Minors have the capacity to contract, although it could subsequently be disaffirmed. If a minor does disaffirm a partnership agreement, (s)he may be required to leave his/her capital in the business if withdrawal imperils the creditors. Answer (b) is incorrect because the aunt may have been adjudicated legally incompetent when committed to the mental hospital and if not is presumably factually insane, at least to the point that she does not have contractual capacity. Answer (c) is incorrect because the uncle was extremely intoxicated at the time of entering into the partnership and did not have capacity to enter into a contract if he was unable to understand and appreciate the consequences of the agreement.

12. A joint venture is

a. An association limited to no more than two persons in business for profit.

b. An enterprise of numerous co-owners in a nonprofit undertaking.

c. A corporate enterprise for a single undertaking of limited duration.

d. An association of persons engaged as co-owners in a single undertaking for profit.

The correct answer is (d). *(CPA 1189 L-4)*

REQUIRED: The correct definition of a joint venture.

DISCUSSION: A joint venture is similar to a partnership except that it does not entail carrying on a business. The joint venture is an association of persons to undertake a specific business project for profit.

Answer (a) is incorrect because the association is not limited to two persons, and the venture involves only a specific project, not a business. Answer (b) is incorrect because a joint venture is undertaken for profit. Answer (c) is incorrect because a corporation formed for a single undertaking, whatever it may be called, is not a joint venture and is governed by corporate, not partnership, law. Joint ventures are not incorporated.

13. A major similarity between the legal rights of a corporate shareholder and a general partner is that each can

a. Control the continuity of a business enterprise.

b. Hold title to the real property of the enterprise in his/her name.

c. Be held liable for the obligations of the enterprise and dispose of his/her ownership interest at any time.

d. None of the above.

The correct answer is (d). *(CIA 976 IV-7)*

REQUIRED: The major similarity between a corporate shareholder and a general partner.

DISCUSSION: None of the other statements is true for both corporate shareholders and general partners.

Answer (a) is incorrect because a corporation usually has continuous life, but a partnership terminates for many reasons, such as the death of a partner. Answer (b) is incorrect because a general partner but not a shareholder has the right to hold title to corporate real property in his/her own name because (s)he is a fiduciary and an agent of the partnership. Answer (c) is incorrect because a shareholder ordinarily cannot be held liable for the obligations of a corporation, but a general partner can be held liable for partnership obligations.

14. Many states require partnerships to file the partnership name under laws known as fictitious name statutes. These statutes

a. Require a proper filing as a condition precedent to the valid creation of a partnership.

b. Are designed primarily to provide registration for tax purposes.

c. Are designed to clarify the rights and duties of the members of the partnership.

d. Have little effect on the creation or operation of a partnership other than the imposition of a fine or other minor penalty for noncompliance.

The correct answer is (d). *(CPA 1183 L-15)*

REQUIRED: The true statement about fictitious name statutes.

DISCUSSION: Fictitious name statutes have been enacted in most states for the protection of creditors. Registration permits creditors to discover the persons liable for the debts of the enterprise. The creation and operation of a partnership is little affected by the requirement because a partnership need not adopt a name, although use of a name may help to distinguish a partnership action from that of a partner. Moreover, the use of a name does not necessarily indicate the existence of a partnership or that a named person is a member of the firm.

Answer (a) is incorrect because creation of a general partnership requires no legal formalities. Answers (b) and (c) are incorrect because the fictitious name statutes are designed to protect creditors.

15.2 Partners' Rights and Authority

15. The distinction between specific partnership property and a partner's property is important not only to the partners and the partnership but also to creditors, heirs, and others. Which of the following is correct?

a. Real property held in the name of a partner is conclusively presumed to be the partner's.

b. Property held in the partnership name is presumed to be partnership property.

c. The form of title to property controls over the partners' intent.

d. A personal creditor of a partner may proceed against partnership property held by the partners together.

The correct answer is (b). *(Publisher)*

REQUIRED: The true statement about partnership property.

DISCUSSION: Under Section 8 of the UPA, "All property originally brought into the partnership...or subsequently acquired by purchase or otherwise, on account of the partnership, is partnership property. Unless the contrary intention appears, property acquired with partnership funds is partnership property." This includes that property created by the partnership and profits. Therefore, when title is held by the partnership, the presumption is that the property is partnership property.

Answer (a) is incorrect because partnership property may be held in the name of a partner. Answer (c) is incorrect because the partners' intent controls over the form of title. Answer (d) is incorrect because a personal creditor of a partner cannot reach the specific partnership property (but can attach the partner's interest in the partnership).

16. The term "partnership property" is significant in partnership law. Which of the following is not partnership property?

a. Capital contributed by partners which is to be returned to them after five years.

b. The name of the partnership which is simply made up of the surnames of the three partners.

c. Realty contributed by a partner but left in his/her name.

d. Accumulated and undistributed profits of the partnership.

The correct answer is (d). *(Publisher)*

REQUIRED: The item which is not partnership property.

DISCUSSION: Accumulated and undistributed profits of a partnership are the property of the individual partners based on their sharing ratio. Partnership property is a term which refers to the assets used to make profits.

Answer (a) is incorrect because capital contributions by partners is partnership property regardless of an obligation to return it sometime in the future. Answer (b) is incorrect because the name of a partnership is also partnership property in which all the partners have an interest but not an individual right. Answer (c) is incorrect because realty contributed by a partner is partnership property regardless of the name in which title is held.

17. Johnelle and Reba formed J&R, a partnership. A year after formation, partnership funds were used to acquire an automobile but title was taken in Reba's name. The property was used for Reba's own purposes except during business hours. Reba paid the sales tax on the acquisition, the insurance premiums, and the fuel and maintenance costs. Reba has been petitioned into bankruptcy, and the trustee has asserted a claim to the vehicle. Which of the following is true if the partners had no specific agreement about partnership property?

a. The trustee will prevail because title to the property is controlling.

b. The trustee will prevail because the objective intent of the partners is controlling.

c. The partnership will prevail because the property was acquired with partnership funds.

d. The partnership will prevail because the property was used for partnership purposes.

The correct answer is (b). *(Publisher)*

REQUIRED: The party entitled to property used by a partnership.

DISCUSSION: "Unless the contrary intention appears, property acquired with partnership funds is partnership property" (UPA Section 8). The intention of the partners is controlling. It may be expressed in the partnership agreement or appear from other writings, such as accounting records. Intent may be inferred from still other indicators, for example, payment of taxes, insurance premiums, and maintenance costs. Title and use of the property are also significant indicators. Since Reba held title, etc., the presumption created by acquisition with partnership funds is rebutted by the apparent intent of the partners that the automobile should be hers.

Answer (a) is incorrect because holding title does not create an irrebuttable presumption. Answer (c) is incorrect because intent controls even over acquisition with partnership funds. Answer (d) is incorrect because use by the partnership is not as significant as the other factors since partners commonly use their own property in partnership activities.

18. Allen, Burton, and Carter were equal partners for the purpose of buying and selling real estate for profit. For convenience, title to all property purchased was taken in the name of Allen. Allen died with partnership real estate and partnership personal property standing in his name valued at $250,000 and $5,000, respectively. The partnership had no debts. Allen's wife claims a dower right in the real property. Allen had bequeathed all his personal property to his children who claim an absolute one-third interest in the $5,000 of personal property. In this situation

a. Allen's wife has a valid dower right to all the real property held in her deceased husband's name.

b. Partnership property is subject to a right of survivorship in the surviving partners; hence, Allen's wife is entitled only to his share of undistributed partnership profits.

c. Allen's children are entitled to one-third of all partnership personal property.

d. Allen's estate is entitled to settlement for the value of his partnership interest.

The correct answer is (d). *(CPA 1174 L-6)*

REQUIRED: The correct statement regarding partnership property standing in the name of the decedent.

DISCUSSION: Under the UPA, each partner is a co-owner with respect to specific partnership property, and no partner has a right to use the partnership property for him/herself even if title is in his/her name. Upon the death of a partner, the partnership property rights vest in the other partners. The decedent's estate is only entitled to the value of the deceased partner's interest in the partnership, not any of the specific partnership real or personal property.

Answer (a) is incorrect because a partner's right in specific partnership property is not subject to dower, curtesy, or allowances to widows, heirs, or next-of-kin. Answer (b) is incorrect because although partnership property is subject to a right of survivorship in the surviving partners, the value of the partnership interest, not just the undistributed profits, becomes part of the decedent's estate. Answer (c) is incorrect because the surviving partners have survivorship rights in the partnership personal property as well as the realty.

19. James Quick was a partner in the Fast, Sure, and Quick Factors partnership. He subsequently died. His will left everything to his wife including a one-third interest in the land and building owned by Fast, Sure, and Quick.

a. Mrs. Quick is a one-third owner of Fast, Sure, and Quick's land and building.

b. The real property in question was held by the partnership as a tenancy in common.

c. Mrs. Quick automatically becomes the partner of Fast and Sure upon her husband's death.

d. Mrs. Quick has the right to receive a settlement for her husband's interest in the partnership.

The correct answer is (d). *(CPA 1173 L-39)*

REQUIRED: The correct statement regarding the partnership interest of a deceased partner.

DISCUSSION: A partnership interest is the right to profits and surplus. Upon a partner's death and dissolution of the partnership, his/her estate (or beneficiaries) is entitled to the value of the decedent's partnership interest but not to any specific partnership property.

Answer (a) is incorrect because the surviving partners have survivorship rights to the partnership property. Answer (b) is incorrect because the partnership owned the entire interest in the property and there was no tenancy in common. Ownership of partnership property is sometimes referred to as a tenancy in partnership. Answer (c) is incorrect because all partners must agree to accept a new partner.

20. Daniels, Beal, and Wade agreed to form the DBW Partnership to engage in the import-export business. They had been life-long friends and had engaged in numerous business dealings with each other. It was orally agreed that Daniels would contribute $20,000, Beal $15,000 and Wade $5,000. It was also orally agreed that in the event the venture proved to be a financial disaster all losses above the amounts of capital contributed would be assumed by Daniels and that he would hold his fellow partners harmless from any additional amounts lost. The partnership was consummated with a handshake and the contribution of the agreed-upon capital by the partners. There were no other express agreements. Under these circumstances, which of the following is correct?

a. Profits are to be divided in accordance with the relative capital contributions of each partner.

b. Profits are to be divided equally.

c. The partnership is a nullity because the agreement is not contained in a signed writing.

d. Profits are to be shared in accordance with the relative time each devotes to partnership business during the year.

The correct answer is (b). *(CPA 1181 L-18)*

REQUIRED: The correct statement regarding profit sharing in the partnership.

DISCUSSION: Unless the partnership agreement specifies otherwise, profits are shared equally based on the number of partners. Unless agreed otherwise, losses are shared in the same way profits are shared. All partners are jointly liable to firm creditors and this liability cannot be changed by the partnership agreement. However, an indemnification agreement is valid among the partners.

Answer (a) is incorrect because in the absence of an express agreement, the partnership profits are divided equally and not based on capital contributions. Answer (c) is incorrect because most partnership agreements need not be contained in a signed writing. Answer (d) is incorrect because in the absence of an express agreement to the contrary, the profits are to be divided equally, not based on the amount of time that the individual partners devote to the business.

21. Skip & Trip decide to start a boutique selling preppy clothing. They sign a partnership agreement providing that Skip will contribute $6,000 toward the necessary $10,000 in start-up capital, and Trip will contribute $4,000. If the agreement is silent as to management and profits, Skip should receive

a. 60% of the profits and share management equally with Trip.

b. 60% of the profits and control 60% of the management functions.

c. 50% of the profits and share management equally with Trip.

d. 50% of the profits and control 60% of the management functions.

The correct answer is (c). *(I. Schwartz)*

REQUIRED: The partners' rights respecting profits and the management of the partnership business.

DISCUSSION: Partners have equal rights in the management of the partnership business even if, pursuant to their partnership agreement, they are to share profits unequally. In addition, absent an agreement to the contrary, each partner has the right to share equally in partnership profits even if their contributions are unequal. Skip and Trip had no such contrary agreement.

Answers (a) and (b) are incorrect because Trip is entitled to an equal share of the profits. Answers (b) and (d) are incorrect because Trip is also entitled to equal rights in the management of the business.

22. In the absence of a specific provision in a general partnership agreement, partnership losses will be allocated

a. Equally among the partners irrespective of the allocation of partnership profits.

b. In the same manner as partnership profits.

c. In proportion to the partners' capital contributions.

d. In proportion to the partners' capital contributions and outstanding loan balances.

The correct answer is (b). *(CPA 1187 L-21)*

REQUIRED: The correct statement regarding the allocation of partnership losses.

DISCUSSION: In the absence of an agreement to the contrary, the UPA requires that each partner contribute toward the losses of the partnership according to his/her share in the profits. This rule applies only among the partners. All partners remain fully liable to third parties.

Answer (a) is incorrect because losses are allocated in the same was as profits when no other allocation is specified by the partnership agreement. Answers (c) and (d) are incorrect because the partners' capital contributions and outstanding loan balances do not affect the allocation of losses unless the partnership agreement so provides.

23. Donovan, a partner of Monroe, Lincoln, and Washington, is considering selling or pledging all or part of his interest in the partnership. The partnership agreement is silent on the matter. Donovan can

a. Sell part but not all of his partnership interest.

b. Sell or pledge his entire partnership interest without causing a dissolution.

c. Pledge his partnership interest, but only with the consent of his fellow partners.

d. Sell his entire partnership interest and confer partner status upon the purchaser.

The correct answer is (b). *(CPA 583 L-4)*

REQUIRED: The validity of the sale or pledge of all or part of a partnership interest.

DISCUSSION: An assignment of a partnership interest, whether temporarily as security (a pledge) or permanently (a sale), does not of itself dissolve the partnership (UPA Section 27). Death, voluntary withdrawal, bankruptcy, or bona fide expulsion of a partner are some of the causes of dissolution (UPA Section 31).

Answer (a) is incorrect because the entire interest may be sold. Answer (c) is incorrect because consent is not required since the pledgee (temporary assignee) is only entitled to receive the profits from the interest, not to exercise any other rights of a partner. Answer (d) is incorrect because consent of the other partners is required to grant partner status.

24. Unless otherwise provided for in the partnership agreement, the assignment of a partner's interest in a general partnership will

a. Result in the termination of the partnership.

b. Not affect the assigning partner's liability to third parties for obligations existing at the time of the assignment.

c. Transfer the assigning partner's rights in specific partnership property to the assignee.

d. Transfer the assigning partner's right to bind the partnership to contracts to the assignee.

The correct answer is (b). *(CPA 1187 L-20)*

REQUIRED: The true statement about the assignment of a partner's interest.

DISCUSSION: The UPA allows the assignment of partnership rights without the dissolution of the partnership. The assignee is entitled to receive the assignor's profits, but the assignee does not replace the assigning partner in the partnership. The assigning partner's liability to third parties as a partner will not be affected by the assignment.

Answer (a) is incorrect because the assignment of a partner's interest is specifically allowed by the UPA. Answer (c) is incorrect because partners may not assign rights in specific partnership property. Answer (d) is incorrect because the assignment of a partnership interest does not entitle the assignee to participate in the management of the partnership or act as its agent.

25. A partner's interest in specific partnership property is

	Assignable to the Partner's Individual Creditors	Subject to Attachment by the Partner's Individual Creditors
a.	Yes	Yes
b.	Yes	No
c.	No	Yes
d.	No	No

The correct answer is (d). *(CPA 1189 L-7)*

REQUIRED: The correct assessment of a partner's interest in specific partnership property.

DISCUSSION: Partnership property is held by the partners as tenants in partnership. Each partner co-owns all partnership property with the other partners, but has no right to possess that property without their consent. A partner may assign his/her interest in the partnership, but is not allowed to assign rights in specific partnership property. Similarly, only a claim against the entire partnership allows specific partnership property to be attached. A partner's individual creditors may not attach partnership property, but may charge a partner's interest in the partnership.

Answers (a), (b), and (c) are incorrect because a partner's interest in specific partnership property cannot be assigned or attached by a partner's individual creditors.

26. Partners have a fiduciary relationship with each other. Accordingly, a partner

a. May engage in a business that competes with the partnership if it is operated with his/her own resources.

b. May take advantage of a business opportunity within the scope of the partnership enterprise if the partnership agreement will terminate before the benefit will be received.

c. Must exercise a degree of care and skill as a professional.

d. May not earn a secret profit in dealings with the partnership or partners.

The correct answer is (d). *(Publisher)*

REQUIRED: The true statement about the duties owed by partners to each other.

DISCUSSION: A partner is an agent of the partnership and the other partners and thus owes a fiduciary duty to act on their behalf with the utmost loyalty and good faith. In dealings with the partnership or other partners, a partner may not earn a secret profit. (S)he must make full disclosure before earning any profit on such transactions.

Answers (a) and (b) are incorrect because a partner's duty of loyalty precludes competition with the partnership. In one famous case, for example, a partner was prevented from receiving a partnership lease in his own name although the lease term would not begin until after termination of the partnership. Answer (c) is incorrect because a partner only has a duty of care to use his/her best efforts and to avoid culpable negligence. (S)he is not liable for ordinary negligence to fellow partners if his/her honest errors of judgment are not intended and do not result in personal benefit.

27. Assuming the partnership agreement is silent as to such matters, which of the following is a true statement about the rights and duties of partners?

a. A partner has a right to be paid a salary for acting in the partnership business.

b. Differences arising as to ordinary business matters are decided by a majority vote based on ownership interests of the partners.

c. Access to inspect and copy partnership books and records may be granted by majority vote of the partners.

d. All partners have equal rights in management.

The correct answer is (d). *(Publisher)*

REQUIRED: The true statement about the rights and duties of partners.

DISCUSSION: Under UPA Section 18, "All partners have equal rights in the management and conduct of the partnership business." Partners also have a duty to serve. In the absence of agreement, partners are expected to devote full time to the partnership business.

Answer (a) is incorrect because unless agreed otherwise, no partner is entitled to remuneration for acting in the partnership business except a surviving partner for winding up the partnership affairs. Answer (b) is incorrect because a majority vote of the partners decides ordinary matters without regard to proportionate interests, but unanimity is necessary to act in contravention of the partnership agreement. Answer (c) is incorrect because every partner has the right to access to the partnership books and records without a vote of the other partners.

28. Wilson and Levy entered into a partnership for a 5-year period to repair appliances. Wilson did the work in the store and Levy made the service calls. Wilson discovered that Levy has been pocketing some of the payments for the service calls and not turning them all in to the partnership. Wilson can

a. Sue Levy for breach of the partnership contract.

b. Demand a formal accounting and dissolution of the partnership.

c. Sue Levy in tort for fraud.

d. Take all of the funds (to make up for Levy's dishonesty) and walk away from the partnership.

The correct answer is (b). *(Publisher)*

REQUIRED: The remedies of a partner against another partner.

DISCUSSION: Under the UPA, a partner has a right to a formal accounting whenever the circumstances render it just and reasonable. The discovery of a partner stealing partnership funds is a proper occasion for a formal accounting and possibly dissolution of the partnership. A formal accounting and dissolution of the partnership are generally done in connection with each other. Reimbursement for the funds stolen and any other claims among the partners would be settled in the accounting.

Answer (a) is incorrect because a partner cannot sue another partner for breach of the partnership contract. A proper remedy is an accounting and dissolution. Answer (c) is incorrect because a partner cannot sue another partner for a tort committed in connection with the partnership business. Again, the correct remedy is a formal accounting and dissolution. Answer (d) is incorrect because Wilson would be in breach of the partnership agreement if he takes all of the funds and leaves the partnership (in effect a dissolution at will).

29. Which of the following actions taken by a general partner without express or implied authority will bind the partnership?

a. Renewing a previously negotiated, existing supply contract that the partners had specifically voted not to renew.

b. Submitting a claim against the partnership to binding arbitration.

c. Taking an action known by the party with whom the partner dealt to be in contravention of a restriction on his/her authority.

d. Signing the firm name as an accommodation co-maker on a promissory note not in furtherance of firm business.

The correct answer is (a). *(CPA 582 L-2)*

REQUIRED: The actions of a general partner taken without express or implied authority that will bind the partnership.

DISCUSSION: A general partner is an agent of the partnership. Agents may have express, implied, and apparent authority. Apparent authority is authority that a reasonable third person believes the agent to have. Renewal of an existing contract, previously negotiated, is a situation in which the partner had apparent authority unless the other party had specific knowledge the partners had voted not to renew the contract. Limitations imposed on an agent by the principal are ineffective as to third persons who have relied on the agent's apparent authority.

Answer (b) is incorrect because submitting a partnership liability to binding arbitration requires by law unanimous consent by all the partners who have not abandoned the business. No apparent authority can exist because everyone is considered to have knowledge of the law. Answer (c) is incorrect because apparent authority cannot exist if the third party knows the partner is exceeding his/her authority. Answer (d) is incorrect because signing the firm name as an accommodation party not in furtherance of firm business requires authorization by all the partners.

30. The apparent authority of a partner to bind the partnership in dealing with third parties

a. Will permit a partner to submit a claim against the partnership to arbitration.

b. Must be derived from the express powers and purposes contained in the partnership agreement.

c. Will be effectively limited by a formal resolution of the partners of which third parties are aware.

d. Will be effectively limited by a formal resolution of the partners of which third parties are unaware.

The correct answer is (c). *(CPA 1187 L-22)*

REQUIRED: The true statement about the apparent authority of a partner.

DISCUSSION: The apparent authority of an agent is manifested in the reasonable perceptions of a third party about the agent's authority to act on behalf of the partnership. If a third party is aware of a resolution by the partners limiting a particular partner's express authority to act as agent for the partnership, that partner's apparent authority will also be limited.

Answer (a) is incorrect because submitting a claim against the partnership to arbitration requires unanimous consent of the partners. It is not included in the apparent authority of an individual partner. Answer (b) is incorrect because apparent authority is derived from the reasonable expectations of third parties, not from the partnership agreement. Answer (d) is incorrect because apparent authority is only effectively limited when third parties are made aware of the limitation.

31. Kroll, Inc., a partner in JKL Partnership, assigns its interest in the partnership to Trell, who is not made a partner. After the assignment, Trell asserts the rights to

I. Receive Kroll's share of JKL's profits and
II. Inspect JKL's books and records.

Trell is correct as to which of the rights?

a. I only.

b. II only.

c. I and II.

d. Neither I nor II.

The correct answer is (a). *(CPA 589 L-16)*

REQUIRED: The rights of an assignee of a partnership interest.

DISCUSSION: The assignment of a partner's interest does not result in the assignee becoming a new partner in the business. The assignee is entitled only to receive those profits the assignor would normally receive. As assignee, Trell would not receive the right to participate in managing the business or to inspect the books of the partnership.

Answers (b), (c), and (d) are incorrect because Trell may receive Kroll's share of the profits but not its rights to inspect books and records.

32. Grand, a general partner, retired. The partnership held a testimonial dinner for him and invited ten of its largest customers. A week later a notice was placed in various trade journals indicating that Grand had retired and was no longer associated with the partnership in any capacity. After the appropriate public notice of Grand's retirement, which of the following best describes his legal status?

a. The release of Grand by the remaining partners and the assumption of all past and future debts of the partnership by them via a "hold harmless" clause constitutes a novation.

b. Grand has the apparent authority to bind the partnership in contracts he makes with persons unaware of his retirement who have previously dealt with the partnership.

c. Grand has no liability to past creditors upon his retirement from the partnership if they all have been informed of his withdrawal and his release from liability, and if they do not object within 60 days.

d. Grand has the legal status of a limited partner for the 3 years it takes to pay him the balance of the purchase price of his partnership interest.

The correct answer is (b). (CPA 1176 L-10)

REQUIRED: The best description of the legal status of a retired partner.

DISCUSSION: A retired partner has no actual authority, but continues to have the apparent authority to bind the partnership with respect to parties who have no notice or knowledge of the retirement and who have extended credit to the partnership prior to the partner's retirement. This concept of continuing apparent authority is based on agency law.

Answer (a) is incorrect because the release or indemnification of Grand by the remaining partners does not constitute a novation. A novation requires the creditors to agree to release Grand and accept the others in his place. Answer (c) is incorrect because a retiring partner is still liable on existing (past) debts unless the creditors agree to release him. Answer (d) is incorrect because Grand has the legal status of creditor (and no status as a partner) during the time it takes to pay him the balance of the purchase price of his partnership interest.

33. Buster and Rover formed a partnership to invest in real estate. However, Buster also decided to sell TVs on the side. Buster went to Harold, a wholesaler, and purchased 20 TVs on credit in the name of the partnership. Harold knew the partnership was formed for the purpose of investing in real estate as he had been solicited to be one of the partners. When Buster did not pay for the TVs, Harold wants to know who can be held liable.

a. Buster had apparent authority to sign for the TVs as a partner.

b. Rover is personally liable as a partner to Harold.

c. Harold can simply seize Buster's partnership and collect his/her profits.

d. The partnership is not liable because it is not a trading partnership.

The correct answer is (d). *(Publisher)*

REQUIRED: The correct statement regarding liability on a debt incurred by a partner of a nontrading partnership.

DISCUSSION: A partner has express, implied, and apparent authority to act on behalf of the partnership. In this case, Buster had no actual or implied authority, so Harold would have to rely on apparent authority to hold the partnership liable. The partner of a trading partnership (one that normally buys and sells goods) does have apparent authority to contract in the name of the partnership for the purchase of goods. However, a partner of a nontrading partnership does not have such apparent authority if the third party specifically knows the nature of the partnership. Harold has no reason to believe the goods are being purchased for partnership business, i.e., for resale.

Answer (a) is incorrect because the partnership was not a trading partnership and Harold knew this. Answer (b) is incorrect because Rover is not liable as a partner since the partnership is not liable to Harold. Answer (c) is incorrect because a creditor must obtain a charging order from a court in order to seize a partnership interest.

34. Cass is a general partner in Omega Company general partnership. Which of the following unauthorized acts by Cass will bind Omega?

a. Submitting a claim against Omega to arbitration.

b. Confessing a judgment against Omega.

c. Selling Omega's goodwill.

d. Leasing office space for Omega.

The correct answer is (d). *(CPA 589 L-15)*

REQUIRED: The unauthorized act of a partner binding on the partnership.

DISCUSSION: Because a general partner is an agent of the business, (s)he has apparent authority to bind the partnership to contracts with third parties formed while carrying on the partnership business in the usual way. Thus, a partner ordinarily need not be explicitly authorized to make an agreement to lease office space.

Answers (a), (b), and (c) are incorrect because the UPA requires the authorization of all partners to submit a partnership claim to arbitration, to confess a legal judgment against the partnership, or to dispose of the goodwill of the partnership.

Questions 35 and 36 are based on the following information: Ted Fein, a partner in the ABC Partnership, wishes to withdraw from the partnership and sell his interest to Gold. All of the other partners in ABC have agreed to admit Gold as a partner and to hold Fein harmless for the past, present, and future liabilities of ABC. A provision in the original partnership agreement states that the partnership will continue upon the death or withdrawal of one or more of the partners.

35. The agreement to hold Fein harmless for all past, present, and future liabilities of ABC will

a. Prevent partnership creditors from holding Fein personally liable only as to those liabilities of ABC existing at the time of Fein's withdrawal.

b. Prevent partnership creditors from holding Fein personally liable for the past, present, and future liabilities of ABC.

c. Not affect the rights of partnership creditors to hold Fein personally liable for those liabilities of ABC existing at the time of his withdrawal.

d. Permit Fein to recover from the other partners only amounts he has paid in excess of his proportionate share.

The correct answer is (c). *(CPA 586 L-56)*

REQUIRED: The effect of an agreement among the remaining partners releasing a retiring partner from liability.

DISCUSSION: The agreement of the other partners to release Fein from liability will only limit his personal liability to those partners. They cannot relieve him from liability to third parties, such as partnership creditors, for those liabilities existing at the time of Fein's withdrawal.

Answers (a) and (b) are incorrect because Fein will remain liable to partnership creditors for those liabilities of ABC outstanding at the time of his withdrawal. Answer (d) is incorrect because the agreement would allow Fein to recover from the other partners all amounts he paid to partnership creditors.

36. As a result of Fein's withdrawal and Gold's admission to the partnership, Gold

a. Is personally liable for partnership liabilities arising before and after his admission as a partner.

b. Has the right to participate in the management of ABC.

c. Acquired only the right to receive Fein's share of the profits of ABC.

d. Must contribute cash or property to ABC to be admitted with the same rights as the other partners.

The correct answer is (b). *(CPA 586 L-55)*

REQUIRED: The true statement about the rights and obligations of a new partner.

DISCUSSION: Absent a contrary agreement, a new partner is entitled to all of the rights of the previously existing partners. Gold therefore has the right to participate in ABC's management.

Answer (a) is incorrect because the liability of a new partner for liabilities existing at the time of his admission is limited to the amount of his capital contribution. Answer (c) is incorrect because Gold was admitted as a new partner, not merely assigned Fein's partnership interests. Answer (d) is incorrect because capital contributions are not required for admittance into a partnership with the same rights as other partners. A partner may contribute expertise, for example, and be regarded as an equal partner.

37. Gillie, Taft, and Dall are partners in an architectural firm. The partnership agreement is silent about the payment of salaries and the division of profits and losses. Gillie works full-time in the firm, and Taft and Dall each work half-time. Taft invested $120,000 in the firm, and Gillie and Dall invested $60,000 each. Dall is responsible for bringing in 50% of the business, and Gillie and Taft 25% each. How should profits of $120,000 for the year be divided?

	Gillie	Taft	Dall
a.	$60,000	$30,000	$30,000
b.	$40,000	$40,000	$40,000
c.	$30,000	$60,000	$30,000
d.	$30,000	$30,000	$60,000

The correct answer is (b). *(CPA 1189 L-6)*

REQUIRED: The division of partnership profits when the partnership agreement is silent about salaries and the division of profits and losses.

DISCUSSION: Partners are not entitled to compensation for their actions on behalf of the partnership, except when such an arrangement is explicitly provided for in the partnership agreement. The partnership agreement is silent on this point, so salaries are not paid to the partners. Profits and losses may be divided among the partners according to any formula stipulated in the partnership agreement. In the absence of such a stipulation, partners are to share equally in the profits. Thus, each partner will receive $40,000.

Answers (a), (c), and (d) are incorrect because an equal division is required absent a contrary agreement.

38. Chester contributed realty to the ABC partnership. However, Chester kept the title in his name in order to avoid the legal fees associated with the transfer of property. Some months later, Chester was in need of cash and decided to sell the property.

a. Chester cannot transfer good title because the property is owned by the partnership.

b. Chester will not have breached his duty to the partnership if one of the other partners agreed to the sale and determined that Chester would merely be receiving a return of capital.

c. Chester has violated his fiduciary duty to the partnership and is liable for damages.

d. Whether the property was held in Chester's or the partnership's name makes no difference in Chester's ability to sell.

The correct answer is (c). *(Publisher)*

REQUIRED: The correct statement concerning the transfer of partnership realty.

DISCUSSION: Partnership realty is partnership property and should not be transferred without unanimous consent of the partners. To sell partnership realty without the consent of the rest of the partners is a violation of a partner's fiduciary duty. This would be true whether or not the property was held in the partner's individual name. Of course, real property held as inventory or for resale can be sold by any partner since this is an act of apparently carrying on the partnership business in its usual way.

Answer (a) is incorrect because Chester can transfer good title since the property was left in his name. This is a risk a partnership takes by not recording title to real property in the partnership name or in all partners' names. Answer (b) is incorrect because unanimous consent is required to sell real property or to return capital contributions. The approval of one other partner would not be sufficient. Answer (d) is incorrect because Chester has the ability (although not the right) to sell property held in his own name. In contrast, a third party would be on notice if Chester were trying to sell property that had been recorded in the partnership name.

39. Partnership goodwill is a term that is not specifically defined. However, with respect to partnership goodwill, which of the following is false?

a. Goodwill is partnership property.

b. Like any other partnership asset, it can be sold by a majority of the partners.

c. A sale of the partnership and the goodwill includes the right to use the partnership name.

d. The personal representative of the deceased partner can require an accounting of the value of the goodwill.

The correct answer is (b). *(Publisher)*

REQUIRED: The false statement regarding partnership goodwill.

DISCUSSION: Partnership goodwill is an asset, the disposal of which requires prior unanimous consent of the partners. With unanimous consent, goodwill can be sold, assigned, etc.

Answer (a) is incorrect because goodwill is intangible partnership property. Answer (c) is incorrect because sale of the partnership and the goodwill does include the right to use the partnership name. The partnership name is commonly considered to be a part of goodwill. Answer (d) is incorrect because goodwill is partnership property for which the personal representative is entitled to an accounting to determine the value of the deceased partner's interest.

15.3 Partners' Relations to Third Parties

40. Partners are considered agents of the partnership and as such are liable for many of the acts of their partners. Which of the following statements is correct with regard to partners' liability?

a. An innocent partner is liable for the crimes of another partner committed while conducting legal partnership business.

b. Partners are liable for all torts committed by another partner.

c. Partners are not liable for contracts entered into by a partner in his/her own name even if made to benefit the partnership.

d. Partners are jointly liable for partnership contracts, and jointly and severally liable for torts in connection with the partnership committed by another partner.

The correct answer is (d). *(Publisher)*

REQUIRED: The correct statement regarding the liability of partners for each other's acts.

DISCUSSION: Partners are considered jointly liable for partnership contracts. This means that all of the partners are liable together and must be sued together. Partners are jointly and severally liable for the torts and breaches of trust committed by another partner. This means that all the partners are liable, but third parties may hold any one of them liable for the entire amount.

Answer (a) is incorrect because a crime is a personal act. An innocent partner has no liability for another partner's crime so long as the business of the partnership was not illegal. Innocent means one did not plan, execute, aid, or conceal the crime. Answer (b) is incorrect because partners are liable for the torts of other partners only if committed within the scope of the partnership business. Answer (c) is incorrect because partners are liable for partnership contracts, no matter whose name was used.

41. Daniels, Beal, and Wade agreed to form the DBW Partnership to engage in the import-export business. It was orally agreed that Daniels would contribute $20,000, Beal $15,000 and Wade $5,000. It was also orally agreed that in the event the venture proved to be a financial disaster all losses above the amounts of capital contributed would be assumed by Daniels and that he would hold his fellow partners harmless from any additional amounts lost. If the partnership becomes insolvent and the partnership debts exceed assets by $15,000, which of the following is correct insofar as the rights of partnership creditors are concerned?

a. Daniels is a surety insofar as partnership debts in excess of $40,000 are concerned.

b. Those creditors who were aware of the oral agreement among the partners regarding partnership liability are bound by it.

c. Partnership creditors must first proceed against Daniels and have a judgment returned unsatisfied before proceeding against Beal or Wade.

d. Each partner may be held jointly liable to firm creditors.

The correct answer is (d). *(CPA 1181 L-19)*

REQUIRED: The rights of creditors of an insolvent partnership.

DISCUSSION: Each member of the partnership is jointly liable for the debts and obligations of the partnership. Even though Daniels has agreed to hold his fellow partners harmless with respect to losses in excess of their capital contributions, that agreement does not bind the creditors of the partnership, who may hold Beal and Wade as well as Daniels jointly liable for the partnership debts. Joint liability means all partners must be named and held liable together in a lawsuit; however, the judgment can be enforced against any of them.

Answer (a) is incorrect because Daniels is not a surety; rather, he is a principal debtor. A surety is a person who binds him/herself to a creditor for the payment of an obligation of another. Answer (b) is incorrect because partners cannot limit their liability to creditors by an agreement among themselves. The creditors must also agree. Answer (c) is incorrect because the partnership creditors must proceed against the partners jointly; i.e., the creditors must join all the partners in the same lawsuit in order to recover on the partnership debts.

42. A general partner will not be personally liable for which of the following acts or transactions?

a. The gross negligence of one of the partnership's employees while carrying out the partnership business.

b. A contract entered into by the majority of the other partners but to which the general partner objects.

c. A personal mortgage loan obtained by one of the other partners on his residence to which that partner, without authority, signed the partnership name on the note.

d. A contract entered into by the partnership in which the other partners agree among themselves to hold the general partner harmless.

The correct answer is (c). *(CPA 1177 L-12)*

REQUIRED: The act or transaction for which a general partner will not be personally liable.

DISCUSSION: A general partner will not be personally liable if another partner signs the partnership name to a note securing a mortgage on his/her personal residence. Such an act is not apparently for the carrying on of the business of the partnership in the usual way and therefore would require the unanimous consent of all the partners. Reasonable third parties should realize that the partner lacked the apparent authority to bind the partnership for personal benefit and therefore should require proof of express authority.

Answer (a) is incorrect because the ordinary rules of agency would apply to make the partnership and the partners liable for the tortious conduct of an employee acting within the course and scope of his/her employment. Answer (b) is incorrect because, in the absence of an agreement to the contrary, partnership management is decided by a majority of the partners if the action taken is ordinary. Extraordinary action requires unanimous approval. Answer (d) is incorrect because a contract entered into among the partners is not binding on creditors.

43. Harry, Harriet, and Horance operate the Triple H used car lot as a general partnership. Pursuant to their agreement, each drives a Triple H vehicle to and from work, makes various business trips about the city either from home or the lot, and keeps a "for sale" sign displayed in the vehicle's windshield. Each car is for sale at all times of the day and night and at any location. One afternoon, Harriet was driving on a business trip when her car collided with one driven by Paine, who was seriously injured. Harriet's conduct was criminally negligent. In a tort action by Paine against Harry, Harriet, and Horance, both individually and operating as the Triple H partnership, who is liable?

a. All defendants because Harriet was acting within the ordinary course of the partnership business.

b. Only Harriet because her tort was not authorized by the other partners.

c. Only Harriet because a crime cannot be imputed to the partnership.

d. Only Harriet and Triple H.

The correct answer is (a). *(Publisher)*

REQUIRED: The liability in a tort action against a partnership and its partners for an act of one partner.

DISCUSSION: Loss or injury caused to any person not a partner by the wrongful act of a partner acting in the ordinary course of the partnership business or with the authorization of his/her copartners results in liability to the partnership (UPA Section 13). If the partnership is liable, each partner has joint and several personal liability for the partnership obligation (UPA Section 15). Since the Triple H partnership business was not transacted solely at the lot but was carried on wherever the partners and their cars happened to be, Harriet was acting within the scope of the partnership business, and the partnership and the partners are thus liable in tort.

Answer (b) is incorrect because partners are jointly and severally liable for the torts of each other committed when acting within the scope of partnership business. Answer (c) is incorrect because the wrong also constituted a tort. Moreover, the partnership and the partners can be criminally liable for illegal partnership activities, although not for other crimes by partners. Answer (d) is incorrect because torts may be imputed to the partnership, and the partners are jointly and severally liable therefor.

44. Stanley and Martin formed a partnership to engage in the trucking business. Stanley contributed the capital and Martin was to contribute the labor. However, Stanley did not want his name associated with the partnership due to interests in other trucking businesses. Martin was involved in an accident while carrying goods on behalf of the partnership. Which of the following would Stanley not be liable for as a result of the accident?

a. Damages caused by the accident.

b. Illegal drug activities when the police discovered their business was transporting illegal drugs.

c. Rental of the truck when the lessor thought it was dealing with Martin individually.

d. Illegal drug activities when Martin was also carrying illegal drugs in the truck unknown to Stanley.

The correct answer is (d). *(Publisher)*

REQUIRED: The activity for which a silent partner is not liable.

DISCUSSION: Stanley is an undisclosed and dormant partner. An undisclosed partner is one who is not held out as a partner; a dormant partner is one who does not take an active part in the business. A partner, whether or not (s)he is undisclosed or dormant, is always liable for the contracts and torts of the partnership. However, a partner is not liable for the crimes of another partner which are not committed as an illegal partnership activity.

Answer (a) is incorrect because Stanley is liable for the damages caused by the accident since it occurred during the course of the partnership business. Answer (b) is incorrect because a partner is liable for crimes (illegal drug activities) that are the business of the partnership. Answer (c) is incorrect because a partner is liable for contractual obligations of the partnership even if the contract was entered into by another partner in his/her own name.

45. Which of the following is not imputed to a partnership?

a. An admission of a partner concerning partnership affairs within the scope of his/her authority.

b. A representation of a partner constituting a fraud on the partnership.

c. Notice received by a partner regarding partnership affairs.

d. Knowledge of a partner regarding partnership affairs.

The correct answer is (b). *(Publisher)*

REQUIRED: The item that is not imputed to a partnership.

DISCUSSION: Under UPA Section 12, notice concerning partnership matters given to a partner and a partner's knowledge of such matters are both imputed to the partnership. The rule reflects normal agency principles based on the reality that a partnership functions through its partners. An exception is made "in the case of a fraud on the partnership committed by or with the consent of that partner."

Answer (a) is incorrect because admissions and representations by a partner concerning partnership affairs within his/her authority are evidence against the partnership (UPA Section 11). Answers (c) and (d) are incorrect because knowledge of and notice to a partner are imputed to the partnership.

46. Major Supply, Inc. is seeking a judgment against Danforth on the basis of a representation made by Coleman, in Danforth's presence, that they were in partnership together doing business as the D & C Trading Partnership. Major Supply received an order from Coleman on behalf of D & C and shipped $800 worth of goods to Coleman. Coleman has defaulted on payment of the bill and is insolvent. Danforth denies he is Coleman's partner and that he has any liability for the goods. Insofar as Danforth's liability is concerned, which of the following is correct?

a. Danforth is not liable if he is not in fact Coleman's partner.

b. Since Danforth did not make the statement about being Coleman's partner, he is not liable.

c. If Major Supply gave credit in reliance upon the misrepresentation by Coleman, Danforth is a partner by estoppel.

d. Since the "partnership" is operating under a fictitious name (the D & C Partnership) a filing is required and Major Supply's failure to ascertain whether there was in fact such a partnership precludes it from recovering.

The correct answer is (c). *(CPA 1180 L-22)*

REQUIRED: The correct statement regarding an ostensible partner's liability.

DISCUSSION: Even though Danforth and Coleman are not in fact partners, if Major relied on the statement by Coleman made in Danforth's presence and not objected to by Danforth, then Danforth will be estopped or prevented from asserting that no partnership relationship existed and will be liable to Major. This is called a partnership by estoppel.

Answer (a) is incorrect because one may be a partner by estoppel even though one is not a partner in fact. Answer (b) is incorrect because Danforth's conduct in failing to object to the misrepresentation is sufficient to establish liability when the misrepresentation was relied upon by Major. Answer (d) is incorrect because not all states require filing under a fictitious name statute, nor does failure to file where so required affect the finding of partnership liability. In any case, compliance with the statute would be the responsibility of the partners, not their customers.

47. Darla, Jack, and Sam have formed a partnership with each agreeing to contribute $100,000. Jack and Sam each contributed $100,000 cash. Darla contributed $75,000 cash and agreed to pay an additional $25,000 two years later. After one year of operations the partnership is insolvent. The liabilities and fair market value of partnership assets are

Assets	
Cash	$ 40,000
Trade accounts receivable	35,000
Receivable from Darla	25,000
Equipment	100,000
	$200,000
Liabilities	
Trade accounts payable	$410,000

Both Jack and Sam are personally insolvent. Darla has a net worth of $750,000. If Darla is a general partner, what is her maximum potential liability?

a. $ 95,000.

b. $185,000.

c. $210,000.

d. $235,000.

The correct answer is (d). *(CPA 1184 L-12)*

REQUIRED: The maximum liability of a general partner.

DISCUSSION: A general partner has unlimited joint and several personal liability for the debts of the partnership. Because the assets excluding the receivable from Darla equal $175,000 and the liabilities are $410,000, Darla's potential liability is the difference, or $235,000.

48. Perone was a member of Cass, Hack & Perone, a general trading partnership. He died and the partnership is insolvent, but Perone's estate is substantial. The creditors of the partnership are seeking to collect on their claims from Perone's estate. Which of the following statements is correct insofar as their claims are concerned?

a. The death of Perone caused a dissolution of the firm, thereby freeing his estate from personal liability.

b. If the existing obligations to Perone's personal creditors are all satisfied, then the remaining estate assets are available to satisfy partnership debts.

c. The creditors must first proceed against the remaining partners before Perone's estate can be held liable for the partnership's debts.

d. The liability of Perone's estate cannot exceed his capital contribution plus that percentage of the deficit attributable to his capital contribution.

The correct answer is (b). *(CPA 1180 L-19)*

REQUIRED: The correct statement regarding the claims of partnership creditors against the estate of a deceased partner.

DISCUSSION: The estate of a deceased partner is liable for partnership debts (just as each living partner is liable) and the estate assets may be reached by creditors to satisfy their claims. The Bankruptcy Code makes a significant change in priorities between creditors of a bankrupt partnership and a bankrupt partner. The partnership creditors have first claim to partnership assets and, to the extent their claims are not satisfied, they are also entitled to share pro rata with the general unsecured creditors of bankrupt individual partners against the partners' personal assets. Under the UPA, however, a partnership's unpaid creditors have no claim against a partner's personal assets until all the personal creditors have been paid in full. Because the Bankruptcy Code is federal law, it prevails over the UPA (state law) when the parties are in bankruptcy.

Answer (a) is incorrect because while the death of a partner dissolves the partnership, it does not extinguish the liability of the estate. Answer (c) is incorrect because the estate of the deceased partner stands on an equal footing with the surviving partners with respect to the firm's debts. Answer (d) is incorrect because the deceased partner's estate may be held liable for the entire amount of the firm's debts; however, the estate would have a right of contribution against the surviving partners.

49. The partnership of Baker, Green, and Madison is insolvent. The partnership's liabilities exceed its assets by $123,000. The liabilities include a $25,000 loan from Madison. Green is personally insolvent. His personal liabilities exceed his personal assets by $13,500. Green has filed a voluntary petition in bankruptcy. Under these circumstances, partnership creditors

a. Must proceed jointly against the partnership and all the general partners so that losses may be shared equitably among the partners.

b. Rank first in payment and all (including Madison) will share proportionately in the partnership assets to be distributed.

c. Will have the first claim to partnership property to the exclusion of the personal creditors of Green.

d. Do not have the right to share pro rata with Green's personal creditors in Green's personal assets.

The correct answer is (c). *(CPA 575 L-23)*

REQUIRED: The status of partnership creditors when the partnership and one partner are insolvent.

DISCUSSION: The creditors of the partnership will have first priority in the distribution of the assets of the partnership. The personal creditors of Green can only reach Green's partnership interest (not specific partnership assets) through a "charging order."

Answer (a) is incorrect because while the creditors must sue the partners' jointly, a successful judgment-creditor could collect all of the judgment from any one of the partners. Answer (b) is incorrect because a partner who is a creditor of the partnership has a claim which is subordinate to that of the other creditors of the partnership. Answer (d) is incorrect because partnership creditors have the right to share pro rata with Green's personal creditors under the new Bankruptcy Code.

50. The effect of dissolution of a partnership on the liability of a partner is to discharge

a. A partner who does not continue in the business.

b. All the partners if the partnership business is to be terminated.

c. A retiring partner if a novation may be inferred from a subsequent course of dealing with creditors.

d. A retiring partner with regard to all liabilities incurred after his/her withdrawal regardless of whether notice is given to creditors.

The correct answer is (c). *(Publisher)*

REQUIRED: The effect of dissolution on partners' liability.

DISCUSSION: Under UPA Section 36, an express novation among the creditors, the persons continuing the partnership business, and a withdrawing partner will terminate the liability of such partner. Moreover, the agreement may be inferred from a course of dealing between a creditor with knowledge of the dissolution and the persons continuing the enterprise. For example, a subsequent extension of credit or the acceptance of a negotiable instrument in full payment of a debt may constitute such a course of dealing.

Answers (a) and (b) are incorrect because the dissolution of the partnership does not discharge the existing liability of any partner. Answer (d) is incorrect because in the absence of the appropriate notice of dissolution given to creditors, a withdrawing partner or the estate of a deceased partner will be liable for debts incurred after dissolution.

51. Millie Dill was properly admitted as a partner in the ABC Partnership after purchasing Jim Ard's partnership interest. Ard immediately withdrew from the partnership. The partnership agreement states that the partnership will continue on the withdrawal or admission of a partner. Unless the partners otherwise agree,

a. Dill's personal liability for existing partnership debts will be limited to Dill's interest in partnership property.

b. Ard will automatically be released from personal liability for partnership debts incurred before Dill's admission.

c. Ard will be permitted to recover from the other partners the full amount that Ard paid on account of partnership debts incurred before Dill's admission.

d. Dill will be subjected to unlimited personal liability for partnership debts incurred before being admitted.

The correct answer is (a). *(CPA 588 L-7)*

REQUIRED: The effect of admitting a new partner after her purchase of an existing partnership interest.

DISCUSSION: As a new partner, Dill's liability for previously existing partnership debts is limited to the amount of her capital contribution, which is Dill's interest in partnership property.

Answer (b) is incorrect because in the absence of a novation, a withdrawing partner remains liable for debts incurred prior to withdrawal. Answer (c) is incorrect because Ard is liable for his share of the debts incurred while he was a partner, and would only be permitted to recover amounts he paid in excess of his share. Answer (d) is incorrect because Dill's liability is limited to his capital contribution.

15.4 Dissolution and Winding Up

52. Grey and Carr entered into a written partnership agreement to operate a hardware store. Their agreement was silent as to the duration of the partnership. Grey wishes to dissolve the partnership. Which of the following is true?

a. Unless Carr consents to a dissolution, Grey must apply to a court and obtain a decree ordering the dissolution.

b. Grey may not dissolve the partnership unless Carr consents.

c. Grey may dissolve the partnership only after notice of the proposed dissolution is given to all partnership creditors.

d. Grey may dissolve the partnership at any time.

The correct answer is (d). *(CPA 588 L-14)*

REQUIRED: The true statement about dissolution of a partnership with no specified duration.

DISCUSSION: Partners always have the power to dissolve a partnership, although they do not always have the right to do so. Dissolution in violation of a partnership agreement is wrongful, and carries with it certain penalties. When the partnership agreement does not specify a duration or objective, the partnership is at will and may be rightfully dissolved at any time.

Answers (a) and (b) are incorrect because a partner desiring to dissolve a partnership need not obtain a court decree or the consent of the other partner(s). Answer (c) is incorrect because notice of the dissolution is not a requirement of the dissolution, although it will be necessary to rescind Grey's apparent authority.

53. Which of the following is a true statement about the key concepts related to ending a partnership's existence?

a. The winding up process follows termination of the partnership's existence.

b. Dissolution is the process of liquidating and distributing partnership assets.

c. The dissolution process follows termination of the partnership's existence.

d. Termination but not liquidation must follow dissolution.

The correct answer is (d). *(Publisher)*

REQUIRED: The true statement about winding up, termination, and dissolution.

DISCUSSION: The end of partnership existence begins with dissolution. Dissolution of a partnership is the change in the relation of the partners caused by any partner's ceasing to be associated in the carrying on of the business. Winding up is the liquidation of the business in an orderly manner: completion of contracts, collection and payment of debts, and distribution of assets. Termination is the formal end of the partnership's existence, although not necessarily that of the business. If the business is to be continued by the surviving partners or others, winding up is omitted. Continuation avoids a forced sale and loss of goodwill.

Answers (a) and (c) are incorrect because termination is the last event. Answer (b) is incorrect because it defines winding up.

54. Which of the following will not result in a dissolution of a partnership?

a. The bankruptcy of a partner as long as the partnership itself remains solvent.

b. The death of a partner as long as his/her will provides that his executor shall become a partner in his/her place.

c. The wrongful withdrawal of a partner in contravention of the agreement between the partners.

d. The assignment by a partner of his/her entire partnership interest.

The correct answer is (d). *(CPA 1179 L-17)*

REQUIRED: The circumstance which will not result in a dissolution of a partnership.

DISCUSSION: A conveyance by a partner of his/her interest in the partnership does not in itself dissolve the partnership. The partnership continues and the assignee is entitled to the assignor partner's share of profits.

Answer (a) is incorrect because the bankruptcy of either a partner or the partnership itself serves to dissolve the partnership. Answer (b) is incorrect because the death of a partner automatically dissolves the partnership and the executor can become a partner only if all the other partners agree. Answer (c) is incorrect because a partnership may be dissolved by the express will of any partner at any time even though in contravention of an agreement between the partners. The breaching partner must pay damages.

55. Braudy and Jones are partners and wish to admit Halsey to the partnership. If Halsey is admitted,

a. He is liable for preexisting obligations of the partnership to the same extent as Braudy and Jones.

b. Only Braudy and Jones are liable for preexisting obligations of the partnership.

c. The old partnership is dissolved.

d. The old partnership must be wound up and liquidated.

The correct answer is (c). *(CPA 1173 L-45)*

REQUIRED: The correct statement regarding the admission of a new partner.

DISCUSSION: The admission of a new partner, like the withdrawal or death of an existing partner, has the effect of dissolving the partnership. A new partnership must be formed to continue the same business.

Answer (a) is incorrect because an incoming partner is liable for preexisting obligations of the partnership only to the extent of the partnership assets (i.e., his capital contribution). Answer (b) is incorrect because Halsey is also liable, but only to the extent of his capital. Answer (d) is incorrect because although the old partnership has been dissolved, winding up and liquidation are unnecessary if the parties wish to continue the same business.

56. Which of the following will dissolve a partnership and cause a breach of the partnership agreement?

a. Mutual agreement of the partners.

b. Attainment of a time designated for dissolution in the partnership agreement, but before a partnership project had been completed.

c. Expulsion of a partner under the authority of a partnership agreement.

d. An arbitrary decision of any partner to terminate the partnership.

The correct answer is (d). *(Publisher)*

REQUIRED: The action which will both dissolve a partnership and cause a breach of the partnership agreement.

DISCUSSION: A partnership can be dissolved by the will of a partner at any time. The dissolution may or may not be in violation of the partnership agreement, depending on whether such agreement contemplated that the partnership be dissolved at any time.

Answer (a) is incorrect because mutual agreement of the partners would be a modification, not a breach, of the partnership agreement. Answer (b) is incorrect because a partnership may be dissolved at the time which is designated in the partnership agreement and the fact that some partnership project had not been completed does not cause a breach. Answer (c) is incorrect because expulsion of a partner pursuant to a power in the partnership agreement, although dissolving the partnership, will not cause a breach.

57. A partner has the power to dissolve a partnership but may not have the right. In some circumstances, the dissolution may be wrongful. One consequence that does not follow from causing a wrongful dissolution is the loss of the

a. Value of one's partnership interest.

b. Right to wind up.

c. Right to continue the business.

d. Right to have goodwill included in the value of one's partnership interest.

The correct answer is (a). *(Publisher)*

REQUIRED: The consequence not accruing to a wrongfully dissolving partner.

DISCUSSION: A dissolution is wrongful when it is in breach of the partnership agreement, e.g., when a partner withdraws prior to expiration of the partnership's definite term. A dissolution by court decree may also be wrongful when the judicial action is the result of a partner's conduct that prejudicially affects the carrying on of the business. The wrongdoer is nevertheless entitled to the value of his/her partnership interest, less damages for breach. Goodwill is not included in calculating this value (UPA Section 38).

Answers (b), (c), and (d) are incorrect because each right may be exercised only by a partner who has not wrongfully dissolved the partnership (UPA Sections 37, 38).

58. A partnership may be dissolved by a decree of a court. Which of the following will a court not dissolve a partnership for?

a. Insanity of a partner.

b. A partner's continual and serious breaches of the partnership agreement.

c. Insolvency of a partner.

d. The failure of a business without any chance of profits in the future.

The correct answer is (c). *(Publisher)*

REQUIRED: The event for which a court will not dissolve a partnership.

DISCUSSION: A court has the power to dissolve a partnership if the circumstances so require. However, such circumstances do not include insolvency of a partner. There is no reason why a partnership cannot continue business if a partner is insolvent, especially if that partner has a chance to recover.

Answer (a) is incorrect because insanity of a partner is a reason for a court to dissolve a partnership. Answer (b) is incorrect because serious and continual breaches of the partnership agreement by a partner does give the court reason to dissolve a partnership. Answer (d) is incorrect because a court may dissolve a partnership which can be carried on only at a loss.

59. Kimball, Thompson, and Darby formed a partnership. Kimball contributed $25,000 in capital and lent the partnership $20,000; he performed no services. Thompson contributed $15,000 in capital and part-time services, and Darby contributed only his full-time services. The partnership agreement provided that all profits and losses would be shared equally. Three years after the formation of the partnership, the three partners agreed to dissolve and liquidate the partnership. Firm creditors, other than Kimball, have bona fide claims of $65,000. After all profits and losses have been recorded there are $176,000 of assets to be distributed to creditors and partners. When the assets are distributed,

a. Darby receives nothing since he did not contribute any property.

b. Thompson receives $45,333 in total.

c. Kimball receives $62,000 in total.

d. Each partner receives one-third of the remaining assets after all firm creditors, including Kimball, have been paid.

The correct answer is (c). *(CPA 575 L-19)*

REQUIRED: The proper distribution of the partnership assets.

DISCUSSION: Partnership assets are distributed in the following order:

1) Claims of outside creditors.
2) Claims of partners as creditors.
3) Claims of partners for capital.
4) Claims of partners for profits.

Under these rules, the first $65,000 of the partnership assets goes to the outside creditors. The next $20,000 will be distributed to the partner-creditor, Kimball. $40,000 will be distributed to Kimball and Thompson as a return of their capital contributions. The balance of $51,000 will be divided equally between the three partners, $17,000 to each. Kimball should thus receive $62,000 ($20,000 as repayment of his loan to the partnership, $25,000 as a return of his capital contribution, and $17,000 as his share of the profits).

Answer (a) is incorrect because Darby should receive $17,000 as his share of the profits. Answer (b) is incorrect because Thompson should receive $32,000 ($15,000 in capital and $17,000 in profits). Answer (d) is incorrect because partners are entitled to receive repayment of any loan and their capital contribution before sharing profits on liquidation.

60. Concerning the order of distribution for satisfying firm debts upon the dissolution and winding up of a general partnership, which of the following is a correct statement?

a. General creditors, including partners who are also general creditors, are ranked first.

b. Profits are distributed only after all prior parties, including partners, have had their various claims satisfied.

c. Secured obligations are disregarded entirely insofar as the order of distribution.

d. Capital contributions by the partners are distributed before unsecured loans by the partners.

The correct answer is (b). *(CPA 1177 L-8)*

REQUIRED: The correct statement regarding the order of distribution for satisfying debts upon winding up of a general partnership.

DISCUSSION: Upon the winding up of a partnership, the following order of distribution of the partnership assets applies:

1) Claims of outside creditors.
2) Claims of partners as creditors.
3) Claims of partners for capital.
4) Claims of partners for profits.

Answer (a) is incorrect because outside creditors have priority over partners who are also creditors. Answer (c) is incorrect because an outside creditor with a security interest in a partnership asset has priority over all other creditors. Answer (d) is incorrect because claims by partners for loans have priority over claims by partners for the return of their capital contribution.

61. X, Y, and Z have capital balances of $30,000, $15,000, and $5,000, respectively, in the XYZ Partnership. The general partnership agreement is silent as to the manner in which partnership losses are to be allocated but does provide that partnership profits are to be allocated as follows: 40% to X, 25% to Y, and 35% to Z. The partners have decided to dissolve and liquidate the partnership. After paying all creditors, the amount available for distribution will be $20,000. X, Y, and Z are individually solvent. Z will

a. Receive $7,000.

b. Receive $12,000.

c. Personally have to contribute an additional $5,500.

d. Personally have to contribute an additional $5,000.

The correct answer is (c). *(CPA 588 L-13)*

REQUIRED: The correct distribution of assets after partnership dissolution and liquidation.

DISCUSSION: Upon termination, a partnership must first pay all creditors and then distribute the remaining assets to the partners. In this case, $20,000 is available for distribution. However, the total of capital contributions is $50,000, and a $30,000 loss must be allocated among the partners. When the partnership agreement does not specify otherwise, losses are allocated in the same ratio as profits. Thus, Z is properly allocated 35% of the loss, or $10,500 (35% x $30,000). Z's capital contribution of $5,000 is less than Z's share of the loss. Hence, Z must contribute an additional $5,500 to the partnership.

62. The Marvel Partnership was dissolved when one of the partners died. Which of the following is correct regarding liability?

a. The authority of the remaining partners to bind the partnership is terminated upon the partner's death.

b. If the remaining partners continue the business by forming a new partnership, they cannot use the deceased partner's name.

c. Notice of the dissolution by publication in a newspaper will terminate potential liability.

d. If the partners continue the business, the creditors of the old partnership become creditors of the new partnership.

The correct answer is (d). *(Publisher)*

REQUIRED: The correct statement regarding liability after dissolution of a partnership.

DISCUSSION: Partners of a dissolved partnership may continue the business without interruption by forming a new partnership. However, all creditors of the old partnership become creditors of the new partnership.

Answer (a) is incorrect because the apparent authority of the remaining partners continues until notice of dissolution is given to third parties. Answer (b) is incorrect because the partnership name is a partnership asset which can be retained by the continuing partnership. However, the deceased partner's estate may demand compensation for the decedent's name. Answer (c) is incorrect because publication in a newspaper only gives constructive notice of the dissolution. Actual notice must be given to creditors who have dealt with the partnership and with whom the old partners have apparent authority.

63. The partnership agreement of one of your clients provides that upon death or withdrawal, a partner shall be entitled to the book value of his or her partnership interest as of the close of the year preceding such death or withdrawal and nothing more. It also provides that the partnership shall continue. Regarding this partnership provision, which of the following is a correct statement?

a. It is unconscionable on its face.

b. It has the legal effect of preventing a dissolution upon the death or withdrawal of a partner.

c. It effectively eliminates the legal necessity of a winding up of the partnership upon the death or withdrawal of a partner.

d. It is not binding upon the spouse of a deceased partner if the book value figure is less than the fair market value at the date of death.

The correct answer is (c). *(CPA 1180 L-20)*

REQUIRED: The correct statement regarding the partnership agreement.

DISCUSSION: The termination of a partnership requires two preliminary stages: dissolution and winding up (liquidation). The agreement in the question is not effective to prevent dissolution of the partnership since the withdrawal of any partner dissolves the partnership. It is effective, however, to prevent the winding up (liquidation) process and to permit the continuation of the business as a going concern.

Answer (a) is incorrect because such contracts are commonly enforced and are not deemed to be unreasonably unfair. Book value may or may not be less than fair market value. Answer (b) is incorrect because the death or withdrawal of a partner automatically dissolves the partnership irrespective of any agreement. Answer (d) is incorrect because the estate (or spouse as beneficiary) can have no greater interest in the partnership than the partner had. If the partner was only entitled to the book value, then the estate is entitled to that and no more.

64. After dissolution, a partner who is winding up the business of the partnership lacks express or implied authority to carry on the partnership business in the usual way. The only actual authority (s)he has is that needed to liquidate the partnership's affairs. The apparent authority of a winding-up partner continues with regard to which of the following persons?

a. Prior creditors of the partnership who had knowledge of the dissolution but did not receive notice of the dissolution from the partnership.

b. Persons who had not previously extended credit, knew of the partnership, and had no knowledge or notice of dissolution.

c. Any person who had neither knowledge nor any form of notice of dissolution.

d. Persons who had not previously dealt with the partnership, but knew of its existence and had only constructive notice of dissolution.

The correct answer is (b). *(Publisher)*

REQUIRED: The apparent authority of a partner after dissolution.

DISCUSSION: A winding up partner has apparent authority to carry on the business in the usual way with regard to prior creditors who have no knowledge or notice of dissolution. Apparent authority also extends to transactions with persons who did not previously extend credit but who prior to dissolution knew of the partnership's existence and who have no knowledge, actual notice, or constructive notice by publication of dissolution (UPA Section 35).

Answer (a) is incorrect because knowledge defeats apparent authority. Answer (c) is incorrect because a partner has no apparent authority to carry on business in the usual way with regard to persons who did not know of the partnership prior to its dissolution. Answer (d) is incorrect because constructive notice by publication in a newspaper of general circulation in the places where the partnership business was regularly carried on suffices with regard to such persons.

65. A partner will not be liable to the partnership or the partners

a. For a loss arising from use of his/her apparent authority to enter into a contract without actual authority.

b. For indemnification for a loss arising from his/her commission of a tort committed in the partnership business.

c. For benefits received from purchase of the partnership property during the winding-up process if (s)he has made full disclosure.

d. In an action for an accounting when (s)he has improperly performed winding-up duties.

The correct answer is (c). *(Publisher)*

REQUIRED: The instance when a partner is not liable to the partnership or the partners.

DISCUSSION: A partner is a fiduciary who is held to a standard of the utmost honesty and loyalty. However, (s)he is not precluded from all dealings with the partnership. When a partnership is being liquidated, a partner may be a purchaser. A partner who deals fairly with the partnership by making full disclosure concerning whatever (s)he knows about the property's value will not have liability based on breach of a fiduciary duty.

Answer (a) is incorrect because losses from unauthorized contracts are reimbursable. Each partner has a duty to the other partners and the partnership not to act outside his/her actual authority. Answer (b) is incorrect because a partner who causes loss to the partnership by commission of a tort will be liable to the other partners. Answer (d) is incorrect because an action for an accounting may be maintained by a partner whenever the circumstances render it just and reasonable; e.g., breach of the fiduciary duties involved in the winding-up process.

15.5 Limited Partnerships

66. In general, which of the following statements is true with respect to a limited partnership?

a. A limited partner will be personally liable for partnership debts incurred in the ordinary course of the partnership's business.

b. A limited partner is unable to participate in the management of the partnership in the same manner as general partners and still retain limited liability.

c. A limited partner's death or incompetency will cause the partnership to dissolve.

d. A limited partner is an agent of the partnership and has the authority to bind the partnership to contracts.

The correct answer is (b). *(CPA 1187 L-19)*

REQUIRED: The true statement about a limited partner's relationship to a limited partnership.

DISCUSSION: A primary characteristic of limited partnerships is that they must have both general and limited partners. General partners have unlimited liability for the obligations of the partnership and are entitled to manage the business. A limited partner's liability is ordinarily limited to the amount of the capital contribution to the partnership, and a limited partner does not have a right to participate in management. A limited partner who nevertheless takes an active role in managing the business may become personally liable for partnership obligations to third parties aware of that role.

Answer (a) is incorrect because limited partners are personally liable for partnership debts only if they participate in the management of the partnership. Answer (c) is incorrect because the withdrawal of a limited partner does not automatically dissolve the partnership. The withdrawal of a general partner, however, does dissolve the partnership absent a contrary agreement. Answer (d) is incorrect because a limited partner is not considered an agent of the partnership, and thus cannot bind it to contracts.

67. A limited partner

a. Is liable for obligations of the partnership to the extent of his/her capital contribution.

b. Has no voting rights.

c. May freely transfer his/her interest in the partnership and substitute the transferee as a limited partner.

d. May not demand the return of his/her contribution.

The correct answer is (a). *(Publisher)*

REQUIRED: The true statement about a limited partner.

DISCUSSION: One of the principal advantages of the limited partnership is that persons who invest but who do not take part in management have limited personal liability. A limited partner is liable only to the extent of his/her agreed-upon contribution of cash or other property.

Answer (b) is incorrect because a limited partner may vote on certain important matters, such as the admission of new partners. Answer (c) is incorrect because an assignee of a limited partner does not automatically become a limited partner. All partners must consent or the assignor must have a power conferred by the certificate to designate the assignee a limited partner. Answer (d) is incorrect because a limited partner may withdraw under terms specified in the certificate or upon giving six months' written notice.

68. A valid limited partnership

a. Created pursuant to state law cannot be treated as an "association" for federal income tax purposes.

b. May have an unlimited number of partners.

c. Is exempt from all Securities and Exchange Commission regulations.

d. Must designate in its certificate the name, residence, and capital contribution of each general partner but need not include this information in respect to limited partners.

The correct answer is (b). *(CPA 1176 L-14)*

REQUIRED: The correct statement regarding a valid limited partnership.

DISCUSSION: There is no maximum limit as to the number of partners (limited or general). The only requirement is that there be at least one limited and one general partner. This differs from S corporations which currently have a limit of 35 shareholders.

Answer (a) is incorrect because a partnership will be treated as an association (and taxed as a corporation) if it has more corporate than partnership attributes. Answer (c) is incorrect because a limited partnership interest is considered a security and generally subject to SEC regulations. Answer (d) is incorrect because under the ULPA, the name, business address, and capital contribution of all partners (limited and general) must be included in the certificate.

69. Which of the following statements is correct with respect to the differences and similarities between a corporation and a limited partnership?

a. Directors owe fiduciary duties to the corporation, and limited partners owe such duties to the partnership.

b. A corporation and a limited partnership may be created only pursuant to a state statute, and a copy of its organizational document must be filed with the proper state agency.

c. Shareholders may be entitled to vote on corporate matters, whereas limited partners are prohibited from voting on any partnership matters.

d. Stock of a corporation may be subject to registration under federal securities laws, but limited partnership interests are automatically exempt from such requirements.

The correct answer is (b). *(CPA 1188 L-5)*

REQUIRED: The correct statement comparing corporations and limited partnerships.

DISCUSSION: Both corporations and limited partnerships can be created and exist only under the authority of statutes. Common law cannot be a basis for their formation. Both require the filing with appropriate state authorities of organizational documents (articles of incorporation or certificates of limited partnership).

Answer (a) is incorrect because limited partners are not fiduciaries and owe no such duty to the partnership. Answer (c) is incorrect because although not allowed to participate in management, limited partners may still vote on such partnership matters as dissolution of the partnership or the removal of a general partner. Answer (d) is incorrect because limited partnership interests are subject to registration requirements.

70. Unless otherwise provided in the limited partnership agreement, which of the following statements is correct?

a. A general partner's capital contribution may not consist of services rendered to the partnership.

b. Upon the death of a limited partner the partnership will be dissolved.

c. A person may own a limited partnership interest in the same partnership in which (s)he is a general partner.

d. Upon the assignment of a limited partner's interest, the assignee will become a substituted limited partner if the consent of two-thirds of all partners is obtained.

The correct answer is (c). *(CPA 1184 L-11)*

REQUIRED: The true statement about limited partnerships.

DISCUSSION: A person may be a general and limited partner in the same partnership at the same time. Such a person has all the rights, powers, restrictions, and liabilities of a general partner with respect to his/her general partnership interest. (S)he also has the rights and limitations of a limited partner with respect to his/her limited partnership interest.

Answer (a) is incorrect because a general and a limited partner may contribute services. Answer (b) is incorrect because one advantage of the limited partnership is that withdrawal or death of a limited partner is not a basis for dissolution. Answer (d) is incorrect because unanimous consent of the partners is needed unless the limited partnership certificate provides otherwise.

71. In general, which of the following statements is correct with respect to a limited partnership?

a. A limited partner has the right to obtain from the general partner(s) financial information and tax returns of the limited partnership.

b. A limited partnership can be formed with limited liability for all partners.

c. A limited partner may not also be a general partner at the same time.

d. A limited partner may hire employees on behalf of the partnership.

The correct answer is (a). *(CPA 1188 L-4)*

REQUIRED: The correct statement about a limited partnership.

DISCUSSION: Both general and limited partners have the right to examine the books of the partnership, thus allowing them to obtain financial information and tax returns of the limited partnership.

Answer (b) is incorrect because all limited partnerships must have at least one general partner with unlimited liability for partnership obligations. Answer (c) is incorrect because it is possible for one person to be both a general and a limited partner in the partnership. Answer (d) is incorrect because a limited partner is not an agent of the partnership or allowed to participate in management.

72. Marshall formed a limited partnership for the purpose of engaging in the export-import business. Marshall obtained additional working capital from Franklin and Lee by selling them each a limited partnership interest. Under these circumstances, the limited partnership

a. Will generally be treated as a taxable entity for federal income tax purposes.

b. Will lose its status as a limited partnership if there is ever more than one general partner.

c. Can limit the liability of all partners.

d. Can only be availed of if the state in which it is created has adopted the original or revised Uniform Limited Partnership Act or similar statute.

The correct answer is (d). *(CPA 1177 L-7)*

REQUIRED: The correct statement regarding a limited partnership.

DISCUSSION: The limited partnership is not available as a form of business organization under the common law. An organization purporting to be a limited partnership created in a state with no statutory authority for such a form of business organization will very likely be treated as a general partnership.

Answer (a) is incorrect because a partnership is not a taxable entity for federal income tax purposes. Partnerships are required to file informational returns only. Answer (b) is incorrect because a limited partnership may have more than one general partner. There is simply a minimum of at least one limited and one general partner. Answer (c) is incorrect because there must be at least one general partner with unlimited personal liability.

73. Dowling is a promoter and has decided to use a limited partnership for conducting a securities investment venture. Which of the following is unnecessary in order to validly create such a limited partnership?

a. All limited partners' capital contributions must be paid in cash.

b. There must be a state statute that permits the creation of such a limited partnership.

c. A limited partnership certificate must be signed by the participants and filed in the proper office in the state.

d. There must be one or more general partners and one or more limited partners.

The correct answer is (a). *(CPA 1179 L-14)*

REQUIRED: The item unnecessary to validly create a limited partnership.

DISCUSSION: The capital contribution of a limited partner may be paid in other property as well as in cash. The rendition of services is also a proper contribution by a limited partner now. This is a change from prior versions of the ULPA that did not allow services by limited partners as capital contributions.

Answers (b), (c) and (d) are incorrect because each is a requirement in order to validly create a limited partnership.

74. The XYZ Limited Partnership has two general partners, Smith and Jones. A provision in the partnership agreement allows the removal of a general partner by a majority vote of the limited partners. After a falling out between Smith and Jones, the conduct of partnership business reaches an impasse. The limited partners vote to remove Jones as a general partner. Which of the following statements is true?

a. The limited partners are now liable to third parties for partnership obligations.

b. Limited partners may vote to remove a general partner without losing their status as limited partners.

c. By voting to remove a general partner, the limited partners are presumed to exercise control of the business.

d. Limited partners may participate in management decisions without limitation as long as this right is provided for in the limited partnership agreement.

The correct answer is (b). *(D.B. MacDonald)*

REQUIRED: The effect on the status of limited partners of voting for removal of a general partner.

DISCUSSION: Under Section 303 of the Revised Uniform Limited Partnership Act, a limited partner is not liable to third parties for partnership obligations as long as the limited partner does not take part "in the control of the business." The RULPA lists several activities in which a limited partner may engage without being considered "in the control of the business," among them, voting on the removal of a general partner.

Answers (a) and (c) are incorrect because voting on the removal of a general partner is allowed by the RULPA. Answer (d) is incorrect because excessive involvement in the management of the business may constitute taking part "in the control of the business." The result would be liability to those parties who have knowledge of the limited partner's participation in control or, if the limited partner is exercising the powers of a general partner, to all third parties.

75. Which of the following statements regarding a limited partner is(are) usually correct?

I. The limited partner is subject to personal liability for partnership debts.
II. The limited partner has the right to take part in the control of the partnership.

a. I and II.

b. I only.

c. II only.

d. Neither I nor II.

The correct answer is (d). *(CPA 1189 L-5)*

REQUIRED: The liabilities and rights of a limited partner.

DISCUSSION: A characteristic of limited partnerships is the limited partners' limited liability for partnership obligations. A limited partner's liability is limited to his/her capital contribution to the business, whereas a general partner retains unlimited personal liability for partnership debts. Coincident with limited liability, the limited partner is also restricted in the right to control the partnership. A limited partner is not allowed to participate in the management of the partnership business.

Answers (a), (b), and (c) are incorrect because neither statement is true.

76. Williams, Watkins, and Glenn is a limited partnership. At present, there are three general partners and sixteen limited partners. The partnership is engaged in the grain-futures business. The general partners decided to expand the business substantially by offering $2,000,000 of limited-partner interests to the investing public in several states at $5,000 per limited-partner interest. A majority of the existing limited partners object to the proposition. Under the circumstances, the limited partnership

a. Has been dissolved.

b. Must file a registration statement with the SEC if it is going to offer the two million dollars of limited-partner interests to prospective buyers.

c. Is exempt from federal registration because a limited-partner interest is not a "security."

d. Is recognized as a general partnership as a result of the dispute between the general and limited partners and each is entitled to an equal vote in the management of the partnership.

The correct answer is (b). *(CPA 1174 L-8)*

REQUIRED: The proper statement regarding a limited partnership that desires to sell limited partnership interests in several states.

DISCUSSION: An offering of in excess of $1,500,000 worth of limited partnership interests to the public in several states would require that a registration statement be filed with the SEC. Limited partnership interests are considered securities and their issuance is subject to regulation by the SEC. No exemption from registration applies since this is a public, interstate offering of securities with an aggregate offering price in excess of $1,500,000 in a period of one year.

Answer (a) is incorrect because no event has occurred which would cause the dissolution of the partnership, e.g., the death, retirement, or insanity of a general partner. Answer (c) is incorrect because a limited partnership interest is regarded as a "security" under federal securities laws. Answer (d) is incorrect because the opposition of the existing limited partners to the admission of new limited partners does not constitute participating in the control and management of the business and therefore would not alter the limited partners' status. They will continue to have no voice in the management of the partnership.

77. Martin Cosgrove induced Harold Watts, Charles Randall, and James Howard to join him in a partnership venture. Cosgrove is a sophisticated investor. He proposed that Watts, Randall, and Howard each contribute $100,000 to a limited partnership which would consist of himself as general partner and the others as limited partners. Cosgrove was to contribute $50,000, but he was to share equally in all profits and assume all losses in excess of $50,000 upon dissolution. Under these circumstances,

a. The purported creation of a limited partnership is invalid because there must be at least two general partners.

b. Creditors of the limited partnership would have to sue Cosgrove for any deficiency of assets in liquidation in excess of $50,000 before being able to resort to limited-partnership property above this amount.

c. If one of the limited partners agreed in the certificate to contribute $90,000 in cash and $10,000 in services but has not provided the services as agreed, he may be held liable for $10,000 cash.

d. The limited partnership can properly be called the Cosgrove, Watts, Randall & Howard Investing Company, Limited Partnership.

The correct answer is (c). *(CPA 575 L-18)*

REQUIRED: The correct statement regarding a limited partnership.

DISCUSSION: A limited partner's contribution may consist of cash or other property, including services. These services must not include partnership management or (s)he will become liable as a general partner. A limited partner will be liable to the partnership for the difference between his/her contribution as made and that agreed to. When promised services have not been provided, cash equal to the value of the promised services may be required.

Answer (a) is incorrect because a valid limited partnership may be formed with only one general partner. Answer (b) is incorrect because the creditors of the limited partnership could and would have to proceed against the partnership assets before attempting to reach Cosgrove's personal assets. Answer (d) is incorrect because the surname of a limited partner may not appear in the partnership name unless it is also the surname of a general partner or it appeared in the name prior to the time when the limited partner became such. Otherwise, a limited partner whose name appears in the partnership name will be liable as a general partner to creditors who extend credit without actual knowledge that (s)he is not a general partner.

78. Darla, Jack, and Sam have formed a partnership with each agreeing to contribute $100,000. Jack and Sam each contributed $100,000 cash. Darla contributed $75,000 cash and agreed to pay an additional $25,000 2 years later. After 1 year of operations the partnership is insolvent. The liabilities and fair market value of the assets of the partnership are as follows:

Assets	
Cash	$ 40,000
Trade accounts receivable	35,000
Receivable from Darla	25,000
Equipment	100,000
	$200,000
Liabilities	
Trade accounts payable	$410,000

Both Jack and Sam are personally insolvent. Darla has a net worth of $750,000. If Darla is a limited partner, what is her maximum potential liability?

a. $0.

b. $25,000.

c. $210,000.

d. $235,000.

The correct answer is (b). *(CPA 1184 L-13)*

REQUIRED: The maximum liability of a limited partner.

DISCUSSION: The liability of a limited partner extends only to the amount of his/her agreed upon capital contribution. At the time of insolvency 1 year after creation of the partnership, Darla's liability to make further payments will be a maximum of $25,000, the amount that she agreed to contribute 2 years after formation. A limited partner may lose his/her limited liability:

1. If (s)he agrees to be a surety on a particular partnership debt.
2. If (s)he knowingly permits his/her name to be included in the firm name or in association with promoting the firm, and creditors are without actual knowledge that (s)he is a limited partner.
3. If (s)he participates in management or control of the partnership and misleads a creditor into believing (s)he is a general partner at the time of the transaction.

Questions 79 through 81 are based on the following information: White, Grey, and Fox formed a limited partnership. White is the general partner and Grey and Fox are the limited partners. Each agreed to contribute $200,000. Grey and Fox each contributed $200,000 in cash, and White contributed $150,000 in cash and $50,000 worth of services already rendered. After 2 years, the partnership is insolvent. The fair market value of the assets of the partnership is $150,000 and the liabilities total $275,000. The partners have made no withdrawals.

79. If Fox is insolvent and White and Grey each has a net worth in excess of $300,000, what is White's maximum potential liability in the event of a dissolution of the partnership?

a. $62,500.

b. $112,500.

c. $125,000.

d. $175,000.

The correct answer is (c). *(CPA 587 L-7)*

REQUIRED: The potential liability of a general partner in the event of dissolution.

DISCUSSION: As limited partners, the liability of Grey and Fox for partnership obligations is limited to their capital contributions. Fox's insolvency is irrelevant. Neither Grey nor Fox is liable for any losses realized during dissolution. The general partner (White) is personally responsible for all obligations of the partnership. In this case, liabilities exceed the fair market value of the assets by $125,000, and that is White's maximum potential liability.

80. Unless otherwise provided in the certificate of limited partnership, which of the following is correct if Fox assigns her interest in the partnership to Barr, and White but not Grey consents to Barr's admission as a limited partner?

a. Barr will not become a substituted limited partner unless Grey also consents.

b. Barr will have the right to inspect the partnership's books.

c. The partnership will be dissolved.

d. Barr will become a substituted limited partner because White, as general partner, consented.

The correct answer is (a). *(CPA 587 L-8)*

REQUIRED: The true statement about the assignment of a limited partnership interest.

DISCUSSION: As in regular partnerships, the assignment of a limited partnership interest entitles the assignee to the assigning partner's share of capital and profits, but does not make the assignee a partner. Only the unanimous consent of all existing partners allows an assignee to become a substituted limited partner.

Answer (b) is incorrect because without Grey's consent, Barr cannot become a partner or gain all of the rights of a limited partner, such as the right to inspect the partnership's books. Answer (c) is incorrect because the assignment of a limited partnership interest does not dissolve the partnership. Answer (d) is incorrect because the election of a substitute limited partner requires the consent of all partners, both general and limited.

81. Unless otherwise provided in the certificate of limited partnership, which of the following is correct if Grey dies?

a. Grey's personal representative will automatically become a substituted limited partner.

b. Grey's personal representative will have all the rights of a limited partner for the purpose of settling the estate.

c. The partnership will automatically be dissolved.

d. Grey's estate will be free from any liabilities incurred by Grey as a limited partner.

The correct answer is (b). *(CPA 587 L-9)*

REQUIRED: The effect of the death of a limited partner.

DISCUSSION: The death of a limited partner does not result in dissolution of the partnership. The limited partner's estate would retain all of Grey's rights and liabilities as a limited partner, and Grey's personal representative would act as limited partner for the purpose of settling the estate.

Answer (a) is incorrect because a limited partner's personal representative is not actually made a limited partner, but is only entitled to act in that capacity for purposes of settling the estate. Answer (c) is incorrect because a partnership is not automatically dissolved upon the death of a limited partner. Answer (d) is incorrect because the estate retains both the rights and liabilities that would accrue to Grey as a limited partner.

82. The certificate of limited partnership filed in the public records need not contain

a. The name of the partnership and the names of the general and limited partners separately designated.

b. The general character of the business.

c. The contribution of each partner (general and limited).

d. The amount of each limited partner's liability.

The correct answer is (d). *(Publisher)*

REQUIRED: The item not contained in the limited partnership certificate.

DISCUSSION: Limited partners are not liable beyond their capital contribution (amount made and amount promised to be made in the future). Therefore, there is no liability to be disclosed in the certificate.

Answers (a), (b), and (c) are incorrect because each is required to be included in the certificate.

83. Stanley is a well-known retired movie personality who purchased a limited partnership interest in Terrific Movie Productions upon its initial syndication. Terrific has three general partners, who also purchased limited partnership interests, and 1,000 additional limited partners located throughout the United States. Which of the following is correct?

a. If Stanley permits his name to be used in connection with the business and is held out as a participant in the management of the venture, he will be liable as a general partner.

b. The sale of these limited partnership interests would not be subject to SEC registration.

c. This limited partnership may be created with the same informality as a general partnership.

d. The general partners are prohibited from also owning limited partnership interests.

The correct answer is (a). *(CPA 582 L-3)*

REQUIRED: The correct statement concerning a limited partnership.

DISCUSSION: A limited partner who permits his/her name to be used in the name of the partnership or in connection with the business will be liable to creditors who give credit without actual knowledge that (s)he is not a general partner. Such a limited partner will forfeit his/her limited liability because the use of his/her name may have led unsuspecting creditors to believe that (s)he was a general partner with unlimited liability.

Answer (b) is incorrect because limited partnership interests are considered to be securities and will be subject to registration with the SEC unless there are grounds for exemption. Answer (c) is incorrect because a limited partnership can only be formed pursuant to a statute permitting the formation and existence of limited partnerships, and such statutes require many formalities. Answer (d) is incorrect because a general partner may also be a limited partner.

84. Teal and Olvera were partners of the T & O Real Estate Investment Company. They decided to seek more capital in order to expand their participation in the booming real estate business in that area. They obtained five individuals to invest $100,000 each in their venture as limited partners. Assuming the limited partnership agreement is silent on the point, which of the following acts may Teal and Olvera engage in without the written consent of all limited partners?

a. Admit an additional person as a general partner.

b. Continue the partnership business upon the death or retirement of a general partner.

c. Invest the entire amount ($500,000) of contributions by the limited partners in a single venture.

d. Admit additional limited partners from time to time in order to obtain additional working capital.

The correct answer is (c). *(CPA 1179 L-18)*

REQUIRED: A general partner's act not requiring written consent of all the limited partners.

DISCUSSION: Investment of the contributions of the limited partners by the general partners is an action that does not require the consent of limited partners. Limited partners are not allowed to take part in the control and management of the business; therefore, their consent could not be required. General partners may invest the partnership funds in one or more ventures, as long as the partnership agreement is complied with.

Answers (a), (b) and (d) are incorrect because they represent actions specifically enumerated in the ULPA as requiring the unanimous consent of the limited partners when the partnership agreement does not grant authority.

85. Vast Ventures is a limited partnership. The partnership agreement does not contain provisions dealing with the assignment of a partnership interest. The rights of the general and limited partners regarding the assignment of their partnership interests are

a. Determined according to the common law of partnerships as articulated by the courts.

b. Basically the same with respect to both types of partners.

c. Basically the same with the exception that the limited partner must give ten days' notice prior to the assignment.

d. Different in that the assignee of the general partnership interest does not become a substituted partner, whereas the assignee of a limited partnership interest automatically becomes a substituted limited partner.

The correct answer is (b). *(CPA 1183 L-18)*

REQUIRED: The rights of all partners to assign their interests in a limited partnership.

DISCUSSION: Unless the partnership agreement provides otherwise, both general and limited partners may assign their interests to creditors or others without dissolving the partnership. The interest of either kind of partner is personal property against which a charging order may be obtained. The assignee does not become a partner but is merely entitled to receive the partner's distributions. If the agreement provides, however, the assignee of a general or a limited partner may be designated a limited partner by the assignor. Assignment also terminates either a general or a limited partner's status as a partner.

Answer (a) is incorrect because limited partnerships are statutory creations. The partners' rights are essentially determined with regard to the ULPA, which has been adopted in most states. Answer (c) is incorrect because the ULPA imposes no such requirement. Answer (d) is incorrect because the right to confer limited partner status on an assignee must be expressly granted in the certificate. If granted, either a general or a limited partner may exercise the right.

86. Which of the following is a correct statement with respect to the rights of a limited partner?

a. The limited partner will only have taxable income if the limited partnership makes a distribution in the tax year.

b. The partnership is required to purchase the limited partnership interest at the book value if the limited partner demands this.

c. The limited partner may assign his/her partnership interest to whomsoever (s)he wishes at any time.

d. The limited partner must first offer his/her interest to the partnership before (s)he may sell to another party.

The correct answer is (c). *(CPA 1178 L-26)*

REQUIRED: The correct statement with respect to the rights of a limited partner.

DISCUSSION: The partnership interest of a limited partner is personal property which may be freely assigned. An assignee will not become a substituted limited partner, however, unless all members of the partnership agree, or unless the certificate gives the assignor the right to confer substituted limited partner status upon the assignee.

Answer (a) is incorrect because a limited partner may have taxable income from the limited partnership even though no distribution is made. Answer (b) is incorrect because if a limited partner withdraws, (s)he is entitled within a reasonable time to receive the fair value (not book value) of his/her interest. Answer (d) is incorrect because a limited partner may assign his/her interest to whomever (s)he pleases, unless the partnership agreement provides otherwise.

87. Ms. Walls is a limited partner of the Amalgamated Limited Partnership. She is insolvent and her debts exceed her assets by $28,000. Goldsmith, one of Walls' largest creditors, is resorting to legal process to obtain the payment of Walls' debt to him. Goldsmith has obtained a charging order against Walls' limited partnership interest for the unsatisfied amount of the debt. As a result of Goldsmith's action, which of the following will happen?

a. The partnership will be dissolved.

b. Walls' partnership interest must be redeemed with partnership property.

c. Goldsmith automatically becomes a substituted limited partner.

d. Goldsmith becomes in effect an assignee of Walls' partnership interest.

The correct answer is (d). *(CPA 1180 L-24)*

REQUIRED: The result of a creditor obtaining a charging order against an insolvent limited partner's interest.

DISCUSSION: A charging order is a court order which has the effect of an involuntary assignment of the limited partner's interest to the judgment-creditor (or an independent third party called a receiver). The limited partner's interest may be temporarily assigned until the profits distributed pay off the debt, or may be permanently assigned using its fair market value to pay off the debt.

Answer (a) is incorrect because a limited partnership is not dissolved by the bankruptcy of a limited partner or by assignment of his/her interest. Answer (b) is incorrect because Walls' partnership interest is not required to be redeemed. Answer (c) is incorrect because an assignee of a limited partnership interest does not become a substituted limited partner unless the assignor gives the assignee that right pursuant to the limited partnership agreement, or all the members of the partnership agree.

88. A limited partner's capital contribution to the limited partnership

a. Creates an intangible personal property right of the limited partner in the limited partnership.

b. Can be withdrawn at the limited partner's option at any time prior to the filing of a petition in bankruptcy against the limited partnership.

c. Can only consist of cash or marketable securities.

d. Need not be indicated in the limited partnership's certificate.

The correct answer is (a). *(CPA 1176 L-15)*

REQUIRED: The correct statement regarding a limited partner's capital contribution.

DISCUSSION: A limited partner's interest in the partnership is personal property. Furthermore, that interest constitutes an intangible since the limited partner has no right to specific partnership property. The limited partner's interest is an investment in the entity as a whole.

Answer (b) is incorrect because a limited partner's right of withdrawal of his/her capital contribution is restricted. It may be withdrawn upon the dissolution of the partnership, at the date specified in the certificate, upon six months' notice in writing to all the members, or with the consent of all the members but only if all creditors are paid or there are sufficient assets left for creditors. Answer (c) is incorrect because a limited partner's capital contribution may consist of cash, other property, and services also. Answer (d) is incorrect because a limited partner's contribution must be described in the certificate.

89. Link and Stover were partners of the Hot Springs Limited Partnership. They decided to seek more capital in order to expand their participation in the real estate business in that area. They obtained five individuals to invest $100,000 each in their venture as limited partners. Which of the following rights would the limited partners not have?

a. The right to have a dissolution and winding up by court decree where such is appropriate.

b. The right to remove a general partner by a majority vote if provided for in the partnership agreement.

c. The right to vote on management decisions proposed by the general partners.

d. The right to have the partnership books kept at the principal place of business and to have access to them.

The correct answer is (c). *(CPA 1179 L-19)*

REQUIRED: The right which a limited partner would not have.

DISCUSSION: Limited partners have no authority to manage the affairs of the business. If they do participate in management, they lose their limited liability. But if the participation by the limited partner in management (control of the business) is not substantially the same as the general partners', the limited partner only becomes liable to persons who know of the participation in management.

Answers (a), (b), and (d) are incorrect because each represents a right possessed by a limited partner under the ULPA.

90. Fox, Harrison, and Dodge are the general partners of Great Expectations, a limited partnership. There are 20 limited partners. The general partners wish to add two more general partners and sell additional limited partnership interests to the public. The limited partnership certificate is silent on these matters. The general partners

a. Can admit the two additional partners as general partners without the consent of the limited partners if the general partners vote unanimously to do so.

b. Cannot admit additional limited partners unless there is unanimous written consent or ratification of their action by the limited partners.

c. Can admit additional limited partners if a majority of the general and limited partners consent to do so.

d. Cannot admit any general or limited partners without amending the written partnership agreement.

The correct answer is (b). *(CPA 575 L-5)*

REQUIRED: The correct statement regarding the admission of new general and limited partners to a limited partnership.

DISCUSSION: In the absence of a provision to the contrary in the partnership agreement, the general partners cannot admit additional limited partners without the unanimous written consent or ratification of all partners (limited and general). This protects the existing partners' proportionate interest in the partnership.

Answer (a) is incorrect because the general partners may not admit additional general partners without the unanimous consent of the limited partners. Answer (c) is incorrect because in the absence of a provision to the contrary in the partnership agreement, admission of new limited partners requires the unanimous consent of all partners. Answer (d) is incorrect because only the certificate filed with the state needs to be amended when new partners are admitted.

91. A limited partner

a. May not withdraw his/her capital contribution unless there is sufficient limited-partnership property to pay all general creditors.

b. Must not own limited-partnership interests in other competing limited partnerships.

c. Is automatically an agent for the partnership with apparent authority to bind the limited partnership in contract.

d. Has no liability to creditors even if (s)he takes part in the control of the business as long as (s)he is held out as being a limited partner.

The correct answer is (a). *(CPA 1176 L-11)*

REQUIRED: The correct statement concerning a limited partner.

DISCUSSION: Under the ULPA, outside creditors have priority over liabilities to limited partners for the return of their capital contributions. Therefore, a limited partner may not withdraw his/her capital contribution if it would impair the creditors' rights.

Answer (b) is incorrect because a limited partner may own an interest in competing partnerships or compete in other ways since a limited partner does not engage in the management of the partnership. Answer (c) is incorrect because limited partners are not agents of the partnership and have no apparent or other authority to bind the partnership. Answer (d) is incorrect because a limited partner who takes part in the control of the business will become personally liable to creditors, even if held out as a limited partner.

92. Cavendish is a limited partner of Custer Venture Capital. He is extremely dissatisfied with the performance of the general partners in making investments and managing the portfolio. He is contemplating taking whatever legal action may be appropriate against the general partners. Which of the following rights would Cavendish not be entitled to assert as a limited partner?

a. To have a formal accounting of partnership affairs whenever the circumstances render it just and reasonable.

b. To have the same rights as a general partner to a dissolution and winding up of the partnership.

c. To have reasonable access to the partnership books and to inspect and copy them.

d. To have himself elected as a general partner by a majority vote of the limited partners in number and amount.

The correct answer is (d). *(CPA 582 L-4)*

REQUIRED: The right that a limited partner is not entitled to assert.

DISCUSSION: A new general partner may be admitted to a limited partnership only with the specific written consent of each and every partner (both limited and general). The limited partners thus do not have the power to admit new general partners, and unanimous consent is needed unless the partnership agreement provides otherwise.

Answers (a), (b), and (c) are incorrect because each represents a right which may be asserted by a limited partner. In general, a limited partner has such rights as are reasonably necessary to protect his/her investment, but not those which would give him/her the power to manage or control the enterprise.

93. Bonanza Real Estate Ventures is a limited partnership created pursuant to the law of a state which has adopted the Uniform Limited Partnership Act. It has three general partners and 1,100 limited partners living in various states. The limited partnership interests were offered to the general public at $5,000 per partnership interest. Johnson purchased a limited-partnership interest in the Bonanza Real Estate Ventures. As such, he

a. Cannot assign his limited-partnership interest to another person without the consent of the general partners.

b. Is entitled to interest on his capital contribution.

c. Is a fiduciary vis-a-vis the limited partnership and its partners.

d. Must include his share of the limited-partnership taxable profits in his taxable income even if he does not withdraw anything.

The correct answer is (d). *(CPA 575 L-20)*

REQUIRED: The proper statement regarding a limited partnership interest.

DISCUSSION: Partnerships are tax-reporting rather than taxpaying entities. The taxable profits of the enterprise "flow through" to the partners. Accordingly, a limited partner must include his/her share of the partnership profits in his/her taxable income even though no distribution has been received.

Answer (a) is incorrect because under the ULPA, a limited partner has an absolute right to assign his/her partnership interest. Answer (b) is incorrect because a partner is entitled to interest on his/her capital contribution only after the date it is required to be returned. Answer (c) is incorrect because a limited partner, having no management responsibilities, is not a fiduciary vis-a-vis the partnership and the partners. The limited partner is only an investor.

94. Absent any contrary provisions in the agreement, under which of the following circumstances will a limited partnership be dissolved?

a. A limited partner dies and his/her estate is insolvent.

b. A personal creditor of a general partner obtains a judgment against the general partner's interest in the limited partnership.

c. A general partner retires and all the remaining general partners do not consent to continue.

d. A limited partner assigns his/her partnership interest to an outsider and the purchaser becomes a substituted limited partner.

The correct answer is (c). *(CPA 1176 L-13)*

REQUIRED: The circumstance in which a limited partnership will be dissolved.

DISCUSSION: Retirement of a general partner will generally dissolve a limited partnership just as it would dissolve a general partnership. However, dissolution can be avoided if the business is continued by the remaining general partners either with the consent of all partners or pursuant to a stipulation in the partnership agreement.

Answer (a) is incorrect because the death of a limited partner, regardless of the solvency of the estate, does not dissolve the partnership. Answer (b) is incorrect because a judgment against the interest of a general partner is similar to an assignment of that interest, which does not dissolve the partnership. Answer (d) is incorrect because the assignment of a limited partnership interest does not dissolve the partnership. It makes no difference whether the assignee becomes a substituted limited partner.

95. Wichita Properties is a limited partnership created in accordance with the provisions of the Uniform Limited Partnership Act. The partners have voted to dissolve and settle the partnership's accounts. Which of the following will be the last to be paid?

a. General partners for unpaid distributions.

b. Limited partners in respect to capital.

c. Limited and general partners in respect to their undistributed profits.

d. General partners in respect to capital.

The correct answer is (c). *(CPA 1181 L-23)*

REQUIRED: The lowest priority of distribution upon liquidation of a limited partnership.

DISCUSSION: Under the RULPA, limited and general partners are treated equally. Unless the partnership agreement provides otherwise, assets are distributed as follows:

1) creditors (including all partners)
2) partners for unpaid distributions (i.e., declared but not paid)
3) partners for capital
4) partners for remaining assets (i.e., undistributed profits) in proportions for sharing distributions

96. Donald Fisk is a limited partner of Sparta Oil Development. He paid $10,000 for his limited-partnership interest. In addition, he lent Sparta $7,500. Sparta failed to find oil and is in financial difficulty. Upon dissolution and liquidation,

a. Fisk and all outside general creditors will receive repayment of their loans prior to any other distributions.

b. Fisk will receive repayment, along with the other limited partners, in respect to his capital and loan after all other creditors have been satisfied.

c. The last distribution, if anything remains, is to the general partners in respect to capital.

d. If Fisk holds partnership property as collateral, he may resort to it to satisfy any deficiency if other partnership assets are insufficient to meet creditors' claims.

The correct answer is (a). *(CPA 575 L-21)*

REQUIRED: The proper statement regarding liquidation of a limited partnership.

DISCUSSION: Under the RULPA, a limited (or general) partner is entitled to the same priority for repayment of a loan by the partnership as outside creditors. This is the first priority in the distribution of partnership assets.

Answer (b) is incorrect because Fisk is entitled to receive repayment of his loan at the same time as outside creditors. Answer (c) is incorrect because the last distribution is to partners (general and limited) for undistributed profits. Answer (d) is incorrect because if the other assets are insufficient to meet the claims of creditors, a partner's resorting to partnership property held as collateral to satisfy a claim for capital and profits would be a fraud on creditors. However, Fisk could share in this property to the extent that he is a general creditor.

CHAPTER SIXTEEN
CORPORATIONS

Because the Model Business Corporation Act has been adopted in the majority of states (with varying changes), it is the basis for most of the answer explanations in this chapter. When no provision of the Act is applicable, the general rules developed over the years are the source of the answer explanation. The version of the Act resulting from a substantial revision in 1984 is followed in the discussions of corporate law in current editions of many business law textbooks. It will be cited here as the RMBCA.

16.1 General Characteristics of Corporations

1. The corporation and the general partnership are primary forms of business organization. Both

a. Exist in perpetuity.

b. Are treated for most purposes as entities distinct from their owners.

c. Are regarded as distinct entities for litigation, bankruptcy, and tax purposes.

d. Can hold and convey property.

The correct answer is (d). *(Publisher)*

REQUIRED: The respect in which a general partnership resembles a corporation.

DISCUSSION: A corporation is nearly always regarded as a separate legal entity, while a partnership is for many purposes treated as an aggregate of individuals. One similarity is that both may hold and convey property.

Answer (a) is incorrect because a partnership terminates upon the death or withdrawal of a partner. Answer (b) is incorrect because partnerships are not distinct from their owners for many purposes, e.g., legal liability, duration of existence, and taxation. Answer (c) is incorrect because partnerships are not taxed, but the Federal Rules of Civil Procedure and some states regard partnerships as capable of suing and being sued. Moreover, the Bankruptcy Code permits a partnership to be adjudicated a bankrupt.

2. A corporation is an artificial being, existing only in contemplation of law. Nevertheless, this legal fiction possesses many of the rights and is subject to many of the obligations of a natural person. Which of the following states a right or rights that can be exercised only by an individual?

a. The right to contract and to own and transfer property.

b. The right to due process, the equal protection of the laws, and freedom from unreasonable searches and seizures.

c. The right to freedom of expression, protection from self-incrimination, and the privileges and immunities of citizens in the several states.

d. The right to sue or be sued, to pay taxes, and to be treated as a citizen for some purposes.

The correct answer is (c). *(Publisher)*

REQUIRED: The right(s) exercisable only by a natural rather than a corporate person.

DISCUSSION: Freedom of expression by corporations is protected by the First Amendment, but the Fifth Amendment's provision that no person "shall be compelled in any criminal case to be a witness against himself" has not been applied to corporations. Thus, an officer or director could be compelled to give testimony that would incriminate the corporation, and a corporation's records can be subpoenaed.

Answer (a) is incorrect because corporations would have little reason for being if they had no contractual capacity and could not hold, buy, and sell property. Answer (b) is incorrect because these constitutional protections do apply to corporations. Answer (d) is incorrect because along with the right to contract and to buy and sell property is the right to sue and be sued. The corporation is also a taxable entity and is regarded as a citizen of the state of incorporation.

3. A corporation is a separate legal entity for most purposes. Accordingly, one significant issue is whether it is also separate from its owners for tax purposes. Which of the following is true?

a. Certain corporations may elect to avoid federal income taxation.

b. Corporations file information returns but are not taxpayers.

c. All for-profit corporations pay federal taxes on their income.

d. If the corporation pays tax on its income, dividends distributed out of that income are not taxable.

The correct answer is (a). *(Publisher)*

REQUIRED: The true statement about taxation of corporations.

DISCUSSION: Unlike partnerships, corporations are usually subject to taxation at the local, state, and federal levels. But certain closely held corporations may choose to avoid federal income tax by electing S corporation status under the Internal Revenue Code. An S corporation election is available when the stock is held by no more than 35 shareholders, all shareholders are individuals (or certain trusts and estates), no nonresident alien owns the stock, and the firm has only one class of stock.

Answer (b) is incorrect because it is true of partnerships but not corporations. Answer (c) is incorrect because an S corporation may be taxed similar to a partnership. Answer (d) is incorrect because corporate taxation results in double taxation: the corporate tax is levied on corporate income before dividends and most dividends are taxable to the recipients.

4. A corporation is most likely to elect S corporation status when

a. A corporation needs to issue preferred stock.

b. A closely held corporation desires to "go public."

c. A creditor demands personal liability on the part of the shareholders for inventory to be sold to the corporation.

d. A loss is anticipated especially during the start-up of a business.

The correct answer is (d). *(P. Karl III)*

REQUIRED: When a corporation is most likely to elect S corporation status.

DISCUSSION: Unlike most corporations, the taxable income or losses of an S corporation flow through to the shareholders. Therefore, losses, which are quite common in the start-up of a corporation, can be utilized by the shareholders on their individual tax returns in order to reduce their own tax liability.

Answer (a) is incorrect because an S corporation can only have one class of stock. Answer (b) is incorrect because an S corporation is limited to 35 shareholders. Answer (c) is incorrect because the S corporation election does not create personal liability on the part of the shareholders for the debts of the corporation. But a shareholder who is required to sign personally on a corporation obligation does have personal liability.

5. Skipper was for several years the principal stockholder, director, and chief executive officer of the Canarsie Grocery Corporation. Canarsie is in bankruptcy. Several creditors are seeking to hold Skipper personally liable as a result of his stock ownership and as a result of his being an officer-director. Skipper in turn filed with the bankruptcy judge a claim for $1,400 salary due him. Which of the following is correct?

a. Skipper's salary claim will be allowed and he will be entitled to a priority.

b. Skipper has no personal liability to the creditors as long as Canarsie is recognized as a separate legal entity.

c. Skipper can not personally file a petition in bankruptcy for seven years.

d. Skipper is personally liable to the creditors for Canarsie's losses.

The correct answer is (b). *(CPA 582 L-17)*

REQUIRED: The personal liability and status as a creditor of a stockholder-director-officer of a bankrupt corporation.

DISCUSSION: A fundamental characteristic of the corporation is that it is a separate legal entity apart from its stockholders. The stockholders have no personal liability for corporate debts. Therefore, Skipper will have no personal liability as long as the corporation is considered a separate legal entity.

Answer (a) is incorrect because as a principal stockholder-director-officer, Skipper qualifies as an insider. The claims of insiders are not allowed priority in bankruptcy. Answer (c) is incorrect because the bankruptcy of the corporation has no effect on Skipper's ability to file bankruptcy. Answer (d) is incorrect because Skipper has no personal liability to the creditors unless he agreed to become personally liable.

6. The corporate veil is most likely to be pierced and the shareholders held personally liable if

a. An ultra vires act has been committed.

b. The corporation has elected S corporation status under the Internal Revenue Code.

c. A partnership incorporates its business solely to limit the liability of its partners.

d. The shareholders have commingled their personal funds with those of the corporation.

The correct answer is (d). *(CPA 586 L-1)*

REQUIRED: The most likely reason to disregard the corporate entity.

DISCUSSION: A court will "pierce the corporate veil" when the corporation is merely an alter ego of the shareholders. A corporation will not be considered a separate entity if it is not treated as such by its shareholders. Indications that a corporation is not considered a separate entity include corporate formalities not being followed, commingling of assets, and corporate transactions based on personal motives.

Answer (a) is incorrect because under modern statutes, the validity of corporate action may not be challenged on the ground that the corporation lacks or lacked authority to act (that is, the act was ultra vires) except in limited circumstances. Answer (b) is incorrect because an action in accordance with federal tax law provides no basis for disregarding the corporate entity. Answer (c) is incorrect because limitation of liability is a permissible objective of incorporation.

7. The limited liability of the shareholders of a closely held corporation will most likely be disregarded if the shareholders

a. Lend money to the corporation.

b. Are also corporate officers, directors, or employees.

c. Undercapitalized the corporation when it was formed.

d. Formed the corporation solely to limit their personal liability.

The correct answer is (c). *(CPA 1188 L-7)*

REQUIRED: The reason for disregarding the limited liability of the shareholders of a close corporation.

DISCUSSION: The shares of a closely held corporation are owned by just a few shareholders. Whereas state corporate law ordinarily apply whether or not the entity is publicly held, special statutes often permit closely held corporations to dispense with the usual formalities (board meetings, etc.) and to be managed as if they were partnerships. Nevertheless, the integrity of the corporate form must be maintained. If the shareholders do not treat the corporation as a genuinely separate entity, however, they will incur personal liability. One way in which the shareholders may disregard the corporate entity is by thin capitalization. Undercapitalization results in a potential fraud on creditors because a corporation is expected to have enough assets to meet its obligations.

Answer (a) is incorrect because a corporation may borrow from shareholders as long as the objective is not to defraud other creditors. Answer (b) is incorrect because shareholders of close corporations necessarily serve in these positions Answer (d) is incorrect because limited liability is a major reason for incorporation.

8. A major characteristic of the corporation is its recognition as a separate legal entity. As such it is capable of withstanding attacks upon its valid existence by various parties who would wish to disregard its existence or "pierce the corporate veil" for their own purposes. The corporation will normally be able to successfully resist such attempts except when

a. The corporation was created with tax savings in mind.

b. The corporation was created in order to insulate the assets of its owners from personal liability.

c. The corporation being attacked is a wholly owned subsidiary of its parent corporation.

d. The creation of and transfer of property to the corporation amounts to fraud upon creditors.

The correct answer is (d). *(CPA 580 L-9)*

REQUIRED: The situation in which it is possible to "pierce the corporate veil."

DISCUSSION: A corporation is a separate legal entity which may be organized and used for a variety of purposes. The corporate form may be disregarded, however, if it is used in a manner contrary to public policy, e.g., to defraud creditors.

Answers (a) and (b) are incorrect because each represents a valid reason for incorporation. Answer (c) is incorrect because if the wholly owned subsidiary maintains a reasonably separate existence from its parent corporation, it will be recognized as a separate legal entity.

9. A corporation formed by a political unit to effectuate a governmental purpose is best described as

a. Quasi-public.

b. Public.

c. Nonprofit.

d. Publicly held.

The correct answer is (b). *(Publisher)*

REQUIRED: The best term for a corporation formed by a government to achieve its purposes.

DISCUSSION: A public corporation is formed and funded by a local, state, or federal political unit to achieve some governmental purpose. Examples are incorporated cities, school and water districts, state universities, and the Tennessee Valley Authority. Public corporations are distinguished from private corporations, which are formed by private persons for private purposes, whether for-profit or not-for-profit.

Answer (a) is incorrect because a quasi-public corporation is formed privately and is for-profit, but is often heavily regulated because of its substantial effect on the public interest and its special privileges. Examples are banking and thrift institutions, railroads, and utilities. Answer (c) is incorrect because nonprofit corporations are created to achieve a charitable, educational, social, religious, or philanthropic purpose. Answer (d) is incorrect because a company is publicly held if its ownership is widely distributed and management is distinct from the stockholders. Most but not all large corporations are publicly held.

10. JBR Corporation was organized in the United States and incorporated in State Q. It wishes to do business in State R. The shareholders all reside in State X. From State R's perspective, the corporation is best described as

a. Alien.

b. Domestic.

c. Foreign.

d. Multinational.

The correct answer is (c). *(Publisher)*

REQUIRED: The best term for a corporation organized in another state.

DISCUSSION: A corporation is a domestic corporation in the state of incorporation. Hence, JBR is a domestic corporation in State Q. In every other state it is deemed a foreign corporation.

Answer (a) is incorrect because an alien corporation is one formed in another country. Answer (b) is incorrect because with respect to a given state, a domestic corporation is one incorporated in that state. Answer (d) is incorrect because multinational is a business term describing a corporation with widespread operations.

11. The close corporation furnishes not only the usual advantages of the corporate form but also various advantages of partnerships, such as active participation in the business by owners, security of control, and choice of present and future associates. Disadvantages include all but which of the following?

a. Difficulties in raising equity capital when shares are not traded publicly.

b. Potential deadlocks concerning vital corporate activities when a minority interest has veto power.

c. Problems encountered by owners who wish to withdraw their capital.

d. Inability to enter into contracts in its own name.

The correct answer is (d). *(Publisher)*

REQUIRED: The disadvantage that is not present in a close corporation.

DISCUSSION: A close corporation has relatively few shareholders, the shares are not publicly traded, and the owners are usually involved in management. One disadvantage is that many state statutes are not drafted to allow the flexibility and simplicity needed by organizers of a close corporation. However, the close corporation is a separate legal entity, the same as a publicly held corporation. It may sue and be sued, own property, make contracts, and exercise a wide range of rights in its own name.

Answer (a) is incorrect because equity investment may be difficult to obtain since shares are not publicly traded and capital must generally come from the existing stockholders or loans guaranteed by them. Answer (b) is incorrect because minority shareholders often insist upon voting provisions giving them a veto over corporate actions. The result may be an impasse in which no corporate action may be taken because of disagreements among the shareholders. Answer (c) is incorrect because in the absence of a market for the stock, shareholders may find themselves without the means to liquidate their investment through sale to others.

12. An important trend in corporate law is the recognition that traditional concepts applicable to large publicly held corporations often do not meet the needs of those closely held. Accordingly, many states have enacted statutes that address these needs, and a Statutory Close Corporation Supplement has been added to the MBCA. Under the Supplement,

a. A qualifying entity is automatically treated as a close corporation if it has fewer than 50 shareholders.

b. A shareholder may have power to dissolve the corporation that is similar to a partner's.

c. Transfer of shares is restricted by means of a statutory buy-and-sell arrangement.

d. A board of directors is required but shareholders have absolute power to restrict its discretion.

The correct answer is (b). *(Publisher)*

REQUIRED: The true statement about the Close Corporation Supplement.

DISCUSSION: In substance, many close corporations are partnerships in which all of the shareholders are active in management or are friends and relatives of those who are. In a partnership, a partner's interest is protected by his/her power to dissolve the association at any time and receive the value of his/her interest. Traditional corporate law did not provide that option for minority shareholders. The Supplement allows the articles to include a provision enabling any shareholder to dissolve the corporation either at will or upon the happening of a certain event.

Answer (a) is incorrect because, if a qualifying entity fails to elect this status, the regular corporate statutes and cases will govern. Answer (c) is incorrect because the Supplement provides a statutory right of first refusal but no buy-and-sell arrangement. Answer (d) is incorrect because no board is required.

13. Hobson, Jones, Carter, and Wolff are all medical doctors who have worked together for several years. They decided to form a corporation and their attorney created a typical professional corporation for them. Which of the following is correct?

a. Such a corporation will not be recognized for federal tax purposes if one of its goals is to save taxes.

b. The state in which they incorporated must have enacted professional corporation statutes permitting them to do so.

c. Upon incorporation, the doctor-shareholder is insulated from personal liability beyond his capital contribution.

d. The majority of states prohibit the creation of professional corporations by doctors.

The correct answer is (b). *(CPA 1178 L-22)*

REQUIRED: The correct statement regarding the formation of a professional corporation.

DISCUSSION: Until recently, professionals were not permitted to incorporate. Now most states have enacted special statutes permitting members of professions such as law, medicine, and public accounting to use the corporate form. Medical doctors can only incorporate in states which have enacted such professional corporation statutes. They would not be permitted to incorporate under general incorporation statutes.

Answer (a) is incorrect because one of the underlying policies of allowing professionals to incorporate is to provide them equal tax treatment. The IRS has agreed to recognize such corporations. Answer (c) is incorrect because the practitioner remains personally liable for his/her professional actions. The ordinary corporate insulation from personal liability extends only to the non-professional activities of the shareholder-practitioners. Answer (d) is incorrect because the majority of states now permit the creation of professional corporations by doctors and other professionals.

16.2 Formation of Corporations

14. As a general rule, a business corporation can be formed only by

a. Simple agreement of investors.

b. Adoption of a special act of a state legislature.

c. Decree of a court of equity.

d. Grant of state pursuant to state law.

The correct answer is (d). *(CMA 679 1-34)*

REQUIRED: The correct statement of how business corporations can be formed.

DISCUSSION: Business corporations only exist pursuant to state statutes. They did not exist at common law. Each state has a general incorporation statute permitting a state official to issue a corporate charter (articles of incorporation) when the applicant complies with the terms of the statute.

Answer (a) is incorrect because a corporation cannot be created solely by private action. Answer (b) is incorrect because a special act is no longer needed. Answer (c) is incorrect because although they can dissolve a corporation, courts lack authority to form a corporation.

15. In general, which of the following must be contained in articles of incorporation?

a. The names of states in which the corporation will be doing business.

b. The name of the state in which the corporation will maintain its principal place of business.

c. The names of the initial officers and their terms of office.

d. The classes of stock authorized for issuance.

The correct answer is (d). *(CPA 587 L-3)*

REQUIRED: The information required in the articles of incorporation.

DISCUSSION: Under the RMBCA, the articles must contain the name of the corporation, the authorized shares and details of their division into classes and issuance in series, the address of the initial registered office of the corporation and the name of its first registered agent at that address, and the names and addresses of the incorporators. The articles may also include the names and addresses of the initial directors; the purpose and duration of the corporation; the par value of shares; provisions for managing the corporation and regulating its internal affairs; the powers of the corporation, its board, and its shareholders; the liability of shareholders for corporate debts; and any provision that may be set forth in the bylaws.

Answers (a), (b), and (c) are incorrect because these matters need not be included. The RMBCA prescribes few requirements so as to facilitate the drafting of the articles.

16. Corporations are creatures of state statutory law. Which of the following is a true statement about attempts to unify state corporate law?

a. Most states have adopted the Uniform Corporation Act drafted by the American Law Institute.

b. Unlike commercial law, corporate law has not been subject to the unifying effect of a widely adopted model or uniform Act.

c. The Revised Model Business Corporation Act has been substantially adopted in almost all states.

d. Most states have used the Model Business Corporation Act as a guide for their incorporation statutes.

The correct answer is (d). *(Publisher)*

REQUIRED: The true statement about state corporate law.

DISCUSSION: Unlike commercial law, incorporation statutes need not be substantially uniform. Accordingly, the American Bar Association's Model Business Corporation Act (revised in 1984) is intended as a guide to improve the quality of state statutes, especially for small corporations. Today, at least 39 states have partially or substantially enacted the MBCA.

Answer (a) is incorrect because no such Act has been published. Answer (b) is incorrect because the MBCA has been at least partially enacted in a large majority of states. Answer (c) is incorrect because the RMBCA has been adopted in some states and is under consideration in others but has not yet been widely influential. However, many of its rules reflect majority practice, and others are expected to be widely adopted.

17. The corporate existence is most likely to begin when

a. The certificate of incorporation is issued.

b. The articles of incorporation are signed by the incorporators.

c. Corporate officers are elected at the organization meeting.

d. Corporate directors are elected at the organization meeting.

The correct answer is (a). *(Publisher)*

REQUIRED: When corporate existence may begin.

DISCUSSION: Under the MBCA, corporate existence begins upon issuance of the certificate of incorporation. Under the RMBCA, the corporation comes into existence when the articles are filed. The RMBCA rule has usually been followed in states that do not require issuance of a certificate. Also, some states that issue certificates observe the time-of-filing principle.

Answer (b) is incorrect because the date of filing is the earliest possible time when the corporate existence can commence. Answer (c) is incorrect because the corporation should already be in existence at this time since acts binding on it are taken at the meeting. Answer (d) is incorrect because the initial directors are usually named in the articles and are thus selected prior to the official commencement of corporate existence. Changes in the board can occur at an organizational meeting. In no event does election of the board mark the beginning of corporate existence.

18. State incorporation statutes prescribe certain formalities as conditions precedent to the creation of a corporation. Which of the following is a true statement about the effect of defective formation?

a. A de jure corporation is formed when all statutory provisions are not complied with, but a good faith effort was made to do so.

b. In most states that have followed the MBCA, the significance of the de facto incorporation doctrine has been reduced.

c. A corporation by estoppel will be found when a good faith effort has been made to comply with the incorporation law.

d. A de facto corporation is formed if the mandatory provisions of the statute have been complied with.

The correct answer is (b). *(Publisher)*

REQUIRED: The true statement about defective corporate formation.

DISCUSSION: Traditionally, a de facto corporation was formed when a good faith effort was made to comply with the statutory provisions but some statutory provisions were not complied with. Under the MBCA, however, the issuance of a certificate is conclusive evidence against all parties except the state that a corporation has been formed. The RMBCA treats the filing of the articles (an official act done by the secretary of state) as conclusive proof that all conditions have been satisfied. The effect is to treat a corporation as de jure even though a mandatory provision was not complied with.

Answer (a) is incorrect because it describes a de facto corporation. Answer (c) is incorrect because it describes one requirement of a de facto corporation. The estoppel doctrine creates no corporation but instead prevents certain persons from denying corporateness. For example, a person who has dealt with a business association in reliance on its representation of corporate status may assert the estoppel doctrine. Answer (d) is incorrect because a de jure corporation is formed.

19. The Zebra Corporation is neither de jure nor de facto but has done business and held itself out as a corporation.

a. Zebra can nevertheless recover on a loan which it made to one of its suppliers.

b. Zebra cannot be held liable for torts committed by its agents.

c. The shareholders and officers will incur no personal liability.

d. Zebra can nevertheless validly continue to do business as a corporation without fear of legal action by the state as long as it is solvent and pays taxes.

The correct answer is (a). *(CPA 1174 L-39)*

REQUIRED: The correct statement regarding a company which is neither de jure nor de facto.

DISCUSSION: A de jure corporation is one that meets all the requirements for valid corporate organization. A de facto corporation is one that, although defectively formed, represents a substantial good-faith attempt to comply. An entity which does not even qualify as a de facto corporation may recover on its claims against third parties as long as the third parties thought they were dealing with a corporation. The debtors are estopped from proving that no corporation was formed to prevent these third parties from being unjustly enriched.

Answer (b) is incorrect because a defective corporation could be held liable for torts committed by its agents to prevent unfairness to third parties. Answer (c) is incorrect because all participants may under certain circumstances be held jointly and severally liable. Answer (d) is incorrect because the state of incorporation can bring a legal action to prohibit Zebra from holding itself out as a corporation until it fully complies with state incorporation statutes.

20. The United States is a federal entity with independent state legal systems. Because corporate law is a state matter, a business may choose among 50 jurisdictions in which to incorporate. Which of the following factors is least apt to influence a firm to incorporate in a particular state?

a. The state restricts dividend payments.

b. The state has no corporate income tax.

c. Organization fees are relatively high.

d. The incorporation statute provides few restrictions on corporate management.

The correct answer is (c). *(Publisher)*

REQUIRED: The least likely reason for choosing a state in which to incorporate.

DISCUSSION: If operations are confined to one state, incorporation generally occurs there. But when operations extend to several states, many factors should be considered in choosing the appropriate jurisdiction. The amount of flexibility accorded to management, voting and other rights of shareholders, limitations on issuance of shares and on dividends, taxation, and organization costs (stock issuance taxes, organization fees, franchise taxes, etc.) are all issues of significance. If a company has a genuine choice of states, the fee to organize the corporation will be nominal compared to the economic impact of the other factors.

21. Phillips was the principal promoter of the Waterloo Corporation, a corporation which was to have been incorporated not later than July 31. Phillips obtained written subscriptions for $1.4 million of common stock from 17 individuals. He hired himself as the chief executive officer of Waterloo at $200,000 for 5 years and leased three floors of office space from Downtown Office Space, Inc. The contract with Downtown was made in the name of the corporation. Phillips had indicated orally that the corporation would be coming into existence shortly. The corporation did not come into existence through no fault of Phillips. Which of the following is correct?

a. The subscribers have a recognized right to sue for and recover damages.

b. Phillips is personally liable on the lease with Downtown.

c. Phillips has the right to recover the fair value of his services rendered to the proposed corporation.

d. The subscribers were not bound by their subscriptions until the corporation came into existence.

The correct answer is (b). *(CPA 582 L-9)*

REQUIRED: The correct statement concerning the pre-incorporation activity for a corporation which did not come into existence.

DISCUSSION: A promoter is personally liable on contracts entered into on behalf of nonexistent corporations, unless such liability is excluded or performance is conditioned on adoption by the corporation. Therefore, Phillips is personally liable on the lease.

Answer (a) is incorrect because the subscribers have no right to recover damages if Phillips was not at fault. They would have a right to a refund of their subscriptions. Answer (c) is incorrect because a promoter has no right to compensation for services unless the corporation comes into existence and so agrees. The same is generally true of pre-incorporation expenses. Answer (d) is incorrect because the subscribers are bound to their subscriptions for 6 months.

22. Grandiose secured an option to purchase a tract of land for $100,000. He then organized the Dunbar Corporation and subscribed to 51% of the shares of stock of the corporation for $100,000, which was issued to him in exchange for his three-month promissory note for $100,000. Controlling the board of directors through his share ownership, he had the corporation authorize the purchase of the land from him for $200,000. He made no disclosure to the board or to other shareholders that he was making a $100,000 profit. He promptly paid the corporation for his shares and redeemed his promissory note. A disgruntled shareholder subsequently learned the full details of the transaction and brought suit against Grandiose on the corporation's behalf. Which of the following is a correct statement?

a. Grandiose breached his fiduciary duty to the corporation and must account for the profit he made.

b. The judgment of the board of directors was conclusive under the circumstances.

c. Grandiose is entitled to retain the profit since he controlled the corporation as a result of his share ownership.

d. The giving of the promissory note in exchange for the stock constituted payment for the shares.

The correct answer is (a). *(CPA 580 L-13)*

REQUIRED: The correct statement concerning a profit made by a promoter and 51% shareholder in dealing with a newly formed corporation.

DISCUSSION: A promoter is a fiduciary with respect to the newly organized corporation. Grandiose breached this fiduciary obligation. He had a duty to act in good faith, to make full disclosure, and to not make a secret profit at the expense of the corporation. The corporation can recover the profits for violation of this duty. The fact that the property is sold at fair market value does not eliminate the promoter's profit.

Answer (b) is incorrect because the board of directors acted without full knowledge and subject to Grandiose's control. Answer (c) is incorrect because Grandiose is accountable to the corporation for the secret profit. Answer (d) is incorrect because a promissory note is not usually considered proper consideration for the issuance of stock (but the RMBCA allows it).

23. Rice is a promoter of a corporation to be known as Dex Corp. On January 1, Rice signed a 9-month contract with Roe, a CPA, which provided that Roe would perform certain accounting services for Dex. Rice did not disclose to Roe that Dex had not yet been formed. Dex was incorporated on February 1. Prior to the incorporation, Roe rendered accounting services pursuant to the contract. After rendering accounting services for an additional period of 6 months pursuant to the contract, Roe was discharged without cause by the board of directors of Dex. In the absence of any agreements to the contrary, who will be liable to Roe for breach of contract?

a. Both Rice and Dex.

b. Rice only.

c. Dex only.

d. Neither Rice nor Dex.

The correct answer is (a). *(CPA 1185 L-5)*

REQUIRED: The liability of a corporation and a promoter on a pre-incorporation agreement.

DISCUSSION: A promoter who contracts for a nonexistent corporation is personally liable on such contracts. A novation, not subsequent adoption by the corporation, releases the promoter from liability. Dex is also liable because it impliedly adopted the contract by accepting Roe's performance.

24. Watson entered into an agreement to purchase 1,000 shares of the Marvel Corporation, a corporation to be organized in the near future. Watson has since had second thoughts about investing in Marvel. Under the circumstances, which of the following is correct?

a. A written notice of withdrawal of his agreement to purchase the shares will be valid as long as it is received prior to incorporation.

b. A simple transfer of the agreement to another party will entirely eliminate his liability to purchase the shares of stock.

c. Watson may not revoke the agreement for a period of 6 months in the absence of special circumstances.

d. Watson may avoid liability on his agreement if he can obtain the consent of the majority of other individuals committed to purchase shares to release him.

The correct answer is (c). *(CPA 1178 L-15)*

REQUIRED: The correct statement regarding a pre-incorporation stock subscription agreement which the investor wishes to repudiate.

DISCUSSION: Under the RMBCA, such an agreement may not be revoked for 6 months unless otherwise provided by the terms of the subscription agreement or unless all other subscribers agree. The rationale is that the subscription agreement represents an irrevocable continuing offer for the administrative convenience of the promoter.

Answer (a) is incorrect because even a written notice of withdrawal of the agreement will not be valid until the expiration of 6 months. Answer (b) is incorrect because an assignment of the agreement to a third party will not eliminate the liability of the assignor if the assignee fails to perform. Answer (d) is incorrect because Watson can avoid liability only by obtaining the consent of all the other subscribers to release him/her.

16.3 Corporate Operations

25. Blanche was vice president of the Saturn Corporation, a major weapons dealer. She used corporate funds to bribe a government official of Sparta, a small European country, to use his influence to secure a contract for Saturn. Blanche also caused advertisements to be published in the U.S. press which defamed Saturn's chief competitor.

a. Saturn cannot be found guilty of a crime since a corporation cannot form the requisite intent.

b. Saturn will prevail on a defense of ultra vires.

c. Both Saturn and Blanche are liable in tort and guilty of a crime.

d. Blanche is guilty of a crime but is not liable in tort.

The correct answer is (c). *(Publisher)*

REQUIRED: The liability of a corporation for torts and crimes.

DISCUSSION: The facts indicate that Blanche, acting as an agent for Saturn, committed the tort of defamation and the crime of bribing a foreign governmental official. An agent is personally liable for his/her crimes and torts. Under agency law, Saturn is liable for the torts of its agents. Saturn, as well as Blanche, is also criminally liable for the bribe under the Foreign Corrupt Practices Act of 1977.

Answer (a) is incorrect because the necessary intent for the commission of a crime may be imputed to the corporation from the agent who actually committed the crime. Answer (b) is incorrect because a corporation is liable for actions which are beyond its powers (ultra vires). But the officers might be liable for acting beyond their powers. Answer (d) is incorrect because an agent is individually liable for his/her torts even though the principal may also be liable.

26. The bylaws of a corporation provide for officers and define their rights and duties. An officer can bind the corporation

a. Only if (s)he acts within the authority granted in the bylaws.

b. Only if (s)he acts within a resolution approved by the directors.

c. Because officers and directors are regarded as principals, not mere agents.

d. Because (s)he is an agent whose authority is governed by the law of agency.

The correct answer is (d). *(Publisher)*

REQUIRED: The true statement about an officer's authority to bind the corporation.

DISCUSSION: Officers are agents of a corporate principal, and agency law prescribes their real and apparent authority to bind the corporation. The bylaws and resolutions by the board of directors may specifically limit that authority, but the usual duties of an officer operate to define the officer's capacity to enter agreements enforceable against the corporation. A corporation may be estopped from asserting a lack of actual authority on the part of its employees who have apparent authority.

Answers (a) and (b) are incorrect because an agent with apparent authority may bind the principal. Answer (c) is incorrect because an officer is an agent and the corporation is the principal. But a director is not clearly one or the other. Directors individually cannot bind the principal and thus are not agents. When acting collectively, they control the corporation, which is not an activity of an agent.

27. Modern corporations wield a wide variety of powers. A corporation

a. Can do anything permitted by the incorporation statute.

b. Can exercise any power as long as it is expressly conferred by statute or the articles.

c. Has the powers expressly or impliedly conferred by the bylaws.

d. Has the powers expressly or impliedly conferred by resolutions of the board.

The correct answer is (a). *(Publisher)*

REQUIRED: The true statement about the source of corporate powers.

DISCUSSION: Subject to the limitations imposed by the federal or state constitution, a state incorporation statute is the source of a corporation's powers. The articles of incorporation may narrow the grant of authority but cannot broaden it. The powers include not only those expressed in the statute or articles but also those implied as reasonably necessary to carry out the expressed powers and purposes.

Answer (b) is incorrect because the RMBCA grants to the corporation all powers necessary or convenient to effect its purposes. Answer (c) is incorrect because bylaws are the rules adopted by a corporation to regulate its internal affairs. Answer (d) is incorrect because the board must act within limits set by the state incorporation statute, the articles, and the bylaws.

28. Corporations generally may

a. Make political contributions to candidates for federal office.

b. Make contributions for charitable, scientific, or educational purposes.

c. Not lend money.

d. Not act as a surety.

The correct answer is (b). *(Publisher)*

REQUIRED: The true statement about specific corporate powers.

DISCUSSION: Corporations today exercise many powers. The RMBCA, for example, states that a corporation "has the same powers as an individual to do all things necessary or convenient to carry out its business and affairs." One specific power formerly denied but now generally permitted to a corporation is the right "to make donations for the public welfare or for charitable, scientific, or educational purposes."

Answer (a) is incorrect because contributions to federal election campaigns are prohibited (but in some states, corporations can make contributions to state and local political campaigns). Answer (c) is incorrect because the MBCA permits a corporation to lend money for its corporate purposes. Answer (d) is incorrect because the MBCA specifically grants the power to make contracts and guarantees, and also to incur liabilities.

29. The board of directors of Wilcox Manufacturing Corporation, a publicly held corporation, has noted a significant drop in the stock market price of its 7% preferred stock and proposes to purchase some of the stock. The proposed purchase price is substantially below the redemption price of the stock. The board has decided to acquire 100,000 shares of said preferred stock and either place it in the treasury or retire it. Under these circumstances, which of the following is a correct statement?

a. The corporation will realize a taxable gain as a result of the transaction.

b. The preferred stock so acquired must be retired and may not be held as treasury stock.

c. The corporation may not acquire its own shares unless the articles of incorporation so provide.

d. Such shares may be purchased by the corporation to the extent of unreserved and unrestricted earned surplus available therefor.

The correct answer is (d). *(CPA 580 L-8)*

REQUIRED: The correct statement regarding the reacquisition of a corporation's own stock.

DISCUSSION: A corporation may reacquire its own stock (called a redemption), provided certain conditions are met. The redemption of stock must not render the corporation insolvent, and generally must not be made out of legal or stated capital; i.e., redemptions may only be made out of contributed or earned surplus which is not restricted.

Answer (a) is incorrect because the redemption of stock is a taxable event to the corporation only if appreciated property is used to purchase the stock. Answer (b) is incorrect because either common or preferred stock may be held as treasury shares. Answer (c) is incorrect because a corporation may acquire its own shares even if the articles of incorporation do not specifically address the matter.

30. In general, which of the following statements concerning treasury stock is correct?

a. A corporation may not reacquire its own stock unless specifically authorized by its articles of incorporation.

b. On issuance of new stock, a corporation has preemptive rights with regard to its treasury stock.

c. Treasury stock may be distributed as a stock dividend.

d. A corporation is entitled to receive cash dividends on its treasury stock.

The correct answer is (c). *(CPA 588 L-15)*

REQUIRED: The true statement about treasury stock.

DISCUSSION: Unless the articles provide otherwise, shares may be issued pro rata and without consideration to the shareholders by an action of the directors (RMBCA). Treasury shares have the status of authorized but unissued shares, which may be used for stock dividends.

Answer (a) is incorrect because a corporation may acquire its own shares according to the RMBCA provided it remains solvent. Answers (b) and (d) are incorrect because a corporation has no dividend or preemptive rights regarding treasury stock.

31. In their relationships with the U.S. government, business corporations are prohibited from

a. Encouraging employees and stockholders to register and to vote or providing them with information about the candidates.

b. Providing off-the-record information to regulatory agencies and employing lobbyists.

c. Donating to political election campaigns.

d. Publicizing the corporation's position on public issues affecting the corporation.

The correct answer is (c). *(CMA 680 1-15)*

REQUIRED: The action prohibited to business corporations in dealings with the U.S. government.

DISCUSSION: Federal law prohibits business corporations from donating to political election campaigns at the federal level. Note that this does not prohibit donations to state election campaigns, although some states have similar laws.

Answer (a) is incorrect because corporations are entitled to encourage employees and stockholders to register and vote, and to provide them with political information. Answer (b) is incorrect because corporations are encouraged to provide information to regulatory bodies, and they are allowed to employ lobbyists, and major corporations do so frequently. Answer (d) is incorrect because corporations have the constitutional right to publicize their positions on various public issues.

32. Which one of the following statements is a correct characterization of current federal policy toward political action committees (PACs)?

a. Corporations may use company funds to organize and administer a PAC.

b. Corporations may make corporate contributions to PACs.

c. Unions may help organize PACs, but corporations may not.

d. Individuals may only make political contributions through PACs.

The correct answer is (a). *(CMA 1286 1-28)*

REQUIRED: The true statement about political action committees (PACs).

DISCUSSION: Federal law prohibits business corporations from donating to political election campaigns at the federal level. But this law does not prohibit donations to state election campaigns, although some states have such laws. Political action committees (PACs) have therefore grown in importance over the past decade as a means of circumventing this prohibition.

Answers (b) and (c) are incorrect because direct corporate contributions are not allowed. However, corporations, trade associations, and unions may form PACs and encourage employees to participate, and company funds may be used to organize and administer the PAC. Answer (d) is incorrect because individuals may give funds either directly to candidates or to PACs.

33. Golden Enterprises, Inc. entered into a contract with Hidalgo Corporation for the sale of its mineral holdings. The transaction proved to be ultra vires. Which of the following parties may properly assert the ultra vires doctrine and why?

a. Golden Enterprises to avoid performance.

b. A shareholder of Golden Enterprises to enjoin the sale.

c. Hidalgo Corporation to avoid performance.

d. Golden Enterprises to rescind the consummated sale.

The correct answer is (b). *(CPA 580 L-12)*

REQUIRED: The party that may properly assert the transaction was ultra vires.

DISCUSSION: The doctrine of ultra vires states that a corporation may not act beyond the powers inherent in the corporate existence or which are provided in the articles of incorporation and the incorporation statutes. Ultra vires has been eliminated as a defense, but is available as a cause of action in three instances: (1) a shareholder can seek an injunction; (2) corporations can proceed against directors or officers; (3) the state attorney general can proceed against the corporation.

Answers (a) and (c) are incorrect because the parties who entered into the contract will not be allowed to get out of it by asserting ultra vires. Answer (d) is incorrect because courts will not use the ultra vires doctrine to rescind a contract which has been fully executed.

34. Destiny Manufacturing, Inc. is incorporated under the laws of Nevada. Its principal place of business is in California and it has permanent sales offices in several other states. Under the circumstances, which of the following is correct?

a. California may validly demand that Destiny incorporate under the laws of the state of California.

b. Destiny must obtain a certificate of authority to transact business in California and the other states in which it does business.

c. Destiny is a foreign corporation in California, but not in the other states.

d. California may prevent Destiny from operating as a corporation if the laws of California differ regarding organization and conduct of the corporation's internal affairs.

The correct answer is (b). *(CPA 580 L-14)*

REQUIRED: The correct statement regarding the operations of a corporation outside the state of incorporation.

DISCUSSION: Since Destiny has its principal place of business in California, it has sufficient contact with the state to qualify as "doing business there." A corporation "doing business" but not incorporated in that state is considered a "foreign corporation" and must obtain a certificate of authority to transact business there.

Answer (a) is incorrect because no state may require an existing corporation to incorporate under its laws simply because it is doing business within the state. Answer (c) is incorrect because Destiny is a foreign corporation in all states in which it is not incorporated. Therefore, Destiny is a domestic corporation in Nevada and a foreign corporation in all other states. Answer (d) is incorrect because if Destiny is validly incorporated in the state of Nevada, California may not prevent Destiny from doing business there, even if California's corporation law varies from Nevada's. Full faith and credit means that a corporation validly formed in one state must be recognized as a corporate entity in all other states.

Questions 35 and 36 are based on Dexter, Inc., which was incorporated in its home state. It expanded substantially and now does 20% of its business in a neighboring state in which it maintains a permanent facility. It has not filed any papers in the neighboring state.

35. Which of the following statements is correct?

a. Since Dexter is a duly incorporated domestic corporation in its own state, it can transact business anywhere in the United States without further authority as long as its corporate charter so provides.

b. As long as Dexter's business activities in the neighboring state do not exceed 25%, it need not obtain permission to do business in the neighboring state.

c. Dexter must create a subsidiary corporation in the neighboring state to continue to do business in that state.

d. Dexter is a foreign corporation in the neighboring state and as such must obtain a certificate of authority or it will not be permitted to maintain any action or suit in the state with respect to its intrastate business.

The correct answer is (d). *(CPA 1178 L-9)*

REQUIRED: The correct statement regarding a corporation doing substantial business outside the state of incorporation.

DISCUSSION: Dexter is a foreign corporation in the neighboring state because it is not incorporated there. Foreign corporations have a constitutional right to engage in interstate commerce, but when they engage in intrastate commerce (called "doing business"), they are subject to regulation and jurisdiction by the state. A foreign corporation doing business in a state must obtain a certificate of authority or it will not be permitted to maintain a lawsuit in that state with respect to its business there. Dexter is "doing business" in the neighboring state since it does 20% of its business and maintains a permanent facility there.

Answer (a) is incorrect because if Dexter is "doing business" within the state, its intrastate activity falls within the regulatory authority of that state. Answer (b) is incorrect because Dexter needs permission by the neighboring state to transact business if it is "doing business" within that state. The requirement applies when intrastate business amounts to more than an occasional transaction and is not based on any set percentage. Answer (c) is incorrect because Dexter may do business within the neighboring state simply by obtaining a certificate of authority there; it need not form a new corporation.

36. Which of the following statements is incorrect?

a. Dexter has automatically appointed the secretary of state of the neighboring state as its agent for the purpose of service of legal process if it failed to appoint or maintain a registered agent in that state.

b. Dexter will be able to maintain an action or suit in the neighboring state if it subsequently obtains a certificate of authority.

c. Dexter can not defend against a suit brought against it in the neighboring state's courts.

d. The attorney general of the neighboring state can recover all back fees and franchise taxes which would have been imposed plus all penalties for failure to pay same.

The correct answer is (c). *(CPA 1178 L-10)*

REQUIRED: The false statement regarding a corporation doing business outside the state of incorporation.

DISCUSSION: Because of the constitutional provision of due process, a corporation cannot be prevented from defending a lawsuit regardless of its failure to comply with local laws. Therefore, Dexter would be permitted to defend against a lawsuit, even though it did not comply with the statute governing operations of foreign corporations and would not be allowed to bring an action regarding its intrastate business.

Answers (a), (b), and (d) are incorrect because each is a correct statement concerning the law governing foreign corporations.

37. Acme Corp. is incorporated in Delaware. Its principal place of business is in Miami, Florida, and Acme Corp. does business in all 50 states. For purposes of diversity of citizenship, Acme Corp. is considered to be a citizen of

a. Delaware only.

b. Florida only.

c. Delaware and Florida.

d. All 50 states.

The correct answer is (c). *(K.J. Elwell)*

REQUIRED: The citizenship of a corporation.

DISCUSSION: For the purpose of federal court jurisdiction in cases involving parties with diverse citizenship, a corporation is a citizen of the state in which it is incorporated and of the state in which it has its principal place of business. If these are different states, the corporation is a citizen of both states.

Answers (a) and (b) are incorrect because the corporation is a citizen of both states. Answer (d) is incorrect because the corporation cannot be a citizen of more than two states.

38. Business activity in interstate commerce often presents the question of when a corporation will be subject to suit in a state court. The in personam jurisdiction of a state court will extend to a corporation only when

a. The corporation maintains an office or registered agent within the state.

b. The corporation is incorporated in the state.

c. The corporation has sufficient minimum contacts with the state that suits would not be unfair to the defendant.

d. The corporation is subject to taxation by the state.

The correct answer is (c). *(Publisher)*

REQUIRED: When a corporation may be sued in a court of a given state.

DISCUSSION: The U.S. Supreme Court has held that due process is not violated when a corporation is compelled to be a defendant in a state court if the corporation has sufficient minimum contacts with that state that it would not be unfair for the courts of that state to exercise power over it. How extensive the contacts must be for the state court to exercise its jurisdiction depends on the facts of the case. The court would consider the number and extent of contacts and whether the action arose out of those contacts.

Answer (a) is incorrect because although maintaining an office or an agent within the state would result in personal jurisdiction, lesser contacts could be sufficient, e.g., committing a tortious act within the state. Answer (b) is incorrect because although incorporation in the state would permit a corporation to be sued there, it is not necessary for a finding of jurisdiction. Answer (d) is incorrect because while a corporation that is subject to taxation in a state is usually subject to that state's jurisdiction, many corporations not subject to such taxation would still be subject to its personal jurisdiction.

39. The Foreign Corrupt Practices Act of 1977 has enormous significance for U.S. corporations doing business abroad. The Act

a. Only applies to bribery of foreign officials.

b. Imposes heavy civil but not criminal sanctions upon violators.

c. Does not apply to U.S. firms doing business solely in the United States if they are subject to the Securities Exchange Act of 1934.

d. Applies to all U.S. firms.

The correct answer is (d). *(Publisher)*

REQUIRED: The correct statement concerning the Foreign Corrupt Practices Act of 1977.

DISCUSSION: The Foreign Corrupt Practices Act of 1977 attempted to put an end to bribery of foreign officials by U.S. corporations and their subsidiaries. It also imposes stringent accounting requirements on firms subject to the Securities Exchange Act of 1934 to promote accountability for assets. The bribery provisions of the Act apply to all U.S. firms.

Answer (a) is incorrect because in addition to prohibiting bribery of foreign officials, the Act requires an adequate system of internal control to maintain accountability for assets. Answer (b) is incorrect because violators may be liable for criminal penalties of up to $10,000 in fines and five years in prison. Answer (c) is incorrect because the accounting provisions of the Act apply to all U.S. firms subject to the 1934 SEC Act.

16.4 Directors and Officers

40. In general, corporate officers

a. Are elected directly by the shareholders.

b. May not hold more than one office.

c. Cannot be removed before their terms expire except for cause.

d. Manage the corporation.

The correct answer is (d). *(Publisher)*

REQUIRED: The true statement about corporate officers.

DISCUSSION: Directors are elected by the corporate shareholders. They establish policy but elect officers to manage the corporation. The bylaws generally determine what duties the officers will perform.

Answer (a) is incorrect because officers are elected by the directors. Answer (b) is incorrect because the MBCA requires corporations to have a president, at least one vice-president, a secretary, and a treasurer. Two or more offices may be held by the same person except those of president and secretary. The RMBCA is silent on this issue except to state that a corporation has only those officers described by the bylaws and appointed by the board in accordance therewith. Answer (c) is incorrect because the board may remove an officer at any time without cause.

41. Generally, officers of a corporation

a. Are elected by the shareholders.

b. Are agents and fiduciaries of the corporation, having actual and apparent authority to manage the business.

c. May be removed by the board of directors without cause only if the removal is approved by a majority vote of the shareholders.

d. May declare dividends or other distributions to shareholders as they deem appropriate.

The correct answer is (b). *(CPA 585 L-14)*

REQUIRED: The true statement about corporate officers.

DISCUSSION: Officers are agents of a corporate principal, and agency law prescribes their real and apparent authority to bind the corporation. The bylaws and board resolutions may specifically limit that authority, but the usual duties of an officer operate to define the officer's capacity to enter agreements enforceable against the corporation. Any principal, including a corporation, may be estopped from asserting a lack of actual authority on the part of its officers and other employees. Officers are also fiduciaries. Like directors, they owe a duty of loyalty, good faith, and fair dealing when transacting business with or on behalf of the corporation.

Answer (a) is incorrect because officers are elected by the directors. Answer (c) is incorrect because officers are removable at any time without cause by the board of directors. Answer (d) is incorrect because the directors declare dividends.

42. Fairwell is executive vice-president and treasurer of Wonder Corporation. He was named as a party in a shareholder derivative action in connection with certain activities he engaged in as a corporate officer. In the lawsuit, it was determined that he was liable for negligence in performance of his duties. Fairwell seeks indemnity from the corporation for his liability. The board of directors would like to indemnify him. The articles of incorporation do not contain any provisions regarding indemnification of officers and directors. Indemnification

a. Is not permitted since the articles of incorporation do not so provide.

b. Is permitted only if he is found not to have been grossly negligent.

c. Cannot include attorney's fees since he was found to have been negligent.

d. May be permitted by court order despite the fact that Fairwell was found to be negligent.

The correct answer is (d). *(CPA 582 L-10)*

REQUIRED: Whether a negligent officer of a corporation may be indemnified for his/her liability.

DISCUSSION: Usually an officer found negligent in the performance of his/her duties is not entitled to indemnification. However, a court may order indemnification of an officer of a corporation (even though found negligent) if the court determines (s)he is reasonably entitled to it under the circumstances. There is no set rule as to when this may occur.

Answer (a) is incorrect because indemnification is permitted unless the articles expressly prohibit it. Answer (b) is incorrect because a court may order indemnification if it determines that the officer is reasonably entitled to it in view of all the relevant circumstances, even if the officer was negligent. Answer (c) is incorrect because if an officer is entitled to indemnification, it may include attorney's fees.

43. At their annual meeting, shareholders of the Bones Corp. approved several proposals made by the board of directors. Among them was the ratification of the salaries of the executives of the corporation. In this connection, which of the following is correct?

a. The salaries ratified are automatically valid for federal income tax purposes.

b. Such ratification by the shareholders is required as a matter of law.

c. The action by the shareholders serves the purpose of confirming the board's action.

d. The shareholders cannot legally ratify the compensation paid to director-officers.

The correct answer is (c). *(CPA 1183 L-19)*

REQUIRED: The true statement about shareholder ratification of officers' salaries.

DISCUSSION: Under the RMBCA, all corporate powers are exercised by or under the authority of the board of directors. Unless the articles provide otherwise, the directors are thus responsible for setting the compensation of officers and shareholder approval is not necessary.

Answer (a) is incorrect because the IRS is not bound by the action of the directors and may decide the salaries are excessive and not deductible for federal income tax purposes. Answer (b) is incorrect because the typical corporation statute does not require shareholder action on this matter. Answer (d) is incorrect because the articles of incorporation or bylaws may require shareholder ratification.

44. Mark Corporation is a moderate-sized closely held corporation which is 80% owned by Joseph Mark. The remaining 20% of stock is owned by Mark's wife, sons, daughter, and parents. One son, David Mark, who recently graduated from business school, has been hired by the corporation as financial vice-president at a salary of $60,000 per year. Other members of the family are either officers or directors of the corporation and are all generously compensated. Joseph Mark is paid $300,000 as chairman of the board and chief executive officer. The corporation is profitable, solvent, and meeting all claims as they become due. Who of the following would have standing to attack the reasonableness of the salary payments?

a. The creditors of the corporation.

b. The attorney general of the state in which Mark is incorporated.

c. The Internal Revenue Service.

d. The Securities and Exchange Commission.

The correct answer is (c). *(CPA 580 L-7)*

REQUIRED: Who has standing to attack reasonableness of salary payments to the officers and directors of a closely held corporation.

DISCUSSION: If the compensation paid to a director or officer (who is also a shareholder or is related to one) is disproportionate to the fair value of the services rendered, the IRS may attack the compensation as constituting a disguised dividend. The effect would be to prevent the corporation from claiming the excess payment as a deduction for compensation expense on the corporate tax return.

Answer (a) is incorrect because the creditors have no standing to attack the reasonableness of compensation as long as the corporation is solvent. Answers (b) and (d) are incorrect because such parties have no standing to attack the reasonableness of compensation unless criminal or fraudulent conduct is involved.

45. Which of the following is a true statement about the directors of a corporation?

a. The MBCA permits a corporation to have only one director.

b. Directors may serve only from one annual meeting to the next.

c. Directors may only be elected by the shareholders.

d. The number of directors may not exceed the number of shareholders.

The correct answer is (a). *(Publisher)*

REQUIRED: The true statement about corporate directors.

DISCUSSION: Because of an awareness of the needs of close corporations, the RMBCA permits only one director. Some states require a minimum of three directors but permit the number of directors to equal the number of shareholders if less than three. Other states still require at least three directors.

Answer (b) is incorrect because a director usually serves for one year, but staggered, multiyear terms are also allowed. Answer (c) is incorrect because the remaining directors may fill vacancies resulting from the death, removal, or resignation of directors until the next shareholders' meeting. They may also be empowered to fill vacancies created when new positions are created through amendment of the bylaws or articles. Answer (d) is incorrect because no such requirement exists.

46. A director of a corporation

a. Must usually be a resident of the state of incorporation.

b. Is often removable for cause by the other directors.

c. Must generally be a shareholder.

d. Must usually be at least 21 years old.

The correct answer is (b). *(Publisher)*

REQUIRED: The true statement about a corporate director.

DISCUSSION: The RMBCA allows the shareholders to remove a director with or without cause at a meeting called for that purpose, and the board itself is permitted in many states to remove a director for cause, e.g., insanity or conviction of a felony. Such action is subject to shareholder review.

Answers (a) and (d) are incorrect because age and residency requirements are imposed by statute in only a few states. Answer (c) is incorrect because while directors may be shareholders, they generally are not required to be.

47. A director of a corporation is best characterized as

a. An agent.

b. A trustee.

c. A fiduciary.

d. A principal.

The correct answer is (c). *(Publisher)*

REQUIRED: The best characterization of a corporate director.

DISCUSSION: Officers and employees as well as directors are fiduciaries with regard to the corporation. They owe a duty of loyalty, good faith, and fair dealing when transacting business with or on behalf of the company. This duty requires full disclosure of any personal interest in transactions with the corporation, avoidance of conflicts of interest and the making of secret profits, and placing the corporate interest ahead of personal gain.

Answer (a) is incorrect because a director is not an agent since (s)he cannot act alone to bind the corporation. As a group, directors control the corporation in a manner that agents could not. Answer (b) is incorrect because a trustee holds legal title to property used for the benefit of others. Answer (d) is incorrect because the corporation itself is the principal.

48. Delegation of the powers of the board of directors is generally

a. Prohibited.

b. Allowed with regard to any matter upon which the board may act.

c. Prohibited except when required by an outside agency, for example, a stock exchange that requires members to have audit committees.

d. Allowed except with regard to specified important transactions.

The correct answer is (d). *(Publisher)*

REQUIRED: The true statement about delegation of directors' authority.

DISCUSSION: If the articles or bylaws permit, the directors may by majority vote of the full board delegate authority to specified directors constituting an executive or other committee. Such a committee may exercise all the powers of the board except with regard to significant or extraordinary transactions such as declaring dividends, issuing stock, or amending bylaws. The committee must consist only of directors.

Answer (a) is incorrect because executive, audit, finance, and other committees are normally allowed. Answer (b) is incorrect because certain powers may not be delegated. Answer (c) is incorrect because board committees are established but not solely to meet external requirements such as the New York Stock Exchange's rule requiring members to establish audit committees of outside directors.

49. Iago and Desdemona are the sole directors, officers, and shareholders of the ID Corporation, a theatrical group incorporated in Florida. They regularly hold board meetings outside of Florida or by long distance telephone calls. Recently, without a meeting, Desdemona increased compensation of the directors and declared the regular dividend. Iago later filed in the minutes a signed, written consent to the actions taken. The articles and bylaws are silent on these matters.

a. Board meetings must be held in the state of incorporation or where the corporation has its principal business and must be conducted in person.

b. The board may declare dividends but may not fix its own compensation.

c. ID is in violation of the Model Business Corporation Act because it has fewer than three directors.

d. Unanimous written consent of all directors may substitute for a meeting.

The correct answer is (d). *(Publisher)*

REQUIRED: The correct statement concerning the formalities required of a close corporation.

DISCUSSION: Traditionally, the board of directors could act only after a formal meeting at which a quorum was present. Under modern statutes, unanimous written consent filed in the minutes is a sufficient basis for action by the board.

Answer (a) is incorrect because board meetings may be conducted anywhere and are not required to be in person; e.g., the meetings may be held by conference telephone call. Answer (b) is incorrect because the board of directors may routinely declare dividends and may also fix its own compensation unless the articles provide otherwise. Answer (c) is incorrect because the MBCA provides for as few as one director on the board. Some modern statutes (and the RMBCA) allow the board to be dispensed with entirely.

50. Derek Corporation decided to acquire certain assets belonging to the Mongol Corporation. As consideration for the assets acquired, Derek issued 20,000 shares of its no-par common stock with a stated value of $10 per share. The value of the assets acquired subsequently turned out to be much less than the $200,000 in stock issued. Under the circumstances, which of the following is correct?

a. It is improper for the board of directors to acquire assets other than cash with no-par stock.

b. Only the shareholders can have the right to fix the value of the shares of no-par stock exchanged for assets.

c. In the absence of fraud in the transaction, the judgment of the board of directors as to the value of the consideration received for the shares shall be conclusive.

d. Unless the board obtained an independent appraisal of the acquired assets' value, it is liable to the extent of the overvaluation.

The correct answer is (c). *(CPA 1178 L-19)*

REQUIRED: The correct statement regarding the issuance of stock for property when the property has a value significantly less than the stated value of the stock issued.

DISCUSSION: The board of directors has the authority to issue stock of the corporation. In the absence of fraud, the judgment of the board of directors is conclusive in determining the value of the consideration received for the issuance of stock.

Answer (a) is incorrect because assets other than cash can be acquired with no-par stock. Answer (b) is incorrect because it is within the authority of the board of directors to fix the value of no-par stock (as well as of par stock). Answer (d) is incorrect because an independent appraisal is not required, but it may be a factor in determining whether the directors exercised reasonable business judgment.

51. Shares of stock without par value may be issued for such consideration (in dollars) as may be fixed by a corporation's

a. Creditors.

b. Officers.

c. Board of directors.

d. Minority shareholders.

The correct answer is (c). *(CPA 576 L-18)*

REQUIRED: Who may fix consideration for issuance of no-par stock.

DISCUSSION: The board of directors has authority to fix the amount of consideration to be received for the issuance of no-par stock, as well as all other stock. The board is obligated to exercise reasonable business judgment.

Answers (a), (b), and (d) are incorrect because only the board of directors has this power. Creditors have no management rights, officers only manage day-to-day business, and minority shareholders only vote to elect directors, approve fundamental corporate changes, etc.

52. Seymore was recently invited to become a director of Buckley Industries, Inc. If Seymore accepts and becomes a director, he along with the other directors will not be personally liable for

a. Lack of reasonable care.

b. Honest errors of judgment.

c. Declaration of a dividend which the directors know will impair legal capital.

d. Diversion of corporate opportunities to themselves.

The correct answer is (b). *(CPA 1173 L-20)*

REQUIRED: The situation in which a director will not be held personally liable.

DISCUSSION: The directors of a corporation owe a fiduciary duty to the corporation and the shareholders. They are also expected to exercise reasonable business judgment. The law does recognize human fallibility and allows for directors to be safe from liability for honest mistakes of judgment.

Answer (a) is incorrect because directors are personally liable for failure to exercise reasonable care. Answer (c) is incorrect because directors are prohibited from declaring dividends which would impair legal capital. Answer (d) is incorrect because a director may not exploit opportunities presented to him/her in his/her capacity as a director for his/her own benefit without first offering them to the corporation.

53. After proper incorporation of Bryan, it was decided to purchase a plant site. Shephard, a newly elected director, has owned a desirable site for many years. He purchased the property for $60,000, and its present fair value is $100,000. What would be the result if Shephard offered the property to Bryan for $100,000 in an arm's-length transaction with full disclosure at a meeting of the seven directors of the corporation?

a. The sale would be proper only upon requisite approval by the appropriate number of directors and at no more than Shephard's cost, thus precluding his profiting from the sale to the corporation.

b. The sale would be void under the self-dealing rule.

c. The sale would be proper and Shephard would not have to account to the corporation for his profit if the sale was approved by a disinterested majority of the directors.

d. The sale would not be proper, if sold for the present fair value of the property, without the approval of all of the directors in these circumstances.

The correct answer is (c). *(CPA 574 L-41)*

REQUIRED: The result if a director makes full disclosure and sells property to his/her corporation at a profit.

DISCUSSION: The fiduciary duty of directors to the corporation does not prohibit them from dealing with the corporation. The view has been that the director must disclose the conflict and refrain from voting. Under the RMBCA, if the contract is fair and reasonable to the corporation, self-dealing contracts between directors and corporations are not voidable even if the interested director is counted for the quorum and votes for the contract. If the interested director discloses the interest, refrains from voting, and leaves the decision to a disinterested majority, there is no secret profit and no breach of fiduciary duty.

Answer (a) is incorrect because a director may profit on transactions with his/her corporation as long as there is full disclosure and approval by sufficient disinterested directors. Answer (b) is incorrect because a director is not considered to be self-dealing when the transaction is conducted openly and approved by a majority of the disinterested directors. Answer (d) is incorrect because only a majority of the directors, not unanimity, is required.

54. Laser Corporation lent $5,000 to Mr. Jackson, a member of its board of directors. Mr. Jackson was also vice-president of operations. The board of directors, but not the stockholders, of Laser authorized the loan on the basis that the loan would benefit the corporation. The loan made to Mr. Jackson is

a. Improper because Mr. Jackson is both a director and an employee.

b. Improper because Mr. Jackson is an employee.

c. Improper because Mr. Jackson is a director.

d. Proper.

The correct answer is (d). *(CPA 1175 L-31)*

REQUIRED: The propriety of a loan made by a corporation to a director-officer.

DISCUSSION: Approval of a loan to a fellow director is not a per se violation of the director's fiduciary obligation to the corporation. Subject to that obligation and the duty to act with reasonable care, the board of directors may approve a loan which in their judgment would benefit the corporation. It would be inappropriate for Jackson to vote on the loan resolution, but his vote would not necessarily make it voidable. The stockholders need not authorize the loan.

Answers (a), (b), and (c) are incorrect because a loan is not prohibited solely because it is made to an employee, a director, or both.

55. A corporate director commits a breach of duty if

a. The director's exercise of care and skill is minimal.

b. A contract is awarded by the company to an organization owned by the director.

c. An interest in property is acquired by the director without prior approval of the board.

d. The director's action, prompted by confidential information, results in an abuse of corporate opportunity.

The correct answer is (d). *(CIA 580 IV-21)*

REQUIRED: When a corporate director commits a breach of duty.

DISCUSSION: Corporate directors are under a fiduciary duty to provide the corporation with business opportunities which come to them in their positions as directors of the corporation. A director who personally takes such a business opportunity has breached his/her duty.

Answer (a) is incorrect because a director is under a duty to use good business judgment, but is not responsible for the highest standard of care and skill. Answer (b) is incorrect because a director is not prohibited from entering into transactions with the corporation as long as full disclosure is made to the board. Answer (c) is incorrect because a director is under no duty to report personal property investments unless they relate to corporate business.

16.5 Stockholders

56. Portavoy and Bredstock are the major shareholders of and active participants in the management of Port-a-Stock Corporation. Mann is an investor who owns 10% of the shares but is otherwise uninvolved. Kalik is a promoter and 5% shareholder who has no voice in management. Unfortunately, Port-a-Stock was defectively formed and does not even qualify as a de facto corporation. The majority of states would impose personal liability

a. On all the shareholders.

b. Only on Portavoy, Bredstock, and Kalik.

c. On no one.

d. Only on those active in management.

The correct answer is (a). *(Publisher)*

REQUIRED: The liability of shareholders of a defectively formed corporation.

DISCUSSION: Because the corporation lacks even de facto status, many state statutes still adhere to an earlier MBCA position: "All persons who assume to act as a corporation without authority so to do shall be jointly and severally liable for all debts and liabilities incurred or arising as a result thereof." The liability is that imposed on the partners of a general partnership. No distinction is made between the active and inactive participants. The new RMBCA imposes liability on "all persons purporting to act as or on behalf of a corporation, knowing that there was no incorporation under this Act." The RMBCA, which does not yet state the majority view on this issue, thus excuses inactive parties and those not knowing of the defective incorporation.

Answers (b) and (d) are incorrect because the minority of courts would impose joint and several liability only on those active in the promotion or operation of the entity. Answer (c) is incorrect because most states impose liability in these cases even on innocent shareholders.

57. Limited liability of shareholders is one of the advantages of incorporation. Generally, a shareholder is personally liable

a. For torts of the corporation although (s)he did not participate in them.

b. For crimes of the corporation although (s)he did not participate in them.

c. Only for his/her investment in the corporation.

d. For the corporation's debts.

The correct answer is (c). *(Publisher)*

REQUIRED: The true statement about personal liability of a shareholder.

DISCUSSION: One of the principal advantages of incorporation is limited liability. If the corporation is properly formed and operated as an entity distinct from its owners, the shareholders will ordinarily have no personal liability beyond the amount of their investment. The corporation is a separate legal person capable of being held liable for its independent actions.

Answers (a) and (b) are incorrect because a corporation can be held liable for torts and crimes, but a shareholder who did not participate in the wrongful conduct or to whom the actions are not otherwise attributable is insulated from liability. Answer (d) is incorrect because shareholders are not answerable for corporate debts or vice versa.

58. An officer shareholder of a corporation could be held personally liable for which one of the following debts?

a. Unpaid U.S. corporate income taxes.

b. A bank note signed by a shareholder in his/her capacity as president of the corporation.

c. Federal payroll taxes that were withheld from the employees' wages but never remitted to the IRS.

d. A judgment against the corporation stemming from a tort committed by a former employee.

The correct answer is (c). *(P. Karl III)*

REQUIRED: The debts for which an officer shareholder can be held personally liable.

DISCUSSION: An employer is required to withhold from an employee's salary income taxes and Social Security taxes (FICA). If an officer shareholder is deemed to be a "responsible party" by the IRS, (s)he can be held personally liable for these taxes since they are considered to be held "in trust" for the benefit of the employee until remitted to the IRS.

Answer (a) is incorrect because personal liability is not extended to unpaid U.S. corporate income taxes. Answer (b) is incorrect provided that the officer shareholder was not required to also sign personally on the bank note. It should be noted that in closely held corporations, two signatures are often required: once as an agent for the corporation and the other in an individual capacity. Answer (d) is incorrect because the corporation insulates owners from the liability emanating from the torts of their employees.

59. The most accurate statement about managerial control of traditional corporations is that shareholders

a. Are similar to general partners in that they have direct managerial authority.

b. Of large corporations have no legal power to exercise any effective control over management.

c. Can exert control over the corporation only by choosing directors.

d. Have little management control of a corporation.

The correct answer is (d). *(Publisher)*

REQUIRED: The most accurate statement about shareholder control over corporate management.

DISCUSSION: In principle, the board of directors is responsible for conducting the corporate business. The directors make decisions about policy and certain major transactions but delegate day-to-day operational control to officers and other employees. The directors are chosen by and are accountable to the shareholders, who thus exert only indirect control over the corporation. However, the reality in most publicly held companies is that management uses the proxy solicitation process to nominate and secure the election of directors favorable to its policies. Hence, management is usually in effective control of the company.

Answer (a) is incorrect because general partners operate the business while shareholders who are not directors or officers have only an indirect effect on management of the enterprise. Answers (b) and (c) are incorrect because shareholders have the right to exercise indirect control by electing or removing directors; by adoption, amendment, or repeal of bylaws; by amending the corporate charter; or by effecting other fundamental changes. By these means, shareholders can effectively override the actions of the directors or managers of the entity.

60. Donald Walker is a dissident stockholder of the Meaker Corporation which is listed on a national stock exchange. Walker is seeking to oust the existing board of directors and has notified the directors that he intends to sue them for negligence. Under the circumstances, Walker

a. Can be validly denied access to the corporate financial records.

b. Can be legally prohibited from obtaining a copy of the stockholder list because his purpose is not bona fide.

c. Must show personal gain on the part of the directors if he is to win his lawsuit.

d. Can insist that the corporation mail out his proxy materials as long as he pays the cost.

The correct answer is (d). *(CPA 1174 L-36)*

REQUIRED: The correct statement regarding the activities of a dissident stockholder seeking to oust the existing board.

DISCUSSION: Under federal securities law, a dissident stockholder may require the corporation to furnish a list of the stockholders and mail out proxy materials to those stockholders, as long as the dissident stockholder pays the cost of the mailing.

Answer (a) is incorrect because a stockholder has the right to inspect corporate records if the purpose is valid and reasonable time and place requirements are met. Answer (b) is incorrect because it is valid to seek to obtain a stockholder list for purposes of contesting control of the corporation. Answer (c) is incorrect because a stockholder suing the board of directors for negligence need not show that they personally benefited from the contested actions.

61. Which of the following is the most accurate listing of the sources of shareholder rights?

a. The articles of incorporation, state and federal statutes, and the common law.

b. The articles of incorporation and statutory law only.

c. State and federal statutes and the common law only.

d. The articles of incorporation and state law only.

The correct answer is (a). *(Publisher)*

REQUIRED: The most accurate list of the sources of shareholder rights and duties.

DISCUSSION: Corporations are created through the authority of state statutes. Unlike partnerships, they have no common law basis for existence. Accordingly, the incorporation statute of a state is one source for shareholder rights. However, some shareholder rights have common law origins, for example, the power to remove directors for cause, the right to inspect corporate records, and the preemptive right. The articles of a corporation may also enumerate specific shareholder rights not detailed in the general language of a statute. Federal law is still another source of shareholder rights, for instance, regulation of the issuance and subsequent trading of securities.

62. A shareholder of a corporation

a. Has no right to a stock certificate because ownership rights are intangible.

b. Generally has a preemptive right to the extent permitted by the articles.

c. Has an absolute right to dividends in any year when the corporation is profitable.

d. Has no right to have his/her name recorded in the corporation's stock record book.

The correct answer is (b). *(Publisher)*

REQUIRED: The true statement about the specific rights of a shareholder.

DISCUSSION: A preemptive right gives a shareholder an opportunity to purchase a proportionate share of a new stock issue so that his/her percentage interest in the entity can be maintained. Some statutes grant the preemptive right but allow it to be denied in the articles, while other statutes deny the right but allow it to be granted in the articles. The articles are therefore generally determinative. The right does not apply to the reissuance of treasury shares and is only exercisable for a specified time.

Answer (a) is incorrect because shareholders generally have the right to evidence of their ownership. However, the advent of computers and their use in recording stock transactions is responsible for a trend toward uncertificated shares. Answer (c) is incorrect because the directors have broad discretion to withhold declaration of dividends even if ample funds are available. Answer (d) is incorrect because recordation of stockholders' names in the corporate books is the basis for voting rights, notice of meetings, payment of dividends, and distribution of reports.

63. A shareholder of a corporation has

a. The right to inspect the corporate records for any purpose.

b. The right to vote for directors but not on corporate transactions, including extraordinary ones.

c. An absolute right to transfer his/her shares.

d. The right to a pro rata distribution of assets upon dissolution.

The correct answer is (d). *(Publisher)*

REQUIRED: The true statement about the specific rights of a shareholder.

DISCUSSION: After payment of creditors' claims, the assets of a dissolving corporation are generally distributed to the shareholders in proportion to their percentage ownership. Preferred shareholders, however, may be granted a preference in dissolution based upon their contract with the corporation.

Answer (a) is incorrect because upon 5 business days' written notice, the RMBCA provides an absolute right of inspection of some records (e.g., the articles and bylaws), but the right is conditional with regard to certain other matters, such as accounting records and minutes of various meetings. The conditions are good faith, a proper purpose, a description of such purpose and the desired records with reasonable particularity, and a direct connection of the records to the purpose. Answer (b) is incorrect because shareholders may vote on certain major transactions, such as voluntary dissolutions, mergers and consolidations, and disposal of substantially all assets other than in the regular course of business. Answer (c) is incorrect because especially in close corporations, transferability of stock may be limited by contract, the bylaws, or otherwise.

64. A shareholder of a professional corporation has committed malpractice. Which of the following is the rule least likely to be adopted by a state regarding personal liability?

a. Only the corporation will be liable.

b. Only the corporation and the wrongdoer are liable.

c. All the shareholders are liable as if they were partners.

d. The other shareholders are liable but only in the amount of the required insurance.

The correct answer is (a). *(Publisher)*

REQUIRED: The least likely rule of liability applied to professional corporation shareholders.

DISCUSSION: Incorporation does not limit the liability that a professional would otherwise have incurred for malpractice as a sole practitioner. Whether the professional-shareholder-employee is protected from personal liability for the malpractice of others in which (s)he did not participate is an issue yet to be clarified. The shareholder will usually not be personally liable for the torts of others that are not related to malpractice.

Answers (b), (c), and (d) are incorrect because each is a possibility.

65. Bassel Hardheart is the majority shareholder and chairman of the board of Close Corporation. Carter and Kelly are respectively a minority common shareholder and a holder of nonvoting preferred stock. Bassel has diverted corporate assets to personal use. Bassel has also caused the board to declare and pay common stock dividends without paying preferred dividends. Under these circumstances,

a. Carter may bring a representative action against Close Corporation based on Hardheart's diversion of assets.

b. Kelly may bring a representative action against Close Corporation based on Hardheart's diversion of assets.

c. Carter may bring a derivative action against the corporation for withholding the preferred dividends.

d. Kelly may bring a representative action against the corporation for withholding the preferred dividends.

The correct answer is (d). *(Publisher)*

REQUIRED: The appropriate legal action given certain causes of action.

DISCUSSION: Both representative and derivative suits are shareholder suits in which the plaintiff represents a class of (or all) stockholders. The representative suit is brought directly against the corporation for a wrong done by the corporation itself. The derivative action is brought on behalf of the corporation for a wrong done to the corporation. The withholding of the preferred dividends would give rise to a right of action by the preferred shareholders against the corporation. Therefore, Kelly could bring a representative action as a preferred shareholder.

Answers (a) and (b) are incorrect because the diversion of corporate assets by Hardheart would be the basis for a derivative suit (by either Carter or Kelly) against Hardheart, not against the corporation. Answer (c) is incorrect because the suit for withholding the preferred dividend would be a representative suit, and could not be brought by Carter since she is not a preferred shareholder.

66. Which of the following would be a true statement in most jurisdictions regarding a stockholder derivative suit?

a. The directors have no right to ask the court to dismiss the action.

b. The plaintiff must usually have been a stockholder when the transaction complained of occurred.

c. Any out-of-court settlement need not be approved by the court.

d. Any recovery will belong to the plaintiff.

The correct answer is (b). *(Publisher)*

REQUIRED: The true statement about a derivative suit.

DISCUSSION: A derivative suit is brought on behalf of the corporation by one or more stockholders when the directors have failed to initiate an action to redress a wrong done to the corporation. The plaintiff is required to have owned his/her shares when the transaction complained of occurred, to show that (s)he demanded that the directors take action, that they did not, and that such inaction was in bad faith (the last three steps may be waived if the plaintiffs prove they would have been futile).

Answer (a) is incorrect because the directors may have a right to have a derivative action dismissed if their action was within the business judgment rule. Answer (c) is incorrect because generally settlements must be court-approved, and all shareholders must be notified. Answer (d) is incorrect because the recovery belongs to the corporation.

67. The board of directors of the Garrett Co. wishes to call a special meeting of shareholders to consider a proposed merger.

a. The shareholders must be given specific notice of the meeting and the issues on the agenda.

b. At least one week's notice must be given.

c. If notice is not given to shareholders entitled to vote at the record date, action taken at the meeting will be invalid even if all the shareholders attend and participate in the meeting.

d. A majority of shareholders entitled to vote must be represented in person at the meeting to constitute a quorum, unless otherwise provided in the articles.

The correct answer is (a). *(Publisher)*

REQUIRED: The legal requirements for special shareholders' meetings.

DISCUSSION: Notice is not usually required for regular meetings since the time and place of such meetings are normally specified in the bylaws. The ordinary business of the corporation may be transacted at regular meetings without specific notice being given to shareholders. Special meetings, on the other hand, must be the subject of a timely notice specifying the time, place, and issues on the agenda.

Answer (b) is incorrect because under the MBCA at least 10 days' notice must be given. Answer (c) is incorrect because while notice must usually be given to shareholders, attendance and participation in the meeting by shareholders who did not receive notice will constitute a waiver of the right to notice. Answer (d) is incorrect because a majority of the shares entitled to vote must be represented to constitute a quorum, but they may be represented in person or by proxy.

68. Shareholder meetings must be held annually but special meetings may also be convened. If a quorum is present at a meeting, the shareholders may act by voting to approve or disapprove resolutions. Which of the following is a true statement about this process?

a. Shareholders cannot act without a meeting.

b. Notice of meetings must be given and a waiver of the requirement can only be by a signed writing.

c. Certain shareholder actions may require more than a simple majority.

d. All holders of voting shares at the date of the meeting are entitled to vote.

The correct answer is (c). *(Publisher)*

REQUIRED: The true statement about shareholder action at meetings.

DISCUSSION: If a quorum is present (under the RMBCA, 50% of the outstanding shares must be represented in person or by proxy), resolutions may generally be adopted by a simple majority of the voting shares. For the protection of minority shareholders, however, the bylaws, articles, or a statute may require more than a simple majority when action is taken with regard to extraordinary matters.

Answer (a) is incorrect because most states allow shareholders to act without a meeting if unanimous written consent is given. Answer (b) is incorrect because attendance at the meeting is also an effective waiver. Answer (d) is incorrect because only those owning stock at the record date may vote. The record date is a date prior to the meeting used to determine those eligible to vote.

69. Shareholder voting

a. Is required to be cumulative in most states.

b. May usually be accomplished by oral or written proxy.

c. May usually be by proxy, but the agency thus created is generally limited to a specific issue.

d. May be by proxy, but a proxy may be revoked if the shareholder signs a later proxy.

The correct answer is (d). *(Publisher)*

REQUIRED: The true statement about shareholder voting.

DISCUSSION: A proxy is a written authorization to vote another person's shares. Voting by proxy may be a practical necessity when shares of a corporation are held by many thousands of persons. In these circumstances, successful solicitation of proxies determines control of the enterprise. The rule that the last proxy signed by a shareholder revokes prior proxies is a significant issue in proxy battles. A proxy is also revoked when the shareholder actually attends the meeting and votes his/her shares or when (s)he dies.

Answer (a) is incorrect because cumulative voting is allowed but not required in most states. This method of voting facilitates minority representation on the board by permitting a shareholder to cast all of his/her votes for one candidate. For example, if three directors are to be elected and a shareholder has 40 of the 100 outstanding shares, (s)he has 120 votes, which can all be cast for one director. Answer (b) is incorrect because a proxy must usually be written. Answer (c) is incorrect because proxies commonly authorize action regarding all matters presented at the shareholders' meeting.

70. Shareholders representing a majority of the voting shares of Nadier, Inc. have transferred their shares to Thomasina Trusty to hold and vote irrevocably for ten years. Trusty has issued certificates to the shareholders and pays over to them the dividends received.

a. The agreement is an illegal voting trust, and is void because it is against public policy.

b. The arrangement is valid if entered into pursuant to a written voting trust agreement.

c. The agreement need not be filed with the corporation.

d. The agreement may be revoked because it is in essence a proxy.

The correct answer is (b). *(Publisher)*

REQUIRED: The legal status of a voting trust agreement.

DISCUSSION: The RMBCA provides that irrevocable voting trust agreements authorizing a trustee to hold and vote shares for up to 10 years are valid if written and filed with the corporation where they are available for inspection by shareholders.

Answer (a) is incorrect because the voting trust is a legal arrangement which has a statutory or case law basis in most states. Answer (c) is incorrect because one of the statutory requirements for a valid voting trust is that the agreement be filed with the corporation and be available for inspection. Answer (d) is incorrect because the voting trust differs substantially from a proxy since it is irrevocable for the agreed period.

71. Ambrose purchased 400 shares of $100 par value original issue common stock from Minor Corporation for $25 a share. Ambrose subsequently sold 200 of the shares to Harris at $25 a share. Harris did not have knowledge or notice that Ambrose had not paid par. Ambrose also sold 100 shares of this stock to Gable for $25 a share. At the time of this sale, Gable knew that Ambrose had not paid par for the stock. Minor Corporation became insolvent and the creditors sought to hold all the above parties liable for the $75 unpaid on each of the 400 shares. Under traditional view,

a. The creditors can hold Ambrose liable for $30,000.

b. If $25 a share was a fair value for the stock at the time of issuance, Ambrose will have no liability to the creditors.

c. Since Harris acquired the shares by purchase, he is not liable to the creditors, and his lack of knowledge or notice that Ambrose paid less than par is immaterial.

d. Since Gable acquired the shares by purchase, he is not liable to the creditors, and his knowledge that Ambrose paid less than par is immaterial.

The correct answer is (a). *(CPA 1183 L-24)*

REQUIRED: The legal effect of purchasing and later selling stock at less than par.

DISCUSSION: The traditional rule is that the purchaser of "discount" stock for cash (less than the par value) is liable for the difference between the amount paid and par. Under a statute following this rule, Ambrose would be liable to the corporation and thus the creditors for $30,000 [400 shares x ($100 par - $25 paid)].

Answer (b) is incorrect because it reflects the newer RMBCA rule. The RMBCA recommends eliminating the concepts of par and stated value and makes the good faith judgment of the directors conclusive as to the consideration to be paid for shares. Answers (c) and (d) are incorrect because under the old rule, a subsequent purchaser was liable only if (s)he knew that the seller had been issued the shares for less than the par or stated value.

72. Pursuant to a pre-incorporation agreement, Canyon Company, in good faith and in reliance on certain false representations, originally issued stock with a value of $70,000 to Scratch for a parcel of realty. Subsequently, the directors inquired about the value of the land. A broker estimated that it was worth $20,000. Canyon then gave notice of rescission of the stock transfer and offered to reissue $20,000 of stock or whatever a court deemed to be the true value. At trial, the court ordered the return of the $70,000 worth of stock and the issuance of $10,000 worth of stock because, unknown to Canyon, Scratch had recently paid only $10,000 for the land. On appeal, a court will most likely find that Scratch is entitled to

a. $10,000 worth of stock.

b. $20,000 worth of stock.

c. $70,000 worth of stock.

d. $0.

The correct answer is (a). *(Publisher)*

REQUIRED: The proper valuation of consideration given for stock.

DISCUSSION: The stock originally issued to Canyon was clearly watered. The true value of the property received for it was substantially less than the issuance price. The difference is commonly known as "water." The shareholder is ordinarily held liable for this difference, but the corporation may choose to rescind the transaction. However, the RMBCA states, "In the absence of fraud in the transaction, the judgment of the board as to the value of the consideration received for shares shall be conclusive."

Scratch could argue that the board's good faith resolution offering $20,000 worth of stock was a conclusive valuation. The refutation of that argument is that the board only relied on an estimate and was as yet unaware of the full extent of the fraud when its $20,000 offer was made. Since Canyon chose to rescind but made an offer that was still tainted by the fraud, the court's determination of a value of $10,000 is binding.

73. As the owner of common stock in a corporation, you will not have liability (under the traditional view) beyond actual investment even if you

a. Paid less than par value for stock you purchased in connection with an original issue.

b. Fail to pay the full amount owed on a subscription contract for no-par stock.

c. Purchased treasury stock for less than par value.

d. Received a dividend distribution which impaired the legal capital of the corporation.

The correct answer is (c). *(CPA 1174 L-34)*

REQUIRED: When the owner of common stock will not have liability beyond actual investment.

DISCUSSION: Unlike the purchaser of originally issued shares of stock, the purchaser of treasury shares at a price below the par value will not be liable for the difference between par value and the purchase price.

Answer (a) is incorrect because under the traditional view, the purchaser of stock may be liable for the difference between par value and the purchase price, if the price is less than par. Answer (b) is incorrect because a subscriber who has failed to perform under a subscription contract will be liable for the unpaid balance. Answer (d) is incorrect because the recipient of an unlawful dividend will usually be liable for the amount of the dividend distribution, although this liability usually exists only if the shareholder had knowledge of the impairment of stated capital.

74. The articles of incorporation of Divy Company prohibit dividends in any year in which the corporation has not earned an after-tax profit. For the year just ended, Divy had a net loss. Nevertheless, the board declared a dividend since it has a substantial surplus from prior years. Which of the following is true?

a. The directors are personally liable only if the dividend was statutorily prohibited.

b. Shareholders who knew that the dividend was improper will be liable.

c. All shareholders who received a dividend will be liable.

d. The directors are personally liable only if the dividend rendered the corporation insolvent.

The correct answer is (b). *(Publisher)*

REQUIRED: The true statement about liability for an unlawful dividend.

DISCUSSION: Dividends may be restricted both contractually and statutorily. Agreements with lenders, bondholders, and preferred shareholders as well as the articles, stock exchange rules, and statutes affect dividends. The common law rule is that a dividend may not impair capital. The majority view is that a corporation must have earned surplus (retained earnings) before declaring a dividend. Moreover, all states prohibit a dividend that renders the corporation insolvent. The directors have joint and several personal liability to the corporation or its creditors for illegal or improper dividends, and shareholders who knew of the impropriety can also be held liable.

Answers (a) and (d) are incorrect because the directors are liable for any improper distribution. Answer (c) is incorrect because innocent shareholders are generally not liable unless the corporation is insolvent.

75. Which of the following statements is correct regarding the fiduciary duty?

a. A director's fiduciary duty to the corporation may be discharged by merely disclosing his/her self-interest.

b. A director owes a fiduciary duty to the shareholders but not to the corporation.

c. A promoter of a corporation to be formed owes no fiduciary duty to anyone, unless the contract engaging the promoter so provides.

d. A majority shareholder as such may owe a fiduciary duty to fellow shareholders.

The correct answer is (d). *(CPA 585 L-12)*

REQUIRED: The fiduciary duty of directors, promoters, and shareholders.

DISCUSSION: Directors and officers owe a fiduciary duty to the corporation to act in its best interests, to be loyal, to use due diligence in carrying out their responsibilities, and to disclose conflicts of interest. Controlling as well as majority shareholders owe a similar duty. Courts will often protect the interests of minority shareholders by ordering the payment of dividends that were withheld in bad faith or by compelling a seller of a controlling block of shares to distribute ratably among all shareholders any "control premium" paid in excess of the fair value of the stock.

Answer (a) is incorrect because the fiduciary duty is far more extensive. Answer (b) is incorrect because the duty is owed to the corporation, not the shareholders. Answer (c) is incorrect because a promoter owes a fiduciary duty of fair dealing, good faith, and full disclosure to subscribers, shareholders, and the corporation.

76. Young owns 200 shares of stock of Victory Manufacturing Company. Victory is listed on a national stock exchange and has in excess of one million shares outstanding. Young claims that Truegood, a 10% shareholder, has purchased and sold shares in violation of the insider trading provisions of the Securities Exchange Act of 1934. Young has threatened legal action. Which of the following statements is correct?

a. Truegood will have a valid defense if he can show he did not have any insider information which influenced his purchases or sales.

b. Young can sue Truegood personally, but his recovery will be limited to his proportionate share of Truegood's profits plus legal expenses.

c. In order to prevail, Young must sue for and on behalf of the corporation and establish that the transactions in question occurred within less than 6 months of each other and at a profit to Truegood.

d. Since Young's stock ownership is less than 1%, his only recourse is to file a complaint with the SEC or obtain a sufficient number of other shareholders to join him so that the 1% requirement is met.

The correct answer is (c). *(CPA 1178 L-33)*

REQUIRED: The liability of a 10% shareholder for insider trading.

DISCUSSION: Under Section 16(b) of the Securities Exchange Act of 1934, any shareholder of a corporation may bring a shareholder derivative action against an insider of the corporation who made short-swing profits trading in the shares of the corporation. Truegood is an insider as a 10% shareholder of the company. If Truegood has purchased and sold (or sold and purchased) stock of Victory within a 6-month period, Truegood will be liable to Victory for any profits earned.

Answer (a) is incorrect because the 1934 Act establishes absolute liability for short-swing profits made by insiders regardless of whether inside information was used. Answer (b) is incorrect because Young cannot sue Truegood personally, only for and on behalf of the corporation. The recovery will extend to the full amount of the short-swing profits with no offset for losses. Answer (d) is incorrect because any shareholder may enforce the insider trading provisions of the 1934 Act.

77. Rocco Pierre was an 80% shareholder of La Bos Company, which was formed with his contribution of $2,000 of assets. His sister, Petra, provided $500 worth of assets and held the remaining stock. As the need for operating capital arose, Rocco and Petra advanced funds to the company. These advances eventually totaled $250,000. Annual sales averaged $300,000. When La Bos went into receivership, Rocco and Petra asserted their position as creditors of equal dignity with the other general creditors for the purpose of distribution of assets. They cited the existence of promissory notes signed by the corporate officers as evidence of their standing. The most likely result is that Rocco and Petra

a. Have the status of creditors.

b. Have no standing as creditors because loans by controlling shareholders are per se capital contributions.

c. Will be liable for all the debts of the corporation.

d. Have no standing as creditors under the Deep Rock doctrine.

The correct answer is (d). *(Publisher)*

REQUIRED: The effect of too thin capitalization.

DISCUSSION: If the debt to equity ratio is unreasonably high given its needs, nature, and size, a corporation is thinly capitalized. The potential tax advantages are that the corporation can deduct interest expense and repayments are not taxed to the lender as dividends. A further advantage is that in bankruptcy proceedings the claims of creditors are superior to those of owners. Under the Deep Rock doctrine (established in a Supreme Court decision), loans made by insiders to a too thinly capitalized corporation are treated as contributions of capital. The lenders, Rocco and Petra, controlled the corporation based on a nominal capital investment grossly disproportionate to its need for funds. Hence, they should not have standing as creditors.

Answer (a) is incorrect because they are owners since the loans were effectively capital contributions. Answer (b) is incorrect because controlling shareholder loans are not capital contributions per se, but they are strictly scrutinized by courts to determine their true substance. Answer (c) is incorrect because it is unusual for a corporation to be disregarded and the shareholders held liable similar to partners. But it can happen when there is thin capitalization, commingling of personal and company assets, and failure to observe the formalities of corporate life.

16.6 Investment Security Rules

78. An investor purchased a certificate representing 500 shares of common stock of the Sims Corporation from a former clerk of the corporation. It was the duty of the clerk to prepare stock certificates from a supply of blanks for signature of the corporate secretary. The clerk forged the corporate secretary's signature on a bearer certificate and delivered the certificate for value to the investor who did not have notice of the forgery and who now demands a reissued certificate in the investor's name from the corporation. The corporation asserts that it has no liability to reissue a certificate in the name of the investor and that the investor's bearer certificate is null and void. Which of the following is correct?

a. The certificate is valid and the investor is entitled to a reissued certificate.

b. The certificate issued is invalid and the corporation has no liability to reissue.

c. An appropriate recourse for the investor is to sue the corporation and clerk for dollar damages and to sue the clerk for the crime of forgery.

d. The corporation is required to reissue a certificate only if appropriately compensated by the investor.

The correct answer is (a). *(CPA 582 L-44)*

REQUIRED: The legal effect of an unauthorized issue of an investment security.

DISCUSSION: An unauthorized signature placed on a security prior to or in the course of issue is effective for a bona fide purchaser if the signing has been done by an employee of the issuer entrusted with responsible handling of the security (UCC 8-205). The certificate is therefore valid, and the investor is entitled to a reissued certificate.

Answer (b) is incorrect because the certificate is valid and the corporation must reissue a certificate in proper form. Answer (c) is incorrect because persons who perpetrate crimes are prosecuted by the government, not by private citizens. Answer (d) is incorrect because the corporation has the duty to issue its stock certificates in proper form and is not entitled to additional compensation.

79. In order to qualify as an investment security under the Uniform Commercial Code, an instrument must be

a. Issued in registered form, and not bearer form.

b. Of a long-term nature not intended to be disposed of within one year.

c. Only an equity security or debenture security, and not a secured obligation.

d. In a form that evidences a share, participation, or other interest in property or in an enterprise, or evidences an obligation of the issuer.

The correct answer is (d). *(CPA 1183 L-48)*

REQUIRED: The characteristic of an investment security under the UCC.

DISCUSSION: Under UCC 8-102, an investment security is a share, participation, or other interest in property of or an enterprise of the issuer or an obligation of the issuer of a type commonly dealt in on securities exchanges or markets or commonly recognized in any area in which it is issued or dealt in as a medium for investment. A certificated security is represented by an instrument in bearer or registered form. An uncertificated security is not represented by an instrument and the transfer is registered upon the corporate books.

Answer (a) is incorrect because the instrument may be in bearer form. Answer (b) is incorrect because an investment security may be short-term. Answer (c) is incorrect because an investment security may be an interest in property, an enterprise, or an obligation of the issuer.

80. Assuming all other requirements have been met, which of the following terms ordinarily must be included in a writing in order to satisfy the UCC Statute of Frauds regarding the sale of securities?

	Price	Quantity	Time of Payment
a.	Yes	Yes	Yes
b.	No	Yes	No
c.	Yes	No	Yes
d.	Yes	Yes	No

The correct answer is (d). *(CPA 587 L-47)*

REQUIRED: The term(s) ordinarily required in a writing evidencing a sale of securities.

DISCUSSION: Under UCC 8-319, such a contract is usually unenforceable absent a writing 1) signed by the party sought to bound, 2) sufficient to indicate a contract has been entered into, 3) stating a quantity of described securities, and 4) defining or stating a price. Time of payment is not a term required to be expressed in the writing. Payment within a reasonable time is implied if no express term is given.

81. Wilberforce & Company has in its possession certain securities which it took in good faith and for value from Dunlop. An adverse claim or defense has been asserted against the securities. Which of the following warranties may Wilberforce validly assert against Dunlop, its prior transferor?

a. There is no defect in the prior chain of title.

b. The securities are genuine and have not been materially altered.

c. There is no defect which might impair the validity of the securities.

d. Dunlop will defend the purchaser's title from adverse claim or defects which would impair the validity of the securities.

The correct answer is (b). *(CPA 582 L-45)*

REQUIRED: The warranties made by a person transferring a security for value.

DISCUSSION: Under UCC 8-306, a person who transfers a security (such as a stock certificate) to a purchaser for value warrants that the transfer is effective and rightful, that the security is genuine and has not been materially altered, and that (s)he knows no fact which might impair the validity of the security.

Answers (a), (c), and (d) are incorrect because a transferor is not an absolute guarantor of the validity of a security. Since it is not feasible for the holder of a security which circulates freely in commercial channels to be aware of all aspects of prior transactions involving the security, the transferor is held only to warranties of those aspects of transactions which are within his/her control.

82. Hargrove lost some stock certificates of the Apex Corporation which were registered in his name, but which he had endorsed in blank. Flagg found the securities and sold them through a brokerage house to Waldorf. Apex, unaware of Hargrove's problem, transferred them to Waldorf. Hargrove is seeking to recover the securities or damages for their value. Which of the following is correct?

a. The stock in question is transferable but Waldorf takes subject to Hargrove's claim of title.

b. Waldorf is a holder in due course of a negotiable instrument and therefore will prevail.

c. Apex is liable for wrongfully transferring Hargrove's stock to Waldorf.

d. Waldorf qualifies as a bona fide purchaser and acquires the stock free of Hargrove's adverse claim.

The correct answer is (d). *(CPA 1180 L-10)*

REQUIRED: The legal effect of the transfer of lost securities in bearer form.

DISCUSSION: Waldorf is a bona fide purchaser for value, in good faith, and without notice of any adverse claim (UCC 8-302). Bearer certificates need only be delivered; i.e., no endorsement is necessary. A bona fide purchaser acquires the security free of any adverse claims under UCC 8-301.

Answer (a) is incorrect because Waldorf, as a bona fide purchaser, takes free of any adverse claims. Answer (b) is incorrect because while the security in question is a negotiable instrument (UCC 8-105), Article 8 on investment securities governs the transaction. Under Article 8, Waldorf is a bona fide purchaser rather than a holder in due course (the concepts are similar). Answer (c) is incorrect because when a security has been lost and the owner fails to notify the issuer, the issuer may register a transfer of the security and the owner is precluded from asserting any claim for wrongful registration (UCC 8-405).

83. The good-faith purchaser of a stolen stock certificate will defeat the claims of the prior owner(s)

a. Even though the certificate bears the forged endorsement of the prior owner.

b. Provided the certificate was endorsed in blank by the prior owner.

c. If the certificate is registered and contains no endorsement whatsoever.

d. If the certificate contains the full endorsement of one of the two prior joint owners.

The correct answer is (b). *(CPA 1175 L-32)*

REQUIRED: When a good faith purchaser of a stolen stock certificate will defeat the claims of prior owners.

DISCUSSION: The good faith purchaser of a stolen stock certificate who has taken for value and without notice of any adverse claim will be a "bona fide purchaser" if (s)he takes delivery of a security in bearer form or in registered form which is endorsed in blank (UCC 8-302). A "bona fide purchaser" will defeat the claims of any prior owner with respect to a stolen stock certificate (UCC 8-301).

Answer (a) is incorrect because a good faith purchaser takes subject to the claim of forgery. Answer (c) is incorrect because a purchaser of a registered stock certificate which has not been endorsed cannot qualify as a "bona fide purchaser" and will take subject to the claim of a prior owner. Answer (d) is incorrect because both signatures of two joint owners are required for a purchaser to qualify as a "bona fide purchaser" and take free of the claim of theft.

84. Able was the owner of investment securities issued in registered form by Jay Company. Ben found them, forged a blank endorsement, and transferred them to Chip, who had no knowledge of the forgery. Chip in turn sold the securities to Denise, who took for value, in good faith, and without notice of any adverse claim. Denise then sent the certificates to Jay's stock transfer agent, who canceled the old certificates and issued new ones to Denise. As a result of these events

a. Able has a right of action against Jay.

b. Denise has no claim to the new certificates because of the forgery.

c. Denise had a valid claim to the old certificates because she was a bona fide purchaser.

d. Jay has a right of action against Denise.

The correct answer is (a). *(Publisher)*

REQUIRED: The legal effect of issuing new stock certificates to a bona fide purchaser.

DISCUSSION: A security in registered form is transferred by endorsement and delivery. Under UCC 8-311, the owner of lost or stolen certificates may not assert the ineffectiveness of an unauthorized endorsement against a bona fide purchaser who has in good faith received a new, reissued, or reregistered certificated security on registration of transfer. Denise will thus prevail over Able. But an issuer who registers the transfer upon the unauthorized endorsement is subject to liability for improper registration. Able may therefore hold Jay liable.

Answer (b) is incorrect because a bona fide purchaser owns new certificates obtained from the stock transfer agent. Answer (c) is incorrect because the owner would prevail against the bona fide purchaser with respect to the old certificates since the transfer was by means of an unauthorized endorsement. Answer (d) is incorrect because as a bona fide purchaser who received new certificates from the stock transfer agent after presentment of the old, Denise warranted only that she had no knowledge of any unauthorized signature (UCC 8-306).

85. Glenn Corporation is closely held by two shareholders, Jenny and Garp, who entered an agreement giving each other a right of first refusal if either wished to sell the stock. The restriction on transfer of shares was conspicuously noted in their written contract. In violation of the agreement, Garp sold his shares to Fields. The stock transfer restriction is most likely to be disregarded by a court

a. If neither the bylaws nor the articles mentioned it.

b. If it was not conspicuously noted on the certificates.

c. Because it was unreasonable.

d. Even though the transferee knew of it.

The correct answer is (b). *(Publisher)*

REQUIRED: The best reason for disregarding a stock transfer restriction.

DISCUSSION: Under UCC 8-204, a stock transfer restriction "is ineffective against any person without actual knowledge of it unless the security is certificated and the restriction is noted conspicuously thereon."

Answer (a) is incorrect because the restriction may be included in an agreement among the shareholders in addition to the articles or bylaws. Answer (c) is incorrect because a restriction must be reasonable and not absolute. The desire to maintain control of a close corporation is a reasonable purpose, and the provision for a right of first refusal is reasonable. Answer (d) is incorrect because knowledge by the transferee makes a reasonable restriction valid even if not noted on the certificates.

16.7 Financing Structure and Dividends

86. In most states, what must be stated in the articles of incorporation regarding the financial structure of the entity?

a. The number of authorized shares of each class of stock.

b. The par value of authorized shares.

c. Restrictions on transfer of stock.

d. The minimum initial capital investment.

The correct answer is (a). *(Publisher)*

REQUIRED: The item required in most states to be included in the articles.

DISCUSSION: Under the RMBCA, the total authorized shares, including the number for each class, must be stated. The designation of each class and a statement of its rights and limitations must be given. Also, if a preferred or special class of shares is to be issued in series, information about the rights and limitations of each series and the authority of the board with regard thereto must be stated.

Answers (b) and (c) are incorrect because each is a specific provision cited by the RMBCA as permitted but not required to be included. However, any provision not inconsistent with law may be included. Answer (d) is incorrect because the RMBCA, unlike prior law, does not require a minimum capital investment.

87. Which of the following is a true statement about financing a for-profit corporation?

a. Stocks and bonds are the exclusive means of financing used by corporations.

b. Some corporations rely entirely on debt financing.

c. Large corporations usually have a blend of debt and equity financing.

d. Small corporations and governmental units rely on the issuance of bonds.

The correct answer is (c). *(Publisher)*

REQUIRED: The true statement about financing a corporation.

DISCUSSION: A for-profit corporation can raise capital by issuing equity securities (stock) or by incurring debt. The advantage of equity is that it does not have to be repaid and it does not result in periodic fixed charges. The advantage of debt is that it does not give voting control to the creditor and may permit trading on leverage (borrowing is favorable if the cost of capital is less than the company's return). Large corporations and many small ones prefer a combination of these financing methods.

Answer (a) is incorrect because corporations of all sizes also finance their operations by such means as accounts and notes payable, leases, and retained earnings. Answer (b) is incorrect because all for-profit corporations must issue stock. Answer (d) is incorrect because large corporations are far more likely than small ones to issue bonds, which are long-term debt securities paying a fixed amount of interest at specified periods and with a fixed maturity date for repayment of principal. Bonds are a means of dividing large-scale borrowing into small units to facilitate marketing.

88. If a corporation wishes to issue securities to the public, it must comply with the applicable securities laws. Which of the following is true?

a. The enactment of federal securities laws preempted state regulation.

b. Few states have adopted the Uniform Securities Act.

c. A sale of securities may not be concurrently subject to both state and federal regulation.

d. Some states have statutes permitting regulators to pass on the merits of securities.

The correct answer is (d). *(Publisher)*

REQUIRED: The true statement about state securities laws.

DISCUSSION: Most state "blue-sky" laws require registration of nonexempt securities, provide for licensing or registration of brokers and dealers, prohibit fraud in the issuance and subsequent trading of securities, and impose full disclosure standards. These provisions are similar in many ways to federal law. However, some states have also established merit or fairness standards for the issuance of securities; that is, securities may not qualify for registration until a state regulator has evaluated them to determine whether they are unduly risky. By contrast, federal law assumes that full disclosure is sufficient to protect investors.

Answer (a) is incorrect because the federal securities law recognizes concurrent state power over securities issues and trading. Answer (b) is incorrect because the majority of states have passed the Uniform Securities Act to provide consistency. Answer (c) is incorrect because a sale of securities in interstate commerce usually is subject to both federal law and the laws of various states.

89. Authorized shares means the shares of all classes of stock which a corporation

a. Has legally outstanding.

b. Is legally permitted to issue.

c. Has issued including treasury shares.

d. Has issued excluding treasury shares.

The correct answer is (b). *(CPA 1175 L-24)*

REQUIRED: The meaning of authorized shares of stock.

DISCUSSION: Authorized shares are those which a corporation is legally permitted to issue under its articles of incorporation. The articles of incorporation may be amended to change the number of authorized shares.

Answer (a) is incorrect because a corporation may not have issued all of its authorized stock; therefore, it would not be outstanding. Answers (c) and (d) are incorrect because whether stock has been reacquired as treasury stock is irrelevant to the number of authorized shares.

90. Which of the following most accurately states an advantage or disadvantage of preferred stockholders?

a. They incur more risk than common stockholders.

b. They incur less risk than bondholders.

c. They have less opportunity for benefiting from the growth of the corporation than common stockholders.

d. They have a stronger position upon dissolution than bondholders or common stockholders.

The correct answer is (c). *(Publisher)*

REQUIRED: The advantage or disadvantage of preferred stock.

DISCUSSION: Preferred stock offers a fixed return whereas common stock dividends may grow as the firm prospers. Preferred stock is also frequently redeemable for a fixed price at the corporation's option. Common stockholders thus are more likely to benefit from appreciation of the value of their shares. Preferred shareholders, however, may have participation or conversion rights that often offset these disadvantages.

Answer (a) is incorrect because preferred stock is less risky than common. It has preferences regarding both dividends and dissolution. Answer (b) is incorrect because preferred stock is more risky than bonds. The latter are long-term debt instruments that pay a return regardless of dividends. Bondholders are creditors with priority of payment over all shareholders in dissolution. Answer (d) is incorrect because creditors, including bondholders, are paid before shareholders when the corporation is liquidated.

91. The owner of cumulative preferred stock has the right to

a. Convert preferred stock into common stock.

b. A residual share in profits after a fixed dividend has been paid to both common and preferred stockholders.

c. The carryover of fixed dividends to subsequent periods from years in which they were not paid.

d. Receive the par value of their shares but not unpaid dividends before common stockholders receive anything in liquidation.

The correct answer is (c). *(Publisher)*

REQUIRED: The rights of the owner of cumulative preferred stock.

DISCUSSION: Normally, a preferred shareholder is entitled to a fixed dividend that must be paid before dividends are received by the common shareholders. If the preferred stock is cumulative, any dividends not paid in preceding years will be carried over and must be paid before the common shareholders may receive anything. Under case law, preferred stock dividends are impliedly cumulative unless stated otherwise, but the RMBCA suggests that whether stock is cumulative or noncumulative should be included in the articles.

Answer (a) is incorrect because the right of cumulation does not apply to convertibility of one class of security into another. Answer (b) is incorrect because it describes participating rather than cumulative preferred stock. Answer (d) is incorrect because the liquidation preference of cumulative preferred shareholders extends both to the par value of their shares and to unpaid dividends.

92. Delray Corporation has a provision in its corporate charter as follows: "Holders of the noncumulative preferred stock shall be entitled to a fixed annual dividend of 8% before any dividend shall be paid on common stock." There are no further provisions relating to preferences or statements regarding voting rights. The preferred stock apparently

a. Is noncumulative, but only to the extent that the 8% dividend is not earned in a given year.

b. Is nonvoting unless dividends are in arrears.

c. Has a preference on the distribution of the assets of the corporation upon dissolution.

d. Is not entitled to participate with common stock in dividend distributions beyond 8%.

The correct answer is (d). *(CPA 1174 L-33)*

REQUIRED: The rights of holders of the preferred stock.

DISCUSSION: The preferred stock is noncumulative and entitled to a fixed annual dividend of 8% before any dividend is paid on the common. Preferred stock is nonparticipating unless specified otherwise. Here, since there are no further provisions, it is not entitled to participate after 8% dividends.

Answer (a) is incorrect because the stock is specified to be noncumulative, regardless of earnings. Answer (b) is incorrect because all classes of stock, including preferred, are voting unless the articles of incorporation specify otherwise (which they usually do). Answer (c) is incorrect because the preferred stock has no preference on the distribution of assets in dissolution unless the articles of incorporation specify otherwise (which they usually do).

93. West owns 5,000 shares of $7 cumulative preferred stock of Sky Corp. During the first year of operations, cash dividends of $7 per share were declared on Sky's preferred stock but were never paid. In the second year of operations, dividends on Sky's preferred stock were neither declared nor paid. If Sky is dissolved, which of the following statements is correct?

a. West will have priority over the claims of Sky's debenture bond owners.

b. West will have priority over the claims of Sky's unsecured judgment creditors.

c. Sky will be liable to West as an unsecured creditor for $35,000.

d. Sky will be liable to West as an unsecured creditor for $70,000.

The correct answer is (c). *(CPA 587 L-2)*

REQUIRED: The position of a preferred shareholder upon dissolution.

DISCUSSION: Dividends do not become legal obligations (debts) of the corporation until they are declared. This principle applies to dividends on common stock and on both noncumulative and cumulative preferred stock. West therefore became a creditor of Sky only with respect to the $35,000 (5,000 X $7) dividend that was declared but not paid. Because this debt was not collateralized, West is an unsecured creditor.

Answers (a) and (b) are incorrect because these unsecured creditors have the same priority as West. Debentures are unsecured bonds. Beyond the $35,000 claim, however, West's priority in the assets of Sky is subordinate to that of a creditor. In a dissolution, creditors must be paid before preferred shareholders, but holders of preferred stock are paid before the common shareholders. Answer (d) is incorrect because no dividends were declared for the second year, so Sky's dividend liability to West is $35,000, not $70,000.

94. The number of shares actually held by shareholders are best described as

a. Authorized shares.

b. Issued shares.

c. Treasury shares.

d. Outstanding shares.

The correct answer is (d). *(Publisher)*

REQUIRED: The term best describing shares actually held by shareholders.

DISCUSSION: Shares are outstanding if they are authorized and issued to shareholders but have not been reacquired by the corporation.

Answer (a) is incorrect because authorized shares are those permitted by the articles to be issued. Corporate law places no limit on the amount that may be authorized. Answer (b) is incorrect because issued shares are those actually issued, including shares reacquired by the corporation. Answer (c) is incorrect because treasury shares are authorized and issued, but not outstanding.

95. The preemptive right of a shareholder is the right to acquire a pro rata amount of newly issued stock to maintain his/her proportionate ownership of the corporation.

a. The right is generally inapplicable to shares issued in mergers.

b. Most states prohibit denial of the right in the articles.

c. If the right is denied in the articles, a new issue intended to dilute the voting power of minority shareholders will be upheld.

d. The right is generally applicable to sales of treasury stock, shares issued as compensation, and shares issued for noncash consideration.

The correct answer is (a). *(Publisher)*

REQUIRED: The true statement about the preemptive right.

DISCUSSION: The preemptive right does not apply to issues of stock to effect mergers or consolidations, for noncash consideration, or to provide compensation to employees. It also does not apply to sales of treasury stock. Under the RMBCA, the right does not apply to shares issued within 6 months of incorporation.

Answer (b) is incorrect because almost all states recognize the right but permit its limitation or denial in the articles. Most publicly held companies do not grant preemptive rights because they place an undue burden on stock issuances. Stockholders must be notified as to the number of shares they can purchase, when the option is exercisable, and the price. The issuance must then be delayed until the company knows how many shareholders have exercised their rights. Answer (c) is incorrect because courts often grant relief to the minority shareholders in circumstances that are basically unfair. Answer (d) is incorrect because the right does not apply to these issues.

96. Treasury shares of a corporation are its shares that are

a. Issued and outstanding.

b. Issued but not outstanding.

c. Outstanding but not issued.

d. Neither outstanding nor issued.

The correct answer is (b). *(CPA 1175 L-25)*

REQUIRED: The definition of treasury shares of a corporation.

DISCUSSION: Treasury shares are those which were issued and then reacquired by the corporation. Therefore, they are issued but no longer outstanding.

Answer (a) is incorrect because treasury shares are not outstanding. Answer (c) is incorrect because shares cannot be outstanding without having first been issued. Answer (d) is incorrect because shares neither outstanding nor issued are simply authorized but unissued.

97. The consideration for the issuance of shares by a corporation may not be paid in

a. Tangible property.

b. Intangible property.

c. Services to be performed for the corporation.

d. Services actually performed for the corporation.

The correct answer is (c). *(CPA 581 L-22)*

REQUIRED: The form of consideration that is not allowed for the issuance of shares.

DISCUSSION: Corporation statutes usually require that consideration for the issuance of shares be paid only in the form of cash, property, or past services rendered for the corporation. Future services and promissory notes are not proper consideration under most current laws (but are under the RMBCA).

Answers (a), (b), and (d) are incorrect because each represents a valid form of consideration for the issuance of shares.

98. The term "watered stock" typically refers to

a. The decline in value of a share of stock following a stock split.

b. The issuance of stock as fully paid in exchange for over-valued property or services.

c. The issuance of stock at less than the proportionate book value of the corporation.

d. The difference between the amount received by the corporation and the amount subscribed.

The correct answer is (b). *(Publisher)*

REQUIRED: The statement which describes watered stock.

DISCUSSION: When a corporation issues stock as fully paid when in fact full payment has not been made, the stock is said to be "watered." This situation can arise when stock is issued in exchange for property or services held out to have value equivalent to the stock, but actually is substantially overvalued.

Answer (a) is incorrect because stock splits have no effect on the capitalization of the corporation. A stock split increases the number of shares without altering the proportionate ownership. Answer (c) is incorrect because the directors may fix the price at which stock will be sold; there is no "water" as long as the price is fully paid. Book value is not relevant to the issue of stock. Answer (d) is incorrect because it describes the unpaid portion of a stock subscription which is an enforceable debt.

99. The consideration received by a corporation when issuing shares of stock shall constitute stated capital to the extent of the par value of the shares, and any excess shall constitute

a. Treasury shares.

b. Earned surplus.

c. Restricted surplus.

d. Capital surplus.

The correct answer is (d). *(CPA 577 L-10)*

REQUIRED: The term describing the amount paid for shares in excess of the par value.

DISCUSSION: When stock with a par value is issued, consideration equal to the par value is allocated to stated capital. Consideration in excess of the par value constitutes capital surplus.

Answer (a) is incorrect because the term treasury shares refers to stock of the corporation which was issued and then repurchased by the corporation. Answer (b) is incorrect because the term earned surplus refers to earnings of the corporation which have been retained. Answer (c) is incorrect because the term restricted surplus refers to earned or capital surplus which is restricted in its use, e.g., to repay bonds.

100. Needham Corporation has issued 10,000 shares of stock for a consideration of $10 per share. The par value is $1 per share. Its total stated capital amounts to

a. $10,000.

b. $90,000.

c. $100,000.

d. $110,000.

The correct answer is (a). *(CPA 576 L-22)*

REQUIRED: The amount of the total stated capital of the corporation.

DISCUSSION: If a corporation issues par value shares, the stated capital is equal to the par value of the shares issued. If 10,000 shares are issued at $1 par, the stated capital will be $10,000.

Answer (b) is incorrect because $90,000 is the amount of capital surplus. Answer (c) is incorrect because $100,000 is the total capital. Answer (d) is incorrect because only $100,000 was received.

101. Surplus of a corporation means

a. Net assets in excess of stated capital.

b. Liquid assets in excess of current needs.

c. Total assets in excess of total liabilities.

d. Contributed capital.

The correct answer is (a). *(CPA 1175 L-22)*

REQUIRED: The meaning of the term surplus of a corporation.

DISCUSSION: Surplus of a corporation is defined as the excess of net assets over stated capital. This is also equivalent to the total of capital surplus and earned surplus. Note that net assets equal total assets less total liabilities.

Answer (b) is incorrect because the excess of liquid assets over current liabilities is the accounting definition for "net quick assets." Answer (c) is incorrect because total assets in excess of total liabilities is the total capital of the corporation. Answer (d) is incorrect because contributed capital includes both stated capital and capital surplus.

102. Capital surplus of a corporation means

a. The portion of its entire surplus other than earned surplus.

b. Contributed capital.

c. Working capital.

d. Stated capital.

The correct answer is (a). *(CPA 1175 L-27)*

REQUIRED: The definition of capital surplus of a corporation.

DISCUSSION: Surplus of a corporation consists of capital and earned surplus. Therefore, capital surplus is the surplus which is not earned. It is also the contributed capital in excess of the stated value of the shares.

Answer (b) is incorrect because contributed capital includes both stated capital and capital surplus. Answer (c) is incorrect because working capital is the excess of current assets over current liabilities. Answer (d) is incorrect because stated capital is equal to the par value of shares issued.

103. Dora Roe reached a pre-incorporation agreement with Nora for the purchase of shares in a corporation that she planned to form to sell pizza. Dora later formed the corporation, which promptly went into the sportswear business as Dolsports, Inc. After incorporation, Dolsports accepted Nora's subscription and entered into a subscription agreement with Phoebe. It also signed an executory contract to sell shares to Susan. Who is not liable on their agreement?

a. Phoebe, because a post-incorporation subscription is not binding.

b. Nora, because the actual corporation differed from the one subscribed to.

c. Susan, because an executory contract to sell shares is not binding.

d. Dolsports, because agreements to sell shares are not binding on a corporation.

The correct answer is (b). *(Publisher)*

REQUIRED: The person not liable on a subscription agreement or executory contract.

DISCUSSION: A subscription agreement may be reached by potential shareholders with a promoter prior to incorporation. A corporation also may enter into subscription agreements. A subscription is an undertaking to sell shares for a specified price. An executory contract differs from a post-incorporation subscription in that the parties do not intend for the investor to have the rights of a shareholder at the time the contract is entered into.

Nora's pre-incorporation subscription is not binding although accepted by Dolsports because the corporation formed was materially different from the one contemplated in the agreement.

Answers (a) and (c) are incorrect because post-incorporation subscriptions and executory contracts are valid and are used much more often than pre-incorporation subscriptions. They must be in writing. Answer (d) is incorrect because a corporation has contractual capacity.

104. When no-par shares are issued in a corporation, the value that must be allocated to capital surplus as distinct from stated capital is

a. The book value of the shares.

b. The fair market value of the shares.

c. The entire amount of the consideration received.

d. Any portion of the proceeds so directed by the board of directors.

The correct answer is (d). *(Publisher)*

REQUIRED: The amount that must be allocated to capital surplus for no-par shares.

DISCUSSION: If the state statute requires that the corporation maintain a stated or legal capital account, and if no-par shares are issued, the entire consideration received for the shares must be allocated to the stated capital of the corporation except to the extent that the directors in their discretion allocate (within 60 days) any part of the proceeds to capital surplus.

Answers (a), (b), and (c) are incorrect because the allocation is in the directors' discretion.

105. For legal purposes, net assets of a corporation means the amount

a. By which current assets exceed its current liabilities.

b. By which liquid assets exceed its current liabilities.

c. By which total assets exceed its total liabilities.

d. Of its current assets.

The correct answer is (c). *(CPA 1175 L-26)*

REQUIRED: The definition of net assets of a corporation for legal purposes.

DISCUSSION: The accounting definition of net assets is applicable for legal purposes: the amount by which total assets exceed total liabilities of the corporation.

Answer (a) is incorrect because the amount by which current assets exceed current liabilities is known as working capital. Answer (b) is incorrect because it defines the "net quick assets" of the corporation. Answer (d) is incorrect because the calculation of net assets includes not only current assets, but also all other assets and liabilities.

106. The issuance of a stock certificate

a. Is a condition precedent to a person's becoming a shareholder.

b. Is void and the corporation will have no liability if the result would be an overissuance.

c. Provides evidence of ownership but the certificate is not the stock.

d. Is required under the revised Model Business Corporation Act.

The correct answer is (c). *(Publisher)*

REQUIRED: The significance of the issuance of a stock certificate.

DISCUSSION: The certificate is merely evidence that a person is a shareholder. If it is lost or destroyed or if it has not yet been issued to a stock subscriber, the person is nevertheless deemed to be a shareholder.

Answers (a) and (d) are incorrect because the intangible ownership interest exists independent of the certificate. In recognition of the advantages of computerized transfers of stock, the RMBCA and Article 8 of the UCC (Investment Securities) allow for uncertificated shares. Answer (b) is incorrect because according to UCC 8-104, if an issuance of new shares would result in exceeding the number of authorized shares, a person otherwise entitled to the shares may require the corporation to acquire identical shares, if reasonably available, or to refund the price that the last purchaser paid for the stock plus interest.

107. When does the board of directors have a right to declare and pay dividends?

a. Only in years that the corporation is profitable.

b. Never out of capital surplus.

c. As a stock dividend of authorized but unissued shares if there are no available retained earnings or capital surplus.

d. When the corporation has both capital surplus and retained earnings.

The correct answer is (d). *(Publisher)*

REQUIRED: When the board of directors has the right to declare and pay dividends.

DISCUSSION: The financial requirements of the corporation vary as to when dividends are proper. They are almost always proper if paid out of earned surplus (retained earnings). In addition, dividends are never proper if the corporation is or would become insolvent.

Answer (a) is incorrect because dividends may be paid out of prior years' earned surplus even if there are no current earnings. Answer (b) is incorrect because many states permit the payment of dividends out of capital surplus with approval of the shareholders or pursuant to the bylaws. Answer (c) is incorrect because a dividend of authorized but previously unissued shares is possible only if a transfer can be made from capital surplus or retained earnings to stated capital to cover the par or stated value of the stock issued.

108. Freud Rotor Company was created 10 years ago and was immediately successful. Nevertheless, Freud paid only its regular dividend and no special dividend. The announced purpose of the limited dividend policy was to set aside funds for a substantial expansion. If minority shareholders sue for a court order requiring payment of increased dividends, the directors will most likely

a. Win because the declaration of dividends is solely in the discretion of the directors.

b. Lose even though a bond indenture limits dividend payments.

c. Lose if similar companies pay substantially higher dividends.

d. Lose because the refusal of higher dividends was not protected by the business judgment rule.

The correct answer is (d). *(Publisher)*

REQUIRED: The likely result of a suit to compel payment of dividends.

DISCUSSION: The directors and not the courts or shareholders are customarily deemed to be in the best position to judge what is best for the corporation. A court will not substitute its business judgment for that of the board if the directors have acted in good faith, without fraud, have avoided conflicts of interest, and have generally complied with their fiduciary duties, including that of due care. But if the directors have not acted in good faith, then the minority shareholders have a good chance of winning.

Answer (a) is incorrect because the directors may not abuse their discretion at the expense of minority shareholders. Answer (b) is incorrect because bond or debenture indentures or loan agreements provide valid contractual reasons for nondeclaration of dividends. Answer (c) is incorrect because the actions of similar companies provide an insufficient reason for overcoming the strong presumption in favor of upholding the directors' business judgment.

109. Randolph Corporation would like to pay cash dividends on its common shares outstanding. Under corporate law, Randolph may not pay these dividends if it is insolvent or would be rendered so by the payment. For this purpose, an insolvent corporation is one which

a. Is unable to pay its debts as they become due in the usual course of its business or has an excess of liabilities over assets.

b. Has an excess of liabilities over assets.

c. Has an excess of current liabilities over current assets.

d. Has a deficit in earned surplus.

The correct answer is (a). *(CPA 577 L-15)*

REQUIRED: The definition of insolvency for the payment of dividends.

DISCUSSION: Corporations are not permitted to pay cash dividends if the corporation would be unable to pay debts as they become due in the usual course of business or if the corporation's total assets are less than its total liabilities.

Answer (b) is incorrect because insolvency as a restriction on the payment of cash dividends includes insolvency in the equity sense, as well as an excess of liabilities over assets. Answer (c) is incorrect because a firm may have an excess of current liabilities over current assets and still be able to pay debts as they become due. Answer (d) is incorrect because solvency has no direct relationship to a deficit in earned surplus, but many states do prohibit dividends if there is a deficit in surplus.

110. Assuming no agreement on the matter between the buyer and seller of stock, who is entitled to a declared dividend?

a. If the stock is listed on a stock exchange, the buyer if the purchase was 6 days before the record date.

b. If the stock is not listed on a stock exchange, the seller if the purchase was between the ex dividend and record dates.

c. If the stock is listed on a stock exchange, the buyer if the purchase was after the record date.

d. If the stock is not listed on a stock exchange, the shareholder of record at the ex dividend date.

The correct answer is (a). *(Publisher)*

REQUIRED: The party entitled to a declared dividend.

DISCUSSION: When the dividend is declared, the board sets a date of record. The corporation will have no liability to third parties if it pays the dividend to the recorded shareholders at that date. Between the transferor and transferee of shares, their contractual agreement controls disposition of the dividend. In the absence of an agreement, the transferor receives the dividend if the transfer occurred after the record date.

But if the stock is listed on a stock exchange, the transferor is entitled to the dividend if the transfer occurred after the ex dividend date (5 business days before the record date). Accordingly, a buyer 6 days prior to the record date has a right to the dividend.

Answers (b) and (d) are incorrect because if the stock is not listed, the ex dividend date is not relevant. A transferee before the record date is entitled to the dividend. Answer (c) is incorrect because whether or not the stock is listed, the transferor has a right to the dividend if the transfer is after the record date.

111. The essential difference between a stock dividend and a stock split is that a

a. Stock split will increase the amount of stockholders' equity.

b. Stock split will increase a stockholder's percentage of ownership.

c. Stock dividend must be paid in the same class of stock as held by the stockholder.

d. Stock dividend of newly issued shares will result in a decrease in retained earnings.

The correct answer is (d). *(CPA 585 L-15)*

REQUIRED: The difference between a stock dividend and a stock split.

DISCUSSION: A stock dividend is an issuance of additional shares of the company's stock proportionate to current holdings. Total stockholders' equity is unaffected since it is merely represented by a greater number of shares. Generally accepted accounting principles require a transfer from retained earnings to stated capital of the fair value of the shares distributed as a stock dividend.

A stock split differs in that par value rather than retained earnings is reduced and the number of authorized shares is increased.

Answer (a) is incorrect because a stock dividend requires a transfer between capital accounts; a split results in a reduction of par value. Answer (b) is incorrect because the distribution is proportionate to existing holdings. Answer (c) is incorrect because a preferred shareholder may, for example, receive a dividend of common stock.

112. The Larkin Corporation is contemplating a two-for-one stock split of its common stock. Its $4 par value common stock will be reduced to $2 after the split. It has 2 million shares issued and outstanding out of a total of 3 million authorized.

a. The transaction will require both authorization by the board of directors and approval by the shareholders.

b. The distribution of the additional shares to the shareholders will be taxed as a dividend to the recipients.

c. Surplus equal to the par value of the existing number of shares issued and outstanding must be transferred to the stated capital account.

d. The trustees of trust recipients of the additional shares must allocate them ratably between income and corpus.

The correct answer is (a). *(CPA 581 L-27)*

REQUIRED: The correct statement regarding the legal or tax consequences of a two-for-one stock split of common stock.

DISCUSSION: The effect of the stock split will be to increase the number of shares issued and outstanding from two million to four million, which will exceed the number of authorized shares. Such a transaction is a fundamental change in the corporate financial structure and therefore must be approved by the shareholders as well as by the Board of Directors.

Answer (b) is incorrect because stock splits are normally nontaxable since the proportional ownership of the corporation remains the same. Answer (c) is incorrect because no retained earnings need be transferred to the stated capital account since the stock split does not change the aggregate par value of the shares issued and outstanding. Answer (d) is incorrect because stock dividends and splits are allocated solely to the principal (corpus) of the trust.

113. Miller Corporation declared a common stock dividend of 1 share for every 10 shares outstanding. The owner's equity accounts of the corporation immediately prior to the declaration of the common stock dividend were as follows:

Stated capital (10,000 shares of common stock issued and outstanding, $1 par value per share)	$10,000
Earned surplus (retained earnings)	$4,000

Immediately after the issuance of the common stock dividend, stated capital will amount to

a. $11,000.

b. $10,000.

c. $9,000.

d. $1,000.

The correct answer is (a). *(CPA 1175 L-30)*

REQUIRED: The amount of stated capital after the issuance of the stock dividend.

DISCUSSION: The issuance of a stock dividend requires the transfer from surplus (either earned or capital) to stated capital of an amount equal to the par value of the shares issued as the stock dividend. The issuance of a 10% stock dividend when 10,000 shares are outstanding at a $1 par value per share requires that stated capital be increased by $1,000 to $11,000.

114. A shareholder is personally liable to creditors for all but which of the following?

a. For an unpaid subscription balance when the corporation is insolvent.

b. For illegal dividends paid by an insolvent corporation.

c. For the fair market value of shares subscribed.

d. For amounts owed by the entity when the corporate veil has been pierced.

The correct answer is (c). *(Publisher)*

REQUIRED: When a shareholder is not personally liable to creditors.

DISCUSSION: The amount to be paid for stock is determined by the board of directors, subject to the requirements of good faith and business judgment. The amount for which stock is issued may be less than the fair market value at the date of issuance, and the shareholder would have no liability. Traditionally, a purchaser who pays less than par value could be liable for the difference between the amount paid and par. This rule has been revised by the RMBCA.

Answer (a) is incorrect because a subscription is a binding promise to pay which can be enforced by the creditors of an insolvent corporation. Answer (b) is incorrect because both the board of directors (which has declared and paid an illegal dividend) and the recipient are liable to creditors if the corporation is insolvent. Answer (d) is incorrect because if the corporate veil is pierced, the shareholders will no longer have the benefit of limited liability and will be directly liable to creditors.

16.8 Fundamental Corporate Changes

115. Shareholders must vote on certain fundamental corporate changes. Which of the following ordinarily does not require shareholder approval?

a. The sale of corporate assets even in the regular course of business.

b. An exchange of shares for those of another corporation.

c. A dissolution.

d. A merger.

The correct answer is (a). *(Publisher)*

REQUIRED: The true statement about approval of extraordinary transactions by shareholders.

DISCUSSION: Shareholders invest in a corporation with the expectation that the directors and officers will manage it and approve ordinary business transactions such as the sale of corporate assets in the regular course of business. Only if it was a sale of substantially all the corporate assets would shareholder approval be needed since that would be an extraordinary matter.

Answers (b), (c), and (d) are incorrect because each is generally an extraordinary matter substantially affecting the shareholders' rights, so their approval is needed.

116. Fundamental corporate changes require shareholder approval. Based on the procedure required by the RMBCA, which of the following is false?

a. Notice must be given to shareholders whether or not entitled to vote.

b. The articles may require a supermajority vote.

c. The board of directors usually gives prior approval to the change.

d. At least a majority of each class must approve even though the rights of a class may not be affected.

The correct answer is (d). *(Publisher)*

REQUIRED: The false statement about the general procedure for making fundamental changes.

DISCUSSION: Under the RMBCA, the first step is approval of the change by the board. All shareholders must then be notified, including those without voting rights regarding the matter. A majority vote of the shareholders taken at an annual or special meeting is sufficient to pass the proposal unless the articles require a greater percentage. Voting by class is required by the RMBCA for share exchanges and mergers if the interests of a class are significantly affected. The articles may provide that class voting is required on other transactions.

Answer (a) is incorrect because all shareholders must be notified. Answer (b) is incorrect because a greater-than-majority vote may be required by the articles. Answer (c) is incorrect because approval by the directors is the initial step.

117. Shareholder action on fundamental changes in a large publicly held corporation generally requires that a meeting be convened. Under the RMBCA, and unless the articles or bylaws stipulate otherwise,

a. Holders of not less than 10% of the shares entitled to be voted may call a special meeting.

b. Action on extraordinary transactions may only be taken at the annual meeting.

c. Notice of a special but not an annual meeting must include an agenda if extraordinary transactions are to be approved.

d. Action on extraordinary transactions taken at special but not annual meetings is void in the absence of notice, waiver of notice, or attendance without objection.

The correct answer is (a). *(Publisher)*

REQUIRED: The true statement about shareholders' meetings.

DISCUSSION: When shareholder action is required concerning a fundamental corporate change, a meeting must be held. If the issue must be resolved before the annual meeting, a special meeting may be called by the board, by a person authorized by the bylaws (e.g., the president), or by holders of not less than 10% of the shares entitled to be voted at the meeting.

Answer (b) is incorrect because action may also be taken at special meetings. Answers (c) and (d) are incorrect because notice must be given prior to any meeting or the action taken is void. If extraordinary changes are to be voted on, the purposes must be stated in the notice, including that for an annual meeting.

118. Under the MBCA, which of the following is a true statement about involuntary dissolution of a corporation?

a. The attorney general, shareholders, and directors but not creditors may dissolve a corporation through court action.

b. Administrative dissolution by the secretary of state may be achieved for failure to pay franchise taxes or to deliver an annual report.

c. If otherwise properly formed, the corporation cannot be dissolved on the grounds that its articles were obtained by fraud.

d. A creditor may seek dissolution but only if (s)he has reduced a claim to judgment.

The correct answer is (b). *(Publisher)*

REQUIRED: The true statement about involuntary dissolution.

DISCUSSION: Administrative dissolution in a proceeding commenced by the secretary of state may be effected on grounds of failure to pay any franchise tax or penalty, to deliver an annual report, or to maintain a registered office or agent in the state. Expiration of the period of duration stated in the articles is also grounds for such action.

Answers (a) and (d) are incorrect because creditors of an insolvent corporation may sue for its dissolution if a judgment has been returned unsatisfied or the corporate debt has been admitted in writing. Answer (c) is incorrect because the attorney general may sue for dissolution if the articles were obtained by fraud or if the corporation is exceeding or abusing its authority or is corrupt.

119. Which of the following would be grounds for the judicial dissolution of a corporation on the petition of a shareholder?

a. Refusal of the board of directors to declare a dividend.

b. Waste of corporate assets by the board of directors.

c. Loss operations of the corporation for three years.

d. Failure by the corporation to file its federal income tax returns.

The correct answer is (b). *(CPA 584 L-6)*

REQUIRED: The grounds for judicial dissolution by a shareholder.

DISCUSSION: Under the RMBCA, shareholders may seek a court-ordered dissolution if a corporate deadlock develops; if those in control have acted, are acting, or will act illegally, oppressively, or fraudulently; or if assets are being misapplied or wasted.

Answer (a) is incorrect because if the directors comply with their fiduciary duties and do not abuse their discretion, their business judgment will not be questioned by a court. Answer (c) is incorrect because net operating losses are not grounds for dissolution since many corporations may survive to become consistently profitable. Answer (d) is incorrect because failure to file results in assessment of a penalty, not dissolution.

120. A corporation may be voluntarily dissolved

a. By the unanimous written consent of all voting shareholders.

b. By resolution of the board of directors.

c. By resolution of the board of directors approved by an absolute majority of all voting shares or of such greater proportion as is provided in the articles.

d. By a majority vote of all shareholders.

The correct answer is (c). *(Publisher)*

REQUIRED: When a corporation may be voluntarily dissolved.

DISCUSSION: The legal termination of a corporation may be brought about by action of the corporation itself. This requires a resolution by the board of directors which is approved by a majority of all voting shareholders, or if so provided in the articles, by a supermajority of the voting shareholders. If voting is by classes of stock, each class of stock with voting rights must approve the dissolution by at least a majority vote. A court could enjoin an otherwise proper dissolution on the ground that public policy required the corporation's continuation.

Answer (a) is incorrect because the voluntary dissolution of the corporation by consent of the shareholders (without approval of the board of directors) requires unanimous written consent of all shareholders, not merely those entitled to vote. Answer (b) is incorrect because the board of directors does not have the power to dissolve the corporation without shareholder approval. Answer (d) is incorrect because the voluntary dissolution of the corporation requires either unanimous written consent of all shareholders or a resolution of the board of directors plus approval of at least a majority of all shareholders entitled to vote.

121. Under the federal Racketeer Influenced and Corrupt Organizations Act (RICO)

a. A legitimate business corporation may be seized if its control was acquired with the proceeds of illicit activities.

b. The government may bring criminal but not civil actions to enforce the Act.

c. Illegitimate associations, illegal profits, but not legitimate enterprises may be forfeited.

d. A pattern of racketeering may consist of one criminal act, such as extortion, bribery, or mail fraud.

The correct answer is (a). *(Publisher)*

REQUIRED: The true statement about RICO.

DISCUSSION: The purpose of RICO is to reach organized crime's interests in legitimate businesses. The Act is to be construed broadly for the purpose of prohibiting a pattern of racketeering, which is defined as at least two acts of criminal conduct of specified types, e.g., mail and securities fraud, bribery, extortion, illegal gambling, and narcotics violations, within a 10-year period. The Act provides for both criminal and civil sanctions. The federal government can also trace illegal profits and proceeds and confiscate legitimate businesses as well as illegal goods and profits.

Answer (b) is incorrect because the Act's civil suit provisions have been controversial since they have been broadly applied to activities not connected to organized crime. Answer (c) is incorrect because legitimate enterprises may also be confiscated. Answer (d) is incorrect because commission of at least two of a wide variety of crimes constitutes a pattern of racketeering.

122. Under which of the following circumstances would a corporation's existence terminate?

a. The death of its sole owner-shareholder.

b. Its becoming insolvent.

c. Its legal consolidation with another corporation.

d. Its reorganization under the federal bankruptcy laws.

The correct answer is (c). *(CPA 1174 L-35)*

REQUIRED: The circumstances under which a corporation's existence would terminate.

DISCUSSION: In a legal consolidation with another corporation, the existence of both corporations terminates. The succeeding entity is a new corporation, requires a new charter, and is responsible to the creditors of both dissolved corporations.

Answer (a) is incorrect because one of the fundamental characteristics of the corporate form is that it is a separate legal entity not affected by the death of its shareholders. Answer (b) is incorrect because a corporation may continue its existence even though insolvent. Answer (d) is incorrect because neither reorganization nor straight bankruptcy (no discharge for a corporation or partnership) under bankruptcy law terminates the existence of a corporation. All bankruptcy proceedings are intended to save the corporation.

123. The boards of directors of Anchor Corp. and Bridge, Inc., two corporations whose shares are listed on a major stock exchange, have discussed the possibility of merging the companies. Considering such a merger

a. Unanimous approval by both boards of directors of the merger would permit the merger without approval of shareholders of the corporations.

b. Approval by at least a two-thirds majority of the board of directors of each corporation would permit merger without shareholder approval.

c. If the merger were validly accomplished by an exchange of Anchor stock for Bridge stock with Bridge surviving, creditors of Anchor could look to Bridge for payment of their claims.

d. The new board of directors immediately after the merger of Anchor into Bridge automatically consists of the previous boards of the two corporations.

The correct answer is (c). *(CPA 574 L-37)*

REQUIRED: The correct statement regarding a merger of two corporations.

DISCUSSION: In a merger, two or more corporations are combined so that one corporation survives and absorbs the other(s). Unlike a consolidation, no new corporation comes into being. But like a consolidation, the successor entity will be liable to the creditors of its predecessors.

Answers (a) and (b) are incorrect because a merger is such a fundamental change in the corporate entity that shareholder approval of each corporation is required. Since the change is so fundamental, stockholders who do not wish to maintain their investment in a substantially different firm are given the right to a mandatory buy-out of their stock. Answer (d) is incorrect because the composition of the board of directors of the survivor of a merger would be determined pursuant to the plan of merger approved by the shareholders.

124. Barton Corporation and Clagg Corporation have decided to combine their separate companies pursuant to the provisions of their state corporation laws. After much discussion and negotiation, they decided that a consolidation was the appropriate procedure to be followed. Which of the following is an incorrect statement with respect to the contemplated statutory consolidation?

a. A statutory consolidation pursuant to state law is recognized by the Internal Revenue Code as a type of tax-free reorganization.

b. The larger of the two corporations will emerge as the surviving corporation.

c. Creditors of Barton and Clagg will have their claims protected despite the consolidation.

d. The shareholders of both Barton and Clagg must approve the plan of consolidation.

The correct answer is (b). *(CPA 580 L-6)*

REQUIRED: The false statement regarding the consolidation of two corporations.

DISCUSSION: In a consolidation, two or more corporations combine to form a new corporate entity. The old corporations are dissolved in the process of forming the new corporation. Thus, neither of the original corporations in this instance would survive. The newly consolidated corporation must obtain a new charter and is liable for the debts of the dissolved corporations.

Answers (a), (c), and (d) are incorrect because each is a correct statement regarding statutory consolidations.

125. All but which of the following would have potential ramifications which would be in violation of the antitrust laws?

a. The merger of a financially sound corporation with a competitor in a failing condition.

b. The acquisition of substantially all of the assets of a competing corporation.

c. The acquisition of a controlling stock interest in a directly competing corporation.

d. A horizontal merger of competing corporations.

The correct answer is (a). *(Publisher)*

REQUIRED: The fundamental corporate change not involving an antitrust violation.

DISCUSSION: The antitrust laws generally prohibit mergers among corporations which might diminish competition in the industry. An exception is provided, however, for mergers and acquisitions to save a failing corporation.

Answers (b), (c), and (d) are incorrect because the Clayton Act, as amended, prohibits the acquisition of a controlling stock interest, the acquisition of substantially all the assets, and the merger of competing corporations where the effect may be to substantially lessen competition.

CHAPTER SEVENTEEN
SECURED TRANSACTIONS

The explanations of the answers in this chapter are based almost solely on Article 9 of the Uniform Commercial Code (UCC). References to the relevant UCC Sections are provided for those interested in the source of the law. These references are only given for the major UCC Sections supporting the answer, however, so as not to inundate the explanation with citations.

Secured transactions overlaps with consumer and credit law, mortgages, bankruptcy, and suretyship. Hence, this chapter should be read with the chapters on those topics.

17.1 Secured Transactions: Introduction and Definitions

1. For purposes of the Secured Transactions Article of the Uniform Commercial Code, a security interest includes

a. An interest in any property that secures payment or performance of an obligation.

b. An interest in personal property or fixtures that secures payment or performance of an obligation.

c. The special interest of a buyer of goods acquired on identification of the goods to a contract for sale.

d. The interest of a consignor when title is retained regardless of whether the arrangement is intended as security.

The correct answer is (b). *(Publisher)*

REQUIRED: The interest treated as a security interest under Article 9.

DISCUSSION: Under UCC 1-201, a security interest is "an interest in personal property or fixtures that secures payment or performance of an obligation. The retention or reservation of title by a seller of goods notwithstanding, shipment or delivery to the buyer is limited in effect to a reservation of a security interest." This broad definition encompasses currently existing security devices and any new ones that may evolve.

Answer (a) is incorrect because the interest must be in personal property or fixtures. Answer (c) is incorrect because the UCC states that this special interest is not a security interest. Answer (d) is incorrect because reservation of title is not a security interest unless a lease or consignment is intended as security. This is consistent with the general UCC approach of de-emphasizing concern about location of title.

2. Which of the following is included within the scope of the Secured Transactions Article of the UCC?

a. The outright sale of accounts receivable.

b. A landlord's lien.

c. The assignment of a claim for wages.

d. The sale of chattel paper as a part of the sale of a business out of which it arose.

The correct answer is (a). *(CPA 1180 L-38)*

REQUIRED: The transaction included within the scope of Article 9 of the UCC.

DISCUSSION: Article 9 of the UCC explicitly applies not only to transactions intended to create security interests in personal property or fixtures, but also to the sale of accounts or chattel paper (UCC 9-102).

Answers (b), (c), and (d) are incorrect because each states a transaction explicitly excluded from Article 9 (UCC 9-104).

3. Migrane Financial does a wide variety of lending. It provides funds to manufacturers, middlemen, retailers, consumers, and home owners. In all instances it intends to create a security interest in the loan transactions it enters into. To which of the following will Article 9 (Secured Transactions) of the Uniform Commercial Code not apply?

a. A second mortgage on the borrower's home.

b. An equipment lease.

c. The sale of accounts.

d. Field warehousing.

The correct answer is (a). *(CPA 579 L-18)*

REQUIRED: The transaction to which Article 9 of the UCC will not apply.

DISCUSSION: Except for security interests in fixtures, Article 9 of the UCC does not apply to transactions in real estate. Mortgages are discussed in Chapter 21 of this book. There is no uniform act covering mortgages because they are local transactions.

Answer (b) is incorrect because Article 9 does apply to an equipment lease if the lease is intended to create a security interest rather than a true lease (see question 5). Answer (c) is incorrect because Article 9 explicitly applies to the sale of accounts. Answer (d) is incorrect because field warehousing is a method by which a secured party may both attach and perfect a security interest. In a field warehousing arrangement, the creditor advances funds and takes possession of the collateral by locking it up (warehouse, shed, or fenced area) on the debtor's property. It can then easily be released a portion at a time as the debtor needs it and pays off the debt.

4. The scope of secured transactions in the Uniform Commercial Code does not include

a. Pledges.

b. Transactions in which title has not passed.

c. After-acquired collateral.

d. Sale of corporate debentures.

The correct answer is (d). *(CPA 1175 L-35)*

REQUIRED: The transaction excluded from Article 9 of the UCC.

DISCUSSION: Article 9 applies to security interests in personal property and fixtures, and also to sales of accounts or chattel paper. It does not apply to a sale of corporate debentures. These are governed by Article 8 of the UCC, other state statutes, and possibly the federal security laws.

Answers (a), (b), and (c) are incorrect because each is within the scope of Article 9 of the UCC.

5. The Wu Wei Company is a giant conglomerate which manufactures abacuses. Wu Wei has just begun to market its latest model, the Yin and Yang, which is the product of years of research and is the best and most complex abacus ever made. The agreements with Wu Wei's customers take the form of leases. Wu Wei expressly retains title but grants the customer an option to purchase at the end of the lease period for an additional sum equal to 1% of the aggregate lease payments. Does Article 9 of the UCC on secured transactions govern the lease?

a. Yes. The inclusion of the option to purchase in itself makes the lease one intended for security.

b. Yes. The lease is one intended for security because the lessee has the option to become the owner of the property for a nominal consideration.

c. No. The express retention of title indicates that the transaction is a true lease and not a sale with retention of a security interest.

d. No. In order for the UCC to apply, Wu Wei would have had to have filed a financing statement.

The correct answer is (b). *(Publisher)*

REQUIRED: Whether Article 9 of the UCC on secured transactions governs the lease.

DISCUSSION: UCC 9-102 states that Article 9 applies to a lease intended as security. The form of the transaction or the name by which the parties have called it is irrelevant if the parties have intended the creation of a security interest. Under UCC 1-201, whether a lease is intended as security is to be determined by the facts of each case. If the agreement states that upon compliance with its terms, the lessee shall become the owner of the property for nominal consideration, then the lease is deemed to be one intended for security. Wu Wei's "lease" is therefore governed by Article 9.

Answer (a) is incorrect because UCC 1-201 states that the inclusion of an option to purchase does not in and of itself make the lease one intended for security. Answer (c) is incorrect because under the UCC the particular facts of each case will govern whether Article 9 applies to a "lease." The general policy of the UCC is to ignore location of title in determining the rights and duties of the parties. Answer (d) is incorrect because the application of Article 9 is determined by the nature of the underlying transaction as discussed above. Financing statements are provided for in Article 9, but it is not a financing statement that makes the UCC apply.

6. Article 9 of the UCC applies to any transaction intended to create a security interest in personal property or fixtures. Which is the incorrect statement concerning the forms of property in which a security interest may be created?

a. An account is any right to payment for goods sold or leased or for services rendered, not evidenced by an instrument or chattel paper, whether or not earned by performance.

b. General intangibles include patents, trademarks, and copyrights.

c. Documents include bills of lading, warehouse receipts, and promissory notes.

d. Chattel paper is a writing or writings which evidence both a monetary obligation and a security in or lease of specific goods.

The correct answer is (c). *(Publisher)*

REQUIRED: The false statement of property in which a security interest may be created.

DISCUSSION: Article 9 of the UCC governs the creation of security interests in any form of personal property as well as fixtures. "Document" means document of title and includes bills of lading and warehouse receipts that evidence rights in specific goods (UCC 9-105 and 1-201). Promissory notes are negotiable instruments and are not properly classified under documents.

Answer (a) is incorrect because it correctly defines the term "account" (UCC 9-106). Answer (b) is incorrect because a "general intangible" is any personal property other than goods, accounts, chattel paper, documents, instruments, and money (UCC 9-106). To the extent that a U.S. statute governs, however, the UCC is inapplicable to patents, trademarks, and copyrights. Answer (d) is incorrect because it states the proper definition of "chattel paper" (UCC 9-105).

7. Which is the correct classification of goods under UCC 9-109?

a. Consumer goods, instruments, and inventory.

b. Accounts, equipment, inventory, unextracted minerals.

c. Consumer goods, equipment, farm products, inventory.

d. Accounts, consumer goods, equipment, inventory.

The correct answer is (c). *(Publisher)*

REQUIRED: The correct classification of goods under UCC 9-109.

DISCUSSION: UCC 9-109 classifies goods into four categories. Consumer goods are those used or bought for use primarily for personal, family, or household purposes. Equipment is used primarily in business but excludes inventory, farm products, and consumer goods. Farm products are crops, livestock, supplies used or produced in farming operations, or products of crops or livestock in their unmanufactured states. They must be in the hands of one engaged in farming operations. If goods are farm products, they are not equipment or inventory. Inventory consists of goods held by one who holds them for sale or lease or to be furnished under contracts of service or as raw material, work-in-process, or materials used or consumed in a business.

Answers (a), (b), and (d) are incorrect because UCC 9-105 defines goods as all things that are movable but not accounts, money, documents, instruments, chattel paper, general intangibles, or minerals before extraction.

8. Case Corporation manufactures electric drills and sells them to retail hardware stores. Under the Uniform Commercial Code, it is likely that

a. The drills are inventory in Case's hands.

b. The drills are equipment in Case's hands.

c. The raw materials on hand to be used in the manufacturing of the drills are not inventory in Case's hands.

d. The drills are considered equipment in the hands of the hardware stores who purchased them.

The correct answer is (a). *(CPA 575 L-45)*

REQUIRED: The correct statement regarding the classification of property.

DISCUSSION: The classification of property depends on who holds the property and the use to which it is put (UCC 9-109). Electric drills are inventory in the hands of their manufacturer (or a retailer) since they are held for sale. The drills would be consumer goods, however, in the hands of someone using them primarily for personal, family, or household purposes. They would be equipment in the hands of someone using them in his/her business.

Answer (b) is incorrect because the drills are inventory in Case's hands. Case holds the drills for sale rather than for use in its business. Answer (c) is incorrect because the definition of inventory includes raw materials consumed by a manufacturer in the course of its business. Answer (d) is incorrect because the drills would be considered inventory in the hands of the hardware stores so long as they are held for sale to others.

17.2 Formation of Security Interests

9. Attachment under Article 9 of the Uniform Commercial Code applies primarily to the rights of

a. Third party creditors.

b. Parties to secured transactions.

c. Holders in due course.

d. Warehousemen.

The correct answer is (b). *(CPA 583 L-50)*

REQUIRED: The parties to whose rights attachment primarily applies.

DISCUSSION: Attachment is the process by which a security interest becomes enforceable against a debtor by a secured party. Three events must occur: collateral is in the hands of the secured party or the debtor has signed a security agreement describing the collateral; value has been given; and the debtor has rights in the collateral. When these events have taken place, the security interest will be enforceable against the debtor with respect to the collateral and attachment will have occurred (UCC 9-203).

Answers (a), (c), and (d) are incorrect because perfection, not attachment, is the process by which a security interest is made effective against third parties. However, a holder in due course of an instrument or a warehouseman with a lien arising out of the rendition of services with respect to goods will prevail against even a perfected security interest (UCC 9-309 and 310).

10. In order for a security interest in goods to attach, one of the requirements is that the debtor

a. Sign a financing statement that adequately describes the goods.

b. Sign a security agreement that adequately describes the goods.

c. Receive the goods from the creditor.

d. Have rights in the goods.

The correct answer is (d). *(CPA 1187 L-42)*

REQUIRED: The requirement for attachment of a security interest in goods.

DISCUSSION: UCC 9-203 states the requirements for attachment of a security interest. Among them is that a debtor have rights in the collateral. Before a security interest will attach all of the requirements for attachment must be met.

Answer (a) is incorrect because a financing statement is not required for attachment, but may be required for perfection. Answer (b) is incorrect because the debtor need not sign a security agreement if the secured party has possession of the collateral pursuant to agreement. Answer (c) is incorrect because the requirement that value be given may be satisfied by the creditor's giving a promise to deliver goods.

11. Under the UCC Secured Transactions Article, for a security interest to attach, the

a. Debtor must agree to the creation of the security interest.

b. Creditor must properly file a financing statement.

c. Debtor must be denied all rights in the collateral.

d. Creditor must take and hold the collateral.

The correct answer is (a). *(CPA 1189 L-50)*

REQUIRED: The correct statement about the event necessary for attachment of a security interest.

DISCUSSION: Article 9 of the UCC governs secured transactions and sales of accounts and chattel paper. UCC 9-203 specifically addresses the issue of attachment of a security interest. It states that attachment occurs when all of the following events have taken place unless the time is postponed by an explicit agreement: value has been given; the debtor has rights in the collateral; and the collateral is in the possession of the secured party pursuant to agreement, or the debtor has signed a security agreement containing a description of the collateral.

Answer (b) is incorrect because a financing statement puts people other than those party to the secured transaction on notice of the secured party's interest. A financing statement is not mandatory for attachment, but it may be necessary to perfect a security interest. Answer (c) is incorrect because the debtor must have rights in the collateral. Answer (d) is incorrect because the secured party may have possession of the collateral pursuant to the agreement, but it is not required to obtain and hold the collateral.

12. Dart Co., which is engaged in the business of selling appliances, borrowed $8,000 from Arco Bank. Dart executed a promissory note for that amount and pledged all of its customer installment receivables as collateral for the loan. Dart executed a security agreement that described the collateral, but Arco did not file a financing statement. With respect to this transaction,

a. Attachment of the security interest took place when Dart executed the security agreement.

b. Attachment of the security interest did not occur because Arco failed to file a financing statement.

c. Perfection of the security interest occurred despite Arco's failure to file a financing statement.

d. The UCC Secured Transactions Article does not apply because Arco failed to file a financing statement.

The correct answer is (a). *(CPA 1188 L-53)*

REQUIRED: The correct statement about the timing of attachment of a security interest.

DISCUSSION: According to UCC 9-203, attachment of a security interest occurs upon the completion of all of the following requirements. The requirements include the debtor having rights in the collateral, the giving of value by the creditor, and the existence of a security agreement. Because Arco gave value of $8,000 and Dart had rights in the installment receivables, attachment occurred upon Dart's execution of the security agreement.

Answer (b) is incorrect because the filing of a financing statement is not required by Article 9 for attachment to occur. However, it may be required for perfection of the security interest. Answer (c) is incorrect because under UCC 9-302, which governs filing to perfect a security interest, most security interests are required to be perfected through filing. One of the stated exceptions is for accounts, but it applies only to an assignment that alone or in conjunction with others to the same assignee does **not** transfer a significant part of the assignor's accounts. This pledge was for all the customer receivables. Answer (d) is incorrect because Article 9 does not require the filing of a financing statement. A financing statement puts parties other than those party to the security transaction on notice of the secured party's security interest in the collateral.

13. Retailer Corp. was in need of financing. To secure a loan, it made an oral assignment of its accounts receivable to J. Roe, a local investor, under which Roe loaned Retailer, on a continuing basis, 90% of the face value of the assigned accounts receivable. Retailer collected from the account debtors and remitted to Roe at intervals. Before the debt was paid, Retailer filed a petition in bankruptcy. Which of the following is correct?

a. As between the account debtors and Roe, the assignment is not an enforceable security interest.

b. Roe is a secured creditor to the extent of the unpaid debt.

c. Other unpaid creditors of Retailer Corp. who knew of the assignment are bound by its terms.

d. An assignment of accounts, to be valid, requires the debtors owing the accounts to be notified.

The correct answer is (a). *(CPA 1180 L-36)*

REQUIRED: The correct statement concerning an oral assignment of accounts receivable.

DISCUSSION: Retailer's assignment does not constitute an enforceable security interest between the account debtors and Roe because a security interest does not attach until the collateral is either in the possession of the secured party or the debtor has signed a security agreement describing the collateral (UCC 9-203). Attachment of a security interest in accounts receivable requires that the debtor sign a security agreement since it is impossible for the secured party to take physical possession of the intangible collateral.

Answer (b) is incorrect because the security interest failed to attach since Retailer did not sign a security agreement. Answer (c) is incorrect because other unpaid creditors are not bound by the terms of the assignment since it was not even effective between the parties to it and also since they did not agree to it. Answer (d) is incorrect because an assignment of accounts receivable is valid even though the account debtors are not notified. However, their debts will be discharged if they pay the original creditor.

14. Maxim Corporation, a wholesaler, was indebted to the Wilson Manufacturing Corporation in the amount of $50,000 arising out of the sale of goods delivered to Maxim on credit. Wilson and Maxim signed a security agreement creating a security interest in certain collateral of Maxim. The collateral was described in the security agreement as "the inventory of Maxim Corporation, presently existing and thereafter acquired." In general, this description of the collateral

a. Applies only to inventory sold by Wilson to Maxim.

b. Is sufficient to cover all inventory.

c. Is insufficient because it attempts to cover after-acquired inventory.

d. Must be more specific for the security interest to be perfected against subsequent creditors.

The correct answer is (b). *(CPA 1175 L-33)*

REQUIRED: The correct statement concerning the description of the collateral.

DISCUSSION: Unless the secured party takes possession of the collateral, the security interest will not attach unless the debtor has signed a security agreement which adequately describes the collateral. Such a description is sufficient if it reasonably identifies what is described even though the language is not specific (UCC 9-110).

Answer (a) is incorrect because the security interest attaches to inventory sold to the debtor by other parties as well as by the secured party. It covers all inventory owned by Maxim at any time while the security agreement is in effect; i.e., while Maxim owes Wilson money. Answer (c) is incorrect because a security interest (and the agreement) may cover after-acquired property. Answer (d) is incorrect because a description is sufficient if it reasonably identifies what is described. Here, the description is adequate to allow interested parties to identify the collateral, i.e., all inventory.

15. Lombard, Inc. manufactures exclusive designer apparel. It sells through franchised clothing stores on consignment, retaining a security interest in the goods. Gifford is one of Lombard's franchisees pursuant to a detailed contract signed by both Lombard and Gifford. In order for the security interest to be valid against Gifford with respect to the designer apparel in Gifford's possession, Lombard

a. Must retain title to the goods.

b. Does not have to do anything further.

c. Must file a financing statement.

d. Must perfect its security interest against Gifford's creditors.

The correct answer is (b). *(CPA 1182 L-52)*

REQUIRED: The action the secured party must take for the security interest to be effective against the debtor.

DISCUSSION: A security interest becomes enforceable against the debtor (attaches) when the secured party holds the collateral or the debtor has signed a security agreement describing the collateral; when value has been given; and when the debtor has rights in the collateral (UCC 9-203). Here, all these conditions have been satisfied. The detailed contract was a "security agreement" because it created or provided for a security interest (UCC 9-105). Value has been given because Lombard has effectively sold the goods on credit to Gifford. The debtor has rights in the goods because it has the power to sell the goods at a profit. Consequently, the security interest has attached and Lombard need not do anything further to protect itself against Gifford.

Answer (a) is incorrect because the provisions of Article 9 apply regardless of the location of title. Answer (c) is incorrect because filing is a means of perfecting a security interest so as to gain priority over third parties. Answer (d) is incorrect because attachment is sufficient against the debtor.

16. Even if provided for in a security agreement, the secured party will generally have no right in

a. Proceeds received from the disposition of the original collateral.

b. Collateral to the extent it secures future advances.

c. Consumer goods acquired more than 10 days after the security interest attached.

d. Inventory or accounts acquired in the future.

The correct answer is (c). *(Publisher)*

REQUIRED: The right not given to a secured party.

DISCUSSION: Under UCC 9-204, a security agreement may include after-acquired property as collateral for the obligation secured. But it does not apply to consumer goods given as additional security unless the debtor acquires rights in them within ten days after the secured party gives value.

Answer (a) is incorrect because UCC 9-203 provides that the secured party has rights in the proceeds from the sale, exchange, collection, or other disposition of collateral or proceeds unless otherwise agreed. Answer (b) is incorrect because obligations covered by a security agreement may include future advances (UCC 9-204). Answer (d) is incorrect because after-acquired property clauses are generally effective except for the limitation discussed above with regard to consumer goods.

17. On January 1, Shemwell Co. signed a security agreement giving Jones a security interest in a crane Shemwell was planning to buy for its business. In exchange for the security agreement, Jones signed a contract to lend Shemwell $10,000 on request. On January 9, Shemwell purchased the crane. On January 15, Jones delivered $10,000 to Shemwell. On January 20, Jones filed the security agreement with the appropriate public officials. Under the UCC, when did Jones's security interest in Shemwell's crane attach?

a. On January 1, when the security agreement was signed.

b. On January 9, when Shemwell purchased the crane for its business.

c. On January 15, when Jones delivered $10,000 to Shemwell.

d. On January 20, when Jones filed the security agreement.

The correct answer is (b). *(J. Pittman)*

REQUIRED: The time of attachment of a security interest.

DISCUSSION: Under the UCC, a security interest attaches when all the following are present: the debtor has signed a security agreement (or the secured party is in possession of the collateral), the secured party has given value, and the debtor has rights in the collateral (UCC 9-203). These requirements were all met on January 9.

Answer (a) is incorrect because on January 1 Shemwell did not have rights in the crane. Answer (c) is incorrect because Jones had given value before the loan proceeds were delivered. Value includes binding commitments to extend credit (UCC 1-201). Hence, Jones gave value on January 1. Answer (d) is incorrect because filing is not necessary for attachment of a security interest.

18. Unless otherwise agreed, when collateral covered under the Secured Transactions Article of the UCC is in the secured party's possession,

a. The risk of accidental loss is on the debtor to the extent of any deficiency in any effective insurance coverage.

b. The secured party will lose his/her security interest if (s)he commingles fungible collateral.

c. Reasonable expenses incurred to preserve the collateral are chargeable to the secured party.

d. Any repledge of the collateral by the secured party will be unenforceable.

The correct answer is (a). *(CPA 1184 L-60)*

REQUIRED: The parties' rights and duties when the secured party holds the collateral.

DISCUSSION: A secured party must use reasonable care in the custody and preservation of collateral in his/her possession and is liable for any loss caused by failure to meet this obligation. But unless otherwise agreed, UCC 9-207 states that "the risk of accidental loss or damage is on the debtor to the extent of any deficiency in any effective insurance coverage of the party in possession."

Answer (b) is incorrect because the secured party must keep the collateral identifiable but fungible collateral may be commingled. Answer (c) is incorrect because the expenses, including insurance and taxes, are chargeable to the debtor and are secured by the collateral. Answer (d) is incorrect because repledging the collateral is permitted on terms not impairing the debtor's right to redeem it.

19. Charlotte O'Hare was the holder of a negotiable instrument which had been endorsed by Clark Fable. She also owned stock in Plantation Parties, Inc. which was a large Georgia corporation engaged in nostalgia revival. Charlotte pledged the instrument and the stock as security for a loan from the Ante-Bellum Bank. Subsequently, the instrument became due but neither Charlotte nor the bank presented it for payment, and as a result Clark was discharged from liability. Also, both cash and stock dividends were declared on the stock and there was a disagreement as to who had rights thereto. Charlotte had a right to

a. The cash dividend, but had a duty to preserve rights against the endorser of the instrument.

b. Both the cash and stock dividends but was under a duty to preserve rights against the endorser.

c. The stock dividend, and had no duty to preserve rights against the endorser.

d. The cash dividend, but had no duty to preserve rights against the endorser.

The correct answer is (d). *(Publisher)*

REQUIRED: The rights and duties of the parties when collateral is in the secured party's possession.

DISCUSSION: UCC 9-207 defines the rights and duties of the parties when collateral is in the secured party's possession. The secured party may hold as additional security any increase or profits received from the collateral except money. A cash dividend would belong to Charlotte and would have to be remitted to her or applied in reduction of the obligation.

The secured party, not the debtor, must use reasonable care in the custody and preservation of collateral in its possession. In the case of an instrument, reasonable care includes taking those steps necessary to preserve rights against prior parties; e.g., the bank should have presented the instrument for payment.

Answer (a) is incorrect because the bank had the duty to preserve rights against the endorser. Answers (b) and (c) are incorrect because the bank is entitled to retain the property dividend as additional security.

20. Shemwell Co., in purchasing a punch press from Jones Equipment, Inc., signed a promissory note for the purchase price. In addition, Shemwell signed a security agreement granting Jones a security interest in the punch press. The security agreement stated, "The buyer hereby waives as against any assignee of the security interest any claim or defense that the buyer may have against the seller." Jones assigned the promissory note and security agreement to 1st Bank and Trust. Later, the punch press malfunctioned and Shemwell refused to continue payments to 1st Bank. The waiver of defenses clause is not enforceable against Shemwell if

a. Jones had issued a written warranty on the punch press.

b. 1st Bank did not give value for the assignment from Jones.

c. Jones knew the punch press could malfunction.

d. After the assignment 1st Bank learned the punch press had malfunctioned.

The correct answer is (b). (J. Pittman)

REQUIRED: The correct statement about enforceability of a waiver of defenses clause.

DISCUSSION: A waiver of defenses clause contained in a security agreement is not always binding. For personal defenses (here, breach of contract) in business transactions, the debtor is bound by the waiver only when the assignee has taken the assignment for value, in good faith, and without notice of a claim or defense. A buyer who as part of one transaction signs both a negotiable instrument and a security agreement makes such an agreement (UCC 9-206).

Answers (a) and (c) are incorrect because neither has a bearing on whether 1st Bank received the assignment under the terms of UCC 9-206. Answer (d) is incorrect because knowledge of possible defenses is immaterial if it is learned after the assignee has given value in good faith.

17.3 Perfection

21. Two Uniform Commercial Code concepts relating to secured transactions are "attachment" and "perfection." Which of the following is correct in connection with the similarities and differences between these two concepts?

a. They are mutually exclusive and wholly independent of each other.

b. Attachment relates primarily to the rights against the debtor and perfection relates primarily to the rights against third parties.

c. Satisfaction of one automatically satisfies the other.

d. It is not possible to have a simultaneous attachment and perfection.

The correct answer is (b). *(CPA 1182 L-54)*

REQUIRED: The correct statement comparing "attachment" and "perfection."

DISCUSSION: The concept of "attachment" involves the creation of an enforceable security interest by the creditor in the debtor's property (UCC 9-203). The concept of "perfection" involves establishing the priority of the secured party's security interest against other security interest in the collateral and purchasers thereof (UCC 9-312). Therefore, attachment involves rights between the creditor and debtor, while perfection involves rights between the creditor and other creditors or purchasers.

Answer (a) is incorrect because perfection cannot occur until the security interest attaches. Answer (c) is incorrect because attachment is the creation of an enforceable security interest, and perfection is an additional step to obtain greater rights. Answer (d) is incorrect because it is possible to have a simultaneous attachment and perfection simply by taking possession or filing when the security interest is created (and in a very few instances, attachment is automatic perfection).

22. The Secured Transactions Article of the UCC recognizes various methods of perfecting a security interest in collateral. Which of the following is not recognized by the UCC?

a. Filing.

b. Possession.

c. Consent.

d. Attachment.

The correct answer is (c). *(CPA 1180 L-37)*

REQUIRED: The method of perfection not recognized by the UCC.

DISCUSSION: Perfection is a term used to describe when certain steps have been taken with respect to a security interest to give the creditor priority over other secured creditors. It generally consists of a means of giving notice to other potentially secured creditors. Possession of the collateral or filing a financing statement can be used most of the time. Attachment alone suffices in a few limited circumstances. However, consent is never sufficient.

Answers (a), (b), and (d) are incorrect because each is a method of perfection recognized by the UCC.

23. Perfection of a security interest permits the secured party to protect its interest by

a. Avoiding the need to file a financing statement.

b. Preventing another creditor from obtaining a security interest in the same collateral.

c. Establishing priority over the claims of most subsequent secured creditors.

d. Denying the debtor the right to possess the collateral.

The correct answer is (c). *(CPA 1189 L-53)*

REQUIRED: The correct statement about the rights of a perfected secured party.

DISCUSSION: In order for a secured party to gain rights superior to the rights of a subsequent secured creditor, a secured party must give constructive notice of its security interest in the collateral by perfecting its security interest. The secured party maximizes rights with respect to the collateral by establishing priority over prior unperfected security interests and subsequent secured parties.

Answer (a) is incorrect because filing a financing statement is required to perfect an interest in certain types of collateral, such as accounts receivable. Answer (b) is incorrect because perfection of a security interest does not bar other creditors from obtaining a security interest in collateral. Answer (d) is incorrect because possession is one means of perfecting a security interest, but the parties ordinarily contemplate that the debtor will have possession.

24. Perfection of a security interest in personal property may be accomplished in many cases by filing a financing statement. A financing statement is

a. Any writing evidencing both a monetary obligation and a security interest in specific goods.

b. An agreement that creates or provides for a security interest.

c. Any writing evidencing a contractual agreement by which a debtor acquires possession of goods and the seller retains title until payment is made.

d. Any writing filed in the public records that provides notice of a security interest in collateral.

The correct answer is (d). *(Publisher)*

REQUIRED: The correct definition of a financing statement.

DISCUSSION: A secured party may protect his/her interest in many kinds of personal property held by the debtor by filing a financing statement in the appropriate public records. This writing gives notice of the security interest in the types of collateral listed or in the items of collateral described. The financing statement must be signed by the debtor, contain the names of the debtor and the secured party, an address of the secured party, a mailing address of the debtor, and a statement describing the collateral (UCC 9-402).

Answer (a) is incorrect because it defines chattel paper. Answer (b) is incorrect because it defines the security agreement itself. This agreement may be filed as a financing statement if it meets the requirements of UCC 9-402. Answer (c) is incorrect because it defines a conditional-sale contract.

25. The perfection of a security interest by filing a financing statement

a. Serves to protect the secured party's interest in the collateral against most creditors who acquire a security interest in the same collateral after the filing.

b. Is necessary to enable the secured party to enforce its security interest against the debtor.

c. Serves to give the public actual notice.

d. Gives the secured party priority over all other parties who acquire an interest in the collateral after the filing.

The correct answer is (a). *(CPA 1186 L-50)*

REQUIRED: The correct statement about perfection of a security interest through filing a financing statement.

DISCUSSION: Perfection of a security interest maximizes a secured party's rights with respect to the collateral. Although perfection by filing a financing statement will not give the secured party priority over all subsequent secured parties, it will give priority over all unperfected interests and over most subsequent secured interests.

Answer (b) is incorrect because perfection is needed to put those not privy to the secured transaction on notice of the secured party's interest. However, it is not required to enforce the secured party's rights against the debtor. Answer (c) is incorrect because perfection by filing a financing statement gives the public constructive notice. Answer (d) is incorrect because perfection by filing a financing statement will give the secured party priority over all unperfected creditors and some, but not all, subsequent secured parties.

26. Burn Manufacturing borrowed $500,000 from Howard Finance Co., secured by Burn's current and future inventory, accounts receivable, and the proceeds thereof. The parties signed a financing statement that described the collateral and was filed in the appropriate state office. Burn subsequently defaulted on the repayment of the loan, and Howard attempted to enforce its security interest. Burn contended that Howard's security interest was unenforceable. In addition, Green, who subsequently gave credit to Burn without knowledge of Howard's security interest, is also attempting to defeat Howard's alleged security interest. The security interest in question is valid with respect to

a. Both Burn and Green.

b. Neither Burn nor Green.

c. Burn but not Green.

d. Green but not Burn.

The correct answer is (a). *(CPA 589 L-60)*

REQUIRED: The correct statement about the validity of a security interest.

DISCUSSION: Before attachment of the security interest, Article 9 of the UCC requires the creditor to give value, the debtor to have rights in the collateral, and a security agreement to exist. In this case, Howard has given value ($500,000), Burn has rights in the inventory and accounts receivable, and a security agreement exists. Thus, attachment has occurred, and the security interest is enforceable between the debtor and the secured party. Because Howard's security interest was perfected by filing a financing statement, notice of Howard's security interest is imputed to Green, and Howard's claim has priority over Green's.

Answers (b), (c), and (d) are incorrect because the security interest is enforceable against both Burn and Green.

27. The filing of a financing statement in the public records is often crucial to the perfection of a security interest. Which is the correct statement concerning the appropriate place of filing under the UCC?

a. The UCC provides that filing will be made exclusively in the office where a mortgage on real estate would be filed or recorded.

b. The UCC provides for filing exclusively in the office of the secretary of state or the equivalent.

c. The UCC provides for dual filing with regard to all forms of security: in the county where the security is kept and in the county where the debtor has its principal place of business.

d. The UCC provides for alternative systems of filing from which each state can choose.

The correct answer is (d). *(Publisher)*

REQUIRED: The appropriate place(s) for filing a financing statement.

DISCUSSION: The UCC does not attempt to resolve the dispute over whether a local or a centralized filing system is preferable. UCC 9-401 provides alternative subsections to be adopted by individual states according to local needs. If credit inquiries come principally from local sources about local debtors, then a county filing system is advantageous. Otherwise most filings in one central state office can be very useful.

Answer (a) is incorrect because all three alternatives provided by the UCC provide for filing in the real property records, but only when the collateral is timber, minerals, or fixtures. Answers (b) and (c) are incorrect because the UCC provides various alternatives for dual filing, local filing, and centralized filing.

28. For obvious commercial reasons, a debtor who has satisfied an obligation with respect to which a security interest was created and a financing statement filed may wish the record to reflect that the creditor no longer claims a security interest in the property of the debtor. Accordingly, the UCC provides for the filing of termination statements. Which of the following is true?

a. The requirements for filing termination statements are the same for all forms of property of the debtor.

b. In the case of inventory, the secured party must file a termination statement within one month after termination of any obligation.

c. Regardless of the nature of the property, when no further obligation exists, the secured party must upon written demand provide a termination statement within 10 days.

d. A termination statement need not be filed with respect to consumer goods.

The correct answer is (c). *(Publisher)*

REQUIRED: The correct statement concerning termination statements.

DISCUSSION: Since most financing statements last no more than 5 years unless a continuation statement is filed, the secured party is under no obligation to file a termination statement unless the collateral consists of consumer goods. In that case, after there is no further obligation, the secured party must file a termination statement within 1 month or within 10 days following written demand by the debtor (UCC 9-404). If the collateral is not consumer goods, the secured party is not required to file a termination statement. Rather, upon written demand by the debtor after no further obligation exists, the secured party must send the debtor a termination statement within 10 days, which the latter may file in the appropriate place. The penalty for noncompliance with UCC 9-404 is $100 payable to the debtor, who may also recover any loss caused by the secured party's noncompliance.

Answer (a) is incorrect because the UCC makes a distinction between consumer goods and other collateral as discussed above. Answer (b) is incorrect because it describes the requirement in the case of consumer goods, but not for any other collateral. Answer (d) is incorrect because the filing of a termination statement is required with respect to consumer goods.

29. On October 1, Winslow Corporation obtained a loan commitment of $250,000 from Liberty National Bank. Liberty filed a financing statement on October 2. On October 5, the $250,000 loan was consummated and Winslow signed a security agreement granting the bank a security interest in inventory, accounts receivable, and proceeds from the sale of the inventory and collection of the accounts receivable. Liberty's security interest was perfected

a. On October 1.

b. On October 2.

c. On October 5.

d. By attachment.

The correct answer is (c). *(CPA 1182 L-56)*

REQUIRED: The time a security interest attached and was perfected.

DISCUSSION: Under UCC 9-303, a security interest is perfected when it has attached and when all of the necessary steps required for perfection have been taken. The security interest did not attach until October 5 when the security agreement was signed. Since the financing statement had already been filed, October 5 was also the date when perfection occurred.

Answers (a) and (b) are incorrect because the security interest was perfected on October 5 as discussed above. Answer (d) is incorrect because a security interest in inventory, accounts, and their proceeds must be perfected by filing rather than attachment alone.

30. Attachment and perfection will occur simultaneously when

a. The security agreement so provides.

b. There is a purchase money security interest taken in inventory.

c. Attachment is by possession.

d. The goods are sold on consignment.

The correct answer is (c). *(CPA 583 L-47)*

REQUIRED: The situation in which attachment and perfection occur simultaneously.

DISCUSSION: Attachment occurs when the collateral is in the hands of the secured party by agreement or the debtor has signed a proper security agreement, value has been given, and the debtor has rights in the collateral (UCC 9-203). Most types of collateral may be perfected by the secured party's taking possession (UCC 9-305). Hence, attachment and perfection may occur simultaneously by possession.

Answer (a) is incorrect because attachment and perfection are not determined merely by agreement of the parties. They occur when the statutorily required steps have been taken. Answers (b) and (d) are incorrect because in each of these cases perfection is generally by filing. Although a financing statement can be filed before attachment (in which case attachment and perfection would occur simultaneously), this will not happen in all instances.

31. Mern Corp. is in the business of selling computers and computer software to the public. Mern sold and delivered a personal computer to Whyte on credit. Whyte executed and delivered to Mern a promissory note for the purchase price and a security agreement covering the computer. If Whyte purchased the computer for personal use and Mern fails to file a financing statement, which of the following statements is correct?

a. The computer was a consumer good while in Mern's possession.

b. Perfection of Mern's security interest occurred at the time of attachment.

c. Mern's security interest is not enforceable against Whyte because Mern failed to file a financing statement.

d. Mern does not have a perfected security interest because it failed to file a financing statement.

The correct answer is (b). *(CPA 1188 L-52)*

REQUIRED: The correct statement about perfection of a purchase money security interest.

DISCUSSION: A purchase money security interest is an interest taken in collateral to secure payment of the purchase price of that collateral. UCC 9-302 lists the types of security interests that are perfected without the filing of a financing statement. Included in this list is a purchase money security interest in consumer goods. Mern's security interest is a purchase money security interest, the computer is a consumer good because it is intended for personal use, and the interest was perfected automatically upon attachment.

Answer (a) is incorrect because the computer was inventory. Mern was in the business of selling computers. Answer (c) is incorrect because perfection of a security interest is not required for the secured party to enforce it against the debtor. Perfection has the effect of putting those not privy to the secured transaction on notice of the security interest. Attachment was the only requirement for enforceability of the security interest, and attachment occurred when Mern gave value, Whyte had rights in the collateral, and the security agreement was made. Answer (d) is incorrect because perfection is automatic upon attachment when a purchase money security interest in consumer goods is created.

32. Wurke, Inc. manufactures and sells household appliances on credit directly to wholesalers, retailers, and consumers. Wurke can perfect its security interest in the appliances without having to file a financing statement or take possession of the appliances if the sale is made by Wurke to

a. Retailers.

b. Wholesalers that then sell to distributors for resale.

c. Consumers.

d. Wholesalers that then sell to buyers in the ordinary course of business.

The correct answer is (c). *(CPA 1187 L-41)*

REQUIRED: The correct statement about perfection of security interest upon attachment.

DISCUSSION: UCC 9-302 lists the circumstances in which filing is not required to perfect a security interest. Included in the exceptions to filing is a purchase money security interest in consumer goods other than motor vehicles. A purchase money security interest is any interest taken in collateral to secure payment of the purchase price of that collateral. Thus, Wurke's perfection of a security interest is automatic upon attachment when the sale is made to consumers.

Answers (a), (b), and (d) are incorrect because goods held by retailers and wholesalers are considered inventory. Inventory is not an exception to the filing requirement, and Wurke would be required to file a financing statement in order to perfect a security interest in collateral held by retailers and wholesalers.

33. The Town Bank makes collateralized loans to its customers at 1% above prime on securities owned by the customer, subject to existing margin requirements. In doing so, which of the following is correct?

a. Notification of the issuer is necessary in order to perfect a security interest.

b. Filing is a permissible method of perfecting a security interest in the securities if the circumstances dictate.

c. Any dividend or interest distributions during the term of the loan belong to the bank.

d. A perfected security interest in the securities can only be obtained by possession.

The correct answer is (d). *(CPA 1180 L-34)*

REQUIRED: The correct statement concerning loans using securities as collateral.

DISCUSSION: The definition of instruments includes securities (UCC 9-105) and a security interest in instruments can be perfected only by the secured party's taking possession (UCC 9-304). Exceptions are automatic perfection for 21 days if new value is given, and temporary surrender of the securities to the debtor for a period of 21 days without loss of the perfected status. But even then a bona fide purchaser or a holder in due course will take priority.

Answer (a) is incorrect because notification of the issuer (e.g., a corporation) is not necessary for the perfection of a security interest in securities. Answer (b) is incorrect because filing is not a permissible method of perfecting a security interest in the securities due to their ease of transfer. Answer (c) is incorrect because cash distributions during the term of the loan belong to the debtor.

34. Field warehousing is a well-established means of securing a loan. It resembles a pledge in many legal respects. Which of the following is correct?

a. The field warehouseman must maintain physical control of and dominion over the property.

b. A filing is required in order to perfect such a financing arrangement.

c. Temporary relinquishment of control for any purpose will suspend the validity of the arrangement insofar as other creditors are concerned.

d. The property in question must be physically moved to a new location although it may be a part of the borrower's facilities.

The correct answer is (a). *(CPA 1177 L-24)*

REQUIRED: The correct statement concerning field warehousing.

DISCUSSION: A pledge is a security arrangement in which the secured party takes physical possession of property of the debtor as collateral for the debt. Field warehousing is similar, but it differs in that possession of the debtor's property (collateral) is taken on the premises of the debtor. A secured party or his/her agent who maintains physical control of and dominion over the property in the field warehouse meets the requirement of possession for the perfection of a security interest.

Answer (b) is incorrect because such a financing arrangement is perfected by the act of taking possession of the collateral. Answer (c) is incorrect because the UCC contemplates the temporary relinquishment of control for a variety of legitimate purposes (e.g., processing, packaging, etc.) without impairment of the security interest (UCC 9-304). Answer (d) is incorrect because the property need not be physically moved to another location so long as the secured party or his/her agent acquires physical control over the property.

35. Tawney Manufacturing approached Worldwide Lenders for a loan of $50,000 to purchase vital components it used in its manufacturing process. Worldwide decided to grant the loan but only if Tawney would agree to a field warehousing arrangement. Pursuant to their understanding, Worldwide paid for the purchase of the components, took a negotiable bill of lading for them, and surrendered the bill of lading in exchange for negotiable warehouse receipts issued by the bonded warehouse company that had established a field warehouse in Tawney's storage facility. Worldwide did not file a financing statement. Under the circumstances, Worldwide

a. Has a security interest in the goods that has attached and is perfected.

b. Does not have a security interest that has attached since Tawney has not signed a security agreement.

c. Must file an executed financing statement in order to perfect its security interest.

d. Must not relinquish control over any of the components to Tawney for whatever purpose, unless it is paid in cash for those released.

The correct answer is (a). *(CPA 1182 L-55)*

REQUIRED: The position of a creditor secured by goods held in a field warehouse.

DISCUSSION: The requirements of attachment have been satisfied. Even if the debtor did not sign a security agreement, the collateral is in the possession of the secured party pursuant to agreement since the warehouse company is an agent of the secured party. Also, value was given when Worldwide paid for the parts, and the debtor has rights in the collateral (use of the components in manufacturing) (UCC 9-203). Perfection has occurred because possession of the goods is a means of perfecting a security interest in them without filing (UCC 9-305).

Answer (b) is incorrect because the goods are in the possession of the secured party pursuant to agreement. Possession substitutes for the requirement of a written and signed security agreement. Answer (c) is incorrect because the security interest is perfected by possession of the goods. Answer (d) is incorrect because Worldwide's security interest in the goods will be perfected for a period of 21 days without filing after making them available to the debtor (UCC 9-304).

36. Mansfield Financial lends money on the strength of negotiable warehouse receipts. Its policy is always to obtain a perfected security interest in the receipts against the creditors of the borrowers and to maintain it until the loan has been satisfied. Insofar as this policy is concerned, which of the following is correct?

a. Mansfield cannot transfer the warehouse receipts to another lending institution without the debtor's consent.

b. Relinquishment of the receipts is not permitted under any circumstances without the loss of the perfected security interest in them.

c. Mansfield has a perfected security interest in goods which the receipts represent.

d. If the receipts are somehow wrongfully duly negotiated to a holder, Mansfield's perfected security interest will not be prejudiced.

The correct answer is (c). *(CPA 582 L-46)*

REQUIRED: The correct statement concerning perfection of a security interest in negotiable warehouse receipts.

DISCUSSION: A warehouse receipt is a form of document of title issued by a person engaged in the business of storing goods. A warehouse receipt is negotiable if by its terms the goods which it represents are to be delivered to the bearer or to the order of a named person. During the period that goods represented by a document of title are in the possession of the issuer (bailee), a security interest in the goods may be perfected by perfecting a security interest in the document (UCC 9-304).

Answer (a) is incorrect because a secured party may repledge the collateral upon terms which do not impair the debtor's right to redeem it (UCC 9-207). Answer (b) is incorrect because a security interest perfected by possession of negotiable documents will remain perfected for a 21-day period without filing when a secured party makes a temporary surrender of the documents to the debtor for purposes of dealing with them prior to ultimate sale or exchange. But a bona fide purchaser will take priority. Answer (d) is incorrect because the due negotiation to a holder (by purchase in good faith) passes title to the document and the goods represented by it (UCC 7-502).

37. A filing requirement applies to which of the following transactions under Article 9 (Secured Transactions) of the Uniform Commercial Code?

a. The factoring of accounts receivable.

b. A collateralized bank loan, with securities serving as the collateral.

c. The transfer of an interest in an insurance policy to secure a loan.

d. The retention of title by a seller of land to secure payment under the terms of a land contract.

The correct answer is (a). *(CPA 1181 L-50)*

REQUIRED: The transaction with a filing requirement under Article 9.

DISCUSSION: The factoring of accounts receivable involves their outright sale and is governed by Article 9 (UCC 9-102). In standard commercial practice, the distinction between transactions in accounts which are secured transactions and those which are sales is often obscure, so the UCC treats both as secured transactions. Perfection of a security interest in accounts may only be achieved by filing since there is nothing to effectively possess. An outright purchaser of accounts would thus also be required to file a financing statement in order to perfect his/her ownership interest.

Answer (b) is incorrect because no filing is required when possession of securities is taken as collateral. Answers (c) and (d) are incorrect because each is a transaction explicitly excluded from the coverage of Article 9 (UCC 9-104).

38. Bigelow manufactures mopeds and sells them through franchised dealers who are authorized to resell them to the ultimate consumer or return them. Bigelow delivers the mopeds on consignment to these retailers. The consignment agreement clearly states that the agreement is intended to create a security interest for Bigelow in the mopeds delivered on consignment. Bigelow wishes to protect itself against the other creditors of and purchasers from the retailers who might assert rights against the mopeds. Under the circumstances, Bigelow

a. Must file a financing statement and give notice to certain creditors in order to perfect its security interest.

b. Will have rights against purchasers in the ordinary course of business who were aware that Bigelow had filed.

c. Need take no further action to protect itself because the consignment is a sale or return and title is reserved in Bigelow.

d. Will have a perfected security interest in the mopeds upon attachment.

The correct answer is (a). *(CPA 579 L-20)*

REQUIRED: The true statement about a consignor's rights against other creditors of and purchasers from retailers.

DISCUSSION: A consignment intended as security for the sales price is treated as a security interest. To perfect its interest, the consignor must file a financing statement and give actual notice in writing to existing secured creditors who have already filed a financing statement covering the same types of goods (UCC 9-114). The notice must be received by the holders of security interests within 5 years before the consignee takes possession. The consignor will then be as fully protected as possible.

Answer (b) is incorrect because a buyer in the ordinary course of business takes free of the security interest created by the seller even though the security interest is a perfected purchase money security interest and the buyer knows of its existence. It is expected that retailers will have authority to sell their inventory, and the purchaser should take free of any other interests. Answer (c) is incorrect because the UCC provides that in a sale or return the buyer's creditors may reach the goods while in the hands of the buyer unless further steps (e.g., filing and notice) are taken by the consignor. Answer (d) is incorrect because the mopeds are inventory in the hands of the dealers, and a security interest in inventory is perfected by filing a financing statement.

39. Milo Manufacturing Corp. sells baseball equipment to distributors, who in turn sell it to various retailers throughout the United States. The retailers then sell the equipment to consumers who use it for their own personal use. In all cases, the equipment is sold on credit with a security interest taken in the equipment by each of the respective sellers. Which of the following is correct?

a. The security interests of all of the sellers remain valid and will take priority even against good faith purchasers for value, despite the fact that resales were contemplated.

b. The baseball equipment is inventory in the hands of all the parties concerned.

c. Milo's security interest is automatically perfected since Milo qualifies as a purchase money secured party.

d. Milo and the distributors must file a financing statement or take possession of the baseball equipment to perfect their security interests.

The correct answer is (d). *(CPA 1184 L-58)*

REQUIRED: The true statement about security interests held by sellers in the chain of distribution.

DISCUSSION: The equipment is inventory in the hands of the distributors and the retailers. Milo and the distributors must therefore either take possession of the goods (UCC 9-305) or file a financing statement (UCC 9-302) to perfect their security interests.

Answer (a) is incorrect because a distributor or retailer is a buyer in the ordinary course of business (UCC 1-201) and takes free of a security interest created by his/her seller even though the security interest is perfected and even though the buyer knows of its existence (UCC 9-307). Answer (b) is incorrect because the equipment is classified as consumer goods in the hands of buyers who purchase for personal, family, or household use (UCC 9-109). Answer (c) is incorrect because the only purchase money security interest that is automatically perfected is one in consumer goods.

40. Bass, an automobile dealer, had an inventory of 40 cars and ten trucks. He financed the purchase of this inventory with County Bank under an agreement dated January 5 that gave the bank a security interest in all vehicles on Bass's premises, all future-acquired vehicles, and the proceeds from their sale. On January 10, County Bank properly filed a financing statement that identified the collateral in the same way that it was identified in the agreement. On April 1, Bass sold a passenger car to Dodd for family use and a truck to Diamond Company for its hardware business. Which of the following is correct?

a. The security agreement may not provide for a security interest in after-acquired property even if the parties so agree.

b. County Bank's security interest is perfected as of January 10.

c. The passenger car sold by Bass to Dodd continues to be subject to the security interest of County Bank.

d. The security interest of County Bank does not include the proceeds from the sale of the truck to Diamond Company.

The correct answer is (b). *(CPA 1181 L-45)*

REQUIRED: The correct statement regarding a security interest in inventory.

DISCUSSION: A security interest is perfected when it has attached and all steps necessary for perfection have been taken (UCC 9-303). The security interest attached on January 5, when the security agreement was signed, value was given, and Bass had the cars and trucks. It was perfected on January 10, when the financing statement was filed. Note that if the collateral had not been inventory, the perfection would have effectively related back to January 5 because the perfection took place within 10 days after creation of a purchase money security interest (UCC 9-312).

Answer (a) is incorrect because security agreements may (and often do) validly cover after-acquired property. Answer (c) is incorrect because a purchaser in the ordinary course of business (e.g., of inventory) takes free of the security interest. It can also be assumed that County Bank authorized the sale (which releases the security interest) since the collateral is inventory. Answer (d) is incorrect because the security agreement expressly applied to proceeds, and even if it did not, proceeds are covered unless expressly excluded by the agreement.

41. Vista Motor Sales, a corporation engaged in selling motor vehicles at retail, borrowed money from Sunshine Finance Company and gave Sunshine a properly executed security agreement in its present and future inventory and in the proceeds therefrom to secure the loan. Sunshine's security interest was duly perfected under the laws of the state where Vista does business and maintains its entire inventory. Thereafter, Vista sold a new pickup truck from its inventory to Archer and received Archer's certified check in payment of the full price. Under the circumstances, which of the following is correct?

a. Sunshine must file an amendment to the financing statement every time Vista receives a substantial number of additional vehicles from the manufacturer if Sunshine is to obtain a valid security interest in subsequently delivered inventory.

b. Sunshine's security interest in the certified check Vista received is perfected against Vista's other creditors.

c. Unless Sunshine specifically included proceeds in the financing statement it filed, it has no rights to them.

d. The term "proceeds" does not include used cars received by Vista since they will be resold.

The correct answer is (b). *(CPA 1179 L-26)*

REQUIRED: The correct statement concerning the sale of an item of inventory which was subject to a perfected security interest.

DISCUSSION: The certified check received by the debtor constitutes proceeds from the sale of the inventory. At a minimum, the security interest in the proceeds remains perfected for 10 days after receipt by the debtor (UCC 9-306). However, in many circumstances, identifiable proceeds will remain perfected after 10 days without any action by the secured party.

Answer (a) is incorrect because the after-acquired property (future inventory) clause in the perfected security agreement renders it unnecessary for Sunshine to file an amendment every time Vista receives additional vehicles from the manufacturer. Answer (c) is incorrect because a security interest continues in proceeds unless the security agreement provides otherwise, and the interest is perfected for a minimum of 10 days. Answer (d) is incorrect because the term "proceeds" includes whatever is received upon the sale, exchange, collection, or other disposition of collateral or proceeds. It includes cash, checks, notes, deposit accounts, exchanged property, insurance property, etc.

42. A fixture is an item of personal property that has become permanently affixed to real estate. Perfection of a security interest in a fixture requires

a. Filing of a financing statement in the office where a mortgage on the real estate would be recorded.

b. Filing in the office where financing statements covering other kinds of goods are recorded.

c. No filing if the fixture was initially a consumer good and the secured party has a purchase money security interest.

d. Filing in both the personal property and real estate records.

The correct answer is (a). *(Publisher)*

REQUIRED: The true statement about the requirements of a fixture filing.

DISCUSSION: A "fixture filing" is required to obtain priority over conflicting interests in fixtures (UCC 9-302). The filing must be in the office where a mortgage on the real estate would be filed or recorded, and the financing statement covering goods that are or are to become fixtures should conform to the requirements of UCC 9-402 (UCC 9-313).

Answers (b) and (d) are incorrect because the filing must be in the real estate records, but a dual filing is not necessary. Answer (c) is incorrect because motor vehicles required to be registered and fixtures are exceptions to the principle that a purchase money security interest in consumer goods is perfected without filing.

43. Mozart Manufacturers of Florida manufactured and sold three pianos to Virtuoso Piano School of Caliban, Florida in a credit transaction. Mozart properly filed a 5-year financing statement with regard to the pianos in Florida on February 2, the day after the sale. Finding its business a trifle slow in Caliban, Virtuoso packed up its pianos and moved to Atlanta, Georgia on May 2 of the same year. On September 1, Mozart properly filed a financing statement in Georgia.

a. Mozart's security interest was continuously perfected.

b. Mozart's security interest was unperfected during the interval of May 2 through September 1.

c. Mozart's filing on September 1 was retroactive to May 2.

d. Mozart's Georgia filing was unnecessary in order to continue perfection.

The correct answer is (a). *(Publisher)*

REQUIRED: The status of the perfection of a security interest in goods moved from one state to another.

DISCUSSION: The perfection of the security interest continues for the unexpired period in the original jurisdiction or 4 months after removal from the jurisdiction in which perfection was obtained, whichever period first expires. Here, the security interest was perfected from February 2 to May 2, the day of removal. It would have continued perfected from May 2 until September 2 without any action by Mozart. By taking the appropriate steps to perfect the security interest in the new jurisdiction, Mozart ensured itself of a continuously perfected security interest (UCC 9-103).

Answer (b) is incorrect because perfection continues for a 4-month period after removal from the jurisdiction in which perfection was obtained or until the expiration of the period of perfection in the original jurisdiction, whichever occurs first. Answer (c) is incorrect because no provision in Article 9 creates retroactive perfection. Answer (d) is incorrect because if Mozart had failed to file in Georgia before the expiration of the 4-month period, its security interest would have been unperfected as of the end of that period. Please read UCC 9-103 for additional details.

17.4 Priorities

44. Assuming that the special priority rules do not apply, which of the following is the most accurate statement regarding conflicts between competing security interests?

a. The secured party who has not perfected has no priority over an unsecured party.

b. The first to attach has priority if neither security interest is perfected.

c. The first to file has priority.

d. The first to perfect has priority.

The correct answer is (b). *(Publisher)*

REQUIRED: The most accurate statement about priorities among security interests.

DISCUSSION: Under UCC 9-312, "so long as conflicting security interests are unperfected, the first to attach has priority," assuming special priority rules do not apply. For example, if Q's interest in the collateral attached on July 1 and X's interest attached on July 15, Q has priority. But if X perfects his/her interest on August 1 and Q perfects on August 5, Q will lose priority to X.

Answer (a) is incorrect because the secured party who has not perfected has priority over a general creditor (unsecured party). A perfected security interest will provide protection against this eventuality. Answers (c) and (d) are incorrect because the first to perfect generally has priority, but the first to file has priority if his/her date of filing preceded filing and perfection by the other party.

45. On May 2, Safe Bank agreed to loan Tyler Corp. $50,000. Tyler signed a security agreement and financing statement covering its existing equipment. On May 4, Safe filed the financing statement. On May 7, State Bank loaned Tyler $60,000. State had notified Safe on May 5 of its intention to make the loan. Tyler signed a security agreement and financing statement covering the same existing equipment. On May 8, State filed the financing statement. On May 10, Safe loaned Tyler $50,000. If Tyler defaults on both loans, who will have a priority security interest in the equipment?

a. State. It was the first to perfect its security interest.

b. State. It properly notified Safe prior to making the loan.

c. Safe. It was the first to file.

d. Safe. It has a purchase money security interest in the equipment that was perfected within the permissible time limits.

The correct answer is (c). *(CPA 1186 L-51)*

REQUIRED: The correct statement about the order of priority of perfected security interests.

DISCUSSION: To perfect a security interest in collateral, the three requirements for attachment must first be met. The requirements for attachment are that the debtor have rights in the collateral, the creditor has given value, and a security agreement exists. In this case, Tyler has rights in the equipment, Safe's agreement to the loan is considered value given, and a security agreement was signed. Thus, attachment has occurred. After attachment, UCC 9-312 states that conflicting security interests in the same collateral rank in priority according to the time of filing or of automatic perfection. Safe filed its financing statement first, and it will have priority over State.

Answer (a) is incorrect because Safe was first to perfect its security interest by filing on May 4. Answer (b) is incorrect because by the time State perfected its security interest, Safe's had already been perfected. Answer (d) is incorrect because a purchase money security interest is an interest taken in collateral to secure payment of the purchase price of that collateral. The loan proceeds were not used to purchase the equipment in which Safe had a security interest, and it would not have a purchase money security interest in that equipment.

46. Roth and Dixon both claim a security interest in the same collateral. Roth's security interest attached on January 1, 1989, and it was perfected by filing on March 1, 1989. Dixon's security interest attached on February 1, 1989, and it was perfected on April 1, 1989 by taking possession of the collateral. Which of the following statements is correct?

a. Roth's security interest has priority because Roth perfected before Dixon perfected.

b. Dixon's security interest has priority because Dixon's interest attached before Roth's interest was perfected.

c. Roth's security interest has priority because Roth's security interest attached before Dixon's security interest attached.

d. Dixon's security interest has priority because Dixon is in possession of the collateral.

The correct answer is (a). *(CPA 1189 L-54)*

REQUIRED: The correct statement about the priority of perfected security interests.

DISCUSSION: UCC 9-312 states that conflicting security interests in the same collateral will rank in priority according to the time of filing. Perfection of a security interest can only occur after the attachment requirements have been met. Attachment has occurred for both parties, and the party whose security interest was perfected first will have priority. Roth's security interest was perfected 1 month prior to the perfection of Dixon's security interest, so Roth has priority.

Answers (b) and (c) are incorrect because attachment is only used to establish priority when the conflicting security interests are unperfected. Answer (d) is incorrect because Dixon's security interest was perfected by possession only after Roth's was perfected.

47. Ace Auto Sales sold a 1986 Skylark Magnificent to Marcus on the installment basis for his own personal use. Marcus signed an installment agreement for the balance due ($2,000) on the purchase price. Ace's policy was not to file a financing statement in the appropriate recordation office. Marcus subsequently sold the car to Franks without disclosing the debt owed to Ace. Franks purchased the car in good faith, knowing nothing about the debt owed by Marcus to Ace. Marcus is bankrupt. Wallace, a general creditor of Marcus, has asserted rights to the car in question. Under the circumstances

a. Marcus takes title free and clear of any claims because Ace did not file.

b. Ace can defeat the claim of Franks in that Franks is a mere third party beneficiary.

c. Ace's rights against Marcus under the contract of sale are unimpaired despite the lack of filing.

d. In the final analysis Wallace will prevail.

The correct answer is (c). *(CPA 1175 L-39)*

REQUIRED: The correct statement concerning the rights of the various parties.

DISCUSSION: Ace sold an automobile to Marcus and financed part of the purchase price. Presumably, Ace took a security interest in the automobile as collateral. This security interest is good against Marcus regardless of perfection. Note that Ace's purchase money security interest in consumer goods is not perfected. A filing is required for motor vehicles required to be registered (UCC 9-302).

Answer (a) is incorrect because Ace's security interest is good against the debtor (Marcus) without filing or other method of perfection. Answer (b) is incorrect because Franks is a buyer of consumer goods (not from a dealer) who has given value and received delivery of the collateral without knowledge of the security interest. He takes free of Ace's security interest since no financing statement was filed and apparently the security interest was not noted on the certificate of title (or Franks would have had knowledge). Answer (d) is incorrect because a secured creditor (whether perfected or not) will prevail over an unsecured (general) creditor.

48. Fogel purchased a TV set for $900 from Hamilton Appliance Store. Hamilton took a promissory note signed by Fogel and a security interest for the $800 balance due on the set. It was Hamilton's policy not to file a financing statement until the purchaser defaulted. Fogel obtained a loan of $500 from Reliable Finance, which took and recorded a security interest in the TV set. A month later, Fogel defaulted on several loans outstanding and one of his creditors, Harp, obtained a judgment against Fogel that was properly recorded. After making several payments, Fogel defaulted on a payment due to Hamilton, who then recorded a financing statement subsequent to Reliable's filing and the entry of the Harp judgment. Subsequently, at a garage sale, Fogel sold the set for $300 to Mobray. Which of the parties has the priority claim to the set?

a. Reliable.

b. Hamilton.

c. Harp.

d. Mobray.

The correct answer is (b). *(CPA 583 L-51)*

REQUIRED: The party who will have priority in collateral consisting of consumer goods.

DISCUSSION: Hamilton's security interest was automatically perfected when Fogel purchased the TV set and signed a security agreement. A purchase money security interest in consumer goods is perfected without filing except with respect to a subsequent consumer purchaser (UCC 9-302). Later, Reliable perfected a security interest in the set by filing and Harp became a judgment creditor. Harp did not perfect a security interest in the set. After these events, Hamilton filed and still later Fogel sold the set to Mobray, presumably a good faith purchaser for value and for personal, household, or family use.

Answer (a) is incorrect because Hamilton has priority over Reliable because Hamilton was the first to perfect (UCC 9-312). Answer (c) is incorrect because Hamilton has priority over Harp because Harp did not perfect or even obtain a security interest. Answer (d) is incorrect because Hamilton has priority over Mobray because it filed prior to the sale by Fogel. Otherwise, Mobray would have defeated the automatically perfected purchase money security interest (UCC 9-307).

49. Forward Motors, Inc. is a franchised automobile dealer for National Motors. National provides the financing of the purchase of its automobiles by Forward. It sells Forward 25 to 50 automobiles at a time and takes back promissory notes, a security agreement, and a financing statement on each sale. The financing statement covering this revolving inventory has been duly filed.

a. Each automobile sold to Forward must be described and the serial number listed on the financing statement.

b. Sales by Forward to bona fide purchasers for value in the ordinary course of business will be subject to the rights of National.

c. No filing is required against the creditors of Forward since the automobiles are "consumer goods" in its hands.

d. As against the creditors of Forward, National has a valid "floating lien" against the automobiles and the proceeds from their sale.

The correct answer is (d). *(CPA 1173 L-7)*

REQUIRED: The correct statement concerning the financing of an automobile dealer's inventory.

DISCUSSION: A "floating lien" is one which the secured party retains against the inventory of a debtor even though the individual items comprising the inventory change over time. Such a lien is created pursuant to an after-acquired property clause in the security agreement (UCC 9-204). National Motors, as a purchase money secured creditor with a perfected "floating lien," has priority in the inventory against other creditors of Forward.

Answer (a) is incorrect because under UCC 9-402, a financing statement covering property which is inventory in the hands of the debtor only needs to indicate the type of collateral. Answer (b) is incorrect because a sale by an automobile dealer of an auto in the ordinary course of business would not be subject to the rights of the inventory financier. National would continue to have rights in the proceeds possessed by Forward, but would not be able to proceed against the automobile in the hands of a purchaser in the ordinary course of business. Answer (c) is incorrect because the automobiles are inventory in the hands of Forward and National needs to file a financing statement in order to protect itself against Forward's creditors.

50. A purchase money security interest

a. May be taken or retained only by the seller of collateral.

b. Is exempt from the Uniform Commercial Code's filing requirements.

c. Entitles the person who is the original purchase money lender to certain additional rights and advantages, which are nontransferable.

d. Entitles the purchase money lender to priority through a 10-day grace period for filing in many cases.

The correct answer is (d). *(CPA 1181 L-46)*

REQUIRED: The correct statement concerning a purchase money security interest.

DISCUSSION: A purchase money secured party is given priority over other perfected creditors of the debtor including those with after-acquired clauses. The requirements of this special priority differ between transactions involving inventory and those involving other collateral. If a secured party files with respect to a purchase money security interest before or within 10 days after the debtor receives possession of collateral other than inventory, the purchase money secured party will have priority.

In general, the 10-day grace period does not apply to a purchase money security interest in inventory in the debtor's possession. To acquire priority, the secured party must both file and give written notice to other secured parties before delivering possession. The 10-day grace period for inventory only applies with regard to the rights of a bulk transferee or a lien creditor which arise between the time of the attachment of the security interest and the time of filing (UCC 9-301 and 9-312).

Answer (a) is incorrect because a purchase money security interest may also be taken or retained by any person who gives value (e.g., a lender) to enable the debtor to acquire rights in the collateral if such value is in fact so used. Answer (b) is incorrect because only a purchase money security interest in consumer goods may be perfected without possession or filing. Answer (c) is incorrect because there is no prohibition against transfer of the rights of a purchase money secured party.

51. On January 5, Wine purchased and received delivery of new machinery from Toto Corp. for $50,000. The machinery was to be used in Wine's production process. Wine paid 30% down and executed a security agreement for the balance. On January 9, Wine obtained a $150,000 loan from Safe Bank. Wine signed a security agreement that gave Safe a security interest in Wine's existing and after-acquired machinery. The security agreement was duly filed by Safe that same day. On January 10, Toto properly filed its security agreement. If Wine defaults on both loans and funds are insufficient to pay Toto and Safe, which party will have a superior security interest in the machinery purchased from Toto?

a. Safe, since it was the first in time to file and perfect its security interest.

b. Safe, since Toto perfected its security interest by filing after Wine took possession.

c. Toto, since it filed its security agreement within the permissible time limits.

d. Toto, since it acquired a perfected purchase money security interest without filing.

The correct answer is (c). *(CPA 584 L-58)*

REQUIRED: The priority between a PMSI and an earlier filed security interest.

DISCUSSION: "A purchase money security interest (PMSI) in collateral other than inventory has priority over a conflicting security interest in the same collateral or its proceeds if the purchase money security interest is perfected at the time the debtor receives possession of the collateral or within 10 days thereafter" (UCC 9-312). The collateral was equipment, the debtor received possession on January 5, and Toto properly filed five days later. Toto thus has priority even though Safe Bank was the first to both file and perfect.

Answer (a) is incorrect because the general rule that conflicting security interests rank according to priority in time of filing or perfection does not apply since the UCC gives special protection to a PMSI. Answer (b) is incorrect because a PMSI will prevail over a prior perfected interest if a proper filing is made within 10 days of the debtor's receiving possession. Answer (d) is incorrect because a PMSI in consumer goods, not equipment, is perfected without filing.

52. In respect to obtaining a purchase money security interest, which of the following requirements must be met?

a. The property sold may only be consumer goods.

b. Only a seller may obtain a purchase money security interest.

c. Such a security interest must be filed in all cases to be perfected.

d. Credit advanced to the buyer must be used to obtain the property which serves as the collateral.

The correct answer is (d). *(CPA 1179 L-25)*

REQUIRED: The requirement for obtaining a purchase money security interest.

DISCUSSION: A security interest qualifies as a purchase money security interest if the credit advanced to the buyer by the secured party is in fact used to obtain the collateral (UCC 9-107). The purchase money secured party may be the seller or any other lender who furnishes credit which enables the debtor to acquire rights in the collateral.

Answer (a) is incorrect because a purchase money security interest may be created in any property. Answer (b) is incorrect because the seller or any lender may obtain a purchase money security interest if (s)he gives value which is used by the debtor to acquire rights in the collateral. Answer (c) is incorrect because a security interest need not be filed in all cases to be perfected. For example, possession of the collateral in most instances is a substitute for filing.

53. Perfection of a security interest under the UCC by a creditor provides added protection against other parties in the event the debtor does not pay his/her debts. Which of the following is not affected by perfection of a security interest?

a. The trustee in a bankruptcy proceeding.

b. A buyer in the ordinary course of business.

c. A subsequent personal injury judgment creditor.

d. Other prospective creditors of the debtor.

The correct answer is (b). *(CPA 585 L-46)*

REQUIRED: The party not affected by perfection of a security interest.

DISCUSSION: A buyer in the ordinary course of business means "a person who in good faith and without knowledge that the sale to him/her is in violation of the ownership rights or security interest of a third party in the goods buys in the ordinary course from a person in the business of selling goods of that kind but does not include a pawnbroker" (UCC 1-201). Such a buyer takes free of a perfected security interest created by the seller even though the buyer knows of its existence (UCC 9-307).

Answer (a) is incorrect because although a trustee in bankruptcy is hypothetically a lien creditor, a secured party with a prior perfected security interest will prevail. An unperfected security interest is subordinate to the rights of a person who becomes a lien creditor before perfection (UCC 9-301). Answers (c) and (d) are incorrect because each subsequent creditor is affected.

54. With regard to a prior perfected security interest in goods for which a financing statement has been filed, which of the following parties is most likely to have a superior interest in the same collateral?

a. A buyer in the ordinary course of business who purchased the goods from a merchant.

b. A subsequent buyer of consumer goods who purchased the goods from another consumer.

c. The trustee in bankruptcy of the debtor.

d. Lien creditors of the debtor.

The correct answer is (a). *(CPA 1188 L-54)*

REQUIRED: The correct statement about the party who will have a superior interest in the collateral of a perfected security interest.

DISCUSSION: According to Article 1 and Article 9 of the UCC, a buyer in the ordinary course of business takes the goods free of any security interest if (s)he buys the goods from a seller of that kind of goods. This right is extended to the buyer regardless of whether the security interest is perfected or the buyer has knowledge of its existence.

Answer (b) is incorrect because a subsequent bona fide purchaser will not have priority over a prior perfected security interest in consumer goods if the interest was perfected by filing a financing statement, but (s)he will have priority over any interest that was perfected automatically upon attachment. Answer (c) is incorrect because a trustee in bankruptcy has priority over any unperfected security interests or any perfected security interests created subsequent to the filing of the petition for relief. However, the trustee's rights are subordinate to those of a prior perfected security interest. Answer (d) is incorrect because a lien creditor has an interest superior to an unperfected security interest or to a perfected security interest created after attachment of the lien.

55. Acorn Marina, Inc. sells and services boat motors. On April 1, 1989, Acorn financed the purchase of its entire inventory with GAC Finance Company. GAC required Acorn to execute a security agreement and financing statement covering the inventory and proceeds of sale. On April 14, 1989, GAC properly filed the financing statement pursuant to the UCC Secured Transactions Article. On April 27, 1989, Acorn sold one of the motors to Wilks for use in her charter business. Wilks, who had once worked for Acorn, knew that Acorn regularly financed its inventory with GAC. Acorn has defaulted on its obligations to GAC. The motor purchased by Wilks is

a. Subject to the GAC security interest because Wilks should have known that GAC financed the inventory purchase by Acorn.

b. Subject to the GAC security interest because Wilks purchased the motor for a commercial use.

c. Not subject to the GAC security interest because Wilks is regarded as a buyer in the ordinary course of Acorn's business.

d. Not subject to the GAC security interest because GAC failed to file the financing statement until more than 10 days after April 1, 1989.

The correct answer is (c). *(CPA 589 L-47)*

REQUIRED: The correct statement about the rights of a buyer in the ordinary course of business.

DISCUSSION: Articles 1 and 9 of the UCC explicitly state that a buyer of goods from a person in the business of selling goods of that kind will take the goods free of any security interest in the goods whether or not the interest was perfected or the buyer had knowledge of the interest. Because boat motors constitute the regular inventory of Acorn Marina, Inc., Wilks is a buyer in the ordinary course of business and takes the motor free of GAC's security interest.

Answer (a) is incorrect because Article 9 specifically states that the buyer will take the goods free of any security interest even though (s)he may have known of its existence. Answer (b) is incorrect because the purpose for which a good is purchased is irrelevant if the buyer purchases in the ordinary course of business. Answer (d) is incorrect because buyers in the ordinary course of business will prevail over perfected as well as unperfected security interests.

56. Rock N. Roller buys a new C.D. player for his personal enjoyment from Sounds R Us, a local stereo dealer. Unbeknownst to Rock, Sounds has financed the purchase of all its inventory, including his new C.D. player, through Bug Bux Finance Co., and given Bux a security interest in the inventory that Bux perfected by filing. On these facts,

a. Bux loses its security interest because Rock was a buyer in the ordinary course of business.

b. Bux may repossess the collateral.

c. Bux loses its security interest because the C.D. player is a consumer good.

d. Rock gets the C.D. player free of any perfected security interests, but subject to any unperfected ones.

The correct answer is (a). *(I. Schwartz)*

REQUIRED: The rights of a secured party and of a purchaser of collateral.

DISCUSSION: A "buyer in the ordinary course of business" is one who in good faith and without knowledge that the sale violated a security interest of a third party bought from someone in the business of selling goods of the kind involved in the transaction. Such a buyer takes the collateral free of perfected or unperfected security interests even if the secured party did not authorize the sale.

Answer (b) is incorrect because Sounds no longer has possession of the C.D. player, and Rock acquired it free of the security interest of Bux. Answer (c) is incorrect because in order for Bux to lose its security interest, Rock must be a buyer in the ordinary course of business, regardless of the collateral's status as a consumer good. Answer (d) is incorrect because Rock takes the C.D. player free of all security interests, perfected or unperfected.

57. In the case of consumer goods, a buyer from the original purchaser takes the goods free of a perfected security interest if (s)he buys

a. Without knowledge of the security interest, for value, for personal purposes, and the secured party has not filed a financing statement covering such goods.

b. Without knowledge of the security interest, for value, for personal purposes, and prior to the purchase the secured party has filed a financing statement covering such goods.

c. With knowledge of the security interest, and after the purchase the secured party files a financing statement covering such goods.

d. With knowledge of the security interest, and the secured party has not filed a financing statement covering such goods prior to delivery of the goods.

The correct answer is (a). *(CPA 1175 L-34)*

REQUIRED: When a buyer of consumer goods takes free of a perfected security interest.

DISCUSSION: A buyer from the original purchaser of consumer goods will have priority over a secured party whose security interest is perfected by attachment if the buyer has no knowledge of the security interest, gives value, and buys for his/her personal, family, or household purposes. If a financing statement has been filed, constructive knowledge of the security interest is imputed to the buyer and the secured party will prevail. Note that a person who buys from the original purchaser is a casual purchaser, not a buyer in the ordinary course of business who would prevail even with actual knowledge of the security interest (UCC 9-307).

Answer (b) is incorrect because the rights of a buyer of consumer goods from the original purchaser will be subordinate to those of a secured party who has filed a financing statement. Answers (c) and (d) are incorrect because a buyer from the original purchaser of consumer goods who takes with knowledge of a prior perfected security interest will be subordinate to the secured party whether a financing statement is filed or not.

58. Edie owned and operated a bowling alley. She obtained a loan from Bank secured by "the equipment and all other chattels and personal property used in the business." Bank properly filed a financing statement. Edie then borrowed funds from S & L, giving a first mortgage on "all real property used in the business." Edie became insolvent and filed a petition in bankruptcy. Which of the following is true?

a. Bank is entitled to resort to the personal property even against a trustee in bankruptcy.

b. Bank has a priority in bankruptcy and is entitled to defeat the claims of all creditors that are asserted against the personal property.

c. Bank has a security interest in Edie's central air conditioning system.

d. Edie's sale of all the business property to a bona fide purchaser will defeat Bank's security interest.

The correct answer is (a). *(Publisher)*

REQUIRED: The true statement about the rights given by a perfected security interest.

DISCUSSION: Even in bankruptcy proceedings, a secured creditor with a perfected security interest may pursue its remedy against the particular property. The secured party has a property right in the property and the proceeds flowing from disposition of the collateral. However, the trustee in bankruptcy has the status of a hypothetical lien creditor and can defeat a nonperfected security interest in personal property (UCC 9-301).

Answer (b) is incorrect because Bank has a property right in the goods that it is entitled to assert before the goods become available to other creditors, whether they have a priority or not. Bank's interest is thus not a "priority." Answer (c) is incorrect because Bank's security interest covers only personal property. The central air conditioning system is a fixture and covered by the mortgage. With respect to real property, a trustee in bankruptcy has the rights of a good faith purchaser at the time the petition is filed. Answer (d) is incorrect because while a transferee in bulk who gives value and has no knowledge of the security interest will prevail against a secured party who has not perfected, Bank's perfected security interest extends to the proceeds of the sale of the personal property.

59. On May 8, Westar Corp. sold 20 typewriters to Saper for use in Saper's business. Saper paid for the typewriters by executing a promissory note that was secured by the typewriters. Saper also executed a security agreement. On May 9, Saper filed a petition in bankruptcy and a trustee was appointed. On May 16, Westar filed a financing statement covering the typewriters. Westar claims that it has a superior interest in the typewriters. The trustee in bankruptcy disagrees. Which of the parties is correct?

a. The trustee, because the filing of a petition in bankruptcy cuts off Westar's rights as of the date of filing.

b. The trustee, because the petition was filed prior to Westar's filing of the financing statement.

c. Westar, because it perfected its security interest within 10 days after Saper took possession of the typewriters.

d. Westar, because its security interest was automatically perfected upon attachment.

The correct answer is (c). *(CPA 1187 L-43)*

REQUIRED: The correct statement about the priority of a purchase money security interest.

DISCUSSION: UCC 9-312 sets priorities among conflicting security interests in the same collateral. This section states that "a purchase money security interest in collateral other than inventory has priority over a conflicting security interest in the same collateral or its proceeds if the purchase money security interest is perfected at the time the debtor receives possession of the collateral or within 10 days thereafter." Because Westar has a purchase money security interest in the typewriters, and the typewriters are classified in Saper's business as equipment, not inventory, Westar will have superior rights in the collateral because it filed 8 days after Saper took possession.

Answer (a) is incorrect because the right of perfection is unaffected by the filing of the petition for relief in bankruptcy. Answer (b) is incorrect because Westar's filing within the 10-day limit meant that perfection of its security interest related back to the day Saper took possession (May 8), which was 1 day prior to the filing of the bankruptcy petition. Answer (d) is incorrect because automatic perfection upon attachment is only possible when the purchase money security interest is in consumer goods. Saper used the typewriters as equipment, and Westar was required to file a financing statement to perfect its interest.

60. Mozart Manufacturers has a perfected security interest in pianos owned by the Virtuoso Piano School. Virtuoso sends one of the pianos to Rachmaninoff Repair Service, which makes extensive repairs to the instrument. Virtuoso is unable to make payment for the repairs, and the piano remains in Rachmaninoff's possession. A state statute creates a mechanic's lien but is silent with regard to priority as against a perfected security interest.

a. Rachmaninoff will prevail in a priority contest because the statute did not expressly provide that the security interest took priority.

b. Mozart will prevail because its interest was perfected before Rachmaninoff gained possession.

c. Mozart will prevail because its interest was first in time.

d. Rachmaninoff will prevail because it has perfected by possession which is superior to perfection by filing.

The correct answer is (a). *(Publisher)*

REQUIRED: The priority between a mechanic's lien and a prior perfected security interest.

DISCUSSION: Under UCC 9-310, certain liens have priority over even a perfected security interest. If a state statute creates a lien in favor of a person who, in the ordinary course of business, furnishes services or materials with respect to goods subject to a security interest and such person retains possession of the goods, the lien will have priority over a perfected security interest unless the statute creating the lien expressly provides otherwise.

Answers (b) and (c) are incorrect because neither prior perfection nor prior creation of the security interest is relevant against a mechanic's lien unless the statute creating the lien expressly provides otherwise. Answer (d) is incorrect because perfection by filing is not necessarily inferior to perfection by possession. In any event, the contest here is not between two secured parties who have perfected, but between a mechanic's lienor and a secured party.

61. Cross has an unperfected security interest in the inventory of Safe, Inc. The unperfected security interest

a. Is superior to the interest of subsequent lenders who obtain a perfected security interest in the property.

b. Is subordinate to lien creditors of Safe who become such prior to any subsequent perfection by Cross.

c. Causes Cross to lose important rights against Safe as an entity.

d. May only be perfected by filing a financing statement.

The correct answer is (b). *(CPA 586 L-39)*

REQUIRED: The correct statement about the rights of an unperfected security interest.

DISCUSSION: UCC 9-301 states the interests that take priority over unperfected security interests. Included is a lien creditor, that is, a creditor who has acquired a lien on the property involved by attachment, levy, or the like. The lien creditor takes the property subject to any security interest perfected before the lien attached, but its rights are superior to any security interest perfected after the lien attached.

Answer (a) is incorrect because a subsequent creditor who perfects its security interest will have priority over an unperfected security interest unless the perfected creditor had knowledge of the competing interest prior to perfection. Answer (c) is incorrect because perfection maximizes the rights of the creditor with respect to third parties. Perfection has no effect on the relationship between debtor and creditor. Answer (d) is incorrect because inventory is one type of collateral that can be perfected by taking possession of the property.

62. Donaldson, Inc. lent Watson Enterprises $50,000 secured by a real estate mortgage which included the land, buildings, and "all other property which is added to the real property or which is considered as real property as a matter of law." Star Company also loaned Watson $25,000 and obtained a security interest in all of Watson's "inventory, accounts receivable, fixtures, and other tangible personal property." There is insufficient property to satisfy the two creditors. Consequently, Donaldson is attempting to include all property possible under the terms and scope of its real property mortgage. If Donaldson is successful in this regard, then Star will receive a lesser amount in satisfaction of its claim. What is the probable outcome of Donaldson's action?

a. Donaldson will not prevail if the property in question is detachable trade fixtures.

b. Donaldson will prevail if Star failed to file a financing statement.

c. Donaldson will prevail if it was the first lender and duly filed its real property mortgage.

d. The problem will be decided by taking all of Watson's property (real and personal) subject to the two secured creditors' claims and dividing it in proportion to the respective debts.

The correct answer is (a). *(CPA 578 L-29)*

REQUIRED: The probable outcome of the attempt of a real estate mortgagee to include all possible property under its mortgage.

DISCUSSION: Donaldson's loan is secured by Watson's real property and Star's loan is secured by Watson's personal property. The problem here arises with respect to the classification of property which may be deemed either realty or personalty. If the property is classified as realty then Donaldson will prevail. If the property in question is classified as detachable trade fixtures, however, Star will prevail because trade fixtures are regarded as personal property and therefore not subject to a real estate mortgage. Ordinary fixtures are treated as realty.

Answers (b) and (c) are incorrect because the classification of property as real or personal is the issue. If the property is classified as personal, it will not fall under Donaldson's real estate mortgage. Answer (d) is incorrect because each creditor can have rights only in the property subject to its security agreement.

63. Owner planned to add a wing to his house and to install central air conditioning. He obtained a loan from Bank to finance the construction and gave a mortgage on the realty as security. Bank recorded the mortgage on August 1. On July 29, Owner purchased on credit a central air conditioning unit from Seller. Seller took a security interest in the unit and made a proper fixture filing of a financing statement on August 2. The air conditioning unit was permanently installed on August 15th and construction of the house was completed on August 30th.

a. Bank has priority over Seller because it has a recorded real estate mortgage against a perfected security interest in a fixture.

b. Bank has priority over Seller because the conditions for priority of a construction mortgage have been met.

c. Seller has priority over Bank because it recorded first.

d. Seller has priority over Bank because it has a perfected purchase money security interest in fixtures which was perfected by a fixture filing before the goods became fixtures.

The correct answer is (b). *(Publisher)*

REQUIRED: The priority between a holder of a construction mortgage and a secured party with a perfected purchase money security interest.

DISCUSSION: Seller has a purchase money security interest in the air conditioning unit which was perfected by a proper fixture filing on August 2. The goods subsequently became fixtures on August 15. Nevertheless, UCC 9-313 gives Bank priority because the construction mortgage was recorded (August 1) before the goods became fixtures, and the goods became fixtures (August 15) before completion of construction (August 30).

Answer (a) is incorrect because a perfected purchase money security interest in fixtures generally has priority over real estate mortgages. It is only against construction mortgages meeting the conditions of UCC 9-313 that the priority is lost. Answer (c) is incorrect because Bank recorded first. Answer (d) is incorrect because the priority of a purchase money security interest in fixtures is not applicable against a construction mortgage which meets the conditions of UCC 9-313.

17.5 Default and Remedies

64. Under the UCC Secured Transactions Article, if a debtor is in default under a payment obligation secured by goods, the secured party has the right to

	Reduce the Claim to a Judgment	Sell the Goods and Apply the Proceeds Toward the Debt	Take Possession of the Goods Without Judicial Process
a.	Yes	Yes	No
b.	Yes	No	Yes
c.	No	Yes	Yes
d.	Yes	Yes	Yes

The correct answer is (d). *(CPA 1189 L-55)*

REQUIRED: The rights of a secured party when a debtor defaults under a payment obligation.

DISCUSSION: Part 5 of Article 9 of the UCC governs default by debtors and the remedies afforded to secured parties. Although default by a debtor does not require a secured creditor to take action, there are essentially three options given to a secured party. The secured party can sue the debtor for the amount owed, foreclose on the collateral, or repossess the collateral privately through the self-help provision of Article 9.

Answer (a) is incorrect because the secured party has the right to repossess the collateral either privately or with judicial assistance. Answer (b) is incorrect because the secured party has the right to foreclose on the collateral and have the proceeds of a judicial sale applied to repayment of the debt. Answer (c) is incorrect because the secured party has the right to sue the debtor for the amount paid.

65. Gilbert borrowed $10,000 from Merchant National Bank and signed a negotiable promissory note containing an acceleration clause. In addition, securities valued at $11,000 at the time of the loan were pledged as collateral. Gilbert has defaulted on the loan repayments. At the time of default, $9,250 plus interest of $450 was due, and the securities had a value of $8,000. Merchant

a. Must first proceed against the collateral before proceeding against Gilbert personally on the note.

b. Cannot invoke the acceleration clause in the note until 10 days after the notice of default is given to Gilbert.

c. Must give Gilbert 30 days after default in which to refinance the loan.

d. Is entitled to proceed against Gilbert on either the note or the collateral or both.

The correct answer is (d). *(CPA 583 L-52)*

REQUIRED: The action available to a secured party after the debtor's default.

DISCUSSION: After the debtor's default, the secured party may reduce the claim to judgment, foreclose, or otherwise enforce the security interest by any available procedure (UCC 9-501). The secured party also has the right to take possession of the collateral without judicial process if this can be done without a breach of the peace (UCC 9-503).

Answer (a) is incorrect because the secured party may pursue both remedies. Answers (b) and (c) are incorrect because the UCC provides no such limitations on the secured party's remedies.

66. Thrush, a wholesaler of television sets, contracted to sell 100 sets to Kelly, a retailer. Kelly signed a security agreement with the 100 sets as collateral. The security agreement provided that Thrush's security interest extended to the inventory, to any proceeds therefrom, and to the after-acquired inventory of Kelly. Thrush filed his security interest centrally. Later, Kelly sold one of the sets to Myra Haynes who purchased with knowledge of Thrush's perfected security interest. Haynes gave a note for the purchase price and signed a security agreement using the set as collateral. Kelly is now in default. Thrush can

a. Not repossess the set from Haynes, but is entitled to any payments Haynes makes to Kelly on her note.

b. Repossess the set from Haynes as he has a purchase money security interest.

c. Repossess the set as his perfection is first, and first in time is first in right.

d. Repossess the set in Haynes's possession because Haynes knew of Thrush's perfected security interest at the time of purchase.

The correct answer is (a). *(CPA 1182 L-57)*

REQUIRED: The remedy available to a secured party after the defaulting debtor has sold the collateral.

DISCUSSION: Assuming Haynes bought in good faith, without knowledge that the sale was in violation of Thrush's security interest, in the ordinary course, and from a person in the business of selling television sets (not a pawnbroker), she qualifies as a buyer in the ordinary course of business. She therefore takes free of a security interest created by Kelly even though it was perfected and she knew of its existence (UCC 1-201 and 9-307). However, the security interest will continue in any identifiable proceeds including collections received by the debtor (UCC 9-306), so Thrush may recover payments made by Haynes to Kelly.

Answer (b) is incorrect because a purchase money security interest confers certain special protections but not against a buyer in the ordinary course. Answer (c) is incorrect because the priority contest here is not between two parties with perfected security interest. In any case, "first in time, first in right" is a principle with numerous exceptions. Answer (d) is incorrect because mere knowledge of the interest does not prevent Haynes from qualifying as a buyer in the ordinary course of business.

67. Bean defaulted on a promissory note payable to Gray Co. The note was secured by a piece of equipment owned by Bean. Gray perfected its security interest on May 29, 1987. Bean had also pledged the same equipment as collateral for another loan from Smith Co. after she had given the security interest to Gray. Smith's security interest was perfected on June 30, 1987. Bean is current in her payments to Smith. Subsequently, Gray took possession of the equipment and sold it at a private sale to Walsh, a good faith purchaser for value. Walsh will take the equipment

a. Free of Smith's security interest because Bean is current in her payments to Smith.

b. Free of Smith's security interest because Walsh acted in good faith and gave value.

c. Subject to Smith's security interest because the equipment was sold at a private sale.

d. Subject to Smith's security interest because Smith is a purchase money secured creditor.

The correct answer is (b). *(CPA 1187 L-44)*

REQUIRED: The correct statement about the rights of a good faith purchaser for value.

DISCUSSION: UCC 9-504 states that when a secured party disposes of collateral after default, the purchaser for value takes the property free of any subordinate security interests or liens and free of the security interest under which the sale was made. As long as the purchaser acts in good faith, the purchaser will receive the property free of any security interest even if the secured party does not comply with the requirements for the sale under Article 9. Thus, Walsh will take the equipment free of Smith's security interest as one who acted in good faith and was a purchaser for value.

Answer (a) is incorrect because that Bean is current in her payments to Smith is not a basis for survival of Smith's interest after disposition to a purchaser for value. Answer (c) is incorrect because the type of sale, either public or private, is irrelevant as long as the buyer is a good faith purchaser for value. Answer (d) is incorrect because a purchase money security interest arises when the proceeds of the transaction are used to purchase the collateral of the security interest. In this case, the loan from Smith was not used to purchase Bean's equipment.

68. Bonn, a secured party, sells collateral at a private sale to a good faith purchaser for value after the debtor defaults. Which of the following statements is correct under the UCC Secured Transactions Article?

a. In all cases, the collateral will remain subject to the security interests of subordinate lien creditors.

b. The security interest under which the sale was made and any security interest or lien subordinate to it will be discharged.

c. In all cases, Bonn may not buy the collateral at a private sale.

d. Bonn will be entitled to receive a first priority in the sale proceeds.

The correct answer is (b). *(CPA 1188 L-55)*

REQUIRED: The correct statement under the UCC Secured Transactions Article concerning good faith purchasers for value.

DISCUSSION: UCC 9-504 states that a purchaser for value will take property free of the security interest under which the sale is made and free of any subordinate security interests and liens when the secured party disposes of the collateral after default. Even if the secured party fails to comply with the requirements for the sale under Article 9, the purchaser will take the property free of these interests if (s)he acts in good faith.

Answer (a) is incorrect because the purchaser who acts in good faith will take the property free of any subordinate lien creditors' security interests. Answer (c) is incorrect because a secured party is permitted to buy the collateral at a private sale as long as the debtor is given reasonable notification and the sale is conducted in a commercially reasonable manner. Answer (d) is incorrect because the secured party will take the sale proceeds subject to any superior interests that exist in the collateral.

69. Under the UCC, collateral sold at a public sale by a secured party to a good faith purchaser for value after the debtor's default

a. Transfers to the purchaser marketable and insurable title to the collateral.

b. May be redeemed by the debtor within 30 days after the sale.

c. Remains subject to security interests that are senior to that being discharged at the sale.

d. May be redeemed by judicial lien creditors whose claims are subordinate to that being discharged at the sale.

The correct answer is (c). *(CPA 587 L-57)*

REQUIRED: The correct statement about the rights of a good faith purchaser for value after a debtor's default.

DISCUSSION: When a secured party disposes of collateral after a debtor defaults, the purchaser for value receives all of the debtor's rights in the collateral. (S)he also receives the collateral free of any subordinate security interests or liens. However, the purchaser remains subject to all security interests superior to the security interest being discharged by the sale.

Answer (a) is incorrect because the purchaser will receive the debtor's title, which may or may not be marketable and insurable. Answer (b) is incorrect because the debtor's right of redemption is lost once the collateral has been sold to a good faith purchaser for value. Answer (d) is incorrect because the subordinate creditors' claims are considered only after the sale proceeds have been distributed to the secured party to cover his/her secured debt and reasonable expenses. The subordinate creditors may not redeem the collateral once the secured party has disposed of it.

70. Brian purchased an electric typewriter from Robert under a written contract. The contract provided that Robert retained title until the purchase price was fully paid and granted him the right to repossess the typewriter if Brian failed to make any of the required ten payments. Arthur, an employee of Robert, was instructed to repossess the machine on the grounds that Brian had defaulted in making the third payment. Arthur took possession of the typewriter and delivered it to Robert. It was then discovered that Brian was not in default. Which of the following conclusions is supported by the above facts?

a. Arthur is not liable to Brian.

b. Brian can sue either Arthur or Robert or both for damages, but can collect only once.

c. Neither party is liable since it was apparently an honest mistake.

d. If Arthur is sued and must pay the judgment obtained against him, he has no rights against Robert.

The correct answer is (b). *(CPA 577 L-24)*

REQUIRED: The correct statement concerning the legal effect of a wrongful repossession.

DISCUSSION: A secured party has the general right upon default to take possession of the collateral, which may be done without recourse to judicial process if this can be accomplished without breach of the peace (UCC 9-503). If such repossession is wrongful, however (e.g., if the debtor is not truly in default), the secured party and an agent employed by the secured party to effect the repossession will both be liable to the debtor in tort for damages. However, Brian is allowed only one recovery of his damages.

Answer (a) is incorrect because agents are liable for their torts committed within the course and scope of their agency even though their principal is also liable. Answer (c) is incorrect because Brian is entitled to damages for the wrong of trespass or conversion caused by Robert and Arthur even if it was an honest mistake. Answer (d) is incorrect because an agent has the right to indemnification by his/her principal for any liability which the agent incurred as the result of doing an act, without knowledge of its unlawfulness, which was directed by the principal.

71. Pine has a security interest in certain goods purchased by Byron on an installment contract. Byron has defaulted on the payments resulting in Pine's taking possession of the collateral. Which of the following is correct?

a. Byron may waive his right of redemption at the time he executes the security agreement.

b. Pine must sell the collateral if Byron has paid more than 60% of the cash price on a purchase money security interest in business equipment.

c. The collateral may be sold by Pine at a private sale and, if it is consumer goods, without notice to other secured parties.

d. Unless otherwise agreed, Pine must pay Byron for any increase in value of the collateral while it is in Pine's possession.

The correct answer is (c). *(CPA 1184 L-57)*

REQUIRED: The rights and duties of the parties after default and repossession.

DISCUSSION: The secured party may dispose of the collateral at a public or private sale provided that every aspect of the disposition is commercially reasonable. Unless the collateral is perishable, threatens to decline rapidly in value, or is of a type customarily sold on a recognized market, reasonable notice must be given to the debtor unless (s)he has waived that right. In the case of consumer goods, no other notification need be sent to other secured parties because many PMSI in consumer goods are perfected by attachment alone (UCC 9-504).

Answer (a) is incorrect because except for a debtor's agreement in writing after default, the right of redemption cannot be waived or varied (UCC 9-501 and 9-506). Answer (b) is incorrect because disposition is compulsory if the debtor has paid 60% in the case of a security interest in consumer goods, not equipment. Answer (d) is incorrect because, under UCC 9-207, "The secured party may hold as additional security any increase or profits (except money) received from the collateral, but money so received, unless remitted to the debtor, shall be applied in reduction of the secured obligation."

72. Vega Manufacturing, Inc., manufactures and sells hi-fi systems and components to the trade and at retail. Repossession is frequently made from customers who are in default. Which of the following statements is correct concerning the rights of the defaulting debtors who have had property repossessed by Vega?

a. Vega has the right to retain all the goods repossessed as long as it gives notice and cancels the debt.

b. It is unimportant whether the goods repossessed are defined as consumer goods, inventory, or something else in respect to the debtor's rights upon repossession.

c. If the defaulting debtor voluntarily signs a statement renouncing his/her rights in the collateral, the creditor must nevertheless resell them for the debtor's benefit.

d. If a debtor has paid 60% or more of the purchase price of consumer goods in satisfaction of a purchase money security interest, the debtor has the right to have the creditor dispose of the goods.

The correct answer is (d). *(CPA 578 L-50)*

REQUIRED: The correct statement concerning the rights of defaulting debtors who have had property repossessed by the secured party.

DISCUSSION: In order to protect the equity interest of debtors who have had property repossessed by secured parties, the UCC provides for compulsory disposition of the collateral in certain cases. In other cases, a secured party may retain the collateral if appropriate notice is given to the debtor and other secured parties and no objection is made within 21 days. If the debtor has paid at least 60% of the debt in the case of consumer goods, the secured party must dispose of the goods unless the debtor renounces his/her rights in a writing signed after the default (UCC 9-505).

Answer (a) is incorrect because Vega may be compelled to dispose of the collateral in the case of consumer goods 60% paid for or if timely objection is made to Vega's retaining the collateral. Answer (b) is incorrect because the secured party is subject to compulsory disposition of certain consumer goods. Answer (c) is incorrect because a defaulting debtor may renounce or modify his/her rights to disposition of the collateral, in which case the secured party may elect to sell or retain it. If the collateral is sold, the debtor receives any surplus and remains liable for any deficiency.

73. The Uniform Commercial Code contains numerous provisions relating to the rights and remedies of the parties upon default. With respect to a buyer, these provisions may

a. Not be varied even with the agreement of the buyer.

b. Only be varied if the buyer is apprised of the fact and initials the variances in the agreement.

c. Not be varied insofar as they require the secured party to account for any surplus realized on the disposition of collateral securing the obligation.

d. All be varied by agreement as long as the variances are not manifestly unreasonable.

The correct answer is (c). *(CPA 582 L-49)*

REQUIRED: When the rights and remedies of the parties upon default may be varied.

DISCUSSION: Under UCC 9-504, if the security interest secures an indebtedness, the secured party must account to the debtor for any surplus on disposition of the collateral after default. This is an absolute right of the buyer-debtor when the collateral is sold after default because the risk remains with the debtor (but it would not apply if the secured party is allowed to retain the collateral and later sells it at a profit).

Answer (a) is incorrect because many provisions may be varied with the agreement of the buyer; e.g., under certain circumstances a buyer in default has a right to a compulsory disposition of collateral which may be waived. Answer (b) is incorrect because certain provisions for rights and remedies of the buyer upon default may not be waived. Answer (d) is incorrect because certain rights and remedies of the buyer upon default may not be varied by agreement regardless of the reasonableness of the variance.

74. Kelcar, Inc. designs and markets anti-pollution devices. It has developed several patents, one of which it has licensed to a major processor of cloves. To finance expansion, Kelcar has taken out a loan from Incensed Finance Co. and given its accounts, rights under the patent license, and chattel paper as collateral. If Kelcar defaults

a. Incensed is entitled to whatever it can collect from the collateral after proper notification to the debtors or obligors.

b. Incensed has no collection rights with respect to licensing of the patent since patents are not subject to the UCC.

c. Kelcar is entitled to any surplus of collections made by Incensed after deduction of expenses.

d. Incensed has no recourse against Kelcar beyond the collateral.

The correct answer is (c). *(Publisher)*

REQUIRED: The correct statement concerning the collection rights of a secured party upon default.

DISCUSSION: Under UCC 9-502, if the security agreement secures a debt, the secured party must account to the debtor for any surplus collections, less reasonable expenses incurred in the collection. Incensed is entitled (upon default) to notify account debtors or obligors to make payment to it regardless of any agreement with Kelcar.

Answer (a) is incorrect because Incensed is liable for surplus to Kelcar, since the security interest secures an indebtedness. Had the underlying transaction been a sale of accounts or chattel paper, Kelcar would have been entitled to the surplus only if explicitly agreed. Answer (b) is incorrect because if Kelcar has amounts owing to it as a result of licensing the patent, it could assign such rights as security and Incensed would have collection rights upon default. Answer (d) is incorrect because if the collections are insufficient to pay the indebtedness, Kelcar will be liable for the deficiency. Furthermore, a secured party after default may seek the remedy of judgment rather than repossession of the collateral.

75. If a secured party does not comply with the UCC rules with respect to collateral after a debtor's default, the secured party will

a. Lose his/her security interest.

b. Be required to sell the collateral.

c. Be liable for any better price available by any other method of sale.

d. Be liable to another known secured party for losses resulting from not sending notification of sale.

The correct answer is (d). *(Publisher)*

REQUIRED: A secured party's liability for not properly disposing of collateral.

DISCUSSION: In general, a secured party is liable for losses to the debtor or other secured parties as a result of not following the UCC rules for disposing of collateral. If another secured party ought to have been notified of a sale but was not, any losses resulting are recoverable.

Answer (a) is incorrect because it is not a penalty provided for by the UCC. Answer (b) is incorrect because the secured party also may be restrained from selling depending on the circumstances. Answer (c) is incorrect because a secured party need not sell at the very best price, just in a commercially reasonable manner.

CHAPTER EIGHTEEN
SURETYSHIP

Suretyship overlaps with bankruptcy, consumer law, credit law, mortgages, and secured transactions. Thus, this chapter should be read with the chapters on those topics.

18.1 Basic Concepts of Suretyship

1. The best definition of a surety is one who

a. Insures against a risk in return for compensation.

b. Holds an interest in collateral that secures payment or performance of an obligation.

c. Promises to answer to a third person for the debt or performance of another.

d. Signs an instrument in any capacity for the purpose of lending his/her name to it.

The correct answer is (c). *(Publisher)*

REQUIRED: The best description of the nature of a surety.

DISCUSSION: A surety is contractually obligated to a creditor to pay a debt or to perform an obligation owed by the principal debtor to the creditor if the principal fails to pay or otherwise perform. Suretyship is therefore a security device.

Answer (a) is incorrect because it describes an indemnification agreement of an insuror. Answer (b) is incorrect because it is the definition of a secured party. Answer (d) is incorrect because it defines an accommodation party. Although this is a specific kind of surety for negotiable instruments, answer (c) is a better definition of a surety.

2. Which of the following is the most accurate statement of a reason for using a surety?

a. All work done for a governmental entity must be protected by a surety.

b. The costs of using a secured transaction may be excessive.

c. The contracts of a minor may be ratified when (s)he reaches his/her majority and certain other contracts are enforceable in spite of the party's infancy.

d. A building contractor for a commercial project may seek a performance bond to protect against failure of the owner to pay the contract price.

The correct answer is (b). *(Publisher)*

REQUIRED: The most accurate statement of a reason for using a surety.

DISCUSSION: A surety may be used in addition to a secured transaction to provide further security. A surety may also be used instead of a secured transaction to avoid the trouble and expense of attaching, perfecting, and enforcing a security interest. Perfection by taking possession of the collateral, for example, may be especially costly and inconvenient.

Answer (a) is incorrect because statutes require only certain kinds of work done for a governmental unit to have a surety. Answer (c) is incorrect because minors may disaffirm many of their contracts. The advantage of a surety is to have someone with contractual capacity bound on the obligation. Answer (d) is incorrect because the performance bond is usually sought by the owner rather than the contractor.

3. Nolan Surety Company has agreed to serve as a guarantor of collection (a form of conditional guaranty) of the accounts receivable of the Dunbar Sales Corporation. The duration of the guarantee is one year and the maximum liability assumed is $3,000. Nolan charged the appropriate fee for acting in this capacity. Which of the following statements best describes the difference between a guarantor of collection and the typical surety relationship?

a. A guaranty need not be in writing provided the duration is less than a year.

b. The guarantor is not immediately liable upon default; the creditor must first proceed against the debtor.

c. A guaranty is only available from a surety who is a compensated surety.

d. A guaranty is only used in connection with the sale of goods which have been guaranteed by the seller.

The correct answer is (b). *(CPA 580 L-39)*

REQUIRED: The distinction between a surety and guarantor of collection.

DISCUSSION: A person who guarantees the payment of the debt of another without qualification is required to pay the debt upon default. Such a person is normally called a surety. The guarantor of collection is a person who guarantees a debt upon the condition that the creditor first make use of ordinary legal means to collect it from the debtor.

Answer (a) is incorrect because as a general rule, both a guaranty and a surety arrangement are within the Statute of Frauds and are required to be in writing. Answer (c) is incorrect because as stated above, a guaranty is not the same as a surety arrangement, and the guarantor may be compensated or uncompensated. Answer (d) is incorrect because a guaranty is used as a conditional surety arrangement and is not limited to sales of goods.

4. When the debtor has defaulted on its obligation, the creditor is entitled to recover from the surety unless which of the following is present?

a. The surety is in the process of exercising its right of exoneration against the debtor.

b. The debtor had died or become insolvent.

c. The creditor could collect the entire debt from the debtor's collateral in its possession.

d. The surety is a guarantor of collection and the creditor failed to exercise due diligence in enforcing its remedies against the debtor.

The correct answer is (d). *(CPA 1181 L-25)*

REQUIRED: The situation that will prevent a creditor from recovering from a surety.

DISCUSSION: The general rule is that a surety is liable to the creditor immediately upon the debtor's default without the necessity of notice or demand. When the surety has conditioned the obligation to pay by requiring the creditor to first proceed against the debtor, the surety is described as a guarantor of collection and is not liable until the creditor exercises due diligence in enforcing its remedies against the debtor.

Answer (a) is incorrect because the surety's right to exoneration from the debtor (compel the debtor to pay) does not suspend the creditor's right to recover from the surety. Answer (b) is incorrect because the death or insolvency of the debtor does not release the surety. Answer (c) is incorrect because a creditor can proceed directly against the surety without first exercising any rights against collateral in the creditor's possession.

5. Guaranty agreements are classified variously. Under a general guaranty,

a. The creditor can proceed directly against the guarantor.

b. The creditor must have made a reasonable effort to collect from the principal debtor before proceeding against the guarantor.

c. The guarantor agrees to be liable only to a single creditor and/or on a single debt.

d. The guarantor extends the promise to more than one transaction or creditor.

The correct answer is (d). *(Publisher)*

REQUIRED: The definition of a general guaranty.

DISCUSSION: The promise by a general guarantor may extend to multiple debts and creditors. An example is an open line of credit.

Answer (a) is incorrect because it describes an absolute guarantee. Answer (b) is incorrect because it describes a conditional guaranty. Answer (c) is incorrect because it describes a special guaranty.

6. Ace Corporation lent $10,000 to King Enterprises, Inc., one of its best customers. The loan was for three years and was evidenced by a note. In addition, Walsh and Paxton, King's principal shareholders, had orally guaranteed the repayment of the loan. With respect to Walsh and Paxton, which of the following is a correct statement?

a. Unless otherwise indicated, each guaranteed $5,000 of the loan.

b. They will be denied the usual surety defenses.

c. They are cosureties and, as such, their surety undertaking must be in a signed writing.

d. Some additional consideration, independent of the making of the loan by Ace, must pass directly to Walsh and Paxton.

The correct answer is (c). *(CPA 1178 L-24)*

REQUIRED: The correct statement regarding an oral guaranty by two shareholders.

DISCUSSION: Walsh and Paxton each guaranteed the loan in full. This direct guaranty makes them sureties. Two or more persons who are sureties on the same obligation are known as cosureties. A valid defense of the shareholders in this situation is that the suretyship agreement was not in writing and signed as required.

Answer (a) is incorrect because cosureties are jointly and severally liable. Each cosurety is liable to the creditor for the full amount of the debt. Answer (b) is incorrect because the facts do not indicate that they should be denied the usual surety defenses. Answer (d) is incorrect because these surety obligations arose at the time the loan was made, so the consideration given by the creditor to the debtor is considered extended to the cosureties.

7. In order to establish a cosurety relationship the two or more sureties must

a. Be aware of each other's existence at the time of their contract.

b. Sign the same contract creating the debt and the cosurety relationship.

c. Be bound to answer for the same debt or duty of the debtor.

d. Be bound for the same amount and share equally in the obligation to satisfy the creditor.

The correct answer is (c). *(CPA 1176 L-31)*

REQUIRED: The statement required to establish a cosurety relationship.

DISCUSSION: Cosureties exist when more than one surety is bound to answer for the same debt or duty of a debtor. Without an agreement to the contrary, cosureties share equally the loss caused by the debtor's default.

Answer (a) is incorrect because cosureties are not required to know of each other at the time of their contract. They may also become sureties at different times. Answer (b) is incorrect because it is not necessary for a surety to sign the same contract signed by the debtor or the other cosurety. The surety must only contract to pay the debt if the debtor does not pay. Answer (d) is incorrect because cosureties can guarantee unequal amounts of a debt. Each can guarantee any part of a debt.

8. Lester Dunbar sold to Walter Masters real property on which Charles Endicott held a first mortgage which had been created at the time Dunbar purchased the property. Under the terms of the written purchase agreement, Masters expressly assumed the mortgage debt. Subsequent to the purchase, Masters defaulted in his payment of the mortgage debt. Endicott thereupon sought to enforce payment of the mortgage debt against Masters personally. Masters contends that Endicott should have proceeded against Dunbar, the original mortgagor, because he is primarily liable for the mortgage debt. Based upon the above facts

a. Masters is correct in his assertion.

b. Endicott lost all rights against Dunbar upon learning of the sale to Masters and having made no objection thereto.

c. Dunbar is, in fact, a surety and must satisfy the mortgage if Masters does not.

d. Upon default, Endicott must elect to proceed against one of the parties involved and by so doing has made a binding election, thereby releasing the other.

The correct answer is (c). *(CPA 1174 L-27)*

REQUIRED: The correct statement concerning a mortgage assumed by a buyer of real property.

DISCUSSION: When a buyer of real estate assumes an existing mortgage, the seller remains liable because there has been no novation. Between the seller and buyer, the buyer has become the primary debtor, and the seller is a surety. Since Dunbar is a surety of the assumed mortgage, he must pay if Masters does not.

Answer (a) is incorrect because Masters is primarily liable for the mortgage debt after assuming it. Dunbar is only a surety obligated to pay if Masters does not. Answer (b) is incorrect because the creditor, Endicott, lost no rights when the mortgage was assigned and assumed. In fact, he gained additional rights against the purchaser. Answer (d) is incorrect because the creditor need not elect to proceed against only one of the parties since they are jointly and severally liable. Endicott can sue either or both without making a binding election until a final judgment is obtained.

9. Sims became an agent for Paul with the power to sell goods furnished by Paul but with the requirement that Sims would guarantee payment to Paul for all credit sales made by Sims. Under the circumstances

a. Sims is an agent coupled with an interest.

b. The Statute of Frauds applies to the above arrangement regardless of the amount of sales Sims makes.

c. Sims is a surety vis-a-vis any credit sales he makes on Paul's behalf.

d. The relationship between Sims and Paul is subject to the federal Fair Labor Standards Act.

The correct answer is (c). *(CPA 1175 L-12)*

REQUIRED: The correct statement regarding an agent's guaranty of his/her credit sales.

DISCUSSION: When an agent guarantees his/her credit sales (i.e., that the customer will pay), the agent is a surety for those accounts. (S)he is called a del credere agent.

Answer (a) is incorrect because the facts do not indicate Sims is an agent coupled with an interest. An agent coupled with an interest has a property right in the subject matter of the agency which may take the form of an ownership interest or security interest. Since it is property, the agency is not cancelable by the principal. Answer (b) is incorrect because a del credere agent's relationship is by custom not subject to the Statute of Frauds (under the theory that it is made before the debtors exist and is therefore a direct promise of the agent). Answer (d) is incorrect because Sims is an outside salesman and not considered an employee under the federal Fair Labor Standards Act.

10. Which of the following contractual prerequisites is not usually necessary to establish a legally enforceable surety relationship?

a. A signed writing.

b. The solvency of the principal debtor.

c. Separate consideration for the surety's promise.

d. The legal capacity of the surety.

The correct answer is (b). *(CPA 1178 L-25)*

REQUIRED: The item not required for a creditor to recover from a surety.

DISCUSSION: A suretyship is a relationship in which one person agrees to answer for the debt or default of another person. Whether the principal debtor is solvent at the time the promise is made is immaterial. An insolvent person can incur debts and a surety can guarantee them.

Answers (a), (c), and (d) are incorrect because each is ordinarily necessary to establish a legally enforceable surety relationship. Separate consideration for the surety's promise is required unless the promise is made at the same time the creditor extends consideration to the debtor.

11. Payne borrowed $500 from Onest Bank. At the time the loan was made to Payne, Gem orally agreed with Onest that Gem would repay the loan if Payne failed to do so. Gem received no personal benefit as a result of the loan to Payne. Under the circumstances

a. Gem is secondarily liable to repay the loan.

b. Both Gem and Payne are primarily liable to repay the loan.

c. Gem is free from liability concerning the loan.

d. Gem is primarily liable to repay the loan.

The correct answer is (c). *(CPA 1188 L-14)*

REQUIRED: The correct statement concerning the formation of a surety contract.

DISCUSSION: A surety contract is an agreement to answer for the debt or default of another. As such, it is required to be in writing by the Statute of Frauds whatever its amount. If the contract is not in writing, it will not be enforceable.

Answer (a) is incorrect because the surety would have been primarily liable if the agreement had been written. Answers (b) and (d) are incorrect because the surety has no liability on an oral promise.

12. Which of the following best describes what is required of an uncompensated surety?

a. The uncompensated surety must have the legal capacity to make contracts generally.

b. The uncompensated surety cannot be a corporation.

c. The uncompensated surety benefits by a rule that requires a creditor to first proceed against the principal debtor before the surety can be held liable.

d. The uncompensated surety must not directly or indirectly benefit from the undertaking.

The correct answer is (a). *(CPA 1177 L-18)*

REQUIRED: The best statement describing the requirement of an uncompensated surety.

DISCUSSION: All parties to suretyship agreements (including both compensated and uncompensated sureties) are ordinarily required to have the legal capacity to make contracts. A suretyship agreement is a contract.

Answer (b) is incorrect because a corporation can be an uncompensated surety. Answer (c) is incorrect because a creditor need not proceed first against the principal debtor before the uncompensated surety can be held liable. A compensated and an uncompensated surety have the same liability. Answer (d) is incorrect because the uncompensated surety is permitted to benefit directly or indirectly from the undertaking (and frequently does so).

13. Which of the following transactions does not establish Samp as a surety?

a. Samp says: "Ship goods to my son and I will pay for them."

b. Samp signs commercial paper as an accommodation endorser for one of his suppliers.

c. Samp guarantees a debt of a corporation he controls.

d. Samp sells an office building to Park and, as a part of the consideration, Park assumes Samp's mortgage on the property.

The correct answer is (a). *(CPA 1182 L-22)*

REQUIRED: The transaction not establishing a person as a surety.

DISCUSSION: A surety makes a secondary promise (Sarah promises to pay if Doug does not), not a primary promise (Sarah promises to pay if Pete will send consideration to Doug). Samp's statement is of the latter variety because Samp is establishing his own debt and is not promising to answer for the debt or performance of another.

Answer (b) is incorrect because an accommodation endorser of commercial paper may be liable if another fails to pay (UCC 3-415), so an accommodation party is a surety. Answer (c) is incorrect because Samp qualifies as a surety since the corporation is the primary obligor on a debt. Answer (d) is incorrect because the party who assumes the mortgage becomes the primary debtor and the seller becomes a surety.

14. Anthony is a surety on a debt owed by Victor to Day. Which of the following is correct?

a. Day must satisfy the Uniform Commercial Code's filing requirements in order to perfect his security interest.

b. The surety undertaking need not be in writing if the surety is obtained by Victor at Day's request.

c. The extension of credit by Day to Victor, contingent upon Anthony's agreeing to act as a surety, provides the consideration for Anthony's promise.

d. Upon default, Anthony would be allowed to deduct a personal claim that he has against Victor from his required payment to Day.

The correct answer is (c). *(CPA 1176 L-26)*

REQUIRED: The correct statement regarding a surety arrangement.

DISCUSSION: The extension of credit by the creditor to the debtor, contingent upon the surety's agreeing to act as a surety, supports the promises of both the debtor and the surety. Thus, separate consideration is not required.

Answer (a) is incorrect because surety arrangements are not security interests and are not governed by the UCC. Answer (b) is incorrect because surety arrangements are required by the Statute of Frauds to be in writing to be enforceable. Answer (d) is incorrect because when the debt is in default, the surety must pay it in full without set-off by any amount owed by the debtor to the surety. A surety could use as a set-off amounts owed by the creditor to either the surety or the debtor.

18.2 Creditors and Sureties: Defenses of a Surety

15. Which of the following defenses by a surety will be effective to avoid liability?

a. Lack of consideration to support the surety undertaking.

b. Insolvency in the bankruptcy sense by the debtor.

c. Incompetency of the debtor to make the contract in question.

d. Fraudulent statements by the principal debtor which induced the surety to assume the obligation and which were unknown to the creditor.

The correct answer is (a). *(CPA 582 L-23)*

REQUIRED: The defense by a surety that will be effective to avoid liability.

DISCUSSION: The contract of a surety must be supported by consideration or a legal substitute as must any other contract. If the surety enters into the agreement when the obligation is assumed by the debtor, the consideration given by the creditor to the debtor is extended to the surety. If the surety's promise is given later, separate consideration is required.

Answer (b) is incorrect because the possibility of the debtor's insolvency is one purpose for the creditor requiring a surety. Answer (c) is incorrect because a person may validly enter into a contract to answer for the debt of a person who is not competent to make the contract in question; e.g., a grandparent acts as a surety for a loan to a minor grandchild. Answer (d) is incorrect because while the fraud of the creditor would release the surety, fraud by the principal debtor upon the surety without the creditor's knowledge would not be a defense.

16. Young, a minor, purchased a car from Ace Auto Sales by making a down payment and signing a note for the balance. The note was guaranteed by Rich. Subsequently, Young sought to return the car and not pay off the note because Ace made false representations concerning the car's mileage at the time of sale. Which of the following best describes the legal implications in these circumstances?

a. Neither Young nor Rich is liable on the note solely because Young is a minor.

b. Young's attempt to return the car, in and of itself, released Rich of any liability.

c. The fraud perpetrated upon Young is a valid defense to Rich's guaranty.

d. There are no valid defenses for Rich and Young and the only recourse is to seek to reduce the amount owed based upon a counterclaim for fraud.

The correct answer is (c). *(CPA 576 L-16)*

REQUIRED: The legal implications of creditor fraud on the suretyship relation.

DISCUSSION: Upon discovery of fraud by the creditor, the debtor can elect either to rescind the contract or to affirm it. If the debtor rescinds, as in this situation, the surety may avail him/herself of the defense of fraud. Thus, the fraud perpetrated upon Young is a valid defense to Rich's guaranty.

Answer (a) is incorrect because infancy of the principal debtor has no legal effect on a surety's obligation. Answer (b) is incorrect because the actions of the debtor after the surety arrangement was formed had no effect on the surety's liability. Only acceptance of the car by Ace would have constituted a defense for Rich. Answer (d) is incorrect because the fraud of Ace Auto Sales is a valid defense for the surety and the debtor, not a counterclaim.

17. A surety will not be liable on an undertaking if

a. The principal is a minor.

b. The underlying obligation was illegal.

c. The principal was insolvent at the time of the surety's agreement to act as surety.

d. The surety was mistaken as to the legal implications of the surety agreement.

The correct answer is (b). *(CPA 577 L-31)*

REQUIRED: The situation in which a surety will not be liable.

DISCUSSION: The obligation for which the surety assumes liability must be legal. A suretyship agreement is a contract, and one of the requirements for a valid contract is that the subject be legal.

Answer (a) is incorrect because the infancy of the principal debtor has no effect on a suretyship arrangement. Such incapacity is one of the reasons for use of the suretyship device. Answer (c) is incorrect because the principal debtor's insolvency at the time the surety agrees to act as surety has no effect on the surety's liability. Answer (d) is incorrect because a surety's mistake as to the legal implications of the surety agreement is a unilateral mistake which does not release him/her.

18. Don loaned $10,000 to Jon, and Robert agreed to act as surety. Robert's agreement to act as surety was induced by 1) fraudulent misrepresentations made by Don concerning Jon's financial status and 2) a bogus unaudited financial statement of which Don had no knowledge, and which was independently submitted by Jon to Robert. Which of the following is correct?

a. Don's fraudulent misrepresentations will not provide Robert with a valid defense unless they were contained in a signed writing.

b. Robert will be liable on his surety undertaking despite the facts because the defenses are personal defenses.

c. Robert's reliance upon Jon's financial statements makes Robert's surety undertaking voidable.

d. Don's fraudulent misrepresentations provide Robert with a defense that will prevent Don from enforcing the surety undertaking.

The correct answer is (d). *(CPA 581 L-36)*

REQUIRED: The correct statement concerning the legal effect of fraudulent misrepresentations made to the surety.

DISCUSSION: A surety may take advantage of all his/her available personal defenses on a contract, e.g., fraud or intentional misrepresentation. Here, the creditor's fraudulent misrepresentations provide the surety with a defense that will prevent the creditor from enforcing the surety undertaking.

Answer (a) is incorrect because the law does not require that fraudulent misrepresentation be in writing in order to be assertible as a defense. Answer (b) is incorrect because while the surety may not exercise the debtor's personal defenses, (s)he may exercise his/her own personal defenses. Answer (c) is incorrect because the fraud committed by the debtor upon the surety has no effect on the surety's liability to the creditor unless the creditor had knowledge of it. The creditor is entitled to recover independently of the debtor's acts.

19. Surety agreed with Creditor and several other lenders to guarantee payment of all liabilities incurred by Principal to Creditor, but reserved the right to revoke her promise by written notice at any time. Creditor extended credit to Principal on several occasions and was repaid. At a time when no amounts were owed by Principal to Creditor, Surety severed her business relationship with Principal. She also gave written notice of revocation of her continuing guarantee to all parties but mistakenly omitted Creditor, an error that was known by Creditor. Subsequently, Creditor again extended credit to Principal, although it had learned of Principal's insolvency. Surety did not know of the insolvency, and Creditor was aware of her ignorance. Creditor had a reasonable opportunity to notify Surety prior to granting the loan to Principal but did not. In an action by Creditor against Surety to recover on Principal's debt, who will prevail and why?

a. Surety. Creditor knew that Surety was unaware of Principal's insolvency.

b. Surety. Courts do not enforce continuing guarantees.

c. Creditor. Surety failed to revoke the guarantee.

d. Creditor. The mistaken failure to notify Creditor was a unilateral mistake and was not grounds for voiding Surety's obligation.

The correct answer is (a). *(Publisher)*

REQUIRED: The outcome of a suit on a continuing guarantee that the surety mistakenly failed to revoke.

DISCUSSION: Surety should prevail on two grounds. First, Creditor breached its fiduciary duty to notify Surety of a fact that materially increased Surety's obligation beyond what Creditor had reason to believe Surety intended to assume. Creditor knew that Surety was ignorant of Principal's insolvency but did not avail itself of a reasonable opportunity to inform Surety. A duty of good faith and fair dealing is owed by all parties to the suretyship arrangement. Second, a unilateral mistake made by one party to a contract that is known by the other party is sufficient to render the agreement voidable. A continuing guarantee can be analogized to a continuing offer that is serially accepted by each extension of credit. Creditor knew that Surety did not intend to make an offer to guarantee the latest debt because Creditor was aware that Surety had mistakenly failed to send it a notice of revocation.

Answer (b) is incorrect because a general guarantor may make a continuing or general guarantee extending to more than one transaction and to multiple creditors. Answers (c) and (d) are incorrect because Creditor knew of Surety's mistaken failure to revoke the guarantee as well as of Surety's ignorance of Principal's insolvency.

20. State Bank loaned Barr $80,000 and received securities valued at $20,000 from Barr as collateral. At the request of State, Barr entered into an agreement with Rice and Noll to act as cosureties on the loan. The agreement provided that Rice and Noll's maximum liability would be $80,000 each. Which of the following defenses asserted by Rice will completely release Rice from liability to State?

a. State and Barr entered into a binding agreement to extend the time for payment that increased the sureties' risk and was agreed to without the sureties' consent.

b. Fraud by Barr that induced Rice to enter into the surety contract and was unknown to State.

c. Release of Barr's obligation by State without Rice's or Noll's consent but with State's reservation of its rights against Rice.

d. Return of the collateral to Barr by State without Rice's or Noll's consent.

The correct answer is (a). *(CPA 587 L-26)*

REQUIRED: The defense of a surety that results in a complete release.

DISCUSSION: An extension of time of payment or performance given by the creditor to the debtor that meets the requirements of a contract ordinarily releases the surety. This is particularly true when the surety is not compensated and does not consent. When the surety is compensated, the burden is on the surety to prove that damages resulted from the change or modification. If the creditor expressly reserves his/her rights against the surety in the extension agreement, the surety is not released. The rationale for the rule is that if the surety disapproves of the extension, (s)he may pay the debt and seek reimbursement.

Accordingly, Rice is discharged by the binding extension agreement whether or not Rice was compensated. If Rice is uncompensated and State made no reservation of rights, Rice would be discharged as a nonconsenting surety, even if the increase in risk is immaterial. If Rice is compensated and did not consent, Rice would be discharged if the change in the binding extension agreement is both material and prejudicial.

Answer (b) is incorrect because if the creditor acted in good faith, the principal debtor's fraud will not discharge the surety. Answer (c) is incorrect because the release with reservation of rights serves only as a covenant by the creditor not to sue the principal debtor. The creditor can still proceed against the surety, and the surety can still seek reimbursement from the principal debtor and contribution from the cosurety. Answer (d) is incorrect because the return of the collateral releases the surety only to the extent of the value returned.

21. Ford was unable to repay a loan to City Bank when due. City refused to renew the loan unless an acceptable surety could be provided. Ford asked Owens, a friend, to act as surety on the loan. To induce Owens to agree to become a surety, Ford made fraudulent representations about Ford's financial condition and promised Owens discounts on merchandise sold at Ford's store. Owens agreed to act as surety and the loan was made to Ford. Subsequently, Ford's obligation to City was discharged in Ford's bankruptcy and City wishes to hold Owens liable. Owens may avoid liability

a. Because the arrangement was void at the inception.

b. If Owens was an uncompensated surety.

c. If Owens can show that City Bank was aware of the fraudulent representations.

d. Because the discharge in bankruptcy will prevent Owens from having a right of reimbursement.

The correct answer is (c). *(CPA 1188 L-20)*

REQUIRED: The defense of a surety if the principal debtor has committed fraud.

DISCUSSION: A principal debtor's fraudulent misrepresentation is a material fact that the creditor has a duty to disclose to the surety. Because the surety arrangement is between the surety and the creditor, concealment or nondisclosure is a form of fraud against the surety by the creditor and is a personal defense of the surety. However, the principal debtor's fraud is not a defense against an innocent creditor.

Answer (a) is incorrect because the arrangement was voidable, not void. Answer (b) is incorrect because the loan renewal agreement and the suretyship contract were created at the same time, so no separate consideration was required to bind the surety. Answer (d) is incorrect because a surety may not exercise certain defenses of the principal debtor. The main exceptions are discharge in bankruptcy, expiration of the statute of limitations, and the principal debtor's lack of capacity. Discharge in bankruptcy is not a permissible defense because protection from the debtor's nonperformance is the essence of suretyship.

22. Dinsmore & Company was a compensated surety on the construction contract between Victor (the owner) and Gilmore Construction. Gilmore has defaulted and Victor has released Dinsmore for a partial payment and other consideration. The legal effect of the release of Dinsmore is

a. To release Gilmore as well.

b. Contingent on recovery from Gilmore.

c. Binding upon Victor.

d. To partially release Gilmore to the extent that Dinsmore's right of subrogation has been diminished.

The correct answer is (c). *(CPA 582 L-24)*

REQUIRED: The legal effect of the release of the surety by the creditor.

DISCUSSION: Victor will be bound by the release of the surety. The contractual obligation of the surety to the creditor may be discharged by a release that meets the requirements of a contract (especially consideration). The partial payments and other consideration will thus support Victor's promise to release Dinsmore.

Answer (a) is incorrect because the release of a surety will not release the principal debtor. Answer (b) is incorrect because unless otherwise stated, a release is not contingent upon any other factor. Answer (d) is incorrect because Gilmore has not been released from the obligation to any extent. Gilmore is the debtor in default and has no subrogation rights.

23. Quinn was the sole owner of Sunnydale Farms, Inc. The business was in dire need of additional working capital in order to survive. Click Company was willing to loan Sunnydale $12,000, but only if Click obtained a security interest in Sunnydale's machinery and equipment and a promise from Quinn to guarantee repayment of the loan. Click obtained both. Sunnydale was subsequently adjudged bankrupt. Click filed a reclamation claim for the machinery and equipment which was denied by the trustee in bankruptcy. The property was sold at public auction for $10,500. Click negotiated a settlement with the trustee whereby it received the $10,500 proceeds on the sale in full settlement of its claim against the bankrupt. Which of the following is a correct statement?

a. Where a surety is the sole owner of the stock of the corporation whose debt he guarantees, he is a compensated surety.

b. Click first had to exhaust its remedies against the property before sueing Quinn.

c. Quinn must pay Click the $1,500 difference, plus interest.

d. The settlement released Quinn from his surety obligation.

The correct answer is (d). *(CPA 579 L-6)*

REQUIRED: The legal effect of the release of the debtor by the creditor.

DISCUSSION: After a surety's payment to a creditor, the surety steps into the place of the creditor and may recover from the debtor to the same extent and in the same manner as the creditor could have recovered. When Click released Sunnydale from the remaining part of the debt, it interfered with Quinn's potential rights. Therefore, the settlement released Quinn from his obligation to Click.

Answer (a) is incorrect because the fact that a surety of the debt of a corporation is the sole stockholder does not establish that (s)he is a compensated surety. The benefit of the guaranty to the stockholder is only indirect. Answer (b) is incorrect because the creditor need not exhaust his/her remedies against collateral before seeking recovery from the surety. Answer (c) is incorrect because Quinn need not pay Click anything since the release of Sunnydale released Quinn from further obligation.

24. Which of the following will release a surety from liability?

a. Release of the principal debtor from liability with the consent of the surety.

b. Delegation of the debtor's obligation to another party with the acquiescence of the creditor.

c. Lack of capacity because the debtor is a minor.

d. Discharge of the debtor in bankruptcy.

The correct answer is (b). *(CPA 1182 L-25)*

REQUIRED: The situation in which a surety is released from liability.

DISCUSSION: Unless the surety agrees, a change in the debtor's duty under the contract releases the surety because of the possible effect on the surety's rights and liabilities. The delegation of the duty to perform alters the conditions under which the surety agreed to assume an obligation, so the surety is released.

Answer (a) is incorrect because the surety is not discharged if (s)he consents to the release or if the creditor reserves rights against the surety. Answer (c) is incorrect because the principal debtor's incapacity is a reason for using the suretyship arrangement since incapacity is a personal defense of the debtor but not the surety. Answer (d) is incorrect because discharge of the debtor in bankruptcy is only a personal defense of the debtor.

25. Dustin is a very cautious lender. When approached by Lanier regarding a $2,000 loan, he not only demanded an acceptable surety but also collateral equal to 50% of the loan. Lanier obtained King Surety Company as his surety and pledged rare coins worth $1,000 with Dustin. Dustin was assured by Lanier one week before the due date of the loan that he would have no difficulty in making payment. He persuaded Dustin to return the coins since they had increased in value and he had a prospective buyer. What is the legal effect of the release of the collateral upon King Surety?

a. It totally releases King Surety.

b. It does not release King Surety if the collateral was obtained after its promise.

c. It releases King Surety to the extent of the value of the security.

d. It does not release King Surety unless the collateral was given to Dustin with the express understanding that it was for the benefit of King Surety as well as Dustin.

The correct answer is (c). *(CPA 1181 L-24)*

REQUIRED: The legal effect on the surety of the release of the collateral by the creditor.

DISCUSSION: When a debtor has put up security or collateral, the surety (after payment) succeeds to it if the creditor has not sold it to satisfy the debt. Hence, a creditor who releases collateral interferes with the subrogation rights of the surety to the collateral. This interference releases the surety. Therefore, when Dustin released the $1,000 coin collection, he also released King Surety to that extent.

Answer (a) is incorrect because release of security by the creditor only releases the surety to the extent of its value. Answer (b) is incorrect because a surety has subrogation rights to the collateral no matter when pledged. Therefore, its release prejudices the surety, and (s)he is released. Answer (d) is incorrect because the surety has subrogation rights to the collateral automatically under law.

26. At the request of Pax, Somes and Tabor became cosureties on a loan from Cox to Pax. At the time they agreed to become sureties, Somes placed a limit of $30,000 on his liability and Tabor placed a limit of $20,000 on his; the loan was in the amount of $30,000. Somes and Tabor mutually intended to be cosureties and each promised to pay the loan to the extent of the limit placed should Pax default on payment at maturity. Based on these facts

a. A release of Tabor by Cox would result in a complete discharge of Somes.

b. A release of Somes by Cox, reserving Cox's rights against Tabor, would not reduce Tabor's obligations.

c. Insolvency of Somes would discharge Tabor.

d. Bankruptcy of Tabor before maturity of the note would limit Somes' potential liability to $18,000.

The correct answer is (b). *(CPA 574 L-17)*

REQUIRED: The correct statement regarding the liability of a cosurety.

DISCUSSION: If the creditor releases one cosurety, the others are released to the extent of the released cosurety's liability for contribution. The rule, however, is not applicable when the creditor reserves his/her rights against the remaining cosureties. The rationale of the exception is that the release with reservation of rights is a promise or covenant by the creditor not to sue the released cosurety and thus leaves the other cosureties' rights of reimbursement from the principal debtor and contribution from all the other cosureties intact. Thus, the release of Somes by Cox reserving Cox's rights against Tabor would not reduce Tabor's obligation because Tabor could still seek contribution from Somes and reimbursement from Pax.

Answer (a) is incorrect because a release of a cosurety does not result in a complete discharge of other cosureties but merely reduces their liability to the extent of the released cosurety's obligation of contribution. Answer (c) is incorrect because the insolvency of a cosurety would not discharge any other cosureties. Answer (d) is incorrect because bankruptcy of a cosurety does not affect the liability of the remaining solvent cosureties.

27. Ott and Bane agreed to act as cosureties on an $80,000 loan that Cread Bank made to Dash. Ott and Bane are each liable for the entire $80,000 loan. Subsequently, Cread released Ott from liability without Bane's consent and without reserving its rights against Bane. If Dash subsequently defaults, Cread will be entitled to collect a maximum of

a. $0 from Bane.

b. $0 from Dash.

c. $40,000 from Bane.

d. $40,000 from Dash.

The correct answer is (c). *(CPA 1188 L-21)*

REQUIRED: The liability of a cosurety after the creditor releases the other cosurety without consent and without reserving rights.

DISCUSSION: The unconsented to release of Ott by Cread without reservation of rights against Bane is regarded as a true release. Consequently, Bane will also be released to the extent that Bane cannot obtain contribution from Ott. Because both cosureties agreed to be liable for the entire loan, Ott's pro rata contributive share was $40,000. Hence, Bane's potential liability to Cread will be reduced from $80,000 to $40,000.

28. Which of the following defenses will release a surety from liability?

a. Insanity of the principal debtor at the time the contract was entered into.

b. Failure by the creditor to promptly notify the surety of the principal debtor's default.

c. Refusal by the creditor, with knowledge of the surety relationship, to accept the principal debtor's unconditional tender of payment in full.

d. Release by the creditor of the principal debtor's obligation without the surety's consent but with the creditor's reservation of rights against the surety.

The correct answer is (c). *(CPA 584 L-24)*

REQUIRED: The defense releasing a surety from liability.

DISCUSSION: The surety is released when the creditor refuses tender either by the debtor or by the surety. The debtor is not completely discharged by refusal of his/her tender, but accrual of interest on the obligation stops and the creditor will be unable to recover costs in a later suit on the debt.

Answer (a) is incorrect because incapacity of the principal debtor is a personal defense only of the debtor since such incapacity may create a need for a suretyship arrangement. Answer (b) is incorrect because lack of notice by the creditor is not a defense. Answer (d) is incorrect because the reservation of rights results in the release being treated merely as a covenant not to sue and thus not as a defense of the surety.

29. Knott obtained a loan of $10,000 from Charles on January 1, payable on April 15. At the time of the loan, Beck became an uncompensated surety thereon by written agreement. On April 15, Knott was unable to pay and wrote to Charles requesting an extension of time. Charles made no reply, but did not take any immediate action to recover. On May 30, Charles demanded payment from Knott and, failing to collect from him, proceeded against Beck. Based upon the facts stated

a. Charles was obligated to obtain a judgment against Knott returned unsatisfied before he could collect from Beck.

b. Beck is released from his surety obligation because Charles granted Knott an extension of time.

c. Charles may recover against Beck although Beck was an uncompensated surety.

d. Beck is released because Charles delayed in proceeding against Knott.

The correct answer is (c). *(CPA 1182 L-24)*

REQUIRED: The liability of an uncompensated surety upon default.

DISCUSSION: If the promise of the surety is made at the same time as that of the principal debtor, the same consideration that supports the latter promise will support the former. That Beck was not compensated thus has no effect on his/her liability.

Answer (a) is incorrect because only if the surety is a conditional guarantor of collection must the creditor exhaust legal remedies against the principal debtor before proceeding to collect from the surety. Answer (b) is incorrect because although an extension of time without reservation of rights does release the surety, no such agreement was made by Charles, and a simple delay of 45 days in demanding payment has no effect on the creditor's rights against either the principal debtor or the surety. Answer (d) is incorrect because the delay was too brief to affect anyone's rights or duties.

18.3 Rights of a Surety Against Debtors and Cosureties

30. Queen paid Pax & Co. to become the surety on a loan that Queen obtained from Squire. The loan is due and Pax wishes to compel Queen to pay Squire. Pax has not made any payments to Squire in its capacity as Queen's surety. Pax will be most successful if it exercises its right to

a. Reimbursement (Indemnification).

b. Contribution.

c. Exoneration.

d. Subrogation.

The correct answer is (c). *(CPA 1186 L-28)*

REQUIRED: The right that can be exercised by a surety that has not paid the creditor.

DISCUSSION: The principal debtor is expected to perform so that the surety will not be required to pay the creditor. The surety therefore has a right (exoneration) to compel performance by the principal debtor by obtaining a decree from a court.

Answer (a) is incorrect because reimbursement is the right of a surety who has paid the debt to be paid by the principal debtor. Indemnification is not the same as reimbursement. It arises from an agreement by one party to protect an obligor (debtor), not an obligee (creditor), from loss. An example is an insurance contract. Answer (b) is incorrect because contribution is the right of a cosurety who has paid more than his/her proportionate or agreed share of the debt to proceed against the other cosureties for their share. Answer (d) is incorrect because subrogation is the right of a surety who has paid the principal debtor's full obligation to exercise all the rights that the creditor had against or through the principal debtor.

31. A surety paid the creditor upon default and then brought suit against the principal debtor for the amount paid. The surety exercised the right of

a. Subrogation.

b. Contribution.

c. Exoneration.

d. Reimbursement.

The correct answer is (d). *(Publisher)*

REQUIRED: The right of a surety who has paid the creditor to receive payment from the principal debtor.

DISCUSSION: A surety who has paid the creditor has a right to be paid by the principal debtor. This right of reimbursement accrues only after actual payment and only for the amount paid.

Answer (a) is incorrect because subrogation is the right of a surety who has paid the principal debtor's full obligation to exercise all the creditor's rights. Answer (b) is incorrect because contribution is the right of a cosurety who has paid more than his/her proportionate or agreed share of the debt to proceed against the other cosureties for their share. Answer (c) is incorrect because exoneration is the surety's right to compel performance by the principal debtor.

32. Baker was the surety on an obligation owed by Swanson to Libby. Swanson defaulted on the debt but Libby had never requested payment from Baker. Several years later, Libby came to Baker and requested payment. Baker paid Libby, not realizing that the statute of limitations had run on Swanson's obligation. Which statement is correct concerning the rights of Baker?

a. Because the statute of limitations had run, Baker is entitled to a return of the funds from Libby.

b. Because Baker had obligated him/herself to pay Swanson's debt, Baker is entitled to reimbursement from Swanson even though the statute of limitations had run.

c. Baker was required to pay the debt because, although the statute of limitations may have run with regard to Swanson, it could not have run with regard to Baker given that Libby had never made a demand of payment.

d. Baker cannot recover from either Swanson or Libby.

The correct answer is (d). *(Publisher)*

REQUIRED: The correct statement concerning a surety who pays after the statute of limitations has run.

DISCUSSION: Because the statute of limitations had run on Swanson's debt, Swanson was no longer liable to Libby, so Baker has no right of recourse against Swanson. Moreover, Baker may not have been legally obligated to pay Libby because the statute of limitations may have run regarding the suretyship promise. But a surety who pays a creditor is not entitled to repayment by the creditor whether or not the statute of limitations has run. The statute of limitations is merely a bar that can be waived by payment.

Answer (a) is incorrect because if the statute of limitations had run, Baker's payment was a waiver of the defense of the statute of limitations. Answer (b) is incorrect because Swanson is entitled to the defense of the statute of limitations. Answer (c) is incorrect because a surety is liable immediately upon default of the debtor. When the statute of limitations began running for Swanson, it also began for Baker even though no demand for payment was made. Thus, Baker might not have been required to pay because the separate statute of limitations applicable to the surety's promise may also have elapsed.

33. If a debtor defaults and the debtor's surety satisfies the obligation, the surety acquires the right of

a. Subrogation.

b. Primary lien.

c. Indemnification.

d. Satisfaction.

The correct answer is (a). *(CPA 1189 L-21)*

REQUIRED: The surety's right arising from satisfaction of the principal debtor's obligation.

DISCUSSION: Subrogation is the right of a surety, after payment upon default of the debtor, to step into the creditor's shoes and recover from the debtor in the same manner as the creditor. Thus, subrogation allows a surety to succeed to the creditor's rights.

Answer (b) is incorrect because the surety stands in the shoes of the creditor, who may or may not have had a security interest or a priority in bankruptcy. Indeed, even a secured party may have had a junior lien. Answer (c) is incorrect because a right of indemnification arises from a contract by which one party agrees to hold another party harmless, that is, to protect that party from loss. A contract of indemnity (e.g., insurance) involves a promise to protect a debtor. A suretyship contract protects a creditor. Answer (d) is incorrect because satisfaction is the creditor's acceptance of a performance stipulated in an accord, which is an agreement to accept some performance by the debtor that is different from and usually less than what was originally agreed.

34. Susan is a surety on an obligation owed by Paul to Bank. Paul has transferred possession of 1,000 shares of common stock to Susan as collateral. Which of the following is true?

a. Susan is subrogated to Bank's rights against Paul, but Bank has no subrogation rights.

b. Bank may enforce Susan's rights against Paul.

c. If Susan returns the stock to Paul, the Bank's subrogation rights are voided.

d. Bank is powerless to prevent the return of the stock to Paul prior to the time the debt is due.

The correct answer is (b). *(Publisher)*

REQUIRED: The creditor's rights in collateral held by the surety.

DISCUSSION: A creditor as well as a surety has subrogation rights. Thus, a creditor may "step into the shoes" of the surety and enforce whatever rights the surety may have against the debtor. If the debtor places assets in the hands of the surety to provide against default, the creditor has the right to assert the surety's rights against those assets. Hence, Bank may enforce Susan's rights to the stock.

Answer (a) is incorrect because both creditors and sureties have subrogation rights. Answer (c) is incorrect because if the stock is returned, the creditor may nevertheless obtain a lien against it. Answer (d) is incorrect because Bank can obtain an injunction to prevent the return. In effect, the stock can be held by the court until the due date and sold if the principal debt is not paid.

35. Burns borrowed $240,000 from Dollar Bank as additional working capital for his business. Dollar required that the loan be collateralized to the extent of 20%, and that an acceptable surety for the entire amount be obtained. Surety Co. agreed to act as surety on the loan and Burns pledged $48,000 of negotiable bearer bonds. Burns defaulted. Which of the following statements is correct?

a. Dollar must first liquidate the collateral before it can proceed against Surety.

b. Surety is liable in full immediately upon default by Burns, but will be entitled to the collateral upon satisfaction of the debt.

c. Dollar must first proceed against Burns and obtain a judgment before it can proceed against the collateral.

d. Surety may proceed against Burns for the full amount of the loan even if Surety settles with Dollar for a lower amount.

The correct answer is (b). *(CPA 1189 L-20)*

REQUIRED: The rights of a surety after default on a partially collateralized debt.

DISCUSSION: Subrogation is the right of a surety, after payment upon default of the debtor, to step into the creditor's shoes and recover from the debtor in the same manner as the creditor. This includes rights in the collateral provided by the principal debtor, a priority in bankruptcy, rights against other parties indebted on the same obligation, and rights against cosureties. Surety is therefore subrogated to Dollar's rights against the bonds.

Answer (a) is incorrect because unless otherwise agreed, Dollar may proceed directly against Surety after default. Answer (c) is incorrect because only if the surety is a conditional guarantor of collection must the creditor exhaust legal remedies against the principal debtor before proceeding to collect from the surety. Answer (d) is incorrect because the surety's right of reimbursement is limited to amounts paid to the creditor.

36. Clark is a surety on a $100,000 obligation owed by Thompson to Owens. The debt is also secured by a $50,000 mortgage to Owens on Thompson's factory. Thompson is in bankruptcy. Clark has satisfied the debt. Clark is

a. Only entitled to the standing of a general creditor in bankruptcy.

b. A secured creditor to the extent of the $50,000 mortgage and a general creditor for the balance.

c. Entitled to nothing in bankruptcy since this was a risk he assumed.

d. Not entitled to a priority in bankruptcy, even though Owens could validly claim it.

The correct answer is (b). *(CPA 582 L-22)*

REQUIRED: The status of a surety on a partially secured obligation.

DISCUSSION: When a surety has satisfied the debt, (s)he becomes subrogated to the rights of the creditor against the debtor. Thus, the surety will have the same standing in bankruptcy as the creditor would have had. Owens was a secured creditor to the extent of the $50,000 mortgage and a general creditor for the balance, and Clark will have the same standing.

Answer (a) is incorrect because Clark will be subrogated to the security of the $50,000 mortgage. Answer (c) is incorrect because a surety becomes a creditor of the principal debtor upon paying the original creditor. Answer (d) is incorrect because Clark will be subrogated to Owens' priority also.

37. Dunlop loaned Barkum $20,000 which was secured by a security agreement covering Barkum's machinery and equipment. A financing statement was properly filed covering the machinery and equipment. In addition, Delson was a surety on the Barkum loan. Barkum is now insolvent and a petition in bankruptcy has been filed against him. Delson paid the amount owed ($17,000) to Dunlop. The property was sold for $12,000. Which of the following is correct?

a. Delson has the right of a secured creditor to the $12,000 via subrogation to Dunlop's rights and the standing of general creditor for the balance.

b. To the extent Delson is not fully satisfied for the $17,000 he paid Dunlop, his claim against Barkum will not be discharged in bankruptcy.

c. Delson's best strategy would have been to proceed against Barkum in his own right for reimbursement.

d. Delson should have asserted his right of exoneration.

The correct answer is (a). *(CPA 579 L-5)*

REQUIRED: The rights of a surety against a bankrupt debtor after payment to the creditor.

DISCUSSION: A surety, after payment of the debt, is subrogated to the creditor's rights against the debtor, including the right to any collateral or security interest held by the creditor. Here, Delson is entitled to the $12,000 proceeds from the collateral, and since the collateral has been exhausted, (s)he becomes a general creditor for the balance.

Answer (b) is incorrect because a surety's claim against a bankrupt is dischargeable in bankruptcy. Answers (c) and (d) are incorrect because the petition in bankruptcy suspends further legal proceedings against Barkum. Therefore, Delson could only file a claim in bankruptcy after payment to Dunlop.

38. In relation to the principal debtor, the creditor, and a fellow cosurety, the cosurety is not entitled to

a. Exoneration against the debtor under any circumstances.

b. A pro rata contribution by fellow sureties if (s)he pays the full amount.

c. Be subrogated to the rights of the creditor upon satisfaction of the debt.

d. Avoid performance because the cosurety refuses to perform.

The correct answer is (d). *(CPA 582 L-25)*

REQUIRED: The right not held by a cosurety against the other parties.

DISCUSSION: The obligation of a cosurety to perform under the suretyship agreement is not contingent upon the performance of another cosurety. Instead, a cosurety who pays is entitled to contribution from the other cosurety.

Answer (a) is incorrect because a cosurety is entitled to exoneration against the debtor (to bring a suit to compel the debtor to pay). Answer (b) is incorrect because a cosurety is entitled to contribution from another cosurety to the extent that (s)he has paid more than his/her pro rata share. Answer (c) is incorrect because a cosurety who has paid the creditor steps into the shoes of the creditor and may assert all rights that the creditor had.

39. A distinction between a surety and a cosurety is that only a cosurety is entitled to

a. Contribution.

b. Exoneration.

c. Subrogation.

d. Reimbursement (Indemnification).

The correct answer is (a). *(CPA 587 L-29)*

REQUIRED: The distinction between a surety and a cosurety.

DISCUSSION: A cosurety who has paid more than his/her proportionate or agreed share of the debt has a right to proceed against the other cosureties for their proportionate or agreed share. By definition, this right of contribution exists only when cosureties are involved.

Answers (b) and (c) are incorrect because both are entitled to the rights of subrogation and exoneration. Answer (d) is incorrect because both are entitled to reimbursement. However, indemnification is not the same as reimbursement. It arises from an agreement to hold an obligor (debtor) harmless, that is, to protect a debtor who is to perform an act or pay an amount from any loss as a result of nonperformance.

40. Prior to making payment, cosureties may seek the remedy of

a. Contribution.

b. Reimbursement.

c. Subrogation.

d. Exoneration.

The correct answer is (d). *(CPA 584 L-22)*

REQUIRED: The remedy that may be sought by the cosureties prior to payment.

DISCUSSION: The principal debtor is expected to perform so that the surety will not be required to pay the creditor. The surety therefore has a right (exoneration) to compel performance by the principal debtor by obtaining a decree from a court exercising its equity powers.

Answer (a) is incorrect because contribution is the right of a cosurety who has paid more than his/her proportionate or agreed share of the debt to proceed against the other cosureties for their proportionate or agreed share. Answer (b) is incorrect because it is the right of a surety who has paid the creditor to be paid by the principal debtor. Answer (c) is incorrect because subrogation is the right of a surety who has paid the principal debtor's full obligation to exercise all the rights that the creditor had against or through the principal debtor.

41. Sklar borrowed $360,000 from Rich Bank. At Rich's request, Sklar entered into an agreement with Aker, Burke, and Cey to act as cosureties on the loan. The agreement between Sklar and the cosureties provided that the maximum liability of each cosurety was: Aker $72,000, Burke $108,000, and Cey $180,000. After making several payments, Sklar defaulted on the loan. The balance was $240,000. If Cey pays $180,000 and Sklar subsequently pays $60,000, what amounts may Cey recover from Aker and Burke?

a. $0 from Aker and $0 from Burke.

b. $60,000 from Aker and $60,000 from Burke.

c. $48,000 from Aker and $72,000 from Burke.

d. $36,000 from Aker and $54,000 from Burke.

The correct answer is (d). *(CPA 588 L-26)*

REQUIRED: The amounts recoverable from cosureties by one who has paid the full amount.

DISCUSSION: A cosurety who has paid more than his/her proportionate or agreed share of the debt has a right to proceed against the other cosureties for their proportionate or agreed share. A cosurety's contributive share is determined by dividing the maximum liability of each surety by the sum for all the cosureties and then multiplying by the amount of the default

Aker	$ 72 ÷ ($72 + $108 + $180)	=	1/5 x $180	= $36
Burke	$108 ÷ ($72 + $108 + $180)	=	3/10 x $180	= $54
Cey	$180 ÷ ($72 + $108 + $180)	=	1/2 x $180	= $90

Hence, Cey should receive contributions of $36,000 and $54,000 from Aker and Burke, respectively.

CHAPTER NINETEEN
PERSONAL AND INTELLECTUAL PROPERTY AND BAILMENTS

19.1 Introduction to Property

1. Which of the following is false with respect to the concept called property?

a. Property rights are created by law. No form, color, or visible trace expresses the relationship that constitutes the rights of property.

b. Property includes every interest anyone may have in anything that may be the subject of ownership, including the right to freely possess, use, enjoy, and dispose of the same. The sum of these rights is designated "title" to property.

c. Currently, in the United States, a societal theory of land use prevails over individual determination of property use. The traditional freedom of private decision is now within governmental control that promotes the welfare of society at the expense of the rights of private property.

d. Property is whatever a person is legally entitled to do. Such a right may not be contrary to public policy, and legal redress must be available for interference with it.

The correct answer is (d). *(Publisher)*

REQUIRED: The false statement regarding the concept of property.

DISCUSSION: Property is difficult to define. The traditional definition is that property is a bundle of legally enforceable rights capable of being valued, owned, and transferred. The bundle may relate to something tangible (land or a television set) or intangible (a share of stock or a patent). In constitutional law, however, property is also deemed to include entitlements, such as welfare benefits, that have value but cannot be transferred. But not every legal right is property. Free speech, for example, is a right enjoyed by the people of the United States. Its infringement may be redressed through recourse to the legal system, but it is not amenable to valuation, capable of being owned, or transferrable.

Answers (a) and (b) are incorrect because each illustrates that no property rights exist without a government and a legal system to create and enforce them. Private property rights do not exist without some method of keeping the rights and restoring them to the owner when (s)he is deprived of them. Answer (c) is incorrect because it illustrates that no owner has unlimited rights. The law limits use of private property to accommodate the public interest. In many ways, the promotion of the welfare of society by the government is at the expense of the ownership of property. However, property rights are protected by the 5th and 14th Amendments to the U.S. Constitution as well as by state constitutions. The due process clauses in the Constitution state that government may not deprive a person of life, liberty, or property without due process of law.

2. Property is traditionally viewed by the law as a "bundle of rights" related to a thing capable of being owned. Property is defined very broadly because it is a category that is constantly expanding to recognize new interests. Property may be classified very generally as tangible or intangible or as real or personal. Which of the following is true?

a. Personal property is tangible but real estate may be either tangible or intangible.

b. The bundle of rights may not be held by more than one person at a time.

c. Personal property cannot exist independently of the evidence of its ownership.

d. Real property is the bundle of rights a person may have in land, things attached to the land, and the spaces above and below the surface.

The correct answer is (d). *(Publisher)*

REQUIRED: The true statement about property.

DISCUSSION: Real property itself consists of the surface of land, the airspace above, things attached to the surface, such as buildings or trees, and the space below the land, including minerals. The law of real property involves legal rights in the property (e.g., mineral, air, and water rights) and, in general, the right freely to use, possess, enjoy, and transfer any interest in real estate.

Answer (a) is incorrect because tangible property has a physical existence, e.g., real estate and goods, while intangible property has value and is transferable but has no physical form, e.g., accounts, patents, copyrights, goodwill, trademarks, and stock. Answer (b) is incorrect because the "bundle of rights" concept includes different persons having rights in the same property. For example, one person may own property for his/her life, a second may lease it for a specified term, a third may own the mineral rights, a fourth may have a right to cross the land. Answer (c) is incorrect because intangible personal property exists even though its physical representation is destroyed. An ownership interest in a corporation, for instance, continues although the certificate of stock is lost in a fire.

3. Which of the following is a false statement about the common law and property?

a. The law of real property was highly developed by the common law.

b. The common law was originally unresponsive to the personal property problems of commercial paper.

c. Common law legal rights in property include the absolute ability to possess, enjoy, transfer, or exclude others from using or possessing property.

d. Much of the common law of personal property has been supplemented by state statutes.

The correct answer is (c). *(Publisher)*

REQUIRED: The false statement about the common law and property.

DISCUSSION: Property rights of any kind are never absolute. One may not exercise rights in property so as to injure another, including society at large. Rights are relative because of the constant need to balance individual and societal needs and interests. For example, one's use and enjoyment of property is always subject to the government's police power when reasonably invoked to protect the public health, safety, welfare, and morals. Zoning laws are an illustration.

Answer (a) is incorrect because the law of real property was highly developed by the early common law. Realty was the principal form of wealth in feudal society prior to the industrial revolution. Answer (b) is incorrect because the early common law courts were ill-equipped to handle the legal problems of the trading class, so those engaged in commerce formed guilds, established private courts, and developed their own law, which is the origin of today's commercial law. Answer (d) is incorrect because much of today's property law is statutory.

4. Which of the following is classified as personal property, not real property?

a. Chattels real.

b. Fruit of nature such as trees, perennial crops, and grazing grass.

c. Fixtures.

d. One season's crops.

The correct answer is (a). *(Publisher)*

REQUIRED: The example of personal property.

DISCUSSION: Personal property was traditionally divided into two main classes: chattels real and chattels personal. Chattels real generally include leases of real property. Chattels personal are typical personal property such as goods and intangibles.

Answer (b) is incorrect because fruit of nature, such as grazing grass, trees, and perennial crops that do not require annual seeding, are usually treated as part of the land and classified as real property. Answer (c) is incorrect because a fixture is personal property which has become so attached to or used with real estate that it is considered to be part of the real estate. A trade fixture is one attached by a business tenant and does not become a true fixture. It is personal property. Answer (d) is incorrect because crops attached to the land are considered to be real property unless a statute provides otherwise.

5. The distinction between the compensable taking under eminent domain and a noncompensable regulation under police power is

a. Spelled out in detail in the U.S. Constitution, particularly the 5th Amendment.

b. Determined by the class of property involved and its value.

c. The difference between government action in its enterprise capacity to take private resources for a common good, and action in its regulatory capacity to limit uses of property that are injurious to others.

d. Dependent on the intent of the governing body taking the action complained of.

The correct answer is (c). *(Publisher)*

REQUIRED: The distinction between eminent domain and police power.

DISCUSSION: There are several important restrictions on the use and enjoyment of private property. First, under the Constitution, the government retains the right to take privately owned property for a public use (eminent domain) by paying just compensation to the owner. Second, state government has the sovereign right to enact rules and regulations which may have an impact on property provided they are reasonably related to public health, safety, and general welfare. Compensation is paid under eminent domain when the government is acting in an enterprise capacity, while no compensation is paid under the police power when the government is acting in a regulatory capacity.

Answer (a) is incorrect because the distinction between eminent domain and police power is not spelled out in the U.S. Constitution. It has been decided by judicial interpretation. Answer (b) is incorrect because the distinction is not determined by class of property involved or its value. Answer (d) is incorrect because the distinction is dependent on the effect rather than the intent. A political institution may believe that it is properly exercising police power but a court may determine that there has been a taking in the constitutional sense of eminent domain.

6. The city of Nirvana determined that a particular railroad street crossing was hazardous and constructed an underpass below the tracks. In doing so, the plaintiff was cut off from entry and exit to the street from his property.

a. There has been a taking of the plaintiff's property in the constitutional sense for which (s)he is entitled to compensation.

b. The action of the city was a constitutional exercise of police power for which no compensation is payable.

c. Since the plaintiff's land was left intact and none was physically taken, there was no taking in the constitutional sense.

d. The city's action cannot be a valid eminent domain action because the use did not involve a public use since only a small percentage of the public can be expected to use the underpass.

The correct answer is (a). *(Publisher)*

REQUIRED: The legal implications of a governmental body's constructing an underpass.

DISCUSSION: When a city makes roadway improvements and thereby cuts off a property owner from access to the nearest public street, a taking of property in the constitutional sense has occurred. The owner is entitled to compensation although no physical taking was involved; the courts would interpret ownership of property to include the right of access to the nearest public road.

Answer (b) is incorrect because building an underpass and cutting off access to a public street is not an exercise of police power. It goes beyond rules or activities reasonably regulating the general welfare of the public. Answer (c) is incorrect because physical taking is not legally necessary for eminent domain to occur. A taking can occur in the constitutional sense without a physical taking. Answer (d) is incorrect because governmental action involving eminent domain need not benefit all or substantially all of the public as long as the number who are benefited is not insignificant.

7. The exercise of the power of eminent domain

a. Must be by a governmental unit but the actual user of the condemned property may be private.

b. Is constitutionally limited to the taking of real property.

c. Must be by a governmental unit for its own direct use.

d. Is subject to a rational basis test of what constitutes a public use.

The correct answer is (d). *(Publisher)*

REQUIRED: The correct statement concerning the power of eminent domain.

DISCUSSION: Eminent domain is the right of the government to take privately owned property for "public use." In a 1984 decision, the Supreme Court stated a test that apparently defines "public use" very broadly. It held that if "the exercise of the eminent domain power is rationally related to a conceivable public purpose," the court would not proscribe a compensated taking.

Answers (a) and (c) are incorrect because a governmental entity may entrust the power to a private entity (e.g., a utility to acquire property for utility lines, and the use itself need not be directly governmental). Answer (b) is incorrect because eminent domain is the power to take "private property," not merely real property. The limitations are that it must be for a public use and compensated.

19.2 Personal and Intellectual Property

8. If personal property is viewed as a collection of legal rights in a thing, it will be apparent that the category will expand to include new rights recognized by the law. Which of the following is not a relatively recent addition to the category?

a. Commercial paper.

b. Computer programs.

c. Company records.

d. The right to governmental benefits.

The correct answer is (a). *(Publisher)*

REQUIRED: The item of personal property not a relatively recent development.

DISCUSSION: Forms of commercial paper such as drafts and notes have been used for centuries and thus are not new developments.

Answers (b), (c), and (d) are incorrect because each may represent a right of recent creation that has at least some of the qualities traditionally associated with personal property. For example, utility services (telephone, gas, water, computer facilities) and computer programs are all regarded as personal property for criminal law purposes when stolen or used without consent. Illegally copying records or tapes and selling them is likewise a crime. The courts have recognized a species of constitutional property rights in governmental benefits (welfare, licenses, employment, education) on the part of qualifying persons that may not be deprived without due process.

9. Personal property is

a. Minerals to be mined by the buyer.

b. Immovable.

c. Something that is not real property but is firmly attached to land.

d. Something capable of being owned, but not real property.

The correct answer is (d). *(Publisher)*

REQUIRED: The correct statement which describes personal property.

DISCUSSION: The legal definition of personal property is negative. Personal property is classified as anything capable of being owned that is not real property.

Answer (a) is incorrect because a mineral which is to be mined and removed from the ground by the buyer is part of the soil and therefore real property. It would not become personal property until actually severed from the land. Answer (b) is incorrect because personal property is characterized by mobility while real property is immovable. Answer (c) is incorrect because something which is not real property but is firmly attached to land is generally classified as a fixture and considered to be real property.

10. Intellectual property is a type of intangible personal property interest that may take all of the following forms except a

a. Patent.

b. Trademark.

c. Copyright.

d. College degree.

The correct answer is (d). *(Publisher)*

REQUIRED: The personal property that is not a form of intellectual property.

DISCUSSION: Intellectual property is intangible personal property that is a direct expression of the human intellect and that entitles the owner to its exclusive use. Patents, copyrights, and trademarks are the major forms of intellectual property, but other forms, such as trade secrets and rights of publicity, also exist. A college degree is arguably a form of property and is presumably the result of intellectual endeavor, but it is not a specific, direct expression thereof. A degree is a title conferred by an academic institution to signify completion of a course of study. It may have value, but it cannot be transferred and does not represent an exclusive right to use some specific, direct expression of intellect.

Answers (a), (b), and (c) are incorrect because each is a major form of intellectual property.

11. Intangible personal property includes intellectual property. The law gives protection to those who engage in creative or learned endeavor, including research and development, or who invest resources in establishing goodwill signified by various trade symbols. Which of the following is true?

a. A patent gives a nonrenewable monopoly to an inventor for the duration of his/her life, including the right to license its use.

b. Trade secrets may be protected by federal registration from industrial espionage or disclosure by disloyal employees.

c. The Copyright Act protects original works fixed in any tangible medium, but it does not protect ideas or prohibit fair use.

d. Trademarks and trade names are safeguarded from infringement if they are registered with the Patent Office.

The correct answer is (c). *(Publisher)*

REQUIRED: The true statement about intellectual property.

DISCUSSION: The Federal Copyright Act provides broad rights (in most cases, for the life of the author plus 50 years) for original works in any tangible medium or expression. The works protected include but are not limited to literary, musical, and dramatic works, sound recordings, motion pictures, computer programs, and other audiovisual works. The author has extensive rights exclusively to reproduce, distribute, perform, display, and prepare derivative works from copyrighted material. Limited exceptions are allowed for library or archive reproduction and fair use for purposes of comment, criticism, news coverage, teaching, scholarship, or research. The Copyright Act does not protect ideas, processes, discoveries, principles, etc.

Answer (a) is incorrect because an invention or discovery is patentable for 17 years. Upon expiration, the invention or discovery may be used by anyone. Answer (b) is incorrect because trade secrets cannot be registered unless they are patentable. However, if a company makes reasonable efforts to protect its secret information, such as processes, formulas, and customer lists, it will receive legal protection. Answer (d) is incorrect because trade names are protected but cannot be registered. Trademarks can be registered with the Patent Office but are partially protected even if not registered. Trademarks and trade names are safeguarded because their wrongful use is a deceptive appropriation of the goodwill and reputation of competitors.

12. Under federal patent law,

a. An inventor granted a patent has unlimited monopoly power regarding the invention.

b. Patentable items include any new and useful process, machine, manufacture, composition of matter, or scientific principle.

c. The doctrine of equivalents holds that a patent infringement need not be identical to the patented invention.

d. Any patent resulting from an invention made by an employee on company time belongs to the employer.

The correct answer is (c). *(Publisher)*

REQUIRED: The true statement about patents.

DISCUSSION: A patent is the exclusive legal right to use or sell an invention, such as a device or process. Patent law provides that a patent may be given to any new and useful process, machine, manufacture, or composition of matter, and any infringement upon a patent is valid ground for a lawsuit. An infringing item need not be identical to the device or process patented. The doctrine of equivalents states that infringement occurs whenever two devices work in substantially the same manner, and accomplish substantially the same result.

Answer (a) is incorrect because a patent is limited to 17 years, and inventors are also not allowed to "misuse" their patents through such acts as tying a patented good to an unpatented one. Answer (b) is incorrect because a scientific principle is not patentable. Answer (d) is incorrect because a person not hired to do creative or inventive work will own patents (s)he obtains even if the work was done on company time and using company facilities. Under the shop rights doctrine, however, the employer has a nonexclusive, royalty-free license to use any invention created by an employee in such circumstances.

13. Which of the following is subject to copyright protection?

a. Choreography.

b. Corporate symbols.

c. Trade secrets.

d. A new hybrid form of plant life.

The correct answer is (a). *(Publisher)*

REQUIRED: The item subject to copyright protection.

DISCUSSION: A copyright is a form of legal protection for the tangible expression of ideas, but it does not protect the underlying ideas themselves. Thus, copyrights are used to protect literary works, music, recordings, art, films, and even choreography. The copyright covers the expression of the idea, and gives the copyright holder exclusive rights to reproduce it, perform it, or display it.

Answer (b) is incorrect because corporate symbols are subject to trademark, not copyright, protection. Answer (c) is incorrect because trade secrets may only be ideas or information, not the tangible expression of an idea. Answer (d) is incorrect because a new hybrid plant is patentable, not copyrightable.

14. The loss of trademark rights does not follow from

a. Failure to put the word "Trademark" or a similar term next to the mark itself.

b. The expiration of a patent or copyright on which a mark is based.

c. The general usage of the mark as a generic term by the public.

d. Abandonment of the mark.

The correct answer is (a). *(Publisher)*

REQUIRED: The act or event that does not cause the loss of trademark rights.

DISCUSSION: According to the Lanham Act of 1946, a trademark is a word, name, symbol, or device used by a manufacturer or merchant to identify its goods and distinguish them from the goods of others. Trademarks can be registered and protected from infringement, but rights to a trademark must first be established through use in commerce, providing that the mark does not infringe on a trademark already in use. A trademark holder should place the words "Trademark" or "Registered Trademark" next to the mark itself to protect it from becoming generic, but failure to do so does not automatically result in loss of trademark rights.

Answers (b), (c), and (d) are incorrect because each act or event results in the loss of trademark rights.

15. Barry Mason wrote to author Ella Street to convey an idea for Street's next novel. Mason suggested that it concern a lawyer who leaves her practice and moves to Australia. Street phoned Mason to tell him that the idea was ridiculous. Two years later, however, Street's novel about law practice in Australia, "Outback Lawyer," was a best-seller. Does Mason have a probable legal claim against Street?

a. Yes, because Mason's idea was so original that it was protected.

b. No, because Mason has no evidence that Street ever read his suggestion.

c. Yes, because Mason's letter to Street is sufficient to show his ownership of the idea.

d. No, because after voluntary communication to others, ideas become available for common use.

The correct answer is (d). *(Publisher)*

REQUIRED: The likelihood of winning a lawsuit based on the use of an unsolicited idea.

DISCUSSION: The courts have ordinarily held that voluntary communication of ideas, conceptions, and truths to others results in their becoming freely available to others. An idea will only be protected if it is original, expressed in some tangible form, and if the parties involved have a contractual or other relationship. An unsolicited idea is not protected.

Answers (a) and (c) are incorrect because the unsolicited nature of the idea, as well as its unfinished form, mean that Mason's idea is not protected. Answer (b) is incorrect because the lack of protection for the idea means that it is irrelevant whether Street actually read Mason's letter.

16. Albert, who is the owner of a house and lot, leased it to Marvin Barnes for a term of 5 years. There was also an unattached brick two-car garage. For his hobbies, Barnes installed a work bench, electric lights, and radiator in the garage. He also laid pipes connecting the radiator with the heating plant inside the house. Thereafter, Albert mortgaged the premises to Good Bank to secure a loan. Barnes was not given notice of the mortgage, but it was recorded. Later, Albert defaulted on his mortgage payments, and Good Bank began foreclosure proceedings. By this time Barnes's lease had almost expired. Barnes began the removal of equipment he had installed in the garage. Good Bank brought an action to enjoin the removal of the equipment mentioned above. If the court refuses the injunction, it will be because

a. Barnes was without notice of the mortgage.

b. The circumstances reveal that the equipment was installed for Barnes's exclusive benefit.

c. In the absence of a contrary agreement, a residential tenant is entitled to remove any personal property (s)he voluntarily brings upon the premises.

d. The Statute of Frauds precludes the bank from claiming any interest in the equipment.

The correct answer is (b). *(MBE Part I-163)*

REQUIRED: The reason for refusal of an injunction against removal of equipment.

DISCUSSION: If the items of equipment are deemed to be fixtures, they will be subject to the real estate mortgage. The exception for trade fixtures does not apply since Barnes was not carrying on a trade or business on the leased premises. Accordingly, denial of the injunction must rest upon a finding that the items were not fixtures. The most important factor in this determination is the intent of the parties. Because a lessee rarely intends to benefit the lessor when (s)he attaches an item to the lessor's realty, the presumption is that the lessee intended the items to be removable. The best reason for denial of an injunction is therefore that Barnes intended the items to be for his exclusive benefit.

Answer (a) is incorrect because Barnes had constructive notice as a result of Good Bank's recording of the mortgage. Answer (c) is incorrect because the intention of the parties, the physical relation of the items to the realty, and the purposes they serve are factors that may dictate otherwise. Answer (d) is incorrect because the facts indicate that the mortgage was contained in a writing signed by Albert. The issue is whether Barnes's equipment is considered permanently attached to Albert's property.

17. Ada was in a serious accident and was hospitalized in critical condition. Just before going into surgery, she gave Bea, her sister, a check for $20,000, remarking that her chances of survival were not good and she wanted Bea to have the money in the event of her death. Ada survived the operation but died a month later from a cause unrelated to her original injury. She did not specifically revoke the gift.

a. Ada made a valid inter vivos gift.

b. The donee has no right to the money since the donor did not die from the contemplated cause.

c. A valid gift causa mortis was made since the gift was not revoked.

d. A valid gift causa mortis was not made since the gift was not properly delivered.

The correct answer is (b). *(Publisher)*

REQUIRED: The requirements of gifts inter vivos and causa mortis.

DISCUSSION: A gift causa mortis (in contemplation of death) is a conditional gift. It must be made in view of impending death from some specific illness or peril; the donor must die from the illness or peril without having revoked the gift; the donee must survive the donor; and the subject matter must have been delivered to the donee. Since Ada died from an unrelated cause, the gift was ineffective (automatically revoked) despite the lack of an express revocation.

Answer (a) is incorrect because a gift inter vivos is between the living, and not conditional upon death. Answers (c) and (d) are incorrect because failure to die from the specific cause automatically revoked the gift. The money must be returned to the estate.

18. Donor was in a hospital suffering from a serious illness. The doctor and a friend, Donee, were nearby when Donor told them she wanted to give her bank account to Donee. She wanted the doctor to give her savings bank book to Donee. The doctor, a member of the hospital staff and agent of the hospital, said the bank book and other personal effects were locked in the cashier's office, which would not be open until 8:00 a.m. the next morning. However, the doctor informed Donor and Donee that if Donee came by the next morning, the doctor would see that the bank book was given to him. Donee said that would be fine. Donor did not live through the night. When Donee appeared the next morning, the doctor went with him to the cashier's office and gave him the bank book.

a. If Donor died intestate, the money in the savings account will go to her heirs.

b. The delivery of a deposit book of a savings account is not sufficient to effect a gift of the funds on deposit because there has been no delivery.

c. A gift causa mortis is irrevocable once it is made.

d. All the elements of a valid gift were present, so the attempted gift is valid.

The correct answer is (d). *(Publisher)*

REQUIRED: The correct statement regarding the validity of an attempted gift.

DISCUSSION: A valid gift requires intent of the donor, acceptance by the donee, and delivery. These requirements must occur during the lifetime of the donor. Here, the elements of intent and acceptance are clearly present. The depositing of the bank book with the hospital created a bailment. Delivery of personal property in the possession of a bailee becomes effective as soon as the bailee agrees to hold it for a donee or a purchaser. Since the doctor is an agent for the hospital (bailee), his agreement to hold the bank book for Donee constituted a delivery during the lifetime of the decedent. A delivery of a deposit book of a savings account is considered a constructive delivery of the balance of the funds in the account.

Answer (a) is incorrect because the inter vivos gift was valid and the money in the savings account will not go to Donor's heirs. Answer (b) is incorrect because the delivery of a deposit book of a savings account is considered a constructive delivery of the funds in the account, although the delivery of a book for a checking account would not have the same effect. Answer (c) is incorrect because a gift causa mortis is revocable but an inter vivos gift is not.

19. William knew he was fatally wounded, so he gave his valuable ring to a young man who had administered first aid, stating, "I am going fast. I'd like for you to have this." William died a few minutes later in the emergency room of the hospital. As the young man was leaving the hospital, the ring slipped through a hole in his pocket and a nurse found the ring in the hallway just inside the hospital entrance. The young man has never been located. The hospital administrator, the executor of William's estate, and the nurse all claim the ring.

a. The hospital has the best claim since the property was lost and found on its premises.

b. The nurse has the best claim because the property was lost in a public place.

c. William's estate has the best claim since William lacked donative intent.

d. At common law, the young man has the best claim.

The correct answer is (d). *(Publisher)*

REQUIRED: The ownership of a ring transferred by gift and lost.

DISCUSSION: At common law, an owner of personal property who loses or mislays it retains title against the finder and any other claimant. Title appears to have been vested in the young man by a valid gift from William. The three elements of a valid gift are intent, acceptance, and delivery.

Answer (a) is incorrect because the hospital's claim is not as valid as the young man's. One common law test gives the right to possession of lost property to the finder, and mislaid property to the landowner. A newer test gives possession to the finder if in a public place, and to the landowner if in a private place. The hospital entrance is probably a public-type place, so the nurse would prevail over the hospital. Answer (b) is incorrect because her claim is secondary to the young man's, but ahead of the hospital's. Answer (c) is incorrect because it does not appear that William's estate has any further claim to the ring.

20. Which of the following is a true statement about the forms of ownership of personal property?

a. Property is held in severalty when two or more persons have concurrent rights to it.

b. In a community property state, each spouse owns half of all property acquired before, during, but not after the marriage.

c. A valid tenancy in common may be created even though the tenants have unequal interests.

d. A joint tenant with a right of survivorship has no power to sever the tenancy.

The correct answer is (c). *(Publisher)*

REQUIRED: The true statement about the forms of personal property ownership.

DISCUSSION: In a tenancy in common, each co-owner has an undivided interest in the whole property with a right of possession but no right of survivorship. The tenants need not have equal interests. The interest of the tenant may pass by bequest, intestate succession, sale, gift, etc., none of which severs the tenancy in common. When property is transferred to two or more persons, a tenancy in common is presumed absent an express statement to the contrary.

Answer (a) is incorrect because severalty is ownership by one person. Answer (b) is incorrect because only property acquired during marriage is community property. Answer (d) is incorrect because a joint tenant may transfer his/her interest unless the property is held by spouses in a tenancy by the entirety. The transfer severs the joint tenancy with right of survivorship and creates a tenancy in common.

21. The Uniform Transfers to Minors Act (UTMA)

a. Provides that a gift is revocable if the donor fully complies.

b. Concerns only gifts of securities.

c. Requires that an account be established in a name other than that of the donor if an irrevocable gift is to be made.

d. Vests the custodial property in the custodian.

The correct answer is (d). *(Publisher)*

REQUIRED: The true statement about operation of the UTMA.

DISCUSSION: The UTMA has been enacted in the majority of states to provide a means for making legal gifts or other transfers to minors, e.g., from estates, trusts, insurance companies, guardianships, and judgment debtors. The UTMA is a revision of the Uniform Gifts to Minors Act, which was adopted in all jurisdictions. One method is to deposit money in an account in a bank or other financial institution in the name of the custodian for the minor under the UTMA. The Act may be viewed as creating a statutory form of trust or guardianship until the minor attains the age of 21. However, the custodianship created is not a separate legal entity or taxpayer, and the property is indefeasibly vested in the minor.

Answer (a) is incorrect because compliance results in an irrevocable gift. Answer (b) is incorrect because the UTMA concerns gifts of any kind of property. Answer (c) is incorrect because the donor may be the custodian.

22. Chukar owns 200 acres of Florida woodlands, most of which has the wild plant, Deer Tongue, growing on it. Bob White trespassed and picked 10,000 pounds of Deer Tongue, worth $8,000 after being picked and sacked. The value of the leaves standing in the woods was about 10 mills per pound or $100 for the amount picked. White sold the leaves to Don Deiler who dried and cured them, and thus made them worth about $16,000. Deiler used the Deer Tongue to flavor $250,000 of Dawgweed, a powerful aphrodisiac.

a. Chukar can recover the Dawgweed only if Bob White was an innocent trespasser.

b. The type of trespass is not material because Chukar, the owner, can always recover property wrongfully taken from him/her.

c. Wildlife is ownerless and title may be acquired by taking possession and control as Bob White did. Thus, Chukar cannot recover.

d. Chukar can recover the Dawgweed if Bob White was a willful trespasser.

The correct answer is (d). *(Publisher)*

REQUIRED: The landowner's right to personal property taken by a trespasser and changed in nature or greatly enhanced in value.

DISCUSSION: In accession by specification, new property is created from the property of one person by the labor and materials of a wrongful taker so that the original property no longer exists. Where accession has occurred in such circumstances, the owner is entitled to the value of his/her property at the time and place of taking. The prevailing rule with respect to willful trespass, however, is that title to the finished product passes to the owner of the original materials. A bona fide purchaser takes no greater rights to the finished product than the trespasser. Thus, if White was a willful trespasser, Chukar should be entitled to recover the finished product.

Answer (a) is incorrect because the owner of property taken can recover damages but cannot recover the finished item if the taker is an innocent trespasser and has changed the property or enhanced its value sufficiently so the court will say the original item is no longer in existence. Answer (b) is incorrect because recovery of the property depends on the type of trespass. Answer (c) is incorrect because plants are not wildlife, and a trespasser does not acquire title except when the trespass is innocent and the substantial change or enhancement of value test is met.

23. Ann cut 1,000 logs belonging to Bob. Upon discovery that she had trespassed, Ann nevertheless marked the logs as hers, mixed them with 100 of her own and started them down river to market. The logs of Ann and Bob cannot be distinguished.

a. If Bob seizes the logs and sells them to Carol, Ann will be unable to recover any logs if Carol is a bona fide purchaser.

b. Ann and Bob are owners in common of the mass of logs.

c. Accession of personal property has occurred.

d. Ann should be entitled to half the logs if in cutting the logs, she was an innocent trespasser.

The correct answer is (a). *(Publisher)*

REQUIRED: The correct statement concerning the confusion of logs by a trespasser.

DISCUSSION: Confusion is a legal term describing the intermingling of property of different owners. If confusion of personal property results from an innocent act or accident and the goods are of the same kind, each person is an owner of a proportionate share of the confused mass. However, where the confusion results from wrongdoing or intentional trespass, most courts vest title to the entire mass in the innocent party until the wrongdoer proves a portion is his/hers. Ann willfully confused the logs with her own after discovery of trespass. Thus, title is vested in Bob, and Carol has title free of any claim of Ann if Carol is a bona fide purchaser.

Answer (b) is incorrect because Ann and Bob are not owners in common of the mass since Ann was a willful confuser and title vested in Bob. Answer (c) is incorrect because the problem concerns confusion, not accession. Accession occurs when one person's personal property is taken by another and changed into new property. Answer (d) is incorrect because this was not an innocent confusion even though the cutting may have been, so Ann must prove her proportionate ownership.

24. Colonel Bulls Hit, a famous horse trader and descendant from two royal English families, purchased a Clodsdale horse by giving the seller, Nan Needy, a worthless check. Bulls Hit immediately sold the horse to Bud Wiser.

a. Nan Needy can rescind the sale and reclaim her horse.

b. The outcome of a dispute would not be affected by whether Bulls Hit stole the horse from Nan or obtained it by fraud.

c. Bud will prevail over Nan if he is an innocent purchaser for value.

d. If Nan recovers her horse, she will be required to pay Bulls Hit and Bud for its feed during the subject period.

The correct answer is (c). *(Publisher)*

REQUIRED: The legal result of obtaining property with a worthless check and immediately reselling it.

DISCUSSION: A seller's passing title to sold goods is impliedly conditional on the validity of the check. Because the check is worthless, the seller has a right to rescind. However, a good faith purchaser for value obtains a valid title from a seller who has a voidable title that has yet to be rescinded. Hence, Bud will prevail.

Answer (a) is incorrect because Nan cannot rescind the sale and reclaim her horse. The voidable title of Hit became valid in the hands of Bud, a bona fide purchaser. Answer (b) is incorrect because the result of a dispute is affected by the distinction between fraud and theft. In the case of theft, there would be no voidable title to pass because a thief can pass no title. Answer (d) is incorrect because Nan will not recover the horse and no court will award a fraud, such as Hit, the cost of feeding the animal.

25. A claim has been made by Donnegal to certain goods in your client's possession. Donnegal will be entitled to the goods if it can be shown that Variance, the party from whom your client purchased the goods, obtained them

a. By deceiving Donnegal as to his identity at the time of the purchase.

b. By giving Donnegal his check that was later dishonored.

c. From Donnegal by fraud, punishable as larceny under criminal law.

d. By purchasing goods that had been previously stolen from Donnegal.

The correct answer is (d). *(CPA 582 L-47)*

REQUIRED: The basis upon which goods may be recovered from a bona fide purchaser.

DISCUSSION: A thief cannot pass good title to goods. Consequently, even a good faith purchaser for value will not prevail against the rightful owner when the goods are stolen. The general principle is that when the transferor obtained the property in a transaction that was void, (s)he can transfer no rights to a third party.

Answers (a), (b), and (c) are incorrect because deception as to the identity of a contracting party, dishonoring a check, and fraud in the inducement of a bargain each gives rise to a voidable transaction. In each case, a bona fide purchaser may obtain rights that his/her transferor did not have.

19.3 Bailments

26. A bailment arises when personal property is transferred and the transferee must return it or dispose of it at the owner's direction. Which of the following is false?

a. The property bailed might be returned in altered form to the owner.

b. The owner of the property is the bailee and the party in possession is the bailor.

c. Strict liability is sometimes imposed in bailments.

d. If the party in possession of bailed property returns it damaged, a prima facie case of negligence is created.

The correct answer is (b). *(Publisher)*

REQUIRED: The false statement concerning a bailment transaction.

DISCUSSION: A bailment is the legal relationship resulting from the transfer of possession of personal property from one person (the bailor) to another person (the bailee) under such circumstances that the bailee is under a duty to return the item to the bailor or dispose of it as directed by the bailor.

Answer (a) is incorrect because a bailment results when the identical property is to be returned in the same or in an altered form, e.g., repaired goods. Answer (c) is incorrect because strict liability may be imposed in bailments of goods regardless of the bailor's fault if the goods prove to be unreasonably dangerous. Answer (d) is incorrect because the failure of the bailee to return the bailed property undamaged establishes a prima facie case of negligence.

27. The employees of Company must wear special clothing in the work area. Accordingly, Company provides a locker room with an attendant for storing personal items. Which of the following statements is correct?

a. A gratuitous bailment has been formed because it is for the sole benefit of the bailee when a worker leaves his/her property in the storage room.

b. A mutual benefit bailment has been formed.

c. Company can avoid all liability for its workers' property by including an exculpatory clause in their contracts that states, "Not responsible for any property left in the locker room."

d. When a worker leaves his/her property in the locker room, (s)he is a mere lessee or licensee.

The correct answer is (b). *(Publisher)*

REQUIRED: The correct statement concerning storage of personal property by employees.

DISCUSSION: Mutual benefit bailments occur when both the bailor and bailee receive a benefit. The employees (bailors) benefit from the storage facilities. The employer (bailee) benefits from uncluttered work areas and possibly decreasing the chances of accidents.

Answer (a) is incorrect because the arrangement is a mutual benefit bailment. Answer (c) is incorrect because while exculpatory clauses are permitted in bailment agreements, they are unenforceable if, as here, they are so broad as to be unconscionable or in violation of public policy. Answer (d) is incorrect because a bailment has been formed. The legal test is whether the person leaving the property (the worker) has made such a delivery to the owner of the premises (Company through its agent) as to amount to a temporary relinquishment of exclusive possession, control, and dominion over the property. Otherwise, it is generally held that the owner of the goods is a tenant or lessee of the space upon the premises where they are left.

28. Which of the following statements concerning bailments is true?

a. Bailor asked Neighbor to take care of his car while he was away on business. No compensation was involved. Neighbor is only required to exercise ordinary care under the traditional rule.

b. E is a bailee of R's goods. While the bailment is still in effect, Thief steals the bailed property. Both E and R have an action against Thief.

c. Lessor leased a truck to Lessee who was injured owing to mechanical failure of the truck. Lessee cannot recover on an implied warranty since no sale occurred.

d. A customer checks his coat with an attendant at a restaurant. In the pocket of the coat is a ring. A bailment exists for both the coat and ring because taking reasonable care of the coat results in reasonable care of the ring.

The correct answer is (b). *(Publisher)*

REQUIRED: The true statement concerning bailment transactions.

DISCUSSION: The bailor and bailee have a right of action against a third party who wrongfully interferes with the bailed property. The bailor and bailee both have a property interest in the bailed goods.

Answer (a) is incorrect because a gratuitous bailee is required to use only slight care to preserve or protect bailed property under the traditional rule. The modern rule requires reasonable care under the circumstances. Answer (c) is incorrect because in a bailment for hire, the bailor has an obligation to see that the bailed property is reasonably fit for its intended use. Lessor impliedly warranted the fitness of the vehicle. Answer (d) is incorrect because a party cannot be held to the obligations of a bailee unless (s)he has notice of his/her possession of the bailed property. No bailment of the ring exists, so the restaurant is not liable.

29. Mimi came into the Lead Palace Barber & Beauty Shop wearing an expensive fur coat. The shop consisted of a waiting room in front, the beauty shop in the middle, and the barber shop in the rear. On prior occasions, Mimi had asked the proprietor if it was safe to leave coats and other articles of property on the coat rack of the waiting room and she had been assured that it was perfectly safe--"nothing has been stolen in our 20 years here." The coat was stolen from the waiting room while Mimi was in the beauty shop. With respect to the elements needed to establish a bailment, which of the following is correct?

a. All elements of a valid bailment are present.

b. The element of consideration by the bailor, Mimi, is missing.

c. The element of delivery of possession and control to the shop is missing.

d. The shop could successfully defend Mimi's claim of bailment by showing that Mimi did not own the coat.

The correct answer is (c). *(Publisher)*

REQUIRED: Whether the elements necessary to establish a bailment are present.

DISCUSSION: To establish a bailment, the owner of personal property must make delivery of possession and control of the property to the bailee who must accept. Here, there was no change of possession by delivery or acceptance, so no bailment was created.

Answer (a) is incorrect because all the elements of a valid bailment are not present, since the owner of the coat did not deliver possession and control to the beauty shop. Answer (b) is incorrect because consideration is not required to establish a bailment. If it had been a bailment, a court would consider the bailment part of the overall transaction and Mimi's promise to pay the charges of the shop would have been considered made in exchange for the promise of the shop to render the services and to safeguard her coat. Answer (d) is incorrect because a possessor of personal property has a sufficient property interest (without ownership) to enter into a bailment contract and recover damages for its breach.

30. Eleanor Means had a dairy products factory. She contracted with many dairymen to accept their surplus milk which she agreed to manufacture into dairy products such as butter, cottage cheese, sour cream, etc.; market the products; deduct her commissions; and divide the remaining proceeds among the dairymen in proportion to the amount of milk each contributed. Means' factory and its contents burned. Which of the following is correct?

a. The transaction is not a sale but a bailment with a power of sale granted to the bailee.

b. The transaction is a sale because the same item of property is not to be returned.

c. Until Means sold the dairy products, title and risk of loss was on Means.

d. Means, as the party in possession of goods owned by another, is an insurer of the safety of the goods.

The correct answer is (a). *(Publisher)*

REQUIRED: The correct statement as to whether a bailment contract has been formed.

DISCUSSION: Title does not pass in a bailment. Here, there is a bailment because the property is to be returned, even though in a changed form as proceeds. The proceeds of sale were being divided among the milk suppliers in proportion to milk supplied. Means was only providing services and receiving compensation for them. The transaction should thus be classified as a bailment (not a sale) with a power of sale granted to the bailee.

Answer (b) is incorrect because the transaction is not a sale, even though the same item of property is not to be returned. Means was merely authorized to sell the property after processing it and required to strictly account for the proceeds received from the sale. Answer (c) is incorrect because the title and risk of loss in this transaction was never on Means but remained in the dairymen at all times. A bailee has neither title nor risk of loss (provided (s)he acts in a nonnegligent manner). Answer (d) is incorrect because a person in possession of goods owned by another is not an insurer, but must only exercise reasonable care for their safety.

31. Minni Mild had 200 logs which she wanted processed into lumber of various sizes. She entered into an agreement with Ralph Ruff for Ruff to receive Minni's logs and Ruff agreed to deliver to Minni a certain number of pieces of lumber of the various sizes she wanted cut from her logs or logs of equivalent quality. While the transaction was in process, fire of an undetermined cause destroyed the mill, all logs, and all lumber. Which statement is correct with respect to the party that must bear the loss?

a. Ralph Ruff must bear the loss since he is the owner of the mill, the logs, and the lumber.

b. Minni Mild must bear the loss since she is the owner of either the logs and/or the lumber.

c. Mild and Ruff are co-owners of the logs and lumber, and each must bear his/her proportionate share of loss.

d. A bailment of the logs had been formed between Minni and Ralph, and since Minni is unable to prove lack of reasonable care by Ralph, the destruction of her logs is her loss.

The correct answer is (a). *(Publisher)*

REQUIRED: The correct statement regarding certain logs and lumber destroyed in a fire.

DISCUSSION: The essential requirement of a bailment is that the property (even if in an altered form) be returned to the bailor. But if the party receiving personal property has an option to return the same item or one of equivalent value or quality, the transaction is considered to be a sale and not a bailment. Since Ralph could pay Minni in lumber from any logs of equivalent quality, the legal effect is that Ralph has purchased Minni's logs and is responsible to her for their purchase price. Since he has not delivered the finished lumber, he also bears the risk of loss (as a purchaser).

Answer (b) is incorrect because Minni was not the owner of either the logs or the lumber at the time of the fire. She had sold the logs and transferred risk and title to Ralph. Answer (c) is incorrect because Minni Mild and Ralph Ruff are not co-owners of the logs and lumber. Therefore, the loss will not be apportioned between them. Answer (d) is incorrect because a bailment of the logs has not been formed since, as explained above, the transaction resulted in a sale. If a bailment had been formed and the bailor was unable to prove lack of reasonable care, the bailor would bear the risk of loss.

32. Marrieo and Dreddy built a fancy custom roadster. They drove it through an automatic gate into a parking lot, received a ticket from a machine, parked, and took their keys with them. To leave they are required to drive to the exit and present the ticket to an attendant who collects the parking fee. Which of the following statements is incorrect?

a. If this arrangement were a bailment, the parking lot would be responsible for a spare tire, jack, and tools locked in the trunk.

b. Marrieo and Dreddy have rented a parking space since they retained control of their car.

c. The most important factor in deciding whether this is a bailment is the fact that Marrieo and Dreddy received the ticket from a machine and not an attendant.

d. If a third person wrongfully damages personal property in the possession and control of a bailee, the bailee may bring suit for him/herself and for the bailor.

The correct answer is (c). *(Publisher)*

REQUIRED: The false statement concerning parking a car in an automated lot.

DISCUSSION: In the cases deciding whether a parking lot transaction is a bailment or lease of space, courts have determined that the most important factor is whether the keys are retained by the owner. Constructive delivery of possession and acceptance is generally construed by giving the keys to a parking attendant or leaving them in the car at the parking attendant's direction. However, a bailment of a parked vehicle can occur other than through delivery of keys (e.g., premises locked up).

Answer (a) is incorrect because when a bailment of an automobile exists, the bailee-parking lot would be responsible for the automobile and other items of personal property which they know are in the automobile or which they could reasonably anticipate, e.g., a spare tire, jack, and tools. Answer (b) is incorrect because courts interpret retention of keys as retention of control of the car, resulting in a rental or lease of a parking space. Answer (d) is incorrect because the bailee's rights are generally held broad enough to permit him/her to bring an action against the third party for damages to the bailor's reversionary interest in the bailed property in addition to the bailee's interest. This is not a duty of the bailee but is permitted. If the bailee settles for the bailor, the bailor is bound by the settlement, but may have an action against the bailee for an inadequate settlement.

33. With respect to involuntary bailments, which of the following is correct?

a. An involuntary bailee has no liability to the bailor-owner because (s)he is only a custodian.

b. The liability of an involuntary bailee will be the same as the liability of an ordinary bailee.

c. Common examples of involuntary bailment would be finding a lost wallet, a horse straying onto your property, or a storm depositing property on your land.

d. An involuntary bailee should not be entitled to recover for the value of his/her services in quantum meruit.

The correct answer is (c). *(Publisher)*

REQUIRED: The correct statement regarding an involuntary bailment.

DISCUSSION: Finding a lost wallet, having an animal stray onto your property, or having property of another deposited by an act of God on your property are examples of incidents which the courts refer to as involuntary bailments. The term involuntary is used because the transactions do not fit within bailment contracts, but nevertheless the bailee has voluntarily taken legal possession and control of the property of another due to the circumstances.

Answer (a) is incorrect because an involuntary bailee has a legal responsibility to the owner to exercise reasonable care under the circumstances. Answer (b) is incorrect because the courts will not impose the same liability on an involuntary bailee as on an ordinary one. Answer (d) is incorrect because an involuntary bailee, without the benefit of a contract, should be entitled to recover the value of his/her services to the bailed property. This equitable remedy is called quantum meruit.

34. Grooms took his new wedding suit to Quick & Easy Dry Cleaners to be pressed. When Grooms returned for his suit on the morning of his wedding, the owner of Quick & Easy was standing beside the smoldering ruins of the dry cleaning shop. Which of the following statements is incorrect?

a. Quick & Easy can collect for pressing the suit if they establish that the suit was pressed and waiting for pickup before the fire and the fire was not its fault.

b. Dry cleaners like Quick & Easy routinely carry insurance that covers such losses.

c. The cause or source of the fire is an important factor in determining the liability for the loss of Grooms's suit.

d. A disclaimer of liability printed on the claim receipt that Quick & Easy gave to Grooms would probably not be considered to be a part of the contract between the bailor and bailee.

The correct answer is (b). *(Publisher)*

REQUIRED: The false statement concerning a bailment for dry cleaning.

DISCUSSION: Dry cleaners do not routinely carry insurance that covers losses to customers' property for which the dry cleaners are not legally responsible. Although such insurance can be purchased, most businesses would limit their coverage to liability insurance which indemnifies the dry cleaners for damages which are their fault.

Answer (a) is incorrect because a bailee-service person is entitled to collect for services rendered to bailed property before its destruction. The requirement that a bailee return the goods to the bailor is excused if the bailee exercised reasonable care. Answer (c) is incorrect because a fire caused by the bailee or its employees would not meet the duty of reasonable care. Answer (d) is incorrect because courts eliminate printed disclaimers by holding that the claim receipt is not part of the contract unless it was read by the bailor or called to the bailor's attention by conspicuous print, a sign, or the bailee's employee.

35. Brenda McOwns took her property to Security Storage and Warehouse to be kept at 1220 South Main Street for storage. She paid a fee and was given a warehouse receipt in usual form. Later the warehousemen moved the goods from the original storage place to a different but equally safe building. The goods were destroyed by a fire set by an unknown arsonist. With respect to liability,

a. The warehouse has no liability to McOwns because title and risk of loss remained with the bailor.

b. The standard of care imposed on the warehouse is ordinary care under the circumstances.

c. A bailee cannot move goods from the agreed place of storage for any reason.

d. The warehouse deviated from the terms of the contract when it moved the goods and is therefore strictly liable for any harm to McOwns's goods.

The correct answer is (d). *(Publisher)*

REQUIRED: The correct statement concerning the liability of a warehouse.

DISCUSSION: A warehouse, when it receives goods, is acting in the capacity of a bailee, and is subject to the general rules of bailment. When a bailee deviates from the terms of the contract, the law imposes strict liability for any harm to the bailor's goods instead of the usual standard of reasonable care. It appears a contract was made to store the goods at a particular location and the bailee, without the bailor's consent, moved them to a different, although equally safe place. Even though the goods were destroyed through no fault of the bailee, the bailee is liable for the value of the goods under the strict liability rule.

Answer (a) is incorrect because the warehouse is under an obligation to adhere to the contract and exercise reasonable care. These duties are imposed without regard to title and risk remaining with the bailor. Since the warehouse did not adhere to the terms of the contract, it is liable. Answer (b) is incorrect because it states the usual standard imposed on a bailee; however, the warehouse deviated from the terms of the contract which results in strict liability. Answer (c) is incorrect because a bailee may move goods from the agreed place of storage, despite the contract, but only for reasons of safety.

36. A bailee was instructed by the bailor to return the bailed property by means of Quickie Express. A man dressed similarly to the usual Quickie Express employee came into the bailee's office and called out, "Quickie Express." Bailee delivered the bailed property to him and had him sign an official Quickie Express receipt in a book furnished to the bailee by Quickie Express. Bailee properly forwarded copies of the signed receipt to Quickie Express and to the bailor. Despite the care of bailee and the good faith belief that he was dealing with a Quickie Express agent, the person taking the bailed property was an impostor. Which of the following is a correct legal conclusion?

a. Quickie Express is liable because the bailee acted in good faith in delivering to a person dressed similarly to a Quickie Express employee and claiming to work for it.

b. The bailee is liable, good faith or not.

c. The bailor must bear the loss because (s)he owns the property and the bailee acted with reasonable care.

d. The bailee would have less liability if this were a bailment for the sole benefit of the bailor.

The correct answer is (b). *(Publisher)*

REQUIRED: The correct legal conclusion regarding misdelivery of bailed property.

DISCUSSION: The usual standard of care imposed on bailees is reasonable care. However, the bailee owes a strict duty to return the bailed property to the bailor. Misdelivery of the bailed property to a third party who is not legally entitled to it results in strict liability to the bailee and cannot be justified by reasonable care and good faith.

Answer (a) is incorrect because Quickie Express is not liable for the actions of impostors unless it has been negligent in permitting uniforms to remain in the hands of ex-employees. The courts ask whom the impostor intended to deceive. The answer is the victim of the fraud. Answer (c) is incorrect because even though the bailor owns the property and the bailee may have acted with reasonable care, a bailee is strictly liable to the bailor for misdelivery. Answer (d) is incorrect because strict liability for misdelivery applies to a gratuitous bailee also.

37. Gal lends Guy her car so that he may run errands for her. Subsequently, Gal lends Guy her lawn mower so that he may mow his own yard. Which is the correct statement concerning the traditional duties of care owed by the parties?

a. Guy is required to exercise ordinary care with respect to his use of the lawn mower.

b. If Guy had rented the lawn mower from Gal, he would have owed a duty to her to inform regarding defects which would have been discovered by the exercise of reasonable care.

c. Guy must exercise great care in the use of the car.

d. If Guy had been compensated by Gal for running the errands, he would have been required to exercise great care in the use of the automobile.

The correct answer is (b). *(Publisher)*

REQUIRED: The duties of care traditionally imposed in bailments.

DISCUSSION: Under traditional tort principles, the duty of care owed by a party to a bailment depends upon the party benefited. When a bailment is for the mutual benefit of the bailor and the bailee, the duty owed by the bailor (Gal) is that of ordinary care. Exercise of ordinary or due care includes an affirmative obligation to use reasonable care to discover dangerous defects in the goods. These duties have generally been replaced with the standard of reasonable care.

Answer (a) is incorrect because in a bailment for the bailee's sole benefit, (s)he is required to use great care. Answer (c) is incorrect because if the bailment is for the sole benefit of the bailor and the bailee is uncompensated, the bailee is required to exercise only slight care. Answer (d) is incorrect because if Guy had been compensated by Gal for running the errands, the bailment would have been mutually beneficial and he would have only been required to use ordinary care.

38. Jon Hailey deposited his suitcase (and contents) valued at $300 with the clerk of the New York Middle Railroad after being informed that the price was only $1. He received a check stub or claim receipt upon which was printed a limitation for loss of $25. Which statement is correct?

a. The parties to a bailment may by contract limit the liability of the bailee, but that rule is not applicable here because Hailey never agreed to the limitation.

b. The claim check is part of the agreement whether Hailey read the limitation or not.

c. Railroads, as common carriers, are not permitted to limit their liability.

d. The railroad was merely a custodian and not a bailee of Hailey's suitcase.

The correct answer is (a). *(Publisher)*

REQUIRED: The correct statement concerning a bailment contract that attempts to limit or modify the liability of the bailee.

DISCUSSION: Parties to a bailment may limit their liability, but any such limitation must be part of the contract (agreed to by each). No such agreement was reached because Hailey never agreed to the limitation; it was merely printed on a receipt delivered to him after the contract was entered into. The courts are strict in their interpretation of modification of liability and require that the limitation be called to the attention of the bailee prior to the contract being formed. This could be done by specific mention, a sign, or by the limitation being conspicuously printed in a place where it is seen and agreed to before the contract is formed.

Answer (b) is incorrect because a claim check is generally not considered by the courts to be part of the agreement; it is merely a receipt or form of identification for return of the bailed property. Answer (c) is incorrect because even though railroads are common carriers, and in many instances in their capacity as carriers are held to strict liability, they are permitted to limit their liability by contract unless unconscionable. Answer (d) is incorrect because the railroad was a bailee since it had received and accepted physical possession and legal control.

39. To recover when bailed property is damaged or lost while in the possession of the bailee, the plaintiff-bailor

a. Must prove fault.

b. Need not prove fault because the bailee is presumed to have been negligent.

c. Need not prove fault because the bailee is presumed to have been an insurer.

d. Must prove fault if the bailee explains the exact cause of the damage or loss.

The correct answer is (b). *(Publisher)*

REQUIRED: The proof required in an action by a bailor against a bailee.

DISCUSSION: When the bailed item is damaged or lost, the presumption is that the bailee was at fault. Accordingly, (s)he has the burden of proving that (s)he exercised due care and of providing an explanation of the exact cause of the damage or loss. The burden is placed on the bailee because the item was in his/her possession and the bailor would have obvious difficulties in obtaining proof of negligence. The legal principle involved is res ipsa loquitur ("the thing speaks for itself"). For more on this doctrine, see Chapter 9, Question 58.

Answer (a) is incorrect because the bailee's fault is rebuttably presumed. Answer (c) is incorrect because absent an explicit agreement, the bailee is only liable for not acting with the care required in the circumstances. Answer (d) is incorrect because the bailee also has the burden of proving that (s)he was not negligent.

40. In a bailment, the bailee

a. Has a right to a possessory lien if just compensation is not paid.

b. Has a right to a possessory lien but not to sell the goods at public auction.

c. Retains a lien on the bailed property only if (s)he retains the property.

d. Must bear the expenses of the bailment.

The correct answer is (a). *(Publisher)*

REQUIRED: The rights of a bailee against a bailor.

DISCUSSION: If a bailment requires the bailee to perform services in regard to the bailed item, (s)he will be entitled to reasonable compensation. To secure payment, the bailee is ordinarily entitled to a possessory lien. Most states allow a bailee to foreclose the lien and sell the property at a public sale if the bailor does not pay.

Answer (b) is incorrect because the bailee may usually sell the property at auction if the bailor fails to pay. Answer (c) is incorrect because many states also permit the bailee to retain the lien even if possession of the property has been returned to the bailor. Answer (d) is incorrect because an apportionment of expenses depends on whether the bailment is for the sole benefit of the bailor or the bailee or for their mutual benefit. Who pays also may depend on custom regarding the bailed goods, the intent of the parties, whether the expenses are ordinary or extraordinary, and whether they were caused by the fault of one or the other.

41. Molly Tiff visited Happy Landing Riding Stables and rented a horse. The stable was busy and Tiff was mistakenly given a spirited horse suitable only for excellent riders which Tiff was not. Hondo, an employee of Riding Stables, in saddling the horse failed to tighten the saddle. Tiff fell when the saddle slipped.

a. Tiff cannot recover unless she clearly told the riding stable of her limited riding skills.

b. Tiff assumed those risks that are the natural dangers inherent in a particular activity and, since falling off a horse was the obvious danger, Tiff cannot collect.

c. Riding stables such as Happy Landing impliedly warrant their horse's suitability and its tack.

d. If Tiff ever returns to Happy Landing Stables, Happy Landing could avoid all liability by requiring Tiff to sign a disclaimer of liability.

The correct answer is (c). *(Publisher)*

REQUIRED: The relationship between a riding stable and its customer.

DISCUSSION: The rental of the horse was a bailment. A bailor, unless agreed otherwise, impliedly warrants that the subject of the bailment is reasonably fit for its intended use or purpose. A spirited horse suitable only for an excellent rider is not reasonably fit for rental to the general public. The riding stable also impliedly warranted that the saddle and other equipment was in proper repair and correctly adjusted.

Answer (a) is incorrect because the burden is on the riding stable to furnish a horse that is suitable to the skills of the rider-customer. Answer (b) is incorrect because a customer of a riding stable does not assume the risk of being assigned a highly spirited horse, nor one whose saddle has not been properly attached. A rider only assumes the risks of natural dangers inherent in horseback riding. Answer (d) is incorrect because such a disclaimer of liability is probably against public policy and would not be upheld by the courts when the horse was known to be spirited and it was improperly saddled.

42. Juan Solo enrolled as a student in a flight training school operated by Fly-By-Nite Flight School. The plane Solo was flying went out of control and crashed, severely injuring him. When the plane was dismantled, it was discovered that a large screwdriver apparently left by a mechanic at an unknown time had jammed some of the controls and caused the crash. The basis of the School's liability will rest primarily on

a. The standard of care expressed by the parties in the contract.

b. Negligence in furnishing the plane with a screwdriver in the control panel which the court will presume was placed there by the School's employees.

c. The legal doctrine of assumption of risk, since it is a known fact that small planes frequently crash without negligence on the part of anyone concerned.

d. The duty of the School to furnish its student with a plane reasonably fit for the use or purpose intended, or one free of defects.

The correct answer is (d). *(Publisher)*

REQUIRED: The basis of a lessor's liability for an airplane crash.

DISCUSSION: A bailor in a mutual benefit bailment is under a duty to inform a bailee of hidden defects in the bailed property. A gratuitous bailee would not have an affirmative duty to inspect to see if the property is free from defects. In a mutual benefit bailment for hire, the bailor has an obligation to see that the bailed property is reasonably fit for the purposes intended. This rule has been replaced in some jurisdictions by the doctrine of strict liability in tort, under which the bailor is liable for any defects.

Answer (a) is incorrect because in a majority of jurisdictions, the bailor may not limit his/her liability on the grounds that such agreements are opposed to public policy. Also, unless the bailor expressly informs the bailee of the limitation, it is not effective. Answer (b) is incorrect because it would be very difficult to establish negligence since it is not known when or how the screwdriver was left in the controls. Answer (c) is incorrect because the airplane is required to be at least reasonably fit to fly and assumption of the risk is not relevant.

43. Hurts Corporation leases a car to Benny Bailey for 30 days. The lease can be terminated except by

a. Performance or the expiration of 30 days.

b. Mutual rescission of the parties.

c. The will of either party who gives notice of termination and agrees to pay damages to the other party.

d. Notification by Hurts to Benny that the lease is canceled because Benny has engaged in an unauthorized use (and abuse) of the vehicle.

The correct answer is (c). *(Publisher)*

REQUIRED: The correct statement concerning proper termination of a bailment.

DISCUSSION: A bailment for a definite time or purpose cannot, as a general rule, be terminated at the will of either party since a bailment of specific property gives the bailee a property interest that will be protected against everyone including the bailor. The bailment contract may be terminated at the will of the bailee if the bailee voluntarily surrenders his/her property interest in the bailed property.

Answer (a) is incorrect because it contains two proper methods of termination of a bailment. Answer (b) is incorrect because a bailment (like any other contract) may be terminated by mutual rescission. Answer (d) is incorrect because the bailor can notify the bailee that the bailment is canceled if the bailee has misused or abused the bailed property.

44. Andy Handy rented a power tool from Together Rent All and agreed to return it not more than five days later. He failed to return it and communicated no reason for this action. When reached by phone, he offered no explanation but simply hung up on Rent All's employee twice. Which of the following is not true?

a. A suit based on replevin will get the tool back.

b. A suit based on trespass will get the tool back or its value plus any profits Handy may have realized from the expended and unpermitted use of the tool.

c. Damage caused by a defect in the tool's wheel housing could be used as an offset against a claim by Rent All.

d. A suit to quiet title will settle the question of ownership.

The correct answer is (d). *(Publisher)*

REQUIRED: The false statement of legal options involving a tortious bailee.

DISCUSSION: A suit to quiet title is an action to determine ownership of real property. It is not applicable to personal property.

Answer (a) is incorrect because replevin is a legal remedy to get unlawfully withheld property returned to the owner. Answer (b) is incorrect because a suit based on trespass also will get the property, or the value of the property, returned to the owner, plus any profits the wrongdoer may have realized from the unpermitted use of the property. Answer (c) is incorrect because damage caused by a defect in the bailed property can be used as an offset by the bailee against a claim for trespass or damages by the bailor. The fact that the bailee is tortious should not change this result.

45. With respect to a carrier, which of the following is incorrect?

a. Carriers are classified as contract or private carriers, and as common carriers.

b. Common law provides that a common carrier is an insurer of the goods entrusted to it as a carrier without exception.

c. The liability of a carrier frequently changes to that of a warehouseman.

d. A common carrier and a contract carrier both acquire a possessory lien on the goods to secure the shipping and storage charges.

The correct answer is (b). *(Publisher)*

REQUIRED: The false statement regarding a carrier.

DISCUSSION: While the common law does provide as a general rule that a common carrier is an insurer of the goods entrusted to it, this rule is not without exceptions. Acts of God, acts of public enemy, acts of public authority, acts of the shipper, and damage due to the inherent nature of the goods themselves are excepted matters for which the common carrier is not liable. The carrier can also reduce its liability by contract.

Answer (a) is incorrect because carriers are classified as contract or private, and as common carriers. A contract carrier engages to transport goods or passengers in a particular situation and does not offer to serve the public generally. The liability of a contract carrier is that of an ordinary bailee. A common carrier engages to transport freight and passengers without discrimination and is subject to legal liability for failure to carry out this duty. Answer (c) is incorrect because the liability of a common carrier changes to that of a warehouseman after the carrier has fulfilled the carriage contract and is holding the goods for the consignee. Answer (d) is incorrect because both common carriers and contract carriers acquire a possessory lien on the goods they handle to secure shipping and storage charges.

46. Ted and Alice are seeking to check in at the Zestful Night Hotel. Which is the correct statement with respect to the Hotel's legal rights and obligations?

a. The hotel may turn away Ted, Alice, and other unwanted guests by stating that all of its accommodations have been filled or reserved.

b. The hotel is not an insurer of the safety of guests on the hotel's premises and therefore is not liable for an injury to Alice caused by another guest.

c. If Ted and Alice run up a bill of $650 during their stay at Zestful Night, the hotel may take possession of their luggage and contents until they pay.

d. If the hotel sprinkler system malfunctions and damages Ted and Alice's property, they can recover but only by proving negligence by the hotel or its employees.

The correct answer is (c). *(Publisher)*

REQUIRED: The correct statement regarding a hotel's obligations to guests.

DISCUSSION: An innkeeper is given a lien on all goods brought onto the premises by guests to secure charges for the accommodations and services. At common law, this lien was only possessory, but under modern statutes the innkeeper may ultimately sell such goods to enforce the lien.

Answer (a) is incorrect because a hotel owner or innkeeper is generally obligated to serve the public, and, while a hotel may turn away guests, it must not be as a result of discrimination. Answer (b) is incorrect because unlike at common law, the modern hotel or innkeeper is not an insurer of the safety of guests on the hotel's premises, although they are held to a high standard of care and may be liable for an injury caused by another guest. Answer (d) is incorrect because the liability of hotels for damage to their guests' property has been amended by statute relieving the innkeeper of strict liability. However, a malfunctioning hotel fire sprinkler system may be a res ipsa loquitur case and thus shift the burden to the hotel to show lack of negligence.

CHAPTER TWENTY
REAL PROPERTY LAW AND LAND USE CONTROL

20.1 Nature, Interests, and Estates in Real Property

1. Which of the following statements about property is false?

a. The material wealth of the world consists of the legal rights collectively known as property.

b. Only a small percentage of civil lawsuits arise out of disputes over property or property rights.

c. Real property is limited to land and most things attached to it; personal property is all other property.

d. In the legal sense, property is a group of rights guaranteed by governmental authority.

The correct answer is (b). *(Publisher)*

REQUIRED: The false statement about property.

DISCUSSION: Property law is of critical importance to society. It affects the rights of litigants in most "things" about which a dispute may arise. Since property rights are involved in all economic activity and are affected by much noneconomic activity, they are the subject of much litigation.

Answer (a) is incorrect because property consists of legally protected rights to use, possess, control, and transfer "things." Without these rights, the things owned would lack value. Answer (c) is incorrect because real property includes the land, buildings, permanent improvements, fixtures, the airspace above, and the soil and minerals below. Personal property is all property that is not realty. Answer (d) is incorrect because property rights cannot exist without law backed by the coercive power of government. (See Chapter 19 for further discussion of property.)

2. Ole McDonald owns a small farm located on the edge of a small creek that he uses for irrigation. Grubb, Inc. has purchased the land just upstream from McDonald and is building a 20-story condominium project. In the construction, the creek was blocked and detoured to another creekbed one mile away. The building will also cut off the sunlight needed to grow crops on McDonald's land. Which of the following rights does McDonald have?

a. The right to have the water continue to flow in its natural course.

b. The right to the sunlight in order to grow crops.

c. The right to be free from the construction dust and later from automobile exhaust.

d. The right to the magnificent mountain view that previously existed from McDonald's land.

The correct answer is (a). *(Publisher)*

REQUIRED: The rights of a landowner when a new use is made of neighboring property.

DISCUSSION: A riparian landowner (one who owns land along a waterway) may make reasonable use of the water. However, a lower riparian owner has the right to the continued flow of the water without unreasonable diminution. The "natural flow" theory allows use of the water as long as the natural condition of the waterway is retained. The "reasonable use" theory allows use of the water as long as it does not interfere with other riparian owners. Under either theory, the blocking of the creek by Grubb is a violation of McDonald's right that may require the creek to be rediverted to its natural course.

Answer (b) is incorrect because there is no general right to have direct sunlight on one's property. Answer (c) is incorrect because there is no right to be free of air contaminants, although if the air contamination is too great it could constitute a private nuisance. Answer (d) is incorrect because no general right to retain a view is recognized in the absence of an express agreement no matter how long it may have existed.

3. Interests in real property include the airspace above the surface of the land. Which of the following is true?

a. The landowner owns all the airspace extending upward indefinitely from the surface of the land.

b. Airspace is not separately transferable.

c. No trespass occurs if an aircraft flies 1,000 feet above land in a populated area.

d. Because of the public interest in air transportation, no trespass is recognized for entry into a landowner's airspace.

The correct answer is (c). *(Publisher)*

REQUIRED: The true statement about the rights of a landowner in airspace.

DISCUSSION: The modern rule is that a landowner owns the airspace necessary to the beneficial enjoyment of the land surface. Since airspace is regarded as a public resource, no trespass occurs as a result of an overflight if it is at a reasonable height and in accordance with governmental regulations. For example, the FAA does not ordinarily permit flight below 1,000 feet over populated areas or 500 feet over unpopulated areas.

Answer (a) is incorrect because the rule today greatly restricts the common law principle allowing unlimited rights in the airspace above the land. Answer (b) is incorrect because airspace is often transferred separately, e.g., to one who wishes to build over an existing structure, such as over a railroad track. Answer (d) is incorrect because a landowner has a right to beneficial and convenient enjoyment of his/her property. If an intrusion into the airspace above the land is deemed to interfere with the right, an action for trespass may be brought.

4. Interests in real property include certain subsurface rights. Which of the following is true?

a. Subsurface rights are not separately transferable.

b. Materials below the surface are not part of the realty.

c. Subsurface rights may have little value since the owner of the surface controls entry upon the land to remove materials below.

d. The usual rule regarding oil and gas is that the landowner does not have a specific right in any such materials beneath the surface.

The correct answer is (d). *(Publisher)*

REQUIRED: The true statement about subsurface rights.

DISCUSSION: The general principle is that the landowner has a right to the materials beneath the land unless subsurface rights have been separately conveyed. Because they flow from one location to another, oil and gas are exceptions. The majority rule is that the landowner does not own the oil and gas but simply has an exclusive right to drill on the property and extract what is found, regardless of the extent of the underground pool. Complex state and federal laws restrict the amounts that may be removed.

Answer (a) is incorrect because subsurface rights are often transferred apart from those to the surface. Answer (b) is incorrect because except for oil and gas, underground materials are clearly part of the realty unless separately conveyed. Answer (c) is incorrect because if subsurface rights are transferred separately, the grantee also acquires a right of entry.

5. Which of the following is a true statement about the classification of timber and growing crops?

a. Unless agreed otherwise, a sale of the real property on which they are growing includes timber and crops.

b. Timber to be cut and growing crops are personal property whether or not they are sold apart from the land and regardless of who does the securing.

c. Growing crops sold apart from the land are personal property only if secured by the seller.

d. Timber to be cut and sold apart from the land is classified as goods only if secured by the buyer.

The correct answer is (a). *(Publisher)*

REQUIRED: The correct statement about the status of timber and growing crops.

DISCUSSION: Whether or not cultivated, the vegetation on the land is transferred with the real property unless the seller expressly reserves rights thereto. A seller who failed to do so thus could not harvest crops or timber growing on the land. If the timber has been felled or the crops have been harvested, however, they do not pass with the land.

Answers (b), (c), and (d) are incorrect because a contract for the sale of 1) growing crops or 2) timber to be cut is a contract for the sale of goods (UCC 2-107). But minerals and a structure or its materials to be removed from the realty are goods only if severance is to be by the seller.

Questions 6 through 8 are based on the following information. After Allen had built a four-story building on his own land, survey revealed that one of the eaves extended 6 inches over the land of his neighbor, Bates. The guttering and spouting were so constructed that no water from the building fell upon Bates's land. Bates's land was unoccupied and unimproved at the time, but shortly thereafter Bates began the erection of a two-story building on his land. In doing so he excavated to a depth of several feet up to but not over the line between Allen and Bates. Bates did not give Allen any advance notice of the excavation. The excavation was performed in a careful and workmanlike manner except that no steps were taken to shore up Allen's building. As a result of the excavation, Allen's building settled and cracked and was damaged before the excavation came to Allen's personal attention.

6. Bates sued Allen in trespass requesting damages caused by the overhanging eaves. Judgment for

a. Allen, because Bates has suffered no damages.

b. Allen, because Allen acted in good faith and was unaware of the overhang until after the building was completed.

c. Allen, because the overhang does not touch or concern any present or contemplated use of Bates's land.

d. Bates, without regard to whether or not Bates is able to show any actual harm to himself.

The correct answer is (d). *(MBE 272 197)*

REQUIRED: Whether eaves overhanging neighboring land is a trespass.

DISCUSSION: The tort of trespass is committed by a physical intrusion upon another's land without permission or legal excuse. Actual damages do not have to be proven in order to prevail. Moreover, the physical intrusion need not be upon the surface of the land. It may be an intrusion in the airspace above the ground.

Answer (a) is incorrect because damages need not be proven in a trespass action, though lack of damages will limit the monetary recovery. Answer (b) is incorrect because the only intent required is that the eaves were built in that spot. Intent to, or knowledge of, trespass is not necessary. Answer (c) is incorrect because Bates need only show that a physical intrusion occurred.

7. Allen sued Bates for damages to Allen's building but was unable to show that there would not have been any settling or falling of Allen's land if it had been in its natural condition without the weight of the building upon it. Judgment for

a. Allen, because Allen is entitled as a matter of right to lateral support from adjoining lands.

b. Allen, because of Bates's failure to give Allen notice of the excavation, if there is a jury finding that such failure was negligence and that the negligence was the proximate cause of the injury suffered.

c. Bates, because a landowner has no obligation to provide support to artificial structures on his neighbor's land.

d. Bates, because his duty extends no further than to perform the excavation in a careful and workmanlike manner.

The correct answer is (b). *(MBE 272 198)*

REQUIRED: Who should prevail in a suit for damages caused by excavation of adjacent property.

DISCUSSION: A landowner has an absolute right to lateral support for his land from adjacent landowners. This absolute right extends only to the land in its natural condition. To allow the owner of the building to take any necessary steps, the excavator has the duty to give notice to the adjoining owner. A landowner also has a right that his/her buildings be free of damage from another's negligence. Thus, Allen can win by proving negligence and resulting damages.

Answer (a) is incorrect because Allen's right of lateral support is only for the land in its natural condition, not for the building. Answer (c) is incorrect because a landowner is obligated not to cause damage on adjacent land through negligent actions (e.g., excavations near another's building without notice). Answer (d) is incorrect because Bates also has a duty of reasonable care which in the circumstances might extend to giving notice of the excavation.

8. In an action brought by Allen against Bates for damage to Allen's building it was shown that, even if there had been no building on the land, Allen's land would have subsided as a result of Bates's excavation. This was because of an especially pliable clay soil condition of which Bates was unaware prior to the excavation. Judgment for

a. Allen, because Allen is entitled to support for his land in its natural condition.

b. Allen, because Allen is entitled to support for his land in its improved condition.

c. Bates, because Bates is not liable for the peculiar condition of the soil.

d. Bates, because there was no showing of malice or ill will toward Allen.

The correct answer is (a). *(MBE 272 199)*

REQUIRED: Who should prevail if land would have subsided in its natural state as a result of excavation of adjacent property.

DISCUSSION: Bates has an absolute duty to provide lateral support for Allen's land in its natural state. The duty is imposed regardless of the standard of care observed. If this duty is violated, Allen can also recover for damages to the building.

Answer (b) is incorrect because Allen is only entitled to support for the land in the natural state. Answer (c) is incorrect because Bates must provide lateral support for Allen's land in its natural condition regardless of the conditions of the soil. Answer (d) is incorrect because the duty of lateral support for land in its natural condition is imposed regardless of the mental state of the defendant.

Questions 9 through 13 are based on the following information. In 1976 Owen, owner of both Blackacre and Whiteacre, executed and delivered two separate deeds by which he conveyed the two tracts of land as follows: Blackacre was conveyed "To Alpha and his heirs as long as it is used exclusively for residential purposes, but if it is ever used for other than residential purposes, to the American Red Cross." Whiteacre was conveyed "To Beta and his heirs as long as it is used exclusively for residential purposes, but if it is used for other than residential purposes prior to 1996, then to the Salvation Army." In 1981 Owen died leaving a valid will by which he devised all his real estate to his brother, Bill. The will had no residuary clause. Owen was survived by Bill and by Owen's son, Sam, who was Owen's sole heir.

9. In 1986 Alpha and Sam entered into a contract with John whereby Alpha and Sam contracted to sell Blackacre to John in fee simple. After examining title, John refused to perform on the grounds that Alpha and Sam could not give good title. Alpha and Sam joined in an action against John for specific performance. Specific performance will be

a. Granted, because Alpha and Sam together own a fee simple absolute in Blackacre.

b. Granted, because Alpha alone owns the entire fee simple in Blackacre.

c. Denied, because Bill has a valid interest in Blackacre.

d. Denied, because the American Red Cross has a valid interest in Blackacre.

The correct answer is (c). *(MBE 272 38)*

REQUIRED: Whether Alpha and Sam will prevail in their suit to sell the property.

DISCUSSION: Alpha and his/her heirs received a fee simple determinable subject to a future interest. Since the future interest might not vest in the Red Cross until well after the perpetuity period of a life in being plus 21 years, the future interest was void under the Rule Against Perpetuities. This left a valid fee simple determinable with a possibility of reverter in the grantor and his/her heirs. This possibility of reverter was a future interest in real estate which would have been effectively devised to Bill in the 1981 will, and not to Sam. John will win the suit since Alpha and Sam are unable to fulfill their contractual promise to sell the fee simple without Bill's joining in the sale.

Answer (a) is incorrect because Alpha and Bill together own a fee simple absolute in Blackacre. Answer (b) is incorrect because Alpha owns only the fee simple determinable which may be divested whenever it is used for purposes other than residential. Answer (d) is incorrect because the Red Cross has no interest in Blackacre since the Rule Against Perpetuities invalidated its executory interest conveyed by Owen.

10. In 1977 the interest of the American Red Cross in Blackacre could be best described as a

a. Valid contingent remainder.

b. Void executory interest.

c. Valid executory interest.

d. Void contingent remainder.

The correct answer is (b). *(MBE 272 39)*

REQUIRED: The best description of the Red Cross's interest in Blackacre.

DISCUSSION: The conveyance by Owen created a valid fee simple determinable in Alpha and a void executory interest in the Red Cross. It was void because it violated the Rule Against Perpetuities as discussed in the answer above. The future interest was an executory interest because it was in a transferee (as opposed to a reversionary interest in the transferor) and it divests the preceding estate (as opposed to taking effect upon the natural termination of the preceding estate as a remainder).

Answer (a) is incorrect because the interest of the Red Cross was invalid under the Rule Against Perpetuities and was not a remainder. A remainder cannot follow an interest which may never terminate. Answer (c) is incorrect because the executory interest of the Red Cross is void under the Rule Against Perpetuities. Answer (d) is incorrect because the interest is not a remainder.

11. In 1982 the interest of Bill in Blackacre could best be described as

a. A possibility of reverter.

b. An executory interest.

c. An executory interest in a possibility of reverter.

d. None of the above.

The correct answer is (a). *(MBE 272 40)*

REQUIRED: The best description of Bill's interest in 1982.

DISCUSSION: The conveyance by Owen created a valid fee simple determinable and a void executory interest. The failure of the executory interest left a possibility of reverter in Owen which passed to Bill under the will. A possibility of reverter is a reversionary interest in the grantor which follows the termination of a fee simple determinable.

Answers (b) and (c) are incorrect because an executory interest can only be created in a transferee, not in a transferor. Bill's interest was taken through Owen, the original transferor.

12. In 1979 a contract was entered into whereby Beta and the Salvation Army contracted to sell Whiteacre to Yates in fee simple. After examining title, Yates refused to perform on the ground that Beta and the Salvation Army could not convey marketable title. Beta and the Salvation Army joined in an action for specific performance. Specific performance will be

a. Denied, because Beta and the Salvation Army cannot convey marketable title without Owen's joining in the deed.

b. Granted, because Beta and the Salvation Army together own a fee simple absolute in Whiteacre.

c. Granted, because the attempted restrictions on the use of Whiteacre are void as a violation of the Rule against Perpetuities.

d. Granted, because the attempted restrictions on the use of Whiteacre are void as a violation of the rule against restraints on alienation.

The correct answer is (a). *(MBE 272 41)*

REQUIRED: The result of an action by Beta and the Salvation Army to sell the property.

DISCUSSION: A marketable title is usually considered a fee simple title. Beta and the Salvation Army together do not have a fee simple title in Whiteacre. Beta has a fee simple determinable subject to an executory interest, the Salvation Army holds the executory interest, and Owen has a possibility of reverter. Owen has a possibility of reverter if the property is used for other than residential purposes after 1996 (if used for other than residential purposes before 1996, it goes to the Salvation Army).

Answer (b) is incorrect because Beta and the Salvation Army own less than a fee simple absolute since Owen retains a possibility of reverter. Answer (c) is incorrect because none of the interests is void under the Rule Against Perpetuities. The executory interest will vest or fail to vest within 20 years, and interests retained by the grantor are not subject to the rule. Answer (d) is incorrect because the restrictions are upon use, not upon alienation (the power to transfer the interest).

13. In 1977 the interest of Beta in Whiteacre could best be described as a

a. Determinable fee.

b. Fee simple subject to a condition subsequent.

c. Fee simple subject to an executory interest.

d. Determinable fee subject to an executory interest.

The correct answer is (d). *(MBE 272 42)*

REQUIRED: The best description of Beta's interest in Whiteacre in 1977.

DISCUSSION: Beta received a fee simple that would automatically terminate upon the subsequent occurrence of an event (failure to use the property for residential purposes). This is a determinable fee (or fee simple determinable). It is subject to an executory interest because it is a future interest in a transferee (Salvation Army) which divests the previous estate.

Answer (a) is incorrect because it is subject to an executory interest. Answer (b) is incorrect because a condition subsequent does not terminate the previous estate automatically; e.g., "If Whiteacre is not used for residential purposes, the Salvation Army may enter and take title." Answer (c) is incorrect because Beta's interest in 1977 was a determinable fee subject to an executory interest.

14. Which of the following factors is least significant in determining whether an item of personal property has become a fixture?

a. The extent of injury that would be caused to the real property by the removal of the item.

b. The value of the item.

c. The manner of attachment.

d. The adaptability of the item to the real estate.

The correct answer is (b). *(CPA 1187 L-53)*

REQUIRED: The least significant factor in deciding whether personal property is a fixture.

DISCUSSION: Intent is the criterion. If the intention of the party who attached the personal property to the realty is unclear, the court will examine other factors to deduce that intent. For example, the property need not be physically affixed to the realty to be a fixture, but the mode of annexation and the injury caused by removal are important factors in determining intent. Accordingly, a central heating system is usually deemed to be a fixture. If an item is beneficial or necessary (adapted) to the ordinary uses to which the realty is put, the court will usually infer an intent to make it a fixture even though it is easily removable. A hot water heater is an example. Intent may also be inferred from the parties' relationship. For instance, a lessee seldom intends to make a gift of a fixture to a lessor upon vacating the premises. Value, however, is not significant in determining whether personal property has become a fixture. A key, for example, has been held to be a fixture because of its adaptation to the realty.

Answers (a), (c), and (d) are incorrect because each is a significant factor in determining intent as discussed above.

15. Abrams owned a fee simple absolute interest in certain real property. Abrams conveyed it to Fox for Fox's lifetime with the remainder interest upon Fox's death to Charles. What are the rights of Fox and Charles in the real property?

a. Charles may not sell his interest in the property until the death of Fox.

b. Fox has a possessory interest in the land and Charles has a future interest.

c. Charles must outlive Fox to obtain any interest in the real property.

d. Any conveyance by either Fox or Charles must be joined in by the other party to be valid.

The correct answer is (b). *(CPA 577 L-40)*

REQUIRED: The rights of the life tenant and the remainderman in the real property.

DISCUSSION: A fee simple absolute interest includes the full rights allowed by law. Abrams' conveyance split the ownership into two types: a life estate to Fox and a remainder interest to Charles. The life estate gives Fox the right to possess and enjoy the property for the duration of his life. The remainder interest gives Charles a future interest in the property, which will become a fee simple absolute upon termination of Fox's life estate.

Answer (a) is incorrect because both a life estate and a remainder interest may be transferred at any time. Answer (c) is incorrect because Charles has a vested interest in the property that will become possessory upon the conclusion of the life estate. Charles' interest is both assignable and inheritable. Answer (d) is incorrect because both Fox and Charles may separately convey their respective interests.

16. A life estate is the right of a person to use property for the rest of his/her life. This person is known as a life tenant. Certain duties and limitations of rights are imposed on the life tenant to safeguard the remainderman's rights.

a. The life tenant is entitled to the use of the land, but must not take profits from it which are to be saved for the remainderman.

b. The remainderman is responsible for taxes on the land since (s)he is to receive the long-term benefits from the land.

c. The life tenant may exploit natural resources of the land in reasonable amounts if the land was so used when the life estate was granted.

d. The life tenant is responsible to preserve the land in the same repair as when the life estate was granted.

The correct answer is (c). *(Publisher)*

REQUIRED: The correct statement concerning the rights and duties of a life tenant.

DISCUSSION: A life tenant is entitled to reasonable use of the land, including the profits. As a general rule, the life tenant is not entitled to exploit the natural resources of the land such as timber, minerals, and oil. But if the land was so used when the life estate was granted, the grantor is deemed to have intended continued reasonable use by the life tenant.

Answer (a) is incorrect because the life tenant is entitled to the profits from the land so long as waste is not committed. Answer (b) is incorrect because the life tenant is responsible to pay ordinary taxes on the land, but not those constituting assessments for permanent improvements. Answer (d) is incorrect because the life tenant is only responsible to maintain the land and structures on it in a reasonable state of repair, not necessarily the same as when the life estate was granted; i.e., reasonable depreciation is allowed.

17. Paul Good's will left all of his commercial real property to his wife Dorothy for life and the remainder to his two daughters, Joan and Doris, as tenants in common. All beneficiaries are alive and over 21 years of age. Regarding the rights of the parties, which of the following is a correct statement?

a. Dorothy may not elect to take against the will and receive a statutory share instead.

b. The daughters must survive Dorothy in order to receive any interest in the property.

c. Either of the daughters may sell her interest in the property without the consent of their mother or the other daughter.

d. If only one daughter is alive upon the death of Dorothy, she is entitled to the entire property.

The correct answer is (c). *(CPA 1180 L-50)*

REQUIRED: The correct statement concerning the rights of the parties.

DISCUSSION: Even though their interests will not become possessory until the death of Dorothy, the daughters have vested future interests in the property that cannot be defeated by any subsequent event. Their interests (as tenants in common) may be transferred without the permission of the life tenant or of each other.

Answer (a) is incorrect because the surviving spouse of a testate decedent may choose to take under the will or under the state statute which provides for a minimum elective share. Answer (b) is incorrect because the daughters' remainder interests are not contingent upon surviving the life tenant. They vested in the daughters upon the death of the testator. Answer (d) is incorrect because the daughters took as tenants in common, not as joint tenants with rights of survivorship. The rights of a tenant in common are inheritable and the surviving daughter would have to share the property with her sister's heirs.

18. Jane and her brother each owns a half interest in certain real property as tenants in common. Jane's interest

a. Is considered personal property.

b. Will pass to her brother by operation of law upon Jane's death.

c. Will pass upon her death to the person Jane designates in her will.

d. May not be transferred during Jane's lifetime without her brother's consent.

The correct answer is (c). *(CPA 1185 L-53)*

REQUIRED: The characteristic of the interest of a tenant in common.

DISCUSSION: The two tenants in common are each entitled to possession and an undivided interest in the whole property. The interest of a tenant in common may be transferred by deed or by will. In contrast, a joint tenant's interest contains a right of survivorship and cannot be transferred by will.

Answer (a) is incorrect because the nature of the interest of a tenant in common depends on the underlying property. Here, that property is realty. Answer (b) is incorrect because Jane's interest may be transferred by sale, gift, assignment, or will. Answer (d) is incorrect because a tenant in common may convey his/her interest without the approval of other co-tenants absent an agreement to the contrary.

19. Dombres is considering purchasing Blackacre. The title search revealed that the property was willed by Adams jointly to his children, Donald and Martha. The language contained in the will is unclear as to whether a joint tenancy or a tenancy in common was intended. Donald is dead (leaving children), and Martha has agreed to convey her entire interest by quitclaim deed to Dombres. The purchase price is equal to the full fair market price of the property. Dombres is not interested in anything less than the entire title to the tract. Which of the following is correct?

a. There is a legal preference for a joint tenancy.

b. Whether the will created a joint tenancy or a tenancy in common is irrelevant because Martha is the only survivor.

c. Dombres will not obtain complete title to the land by Martha's conveyance.

d. There is no way or means whereby Dombres may obtain a clear title under the circumstances.

The correct answer is (c). *(CPA 580 L-26)*

REQUIRED: The correct statement regarding title to the land.

DISCUSSION: If Donald and Martha had held the land as joint tenants, Martha, upon Donald's demise, would have acquired the entire tract by right of survivorship. She would then have been able to convey the entire ownership interest. Unless a joint tenancy is expressly created, however, it is presumed that a conveyance to two or more persons creates a tenancy in common. Here, a tenancy in common was created and Donald's heirs succeeded to his interest in the property. Thus, Dombres will not obtain title to the entire tract through Martha's quitclaim deed.

Answer (a) is incorrect because the legal preference is for a tenancy in common. Answer (b) is incorrect because an interest in a tenancy in common is inheritable, and Donald's interest passed to his heirs. Answer (d) is incorrect because Dombres could obtain clear title by purchasing the interest held by Donald's heirs as well as that held by Martha, or he could bring a suit to quiet title to determine ownership.

Questions 20 and 21 are based on the following information. Boch and Kent are equal owners of a warehouse. Boch died leaving a will that gave his wife all of his right, title, and interest in his real estate.

20. If Boch and Kent owned the warehouse at all times as joint tenants with the right of survivorship, Boch's interest

a. Will pass to his wife after the will is probated.

b. Will not be included in his gross estate for federal estate tax purposes.

c. Could not be transferred before Boch's death without Kent's consent.

d. Passed to Kent upon Boch's death.

The correct answer is (d). *(CPA 588 L-53)*

REQUIRED: The effect of the death of a joint tenant.

DISCUSSION: One characteristic of a joint tenancy is the right of survivorship. The surviving joint tenant (Kent) succeeds to the entire interest of the decedent. Hence, the interest of a joint tenant cannot be transferred under a will or pass by intestate succession. However, a joint tenancy may be created by various means, e.g., under a will or by judicial sale. Each tenant's interest in a joint tenancy must be created at the same time and under the same instrument.

Answer (a) is incorrect because a joint tenant's interest can be transferred by an inter vivos gift (one during life) but not by a testamentary gift (a disposition by will), or otherwise as part of the probate estate. Answer (b) is incorrect because a joint tenant's gross estate includes his/her interest, but 50% of the value is excluded if the other joint tenant is the surviving spouse. Answer (c) is incorrect because the interest can be transferred by sale or gift or it can be encumbered. However, the effect is to sever the joint tenancy and create a tenancy in common with respect to the interest transferred.

21. If Boch and Kent owned the warehouse at all times as tenants in common, which of the following statements is correct?

a. Boch's interest will pass to his wife after the will is probated.

b. Upon Boch's death, all tenancies in common terminated.

c. Boch's interest will not be included in his gross estate for federal estate tax purposes.

d. Upon Boch's death, his interest passed to Kent.

The correct answer is (a). *(CPA 588 L-54)*

REQUIRED: The effect of the death of a tenant in common.

DISCUSSION: The essential aspect of a tenancy in common is that each of the co-tenants owns an undivided interest in the whole. Rather than owning a specific portion of the land, each co-tenant is considered to own a right to the entire property. But unlike a joint tenancy, the tenancy in common does not include a right of survivorship. The interest of a deceased co-tenant passes to his/her heirs. Thus, it may pass by intestate succession or by will.

Answer (b) is incorrect because the decedent's estate will have the same interest as the decedent, so the tenancy in common is not terminated. Answer (c) is incorrect because the interest of a deceased joint tenant or a tenant in common will be included. Answer (d) is incorrect because the interest would have passed to Kent if the property had been held in a joint tenancy.

Questions 22 and 23 are based on Hill, Knox, and Lark, who own a building as joint tenants with the right of survivorship. Hill donated her interest in the building to Care Charity by executing and delivering a deed to Care. Both Knox and Lark refused to consent to Hill's transfer to Care. Subsequently, Hill and Knox died.

22. As a result of Hill's transfer to Care, Care acquired

a. A 1/3 interest in the building as a joint tenant.

b. A 1/3 interest in the building as a tenant in common.

c. No interest in the building because Knox and Lark refused to consent to the transfer.

d. No interest in the building because it failed to qualify as a bona fide purchaser for value.

The correct answer is (b). *(CPA 1187 L-54)*

REQUIRED: The result of a gift of a joint tenant's interest prior to her death.

DISCUSSION: The gift of the joint tenant's interest made during life severed the joint tenancy only with respect to the interest transferred. The effect was to create a tenancy in common with a 1/3 interest held by the donee (Care) and a 2/3 interest held by Knox and Lark. The latter parties held their interest in the tenancy in common as joint tenants with rights of survivorship; that is, the gift did not sever the portion of the joint tenancy not transferred.

Answer (a) is incorrect because the gift severed the joint tenancy with respect to the donor's interest. Answer (c) is incorrect because their consent was unnecessary. Answer (d) is incorrect because a gift as well as a sale severs a joint tenancy.

23. As a result of Hill's and Knox's death,

a. Lark owns the entire interest in the building.

b. Lark owns a 2/3 interest in the building as a tenant in common.

c. Care and Lark each own a 1/2 interest in the building as joint tenants.

d. Knox's heirs and Lark each own a 1/3 interest in the building as tenants in common.

The correct answer is (b). *(CPA 1187 L-55)*

REQUIRED: The effect of the deaths of two of the original joint tenants.

DISCUSSION: After the gift to Care, Knox and Lark held as joint tenants with right of survivorship a 2/3 interest in a tenancy in common. Consequently, Knox's death resulted in the passage to Lark of full ownership of the 2/3 interest.

Answers (a) and (c) are incorrect because Hill's gift during life transferred a 1/3 interest to Care. Knox's death had no effect on that interest. Answer (d) is incorrect because Knox's interest in the remnant of the joint tenancy passed to the surviving joint tenant, not to the heirs.

24. Lawnacre was conveyed to Celeste and Donald by a deed which, in the jurisdiction in which Lawnacre is situated, created a co-tenancy in equal shares and with right of survivorship. The jurisdiction has no statute directly applicable to any of the problems posed. Celeste, by deed, conveyed "my undivided one-half interest in Lawnacre" to Paul. Celeste has since died. In an appropriate action between Paul and Donald in which title to Lawnacre is at issue, Donald will

a. Prevail, because he is the sole owner of Lawnacre.

b. Prevail only if the co-tenancy created in Celeste and Donald was a tenancy by the entirety.

c. Not prevail if he had knowledge of the conveyance prior to Celeste's death.

d. Not prevail, because Paul and Donald own Lawnacre as tenants in common.

The correct answer is (b). *(MBE Part I-123)*

REQUIRED: Whether Donald will prevail in the action and why.

DISCUSSION: If the grantees were married to each other, a presumption of tenancy by the entirety would arise if both names were included on the deed or other title documents. If they held as tenants by the entirety, the conveyance by Celeste was ineffective because a tenancy by the entirety may not be severed by a unilateral conveyance. If Celeste and Donald had held merely as joint tenants with the right of survivorship, however, the conveyance would have severed the joint tenancy and resulted in a tenancy in common between Paul and Donald.

Answer (a) is incorrect because Donald will prevail only if one assumes that he and Celeste were married. Answer (c) is incorrect because Donald's knowledge of the conveyance is irrelevant. The effectiveness of the conveyance is contingent on whether Donald and Celeste were tenants by the entirety. Answer (d) is incorrect because Paul and Donald can own Lawnacre as tenants in common only if Donald and Celeste were not married, which the question did not assume.

25. The following events took place in a state that does not recognize the common-law marriage. The state does recognize the common-law estate of tenancy by the entirety and has no statute on the subject.

Wade Sloan and Mary Isaacs, who were never formally married, lived together over a seven year period. Within this period Wade decided to buy a home. The deed was in proper form and identified the grantees as "Wade Sloan and Mary Sloan, his wife, and their heirs and assigns forever as tenants by the entirety." Both Wade and Mary signed the note and mortgage as husband and wife. Wade made the monthly payments as they became due until he and Mary had a disagreement and he abandoned her and the house. Mary then made the payments for three months. She then brought an action against Wade for partition of the land in question. The partition should be

a. Denied, because a tenant by the entirety has no right to partition.

b. Denied, because Wade has absolute title to the property.

c. Granted, because the tenancy by the entirety that was created by the deed was severed when Wade abandoned Mary.

d. Granted, because the estate created by the deed was not a tenancy by the entirety.

The correct answer is (d). *(MBE Part I-96)*

REQUIRED: Whether a suit for partition should be successful and why.

DISCUSSION: A tenancy by the entirety is a form of joint ownership of property with right of survivorship, but it exists only for married couples. It is not subject to partition without the consent of both. Since Wade and Mary were not legally married, the law would probably consider them to be tenants in common. A tenancy in common may be partitioned.

Answer (a) is incorrect because Wade and Mary are not tenants by the entirety. Answer (b) is incorrect because Wade does not have absolute title since Mary is a grantee named in the deed. Answer (c) is incorrect because a tenancy by the entirety was not created and, furthermore, could not have been severed by the act of one party even if it had been.

26. In 1959, Harold bought a house from Sydney. In 1960, Harold married Wilma, and they have lived continuously in the house together since then. Bart is now negotiating with Harold for the purchase of the house. Which of the following is true?

a. Bart should have Wilma sign the deed because she has acquired an interest by adverse possession.

b. Bart should have Wilma sign the deed because she may have rights in this property by virtue of her status as a spouse.

c. Since Harold owns the property in his name only, his signature will suffice to transfer the property.

d. If this house is in California, Bart should have Harold's children sign the deed because a house is community property.

The correct answer is (b). *(M. Levin)*

REQUIRED: The spouse's right in real property.

DISCUSSION: At common law, a wife acquired a legal interest, typically a life estate, in land owned by her husband during their marriage. The interest was known as dower. In some states, a husband had a similar right (curtesy) in his wife's land. Today, many states recognize similar spousal rights by statute. Thus, if a husband conveys without his wife's joining in the deed, and his wife survives him, she may succeed to an interest in the land, even though a purchaser from the husband acted innocently.

Answer (a) is incorrect because the wife's interest is not one of adverse possession. Wilma's use of their residence is clearly permissive. Answer (c) is incorrect because a wife's interest may prevent conveyance solely by a husband. Answer (d) is incorrect because the community property system, which is followed in California, recognizes that the husband and wife should share equally in property acquired by their joint efforts during marriage. It imparts no special interest to children, however.

27. Community property is a form of property ownership in eight Western states. There are several ways in which community property law differs from the law determining ownership of property in the rest of the United States.

a. Community property law operates similar to a condominium association in which each person owns a part of the property but is subject to the rules determined by the group.

b. Under community property law, a husband and wife each own a 1/2 interest in the property acquired during their marriage.

c. Community property law is not a widespread concept because it is generally thought of as a step towards socialism.

d. People who move from a community property state to a noncommunity property state are relieved from the ownership which had been imposed upon them.

The correct answer is (b). *(Publisher)*

REQUIRED: The correct statement concerning the community property form of ownership.

DISCUSSION: Community property law directly affects only the ownership of property between a husband and wife. Each owns a 1/2 interest in property acquired during their marriage. It applies to both real and personal property. It is similar to a tenancy in common, but the rights and duties of the husband and wife vary from state to state.

Answer (a) is incorrect because community property law only exists between a husband and wife, and is more similar to a tenancy in common than to condominium ownership. Answer (c) is incorrect because community property is not considered a step toward socialism; rather it is a means of providing each party with equal benefits from his/her contributions to the marital family. Answer (d) is incorrect because the community property (or 1/2 each ownership) retains that status when people move from a community property state to a noncommunity property state.

28. Condominiums and cooperatives are two forms of common ownership of buildings. They have been traditionally used for residential purposes, although there is an increasing trend to use them for business purposes. Cooperatives and condominiums differ in that

a. Cooperative interests are freely transferable while condominiums are not.

b. Condominium owners individually finance their units, while cooperatives finance through a blanket mortgage on the entire property.

c. Condominium owners pay their own taxes while the individuals have no liability for the taxes on a cooperative.

d. In a cooperative the residents own the common areas, while in a condominium they do not.

The correct answer is (b). *(Publisher)*

REQUIRED: The manner in which cooperatives and condominiums differ.

DISCUSSION: Condominium owners individually own their units. They obtain whatever financing is necessary on the unit and are solely responsible for the payments. A cooperative is generally set up as a corporation which owns the building and rents to the shareholders. The corporation holding title to the building finances it with a blanket mortgage.

Answer (a) is incorrect because condominiums are freely transferable while cooperatives sometimes impose restrictions on the assignment or sublease of the apartments. Answer (c) is incorrect because the taxes are paid by the cooperative corporation, but the individuals are in turn liable to the corporation. Answer (d) is incorrect because in a cooperative the corporation owns the common areas, while in a condominium the individuals own the common areas through the condominium association.

29. Glover Manufacturing, Inc. purchased a 4-acre tract of commercially zoned land. A survey of the tract was made prior to the closing, and it revealed an unpaved road which passed across the northeast corner of the land. The title search did not indicate the existence of any other adverse interest which would constitute a defect in title. There was no recordation made in connection with the unpaved road. Which of the following statements is correct regarding Glover's title and rights to the land against adverse claims?

a. The unpaved road poses no potential problem if Glover promptly fences off the property and puts up "no trespassing" signs.

b. Glover does not have to be concerned with the unpaved road since whatever rights the users might claim were negated by failing to record.

c. The mere use of the unpaved road as contrasted with the occupancy of the land cannot create any interest adverse to Glover.

d. The unpaved road revealed by the survey may prove to be a valid easement created by prescription.

The correct answer is (d). *(CPA 581 L-52)*

REQUIRED: The buyer's rights to the land against adverse claims.

DISCUSSION: An easement is a non-ownership interest in land belonging to someone other than the landowner. It is a right to use the land which may be acquired either by conveyance, which is unlikely on these facts since there was no recorded easement, or by prescription, which bears some similarity to the acquisition of an ownership interest in land by means of adverse possession. A valid easement might have been created by prescription if someone had continuously used the road, without the permission of the owner, in an open and notorious manner for the statutory period. "Open and notorious" means that the use would have had to have been in such a manner that the owner would have known or had the means of knowing of the use.

Answer (a) is incorrect because promptly fencing off the property and putting up signs will be ineffective if a valid easement by prescription has already been created. Answer (b) is incorrect because a valid easement by prescription may be created without recordation. Answer (c) is incorrect because while adverse possession of the land would create an ownership interest, use of the road could create a right to continued use of the land.

30. Oxnard owned Goldacre, a tract of land, in fee simple. At a time when Goldacre was in the adverse possession of Amos, Eric obtained the oral permission of Oxnard to use as a road or driveway a portion of Goldacre to reach adjoining land, Twin Pines, which Eric owned in fee simple. Thereafter, during all times relevant to this problem, Eric used this road across Goldacre regularly for ingress and egress between Twin Pines and a public highway. Amos quit possession of Goldacre before acquiring title by adverse possession. Without any further communication between Oxnard and Eric, Eric continued to use the road for a total period, from the time he first began to use it, sufficient to acquire an easement by prescription. Oxnard then blocked the road and refused to permit its continued use. Eric brought suit to determine his right to continue use of the road. Eric should

a. Win, because his use was adverse to Amos and once adverse it continued adverse until some affirmative showing of a change.

b. Win, because Eric made no attempt to renew permission after Amos quit possession of Goldacre.

c. Lose, because his use was with permission.

d. Lose, because there is no evidence that he continued adverse use for the required period after Amos quit possession.

The correct answer is (c). *(MBE Part I-15)*

REQUIRED: The result of the suit to determine the right to use the road.

DISCUSSION: An easement by prescription requires a use hostile to the owner's rights. Hostile use does not exist if the owner gives permission to use the land. Although Amos was adversely possessing the land, Oxnard was the owner and gave Eric permission to use it.

Answer (a) is incorrect because Amos was not the owner of the land and Eric's use was not hostile to Oxnard. Answer (b) is incorrect because Oxnard's permission did not need to be renewed since Amos never owned the land. Answer (d) is incorrect because whether Eric continued the use for the required period is irrelevant since it was not adverse to Oxnard's rights.

31. An easement by necessity is created when

a. A grant of land has created a parcel of realty that is inaccessible or accessible only by a difficult route.

b. A grantee but not a grantor is left with a difficult access to realty as a result of a conveyance.

c. A landlocked parcel of realty is conveyed.

d. A grantor but not a grantee is left with a difficult access to realty as a result of a conveyance.

The correct answer is (c). *(Publisher)*

REQUIRED: The condition necessary for recognition of an easement by necessity.

DISCUSSION: If the grantor conveys part of his/her realty without providing the grantee a means of access, a court will find that an easement across the grantor's remaining land was implied by necessity. This easement is created only if the parcel would otherwise be landlocked. Access by a difficult, circuitous, or otherwise inconvenient route defeats an application for such for easement. Similarly, an easement by necessity may arise through an implied reservation when a conveyance leaves the grantor's property landlocked.

Answers (a), (b), and (d) are incorrect because an easement by necessity arises only when a conveyance creates a landlocked parcel of real property. Also, either a grantor or a grantee may be entitled to such an easement.

32. An easement cannot be

a. Created by reservation.

b. The mere right to the use of another's land but must be obtained for the benefit of the land owned by the party obtaining the easement.

c. Obtained by prescription if the claimant's use of the land has been interrupted by the prompt action of the landowner.

d. Conveyed by the easement owner to another party who purchases the land owned by the easement owner.

The correct answer is (c). *(CPA 1176 L-42)*

REQUIRED: The correct statement regarding an easement.

DISCUSSION: Easements may be obtained by prescription if the use of the land proceeds continuously for the statutory period, is without the permission of the owner, and is open and notorious. If the use is interrupted before the statutory period has run, no easement by prescription can be created because the continuity requirement will not have been met.

Answer (a) is incorrect because an easement may be created by reservation, e.g., a sale of land by a grantor who reserves the right to use a road crossing the land conveyed. Answer (b) is incorrect because an easement may be in gross as well as appurtenant. An easement is in gross if it is for the benefit of a particular person and does not relate to any specified parcel of real property. An easement is appurtenant if it benefits a particular parcel of land. Answer (d) is incorrect because if the easement is appurtenant, then a conveyance of the land benefited by the easement customarily also conveys the easement.

33. Which of the following is true with respect to an easement created by an express grant?

a. The easement will be extinguished upon the death of the grantee.

b. The easement cannot be sold or transferred by the owner of the easement.

c. The easement gives the owner of the easement the right to the physical possession of the property subject to the easement.

d. The easement must be in writing to be valid.

The correct answer is (d). *(CPA 577 L-36)*

REQUIRED: The correct statement regarding an easement created by express grant.

DISCUSSION: An easement is a nonpossessory interest in land which confers the right to use that land. The express grant of an easement is a transfer of an interest in land and therefore must be in writing and signed by the grantor to comply with the Statute of Frauds.

Answer (a) is incorrect because the typical easement created by express grant will not be extinguished upon the death of the grantee. The easement could provide, however, for termination on the death of the grantee. Answer (b) is incorrect because easements appurtenant are assignable as well as inheritable, but easements in gross are not. The typical easement appurtenant is transferred when the land to which it relates is sold or transferred. Answer (c) is incorrect because an easement is a nonpossessory right to use the land.

34. Franklin and Jefferson own adjacent properties. There is a party wall down their property line that existed before each purchased his property. Jefferson wants the wall to be torn down, but Franklin does not.

a. Jefferson is entitled to have the wall torn down since it extends over his property line.

b. Franklin must compensate Jefferson if he does not agree to tear down the wall.

c. Franklin and Jefferson each have an undivided interest in the entire wall.

d. Franklin has an easement of support from Jefferson's side of the wall.

The correct answer is (d). *(Publisher)*

REQUIRED: The rights and duties with respect to a party wall between adjacent landowners.

DISCUSSION: Each party is entitled to the use of a party wall and also has an easement of support from the other side. Without the easement, the right to retain an existing wall would be illusory.

Answer (a) is incorrect because there is no right to tear down a party wall unless such a right existed by agreement or has been acquired by adverse possession. Answer (b) is incorrect because Franklin is under no obligation to have the wall torn down or to agree to do so. Answer (c) is incorrect because they are not tenants in common. In most states, each is considered to own the part on his/her side and to have an easement of support from the other side.

35. Maria is the owner and possessor of Goodacre, on which there is a lumber yard. Maria conveyed to Reliable Electric Company the right to construct and use an overhead electric line across Goodacre to serve other properties. The conveyance was in writing, but the writing made no provision concerning the responsibility for repair or maintenance of the line. Reliable installed the poles and erected the electric line in a proper and workmanlike manner. Neither Maria nor Reliable took any steps toward the maintenance or repair of the line after it was built. Neither party complained to the other about any failure to repair. Because of the failure to repair or properly maintain the line, it fell to the ground during a storm. In doing so, it caused a fire in the lumber yard and did considerable damage. Maria sued Reliable to recover for damages to the lumber yard. The decision should be for

a. Maria, because the owner of an easement has a duty to maintain the easement.

b. Maria, because the owner of an easement is absolutely liable for any damage caused by the easement.

c. Reliable, because the property owner has a duty to give the easement holder notice of defective conditions.

d. Reliable, because an easement holder's right to repair is a right for his/her own benefit only.

The correct answer is (a). *(MBE Part I-187)*

REQUIRED: The result of a suit by the fee simple owner against the user of an easement.

DISCUSSION: An easement is a nonpossessory right to use the land of another. The owner of an easement is responsible for its maintenance. Therefore, Reliable had an implied duty to take reasonable steps to keep the utility lines in good repair. Failure to do so results in liability for damages caused.

Answer (b) is incorrect because Reliable would not be liable for reasonable, nonnegligent use of the easement. However, an owner of an easement used for an inherently dangerous activity might be strictly liable. Answer (c) is incorrect because Reliable, as the user of the easement, has the duty to inspect and maintain the utility lines. Answer (d) is incorrect because the easement holder's duty to repair arises from the duty to prevent interference with the rights of the owner of the land.

36. An easement is terminated when

a. It is deeded back to the owner of the dominant tenement.

b. Its owner ceases to use it, although (s)he has no intent to abandon it.

c. The owner of the servient tenement merges his/her land with the adjacent property of a third party.

d. The requirements of adverse possession are met.

The correct answer is (d). *(Publisher)*

REQUIRED: The correct statement about one method of terminating an easement.

DISCUSSION: An easement may be terminated by adverse possession. The owner of the servient tenement must occupy the property openly and notoriously and in such a manner as to deny the rights of the owner of the easement. This conduct must continue for the statutory period.

Answer (a) is incorrect because a deed by the easement owner to the owner of the servient tenement (the realty subject to the easement) is the most usual means of termination. Answer (b) is incorrect because abandonment results in termination only when nonuse is coupled with intent to abandon. Answer (c) is incorrect because termination by merger occurs when the easement owner acquires the servient tenement.

37. Rogers has a large lot on which he collected old cars. He gave permission to Thomas to enter on his land and remove them. Thomas sells them, keeping all proceeds for himself. If after a month Rogers decides he wants Thomas to remove no more cars, his best legal argument is that Thomas

a. Is a trespasser.

b. Is a licensee.

c. Has a license coupled with an interest.

d. Has an easement.

The correct answer is (b). *(Publisher)*

REQUIRED: The best legal argument to terminate another's right to use land.

DISCUSSION: A license is the mere right to be on the land of another without being a trespasser. It is revocable at any time. When the right is retracted, the licensee is required to leave the premises.

Answer (a) is incorrect because Rogers gave Thomas permission to enter his land, so Thomas cannot be a trespasser. Answer (c) is incorrect because a license coupled with an interest is not revocable. If Thomas had paid for the right to remove all the cars, he would have a license coupled with an interest to enter on Rogers' land. Answer (d) is incorrect because an easement is not terminable at will.

38. Which of the following is a true statement about liens on real property created without the owner's consent?

a. An attachment lien is generally obtained by a secured creditor while an action is pending against the debtor.

b. A judgment lien is automatically created on behalf of the plaintiff when a judgment is rendered against the defendant.

c. An execution lien is directed to a specific parcel, not to all the realty of the debtor in the county where the lien is recorded.

d. A tax lien is automatically created when state or federal real property or income taxes are not paid.

The correct answer is (c). *(Publisher)*

REQUIRED: The true statement about involuntary liens on realty.

DISCUSSION: When a judgment has been entered, the successful party becomes a judgment creditor. If the judgment is not paid, (s)he may then obtain a judgment lien on all real property of the judgment debtor in a given county by recording the judgment in that county. If further measures are necessary, the judgment creditor may then seek a writ of execution from a court directing the sheriff to seize and sell a specified parcel of property.

Answer (a) is incorrect because an unsecured creditor would seek an attachment lien. A secured creditor already has a legal interest in the specific property. An attachment lien is recorded in the real property records pending the conclusion of the suit. Answer (b) is incorrect because the lien must be recorded where the debtor has real property before it is effective to encumber the property. Answer (d) is incorrect because real property tax liens are created automatically without court action, but an income, sales, or other nonproperty tax lien generally arises only after filing of a notice in the county records.

39. Jansa is the owner of real property. She will most likely not be liable in which of the following cases?

a. She has a swimming pool in her backyard that she knows is attractive to the four-year old next door. On a warm summer afternoon, the child walked through an unlocked steel gate, the only entry to the property, fell in the pool, and drowned.

b. Ivan was a party guest at Jansa's country place. Wandering half a mile away from the part of the property where the party was held, Ivan fell into covered pit recently dug by workmen and was injured.

c. She owns a country place mostly covered with woods. One afternoon she saw a strange man walking on the property without permission. She shot and seriously wounded the stranger.

d. Nicholas is a customer who entered Jansa's two-story furniture store to shop. While climbing the stairway, he slipped on a piece of loose carpeting, fell, and was injured.

The correct answer is (b). *(Publisher)*

REQUIRED: The case in which the owner of realty will not be liable to a visitor.

DISCUSSION: A licensee is one, such as a social guest, who is privileged to enter or remain on the property by the consent of the lawful possessor. The duty of the owner or occupant is to refrain from intentional injury and to warn of known dangerous conditions. A licensee who strays without permission from the part of the property where (s)he is privileged to be becomes a trespasser. The duty to a trespasser is merely to avoid intentional infliction of injury. When Ivan left the area of the party, he became a trespasser, and Jansa had no duty to warn of known dangerous conditions.

Answer (a) is incorrect because the possessor must use reasonable care to prevent an unreasonably dangerous condition on one's property from being accessible by children who cannot appreciate the danger. Answer (c) is incorrect because the lawful owner or occupant of property has a duty not to cause intentional harm to a trespasser. Answer (d) is incorrect because a higher duty is owed to an invitee than to a licensee or trespasser. The lawful possessor must use reasonable care to protect against dangerous conditions that the invitee is unlikely to discover. Invitees include those who are invited to the property for the benefit of the owner or occupant, e.g., customers.

20.2 Land Use Control

40. Cardosa purchased a ranch style house near the edge of town but within the city limits. She had a fee simple title and had paid the purchase price in full. Cardosa placed a sign by the road that read "Bulls Hit Ranch." Cardosa had many friends living at the house in violation of local zoning. They partied until dawn making a lot of noise. The garbage in the yard also began to pile up. The city council tried to have Cardosa correct these problems, but Cardosa says she can do anything with the land since she owns it in fee simple. Which of the following can the city council or appropriate governmental body do?

a. Hold a sheriff's sale of Cardosa's land since she has not complied with the applicable zoning laws.

b. Prohibit the occupancy of the property if the garbage constitutes a health hazard.

c. Tear down the sign as a violation of the city sign ordinance.

d. Confiscate Cardosa's stereo equipment to reduce the noise level for the neighbors.

The correct answer is (b). *(Publisher)*

REQUIRED: The action available to an appropriate governmental body to abate a nuisance.

DISCUSSION: Although a landowner ordinarily may use the land for any purpose, (s)he must not substantially and unreasonably interfere with neighboring landowners. Under the police power, a governmental body could take necessary steps to prevent a health hazard. If Cardosa did not clean up garbage that constituted a health hazard, the city might be able to prohibit occupancy of the property.

Answer (a) is incorrect because noncompliance with the zoning laws is not a basis for a sheriff's sale; rather it would be a basis for a court order prohibiting the violations. Answer (c) is incorrect because the city would first have to obtain a court order to remove the sign. Answer (d) is incorrect because Cardosa's personal property could not be confiscated without a court order. But a court would probably issue an injunction which, if ignored, could lead to a citation for contempt of court.

41. A court rules that city government regulations are overly restrictive of Mary's use of her land. For the city government to achieve its purposes, it must

a. Condemn the land under its power of eminent domain and pay Mary reasonable compensation.

b. Condemn the land under its police power and provide Mary with an equivalent parcel of land elsewhere.

c. File a comprehensive plan with the court as a basis for seizing Mary's land.

d. Attempt to bargain with Mary to purchase the property because the court has ruled against the city.

The correct answer is (a). *(Publisher)*

REQUIRED: The remedy available to a local government if its regulations are overly restrictive.

DISCUSSION: Public controls of land use fall under two basic types: the power of eminent domain and police power. Eminent domain is the power of government to take land from private owners through condemnation when the taking is for a public purpose and the private owner is reasonably compensated. Police power is the broad power of state and local governments to promote the public health, safety, and welfare, for example, through land use regulation. Under the police power, land is not appropriated by the government and compensation is not paid to the owner. If a court rules that regulations are so restrictive that the owner is deprived of all reasonable use of the land, the regulations are not binding, and the government must resort to condemnation.

Answer (b) is incorrect because condemnation is based on the power of eminent domain. Answer (c) is incorrect because a comprehensive plan is a set of standards that forms the basis of a zoning code. It is not necessarily a specific document and is not filed with a court, although a court may use it to evaluate the propriety of a zoning administration's actions. A comprehensive plan is not a basis for seizing property. Answer (d) is incorrect because the court's unfavorable ruling does not prevent the city from pursuing condemnation of the property.

42. The limitations, restrictions, and conditions on the ownership of real property are many and diverse. Which of the following is a false statement with respect to such limitations, restrictions and conditions of real property ownership?

a. Compensation for a taking of property under eminent domain is paid only to possessory interests in property.

b. Property is taxed according to its highest and best use.

c. A mortgagee who has paid the real property taxes may recover them from the mortgagor.

d. Zoning ordinances may prohibit the most profitable use of the property.

The correct answer is (a). *(Publisher)*

REQUIRED: The limitation not placed on real estate ownership.

DISCUSSION: Eminent domain is the power of a governmental unit to take private property for a public purpose for which the owners must be paid compensation. Those entitled to compensation include not only the persons in possession but also those with vested interests, e.g., one who has a remainder following a life estate. But contingent future interests are not compensable.

Answer (b) is incorrect because real property appraisals based on the highest and best use are the basis for taxation. Answer (c) is incorrect because the owner-mortgagor has a duty not to impair the value of the security and must pay property taxes to avoid a tax sale of the property. If the mortgagee pays the taxes, it may add the amount paid to its claim against the debtor. Answer (d) is incorrect because a reasonable zoning ordinance will be upheld although it prohibits the most profitable use of a person's property.

43. Public control of the use of real property is achieved principally through zoning. Which of the following is true?

a. Zoning is an exercise of the inherent police power of the state to take private property to promote public health, morals, safety, and welfare.

b. A zoning ordinance allows for nonconforming uses and variances.

c. Zoning is an inherent power of municipalities and its use must have a rational relationship to its basis in public policy.

d. Creation of floating zones has been held to be an unconstitutional use of the police power.

The correct answer is (b). *(Publisher)*

REQUIRED: The true statement about zoning.

DISCUSSION: Zoning is used to plan and control the development of real property. The passage of a zoning ordinance, however, may not prohibit a lawful preexisting use. A nonconforming use must be allowed to continue for a reasonable time. The statute must also allow for variances. Zoning variances are granted upon the petition of a landowner if (s)he cannot make reasonable use of his/her land, if the adverse effect of the ordinance is unique to the petitioner, and if the character of the zone will not be substantially changed. Also, special use permits are used by local governments to control the location of some special types of development that may not be included in the regular zoning plan, such as churches and schools.

Answer (a) is incorrect because the police power may be used to regulate but not take property. Eminent domain is a basis for a compensated taking for a public purpose. Answer (c) is incorrect because ordinarily, local governments may not enact a zoning ordinance without an enabling statute (a state statute granting such authority to local governments). Answer (d) is incorrect because floating zones are permissible. Under this flexible approach, the amount of land to be designated for various uses is determined at the beginning, but classifications are assigned to particular parcels only at a later time and upon the request of landowners.

44. Fifteen years ago, Mr. Xavier violated the zoning of his real estate in Allentown by erecting a gas station. The authorities have never proceeded against him because of the violation, and he operated his gas station without incident until he was ready to retire. Xavier tells the prospective buyer that he has a "pre-existing, nonconforming use," and that the buyer can continue to use the property for a gas station despite the violation of the zoning law.

a. Pre-existing, nonconforming uses are those legal uses of property that preceded the enactment of a zoning law. The buyer therefore cannot continue the use.

b. The illegality of the use was cured by the passage of time.

c. Allentown is unable to use zoning laws to attack the current use of the property and curtail it.

d. Zoning laws can be defeated by showing that the illegal use of the property did not harm adjacent landowners.

The correct answer is (a). *(E. O'Connor)*

REQUIRED: The status of a long-term use of property that has always been in violation of the zoning laws.

DISCUSSION: Zoning codes do not have retroactive effect. Hence, an existing legal use cannot be invalidated by enactment of a zoning ordinance or an amendment thereto. Such a nonconforming use may therefore continue, but it may not be expanded. Moreover, it runs with the land; that is, a subsequent buyer may continue the use. But if it terminates, for example, because of destruction of a building, it may not be resumed. Mr. Xavier's use, however, was simply illegal, not nonconforming, and neither Mr. Xavier nor a buyer has a right to continue the use.

Answer (b) is incorrect because no principle analogous to adverse possession applies to zoning violations. Answer (c) is incorrect because the municipality could immediately end an illegal use and require a nonconforming use to be stopped in a reasonable time. Answer (d) is incorrect because absence of harm to owners of adjacent property does not validate an illegal use. A zoning ordinance will be defeated only if it is an invalid use of the police power, e.g., one that constitutes an uncompensated taking of the property.

45. A specialized type of zoning that has been found to be prima facie illegal by some states is

a. Regional zoning.

b. Limited-density zoning.

c. Performance standards zoning.

d. Large-lot zoning.

The correct answer is (d). *(Publisher)*

REQUIRED: The type of zoning found by some courts to violate public policy.

DISCUSSION: Zoning and land use regulations are intended to give communities some control over their growth and development. These regulations must promote a valid purpose and not violate public policy. Large-lot zoning sets excessively large minimum lot size standards for new construction. Whether intentionally or not, such standards discriminate against low and middle income housing. Some state courts, most notably in Pennsylvania, have ruled large-lot zoning to be prima facie illegal.

Answer (a) is incorrect because regional zoning allows more comprehensive planning for regional needs and has been encouraged by various courts. Answer (b) is incorrect because zoning is commonly used to control the density of development within reasonable limits. Limited-density zoning has also been used to provide a minimum of "green space" within a community. Answer (c) is incorrect because performance standards zoning is a valid use of a community's police power to regulate public nuisances such as toxic wastes, noise, odors, and traffic. For example, a standard may specify the decibel level or the amount of vehicular traffic.

46. Most municipalities regulate the subdivision of land into residential developments. Which of the following is a true statement about subdivisions?

a. The government's power of eminent domain allows municipalities to regulate subdivision development.

b. A local planning board must approve future subdivisions, even though all subdivision regulations will be met.

c. A planned unit development (PUD) is a larger version of a subdivision.

d. The infrastructure of a subdivision located inside the city limits must be maintained by the city.

The correct answer is (b). *(Publisher)*

REQUIRED: The true statement about the regulation and maintenance of a subdivision.

DISCUSSION: Municipal subdivision regulations are intended to assure that new developments conform to local requirements regarding roads, sewers, parks, and other infrastructure needs. Compliance with these requirements is monitored by a planning board, which must approve all plans for future subdivisions. When all regulations and requirements have been met, the municipality will ordinarily accept responsibility for maintenance of the subdivision's infrastructure.

Answer (a) is incorrect because the police power underlies subdivision regulation. Answer (c) is incorrect because a PUD also provides for various kinds of land use. It may have commercial and industrial as well as residential uses. Answer (d) is incorrect because the city is not required to accept maintenance responsibility for the infrastructure if, for example, the developer fails to faithfully execute the plan submitted to the planning board.

47. Wetlands have recently come to be seen as valuable natural resources that contribute greatly to society. Which of the following is a true statement concerning land use controls instituted to protect wetlands?

a. Zoning is the control most widely used to protect wetlands.

b. Wetland protection controls are designed to stop all further destruction of wetlands as soon as possible.

c. Wetland protection controls are exempt from the prohibition against depriving property owners of all reasonable uses of their land.

d. Permitting is the control most widely used to protect wetlands.

The correct answer is (d). *(Publisher)*

REQUIRED: The true statement about the protection of wetlands.

DISCUSSION: Preservation of certain special environments (such as wetlands and historic districts) has become more important as society's environmental awareness has grown. Wetlands in particular have been found to be vital for wildlife, flood control, and ground water maintenance. Various methods have been used to limit wetland destruction, but the most widely used control is permitting. For example, the Clean Water Act of 1972 requires a permit from the Corps of Engineers for dredging and filling operations.

Answer (a) is incorrect because permitting, not zoning, predominates as a method to protect wetlands. Answer (b) is incorrect because the controls are designed to limit further destruction, not stop it entirely. Answer (c) is incorrect because there are no exemptions to the prohibition against "taking."

48. Williamsville has adopted a transferable development rights (TDRs) scheme to protect its historic district, which includes recent structures as well as landmarks. The municipality designated a transfer zone and a preservation zone. Under this arrangement, the most likely result is that

a. Development in the transfer zone will be allowed to the limit imposed by the zoning code without any transfer of rights.

b. No TDRs will be assigned to property in the preservation zone.

c. The holder of property in the preservation zone will be able to secure a return despite not being able to develop the site.

d. TDRs will be assigned to property in the preservation zone, but development therein will be limited to the rights initially received or subsequently purchased.

The correct answer is (c). *(Publisher)*

REQUIRED: The true statement about a transferable development rights arrangement.

DISCUSSION: The use of TDRs is a device to protect special environments, such as historic places, wetlands, and open space. This approach allocates TDRs to different parcels in amounts that restrict development to less than that allowed in the zoning regulations. Development may be forbidden in some areas (preservation zones), but TDRs will nevertheless be assigned to those properties. Landowners in other areas (transfer zones) are permitted to develop their parcels but must acquire additional TDRs to take maximum advantage of zoning designations, such as density allowances. Hence, an owner in a preservation zone could sell TDRs to a party in a transfer zone and receive an economic return for the property despite not being able to develop it.

Answer (a) is incorrect because the TDRs initially assigned to the transfer zone will be insufficient for full development. Answer (b) is incorrect because TDRs assigned to the preservation zone effectively compensate landowners for their inability to develop. Answer (d) is incorrect because development in the preservation zone may be prohibited altogether.

49. Joe purchased property fronting a river that is known to flood its banks approximately every 10 years. Joe loves the view, however, and intends to build a house there. Which of the following is a true statement about the effect land use regulations of floodplains will have on Joe's plans?

a. Local government zoning regulations are most likely the principal obstacle to construction.

b. Joe's bank will be prohibited from lending him money to construct a house on his new property.

c. Joe may purchase transferable development rights (TDRs) from other property owners in the area that will allow him to build on his property.

d. In general, the regulations to which Joe's property is subject are essentially the same as regulations protecting wetlands.

The correct answer is (b). *(Publisher)*

REQUIRED: The true statement about the regulation of floodplain development.

DISCUSSION: Development of lands subject to flooding by nearby waterways frequently exacerbates the flooding problem and leads to greater destruction and higher disaster relief costs. Thus, controls have been devised to limit further floodplain development. The principal source of these controls is the federal government. Only communities that act to protect the floodplain are eligible for the National Flood Insurance Program. Also, financial institutions are not allowed to lend money for construction on floodplains (flood hazard areas).

Answer (a) is incorrect because federal legislation is the main source of flood plain protection. Answer (c) is incorrect because the use of transferable development rights is a control device to curtail development in a designated preservation zone while allowing property owners to recover some economic value. Answer (d) is incorrect because wetlands are largely protected through permitting.

50. The Civil Rights Act of 1968 is commonly known as the Federal Fair Housing Act. Under the Act, it is illegal to refuse to rent to someone because (s)he is

a. Married.

b. Handicapped.

c. A certain age.

d. From a certain country.

The correct answer is (d). *(Publisher)*

REQUIRED: The illegal act under the Civil Rights Act of 1968.

DISCUSSION: The Federal Fair Housing Act was designed to end private discrimination in housing. The Act is concerned with discrimination based on race, color, religion, national origin, and sex. Refusal to sell, rent, or negotiate because of any of these factors is illegal.

Answers (a), (b), and (c) are incorrect because discrimination in housing based on marital status, infirmities, and age are not addressed by the Act. Discrimination based on these factors is commonly addressed by state and local fair housing laws.

51. Land use controls may be public or private. They may be imposed by law or arise by agreement. Which of the following is a true statement about private means of control?

a. An equitable servitude is a promise that is enforceable only if the parties are in privity of estate.

b. An equitable servitude is enforceable although the promise is oral.

c. A covenant running with the land is enforceable by an action for damages brought by a successor of the covenantee against a successor of the covenantor.

d. A covenant running with the land must touch and concern the land but the original parties need not have intended that successors be bound.

The correct answer is (c). *(Publisher)*

REQUIRED: The true statement about private methods of land use control.

DISCUSSION: A covenant runs with the land if it touches and concerns the land, if the original parties intended it to bind their successors, if it is contained in a writing, and if the original parties were in privity of estate (e.g., grantor-grantee or testator-devisee). If X is a developer who sells a lot in a subdivision to Y and the deed contains the restriction that Y and his/her successors, heirs, and assigns may use the property only for residential purposes, the restriction meets the criteria for a covenant that will run with the land. It will be enforceable by successors of X (other purchasers of lots in the subdivision) against a successor of Y (such as a person to whom Y sold the lot).

Answers (a) and (b) are incorrect because an equitable servitude is a restrictive covenant that is similar to a covenant running with the land except that no privity of estate is necessary. An equitable servitude will be enforced against successors who have actual or constructive notice provided that the promise touches and concerns the land, is in writing, and was intended by the original parties to restrict the use of the land. Answer (d) is incorrect because intent is a requirement.

52. Ralph owned 73 apartments that he rented on an annual basis. Ralph advertised one of the available apartments in the local paper. Tom saw the ad, contacted Ralph, and arranged to see the apartment. Upon meeting Tom, Ralph quickly explained that the apartment was unavailable. In reality, the apartment was available but Ralph did not like the color of Tom's skin. Ralph's action is commonly known as

a. Steering.

b. Blockbusting.

c. Panic selling.

d. Gerrymandering.

The correct answer is (a). *(Publisher)*

REQUIRED: The name for falsely representing that a dwelling is unavailable because of the potential occupant's skin color.

DISCUSSION: Falsely representing that a dwelling is unavailable because of race, color, national origin, religion, or sex is illegal under the Civil Rights Act of 1968. This practice is known as steering.

Answers (b) and (c) are incorrect because blockbusting and panic selling are both names for the practice of enticing a person to sell property because people of a certain race, sex, color, religion, or national origin are moving into the neighborhood. Answer (d) is incorrect because gerrymandering is the practice of drawing election or school district lines in order to benefit one group of people to the detriment of another group.

53. The Civil Rights Act of 1968 contains exemptions from its housing provisions for certain persons and organizations. Which of the following may be exempt?

a. An owner who sells his/her home through a broker.

b. An owner who sells his/her home while owning an interest in a new home.

c. The owner of a rental property containing six units who resides in one of the units.

d. A religious organization that operates rental property and discriminates against a particular religion.

The correct answer is (b). *(Publisher)*

REQUIRED: The person or organization exempt from the provisions of the Civil Rights Act of 1968 that relate to housing.

DISCUSSION: Ordinarily, an owner who sells his/her home is not subject to the Act. This is true even if the owner has already acquired a new home or owns a second home prior to offering the residence for sale.

Answer (a) is incorrect because the exemption does not apply to an owner who uses a broker in the sales transaction. Answer (c) is incorrect because the rental property must contain four units or less to be exempt. Answer (d) is incorrect because a religious organization operating rental property may only discriminate in favor of a particular religion.

54. A person injured by an action prohibited by the Federal Fair Housing Act may file a complaint with the Secretary of Housing and Urban Development (HUD). If HUD refers the case to the U.S. Attorney General for prosecution, several remedies are available. Which of the following is not an available remedy?

a. Compensatory damages.

b. Punitive damages limited to $10,000.

c. Injunctive relief.

d. Attorney's fees and costs.

The correct answer is (b). *(Publisher)*

REQUIRED: The remedy not available under the Federal Fair Housing Act.

DISCUSSION: Punitive damages are awarded to the injured party and assessed against the party who violated the Act in order to punish the violator. The Act limits punitive damages to $1,000. The limit does not affect the award of compensatory damages.

Answers (a), (c), and (d) are incorrect because compensatory damages, injunctive relief, and attorney's fees and costs may be awarded to the plaintiff by the court.

20.3 Contracts, Conveyances, and Title

55. A seller of real property may engage another person to locate a buyer. A real estate broker will generally serve as the seller's agent for this purpose. Which of the following is true?

a. Since the broker has no interest in the real estate, the brokerage contract need not be written.

b. The broker may not prepare the buyer's offer to purchase because of the prohibition against the unlicensed practice of law.

c. The broker's essential task is to bind a buyer and enter into a binding contract on behalf of the seller.

d. The listing contract determines when the seller must compensate the broker. It may provide for an open listing, an exclusive agency, or an exclusive right to sell.

The correct answer is (d). *(Publisher)*

REQUIRED: The true statement about real estate brokers.

DISCUSSION: The listing agreement specifies the duration of the listing, the seller's terms of sale, and the compensation due the broker. In an open listing, an agent who produces a ready, willing, and able buyer will receive the commission. If the seller finds the buyer, no commission need be paid. In an exclusive agency, only the specified broker can receive the commission, but if the seller finds a buyer no commission is owed. In exclusive-right-to-sell listing, the broker must be paid regardless of who produces the buyer.

Answer (a) is incorrect because many states require that real estate broker commission arrangements be in writing. Answer (b) is incorrect because many states allow the broker to perform this task, but an attorney must prepare the deed and other closing documents. Answer (c) is incorrect because the broker is generally authorized to find a ready, willing, and able buyer and to negotiate on behalf of the seller, but not to sign a contract binding the seller.

56. The real estate binder

a. Must satisfy the general requirements applicable to all contracts as well as the Statute of Frauds.

b. Does not transfer risk of loss to the buyer until the closing unless the parties expressly agree otherwise.

c. Transfers title but not possession.

d. Is not effective unless recorded.

The correct answer is (a). *(Publisher)*

REQUIRED: The true statement about a contract to sell real estate.

DISCUSSION: A real estate binder is a contract so the elements of a valid contract must be present: offer and acceptance, consideration, legality, and competent parties. The contract to sell must also be in writing and signed by the party to be bound. The contract should contain a description of the property, the time for conveyance, the kind of deed, the price, the mode of financing, the closing date, the date of possession, the date of prorating taxes, insurance, etc., and a provision for title insurance or an abstract of title.

Answer (b) is incorrect because the majority rule is that risk of loss passes to the buyer upon formation of the contract, but contracts for sale of real property frequently make other arrangements. Answer (c) is incorrect because transfer of title by deed commonly occurs at the closing. Answer (d) is incorrect because the contract is effective between the parties when formed. Recording puts the third parties on notice of the existence of the contract.

57. Moss entered into a contract to purchase certain real property from Shinn. Which of the following statements is not correct?

a. If Shinn fails to perform the contract, Moss can obtain specific performance.

b. The contract is nonassignable as a matter of law.

c. The Statute of Frauds applies to the contract.

d. Any amendment to the contract must be agreed to by both Moss and Shinn.

The correct answer is (b). *(CPA 1189 L-18)*

REQUIRED: The false statement concerning a contract for the purchase of real property.

DISCUSSION: The general rule is that contracts of an impersonal nature (such as those for the purchase and sale of land) are assignable unless otherwise provided. Contracts for personal services, that involve a confidential relationship, or that have some other personal elements tend not to be assignable.

Answers (a), (c), and (d) are incorrect because each is a correct statement concerning contracts for the purchase and sale of real property.

58. A clause in a contract for the purchase of real estate providing that the seller shall be entitled to retain the purchaser's down payment as liquidated damages should the purchaser fail to close the transaction will usually be enforceable

a. In addition to the seller's right to recover compensatory damages.

b. As a penalty if the purchaser has intentionally defaulted.

c. If the amount of the down payment bears a reasonable relationship to the probable loss.

d. In all cases provided the parties have agreed in a signed writing.

The correct answer is (c). *(CPA 587 L-24)*

REQUIRED: The enforceability of a liquidated damages clause in a real estate contract.

DISCUSSION: Liquidated damages are those provided for in the contract. A liquidated damages clause may save the trouble and expense of litigation, but the amount must have a reasonable relationship to the loss expected to result from breach.

Answer (a) is incorrect because the election of remedies doctrine provides that inconsistent remedies may not be sought. Both liquidated and compensatory damages cannot be sought. Answer (b) is incorrect because a penalty is not a proper contract remedy. The purpose of contract remedies is not to punish the breacher but to put the nonbreacher in as good a position as (s)he would have occupied if the contract had been fully performed. Answer (d) is incorrect because a writing would not save an excessive liquidated damages clause.

59. Buyer, under a valid contract to purchase real property, dies before closing, there being no breach of the agreement by either party. Which of the following is appropriate in most jurisdictions?

a. Buyer's heirs may specifically enforce the agreement.

b. Seller has the right to return the down payment and cancel the contract.

c. Death terminates the agreement.

d. Any title acquired would be unmarketable by reason of Buyer's death.

The correct answer is (a). *(MBE Part IV-12)*

REQUIRED: The correct statement if a buyer of real property dies after execution of the contract but before closing.

DISCUSSION: Either Buyer or Seller under a purchase agreement for real estate can obtain specific performance. In the event of death their contract rights descend to their heirs. Thus, Buyer's heirs may specifically enforce the agreement.

Answer (b) is incorrect because Buyer's contractual right to purchase the real estate passes to his/her estate as both an obligation and an enforceable right. Answer (c) is incorrect because death does not terminate an agreement to buy/sell. It only terminates personal service contracts. Answer (d) is incorrect because the marketability of the title is unrelated to Buyer's death.

60. Fulcrum Enterprises, Inc. contracted to purchase a 4-acre tract of land from Devlin as a site for its proposed factory. The contract of sale is silent as to the type of deed to be received by Fulcrum and does not contain any title exceptions. The title search revealed that 15 zoning laws affect Fulcrum's use of the land and that back taxes are due. A survey revealed a stone wall encroaching upon a portion of the land Devlin is purporting to convey. A survey made 23 years ago also had revealed the wall. Regarding the rights and duties of Fulcrum, which of the following is correct?

a. The contract is invalid because it does not specify the type of deed.

b. The existence of the zoning laws will permit Fulcrum to avoid the contract.

c. Fulcrum must take the land subject to the back taxes.

d. The wall suggests a potential breach of the implied warranty of marketability.

The correct answer is (d). *(CPA 582 L-53)*

REQUIRED: The rights and duties of a party contracting to purchase realty.

DISCUSSION: In the absence of an express provision to the contrary, every contract for the sale of real property contains an implied warranty of marketability. The seller warrants that the title is free from defects that would prevent a reasonable buyer from purchasing. The encroachment is a circumstance that would render the title unmarketable because it suggests that someone has acquired part of the property by adverse possession.

Answer (a) is incorrect because the contract is valid. When the contract is silent, the courts infer the intent is to provide the customary deed used in that community. This may be a full warranty deed, special warranty deed, or quitclaim deed. Answer (b) is incorrect because zoning laws are public restrictions assumed to be known by all parties and do not affect marketability of title. Answer (c) is incorrect because the existence of back taxes would be a breach of the implied warranty of marketability and would relieve Fulcrum of performing if they are not paid before the closing.

61. Vic Venner, the owner of Greenacre, a tract of land, entered into an enforceable written agreement with Bill Brier providing that Venner would sell Greenacre to Brier for an agreed price. At the place and time designated for the closing, Venner tendered an appropriate deed, but Brier responded that he had discovered a mortgage on Greenacre and would not complete the transaction, because Venner's title was not free of encumbrances, as the contract required. Venner said that it was his intent to pay the mortgage from the proceeds of the sale, and he offered to put the proceeds in escrow for that purpose with any agreeable, responsible escrowee. The balance due on the mortgage was substantially less than the contract purchase price. Brier refused Venner's proposal. Venner's best legal argument in support of his claim for relief is that

a. As the seller of real estate, he had an implied right to use the contract proceeds to clear the title being conveyed.

b. The lien of the mortgage shifts from Greenacre to the contract proceeds.

c. Under the doctrine of equitable conversion, title has already passed to Brier, and the only issue is how the purchase price is to be allocated.

d. No provision of the contract has been breached by Venner.

The correct answer is (a). *(MBE Part I-109)*

REQUIRED: The best legal argument for a seller of real estate to enforce a sale.

DISCUSSION: Venner's best argument is that by placing the proceeds in escrow and satisfying the mortgage from the escrow account he would be able to convey a title free of encumbrances. Use of proceeds for such purposes is a routine incident of real estate transactions and an argument could be made it is an implied right. Often the buyer applies part of the purchase price to mortgages and other liens in order to clear the title to the property.

Answer (b) is incorrect because the lien of a real estate mortgage continues in the real property rather than in the sale proceeds. Answer (c) is incorrect because legal title does not pass until the deed is delivered. Equitable title does pass to the buyer upon execution of the contract, but the buyer is still entitled to enforce the terms of the agreement. Answer (d) is incorrect because Venner breached the contractual duty to deliver a title free of encumbrances.

62. Taylor entered into an agreement to purchase a tract of land. The agreement specified that the seller was to provide title insurance, an attorney's opinion, or a title abstract at the purchaser's option. Which of the following is a correct statement of the benefits of and differences between these three methods of title assurance?

a. An attorney's opinion is usually the safest assurance because (s)he will be liable for malpractice if the opinion is incorrect.

b. Title insurance from a licensed company usually provides the greatest protection against risk of loss.

c. An abstract of title is a guarantee that the title is held by the person named.

d. All of these methods are unnecessary because a seller warrants both title and the obligation of the seller to defend against claims of others in a general warranty deed.

The correct answer is (b). *(Publisher)*

REQUIRED: The correct statement concerning various methods of title assurance.

DISCUSSION: Title insurance obtained from a licensed company usually provides the greatest protection against risk of loss. These companies are licensed by the state and have certain requirements as to financial condition and maintenance of reserves. Title insurance companies indemnify against defects whereas abstract companies and title examiners are required to not be negligent.

Answer (a) is incorrect because if an attorney does not maintain malpractice insurance, there may be no source of funds in the event (s)he becomes insolvent. Answer (c) is incorrect because an abstract of title is merely a collection of copies of all the recorded documents affecting a piece of property. An abstract is used to determine the status and quality of the title but is not a guaranty or assurance in itself. Answer (d) is incorrect because although a seller does make such warranties in a warranty deed, (s)he may have left the jurisdiction or not be able to pay.

63. One method of assuring title to real property is to obtain an attorney's opinion. Which of the following is true?

a. The attorney will in most cases conduct a search of the public land records related to the title.

b. The attorney will be liable for negligence but not for damage covered by every undisclosed defect in the title.

c. The attorney will usually prepare an abstract of title and render an opinion thereon.

d. Failure to discover all defects in the title is grounds for a malpractice suit.

The correct answer is (b). *(Publisher)*

REQUIRED: The true statement about an attorney's role in title assurance.

DISCUSSION: The attorney must exercise the care expected of ordinarily competent members of the profession in the locality where (s)he practices. (S)he will therefore not be liable for any injury arising from a defect in the title but only for that caused by failure to use due care.

Answers (a) and (c) are incorrect because in most states, abstract companies maintain records and prepare listings (abstracts) of events affecting title to realty. An attorney may then be called upon to render an opinion based on the abstract. Answer (d) is incorrect because the attorney who renders an opinion is not an insurer. (S)he will not be liable if a defect could not be discovered by the exercise of due care.

64. Smith purchased a tract of land. To protect himself, he ordered title insurance from Valor Title Insurance Company. The policy was the usual one issued by title companies. Accordingly,

a. Valor will not be permitted to take exceptions to its coverage if it agreed to insure and prepared the title abstract.

b. The title policy is assignable in the event Smith subsequently sells the property.

c. The title policy can provide protection against defects in record title only.

d. Valor will be liable for any title defect that arises, even though the defect could not have been discovered through the exercise of reasonable care.

The correct answer is (d). *(CPA 583 L-55)*

REQUIRED: The true statement about title insurance.

DISCUSSION: The title insurer searches the public records before issuing the policy, but title insurance goes beyond the matters covered in an attorney's title opinion. A title policy, like other insurance, is a contract of indemnification and is not based on fault or negligence. The policy gives protection if title is actually in another person, if title is subject to an encumbrance or other kind of defect, if the insured has no access to his/her land, and possibly if (s)he suffers loss from nonmarketability of the title. Unlike an attorney, a title insurer may be liable without having been negligent.

Answer (a) is incorrect because exceptions are allowed, for example, a taking under eminent domain, defects created by the insured, or those known by the insured but not by the company. Mechanic's liens, unpaid taxes, and utility easements may also be excepted. Answer (b) is incorrect because the buyer must secure a new policy based on an updated title search. Answer (c) is incorrect because other risks may be insured, for instance, lack of access, but it is common for the title policy to apply only to record title.

65. A buyer of real estate who receives a title insurance policy will

a. Take title free of all defects.

b. Be able to transfer the policy to a subsequent buyer of the real estate.

c. Not have coverage for title exceptions listed in the insurance policy.

d. Not have coverage greater than the amount of any first mortgage.

The correct answer is (c). *(CPA 1189 L-56)*

REQUIRED: The right obtained or the coverage not received by the buyer of title insurance.

DISCUSSION: Possible exceptions in a title policy include a taking under eminent domain, defects created by the insured, or those known by the insured but not by the company. Mechanic's liens, unpaid taxes, and utility easements may also be excepted.

Answer (a) is incorrect because title insurance does not clear the title. It merely indemnifies the buyer if (s)he suffers loss. Answer (b) is incorrect because title insurance is not assignable to a subsequent buyer. A new title examination is necessary before such a buyer can receive title insurance. Answer (d) is incorrect because title insurance for the benefit of an owner usually covers the purchase price. But a policy written to protect a mortgagee, such as a leader-bank, may be for the amount of the mortgage. The leader usually requires the buyer to obtain a separate policy for this purpose.

66. Buyer purchased a rural lot from a person purporting to be Grantor 10 years ago and recorded the deed. Buyer paid the property taxes but had not seen the lot in years. On a vacation trip in the area, Buyer inspected the lot and found it to be occupied. Occupant stated that she had received the land 5 years ago in a testamentary transfer from Grantor. The signatures on the deed and the will by Grantor were dissimilar. Under these circumstances,

a. Buyer has a valid title insurance claim.

b. Occupant has a valid title insurance claim.

c. Buyer and Occupant are tenants in common.

d. Occupant would have priority even if Grantor had actually given Buyer a deed 10 years ago.

The correct answer is (a). *(Publisher)*

REQUIRED: The outcome of a contest between an inter vivos transferee and a beneficiary under a will.

DISCUSSION: The deed received by Buyer was apparently a forgery. Accordingly, it conveyed no interest in the property, and recording it gave Buyer no rights against a subsequent transferee. This case should be distinguished from that in which an owner conveys the same property to more than one person. In that event, a subsequent bona fide purchaser for value who has no notice of the earlier conveyance will usually prevail. Thus, Buyer has incurred a loss of the kind that title insurance is meant to indemnify, that is, the loss resulting when title is actually in another person.

Answer (b) is incorrect because Occupant has a valid title obtained through Grantor's will. Answer (c) is incorrect because Buyer has no interest in the property. Answer (d) is incorrect because if Grantor had actually given Buyer a valid deed, Grantor could not have made an effective testamentary transfer even if Buyer had not recorded. Occupant would not have been a bona fide purchaser.

Questions 67 through 69 are based on the following information. Sue owned a 5-acre tract of land, 1 acre of which had previously been owned by Opal, but to which Sue had acquired title by adverse possession. Sue contracted to convey the full 5-acre tract to Peg, but the contract did not specify the quality of title Sue would convey.

67. Suppose Peg pays the purchase price and accepts the deed. Subsequently, Sue's title to the 1 acre proves inadequate and Opal ejects Peg from that acre. Peg sues Sue for damages. Which of the following statements applies most accurately to the determination of Peg's rights?

a. Sue's deed was fraudulent.

b. The terms of the deed control Sue's liability.

c. The only remedy available for breach of warranty of title is rescission.

d. Peg's rights are based on the implied covenant that the title conveyed shall be marketable.

The correct answer is (b). *(MBE Part II-5)*

REQUIRED: The rights of a buyer when the seller's title has proven inadequate.

DISCUSSION: A seller's liability for inadequate title depends on the terms of the deed given. For example, a warranty deed subjects the seller to full liability but a quitclaim deed subjects the seller to no liability.

Answer (a) is incorrect because in order for the deed to have been fraudulent, Sue must have conveyed it with knowledge that she was making a false representation and with an intention to deceive. Answer (c) is incorrect because damages are available for breach of warranty of title. Answer (d) is incorrect because the contract for sale does not survive closing unless expressly agreed; i.e., the deed merges the prior agreements and a lawsuit can only be based on the deed.

68. Suppose Sue's contract had called for the conveyance of a "good and marketable title." Pursuant to that contract, Peg paid the purchase price and accepted a deed from Sue containing no covenants of title. Sue's title to the 1 acre subsequently proved defective and Peg was ejected by Opal. Peg sued Sue. Which of the following results is most likely?

a. Peg will win because Sue's deed was fraudulent.

b. Peg will win because the terms of the deed control Sue's liability.

c. Sue will win because the terms of the deed control her liability.

d. Sue will win because the deed incorporates the terms of the contract.

The correct answer is (c). *(MBE Part II-6)*

REQUIRED: The result of a suit against the grantor when the grantee's title is defective.

DISCUSSION: The agreements in the contract for sale do not survive closing unless expressly agreed by the parties. By accepting a deed containing no covenants of title, Peg lost her right to a marketable title. Sue will have no liability since she made no covenants of title in the deed.

Answer (a) is incorrect because the absence of covenants of title is not fraudulent. It is common. Answer (b) is incorrect because although the terms of the deed control liability, Sue's deed made no covenants of title. Answer (d) is incorrect because a deed does not incorporate the terms of the contract; rather it merges any prior agreements.

69. Suppose that before closing, the house on the property had been totally destroyed by fire. In determining the rights of Sue and Peg, the court would most likely consider the doctrine of equitable

a. Marshaling.

b. Sequestration.

c. Subrogation.

d. Conversion.

The correct answer is (d). *(MBE Part II-7)*

REQUIRED: The doctrine most likely to be considered when real property is destroyed before closing.

DISCUSSION: Under the doctrine of equitable conversion, many states place the risk of loss by destruction on the purchaser after the contract is entered into. This transfer of risk of loss prior to the conveyance of legal title is based on the theory that the purchaser's contract right has been equitably converted to title since the contract is specifically enforceable. Since in equity the equitable title holder will prevail over the legal title holder (seller), it follows that the equitable title holder (buyer) has the risk of loss.

Answer (a) is incorrect because marshaling refers to the separation of assets into different categories so that they may be applied to claims according to an order of priority. Answer (b) is incorrect because sequestration is the seizure and holding of property until claims are satisfied. Answer (c) is incorrect because subrogation is the succession to the rights of another after paying the other's claim.

70. Seller and Buyer execute an agreement for the sale of real property. The jurisdiction in which the property is located recognizes the principle of equitable conversion and has no statute pertinent to this problem. Seller dies before closing and his will leaves his personal property to Perry and his real property to Rose. Which of the following is correct?

a. Death, an eventuality for which the parties could have provided, terminates the agreement if they did not so provide.

b. Rose is entitled to the proceeds of the sale when it closes, because the doctrine of equitable conversion does not apply to these circumstances.

c. Perry is entitled to the proceeds of the sale when it closes.

d. Title was rendered unmarketable by Seller's death.

The correct answer is (c). *(MBE Part IV-11)*

REQUIRED: The correct statement when a seller of real property dies after execution of the contract but before closing.

DISCUSSION: The doctrine of equitable conversion operates to transform the seller's interest into personal property. The underlying theory is that the buyer has acquired equitable title and the seller only has a contract right since the contract is specifically enforceable by the buyer. Perry, as the beneficiary of the personal property, would be entitled to the proceeds of the contract.

Answer (a) is incorrect because death does not automatically terminate an agreement to sell real property. The contract is enforceable against the estate. Answer (b) is incorrect because the doctrine applies to such circumstances as well as to the situation in which the realty is destroyed after the execution of the contract. Answer (d) is incorrect because the personal representative of the estate can convey a marketable title.

71. Which of the following warranty(ies) is(are) given by a general warranty deed?

I. The grantor owns the property being conveyed.
II. The grantee will not be disturbed in her possession of the property by the grantor or some third party's lawful claim of ownership.
III. The grantor has the right to convey the property.

a. I only.

b. I, II, and III.

c. I and III only.

d. II and III only.

The correct answer is (b). *(CPA 1186 L-58)*

REQUIRED: The warranty coverage given by a general warranty deed.

DISCUSSION: Of the deeds customarily used in modern conveyances, the warranty deed with full covenants (general warranty deed) provides the greatest protection for the buyer. The seller who gives such a deed warrants that (s)he has the authority to convey the property, that there are no undisclosed encumbrances, and that (s)he will defend the rights of the buyer against the claims of any other person.

Answers (a), (c), and (d) are incorrect because all these warranties are contained in a general warranty deed.

72. Park purchased Marshall's department store. At the closing, Park delivered a certified check for the balance due and Marshall gave Park a warranty deed with full covenants to the property. The deed

a. Must be recorded to be valid between the parties.

b. Must recite the actual consideration given by Park.

c. Must be in writing and contain the signature of both parties duly witnessed.

d. Usually represents an exclusive integration of the duties of the seller.

The correct answer is (d). *(CPA 582 L-52).*

REQUIRED: The effect of a warranty deed with full covenants.

DISCUSSION: The usual effect of a deed is to represent the complete and exclusive duties between the buyer and seller. A document intended to be complete and containing all the elements of an agreement is called an exclusive integration. Therefore, none of the provisions of the binder contract survive the delivery of the deed unless agreed to by the parties.

Answer (a) is incorrect because recording a deed has no effect on the agreement between the parties. It only protects the buyer against third parties. Delivery of the deed is essential to its effectiveness. Answer (b) is incorrect because a deed is valid without consideration. Answer (c) is incorrect because a deed need only contain the signature of the grantor.

73. A deed is used to convey real property. Which of the following statements is correct with respect to deeds?

a. A deed purporting to convey real property, but that omits the day of the month, is invalid.

b. A deed that lacks the signature of the grantor is valid.

c. A quitclaim deed that purports to transfer to the grantee "whatever title the grantor has" is invalid.

d. A deed that purports to convey real property and recites a consideration of $1 and other valuable consideration is valid.

The correct answer is (d). *(CPA 578 L-31)*

REQUIRED: The correct statement concerning a deed to real property.

DISCUSSION: A deed may convey effective title to real property even though no consideration is involved in the transaction. Therefore, a statement of "$1 and other valuable consideration" is sufficient. Furthermore, this is a common practice so as not to reveal (in the public records) the actual consideration. Binder contracts require consideration and more care must be exercised to satisfy the requirements of consideration.

Answer (a) is incorrect because omission of the day of the month of the conveyance from the deed does not invalidate the deed. Lack of a specific date simply means someone else may produce a deed with a specific date in that month, and claim his/her deed was earlier. Answer (b) is incorrect because a deed not signed by the grantor is invalid. Answer (c) is incorrect because all states recognize the validity of quitclaim deeds. In a quitclaim deed, the grantor simply conveys whatever title (s)he may have without making any warranties.

74. Which of the following deeds gives the grantee the least amount of protection?

a. Bargain and sale deed.

b. Grant deed.

c. Quitclaim deed.

d. Warranty deed.

The correct answer is (c). *(CPA 1188 L-58)*

REQUIRED: The deed that gives the grantee the least amount of protection.

DISCUSSION: A quitclaim deed merely relinquishes to the grantee whatever interest the grantor may have. Such a deed contains no covenants (warranties). Thus, it does not warrant that the grantor has a clear title or any title at all. If an adverse claimant prevails, the grantee will have no recourse against the grantor.

Answer (a) is incorrect because a bargain and sale deed is essentially a contract, and the seller is considered to imply that (s)he has a right to convey the property. It may also contain a covenant that the seller has not impaired the title. Answer (b) is incorrect because a grant (special warranty) deed provides warranty protection but only with respect to events occurring after the grantor acquired the property. Answer (d) is incorrect because a general warranty provides the fullest possible protection.

75. In order for a deed to be effective between the purchaser and seller of real estate, the deed must be

a. Delivered by the seller with an intent to transfer title.

b. Recorded within the permissible statutory time limits.

c. In writing and signed by the seller and purchaser.

d. Essentially in the same form as the contract for purchase and sale and include the actual sales price.

The correct answer is (a). *(CPA 586 L-42)*

REQUIRED: The condition for a deed to be effective between the purchaser and seller of real estate.

DISCUSSION: Real property cannot be conveyed unless a valid delivery and acceptance of the deed have occurred. The grantor must intend to transfer title and surrender control of the document. Subsequent return of the deed or destruction of the deed, even if intentional, is not sufficient to rescind the conveyance. A reconveyance is required.

Answer (b) is incorrect because recording protects against claims by third parties but has no effect on the grantor-grantee relationship. Answer (c) is incorrect because only the seller must sign. Answer (d) is incorrect because the deed must contain a recital of consideration but not the actual price; e.g., the phrase "$1 and other valuable consideration" is sufficient. Also, a deed's form is quite different from that of a contract of purchase and sale.

76. The special warranty deed

a. Makes no warranties but simply conveys whatever interest the grantor has.

b. Warrants that the grantor has not encumbered the property or transferred any interest in it to another person.

c. Includes a covenant that the owner has the right to transfer a fee simple title.

d. Warrants that the grantee will have quiet enjoyment of the property.

The correct answer is (b). *(Publisher)*

REQUIRED: The true statement about a special warranty deed.

DISCUSSION: A special warranty deed is one that contains some warranties but less than a full warranty deed (which warrants against all lawful claims). Answer (b) is an example of one that transfers the grantor's interest and warrants that (s)he has not encumbered the property or transferred any interest in it to another person. It does not contain a warranty that the acts of others have not created a defect in the title.

Answer (a) is incorrect because it describes a quitclaim deed. Answers (c) and (d) are incorrect because a general warranty deed provides such warranties.

77. In the majority of states, a deed must be signed by

a. The grantor and grantee but not witnessed or acknowledged.

b. The grantor and grantee and acknowledged.

c. The grantor but not the grantee.

d. The grantor and the grantee and both witnessed and acknowledged.

The correct answer is (c). *(Publisher)*

REQUIRED: The true statement about execution of a deed.

DISCUSSION: While the names of both appear on the deed, the grantor but not the grantee is generally required to sign. Many states also require the deed to be witnessed and acknowledged before a notary. Notarization is useful in establishing the validity of any required signature.

Answers (a), (b), and (d) are incorrect because the grantee need not sign the deed. The requirements of witnesses and acknowledgment before a notary vary among the states.

78. The failure to record a deed will

a. Not affect the rights between the parties to the deed.

b. Constitute a fraud upon the creditors of the seller.

c. Defeat the rights of the buyer if the seller subsequently conveys the property to a third party who has actual knowledge of the prior conveyance.

d. Be disregarded in respect to the rights of subsequent third parties if the deed is a mere quitclaim.

The correct answer is (a). *(CPA 1176 L-43)*

REQUIRED: The effect of failure to record a deed.

DISCUSSION: The failure to record a deed does not affect the rights between the grantor and grantee. The lawful delivery of a valid deed is sufficient to establish the rights between the parties to the transaction. The purpose of recording a deed is to protect against third parties.

Answer (b) is incorrect because failure to record is not a fraud upon any parties unless it is accompanied by some fraudulent conduct. Answer (c) is incorrect because a subsequent purchaser with knowledge will not prevail over an unrecorded deed in most jurisdictions. Only a subsequent good faith purchaser without knowledge will usually prevail over an unrecorded deed. Answer (d) is incorrect because the type of deed is irrelevant to the recording requirement. A subsequent innocent purchaser from the same grantor would, under most recording statutes, take free of the interests of a preceding grantee regardless of who may have received a quitclaim deed.

79. Purdy purchased real property from Hart and received a warranty deed with full covenants. Recordation of this deed is

a. Not necessary if the deed provides that recordation is not required.

b. Necessary to vest the purchaser's legal title to the property conveyed.

c. Required primarily for the purpose of providing the local taxing authorities with the information necessary to assess taxes.

d. Irrelevant if the subsequent party claiming superior title had actual notice of the unrecorded deed.

The correct answer is (d). *(CPA 583 L-56)*

REQUIRED: The true statement about recordation of a deed.

DISCUSSION: Recordation gives constructive notice to a subsequent purchaser who then cannot qualify as a bona fide purchaser and take despite the earlier transfer. If the deed is not recorded, a purchaser without actual notice or another form of constructive notice may prevail over an earlier grantee of the same grantor.

Answer (a) is incorrect because the language of the deed does not determine the need to have it recorded. Answer (b) is incorrect because recordation has no effect on the rights of the parties to the transaction against each other. It is a means of giving notice to third parties who lack actual notice. Answer (c) is incorrect because notice is the primary purpose of recordation.

Questions 80 and 81 are based on Bean, who on July 1 deeded her home to Park. The deed was never recorded. On July 5, Bean deeded the same home to Noll. On July 9, Noll executed a deed, conveying his title to the same home to Baxter. On July 10, Noll and Baxter duly recorded their respective deeds.

80. If Noll and Baxter are bona fide purchasers for value, which of the following statements is correct?

a. Baxter's interest is superior to Park's.

b. Bean's deed to Park was void as between Bean and Park because it was not recorded.

c. Bean's deed to Noll was void because she had no interest to convey.

d. Baxter can recover the purchase price from Noll.

The correct answer is (a). *(CPA 585 L-53)*

REQUIRED: The true statement about the priority of interests.

DISCUSSION: Three kinds of recording statutes are in force. Under a notice statute, an unrecorded deed is ineffective against a subsequent bona fide purchaser (for value and without notice). Under a notice-race statute, the subsequent bona fide purchaser must record before the prior grantee. In two states, a race is in effect: regardless of notice, the first to record prevails. Since Noll and Baxter were bona fide purchasers, they would prevail in every state since they recorded before Park.

Answer (b) is incorrect because recordation has no effect on the rights of the parties to the conveyance against each other. Answer (c) is incorrect because before Park records, Bean has the power to make an effective conveyance to a subsequent bona fide purchaser who complies with the recording statute. Answer (d) is incorrect because Noll and Baxter are protected by recording. Baxter has a title superior to Park's and no basis for recovery against Noll.

81. In order for Noll's deed from Bean to be effective it must

a. Contain the actual purchase price paid by Noll.

b. Be signed by Noll.

c. Include a satisfactory description of the property.

d. Be recorded with Bean's seal affixed to the deed.

The correct answer is (c). *(CPA 585 L-52)*

REQUIRED: The condition precedent to effectiveness of the deed.

DISCUSSION: A description of the property transferred is required in every deed. The description should provide the precise location of the land. The system used is commonly either rectangular survey, metes and bounds (by landmarks), or plat (a recorded document subdividing a tract).

Answer (a) is incorrect because actual consideration need not be stated. Answer (b) is incorrect because the grantee need not sign. Answer (d) is incorrect because modern deeds need not be sealed.

Questions 82 through 86 are based on the following information. By way of a gift, Pat executed a deed naming his son, Mike, as grantee. The deed contained descriptions as follows:

1) All of my land and dwelling known as 44 Main Street, Midtown, United States, being 1 acre.
2) All that part of my farm, being a square with 200-foot sides, the southeast corner of which is in the north line of my neighbor, John Brown.

The deed contained covenants of general warranty, quiet enjoyment, and right to convey.

Pat handed the deed to Mike who immediately returned it to his father for safekeeping. His father kept it in his safe deposit box. The deed was not recorded.

The property at 44 Main Street covered 7/8 of an acre of land, had a dwelling and a garage situated thereon, and was subject to a right of way, described in prior deeds, in favor of Jack, a neighbor. Pat owned no other land on Main Street. Jack had not used the right of way for ten years and it was not visible on inspection of the property.

---

82. The description of 44 Main Street was

a. Sufficient, because the discrepancy in area is not fatal.

b. Not sufficient, because it contained no metes and bounds.

c. Not sufficient, because the acreage given was not correct.

d. Not sufficient, because a deed purporting to convey more than a grantor owns is void.

The correct answer is (a). *(MBE 272 72)*

REQUIRED: The correct statement regarding the description of 44 Main Street.

DISCUSSION: An effective conveyance of real property requires a legally sufficient description of the land. The description need not conform to any special requirements provided it is sufficient to reasonably locate the property. 44 Main Street is sufficient even with the discrepancy in area because Pat owned no other land with which to confuse it.

Answer (b) is incorrect because the description need not contain a surveyor's description by metes and boundaries. Answer (c) is incorrect because the discrepancy in acreage is not a fatal flaw. Answer (d) is incorrect because such a deed is not void since it would be effective to convey the entire interest actually owned by the grantor.

83. The description of part of Pat's farm

a. Is sufficient if consideration has been paid.

b. Is sufficient because no ambiguity therein appears on the face of the deed.

c. Could be enforced if the deed contained a covenant of seisin.

d. Is insufficient because of vagueness.

The correct answer is (d). *(MBE 272 73)*

REQUIRED: The correct statement concerning the description of part of a farm.

DISCUSSION: The description of part of Pat's farm is legally insufficient since the land conveyed cannot be accurately determined. The description could refer to many 200-foot square parcels. The usual remedy when a deed is defective is to reform it.

Answer (a) is incorrect because consideration does not cure an insufficient description. Answer (b) is incorrect because the description is ambiguous since the land described could not be located with certainty. Answer (c) is incorrect because the covenant of seisin has nothing to do with the sufficiency of the description. The covenant of seisin is a covenant that the grantor owns the interest that (s)he is attempting to convey.

Note: Questions 84-86 are based on information provided on page 511.

84. Ignoring any question of the adequacy of description, the deed

a. Transferred a property interest to Mike which he could enforce against Pat.

b. Transferred nothing to Mike because it was not recorded.

c. Transferred nothing to Mike because it was never accepted by him.

d. Was not delivered to Mike because Pat maintained custody of the deed.

The correct answer is (a). *(MBE 272 74)*

REQUIRED: Whether the deed was effective aside from any inadequacy in the description.

DISCUSSION: Delivery is necessary for a deed to be effective. Delivery occurred when Pat handed the deed to Mike. Once it was delivered, Mike could enforce his interest against Pat.

Answer (b) is incorrect because recording merely protects the grantee against third parties and is unnecessary as between the grantor and grantee. Answer (c) is incorrect because the facts indicate that Mike accepted the deed and returned it to his father only for safekeeping. Answer (d) is incorrect because mere physical custody of the deed by the grantor does not invalidate a prior delivery of the deed.

85. Mike made a title search a few months after Pat showed him the deed and discovered the existence of Jack's right of way. Mike could recover substantial damages from Pat for breach of the covenant of

a. Right to convey.

b. Right to convey if Jack has commenced using the right of way.

c. Quiet enjoyment.

d. Quiet enjoyment if Jack has commenced using the right of way and Mike had given consideration for the deed.

The correct answer is (d). *(MBE 272 75)*

REQUIRED: The covenant for breach of which Mike could recover damages due to the easement.

DISCUSSION: The covenant of quiet enjoyment is a promise by the grantor that the grantee will not be disturbed in possession or enjoyment of the property by the lawful claim of a third party. Until Jack uses the easement, Mike's use of the land is not interfered with, nor is the covenant violated. Furthermore, Mike has no damages unless he gave consideration for the deed.

Answers (a) and (b) are incorrect because the covenant of right to convey is simply a promise by the grantor that he has a right to make the conveyance. Answer (c) is incorrect because a breach of the covenant of quiet enjoyment does not occur until such enjoyment is actually disturbed.

86. Assume that Jack continues not to use his right of way as such but erects a tool shed within the boundaries of the right of way on Mike's lot. Which of the following statements is most accurate?

a. Mike can recover from Pat for breach of the covenant of quiet enjoyment.

b. Mike can obtain an injunction requiring Jack to remove the shed.

c. Jack is entitled to maintain the shed on the right of way so long as it does not become a fixture.

d. The existence of the shed will not inhibit a conveyance of marketable title by Mike.

The correct answer is (b). *(MBE 272 76)*

REQUIRED: The rights of the parties if a tool shed is erected on a right of way.

DISCUSSION: Jack's right of way is a nonpossessory right to cross Mike's land. Such a right would not include the erection of structures within the boundaries of the right of way. Mike could obtain an injunction or order of the court requiring removal of the shed.

Answer (a) is incorrect because the covenant of quiet enjoyment applies to legal claims by third parties, not to improper uses of existing rights. Answer (c) is incorrect because Jack has no right to maintain the shed on the right of way even if it is not a fixture. Answer (d) is incorrect because the presence of the shed suggests the existence of a possessory interest which is otherwise undisclosed. This would indicate title may not be marketable.

87. Joe and Minnie Sixpack just purchased a new house from the contractor who built it. Under the law in their state, the seller of a new house is required to provide a warranty for at least one year against defects in workmanship. Under the typical statute, which of the following would be covered by the warranty?

a. A serious crack in the foundation.

b. A mechanic's lien for work performed on the house by a subcontractor who was not paid by the contractor.

c. Installation of fixtures in the bathrooms different from those agreed upon.

d. Construction of a sidewalk by the city between the house and the road when the Sixpacks thought they had all rights to the land up to the road.

The correct answer is (a). *(Publisher)*

REQUIRED: The legal protection given by a new home warranty against defects in workmanship.

DISCUSSION: It has become more common in recent years for new homes to carry warranties against defects in workmanship. Some state statutes impose these warranties. They generally cover such items as cracks in the foundation and any other flaws in the construction.

Answer (b) is incorrect because a mechanic's lien would not be covered by a warranty against defects in workmanship but would be included in the warranties given in a general warranty deed. Answer (c) is incorrect because installing the wrong fixtures would be a contractual breach rather than a breach of a new home warranty. Answer (d) is incorrect because the Sixpacks would be deemed to have constructive notice of any right of way or easement held by the city (from the real property records). The warranty in question is not against encumbrances.

88. Which of the following is a true statement about the federal Real Estate Settlement Procedures Act (RESPA)?

a. It applies to all sales of residential real estate.

b. Advance payments from borrowers to lenders are prohibited.

c. Lenders cannot specify a title company or require a prepayment penalty.

d. It is intended to prevent abuses such as kickbacks.

The correct answer is (d). *(Publisher)*

REQUIRED: The true statement about RESPA.

DISCUSSION: The Act is a consumer protection measure intended to promote disclosure of information, reduce settlement (closing) costs, and prohibit payment of unearned fees and kickbacks. The lender is required to make certain disclosures to the buyer and to permit the buyer an opportunity to obtain advance estimates of closing costs. The mandated use of the Uniform Settlement Statement helps to clarify what costs are to be paid by the buyer and seller. Abusive practices, such as kickbacks, are generally prohibited. One may not receive payment for providing a referral to a given bank, insurer, or attorney.

Answer (a) is incorrect because the Act only applies when a federally related mortgage loan is made on a residential building other than a large apartment house. Answer (b) is incorrect because lenders may collect reasonable advance payments from borrowers for items such as insurance and taxes. Answer (c) is incorrect because a seller may not specify a title insurer to be used by the buyer but a lender may. Also, a lender is permitted to charge the seller a prepayment penalty if the new mortgage loan is not made with the same institution.

89. Mark has obtained title to land by adverse possession. He

a. Can convey good title to a subsequent purchaser.

b. Must record his interest in the property in order to perfect his interest against the holder of record.

c. Must have occupied the property initially with the permission of the owner of record.

d. Need not have occupied the land for an uninterrupted period of time as long as the sum total of years he has occupied the land is equal to or greater than the prescribed period.

The correct answer is (a). *(CPA 576 L-24)*

REQUIRED: The true statement concerning title by adverse possession.

DISCUSSION: A person who has satisfied the requirements for obtaining title by adverse possession has a fee simple absolute interest in the land. Such a person can therefore convey good title to a subsequent purchaser by ordinary conveyance methods. However, such a title is not marketable because the records will not show the interest of the adverse possessor. A suit to quiet title is usually brought so that the court's judgment can be recorded to prove the adverse possession.

Answer (b) is incorrect because a person who has title by adverse possession can prevail over the holder of record, although a lawsuit may be required to quiet title. Furthermore, there is nothing to record until a judgment is obtained. Answer (c) is incorrect because a person who obtains title by adverse possession must have done so without the permission of the owner of record. Answer (d) is incorrect because adverse possession requires continuous occupation for the prescribed period.

90. Dunbar Dairy Farms, Inc., pursuant to an expansion of its operations in Tuberville, purchased from Moncrief a 140-acre farm strategically located in the general area in which Dunbar wishes to expand. Unknown to Dunbar, Cranston, an adjoining landowner, had fenced off approximately 5 acres of the land in question. Cranston installed a well, constructed a storage shed and garage on the fenced-off land, and continuously farmed and occupied the 5 acres for approximately 22 years prior to Dunbar's purchase. Cranston did this under the mistaken belief that the 5 acres of land belonged to him. Which of the following is a correct answer in regard to the 5 acres occupied by Cranston?

a. Under the circumstances Cranston has title to the 5 acres.

b. As long as Moncrief had properly recorded a deed which includes the 5 acres in dispute, Moncrief had good title to the five acres.

c. At best, the only right that Cranston could obtain is an easement.

d. If Dunbar is unaware of Cranston's presence and Cranston has failed to record, Dunbar can oust him as a trespasser.

The correct answer is (a). *(CPA 1179 L-41)*

REQUIRED: The correct statement concerning land fenced by a neighbor.

DISCUSSION: Title to real property may be acquired by adverse possession if four requirements are satisfied. First, actual and exclusive possession of land must be taken. Cranston's fencing, farming, etc. constituted actual and exclusive possession. Second, the possession must be open and notorious. Cranston did this since his/her possession was in such a manner that the owner knew or should have known of the possession. Third, the possession must be hostile to the rights of the owner. Absent permission from Moncrief, the activities of Cranston would satisfy the requirement of hostile possession. Fourth, possession must continue uninterrupted for the full statutory term, which may be as long as 20 years. Under the circumstances, it appears that Cranston has title to the 5 acres by way of adverse possession.

Answer (b) is incorrect because adverse possession will prevail against a properly recorded deed. Answer (c) is incorrect because Cranston can obtain title to the property by way of adverse possession. Answer (d) is incorrect because as a purchaser of real property, Dunbar is considered to have constructive notice of Cranston's presence. Cranston has acquired title by adverse possession, has nothing to record, and cannot be ousted as a trespasser.

91. Real property may be transferred in many ways other than by private sale. Which of the following is not such a means of transfer?

a. Avulsion and accretion.

b. Eminent domain and escheat.

c. Testamentary disposition and descent.

d. Sale by public official and dedication.

The correct answer is (a). *(Publisher)*

REQUIRED: The methods that do not result in a transfer of realty.

DISCUSSION: Accretion is the gradual increase in the land caused by the deposit of material by water. Avulsion is the sudden increase in the land by action of water, for example, by a flood. Accretion passes title to the riparian owner to whose land the addition has been made. Avulsion does not.

Answer (b) is incorrect because the government may condemn property under its eminent domain power for a public purpose if just compensation is awarded. Escheat is the transfer to the state of the property of one who dies intestate and without heirs. Answer (c) is incorrect because real property may be transferred by will or under the intestacy statute. Answer (d) is incorrect because real property is sometimes sold at a judicial sale to satisfy a judgment, mortgage, or unpaid taxes. Dedication is the gift to a governmental unit for a specified purpose, e.g., a park or street.

92. Which of the following remedies is more likely to be available for a breach of a contract to sell real rather than personal property?

a. Rescission.

b. Specific performance.

c. Damages.

d. Replevin.

The correct answer is (b). *(Publisher)*

REQUIRED: The remedy more likely to be available for a breach involving real rather than personal property.

DISCUSSION: The equitable remedy of specific performance will be granted when the legal remedy of damages is insufficient, for example, because the subject matter is unique. Each parcel of realty is considered unique so contracts to sell real estate are specifically enforceable. While contracts for the sale of antiques, heirlooms, and other rare items are also specifically enforceable, most contracts concerning personal property are not.

Answers (a) and (c) are incorrect because the nonbreaching party may, if the breach is material, elect to rescind and not be bound by the contract or to bring suit for damages. Either remedy is customarily available for personal property. Answer (d) is incorrect because replevin is an action to recover personal property taken unlawfully.

CHAPTER TWENTY-ONE
MORTGAGES AND OTHER SECURITY DEVICES

This chapter overlaps with bankruptcy, consumer and credit law, suretyship, and secured transactions. It should be read with the chapters on those topics.

21.1 Mortgages and Deeds of Trust

1. Which of the following is a true statement about the real estate mortgage?

a. The mortgage is the debt owed by the mortgagor to the mortgagee.

b. The mortgage is security for the debt owed by the mortgagee to the mortgagor.

c. The substance of the transaction is that the mortgagee conveys ownership of the property to the mortgagor subject to nullification by payment of the debt.

d. The mortgagor executes a promissory note and a mortgage evidencing the debt and the conveyance of a security interest, respectively.

The correct answer is (d). *(Publisher)*

REQUIRED: The true statement about a real estate mortgage.

DISCUSSION: Regardless of the words used in the mortgage document (grant, bargain, sell, convey, etc.) purporting to transfer the property to the mortgagee, most states recognize the mortgage as a security interest. The mortgagor-debtor signs a promissory note for the sum borrowed from the mortgagee-creditor. (S)he also signs a mortgage document representing the right of the mortgagee to seek judicial foreclosure of the mortgage and sale of the property upon default. The mortgage is an interest in real property, so it should comply with the requirements of contract law, the Statute of Frauds, and the execution of deeds.

Answer (a) is incorrect because the mortgage is the interest in the realty that is security for the debt. Answer (b) is incorrect because the mortgagor-debtor conveys an interest (the mortgage) in the realty to the mortgagee-lender. Answer (c) is incorrect because regardless of whether title is conveyed to the mortgagee-lender, almost all states treat the mortgagor-debtor as at the least the equitable owner of the realty.

2. Which of the following statements pertaining to a mortgage on a building is incorrect?

a. The mortgagor customarily retains legal title to the building despite the mortgage.

b. The recording of the mortgage is necessary to validate the rights and liabilities of the mortgagor and mortgagee against each other.

c. The mortgage must be in writing and signed by the mortgagor.

d. The mortgage must contain a description of the property subject to the mortgage.

The correct answer is (b). *(CPA 586 L-47)*

REQUIRED: The incorrect statement about a mortgage on a building.

DISCUSSION: Recording the transfer of an interest in realty (whether a deed, mortgage, contract to sell, lien, or judgment) does not affect the rights of the parties to the transaction. Instead, it operates to give constructive notice of the interest to third parties. Thus, recording is only necessary to protect the rights of the mortgagee against third parties who do not have actual notice of the mortgage.

Answer (a) is incorrect because in the majority of states, title is not transferred by a mortgage. The mortgagee is regarded as a secured party and the mortgagor retains all the incidents of ownership. Answer (c) is incorrect because a mortgage is an interest in real property and is therefore within the statute of Frauds. The mortgage must be in writing and signed by the party to be bound (the mortgagor). Answer (d) is incorrect because the mortgage must be executed with the same formalities as a deed. Hence, it must contain a legally sufficient description of the property, that is, one precise enough to accurately determine the location of the land.

3. Trudy purchased a tract of land giving a down payment and a promissory note for the balance. Trudy received a warranty deed for a fee simple title. Another document was filed in the real property records indicating that the seller had a security interest in the land which could be satisfied by foreclosure in the event the promissory note was not paid. This debt arrangement is called

a. A mortgage under the title theory.

b. A mortgage under the lien theory.

c. A deed of trust.

d. An installment land contract.

The correct answer is (b). *(Publisher)*

REQUIRED: The debt arrangement in which a security interest is taken in land.

DISCUSSION: A mortgage is a security interest in real property. Under the lien theory, a mortgagor holds the title and has a right to possession. The mortgagee has a security interest (lien) enforceable against the real property if the mortgagor defaults. Satisfaction of the debt is through a judicially ordered foreclosure and a sale.

Answer (a) is incorrect because under the title theory, the mortgagee has a title that is voidable if the mortgagor makes the proper payments. Upon default, the mortgagee has an immediate right to possession, and the mortgagor has no right to a forced judicial sale or redemption. Today, very few states strictly observe the title theory. Answer (c) is incorrect because a deed of trust creates a lien in favor of a third party (trustee) in trust to hold as the security for the debt owed to the seller. Answer (d) is incorrect because an installment land contract is an agreement between the buyer and the seller that the seller will retain title on default by the purchaser. Traditionally, the seller was also able to keep any payments received, but this is changing in many jurisdictions.

4. Donaldson, Inc. loaned Watson Enterprises $50,000 secured by a real estate mortgage which included the land, buildings, and "all other property which is added to the real property or which is considered as real property as a matter of law." Wilkins also loaned Watson $25,000 and obtained a security interest in all of Watson's "inventory, accounts receivable, fixtures, and other tangible personal property." Watson defaulted and there is insufficient property to fully satisfy the two creditors. There is some doubt as to the nature of certain property and Donaldson is attempting to include all the property under the terms and scope of its real property mortgage. What is the probable outcome for Donaldson?

a. Donaldson will prevail in that real property is preferred over personal property.

b. Assuming Donaldson was the first lender and duly filed its real property mortgage, Donaldson will prevail in respect to all property necessary to satisfy its $50,000 loan.

c. If the fixtures in question are detachable trade fixtures, Donaldson will not prevail in its attempt to include them.

d. The problem will be decided by taking all of Watson's property (real and personal) subject to the two secured creditors' claims and dividing it in proportion to the respective debts.

The correct answer is (c). *(CPA 577 L-37)*

REQUIRED: The property covered by a mortgage on real property.

DISCUSSION: Trade fixtures are personal property and are not subject to a real property mortgage unless expressly covered. Donaldson's mortgage will only apply to realty, buildings, and true fixtures.

Answer (a) is incorrect because real property receives no preference and Donaldson's mortgage does not cover personal property. Answer (b) is incorrect because there is no priority between personal property security interests and mortgages. Donaldson can only recover against the real property. Answer (d) is incorrect because each creditor is only entitled to the property secured by his/her/its lien.

5. Which of the following statements is correct concerning a mortgagee's transfer of the note and mortgage, and the mortgagor's transfer of the property.

a. The mortgagee cannot transfer the note and mortgage because it is a personal contract between the parties.

b. If the mortgagor transfers the property, (s)he will also be relieved of the mortgage.

c. The mortgagee can transfer the note and mortgage by an assignment in a lien theory state.

d. The mortgagor can transfer the property without paying off the mortgage if there is a due on sale clause.

The correct answer is (c). *(Publisher)*

REQUIRED: The correct statement concerning the assignment of a mortgage or the mortgaged property.

DISCUSSION: In a lien theory state, the mortgage is merely a security interest in the real property. Thus, it can be transferred by an assignment rather than by deed as required in a title theory state.

Answer (a) is incorrect because a mortgagee is free to transfer the note and mortgage since they represent only a right to payment and security therefor. Answer (b) is incorrect because a mortgagor who transfers the mortgaged property remains liable on the debt unless the purchaser assumes the mortgage and the mortgagee releases the original mortgagor (e.g., by a novation). Answer (d) is incorrect because due on sale clauses are generally being upheld now, and federally chartered lenders are permitted to require them.

6. In general, which of the following statements is correct with respect to a real estate mortgage?

a. The mortgage must be in writing and signed by both the mortgagor (borrower) and mortgagee (lender).

b. The mortgagee may assign the mortgage to a third party without the mortgagor's consent.

c. The mortgage need not contain a description of the real estate covered by the mortgage.

d. The mortgage must contain the actual amount of the underlying debt and the rate of interest.

The correct answer is (b). *(CPA 588 L-52)*

REQUIRED: The correct statement with respect to real estate mortgages.

DISCUSSION: In a lien theory state, the mortgage is merely a security interest in the real property. Thus, it can be transferred by an assignment without the mortgagor's consent rather than by deed, which would be required in a title theory state. The majority of states adhere to the lien theory. The note and mortgage are assignable in most states because they represent only a right to payment and security therefor.

Answer (a) is incorrect because the mortgage requires the signature of the mortgagor only. Answer (c) is incorrect because a legally sufficient description of the property must be included in the mortgage. Answer (d) is incorrect because even though the amount of indebtedness and the rate of interest are usually included on most mortgages, they are not legally required.

7. Pix borrowed $80,000 from Null Bank. Pix gave Null a promissory note and mortgage. Subsequently, Null assigned the note and mortgage to Reed. Reed failed to record the assignment or notify Pix of the assignment. If Pix pays Null pursuant to the note, Pix will

a. Be primarily liable to Reed for the payments made to Null.

b. Be secondarily liable to Reed for the payments made to Null.

c. Not be liable to Reed for the payments made to Null because Reed failed to record the assignment.

d. Not be liable to Reed for the payments made to Null because Reed failed to give Pix notice of the assignment.

The correct answer is (d). *(CPA 1188 L-18)*

REQUIRED: The consequences if the debtor pays the assignor.

DISCUSSION: The debtor (Pix) will not be held either primarily or secondarily liable to the assignee (Reed) for payments made to the assignor (Null). An assignee's failure to give notice to the debtor of the assignment permits discharge of the obligation by payment to the assignor rather than the assignee. However, the assignor will have a duty to account to the assignee.

Answers (a) and (b) are incorrect because the debtor (Pix) is neither primarily nor secondarily liable to the assignee (Reed) for payments made to the assignor (Null) prior to receiving notice of the assignment. Answer (c) is incorrect because recording gives constructive notice to parties who may have competing interests in the mortgage but is not sufficient against the debtor. An assignee must give some form of actual notice because expecting the mortgage debtor to search the property records before making each payment would be unfair.

8. An acceleration clause in a mortgage

a. Is an unconstitutional restraint on alienation if embodied in a due-on-sale clause.

b. Will be deemed unconscionable if embodied in a due-on-default clause.

c. May prevent the mortgagor from further encumbering the property.

d. That requires full payment on sale is usually accompanied by a prepayment penalty clause.

The correct answer is (c). *(Publisher)*

REQUIRED: The true statement about acceleration clauses.

DISCUSSION: Acceleration clauses permit the mortgagee to require full payment of the obligation upon occurrence of stipulated conditions. Encumbering the property by nonpayment of taxes, creation of a mechanic's lien, giving a second mortgage, establishing an easement, or agreeing to a restrictive covenant are conditions that might give a right of acceleration. Sale of the collateral and default are other possible grounds.

Answer (a) is incorrect because the due-on-sale clause has been upheld by the Supreme Court for use in federally related mortgages. Many states now also permit use of this clause, which operates to protect the mortgagee from a purchaser who is not credit worthy. Answer (b) is incorrect because a standard acceleration clause allows the mortgagee to call the entire loan when a mortgagor defaults in some provision of the mortgage. Answer (d) is incorrect because a prepayment penalty clause in conjunction with a due-on-sale clause would probably be unconscionable.

9. The payment of a mortgage

a. Gives a mortgagee a right to a release enforceable by a court.

b. Imposes a duty on the mortgagee to give a satisfaction of the debt.

c. Ordinarily is not recorded.

d. Gives a mortgagor a right to a reversion of title.

The correct answer is (b). *(Publisher)*

REQUIRED: The effect of payment of a mortgage.

DISCUSSION: Payment of the debt imposes a duty on the mortgagee to give a written release (satisfaction) to the mortgagor. When recorded, the release will remove the encumbrance from the title. Clearing the title obviously increases the property's marketability.

Answer (a) is incorrect because it is the mortgagor who has made the payments and is entitled to a release so the title will be clear. Answer (c) is incorrect because the satisfaction must be recorded to remove the lien from the recorded title. Answer (d) is incorrect because the majority of states recognize the lien theory of mortgages, so the mortgagee has no title to be voided by payment.

10. Land contracts and trust deeds are alternatives to real estate mortgages that may be more beneficial to lenders. Which of the following is true?

a. The principal difference between a trust deed and a mortgage concerns foreclosure.

b. A trust deed permits the lender to hold the deed in trust until the buyer pays the obligation.

c. A land contract permits immediate forfeiture of the premises upon default although title is held by the buyer.

d. Under a land contract, the buyer holds the equitable but not legal title, and, in most states, the relation of lender and buyer is essentially that of landlord and tenant.

The correct answer is (a). *(Publisher)*

REQUIRED: The true statement about land contracts and trust deeds.

DISCUSSION: In most jurisdictions, mortgage foreclosure is a costly and time-consuming procedure. Suit must be brought, the property must be sold at a public auction, and a redemption period is often allowed for. The trust deed's principal difference from the mortgage is the handling of this process. After the buyer receives the deed from the seller, (s)he gives a trust deed to a trustee who holds it on behalf of the lender. Upon default, the trustee sells the property and pays the lender the amount of the debt. The balance is paid to the debtor. This process involves no judicial foreclosure.

Answer (b) is incorrect because a third party acts as trustee. Answers (c) and (d) are incorrect because under the traditional land sale contract (a conditional sale), the lender (who is frequently the seller) retains the deed and legal title until the last installment is paid. The buyer has the right of possession and equitable ownership. Upon default, some states permit the eviction of the debtor, forfeiture of his/her equity, and a resolution of the matter more rapidly than foreclosure of a mortgage or sale of a trust deed. However, the trend is to treat land sale contracts in much the same way as mortgages, e.g., by requiring the return of the debtor's equity and a redemption period.

21.2 Recording and Priorities

11. Lake purchased a home from Walsh for $95,000. Lake obtained a $60,000 loan from Safe Bank to finance the purchase, executing a promissory note and mortgage. The recording of the mortgage by Safe

a. Gives the world actual notice of Safe's interest.

b. Protects Safe's interest against the claims of subsequent bona fide purchasers for value.

c. Is necessary in order that Safe have rights against Lake under the promissory note.

d. Is necessary to protect Safe's interest against the claim of a subsequent transferee who does not give value.

The correct answer is (b). *(CPA 585 L-55)*

REQUIRED: The effect of the mortgagee's recording the mortgage.

DISCUSSION: If the mortgagee's interest is recorded, a subsequent purchaser has notice of the mortgage and will take subject to it. Recording will also give Safe priority over a subsequent mortgagee.

Answer (a) is incorrect because recording only gives constructive notice to everyone. However, actual and constructive notice are equivalent for most purposes. Answer (c) is incorrect because the contract between Safe and Lake is sufficient to establish their rights against each other. Answer (d) is incorrect because bona fide purchasers are protected by a public policy that favors free transferability of realty, but that policy does not protect those who do not take for value, such as heirs, devisees, and donees.

12. Watts gave a mortgage on a vacant lot to Fast to secure payment of a note. Fast assigned the note and mortgage to Beal who paid 85% of the face value for it. Neither Fast nor Beal recorded the mortgage. Subsequently, Fast assigned the same note and mortgage to Rusk who paid 75% of the face value for it and who had no notice of the prior assignment to Beal. Rusk promptly recorded the mortgage and the assignment. Watts has made no payments on the note. The jurisdiction has a notice-type of recordation statute. Under the circumstances

a. The assignments to Beal and Rusk are ineffective because Fast failed to record the mortgage.

b. Equity will require that Beal and Rusk share in the proceeds of the note equally as their interests may appear.

c. Rusk is entitled to recover only 75% of the fact value of the note.

d. Rusk is entitled to the full face amount of the Watts note.

The correct answer is (d). *(CPA 1186 L-54)*

REQUIRED: The effect of successive assignments of the same mortgage in a jurisdiction with a notice-type recording statute.

DISCUSSION: Under a notice-type statute, an unrecorded interest in real property is ineffective against a subsequent bona fide purchaser (for value and without notice) even if such a purchaser does not record. Under a notice-race statute, the bona fide purchaser must record before the prior grantee. Under a pure race statute, the first to record has priority regardless of notice. Accordingly, Rusk would prevail over Beal regardless of the type of recording statute in force. Rusk will be entitled to the full face value of the note despite having paid a discounted amount. Courts ordinarily do not question the value of the consideration unless the contract is oppressively unfair. Such is not the case here because transfer of a note at a discount is customary.

Answer (a) is incorrect because an assignment by a mortgagee-assignor is effective between the parties even though the mortgage is unrecorded. Recording simply protects the mortgagee's interest against parties who subsequently take interests in the property from the mortgagor. Answer (b) is incorrect because Beal's interest was completely extinguished by the transfer to Rusk. Answer (c) is incorrect because Rusk presumably contracted for the full face value and is entitled thereto unless the consideration paid is deemed unconscionable.

13. In a notice-type recordation jurisdiction, failure by the mortgagee to record its mortgage

a. Releases the mortgagor (borrower) from the underlying obligation to pay.

b. Permits a subsequent mortgagee without knowledge of the prior mortgage to have a superior security interest.

c. Permits a subsequent purchaser for value with knowledge of the mortgage to take the property free of the prior security interest.

d. Permits a subsequent mortgagee with knowledge of the prior mortgage to have a superior security interest provided it promptly records the mortgage.

The correct answer is (b). *(CPA 1186 L-55)*

REQUIRED: The effect of failure to record given a notice-type statute.

DISCUSSION: Under a notice-type statute, an unrecorded interest in real property is ineffective against a subsequent bona fide purchaser (for value and without notice) even if such a purchaser does not record.

Answer (a) is incorrect because the recording statute simply protects the mortgagee against third parties, not the mortgagor. Answers (c) and (d) are incorrect because the mortgagee's unrecorded interest is superior to that of any subsequent party with knowledge of the existing mortgage.

14. On April 6, 1988, Walsh purchased a warehouse from Bock for $150,000. Best Title Co. had performed a title search of the property. The results of the title search indicated that a mortgage given to Stone by Bock was duly recorded against the warehouse on March 9, 1988. However, the title search failed to detect a purchase money mortgage dated March 2, 1988, given by Bock to Todd. This mortgage was never recorded. Walsh was unaware of the mortgage to Todd. Under the circumstances

a. Walsh will take title to the warehouse subject to Todd's mortgage because it is a purchase money mortgage.

b. Walsh will take title to the warehouse free of Todd's mortgage.

c. Todd's mortgage is superior to Stone's mortgage.

d. Best will be liable to Walsh because of its failure to detect the Todd mortgage.

The correct answer is (b). *(CPA 588 L-57)*

REQUIRED: The correct statement concerning an unrecorded mortgage asserted against a subsequent purchaser.

DISCUSSION: Walsh qualifies as a bona fide purchaser, that is, a party who gave value and took title without notice of the second mortgage. Walsh will therefore take free of any unrecorded mortgage.

Answer (a) is incorrect because a subsequent bona fide purchaser prevails over an unrecorded purchase money mortgage. Answer (c) is incorrect because if a subsequent buyer does not have knowledge of a first mortgage and records his/her mortgage properly, (s)he will have priority over a first mortgagee who failed to record. Answer (d) is incorrect because the standard title policy only insures against defects of record. Because there was no defect of record and Walsh suffered no damages, no claim can be made against Best.

15. Gray owned a warehouse free and clear of any encumbrances. Gray borrowed $30,000 from Harp Finance and executed a promissory note secured by a mortgage on the warehouse. The state within which the warehouse was located had a notice-race recording statute applicable to real property. Harp did not record its mortgage. Thereafter, Gray applied for a loan with King Bank, supplying King with certified financial statements that disclosed Harp's mortgage. After review of the financial statements, King approved Gray's loan for $25,000, taking an executed promissory note secured by a mortgage on the warehouse. King promptly recorded its mortgage. Which party's mortgage will be superior?

a. Harp's, since King had notice of Harp's interest.

b. Harp's, since it obtained a purchase money security interest.

c. King's, since it was the first to file.

d. King's, since a title search would fail to reveal Harp's interest.

The correct answer is (a). *(CPA 585 L-56)*

REQUIRED: The mortgagee with priority in a notice-race state.

DISCUSSION: A notice-race statute gives priority to the first party to record unless (s)he had actual notice of a preexisting interest. King knew or should have known of Harp's mortgage from the financial statements, so King's interest will be subordinate although recorded first.

Answer (b) is incorrect because Harp did not finance the purchase of the property. Moreover, while a purchase money mortgage generally has priority, it is subject to the requirements of the applicable recording act. Answers (c) and (d) are incorrect because King had actual notice of the mortgage. Only in one of the few states with a pure race statute (one that ignores a party's actual notice of an existing, unrecorded interest if (s)he is the first to record) would King have priority.

16. Moch sold her farm to Watkins and took back a purchase money mortgage on the farm. Moch failed to record the mortgage. Moch's mortgage will be valid against all of the following parties except

a. The heirs or estate of Watkins.

b. A subsequent mortgagee who took a second mortgage and knew of the prior mortgage.

c. A subsequent bona fide purchaser from Watkins.

d. A friend of Watkins to whom the farm was given as a gift and who took without knowledge of the mortgage.

The correct answer is (c). *(CPA 583 L-59)*

REQUIRED: The party against which an unrecorded mortgage will not prevail.

DISCUSSION: If the mortgagee's interest is not recorded, a subsequent good faith purchaser for value without notice of the mortgage (bona fide purchaser) will take free of it. Recording will also give a mortgagee priority over a subsequent mortgagee.

Answers (a) and (d) are incorrect because those who do not take for value (e.g., heirs, devisees, and donees) cannot take free of a prior unrecorded mortgage. Answer (b) is incorrect because in most jurisdictions, a subsequent mortgagee with actual notice takes subject to a prior unrecorded mortgage.

17. Joe Glenn borrowed $80,000 from City Bank. He executed a promissory note and secured the loan with a mortgage on business real estate he owned as a sole proprietor. Glenn neglected to advise City that he had previously mortgaged the property to Ball, who had failed to record the mortgage. City promptly recorded its mortgage. Subsequently, Glenn conveyed his business assets including the property to a newly-created corporation in exchange for all of its stock. Which of the following is correct?

a. Ball's mortgage is prior in time and would take priority over City's mortgage.

b. Glenn's corporation will take the property subject to both mortgages.

c. The corporation will be deemed to have assumed both mortgages.

d. On foreclosure, Glenn could not be called upon to pay City any deficiency.

The correct answer is (b). *(CPA 586 L-49)*

REQUIRED: The true statement about the effects of giving successive mortgages followed by a conveyance of the mortgaged property.

DISCUSSION: Glenn is the sole shareholder, so the corporation is deemed to have Glenn's knowledge of the transactions in question. Hence, the corporation cannot be a bona fide purchaser for value with respect to either Ball or City and will therefore take the property subject to both mortgages. Absent the imputation of Glenn's knowledge to the corporation, it would be deemed to have constructive notice of City's recorded mortgage.

Answer (a) is incorrect because City's recorded mortgage has priority over Ball's unrecorded mortgage. Answer (c) is incorrect because the facts do not indicate that the corporation is genuinely separate from Glenn, so the courts would "pierce the corporate veil" and hold Glenn primarily liable. If an assumption of the mortgages had occurred, Glenn would still be liable but the corporation would be the primary obligor. Answer (d) is incorrect because Glenn is personally liable and must pay any deficiency.

18. Norton owned and operated a trucking business. He was financially hard pressed and obtained a loan from the First State Bank "secured by his equipment and including all other chattels and personal property used in his business." The loan security agreement was properly filed in the county records office. In addition, Norton obtained a loan from the Title Mortgage Company; the loan was secured by a first mortgage on all the real property used in the trucking business. Norton is now insolvent and a petition in bankruptcy has been filed. Which of the following is a correct statement concerning the security interests in the properties?

a. If Title Mortgage failed to record its mortgage, the trustee in bankruptcy will be able to defeat Title's security interest.

b. Norton's central air conditioning and heating system is included in First State's security interest.

c. If Title Mortgage did not record its mortgage, First State is entitled to all fixtures, including those permanently annexed to the land.

d. A sale of all the personal and real business property by Norton to a bona fide purchaser will defeat First State's security interest unless First State recorded its security interest in both the appropriate real and personal property recordation offices.

The correct answer is (a). *(CPA 575 L-12)*

REQUIRED: The correct statement concerning the security interests in the properties.

DISCUSSION: A trustee in bankruptcy can assert the powers of a hypothetical lien creditor. A lien creditor would prevail over an unrecorded mortgage, so the trustee will also prevail.

Answer (b) is incorrect because First State's security interest covers only personal property. A central air conditioning and heating system is ordinarily deemed a fixture and therefore real property covered by the mortgage. Answer (c) is incorrect because regardless of whether Title Mortgage recorded, First State is still entitled only to the collateral described in its security agreement, i.e., personal property. Fixtures are considered part of the real property. Answer (d) is incorrect because First State's security interest extends to the proceeds of the sale of the personal property.

19. Cutter purchased a building and land from Murley. Cutter made a downpayment to Murley and gave a mortgage for the balance of the purchase price. The property was already subject to an existing mortgage that Murley agreed to continue to pay.

a. Murley's mortgage takes priority over a judgment that had been rendered against Cutter prior to the sale.

b. Murley has committed a fraud by taking a mortgage on the property without paying off the existing mortgage.

c. Murley's original mortgage became due immediately on the sale to Cutter.

d. In the event of a default on the mortgages, the mortgage from Cutter to Murley will take priority because it is a purchase-money mortgage.

The correct answer is (a). *(Publisher)*

REQUIRED: The correct statement concerning a wrap-around mortgage.

DISCUSSION: Murley obtained a purchase-money mortgage on the sale of the property. A purchase-money mortgage takes priority over pre- existing debts of the mortgagor. Therefore, a prior judgment against Cutter might become a lien on the real property but would be junior to Murley's mortgage.

Answer (b) is incorrect because it is not fraudulent to sell property taking a mortgage for part of the price while continuing to pay the old mortgage. This is generally called a wrap-around mortgage since the new mortgage wraps around the old and the additional debt. Answer (c) is incorrect because a mortgage will only become due immediately on sale if specifically provided. The validity of due on sale clauses has been upheld in recent years. Answer (d) is incorrect because the original mortgage has priority since it was first in time and presumably first recorded. A purchase-money mortgage does not take priority over preexisting liens on the property.

20. Lusk borrowed $20,000 from Marco Finance. The loan was secured by a mortgage on a four-unit apartment building owned by Lusk. The proceeds of the loan were used by Lusk to purchase a business. The mortgage was duly recorded 60 days after Marco loaned the money to Lusk. Six months after borrowing the money from Marco, Lusk leased one of the apartments to Rudd for $800 per month. Neither Rudd nor Lusk notified Marco of the lease. Subsequently, Lusk defaulted on the note to Marco and Marco has commenced foreclosure proceedings. Under the circumstances

a. Marco's mortgage is junior to Rudd's lease because the mortgage was not a purchase money mortgage.

b. Marco's mortgage is junior to Rudd's lease because Marco failed to record the mortgage for 60 days after the closing.

c. Rudd's lease is subject to Marco's mortgage because Marco recorded its mortgage prior to the time Rudd's leasehold interest arose.

d. Rudd's lease is subject to Marco's mortgage because of the failure to notify Marco of the lease.

The correct answer is (c). *(CPA 1187 L-52)*

REQUIRED: The correct statement concerning foreclosure under a recorded mortgage.

DISCUSSION: Recordation gives constructive notice to third parties that the property is subject to an existing mortgage. Because Marco recorded, Rudd has constructive notice, and the lease is therefore subject to the mortgage.

Answer (a) is incorrect because a mortgage is not required to arise from a purchase transaction to establish priority over other subsequent interests. Answer (b) is incorrect because the only requirement for priority is to record the mortgage prior to the creation of a new interest in the property. There is no statute of limitations for recordation. Answer (d) is incorrect because notice of the lease would not have subordinated Marco's interest.

21. The legal rights of a mortgagee may depend on the nature of the mortgage and of competing claims. Which of the following is false?

a. Jane wins a lawsuit and records a judgment against Dee. Dee subsequently finances the purchase of Redacre by giving a mortgage to Bank. Bank's interest in Redacre has priority over Jane's.

b. Buck mortgages Blueacre and its fixtures to pay a tort judgment. Buck then buys goods from Lindy and gives her a security interest in the goods and Blueacre's furnace. If Lindy properly files before Bank, she has priority in the furnace.

c. Bank finances the construction of White's new home, Blackacre. White then purchases a fixture from Greene who immediately perfects a security interest in it by a proper filing. If the fixture is attached to the realty before the completion of construction and Bank records its mortgage after Greene's filing but before annexation of the fixture, Bank has priority in the fixture.

d. Mary Yello raised business capital by giving a home mortgage to Bank, which it promptly recorded. Later, she purchased a fixture for her home from Paul. He perfected a security interest in it by a proper fixture filing 15 days after its attachment to the realty. Paul has priority in the fixture.

The correct answer is (d). *(Publisher)*

REQUIRED: The false statement about the rights of real estate mortgagees.

DISCUSSION: Under UCC 9-313, a perfected purchase money security interest in fixtures has priority over the conflicting interest of a mortgagee when the security interest is perfected by a fixture filing in the real estate records no later than 10 days after the goods become fixtures. The priority is given although the mortgagee filed first. Since Paul did not file within 10 days after annexation, Bank's earlier recorded real estate mortgage gives it priority in the fixture.

Answer (a) is incorrect because the general rule is that a recorded purchase money mortgage has priority over other liens that attach to the property. It will prevail even over a judgment entered against the mortgagor prior to the purchase. Answer (b) is incorrect because in a contest between a non-purchase money security interest in a fixture and a non-purchase money mortgagee of the realty, the first to make a proper filing has priority. Answer (c) is incorrect because a perfected purchase money security interest in fixtures is subordinate to a construction mortgage recorded before the goods become fixtures if the goods become fixtures before the construction is completed.

22. Emma Perkins was a real estate wheeler-dealer. She owned a tract of land on which she intended to build a shopping center. Perkins obtained a loan from Brown giving a mortgage in return. The mortgage provided that it was intended to secure the present loan and any future advances, and would also apply to any real property acquired by Perkins subsequent to the mortgage until the debt was repaid.

a. The after-acquired property clause is invalid.

b. A mortgage cannot secure future advances. Instead, an additional mortgage must be entered into when the subsequent loan is made.

c. If Perkins acquires additional property and then sells it, Brown will have a priority for his mortgage over any purchasers.

d. In many states Brown can make an additional loan to Perkins, and retain priority over junior liens which have arisen after the mortgage was recorded.

The correct answer is (d). *(Publisher)*

REQUIRED: The correct statement concerning a mortgage with a future advance and after-acquired property clause.

DISCUSSION: In many states, a future advance clause permits the mortgagee to retain the same priority for a future advance as for the original mortgage. This is based on the theory that persons with subsequent liens have notice of the mortgage and the future advance clause.

Answer (a) is incorrect because an after-acquired property clause is valid. Answer (b) is incorrect because a real property mortgage can secure future advances just as readily as a personal property security interest. Answer (c) is incorrect because a subsequent purchaser would check title from Perkins back to her grantor and would not have notice of the after-acquired clause in a mortgage on the first property which is not in the chain of title of the after-acquired property. Such a clause is not effective since the creditor has no adequate protection against third persons unless a separate filing is made.

21.3 Default and Foreclosure

23. Default on a mortgage does not occur when the mortgagor

a. Fails to pay or makes delayed payments.

b. Transfers ownership or leases the premises.

c. Commits waste or maintains no insurance coverage.

d. Extracts minerals or cuts timber without express reservation in the agreement if such activities were not being carried out when the mortgage was created.

The correct answer is (b). *(Publisher)*

REQUIRED: The actions not constituting a mortgage default.

DISCUSSION: The mortgagor has the right to use, possess, enjoy, and transfer the realty, to lease it and collect rent, to borrow money and use the property as security, and to pass the property to heirs or devisees. However, a mortgagor's rights may be limited by acceleration clauses for events that do not constitute a default. A due-on-sale clause requires full payment if the property is sold. A due-on-encumbrance clause accelerates payment when another lien is placed on the realty.

Answers (a), (c), and (d) are incorrect because a mortgagor generally has a duty to repay the debt, to insure the property against fire, to pay real estate taxes and assessments, to refrain from acts that materially diminish the value of the property, and to pay any prior mortgage. Each of the items listed would generally constitute a default.

24. If a promissory note secured by a mortgage on real property is not paid, the creditor is entitled to sell the property to satisfy the debt. This is called a foreclosure sale. Which statement is correct concerning foreclosure in most states?

a. The mortgagee may sell the property at a public auction.

b. The mortgagee is limited to collection of the proceeds from the sale even if they do not satisfy the debt in its entirety.

c. The mortgagee is entitled to the entire proceeds of the foreclosure sale, regardless of the amount of the unpaid debt.

d. The mortgagor is entitled to repurchase the land within a statutory period.

The correct answer is (d). *(Publisher)*

REQUIRED: The correct statement concerning a foreclosure sale.

DISCUSSION: A foreclosure sale occurs when a mortgage is in default and the mortgagee elects to satisfy its debt by sale of the property rather than by obtaining a personal judgment against the mortgagor. After the sale, the mortgagor ordinarily has a right to redeem (to repurchase) the land for a statutory period.

Answer (a) is incorrect because the mortgagee does not sell the property; a trustee, sheriff, or other official sells the property at public auction. Answer (b) is incorrect because the mortgagee is entitled to seek payment from the mortgagor in the event that the foreclosure sale does not satisfy the debt in its entirety. Answer (c) is incorrect because the mortgagee is only entitled to payment of the debt and expenses, and any surplus must be turned over to the mortgagor.

25. Which of the following is a true statement about foreclosure of a mortgage?

a. A power of sale clause creates an agency coupled with an interest that may be revoked by the mortgagor.

b. Strict foreclosure is generally permitted in those states that adhere to the lien theory of mortgages.

c. When the mortgagor gives a deed to the mortgagee in lieu of foreclosure, junior interests are extinguished.

d. Judicial foreclosure and sale is closely supervised by courts and by statute and may result in a deficiency decree.

The correct answer is (d). *(Publisher)*

REQUIRED: The true statement about foreclosure.

DISCUSSION: The most common means of foreclosure is by action of a court. It will authorize sale at a public auction by the sheriff or other public official. The sale process is carefully defined by statute. The proceeds are turned over to the court, which will then confirm the sale. Confirmation results in payment of the debt, interest, and costs, with the balance being given to the mortgagor. The purchaser receives a deed conveying the mortgagor's interest, subject to a statutory right of redemption. If the proceeds are insufficient, usually a deficiency decree will be issued against the mortgagor.

Answer (a) is incorrect because such an agency cannot be revoked by the principal since the agent has a property interest in the subject matter. Some states permit power of sale clauses. Answer (b) is incorrect because strict foreclosure is allowed only in a few states that adhere to the title theory. Strict foreclosure gives title to the mortgagee if the debt is not paid on time. Answer (c) is incorrect because this process does not extinguish the rights of third parties as in a strict foreclosure.

26. Peters defaulted on a purchase money mortgage held by Fairmont Realty. Fairmont's attempts to obtain payment have been futile and the mortgage payments are several months in arrears. Consequently, Fairmont decided to resort to its rights against the property. Fairmont foreclosed on the mortgage. Peters has all of the following rights except

a. To remain in possession as long as his equity in the property exceeds the amount of debt.

b. An equity of redemption.

c. To refinance the mortgage with another lender and repay the original mortgage.

d. A statutory right of redemption.

The correct answer is (a). *(CPA 583 L-60)*

REQUIRED: The right not held by a defaulting mortgagor.

DISCUSSION: The usual procedure is foreclosure by judicial sale. If the court finds such action is appropriate, it will order a public sale of the property by the sheriff or other official. The purchaser will receive a right to possession after the sale (or in some states after the redemption period elapses).

Answer (b) is incorrect because a defaulting mortgagor has a right to redeem the property before the foreclosure proceedings are complete by payment of the debt, interest, and costs. This equity of redemption cannot be barred or "clogged" by the mortgage agreement. Answer (c) is incorrect because redemption might be accomplished by refinancing. Answer (d) is incorrect because numerous states provide by statute for redemption after foreclosure. The redemption period is most commonly six months or one year but may be as much as two years.

27. A mortgagor who defaults on his/her mortgage payments will not be successful if (s)he attempts to

a. Assert the equitable right to redeem.

b. Redeem the property after a judicial foreclosure sale has taken place.

c. Obtain any excess resulting from a judicial foreclosure sale.

d. Contest the validity of the price received at a judicial foreclosure sale by asserting that a higher price could have been received at a later date.

The correct answer is (d). *(CPA 585 L-57)*

REQUIRED: The right not assertible by a mortgagor.

DISCUSSION: Foreclosure by judicial sale is the most common, although the most time consuming and costly, because it provides all parties with maximum protection of their rights. The usual result is a public judicial sale, after notice, conducted by the sheriff or other official. If the legal procedures are satisfied, the parties will have no right to contest the result on the grounds that still further delay would have produced a better price.

Answers (a) and (b) are incorrect because the mortgagor has both an equity of redemption prior to completion of foreclosure and, in many states, a statutory right afterward. Answer (c) is incorrect because the mortgagor has an equity in the process equal to any amount left after payment of the debt, interest, and costs.

28. Ram Corp. owns a warehouse that has a fair market value of $280,000. Area Bank holds a first mortgage and Public Finance holds a second mortgage on the warehouse. Ram has discontinued payments to Area and Public. As a result, Area, which has an outstanding mortgage of $240,000, and Public, which has an outstanding mortgage of $60,000, have foreclosed on their respective mortgages. If the warehouse is properly sold to Quincy at a judicial sale for $280,000, after expenses

a. Public will receive $40,000 out of the proceeds.

b. Area will receive $224,000 out of the proceeds.

c. Public has a right of redemption after the judicial sale.

d. Quincy will take the warehouse subject to the unsatisfied portion of any mortgage.

The correct answer is (a). *(CPA 1189 L-58)*

REQUIRED: The correct statement about the effects of a judicial sale.

DISCUSSION: A first mortgage holder has priority upon foreclosure and must be paid in full prior to payment of subsequent mortgage holder. Thus, Area will receive the first $240,000 of the proceeds, and Public will receive the remaining $40,000. Public will be an unsecured creditor for the remaining $20,000 of its debt.

Answer (b) is incorrect because Area will receive payment in full before the second mortgage holder is paid anything. The proceeds are not prorated. Answer (c) is incorrect because the mortgagor (Ram), not a mortgagee, has the right of redemption after the sale. Answer (d) is incorrect because the purchaser at the judicial sale will take the property free of any claim.

29. In 1984, Smith gave a mortgage to State Bank to secure a $100,000 loan. The mortgage was silent as to whether it would secure any other loans made by State to Smith. In 1986 Smith gave a second mortgage to Penn Bank to secure an $80,000 loan. Both mortgages described the same land and were properly recorded shortly after being executed by Smith. By 1990 Smith had repaid State Bank $40,000 of the $100,000 debt. State Bank then lent Smith an additional $20,000 without taking any new security. Within a few days, Smith defaulted on the loans from both banks and the first and second mortgages were foreclosed. The balance on the Penn loan was $20,000. The net proceeds of the foreclosure sale were $70,000. State is entitled to receive from the proceeds a maximum of

a. $52,500.

b. $56,000.

c. $60,000.

d. $70,000.

The correct answer is (c). *(CPA 1188 L-60)*

REQUIRED: The maximum proceeds to which the first mortgagor is entitled if it made a subsequent loan without new security.

DISCUSSION: When all mortgages on the same property are properly executed and recorded, the first mortgage will have priority over subsequent mortgages. Upon foreclosure, the mortgages must be fully satisfied in order of their priority. In this situation, State Bank holds a first mortgage for $60,000 and Penn Bank holds a second mortgage for $20,000. State Bank is an unsecured creditor for the additional $20,000 loan. Thus, State Bank will receive the first $60,000 from the foreclosure proceeds, and Penn Bank will receive the remaining $10,000. State Bank's unsecured loan will not be considered in the distribution of proceeds. In many states, however, a future advance clause inserted in the first mortgage would have permitted the first mortgagee to retain the same priority for a future advance as for the original mortgage. This practice is based on the theory that persons with subsequent liens have notice of the mortgage and the future advance clause.

21.4 Transfer of Encumbered Real Property

30. Tim Golden sold his moving and warehouse business, including all the personal and real property used therein, to Clark Van Lines, Inc. The real property was encumbered by a duly recorded $300,000 first mortgage upon which Golden was personally liable. Clark acquired the property subject to the mortgage but did not assume the mortgage. Two years later, when the outstanding mortgage was $260,000, Clark decided to abandon the business location because it had become unprofitable and the value of the real property was less than the outstanding mortgage. Clark moved to another location and refused to pay the installments due on the mortgage. What is the legal status of the parties in regard to the mortgage?

a. Clark took the real property free of the mortgage.

b. Clark breached its contract with Golden when it abandoned the location and defaulted on the mortgage.

c. Golden must satisfy the mortgage debt in the event that foreclosure yields an amount less than the unpaid balance.

d. If Golden pays off the mortgage, he will be able to successfully sue Clark because Golden is subrogated to the mortgagee's rights against Clark.

The correct answer is (c). *(CPA 581 L-53)*

REQUIRED: The legal status of the parties when a landowner defaults on a mortgage that (s)he had taken "subject to."

DISCUSSION: By taking "subject to" a mortgage, Clark avoided personal liability either to Golden or to the mortgagee. If Clark had "assumed" the mortgage, Clark would have been personally liable both to Golden and to the mortgagee. In either case, Golden could not avoid liability on his contractual duty to perform. Only if the mortgagee had released Golden (e.g., by a novation) could he have escaped liability.

Answer (a) is incorrect because Clark took encumbered property but without personal liability. Answer (b) is incorrect because Clark did not promise to assume Golden's duty to pay. Answer (d) is incorrect because neither has rights against Clark. Clark merely took "subject to" the mortgage.

31. Miltown borrowed $60,000 from Strauss upon the security of a first mortgage on a business building owned by Miltown. The mortgage has been amortized down to $50,000. Sanchez is buying the building from Miltown for $80,000. Sanchez is paying only the $30,000 excess over and above the mortgage. Sanchez may buy it either "subject to" the mortgage, or he may "assume" the mortgage. Which is a correct statement under these circumstances?

a. The financing agreement ultimately decided upon must be recorded in order to be binding upon the parties.

b. The financing arrangement is covered by the Uniform Commercial Code if Sanchez takes "subject to" the existing first mortgage.

c. Sanchez will acquire no interest in the property if he takes "subject to" instead of "assuming" the mortgage.

d. Sanchez would be better advised to take "subject to" the mortgage rather than to "assume" the mortgage.

The correct answer is (d). *(CPA 1177 L-21)*

REQUIRED: The correct statement concerning a purchase of mortgaged property.

DISCUSSION: By taking "subject to," Sanchez would avoid personal liability to both Strauss and Miltown. If Sanchez stopped making payments, the mortgagee could foreclose on the property and Sanchez would have no liability. On the other hand, by assuming the mortgage, Sanchez would be liable both to Miltown and to Strauss if foreclosure of the property yielded insufficient proceeds to satisfy the debt.

Answer (a) is incorrect because recording is necessary only to protect one's mortgage priority against subsequent mortgagees. Recording is not necessary between the parties to the arrangement. Answer (b) is incorrect because the UCC does not cover transactions in realty (except for certain transactions concerning fixtures). Answer (c) is incorrect because Sanchez would take precisely the same interest whether he took "subject to" or "assumed" the mortgage.

32. Assume the facts are the same as those stated above in question 31, but the property purchased by Sanchez has declined in value and the mortgage is in default. It has now been amortized to $43,000. The property is sold under foreclosure proceedings and $39,000, net of costs, is received. Which is a correct legal conclusion if Sanchez acquired the property "subject to" the mortgage?

a. Sanchez has no further liability after foreclosure.

b. Miltown cannot be held personally liable by Strauss for the $4,000 deficiency.

c. Sanchez is not liable to Strauss, but is personally liable to Miltown if Miltown pays the deficiency.

d. Miltown and Sanchez will have to satisfy the deficiency equally, that is, each owes $2,000.

The correct answer is (a). *(CPA 1177 L-22)*

REQUIRED: The legal status of the parties when foreclosed property was acquired "subject to" a mortgage.

DISCUSSION: Sanchez has not promised to pay the debt and has no liability either to Strauss or Miltown regardless of the insufficiency of the proceeds from the foreclosure sale. If Sanchez had assumed the mortgage, he would be personally liable on a promise to perform Miltown's duty to pay Strauss.

Answer (b) is incorrect because even if Sanchez had assumed the mortgage, Miltown would still be personally liable absent a release. Answers (c) and (d) are incorrect because Sanchez has no further liability since he only took the property "subject to" the mortgage.

33. Ted Nix purchased 2 acres of land from Sally Pine. Nix paid 15% at the closing and gave his note for the balance secured by a 30-year mortgage. Five years later, Nix found it increasingly difficult to make payments on the note and finally defaulted. Pine threatened to accelerate the loan and foreclose if Nix continued in default. Pine told Nix either to get the money or obtain an acceptable third party to assume the obligation. Nix offered the land to Quick Co. for $4,000 less than the equity Nix had in the property. This was acceptable to Pine and at the closing Quick paid the arrearage, executed a new mortgage and note, and had title transferred to its name. Pine surrendered Nix's note and mortgage to him. The transaction is a(n)

a. Third party beneficiary contract.

b. Novation.

c. Purchase of land subject to a mortgage.

d. Assignment and delegation.

The correct answer is (b). *(CPA 586 L-9)*

REQUIRED: The term for the transaction described.

DISCUSSION: A novation is a mutual agreement between concerned parties for the discharge of an existing agreement by substituting a new contract or new debtor. Here the three-way agreement among the parties substitutes for the old agreement. The novation is the substitution of a new promisor (Quick) for the old (Nix).

Answer (a) is incorrect because a third party beneficiary contract intentionally benefits one who is not a party to the agreement. Answer (c) is incorrect because Quick accepted liability by executing a new mortgage, and Nix has been discharged from any liability. A purchaser who takes subject to a mortgage accepts no personal liability thereon. Answer (d) is incorrect because if Nix had assigned his rights and delegated his duties to Quick, he would not have been released from liability.

34. Bond purchased from Spear Corp. an apartment building that was encumbered by a mortgage securing Spear's promissory note to Fale Finance Co. Bond assumed Spear's note and mortgage. Subsequently, Bond defaulted on the note payable to Fale and, as a result, the building was sold at a foreclosure sale. If the proceeds of the foreclosure sale are less than the balance due on the note, which of the following statements is correct?

a. Fale must sue both Spear and Bond to collect the deficiency because they are jointly and severally liable.

b. Spear will be liable for the deficiency.

c. Fale must attempt to collect the deficiency from Bond before suing Spear.

d. Spear will not be liable for the deficiency because Bond assumed the note and mortgage.

The correct answer is (b). *(CPA 1188 L-17)*

REQUIRED: The true statement about the liability of the mortgagor and the buyer of real property.

DISCUSSION: When a buyer of real estate assumes an existing mortgage, the seller remains liable if there has been no novation. Between the seller and buyer, the buyer has become the primary debtor, and the seller is a surety. Because Spear is surety of the assumed mortgage, it will be liable if the proceeds of the foreclosure sale are less than the balance due on the note.

Answers (a) and (c) are incorrect because Fale would not have to sue both Spear and Bond. It may sue either party individually. Answer (d) is incorrect because although Spear has become a surety, it is still personally liable.

35. Tremont Enterprises, Inc. needed some additional working capital to develop a new product line. It decided to obtain intermediate term financing by giving a second mortgage on its plant and warehouse. Which of the following is true with respect to the mortgages?

a. If Tremont defaults on both mortgages and a bankruptcy proceeding is initiated, the second mortgagee has the status of general creditor.

b. If the second mortgagee proceeds to foreclose on its mortgage, the first mortgagee must be satisfied completely before the second mortgagee is entitled to repayment.

c. Default on payment to the second mortgagee will constitute default on the first mortgage.

d. Tremont cannot prepay the second mortgage prior to its maturity without the consent of the first mortgagee.

The correct answer is (b). *(CPA 581 L-54)*

REQUIRED: The correct statement concerning the legal status of first and second mortgages.

DISCUSSION: The nature of the second mortgage is that it represents a claim that is subordinate to the first mortgage. Upon foreclosure and judicial sale of the property, the proceeds would be distributed to all senior liens (the first mortgage) and to expenses of sale before the second mortgagee received anything. In some jurisdictions, foreclosure of a second mortgage leaves the first mortgage intact and unaffected by the foreclosure sale.

Answer (a) is incorrect because the second mortgagee has the much preferable status of secured creditor with rights in specific property. However, the second mortgage only has value to the extent that the value of the property exceeds the first mortgage. Answer (c) is incorrect because default on one mortgage is not default on the other mortgage. They are separate contractual undertakings. However, a provision can be placed in a mortgage agreeing that a breach of one mortgage is also breach of another. Answer (d) is incorrect because prepayment does not require consent of the first mortgagee.

CHAPTER TWENTY-TWO
LANDLORD AND TENANT

22.1 Landlord and Tenant: Basic Concepts

1. Which of the following is the most accurate statement about the nature of a lease?

a. The landlord-tenant relationship is contractual and does not give the tenant an interest in the land.

b. The tenant has a leasehold estate, an interest equivalent to a freehold estate.

c. The tenant has a leasehold estate, an interest that is partly contractual and partly a real property conveyance.

d. Because the tenant's interest is temporary, (s)he has no ownership interests.

The correct answer is (c). *(Publisher)*

REQUIRED: The most accurate statement about the nature of a lease.

DISCUSSION: A lease is a contract and conveys rights to use real property. A tenant also has an estate in land (through the lease) characterized by the right to possession. Hence, a lease is partly a contracted conveyance and partly a real property conveyance.

Answer (a) is incorrect because the tenant receives an estate in land. Answer (b) is incorrect because a leasehold estate is distinct from a freehold since it is intended to be temporary. A freehold estate lasts indefinitely or for life. Answer (d) is incorrect because the tenant-lessee has certain incidents of ownership, e.g., right to possession.

2. Which of the following is a false statement about a lease and its terms?

a. The lessee gives consideration in the form of rent.

b. The lease transfers exclusive possession to the lessee, and the lessor retains a reversionary interest.

c. The lease often contains an exculpatory clause relieving the lessor of tort liability.

d. The lease is real property.

The correct answer is (d). *(Publisher)*

REQUIRED: The false statement about a lease.

DISCUSSION: The leasehold of a tenant is an interest in real property, but the lease itself is a bundle of mutual contract rights and duties. In that respect, the lease is personal property. Accordingly, if a lessee dies, his/her interest will pass under the will to the recipients of the personal property.

Answers (a), (b), and (c) are incorrect because each is a true statement about most leases. However, courts do not favor exculpatory clauses. Some states have prohibited their use in leases because they are usually imposed when the parties lack equal bargaining power.

3. Which of the following is a true statement about the application of the Statute of Frauds to leaseholds?

a. It does not apply.

b. If the lease contract cannot be performed within a specified period, it applies.

c. The majority of states apply it to all leases.

d. Partial performance has no effect on its application.

The correct answer is (b). *(Publisher)*

REQUIRED: The true statement about the relation of the Statute of Frauds to leases.

DISCUSSION: Contracts that cannot be performed within the statutory time are required to be in writing, be signed by the party to be bound, and state essential terms. The usual period is one year.

Answer (a) is incorrect because if the lease is for the statutory period (e.g., one year), it must be in writing. Answer (c) is incorrect because only in the minority of states that treat a lease as the sale of an interest in land must all leases be written. Answer (d) is incorrect because partial performance (possession, payment of rent, improvement of the property) may permit a lessee to enforce an oral lease although the lease is required to be in writing.

4. The Uniform Residential Landlord and Tenant Act (URLTA) has been enacted in many states. It substantially clarifies, modifies, and adds to the common law regarding residential leases. Which of the following is a true statement about the Act's provisions?

a. In some instances, the lessee may make repairs and deduct their costs from the rent.

b. The lessor may generally enter the premises without the lessee's permission.

c. The lessee may use the premises for both residential and commercial purposes.

d. The lessor may hold the lessee's personal property until overdue rent is paid.

The correct answer is (a). *(Publisher)*

REQUIRED: The true statement about URLTA.

DISCUSSION: At common law, the landlord had no duty to repair, but the URLTA and similar statutes place the duty on the lessor to repair. If the lessor fails to do so, the tenant may make minor repairs (not more than the greater of $100 or half the periodic rent) and deduct the cost from the rent if (s)he gives the lessor two weeks' notice. An itemized expense statement must also be provided when the rent is paid.

Answer (b) is incorrect because except in an emergency, the lessor has no right of entry without consent, but the lessee also may not unreasonably withhold consent when the lessor wishes to enter to effect repairs and inspect. Answer (c) is incorrect because the URLTA does not apply to a commercial lease. Answer (d) is incorrect because the URLTA abolishes this common law action. However, if a lessee holds over in bad faith, the lessor may sue for possession and for the greater of three months' rent or triple the lessor's damages.

5. Vance obtained a 25-year leasehold interest in an office building from the owner, Stanfield.

a. Vance's interest is nonassignable.

b. The conveyance of the ownership of the building by Stanfield to Wax will terminate Vance's leasehold interest.

c. Stanfield's death will not terminate Vance's leasehold interest.

d. Vance's death will terminate the leasehold interest.

The correct answer is (c). *(CPA 1176 L-41)*

REQUIRED: The true statement concerning a long-term leasehold interest.

DISCUSSION: The 25-year leasehold interest qualifies as a tenancy for years because it is a leasehold interest for a fixed period of time. Such an interest does not automatically terminate upon the death of the lessor. It is assignable and inheritable.

Answer (a) is incorrect because a leasehold interest is assignable unless expressly made nonassignable by the terms of the lease agreement. Answer (b) is incorrect because a lessor may also transfer his/her interest in the property without terminating the leasehold. The transferee would take subject to Vance's interest. Answer (d) is incorrect because Vance's death also will not terminate the leasehold. A lease is not a personal contract. The death of neither lessor nor lessee will terminate the agreement.

6. Promises in a lease

a. Must be express, not implied.

b. Are construed as covenants.

c. Are often deemed to include an implied warranty of habitability.

d. Ordinarily are treated as conditions. Thus, breach by the lessee does not give the lessor right of eviction but only an action for damages.

The correct answer is (c). *(Publisher)*

REQUIRED: The true statement about the promises in a lease.

DISCUSSION: In many states, courts have found a warranty of habitability to be implied in a residential lease. Whether a defect is a breach of the warranty depends on the circumstances. Factors considered are the existence of violations of building or housing codes and sanitary regulations, the effect on safety and sanitation, the fault of the tenant, and whether the defect is in a vital part of the premises. A breach may be grounds for rent reductions or termination of the lease. Not all states have recognized the warranty, and most that do have not extended it to commercial property.

Answer (a) is incorrect because many leases contain only the most basic terms, so the law will find implied promises, e.g., make repairs, pay utilities, pay property taxes, etc. Answers (b) and (d) are incorrect because promises may be covenants or conditions. If the promise is only a covenant, the breach gives rise only to an action for damages. If it is deemed a condition, breach will also give the nonbreaching party the right not to perform. If a lessee breaches a condition, the lessor may evict the tenant.

7. Which of the following is a true statement about the kinds of leasehold estates?

a. Most states allow self-help dispossession by the lessor if the estate is at sufferance.

b. An estate at will terminates on the death of the lessor but not upon sale of the premises.

c. An estate from period to period does not terminate on the death of a party or sale of the premises, and notice of termination is not required.

d. An estate for years does not terminate on the death of a party or sale of the premises, and notice of termination is not required.

The correct answer is (d). *(Publisher)*

REQUIRED: The true statement about the kinds of leasehold estates.

DISCUSSION: An estate for years is a lease for any definite time (1 week, 90 days, 10 years, etc.) determined by the parties. It arises only by agreement of the parties and requires no notice of termination because the parties know when the lease will end. These leasehold estates may be inherited or pass by will and are not affected by the landlord's death or sale of his/her interest.

Answer (a) is incorrect because most states require notice of termination. Eviction must generally be made by a law enforcement official. An estate at sufferance arises when a lessee holds over without consent. Answer (b) is incorrect because an estate at will is created when a lessee occupies the premises with consent, but without negotiating a lease. The landlord's death or sale of his/her interest terminates the estate. Answer (c) is incorrect because a periodic estate is for an indefinite time although the other terms of the lease have been negotiated. The duration of the estate is for the payment period. It is automatically reserved for another period unless one party gives notice of termination (usually, one full period in advance).

8. Which of the following is considered a periodic tenancy?

a. A lease for a period of 1 year with a right to renew for another year.

b. A lease for an indefinite period of time under which the rent is paid monthly and the lease may be terminated upon 1 month's notice.

c. A lease for a 1 week period that is to recur each year.

d. A lease created when a tenant occupies the premises without permission.

The correct answer is (b). *(Publisher)*

REQUIRED: The statement that correctly describes a periodic tenancy.

DISCUSSION: A periodic tenancy continues from period to period until terminated. The period may be any period, e.g., a week, a month, or a year. If not expressly provided, it may be implied by the regular payment of rent and requirement of a period's notice for termination.

Answer (a) is incorrect because a lease for 1 year is called a tenancy for years despite a right to renew. Answer (c) is incorrect because a lease for 1 week is also a tenancy for years or a definite time, even if only for a week or recurring each year. Answer (d) is incorrect because the occupation of premises without permission is a tenancy at sufferance.

9. Pierre rented an apartment to Natasha for a 1-year period that expired on May 31 of this year. Rent was $300 per month payable on the first day of each month. Natasha decided to remain in the apartment and therefore made the customary monthly rental payment on June 1. Pierre accepted the payment without comment. Which of the following is true?

a. A periodic tenancy has been created.

b. Pierre may evict Natasha at any time.

c. A tenancy at sufferance has been created.

d. If the original term had been for 9 months, a tenancy at will would have been created.

The correct answer is (a). *(Publisher)*

REQUIRED: The true statement about a tenant's holding over.

DISCUSSION: The original lease was a tenancy for a definite period (tenancy for years). When a lessee holds over after such a lease has expired and the lessor continues to treat the lessee as a tenant (for example, by accepting rent), a periodic tenancy is created. The terms of the holdover tenancy are implied from the circumstances if no express agreement is made. If rent payments are monthly, the tenancy is most likely month-to-month.

Answer (b) is incorrect because Pierre has chosen to bind Natasha to a new lease term. When a tenant holds over, the landlord has the option of eviction or permitting creation of a new tenancy. Answer (c) is incorrect because a tenancy at sufferance is created when a tenant wrongfully holds over. Natasha did not wrongfully hold over because Pierre accepted rent. Answer (d) is incorrect because a tenancy at will is for an indefinite time and is terminable by either party. It is usually created expressly and often involves either no rent payments or payment at irregular intervals.

22.2 Rights, Duties, and Liabilities of the Landlord

10. Joe Davis was a tenant in an apartment and invited Sarah Bacon over as a guest. In the living room, Sarah stepped on a loose board that sprang up and hit her in the face. Davis was frightened and ran outside to seek help. On the way, Davis stepped in an old hole in the staircase and fell down the stairs, breaking his arm.

a. The landlord is liable to Sarah for the injury caused by the loose board.

b. The landlord is not liable to Davis for the injuries caused by the hole in the stairwell since Davis knew it was there from prior experience.

c. If the landlord had undertaken to repair the loose board in the living room, Sarah could recover from him.

d. If Sarah recovers from Davis, the landlord is liable to Davis.

The correct answer is (c). (Publisher)

REQUIRED: The liability of a landlord for injuries to a tenant and a guest.

DISCUSSION: In the absence of an agreement otherwise or notice of a defect, a landlord is not responsible for making repairs to the interior of a residential apartment. But when a landlord does undertake to make a repair, (s)he is held liable for its sufficiency. Therefore, Sarah could recover from the landlord for a faulty repair.

Answer (a) is incorrect because the landlord is generally not liable for making repairs inside a residential apartment. Answer (b) is incorrect because the landlord is responsible for making repairs in the common areas of an apartment building and would be liable to Davis for the hole in the stairwell regardless of Davis' prior knowledge. Answer (d) is incorrect because the tenant is usually responsible for repairs within the apartment, but the landlord is liable for hidden defects of which (s)he has knowledge.

11. Which of the following is not a right of a landlord in the majority of states today?

a. To receive rent without apportionment and to recover possession of the premises.

b. To inspect and to sue for waste.

c. To have the tenant make repairs and insure the premises.

d. To sell the reversionary interest.

The correct answer is (c). *(Publisher)*

REQUIRED: The item not stating a landlord's right in the majority of states.

DISCUSSION: Under the common law, the tenant has the duty to repair the premises, but the URLTA places the burden of repair on the landlord. Although the URLTA has been adopted in fewer than half of the states, many other states have statutes modernizing residential landlord-tenant law. Neither party is obligated to obtain insurance.

Answer (a) is incorrect because collection of rent is the landlord's most basic right. Another right is the return of possession of the premises. Also, rent is not apportioned (prorated). A tenant who leaves prior to the end of the rental period cannot receive a partial refund unless (s)he was wrongfully evicted. Answer (b) is incorrect because the landlord may inspect pursuant to the lease. However, the URLTA provides that (s)he may not enter without the tenant's consent. Consent may not be unreasonably withheld. Answer (d) is incorrect because the landlord may sell, but the new owner will ordinarily be bound by existing leases.

12. Which of the following is a true statement about the tort liability of a landlord?

a. The tenants as a group are liable for maintenance of common areas.

b. A landlord owes no duty to the tenant's guests.

c. A landlord generally is held to make an implied warranty that the premises are safe and suitable for the tenant's intended commercial use.

d. A landlord is liable for a third party's assault of a tenant if it is due to an inoperative security system, the existence of which was used to induce the tenant to rent.

The correct answer is (d). *(Publisher)*

REQUIRED: The true statement about a landlord's tort liability.

DISCUSSION: Although landlords do not always have a duty to repair, it certainly exists where the inoperative item was promised to the tenant as an inducement to rent. The landlord can be held liable for injuries resulting when this duty is breached.

Answer (a) is incorrect because the landlord has control of and should properly maintain the common areas. Answer (b) is incorrect because the landlord owes the same duty to a guest that (s)he owes to the tenant. For example, (s)he must give notice of latent defects of which (s)he knows or should know. Moreover, if a landlord has a duty to repair or voluntarily undertakes to repair, (s)he has a duty to act nonnegligently. Answer (c) is incorrect because although an implied warranty of habitability is found by many courts when the premises are residential, the warranty does not extend to commercial property (except as public health and safety codes may require).

13. Rent is the consideration to be paid by a tenant to a landlord for the use and enjoyment of the premises. The tenant and landlord have certain rights and obligations with regard to the rent. Which is a correct statement of these rights and obligations in the absence of a statute?

a. Prepaid rent cannot be recovered if the tenancy is terminated prior to the end of a rent period.

b. The landlord has the right to terminate the lease if the tenant does not pay the rent.

c. The tenant may withhold the rent if the landlord does not perform his/her obligations.

d. If a lease is assigned, the landlord is under no obligation to accept rent from the assignee.

The correct answer is (a). *(Publisher)*

REQUIRED: The correct statement of the rights and obligations of the landlord and tenant in the absence of a statute.

DISCUSSION: Under common law, prepaid rent was not prorated on a daily or other basis less than the period of the lease. A lessee thus could not recover a portion of a rent prepayment.

Answers (b) and (c) are incorrect because under common law, the landlord's obligation to provide the premises and the tenant's obligation to pay rent were separate. Breach by one party did not release the other from his/her obligation. Today, most statutes allow the landlord to terminate the lease if rent is not paid. Answer (d) is incorrect because unless the assignment is wrongful, the landlord must accept rent from the assignee.

22.3 Rights, Duties, and Liabilities of the Tenant

14. Tess occupied an apartment in a building owned by Len. She paid rent of $125 in advance each month. During the second month of occupancy, Tess organized the tenants in the building as a tenants' association and the association made demands of Len concerning certain repairs and improvements the tenants wanted. When Tess tendered rent for the third month, Len notified her that rent for the fourth and subsequent months would be $200 per month. Tess protested and pointed out that all other tenants paid rent of $125 per month. Thereupon, Len gave the required statutory notice that the tenancy was being terminated at the end of the third month. By an appropriate proceeding, Tess contests Len's right to terminate. If Tess succeeds, it will be because

a. A periodic tenancy was created by implication.

b. The doctrine prohibiting retaliatory eviction is part of the law of the jurisdiction.

c. The $200 rent demanded violates the agreement implied by the rate charged to other tenants.

d. The law implies a term of one year in the absence of any express agreement.

The correct answer is (b). *(MBE Part I-136)*

REQUIRED: The true statement about a landlord's actions after a tenant asserted rights to repairs.

DISCUSSION: Under the URLTA, retaliation is forbidden. It consists of eviction, a decrease in services, or raising rent. The action is presumed to be illegal if it occurs within a year after a conflict between the lessor and lessee. Activity in a tenants' union, complaints about maintenance, and reporting violations of building and housing codes to the authorities are defined as conflicts.

Answer (a) is incorrect because the landlord gave the appropriate notice of termination for a month to month periodic tenancy. Answer (c) is incorrect because no rental rate was implied. Answer (d) is incorrect because a periodic tenancy is created if a tenancy is agreed to but no term is stated.

15. Certain rights and duties between landlord and tenant are implied in most leases. Which of the following is an implied right or duty at common law?

a. The tenant's right to possession will be enforced by the landlord.

b. The premises will be reasonably fit for the use for which they are rented.

c. The landlord will make all the necessary repairs to the premises.

d. The tenant must pay rent even if the landlord does not make repairs.

The correct answer is (d). *(Publisher)*

REQUIRED: The implied right or duty between landlord and tenant at common law.

DISCUSSION: At common law, the obligations of a landlord to provide repairs and maintain the premises are separate from the obligation of the tenant to pay rent. Therefore, if repairs are not made by the landlord, a tenant who withholds rent would be in violation of the lease. The common law rights and duties, however, are often modified by statute.

Answer (a) is incorrect because a tenant does have the right to possession, but the landlord generally is not required to enforce it. Answer (b) is incorrect because the landlord does not warrant the condition of the premises. Answer (c) is incorrect because the tenant has traditionally been obligated to make all the necessary repairs to the premises.

16. The rights of a tenant include

a. The landlord's covenant of quiet enjoyment.

b. Exclusive possession and control subject to a common law right of inspection.

c. Return of the security deposit plus interest but minus wear and tear.

d. The power to remove all except trade fixtures.

The correct answer is (a). *(Publisher)*

REQUIRED: The true statement of a right held by a tenant.

DISCUSSION: Every landlord impliedly promises that the tenant will have quiet enjoyment of the premises. The promise is breached when another party has paramount title to the premises such that the tenant will be dispossessed or at least prevented from making the intended use of the premises. Actual or constructive eviction is also a breach.

Answer (b) is incorrect because under the common law, the landlord may enter only to collect rent, but leases commonly reserve a right to inspect. Answer (c) is incorrect because a statute usually requires landlords to pay interest, to itemize charges against a deposit, to return deposits promptly, and not to charge for normal wear and tear. Answer (d) is incorrect because tenants may remove trade fixtures, but generally not other fixtures.

17. Which of the following is a true statement about a tenant's liability?

a. Even a long-term tenant is liable for waste when (s)he changes the nature of the premises, although the change may increase the value of the property.

b. A tenant may be evicted for maintaining a nuisance on the premises.

c. The landlord, not the tenant, is primarily liable for injuries to third parties.

d. The tenant is generally liable for rent if (s)he vacates prior to expiration of the lease and the landlord does not mitigate damages.

The correct answer is (b). *(Publisher)*

REQUIRED: The true statement about a tenant's liabilities.

DISCUSSION: A tenant's basic responsibilities are to pay rent, avoid waste, return possession of the premises, perform the obligations agreed to in the lease, and not to make illegal use of the property. A use of the property that constituted a nuisance (for example, raising hogs in a residential area) or a criminal activity (operating an illegal gambling establishment) would breach the obligation to make lawful use of the premises.

Answer (a) is incorrect because destruction, alteration, or misuse of the premises is impermissible, but an exception may be made when a long-term tenant makes an alteration that is consistent with a change in the character of the neighborhood and the effect is to increase the value of the property. Answer (c) is incorrect because to the extent the tenant is in possession and control, (s)he is more likely than the landlord to be liable for injuries sustained by a third party. Answer (d) is incorrect because the modern approach is that a landlord has a duty to mitigate damages by seeking a new tenant.

18. Wilmont owned a tract of waterfront property on Big Lake. During Wilmont's ownership of the land, several frame bungalows were placed on the land by tenants who rented the land from Wilmont. In addition to paying rent, the tenants paid for the maintenance and insurance of the bungalows, repaired, altered and sold them without permission or hindrance from Wilmont. The bungalows rested on cinderblock and were not bolted to the ground. The buildings could be removed without injury to either the buildings or the land. Wilmont sold the land to Marsh. The deed to Marsh recited that Wilmont sold the land, with buildings thereon, "subject to the rights of tenants, if any." When the tenants attempted to remove the bungalows, Marsh claimed ownership of them. In deciding who owns the bungalows, which of the following is least significant?

a. The leasehold agreement, to the extent it manifested the parties' intent.

b. The mode and degree of annexation of the buildings to the land.

c. The degree to which removal would cause injury to the buildings or the land.

d. The fact that the deed included a general clause relating to the buildings.

The correct answer is (d). *(CPA 583 L-53)*

REQUIRED: The least significant consideration in determining whether an item is a fixture.

DISCUSSION: The quoted clause in the deed is not significant since it makes Marsh's rights subject to those of the tenants. Hence, the question remains as to whether the tenants have rights to the structures. The primary consideration as to whether these items belong to the tenants as personal property or to Marsh as fixtures is the intent of the parties. The actions by the tenants and Wilmont's actions certainly suggested an intention not to treat them as fixtures. That the items were not permanently annexed and could be removed without harm further reinforces the conclusion.

Answers (a), (b), and (c) are incorrect because each is a significant consideration in determining whether the buildings are fixtures, which in turn determines who owns them.

Questions 19 and 20 are based on Mini, Inc. which entered into a 5-year lease with Rein Realtors. The lease was signed by both parties and immediately recorded. The leased building was to be used by Mini in connection with its business operations. To make it suitable for that purpose, Mini attached a piece of equipment to the wall of the building.

19. Which of the following is most important in determining whether the equipment became a fixture?

a. Whether the equipment can be removed without material damage to the building.

b. Whether the attachment is customary for the type of building.

c. The fair market value of the equipment at the time the lease expires.

d. The fact that the equipment was subject to depreciation.

The correct answer is (a). *(CPA 1185 L-51)*

REQUIRED: The most important consideration in determining whether equipment is a fixture.

DISCUSSION: The intent of the parties controls. However, other factors may be considered to determine that intent in the absence of an explicit statement. The most important are the mode of annexation, the amount of damage to the realty and to the item if it is removed, and the degree to which the item is specifically adapted to the realty. Moreover, trade fixtures are presumed to belong to the lessee.

Answers (b), (c) and (d) are incorrect because each is relatively insignificant.

20. Which of the following statements is correct regarding Mini's rights and liabilities?

a. Mini is prohibited from assigning the lease if it is silent in this regard.

b. Mini has a possessory interest in the building.

c. Mini is strictly liable for all injuries sustained by any person in the building during the term of the lease.

d. Mini's rights under the lease are automatically terminated by Rein's sale of the building to a third party.

The correct answer is (b). *(CPA 1185 L-52)*

REQUIRED: The correct statement about a lessee's rights and duties.

DISCUSSION: Mini has a leasehold estate. It has a right to exclusive possession and control of the premises. But Mini must return possession to the owner of the freehold estate at the end of the lease term.

Answer (a) is incorrect because barring a lease term specifically prohibiting such a transfer, the lessee may assign the lease. Answer (c) is incorrect because Mini will have a varying duty of care depending on the status of injured person (invitee, licensee, trespasser) but will not be strictly liable without fault. Answer (d) is incorrect because a lessor may transfer its reversionary interest subject to the rights of the lessee.

22.4 Assignments and Subleases

Questions 21 through 25 are based on the following information. A certain written lease was entered into, the total contents thereof being as follows:

> On the first day of November 1985, Landlord rents his grocery store on Main Street in Crosstown to Tenant for 4 years. The rent shall be $100 per month.
>
> Signed: *Landlord*
> *Tenant*

On February 1, 1986, Landlord conveyed the grocery store to Owner subject to the lease. Tenant had no notice of the conveyance and continued paying rent to Landlord until July 1, 1986, when he learned thereof and assigned the lease to Assignee without Owner's knowledge. Assignee paid no rent. The Statute of Frauds required a lease for more than 3 years to be in writing.

21. If Owner sued Tenant for the rent due for the period February 1, 1986 to July 1, 1986, he would

a. Collect because the conveyance made him the landlord and Tenant cannot dispute his landlord's title.

b. Collect if his conveyance had been recorded because recording is notice to the world.

c. Not collect because the assignment by Tenant was made before Owner commenced suit.

d. Not collect because Tenant did not receive notice of the conveyance.

The correct answer is (d). *(MBE 272 130)*

REQUIRED: Whether Owner can successfully sue Tenant for rent due from February 1 to July 1.

DISCUSSION: Owner is an assignee of the lessor's interest in the leasehold and has the right to collect rent. But a debtor who pays the assignor without notice of the assignment will not be liable to the assignee. It was Owner's obligation to notify Tenant.

Answer (a) is incorrect because Tenant had no notice of the assignment (sale). Answer (b) is incorrect because recording the transaction is not notice to Tenant since (s)he has no duty to search the records. Recording conveyances is deemed constructive notice to subsequent purchasers, not existing tenants. Answer (c) is incorrect because an assignment does not discharge the liability of the assignor.

22. If Owner sued Assignee for the rent due from July 1, 1986 to November 1, 1986, he would collect

a. Because equity requires that to be done which should be done and Assignee should have paid the rent.

b. If Assignee had notice of the conveyance to Owner.

c. Because they stood in privity of estate.

d. If the assignment were in writing.

The correct answer is (c). *(MBE 272 131)*

REQUIRED: The reason a lessor can collect from the assignee after the lessee assigns the lease.

DISCUSSION: An assignee is considered to stand in privity of estate with the landlord and is subject to all the terms of the lease. Privity of estate exists when both have taken their real property interests from a common grantor (or each other). Without privity, Assignee could only be held liable by Tenant.

Answer (a) is incorrect because Assignee has a legal (not equitable) obligation to pay the rent. Answer (b) is incorrect because Assignee is liable for rent without prior notice of the conveyance so long as (s)he did not pay rent to Landlord. Answer (d) is incorrect because a tenant is liable for rent after occupying the premises regardless of whether the assignment was in writing.

23. In the absence of an applicable statute, the assignment of the lease by Tenant to Assignee was

a. Effective, whether or not it was in writing.

b. Effective, because the lease did not prohibit an assignment.

c. Not effective, because the lease contained no clause permitting assignment.

d. Not effective, because Tenant failed to give notice thereof to Owner.

The correct answer is (b). *(MBE 272 132)*

REQUIRED: Whether the assignment by Tenant to Assignee was effective and why.

DISCUSSION: Leases are assignable unless expressly agreed otherwise. Prohibitions against assignment are narrowly construed.

Answer (a) is incorrect because both the original lease and its assignment are required to be in writing under the Statute of Frauds. Answer (c) is incorrect because assignment is permitted unless expressly prohibited. Answer (d) is incorrect because Tenant had no duty to give notice to Owner in the absence of an agreement to that effect.

24. Assume Assignee dies testate. Assignee's interest in the lease

a. Is terminated because a leasehold is not an estate of inheritance and therefore cannot survive the death of the lessee.

b. Is terminated unless the land is located in a state that has a statute abolishing the distinction between freehold and nonfreehold estates.

c. Survives for the remaining portion of the term and is dealt with as an asset in the estate of the deceased Assignee.

d. Reverts to Tenant for the remaining portion of the term.

The correct answer is (c). *(MBE 272 133)*

REQUIRED: Whether an interest in a lease terminates upon death.

DISCUSSION: A leasehold estate is an interest in real property that may be assigned, donated, or devised. If the assignee dies testate (with a will), the leasehold interest will pass to his/her estate and then to the beneficiaries under the will as personalty (as explained in Question 2 on page 529).

Answer (a) is incorrect because a leasehold is a property interest which can be inherited. Answer (b) is incorrect because both freehold (generally outright ownership) and nonfreehold (generally leaseholds) estates would not terminate. Answer (d) is incorrect because Assignee's interest is inheritable and does not revert to Tenant.

25. Assume Assignee was a sublessee and not an assignee. In the absence of an applicable statute, which of the following statements is most accurate?

a. He could not enforce his sublease because it was not authorized by the lease.

b. He could enforce his sublease because it was not prohibited by the lease.

c. His position would be the same as that of an assignee.

d. He would be liable to Owner for rent because of his privity of contract with Owner.

The correct answer is (b). *(MBE 272 134)*

REQUIRED: The legal status of Assignee if (s)he were a sublessee.

DISCUSSION: Both assignments and subleases are permitted unless expressly prohibited by the lease. Public policy favors the transferability of property.

Answer (a) is incorrect because subleases are permitted unless expressly prohibited. Answer (c) is incorrect because an assignee is in privity of estate with the lessor and is bound by all the terms of the lease. A sublessee has taken only a portion of the sublessor's interest and is not in privity of estate with the lessor. The consequence is that sublessee will be liable only to Tenant. Answer (d) is incorrect because the sublessee is in privity of contract only with the sublessor (Tenant).

26. Tell, Inc. leased a building from Lott Corp. Tell paid monthly rent of $500 and was also responsible for paying the building's real estate taxes. On January 1, Vorn Co. and Tell entered into an agreement by which Vorn was entitled to occupy the building for the remainder of the term of Tell's lease in exchange for monthly payments of $600 to Tell. For the year, neither Tell nor Vorn paid the building's real estate taxes, and the taxes are delinquent. Learning this, Lott demanded that either Tell or Vorn pay the delinquent taxes. Both refused, and Lott has commenced an action against them. Lott will most likely prevail against

a. Vorn but not Tell because the lease was assigned to it.

b. Tell and Vorn because they are jointly and severally liable for the delinquent taxes.

c. Tell without Vorn because their January 1 agreement constituted a sublease.

d. Vorn but only to the extent of $100 for each month that it occupied the building during the year.

The correct answer is (b). *(CPA 1188 L-57)*

REQUIRED: The obligations of a lessee and its transferee to the original lessor.

DISCUSSION: The legal relationship between an original lessee and lessor is not altered by an assignment or a sublease. An assignment is a transfer of all of the lessee's rights, whereas a sublease is characterized by a retention of some right(s) by the lessee. If this agreement had constituted a sublease, Tell would remain liable to Lott for any breach of the terms of the original lease. But as sublessee, Vorn would not be in privity of contract or estate with Lott and could not be successfully sued by it for the delinquent taxes. However, the Tell-Vorn agreement apparently conveyed Tell's entire interest. Tell did not have a reversionary interest in possession, even for a few hours, and no mention is made of other rights retained by the lessee. Thus, the agreement is an assignment, Vorn is an assignee who stands in privity of estate with Lott, and both Tell and Vorn will be liable for the full amount of the taxes.

Answers (a) and (d) are incorrect because whether the agreement constituted a sublease or an assignment, Tell remains liable. Answer (c) is incorrect because Vorn is liable as an assignee.

27. Drake Corp. entered into a 5-year lease with Deb Samon that provided for Drake's occupancy of three floors of a high-rise office building at a monthly rent of $16,000. The lease stated, "The lessee may sublease the premises but only with the landlord's (Samon's) prior written consent." The lease was silent as to whether Drake could assign the lease. Which of the following statements is correct?

a. Subleasing of the premises with Samon's consent will relieve Drake from its obligation to pay rent.

b. Assignment of the lease with Samon's consent will relieve Drake from its obligation to pay rent.

c. Samon may refuse to consent to a subsequent sublease even if she has consented to a prior sublease.

d. Subleasing of the premises without Samon's consent is void.

The correct answer is (c). *(CPA 1187 L-56)*

REQUIRED: The correct statement about a lease that required prior written consent to a sublease.

DISCUSSION: The landlord (Samon) retains all rights reserved to her in the terms of the lease. This lease provides that the lessee (Drake) may sublease the property only after obtaining Samon's prior written consent. Thus, Samon must approve every sublease, and Samon retains the right to refuse consent to a sublease even after approving a prior sublease.

Answers (a) and (b) are incorrect because neither a sublease nor an assignment of a lease relieves Drake of its obligations under the lease unless Samon agrees to a novation. Answer (d) is incorrect because a sublease made in violation of the lease would be voidable, not void.

28. Sisk is a tenant of Met Co. and has 2 years remaining on a 6-year lease executed by Sisk and Met. The lease prohibits subletting but is silent as to Sisk's right to assign the lease. Sisk assigned the lease to Kern Corp., which assumed all of Sisk's obligations under the lease. Met objects to the assignment. Which of the following statements is correct?

a. The assignment to Kern is voidable at Met's option.

b. Sisk would have been relieved from liability on the lease with Met if Sisk obtained Met's consent to the assignment.

c. Sisk will remain liable to Met for the rent provided for in the lease.

d. With respect to the rent provided for in the lease, Kern is liable to Sisk but not to Met.

The correct answer is (c). *(CPA 588 L-55)*

REQUIRED: The rights and duties of a lessor and lessee under a lease prohibiting subletting but not assignments.

DISCUSSION: Absent a restriction against assignments in the lease, the lessee will retain the right to assign his/her interest. The prohibition against subletting does not prohibit assignments. Sisk will remain liable to Met for the rent until such time as Met agrees to a novation or a release and allows Kern to assume all of Sisk's legal obligations to Met.

Answer (a) is incorrect because the lease does not specifically limit Sisk's right of assignment, and Met therefore does not have the option to void the assignment. Answer (b) is incorrect because only a novation would relieve Sisk from his/her lease liability. Met's consent to the assignment would not be equivalent to a novation. Answer (d) is incorrect because after an assignment, the assignee is in privity of estate with the original landlord. Thus, Kern is liable to Met for the rent provided for in the original lease. If Kern does not pay and Met recovers the rent from Sisk, Sisk will be able to seek reimbursement from Kern.

22.5 Termination of the Leasehold

29. Which of the following statements is correct concerning the termination or duration of a periodic tenancy?

a. The tenancy is terminated by advance notice usually equivalent to one period of the tenancy.

b. The tenancy must last a minimum of 6 months.

c. A tenancy at sufferance is created when the landlord allows the tenant to remain after terminating a lease.

d. A tenant who remains after termination of a lease without permission of the landlord is a tenant at will.

The correct answer is (a). *(Publisher)*

REQUIRED: The correct statement concerning termination of a periodic tenancy.

DISCUSSION: A periodic tenancy is terminated by advance notice which is usually equivalent to one period of the tenancy. If the tenancy is from month to month, the notice must be given one month prior to termination. If it is an annual tenancy, the notice must be given one year prior to termination. In some states this advance notice has been shortened by statute.

Answer (b) is incorrect because a periodic tenancy has no minimum duration. Answer (c) is incorrect because a tenancy at will is created when the landlord allows the tenant to remain after termination of a lease. Answer (d) is incorrect because a tenancy at sufferance is created when the tenant remains without permission. If the landlord subsequently recognizes the tenant as a tenant, e.g., accepts rent, then a periodic tenancy is established.

30. Termination of the landlord/tenant relationship may occur in many ways, some rightfully and some upon breach by one of the parties. Which of the following causes of termination must have been the result of a breach?

a. Forfeiture.

b. Destruction of the premises.

c. Expiration of the lease term.

d. Surrender.

The correct answer is (a). *(Publisher)*

REQUIRED: The cause of termination which must have been the result of a breach.

DISCUSSION: A forfeiture is the surrendering of one's rights to the premises as a result of a breach of the lease. Frequently, the lease will require the tenant to forfeit the lease at the election of the landlord upon breach by the tenant.

Answer (b) is incorrect because destruction of the premises may occur through no one's fault. If it occurs due to the negligence or wrongful act of the tenant, then there may have been a breach. Answer (c) is incorrect because expiration of the lease term is a common termination of the landlord/tenant relationship without a breach. Answer (d) is incorrect because a surrender occurs when the tenant conveys his/her leasehold interest back to the landlord at any time. There may be a surrender with or without a breach of the lease.

31. Lester, the owner in fee simple of a small farm consisting of thirty acres of land improved with a house and several outbuildings, leased the same to Tanner for a ten-year period. After two years had expired, the government condemned twenty acres of the property and allocated the compensation award to Lester and Tanner according to their respective interests so taken. It so happened, however, that the twenty acres taken embraced all of the farm's tillable land, leaving only the house, outbuildings, and a small woodlot. Tanner quit possession, and Lester brought suit against him to recover rent. Lester will

a. Lose, because there has been a frustration of purpose which excuses Tanner from further performance of his contract to pay rent.

b. Lose, because there has been a breach of the implied covenant of quiet enjoyment by Lester's inability to provide Tanner with possession of the whole of the property for the entire term.

c. Win, because of the implied warranty on the part of the tenant to return the demised premises in the same condition at the end of the term as they were at the beginning.

d. Win, because the relationship of landlord and tenant was unaffected by the condemnation, thus leaving Tanner still obligated to pay rent.

The correct answer is (d). *(MBE Part I-165)*

REQUIRED: The status of the parties after a partial condemnation of leased property.

DISCUSSION: If the government had condemned the entire property, the tenancy would have terminated by operation of law and Tanner would have had no further liability for rent. Since the condemnation was only partial and the lessee received his share of the condemnation award, the tenancy was not terminated. Tanner remains obligated.

Answer (a) is incorrect because a substantial portion of the property remains and Tanner has theoretically received from the condemnation award damages equal to the value of the interest taken. Answer (b) is incorrect because a landlord is not accountable for breach of the covenant of quiet enjoyment when a governmental unit exercises its power of eminent domain. Answer (c) is incorrect because the tenant cannot be held any more accountable for the condemnation of the property than the landlord. Furthermore, Lester was paid for his interest.

32. Which of the following is a true statement about the landlord's right to evict a tenant?

a. Most jurisdictions statutorily permit forcible entry to evict a wrongfully holding over tenant.

b. Self-help repossession is permitted in most states but only pursuant to a specific term in the lease.

c. In most states, the remedy for unlawful detainer is a suit pursuant to a summary procedure after proper notice has been given.

d. If a tenant's lease has been lawfully terminated, the landlord may sue to evict but may not resort to constructive eviction.

The correct answer is (c). *(Publisher)*

REQUIRED: The true statement about eviction.

DISCUSSION: A tenant who wrongfully remains on the premises may be evicted by court action. Most states have a special summary procedure for the swift eviction of such a tenant. The defendant must be given adequate notice, and the plaintiff must prove a right to possession. If (s)he still remains on the premises, the tenant and his/her property will be forcibly removed by a law enforcement agent.

Answers (a) and (b) are incorrect because most states do not allow forcible entry by the landlord (self-help) to evict a tenant. Answer (d) is incorrect because constructive eviction, e.g., turning off utilities, is a permissible remedy.

CHAPTER TWENTY-THREE INSURANCE

23.1 Nature of Insurance and Contract Formation

1. Insurance is best defined as

a. A system for transferring risk through risk avoidance or loss control.

b. Any contract that creates an insurable interest.

c. A form of pure risk called gambling.

d. A means of combining many loss exposures so that losses are shared by all participants.

The correct answer is (d). *(Publisher)*

REQUIRED: The best definition of insurance.

DISCUSSION: In theory, insurance is a method for spreading losses that arise from a risk to which many persons are subject. Loss is an unanticipated diminution in economic value as opposed to normal depreciation. Risk is uncertainty about the occurrence or the amount of loss. For example, buildings are subject to the risk of loss by fire. If the owners all pay small fees (premiums) for insurance coverage, the minority of owners who suffer loss from fire can be reimbursed from the pool of funds created by the payments from all the owners. Every participant bears part of the loss instead of a few bearing all the loss.

Answer (a) is incorrect because risk avoidance and loss control do not transfer risk of loss. For example, one may avoid the risk of liability for driving an automobile by not performing that act. One may control (prevent or reduce) such liability by observing the traffic laws. Answer (b) is incorrect because an insurable interest is a prerequisite for creating an insurance contract. Answer (c) is incorrect because an insured is required to have an insurable interest, which is basically a potential for loss if an event occurs. Gambling occurs when only a bet is at risk.

2. Which of the following is not an important function of insurance?

a. Providing security for commercial undertakings by translating risk into certainty by the payment of a premium.

b. Providing a basis for credit.

c. Providing employment for a large number of people.

d. Promoting general social values by an equitable distribution of losses.

The correct answer is (c). *(Publisher)*

REQUIRED: The statement which is not an important function of insurance.

DISCUSSION: Insurance is very important in our society, performing several valuable functions for individuals and businesses. Although the insurance industry is one of the largest in the United States, the creation of jobs is incidental to its main societal functions.

Answer (a) is incorrect because insurance provides security for commercial undertakings by eliminating risk through a known premium payment. Answer (b) is incorrect because insurance provides a basis for credit. A person who sells on credit is assured that the goods will be protected. Answer (d) is incorrect because equitable distribution of losses promotes social values by providing for those who have extreme losses.

3. Which of the following is the best functional definition of insurance?

a. A legal contract by which the insurer, in return for consideration, agrees to pay another person if a stated loss or injury occurs.

b. A legal contract by which an insurance company, in return for premiums, agrees to pay the policyholder if a certain event occurs.

c. A written promise by the insurer to pay a person holding an insurable interest if loss occurs from the occurrence of a contingent event.

d. A policy or other writing issued by an insurance company, for a consideration, that promises to pay a beneficiary for a loss arising from an existing or after-created risk.

The correct answer is (a). *(Publisher)*

REQUIRED: The best functional definition of insurance.

DISCUSSION: An insurance contract (a policy) must satisfy the usual requirements: offer and acceptance, consideration, legality, and capacity of the parties. The insured must have an insurable interest in the subject matter of the contract. Also, the subject matter generally must exist at the time of contracting. In the contract, the insurer makes a promise to pay a stated amount for loss or injury incurred as a result of a contingent event.

Answer (b) is incorrect because the payee may be a stranger to the contract. A person who insures his/her own life names a third party as a beneficiary. Moreover, not every insurer is an insurance company, and the contingent event insured against must involve a risk. Answer (c) is incorrect because, while some insurance contracts must be written, the requirement is not general since the Statute of Frauds will not apply when performance may occur within 1 year. Also, the payee and the policyholder need not be the same. Answer (d) is incorrect because the contract may often be oral, and, if the risk is not already in existence, the transaction is in essence a wager, not insurance.

4. Which of the following is not a reason generally given to justify insurance regulation by the government?

a. To protect the purchaser of insurance since most insurance contracts are not subject to bargaining and negotiation.

b. The technical and complicated nature of the insurance contract.

c. To prevent the use of insurance for gambling and illegal purposes.

d. To provide protection for the insurer against competition from other unregulated companies.

The correct answer is (c). *(Publisher)*

REQUIRED: The statement not a reason for governmental regulation of insurance.

DISCUSSION: Insurance regulation protects consumers. Regulation is intended to prevent insolvency of and fraud by insurers so that beneficiaries will receive payment. Regulation also seeks to make insurance available at a fair and affordable price, but preventing the use of insurance for gambling and illegal purposes is not generally a reason for regulation. Requirements such as the need for an insurable interest are presumed to protect against such abuses.

Answer (a) is incorrect because insurance contracts are generally considered contracts of adhesion. The greater bargaining power of the insurer gives the insured no choice as to terms of the contract. Answer (b) is incorrect because the complexity of insurance contracts requires regulation to protect the lay consumer. Answer (d) is incorrect because a responsible insurer needs protection from companies that have lower costs when not regulated.

5. The insurance industry is heavily regulated. Which of the following is true?

a. The federal government has regulated the industry since passage of the McCarron Act in 1945.

b. A state administrative agency may issue rules prescribing standard provisions in insurance contracts.

c. Insurers are generally required to maintain reserves for payment of claims, but rates are usually unregulated.

d. Insurers may operate only through licensed agents and brokers and write only one kind of insurance.

The correct answer is (b). *(Publisher)*

REQUIRED: The true statement about insurance regulation.

DISCUSSION: States may require the use of standard policy forms or standard provisions. The latter may be deemed a part of the insurance contract even though not expressly incorporated into the policy by the insurer. Policy forms usually must be approved by the insurance departments of states, which have the authority to prohibit use of deceptive or ambiguous forms.

Answer (a) is incorrect because Congress has the power to regulate the industry but expressly delegated the power to the states in the McCarron Act. Answer (c) is incorrect because rates are somewhat regulated. Some states require approval prior to implementation of new rates, while others simply empower the insurance commissioner to prohibit use of rates that violate the rate standards but do not otherwise control the rate-setting process. Answer (d) is incorrect because the modern trend is to multiple-line underwriting: one insurer can write many kinds of insurance.

6. Which of the following is not a characteristic of an insurance contract?

a. Performance of at least one party is contingent.

b. An insurance company must be granted competence to contract.

c. Performance is generally simultaneous or nearly so.

d. Offer and acceptance.

The correct answer is (c). *(Publisher)*

REQUIRED: The item not characteristic of an insurance contract.

DISCUSSION: The nature of the insurance agreement is that performance by the policyholder (payment of premiums) occurs before performance by the insurer (payment of claims). Indeed, the contract may always remain executory on the insurer's side although executed by the policyholder by the payment of premiums.

Answer (a) is incorrect because the insurance contract is contingent. The claim is paid only upon the happening of an event that is uncertain as to its timing or occurrence. Answer (b) is incorrect because a contracting party must have the capacity to contract. An insurance company is granted that capacity by the charter issued by the state where it was organized. For operations in other states, the capacity is conferred by license. Answer (d) is incorrect because the elements of a contract must be present: agreement, consideration, competent parties, and legality.

7. In which way does the formation of an insurance contract differ from any other contract?

a. The requirement that the insured must have an insurable interest.

b. The insurance contract is not valid unless written.

c. Consideration is not needed for the formation of an insurance contract.

d. In insurance, only the insured can commit a breach.

The correct answer is (a). *(Publisher)*

REQUIRED: The manner in which the formation of an insurance contract differs from other contracts.

DISCUSSION: An insurance contract is very similar to any other. An additional requirement is that the insured must have an insurable interest, i.e., a possibility of pecuniary loss if the event insured against occurs.

Answer (b) is incorrect because there is no general requirement that an insurance contract be written. Oral binders are given every day in the insurance business. State laws frequently provide that the insured must be provided with a written copy of the insurance policy within a reasonable time. Answer (c) is incorrect because consideration is needed for the initial formation of an insurance contract. The premium may not be paid immediately, but there is a promise to pay. Answer (d) is incorrect because the insurance company can also commit a breach by refusing to pay the proceeds of the policy upon the occurrence of the event.

8. An insurance contract is not enforceable if the person insuring lacks an insurable interest in the subject matter of the policy. The presence of an insurable interest is not

a. Consistent with the indemnity principle.

b. Based on the need to provide safeguards against moral hazards.

c. A reflection of a public policy that discourages wagering agreements.

d. Required when a person insures his/her own life.

The correct answer is (d). *(Publisher)*

REQUIRED: The true statement about an insurable interest.

DISCUSSION: The person who takes out an insurance policy must have the potential to sustain financial loss when the risk insured against occurs. If no insurable interest is present, the insurance contract becomes a speculation for gain rather than a means of compensation for loss, and the insuring person has no motive to avoid the event insured against. The exception is insurance of one's own life. Because one who insures his/her life is presumed to be motivated to avoid death, the impossibility of having an insurable interest in one's own life does not contravene the policy basis of the requirement.

Answer (a) is incorrect because the purpose of insurance is to restore a person to the position (s)he held prior to the loss. Absent an insurable interest, a person would improve his/her position if the event insured against occurred. Answer (b) is incorrect because the moral hazard of indifference to or an active desire to cause the loss insured against is limited by the requirement of an insured interest. Answer (c) is incorrect because, lacking a prospect of loss from the event insured against, the insuring person would in effect be wagering the premiums paid in hopes of recovering a profit from the proceeds.

9. Which of the following is a correct statement about a legal doctrine that assists the insured in pressing a claim against an insurer?

a. A general equitable principle is that the law abhors a forfeiture.

b. The insurer acts through agents but is not bound when they go beyond their actual authority.

c. Insurance policies are strictly construed against insured persons.

d. Contract concepts such as estoppel, waiver, or election may not be asserted by the insured who breaches a condition.

The correct answer is (a). *(Publisher)*

REQUIRED: The true statement about a legal doctrine assisting the insured to recover.

DISCUSSION: The typical contract of insurance is a complex document drafted by the insurer that contains many restrictions on the insured's right of recovery. These limitations may prove difficult for the lay consumer to understand and comply with, and may defeat the insured's reasonable expectations for recovery. Consistent with the equitable maxim that the law abhors a forfeiture (in this case, of premiums paid by an insured who has acted in substantial good faith), courts have shown a tendency to favor the insured so as to avoid unfair results.

Answer (b) is incorrect because an agent binds the insurer by acts within his/her apparent as well as actual authority. Answer (c) is incorrect because insurance contracts are contracts of adhesion that involve great disparity of bargaining power. Such contracts are construed in favor of the insured since ambiguities are the responsibility of the insurer, the party who drafted the agreement and imposed its terms on the insured. Answer (d) is incorrect because these concepts can be asserted by insureds. For example, an insurer who accepts a premium after breach of a condition by the insured may have elected to choose its right to further performance rather than to treat the contract as rescinded. Or, an insurer who processes a claim after the time limit for its submission has lapsed may have waived its right to the limitation.

10. Joan Brady applied for a life insurance policy on her own life for $50,000. The application contained the following clause:

> The insurance hereby applied for shall not take effect until 1) a written or printed policy shall have been actually delivered to and accepted by the insured (Brady), while in good health, and 2) the first premium thereon is paid.

What is the legal effect of the above clause?

a. One or both of the above provisions is invalid as a matter of public policy.

b. If Brady paid the premium at the time she took out the policy and was at that time "in good health," the policy is legally binding irrespective of her having suffered a serious accident prior to the insurance policy being written and delivered.

c. If the insurance company wrote the policy and delivered it to a general agent who held it for safekeeping until Brady picked it up, the policy would be in effect if Brady was in good health when the policy was delivered to the agent even though Brady died before picking it up.

d. Under no circumstances will Brady prevail unless she physically picks up the policy while "in good health."

The correct answer is (c). *(CPA 1177 L-10)*

REQUIRED: The legal effect of a clause in a life insurance policy that provides that it will not take effect until the policy is delivered to the insured who is in good health, and the first premium is paid.

DISCUSSION: Under case law, delivery in insurance includes constructive delivery. Thus, when the insurer puts the policy in the possession of the local agent to be delivered to the insured, the courts hold that the agent is holding the policy for the insured. The policy is deemed to have been delivered within the meaning of the clause.

Answer (a) is incorrect because neither provision set out in the clause is invalid as a matter of public policy. Rather, they are legal standard provisions in life insurance policies. Answer (b) is incorrect because, even though the insured may have paid the first premium when (s)he was in good health, the requirement that the delivery of the policy occur while (s)he was in good health is legally binding. Answer (d) is incorrect because, as explained above, the policy will become effective if it is delivered while (s)he is in good health. Delivery can be actual (physical) or constructive.

11. Gertrude went to an insurance agent and completed an application for insurance. She did not pay anything at the time, and the agent said that the contract would not be effective until signed by the insurance company (the carrier) and delivered to her. However, the agent did say that she would have protection for a period of 30 days.

a. If the agent is an independent agent and the insurance was life insurance, Gertrude would not be insured until the contract was signed and actually delivered to her.

b. If the agent worked for a particular insurance company and the insurance was for an automobile, Gertrude would be insured for the 30 days.

c. If the insurance is fire insurance, Gertrude will clearly be insured for 30 days even if the agent is independent.

d. An independent insurance agent can never bind a company.

The correct answer is (b). *(Publisher)*

REQUIRED: The correct statement concerning the ability of an insurance agent to orally provide protection for a 30-day period.

DISCUSSION: An agent who works for a particular automobile insurance company is considered to have apparent authority to bind the company on a temporary basis. This view of authority is based on the right of a property or liability insurer to cancel excessive risks accepted by its agent by giving legal notice and a refund. Gertrude is covered for 30 days by the temporary contract even though she made no payment.

Answer (a) is incorrect because, although delivery is the usual method of communicating acceptance, courts have held that the contract can be completed by constructive delivery (i.e., to the agent), especially when the insured has died prior to delivery. Answer (c) is incorrect because an independent insurance agent may not have the authority to bind a particular company for 30 days. The extent of an independent agent's authority is not clear. Answer (d) is incorrect because an independent agent may be able to bind a company if given express or apparent authority.

12. The time at which insurance coverage becomes effective is obviously important. Delivery of the insurance contract may affect the timing of its formation depending on the nature of the coverage sought and the intent of the parties. Which of the following is true?

a. Delivery of a life insurance policy is generally not required.

b. Delivery of a property insurance policy is generally not required.

c. Delivery is necessary because insurance contracts must be written.

d. Delivery is necessary under general contract law.

The correct answer is (b). *(Publisher)*

REQUIRED: The true statement about delivery of the insurance contract.

DISCUSSION: An insurance contract is formed only after a valid offer and acceptance have occurred. Commonly, the offer is the application by the insured, and the acceptance is the issuance of a policy by the insurer and its delivery to the insured. Life insurance policies often contain a "delivery in good health clause" by which coverage is not made effective (acceptance does not occur) until the policy is delivered to an insured who is in good health and has paid the first premium. In property and liability insurance, the insured may generally receive an oral or written binder issued by an agent that will commit the company before a policy is issued.

Answer (a) is incorrect because delivery is generally required to bind the company to a policy of life insurance. Answer (c) is incorrect because many insurance contracts are oral (but statutes often require a written policy within some period of time). Answer (d) is incorrect because delivery is not a requirement of general contract law, but it may signify acceptance or fulfill a condition precedent to the insurer's duty to perform.

13. Insurance companies are usually either stock or mutual companies. Which of the following is true?

a. Mutual companies are for-profit corporations.

b. Mutual companies are strongest in the property insurance field.

c. Stock and mutual companies have similar operational characteristics.

d. Stock and mutual companies write all the insurance issued in the U.S.

The correct answer is (c). *(Publisher)*

REQUIRED: The true statement about stock and mutual insurance companies.

DISCUSSION: Stock insurance companies are for-profit corporations; stockholders are not necessarily policy-holders. Mutual companies are in principle cooperatives. Policyholders pay a fee for membership, and any profit earned is returned as a rebate on premiums. The everyday business activities of these kinds of companies vary little. They cover the same risks and provide the same services.

Answer (a) is incorrect because mutual companies are a type of nonprofit organization that returns all "profits" to policyholders. Answer (b) is incorrect because stock companies dominate the insurance field except with regard to life insurance. Answer (d) is incorrect because federal governmental agencies provide Social Security benefits, life insurance for members of the military, insurance for bank deposits, and real estate mortgages on residences. State agencies and fraternal organizations are other insurers.

Questions 14 and 15 are based on the following information. In the application for a life insurance policy, Mary answered in the negative to the question, "Have you ever had any heart disease?" Both the application and the insurance policy which was issued provided: "Applicant warrants the truthfulness of the statements made in the application and they are made conditions to the contract of insurance." Unknown to Mary, she had had a heart disease at a very early age. The policy provided that the proceeds were not to be paid over to the named beneficiary, Mary's daughter, Joan, "until she reaches the age of 21." No contingent beneficiary was named in the policy. Mary was killed in an automobile accident 2 months after the policy was issued. Joan died 1 month later at the age of 19 from injuries incurred in the same accident.

14. If the question is raised in an action against the insurance company, how is the court likely to construe the clause dealing with the truthfulness of statements in the application?

a. The clause is a condition, and because the condition was not met, the company will not be liable.

b. The clause is a condition, but it will be interpreted to mean, "truthfulness to the best of my knowledge."

c. The clause is not a condition, and therefore the company may be liable even though Mary's statement was not true.

d. The clause is not a condition but is a promise and therefore the company will have a cause of action against Mary's estate for any loss it suffered because of Mary's misstatement.

The correct answer is (b). *(MBE Part I-154)*

REQUIRED: How a court should construe a clause dealing with the truthfulness of statements in a life insurance application.

DISCUSSION: Information furnished by a life insurance applicant is classified as either a warranty or a representation. A warranty is a condition precedent, considered to be a part of the insurance contract, and presumed to be material without proof by the insurer. A representation is not part of the policy but merely a statement which induces the insurance company to issue the policy. A representation is acceptable if substantially true and made without fraudulent intent. Most states have statutes requiring their courts to interpret statements made in an application to be representations, not warranties.

Answer (a) is incorrect because the clause will not excuse the company from liability since Mary's statement will be interpreted to be a representation. Answer (c) is incorrect because the clause is a condition the failure of which will rescind, amend, or modify the liability of the insurer if Mary's statement is a material misrepresentation of facts or is otherwise fraudulent. Answer (d) is incorrect because a false statement by an insured will either void the policy (if a warranty or a material representation) or not affect the policy (if only a representation). The insurance company has no right to damages in either case.

15. If no objection is made concerning Mary's misstatement in the application, how is the court most likely to construe the clause dealing with the payment of the proceeds to Joan?

a. Joan's reaching the age of 21 is a constructive condition concurrent.

b. Joan's reaching the age of 21 is a condition precedent to the insurance company's duty to pay anyone.

c. Joan's reaching the age of 21 has legal significance only with respect to the time of payment.

d. Joan's reaching the age of 21 has no legal significance.

The correct answer is (c). *(MBE Part I-155)*

REQUIRED: How a court should construe a clause in a life insurance policy dealing with the payment of proceeds.

DISCUSSION: The beneficiary designation is generally revocable and a named beneficiary has no vested interest. However, on the death of the insured, the named beneficiary has a vested contractual right to the proceeds. Restricting payment until age 21 only determines when the beneficiary will actually receive the proceeds. The proceeds are payable to Joan's estate or heirs since she died before receiving them.

Answer (a) is incorrect because Joan's reaching the age of 21 is only a condition as to time of payment, not as to the obligation to pay. Answer (b) is incorrect because Joan's reaching the age of 21 is not a condition precedent to the insurance company's duty to pay. It only directs the time of payment. Answer (d) is incorrect because Joan's reaching the age of 21 has legal significance as to when Joan was entitled to the proceeds.

23.2 Life Insurance

16. Life insurance

a. Is a contract of indemnity.

b. Policies are usually short-term.

c. Covers only the mortality risk.

d. Generally has no cash value.

The correct answer is (a). *(Publisher)*

REQUIRED: The true statement about the characteristics of life insurance.

DISCUSSION: The risk insured against by life insurance is the financial consequences of premature death, an event that will happen only once but is certain to occur. Other forms of insurance concern events that may recur and are often not serious. Life insurance is usually purchased to protect against the cessation of income needed for support of the family and to shield them from the decedent's debts.

Answer (b) is incorrect because life insurance is customarily long-term if not for life. Answer (c) is incorrect because, unlike other forms of insurance, life insurance does not attempt to reimburse for the actual amount of a loss since loss of life is not measurable. Life insurance is intended to replace economic benefits lost by a person's death. Answer (d) is incorrect because except for term policies, life insurance differs from other kinds of coverage in providing cash value.

17. Life insurance is offered in several forms. The kind that offers no investment feature is

a. Whole life.

b. Endowment.

c. Straight life.

d. Term.

The correct answer is (d). *(Publisher)*

REQUIRED: The kind of life insurance not offering an investment feature.

DISCUSSION: Term life insurance provides protection for a specified period. Premiums are level throughout the period. When the term ends, the insured receives no payment. Term insurance may be renewable (possibly at higher premiums) or convertible to another form. It is the cheapest kind of life insurance.

Answers (a) and (c) are incorrect because whole life furnishes lifetime insurance protection with a cash surrender value. A limited payment policy provides for premiums to be paid over a specified term of years or until the insured reaches a certain age. At the end of the period, protection will continue although no further premiums are paid, but no payment is made to the insured unless the policy is cashed in. A straight life or ordinary policy is whole life insurance with level premiums payable for life. It is easily the most common form of whole life insurance. Answer (b) is incorrect because an endowment policy provides life insurance protection for its duration. A cash payment is made (the policy endows) at the end of the term. Premiums for endowment policies are higher than for whole life insurance.

18. A typical term life insurance policy

a. Builds up a cash value during its duration against which the policyholder can borrow.

b. Is assignable.

c. Creates a vested interest in the named beneficiary.

d. Does not require an insurable interest in the person taking out the policy as do other types of life insurance policies.

The correct answer is (b). *(CPA 576 L-31)*

REQUIRED: The correct statement with respect to a typical term life insurance policy.

DISCUSSION: A life insurance policy, including a term policy, is generally assignable. Consent of the insurance company is frequently not required; the effect is to give the assignee the first claim against the proceeds of the policy.

Answer (a) is incorrect because term life insurance policies do not build up cash value. Answer (c) is incorrect because the general rule is that a beneficiary has a contingent expectancy only and can be replaced prior to the death of the insured. Answer (d) is incorrect because the person taking out term life insurance must have an insurable interest, the same as for other life insurance policies.

19. Which of the following is not a common provision with regard to the payment of premiums on a life insurance policy?

a. The insured is entitled to a grace period after the due date of a premium even if adequate advance notice was given by the insurance company.

b. If an insured does not pay the premiums (s)he may be entitled to a reduced amount of paid-up insurance.

c. The insurance policy may be reinstated with renewed evidence of insurability and the payment of all premiums missed.

d. The insurance company must file notice with the state insurance commissioner before canceling a life insurance policy for failure to pay premiums.

The correct answer is (d). *(Publisher)*

REQUIRED: The item not a common provision for payment of life insurance premiums.

DISCUSSION: In the event an insured does not pay premiums, the insurance company may cancel the policy or apply other provisions contained in the insurance policy. The insurance company does not need to file notice with the state insurance commissioner prior to such cancellation.

Answer (a) is incorrect because it is common to have a grace period to pay life insurance premiums even if adequate advance notice was given. Answer (b) is incorrect because it is also common to convert the existing equity in an insurance policy to a reduced amount of paid-up insurance when premiums are no longer paid. Answer (c) is incorrect because insurance policies are commonly reinstated if the insured provides new evidence of insurability and repays all the premiums missed.

20. Arthur Cox purchased a $100,000 20-year life insurance policy. In filling out the application, he erroneously but unintentionally answered one of the questions regarding his prior medical history incorrectly. The question required the applicant to list "any and all occasions within the past 5 years in which he was hospitalized." His response was "none." However, he had in fact been hospitalized 4 years previously in connection with the removal of an impacted wisdom tooth. The policy stated that all representations in the application were to be strictly enforced, constituted warranties, and were incorporated by reference into the policy. It also contained a 2-year incontestable clause. Less than 2 years after obtaining the policy, Cox suffered a fatal heart attack. The insurance company denies liability under the policy and Cox's beneficiary sues for payment. Under the circumstances, what outcome should Cox's beneficiary expect?

a. Win because Cox lived for a period of 1 year after issuance of the policy.

b. Lose because warranties are strictly construed against the warrantor.

c. Win because the misrepresentation was unintentional and immaterial.

d. Lose despite the fact that the misrepresentation was innocent and immaterial in that the law treats such contracts as voidable.

The correct answer is (c). *(CPA 577 L-7)*

REQUIRED: The legal effect of a health misrepresentation on a life insurance application.

DISCUSSION: Statements made in an application for life insurance are required by statute to be interpreted as representations and not warranties in most states. For an insurance company to avoid liability on a policy because of a misrepresentation, it must prove the misrepresentation was material and would have prevented issuance of the policy. Failure of Cox to disclose he had been hospitalized for an impacted wisdom tooth 4 years prior to the application would not be considered material to the risk of the insurance company. The beneficiary should win because this misrepresentation was unintentional and immaterial.

Answer (a) is incorrect because the contestable period here is 2 years, not 1 year. This means that after 2 years, the insurance company cannot contest the policy due to misstatements by the insured. Answer (b) is incorrect because while warranties are strictly construed against the warrantor, courts construe statements of the insured in an application as representations if there is any ambiguity and gives the insurance company the burden of proving their materiality. Answer (d) is incorrect because insurance contracts are not voidable unless the misrepresentations are shown to be material.

21. Jack financed the purchase of a new truck with Acme Financing Co. The financing arrangement requires Jack to make 48 monthly payments of principal and interest. Acme wants to be sure that Jack's obligation will be paid in full if Jack dies before satisfying the obligation. Acme will most likely require Jack to purchase.

a. Ordinary life insurance.

b. Whole life insurance.

c. Credit life insurance.

d. Universal life insurance.

The correct answer is (c). *(Publisher)*

REQUIRED: The type of policy normally used to protect creditors in consumer financing transactions.

DISCUSSION: Credit life insurance is carried by a debtor in connection with a specific credit transaction. The debtor names his/her creditor as the beneficiary of the policy. Credit life policies are a type of decreasing term insurance. The benefit provided by the policy decreases as the debtor's obligation decreases. Thus, the policy expires when the final payment is made and the obligation is satisfied. Whether credit life insurance may be required and the rates charged are subject to insurance department regulations.

Answer (a) is incorrect because ordinary life insurance is designed to remain in effect for the entire life of the insured. Neither a creditor nor a debtor has a legitimate interest in providing insurance for the protection of the creditor once an obligation is satisfied. Answer (b) is incorrect because whole life is another name for ordinary life. Answer (d) is incorrect because universal life is a variation of ordinary life that includes a savings feature.

22. Tom wants to purchase insurance that includes both life insurance protection and a savings feature. Tom should probably purchase

a. Universal life insurance.

b. An endowment contract.

c. Term insurance.

d. Whole life insurance.

The correct answer is (a). *(Publisher)*

REQUIRED: The insurance contract that provides life insurance protection and a savings feature.

DISCUSSION: Universal life insurance is a relatively new variation of ordinary life insurance. First sold in 1979, universal life divides an ordinary life contract into two parts. The first part is life insurance protection that is provided by renewable term insurance. The term insurance is renewed regularly until the end of life. The second part is a savings feature. The savings feature is funded by the portion of the premium payment that exceeds the cost of the term insurance. The excess premiums are invested and accumulate over the insured's life. The tax treatment of these policies is more favorable than that of ordinary investments.

Answer (b) is incorrect because an endowment contract does not provide life insurance protection, but is an agreement by the insurer to pay a lump sum of money to the insured when (s)he reaches a certain age. Answer (c) is incorrect because term insurance pays a benefit only if the insured dies within a specified period, and does not provide a savings feature. Answer (d) is incorrect because whole life does not provide a savings feature, although the insured has the right to borrow an amount up to the cash surrender value of the policy from the insurer. This type of loan is secured by an assignment to the insurer of the policy's proceeds up to the amount of the loan.

23. On October 15, 1986, Pam Golden made a loan of $100,000 to Phillips and obtained a mortgage for $50,000 on Phillips' home as security for the loan. The home was worth $50,000. The following day Golden, to protect herself further, took out a fire insurance policy on Phillips' home in the sum of $50,000 with herself as beneficiary, and also a policy on Phillips' life in the same sum, with herself as beneficiary. Golden paid the premiums on both policies for 1 year. On March 1, 1987, Phillips paid his debt to Golden in full and the mortgage was satisfied and canceled. On April 15, 1987, Phillips' home was completely destroyed by fire, and Phillips died in the flames. At this time, the two policies were still in effect and there had been no change in the beneficiary. On which policy, if any, is Golden entitled to collect?

a. Life insurance policy only.

b. Fire insurance policy only.

c. Both insurance policies.

d. Neither insurance policy.

The correct answer is (a). *(CPA 581 L-45)*

REQUIRED: Whether the named beneficiary has the requisite insurable interest in life and fire policies.

DISCUSSION: To recover on a property insurance policy, the beneficiary must have an insurable interest at the time the loss occurred. In this case, Golden ceased having an insurable interest in Phillips' house when Phillips repaid the mortgage. Thus, she cannot collect on the fire insurance policy. In life insurance, however, the person buying the insurance needs an insurable interest only at the time the policy is issued. Since Golden had an insurable interest in the life of Phillips (as an unsecured creditor) at the time the policy was issued, she can collect on the life insurance policy even after the debt is paid off.

Answer (b) is incorrect because Golden did not have an insurable interest at the time the property loss occurred and therefore cannot collect on the fire insurance policy. Answer (c) is incorrect because Golden can collect only on the life insurance policy. Answer (d) is incorrect because Golden can collect on the life insurance policy since she had the requisite insurable interest when the policy was issued.

24. Carey insured his own life for $25,000 and named Allen, a long-time friend, as the beneficiary. If the life insurance policy was a 10-year term policy, which of the following is correct?

a. Allen could not continue to pay the premium on Carey's life even if he subsequently owns the policy since he lacks the requisite insurable interest.

b. The policy is nonassignable since term insurance normally does not have a cash surrender value.

c. Allen does not have an insurable interest in the life of Carey.

d. Allen owns the policy because he is the designated beneficiary.

The correct answer is (c). *(CPA 1181 L-57)*

REQUIRED: The correct statement concerning a term life insurance policy purchased by the insured who named a friend as beneficiary.

DISCUSSION: The person who initially buys life insurance must have an insurable interest (a relationship so that there is a possibility of loss if the insured dies) in the life of the insured. Each person is treated as having an insurable interest in his/her own life. Allen, a long-time friend, does not have an insurable interest in the life of Carey, but the beneficiary need not have such an interest.

Answer (a) is incorrect because neither a beneficiary nor a subsequent owner need have an insurable interest. Anyone may pay the premiums. Answer (b) is incorrect because, while it is true that term insurance has no cash surrender value, its potential proceeds may be assigned. Answer (d) is incorrect because the person taking out the insurance (or his/her assignee) is the owner, not the beneficiary.

25. Real Life Insurance Company has refused to pay on a $50,000 term life insurance policy taken out by Dodson. The circumstances surrounding Dodson's procuring the policy are as follows: Maxwell, an acquaintance of Dodson's, contacted him one day and asked him if he would like to make $100. Dodson said, "Sure, as long as it is easy money." Maxwell assured Dodson that the only thing Dodson had to do was sign an application for insurance, submit to a physical, name Maxwell as the beneficiary, and subsequently assign the policy to Maxwell. Maxwell paid Dodson the $100 and reimbursed him for the premium. Two years after taking out the policy, Dodson died. Maxwell presented the policy to Real Life for payment and it refused to pay. Which of the following is correct?

a. Real Life must pay the $50,000 to Maxwell since he is the beneficiary.

b. Dodson's estate is entitled to the $50,000 proceeds of the life insurance policy.

c. Maxwell will recover the $50,000 since the policy was assigned to him.

d. Maxwell will recover nothing in that he lacked an insurable interest in Dodson's life.

The correct answer is (d). *(CPA 1180 L-54)*

REQUIRED: The correct statement concerning the validity of a life insurance policy.

DISCUSSION: The person who initially buys life insurance must have an insurable interest in the insured. This requires a relationship so that there is a possibility of loss if the insured dies. Although Dodson had an insurable interest in his/her own life, the transaction was a sham to circumvent the requirement of insurable interest. Maxwell has no insurable interest in Dodson's life and will receive nothing.

Answers (a) and (c) are incorrect because Maxwell will not recover the $50,000 due to the fraud he and Dodson practiced on the company at the time the policy was issued. Answer (b) is incorrect because Dodson was party to the fraud and also because he assigned all his interest in the policy to Maxwell.

26. The doctrine that a person is prohibited from asserting a position that is inconsistent with his/her conduct, if such acts have been justifiably relied upon by another, is

a. Misrepresentation.

b. Concealment.

c. Waiver.

d. Estoppel.

The correct answer is (d). *(Publisher)*

REQUIRED: The doctrine prohibiting a person from asserting a position not consistent with his/her actions.

DISCUSSION: Estoppel prevents a party from suffering a detriment as a result of relying on the acts or conduct of another. For example, if an insurer routinely accepts late premium payments from the insured and does not cancel the policy, the insurer will be prevented from asserting a defense of late payment should the insured try to collect the benefits provided by the policy.

Answer (a) is incorrect because misrepresentation is a false or misleading statement of fact made to induce an insurer to enter into an insurance contract. A misrepresentation may be grounds for contract rescission if it was relied on by the insurer as an inducement to contract and it was substantially false when made, or if it became substantially false and such falsity was known to the insured before the contract was created. Answer (b) is incorrect because concealment is the failure of a party to communicate what (s)he knows and should communicate to the other party. Failure to communicate information material to the insured risk will invalidate the policy. Answer (c) is incorrect because waiver is the intentional relinquishment of a known right.

27. Booth applied to Ace Insurance Company for a life insurance policy on Abe's life. Because Abe already carried a policy on his own life with Ace, Ace had all the requisite medical and other information concerning Abe. Booth represented that he had an insurable interest. When Abe died, it was discovered that Booth killed Abe and had never had an insurable interest in Abe's life.

a. Booth is entitled to recover on the insurance policy since Ace did collect the premiums and issue the policy.

b. Ace may be liable to Booth's estate for wrongfully issuing the insurance policy to Abe.

c. Ace is not liable on the policy.

d. Booth has no liability to Abe's estate.

The correct answer is (b). *(Publisher)*

REQUIRED: Liability when a life insurance policy is issued to a person who has no insurable interest and kills the insured.

DISCUSSION: Any person who is issued a life insurance policy must have an insurable interest in the person whose life is insured. At least one case has held that a murdered person's estate could recover from insurance companies which wrongfully issue life insurance policies to the murderer. The reasonableness of the insurance company's investigation into the insurable interest may be relevant.

Answer (a) is incorrect because Booth is not entitled to recover on the insurance policy since he did not have an insurable interest and it is a violation of public policy for a murderer to collect. Answer (c) is incorrect because Ace may have to pay someone since it issued the policy and collected the premiums. The law is not clear who will collect. Answer (d) is incorrect because Booth is liable to Abe's estate for wrongful death and fraud.

28. Jon Berstock is an employee and minor stockholder of PR, Inc., a public relations firm. During his employment, the corporation's earnings have doubled, largely because of Jon's ability to attract new accounts. PR therefore insured his life for a substantial sum. If Jon meets an untimely end, will PR be able to collect the insurance proceeds?

a. Yes, because a corporation has an insurable interest in all its employees since it can act only through agents.

b. Yes, because PR has a pecuniary interest in Jon's continued life.

c. No, because PR will continue to exist after Jon's death.

d. No, because Jon was not a major stockholder or partner in the business enterprise.

The correct answer is (b). *(Publisher)*

REQUIRED: The true statement about a corporation's ability to collect proceeds from insurance on an employee's life.

DISCUSSION: When one person insures the life of another, the policyholder must have an insurable interest in the insured. That interest is found among persons who have a close family relationship or expect to suffer substantial economic loss from the death. Business entities are thus permitted to insure key people in their organizations whose death might have an adverse effect on profits. Since Jon is apparently responsible for PR's success, the company has an insurable interest in his life.

Answer (a) is incorrect because a corporation only has an insurable interest in its key employees, i.e., those whose death would cause loss to the firm. Answer (c) is incorrect because the required loss need not be so great as to cause cessation of business. Answer (d) is incorrect because one need not be an owner or even an officer to be insurable as a key person.

29. Dobbins insured his life for $100,000, naming his wife as beneficiary. After the policy had been in effect for 10 years and had a cash surrender value in excess of $15,000, Dobbins assigned the policy to Suburban National Bank to secure a $20,000 loan. A copy of the assignment was filed with Suburban at its home office. Dobbins has died and his widow and Suburban are seeking to recover on the $100,000 life insurance policy. Which is correct?

a. Suburban's recovery is limited to the loan outstanding plus interest.

b. The assignment to Suburban was void without the beneficiary's consent.

c. Suburban will be denied recovery due to a lack of an insurable interest.

d. The widow had a vested interest in the insurance policy in question.

The correct answer is (a). *(CPA 579 L-3)*

REQUIRED: An assignee's rights to the proceeds of a life insurance policy.

DISCUSSION: A life insurance policy is generally assignable. The assignee will prevail over a previously named beneficiary. However, an assignment for security (as in the case of Suburban National Bank) will only entitle the assignee to the amount of the loan outstanding plus accrued interest.

Answer (b) is incorrect because the assignment to the Suburban Bank was valid without the beneficiary's consent. It had the effect of subordinating the beneficiary's contingent rights to as much of the policy as needed to secure the loan. Answer (c) is incorrect because a creditor has an insurable interest in the life of his/her debtor, and an assignee does not need an insurable interest. Answer (d) is incorrect because a beneficiary has a contingent, not a vested right, unless the designation is irrevocable.

30. Lincoln loaned Osgood $20,000 and obtained an unsecured negotiable promissory note for that amount. Lincoln wishes to obtain a life insurance policy on Osgood's life as added protection on the loan. With respect to this policy, which of the following is true?

a. Lincoln has an insurable interest in Osgood's life and may legally assign the insurance policy to a transferee of the note.

b. If Osgood consented to Lincoln's insuring him for an amount in excess of the loan, Lincoln would be able to recover the face amount of the policy.

c. Lincoln does not have an insurable interest since the note is negotiable.

d. The only policy that Lincoln may legally obtain is a term policy.

The correct answer is (a). *(CPA 581 L-46)*

REQUIRED: The correct statement regarding a creditor's interest in a debtor's life.

DISCUSSION: As a general rule, an unsecured creditor may insure the life of his/her debtor to the extent of the unpaid debt. Since Lincoln has an insurable interest due to the debtor/creditor relationship, the policy is valid. Furthermore, a validly issued policy may be assigned.

Answer (b) is incorrect because an unsecured creditor has an insurable interest only to the extent of the unpaid debt at the inception of the policy. Answer (c) is incorrect because Lincoln, the creditor, does have an insurable interest and the form of the note is immaterial. Answer (d) is incorrect because a creditor may legally obtain any type of life insurance policy.

31. Abner purchased a life insurance policy on his life and named Barbara as beneficiary. Later he borrowed from Charles and assigned the policy to Charles as security for the debt. Abner died while the debt was unpaid.

a. Barbara will be entitled to the entire proceeds if she had an insurable interest and did not consent to the assignment even if Abner had retained the right to change the beneficiary.

b. If, prior to the loan, Barbara had been named irrevocably as beneficiary, she will be entitled to the entire proceeds.

c. The assignment operates to change the beneficiary of the policy from Barbara to Charles, but Charles is liable to Abner's estate for proceeds in excess of amounts due him.

d. Normally assignment is not permitted to become effective if the value of the policy at the time of assignment exceeds the debt.

The correct answer is (b). *(CPA 574 L-44)*

REQUIRED: The correct answer regarding assignment of a life insurance policy.

DISCUSSION: The general rule is that the insured reserves the right to change the beneficiary and an assignee of the policy takes a priority over the previously named beneficiary. However, if the policy provides that the beneficiary designation is irrevocable, then the beneficiary's interest is vested. Without Barbara's consent, the assignment to Charles as security would be legally ineffective.

Answer (a) is incorrect because, if Abner had retained the right to change the beneficiary, the assignee is entitled to the proceeds. Answer (c) is incorrect because the assignment operates to change the beneficiary to the extent of the outstanding balance on the loan; any excess proceeds after the loan has been repaid belong to Barbara. Answer (d) is incorrect because there are no restrictions on the assignment of a life insurance policy unless the beneficiary's interest is vested.

32. At his death, Filmore owned a $100,000 life insurance policy on his life in which he designated his wife as the beneficiary. The insurer paid the proceeds of the policy directly to Mrs. Filmore after his death. Which of the following is correct?

a. If Filmore's will designates a person other than his wife to receive the proceeds of the insurance policy, such a designation will not be valid.

b. Upon receipt of the proceeds, Mrs. Filmore will have received $100,000 of taxable income, but income averaging is permitted.

c. The insurance proceeds are not includible in Filmore's estate for federal estate tax purposes.

d. Filmore, having designated his wife as the beneficiary of the policy, could not change the beneficiary unless she died or they were divorced.

The correct answer is (a). *(CPA 580 L-45)*

REQUIRED: The correct statement concerning the disposition of proceeds of a life insurance policy upon death of the insured.

DISCUSSION: A person has an insurable interest in his own life and may name anyone (s)he chooses as beneficiary. Whether the insured can replace the initial beneficiary depends on the terms of the policy. In any event, the beneficiary's interest in the proceeds is fixed by contract at the moment of death of the insured. Hence, Filmore cannot change the beneficiary of the policy by a provision in his will.

Answer (b) is incorrect because the proceeds of an insurance policy are not taxable income to the beneficiaries provided the policy was not transferred for valuable consideration. Answer (c) is incorrect because whenever a decedent owns a policy or retains any incident of ownership, the proceeds are included in his/her estate for federal estate tax purposes. Answer (d) is incorrect because the standard life insurance policy reserves the right of the insured to change the designated beneficiary.

Questions 33 through 36 are based on the following information. In 1985, Insured took out a whole life insurance policy, Insurer promising, on condition that Insured paid an annual premium until death, to pay $50,000 to Insured's wife. The policy stated that Insured had power to change the beneficiary and to assign the policy.

In 1986, Insurer, deeming its insurance risks excessive, entered into a contract with Reinsurer which provided that, in exchange for Insurer's promise to pay an annual premium, Reinsurer promised to perform the duties of Insurer under the policy with Insured.

In 1989, Insured changed the beneficiary from his wife to his son. Upon receiving notice of this, the son wrote a letter to his father expressing appreciation and sent notes to Insurer and Reinsurer stating how fortunate he was that his father had named him the beneficiary under the policy with Insurer and Reinsurer, and advising that, in light of this information, he had purchased a lot on which to build a house.

Later in 1989, Insured, being in need of funds, borrowed $5,000 and assigned the policy to Assignee as security.

In 1990, Insurer's financial condition improved. Consequently, Insurer and Reinsurer rescinded the contract of reinsurance.

Later in 1990, Insured died, the premiums on the policy with Insurer having been paid for the years 1985 through 1990 and the policy being in force. The loan from Assignee has not been repaid.

33. Insured's wife sued Insurer to collect the proceeds of the policy. How would the court hold?

a. Judgment on Insured's wife's suit for the proceeds is denied, because the wife is an incidental beneficiary and an incidental beneficiary has no protected rights.

b. Judgment on Insured's wife's suit for the proceeds is denied, because Insured reserved the power to change the beneficiary and exercised the power.

c. Judgment to Insured's wife for the proceeds, because the wife is a donee beneficiary and her right vested when the policy was issued to Insured.

d. Judgment to Insured's wife for the proceeds, because the wife is a creditor beneficiary and bringing suit on the policy was a change of position in reliance.

The correct answer is (b). *(MBE 272 79)*

REQUIRED: The correct statement concerning the rights of a beneficiary.

DISCUSSION: Whether an insured can replace the initial beneficiary depends on the terms of the policy. Here the contract provided for the right to change the beneficiary as well as to assign the policy. The named beneficiary's interest in the proceeds of the policy is only fixed at the moment of the death of the insured. Here, prior to death, Insured changed the beneficiary from his wife to his son. Therefore, the wife's suit for the proceeds should be denied.

Answer (a) is incorrect because the wife's suit for the proceeds should be denied on the basis that she was not the beneficiary at death. Answer (c) is incorrect because the wife's status as a beneficiary had been properly changed prior to the death of the insured. Answer (d) is incorrect because at most the wife had a contingent interest which would have vested only if her husband had not changed the beneficiary.

34. Insured's son sued Insurer to collect the proceeds of the policy. How would the court hold?

a. Judgment in Insured's son's suit for the proceeds is denied, because the son should have sued Reinsurer before proceeding against Insurer.

b. Judgment in Insured's son's suit for the proceeds is denied, because the son should have sued Reinsurer and Insurer jointly.

c. Judgment to Insured's son for the proceeds, because the son has a right against Insurer and Reinsurer and may elect to bring action against Insurer.

d. Judgment to Insured's son for the proceeds, because the son is subrogated to Insurer's right against Reinsurer.

The correct answer is (c). *(MBE 272 80)*

REQUIRED: The correct statement concerning a beneficiary's rights against the insurer to collect the proceeds of a life insurance policy.

DISCUSSION: A beneficiary's interest in the proceeds of a life policy is fixed by contract at the moment of death of the insured. The son was the properly designated beneficiary of the insured at the moment of death and is entitled to collect from the insurance company. The son was also a creditor beneficiary of a second contract between Insurer and Reinsurer (so he could recover from Reinsurer), but elected to bring his action against Insurer.

Answer (a) is incorrect because the son had enforceable rights against both Insurer and Reinsurer and could properly elect to hold either liable. Answer (b) is incorrect because Insurer and Reinsurer were separately liable. Answer (d) is incorrect because judgment for the son against Insurer is based on the insurance contract and not subrogation rights.

35. Insured's son, not having collected from Insurer, sued Reinsurer on the contract of reinsurance. How would the court hold?

a. Judgment for Insured's son is denied, because the son is an incidental beneficiary of the reinsurance contract.

b. Judgment for Insured's son is denied, because the change of beneficiary clause in the insurance contract prevented the son's right under the reinsurance contract from vesting prior to Insured's death and Insured and Reinsurer rescinded their contract.

c. Judgment to Insured's son, because the son is a creditor beneficiary of Reinsurer's promise, notice was given to the son and he assented and changed his position in reliance.

d. Judgment to Insured's son, because the son is a donee beneficiary of Reinsurer's promise and assent is presumed.

The correct answer is (c). *(MBE 272 81)*

REQUIRED: The correct statement of the beneficiary's rights against a reinsurer.

DISCUSSION: A properly named beneficiary can recover from a reinsurer of a life insurance contract because the named beneficiary is a creditor beneficiary of the reinsurer's promise to the insurance company. Reliance on the creditor beneficiary contract was established when the son changed his position (ought real estate) and gave notice to Reinsurer prior to the rescission of the reinsurance contract. The beneficiary is a creditor beneficiary in this instance because, at the moment of death, the insurance company owed the proceeds to beneficiary and was using the contract with the reinsurer to dispose of this liability.

Answers (a) and (d) are incorrect because the son is a creditor beneficiary as discussed above. Answer (b) is incorrect because, although the son's right did not vest prior to Insured's death, it did vest at Insured's death. Reinsurer will be held to its promise because the son changed his position in reliance prior to rescission.

36. Assignee sued Insurer for $5,000. Insured's son intervened, alleging that Assignee did not have a right to any sum under the insurance policy. How would the court hold?

a. Judgment in Assignee's suit is denied, because Insured's son was named beneficiary before Insured made the assignment, and the beneficiary, being first in time, prevails over the assignee.

b. Judgment in Assignee's suit is denied, because Insured's son is a donee beneficiary and the promisee cannot discharge any part of a donee beneficiary's right.

c. Judgment to Assignee for $5,000, because consideration was given for the assignment.

d. Judgment to Assignee for $5,000, because Insured reserved power to change the beneficiary and to assign the policy.

The correct answer is (d). *(MBE 272 82)*

REQUIRED: The correct statement of the respective rights of a life insurance beneficiary and an assignee of the policy.

DISCUSSION: The policy was expressly assignable and, prior to Insured's death, the son had no vested rights. Therefore, the assignee has priority over the beneficiary to the extent of $5,000.

Answer (a) is incorrect because the beneficiary was revocable; his/her rights were not fixed until the death of the insured. Answer (b) is incorrect because the beneficiary's interest at the time the assignment was made was not vested. Furthermore, the son was a creditor beneficiary, not a donee beneficiary. Answer (c) is incorrect because judgment should be granted to the assignee for $5,000, but not because consideration was given for the assignment. Consideration is not generally a requirement for an assignment.

37. A person is treated as having an insurable interest in his/her own life. The obvious desire of most human beings to continue their existence provides protection for the insurer that is otherwise afforded by the pecuniary insurable interest requirement. The standard life insurance contract furnishes an additional safeguard by incorporating a suicide clause. If the insured dies by suicide,

a. Payment only consists of a refund of premiums paid up to the date of death.

b. The beneficiary will receive nothing.

c. The policy will be fully enforceable if death occurs more than 2 years after its effective date.

d. The incontestable clause will override the suicide clause.

The correct answer is (c). *(Publisher)*

REQUIRED: The effect of a suicide clause.

DISCUSSION: A suicide clause is in effect a statute of limitations. The typical clause provides that after 2 years the policy applies to suicide the same as to death from other causes. But if the insured commits suicide within the first 2 years of the policy, the beneficiary will only receive the premiums paid.

Answers (a) and (b) are incorrect because, if death by suicide occurs within 2 years of issuance of the policy, the beneficiary will receive only the premiums paid up to the date of death. After 2 years, death by suicide is not treated differently than death by any other cause. Answer (d) is incorrect because the incontestable clause generally applies to misstatements in the application, not to suicide.

38. The "incontestable clause" in a life insurance policy usually provides that

a. The insured is covered on delivery of the policy regardless of any misstatement in the application.

b. If death occurs after a specified period of time, a misstatement in the application will not constitute a defense by the insurer.

c. Suicide of the named insured will not constitute a defense by the insurer.

d. Only the estate of the insured may contest the named beneficiary's rights to proceeds of the policy.

The correct answer is (b). *(CPA 574 L-51)*

REQUIRED: The usual provisions of an "incontestable clause."

DISCUSSION: The standard life insurance policy provides in an incontestable clause that after the passage of a specified time (usually 2 years), misstatements in the application will not constitute a defense by the insurance company. In other words, the insurer will not contest a policy after a 2-year period.

Answer (a) is incorrect because the policy is clearly contestable until the incontestable period has expired. Answer (c) is incorrect because suicide is not regulated by the incontestable clause. Answer (d) is incorrect because the standard incontestable clause does not determine who may contest the named beneficiary's rights to a policy. However, the insurance company and any party with a contingent interest could contest the beneficiary's right to proceeds.

39. The Devon Insurance Company issued a $50,000 whole life insurance policy to Finn. Finn's age was incorrectly stated in the application. As a result, she paid a smaller premium than that applicable to her age. Devon denies liability asserting as its defense a material misrepresentation by Finn. Under the circumstances, how much will Finn's beneficiary collect?

a. The entire amount of the policy if the incontestable clause applies.

b. Nothing, unless the beneficiary can establish that Finn was unaware of her correct age.

c. The amount of insurance that the premium would have purchased if the correct age had been stated.

d. The amount of premium Finn paid during her lifetime with interest at the legal rate.

The correct answer is (c). *(CPA 577 L-5)*

REQUIRED: The amount of money that the beneficiary can collect when the age of the insured has been misstated on the application.

DISCUSSION: A standard clause in life insurance provides that if the insured's age is misstated, the policy will not be invalidated, but the benefits will be adjusted down based on the amount of insurance that the premium would have purchased if the correct age had been stated.

Answer (a) is incorrect because the incontestable clause does not override the misstatement of age. The policy can be adjusted any time after its discovery. Answer (b) is incorrect because misstatement of age, though material, does not invalidate a standard life insurance policy regardless whether the misstatement is intentional or accidental. Answer (d) is incorrect because the beneficiary will receive the face amount of the policy adjusted as discussed above. Refund of premiums occurs only when the policy is invalid.

40. The Fargo Corporation provides its employees with free group life insurance of $1,000 for each $1,000 of annual salary. Maxwell is an executive vice-president of Fargo and receives a salary of $100,000 a year. Consistent with state laws, Maxwell has assigned the group policy to his wife, Joan. Regarding the group policy and its assignment, which of the following is correct?

a. The assignee of a group policy must have an insurable interest in the life of the insured.

b. The assignment of the policy to Joan transferred all the legal incidents of ownership to her.

c. Maxwell does not have any income for income tax purposes as a result of Fargo's payment of the insurance premiums.

d. The proceeds from the group policy will be an asset of Maxwell's estate upon his death.

The correct answer is (b). *(CPA 1180 L-56)*

REQUIRED: The correct statement concerning the assignment of a group life policy.

DISCUSSION: The assignment of the policy from the husband to the wife transferred all the legal incidents of ownership of the policy. This is unlike the designation of a beneficiary, which only gives the beneficiary the right to proceeds unless the designation is changed. To make the assignment effective against the insurer, a copy of the assignment or other notice must be furnished.

Answer (a) is incorrect because an assignee of a life insurance policy need not have an insurable interest in the life of the insured. Answer (c) is incorrect because only the first $50,000 of group term life insurance provided by an employer is a tax-exempt benefit (Maxwell is getting $100,000 worth). If the insurance is not term, it may not be exempt at all. Answer (d) is incorrect because Maxwell assigned the policy; if he retains no incidents of ownership, it will not be included in his estate.

41. Larkin insured his own life for $40,000 and named his wife as beneficiary. He took out the policy on July 15, 1984. He has paid all premiums as they became due. The policy included the following two provisions:

- The Insured represents that the statements he has made in the application for insurance and in the questionnaire submitted in connection with his physical health are true and are a part of the policy issued to him.
- This Policy shall be incontestable after it has been in force for a period of 2 years from the date of issue, except for failure to pay premiums.

Larkin died on January 10, 1989, and the insurance company cancelled the policy on February 1, 1990, upon learning that Larkin had lied about his health. Larkin's widow seeks recovery of the $40,000 from the insurer. What will be the probable outcome of the dispute between the widow and the insurers?

a. The widow will receive a refund of all the premiums paid.

b. The widow will receive nothing because of the false health statements made by Larkin at the inception of the policy.

c. The widow will receive the full $40,000.

d. The widow will receive a refund of all the premiums paid plus accrued interest.

The correct answer is (c). *(CPA 581 L-47)*

REQUIRED: The probable outcome of a dispute between a beneficiary and a life insurance company arising after the insured misrepresented his/her health.

DISCUSSION: Statements in an application for insurance are classified as representations (except when such statements are made with fraudulent intent). This interpretation is not changed by such provisions as the first one in the question. As a representation (not a warranty), it does not become part of the policy. This leaves the incontestability clause in the second provision to govern any contest by the company concerning material misrepresentations by the insured. Since more than 2 years have passed since the policy was issued, the incontestability clause bars the insurance company from contesting Larkin's misrepresentation, and his widow will receive the full $40,000.

Answer (a) is incorrect because Larkin's widow would have received a refund of all premiums paid only if the company had been successful in legally cancelling the policy. Answer (b) is incorrect because the 2-year incontestability clause bars any further contest concerning concealments or misstatements. Answer (d) is incorrect because Larkin's widow will receive the proceeds of the policy, not a refund.

42. Under a buy-and-sell agreement to be funded by life insurance, each of three partners took out a $50,000 policy on the life of each of his other two partners. The agreement provided that on the death of the first, each of the other two partners was to collect the proceeds of the policy he owned on the life of the decedent and purchase one-half of the decedent's estate for that amount. Each partner paid the premiums on the lives of his fellow partners from his individual funds. In this situation,

a. Prior to the death of any partner, the policies are partnership assets.

b. On the death of a partner, a surviving partner has the right to purchase from the decedent's estate the policy of insurance (on the survivor's life) which had been owned by the decedent.

c. Continued ownership and payment of premiums by the estate of a deceased partner on a policy the decedent had owned on his former partner would probably give rise to a defense of lack of insurable interest if the insured partner later died.

d. On the death of a partner, the estate of the decedent could transfer the policy it held on the life on one surviving partner to the other surviving partner.

The correct answer is (d). *(CPA 574 L-50)*

REQUIRED: The correct statement regarding a buy-and-sell agreement between partners funded by life insurance.

DISCUSSION: A life insurance policy is assignable and usually without approval of the insurance company. Upon a partner's death, the policies (s)he owned on the surviving partners' lives are owned by the estate. The estate could validly transfer one or more policies to any person.

Answer (a) is incorrect because policies purchased by partners with their individual funds are the property of the partners and not partnership assets. Answer (b) is incorrect because after the death of a partner, the policies on the lives of the surviving partners are owned by the estate, and the surviving partners have no rights in them. The surviving partners had no rights in them even while he was living. Answer (c) is incorrect because an insurable interest is only required at the time the policy is issued, not at the time of death.

43. The typical life insurance policy contains

a. No exclusion for death during military service.

b. A clause allowing coverage for death during noncommercial flight.

c. A prohibition on reinstatement.

d. A provision for a grace period for premium payment.

The correct answer is (d). *(Publisher)*

REQUIRED: The true statement about the provisions of a life insurance policy.

DISCUSSION: State statutes generally require a grace period. If a premium is not received by the due date, the policyholder has a grace period, usually a month or 31 days, in which to pay. After the grace period, the cash surrender value is not forfeited but can be withdrawn or used to buy a paid-up policy.

Answers (a) and (b) are incorrect because life insurance policies often do not cover death while in the military or as a result of a noncommercial air flight. Answer (c) is incorrect because a lapsed policy may often be reinstated by payment of overdue premiums plus interest.

23.3 Property Insurance

44. As a fire insurance policy is one common type of contract, it must meet the general requirements necessary to establish a binding contract. In a dispute between the insured and the insurance company, which of the following is correct?

a. The contract is always unilateral.

b. Insurance contracts are specifically included within the general Statute of Frauds.

c. The insured must satisfy the insurable interest requirement.

d. The actual delivery of the policy to the insured is a prerequisite to the creation of the insurance contract.

The correct answer is (c). *(CPA 1181 L-59)*

REQUIRED: The correct statement necessary to establish a binding fire insurance contract.

DISCUSSION: In order for a fire insurance policy to be valid, the insured must satisfy the insurable interest requirement. That is, the insured must have a potential for pecuniary loss if the building is damaged or destroyed. This potential for loss (e.g., ownership, security interest, etc.) must exist at the time of the loss (fire).

Answer (a) is incorrect because, while most insurance contracts are unilateral, that is not a requirement; insurance contracts could be bilateral. Answer (b) is incorrect because insurance contracts are not specifically included within the Statute of Frauds. But the insured is entitled to a written copy of the policy within a reasonable time under state statutes. Answer (d) is incorrect because although delivery of the policy is usually required, constructive delivery (to the agent) will suffice.

45. A fire insurance policy ordinarily indemnifies for losses arising from

a. Friendly but not hostile fires.

b. Hostile but not friendly fires.

c. Both hostile and friendly fires.

d. Smoke produced by friendly or hostile fires.

The correct answer is (b). *(Publisher)*

REQUIRED: The losses caused by fire that will be indemnified.

DISCUSSION: Ordinarily, smoke, water, or other damage caused by hostile but not friendly fires will be indemnified under a fire insurance policy. Hostile fires are those ignited in places where they are not meant to be. A friendly fire is one that burns where it is intended to burn, such as a fireplace or furnace. For example, if a friendly fire is kept within its usual container, damage caused by smoke from it will not be reimbursed.

46. Which of the following is a characteristic of fire insurance?

a. It is more standardized than life insurance.

b. It is written for a relatively short period but usually includes an incontestable clause.

c. A policy must be valued and contain a pro rata clause.

d. The insurable interest must be an ownership interest in the property itself.

The correct answer is (a). *(Publisher)*

REQUIRED: The true statement about fire insurance.

DISCUSSION: Fire insurance is the most standardized kind of insurance. Following the lead of New York, almost all states have enacted a standard policy either by legislative or administrative action.

Answer (b) is incorrect because, since fire insurance is usually written for a 1- to 3-year period, an incontestable clause is not necessary. Answer (c) is incorrect because a policy may state a definite value of the insured property or simply a maximum amount of coverage that is not conclusive as to valuation when loss occurs. A policy may thus be valued or open (unvalued). A pro rata clause is often included (but not required) which requires the loss to be shared pro rata when there is more than one insurer. Answer (d) is incorrect because the insurable interest merely requires the person to suffer a loss if the event insured against occurs, e.g., mortgagee, bailee, etc.

47. The typical fire insurance policy

a. Covers all damages caused by fire whatever the source.

b. Does not cover water damage which results from the fire department extinguishing the blaze.

c. Will not permit recovery for business interruption unless there is a special endorsement.

d. Prohibits the assignment of the policy both before and after a loss.

The correct answer is (c). *(CPA 576 L-32)*

REQUIRED: The correct statement regarding the typical fire insurance policy.

DISCUSSION: The typical fire insurance policy only insures damage to physical property. It does not permit recovery for business interruption, lost profits, or other special matters unless there is a special endorsement or rider attached to the policy.

Answer (a) is incorrect because the typical fire insurance policy does not cover damages caused by intentional acts of the insured or by "friendly" fires, e.g., damage to the insured's chair because the chair is too close to the fireplace (a "friendly" fire). Answer (b) is incorrect because the typical fire insurance policy covers water damage resulting from attempts to extinguish the blaze. Answer (d) is incorrect because the typical fire insurance policy does not and cannot prohibit the assignment of the policy (right to proceeds) after a loss.

48. The usual fire insurance policy does not

a. Have to meet the insurable interest test if this requirement is waived by the parties.

b. Provide for subrogation of the insurer to the insured's rights upon payment of the amount of the loss covered by the policy.

c. Cover losses caused by the negligence of the insured's agent.

d. Permit assignment of the policy prior to loss without the consent of the insurer.

The correct answer is (d). *(CPA 1179 L-45)*

REQUIRED: The correct statement concerning the usual fire insurance policy.

DISCUSSION: The standard fire insurance policy may not be assigned prior to loss without consent of the insurer because of the personal nature of property insurance and inherent risks in the activities of the insured. If not expressed, this restraint is implied. However, proceeds from policies may be assigned after loss without the consent of the insurer.

Answer (a) is incorrect because the parties cannot waive the insurable interest requirement. Answer (b) is incorrect because the insurance company is entitled to subrogation to the insured's rights after payment. Answer (c) is incorrect because the usual fire insurance policy does cover losses caused by negligence of the insured and his/her agents or employees.

49. Which of the following wrongful acts prevents recovery under a policy of fire insurance?

a. Arson by the insured's employees or agents.

b. Arson by third persons unrelated to the insured.

c. An act by the insured intended to cause the damage.

d. Gross negligence but not amounting to recklessness and willful misconduct.

The correct answer is (c). *(Publisher)*

REQUIRED: The wrongful act preventing an insurance recovery.

DISCUSSION: Arson, fraud, or another intentional act of the insured calculated to cause the damage insured against will preclude recovery. The parties to an insurance contract have an implied duty not to bring about the very event that is the subject matter of the policy.

Answer (a) is incorrect because agency rules do not apply; i.e., the intentional act of an agent will not be imputed to the insured under the doctrine of respondent superior. Arson by an agent without the actual knowledge or conspiracy of the insured will not preclude recovery. Answer (b) is incorrect because arson is compensable unless intended by the insured. Answer (d) is incorrect because negligence without fraud will not prevent recovery by an insured who has acted in good faith.

50. Charleston, Inc. had a warehouse destroyed by fire. Charleston's property was insured against fire loss by the Conglomerate Insurance Company. An investigation by Conglomerate revealed that the fire had been caused by a disgruntled employee whom Charleston had suspended for 1 month due to insubordination. Charleston seeks to hold its insurer liable for the $200,000 loss of its warehouse. Which of the following is correct?

a. Since the loss was due to the deliberate destruction by one of Charleston's employees, recovery will be denied.

b. Conglomerate must pay Charleston, but it will be subrogated to Charleston's rights against the wrongdoing employee.

c. The fact that the employee has been suspended for 1 month precludes recovery against Conglomerate.

d. Arson is excluded from the coverage of most fire insurance policies, and therefore Conglomerate is not liable.

The correct answer is (b). *(CPA 1179 L-12)*

REQUIRED: The correct statement concerning recovery for a fire caused by a disgruntled employee.

DISCUSSION: A fire set intentionally by a disgruntled employee is within the insured risk under a standard fire insurance policy. Therefore, the insured could recover from the insurance company. After payment, however, the insurance company would be subrogated to the employer's right against the employee for his/her wrongful act.

Answer (a) is incorrect because recovery would be denied for deliberate destruction only if caused by the insured or at the insured's direction. Answer (c) is incorrect because disciplinary action against employees does not in any way affect the fire insurance policy. Answer (d) is incorrect because arson by third parties such as disgruntled customers, employees, etc. is not excluded; only arson by the insured is excluded. Therefore, the insurance company is liable.

51. To recover under a property insurance policy, an insurable interest must exist

	When the policy is purchased	At the time of loss
a.	Yes	Yes
b.	Yes	No
c.	No	Yes
d.	No	No

The correct answer is (c). *(CPA 1189 L-60)*

REQUIRED: The time(s) an insurable interest in property must exist.

DISCUSSION: The insurable interest in property must be present when the loss occurs but not when the policy is issued. This is the reverse of the requirement for insurance on the life of another. The rule permits the insured to obtain insurance in advance so that coverage will begin immediately upon acquisition of an interest in property. When a loss occurs, the insured party may recover only up to the amount of his/her interest in the property at that time.

Answer (a) is incorrect because the interest need not exist at the purchase date. Answers (b) and (d) are incorrect because the interest must exist at the time of loss.

52. The insurable interest requirement with regard to property insurance

a. May be waived by a writing signed by the insured and insurer.

b. May be satisfied by a person other than the legal owner of the property.

c. Must be satisfied at the time the policy is issued.

d. Must be satisfied by the insured's legal title to the property at the time of loss.

The correct answer is (b). *(CPA 585 L-60)*

REQUIRED: The true statement about the insurable interest in property.

DISCUSSION: An insurable interest is found not only when the insured has a legally or equitably recognized present or vested future interest but also in many other situations in which the insured could incur economic loss. For example, if the insured has a contract with a supplier whose productive property is vital to performance and damage to the property would cause loss to the insured through breach of the contract, an insurable interest exists.

Answer (a) is incorrect because the rule is not waivable. It is based on a public policy designed to prevent wagering contracts and to reduce moral hazards. Answer (c) is incorrect because the requirement is satisfied if the interest exists when loss occurs. Answer (d) is incorrect because anyone who would suffer an economic loss from destruction of the property has an insurable interest.

53. Nabor, Inc. purchased a 3-year fire insurance policy from the Fidelity Insurance Company covering its factory and warehouse. Which of the following statements is correct as a general rule of insurance law?

a. The policy will not cover the intentional destruction of the property by a third party.

b. The policy will not cover the destruction of the property if it is caused by the gross negligence of an employee of Nabor.

c. If Nabor sells the insured property to a third party and assigns the insurance policy to the buyer, it continues in effect.

d. If Nabor sells the insured property but retains the fire insurance policy, it will not be able to collect on the policy in the event of the property's destruction by fire.

The correct answer is (d). *(CPA 1178 L-13)*

REQUIRED: The correct statement of general insurance law.

DISCUSSION: An insured must have an insurable interest at the time the loss occurs under a fire insurance policy. If Nabor sells the insured property and retains the fire insurance policy, it would not be able to collect on the policy in the event of destruction by fire because its insurable interest ended with the sale (unless a legal or equitable interest was retained).

Answer (a) is incorrect because the standard policy will cover intentional destruction of the insured property by a third person. Answer (b) is incorrect because the standard fire insurance policy will cover the destruction of property caused by gross negligence of an employee of the insured. Answer (c) is incorrect because an assignment of a fire insurance policy is not effective unless approved by the insurer.

54. The earliest time a purchaser of existing goods will acquire an insurable interest in those goods is when

a. The purchaser obtains possession.

b. Title passes to the purchaser.

c. Performance of the contract has been completed or substantially completed.

d. The goods are identified to the contract.

The correct answer is (d). *(CPA 1186 L-59)*

REQUIRED: The earliest time a purchaser will have an insurable interest in the goods.

DISCUSSION: Under UCC 2-501, a buyer of goods has an insurable interest in them when they are identified to the contract. This identification can occur when the seller selects goods that correspond to the description in the contract and marks or otherwise designates them as belonging to the contract.

Answer (a) is incorrect because a purchaser can acquire an insurable interest as soon as the goods are identified and need not wait until delivery. Answers (b) and (c) are incorrect because passage of title and contract performance are irrelevant to acquiring an insurable interest.

55. With respect to property insurance, the insurable interest requirement

a. Need only be satisfied at the time the policy is issued.

b. Must be satisfied both at the time the policy is issued and at the time of the loss.

c. Will be satisfied only if the insured owns the property in fee simple absolute.

d. Will be satisfied by an insured who possesses a leasehold interest in the property.

The correct answer is (d). *(CPA 1187 L-59)*

REQUIRED: The correct statement concerning insurable interest.

DISCUSSION: To satisfy the legal requirement of an insurable interest, the insured must have a possibility of monetary loss if the property is damaged. Both the owner and the long-term lessee of property have an insurable interest because each would lose in the event of damage.

Answers (a) and (b) are incorrect because the insurable interest need only exist at the time of the loss, not at the time of issuance. Answer (c) is incorrect because legal interests other than a fee simple absolute will satisfy the requirement (e.g., creditors with a judgment, mortgagees, parties under a contract to purchase, and lessees).

56. Beal occupies an office building as a tenant under a 25-year lease. Beal also has a mortgagee's (lender's) interest in an office building owned by Hill Corp. In which capacity does Beal have an insurable interest?

	Tenant	Mortgagee
a.	Yes	Yes
b.	Yes	No
c.	No	Yes
d.	No	No

The correct answer is (a). *(CPA 588 L-60)*

REQUIRED: The true statement as to whether tenants and mortgagees have an insurable interest.

DISCUSSION: Both a tenant and a mortgagee could suffer monetary loss if the office building were damaged or destroyed, and both also have a valid legal interest in the building. Thus, Beal has an insurable interest in both capacities.

Answers (b) and (d) are incorrect because a mortgagee can have an insurable interest. The destruction of the security for the loan may cause loss to the lender. Answers (c) and (d) are incorrect because a tenant has a possibility of monetary loss.

57. Peters leased a restaurant from Brady with all furnishings and fixtures for a period of five years with an option to renew for two additional years. Peters made improvements and modifications to the interior of the building. He obtained a fire insurance policy for his own benefit insuring his interest in the property for $25,000. The restaurant was totally destroyed by an accidental fire. Peters seeks recovery from his insurer. Subject to policy limits, which of the following is correct?

a. Peters is entitled to recover damages to the extent of the value of his leasehold interest.

b. Peters is entitled to recover for lost profits due to the fire even though the policy is silent on the point.

c. Peters must first seek redress from the owner before he is entitled to recover.

d. Peters will not recover because he lacks the requisite insurable interest in the property.

The correct answer is (a). *(CPA 578 L-20)*

REQUIRED: The correct statement of the rights of a lessee to recover on a fire policy.

DISCUSSION: A lessee is entitled to recover under a fire policy (s)he purchases to the extent of damages to his/her leasehold interest. Here, recovery probably will be $25,000 since the insurance company agreed to a policy in that amount. The amount will be less if the value of the leasehold is determined to be less. If the policy is for a "stated value," however, the insured gets the face value.

Answer (b) is incorrect because fire insurance policies cover damage to the insured property, not lost profits unless specifically provided for. Answer (c) is incorrect because the lessee need not seek redress from the owner since there is a direct contract between the lessee and the insurance company. Answer (d) is incorrect because a long-term lessee will suffer pecuniary damage if the building is destroyed. Therefore, Peters has the requisite insurable interest.

58. The partnership of Cox & Hayes, CPAs is a medium-sized accounting firm. The senior staff member, Jake Walton, is the office manager. The office building is owned by the partnership and title is duly recorded in the partnership name. With regard to life and property insurance, which of the following is true?

a. Only the partnership, not the partners, has an insurable interest in the lives of the partners.

b. The partnership does not have an insurable interest in the life of Walton because he is not a partner.

c. Each individual partner has an insurable interest in the partnership property even though title to the property is in the partnership name.

d. Only the partnership can insure the firm's building against property damage.

The correct answer is (c). *(CPA 1177 L-2)*

REQUIRED: The correct statement of the rights of a partnership and partners with respect to life and property insurance.

DISCUSSION: An office building owned by a partnership with title in the partnership name can be insured by the partnership. Also, each individual partner has an insurable interest in the partnership property because (s)he has an obvious potential for pecuniary loss should the partnership property be destroyed.

Answer (a) is incorrect because both the partnership and the partners have insurable interests in the lives of each partner. Answer (b) is incorrect because the partnership has an insurable interest in the life of its office manager (a key employee) since his death would cause pecuniary damage to the firm. Answer (d) is incorrect because both the partnership and the partners can insure the firm's office building against property damage.

59. The insurable interest requirement for creditors varies between property insurance and life insurance. Which is correct?

a. A general unsecured creditor has an insurable interest in the life of the debtor, while only a secured creditor has an insurable interest in property owned by the debtor.

b. Neither a general unsecured creditor nor a secured creditor has an insurable interest in the life of the debtor.

c. Both a general unsecured creditor and a secured creditor have an insurable interest in the property owned by the debtor.

d. A secured creditor has an insurable interest in the life of the debtor, while a general unsecured creditor has an insurable interest in the property of the debtor.

The correct answer is (a). *(Publisher)*

REQUIRED: The correct statement concerning a creditor's insurable interest in property and life insurance.

DISCUSSION: An unsecured creditor has an insurable interest in the life of the debtor to the extent of the debt. This is because the creditor has a possibility of pecuniary loss in the event the debtor dies. Only a secured creditor has an insurable interest in property owned by the debtor because (s)he has a direct legal interest in that property and could suffer a pecuniary loss if it were destroyed.

Answer (b) is incorrect because both a secured creditor and an unsecured creditor have an insurable interest in the life of the debtor to the extent of their possible pecuniary loss. Answer (c) is incorrect because a general unsecured creditor has no interest in specific property of the debtor, so (s)he would not suffer a direct pecuniary loss in the event of destruction. Answer (d) is incorrect because an unsecured creditor does not have an insurable interest in the property of the debtor.

60. West is seeking to collect on a property insurance policy covering certain described property that was destroyed. The insurer has denied recovery based upon West's alleged lack of an insurable interest in the property. In which of the situations described below will the insurance company prevail?

a. West is not the owner of the insured property but a mere long-term lessee.

b. The insured property belongs to a general trade debtor of West and the debt is unsecured.

c. The insured property belongs not to West but to a corporation which he controls.

d. The property has been willed to West's father for life and, upon his father's death, to West as the remainderman.

The correct answer is (b). *(CPA 1185 L-60)*

REQUIRED: The instance in which no insurable interest will be found.

DISCUSSION: A general creditor has no insurable interest in specific property of the debtor if damage to or destruction of the property will not cause an economic loss to the creditor. Since the debt was unsecured, no collateral has been impaired. Also, the facts do not suggest that any contract rights of the creditor were dependent upon the welfare of the property.

Answer (a) is incorrect because one who has a legal or equitable interest in the property has an insurable interest. A leasehold is a legally recognized interest. Answer (c) is incorrect because a dominant or controlling stockholder has an equitable interest in property owned by the corporation, the legal owner. Answer (d) is incorrect because a vested future interest of a remainderman suffices for an insurable interest.

61. The coinsurance clause with regard to property insurance

a. Prohibits the insured from obtaining an amount of insurance that would be less than the coinsurance percentage multiplied by the fair market value of the property.

b. Encourages the insured to be more careful in preventing losses since the insured is always at least partially at risk when a loss occurs.

c. Permits the insured to receive an amount in excess of the policy amount when there has been a total loss and the insured carried the required coverage under the coinsurance clause.

d. Will result in the insured sharing in partial losses when the insured has failed to carry the required coverage under the coinsurance clause.

The correct answer is (d). *(CPA 585 L-59)*

REQUIRED: The true statement about the coinsurance clause.

DISCUSSION: Coinsurance is a provision in which the owner agrees to insure the property up to a given percentage (usually 80%) of its value. A policyholder who complies with the coinsurance agreement will recover any loss in full up to the face amount of the policy. If the policyholder insures for less than the agreed percentage, (s)he becomes a coinsurer and must bear any partial loss proportionately with the insurance company. The purpose is to prevent the insured from insuring for a minimal amount (and minimal premium) and recovering in full for a partial loss (the most common).

Answer (a) is incorrect because the insured may obtain less insurance than the coinsurance requirement, but (s)he then becomes a coinsurer for partial losses. Answer (b) is incorrect because the insured is not at risk if (s)he meets the coinsurance requirement. Answer (c) is incorrect because the insured cannot recover more than the face value of the policy.

62. The coinsurance feature of property insurance

a. Is fixed at a minimum of 80% by law.

b. Is an additional refinement of the insurable interest requirement.

c. Precludes the insured from insuring for less than the coinsurance percentage.

d. Prevents the insured from insuring for a minimal amount and recovering in full for such losses.

The correct answer is (d). *(CPA 1187 L-58)*

REQUIRED: The true statement about the coinsurance feature.

DISCUSSION: Partial losses are more common than complete losses. Without a coinsurance clause, many insureds would only insure a small value of their property and pay very little for insurance. But insurance companies would still have to pay for all losses up to the face of the policies. A coinsurance clause requires the insured to insure a higher portion of the value of the property, resulting in higher insurance premiums, but not necessarily resulting in substantially higher loss payments by the insurance companies.

Answer (a) is incorrect because the coinsurance percentage is determined by the parties' agreement. Answer (b) is incorrect because the coinsurance and insurable interest requirements are unrelated. Answer (c) is incorrect because an insured may insure for any amount if (s)he is willing to be a coinsurer of partial losses.

63. Carter, Wallace, and Jones are partners. Title to the partnership's office building was in Carter's name. The Carter, Wallace, and Jones partnership procured a $150,000 fire insurance policy on the building from the Amalgamated Insurance Company. The policy contained an 80% coinsurance clause. Subsequently, the building was totally destroyed by fire. The value of the building was $200,000 at the time the policy was issued, and $160,000 at the time of the fire. Under the fire insurance policy, how much can the partnership recover?

a. Nothing, since it did not have legal title to the building.

b. The face value of the policy ($150,000).

c. 80% of the loss ($128,000).

d. The value at the time of the loss ($160,000).

The correct answer is (b). *(CPA 1181 L-56)*

REQUIRED: The amount the partnership can recover under an 80% coinsurance clause.

DISCUSSION: A coinsurance clause requires the insured to maintain insurance equal to or greater than a specified percentage (usually 80%) of the value of the insured property. If the insured has not carried the specified percentage and a partial loss occurs, the insurance company is only liable for a proportionate part of the loss. This is to deter people from paying for insurance on only a small part of the property's value. However, the coinsurance clause has no application when an insured building is totally destroyed. Thus, the partnership can recover the $150,000 face value of the policy.

Answer (a) is incorrect because under the Uniform Partnership Act, a partner may hold title to property on behalf of the partnership without impairing the partnership's rights to the property. Answer (c) is incorrect because the 80% coinsurance clause is not applicable to a total loss of the building. Answer (d) is incorrect because under no circumstances would an insured collect more from an insurance company than the face value of the policy.

64. On May 5, Sly purchased a warehouse for $100,000. Sly immediately insured the warehouse in the amount of $40,000 with Riff Insurance co. Sly later obtained additional fire insurance on the warehouse in the amount of $10,000 from Beek Insurance Co. Both policies contained an 80% coinsurance clause. Sly failed to notify Riff of the policy with Beek. Two years later, while both policies were still in effect, a fire caused by Sly's negligence resulted in $20,000 of damage to the warehouse. At the time of the loss, the warehouse had a fair market value of $50,000. Which of the following will prevent Sly from obtaining the full $20,000 from Riff?

a. Sly's negligence in causing the fire.

b. Sly's failure to satisfy the coinsurance clause.

c. Sly's failure to notify Riff of the policy with Beek.

d. Sly's purchase of insurance from Beek.

The correct answer is (d). *(CPA 1187 L-60)*

REQUIRED: The reason the insured will not recover the full amount of the loss.

DISCUSSION: The pro rate clause provides that a person who is insured with multiple policies can collect from each insurance company only a proportionate amount of the loss based on the amount of insurance carried with each insurer. Thus, Sly could only collect from Riff a proportionate share of the $20,000 loss.

Answer (a) is incorrect because the negligence of the insured is covered by fire policies. Answer (b) is incorrect because Sly's $50,000 of insurance exceeded 80% of the $50,000 fair market value of the building at the time of the fire and therefore satisfied the coinsurance requirement. Answer (c) is incorrect because Sly's failure to notify Riff of the policy with Beek does not excuse Beek from paying legitimate damage claims.

65. Hazard & Company was the owner of a building valued at $100,000. Because Hazard did not believe that a fire would result in a total loss, it procured two standard fire insurance policies on the property. One was for $24,000 with the Asbestos Fire Insurance Company and the other was for $16,000 with the Safety Fire Insurance Company. Both policies contained standard pro rata and 80% coinsurance clauses. Six months later, when the building was still valued at $100,000, a fire occurred that resulted in a loss of $40,000. What is the total amount Hazard can recover on both policies and the respective amount to be paid by Asbestos?

a. $0 and $0.

b. $20,000 and $10,000.

c. $20,000 and $12,000.

d. $40,000 and $20,000.

The correct answer is (c). *(CPA 580 L-48)*

REQUIRED: The amount collectible under two fire insurance policies with coinsurance clauses and standard pro rata clauses.

DISCUSSION: Under a coinsurance clause, the insured agrees to maintain the insurance equal to a specified percentage of the value of his/her property. If a loss occurs, the insurer only pays a proportionate share if the insured has not carried the specified percentage. In this case, the insured agreed to carry 80%, but in fact only carried 40%; thus, it became a 50% insurer, and the insurance companies' liability was reduced to 50% of any loss. The total combined liability of the fire insurance companies in the problem is $20,000.

Under the standard pro rata clause, a person who is insured with multiple policies can collect from each insurance company only a proportionate amount of the loss. Even though Asbestos Fire Insurance Company issued a policy for $24,000, it is only liable for three-fifths (24,000/40,000) of the recoverable loss after applying the coinsurance formula (3/5 x $20,000 = $12,000).

66. Stein bought an office building valued at $200,000. The fire insurance policy contained a 100% coinsurance clause. Stein insured the building for $120,000. Subsequently, a fire caused $40,000 damage to the building. Which of the following is the correct amount Stein will recover?

a. $40,000.

b. $24,000.

c. $13,333.

d. Nothing because the building was not insured for 100% of its value.

The correct answer is (b). *(CPA 1178 L-7)*

REQUIRED: The amount the insured will recover under a fire insurance policy containing a 100% coinsurance clause.

DISCUSSION: A coinsurance clause requires the insured to maintain insurance equal to or greater than the specified percentage of the property's fair market value. Failure to do so makes the insured bear a proportionate amount of the loss. Stein's recovery is limited to $24,000 as shown below:

$$\frac{\text{Amount of insurance}}{\text{Coinsurance requirement}} \times \text{Loss} = \text{Recovery}$$

$$\frac{\$120{,}000}{100\% \times \$200{,}000} \times \$40{,}000 = \$24{,}000$$

67. McArthur purchased a house for $60,000. The house is insured for $64,000 and the insurance policy has an 80% coinsurance provision. Storms caused $12,000 worth of damage when the house had a fair market value of $120,000. What maximum amount will McArthur recover from the insurance company?

a. $8,000.

b. $9,000.

c. $9,600.

d. $12,000.

The correct answer is (a). *(CPA 1189 L-59)*

REQUIRED: The amount of recovery under a policy containing a coinsurance clause.

DISCUSSION: The standard coinsurance clause provides that the insured agrees to maintain insurance equal to a specified percentage of the value of the property. If the insured has not carried the specified percentage and a loss occurs, the insurance company only pays a proportionate share. The coinsurance requirement is $96,000 (80% x $120,000 FMV at the time of the loss). Under the formula below, McArthur will recover $8,000 of the $12,000 loss.

$$\frac{\text{Amount of insurance}}{\text{Coinsurance requirement}} \times \text{Loss} = \text{Recovery}$$

$$\frac{\$64{,}000}{\$96{,}000} \times \$12{,}000 = \$8{,}000$$

68. Jerry's House of Jewelry, Inc. took out an insurance policy with the Old Time Insurance Company which covered the stock of jewelry displayed in the store's windows. Old Time agreed to indemnify Jerry's House for losses due to window smashing and theft of the jewels displayed. The application contained the following provision: "It is hereby warranted that the maximum value of the jewelry displayed shall not exceed $10,000." The insurance policy's coverage was for $8,000. The application was initialed alongside the warranty and attached to the policy. Subsequently, thieves smashed the store window and stole $4,000 worth of jewels. The total value of the display during that week, including the day of the robbery, was $12,000. Which of the following is correct?

a. Jerry's House will recover nothing.

b. Jerry's House will recover $2,000, the loss less the amount in excess of the $10,000 display limitation.

c. Jerry's House will recover the full $4,000 since the warranty will be construed as a mere representation.

d. Jerry's House will recover the full $4,000 since attaching the application to the policy is insufficient to make it a part thereof.

The correct answer is (a). *(CPA 1181 L-55)*

REQUIRED: The amount an insured will recover when a warranty is breached.

DISCUSSION: Conditions precedent, called warranties, are part of the property insurance policy. Breach of a warranty precludes recovery and results in a forfeiture. Since the law disfavors forfeitures, courts construe questions of interpretation favorably to the insured, and against the insurer that drafted the policy. However, if the parties expressly agree that certain statements are warranties, then a court would recognize them as warranties. Since Jerry's House warranted never to display more than $10,000 of jewelry, the breach of warranty prevents recovery.

Answer (b) is incorrect because Jerry's House will recover nothing; it is not entitled to $2,000. Answer (c) is incorrect because the warranty will not be construed as a mere representation; the intention of the parties clearly was to make it a warranty. Answer (d) is incorrect because attachment of the application to the policy is usually sufficient to make it a part thereof. It may also be incorporated into the policy by reference to it.

69. Bernard Manufacturing, Inc. owns a three-story building which it recently purchased. The purchase price was $200,000, of which $160,000 was financed by the proceeds of a mortgage loan from the Cattleman Savings and Loan Association. Bernard immediately procured a standard fire insurance policy on the premises for $200,000 from the Magnificent Insurance Company. Cattleman also took out fire insurance of $160,000 on the property from the Reliable Insurance Company of America. The property was subsequently totally destroyed as a result of a fire which started in an adjacent loft and spread to Bernard's building. Insofar as the rights and duties of Bernard, Cattleman, and the insurers are concerned, which of the following is a correct statement?

a. Cattleman Savings and Loan lacks the requisite insurable interest to collect on its policy.

b. Bernard Manufacturing can only collect $40,000.

c. Reliable Insurance Company is subrogated to Cattleman's rights against Bernard upon payment of Cattleman's insurance claim.

d. The maximum amount that Bernard can collect from Magnificent is $40,000, the value of its insurable interest.

The correct answer is (c). *(CPA 1180 L-53)*

REQUIRED: The correct statement describing the rights of the parties.

DISCUSSION: A fire insurance company that issues a policy on a building in favor of a mortgagee and pays the mortgagee's insurance claim is subrogated to the mortgagee's rights against the insured. Thus, if Cattleman had acquired no insurance and the building had been destroyed, Cattleman would have had the legal right to collect the balance of the $160,000 mortgage from Bernard. These are the rights to which Reliable Insurance Company is subrogated by having paid Cattleman's claim.

Answer (a) is incorrect because Cattleman Savings and Loan did have an insurable interest by virtue of holding a $160,000 mortgage on Bernard's building. Answers (b) and (d) are incorrect because Bernard can collect $200,000, the face amount of the policy, not merely $40,000. Bernard had an insurable interest of $200,000 composed of $40,000 equity and $160,000 of debt.

23.4 Liability Insurance

70. Marcross Corporation owns a fleet of taxicabs it has insured with the Countrywide Insurance Company against liability and collision. Nabor, one of its drivers, deliberately backed one of the cabs into two other parked cabs in the corporation's garage after a heated dispute with the garage manager. While waiting for a traffic signal, another Marcross cab was hit in the rear by a negligently driven truck. Each cab involved had damages in excess of the minimum deductible.

a. Marcross can recover against Countrywide for damages to all the cabs less the minimum deductible.

b. Countrywide has no rights against Nabor.

c. General creditors of Marcross could insure Marcross' cabs aginst collision and other types of loss because in the event of bankruptcy the creditors would have to resort to the corporation's property to satisfy their claims.

d. Marcross must first sue the negligent truck driver, or his principal, for damages to its cab before it can collect against Countrywide.

The correct answer is (a). *(CPA 576 L-28)*

REQUIRED: The correct statement of the rights and liabilities of the parties under an automobile liability and collision policy.

DISCUSSION: An insured under an automobile collision policy can recover against the insurance company for damages to the insured's vehicles so long as the damage is not directed by the insured. This recovery is not denied because the damage was caused by the negligent or even intentional conduct of the insured's employee.

Answer (b) is incorrect because the insurance company under an automobile collision policy is subrogated to the rights of the insured after payment. Thus, the insurance company would have Marcross's rights against the driver who deliberately damaged the three vehicles. Answer (c) is incorrect because general creditors of a business lack the requisite insurable interest to obtain insurance on the property of the debtor. Answer (d) is incorrect because the insured need not sue negligent third parties who cause damage to its property. This is the risk insured against. After Countrywide pays under the policy, it will be subrogated to the rights of Marcross against the negligent third party (the driver of the truck).

71. Tedland Trading Corporation insured its 17 automobiles for both liability and collision. Milsap, one of its salesmen, was in an automobile accident while driving a company car on a sales trip. The facts clearly reveal that the accident was solely the fault of Williams, the driver of the other car. Milsap was seriously injured, and the automobile was declared a total loss. The value of the auto was $3,000. Which of the following is an incorrect statement regarding the rights and liabilities of Tedland, its insurer, Milsap and Williams?

a. Tedland's insurer must defend Tedland against any claims by Milsap or Williams.

b. Tedland's insurer has no liability whatsoever since the accident was the result of Williams' negligence.

c. Milsap has an independent action against Williams for the injuries caused by Williams's negligence even if Milsap receives worker compensation from Tedland.

d. Tedland's insurer is liable to Tedland for $3,000, less any deductible, on the collision policy, but will be subrogated to Tedland's rights.

The correct answer is (b). *(CPA 582 L-59)*

REQUIRED: The false statement of the rights and liabilities of the parties under a liability and collision policy.

DISCUSSION: Even though the facts clearly indicate fault on the part of Williams, Tedland's insurance carrier has certain duties under its liability and collision policy. The typical collision policy would require the insurance carrier to pay the fair market value of the automobile less any deductible. Under the liability provisions, the insurance carrier is responsible for investigating and preparing to defend Tedland against claims which may be brought and to aid in negotiating a settlement against Williams.

Answer (a) is incorrect because the insurance carrier must defend the insured against claims brought by persons injured in an automobile accident. Answer (c) is incorrect because a person driving the insured's car who is injured by the negligence of another driver has an independent action against that driver. Answer (d) is incorrect because the insurance carrier is liable for the damage to an insured automobile less any deductible contained in the policy. An insurance company that pays a claim is subrogated to the legal rights of the party it has paid.

72. Which of the following is not a type of insurance policy which provides liability insurance?

a. Malpractice insurance.

b. Homeowners insurance.

c. Automobile insurance.

d. Fire insurance.

The correct answer is (d). *(Publisher)*

REQUIRED: The type of insurance policy not providing liability coverage.

DISCUSSION: Fire insurance generally protects the insured from damage to the insured property as a result of fire. It does not cover the insured for causing a fire on someone else's property.

Answer (a) is incorrect because malpractice insurance is a special form of liability insurance protecting professionals from lawsuits by third parties for negligence. Answer (b) is incorrect because homeowners insurance generally contains a liability section in the event guests are injured on the premises. Answer (c) is incorrect because a primary purpose of automobile insurance is to protect the owner or driver from liability in the event (s)he is responsible for damage to another person or property.

73. Andrews was home on Saturday, mowing the lawn and doing general yard work. He was hot and tired from the exertion. A particularly obnoxious salesman stopped by. Andrews punched the salesman in the face and broke his nose. The salesman has sued Andrews.

a. Andrews should notify the company which provides his homeowners insurance since such accidents are covered by the liability section.

b. Neither liability nor any other insurance will cover an intentional tort.

c. If Andrews has an umbrella policy, his liability will be covered up to the maximum amount.

d. Andrews will only be covered if he has a specific liability insurance policy.

The correct answer is (b). *(Publisher)*

REQUIRED: The correct statement concerning liability coverage for an intentional tort.

DISCUSSION: Andrews committed a battery in punching the salesman in the face. This is an intentional tort which is excluded from insurance coverage. Insurance will cover negligence and damage from intentional torts by others, but it generally does not cover the insured for his intentional wrongs. To cover such acts would be against public policy.

Answers (a), (c), and (d) are incorrect because no specific liability insurance policy, whether homeowners or umbrella, will cover intentional wrongs.

74. Alphonse, a sole CPA practitioner, obtained a malpractice insurance policy from the Friendly Casualty Company. In regard to this coverage,

a. Issuance of an unqualified opinion by Alphonse when he knows the statements are false does not give Friendly a defense.

b. The policy would automatically cover the work of a new partnership formed by Alphonse and Borne.

c. Friendly will not be subrogated to rights against Alphonse for his negligent conduct of an audit.

d. Coverage includes injury to a client resulting from a slip on a rug negligently left loose in Alphonse's office.

The correct answer is (c). *(CPA 574 L-53)*

REQUIRED: The correct statement regarding coverage on a malpractice insurance policy.

DISCUSSION: Subrogation is the insurer's right after paying a claim to collect from a person who caused the loss. It applies to fire, automobile collision, accident, and most property policies. However, subrogation rights are not created by malpractice or life insurance. An insurance company that pays a claim for the malpractice of a CPA would not be subrogated to any rights against the CPA. Subrogation never confers rights on an insurer against its own injured but only against negligent third parties.

Answer (a) is incorrect because issuance of an unqualified opinion with knowledge of falsity or negligence is fraud, which would not be covered by malpractice insurance. Answer (b) is incorrect because a new malpractice policy would be necessary to cover Borne. Answer (d) is incorrect because malpractice insurance only covers negligence in providing professional services, not personal injury liability.

75. Ralph and Ted live in one of approximately 25 states that have some form of no-fault automobile insurance. Ralph drove his car into the rear of Ted's car. Ralph and Ted each received minor injuries, as did Ted's passenger, John. Sue, a pedestrian, was also injured when the impact drove Ted's car into the crosswalk, knocking Sue to the ground. Sue was treated at the emergency room for minor scrapes and bruises and released. Which of the following is most likely true concerning recovery for personal injuries?

a. Sue cannot recover from either Ralph or Ted because no-fault systems require pedestrians to provide coverage for minor injuries they suffer.

b. Ted can recover from Ralph's insurer because Ted is clearly without fault.

c. John can recover from Ralph's insurer because Ralph is clearly at fault.

d. Ted can recover from his own insurer regardless of who is at fault.

The correct answer is (d). *(Publisher)*

REQUIRED: The correct statement regarding recovery for minor personal injuries in a no-fault automobile insurance state.

DISCUSSION: No-fault automobile insurance systems compensate persons injured in automobile accidents without regard to fault. Up to a tort immunity threshold, the typical no-fault insurance policy covers personal injury sustained by the named insured, members of his/her household, passengers, pedestrians, and authorized operators of the vehicle.

Answer (a) is incorrect because no-fault systems do not require pedestrians to insure against injuries caused by another's negligence. Answers (b) and (c) are incorrect because under a no-fault system, fault is irrelevant in determining which insurer compensates for minor personal injuries.

CHAPTER TWENTY-FOUR
ESTATE PLANNING:
ESTATES, WILLS, AND TRUSTS

24.1 Estate Administration

1. Estate planning is the process by which an individual may determine how his/her assets will be systematically transferred both before and after death to achieve certain goals. The least compelling motive of this process is to

a. Act in accordance with the public policy against excessive accumulation of wealth.

b. Ensure that the owner's intentions are honored.

c. Prevent the forced sale of important assets.

d. Avoid taxes.

The correct answer is (a). *(Publisher)*

REQUIRED: The least important reason for estate planning.

DISCUSSION: Wealth redistribution is one public policy justification for taxes on estates, estate income, inheritance, and gifts. Estate planning is useful precisely because it is a means of preserving an estate and providing for distribution in accordance with the owner's wishes. Effective estate planning increases the amount that can be transferred to private recipients and is therefore in opposition to the policy of wealth redistribution.

Answer (b) is incorrect because the main purpose of estate planning is to comply with the transferor's intent regarding the amount, timing, manner, and transferees of his/her property. Answer (c) is incorrect because planning for their transfer may prevent the sale at disadvantageous terms of important assets such as a farm, business, or home. Answer (d) is incorrect because tax avoidance (not evasion) is a major objective of planning for any sizable estate.

2. The least sophisticated tool that may be used in planning the distribution of an estate is

a. A will.

b. An intestacy statute.

c. Life insurance.

d. Gifts.

The correct answer is (b). *(Publisher)*

REQUIRED: The least sophisticated tool in planning the distribution of an estate.

DISCUSSION: The various devices used in estate planning generally include wills, trusts, gifts, joint ownership, and insurance. A state intestacy statute is the least sophisticated technique used in estate planning. It determines how the property in a decedent's estate will be transferred when (s)he does not leave a valid will. Using an intestacy statute is really estate planning by default and can be used only when the statutory scheme is consistent with the transferor's intent. But there are many other facets of estate planning that cannot be implemented without wills and trusts, e.g., designating a personal representative, saving taxes, liquidity, and providing for management of property.

Answers (a), (c), and (d) are incorrect because each is a useful and sophisticated estate planning tool. Used together, they provide much flexibility in accomplishing the goals of an individual transferor.

3. Estates are administered through a probate process that consists of two essential steps: the determination of the validity of the will (if any) by a probate court and the actual administration of the estate by a court-appointed and supervised personal representative. Which of the following is true?

a. Probate law is uniform throughout the country as a result of the enactment of the federal Probate Code.

b. Probate is a state law matter but is uniform throughout the country because almost all states have adopted the Uniform Probate Code.

c. Probate law varies among the states. The law of the state where realty is located governs its transfer even though different from the law of the decedent's domicile.

d. Personal property generally passes under the law of the state where it is physically located at the moment of the owner's death.

The correct answer is (c). *(Publisher)*

REQUIRED: The true statement about the law governing the probate process.

DISCUSSION: The probate process is controlled by local rather than federal law and thus varies from state to state. Although a movement toward greater uniformity has begun, the variation remains substantial. Accordingly, the answers to this and other questions are intended to reflect only a general pattern. One general rule is that real property passes under the law of the place where it is located, thereby requiring an additional administration in that state if it is different from the decedent's domicile. Personal property, however, generally passes under the law of the decedent's domicile, so it is possible for different probate rules to be applied to different parts of the estate.

Answer (a) is incorrect because probate is a state law issue. There is no federal probate law. Answer (b) is incorrect because unlike the UCC, the UPC has been adopted by only about one-third of the states. Answer (d) is incorrect because personal property generally passes under the law of the decedent's domicile.

4. Which is the best definition of the probate estate?

a. All property in which the decedent had an interest before death.

b. All property subject to the federal estate tax.

c. All property subject to the state inheritance tax.

d. All property transferred under a will or intestacy statute.

The correct answer is (d). *(Publisher)*

REQUIRED: The best definition of the probate estate.

DISCUSSION: For probate purposes, the estate is an artificial entity to hold all the decedent's property that is subject to the jurisdiction of the probate court (i.e., all property which passes under the will or the intestacy statute). The estate assets are distributed after payment of the valid claims, taxes, and fees assessed against it.

Answer (a) is incorrect because not all such property is included in the decedent's estate. For example, property held as a joint tenant with right of survivorship is not included in the probate estate. Answer (b) is incorrect because the taxable estate is not synonymous with the probate estate; e.g., the assets of certain inter vivos trusts established by the decedent may be included in the taxable estate but not in the probate estate. Answer (c) is incorrect because state inheritance taxes are not assessed against the estate but upon the transfer of property from a decedent.

5. Jean Bond's will left various specific property and sums of money to relatives and friends. She left the residue of her estate equally to her favorite niece and nephew. Which of the various properties described below will become a part of Bond's estate and be distributed in accordance with her last will and testament?

a. A joint savings account that listed her sister, who is still living, as the joint tenant.

b. The entire family homestead that she had owned in joint tenancy with her older brother who predeceased her and that was still recorded as jointly owned.

c. Several substantial gifts that she made in contemplation of death to various charities.

d. A life insurance policy that designated a former partner as the beneficiary.

The correct answer is (b). *(CPA 581 L-50)*

REQUIRED: The property included in the decedent's estate.

DISCUSSION: If the homestead was owned in a joint tenancy with an older brother who had predeceased her, Bond would have become the sole owner of the property upon his death and the joint tenancy would have terminated regardless of how it is recorded. Joint tenancy is a form of property ownership in which surviving joint tenants succeed to the decedent's interests. As the sole owner, Bond could transfer the entire property as she wished, including by devise in her will.

Answer (a) is incorrect because an interest in a savings account held as a joint tenancy would pass to the surviving joint tenant under the right of survivorship in the property. Answer (c) is incorrect because gifts made in contemplation of death are valid and would not be included in the donor's estate. Answer (d) is incorrect because the proceeds of a life insurance policy would pass to the designated beneficiary under the insurance contract.

6. Settlor established an irrevocable 15-year trust for her children. The residue was to revert to her upon termination, but she died before the 15-year period expired. Which of the following is true?

a. No interest in the trust will pass under the intestacy statute if the decedent left no will.

b. If Settlor died testate, no interest in the trust passes under the will.

c. If Settlor retained a power to revoke, the assets are included in the decedent's estate even if the reversion was not retained by Settlor.

d. If the residue passed to others upon expiration of the 15-year period (instead of to Settlor), no interest in the trust would pass under Settlor's will.

The correct answer is (d). *(Publisher)*

REQUIRED: Whether trust property will be included in a decedent's estate.

DISCUSSION: A settlor who establishes a trust for a period of years but retains the reversionary interest has a property right (future interest) that will be included in his/her estate at death. If the reversion is in someone other than the settlor, however, the settlor has no property interest to be disposed of in his/her will.

Answers (a) and (b) are incorrect because if the settlor retained the reversionary interest in the trust, it will pass under her will or under the intestacy statute if she did not have a will. Answer (c) is incorrect because the power to revoke would end at her death and she would not have the reversionary interest to include in her estate.

7. An estate was established upon the decedent's death. Which of the following is a true statement about the procedure for administering the estate?

a. If the decedent left a will, the proper procedure is intestate distribution.

b. If the decedent left no will, the proper procedure is testate distribution.

c. Part of a decedent's property might be transferred under testate distribution and the remainder under intestate distribution.

d. If the decedent left a valid will, all estate property left after required payments must pass under its terms.

The correct answer is (c). *(Publisher)*

REQUIRED: The true statement about distribution of estate assets.

DISCUSSION: If the decedent left a valid will, the proper procedure is testate distribution in accordance with its terms and the applicable law. Otherwise, the proper procedure is intestate distribution according to the terms of the intestacy statute. For various reasons, part of the estate may be distributed according to one scheme and the rest by the other. For example, a child left out of a will might take from a deceased parent as if no valid will had been left but the rest of the beneficiaries would take under the will.

Answers (a) and (b) are incorrect because testate means with a will and intestate without a will. Answer (d) is incorrect because for various reasons, assets may be distributed other than by the terms of a valid will. For example, a surviving spouse can elect to take a statutory share of the estate rather than accept his/her provision in the will.

8. In the administration of an estate, sometimes a decedent owns and has left property other than where than (s)he resides. In such a situation there usually is needed a probate administration in the state where the property is located (unless it is only personal property). This is called

a. A summary administration.

b. An ancillary administration.

c. A family administration.

d. A nonintervention administration.

The correct answer is (b). *(Publisher)*

REQUIRED: The term for a probate in a state other than where the decedent resided.

DISCUSSION: An ancillary administration is an auxiliary administration which is needed to administer real property in a state in which the decedent did not reside. It is not required for personal property because jurisdiction over personal property is the decedent's residence.

Answer (a) is incorrect because a summary administration is one done in a summary form in many states where the value of the estate is very small by a simple court hearing to determine the distribution. Answer (c) is incorrect because family administration is a simplified administration in some states where the estate is small and the only beneficiaries are the decedent's family. Answer (d) is incorrect because nonintervention administration is that in which the personal representative may carry out all his/her powers provided under the state statute without approval of each transaction by the court. After the personal representative is approved by the court, (s)he generally only needs to report again when the administration has been completed.

9. The regular administration of a decedent's estate is necessary even though

a. The estate is very small.

b. (S)he died without heirs.

c. All assets of the decedent were held as a tenant by the entireties.

d. The estate consisted only of the decedent's homestead.

The correct answer is (b). *(Publisher)*

REQUIRED: The instance in which regular administration will be necessary.

DISCUSSION: Heirs are those who succeed to property under the intestacy statute. An absence of heirs does not prevent a transfer by will, and even in the absence of a will an estate of a given size or kind must still be administered.

Answer (a) is incorrect because a very small estate may be administered by a simplified procedure or altogether exempted from the probate process. Answer (c) is incorrect because the surviving spouse has a right of survivorship in all such property, so it does not pass through the probate estate. Answer (d) is incorrect because the homestead often passes directly to a surviving spouse or minor child and not through the estate.

10. Waldorf's will named Franklin as the executor. In respect to Franklin's serving as executor, which of the following is correct?

a. He serves without compensation unless the will provides otherwise.

b. He is at liberty to purchase the estate's property the same as any other person dealing at arm's length.

c. Waldorf must have obtained Franklin's consent in writing to serve as executor.

d. Upon appointment by the court, he serves as the legal representative of the estate.

The correct answer is (d). *(CPA 580 L-40)*

REQUIRED: The correct statement concerning service as an executor.

DISCUSSION: The executor (personal representative) is legally responsible for the administration of the estate after appointment by the court. The duties include collecting the estate assets, processing and paying claims against the estate, and distributing estate assets to the beneficiaries.

Answer (a) is incorrect because the personal representative is entitled to reasonable compensation, regardless of any stipulation in the will. Answer (b) is incorrect because a personal representative is a fiduciary, a person who is held to an unusually high standard of trust. Accordingly, a personal representative cannot purchase the estate's property except under special circumstances. Answer (c) is incorrect because the testator may designate anyone as personal representative. The named party may decline to serve, however, or may not be approved by the court.

11. Madison died 15 years after executing a valid will. In it she named her daughter, Janet, as the executrix of the will and bequeathed two-thirds of her estate to her husband after all taxes, expenses, and fees were paid, and the balance equally to her children. The approximate size of Madison's estate is $1 million. Which of the following is correct?

a. Upon Madison's death, Janet does not have the legal right to act for and on behalf of the estate until the will has been admitted to probate and she has been appointed as executrix.

b. Absent instructions in the will, Janet should sell real property to satisfy debts against the estate before she resorts to personal property.

c. Upon execution of her will, Madison's beneficiaries had a vested interest in her property.

d. Had Madison died without making a will, her husband would have received everything.

The correct answer is (a). *(CPA 1181 L-52)*

REQUIRED: The correct statement concerning a will.

DISCUSSION: Even though an executrix (personal representative) is designated in the will, (s)he has no authority until appointed by the court after the will has been admitted to probate. The court will generally honor the designation in the will, provided that the person is willing and legally qualified to act.

Answer (b) is incorrect because personal property should generally be used to satisfy debts before real property is used. In some states, statutes provide for no distinction in the administration of real and personal property. Answer (c) is incorrect because a testamentary disposition may be revoked at any time before the death of the testatrix. Answer (d) is incorrect because if Madison died intestate, the property in her estate would have passed to her heirs under intestate succession. State statutes typically divide the property between the surviving spouse and the children.

12. Marshall died 15 years after executing a valid will. He named his son, Walker, as the executor of his will. He left two-thirds of his estate to his wife and the balance equally to his children. Which of the following is a right or duty of Walker as executor?

a. Walker must post a surety bond even if a provision in the will attempts to exempt him from this responsibility.

b. Once he accepts and is approved, Walker has an affirmative duty to discover, collect, and distribute all the decedent's assets.

c. If the will is silent on the point, Walker has complete discretion insofar as investing the estate's assets during the term of his administration.

d. Walker can sell real property without a court order, even though he has not been expressly authorized to do so.

The correct answer is (b). *(CPA 577 L-41)*

REQUIRED: The correct statement about the rights and duties of a personal representative.

DISCUSSION: The executor (personal representative) must be approved by the court. The executor then has the duty to discover, collect, preserve, and distribute the assets of the decedent to the beneficiaries.

Answer (a) is incorrect because although many states require that the personal representative post a bond, this may frequently be waived on direction from the will or by court approval of a request. Answer (c) is incorrect because the personal representative must exercise reasonable care and is often regulated by investment standards. Answer (d) is incorrect because the sale of real property usually requires court approval unless the will directs otherwise.

13. One of the principal duties of the personal representative in administering the estate is to pay the claims against the decedent. The statutory probate procedure generally requires that

a. Payment of taxes and administration costs take precedence over the family allowance.

b. Personal notice be given to each of the decedent's creditors.

c. Creditors who file valid claims against the estate at any time prior to its closing must be paid.

d. Creditors file their claims within some specified number of months after publication of notice.

The correct answer is (d). *(Publisher)*

REQUIRED: The true statement about payment of claims against the estate.

DISCUSSION: All of the decedent's outstanding debts at the time of death are the responsibility of the estate. State statutes provide that creditors of the estate must file their claims within a specified period (e.g., four months) after the date of publication of the notice to creditors. After the expiration of this period, claims not filed are forever barred.

Answer (a) is incorrect because the statutory family allowance generally has priority over claims against the estate. Other items with priority are taxes, funeral and burial costs, and administration expense. Answer (b) is incorrect because the personal representative generally need only publish a notice in a newspaper of general circulation. Answer (c) is incorrect because the claim period usually expires well before the estate is formally closed.

14. After the will has been admitted to probate and the personal representative has been appointed, the actual administration of a decedent's estate can be undertaken. It does not include

a. An accounting made to the court by the recipients of estate property.

b. Filing of tax returns.

c. Notification of creditors.

d. Payment of an allowance to the surviving spouse.

The correct answer is (a). *(Publisher)*

REQUIRED: The step not taken during administration of a decedent's estate.

DISCUSSION: The personal representative must collect, preserve, inventory, and appraise the assets of the estate. (S)he must give notice to creditors or other claimants against the estate. This notice allows the filing and proof of claims within some specified period. The surviving spouse may be paid an allowance that usually has priority over other claims. Administration also includes payment of funeral and burial expenses, the decedent's medical bills, costs of administration, debts, and taxes. The responsibilities include filing federal estate tax and estate income tax returns. The will may also provide that inheritance taxes are to be paid from the estate funds. After all payments have been made, an accounting is made to the court (by the personal representative, not the beneficiaries). When that is approved, the assets are distributed, the estate is closed, and the personal representative is discharged.

Answers (b), (c), and (d) are incorrect because each is a step during the administration of an estate.

15. One of the duties of the personal representative during administration of a decedent's estate is to pay the claims against the estate. Which of the following generally has the highest priority?

a. Estate taxes.

b. Fees of the personal representative.

c. The family allowance.

d. Funeral expenses.

The correct answer is (c). *(Publisher)*

REQUIRED: The claim against the estate with the first priority.

DISCUSSION: The statutory family allowance generally has priority over the claims against the estate. Other items with priority are taxes, the expenses of the last illness, funeral and burial costs, and administration expense. The family allowance varies from state to state. Under the Uniform Probate Code, the amount paid to the surviving spouse for a family allowance may not exceed $6,000 for one year after death. However, the UPC also allows him/her a homestead allowance of $5,000 and an exemption for personal and household items of $3,500.

16. Which of the following is a correct statement concerning the personal representative of an estate?

a. If the personal representative of an estate is unable to complete his/her administration, the court will appoint a successor.

b. An advantage of naming a corporate personal representative is that a successor need never be appointed.

c. An executor may resign but an administrator must complete the probate.

d. A court-appointed personal representative is called a testatrix.

The correct answer is (a). *(Publisher)*

REQUIRED: The correct statement concerning a personal representative.

DISCUSSION: When a personal representative resigns or is unable to complete the administration of the estate because of death, illness, or other incapacity, the probate court will appoint a successor. The original or the successor may be an individual, corporation, organization, or other legal entity. Moreover, any person appointed as a personal representative must have reached the statutory age and have contractual capacity. Often, the personal representative is a close relative of the decedent.

Answer (b) is incorrect because a corporation can resign or become insolvent or bankrupt, which would require a successor to be appointed. Answer (c) is incorrect because an executor (executrix if female) is a personal representative named in a will. An administrator is one appointed by the court. Either can resign. Answer (d) is incorrect because a testatrix is a person (female) who executes a will (the masculine term is testator).

17. Leo operated a corporation of which he was the only shareholder. When he died intestate, his widow, Leona, was named the personal representative of the estate. The stock of the corporation was worth $100,000 at Leo's death, and the business received $200,000 in insurance proceeds. As personal representative, Leona operated the company at a loss for two years, paying herself a salary and other fringe benefits. At the end of that period, she closed the business without paying its debts or liquidating the assets. Leo's children then sought, received, and objected to an accounting by Leona. If the daughters seek to surcharge her, Leona

a. Will win because a personal representative may operate the decedent's business.

b. Will lose because a personal representative may not be paid for administering the estate.

c. Will lose because the personal representative has no right to operate the decedent's business.

d. Will lose because she breached a fiduciary duty.

The correct answer is (d). *(Publisher)*

REQUIRED: The outcome of a suit against a personal representative who operated the decedent's business.

DISCUSSION: The personal representative of a decedent's estate is in a position of unusual trust and responsibility. (S)he is a fiduciary who is held to the highest good faith and must exercise care and diligence. The personal representative has a duty to preserve and protect the estate assets and to distribute them to the proper persons within a reasonable time. (S)he may not acquire assets from the estate without court approval or make a personal gain from handling its affairs. (S)he is also expected to display ordinary business acumen and may be liable (surcharged) for losses resulting from acting in bad faith, mismanagement, or dereliction of duty. Leona had no duty to operate the business except for a short time to facilitate its sale as a going concern, the winding up of its affairs, the completion of existing contracts, or distribution of its stock to beneficiaries. She is liable for breach of a fiduciary duty on account of her mismanagement, realization of personal gain, and wasting of assets belonging in part to the other heirs.

Answers (a) and (c) are incorrect because a personal representative may operate the decedent's business pursuant to a direction in the will, agreement of all concerned parties, or for a short time for winding up purposes, but not as occurred in this case. Answer (b) is incorrect because reasonable amounts may be paid to compensate the personal representative.

18. A personal representative of an estate would breach fiduciary duties if the personal representative

a. Combined personal funds with funds of the estate so that both could purchase treasury bills.

b. Represented the estate in a lawsuit brought against it by a disgruntled relative of the decedent.

c. Distributed property in satisfaction of the decedent's debts.

d. Engaged a non-CPA to prepare the records for the estate's final accounting.

The correct answer is (a). *(CPA 589 L-19)*

REQUIRED: The action breaching the fiduciary duty of a personal representative.

DISCUSSION: The personal representative is responsible for administering the estate in accordance with the pertinent legal directions. The representative is a fiduciary with respect to the estate, and as such is charged with acting primarily for the benefit of the estate and with accountability for the assets of the estate. Included among a fiduciary's duties is an obligation to keep the estate's property separate from his/her property.

Answer (b) is incorrect because representing the estate in a lawsuit is a proper duty of a fiduciary. Answer (c) is incorrect because the estate is liable for all of the decedent's debts, and settling those debts is a duty of the personal representative. Answer (d) is incorrect because the final accounting of the estate is not required to be performed by an independent public accountant.

19. The normal types of questions relating to estates and trusts which might be referred from a law firm to a CPA firm would include problems which involve

a. The order of distribution under the intestate succession laws.

b. Whether an ancillary proceeding is required.

c. The amount of property or money to be received by the income beneficiaries as contrasted with the amount to be accumulated for the remainderman.

d. Whether a will has been effectively revoked.

The correct answer is (c). *(CPA 1176 L-46)*

REQUIRED: The issue relating to estates and trusts within the competence of a CPA firm.

DISCUSSION: The computation of the allocation of assets between trust income and principal is an accounting problem within the province of a CPA. It is common for law firms to refer such problems to a CPA. A CPA's duties may also include preparing the estate's federal estate tax returns, fiduciary income tax returns, and schedules in rendering an accounting to the court and other interested parties.

Answers (a), (b), and (d) are incorrect because each represents a legal issue properly determinable by an attorney, not a CPA.

20. The federal estate tax is an excise tax on

a. The income of the decedent's estate received during administration.

b. The decedent's right to transfer property after (s)he dies.

c. Taxes accrued on the income of the decedent at the time of death.

d. Amounts received by a beneficiary from a decedent.

The correct answer is (b). *(Publisher)*

REQUIRED: The nature of the federal estate tax.

DISCUSSION: The federal estate tax is an excise tax because it taxes the exercise of a right (the power to direct the disposition of one's property at death). This graduated tax is imposed on the net value of the estate after deductions for the value transferred to the surviving spouse, various expenses, and charitable gifts. The tax is paid by the personal representative from the estate assets prior to distribution to the beneficiaries.

Answer (a) is incorrect because a separate federal income tax is imposed on the estate's income. This tax is also paid by the personal representative. Answer (c) is incorrect because the personal representative must pay from estate assets the income tax owed by the decedent at death, but no tax is levied on the tax owed. Answer (d) is incorrect because it describes an inheritance tax levied by many states.

24.2 Intestate Succession

21. If an individual dies without a valid will, what becomes of his/her property?

a. The property will be transferred under the applicable statute of descent and distribution.

b. All the real property escheats to the state where it is located and the rest to the state of domicile.

c. Real property descends to the heirs but personal property is distributed according to the applicable state statute.

d. The principle of primogeniture applies.

The correct answer is (a). *(Publisher)*

REQUIRED: The disposition of the property of one who dies intestate.

DISCUSSION: In effect, intestate disposition will be according to a statutory will drafted by the state legislature and called a statute of descent and distribution. This intestacy statute is based on a legislative presumption regarding the intent of the decedent to benefit his/her closest relatives. Accordingly, the real and personal property are generally divided between the surviving spouse and the children.

Answer (b) is incorrect because only if the decedent had no heirs will the property be transferred (escheated) to the state. Answer (c) is incorrect because both the real and personal property pass under the intestacy statute. Answer (d) is incorrect because primogeniture is the archaic English common law rule by which real property automatically descended to the eldest son of the decedent.

22. Dan died intestate and was survived by a spouse, three children, two siblings, and one parent. Each of the three surviving children has two children. A fourth child predeceased Dan, leaving one child alive at Dan's death. Under the typical intestacy statute,

a. The surviving spouse will take the entire estate.

b. Only one grandchild will share in the estate.

c. The surviving spouse, the siblings, and the parent of Dan will receive shares.

d. Collateral relatives and lineal ascendants cannot share in an intestate estate.

The correct answer is (b). *(Publisher)*

REQUIRED: The true statement about distribution of an estate under a typical intestacy statute.

DISCUSSION: The usual statutory scheme favors the surviving spouse, the decedent's children, and the grandchildren of the decedent. Often, the spouse will take a specified percentage and the children will divide the remainder. If a child has predeceased the decedent, the children of that child will take his/her share. Dan's spouse, surviving children, and grandchild through the predeceased child will therefore inherit the estate.

Answer (a) is incorrect because intestacy statutes usually provide for the children of the decedent. Answers (c) and (d) are incorrect because the collateral relatives (siblings and their children) and lineal ascendants (parents or grandparents) generally do not share in the estate unless the decedent has no lineal descendants.

23. Woodrow died and left a will that named as co-executors the Fundamental Trust Company and Harlow, who is one of the residuary legatees. The will was silent on various points indicated below. Which of the following is correct?

a. If Woodrow's will was not properly executed, it will not be admitted to probate and his property will be distributed according to the intestate succession laws even though this is contrary to Woodrow's wishes as stated in the will.

b. Since Harlow is one of the residuary legatees, Harlow cannot serve as executor since this would represent a conflict of interest and also would violate Harlow's fiduciary duty.

c. All taxes paid will be allocated to the residuary estate and not apportioned.

d. The executors have complete discretion insofar as investing the estate's assets during the term of their administration.

The correct answer is (a). *(CPA 1179 L-20)*

REQUIRED: The correct statement concerning the administration of an estate.

DISCUSSION: A will must have been properly executed (formalities observed during signing and witnessing) in order to be admitted to probate. The distribution and wishes provided in a will can only be followed if the will is admitted to probate. Otherwise, the property is distributed according to the intestate succession laws.

Answer (b) is incorrect because a beneficiary under a will may also serve as a personal representative. The other beneficiaries of the estate are protected because the administration of the estate is under the supervision of the court. Answer (c) is incorrect because inheritance taxes enacted by states on the act of inheriting are usually apportioned to the beneficiaries unless the will provides otherwise. The federal estate tax, in contrast, is usually borne by the residue. Answer (d) is incorrect because a personal representative must exercise reasonable care and is often regulated as to investment standards.

24. If a person leaves no will and no heirs, his/her property is transferred to the state under the law of

a. Testate succession.

b. Intestate succession.

c. Escheat.

d. Lapse.

The correct answer is (c). *(Publisher)*

REQUIRED: The term for transfer of decedent's property to the state in the absence of a will or heirs.

DISCUSSION: Property must be owned by someone. Consequently, if the decedent has not directed the disposition of his/her property through a valid will or is not survived by heirs qualifying to take under the applicable statute of descent and distribution, the decedent's property will pass to the state.

Answer (a) is incorrect because it is the process of transfer under a will. Answer (b) is incorrect because it is the process of transfer to the heirs when there is no valid will. Answer (d) is incorrect because an anti-lapse statute concerns failed testamentary gifts. For example, if such a gift fails because the beneficiary predeceased the testator, the anti-lapse statute might provide for the gift to pass to a surviving decedent of the intended recipient.

24.3 Wills

25. Which of the following is a true statement about the power to make a will?

a. No one has a constitutional right to make a will.

b. A will takes effect upon proper execution.

c. The right to make a will is given by common law rather than by statute.

d. A state legislature may not take away the right of testamentary disposition.

The correct answer is (a). *(Publisher)*

REQUIRED: The true statement about the power to make a will.

DISCUSSION: The Supreme Court has declared that the right to make a will is not of constitutional dignity. Nor is there any legal principle to prevent a state legislature from limiting or eliminating the power of testamentary disposition. Estate taxes and statutory provisions for surviving spouses are examples of limits on the power to convey one's property at death.

Answer (b) is incorrect because the power to make a will also includes the power to revoke it at any time prior to death. A will therefore takes effect only upon the death of the testator. Answer (c) is incorrect because the common law does not confer the right to make a will, but a statute in every state gives the power to dispose of property by will. Answer (d) is incorrect because a legislature has absolute authority to control testamentary conveyances.

26. Which of the following types of wills is recognized as valid in every state?

a. Written will.

b. Holographic will.

c. Nuncupative will.

d. Soldiers' and sailors' wills.

The correct answer is (a). *(Publisher)*

REQUIRED: The type of will recognized in every state.

DISCUSSION: A written will is recognized as valid in every state. In addition, a written will executed with the formalities required in one's state of residence is usually recognized as valid if the testator later moves to another state.

Answer (b) is incorrect because a holographic will (one which is handwritten and not properly witnessed) is not recognized in many states. Answer (c) is incorrect because a nuncupative will (an oral will) is not recognized in every state and, even where recognized, is generally valid only for disposing of personal property. Answer (d) is incorrect because soldiers' and sailors' wills (handwritten or oral, and only orally attested) are recognized in many states, but not all, and are only effective to dispose of personal property.

27. Every state has detailed requirements for valid execution of a formal will. In general,

a. The will must be dated.

b. A mark may suffice as a signature.

c. The will must be notarized and filed in the public records.

d. The will is invalidated if witnessed by a beneficiary.

The correct answer is (b). *(Publisher)*

REQUIRED: The true statement about execution of a formal will.

DISCUSSION: Any mark or signature will suffice provided that there is proof that it was the mark of the testator and placed on that part of the will with the intention of operating as his/her signature. In many states, a signature to a will must be placed at the end (subscribed), but the signature need not be in any special form and even an "X" is generally sufficient provided it was placed with the proper intent.

Answer (a) is incorrect because a will should be but is not required to be dated. Answer (c) is incorrect because wills are generally not filed in public records until probated and they need not be notarized. However, a notarized affidavit by the witnesses is commonly used in admitting the will into court. Answer (d) is incorrect because this rule has been replaced in almost all states by statutes permitting beneficiaries to act as essential witnesses. In some states, however, the will may be purged of any provision in favor of such a person. Other states limit an essential witness to his/her intestate share.

28. Joe and his wife Minnie requested their attorney to draw up new wills for them. After reviewing several drafts and making the necessary corrections, Joe and Minnie were ready to sign the final wills. Which of the following is a correct statement concerning the valid execution of a will?

a. The will must be signed although the signature may appear any place on the will.

b. Two witnesses are required to attest that the testator signed the will although it does not matter if they sign the will in the testator's presence.

c. The will must be notarized by a notary public.

d. The testator must have testamentary capacity.

The correct answer is (d). *(Publisher)*

REQUIRED: The correct statement concerning the valid execution of a will.

DISCUSSION: In order to make a valid will, a person must generally be the age of majority in that particular state (usually 18 or 21) and must be of sound mind. Sound mind (also called testamentary capacity) means mentally competent and able to understand the extent of one's property and to whom it will pass.

Answer (a) is incorrect because it is common for statutes to require the testator's signature to appear at the end of the will or at least in some place to indicate that everything in the will has been approved by the testator (prior to signature). Answer (b) is incorrect because the witnesses must generally sign a will in the testator's presence and in the presence of each other. Answer (c) is incorrect because the will does not need to be notarized, although a notarized affidavit by the witnesses is commonly required to admit the will into court.

29. One restriction on the power to convey one's property by will is the requirement of testamentary capacity. A will is conclusively presumed to be invalid if

a. Sarah was under legal guardianship when it was executed.

b. Sarah was 17 when she properly executed it and was 77 when she died without having revoked it.

c. No proof of mental testamentary capacity is offered before the will is admitted to probate.

d. Sarah had been adjudicated insane at the time of death but not at the time of execution.

The correct answer is (b). *(Publisher)*

REQUIRED: The instance in which a will is conclusively presumed to be invalid.

DISCUSSION: A person cannot execute a valid will unless (s)he has attained the statutory age (generally 18 or 21) and has the requisite mental capacity. The age requirement applies at the time of execution. Age at the time of death is irrelevant. Accordingly, a will executed at age 17 cannot be admitted to probate.

Answer (a) is incorrect because a person under a legal guardianship may still be able to make a valid will. The mental capacity required for a will is less than that required to contract, but the maker must at least be aware that (s)he is making a will and able to understand the extent of his/her property and to whom it will pass. Answer (c) is incorrect because proof of mental capacity is not required unless an interested party objects. Answer (d) is incorrect because mental capacity must exist when the will is executed, not at death.

30. The elements constituting a will may not always be clear when the will is written on more than one piece of paper. When one document is treated as the will and another is referred to and included therein although it was not formally executed with the will,

a. The doctrine of integration is applied.

b. An act of independent significance has occurred.

c. The second document is incorporated by reference.

d. The second document is treated as a codicil.

The correct answer is (c). *(Publisher)*

REQUIRED: The legal basis for including a document in a will although it was not formally executed with the will.

DISCUSSION: The usual requirements for applying the doctrine of incorporation by reference are the following: the document existed when the will was executed; the document was referred to in the will as existing at the time of execution; the document is clearly identified in the will; and sufficient proof must be offered of the validity of the document. An example of incorporation by reference is the reference in a will to an already existing trust to hold a bequest for beneficiaries.

Answer (a) is incorrect because under the doctrine of integration, separate papers are treated as one formally executed instrument. Answer (b) is incorrect because this doctrine allows the court to fill in the gaps of the will. For example, a bequest to "all the members of my bowling team" can be upheld because the act of belonging to such a team has sufficient significance apart from any interest in directing testamentary conveyance of property. Answer (d) is incorrect because a codicil is an amendment to a will executed with the same formalities as a will.

31. Several months after executing their wills, Husband and Wife wanted to change a beneficiary. They went to their attorney and requested that (s)he prepare the necessary documents to make this change. Which of the following is the correct statement concerning an amendment to a will?

a. No additional documents are necessary since the changes can be made in the existing wills by crossing out the part to be changed, writing in the new change, and initialing the change in the margin.

b. An amendment to a will is called a codicil.

c. The amendment to the will does not have to be witnessed since it can refer to the original will which was witnessed.

d. An amendment to a will is called an ademption.

The correct answer is (b). *(Publisher)*

REQUIRED: The correct statement concerning an amendment to a will.

DISCUSSION: An amendment to a will is called a codicil. It must be executed with the same formalities as the original will. However, deletions in the original will can intentionally be made in some jurisdictions under case law by physically striking out portions of the will.

Answer (a) is incorrect because any physical crossing out in a will may revoke either that part of the will or in some states the entire will. Additions may never be made to the will without the same formalities as the original will. Answer (c) is incorrect because the amendment must be executed with the same formalities as the original will. A reference to the original will does not nullify this requirement. Answer (d) is incorrect because an ademption is the failure of a bequest or devise if specific property referred to in a will is not owned by the decedent at his/her death.

32. About a year after executing their wills, Joe and Minnie decided that they wanted to completely revise and revoke their old wills. Which of the following is not an effective method of revoking a will?

a. A subsequent will which is completely inconsistent with the original will.

b. A written instrument executed with the same formalities as the original will.

c. Destruction of the original will by an accidental fire.

d. Operation of law.

The correct answer is (c). *(Publisher)*

REQUIRED: The action that will not effectively revoke a will.

DISCUSSION: Destruction of a will by physical act will generally revoke a will if the physical act was done with intent to revoke the will. An accidental destruction of the will, however, will not constitute a revocation.

Answer (a) is incorrect because a subsequent will that is completely inconsistent with the original will does revoke the original will. Answer (b) is incorrect because one may revoke a will simply by stating so in a written instrument executed with the same formalities as the original will. Answer (d) is incorrect because operation of law will revoke a will (or part of it) in certain circumstances (e.g., if after the execution of a will the testator marries, divorces, or has new children born to him/her).

33. Tessie executed a valid will bequeathing her personalty to Lock and devising her realty to Ness. She later physically canceled that will after executing a second instrument leaving a parcel of lakeshore property to Scott but otherwise not disturbing the original disposition of the estate. After Tessie's death, the second will was judicially declared to be invalid. Tessie would not have revoked the first document if she had known that the second would not be effective. Which of the following is true?

a. A court may apply the doctrine of dependent relative revocation.

b. Courts can grant no relief for a mistake in the inducement to revoke a will.

c. Tessie is deemed to have died intestate.

d. If the second will was valid before her death, Tessie can revoke it to revive the first will (a copy was kept).

The correct answer is (a). *(Publisher)*

REQUIRED: The true statement about a revocation conditioned upon the validity of a second will.

DISCUSSION: Dependent relative revocation is a doctrine that allows a court to give effect to a revoked will when it appears that the decedent would not have revoked it but for a mistaken belief that a subsequent instrument would effectively dispose of the estate. Consequently, the revocation of the first will may be ignored by the court given sufficient proof of the decedent's intent and of the terms of the original will.

Answers (b) and (c) are incorrect because the theory of dependent relative revocation may be applied when a mistake was made in the inducement to revoke a will. Tessie's estate therefore can pass by testate succession. Answer (d) is incorrect because the revocation of a second will cannot revive a first will already revoked.

34. When Harry and Wilma were having their wills prepared by their attorney, they specified that if one of their children predeceased them, that deceased child's share was to go to his/her children in equal shares, rather than the grandchildren sharing equally with Harry and Wilma's surviving children. The term which refers to this type of distribution is

a. Per capita.

b. Per stirpes.

c. Dower.

d. Demonstrative legacy.

The correct answer is (b). *(Publisher)*

REQUIRED: The pattern of distribution in which the share of a deceased child goes to his/her descendants in equal shares.

DISCUSSION: Per stirpes is a method of distribution in which the share of a deceased child passes to his/her children in equal shares. For example, if a decedent had 3 living children and 1 deceased child who in turn had 2 children, the estate would pass one-fourth to each living child and one-eighth to each child of the deceased child.

Answer (a) is incorrect because per capita means the living descendants share equally regardless of which generation they belong to; e.g., if there were 3 living children and 2 children of a deceased child, each would receive one-fifth of the decedent's estate. Answer (c) is incorrect because dower was a common law right in which the surviving spouse was entitled to a share (e.g., one-third). Answer (d) is incorrect because a demonstrative legacy is one which is payable from particular property or out of the general estate if the particular property is insufficient.

35. John and Jane are spouses. Both die in the same automobile accident. Which of the following is true?

a. If John and Jane die simultaneously, neither person will inherit any property from the other.

b. If John was insured and Jane was the beneficiary, the proceeds are distributed as if the beneficiary had survived.

c. If John had lingered in a coma for 1 week and then died of the injuries sustained in the accident, John and Jane will be deemed to have died simultaneously.

d. If John and Jane held property as tenants by the entireties, each will be deemed to have inherited from the other.

The correct answer is (a). *(Publisher)*

REQUIRED: The effect of the simultaneous death of a beneficiary and owner of property.

DISCUSSION: The Uniform Simultaneous Death Act has been adopted in most states. Under this Act, when the order of death cannot be established, the property of each person is disposed of as if (s)he had survived the other. The purpose of the statute is to avoid the expense of probating the same property twice. This presumption can be overcome by a provision in the will.

Answer (b) is incorrect because the proceeds would be distributed as if the insured had survived the beneficiary. Answer (c) is incorrect because John clearly survived Jane, so the simultaneous death statute does not apply. Answer (d) is incorrect because the joint tenancy is effectively severed. Each person's interest is distributed as if (s)he survived the other.

36. Which of the following is a gratuitous lifetime transfer made to a potential beneficiary under the donor's will with the intent that it will be applied against any share that the donee might receive?

a. Gift in contemplation of death.

b. Advancement.

c. Ademption.

d. Abatement.

The correct answer is (b). *(Publisher)*

REQUIRED: The term for a transfer intended to be applied against the donee's share of the donor's estate.

DISCUSSION: Gifts are sometimes made to children or other relatives as an advance on their share of the donor's estate. Such a gift will only be considered an advancement if the donor intended that it was to reduce the beneficiary's share of his/her estate. Since the intent is a difficult matter to ascertain, most states provide that a gift will not be considered an advancement unless the donor clearly evidences his/her intent as such.

Answer (a) is incorrect because it describes a gift made with the intent that it will take effect only upon the donor's death. Answer (c) is incorrect because ademption is the failure of a bequest or devise when the specific property is not in the decedent's estate at death. Answer (d) is incorrect because abatement is the reduction of testamentary gifts when the estate has insufficient assets to pay all obligations, bequests, and devises.

37. Ademption and abatement are two terms used in the administration and distribution of an estate which are often confused. Which of the following is a correct statement with regard to ademptions and abatements?

a. Abatement refers to the authority for not allowing a bequest to lapse if the beneficiary is no longer living.

b. Abatement refers to the failure of a bequest if the property is not owned by the decedent at the time of death.

c. Abatement refers to the order of payment of bequests while ademption refers to the valuation of the bequests.

d. Abatement is the process of reducing the gifts to beneficiaries when the decedent's estate is not sufficient to pay all of the obligations and bequests under the will.

The correct answer is (d). *(Publisher)*

REQUIRED: The correct statement concerning ademptions and abatements.

DISCUSSION: Sometimes a decedent's estate is not sufficient to pay the existing debts and make all of the distributions to beneficiaries under the will. In such a case, abatement is the process of reducing the gifts to beneficiaries in accordance with the state statute, after all the debts are paid.

Answer (a) is incorrect because the authority for not allowing a bequest to lapse when the beneficiary is no longer living is called an anti-lapse statute. Answer (b) is incorrect because ademption is the failure of a bequest when the property is not owned by the decedent at the time of death. Answer (c) is incorrect because abatement is the reduction of bequests while ademption is the failure of a bequest.

38. The maker of a will does not have unfettered discretion in disposing of the estate. Which of the following is a false statement about the limitations on testamentary transfers?

a. A pretermitted child may inherit under the intestacy statute.

b. A surviving spouse may receive the homestead although it was devised to another party.

c. If a surviving spouse is not satisfied with the deceased spouse's will, (s)he can elect to take under the intestacy statute.

d. A pretermitted spouse may inherit under the intestacy statute.

The correct answer is (c). *(Publisher)*

REQUIRED: The false statement about limitations on transfer of property by will.

DISCUSSION: The intestacy statute only applies if a decedent dies without a valid will. If a surviving spouse is not satisfied with his/her share under a valid will, most states provide for an "elective share." The amount provided for varies among the states. This elective share often replaces the common law dower in which the surviving spouse was entitled only to a share (e.g., one-third) in the deceased spouse's estate.

Answers (a) and (d) are incorrect because a statute may allow a spouse or child not mentioned in the will (pretermitted) to take an intestate share if the marriage, birth, or adoption was after execution of the will. Answer (b) is incorrect because the homestead is generally not subject to devise when the decedent is survived by a spouse or minor child.

39. A will or any part of it is least likely to be revoked by the subsequent

a. Birth of an illegitimate child acknowledged by the decedent.

b. Adoption of a child.

c. Marriage or divorce of the testator.

d. Birth of a third child when the will left everything to the spouse.

The correct answer is (d). *(Publisher)*

REQUIRED: The event least likely to revoke a will by operation of law.

DISCUSSION: Statutes often provide for a child born subsequent to the execution of a will to take an intestate share unless the will indicates a contrary intention. If the decedent had children at the date of executing a will but left the entire estate to the surviving spouse, such intention is shown.

Answer (a) is incorrect because illegitimate children, or at least those legitimized under statutory procedures, have the same inheritance rights as legitimate children. Answer (b) is incorrect because an adopted child is treated as if (s)he were a biological child of his/her parents. Answer (c) is incorrect because statutes often make provision for pretermitted spouses as well as children. Moreover, a subsequent divorce may result in statutory modification of a testamentary provision for the surviving ex-spouse.

40. Which of the following may not inherit from a decedent's estate?

a. An illegitimate child adjudicated to be the child of the decedent.

b. A posthumous child.

c. An heir convicted of murdering the decedent.

d. The half-brother or half-sister of the decedent.

The correct answer is (c). *(Publisher)*

REQUIRED: The person barred from inheriting from the decedent's estate.

DISCUSSION: Most state statutes that prohibit inheritance by a murderer require that the act be intentional and not accidental, and that (s)he actually be convicted of murder and not a lesser offense. However, some states may ignore this technicality and preclude an inheritance by a killer even if not convicted of murder. Another unworthy heir barred from inheriting may be a spouse who intentionally engages in bigamous conduct.

Answer (a) is incorrect because an illegitimate child is a lineal descendant of the decedent if parentage has been established by adjudication before or after the decedent's death. Answer (b) is incorrect because a posthumous heir (one born after the parent's death) has the same rights as those born before the decedent's death. Answer (d) is incorrect because a half-sibling may inherit, although in some states (s)he will take less than a full sibling.

24.4 Trusts

41. Martins created an irrevocable 15-year trust for the benefit of his minor children. At the end of the 15 years, the principal reverts to Martins. Martins named the Bloom Trust Company as trustee and provided that Bloom would serve without the necessity of posting a bond. In understanding the trust and rules applicable to it, which of the following is correct?

a. If Martins dies 10 years after creation of the trust, it is automatically revoked and the property is distributed to the beneficiaries of his trust upon their attaining age 21.

b. Martins may revoke the trust after 11 years, since he created it, and the principal reverts to him at the expiration of the 15 years.

c. The facts indicate that the trust is a separate legal entity for both tax and nontax purposes.

d. The trust is not a separate legal entity for federal tax purposes.

The correct answer is (c). *(CPA 582 L-57)*

REQUIRED: The correct statement concerning an irrevocable trust for the benefit of minors.

DISCUSSION: Any validly created trust is a separate legal entity for nontax purposes. A trust that is to last longer than 10 years is treated as a separate entity for tax purposes. However, during this period the trust must be irrevocable, and the income of the trust must not be used for the settlor (Martins).

Answer (a) is incorrect because a trust irrevocable for a 15-year term would not be terminated by the death of the settlor. At the end of the 15-year period the assets of the trust would revert to the heirs of the deceased settlor. Answer (b) is incorrect because a settlor who creates an irrevocable trust may not revoke it during the term of its existence. Answer (d) is incorrect because the trust is a separate legal entity for tax purposes because it is to last longer than 10 years and is validly created.

42. James Gordon decided to create an inter vivos trust for the benefit of his grandchildren. Gordon wished to bypass his own children and to provide an independent income for his grandchildren. He did not, however, wish to completely part with the assets he would transfer to the trust. Thus, he transferred the assets to the York Trust Company in trust for the benefit of his grandchildren irrevocably for a period of 21 years. In relation to the Gordon trust and the rights and duties of the parties in respect to it,

a. Such a trust is quite useful in skipping generations and tying up the ownership of property, because its duration can be potentially infinite.

b. The trust is not recognized as a legal entity for tax purposes, and Gordon must include the trust income with his own.

c. York has legal title to the trust property, the grandchildren have equitable title, and Gordon has a reversionary interest.

d. If the trust deed is silent on the point, York must not sell or otherwise dispose of the trust assets without Gordon's advice and consent.

The correct answer is (c). *(CPA 1180 L-49)*

REQUIRED: The rights and duties of the parties with respect to a trust created by a settlor for his grandchildren.

DISCUSSION: Gordon, the settlor, has created an inter vivos trust (one formed during the settlor's lifetime) to last for 21 years, at the end of which time the property will revert to him. During the term of the trust, the ownership of the trust property is separated. The trustee holds the legal title and the beneficiaries hold the equitable title.

Answer (a) is incorrect because although sophisticated trust arrangements may result in tying up property for a considerable length of time, the interests created in the trust agreement must conform to the rule against perpetuities. This provides that a future interest in the property is invalid unless it vests or fails to vest within some life in being plus 21 years. Answer (b) is incorrect because a trust is recognized as a separate legal entity, and the settlor does not include the income as his/her own if the trust lasts for more than 10 years and all other requirements are met. Answer (d) is incorrect because the trustee may not only sell or otherwise dispose of trust assets, but may be under an affirmative duty to do so. The trustee has a duty to invest the trust assets to make them productive.

43. To create a valid inter vivos trust to hold personal property, the trust must be

a. In writing and signed by the settlor (creator).

b. Specific concerning the property to be held in trust.

c. Irrevocable.

d. In writing and signed by the trustee.

The correct answer is (b). *(CPA 588 L-10)*

REQUIRED: The characteristic of a valid inter vivos trust.

DISCUSSION: A trust is a legal arrangement by which one party transfers property to a second party to be held for the benefit of a third. All beneficiaries and trustees must be identified in a legally acceptable manner, the property to be held in trust must be sufficiently described so that legal title can pass to the trustee, and the settlor must make an actual delivery of the property with the intent of transferring title.

Answers (a) and (d) are incorrect because a trust may be established orally if it involves only personal property. When real property is held in trust, a writing signed by the settlor must establish an intent to transfer the property into trust. Answer (c) is incorrect because a trust is revocable in most states if the transferor reserves the right to revoke. In some states, it is presumed to be revocable unless the trust states it is irrevocable.

44. Krieg's will created a trust to take effect upon Krieg's death. The will named Krieg's spouse as both the trustee and personal representative (executor) of the estate. The will provided that all of Krieg's securities were to be transferred to the trust and named Krieg's child as the beneficiary of the trust. Under the circumstances

a. Krieg has created a testamentary trust.

b. Krieg's spouse may not serve as both the trustee and personal representative because of the inherent conflict of interest.

c. Krieg has created an inter vivos trust.

d. The trust is invalid because it will not become effective until Krieg's death.

The correct answer is (a). *(CPA 1188 L-6)*

REQUIRED: The true statement concerning a trust created by a will.

DISCUSSION: An express trust created by a will is a testamentary trust. Such a trust becomes effective upon the death of the testator (the person who made the will). A testamentary trust will be valid only if the will creating it was executed in accordance with the numerous requirements applicable to wills generally.

Answer (b) is incorrect because there is no inherent conflict of interest between the trustee of a testamentary trust and the personal representative of the estate. Answer (c) is incorrect because the settlor of an inter vivos trust must be living when the trust takes effect. Answer (d) is incorrect because a testamentary trust becomes effective only upon death of the settlor.

45. Oscar Okun, a major shareholder in Stale Corp., placed all of his shares of stock in a trust for the benefit of his three children. The purpose of the trust was to provide an entity through which the dividends paid on the stock would pass to his children for their lives. The trust instrument was silent as to whether Okun may terminate the trust. If Okun wishes to terminate the trust, in most states he may

a. Not do so because the trust instrument is silent on this point.

b. Not do so because a trust may only be terminated with court permission.

c. Do so because such a right is impliedly reserved by Okun.

d. Do so only if the trustee also agrees to terminate the trust.

The correct answer is (a). *(CPA 586 L-54)*

REQUIRED: The effect of not expressly reserving a power of revocation.

DISCUSSION: An inter vivos trust (one taking effect while the settlor is alive) may be created with a power of revocation retained by the settlor. Most states follow the rule that a trust is irrevocable unless made expressly revocable. Thus, in those states Okun may not terminate the trust because the trust instrument does not expressly reserve that right.

Answer (b) is incorrect because court permission is not required to terminate a trust when the trust agreement expressly reserves the right of revocation. Answer (c) is incorrect because the right to terminate a trust must ordinarily be express, not implied. Answer (d) is incorrect because a settlor may terminate a trust without the agreement of the trustee if the settlor expressly reserves the right.

46. An express trust

a. May be created by anyone.

b. Is created for the benefit of a specially identified person.

c. Administers a corpus that may consist of any property owned by the transferor or that (s)he expects to own.

d. Is created only if some manifestation of an intent to create a trust is made when the transferor owned the trust property.

The correct answer is (d). *(Publisher)*

REQUIRED: The requirement for a valid express trust.

DISCUSSION: A valid express or private trust may be created by will or by an inter vivos conveyance by the settlor. The settlor must manifest an intent to create a trust at a time when (s)he owned the trust property and prior to its conveyance. This expression of intent may be by any words or conduct, but if the corpus consists of real property the Statute of Frauds must be complied with.

Answer (a) is incorrect because the settlor must have the capacity to transfer property, take legal title to property, and enter into contracts on behalf of the trust. Answer (b) is incorrect because the beneficiaries must be definitely identifiable although they need not be specifically named. Answer (c) is incorrect because the trust property may consist of any interest that the settlor is able to convey but not a mere expectancy.

47. A trust was created in 1980 to provide funds for sending the settlor's child through medical school. The trust agreement specified that the trust was to terminate in 1991. The child entered medical school in 1987, took a leave of absence in 1988, and died in 1990. This trust terminated in

a. 1987.

b. 1988.

c. 1990.

d. 1991.

The correct answer is (c). *(CPA 589 L-20)*

REQUIRED: The termination date of an express trust.

DISCUSSION: Termination of a trust may occur in various ways, including expiration of a specific period of time, the occurrence of a specific event, or the impossibility or illegality of carrying out the purpose of the trust. In this case, termination occurred in 1990 when the death of the child made the trust unnecessary. The achievement of the trust purpose is more important than a specified termination date, which may have been set merely to satisfy the rule against perpetuities.

Answer (a) is incorrect because the trust was intended to provide funds to the child for medical school. Answer (b) is incorrect because the child's leave of absence from medical school did not make the trust's purpose unattainable. Answer (d) is incorrect because the death of the child terminated the trust prior to its scheduled termination in 1991.

48. Ed Roth, a retired businessman, plans to travel extensively during the upcoming year. Roth is concerned that he may not be able to handle the daily activities associated with his financial affairs. As a solution, Roth created a trust and transferred most of his investment assets to Long Bank, as trustee, naming himself as the trust's sole beneficiary. Which of the following statements is correct?

a. The trust is invalid under the merger doctrine because the creator and the beneficiary are the same person.

b. Long has a fiduciary duty to the trust but not to Roth as beneficiary.

c. Roth has created a testamentary trust.

d. Roth has created an inter vivos trust.

The correct answer is (d). *(CPA 586 L-51)*

REQUIRED: The true statement about a trust with the same person as settlor and beneficiary.

DISCUSSION: An inter vivos trust is created when the settlor transfers legal title to property to another person as trustee for the benefit of a beneficiary (the settlor or a third person) during the settlor's life. The trust in this question meets these criteria.

Answer (a) is incorrect because the settlor and beneficiary of a trust may be the same person. The merger doctrine prohibits one person from being both the sole trustee and sole beneficiary because the legal and beneficial interests would then be united and the trust would be terminated. However, the existence of even a remote other beneficiary (e.g., an unborn child) precludes merger. Answer (b) is incorrect because the trustee has a fiduciary duty to both the trust and the beneficiaries. Answer (c) is incorrect because a testamentary trust is created only upon the death of the settlor.

49. A trustee is a fiduciary. Accordingly, (s)he

a. Is automatically liable for any self-dealing with the trust.

b. May commingle his/her assets with those of the trust.

c. Is personally liable on contracts entered into on behalf of the trust.

d. Is not exempt from the prudent investor rule even if the settlor included an exculpatory clause in the trust document.

The correct answer is (a). *(Publisher)*

REQUIRED: The true statement about a trustee's duties as a fiduciary.

DISCUSSION: A trustee is not permitted to enter into a transaction with the trust in his/her individual capacity or as a trustee of another trust. Such a transaction is ordinarily an automatic wrong and not subject to a defense. There are a few exceptions, e.g., court approval of the transaction or a provision in the trust instrument permitting the transaction.

Answer (b) is incorrect because the trustee must keep his/her property separate from the corpus. Answer (c) is incorrect because the trustee is usually not personally liable to third parties unless specifically provided in the contract. Answer (d) is incorrect because the settlor may provide in the trust document that the trustee is relieved of liability for breach of duty or lack of prudence. Courts will enforce such a clause except to the extent it seeks to exempt the trustee from liability for bad faith or intentional or reckless breach of trust.

50. Harris is the trustee named in Filmore's trust. The trust named Filmore as the life beneficiary, remainder to his children at age 21. The trust consists of stocks, bonds, and three pieces of rental income property. Which of the following statements best describes the trustee's legal relationships or duties?

a. The trustee has legal and equitable title to the rental property.

b. The trustee must automatically reinvest the proceeds from the sale of one of the rental properties in like property.

c. The trustee is a fiduciary with respect to the trust and the beneficiaries.

d. The trustee must divide among all the beneficiaries any insurance proceeds received in the event the real property is destroyed.

The correct answer is (c). *(CPA 578 L-30)*

REQUIRED: The correct statement concerning the duties of the trustee.

DISCUSSION: A trustee is a fiduciary with respect to the trust and the beneficiaries. As such, (s)he owes a duty of loyalty and must act in their best interests.

Answer (a) is incorrect because the trustee has the legal title to the trust property, but the beneficiaries have the equitable title. This separation of the legal and equitable titles is a basic characteristic of a trust. Answer (b) is incorrect because a trustee normally makes investment decisions in his/her own discretion subject to reasonable care and local fiduciary administration statutes. Answer (d) is incorrect because if property belonging to the corpus of the trust is destroyed, the insurance proceeds would be allocated to the corpus for the benefit of the remainderperson(s) in place of the property destroyed.

51. Assuming that a given trust document is silent on the point, the trustee has certain rights and duties as a matter of law. The trustee

a. Has a fiduciary duty to the trust but not to the beneficiaries.

b. Is not entitled to commissions unless so provided.

c. Can elect to terminate the trust as long as the beneficiaries unanimously concur.

d. Must act in a competent, nonnegligent manner, or face possible removal.

The correct answer is (d). *(CPA 582 L-55)*

REQUIRED: The correct statement concerning the rights and duties of the trustee.

DISCUSSION: A trustee is expected to use the degree of care and skill that an ordinarily prudent person would employ in the conduct of his/her own affairs. A trustee is expected to act with due care, and is subject to removal (upon the beneficiaries' petition to court) if (s)he does not.

Answer (a) is incorrect because the fiduciary duty of the trustee is owed to the beneficiaries as well as the trust. The trustee is in control of the beneficiaries' property rights and owes an affirmative duty of loyalty to them. Answer (b) is incorrect because if the trust document makes no provisions for trustee commissions, the trustee will normally be entitled to reasonable fees for his/her services to be paid out of the trust. Answer (c) is incorrect because termination of the trust would require consent of the settlor as well as all beneficiaries.

52. With respect to trusts, which of the following states an invalid legal conclusion?

a. The trustee must obtain the consent of the majority of the beneficiaries if a major change in the investment portfolio of the trust is to be made.

b. For federal income tax purposes, a trust is entitled to an exemption similar to that of an individual although not equal in amount.

c. Both the life beneficiaries of a trust and the ultimate takers have rights against the trustee and the trustee is accountable to them.

d. A trust may be a separate taxable entity for federal income tax purposes.

The correct answer is (a). *(CPA 581 L-49)*

REQUIRED: The invalid legal conclusion concerning a trust.

DISCUSSION: The trustee ordinarily need not obtain the consent of the beneficiaries to make a major change in the investment portfolio of the trust. The purpose of having a trustee is to have him/her manage the assets and make investment decisions. Beneficiary approval would only be needed if the investment change violated a duty of the trustee. However, it would usually require unanimous consent.

Answer (b) is incorrect because a trust is entitled to an exemption that varies from $100 to $300 depending on the type of trust. Answer (c) is incorrect because it is true that the beneficiaries of a trust have rights against the trustee who has breached his/her duty. Answer (d) is incorrect because it is true that a trust may be a separate taxable entity for federal income tax purposes if it complies with certain tax laws.

53. Although most trusts must be created by an express declaration of a settlor, there are instances where trusts will be implied: resulting trusts and constructive trusts. Which of the following is a correct statement regarding resulting and constructive trusts?

a. A resulting trust arises only when an express trust fails and the settlor did not provide what should be done with the property in that event.

b. A resulting trust arises when someone embezzles property and converts the proceeds to acquire other property. The embezzler then holds the new property in a resulting trust for the benefit of the person embezzled.

c. A resulting trust and a constructive trust are one and the same.

d. A constructive trust will arise when a fiduciary violates his/her duty to deal fairly with the property of another person.

The correct answer is (d). *(Publisher)*

REQUIRED: The correct statement regarding resulting and constructive trusts.

DISCUSSION: Constructive trusts are implied to remedy unjust enrichment in many situations. They arise when a fiduciary violates his/her duty to deal fairly with the property of another person, when an embezzler converts proceeds and acquires other property, and when property is conveyed by fraud, duress, or misrepresentation.

Answer (a) is incorrect because although a resulting trust will arise when an express trust fails, it will also arise when one person purchases property and leaves title in another's name. Answer (b) is incorrect because it describes a constructive trust, not a resulting trust. Answer (c) is incorrect because constructive trusts arise when the "trustee" has been unjustly enriched from a wrongful act, while a resulting trust arises in the purchase-money situation or upon the failure of an express trust.

54. A spendthrift clause is commonly used in trusts which are set up for a testator's dependents in order to help provide a measure of security. A spendthrift clause performs which of the following functions?

a. Limits the trustee to only spend trust funds for absolutely necessary expenditures.

b. Limits the trustee to make distributions to the beneficiaries only for their health, education, and support.

c. Restricts the beneficiaries from transferring their interests and limiting its availability to creditors.

d. Prevents the settlor from modifying or revoking the trust.

The correct answer is (c). *(Publisher)*

REQUIRED: The function which a spendthrift clause performs in a trust.

DISCUSSION: A spendthrift clause is a restraint on alienation to restrict the beneficiaries from transferring their interests in a trust and also to limit the ability of creditors to reach the assets of the trust for claims against the beneficiaries.

Answer (a) is incorrect because a limitation on the trustee to only spend trust funds for absolutely necessary expenditures may be provided in the trust document, but this is not a spendthrift clause. Answer (b) is incorrect because a limitation on distributions for health, education, and support is commonly known as a support trust. Answer (d) is incorrect because the settlor is prevented from modifying or revoking the trust if the trust agreement so specifies and in most states unless it is specifically revocable.

55. A Totten trust has often been referred to as the poor man's trust. Which of the following statements best describes a Totten trust?

a. It is used for the care of graves or animals.

b. It is formed by depositing money in a savings account in the name of the settlor in trust for another.

c. It is a trust set up in a will to dispose of a decedent's remaining assets after creditors are paid.

d. It is a trust containing no assets, but which is to receive a decedent's estate under his/her will.

The correct answer is (b). *(Publisher)*

REQUIRED: The statement which best describes a Totten trust.

DISCUSSION: A Totten trust is formed by depositing money in a savings account in the name of the settlor on behalf of the beneficiary. It is also called a tentative trust because it is entirely revocable during the depositor's lifetime. It has been referred to as a poor man's trust because of its simplicity to set up.

Answer (a) is incorrect because a trust used for the care of graves or animals is an honorary trust. Answer (c) is incorrect because a trust set up in a will to dispose of remaining assets may be called a residuary trust or testamentary trust. Answer (d) is incorrect because a trust to receive a decedent's estate under his/her will is called a pour-over trust.

56. Trusts set up for charitable purposes are usually subject to liberal rules concerning their creation, duration, and management. Which of the following is not a requirement for a trust to qualify as charitable?

a. The settlor's motive must have been charitable.

b. The effect of the trust must be to benefit the public or the community.

c. The beneficiaries must be indefinite.

d. Any profits received by the beneficiary must be applied to the charitable activity.

The correct answer is (a). *(Publisher)*

REQUIRED: The statement not a requirement for a trust to qualify as charitable.

DISCUSSION: The motive of the settlor is generally not important in determining whether a valid charitable trust has been created. If the effect of the trust is to benefit the public, the community, or some indefinite segment thereof, the trust is charitable regardless of the settlor's motive.

Answer (b) is incorrect because the effect must be charitable in that the trust benefits the public; e.g., the furtherance of education, science, recreation, religion, public health and welfare, etc. Answer (c) is incorrect because the beneficiaries may consist of a small or even a fixed class if the membership is indefinite; for instance, a trust to assist victims of a specific flood would qualify as charitable. Answer (d) is incorrect because if the beneficiary receives profits from the trust, they must be applied to the charitable endeavor and not paid to owners.

57. Cy pres is a doctrine that

a. Allows a trustee to make distributions at his/her discretion among a class of beneficiaries.

b. May allow a court to change the beneficiary named by the settlor of a trust.

c. Applies to noncharitable as well as charitable trusts.

d. Is subject to the rule against perpetuities.

The correct answer is (b). *(Publisher)*

REQUIRED: The trust statement about the cy pres doctrine.

DISCUSSION: Cy pres is a doctrine that allows a court to substitute a new charitable beneficiary when a named charitable beneficiary either ceases to exist or ceases to qualify as charitable, or when the bequest is or becomes impractical. The doctrine permits a court to carry out as nearly as possible the settlor's purpose. To apply this doctrine, an equity court must find that the settlor had a broad or general intent to aid charity or a specific type of charity. Absent a showing of such intent, the trust will fail.

Answer (a) is incorrect because cy pres permits a court to effectuate a settlor's charitable intent but does not otherwise give the trustee discretion in distributions. Answer (c) is incorrect because cy pres applies to charitable trusts only. Answer (d) is incorrect because the legal title of a charitable trust must vest in the trustee within the period of the rule, but otherwise cy pres has nothing to do with the rule against perpetuities.

58. A group of real estate dealers has decided to form a Real Estate Investment Trust (REIT) which will invest in diversified real estate holdings. A public offering of $10,000,000 of trust certificates is contemplated. Which of the following is an incorrect statement?

a. Those investing in the venture will not be insulated from personal liability.

b. The entity will be considered an "association" for tax purposes.

c. The offering must be registered under the Securities Act of 1933.

d. If the trust qualifies as an REIT and distributes all its income to the investors, it will not be subject to federal income tax.

The correct answer is (a). *(CPA 580 L-49)*

REQUIRED: The false statement concerning a real estate investment trust.

DISCUSSION: A real estate investment trust is a business trust similar in structure to an ordinary trust, but its purpose is to act as an investment vehicle (like a limited partnership) for real estate ventures. Limited partnerships are now more commonly used; however, the REIT began under common law before statutes existed authorizing limited partnerships. The REIT legally is similar to ordinary trusts and provides limited liability for the beneficiaries (investors).

Answers (b), (c), and (d) are all correct statements regarding the REIT.

24.5 Allocation Between Principal and Income

59. A trust agreement is silent on the allocation of the following trust receipts between principal and income:

Cash dividends on investments in common stock	$1,000
Royalties from property subject to depletion	$2,000

What is the total amount of the trust receipts that should be allocated to trust income?

a. $0.

b. $1,000.

c. $2,000.

d. $3,000.

The correct answer is (d). *(CPA 589 L-18)*

REQUIRED: The correct allocation of cash dividends and royalties if the trust agreement is silent on their allocation.

DISCUSSION: The rules of the Uniform Principal and Income Act apply, except when the terms of the trust specify otherwise. Under the Act, income is the return in money or property from the use of the trust principal, such as common stock or depletable property (mineral deposits and the like). Hence, both cash dividends and royalties are properly allocated to trust income, and the full $3,000 of trust receipts should be so allocated.

60. Wayne & Company, CPAs was engaged by Harding, the trustee of the Timmons Testamentary Trust. The will creating the Timmons Trust gave Harding wide discretion with respect to the investment of the trust principal but was silent on the question of the allocation of receipts and charges to principal or income. Among the assets invested in by Harding is a $500,000 annuity and a $50,000 limited partnership interest in an offshore investment limited partnership. The partnership has reported a $40,000 loss for the year. Regarding the trust in general and the limited partnership loss allocation in particular, which of the following is correct?

a. It is against public policy to permit the investment by the trustee in the offshore investment limited partnership.

b. Because the trust is silent on the allocation question, Harding has wide discretion in making allocations.

c. The loss attributable to the offshore partnership is allocable equally to principal and income.

d. The receipts from the $500,000 annuity must be apportioned between principal and income.

The correct answer is (d). *(CPA 582 L-56)*

REQUIRED: The correct statement concerning the investments of a trust and the allocation of profits and losses.

DISCUSSION: In general, receipts that represent the change in the form of or a return of the trust principal will be allocated to principal. The income beneficiaries are ordinarily entitled to receipts representing income generated by the trust assets. The receipts from an annuity constitute both interest on an investment and a return of principal. The receipts therefore must be apportioned between principal and income.

Answer (a) is incorrect because public policy dictates only that trustees pursue a prudent investment policy. The investment may have been consistent with trustee investment standards, but there is no way to tell from the facts. Furthermore, state statutes may allow such an investment. Answer (b) is incorrect because the trustee is subject to the Uniform Principal and Income Act (or similar local statute) if the trust does not provide otherwise. Answer (c) is incorrect because allocation of the loss from the partnership depends on the composition of the loss. However, an ordinary partnership loss would be allocated to income.

61. Shepard created an inter vivos trust for the benefit of his children with the remainder to his grandchildren upon the death of his last surviving child. The trust consists of both real and personal property. One of the assets is an apartment building. In administering the trust and allocating the receipts and disbursements, which of the following would be improper?

a. The allocation of forfeited rental security deposits to income.

b. The allocation to principal of the annual service fee of the rental collection agency.

c. The allocation to income of the interest on the mortgage on the apartment building.

d. The allocation to income of the payment of the insurance premiums on the apartment building.

The correct answer is (b). *(CPA 581 L-51)*

REQUIRED: The improper allocation between principal and income.

DISCUSSION: The annual service fee of a rent collection agency represents an ordinary operating expense of the trust. Since it is an expense incurred in the production of income, it is properly chargeable to income.

Answer (a) is incorrect because the allocation is proper. A rent security deposit secures the payment of rent, and coverage for minor damages requiring repairs. Since the rent is allocated to income and the repairs are chargeable to income, it follows that the deposits should be allocated to income. Answer (c) is incorrect because interest is properly charged to income. Answer (d) is incorrect because insurance premiums represent an ordinary operating expense properly chargeable to income.

62. Harper transferred assets into a trust under which Drake is entitled to receive the income for life. Upon Drake's death, the remaining assets are to be paid to Neal. In 1990, the trust received rent of $1,000, royalties of $3,000, cash dividends of $5,000, and proceeds of $7,000 from the sale of stock previously received by the trust as a stock dividend. Both Drake and Neal are still alive. How much of the receipts should be distributed to Drake?

a. $ 4,000.

b. $ 8,000.

c. $ 9,000.

d. $16,000.

The correct answer is (c). *(CPA 1189 L-8)*

REQUIRED: The proper allocation of cash receipts between principal and income.

DISCUSSION: Rent, royalties, and cash dividends are all properly allocated to trust income under the Uniform Principal and Income Act. Stock dividends are allocated entirely to principal, as are the proceeds of the subsequent sale of such dividends. The $9,000 income ($1,000 rent + $3,000 royalties + $5,000 cash dividends) should be distributed to the income beneficiary (Drake) under the terms of the trust.

63. Ryan is the trustee of the Carr Family Trust. The assets of the trust are various income-producing real estate properties. The trust instrument is silent as to the allocation of items between principal and income. Among the items to be allocated by Ryan during the first year were depreciation and the cost of a new roof. Which are properly allocable to income?

	Depreciation	Cost of a New Roof
a.	No	No
b.	Yes	No
c.	Yes	Yes
d.	No	Yes

The correct answer is (b). *(CPA 586 L-52)*

REQUIRED: The proper allocation of the cost of improvements and depreciation between principal and income.

DISCUSSION: Trust expenses should be divided into two categories: ordinary expenses incurred in operating and administering the trust, and extraordinary expenses for setting up the trust or improving trust property. Ordinary expenses are chargeable to trust income, whereas extraordinary expenses are allocable to trust principal. Under the Revised Uniform Principal and Income Act, depreciation is a required charge against income unless the trust indenture provides otherwise. However, many state statutes allow for depreciation only at the trustee's discretion. Accordingly, if it is recognized, depreciation is an ordinary expense and is charged to income (reduces it) for the benefit of the remaindermen; i.e., it preserves the principal. The cost of a new roof is an extraordinary expenditure that enhances the value of the principal and should be charged thereto.

64. The Astor Bank and Trust Company is the trustee of the Wayne Trust. A significant portion of the trust principal has been invested in AAA rated public utility bonds. Some of the bonds have been purchased at face value, some at a discount, and others at a premium. Which of the following is a proper allocation of the various items to income?

a. The income beneficiary is entitled to the entire interest without dilution for the premium paid but is not entitled to the proceeds attributable to the discount upon collection.

b. The income beneficiary is entitled to the entire interest without dilution and to the proceeds attributable to the discount.

c. The income beneficiary is only entitled to the interest less the amount of the premium amortized over the life of the bond.

d. The income beneficiary is entitled to the full interest and to an allocable share of the gain resulting from the discount.

The correct answer is (a). *(CPA 580 L-28)*

REQUIRED: The proper allocation of bond premium and discount.

DISCUSSION: Under the Uniform Principal and Income Act, bond premium or discount is not required to be amortized or specially allocated. The income beneficiary is entitled to the entire interest received, and any gain resulting from purchasing the bonds at a discount is allocated to the principal.

Answer (b) is incorrect because the proceeds due to the discount are allocated to principal. Answer (c) is incorrect because the income beneficiary is entitled to all of the interest. Answer (d) is incorrect because all the gain resulting from the discount is allocated to principal.

65. Which of the following receipts should be allocated to income?

a. Rights to subscribe to shares of the distributing corporation.

b. Sale of rights to subscribe to shares of the distributing corporation.

c. A 2% stock dividend.

d. Rights to subscribe to shares of another corporation.

The correct answer is (d). *(CPA 1179 L-46)*

REQUIRED: The receipts which should be allocated to income.

DISCUSSION: The right to subscribe to shares of another corporation is a form of property dividend. Property dividends, like cash dividends, are allocated to income. They represent current earnings.

Answer (a) is incorrect because the receipt of rights to subscribe to shares of the distributing corporation should be allocated to principal just as an actual stock dividend would be. Answer (b) is incorrect because receipts from the sale of such rights are proceeds from the sale of part of the principal, and therefore represent a mere change in the form of the principal. Answer (c) is incorrect because stock dividends are allocated to principal.

CHAPTER TWENTY-FIVE
CREDIT LAW

Credit law overlaps such topics as bankruptcy, consumer credit, mortgages, secured transactions, and suretyship. Accordingly, this chapter should be read with the chapters covering those subjects.

25.1 Common Law and Related Statutory Liens

1. On April 14, Jack Jackson, CPA watched as his copy machine malfunctioned. Jackson delivered the copier to Copy, Inc. for repair. Jackson agreed to pay $150 under terms of 2/10, n/30 for parts and labor if Copy would fix the copier by 8 a.m. on April 15. Jackson arrived at 8 a.m. on April 15 to pick up the copier, but refused to pay for the repairs at that time. Copy is entitled to

a. An artisan's lien.

b. A mechanic's lien.

c. A materialman's lien.

d. Payment in 30 days.

The correct answer is (d). *(Publisher)*

REQUIRED: The correct statement concerning entitlement to a lien.

DISCUSSION: An artisan's lien is a common law possessory lien that arises in favor of a repairer or other improver of personal property as a result of a specific debt. The holder of an artisan's lien ordinarily must have agreed expressly or impliedly to perform the services on a cash basis. Payment terms of 2/10, n/30 are a common extension of credit. Because Copy agreed to bill Jackson for the repairs, the work was done on a credit basis, and Copy is not entitled to an artisan's lien. Moreover, mechanic's and materialman's liens attach to real property, and a copy machine is personal property. Thus, Copy must await performance under the contract and is not entitled to a possessory lien.

Answer (a) is incorrect because Copy agreed to do the repairs and extend credit to Jackson. Answers (b) and (c) are incorrect because mechanic's and materialman's liens attach to real property, and a copy machine is personal property.

2. One night Chris Lee was driving to a client's office when her car collided with another vehicle. Both headlights on Lee's car were smashed in the collision. A police officer quickly arrived on the scene accompanied by a tow truck from XYZ Towing Co. As Lee signed a traffic citation, XYZ towed Lee's car to its lot at the direction of the police officer. The next day Lee went to XYZ to get the car. XYZ charged Lee $100 for two new headlights that had been installed. Lee refused to pay for the headlights. Is XYZ entitled to a common law lien for the value of the headlights?

a. Yes, XYZ is entitled to an artisan's lien for the value of the headlights.

b. No, XYZ is not entitled to a common law possessory lien for the value of the headlights.

c. Yes, XYZ is entitled to a common carrier's lien for the value of the headlights.

d. No, but XYZ is entitled to a mechanic's lien for the value of the headlights.

The correct answer is (b). *(Publisher)*

REQUIRED: The entitlement of a repairer to a common law lien if the owner did not consent to the work.

DISCUSSION: Common law possessory liens (e.g., artisan's, common carrier's, and hotelkeeper's liens) require the owner's consent to performance of the work or service that benefited the property. Lee did not consent to XYZ's installation of new headlights, so XYZ is not entitled to a common law possessory lien.

Answer (a) is incorrect because an artisan's lien is a common law possessory lien and requires consent of the owner. Answer (c) is incorrect because a common carrier's lien typically arises from freight charges for transportation of goods. Answer (d) is incorrect because mechanic's liens attach to real property.

3. Dwight operates a fleet of limousines. Garage, Inc. repairs the limousines on a cash on delivery basis. Dwight delivered Limousines No. 1 and No. 2 to Garage on Thursday. Dwight forgot his wallet when he went to get Limousine No. 1 on Friday, but Garage allowed Dwight to take Limousine No. 1 on condition that payment be made on Monday. Dwight failed to pay for the repairs on Monday. On Tuesday, Garage

a. Has an artisan's lien on Limousine No. 1 because the repairs were requested by Dwight.

b. Has an artisan's lien on Limousine No. 1 because Dwight delivered possession of Limousine No. 1 to Garage.

c. Does not have a lien on Limousine No. 1 because possession was relinquished to Dwight on Friday.

d. Has a lien against Limousine No. 2 for the value of the repairs made to Limousine No. 1.

The correct answer is (c). *(Publisher)*

REQUIRED: The true statement about liens claimed by a repairer of personalty.

DISCUSSION: The repairer or other improver of property must retain possession of the property to assert a common law possessory lien. Once the improver (artisan) voluntarily surrenders possession of the property, (s)he loses the lien. Hence, Garage lost its lien on Limousine No. 1 by relinquishing possession.

Answers (a) and (b) are incorrect because possession of the property is required for an artisan's lien even if work is performed at the request of the owner or the owner delivers possession of the property to the improver. Answer (d) is incorrect because a lien is not created against all the owner's property possessed by the improver. The lien is only created on the specific improved property.

4. Art owns a mobile automobile repair business. Ann's car would not start so she called Art. Art went to Ann's home and replaced the distributor cap on Ann's car. Ann was unable to pay for the repair. Art is not entitled to an artisan's lien because

a. Ann did not relinquish possession of the car.

b. Artisan's liens only attach to improvements to real property.

c. Automobile repairers are essentially mechanics and therefore are entitled to mechanic's liens rather than artisan's liens.

d. The distributor cap did not appreciably increase the value of the car.

The correct answer is (a). *(Publisher)*

REQUIRED: The reason the improver is not entitled to an artisan's lien.

DISCUSSION: An artisan's lien is a possessory lien. If possession of the personal property is not relinquished by the owner and retained by the improver, the lien cannot exist. Because Art repaired the car at Ann's home, Ann retained possession.

Answers (b) and (c) are incorrect because artisan's liens attach to personal property, and mechanic's liens attach to real property. Answer (d) is incorrect because an increase in the value of the personal property is not a necessary condition of an artisan's lien. The lien arises for labor done or value added.

25.2 Mechanic's and Materialman's Liens

5. Contractor purchased shingles for inventory pursuant to a valid written contract with Supplier. Supplier delivered the shingles to Contractor's warehouse. Two weeks later Contractor's crew used all of the shingles on Owner's new office building. Contractor refused to pay for the shingles because of financial difficulties. Supplier

a. Can obtain a mechanic's lien on Owner's office building because Contractor purchased the shingles pursuant to a valid contract.

b. Can obtain a materialman's lien on Owner's office building because Contractor purchased the shingles pursuant to a valid contract.

c. Cannot obtain a mechanic's lien on Owner's office building because the shingles were not purchased for use on specific property.

d. Cannot obtain a materialman's lien on Owner's office building because the shingles were not purchased for use on a specific property.

The correct answer is (d). *(Publisher)*

REQUIRED: The true statement regarding the rights of a supplier of materials used in construction of a building.

DISCUSSION: A supplier of materials may obtain a materialman's lien on real property improved by the materials only if (s)he sells the materials pursuant to a contract made with reference to a specific property. The shingles were sold for inventory and not for use on specific property. Hence, Supplier cannot assert a lien against Owner's office building even though it was improved by the shingles.

Answers (a) and (c) are incorrect because a supplier of materials cannot obtain a mechanic's lien unless services are also performed. Answer (b) is incorrect because the sale must be made in reference to a specific property, even if made pursuant to a valid contract, or the supplier cannot obtain a materialman's lien.

6. Tom planned to dump the excess cement from his cement truck. On the way to the dump he noticed Ann's dirt driveway. Tom quickly drove onto Ann's lawn, dumped the cement, and paved the driveway. The next day Tom sent Ann an invoice for paving. Ann refused to pay the invoice. Which of the following is true?

a. Tom is the holder of a materialman's lien.

b. Tom has an artisan's lien.

c. A mechanic's lien arose in favor of Tom by operation of law.

d. Tom does not have a mechanic's lien.

The correct answer is (d). *(Publisher)*

REQUIRED: The correct statement regarding Tom's right to a lien.

DISCUSSION: A mechanic's lien is created if the improver of real property performs work pursuant to a contract and is not paid. Some jurisdictions require the contract to be in writing. Because Tom paved the driveway without entering into a contract, a mechanic's lien cannot be created.

Answer (a) is incorrect because the supplier of materials pursuant to a contract concerning specific real property has a materialman's lien, and the supplier of labor and materials has a mechanic's lien, but Tom is not entitled to either lien because the parties had no contract. Answer (b) is incorrect because an artisan's lien is a possessory lien that attaches to personal property. Answer (c) is incorrect because a mechanic's lien must be created pursuant to statutory requirements. Mechanic's liens do not arise by operation of law. The lienholder must take affirmative action to create a mechanic's lien.

Questions 7 through 9 are based on Bynow Mortgage Co., which has held a properly recorded mortgage on Mr. Garcia's home since 1987. On June 1, 1990, Mr. Garcia hired Wetsun Pools, Inc. and Screenwall, Inc. to build a pool and a porch, respectively. Wetsun began construction of the pool on June 2, 1990, and completed the pool on June 30, 1990. Screenwall began and completed the porch on June 15, 1990. Mr. Garcia was unable to pay Wetsun and Screenwall. On July 10, 1990 both Wetsun and Screenwall filed a notice of lien.

7. Assume Wetsun properly forecloses on Mr. Garcia's property on September 1, 1990. Among Bynow, Wetsun, and Screenwall, whose security interest has priority?

a. Bynow, because the mortgage was properly recorded in 1987.

b. Wetsun, because construction of the pool began on June 2, 1990, and mechanic's liens have priority over mortgages in foreclosure proceedings.

c. Screenwall, because porch construction was completed before pool construction, and mechanic's liens have priority over mortgages in foreclosure proceedings.

d. No one lien has priority. Proceeds from foreclosure will be allocated between Bynow, Wetsun, and Screenwall on a pro rata basis.

The correct answer is (a). *(Publisher)*
REQUIRED: The lien that has priority in a foreclosure proceeding.
DISCUSSION: Properly recorded mortgages have priority over mechanic's liens that attach after the mortgage is recorded. Virtually all states have statutes providing that mortgages attach when properly recorded. The majority of states have statutes providing that mechanic's liens attach when work first begins. Priority is determined according to when liens attach.
Answers (b) and (c) are incorrect because the mortgage was properly recorded before pool or porch construction began. Answer (d) is incorrect because Bynow's mortgage was properly recorded and attached before the mechanic's liens. Foreclosure proceeds are only shared on a pro rata basis when several liens are considered equal in priority and funds are insufficient to fully satisfy all liens.

8. Assume only Wetsun and Screenwall have liens on Mr. Garcia's property. Which of the following is correct?

a. Wetsun's lien has priority over Screenwall's lien.

b. Screenwall's lien has priority over Wetsun's lien.

c. Neither lien has priority because Mr. Garcia hired both companies on June 1.

d. Neither lien has priority because both are mechanic's liens.

The correct answer is (a). *(Publisher)*
REQUIRED: The correct statement concerning the priority of liens.
DISCUSSION: Mechanic's liens are entitled to priority based on when work is commenced by the lienholder. Thus, Wetsun's lien (June 2) has priority over Screenwall's (June 15).
Answer (b) is incorrect because Screenwall began work after Wetsun, and mechanic's liens are accorded priority based on when work is commenced. Answer (c) is incorrect because the date of hire is irrelevant for purposes of determining priority of mechanic's liens. Answer (d) is incorrect because all mechanic's liens do not have equivalent status. The date of attachment must be considered in determining priority between mechanic's liens.

9. Assume the applicable statute provides for a 60-day period in which a lienholder may perfect a mechanic's lien. On what date does the period for perfecting Wetsun's lien expire?

a. July 31, 1990.

b. August 1, 1990.

c. August 29, 1990.

d. August 13, 1990.

The correct answer is (c). *(Publisher)*
REQUIRED: The date the period for perfecting a mechanic's lien ends.
DISCUSSION: The period for perfecting a lien begins when work is substantially completed. Because Wetsun completed the pool on June 30, 1990, the 60-day period ends on August 29, 1990.
Answer (a) is incorrect because July 31 is 60 days from the date of hire. Answer (b) is incorrect because August 1 is 60 days from the date work was commenced. Answer (d) is incorrect because August 13 is a nonsense answer.

10. Fly-By-Night Contractors, Inc. contracts to sell Buyer a new house, all work to be complete by June 1, the closing date. On June 1, the title search indicates that Fly-By-Night is the record owner and the property is not currently subject to any adverse interests of record. Buyer pays the $45,000 price on June 1 and moves in. On June 25, Buyer receives a notice from Subcontractor indicating that she claims a mechanic's lien in the amount of $30,000 on Buyer's house for work completed on May 25. Subcontractor has a valid direct lien pursuant to a state statute. Which of the following is false?

a. If Buyer does nothing and Subcontractor is not paid, Subcontractor can foreclose the lien, force the sale of Buyer's house, and receive the first $30,000 of proceeds.

b. The lawyer who prepared the title report is not liable for malpractice because the mechanic's lien was not of record on June 1.

c. If no recovery can be had from Fly-By-Night and Buyer desires to keep the house, Buyer may have to pay an additional $30,000.

d. If Subcontractor does not file a foreclosure action within the specified statutory period, she will lose all of her rights.

The correct answer is (d). *(M. Levin)*

REQUIRED: The effect of a mechanic's lien as a hidden interest in property.

DISCUSSION: A mechanic's lien is statutory, and the specific rules vary from state to state. The notice periods under the various statutes range from 30 to 90 days after the last work is performed. A mechanic's lien filed within the allotted period attaches as of the time the first work is done. Consequently, the record may not reveal existence of the lien to third parties (in this case Buyer). Moreover, the foreclosure action must be filed within a limited period. But failure to do so will not impair the lienholder's private contract rights against the party with whom (s)he contracted.

Answers (a) and (c) are incorrect because such is the plight of the buyer who fails to protect against a hidden lien by getting waivers or having funds retained in escrow. Subcontractor, as an unsatisfied lienholder, has typical foreclosure rights. Answer (b) is incorrect because the lawyer has performed his/her contract competently by reporting the absence of any liens of record.

11. The normal procedure for perfecting a mechanic's lien requires the lienholder to file a notice of

a. Attachment.

b. Garnishment.

c. Perfection.

d. Lien.

The correct answer is (d). *(Publisher)*

REQUIRED: The document filed to perfect a mechanic's lien.

DISCUSSION: The holder of a mechanic's lien normally must file a document that identifies the property subject to the lien. This document is called a notice of lien and is filed with a county official in the county office where real estate deeds are recorded.

Answer (a) is incorrect because attachment is a method of ensuring the collection of a judgment and is not pertinent to the perfection of a mechanic's lien. Answer (b) is incorrect because garnishment is a procedure for collecting a judgment from a party owing money to the judgment debtor. Answer (c) is incorrect because perfection is the result of a prescribed statutory scheme to ensure that a mechanic's lien is free from defect.

12. Which of the following is a true statement about foreclosure by the holder of a lien?

a. The holder of a perfected materialman's lien must foreclose within a prescribed period or lose the right.

b. The sales proceeds resulting from foreclosure and sale are awarded to the holder of a materialman's lien regardless of the size of the debt secured by the lien.

c. Very few states have statutes requiring a lienholder to give notice to the property owner prior to foreclosure and sale.

d. The holder of an artisan's lien may foreclose on the real property subject to the lien.

The correct answer is (a). *(Publisher)*

REQUIRED: The correct statement concerning foreclosure by a lienholder.

DISCUSSION: The holder of a perfected materialman's lien must foreclose the lien within a prescribed period. This period is prescribed by statute and begins when the lienholder files a notice of lien. Typical statutes provide for a foreclosure period ranging from 6 months to 2 years. If the lienholder fails to foreclose within the prescribed period, the right to foreclose is lost.

Answer (b) is incorrect because the lienholder is only entitled to satisfaction of the debt secured by the lien. Answer (c) is incorrect because due process of law requires that notice be given prior to depriving the owner of his/her property. Answer (d) is incorrect because an artisan's lien does not attach to real property.

13. Fabs, Inc. has supplied fabricated steel under a contract to ABC Co., which is erecting a building for Mr. Z on land he owns. ABC refused to pay for the delivered materials. Fabs filed its statutory lien on the property and then sued Z to foreclose. Fabs subsequently learned that Z had given an unrecorded deed to X&Y, a partnership, prior to the delivery of the steel. Which of the following is a true statement?

a. Under the recording acts, the true owner of the land is Mr. Z because the deed to X&Y was never recorded in the Clerk's office where the land was located.

b. Delivery of an unrecorded but properly acknowledged deed has no legal validity and the ownership remains in Mr. Z.

c. Recording acts are never intended to protect third party purchasers from fraudulent conveyances by their grantor.

d. An unrecorded but delivered and acknowledged deed conveys title to the realty despite being unrecorded.

The correct answer is (d). *(E. O'Connor)*

REQUIRED: The effect of failing to record a deed.

DISCUSSION: Recording protects the holder of an interest in real property by giving constructive notice to parties who subsequently acquire interests in the same property. But failure to record never affects the conveyance by the grantor to a grantee. Thus, the materialman (Fabs) must proceed against X&Y.

Answer (a) is incorrect because failure to record does not destroy the conveyance to X&Y. The failure to record would only benefit a purchaser who recorded a deed from Z before X&Y. Answer (b) is incorrect because a duly acknowledged deed delivered by the grantor to the grantee is effective. Answer (c) is incorrect because recording acts are in fact intended to prevent fraudulent conveyances prior to selling realty to an innocent purchaser for value.

25.3 Creditor's Rights/Remedies and Debtor Relief

14. Professor Tortmore teaches torts at the University of Nirvana. Ace Trustmenow of Trustmenow's Fine Automobiles sold Professor Tortmore a previously owned sedan. Ace financed the sale. Ace obtained a judgment against Tortmore after Tortmore defaulted on the last $500 installment. Tortmore failed to pay the judgment. Ace brought an action against Tortmore and the University of Nirvana seeking to collect the $500 from wages owed to Tortmore. This action is best described as

a. A writ of execution.

b. Replevin proceedings.

c. Attachment proceedings.

d. Garnishment proceedings.

The correct answer is (d). *(Publisher)*

REQUIRED: The action seeking collection of a debt from property of the debtor held by a third party.

DISCUSSION: After judgment, garnishment proceedings may be instituted to seize specific property of a judgment debtor that is held by a third party. Federal law limits the amount of wages that may be garnished. Any obligation owed to a debtor may be garnished, including wages owed by employers and bank accounts.

Answer (a) is incorrect because a writ of execution is a postjudgment collection remedy that orders the sheriff to seize and sell any of the debtor's property within the court's geographic jurisdiction. Answers (b) and (c) are incorrect because replevin and attachment are prejudgment remedies used to secure satisfaction of pending judgments.

15. A postjudgment remedy that permits the sheriff to seize and sell a debtor's nonexempt property is

a. The writ of execution.

b. Attachment.

c. Garnishment.

d. Sequestration.

The correct answer is (a). *(Publisher)*

REQUIRED: The postjudgment remedy that allows the seizure and sale of property.

DISCUSSION: The writ of execution is a remedy used for collection of judgments. It is issued by the clerk of the court and orders the sheriff to seize and sell any nonexempt property owned by the judgment debtor. The property may be realty or personalty. The debtor has the right to redeem the seized property prior to sale by satisfying the judgment. The judgment debtor's homestead and certain personal effects are examples of exempt property.

Answers (b) and (d) are incorrect because attachment and sequestration are prejudgment remedies. Answer (c) is incorrect because garnishment does not authorize seizure and sale of property. Garnishment is aimed at collecting a judgment from a third party who is indebted to the judgment debtor.

16. Low Point Distributors coerced Acme Manufacturing into withdrawing from distributorship negotiations with Jack. Jack intends to sue Low Point Distributors for intentional interference with potential contractual relations, but fears Low Point will sell its assets and abandon its leased showroom before trial. Jack wants to protect against this potential problem. The most appropriate remedy for Jack to pursue is

a. Replevin.

b. Attachment.

c. Assignment for the benefit of creditors.

d. Garnishment.

The correct answer is (b). *(Publisher)*

REQUIRED: The prejudgment remedy to ensure that the plaintiff will be able to reach the defendant's assets.

DISCUSSION: Attachment, a prejudgment remedy, is the process of seizing a defendant's property pursuant to judicial authorization and placing it in the custody of the court. Attachment is intended to secure satisfaction of a pending judgment.

Answer (a) is incorrect because replevin, although similar to attachment, is a prejudgment remedy intended to secure property subject to repossession by the plaintiff. Answer (c) is incorrect because an assignment for the benefit of creditors is a tool for debtor's relief. The debtor voluntarily transfers property to a trustee who liquidates the property and uses the proceeds to pay the debtor's obligations. Answer (d) is incorrect because garnishment is a postjudgment remedy.

Questions 17 and 18 are based on East Coast Fish Company, which owns real estate worth $6,000,000 that is not used in operations. East Coast Fish owes Dade Bank $8,000,000, Brevard Bank $3,000,000, and Broward Bank $1,000,000. Dade, Broward, and Brevard demand payment. East Coast Fish contacts Dade, Broward, and Brevard and offers to sell the land and settle all claims in full by paying each creditor 50% of the balance owed.

17. Assuming the three banks accept East Coast Fish Company's offer, this agreement is best described as

a. A composition with creditors.

b. An assignment for the benefit of creditors.

c. A liquidation of unliquidated claims.

d. An extension agreement.

The correct answer is (a). *(Publisher)*

REQUIRED: The term for an agreement among a debtor and its creditors to settle claims for less than the amounts owed.

DISCUSSION: A composition with creditors is a contract under which a debtor pays each creditor a pro rata portion of the obligation owed by the debtor to the creditor. Creditors agreeing to the settlement relinquish all rights to pursue the unpaid balance of the obligation.

Answer (b) is incorrect because under an assignment for the benefit of creditors, the debtor voluntarily transfers assets to a trustee. The trustee uses the assets to satisfy the debtor's obligations to creditors. Answer (c) is incorrect because the liquidation of an unliquidated debt occurs when a debtor and a creditor agree on the amount of a previously disputed debt. Answer (d) is incorrect because under an extension agreement, creditors agree to allow the debtor additional time to pay debts.

18. Assume that Dade Bank and Broward Bank accept the composition offer while Brevard Bank rejects the offer. Which of the following is true?

a. Brevard Bank may not pursue its claim against East Coast Fish if Brevard rejects the composition offer.

b. Dade Bank and Broward Bank may pursue the balance of their claims against East Coast Fish because a composition agreement is valid only if all creditors accept the composition offer.

c. Dade Bank and Broward Bank may not pursue the balance of their claims against East Coast Fish because a debtor's obligations are discharged in full under a composition with creditors.

d. Dade Bank, Broward Bank, and Brevard Bank are all bound by the composition with creditors because a majority of the banks accepted the offer to compose.

The correct answer is (c). *(Publisher)*

REQUIRED: The true statement about the rights of creditors under a composition with creditors.

DISCUSSION: Creditors are not required to accept an offer to compose debts, but if they accept, the balance of the debtor's obligations is discharged. Creditors that reject the offer are not bound by the composition and may seek full payment of their claims.

Answer (a) is incorrect because Brevard Bank's right to payment is not affected if Brevard rejects the composition offer. Answer (b) is incorrect because a composition with creditors only requires acceptance by two creditors. Only the creditors accepting the offer to compose are bound by the composition. Answer (d) is incorrect because only the creditors that accept the offer to compose are bound by the composition.

19. Ed offered to compose his debts to Lenny, Roger, and Mike. While Lenny and Roger considered the offer, Mike attached Ed's assets. Which of the following is true?

a. Mike cannot attach the assets after receiving Ed's offer to compose the debts.

b. The offer to compose the debts precludes attachment of Ed's assets.

c. Mike's attachment of Ed's assets is valid only if Lenny and Roger reject Ed's offer to compose.

d. Mike's attachment of Ed's assets illustrates a disadvantage of a composition with creditors.

The correct answer is (d). *(Publisher)*

REQUIRED: The true statement regarding the attachment of assets after the owner offers to compose debts.

DISCUSSION: Normally, a period of bargaining and negotiation precedes the execution of a composition agreement. During this period any creditor may attach the assets of the debtor. Because creditors may not realize the severity of the debtor's financial position, an offer to compose debts may cause concern among creditors and trigger attachment of the debtor's assets.

Answers (a) and (b) are incorrect because a mere offer to compose debts does not affect a creditor's rights to attach the debtor's assets. Answer (c) is incorrect because the validity of one creditor's attachment is not affected by the other creditors' rejecting an offer to compose debts.

20. One advantage of an assignment for the benefit of creditors over a composition with creditors is that the assignment

a. Prevents attachment of the debtor's assets.

b. Discharges the debtor's obligations.

c. Involves the transfer of assets directly to creditors.

d. Requires the consent of creditors.

The correct answer is (a). *(Publisher)*

REQUIRED: The correct statement about the advantage of an assignment for the benefit of creditors.

DISCUSSION: An assignment for the benefit of creditors requires the transfer of the legal title of the assets from the debtor to a trustee. Creditors cannot attach the transferred assets because the debtor does not own the assets. Creditors can attach the debtor's assets prior to the execution of the composition agreement.

Answer (b) is incorrect because an assignment for the benefit of creditors does not discharge the debtor's obligations. Answer (c) is incorrect because an assignment for the benefit of creditors requires the debtor to transfer assets to a trustee. Answer (d) is incorrect because an assignment for the benefit of creditors does not require the creditors' consent.

21. The Double Diamond Ranch has assets of $3,000,000 and liabilities of $8,000,000. The owner of the Double Diamond has decided to make an assignment for the benefit of creditors to satisfy a portion of the liabilities. This arrangement will provide

a. Equal payments to all creditors.

b. Equal payments to the creditors consenting to the arrangement.

c. Pro rata payments to the creditors consenting to the arrangement.

d. Pro rata payments to all creditors.

The correct answer is (d). *(Publisher)*

REQUIRED: The effect of an assignment for the benefit of creditors.

DISCUSSION: An assignment for the benefit of creditors requires the debtor to transfer assets to a trustee. The trustee uses the assets to make payments to all creditors. The payment made to a specific creditor is calculated by multiplying total assets available for payment by the liability to the creditor and dividing the result by the debtor's total liabilities. Thus, all creditors receive pro rata payments.

Answer (a) is incorrect because the payments are not determined based on the number of creditors. Answers (b) and (c) are incorrect because an assignment for the benefit of creditors does not require the creditors' consent.

22. FGC, Inc. is in serious financial trouble. Trade accounts payable total $1,000,000. FGC has not paid its vendors in over 120 days. Although the vendors are anxious for payments, they agree that everyone will benefit if FGC avoids bankruptcy. FGC and all the vendors agree to a plan calling for FGC to make monthly payments on the overdue accounts for 24 months. All vendors will be paid in full. This plan is best described as

a. A composition with creditors.

b. A liquidation of unliquidated claims.

c. An extension agreement.

d. An assignment for the benefit of creditors.

The correct answer is (c). *(Publisher)*

REQUIRED: The best description of an agreement by a debtor and its creditors to delay payment.

DISCUSSION: An extension agreement is a variation of the composition with creditors. Rather than agree to the reduced but immediate payment of debts, the creditors and debtor agree that payments will be made over an extended period. The key characteristic of an extension agreement is the extended payment period. The agreement may provide for a reduction of the debt as well as an extended payment period.

Answer (a) is incorrect because a composition involves the immediate satisfaction of debts by reduced payments. Answer (b) is incorrect because liquidation of unliquidated claims is merely the agreement between the debtor and creditors on the amount of previously disputed claims. Answer (d) is incorrect because an assignment for the benefit of creditors involves the transfer of the debtor's assets to a trustee, and does not involve an agreement for an extended payment period.

25.4 Bulk Sales and Fraudulent Conveyances

23. Which of the following transactions is subject to the Bulk Transfers Article of the UCC?

a. A transfer of substantially all the assets of an accounting firm.

b. A sale of assets by a receiver.

c. A transfer of substantially all the merchandise of a retailer.

d. A general assignment for the benefit of all the creditors of the transferor.

The correct answer is (c). *(CPA 1184 L-29)*

REQUIRED: The applicability of the UCC's Bulk Transfers Article.

DISCUSSION: Under UCC 6-102, a bulk transfer is any transfer not in the ordinary course of the transferor's business of a major part of the materials, supplies, merchandise, or other inventory of an enterprise.

Answer (a) is incorrect because Article 6 does not apply unless the transferor's principal business is the sale of merchandise from stock (UCC 6-102). Answer (b) is incorrect because sales by executors, administrators, receivers, trustees in bankruptcy, or any public officers under judicial process are not subject to Article 6 (UCC 6-103). Answer (d) is incorrect because Article 6 does not apply to general assignments for the benefit of all the creditors of the transferor, and subsequent transfers by the assignee thereunder (UCC 6-103).

24. Rotland, Inc. manufactures faded blue jeans. In July, Rotland completely replaced its production equipment, which consists of sewing machines and washing machines. Rotland purchased the new equipment from Jeans, Inc. Jeans agreed to allow Rotland to pay for the equipment in three installments. Rotland paid two installments before selling the equipment at a profit to a South American company. The equipment sale is

a. Subject to the Bulk Transfers Article of the UCC because Rotland completely replaced its equipment.

b. Subject to the Bulk Transfers Article of the UCC if the sale was made in connection with a bulk transfer of inventory.

c. Exempt from the Bulk Transfer Article of the UCC because the Article never applies to the sale of equipment.

d. Exempt from the Bulk Transfer Article of the UCC because manufacturers are not subject to the Article.

The correct answer is (b). *(Publisher)*

REQUIRED: The correct statement concerning coverage of equipment transactions by the Bulk Transfer Article of the UCC.

DISCUSSION: The Bulk Transfer Article defines a bulk transfer as "any transfer in bulk and not in the ordinary course of the transferor's business of a major part of the materials, supplies, merchandise, or other inventory of an enterprise." The Article also provides that "A transfer of a substantial part of the equipment of such an enterprise is a bulk transfer if it is made in connection with a bulk transfer of inventory, but not otherwise" (UCC 6-102).

Answer (a) is incorrect because the sale was not made in connection with a bulk transfer of inventory. Answer (c) is incorrect because the Article does apply to the sale of equipment if made in connection with the sale of inventory. Answer (d) is incorrect because manufacturers who sell what they make are subject to the Bulk Transfers Article.

25. Which of the following transfers by a retailer of men's clothing is subject to the Bulk Transfers Article of the UCC?

a. A transfer of substantially all of its merchandise in the ordinary course of its business.

b. A transfer of its entire accounts receivable.

c. A transfer of substantially all of its equipment made in connection with a bulk transfer of inventory.

d. A pledge of a substantial portion of its inventory to secure a working capital loan.

The correct answer is (c). *(CPA 1185 L-33)*

REQUIRED: The transfer by a retailer subject to Article 6.

DISCUSSION: Under UCC 6-102, a transfer of a substantial part of the equipment of a business is treated as a bulk transfer only if it is made in connection with a bulk transfer of inventory. The principle underlying bulk sales law is the protection of creditors who have extended unsecured credit on the basis of the debtor's possession of inventory and other assets.

Answer (a) is incorrect because a bulk transfer is one not in the ordinary course of business. Answer (b) is incorrect because the transfer must be "of a major part of the materials, supplies, merchandise, or other inventory." Answer (d) is incorrect because a pledge is a secured transaction governed by Article 9, not a bulk sale.

26. A bulk transfer of assets must meet four requirements under the UCC to be effective against any creditor of the transferor. Which of the following is one of the requirements?

a. The transferee furnishes the transferor with a sworn list of the transferee's existing creditors.

b. The transferor preserves a list of the transferred property for 6 months and allows his/her creditors to inspect the list.

c. The transferor gives notice of the proposed transfer in bulk to each of the transferor's creditors at least 10 days before the transferee takes possession of the assets.

d. The transferee preserves a list of the transferor's creditors for 6 months and permits inspection of the transferred property by any creditor of the transferor.

The correct answer is (d). *(Publisher)*

REQUIRED: The requirement for a bulk transfer to be effective against a creditor.

DISCUSSION: UCC 6-104 provides for the transferee to maintain a list of the transferor's creditors and a schedule of the transferred property for 6 months. The list must be signed and sworn to by the transferor or his/her agent. If the transferor and transferee do not comply with UCC 6-104, the bulk transfer will be ineffective against any creditor of the transferor. For purposes of UCC 6-104, creditors include only those holding claims based on events prior to the transfer.

Answer (a) is incorrect because the transferor is required to furnish the transferee with a list of the transferor's creditors. Answer (b) is incorrect because the transferee must preserve a list of the transferred property. Answer (c) is incorrect because the transferee is required to give notice to the transferor's creditors.

27. Which of the following will render a bulk transfer ineffective with respect to a creditor of the transferor?

a. Failure by the transferee to require the transferor to furnish a list of the transferor's existing creditors.

b. Failure to file in the county clerk's office a schedule of the property to be transferred at least 10 days prior to the transfer.

c. Failure by the transferor to preserve the list of creditors and schedule of property for at least 6 months after the transfer.

d. Without the knowledge of the transferee, the transferor fails to prepare a complete and accurate list of the transferor's creditors.

The correct answer is (a). *(CPA 584 L-20)*

REQUIRED: The omission rendering a bulk transfer ineffective as to a creditor.

DISCUSSION: Under UCC 6-104, a bulk transfer is ineffective against any creditor of the transferor unless the transferee requires the transferor to furnish a list of his/her existing creditors; the parties prepare a schedule of the property transferred sufficient to identify it; and the transferee preserves the list and schedule for 6 months following the transfer and permits inspection of either or both and copying therefrom at all reasonable hours, or files the list and schedule in a public office.

Answer (b) is incorrect because filing in a public office is required only if the transferee does not preserve the list. Answer (c) is incorrect because the transferee, not transferor, must preserve the list. Answer (d) is incorrect because the transferee must demand the transferor to prepare the list, and refuse to complete the purchase if (s)he does not.

28. Scallop, Inc. plans to transfer its entire inventory of frozen seafood to James Bendofer. Scallop and Bendofer agree to comply with all requirements of the UCC Bulk Transfer Article, including the notice-to-creditors requirement. The notice to creditors must include

a. A statement that a bulk transfer was made.

b. The names and business addresses of the transferor's creditors.

c. The name of the transferee's lending institution.

d. Information concerning whether all debts of the seller in bulk are to be paid in full as a result of the transfer.

The correct answer is (d). *(Publisher)*

REQUIRED: The item included in the notice to creditors.

DISCUSSION: The notice is required to state whether all the transferor's debts will be paid in full as a result of the transfer. If the debts are to be paid in full, the notice should include the address to which creditors may send invoices. If the debts are not to be paid in full and on time, the notice must state the location of the property, describe the property, and the address where the sworn list of creditors and schedule of property can be inspected.

Answer (a) is incorrect because the notice must include a statement that a bulk transfer is about to be made. The notice must precede the transfer by at least 10 days to be effective. If the transfer is not effective, the transferee takes the goods subject to the claims of the transferor's creditors. Answer (b) is incorrect because the notice is not required to include a list of the transferor's creditors. Answer (c) is incorrect because the notice is not required to include the name of the transferee's lending institution.

29. Beta Corp. transferred its entire inventory to Alpha. Alpha did not give notice of the transfer to Beta's creditors as required by the Bulk Transfers Article of the UCC. Within 30 days, Alpha transferred the inventory to Lux. As a result

a. Lux will take free of the claims of Beta's creditors under all circumstances.

b. Lux will take subject to the claims of Beta's creditors if Lux had knowledge of Alpha's failure to give notice.

c. Beta may reacquire its inventory from Lux, declaring the original transfer to Alpha invalid.

d. The entire transaction is void as against public policy.

The correct answer is (b). *(CPA 1184 L-30)*

REQUIRED: The result of a bulk transferee's failure to give notice to creditors.

DISCUSSION: UCC 6-105 provides that any bulk transfer except one made by auction sale is ineffective against any creditor of the transferor unless the transferee gives the proper notice. This notice must be given to the transferor's creditors at least 10 days before the transferee takes possession of the goods or pays for them, whichever happens first. Nevertheless, a purchaser for value in good faith and without knowledge of noncompliance by the transferee takes free of the defect in the transferee's title (UCC 6-110).

Answer (a) is incorrect because Lux is not free of the claims if it is not a good faith purchaser for value. Answer (c) is incorrect because only creditors of the transferor have remedies under the bulk sales provisions. Answer (d) is incorrect because Alpha has a voidable title that it can transfer to a good faith purchaser for value.

30. The notice to creditors in a bulk sale

a. Is only required to be sent to creditors who will not be paid in full from the proceeds.

b. Need not state whether the buyer is paying new consideration if a detailed list of assets transferred is provided.

c. Is mailed by the clerk of the court.

d. Must be delivered personally or mailed even if the transfer is by auction.

The correct answer is (d). *(Publisher)*

REQUIRED: The correct statement regarding the notice to creditors.

DISCUSSION: Normally, a transferee of a bulk transfer must demand and receive a sworn schedule of creditors and amounts owed to those creditors by the transferor. All these creditors (and any others known) must be sent a notice by the transferee (delivered personally or sent by certified or registered mail) at least 10 days before the sale stating 1) that a bulk sale is to be made; 2) the names and addresses of the transferor and transferee; 3) whether the debts will be paid in full and where to send bills, but if not, the location and description of the property, where the schedule of creditors is available, who will receive payment, and full disclosure of the consideration for the sale.

In an auction, the auctioneer is responsible to give notice as indicated above or be liable up to the amount of proceeds.

Answer (a) is incorrect because the notice must be sent to all creditors. Answer (b) is incorrect because full disclosure of consideration is required only if all the creditors are not paid in full or if the transferee is in doubt on this point. Answer (c) is incorrect because the transferee (or the auctioneer) must send the notice.

CHAPTER TWENTY-SIX
DEBTOR LAW AND BANKRUPTCY

This chapter overlaps suretyship, consumer and credit law, secured transactions, and mortgages. It should be read with the chapters on those topics.

26.1 Overview of Key Provisions and Alternatives to Bankruptcy

1. The power to regulate bankruptcies is

a. Exercised solely by the federal government.

b. Derived from the federal government's authority over interstate commerce.

c. Based on the authority of Congress to make all laws that are necessary and proper for carrying out the powers conferred upon it by the Constitution.

d. Specifically granted to Congress by the Constitution.

The correct answer is (d). *(Publisher)*

REQUIRED: The basis for the power to regulate bankruptcies.

DISCUSSION: Under Article I, Section 8 of the Constitution, "The Congress shall have power to establish uniform laws on the subject of bankruptcies throughout the United States." Under Article VI, "This Constitution, and the laws of the United States which shall be made in pursuance thereof, shall be the supreme law of the land." Accordingly, power over bankruptcies is specifically conferred upon Congress, and any state law on the subject must defer to federal law.

Answer (a) is incorrect because a state may deny its citizens the use of the exemptions provided by the federal Bankruptcy Act. Answers (b) and (c) are incorrect because the authority is explicitly granted by the Constitution.

2. Federal courts have jurisdiction over bankruptcy proceedings. Bankruptcy courts

a. Are Article III federal courts the judges of which have life tenure.

b. Are special administrative courts under the authority of the U.S. district courts.

c. Have full powers to decide collateral issues affecting the debtor, such as contract and tort claims.

d. Are presided over by trustees in bankruptcy who serve 14-year terms.

The correct answer is (b). *(Publisher)*

REQUIRED: The true statement about bankruptcy courts in the federal system.

DISCUSSION: Bankruptcy courts are units of federal district courts and preside over specified core proceedings that concern the administration of the bankruptcy estate. Orders and judgments of the bankruptcy court are reviewed by the district court or a panel of three bankruptcy judges. Appeals may then be taken to a circuit court. If a matter is not specified in the Bankruptcy Act as belonging to the bankruptcy court's core jurisdiction, and unless the parties agree otherwise, the district court must issue the final order or judgment based upon findings of fact and conclusions of law submitted by the bankruptcy court.

Answer (a) is incorrect because bankruptcy judges do not have life tenure as do district and circuit judges and Supreme Court Justices. Answer (c) is incorrect because bankruptcy courts have jurisdiction to issue final orders and judgments only with respect to certain core proceedings. In other matters, the bankruptcy judge may prepare findings of fact and conclusions of law to be reviewed by the district court prior to issuance of a final order or judgment. However, the district court may not decide related state law claims that could not be independently considered by a federal court in a nonbankruptcy case. Answer (d) is incorrect because bankruptcy judges preside over proceedings specified in the 1984 Act. They are appointed for 14-year terms.

3. Amos owed a substantial amount of debts, was out of work, and was not able to pay his creditors. His creditors would not leave him alone and one in particular was calling him during the middle of the night. Amos decided to file a voluntary bankruptcy petition in hope of obtaining a fresh start.

a. The creditors may continue to seek payment until Amos obtains a discharge in bankruptcy.

b. The petition cannot be filed with the local state court.

c. The creditors may contest the voluntary petition and prevent the bankruptcy.

d. Amos can file under Chapter 13 for an adjustment of debts rather than liquidation.

The correct answer is (b). *(Publisher)*

REQUIRED: The correct statement regarding an individual filing for voluntary bankruptcy.

DISCUSSION: Federal courts have exclusive jurisdiction over bankruptcy cases. Bankruptcy petitions must be filed with, and all the proceedings conducted before, a U.S. Bankruptcy Court, created in each judicial district as a unit of the U.S. District Court. State courts have no authority (jurisdiction) over any bankruptcy matters.

Answer (a) is incorrect because filing a voluntary petition automatically stays all other proceedings. This means that creditors or others can take no further action against a debtor (Amos) except to file claims with the bankruptcy court. Answer (c) is incorrect because anyone may file a voluntary petition in bankruptcy. There are no prerequisites to its validity, including insolvency. Answer (d) is incorrect because a debtor must have a regular income in order to file under Chapter 13 for an adjustment of debts. Since Amos is out of work, he does not meet this requirement.

4. Which of the following was a significant reform made in the reorganization provisions of the Bankruptcy Reform Act of 1978?

a. Separate treatment of publicly held corporations under its provisions.

b. Elimination of the separate and competing procedures contained in the various chapters of the prior Bankruptcy Act.

c. Requirement of a full-scale investigation by the SEC of a firm undergoing bankruptcy reorganization.

d. The exclusion from its jurisdiction of partnerships and other noncorporate entities.

The correct answer is (b). *(CPA 582 L-21)*

REQUIRED: The significant reform made in the reorganization provisions of the 1978 Act.

DISCUSSION: Bankruptcy law prior to 1978 included Chapter 10 and Chapter 11 reorganizations. Chapter 10 conflicted with Chapter 11. The Bankruptcy Reform Act of 1978 brought all reorganizations under Chapter 11 and eliminated the conflict. The Bankruptcy Reform Act also included changes concerning property exempt in liquidations, simplified the filing of a petition for protection under the law, and included provisions allowing trustees to avoid preferential property transfers by the debtor.

Answers (a) and (d) are incorrect because the 1978 Act consolidates the treatment of publicly held corporations and noncorporate entities under Chapter 11. Answer (c) is incorrect because the full-scale SEC investigation previously required in Chapter 10 was eliminated by the 1978 Act.

5. Which of the following is least likely to be an intended result of the federal bankruptcy law?

a. To prevent dissipation of the assets of the estate.

b. To assure equal treatment of similarly situated creditors.

c. To drive financially embarrassed firms out of business.

d. To give relief to honest persons who are hopelessly burdened by debt.

The correct answer is (c). *(Publisher)*

REQUIRED: The purpose least likely to be an intention of bankruptcy law.

DISCUSSION: Rehabilitation of the debtor (freeing the debtor from an impossible debt situation) is one of the two major purposes of bankruptcy law. Assisting individuals and business entities to escape the burden of excessive debt results in allocating resources in a more productive way. The bankruptcy law has extensive provisions that allow potentially viable enterprises to continue in existence. When the entity involved is of significant size, favorable economic effects may follow from keeping the firm in business.

Answers (a) and (b) are incorrect because the second major purpose of the bankruptcy law is to protect the interests of creditors by avoiding transactions that dissipate the estate, by ensuring that some creditors are not unfairly preferred over others, by protecting against baseless claims of creditors, and by denying unlawful exemptions asserted by the debtor. Answer (d) is incorrect because debtor relief (which encourages risk taking) is a major purpose of bankruptcy law.

6. The Bankruptcy Code allows for all but which of the following proceedings?

a. Equity receivership.

b. Reorganization.

c. Regular income adjustment plan.

d. Liquidation.

The correct answer is (a). *(Publisher)*

REQUIRED: The proceeding not provided for in the Bankruptcy Code.

DISCUSSION: The Code does not allow for an equity receivership. This remedy may be given by a local court. A receiver is appointed as a fiduciary to collect and preserve the debtor's assets. The receiver may be instructed to operate the business of the debtor temporarily, conserve the assets pending resolution of issues by the court, or liquidate the assets. Appointment of a receiver or custodian, whether by a state court or by the debtor, is a basis for an involuntary petition under the Code.

Answer (b) is incorrect because Chapter 11 provides for reorganization of debtor enterprises with a view to their continuation in business. Answer (c) is incorrect because Chapter 13 is a voluntary provision that allows individuals with regular incomes to obtain a discharge after complying with a court-approved repayment plan. Answer (d) is incorrect because Chapter 7 concerns straight bankruptcy that is the conversion of the debtor's assets into cash, its distribution to creditors, and a discharge of remaining debts.

7. Most states have legal provisions allowing a receiver to take charge of the debtor's property. A receiver

a. May be appointed by agreement of a majority of the creditors.

b. Protects the debtor from creditors until (s)he can pay.

c. Attempts to pay creditors their debts.

d. May be appointed any time before a debtor receives a discharge in bankruptcy.

The correct answer is (c). *(Publisher)*

REQUIRED: The correct statement concerning the appointment and duties of a receiver.

DISCUSSION: A receiver is appointed by a local court to take charge of the property of a debtor. Such an appointment is made on petition of one or more creditors after a hearing at which the debtor is allowed to object. The receiver collects the debtor's assets and then attempts to pay the creditors under guidance of the court. This involves distributing assets to creditors or selling the assets.

Answer (a) is incorrect because a receiver may only be appointed by the court. Answer (b) is incorrect because the purpose of a receiver is to satisfy the creditors' claims, not to protect the debtor from the creditors (as in bankruptcy). Answer (d) is incorrect because bankruptcy stays all other proceedings. Creditors can take no further action besides filing petitions and claims once the debtor is in bankruptcy.

8. One of your clients is in financial difficulty. He is not able to pay his debts as they become due. It is desirable that he not go into bankruptcy. However, certain aggressive creditors are threatening this. Under the circumstances

a. It would be proper to attempt, in every way possible, to prepare financial statements indicating the client is not insolvent in the bankruptcy sense even though this means not following generally accepted accounting principles.

b. It may be possible to avoid bankruptcy if your client and the creditors can agree to form a creditor's committee with the usual powers incidental to such an arrangement.

c. Your client, even though he owes more than $100,000, cannot be forced into bankruptcy even though a single creditor's claim is in excess of $50,000.

d. Your client can resist involuntary bankruptcy if a custodian has not taken control of his property.

The correct answer is (b). *(CPA 576 L-43)*

REQUIRED: The correct statement concerning a person threatened with involuntary bankruptcy.

DISCUSSION: One alternative to bankruptcy is to place the assets of the business in the hands of a committee of creditors. The committee would have full power to manage the business of the debtor. The advantages of such an arrangement are that it avoids the stigma of bankruptcy, the attendant formalities and legal expenses, and the losses incurred in a forced liquidation.

Answer (a) is incorrect because preparing misleading financial statements is not only a violation of generally accepted accounting principles, but is also unethical and illegal. Answer (c) is incorrect because a debtor is subject to an involuntary petition for bankruptcy if the debtor has fewer than 12 creditors and a single creditor has unsecured claims aggregating more than $5,000, or, if the debtor has 12 or more creditors, three creditors having aggregate unsecured claims of $5,000 or more. Answer (d) is incorrect because not paying one's debts as they become due is sufficient to support a petition for involuntary bankruptcy.

9. Hance, doing business as Hance Fashions, is hopelessly insolvent. As a means of staving off his aggressive creditors and avoiding bankruptcy, Hance has decided to make a general assignment for the benefit of his creditors. Consequently, he transferred all his nonexempt property to a trustee for equitable distribution to his creditors. What are the legal consequences of Hance's actions?

a. A debtor may not make an assignment for the benefit of creditors if he has been adjudicated a bankrupt and discharged within the preceding 6 years.

b. All his creditors must participate in the assignment and distribution of property if a majority in number and amount participate.

c. Upon distribution of all his assigned property to the participating creditors, he is discharged from all liability.

d. He may be petitioned into bankruptcy by his creditors.

The correct answer is (d). *(CPA 579 L-23)*

REQUIRED: The legal consequences of an assignment for the benefit of creditors.

DISCUSSION: An involuntary petition by the required creditors will be upheld (by an order for relief against the debtor) even if contested by the debtor where the debtor is not paying his/her debts as they come due, or if during the preceding 120 days before the filing of the petition, a custodian (trustee, receiver, etc.) was appointed or permitted to take possession of the debtor's property. For this reason, Hance may not be able to avoid bankruptcy.

Answer (a) is incorrect because an assignment for the benefit of creditors under state law is not an official proceeding and is not subject to federal bankruptcy rules. Answer (b) is incorrect because all creditors need not participate in the assignment, and distribution would not discharge any nonassenting creditors' claims. Answer (c) is incorrect because distribution of assigned property to the participating creditors does not discharge the debtor from liability to the nonparticipants.

10. A client has joined other creditors of the Martin Construction Company in a composition agreement seeking to avoid the necessity of a bankruptcy proceeding against Martin. Which statement describes the composition agreement?

a. It provides a temporary delay, not to exceed six months, insofar as the debtor's obligation to repay the debts included in the composition.

b. It does not discharge any of the debts included until performance by the debtor has taken place.

c. It provides for the appointment of a receiver to take over and operate the debtor's business.

d. It must be approved by all creditors.

The correct answer is (b). *(CPA 581 L-40)*

REQUIRED: The correct statement describing a composition among creditors.

DISCUSSION: A composition with creditors is a common law contractual undertaking between the debtor and the creditors. The participating creditors agree to extend time for payment, take lesser sums in satisfaction of the debts owed, or some other plan of financial adjustment. Under general contract law, the original debts will not be discharged until the debtor has performed the new obligations.

Answer (a) is incorrect because although a composition may involve an extension of time, it is not limited to 6 months. Furthermore, the more common composition is to take lesser sums in satisfaction. Answer (c) is incorrect because it describes the appointment of a receiver. A composition agreement is a contractual agreement not involving judicial intervention. Answer (d) is incorrect because a composition agreement need not be approved by all creditors, but is binding only upon those participating.

11. Dexter had assets of $80,000 and liabilities of $100,000, all unsecured. He owed $25,000 to each of the following: Petrie, Dey, Mabley, and Norris. Petrie, Dey, and Mabley agreed with each other and with Dexter to accept 70 cents on the dollar in immediate satisfaction of their debts. Under these circumstances,

a. The agreement is void for lack of consideration.

b. The agreement is a composition with creditors.

c. Norris would be bound by the agreement.

d. The agreement described is an assignment for the benefit of creditors.

The correct answer is (b). *(CPA 1175 L-10)*

REQUIRED: The correct statement concerning an agreement by a debtor with three of four creditors to accept reduced payment.

DISCUSSION: The agreement is a common law composition with creditors. Under general contract law, Dexter's old debts of $25,000 to each of the three will not be discharged until he performs the new obligation of paying 70%. The problem with this arrangement is that Norris can still petition Dexter into involuntary bankruptcy and void the composition.

Answer (a) is incorrect because consideration is found in the mutual promises made among the creditors to accept a lesser payment or excused by the courts on the basis that public policy requires that informal settlement of debts should be encouraged. Answer (c) is incorrect because Norris is a nonparticipant and under general contract principles would not be bound. Answer (d) is incorrect because an assignment for the benefit of creditors occurs when the debtor places his/her assets in the hands of a trustee who distributes the property to the creditors on a proportional basis as the intended beneficiaries.

26.2 Bankruptcy Administration and Proceedings

12. A federal bankruptcy judge

a. Decides all issues that affect the debtor's estate.

b. No longer has authority to appoint trustees.

c. Presides over core proceedings specified by statute.

d. Collects, preserves, and ultimately distributes the debtor's assets.

The correct answer is (c). *(Publisher)*

REQUIRED: The function of a federal bankruptcy judge.

DISCUSSION: Under the Bankruptcy Amendments Act of 1984, the bankruptcy judges may decide specified issues arising from "core" proceedings related to the administration of the debtor's estate, for example, decisions on claims and preferences, confirmation of plans, and discharge of debts. These decisions are reviewed by the district court of which the bankruptcy court is a unit or by a panel of three bankruptcy judges. Unless the parties agree otherwise, final orders or judgments on collateral issues affecting the debtor may not be made by the bankruptcy courts.

Answer (a) is incorrect because such jurisdiction would be unconstitutional if exercised by an Article I court. Moreover, the district court of which the bankruptcy court is a unit must abstain with regard to state matters that are not independently cognizable by a federal court. Answer (b) is incorrect because the bankruptcy judge may for cause appoint a trustee in a Chapter 11 reorganization case. (S)he appoints an interim trustee in a Chapter 7 liquidation case until the creditors choose one. Only a few districts are involved in a pilot program in which the attorney general appoints U.S. trustees. Answer (d) is incorrect because it describes the function of a trustee.

13. A voluntary bankruptcy proceeding is available to

a. All debtors provided they are insolvent.

b. Debtors only if the overwhelming preponderance of creditors have not petitioned for and obtained a receivership pursuant to state law.

c. Corporations only if a reorganization has been attempted and failed.

d. Most debtors even if they are not insolvent.

The correct answer is (d). *(CPA 583 L-21)*

REQUIRED: The persons who may file voluntary petitions.

DISCUSSION: A voluntary petition in bankruptcy under Chapter 7 (liquidation bankruptcy) may be filed by any debtor with the exception of banks, governmental units (including municipal corporations), savings and loan associations, insurance companies, credit unions, railroads, and other regulated organizations. An individual who files a voluntary petition need not be insolvent in any sense.

Answer (a) is incorrect because insolvency is not required, and certain debtors may not file a voluntary petition. Answer (b) is incorrect because the issuance of an order for relief by a bankruptcy court creates an automatic stay of state receivership proceedings and most other legal action affecting the estate. Answer (c) is incorrect because reorganization is never a condition precedent to a Chapter 7 filing. Reorganization is preferable to liquidation for corporations because corporations do not receive a discharge for unpaid debts.

14. Since the passage of the Bankruptcy Reform Act of 1978, voluntary bankruptcy proceedings have become increasingly popular with debtors. The new law

a. Increases availability and eases filing.

b. Increases the amount of exempt property.

c. Reduces the number of creditors necessary for filing.

d. Accepts solvency in the equity sense as the criterion for determining bankruptcy status.

The correct answer is (b). *(CPA 1182 L-18)*

REQUIRED: The reason for the increased popularity of voluntary bankruptcy.

DISCUSSION: The federal exemptions include $7,500 equity in a residence or burial plot, $1,200 equity in a motor vehicle, $4,000 in household furnishings, appliances, clothing, and the like (up to $200 per item), $500 worth of jewelry, $400 of other property plus the unused portion of the residential equity exemption up to $3,750, $750 worth of tools, alimony and child support payments, Social Security and disability benefits, and others. The federal law permits the debtor to choose between federal or state exemptions.

Answer (a) is incorrect because filing requirements are more extensive. For example, the 1984 amendments require a schedule of current income and expenses. Answer (c) is incorrect because no specified number of creditors is needed for a voluntary petition. Answer (d) is incorrect because a voluntary petitioner may be solvent.

15. Insolvency in the bankruptcy sense

a. Is the same as insolvency in the equity sense.

b. Must be present if the debtor seeks to file a voluntary petition in bankruptcy.

c. Is normally easier to establish than insolvency in the equity sense.

d. Is a financial status in which the liabilities exceed the aggregate fair value of the assets.

The correct answer is (d). *(CPA 1174 L-15)*

REQUIRED: The definition of insolvency in the bankruptcy sense.

DISCUSSION: Insolvency in the bankruptcy sense exists if liabilities exceed the current fair market value of total assets. This definition is now used for almost all purposes under the Bankruptcy Act, except when an involuntary petition is contested.

Answer (a) is incorrect because insolvency in the equity sense is the inability or failure to meet one's obligations as they mature. Answer (b) is incorrect because anyone who owes a debt may file a voluntary petition even though (s)he is not insolvent in either the bankruptcy or the equity sense. Answer (c) is incorrect because insolvency in the bankruptcy sense is more difficult to establish due to problems with obtaining accurate appraisals of property.

16. Which of the following assets would be included in a debtor's bankruptcy estate in a liquidation proceeding?

a. Proceeds from a life insurance policy received 90 days after the petition was filed.

b. An inheritance received 270 days after the petition was filed.

c. Property from a divorce settlement received 365 days after the petition was filed.

d. Wages earned by the debtor after the petition was filed.

The correct answer is (a). *(CPA 1189 L-27)*

REQUIRED: The correct statement about the assets that would be included in a debtor's bankruptcy estate.

DISCUSSION: The general rule is that any asset in which the debtor has a legal or equitable interest at the date the proceedings began is included in the estate. There are, however, several other ways in which property may be added to the estate. For example, the estate includes property acquired by the debtor within 180 days of the filing of the petition for relief if the property was acquired by inheritance, as proceeds of a life insurance policy, or from a property settlement in a divorce case. Thus, the proceeds from the life insurance policy should be included because they were acquired within 90 days of filing.

Answers (b) and (c) are incorrect because the property was acquired more than 180 days after filing. Answer (d) is incorrect because wages earned by the debtor after the petition for relief was filed are not included in the estate according to the Bankruptcy Code provisions.

17. The filing of a voluntary petition in bankruptcy

a. Does not result in a stay of legal proceedings until an adjudication of bankruptcy.

b. Automatically stays legal proceedings except by secured creditors.

c. Does not result in an order for relief until the first creditors' meeting has been convened.

d. Constitutes an automatic order for relief if properly submitted.

The correct answer is (d). *(Publisher)*

REQUIRED: The legal effect of filing a voluntary petition.

DISCUSSION: If the voluntary petition has been properly completed, sworn to, and signed by the debtor, it functions as an automatic order for relief. One effect will be to stay most legal proceedings and other activities of creditors seeking to collect from the debtor.

Answer (a) is incorrect because no "adjudication of bankruptcy" is made under current law. A petition in proper form serves as an automatic order for relief except when an involuntary petition is contested. Also, the court may need to decide whether a creditor is entitled to relief from the automatic stay provision on the grounds that it does afford the creditor adequate protection. Answer (b) is incorrect because secured creditors' actions are also stayed, although they may petition the court for relief if their interests will not be given "adequate protection," for example, from loss in value of the security. Answer (c) is incorrect because a proper petition is itself an order for relief.

18. Which of the following statements is correct with respect to a voluntary bankruptcy proceeding under the liquidation provisions of the Bankruptcy Code?

a. The debtor must be insolvent.

b. The liabilities of the debtor must total $5,000 or more.

c. It may be properly commenced and maintained by any person who is insolvent.

d. The filing of the bankruptcy petition constitutes an order for relief.

The correct answer is (d). *(CPA 588 L-32)*

REQUIRED: The correct statement with respect to a voluntary bankruptcy proceeding.

DISCUSSION: Under the liquidation provisions of the Bankruptcy Code, an order for relief is automatically given to the debtor upon the filing of the petition. The voluntary bankruptcy petition is a formal request by the debtor to the court for an order for relief.

Answer (a) is incorrect because insolvency is not required in order for the debtor to file a petition for voluntary bankruptcy. A statement that the debtor has debts is all that is needed. Answer (b) is incorrect because in a voluntary bankruptcy proceeding, there is no minimum requirement for the debtor's liabilities. Answer (c) is incorrect because the court may dismiss a voluntary petition if the debtor's obligations are primarily consumer debts. The amendments to the Bankruptcy Code give the courts this discretion to prevent the granting of relief that would constitute a substantial abuse of the bankruptcy laws. Also, municipalities, railroads, banks, insurance companies, credit unions, and savings and loan associations are not eligible for voluntary bankruptcy.

19. A client is in serious financial trouble. Several creditors filed an involuntary petition in bankruptcy. Which of the following is correct?

a. As long as the client generally can meet current debts as they mature, the court will deny relief against the client in a bankruptcy proceeding.

b. If the client creates a new corporation and transfers most of its assets to the newly created corporation, it can avoid bankruptcy.

c. As long as the client's assets, at fair value, exceed its liabilities, the creditors' petition will be denied.

d. Unless the client is not paying its debts as they become due or a custodian has been appointed or taken possession of the client's property, the creditors cannot force the client into bankruptcy.

The correct answer is (d). *(CPA 582 L-19)*

REQUIRED: The correct statement regarding an involuntary petition in bankruptcy.

DISCUSSION: A debtor may contest an involuntary petition. If contested, an order for relief will only be granted if the debtor is generally not paying its debts as they become due, or if within the preceding 120 days, a custodian was appointed or took possession of the debtor's property. As long as the client does not have these problems, the involuntary petition will be dismissed. If a petition is filed in bad faith, damages (compensatory and punitive) can be awarded for injury to the debtor's reputation.

Answer (a) is incorrect because even though the client is solvent in the equity sense (ability to meet current debts as they mature), the court will grant relief if the client is actually not paying the debts or if a custodian has taken possession as discussed above. Answer (b) is incorrect because such a transfer will not avoid bankruptcy, and is likely to be considered a fraudulent transfer which may be set aside by the trustee in bankruptcy. Answer (c) is incorrect because solvency in the bankruptcy sense (fair market value of assets in excess of liabilities) is not a basis for denial of the creditors' petition.

20. Which of the following statements is correct concerning the voluntary filing of a petition in bankruptcy?

a. The debtor must be insolvent.

b. The petition may be filed by husband and wife jointly.

c. If the debtor has 12 or more creditors, the debtor's unsecured claims must total at least $5,000.

d. If the debtor has fewer than 12 creditors, the debtor's unsecured claims must total at least $5,000.

The correct answer is (b). *(CPA 589 L-24)*

REQUIRED: The correct statement concerning the voluntary filing of a petition in bankruptcy.

DISCUSSION: A bankruptcy case may be commenced voluntarily or involuntarily. In a voluntary case, the debtor files the petition with the bankruptcy court. Debtors can include individuals, partnerships, corporations, and couples, if the husband and wife file together.

Answer (a) is incorrect because insolvency is not a prerequisite for filing a voluntary petition. Answers (c) and (d) are incorrect because the 12-creditor threshold is applicable only to involuntary petitions.

21. Willa Wilk owes a total of $25,000 to eight unsecured creditors and one fully secured creditor. Rusk is one of the unsecured creditors and is owed $7,000. Rusk has filed a petition against Wilk under the liquidation provisions of the Bankruptcy Code. Wilk has been unable to pay her debts as they become due, and Wilk's liabilities exceed her assets. Wilk has filed the papers that are required to oppose the bankruptcy petition. Which of the following statements is correct?

a. The petition will be granted because Wilk is unable to pay her debts as they become due.

b. The petition will be granted because Wilk's liabilities exceed her assets.

c. The petition will be dismissed because three unsecured creditors must join in the filing of the petition.

d. The petition will be dismissed because the secured creditor failed to join in the filing of the petition.

The correct answer is (a). *(CPA 1188 L-22)*

REQUIRED: The correct statement concerning the entry of an order for relief in an involuntary bankruptcy case.

DISCUSSION: In an involuntary bankruptcy case, a single creditor may file a petition for relief if (s)he is owed more than $5,000 and there are fewer than 12 creditors. The petition will be granted, even if it is contested, if the creditor can prove either that the debtor is not paying his/her debts as they become due or that during the 120 days preceding the filing of the petition a custodian took possession of the debtor's property. In this case, Rusk has met the conditions to file the petition and has proved that Wilk was unable to pay her debts as they became due. Thus, even though the petition was contested, it will still be granted.

Answer (b) is incorrect because having liabilities in excess of assets is not a criterion for automatic granting of a petition for relief. Answer (c) is incorrect because three unsecured creditors must join in filing the petition only if there are 12 or more creditors. Answer (d) is incorrect because a secured creditor is not required to join in filing the petition.

22. Mac, doing business as Mac's Restaurant, has an involuntary petition in bankruptcy filed against him. Which of the following is a correct legal statement regarding such a filing?

a. Mac has the right to controvert the validity of the petition and if Mac is successful, the petition will be dismissed and Mac may recover his costs including a reasonable attorney's fee.

b. The filing of the petition by a majority of the creditors creates a binding presumption that Mac is insolvent.

c. A single creditor may file the petition regardless of the number of creditors if its provable claim exceeds $7,500.

d. A trustee is appointed upon the filing of the petition and is vested by operation of law with the bankrupt's title as of the date of the filing.

The correct answer is (a). *(CPA 582 L-18)*

REQUIRED: The correct statement concerning an involuntary petition in bankruptcy.

DISCUSSION: A debtor has the right to controvert an involuntary petition, and it will be dismissed if the statutory requirements are not met. If the dismissal is not with consent of all parties, the debtor may recover his/her costs, a reasonable attorney's fee, and damages.

Answer (b) is incorrect because filing of the petition by a majority of the creditors creates no presumption of insolvency. In regard to preferential transfers a debtor is presumed to be insolvent during the 90 days preceding the filing of the petition. Answer (c) is incorrect because if the debtor has 12 or more creditors, at least three creditors must join in filing the petition. If the debtor has fewer than 12 creditors, then any one creditor whose unsecured claims equal $5,000 or more may file the petition. Answer (d) is incorrect because in ordinary bankruptcy an interim trustee is appointed only upon the issuance of the order for relief. When a meeting of the creditors is held, a permanent trustee is usually elected.

23. An involuntary petition in bankruptcy

a. Will be denied if a majority of creditors in amount and in number have agreed to a common law composition agreement.

b. Can be filed by creditors only once in a 7-year period.

c. May be successfully opposed by the debtor by proof that the debtor is solvent in the bankruptcy sense.

d. If not contested will result in the entry of an order for relief by the bankruptcy judge.

The correct answer is (d). *(CPA 583 L-22)*

REQUIRED: The true statement about an involuntary petition.

DISCUSSION: If the uncontested involuntary petition is in proper form, the court will issue an order for relief. The debtor will be required to furnish the court with the same information as would have been contained in a voluntary petition, an interim trustee will be appointed to take control of the estate, and a creditors' meeting will be called. In general, the procedure is the same whether the bankruptcy is voluntary or involuntary.

Answer (a) is incorrect because 1 creditor (3 if there are 12 or more creditors) with unsecured, noncontingent claims of $5,000 may petition a debtor into bankruptcy. Answer (b) is incorrect because a discharge may be granted to a debtor only once every 6 years. Answer (c) is incorrect because insolvency in the equity sense (not being able to pay debts as they fall due) is a ground for relief.

24. Bar, a creditor of Sy, has filed an involuntary petition in bankruptcy against Sy. Sy is indebted to six unsecured creditors including Bar for $6,000 each. If Sy opposes the petition, which of the following is correct?

a. Bar must be joined by at least two other creditors in filing the petition.

b. The court must appoint a trustee within ten days after the filing of the petition.

c. Bar may be required to file a bond indemnifying Sy for any losses that Sy may incur.

d. The court may not award attorney's fees to Sy because of its limited authority under the Bankruptcy Code.

The correct answer is (c). *(CPA 584 L-19)*

REQUIRED: The true statement about contesting an involuntary petition.

DISCUSSION: An involuntary petition is a means of harassing a debtor, so the court is empowered to require that the petitioner(s) post a bond to indemnify a debtor who successfully contests the petition. Amounts that the debtor may recover include court costs, attorney's fees, and damages caused by the trustee's taking possession of the debtor's property. If the petitioner(s) acted in bad faith, punitive damages may be awarded.

Answer (a) is incorrect because if the debtor has fewer than 12 creditors, one creditor with an unsecured, noncontingent claim of $5,000 may file. Answer (b) is incorrect because if the petition is contested, a trustee is often not appointed until the order for relief is entered at the conclusion of the trial on the issue. In a liquidation case, the naming of an interim trustee is required unless the debtor posts bond. Answer (d) is incorrect because the court may award costs, attorney's fees, and damages.

25. The filing of an involuntary petition in bankruptcy

a. Allows creditors to continue their collection actions against the debtor while the bankruptcy action is pending.

b. Terminates liens associated with exempt property.

c. Stops the enforcement of a judgment lien against property in the bankruptcy estate.

d. Terminates all security interests in property in the bankruptcy estate.

The correct answer is (c). *(CPA 1189 L-23)*

REQUIRED: The effect of filing an involuntary petition in bankruptcy.

DISCUSSION: The automatic stay resulting from filing the petition operates to postpone certain actions against the debtor and his/her property whether the filing is voluntary or involuntary. All acts, with certain exceptions, to create, enforce, or perfect any lien against estate property are stayed when a petition in bankruptcy is filed.

Answer (a) is incorrect because creditors may not continue or commence collection actions against the debtor while the bankruptcy action is pending. Answer (b) is incorrect because the automatic stay does not affect the existence of liens associated with exempt property but postpones efforts to foreclose the liens. Answer (d) is incorrect because the automatic stay does not affect the existence of all security interests in estate property.

26. Filing a valid petition in bankruptcy acts as an automatic stay of actions to

	Garnish the Debtor's Wages	Collect Alimony from the Debtor
a.	Yes	Yes
b.	Yes	No
c.	No	Yes
d.	No	No

The correct answer is (b). *(CPA 1189 L-25)*

REQUIRED: Correct identification of actions affected by the automatic stay.

DISCUSSION: The filing of a valid petition in bankruptcy automatically postpones certain actions and proceedings that involve the debtor or his/her property. This automatic stay operates to give the debtor protection from creditors. Actions and proceedings not covered by the automatic stay include criminal prosecution of the debtor, collection of child support, and collection of alimony.

Answers (a) and (c) are incorrect because the automatic stay does not operate to prohibit collecting alimony from the debtor. Answers (c) and (d) are incorrect because the automatic stay does prohibit garnishing the debtor's wages.

27. In a bankruptcy case, the order for relief is a formal judicial declaration that the debtor is insolvent. After this order is issued,

a. An unsecured creditor may not obtain a judgment and execution against the debtor's property.

b. A creditor may not make a setoff of a debt owed to the debtor prior to the order.

c. The debtor retains his/her property in an involuntary liquidation proceeding until the permanent trustee is appointed.

d. A debtor who contests an involuntary petition nevertheless must surrender control of his/her property upon proper filing.

The correct answer is (a). *(Publisher)*

REQUIRED: The effect of issuing an order for relief.

DISCUSSION: The order for relief results in an automatic stay of most legal proceedings or other collection efforts by creditors of the debtor. New and pending proceedings are stayed. Creditors, whether or not secured, also may not take action to gain possession of the debtor's property or to create, perfect, or enforce a lien thereon. An unsecured creditor thus could not take advantage of a state "grab" law to obtain a judgment and execute it by seizing and selling property of the debtor without concern for the claims of other creditors.

Answer (b) is incorrect because the right of setoff is not stayed by the order for relief, although a setoff intended to prefer a creditor will be disallowed. For example, a creditor-bank may set off the debtor's deposit against a debt incurred before filing unless the deposit was intended to prefer the bank. Answer (c) is incorrect because an interim trustee is appointed promptly after the order is recorded to take control of the debtor's financial affairs. Answer (d) is incorrect because a debtor may usually continue in control until the order for relief is granted.

28. After an order for relief is recorded in a bankruptcy case, the court will call a creditor's meeting. At this meeting,

a. The bankruptcy judge presides.

b. The debtor must submit to examination under oath.

c. A permanent trustee may be elected by qualified creditors unless the proceedings are under Chapter 7 (liquidation).

d. The creditors may by unanimous vote vacate the order for relief.

The correct answer is (b). *(Publisher)*

REQUIRED: The true statement about the creditors' meeting.

DISCUSSION: The creditors' meeting is convened by the court within a reasonable time after entry of the order for relief. The creditors listed in the schedules filed by the debtor may attend, but the bankruptcy judge may not. One purpose of the meeting is to elect a permanent trustee and discharge the interim trustee (often, the latter becomes the permanent trustee). Election must be by at least 20% of the creditors with noncontingent, unsecured claims. If not excused, the debtor must attend and answer questions under oath that are posed by the creditors or trustee regarding relevant matters.

Answer (a) is incorrect because the judge may not attend. Answer (c) is incorrect because the permanent trustee is elected by the creditors under Chapter 7 but is appointed by the court under other provisions. Answer (d) is incorrect because creditors have no such power.

29. The trustee in bankruptcy of a landlord-debtor under a Chapter 7 liquidation

a. Must be elected by the creditors immediately after a bankruptcy petition is filed.

b. May not be appointed by the court after the order for relief has been entered.

c. Must reject the executory contracts of the debtor.

d. May assign the leases of the debtor.

The correct answer is (d). *(CPA 1184 L-28)*

REQUIRED: The true statement about a trustee in bankruptcy.

DISCUSSION: A trustee in bankruptcy has broad powers to administer the estate. (S)he can, for example, assign, assume, or reject the debtor's executory contracts or unexpired leases. The trustee is empowered to breach bad bargains but to retain those that are assumable or assignable under state law. Breach, however, creates a claim against the estate.

Answers (a) and (b) are incorrect because the creditors may elect a permanent trustee at the first creditors' meeting. An interim trustee appointed by the court after entry of the order for relief serves until then. If no election is made, the interim trustee becomes permanent. Answer (c) is incorrect because the trustee may assign, assume, or reject executory contracts.

30. On June 5, 1989, Green rented equipment under a 5-year lease. On March 8, 1990, Green was involuntarily petitioned into bankruptcy under the liquidation provisions of the Bankruptcy Code, and a trustee was appointed. The fair market value of the equipment exceeds the balance of the lease payments due. The trustee

a. Must assume the equipment lease because its term exceeds 1 year.

b. Must assume and subsequently assign the equipment lease.

c. May elect not to assume the equipment lease.

d. May not reject the equipment lease because the fair market value of the equipment exceeds the balance of the payments due.

The correct answer is (c). *(CPA 588 L-34)*

REQUIRED: The true statement about the bankruptcy trustee's choices regarding a lease held by the bankrupt party.

DISCUSSION: The trustee in bankruptcy is given several options under the Bankruptcy Code, all of which are subject to court approval. The options are to assume and perform the unexpired lease, to assume and assign the unexpired lease to a third party, or reject the unexpired lease. The trustee must act to assume the lease within 60 days after the order for relief is entered or it is deemed to be rejected.

Answers (a) and (b) are incorrect because the trustee may but is not required to assume the lease. Answer (d) is incorrect because regardless of the fair market value of the equipment, the trustee may reject the equipment lease.

31. One of the elements necessary to establish that a preferential transfer was made under the Bankruptcy Code by the debtor to a creditor is that the

a. Debtor was insolvent at the time of the transfer.

b. Creditor was an insider and the transfer occurred within 90 days of the filing of the bankruptcy petition.

c. Transfer was in fact a contemporaneous exchange for new value given to the debtor.

d. Transfer was made by the debtor with actual intent to hinder, delay, or defraud other creditors.

The correct answer is (a). *(CPA 587 L-34)*

REQUIRED: The necessary element to establish that a preferential transfer was made by the debtor to a creditor.

DISCUSSION: One of the elements necessary to prove that a preferential transfer was made is the insolvency of the debtor. Under the Bankruptcy Code, the debtor was presumed to be insolvent for 90 days before the filing of a petition.

Answer (b) is incorrect because general as well as insider creditors can receive a preferential transfer. If a transfer to an insider occurred within 12 months prior to the filing of the petition, it may be voided by the trustee. Answer (c) is incorrect because to prove that a preferential transfer has occurred, it must be proven that the transfer involved an antecedent debt. If the contemporaneous exchange was for new value, it cannot be a preferential transfer. Answer (d) is incorrect because to void the transfer as preferential, the trustee must prove only that the creditor received more than (s)he would have under a Chapter 7 liquidation.

32. The trustee of the bankruptcy estate is accountable to the court for protecting the rights of both the debtor and the creditors. The trustee is therefore granted broad powers that include

a. Having the status of a judgment lien creditor but only if such a person exists.

b. Having the status of a bona fide purchaser of real estate who would prevail against even a perfected security interest in fixtures.

c. The capacity to use, sell, and lease property or borrow money.

d. The ability to void fraudulent transfers and preferences but not to breach the debtor's executory contracts.

The correct answer is (c). *(Publisher)*

REQUIRED: The correct statement about the trustee's powers.

DISCUSSION: The trustee's general duty is to collect and preserve the estate and to reduce it to cash for distribution. (S)he has power to compel delivery of any property belonging to the debtor's estate, including property that is exempt or subject to a security interest. To preserve the value of the estate or sustain an existing business, (s)he may also need to use, sell, or lease property or borrow money.

Answers (a) and (b) are incorrect because the trustee has the status both of a hypothetical judgment lien creditor and of a bona fide purchaser of realty even if such persons do not exist. The trustee would thus prevail over unperfected but not perfected security interests. Answer (d) is incorrect because the trustee can void any transaction voidable by the debtor (for fraud, duress, etc.), fraudulent transfers, preferences, and certain statutory liens (a landlord's lien, for example). (S)he can also assign, assume, or reject the debtor's executory contracts or unexpired leases.

33. In a bankruptcy proceeding, the trustee

a. Must be an attorney admitted to practice in the federal district in which the bankrupt is located.

b. Will receive a fee based upon the time and fair value of the services rendered, regardless of the size of the estate.

c. May not have had any dealings with the bankrupt within the past year.

d. Is the representative of the bankrupt's estate and as such has the capacity to sue and be sued on its behalf.

The correct answer is (d). *(CPA 581 L-41)*

REQUIRED: The correct statement concerning the trustee in bankruptcy.

DISCUSSION: The trustee in bankruptcy is the legal representative of the debtor's estate. In liquidation bankruptcy, the court will appoint an interim trustee when the order for relief is granted. The interim trustee serves until the creditors elect a permanent trustee. In other bankruptcy proceedings, the trustee is appointed by the court. The trustee has broad powers to administer the estate, including the right to sue and be sued on behalf of the estate.

Answer (a) is incorrect because a trustee is not required to be an attorney. Answer (b) is incorrect because although the fee of the trustee is based on the criteria mentioned, there is a maximum limit contingent upon the size of the estate. Answer (c) is incorrect because there is no requirement that the trustee not have had any dealings with the bankrupt within the preceding year.

34. Which of the following is a correct statement regarding assets included in a debtor's bankruptcy estate?

a. Transfers voided by the trustee are not included because the assets were not the debtor's when the petition was filed in bankruptcy.

b. Property subject to a security interest is not included because the secured creditor has the right to it.

c. All of the debtor's property is included except that exempt by law.

d. Most legal or equitable property interests of the debtor are included.

The correct answer is (d). *(Publisher)*

REQUIRED: The correct statement regarding the assets included in a debtor's estate.

DISCUSSION: By definition, a debtor's estate includes most of his/her legal or equitable interests as of the commencement of the case. All interests are included whether or not the property is exempt. Exceptions from inclusion are beneficial interests in spendthrift trusts and certain powers over property to be exercised only for the benefit of others.

Answer (a) is incorrect because property reclaimed by a trustee because of preferential or fraudulent transfers is for the benefit of the creditors and is included in the debtor's estate. Answer (b) is incorrect because the debtor has a residual interest in property subject to a security interest. A secured party simply has first rights to the property to satisfy his/her debt. Answer (c) is incorrect because property exempt from liquidation is part of the debtor's estate even though it will not be distributed to creditors.

35. In general, the debtor's estate in bankruptcy includes all his/her legal or equitable interests at the commencement of the case. Which of the following is part of the estate?

a. Wages earned after the date of filing.

b. A beneficial interest in a spendthrift trust.

c. A secured creditor's security interest in the debtor's property.

d. Proceeds from the property of the estate.

The correct answer is (d). *(Publisher)*

REQUIRED: The property belonging to the debtor's estate.

DISCUSSION: The estate consists of most of the debtor's legal and equitable interests at the commencement of the case. It also includes certain property acquired within 180 days after filing: inheritances, property settlements with a spouse, death benefits, and gifts. The estate is also entitled to community property, property recoverable by the trustee through his/her avoidance powers, and exempt property. Proceeds, receipts, or income generated during the bankruptcy proceedings from the property in the estate are also included. Other after-acquired property is not included.

Answer (a) is incorrect because the general rule that after-acquired property is not included applies to the debtor's earnings from employment. Answer (b) is incorrect because certain powers over property exercisable only for the benefit of others and the debtor's interest in a state-recognized spendthrift trust are excluded. Answer (c) is incorrect because only the debtor's equity in collateral is included. The security interest is the creditor's, although the trustee does administer the collateral.

36. Norton owned and operated a trucking business. He was financially hard pressed and obtained a loan from the First State Bank "secured by his equipment and all other personal property used in his business." The loan security agreement was properly filed in the county records office. In addition, Norton obtained a loan from the Title Mortgage Company; the loan was secured by a first mortgage on all the real property used in the trucking business. Norton is now insolvent and a petition in bankruptcy has been filed. Which of the following is a correct statement concerning the security interests in the properties?

a. If Title Mortgage failed to record its mortgage, the trustee in bankruptcy will be able to defeat Title's security interest.

b. Norton's central air conditioning and heating system is included in First State's security interest.

c. If Title Mortgage did not record its mortgage, First State is entitled to all fixtures, including those permanently annexed to the land.

d. A sale of all the personal and real business property by Norton to a bona fide purchaser will defeat First State's security interest unless First State recorded its security interest in both the appropriate real and personal property recordation offices.

The correct answer is (a). *(CPA 575 L-12)*

REQUIRED: The correct statement concerning the security interests in the properties.

DISCUSSION: Even in bankruptcy proceedings, a secured creditor with a perfected security interest may pursue its remedy against the particular property. The secured party has what amounts to a first priority in the property. However, the trustee in bankruptcy has the special status of a hypothetical ideal judgment lien creditor. (S)he has every right that might be conferred by the state upon a creditor who has obtained a lien by judicial proceedings, including the power to defeat a nonperfected security interest. An unrecorded mortgage is subordinate to the claims of a lien creditor and the trustee will win.

Answer (b) is incorrect because First State's security interest covers only personal property. A central air conditioning and heating system is usually deemed to be a fixture and is therefore real property covered by the mortgage. Answer (c) is incorrect because regardless of whether Title Mortgage recorded, First State is still entitled only to the collateral (personal property) described in its security agreement. Fixtures are considered part of the real property. Answer (d) is incorrect because First State's security interest extends only to personal property so it need not be filed in real property records.

37. Burt Burton's business was faltering and the creditors were beginning to demand immediate payment. Burton's brother had recently set up a new corporation for real estate investments. With the intent to save some of his assets, Burton transferred them to the new corporation with an understanding that Burton would receive stock after resolution of his financial problems. Five months later, Burton filed for bankruptcy. The trustee has discovered the transfer of assets and seeks their recovery.

a. The trustee cannot recover the assets because the transfer was more than 90 days before the petition was filed in bankruptcy.

b. The assets can be recovered as a fraudulent conveyance.

c. The assets can be recovered as a preferential transfer.

d. The assets cannot be recovered because the corporation is a separate legal entity.

The correct answer is (b). *(Publisher)*

REQUIRED: The correct statement regarding recovery of assets transferred by a debtor prior to bankruptcy.

DISCUSSION: A fraudulent conveyance is one made with actual intent to hinder, delay, or defraud creditors. A conveyance is also fraudulent if it results in insolvency or if the debtor receives less than a reasonable value while (s)he is insolvent. Fraudulent conveyances are voidable if the transfer is made within 1 year before bankruptcy. Thus, without regard to whether the new corporation had knowledge of Burton's fraud or insolvency, the trustee can recover the assets because Burton transferred them with intent to defraud creditors within 1 year of bankruptcy.

Answer (a) is incorrect because the trustee can recover the assets. They were fraudulently transferred within 1 year prior to the bankruptcy. Answer (c) is incorrect because the transfer was not a preferential transfer, but a fraudulent conveyance. A preferential transfer is made when one creditor is preferred over another. Answer (d) is incorrect because a conveyance which is fraudulent is voidable no matter to whom the transfer was made.

38. Under the Bankruptcy Code, one of the elements that must be established in order for the trustee in bankruptcy to void a preferential transfer to a creditor who is not an insider is that

a. The transferee-creditor received more than (s)he would have received in a liquidation proceeding under the Bankruptcy Code.

b. Permission was received from the bankruptcy judge prior to the trustee's signing an order avoiding the transfer.

c. The transfer was in fact a contemporaneous exchange for new value given to the debtor.

d. The transferee-creditor knew or had reason to know that the debtor was insolvent.

The correct answer is (a). *(CPA 584 L-18)*

REQUIRED: The element present in a preferential transfer.

DISCUSSION: A preference is 1) a transfer to a creditor, 2) on an antecedent debt, 3) made within 90 days before filing, 4) made while the debtor was insolvent, and 5) permitting the creditor to unfairly receive more than (s)he would have obtained in a bankruptcy proceeding. A preference within 1 year of filing is voidable if given to an insider (examples are relatives, directors, controlling parties, and partners).

Answer (b) is incorrect because it is obviously nonsensical. Answer (c) is incorrect because the transfer must have been on an antecedent (preexisting) debt to be a preference. This rule does not apply if the payment was on a current debt incurred in the ordinary course of the debtor's and creditor's business. Answer (d) is incorrect because under the Bankruptcy Act the debtor is presumed to be insolvent during the 90 days preceding the filing of the petition (but for insider preferences the trustee must show the creditor had reasonable cause to know of the debtor's insolvency.)

39. The federal bankruptcy act contains several important terms. One such term is "insider." The term is used in connection with preferences and preferential transfers. Which among the following is not an "insider?"

a. A secured creditor having a security interest in at least 25% or more of the debtor's property.

b. A partnership in which the debtor is a general partner.

c. A corporation of which the debtor is a director.

d. A close blood relative of the debtor.

The correct answer is (a). *(CPA 580 L-3)*

REQUIRED: The statement which does not describe an insider.

DISCUSSION: An insider is one who has a sufficiently close relationship with the debtor so as to benefit from early information about the troubled financial status of the debtor by obtaining a preference. The 90-day period for avoiding preferences is extended to one year for insiders. A secured creditor who otherwise lacks a close relationship with the debtor would not be considered an insider regardless of the size of the interest in the debtor's property.

Answers (b), (c), and (d) are incorrect because each is an example of an insider. Other examples include a general partner of the debtor and officers, directors, and controlling stockholders of debtor corporations.

40. On January 10, 1990, Edwards gave Cantrell a mortgage on her office building to secure a past-due $40,000 obligation owed to Cantrell. Cantrell promptly recorded the mortgage. On March 15, 1990, a petition in bankruptcy was filed against Edwards. Simpson, the trustee in bankruptcy, desires to prevent Cantrell from qualifying as a secured creditor. Which of the following statements is correct?

a. The mortgage cannot be set aside because it is a real property mortgage and recorded.

b. Even if the mortgage is set aside, Cantrell has a priority in respect to the office building.

c. The mortgage can only be set aside if the mortgage conveyance was fraudulent.

d. The mortgage can be set aside regardless of whether it was taken with knowledge that Edwards was insolvent in the bankruptcy sense.

The correct answer is (d). *(CPA 578 L-25)*

REQUIRED: Whether the trustee in bankruptcy can set aside the mortgage.

DISCUSSION: The transaction described is a preference because it was for an antecedent debt and the mortgage would permit Cantrell to obtain a greater return on his/her claim than if the transfer had not been made. The preference is voidable because it was made within 90 days of the filing of the petition. It is irrelevant whether Cantrell knew or did not know that Edwards was insolvent because under the Act the debtor is presumed to be insolvent within 90 days of the filing of the petition.

Answer (a) is incorrect because whether or not recorded, a real property mortgage can be set aside as a voidable preference. But if the mortgage is sold by the creditor to a bona fide purchaser, it could not be canceled. Presumably, the proceeds of the sale of the mortgage could be recoverable by the trustee. Answer (b) is incorrect because once the mortgage is set aside, Cantrell will only be a general unsecured creditor. Answer (c) is incorrect because the mortgage may be set aside as a voidable preference. The trustee in bankruptcy also has power to avoid fraudulent transfers.

41. Emma's creditors filed an involuntary petition in bankruptcy against her. An order for relief was entered and a trustee was elected by the creditors. The trustee wanted Emma to file a list of creditors, a schedule of assets and liabilities, and a statement of her financial affairs. She was upset by being forced into bankruptcy and refused to cooperate. Which of the following is true?

a. Failure to provide the requested information may prevent her discharge.

b. Emma does not have to cooperate since the petition was involuntary.

c. The creditors must provide this information.

d. Since Emma is a citizen of a state, the federal court cannot issue sanctions against her.

The correct answer is (a). *(Publisher)*

REQUIRED: The correct statement regarding a debtor's refusal to provide financial information requested by the trustee.

DISCUSSION: The Bankruptcy Code requires a debtor to file a list of creditors, a schedule of assets and liabilities, a statement of his/her financial affairs, and a list of current items of income and expense. The debtor has a duty to cooperate with the trustee and the court that includes surrendering the property of the estate and any pertinent records. The court can refuse to grant a discharge in bankruptcy if the debtor refuses to obey any lawful order.

Answer (b) is incorrect because the information listed is required whether the petition is voluntary or involuntary. Answer (c) is incorrect because creditors must provide only information needed to verify their claims. Answer (d) is incorrect because once an order for relief is entered, the debtor is subject to the jurisdiction of the bankruptcy court and can be held in contempt or denied a discharge.

42. A debtor may not claim as exempt from liquidation in bankruptcy and distribution to creditors

a. A motor vehicle not to exceed $1,200 in value.

b. $500 in jewelry.

c. The exemptions allowed under both state and federal law.

d. An interest in property used as a residence up to $7,500 in value.

The correct answer is (c). *(Publisher)*

REQUIRED: The property not exempt from liquidation and distribution to creditors.

DISCUSSION: An individual debtor (not corporate, etc.) must file with the court a list of protected property claimed to be exempt. Both state law and the federal Bankruptcy Code list property that an individual debtor may protect from seizure by creditors. Under federal law, a debtor has a choice of claiming either the state or federal exemptions (not both), but it also allows a state to limit its citizens to use of the state exemptions. The majority of states have done so.

Answers (a), (b), and (d) are incorrect because each states a proper exemption under the Bankruptcy Code. Other items which may be exempted are: up to an additional $400 of any property, up to $750 in value of tools of the trade, unmatured life insurance policies, up to $3,750 in cash or other property on the unused part of the homestead allowance, etc.

26.3 Priorities and Claims Against the Estate

43. The issuance of an order for relief by a bankruptcy court affects the creditors in different ways. The most favorable position is held by a secured creditor. (S)he

a. May petition for relief from the automatic stay of proceedings against the debtor.

b. Must nevertheless file a proof of claim.

c. Is a secured party with regard to the whole of any claim if the value of the collateral is at least 50% of the debt.

d. May receive a nonvoidable preference in the form of a security interest given within 90 days of filing although the original debt was intended to be unsecured.

The correct answer is (a). *(Publisher)*

REQUIRED: The true statement about the treatment of secured creditors.

DISCUSSION: A secured creditor receives payment before any other creditors to the extent of the value of the collateral, but the property is nonetheless collected and administered by the trustee. If this arrangement does not give the secured creditor "adequate protection" from a decline in value of the security or other damage to his/her interests, the court may grant a petition to vacate the stay. The secured party might then proceed to repossess the collateral or take other necessary action. Other relief granted by the court might consist of additional liens or collateral, cash payments, or a guarantee by a solvent third person.

Answer (b) is incorrect because a secured creditor need not file a proof of claim. Answer (c) is incorrect because to the extent the collateral is insufficient, the secured party has an unsecured claim and must file a proof of claim. Answer (d) is incorrect because voidable preferences may consist not only of direct transfers of money or property but also of security interests.

44. Robert Cunningham owns a shop in which he repairs electrical appliances. Two months ago Electrical Supply Company sold Cunningham, on credit, a machine for testing electrical appliances and within 10 days perfected a security interest as security for payment of the unpaid balance. Cunningham's creditors have now filed an involuntary petition in bankruptcy against him. What is the status of Electrical in the bankruptcy proceeding?

a. Electrical is a secured creditor and has the right against the trustee if not paid to assert a claim to the electrical testing machine it sold to Cunningham.

b. Electrical must surrender its perfected security interest to the trustee in bankruptcy and share as a general creditor of the bankrupt's estate.

c. Electrical's perfected security interest constitutes a preference and is voidable.

d. Electrical must elect to resort exclusively to its secured interest or to relinquish it and obtain the same share as a general creditor.

The correct answer is (a). *(CPA 579 L-22)*

REQUIRED: The status in bankruptcy of a seller with a perfected security interest.

DISCUSSION: Electrical obtained a purchase-money security interest in equipment which was perfected because Electrical filed a financing statement within 10 days. Thus, Electrical has a valid security interest that cannot be avoided by the trustee, and Electrical may assert a claim to the machine.

Answers (b) and (c) are incorrect because Electrical's security interest is not a voidable preference even though the transaction occurred within 90 days of bankruptcy. The transaction constituted the giving of new value (the machine) for the debt and security interest, and was not on account of an antecedent debt. Answer (d) is incorrect because Electrical may resort to its security interest and, if the proceeds are insufficient, Electrical will become a general unsecured creditor as to the balance of the debt.

45. Which of the following unsecured debts of $500 each would have the highest relative priority in the distribution of a bankruptcy estate in a liquidation proceeding?

a. Tax claims of state and municipal governmental units.

b. Liabilities to employee benefit plans arising from services rendered during the month preceding the filing of the petition.

c. Claims owed to customers who gave deposits for the purchase of undelivered consumer goods.

d. Wages earned by employees during the month preceding the filing of the petition.

The correct answer is (d). *(CPA 1189 L-28)*

REQUIRED: The correct statement about the relative priorities of unsecured debts in a bankruptcy liquidation distribution.

DISCUSSION: The Bankruptcy Code sets priorities for the claims of unsecured creditors in a liquidation proceeding. All of the claims at a higher priority level must be satisfied in full before any lower priority claims will be considered. The list of priorities is as follows: administrative expenses, unsecured claims arising in the ordinary course of business after the petition was filed but before the order for relief was granted, unsecured claims up to $2,000 for wages earned by an individual within 90 days before filing, unsecured claims for contributions to employee benefit plans, unsecured claims of grain producers and fishermen, unsecured claims of depositors of money for the purchase of undelivered consumer goods, and unsecured tax claims of governmental units.

Answers (a), (b), and (c) are incorrect because all of these debts have a lower relative priority in the bankruptcy liquidation distribution scheme.

46. On July 15, 1990, White, a sole proprietor, was involuntarily petitioned into bankruptcy under the liquidation provisions of the Bankruptcy Code. White's nonexempt property has been converted to $13,000 cash, which is available to satisfy the following claims:

Unsecured claim for 1988 state income tax $10,000
Fee owed to Best & Co., CPAs, for services rendered from April 1, 1990 through June 30, 1990 $ 6,000
Unsecured claim by Stieb for wages earned as an employee of White during March 1990 $ 3,000

There are no other claims. What is the maximum amount that will be distributed for the payment of the 1988 state income tax?

a. $4,000.

b. $5,000.

c. $7,000.

d. $10,000.

The correct answer is (d). *(CPA 1188 L-23)*

REQUIRED: The maximum amount that will be distributed for the payment of the state income tax.

DISCUSSION: In a Chapter 7 bankruptcy case, the Bankruptcy Code requires secured claims to be satisfied in full before any unsecured claims can be paid. After all secured claims are satisfied, the unsecured creditors will receive payment according to the system of priorities given in the Code. All higher-ranking unsecured claims must be paid in full before any lower-ranking claims can be paid. According to the system of priorities, the state taxes rank highest among the listed claims. Thus, they must be satisfied in full ($10,000) before any other claims can be satisfied. Next in order is the fee owed to the CPA, which is a claim of a general unsecured creditor. The wages owed to Stieb will also become a claim of a general unsecured creditor and thus be prorated with the other claims at this level.

47. The Bankruptcy Act provides that certain allowed expenses and claims are entitled to a priority. Which of the following is not entitled to such a priority?

a. Claims of governmental units for taxes.

b. Wage claims, but to a limited extent.

c. Rents payable within the four months preceding bankruptcy, but to a limited extent.

d. Unsecured claims for contributions to employee benefit plans, but to a limited extent.

The correct answer is (c). *(CPA 582 L-20)*

REQUIRED: The expense or claim which is not entitled to a priority.

DISCUSSION: To be entitled to a priority, claims must first be "allowed," meaning they are not objected to and are determined to be proper. Certain allowed claims are then given priority in payment. However, there is no priority for rents payable.

Answers (a), (b), and (d) are incorrect because each is entitled to a priority ahead of general unsecured creditors.

48. Which of the following does not constitute a valid debt of a bankrupt which may be proved and allowed against the bankrupt's estate even if objection is made?

a. A workers' compensation award if the injury occurred before the adjudication of bankruptcy.

b. An open account.

c. Unmatured interest.

d. Fixed liabilities evidenced by a written instrument absolutely owing but not due at the time of the filing of a petition.

The correct answer is (c). *(CPA 1177 L-31)*

REQUIRED: The debt that is not valid (not allowable) against the estate of a bankrupt.

DISCUSSION: Under the Bankruptcy Act a claim is a "right to payment, whether or not such right is reduced to judgment, liquidated, unliquidated, fixed, contingent, matured, unmatured, disputed, undisputed, legal, equitable, secured, or unsecured." However, unmatured interest is specifically listed as a claim that is not allowable because it is not a debt at that time. The distinction is between an amount absolutely owing, but not due, and unmatured interest. Because of the possibility of prepayment, unmatured interest is not an obligation that is absolutely owing.

Answers (a), (b), and (d) are incorrect because each represents a claim that may be proved and allowed in bankruptcy.

Questions 49 through 52 are based on the following information: Knox operates an electronics store as a sole proprietor. On April 5, Knox was involuntarily petitioned into bankruptcy under the liquidation provisions of the Bankruptcy Code. On April 20, a trustee in bankruptcy was appointed and an order for relief was entered. Knox's nonexempt property has been converted to cash, which is available to satisfy the claims and expenses presented in the right column as may be appropriate.

The cash available for distribution includes the proceeds from the sale of the stereos.

Claim by Dart Corp. (one of Knox's suppliers) for computers ordered on April 6 and delivered on credit to Knox on April 10	$20,000
Fee earned by the bankruptcy trustee	$15,000
Claim by Boyd for a deposit given to Knox on April 1 for a computer Boyd purchased for personal use but that had not yet been received by Boyd	$ 1,500
Claim by Noll Co. for the delivery of stereos to Knox on credit. The stereos were delivered on March 4 and a financing statement was properly filed on March 5. These stereos were sold by the trustee with Noll's consent for $7,500, their fair market value	$ 5,000
Fees earned by the attorneys for the bankruptcy estate	$10,000
Claims by unsecured general creditors	$ 1,000

49. What amount will be distributed to the trustee as a fee if the cash available for distribution is $15,000?

a. $6,000.

b. $9,000.

c. $10,000.

d. $15,000.

The correct answer is (a). *(CPA 588 L-28)*

REQUIRED: The amount that will be distributed to the trustee as a fee.

DISCUSSION: The Bankruptcy Reform Act of 1978 classifies creditors into several categories according to the priority in which their claims against the debtor will be satisfied. The Code also states that secured creditors' claims will be satisfied in full before unsecured creditors' claims will be considered. Thus, Noll is the only secured creditor and will have first priority in the distribution of the cash. Its $5,000 claim against Knox will be satisfied in full before the other claims are considered. Administrative costs of the estate, which include trustees' and attorneys' fees, receive second priority in the distribution process. However, funds are not adequate to satisfy these claims in full, and a pro rata distribution is therefore necessary. The trustee will receive $6,000 {[$15,000 ÷ ($10,000 + $15,000)] x [$15,000 - $5,000]}, and the attorney will receive the remaining $4,000. All of the unsecured creditors' claims will not be satisfied.

50. What amount will be distributed to Boyd if the cash available for distribution is $50,800?

a. $480.

b. $800.

c. $900.

d. $1,500.

The correct answer is (b). *(CPA 588 L-29)*

REQUIRED: The amount that will be distributed to an unsecured creditor.

DISCUSSION: The Bankruptcy Reform Act of 1978 states the priority in which creditors' claims must be satisfied when distributing the assets of the debtor's estate. All secured creditors' claims must be satisfied in full before any of the other creditors' claims are considered. Because Noll Co. is the only secured creditor, it must receive the full $5,000 to be completely satisfied before the other creditors' claims are considered. The next priority belongs to administrative costs, including trustees' and attorneys' fees. The trustee will receive $15,000 and the attorney $10,000 in full satisfaction of their claims. Debts incurred after the involuntary petition was filed, but before the order for relief was issued will then be satisfied. Dart is the only "gap creditor". Thus, it will receive $20,000 of the remaining $20,800 ($50,800 - $5,000 - $15,000 - $10,000). Among the remaining creditors, Boyd has the highest priority because the Act ranks prepetition deposits of money for undelivered consumer goods ahead of claims by general unsecured creditors. Hence, Boyd will receive the remaining $800, and the other claims will be unsatisfied.

51. What amount will be distributed to Dart if the cash available for distribution is $41,000?

a. $10,100.

b. $11,000.

c. $16,000.

d. $20,000.

The correct answer is (b). *(CPA 588 L-30)*

REQUIRED: The amount that will be distributed to a gap creditor.

DISCUSSION: The Bankruptcy Reform Act of 1978 prescribes the priorities that must be followed by the trustee in the distribution of the assets of a debtor's estate. Because the claims of secured creditors must be satisfied first, Noll Co. will receive the first $5,000. Among unsecured creditors, administrative costs have top priority; thus, the trustee will receive $15,000 and the attorney $10,000. The remaining $11,000 ($41,000 - $5,000 - $15,000 - $10,000) will go to Dart because it is the only creditor whose claim was incurred during the "gap" after the involuntary petition was filed but before the order for relief was granted.

52. If the trustee in bankruptcy wishes to avoid Noll's March 4 transaction with Knox as a preferential transfer, the trustee will

a. Lose, because the transfer was in fact a substantially contemporaneous exchange for new value given.

b. Lose, because there is no evidence that Knox was insolvent on March 4.

c. Prevail, because the transfer occurred within 90 days of the filing of the bankruptcy petition.

d. Prevail, because the financing statement was not filed on the day of delivery.

The correct answer is (a). *(CPA 588 L-31)*

REQUIRED: The outcome of the trustee's attempt to avoid a secured purchase from a supplier as a preferential transfer.

DISCUSSION: The Bankruptcy Code lists the six elements required for a preferential transfer: 1) a transfer of the property of the debtor, 2) to a creditor, 3) for an antecedent debt, 4) made while the debtor was insolvent, 5) made within 90 days before the date of the filing of a petition, and 6) that enables the creditor to receive more than in a liquidation case under Chapter 7. The trustee is granted the power to avoid such transfers to provide for the equal treatment of creditors. There are, however, exceptions to this power including, but not limited to, a security interest given by the debtor to acquire property that is perfected within 10 days after the security interest attaches. This type of transaction is an enabling loan. Thus, Noll's transaction with Knox is an enabling loan that involved a contemporaneous exchange for new value given.

Answer (b) is incorrect because the Bankruptcy Code presumes that a debtor is insolvent 90 days prior to the filing of a petition. Thus, Knox would be considered insolvent on March 4 because the petition was filed within the 90-day period prior to April 5. Answer (c) is incorrect because transfers involving contemporaneous exchanges for new value given are not preferential transfers regardless of when they occurred. Answer (d) is incorrect because to qualify the transaction as an enabling loan, the financing statement must be filed within 10 days after the security interest attaches. Noll filed the financing statement the day after delivery.

53. Bunker Industries, Inc. ceased doing business and is in bankruptcy. Among the claimants are employees seeking unpaid wages. The following statements describe the possible status of such claims in a bankruptcy proceeding or legal limitations placed upon them. Which one is an incorrect statement?

a. They are entitled to a priority.

b. If a priority is afforded such claims, it cannot exceed $2,000 per wage earner.

c. Such claims cannot include vacation, severance, or sick-leave pay.

d. The amounts of excess wages not entitled to a priority are mere unsecured claims.

The correct answer is (c). *(CPA 580 L-10)*

REQUIRED: The incorrect statement concerning claims by employees seeking unpaid wages.

DISCUSSION: Employees seeking unpaid wages are entitled to a priority junior only to the claims of secured creditors, administrative expenses, and gap creditors (those arising in the ordinary course of the debtor's business after the filing of an involuntary petition but before the order for relief or the appointment of a trustee). The claim must have arisen within 90 days of the date of cessation of the debtor's business or the filing of the petition, whichever occurred first. Such claims include vacation, severance, and sick-leave pay.

Answers (a), (b), and (d) are incorrect because each represents a correct statement.

Questions 54 and 55 are based on the following information: On March 10, Rowe, a sole proprietor selling furniture, was involuntarily petitioned into bankruptcy under the liquidation provisions of the Bankruptcy Code. Rowe's nonexempt property has been converted to cash that is available to satisfy the expenses and unsecured claims presented in the right column as may be appropriate.

Expenses	
Costs necessary to preserve the property of the debtor's estate	$20,000
Salary to Rowe for services rendered in operating the furniture business after the commencement of the bankruptcy action	$10,000
Unsecured Claims	
Claims by two of Rowe's employees for wages earned within 90 days of the filing of the bankruptcy petition in the amount of $4,000 and $3,000, respectively	$ 7,000
Claim by Acme Corp. for furniture delivered to Rowe on March 12, which was prior to the appointment of a trustee and the order for relief	$30,000

54. What amount will be distributed as salary to Rowe if the cash available for distribution is $15,000?

a. $0.

b. $5,000.

c. $7,500.

d. $10,000.

The correct answer is (b). *(CPA 587 L-30)*

REQUIRED: The amount that will be distributed as salary to a bankrupt.

DISCUSSION: The Bankruptcy Reform Act of 1978 prescribes the priority in which the claims of creditors are to be satisfied in the distribution of the assets of the debtor's estate. First, all secured creditors' claims must be satisfied in full before any unsecured creditors' claims will be considered. In this case there are no secured creditors. First among the unsecured creditors are the claimants of administrative costs, which include the actual, necessary costs and expenses of preserving the estate. Salaries for services rendered after the commencement of the proceedings are included in these costs. Thus, the expenses for preserving the estate and the salary paid to Rowe will be satisfied before any other unsecured claims. Because the cash available for distribution is inadequate to satisfy the creditors' claims, a pro rata distribution is necessary. Rowe will receive $5,000 {[$10,000 ÷ ($20,000 + $10,000)] x $15,000} of the cash, and the remaining $10,000 will be paid to reimburse the other costs of preserving the estate.

55. What amount will be distributed to Acme if the cash available for distribution is $50,000?

a. $13,000.

b. $16,000.

c. $20,000.

d. $30,000.

The correct answer is (c). *(CPA 587 L-31)*

REQUIRED: The amount that will be distributed to a gap creditor.

DISCUSSION: There are no secured creditors, and the trustee must therefore consider the Bankruptcy Code's list of priorities for unsecured creditors. First priority is given to the administrative costs, which include the costs of preserving the estate and the salaries for services rendered after the commencement of the liquidation proceedings. Thus, the first $30,000 of the available cash will be distributed for these expenses. Next in priority are any debts incurred after the filing of the petition, but before the granting of the order for relief. Acme Corp. is such a "gap creditor", and the remaining $20,000 ($50,000 - $30,000) will be distributed to it.

56. Your client is entitled to a consumer deposit priority in bankruptcy; as such he

a. Will have his claim satisfied prior to those of general creditors even though the general creditors receive little or nothing.

b. Ranks equally with all other parties entitled to priorities.

c. Has a claim superior to the claims of secured creditors.

d. Is precluded from asserting the priority if it was obtained within three months of the filing of the petition in bankruptcy.

The correct answer is (a). *(CPA 1176 L-28)*

REQUIRED: The correct statement regarding a consumer deposit priority.

DISCUSSION: A person entitled to a consumer deposit priority in bankruptcy will have a claim of up to $900 satisfied before the general unsecured creditors receive anything. Such a claim arises on behalf of an individual who prior to the filing of the petition has deposited money for the purchase, lease, or rental of property. Amounts in excess of $900 are treated as a claim of a general creditor.

Answer (b) is incorrect because the priority for consumer deposits is superior to that of claims for taxes, but is junior to other classes of priorities; e.g., expenses of administration, claims of gap creditors, claims for wages, and claims for distribution of employee benefit plans. Answer (c) is incorrect because secured creditors have a direct claim to the collateral ahead of all other parties. Answer (d) is incorrect because there is no time limit with respect to the claim of a consumer deposit.

57. Safety Surety Company, Inc. issued a surety bond for value received which guaranteed: 1) completion of a construction contract Poe had made with Cairns and 2) payment by Poe of his workmen. Poe defaulted and did not complete the contract. The workers were not paid for their last week's work. Poe had in fact become insolvent, and a petition in bankruptcy was filed two months after the issuance of the bond. What is the effect upon Safety as a result of the above events?

a. If Safety pays the workers in full, it is not entitled to the same priority in the bankruptcy proceedings that the workers would have had.

b. If Safety pays damages to Cairns as a result of default on the contract, Safety is entitled to recover in the bankruptcy proceedings the entire amount it paid prior to the payment of the general creditors of Poe.

c. If Safety has another separate claim against Cairns, Safety may not set it off against any rights Cairns may have under this contract.

d. As a compensated surety, Safety would be discharged by Poe's bankruptcy.

The correct answer is (a). *(CPA 578 L-46)*

REQUIRED: The effect on a surety of the bankruptcy of the debtor.

DISCUSSION: A surety which pays the obligations of the debtor becomes subrogated to the creditors' rights against the debtor. If the creditors were entitled to a priority in bankruptcy, the surety becomes subrogated to this priority. However, the Bankruptcy Code specifically denies this right of subrogation to the priority for wages arising within 90 days prior to the commencement of the case. Therefore, Safety would not be entitled to the same priority.

Answer (b) is incorrect because Safety is only entitled to the status that Cairns would have had in the bankruptcy proceeding. Since Cairns would have only been a general unsecured creditor, Safety will only be entitled to share pro rata with other general unsecured creditors after the priority claimants have been paid. Answer (c) is incorrect because the surety has a right to set-off any claims it has against the creditor. Answer (d) is incorrect because a surety, whether compensated or not, is not discharged from its obligation by the debtor's bankruptcy. This means that bankruptcy of the debtor is not a defense of the surety.

58. Clark is a surety on a $100,000 obligation owed by Thompson to Owens. The debt is also secured by a $50,000 mortgage to Owens on Thompson's factory. Thompson is in bankruptcy. Clark has satisfied the debt. Clark is

a. Only entitled to the standing of a general creditor in bankruptcy.

b. A secured creditor to the extent of the $50,000 mortgage and a general creditor for the balance.

c. Entitled to nothing in bankruptcy since this was a risk he assumed.

d. Not entitled to a priority in bankruptcy, even though Owens could validly claim it.

The correct answer is (b). *(CPA 582 L-22)*

REQUIRED: The status of a surety on a partially secured obligation when the debtor is in bankruptcy.

DISCUSSION: Once a surety has satisfied the debt, (s)he becomes subrogated to the rights of the creditor against the debtor. Therefore, the surety will have the same standing and preferences in bankruptcy the creditor would have had except with respect to wages as explained in the previous question. Since Owens was a secured creditor to the extent of the $50,000 mortgage and a general creditor for the balance, Clark will have the same standing.

Answer (a) is incorrect because Clark is a secured creditor to the extent of the $50,000 mortgage. Answer (c) is incorrect because the surety is entitled to whatever the creditor could have recovered in bankruptcy. Answer (d) is incorrect because if Owens could validly claim a priority in bankruptcy, the surety who has satisfied the debt could do so also.

59. Haplow engaged Turnbow as his attorney when threatened by several creditors with a bankruptcy proceeding. Haplow's assets consisted of $85,000 and his debts were $125,000. A petition was subsequently filed and was uncontested. Several of the creditors are concerned that the suspected large legal fees charged by Turnbow will diminish the size of the distributable estate. What are the rules or limitations which apply to such fees?

a. None, since it is within the attorney-client privileged relationship.

b. The fee is presumptively valid as long as arrived at in an arm's-length negotiation.

c. Turnbow must file with the court a statement of compensation paid or agreed to for review as to its reasonableness.

d. The trustee must approve the fee.

The correct answer is (c). *(CPA 581 L-42)*

REQUIRED: The rules or limitations on legal fees charged by an attorney for the bankrupt.

DISCUSSION: An attorney representing a bankrupt must file a statement of compensation paid or agreed to. If the court determines the compensation exceeds the reasonable value of such services, the court may cancel the agreement or order the return of the excessive part of the payment. The approved legal fees are part of the costs of administration and given priority in payment.

Answer (a) is incorrect because the attorney-client privilege does not apply to compensation. Answer (b) is incorrect because the court must specifically review the fee to determine whether it is reasonable. Answer (d) is incorrect because it is the bankruptcy court who must approve the fee, not the trustee.

60. Skipper was for several years the principal stockholder, director, and chief executive officer of the Canarsie Grocery Corporation. Canarsie had financial difficulties and its assets were liquidated under Chapter 7 of the Bankruptcy Code. Several creditors are seeking to hold Skipper personally liable as a result of her stock ownership and position as an officer-director. Skipper in turn filed with the bankruptcy judge a claim for $1,400 salary due her. Which of the following is correct?

a. Skipper's salary claim will be allowed and she will be entitled to a priority.

b. Skipper has no personal liability to the creditors as long as Canarsie is recognized as a separate legal entity.

c. Skipper cannot personally file a petition in bankruptcy for 7 years.

d. Skipper is personally liable to the creditors for Canarsie's losses.

The correct answer is (b). *(CPA 582 L-17)*

REQUIRED: The personal liability and standing as a creditor of a stockholder-director-officer of a bankrupt corporation.

DISCUSSION: A fundamental characteristic of a corporation is that it is a legal entity separate from its stockholders. The stockholders therefore have no personal liability for corporate debts. Accordingly, Skipper will have no personal liability as long as the corporation is considered a separate legal entity.

Answer (a) is incorrect because as a principal stockholder, director, and chief executive officer, Skipper is an insider. The claims of insiders are not allowed priority. Answer (c) is incorrect because the bankruptcy of the corporation has no effect on Skipper's ability to file for bankruptcy. Answer (d) is incorrect because Skipper has no personal liability to the creditors unless she agreed to become personally liable.

61. Marco owns all the shares of stock of Digits Corporation. Digits is currently short of cash and has had to default on some of its current liabilities. Marco loaned Digits $2,000 to tide it over its crisis and obtained a note from Digits for the amount of the loan. If Digits is petitioned into bankruptcy, what is the status of Marco's loan?

a. It is a provable and allowable claim against the bankrupt's estate which is superior to the claims of other general creditors.

b. It is a provable and allowable claim against the bankrupt's estate together with the claims of all other general creditors.

c. It is invalid because the loan by Marco constituted an act of bankruptcy.

d. It is worthless because Marco is personally liable for the debts of Digits since he owns all of its stock.

The correct answer is (b). *(CPA 1176 L-19)*

REQUIRED: The status of a loan made to a bankrupt corporation by a controlling shareholder.

DISCUSSION: Although Marco is a controlling shareholder of Digits, and would qualify as an insider for purposes of the trustee's power to avoid preferences, Marco's status as a creditor is not otherwise impaired. Marco, however, is not a secured creditor and does not belong to a class of claimants entitled to a priority. Marco is a general unsecured creditor entitled to share with the other members of the class on a pro rata basis after the priority creditors have been paid in full.

Answer (a) is incorrect because although the loan is a provable and allowable claim, it has no priority. Claims of insiders are never given priority. Answer (c) is incorrect because under the Bankruptcy Reform Act of 1978, acts of bankruptcy no longer exist. Answer (d) is incorrect because even a sole shareholder of a corporation is entitled to the protection from personal liability that the corporate form affords.

62. In the course of your audit of Baxter Corporation, you discover a claim against Wills, Inc., which is in bankruptcy. The approximate amount of recovery on this claim depends upon the validity of other claims against Wills. Which of the following statements is valid concerning the other claims against Wills?

a. The claims of secured creditors may be disregarded.

b. Priorities are of no importance since equity rules apply.

c. Judgments obtained as of the date of bankruptcy are legitimate claims against the bankrupt's estate (property).

d. Anticipatory breaches of contract can be disregarded in assessing your client's position.

The correct answer is (c). *(CPA 576 L-41)*

REQUIRED: The correct statement concerning other claims against the bankrupt which will affect Baxter's recovery.

DISCUSSION: Generally, judgments entered before the filing of the petition in bankruptcy are provable and allowable even over objection. Judgments are merely one form of allowable claims, and there is no requirement that a judgment be obtained for a claim to be valid.

Answer (a) is incorrect because secured creditors have rights in specific property of the debtor which have priority over the claims of any other creditors. Answer (b) is incorrect because although bankruptcy courts are essentially courts of equity, they must observe the hierarchy of priorities established by statute. Answer (d) is incorrect because an anticipatory breach of contract creates a right of action for damages, and may increase the amount of claims competing with Baxter's.

63. Finn filed a voluntary petition in bankruptcy. She provided a list of creditors and debts to the courts as required. However, Sawyer was unintentionally left out of the list of creditors and debts. The creditors held their first meeting on March 5. It is now July 30 and Sawyer has just learned of the bankruptcy of Finn. She wants to share in the distribution from the estate.

a. It is too late to file a claim in bankruptcy.

b. Sawyer is not entitled to share in the estate assets because (s)he was not listed by Finn.

c. Sawyer's claim will be given priority due to the mistake.

d. Sawyer can file a proof of claim but it must be allowed by the court.

The correct answer is (d). *(Publisher)*

REQUIRED: The correct statement regarding a creditor who learns of the debtor's bankruptcy after being left out of the list of creditors.

DISCUSSION: To share in the distribution of the bankrupt's estate, a creditor must file a proof of claim with the court within 6 months after the first creditors' meeting. The proof of claim is simply a statement signed by the creditor explaining the nature and source of the claim and the date it is due. All claims not objected to are deemed allowed. If objected to, a claim may be allowed after a hearing to determine its validity.

Answer (a) is incorrect because 6 months have not passed since the first creditors' meeting and a claim can still be filed. Answer (b) is incorrect because Sawyer is entitled to share in the estate since (s)he can still file a proof of claim. Answer (c) is incorrect because no priority is allowed a creditor omitted from the list of creditors. However, if Sawyer had not learned of the bankruptcy, Finn would not be discharged as to that debt.

64. The partnership of Jones, Smith, and Lopez was bankrupt. Jones was also in bankruptcy but Smith and Lopez were not. The assets of the partnership are insufficient to pay all the partnership's creditors.

a. If Smith's and Lopez's assets are insufficient to satisfy the partnership's creditors, Jones's assets will be shared by the partnership's creditors and his personal creditors.

b. Jones's assets will be used to satisfy his personal creditors before partnership creditors.

c. The trustee must go after Jones's assets before those of Smith and Lopez because they might be distributed to Jones's personal creditors.

d. Smith and Lopez are liable to Jones's personal creditors.

The correct answer is (a). *(Publisher)*

REQUIRED: Priorities between personal and partnership creditors when both the partnership and a partner are in bankruptcy.

DISCUSSION: The partnership creditors have first right to the partnership assets, and a trustee of the bankrupt partnership then seeks recovery from the solvent general partners. To the extent that the solvent general partners do not have sufficient assets to satisfy the partnership creditors, the partnership's trustee will share in the bankrupt partner's estate as a general unsecured creditor. This is a change made by the Bankruptcy Reform Act of 1978.

Answer (b) is incorrect because it is a statement of the prior law. The new bankruptcy law allows the partnership creditors to share with the personal creditors of a bankrupt partner. Answer (c) is incorrect because the trustee must first seek recovery of the deficiency from the solvent general partners. Answer (d) is incorrect because Smith and Lopez are liable to the partnership creditors, but not to Jones's personal creditors.

65. Southern, Inc. filed a voluntary petition in bankruptcy on January 1, 1990. Which of the following payments is not a preferential transfer that may be avoided by the trustee?

a. A payment made on December 30, 1989 to the local electric company for monthly service through December 20, 1989.

b. A payment made on December 20, 1989 to the local box dealer for boxes received on July 1, 1989.

c. A payment made on December 20, 1989 to the local garage for repairs made to Southern's equipment on September 21, 1989.

d. A payment made on December 30, 1989 for repairs made to Southern's equipment on October 31, 1989.

The correct answer is (a). *(Publisher)*

REQUIRED: The statement that does not describe a preferential transfer.

DISCUSSION: The trustee may not avoid a transfer made in satisfaction of a debtor's obligation if 1) the debt was incurred in the ordinary course of business of the creditor and the debtor, 2) the payment was made within 45 days of the date the debt was incurred, and 3) the payment was made pursuant to ordinary terms.

Answers (b), (c), and (d) are incorrect because the payments were not made within 45 days of the date the debts were incurred.

26.4 Discharge of the Debtor

66. Which of the following provable debts is not discharged by bankruptcy?

a. Hospital bills.

b. Wages earned more than 3 months prior to commencement of bankruptcy proceedings.

c. Liability for breach of a fiduciary duty resulting from a fraud committed by the debtor-fiduciary.

d. Rent payments due which have accrued within 3 months of the filing of the petition in bankruptcy.

The correct answer is (c). *(CPA 1176 L-18)*

REQUIRED: The provable debt not discharged by bankruptcy.

DISCUSSION: Generally, the debts of a qualified debtor are dischargeable in bankruptcy. Certain debts are excepted due to public policy. One such policy is that a fiduciary should not be able to escape the consequences of abusing his/her position. Liability for fraud committed by a fiduciary, therefore, is not dischargeable in bankruptcy.

Answers (a), (b), and (d) are incorrect because each is a debt which may be discharged by bankruptcy.

67. Barkam is starting a new business, Barkam Enterprises, which will be a sole proprietorship selling retail novelties. Barkam recently received a discharge in bankruptcy, but certain proved claims were unpaid for lack of funds. Which of the following would be a claim against Barkam?

a. The unpaid amounts owed to secured creditors who received less than the full amount after resorting to their security interests.

b. The unpaid amounts owed to trade suppliers for goods purchased and sold by Barkam in the ordinary course of his prior business.

c. A personal loan by his father made in an attempt to stave off bankruptcy.

d. The unpaid amount of taxes due to the United States that became due and owing within three years preceding bankruptcy.

The correct answer is (d). *(CPA 579 L-16)*

REQUIRED: The claim that would not have been discharged in bankruptcy.

DISCUSSION: A discharge terminates the dischargeable debts of the debtor as to those claims that have been allowed. It avoids existing judgments and serves as an injunction against further proceedings on the discharged obligations. Its purpose is to permit an honest debtor to make a fresh financial start.

However, not all debts of an honest debtor are dischargeable in bankruptcy. Claims for most U.S. taxes that became due within three years of bankruptcy are not dischargeable in bankruptcy. Other exceptions include debts incurred through false representations; unscheduled debts (those not listing the creditor); or debts for fraud, alimony and child support, intentional torts, or educational loans. The 1984 amendments prohibit discharge of debts incurred just prior to bankruptcy for luxury items of $500 or more or use of consumer credit to obtain cash advances of more than $1,000 or judgments for operating a motor vehicle while intoxicated.

Answers (a), (b), and (c) are incorrect because each is a debt dischargeable in bankruptcy.

68. In general, which of the following debts will be discharged under the voluntary liquidation provisions of the Bankruptcy Code?

a. Debts incurred after the order for relief but before the debtor receives a discharge in bankruptcy.

b. Income taxes due as the result of filing a fraudulent return 7 years prior to the filing of the bankruptcy petition.

c. A debt arising before the filing of the bankruptcy petition caused by the debtor's negligence.

d. Alimony payments owed to the debtor's spouse under a separation agreement entered into prior to the filing of the bankruptcy petition.

The correct answer is (c). *(CPA 588 L-33)*

REQUIRED: The debts that will be discharged under the voluntary liquidation provisions.

DISCUSSION: The Bankruptcy Code lists certain bases for denial of a discharge in a voluntary liquidation proceeding. Certain acts or circumstances of the debtor or the nature of particular debts may provide grounds for denial. For a discharge to be denied, a trustee or creditor must object to the discharge, and one of the necessary bases must exist. Examples of debts that will be statutorily denied a discharge include penalties imposed by government entities, unpaid taxes, and unpaid child support. A debt arising prior to filing that was the result of mere negligence by the debtor is dischargeable. Unless some other reason for objecting exists, it will be discharged.

Answer (a) is incorrect because only debts incurred prior to the order for relief will be discharged. Answer (b) is incorrect because ordinarily, the only tax debts that will not be discharged are income taxes due from the filing of a tax return within the last 3 years. However, any debt that was incurred by fraudulent means will not be discharged regardless of the time the return was filed. Answer (d) is incorrect because the Code specifically denies of a discharge for any unpaid alimony or child support.

Questions 69 through 71 are based on the following: On May 5, Bold obtained a $90,000 judgment in a malpractice action against Aker, a physician. On June 2, Aker obtained a $75,000 loan from Tint Finance Co. by knowingly making certain false representations to Tint. On July 7, Aker filed a voluntary petition in bankruptcy under the liquidation provisions of the Bankruptcy Code. Both Bold and Tint filed claims in Aker's bankruptcy proceeding. Assets in Aker's bankruptcy estate are exempt.

69. Bold's claim will

a. Be excepted from Aker's discharge in bankruptcy.

b. Cause Aker to be denied a discharge in bankruptcy.

c. Be set aside as a preference.

d. Be discharged in Aker's bankruptcy proceeding.

The correct answer is (d). *(CPA 1188 L-25)*

REQUIRED: The treatment of a malpractice claim in a bankruptcy proceeding.

DISCUSSION: The objective of a bankruptcy proceeding is to obtain a discharge, that is, to relieve the debtor of liability on certain debts. The Code states that debts caused by the negligence of the debtor will be dischargeable. Thus, Bold's claim will be discharged. However, if the debt were based on the willful or malicious misconduct of Aker, it would not be dischargeable.

Answer (a) is incorrect because Bold's claim will be discharged. Answer (b) is incorrect because negligence is not a tortious act that restricts the discharge of all debts. Fraud is an example of such an act. Answer (c) is incorrect because a preferential transfer requires a transfer of the debtor's property, for the benefit of the creditor, for an antecedent debt, made while the debtor was insolvent, made within 90 days before the date the petition was filed, and that enables the creditor to receive more than in a liquidation case under Chapter 7. Bold's claim is not a preferential transfer.

70. Tint's claim will

a. Be excepted from Aker's discharge in bankruptcy.

b. Cause Aker to be denied a discharge in bankruptcy.

c. Be set aside as a preference.

d. Be discharged in Aker's bankruptcy proceeding.

The correct answer is (a). *(CPA 1188 L-26)*

REQUIRED: The treatment of a claim arising from the debtor's fraud.

DISCUSSION: The Bankruptcy Code specifies certain types of debts that will not be discharged. They include penalties imposed by governmental entities, unpaid taxes, unpaid alimony and child support, and liabilities arising from obtaining money or property by false pretenses, false representations, or actual fraud. Hence, Tint's claim is not dischargeable because it arose from a loan obtained fraudulently by the debtor.

Answer (b) is incorrect because Aker's intentional misrepresentation to Tint will have an effect only on the dischargeability of that debt and not on all debts. Answer (c) is incorrect because Tint's claim is not a preference as defined by the Code. Answer (d) is incorrect because Tint's claim will not be discharged.

71. For this item only, assume that on June 9, Aker transferred property she owned to her son. The property was collateral for Aker's obligation to Simon. Aker transferred the property with the intent to defraud Simon. Which of the following statements is correct?

a. Only Simon's debt will be excepted from Aker's discharge in bankruptcy.

b. Aker will be denied a discharge in bankruptcy.

c. The transfer will be set aside because it constitutes a preference.

d. Aker will receive a discharge in bankruptcy of all debts.

The correct answer is (b). *(CPA 1188 L-27)*

REQUIRED: The true statement about transfers of property with the intent to defraud.

DISCUSSION: Under the Bankruptcy Code, the court will deny a general discharge of a debtor's liabilities if, within 1 year of filing the petition for relief, the debtor transfers property with the intent to hinder, delay, or defraud any creditor. Because Aker transferred the property with the intent to defraud Simon within 1 year of filing the petition for relief, she will be denied a general discharge.

Answer (a) is incorrect because the fraudulent act will lead to a denial of a general discharge of the debtor's liabilities. Answer (c) is incorrect because one of the elements of a preferential transfer is the transfer of property to a creditor. Aker's son was not a creditor. Answer (d) is incorrect because Aker will be denied a discharge in bankruptcy of all debts.

72. With respect to a bankruptcy offense, which of the following statements is correct?

a. The offense can only occur during the bankruptcy proceedings.

b. The offense includes the action by an officer of a corporation, in contemplation of a corporate bankruptcy proceeding, of concealing any property of the corporation.

c. The offense can only be committed by the bankrupt.

d. The offense cannot result in fines or imprisonment.

The correct answer is (b). *(CPA 1177 L-29)*

REQUIRED: The correct statement regarding a bankruptcy offense.

DISCUSSION: If an officer of a debtor corporation (within 12 months preceding the filing of the petition) concealed or otherwise disposed of property with the intention of hindering or delaying creditors, then such acts would be a bankruptcy offense. Corporations (and partnerships) cannot obtain a general discharge in liquidation bankruptcy (they are simply liquidated).

Answer (a) is incorrect because a bankruptcy offense may occur prior to bankruptcy proceedings; e.g., fraudulent acts in contemplation of bankruptcy. Answer (c) is incorrect because the offense could be committed by an agent; e.g., an officer of a bankrupt corporation. Answer (d) is incorrect because bankruptcy crimes, e.g., perjury or fraud, may be punishable by fines and/or imprisonment.

73. A discharge in bankruptcy

a. Relieves the debtor from all provable debts.

b. Is not available if the debtor was previously discharged within 10 years prior to the present bankruptcy.

c. Cannot be revoked.

d. Is barred if the debtor commits a bankruptcy offense.

The correct answer is (d). *(CPA 1174 L-13)*

REQUIRED: The correct statement concerning a discharge in bankruptcy.

DISCUSSION: A debtor who fails to qualify as an "honest debtor" will not be permitted a general discharge in bankruptcy. The commission of a bankruptcy offense would be disqualifying. In general, a debtor who fails to act truthfully and in good faith will be guilty of a bankruptcy offense; e.g., concealing property, making false statements, or falsifying records.

Answer (a) is incorrect because some debts are not dischargeable; e.g., taxes. Answer (b) is incorrect because a discharge in bankruptcy is not available if the debtor was previously discharged within 6 years prior to the present bankruptcy. Answer (c) is incorrect because a discharge may be revoked within 1 year if it was obtained through fraud of the debtor.

74. Rolf, an individual, filed a voluntary petition in bankruptcy. A general discharge in bankruptcy will be denied if Rolf

a. Negligently made preferential transfers to certain creditors within 90 days of filing the petition.

b. Unjustifiably failed to preserve his books and records.

c. Filed a fraudulent federal income tax return 2 years prior to filing the petition.

d. Obtained a loan by using financial statements that he knew were false.

The correct answer is (b). *(CPA 1189 L-22)*

REQUIRED: The action that is grounds for denying a general discharge in bankruptcy.

DISCUSSION: In many cases, a debtor's primary purpose in entering bankruptcy is to obtain a discharge of debts. Some circumstances will cause a discharge of indebtedness to be denied. Discharge will be denied if the debtor conceals or destroys property with the intent to hinder, delay, or defraud a creditor, or fails to adequately explain the loss of assets. Similarly, the unjustifiable or fraudulent concealment or destruction of the debtor's financial records is a basis for denying discharge of indebtedness.

Answer (a) is incorrect because preferential transfers resulting from the debtor's negligence will only result in avoidance of the transfers. Answers (c) and (d) are incorrect because the debtor's fraudulent actions may result in denial of discharge of the specific debts, but will not affect the general discharge.

75. Eagle Corp. is a general creditor of Dodd. Dodd filed a petition in bankruptcy under the liquidation provisions of the Bankruptcy Code. Eagle wishes to have the bankruptcy court either deny Dodd a general discharge or not have its debt discharged. The discharge will be granted and it will include Eagle's debt even if

a. Dodd filed and received a previous discharge in bankruptcy under the liquidation provisions within 5 years of the filing of the present petition.

b. Eagle's debt is unscheduled.

c. Eagle was a secured creditor not fully satisfied from the proceeds obtained on disposition of the collateral.

d. Dodd unjustifiably failed to preserve the records from which Dodd's financial condition might be ascertained.

The correct answer is (c). *(CPA 1189 L-26)*

REQUIRED: The circumstance that will allow discharge of a general creditor's debt.

DISCUSSION: Chapter 7 contains the liquidation provisions of the Bankruptcy Code. The nature of the debt or debtor or the debtor's conduct may prevent discharge of all or specific debts. However, secured creditor status does not guarantee full satisfaction of a debt. If the secured claim is not fully satisfied by the proceeds resulting from the sale of collateral, the unsatisfied portion of the debt may still be discharged.

Answer (a) is incorrect because discharge will not be granted if an objection is made and the debtor was granted a discharge under Chapter 7 in a case commenced within 6 years of the petition in the current case. Answer (b) is incorrect because unscheduled debts are not discharged. Answer (d) is incorrect because the debtor's unjustifiable failure to preserve the debtor's financial records is reason to deny discharge of all indebtedness.

76. Cole has gone through bankruptcy and all of his nonexempt property has been distributed to creditors. Cole has applied for a discharge but it has been contested by some creditors. Grounds for denial of the discharge are that

a. Cole, now divorced, obtained a discharge in bankruptcy 5 years ago while still married.

b. Cole obtained a discharge under Chapter 13 (adjustment of debts) 2 years ago after 70% of the debts were paid as a result of Cole's best efforts.

c. Cole negligently issued a false financial statement 6 months before commencement of the bankruptcy proceedings.

d. Cole has been criminally convicted of drunk driving during the bankruptcy proceedings.

The correct answer is (a). *(Publisher)*

REQUIRED: The statement containing a ground for denial of a discharge in bankruptcy.

DISCUSSION: A person is entitled to a discharge in bankruptcy only once every 6 years. Until 6 years have passed, a discharge will be denied even if a person has gone through bankruptcy proceedings. Marital status at a given time has no effect on eligibility for discharge.

Answer (b) is incorrect because a discharge under a Chapter 13 proceeding is not a bar to subsequent discharge in bankruptcy if at least 70% of the debts were paid through the debtor's best efforts. Answer (c) is incorrect because the issuance of a false financial statement is not a basis for denial of a general discharge; however, it would be grounds for denial of discharge of a debt induced by the false financial statement. Answer (d) is incorrect because conviction for drunk driving has no relevance to the financial affairs of a debtor or to the ability to obtain a discharge in bankruptcy (but debts for damages caused by drunk driving would not be discharged).

77. Which of the following will not be discharged in a bankruptcy proceeding?

a. Claims resulting out of an extension of credit based upon false representations.

b. Claims of secured creditors that remain unsatisfied after their receipt of the proceeds from the disposition of the collateral.

c. Claims for unintentional torts that resulted in bodily injury to the claimant.

d. Claims arising out of the breach of a contract by the debtor.

The correct answer is (a). *(CPA 1185 L-30)*

REQUIRED: The claims that are not dischargeable.

DISCUSSION: A legal liability arising from the debtor's obtaining money, property, services, or credit by false pretenses, false representations, or actual fraud is not dischargeable. However, the existence of such a liability does not prevent a debtor from receiving a discharge of other obligations.

Answer (b) is incorrect because no general exception to discharge is provided for such claims. Answer (c) is incorrect because claims for willful and malicious torts or for injury caused by driving while intoxicated are not dischargeable, but claims based on negligence are subject to discharge. Answer (d) is incorrect because no general exception to discharge is allowed for breach of contract.

78. A discharge in bankruptcy

a. May not be revoked.

b. May be revoked within one year.

c. May be objected to by a creditor, but the creditor will be liable for costs and attorney's fees if the challenge fails.

d. May be granted although the debtor waives the discharge hearing.

The correct answer is (b). *(Publisher)*

REQUIRED: The true statement about a discharge in bankruptcy.

DISCUSSION: Fraud or dishonesty committed by the debtor during the bankruptcy proceedings is the basis for revocation of discharge by the Bankruptcy Court. Revocation may occur after a request by either the trustee or a creditor, notice, and a hearing. The time limit is 1 year.

Answer (a) is incorrect because the discharge may be revoked on account of debtor misconduct. Answer (c) is incorrect because the creditor will be liable for fees and costs only if the objection was not substantially justified. Answer (d) is incorrect because a discharge may not be granted unless the debtor personally attends a hearing at which (s)he receives the discharge and is informed of the consequences of any agreement to pay a discharged debt.

79. Devlin made innocent misrepresentations concerning the sale of goods to Van Ness. Shortly thereafter Devlin became a bankrupt. Van Ness was permitted to file a claim for $5,000 for the loss sustained, but actually received only a 20% dividend from the bankrupt's estate. Within 180 days after the petition was filed, but after his discharge, Devlin inherited some property. Van Ness desires to collect the remaining $4,000. Which of the following is correct?

a. The misrepresentation relating to the sale of the merchandise precludes discharge of Van Ness's $4,000 unpaid claim.

b. Van Ness is entitled to a priority as a result of the misrepresentations.

c. Van Ness is entitled to recover a proportionate share of the inheritance up to the $4,000 deficiency.

d. Van Ness has irrevocably lost his right to the $4,000 unpaid claim as a result of Devlin's discharge in bankruptcy.

The correct answer is (c). *(CPA 1177 L-23)*

REQUIRED: The correct statement concerning liability of the bankrupt after discharge.

DISCUSSION: A debtor may receive a discharge of most debts (but not those connected with fraud) as a result of the bankruptcy proceeding. A debt connected with a mere innocent misrepresentation would be dischargeable in bankruptcy. However, property inherited within 180 days after the commencement of the case is part of the bankrupt's estate for purposes of distribution. As an unsecured general creditor, Van Ness would be permitted to share proportionately in the additional property up to the amount of his/her claim.

Answer (a) is incorrect because liability for mere innocent misrepresentation is a debt that may be discharged in bankruptcy. Answer (b) is incorrect because acts by the debtor, whether good or bad, never entitle a creditor to a priority. Answer (d) is incorrect because Van Ness is entitled to share in property inherited within 180 days after commencement of the case whether discharge has occurred or not.

80. Bingham received a discharge in bankruptcy. Several months later, a creditor of a debt that was discharged in the bankruptcy met Bingham. The creditor induced Bingham to agree to pay the old debt. However, the next day Bingham rescinded the agreement. The creditor has filed suit to collect the debt.

a. The agreement to pay is not valid.

b. Bingham does not have to respond to the law suit due to the discharge in bankruptcy.

c. Bingham is bound by her agreement to pay the old debt.

d. After 1 year, a debt discharged in bankruptcy can be reaffirmed.

The correct answer is (a). *(Publisher)*

REQUIRED: The correct statement concerning reaffirmation of a discharged debt.

DISCUSSION: A reaffirmation is an agreement to pay a debt discharged in bankruptcy. Under prior law, creditors frequently attempted to convince discharged debtors to reaffirm their debts. The Bankruptcy Reform Act of 1978 provides that reaffirmation agreements must be entered into before the discharge, must be approved by the court, and are rescindable for 30 days. These requirements prevent creditors from harassing debtors after the discharge.

Answer (b) is incorrect because the discharge in bankruptcy must be pleaded as a defense to the debt in the local state court. Otherwise, the court will grant a judgment against Bingham. Answer (c) is incorrect because Bingham is not bound by her reaffirmation under current federal bankruptcy law. Answer (d) is incorrect because the restrictions on reaffirmation do not end after 1 year.

26.5 Business Reorganizations and Adjustment Plans

81. Lux Corp. has been suffering large losses for the past 2 years. Because of its inability to meet current obligations, Lux has filed a petition for reorganization under Chapter 11 of the Bankruptcy Code. The reorganization provisions under the Bankruptcy Code

a. Require that the court appoint a trustee in all cases.

b. Permit Lux to remain in possession of its assets.

c. Apply only to involuntary bankruptcy.

d. Will apply to Lux only if Lux is required to register pursuant to the federal securities laws.

The correct answer is (b). *(CPA 1185 L-26)*

REQUIRED: The consequence of a bankruptcy reorganization.

DISCUSSION: The usual objective of a reorganization is to permit the debtor to remain in business. The debtor and the creditors' committee negotiate a plan whereby the creditors' claims are at least partly satisfied and the business is restructured. In most cases, the debtor is permitted to continue operating the business, but a trustee may be appointed if mismanagement has been proven or if the best interests of the estate will thereby be served. A debtor may thus be able to retain its assets so as to operate its business.

Answer (a) is incorrect because the debtor usually remains in possession, but a party in interest may request the court to appoint a trustee for cause (dishonesty or incompetence). Answer (c) is incorrect because a reorganization may be voluntarily sought. Answer (d) is incorrect because a corporation need not be subject to the federal securities laws to qualify under Chapter 11. Most parties (individuals, partnerships, and corporations) qualifying under Chapter 7 (liquidation) may file under Chapter 11. Railroads are an exception. They qualify under Chapter 11 but not Chapter 7.

82. The Mello Corporation was adjudicated a bankrupt. Shortly thereafter, the corporation filed a petition for reorganization by Chapter 11 of the Bankruptcy Reform Act of 1978. Objection is made to the petition on the ground that it should have been filed prior to adjudication. Which of the following is correct?

a. The objection is valid.

b. Only corporations listed on one of the national securities exchanges are eligible for such relief.

c. The purpose of such a reorganization is to permit a corporation to carry on its business instead of going through a normal bankruptcy proceeding, thereby avoiding the economic waste and losses entailed in bankruptcy.

d. Such a proceeding (a reorganization) normally results in a scaling down of the rights of the common and preferred shareholders but cannot legally change the bondholders' position.

The correct answer is (c). *(CPA 1177 L-30)*

REQUIRED: The correct statement regarding a petition for reorganization.

DISCUSSION: A voluntary or involuntary petition for reorganization is an alternative to liquidation under a Chapter 7 straight bankruptcy proceeding. Reorganization is appropriate when a business has a reasonable chance to operate profitably under a plan of reorganization where the corporation remains in business and its debts are restructured. The plan may also require changes in management. A debtor is no longer "adjudicated bankrupt;" rather, an "order for relief" is entered.

Answer (a) is incorrect because the corporation may convert the case to a reorganization even after an order for relief has been granted. Answer (b) is incorrect because with minor exceptions, any person who may file for straight bankruptcy under Chapter 7 may also file for reorganization under Chapter 11. Answer (d) is incorrect because a reorganization may affect the rights of all classes of claimants; however, either all classes of claimants must approve the plan, or it must meet the judicial test of being "fair, equitable, and feasible," i.e., performable.

83. The creditors play a vital role in the reorganization of a debtor under Chapter 11. Which of the following is true?

a. The creditors' committee selects the trustee.

b. Only one creditors' committee may be appointed by the court.

c. A committee consisting of the unsecured creditors with the largest claims is appointed.

d. Stockholders cannot be represented on a committee.

The correct answer is (c). *(Publisher)*

REQUIRED: The true statement about creditors' committees in a reorganization.

DISCUSSION: A committee of creditors must be appointed as soon as practicable after entry of the order for relief. It usually includes the seven unsecured creditors with the largest claims who are willing to take part. The committee is a party in interest and represents the creditors during administration of the case.

Answer (a) is incorrect because only the court may appoint a trustee in a reorganization case. Answers (b) and (d) are incorrect because additional committees of creditors and others may be named to represent specified interests, for example, those of equity security holders.

84. A plan of reorganization under Chapter 11

a. May be filed by any party in interest for 120 days after entry of the order for relief.

b. Must be filed by the trustee and approved by the creditors within 180 days after entry of the order for relief.

c. Must treat all classes of claims and ownership interests equally.

d. Must treat all claims or interests in the same class equally.

The correct answer is (d). *(Publisher)*

REQUIRED: The true statement about a plan of reorganization.

DISCUSSION: The plan must designate classes of creditors' claims and owners' interests; state the treatment to be given each class; indicate which classes will or will not be impaired; allow for equal treatment of the members within a class unless they agree otherwise; and provide for an adequate method of payment. If the debtor is a corporation, the plan must also protect voting rights, state that no nonvoting stock will be issued, and require that selection of officers and directors be effected in a manner to protect the parties in interest.

Answers (a) and (b) are incorrect because only the debtor may file a plan within 120 days after entry of the order for relief. If the debtor fails to file or if the creditors do not approve of the plan within 180 days of the entry of the order for relief, any party in interest (including the trustee) may file a plan. Answer (c) is incorrect because the plan must be fair and equitable but all classes need not be treated the same. However, no party may receive less than the amount that would have been distributed in a liquidation.

85. A plan of reorganization formulated under Chapter 11 must be submitted to the creditors for acceptance and to the court for confirmation. Which of the following is true?

a. The effect of confirmation is to make the plan binding on all parties and to grant the debtor a discharge from claims not protected by the plan.

b. A plan cannot be confirmed if any impaired class of claims or interests rejects it.

c. If no class of claims or interests accepts a plan, the court may nevertheless confirm it if the plan is in the best interests of the creditors.

d. A class that is not impaired is presumed to accept, but more than half of the claims in a class by amount must accept if the class is impaired.

The correct answer is (a). *(Publisher)*

REQUIRED: The true statement about acceptance and confirmation of a plan.

DISCUSSION: Confirmation is the court's approval of the plan after notice and a hearing. Confirmation makes the plan binding on the creditors, equity security holders, and debtor, whether or not they accepted the plan. It also operates as a discharge of unprotected debts, except for those claims previously denied discharge in a Chapter 7 case, and vests the estate property in the debtor. Confirmation is contingent upon the plan's feasibility, the good faith in which it was proposed, and the provision for cash payment of certain allowed claims, such as administration expenses.

Answer (b) is incorrect because an impaired class may be required to accept a plan over its objection if the court finds that the plan is "fair and equitable," for instance, if the unsecured creditors either receive property equaling the full value of their claims or they receive less but no junior claim or interest receives anything. Answer (c) is incorrect because at least one class of claims (not ownership interests) must accept. Answer (d) is incorrect because a class of claims accepts if approval is given by more than half the allowed claims, provided they represent at least two-thirds of the claims by amount. A class of interests (shareholders) accepts if approval is given by two-thirds in amount of the allowed interests.

86. Which of the following is not a permissible basis for voiding or modifying a collective bargaining agreement made by a corporation in a Chapter 11 reorganization?

a. The proposal satisfies statutory requirements before the confirmation hearing.

b. The employees' authorized bargaining representative, without good cause, refuses to accept a proposal.

c. The employees' authorized bargaining representative refuses to accept a proposal in good faith.

d. The equities balance in favor of rejecting the collective bargaining agreement.

The correct answer is (c). *(Publisher)*

REQUIRED: The false statement about rejection of a collective bargaining agreement under Chapter 11.

DISCUSSION: According to the 1984 amendments to the Chapter 11 reorganization provisions, the debtor or trustee who is seeking to modify or void a collective bargaining agreement must submit a proposal to the union representative that provides details about the "necessary" modifications and gives assurances that all parties are "fairly treated." There must be good faith negotiations between the union representative and debtor in possession or trustee. The collective bargaining agreement can be modified or voided with court approval if the court finds that the proposal satisfied statutory requirements before the hearing, the union's representative refused to accept the proposal without good cause, and the equities are balanced in favoring rejection of the collective bargaining agreement.

Answers (a), (b), and (d) are incorrect because they are conditions for modifying or voiding a collective bargaining agreement under Chapter 11.

87. A Chapter 13 discharge upon completion of a composition plan bars another discharge for

a. 10 years if the debtor made less than 70% of the payments.

b. 10 years if the debtor made at least 70% of the payments.

c. 6 years if the debtor made at least 70% of the payments.

d. 6 years if the debtor made less than 70% of the payments.

The correct answer is (d). *(Publisher)*

REQUIRED: The correct statement about a discharge of a composition plan under Chapter 13.

DISCUSSION: The Chapter 13 discharge of a composition plan bars another discharge for 6 years. But another discharge can occur within 6 years if 70% of the payments have been made by the debtor under the plan, the plan was proposed in good faith, and the plan was the best effort of the debtor.

Answers (a) and (b) are incorrect because a discharge bars another discharge for 6 years. Answer (c) is incorrect because if 70% of the payments under the plan have been made, the 6-year rule will not be applicable.

88. Englebert is a professor of business at a university. He expected a large raise this year and made a lot of expenditures, including a trip around the world, on credit. However, university funding has been reduced and the raise did not go through. Englebert cannot pay his debts as they become due. Englebert

a. Can request an adjustment of debts under Chapter 13 of the Bankruptcy Reform Act of 1978.

b. Cannot request a reorganization under Chapter 11 of the Bankruptcy Reform Act of 1978.

c. Can be required to go through a bankruptcy liquidation.

d. Can be required by creditors to go through an adjustment of debts under Chapter 13 of the Bankruptcy Reform Act of 1978.

The correct answer is (a). *(Publisher)*

REQUIRED: The correct statement concerning an individual who cannot pay his/her debts.

DISCUSSION: Chapter 13 of the Bankruptcy Reform Act of 1978 provides a procedure for an individual with regular income to submit a plan for the payment of a portion of his/her debts while retaining a sufficient amount of income to live and support his/her family. The petitioner must be an individual who owes unsecured debts of less than $100,000 and secured debts of less than $350,000. The court grants a discharge of most remaining debts after the plan has been carried out.

Answer (b) is incorrect because any person who may go through a liquidation bankruptcy (except stockbrokers and commodity brokers) may file for a reorganization under Chapter 11. Answer (c) is incorrect because an individual may request relief under Chapter 11 or Chapter 13 to avoid a bankruptcy liquidation if the requirements of those sections are met. Answer (d) is incorrect because Chapter 13 is a voluntary provision and a creditor of the debtor cannot file an involuntary petition under Chapter 13.

89. Under Chapter 13 of the Bankruptcy Code, an individual debtor or sole proprietor may propose a composition plan to repay his/her debts. Under this plan,

a. The debtor must repay all claims by creditors within 5 years.

b. The debtor is not entitled to injunctive relief against his/her creditors while the plan is being carried out.

c. The debtor pays creditors less than 100% of their claims.

d. No trustee may be appointed.

The correct answer is (c). *(Publisher)*

REQUIRED: The true statement about a composition plan under Chapter 13.

DISCUSSION: A composition plan may be proposed by a debtor under Chapter 13 of the Bankruptcy Code. Under a composition plan, a debtor pays his/her creditors less than 100% of their claims on a pro rata basis for each class of claims. The repayment time for a Chapter 13 plan is 3 years unless the court permits a 5-year payout period. The debtor must give control of future income to a trustee who makes payments on the debtor's claims. Upon approval of the plan, the debtor is granted injunctive relief against creditors while the plan is being carried out, provided the unsecured creditors will receive amounts at least equal to those paid in straight liquidation. Approval of creditors is not required.

Answer (a) is incorrect because extension beyond the 3-year limit is granted only for cause. Answer (b) is incorrect because while a composition plan is being carried out, a debtor is entitled to injunctive relief against his/her creditors. Answer (d) is incorrect because a trustee must be appointed in all Chapter 13 cases.

90. Under Chapter 13, unsecured creditors

a. Vote on Chapter 13 plans.

b. Receive less than they would receive in a Chapter 7 liquidation.

c. Receive at least the amounts they would receive in a Chapter 7 liquidation.

d. Rights are never unilaterally modified.

The correct answer is (c). *(Publisher)*

REQUIRED: The correct statement concerning unsecured creditors under Chapter 13.

DISCUSSION: A Chapter 13 plan is confirmed if, among other conditions, unsecured creditors would receive amounts equivalent to those that would be received under Chapter 7. Thus, the rights of unsecured creditors may unilaterally be modified, as long as all claims in a class receive the same treatment.

Answer (a) is incorrect because unsecured creditors do not vote on Chapter 13 plans. Answer (b) is incorrect because unsecured creditors must receive at least the same amounts as in a Chapter 7 liquidation. Answer (d) is incorrect because a Chapter 13 plan may modify an unsecured creditor's rights, as long as all unsecured creditor's rights are modified.

91. Bruce Bennet was a salaried employee of Selma Company earning $250 per week. He had accumulated unsecured debts of $15,000 to 15 creditors and had assets of $1,000. Although Bennet's wife was well to do and had no debts, Bennet is not paying his debts as they become due. In this situation,

a. Bennet may not be forced into involuntary bankruptcy if his wife has sufficient assets to pay his debts.

b. Bennet as a salaried employee may not be forced into involuntary bankruptcy.

c. A creditor of Bennet with an unsecured claim of $8,000 may force Bennet into involuntary bankruptcy by filing a petition showing his allowable claim.

d. Three of Bennet's creditors having aggregate allowable, unsecured claims of $5,100 may not force Bennet into involuntary bankruptcy under Chapter 7.

The correct answer is (d). *(CPA 574 L-32)*

REQUIRED: The correct statement concerning an insolvent individual with a regular income.

DISCUSSION: Bennet meets all the requirements to be forced into involuntary bankruptcy. However, an individual with regular income and unsecured debts of less than $100,000 and secured debts of less than $350,000 can avoid involuntary bankruptcy by filing for a consumer debt adjustment under Chapter 13. Under Chapter 13, the individual could obtain confirmation of a plan for the repayment of at least part of his/her indebtedness and be free from the harassment of creditors. Bennet meets the requirements of Chapter 13 because he has a regular income and has a total unsecured indebtedness of less than $100,000 and secured debts of less than $350,000. He can therefore petition the court to convert a Chapter 7 proceeding brought by the three creditors to a Chapter 13 proceeding and thus avoid liquidation.

Answer (a) is incorrect because the separate assets belonging to a spouse are not part of the debtor's estate and are irrelevant in determining whether an individual may be forced into involuntary bankruptcy. Answer (b) is incorrect because merely being a salaried employee does not shield that person from involuntary bankruptcy if his/her debts are too great or his/her income is not considered regular. Answer (c) is incorrect because when a debtor has 12 or more creditors, an involuntary petition joined in by at least three of the creditors whose aggregate claims are $5,000 or more may result in an involuntary bankruptcy under Chapter 7.

92. An individual debtor or sole proprietorship may file for an adjustment of debts under Chapter 13 of the Bankruptcy Code. Under this procedure,

a. No trustee need be appointed.

b. The payment period may not exceed 5 years.

c. All debts are discharged upon successful completion of the plan.

d. A plan may not be confirmed without the consent of the creditors.

The correct answer is (b). *(Publisher)*

REQUIRED: The true statement about a consumer debt adjustment under Chapter 13.

DISCUSSION: The plan is filed by the debtor and may not provide for payments extending over more than 3 years unless the court approves. In that event, the duration of the plan cannot exceed 5 years. The plan must provide for full payment of priority claims unless a claimant agrees otherwise, for submission to the trustee of future income necessary to carry out the plan, and for equal treatment of claimants in a class. The rights of creditors may unilaterally be modified, except for a claim secured by the debtor's principal residence. Also, the plan must be feasible, lawful, offered in good faith, and allow for unsecured creditors to receive as of the effective date of the plan at least as much as they would have received in a liquidation proceeding under Chapter 7.

Answer (a) is incorrect because a trustee must be appointed in all Chapter 13 cases. Answer (c) is incorrect because long-term debts extending beyond the duration of the plan and debts for alimony, maintenance, and support are not discharged. Answer (d) is incorrect because unsecured creditors do not vote on such plans, and a secured creditor need not consent if (s)he receives the collateral or if (s)he retains the security interest and will receive the allowed amount of the claim.

CHAPTER TWENTY-SEVEN
ANTITRUST

27.1 Basic Concepts and Policies

1. Which of the following is the best statement concerning the policy in the United States behind legislation and enforcement of antitrust laws?

a. The legal theory is that large concentration of economic power or market dominance is illegal.

b. The economic theory is that large size alone without abusing market power is not illegal.

c. The economic theory is that competition is best protected by letting the market take care of itself without government interference.

d. Both the economic theory and the legal theory are applied, but not consistently.

The correct answer is (d). *(Publisher)*

REQUIRED: The best statement concerning the policy in the U.S. with respect to antitrust.

DISCUSSION: There are two major theories with respect to antitrust and anticompetitive behavior. The legal theory is that large size alone is not illegal. The illegality occurs when there is an abuse of market power. The economic theory is that large concentration of economic power or market dominance is bad and therefore should be illegal. Both of these theories have been applied, but not consistently. As this makes it hard to interpret the laws and court cases, there are swings in the enforcement of the antitrust laws.

Answer (a) is incorrect because it describes the economic theory. Answer (b) is incorrect because it describes the legal theory. Answer (c) is incorrect because it describes the doctrine of laissez-faire which ended as antitrust laws were enacted beginning in the late 1800s.

2. The intent of antitrust laws is to

a. Establish a range of allowable profit rates for firms in oligopolistic industries.

b. Prohibit firms from engaging in joint ventures with foreign firms.

c. Require firms with high earnings to relinquish any exclusive patent rights which they own.

d. Prohibit agreements that limit individual firm output.

The correct answer is (d). *(CMA 1287 1-17)*

REQUIRED: The intent of antitrust laws.

DISCUSSION: Antitrust laws are designed to promote more efficient allocation of resources, greater choice for consumers, greater business opportunities, fairness in economic behavior, and avoidance of concentrated political power resulting from economic power. Competition results in greater output and lower prices than other market structures.

Answer (a) is incorrect because profits and prices are not set by antitrust laws other than to the extent that price discrimination is prohibited. Answer (b) is incorrect because firms may enter into joint ventures with foreign firms. Answer (c) is incorrect because patents are available to all inventors, regardless of size.

3. Which of the following is a correct statement regarding enforcement of the antitrust laws?

a. Any person whose business or property is injured as a direct result of violation of antitrust laws may sue.

b. A consumer may sue for a violation of the antitrust laws regardless of whether (s)he purchased directly from the person violating the antitrust laws.

c. The U.S. Justice Department may enforce all federal antitrust laws except the Federal Trade Commission Act.

d. The Federal Trade Commission may only enforce the Federal Trade Commission Act.

The correct answer is (a). *(Publisher)*

REQUIRED: The correct statement concerning who enforces the antitrust laws.

DISCUSSION: The U.S. government and private parties can both enforce the antitrust laws by maintaining actions against defendants for violations. The Justice Department and the Federal Trade Commission are the primary government enforcers. Any private person (including businesses, corporations, etc.) whose business or property is injured as a direct result of a violation of antitrust laws may sue the violator. Such private person can also recover treble damages under most statutes.

Answer (b) is incorrect because the consumer may sue for a violation of the antitrust laws only if (s)he purchased a product or service directly from the person who violated the antitrust laws. There must be a direct connection. Answer (c) is incorrect because the U.S. Justice Department may enforce all the antitrust laws. Answer (d) is incorrect because the Federal Trade Commission may enforce all antitrust laws except the Sherman Act.

4. Wanton Corporation, its president, and several other officers of the corporation have been found guilty of conspiring with its major competitor to fix prices. Which of the following sanctions would not be applicable under federal antitrust laws?

a. Suspension of corporate right to engage in interstate commerce for not more than one year.

b. Treble damages.

c. Seizure of Wanton's property illegally shipped in interstate commerce.

d. Fines against Wanton and fines and imprisonment of its president and officers.

The correct answer is (a). *(CPA 1179 L-21)*

REQUIRED: The sanction not applicable under federal antitrust laws for price fixing.

DISCUSSION: The sanctions available to the Justice Department and individuals for violation of antitrust laws do not include suspension of a corporation's right to engage in interstate commerce. Presumably, Congress could enact such legislation under its authority to regulate interstate commerce, but it has not done so.

Answers (b), (c), and (d) are incorrect because each is a current sanction applicable under federal antitrust laws for price fixing. A corporate defendant is subject to a maximum fine of $1 million or at the court's discretion twice the illegal profits gained for each offense. Any other defendant is subject to a maximum fine of $100,000, imprisonment for as much as 3 years, or both, for each offense, and injunctions against further wrongful acts.

5. In order for the federal antitrust laws to apply, the illegal activity must affect goods moving in interstate commerce or

a. Be committed by a business engaged in interstate commerce.

b. Affect a business engaged in interstate commerce.

c. Adversely affect the price of goods sold in interstate commerce.

d. Have a significant impact on interstate commerce.

The correct answer is (d). *(Publisher)*

REQUIRED: The interstate commerce requirement for jurisdiction.

DISCUSSION: Under the commerce clause of the U.S. Constitution, Congress has the power to regulate interstate commerce. The antitrust laws apply to activity that either restrains commerce interstate in character itself or if the restraint has a substantial affect on interstate commerce. If the latter, it is enough if interstate commerce is indirectly affected by solely intrastate activity.

Answers (a) and (b) are incorrect because trade restrictions can have a significant impact on interstate commerce regardless of whether the business committing the violation or the business directly affected is in interstate commerce. A reduction of intrastate commerce would affect interstate commerce in many situations. Answer (c) is incorrect because if interstate commerce is significantly affected, a trade restriction is illegal regardless of whether it has an adverse or beneficial impact.

6. With respect to foreign commerce, the antitrust laws

a. Apply only if there is an effect on U.S. commerce.

b. Apply only to activity occurring in the United States.

c. Do not apply.

d. Do not apply to activity which completely takes place in foreign countries.

The correct answer is (a). *(Publisher)*

REQUIRED: The application of the antitrust laws to foreign commerce.

DISCUSSION: The commerce clause of the U.S. Constitution also allows Congress to regulate foreign commerce. Therefore, the antitrust laws apply to foreign commerce, but only to the extent there is an effect on U.S. commerce. Without an effect on U.S. commerce, the courts have ruled that the antitrust laws do not apply. These court decisions were codified in a statute passed in 1982.

Answer (b) is incorrect because U.S. commerce can be affected by activity occurring in foreign countries. For example, a U.S. firm could conspire with a foreign country to manufacture goods in a foreign country which may later be shipped to the United States. Answer (c) is incorrect because antitrust laws do apply to foreign commerce provided there is an effect by U.S. commerce. Answer (d) is incorrect because activities of U.S. citizens completely taking place in a foreign country are covered by the U.S. antitrust laws if such activities would have an effect on U.S. commerce. It could be activity that would increase or reduce the goods coming into the United States.

7. Which one of the following statements regarding the application of antitrust rules to professional fees is true?

a. Most professionals, including physicians, lawyers, engineers, and accountants, are exempt from the antitrust laws.

b. Agreements to increase fees are legal if the quality of services provided improves.

c. Fee discrimination in any form is illegal.

d. Agreements to set either minimum or maximum fees are illegal.

The correct answer is (d). *(CMA 1287 1-18)*

REQUIRED: The true statement about the application of antitrust laws to professional fees.

DISCUSSION: Lawyers, public accountants, and other professionals have received scrutiny from the FTC in recent years concerning pricing policies. In general, professionals cannot make agreements that provide for either minimum or maximum fees because price fixing by collusion among competitors is a per se violation of the Sherman Act.

Answer (a) is incorrect because professionals and their organizations are not exempt from the antitrust laws. Answer (b) is incorrect because agreements among competitors to increase fees are illegal per se. Answer (c) is incorrect because fee discrimination is not illegal per se. Many factors influence the fees that a particular professional might charge. For example, a professional might charge a lower price if a service is to be performed during a normally slow period.

8. With respect to the federal antitrust laws, regulated industries are

a. Not expressly or completely exempt.

b. Covered to the same extent as all other industries.

c. Covered to the extent determined by the applicable regulatory agency.

d. Covered to the extent determined by statute and the courts.

The correct answer is (a). *(CMA 679 I-37)*

REQUIRED: Application of antitrust laws to regulated industries.

DISCUSSION: Regulated industries are not expressly exempt from the antitrust laws. However, there is an implied exemption to the extent of their regulation by federal or state government. Competition among regulated industries is generally not considered feasible. But to the extent that an enterprise of a regulated industry acts in an anticompetitive manner outside of the areas in which it is regulated, then those acts may be illegal. For example, if an industry is price regulated, it would still be illegal to participate in a joint boycott.

Answer (b) is incorrect because regulated industries are not covered like other industries due to the regulation. Answer (c) is incorrect because regulatory agencies do not determine coverage of antitrust laws. Answer (d) is incorrect because regulated industries have an implied exemption to a certain degree.

9. The antitrust prohibitions against mergers that would tend to lessen competition

a. Are enforced solely by the Commerce Department.

b. Are enforced solely by the Federal Trade Commission.

c. Are enforced by the Federal Trade Commission and the Justice Department.

d. Do not apply to hostile corporate takeovers.

The correct answer is (c). *(CMA 1287 1-19)*

REQUIRED: The true statement about the antitrust prohibitions against mergers.

DISCUSSION: The FTC, in conjunction with the antitrust division of the Justice Department, has broad authority to enforce the antitrust laws. Because mergers may lessen competition or tend to create a monopoly under the terms of the Clayton Act, they are scrutinized by the FTC and the Justice Department.

Answer (a) is incorrect because the Commerce Department has no authority to enforce the antitrust laws. Answer (b) is incorrect because the Justice Department also has the authority to enforce antitrust laws. Answer (d) is incorrect because the prohibitions apply to all mergers that would tend to lessen competition.

27.2 Sherman Act, Section One - Restraints of Trade

10. The Sherman Act has been interpreted to apply

a. To only one person acting alone.

b. To only express agreements.

c. Strictly to every restraint of trade.

d. To only unreasonable restraints of trade.

The correct answer is (d). *(Publisher)*

REQUIRED: How the Sherman Act has been interpreted.

DISCUSSION: The Sherman Antitrust Act of 1890 is the foundation of American antitrust regulation. It prohibits contracts, combinations, and conspiracies in restraint of trade and makes monopolizing or attempting to monopolize any part of interstate commerce a criminal offense. The Act has been interpreted to apply to only unreasonable restraints of trade. This is known as the rule of reason. Otherwise, virtually every normal contract or other business transaction could be found to restrain trade.

Answer (a) is incorrect because a contract, combination, or conspiracy requires two or more persons agreeing to act in concert to restrain trade. Answer (b) is incorrect because express agreements, tacit agreements, and even conscious parallelism are covered provided there is evidence sufficient to infer conspiracy. Answer (c) is incorrect because if every restraint of trade was found illegal, few business transactions would be legal.

11. The term "illegal per se" as it is frequently used in antitrust law

a. Applies exclusively to illegal price fixing and other related activities by competitors.

b. Must be established by the Justice Department in order to impose criminal sanctions under the Federal Trade Commission Act.

c. Represents anticompetitive conduct or agreements which are inherently illegal and without legal justification.

d. Applies exclusively to illegal anticompetitive activities by competitors.

The correct answer is (c). *(CPA 1184 L-33)*

REQUIRED: The meaning of the term "illegal per se."

DISCUSSION: Illegal per se means an action is conclusively presumed to be unreasonable and illegal without inquiry as to the harm caused or any business excuse. Agreements that are determined to be illegal per se are those that are so offensive and lacking in redeeming virtue as to be condemned without further inquiry.

Answer (a) is incorrect because many types of agreements besides price fixing are illegal per se. They are discussed in the next several questions. Answer (b) is incorrect because certain activities have already been determined to be illegal per se without action by the Justice Department. They are illegal under various acts, especially the Sherman Act. Answer (d) is incorrect because certain anticompetitive activities between buyers and sellers (vertical) are also per se illegal.

12. What pricing agreement among competitors is legal?

a. An agreement aimed at lowering prices.

b. An agreement aimed at eliminating cutthroat competition by stabilizing prices.

c. An agreement which seeks to fix prices reasonably and fairly for the consumers' benefit.

d. None. Competitors are forbidden to enter into agreements which determine the price of the product they sell.

The correct answer is (d). *(CPA 1176 L-17)*

REQUIRED: The pricing agreement among competitors that is legal.

DISCUSSION: No pricing agreements among competitors are legal because the antitrust laws forbid competitors to agree on the price of the products they sell.

Answer (a) is incorrect because a pricing agreement among competitors, even if aimed at lowering prices, is illegal per se because it is assumed that such an agreement over the long run will substantially lessen competition. Answer (b) is incorrect because pricing agreements aimed at eliminating cutthroat competition and stabilizing prices are also illegal. Answer (c) is incorrect because it is presumed that in the long run even reasonable and fair agreements will contribute to a lessening of competition.

13. Long Corp. entered into agreements with its retailers whereby they agreed not to sell Long batteries beneath the minimum prices determined by Long. In exchange for this agreement, Long promised not to sell batteries at retail in the retailers' respective territories. The agreement did not preclude the retailers from selling competing brands of batteries. The agreement is

a. Legal since the retailers are permitted to sell the competing brands at any price they choose.

b. Legal if the batteries are sold under Long's exclusive trademark.

c. An exception to the price fixing provision of the Sherman Act because Long has given up the right to sell in the various territories.

d. Illegal even though the minimum prices are reasonable.

The correct answer is (d). *(CPA 1184 L-31)*

REQUIRED: The legality of an agreement between the manufacturer and retailer establishing minimum prices.

DISCUSSION: An agreement between a manufacturer and its retailers establishing minimum prices is a form of price fixing, and is per se illegal under antitrust laws even if the minimum prices are considered reasonable. This is a form of vertical price fixing as opposed to horizontal price fixing by competitors.

Answer (a) is incorrect because the free pricing of competitive brands does not justify the price fixing with Long Corp. Answer (b) is incorrect because there is no provision in the antitrust laws allowing resale price maintenance agreements for trademarked or patented products. Answer (c) is incorrect because a minimum price maintenance agreement is not an exception to the price fixing provisions of the Sherman Act. Furthermore, the territorial agreement itself may not serve a legitimate business interest and may constitute an additional violation of the antitrust laws.

14. Sunrise Company has a distribution system composed of distributors and retailers. Each distributor has a defined geographic area in which it has the exclusive right to sell to retailers and to which sales are restricted. Franchised retailers are authorized to sell Sunrise's products only within specified locations. Both distributors and retailers are forbidden to sell to nonfranchised retailers. Under present law, this marketing arrangement will be

a. Judged under the rule of reason, whether or not title passes.

b. Illegal per se if title passes to the distributor or retailer, but judged under the rule of reason if title does not pass (as under an agency or consignment).

c. Illegal per se, whether or not title passes.

d. Illegal per se if title does not pass, but judged under the rule of reason if title passes.

The correct answer is (a). *(CPA 1181 L-31)*

REQUIRED: The legality of restrictions on distributors' sales to nonfranchised retailers.

DISCUSSION: Vertical territorial limitations between a manufacturer and its distributors and retailers are no longer condemned as per se violations. They are examined under the rule of reason to determine if there is an unreasonable impact on competition. Under prior law, vertical restraints were not permissible after title passed. Under current law, the passage of title is relatively unimportant.

Answer (b) is incorrect because under current law, this marketing arrangement is not illegal per se regardless of whether title has passed. Answer (c) is incorrect because the restrictions on resale do not depend on title passing. They will be examined under the rule of reason. Answer (d) is incorrect because as stated above, the passage of title is no longer the determining factor.

15. Grubar is a troublesome appliance price cutter. The other retail appliance dealers dislike Grubar's price cutting and he is equally unpopular with the appliance manufacturers. Grubar's appliance sales constitute less than .001% of the market. The marketplace has an abundance of retailers, and competition is vigorous. The manufacturers and the retailers jointly decided to boycott Grubar, thereby significantly limiting his access to appliances and thus hoping to drive him out of business. Grubar has commenced legal action against the various parties based upon a violation of the Sherman Act. He is seeking injunctive relief and damages. Under the circumstances,

a. Grubar is entitled to the relief requested since the facts indicate a per se violation.

b. Grubar's complaint should be dismissed since it alleges only a private wrong as opposed to a public wrong.

c. Grubar is entitled to the relief requested against the interstate commerce manufacturers, but not the intrastate retailers.

d. Grubar is not entitled to injunctive relief. Only the Department of Justice is entitled to such relief.

The correct answer is (a). *(CPA 583 L-31)*

REQUIRED: The result of the legal action by someone who has been subject to a joint boycott.

DISCUSSION: The manufacturers and retailers jointly boycotted Grubar, which is per se illegal under the Sherman Act. Therefore Grubar will be entitled to the relief requested. That Grubar's sales constitute less than .001% of the market makes no difference when it is a per se violation.

Answer (b) is incorrect because the antitrust laws are public laws, not private laws. Also, injunctive relief under the circumstances should be available regardless of whether it was a private or a public wrong. Answer (c) is incorrect because the intrastate retailers are also subject to antitrust laws if as a group they affect interstate commerce. Answer (d) is incorrect because the Sherman Act may be enforced by individuals as well as the Department of Justice. Either can obtain an injunction. Individuals are also entitled to treble damages.

16. The Flick Corporation sold various interrelated products that it manufactured. One of the items was manufactured almost exclusively by Flick and sold throughout the United States. Realizing the importance of this product to its purchasers, Flick decided to capitalize on the situation by requiring all purchasers to take at least two other products in order to obtain the item over which it has almost complete market control. At Flick's spring sales meeting, its president informed the entire sales force that they were to henceforth sell only to those customers who agreed to take the additional products. As a result of this plan, gross sales of the additional items increased by more than $1 million. Which of the following best describes the legality of the above situation?

a. It is illegal only if the products are patented products.

b. It is an illegal tying arrangement.

c. It is legal as long as the price charged to retailers for the other products is competitive.

d. It is legal if the retailers do not complain about purchasing the other products.

The correct answer is (b). *(CPA 1179 L-6)*

REQUIRED: The legality of requiring customers to purchase two other products in addition to the product they wish to order.

DISCUSSION: A seller's requiring a buyer to take one or more other products to get the desired product is a tying arrangement. If the amount involved is substantial, it is illegal. Because the results of this plan increased gross sales by more than $1 million, the amount involved is substantial and thus an illegal tying arrangement.

Answer (a) is incorrect because the described activity is illegal no matter what products are involved due to the substantial amount involved. Answer (c) is incorrect because a tying arrangement is not legal due to the substantial amount involved even if the prices charged to retailers for the other products are competitive. Answer (d) is incorrect because tying arrangements are illegal if they have a substantial impact on commerce, regardless of whether complaints are filed by the retailers.

17. Blue purchased a travel agency business from Drye. The purchase price included payment for Drye's goodwill. The agreement contained a covenant prohibiting Drye from competing with Blue in the travel agency business. Which statement regarding the covenant is false?

a. The restraint must be no more extensive than is reasonably necessary to protect the goodwill purchased by Blue.

b. The geographic area to which it applies must be reasonable.

c. The time period for which it is to be effective must be reasonable.

d. The value to be assigned to it is the excess of the price paid over the seller's cost of all tangible assets.

The correct answer is (d). *(CPA 1187 L-2)*

REQUIRED: The false statement regarding the covenant not to compete.

DISCUSSION: A covenant not to compete is common in the sale of a business. It is valid as long as it covers a reasonable geographic area and is for a reasonable period of time. The goodwill purchased by Blue and protected by the covenant should be valued at the excess of the purchase price over the fair value of the net identifiable assets acquired. But the covenant is an identifiable intangible asset and thus not included in goodwill. Moreover, the part of the price assignable to the covenant may be amortized for tax purposes. Goodwill amortization, however, is not deductible.

Answers (a), (b), and (c) are incorrect because each is a true statement about covenants in restraint of trade.

18. The difference between exclusive dealing arrangements and reciprocal dealing arrangements is that

a. Exclusive dealing is judged under the rule of reason and reciprocal dealing is per se illegal.

b. Exclusive dealing is per se illegal and reciprocal dealing is judged under the rule of reason.

c. Reciprocal dealing is a violation of the Sherman Act but exclusive dealing is only a violation of the Clayton Act.

d. In reciprocal dealing, a purchaser requires the seller to also buy its product; in exclusive dealing, a seller requires that a buyer not carry products of the seller's competitors.

The correct answer is (d). *(Publisher)*

REQUIRED: The difference between exclusive and reciprocal dealing arrangements.

DISCUSSION: Reciprocal dealing occurs when one company uses its purchasing power to require the company from whom it purchases to buy its products. Exclusive dealing occurs when a supplier conditions its sales such that the buyer will not use or deal in goods of the seller's competitors.

Answers (a) and (b) are incorrect because under the Sherman Act both are considered illegal per se provided the power to exert this pressure exists, based on the relative size and purchasing volume of the parties. Answer (c) is incorrect because both violate the Sherman Act and the Clayton Act. The Sherman Act requires a substantial volume to be affected and applies to a broad range of commercial activity. The Clayton Act applies only to the lease or sale of goods, merchandise, machinery, supplies, and other commodities. It also requires proof only of a tendency to lessen competition.

27.3 Sherman Act, Section Two - Monopolies

19. The U.S. Department of Justice has alleged that Variable Resources, Inc., the largest manufacturer and seller of variable-speed drive motors, is a monopolist. It is seeking an injunction ordering divestiture by Variable of a significant portion of its manufacturing facilities. Variable denies it has monopolized the variable-speed drive motor market. Which of the following is correct?

a. The government must prove that Variable is the sole source of a significant portion of the market.

b. In order to establish monopolization, the government must prove that Variable has at least 75% of the market.

c. If Variable has the power to control prices or exclude competition, it has a monopoly.

d. As long as Variable has not been a party to a contract, combination, or conspiracy in restraint of trade, it cannot be found to be guilty of monopolization.

The correct answer is (c). *(CPA 582 L-27)*

REQUIRED: The correct statement concerning whether Variable has established a monopoly.

DISCUSSION: The purpose of antitrust laws is to preserve and promote competition. The working definition of monopoly in antitrust law is that the defendant has the power to control prices or exclude competition. Under the Sherman Act, formation of or the attempt to form a monopoly is illegal.

Answer (a) is incorrect because many cases have held that 60% or less of the market constitutes monopolistic power. Answer (b) is incorrect because the government need not prove a particular percentage of the market to establish that an illegal monopoly or attempt to monopolize has occurred. However, a percentage share of the market is an important determining factor in monopoly cases. Answer (d) is incorrect because the Sherman Act prohibits monopolies and attempts to monopolize in addition to contracts, combinations, and conspiracies in restraint of trade.

20. The Duplex Corporation has been charged by the U.S. Justice Department with an "attempt to monopolize" the duplex industry. In defending itself against such a charge, Duplex will prevail if it can establish

a. It had no intent to monopolize the duplex industry.

b. Its percentage share of the relevant market was less than 50%.

c. Its activities do not constitute an unreasonable restraint of trade.

d. It does not have monopoly power.

The correct answer is (a). *(CPA 580 L-5)*

REQUIRED: The valid defense to "an attempt to monopolize" charge.

DISCUSSION: The Sherman Act prohibits contracts, combinations, or conspiracies in restraint of trade in addition to the formation of monopolies and the attempt to monopolize. Since the Sherman Act contains criminal sanctions, the Justice Department must prove that the defendant intended to commit an illegal act. If a defendant can show no intent to monopolize, the government will not prevail.

Answer (b) is incorrect because no set percentage of the relevant market constitutes an attempt to monopolize. Furthermore, a much lower percentage may suffice if the charge is attempting to monopolize rather than holding monopoly power. Answer (c) is incorrect because the rule of reason defense does not apply to an attempt to monopolize charge. Answer (d) is incorrect because actual monopoly power is not needed for attempt to monopolize.

21. Gritney, Inc. manufacturers and sells foibles in competition with about four other firms in the United States. It sells about 90% of the foibles sold in the Midwest, but only about 10% nationally. Gritney will probably

a. Be found guilty of monopolization if the relevant product market is determined to be the Midwest.

b. Be found guilty of monopolization regardless of the product market since there are so few competitors.

c. Not be found guilty of monopolization if it has not evidenced an intent to monopolize even if it has been guilty of various predatory practices.

d. Be found guilty of monopolization in the Midwest if the only reason for its market share is that competitors left due to lack of sales in total.

The correct answer is (a). *(Publisher)*

REQUIRED: The result of an action against a firm for monopolization.

DISCUSSION: In determining monopoly power, an important determinant is the relevant market. If the relevant market is determined to be the Midwest, Gritney has 90% of the market, which is usually considered to be monopoly power.

Answer (b) is incorrect because if the relevant product market is the entire United States, Gritney only has 10% of the market. Even if there are few competitors, 10% is not usually considered monopoly power even in an oligopoly. Answer (c) is incorrect because the courts have found a business liable regardless of intent to monopolize if monopoly power exists and if predatory practices accompany the firm's growth to monopoly power. Answer (d) is incorrect because no intent to monopolize can be found if a monopoly is thrust upon a firm, with no intent to monopolize and no predatory practices by the firm.

27.4 Clayton Act

Note that price discrimination is covered solely in Module 27.5, "Robinson-Patman Act."

22. George Corp. entered into contracts to supply all the requirements of 1,000 dealers in New England. In these contracts the dealers agreed not to sell products competitive with those of George. These dealers constituted 20% of the total number of dealers in the area. George may

a. Be enjoined from enforcing the contracts if they might substantially lessen competition.

b. Be enjoined only to the extent that its own outlets operated by its agents are involved.

c. Not be enjoined because 20% of the New England dealers are involved.

d. Be enjoined for violating the Robinson-Patman Act.

The correct answer is (a). *(CPA 1174 L-43)*

REQUIRED: The result of an agreement that buyers will not sell products competing with the supplier's products.

DISCUSSION: The Clayton Act regulates exclusive dealing arrangements in which a seller requires his/her buyers not to deal in the commodities of a competitor. If a substantial dollar amount or percentage of the market is involved, competition is likely to be substantially lessened and a violation will occur.

Answer (b) is incorrect because the injunction will apply to George's exclusive dealing arrangements with any dealer. Answer (c) is incorrect because 20% of the New England dealers is not an insignificant percentage of the market. Answer (d) is incorrect because exclusive dealing arrangements are prohibited by the Clayton Act, not the Robinson-Patman Act.

23. Global Reproductions, Inc. makes and sells high-quality, expensive lithographs of the works of famous artists. It sells to art wholesalers throughout the United States. It requires that its wholesalers not purchase lithographs of competing companies during the three-year duration of the contract. They may sell all other types of pictures, including oil, watercolor and charcoal. The Federal Trade Commission has attacked the legality of this exclusive dealing arrangement. This exclusive dealing arrangement

a. Is legal per se since its duration is less than five years.

b. Could be found to be illegal under the Sherman, Clayton, and Federal Trade Commission Acts.

c. Will be tested under the rule of reason, and will be declared illegal only if found to be unreasonable.

d. Is legal since the wholesalers are permitted to sell all other types of pictures.

The correct answer is (b). *(CPA 581 L-57)*

REQUIRED: The legal implications of an exclusive dealing arrangement.

DISCUSSION: Contracts calling for exclusive dealing are potentially subject to charges under the Sherman Act, which prohibits any contract that is an unreasonable restraint of trade. The Clayton Act directly prohibits exclusive dealing arrangements in which the effect may be to substantially lessen competition or tend to create a monopoly in any line of commerce. The Federal Trade Commission Act prohibits unfair methods of competition. Thus, this exclusive dealing arrangement could be illegal under the three acts discussed.

Answer (a) is incorrect because legal per se is not a term in antitrust law. Furthermore, exclusive dealing arrangements are not judged on their duration. Answer (c) is incorrect because exclusive dealing arrangements need not necessarily be found unreasonable to be declared illegal. The standard under the Clayton Act is whether there may be a substantial lessening of competition. Answer (d) is incorrect because an exclusive dealing arrangement is not made legal by permission to sell all other types of merchandise.

24. Which of the following is a correct statement concerning a tying arrangement under the Clayton Act?

a. The test of whether a tying arrangement is illegal is essentially the same as for exclusive dealing.

b. The test of whether a tying arrangement is illegal is essentially the same as under the Sherman Act.

c. It is not illegal under the Clayton Act because it is an agreement to restrain trade, which is not covered by the Clayton Act.

d. It is not illegal if the tied goods are not sold by the offeror of the desired goods.

The correct answer is (b). *(Publisher)*

REQUIRED: The correct statement concerning a tying arrangement under the Clayton Act.

DISCUSSION: The tying arrangement occurs when a supplier requires a buyer to purchase one or more additional goods in order to obtain the buyer's desired good. Whether this is legal is determined in a similar manner under both the Sherman Act and the Clayton Act. The arrangement must affect more than an insubstantial amount of commerce, and the supplier must have sufficient economic power to accomplish the tying arrangement. The major difference is that it will be found illegal under the Clayton Act if it tends to lessen competition and under the Sherman Act if there is a substantial effect on commerce.

Answer (a) is incorrect because tying arrangements are generally considered per se violations once the required tests are met. Exclusive dealing arrangements are judged more under the rule of reason, i.e., using both qualitative and quantitative tests. Answer (c) is incorrect because the Clayton Act does prohibit activity which tends to substantially lessen competition. Answer (d) is incorrect because if the supplier has an economic interest in the tied goods, the arrangement may still be illegal. For example, the supplier may manufacture the tied goods which were sold by someone else and want more sales so it can manufacture more.

25. Section 7 of the Clayton Act is the primary statutory provision used by the Department of Justice in controlling anticompetitive mergers and acquisitions. In general, the Clayton Act is invoked because

a. It provides for harsher criminal penalties than does the Sherman Act.

b. It enables the Department of Justice to proscribe mergers and acquisitions in their incipiency.

c. It provides for exclusive jurisdiction over such activities.

d. The Sherman Act applies to asset mergers or acquisitions only, not to stock mergers or acquisitions.

The correct answer is (b). *(CPA 583 L-33)*

REQUIRED: Why the Clayton Act is used in controlling mergers and acquisitions.

DISCUSSION: The Clayton Act prohibits the acquisition of stock or the acquisition of assets of another corporation if the effect may be to substantially lessen competition or tend to create a monopoly. This does allow the Department of Justice to attack mergers and acquisitions in their incipiency rather than waiting for the merger or acquisition to occur and then having to prove that it has had the harmful effect.

Answer (a) is incorrect because criminal penalties are provided for under the Sherman Act, not the Clayton Act. Answer (c) is incorrect because in many instances the Sherman Act, the Federal Trade Commission Act and the Clayton Act are all applicable with respect to mergers and acquisitions. Answer (d) is incorrect because the Sherman Act applies to any situation in which a monopoly exists or there is an intent to monopolize, regardless of the method of acquisition.

26. Expansion Corporation is an aggressive, large conglomerate. It is seeking to obtain control of several additional corporations including Resistance Corporation. Expansion does not currently buy from, sell to, or compete with Resistance. Which of the following statements applies to this proposed takeover?

a. Since Expansion does not buy from, sell to, or compete with Resistance, antitrust laws do not apply.

b. If Expansion can consummate the acquisition before there is an objection to it, the acquisition can not subsequently be set aside.

c. The acquisition is likely to be declared illegal if there will be reciprocal buying and there is a likelihood that other entrants into the market would be precluded.

d. The acquisition is legal on its face if cost efficiency will result from combined marketing and advertising.

The correct answer is (c). *(CPA 1179 L-36)*

REQUIRED: The statement applicable to a proposed takeover of a corporation.

DISCUSSION: The Clayton Act of 1914 supplemented the Sherman Act to prohibit a corporation from acquiring the stock of another corporation (merger) if the effect might be to substantially lessen competition or tend to create a monopoly. If, after the acquisition, there is to be reciprocal buying that creates a likelihood that other entrants into the market would be precluded, the acquisition is likely to be declared illegal as a lessening of competition.

Answer (a) is incorrect because mergers are prohibited if they will substantially lessen competition even in conglomerate mergers (unrelated corporations). Answer (b) is incorrect because both the government and private individuals can take action subsequent to a merger. Answer (d) is incorrect because cost efficiencies resulting from combined marketing and advertising do not justify a merger if there is a substantial lessening of competition.

27. In a pure conglomerate merger,

a. The government must establish an actual restraint on competition in the marketplace in order to prevent the merger.

b. The acquiring corporation neither competes with nor sells to/buys from the acquired corporation.

c. The merger is prima facie valid unless the government can prove the acquiring corporation had an intent to monopolize.

d. Some form of additional anticompetitive behavior must be established (e.g., price fixing) to provide the basis for the government's obtaining of injunctive relief.

The correct answer is (b). *(CPA 1183 L-35)*

REQUIRED: The correct statement concerning a pure conglomerate merger.

DISCUSSION: A conglomerate merger is neither a horizontal nor a vertical merger. The corporations neither compete with each other nor sell to/buy from each other. This usually means they must be in completely different industries.

Answer (a) is incorrect because an actual restraint on competition need not be proven. If one of the firms might have been a likely entrant to the marketplace, the merger might be prevented based on a substantial lessening of competition. Answer (c) is incorrect because the Clayton Act requires only a substantial lessening of competition, not an intent to monopolize. Answer (d) is incorrect because additional anticompetitive behavior such as price fixing is sometimes needed under the Sherman Act, but not under the Clayton Act. Substantial lessening of competition alone suffers.

28. In contesting the validity of a previously consummated vertical merger,

a. The Justice Department must proceed within 5 years of the consummation of the merger.

b. That the acquiring corporation deliberately failed to apply for a ruling is presumptive evidence of bad faith.

c. The Justice Department must show the likelihood that competition may be foreclosed in a substantial share of that market.

d. Only a showing of actual substantial lessening of competition will be sufficient to establish illegality.

The correct answer is (c). *(CPA 1183 L-36)*

REQUIRED: The requirements to contest a vertical merger that has already occurred.

DISCUSSION: Vertical mergers are those between buyers and sellers, as opposed to competitors (called horizontal mergers). A horizontal merger is presumed illegal with a smaller market share, but vertical mergers are less likely to be challenged. They will be attacked if the merger makes it more difficult for other firms to enter the industry or market or if the merger would make the company disproportionately large compared with competitors.

Answer (a) is incorrect because no time limit has been set to contest the validity of a vertical merger since the Sherman Act makes monopolization (at any time) illegal. Answer (b) is incorrect because no application for rulings is required for mergers. The merging corporations must notify the Justice Department and the FTC. Answer (d) is incorrect because increased barriers to market entry as well as actual substantial lessening of the competition will make the merger illegal.

29. Gould Machinery builds bulldozers. Prior to 1986, it sold a substantial amount of equipment to Mace Contractors on credit. Mace went into bankruptcy in 1986. To protect its investment, Gould took over Mace. Erhart Contractors now complains that the acquisition harms its business, alleging that its business would have improved had Gould not entered the market as a competitor. Erhart can

a. Not recover damages under the antitrust laws.

b. Recover treble damages.

c. Recover only its actual damages.

d. Obtain injunctive relief ordering divestiture.

The correct answer is (a). *(CPA 582 L-31)*

REQUIRED: The correct statement concerning the legality of a creditor's taking over the business of a substantial debtor.

DISCUSSION: The acquisition of a substantial contractor by a machinery manufacturer could result in a substantial lessening of competition. However, the failing company doctrine provides that a merger that may reduce competition is allowable if the company acquired is failing and there is no other purchaser whose acquisition of the company would reduce competition less. Gould might also defend under the rule of reason by showing the acquisition was for the purpose of furthering a legitimate business interest (protecting its investment and assuring the continuation of a valuable outlet for its equipment) rather than to reduce competition.

Answers (b) and (c) are incorrect because a private claimant under the antitrust laws can recover treble damages but only if able to show that antitrust violations have occurred. Answer (d) is incorrect because a private person may obtain only preliminary injunctive relief; divestiture is a Justice Department remedy.

30. In 1976, Congress passed the Antitrust Improvement Act. This statute made certain significant procedural changes with respect to the Sherman Act and the Clayton Act. Which is a correct statement concerning these changes?

a. Companies considering a major merger must notify the Federal Trade Commission and the Department of Justice in advance.

b. In addition to a merger by the purchase of stocks, mergers by an acquisition of a substantial amount of another corporation's assets are now covered.

c. Individuals will be allowed five (instead of three) times their damages when the violations involve criminal conduct by either or both parties.

d. Mergers with foreign corporations (i.e., international mergers) are now covered in addition to domestic mergers.

The correct answer is (a). *(Publisher)*

REQUIRED: The correct statement concerning the Antitrust Improvement Act of 1976.

DISCUSSION: The Act requires that the FTC and the Department of Justice be notified in advance of a major merger. This only applies to extremely large businesses. In addition, the Act allows state attorneys general to sue for violations of the Sherman Act on behalf of consumers and collect treble damages for them.

Answer (b) is incorrect because the Clayton Act already covered mergers by an acquisition of a substantial amount of assets. Answer (c) is incorrect because individuals are still only allowed three times their damages for violations of the Sherman or Clayton Act. Answer (d) is incorrect because international mergers are still covered only to the extent a U.S. corporation is involved and interstate commerce or foreign commerce with the United States is affected.

31. The U.S. Justice Department has promulgated the Merger Guidelines in order to inform the public of its views on the factors and considerations to be taken into account in ascertaining whether a merger is potentially illegal. The Merger Guidelines are

a. Strongly influenced by the factor of size, that is, of percentage shares of the market of the parties to the proposed merger.

b. Based exclusively upon the decisions of the U.S. Supreme Court.

c. Binding on all parties affected by them subsequent to the date of their promulgation.

d. Not of great importance because they are too indefinite and uncertain to have any meaning in respect to an actual merger.

The correct answer is (a). *(CPA 1181 L-33)*

REQUIRED: The correct statement concerning Merger Guidelines of the Justice Department.

DISCUSSION: The Merger Guidelines drafted by the Justice Department for guidance as to enforcement of antitrust policy are strongly influenced by the factor of size as reflected in the existing market shares of the merging firms and the relative concentration in the market after the merger. However, nonmarket share factors are also considered, such as barriers to entry, post conduct of the firms, and the future ability of the acquired firm to compete (a failing company is easier to acquire). Also, clear and convincing evidence of improved efficiency will be considered.

Answer (b) is incorrect because the Merger Guidelines are based on decisions of the Supreme Court as well as on policy formulated within the Justice Department Antitrust Division. Answer (c) is incorrect because they are not binding. They are not law but merely guidelines to forewarn the public of the current views of the Justice Department with respect to mergers. Answer (d) is incorrect because the guidelines are not law, but they are very important because they provide definite standards for an actual merger.

32. The Justice Department uses the Herfindahl-Hirschman Index to calculate market concentration data. The Department is most likely to challenge a merger if the postmerger HHI is

a. 800.

b. 1,500 and the increase is 100 points.

c. 1,800 and any increase occurs.

d. 2,000 and the increase is more than 100 points.

The correct answer is (d). *(Publisher)*

REQUIRED: The HHI data most likely to result in challenge to a merger.

DISCUSSION: The HHI is found by summing the squares of the market shares of the firms in a market. For example, if each of five firms has a market share of 20%, the HHI is 2,000 ($20^2 + 20^2 + 20^2 + 20^2 + 20^2$). The Justice Department is most likely to challenge a merger if the postmerger HHI is over 1,800 and the increase is more than 100 points.

Answer (a) is incorrect because a postmerger HHI of less than 1,000 is unlikely to result in a challenge. Answer (b) is incorrect because if the postmerger HHI is between 1,000 and 1,800 and the change exceeds 100 points, a challenge is more likely than if the HHI is below 1,000, but an HHI above 1,800 and a change of more than 100 points is still more likely to trigger a response. Answer (c) is incorrect because the change must be more than 100 points.

33. Over a six-year period, Yeats Corporation acquired 46% of the outstanding stock of Glick, Inc. Both Glick and Yeats have capital, surplus, and undivided profits aggregating more than $1,000,000. Yeats' current directors own stock in both corporations and are on the board of directors of each. Yeats used its ownership control to elect the remaining members of the board of directors and its own slate of officers for Glick. Glick and Yeats manufacture goods which are in competition with each other throughout the United States. Since Yeats acquired control of Glick, Yeats' percentage share of the nationwide market has remained relatively stable. Which of the following statements applies to the above situation?

a. Nothing in these facts would constitute a violation of the federal antitrust laws.

b. The interlocking directorate is not illegal because less than 50% of the Glick stock is owned by Yeats.

c. The interlocking directorate is a clear violation of federal antitrust laws.

d. No current violation of the federal antitrust law exists because there has been no marked improvement in the competitive position of Yeats or Glick.

The correct answer is (c). *(CPA 578 L-7)*

REQUIRED: The correct statement concerning stock ownership and interlocking directorates of competitors.

DISCUSSION: Common directors of two or more corporations are referred to as interlocking directorates. The Clayton Act prohibits common directors on the boards of directors of two or more competing corporations where one of the corporations has equity aggregating more than $1 million.

Answer (a) is incorrect because the interlocking directorates violate the antitrust laws. Answer (b) is incorrect because interlocking directorates are illegal regardless of stock ownership. Answer (d) is incorrect because an interlocking directorate is illegal. That there has been no marked improvement in the competitive position does not prove a lack of antitrust violations.

27.5 Robinson-Patman Act

34. Sunk Corp has been charged with a violation of the Robinson-Patman Act involving sales to its customers at different prices. In order to establish a prima facie case under the Robinson-Patman Act based on price discrimination, it must be shown among other things that

a. Sunk made sales of commodities of a like grade and quality to two or more customers.

b. An actual and substantial lessening of competition which arose out of interstate commerce.

c. A monopoly resulted from the alleged violation.

d. Sunk profited from the alleged violation.

The correct answer is (a). *(CPA 1185 L-25)*

REQUIRED: What the plaintiff must prove under the Robinson-Patman Act to establish a prima facie case.

DISCUSSION: The Robinson-Patman Act amends the Clayton Act to strengthen the provisions against price discrimination. Price discrimination in interstate commerce of commodities of like grade and quality is illegal where the effect may be to substantially lessen competition. The purchasers must be competitors in the same market.

Answer (b) is incorrect because an actual lessening of competition is not required, merely that the discrimination may result in a lessening of competition. The requirement of interstate commerce is satisfied when any one purchaser is in commerce. Answer (c) is incorrect because a monopoly need not have resulted, just the tendency to create a monopoly or the probable substantial lessening of competition. Answer (d) is incorrect because the defendant need not have profited from the violation if there was a lessening of competition.

35. Pratt Company manufactures and sells distinctive clocks. Its best-selling item is a reproduction of a rare antique grandfather clock. Taylor Co. purchased 100 of the clocks from Pratt at $99 each. Much to Taylor's chagrin, it discovered that Stewart, one of its competitors, had purchased the same clock from Pratt at $94 per clock. Taylor has complained and threatened legal action. In the event the issue is litigated,

a. Taylor has a presumption in its favor that it has been harmed by price discrimination.

b. Pratt will prevail if it can show it did not intend to harm Taylor.

c. Pratt will prevail if it can show that it sold the clocks at the lower price to all customers such as Stewart who had been doing business with it continuously for ten years or more.

d. Pratt will prevail if it can establish that there were several other clock companies with which Taylor could deal if Taylor was dissatisfied.

The correct answer is (a). *(CPA 583 L-32)*

REQUIRED: The probable outcome of litigation concerning price discrimination.

DISCUSSION: When a person files a complaint alleging price discrimination, the courts presume that competition has been harmed when the price discrimination involves competing purchasers from the same seller. Taylor has this presumption in its favor.

Answer (b) is incorrect because intent is not an essential element of discriminatory pricing policies under the Robinson-Patman Act. Answer (c) is incorrect because price differentials are allowed only if directly related to lower costs or if the purchasers are not competitors. This must be proven by the defendant. Answer (d) is incorrect because it is not a defense to establish that the plaintiff could have dealt with other companies.

36. Super Sports, Inc. sells branded sporting goods and equipment throughout the United States. It sells to wholesalers, jobbers, and retailers who in turn sell the goods to their respective customers. The wholesalers and jobbers, who do not sell at retail, are charged lower prices than retailers, but are required to purchase in larger quantities than retailers with the cost savings inherent in such purchases accounting for the lower prices. The retailers are all charged the same prices but receive discounts for quantity purchases based exclusively upon the cost savings resulting from such quantity purchases. Girard, one of Super's retail customers, has demanded discounts comparable to those available to the wholesalers and jobbers in its vicinity. Super has refused to acquiesce to this demand. Therefore, Girard sues Super alleging an illegal price discrimination in violation of the Robinson-Patman Act. Which defense by Super listed below will be most likely to prevail?

a. Girard does not have the right to sue under the Robinson-Patman Act.

b. The discounts are functional, i.e., Super's wholesalers and jobbers do not compete with retailers such as Girard.

c. Super does not have the requisite intent to discriminate among its purchasers.

d. The prices Super charges are reasonable and its profit margins are low.

The correct answer is (b). *(CPA 578 L-9)*

REQUIRED: The best defense to a price discrimination charge.

DISCUSSION: The Robinson-Patman Act makes it unlawful for any seller engaged in interstate commerce to discriminate in price between purchasers of commodities of like grade and quality where the effect of such discrimination may be to substantially lessen competition or tend to create a monopoly in any line of commerce. Price differentials are allowed if directly related to lower cost caused by production and sales in quantity, or where the buyers are in different markets so there is no injury to competition. These are called functional discounts because the buyers are differentiated by function such as the wholesalers and jobbers who do not compete with the retailers in this question.

Answer (a) is incorrect because the retailer does have the right to have the price differential examined under the provisions of the Robinson-Patman Act. Answer (c) is incorrect because intent is not a prerequisite to a price discrimination charge, so absence of intent is not a defense. Answer (d) is incorrect because the legislative purpose of the Robinson-Patman Act is to eliminate discriminatory pricing policies even if the prices charged are reasonable under the circumstances.

37. Marvel Toys, Inc. manufactures and sells toys to Gem Stores, a large department store chain, and to Fantastic Discounts, a major toy retailer, at prices below its sales price of similar toys to other retailers in the market area. Its pricing policy vis-a-vis Gem is based solely upon the fact that Gem is a new customer and the low prices were quoted in order to obtain its business and thereby eliminate Marvel's unused production capacity. For Fantastic, the lower prices are charged in order to meet the identical prices legally charged by a competitor. In assessing the potential violation of antitrust laws against price discrimination, it would appear that Marvel Toys

a. Has not violated the antitrust laws as long as none of its competitors can show damages.

b. Has a valid defense with respect to its sales to Gem.

c. Has not violated the antitrust laws with respect to its sales to Fantastic.

d. Will not have committed any violation if it was operating at a loss at the time of the sales.

The correct answer is (c). *(CPA 1175 L-46)*

REQUIRED: The correct statement concerning a potential price discrimination.

DISCUSSION: The Robinson-Patman Act prohibits price discrimination between purchasers of goods of like quality and grade. However, price discrimination or differentiation is allowed if the seller meets the burden of proving that the price discrimination is to meet lawful competition.

Answer (a) is incorrect because the courts in antitrust cases presume competition has been harmed when the price discrimination involves competing purchasers from the same seller. Answer (b) is incorrect because selling at a discriminatory price cannot be justified by the fact the purchaser is a new customer and/or the lower prices were quoted to obtain new business to eliminate unused production capacity. Answer (d) is incorrect because operating at a loss is not a defense to a price discrimination charge.

27.6 Federal Trade Commission Act

See Module 30.4 for additional questions concerning the Federal Trade Commission.

38. If a defendant is charged with an unfair method of competition under the Federal Trade Commission Act,

a. The FTC may prevail despite the fact that the conduct alleged to be illegal did not violate either the Sherman or Clayton Act.

b. Criminal sanctions can generally be imposed against a defendant even though the defendant has not violated an FTC order to cease and desist.

c. There can be no violation of the Act unless one or more of the specifically enumerated unfair methods of competition are established.

d. The complaint must be based upon the purchase or sale of goods, wares, or commodities in interstate commerce.

The correct answer is (a). *(CPA 1183 L-37)*

REQUIRED: The correct statement concerning the FTC's power.

DISCUSSION: The Federal Trade Commission Act created the Federal Trade Commission (FTC) to help to provide day-to-day enforcement of the antitrust laws. In addition to having jurisdiction to enforce all of the antitrust laws, the FTC has broad authority to prevent unfair methods of competition and unfair or deceptive acts or practices. Therefore, the FTC's power under Section 5 goes far beyond the Sherman or Clayton Act.

Answer (b) is incorrect because the FTC does not have power to impose criminal sanctions. Criminal sanctions must be enforced by the U.S. Justice Department. Answer (c) is incorrect because the FTC has broad authority with respect to unfair methods of competition; they are not necessarily enumerated. Answer (d) is incorrect because the FTC does have power over unfair methods of competition and deceptive acts or practices which extend to commerce in general, not just the sale of goods or commodities.

39. The Federal Trade Commission (FTC) is an independent and powerful agency. It has the authority to enforce the Sherman Act and the Clayton Act (including practices still in their incipiency), and also to identify and prevent activities which might be unfair methods of competition. Which of the following is not a sanction available to the FTC against offenders?

a. Enter into a consent decree with an offender.

b. Issue a cease and desist order.

c. Impose monetary penalties on a prospective basis.

d. Sentence criminal offenders to up to three years in prison.

The correct answer is (d). *(Publisher)*

REQUIRED: The sanction not within the FTC's authority.

DISCUSSION: The Federal Trade Commission (FTC) has broad powers to enforce the antitrust laws. It does not, however, have the power to sentence criminal offenders to prison. Criminal sanctions must be enforced by the U.S. Justice Department; sentencing can only be done by a court of law.

Answer (a) is incorrect because the FTC is empowered to enter into a consent decree with an offender (the offender agrees to do or not to do some act). Answer (b) is incorrect because the FTC can issue cease and desist orders. The offender can obtain judicial review of such a determination. Answer (c) is incorrect because monetary penalties may be issued by the FTC on a prospective basis; however, they cannot be enforced without judicial review.

CHAPTER TWENTY-EIGHT
FEDERAL SECURITIES REGULATION

28.1 Securities Regulation: Introduction

1. The principal purpose of the federal securities laws is to

a. Prevent public offerings of securities in which management fraud or unethical conduct is suspected.

b. Provide the SEC with the information necessary to determine the accuracy of the facts presented in the financial statements.

c. Assure that investors have adequate information upon which to base investment decisions.

d. Provide the SEC with the information necessary to evaluate the financial merits of the securities being offered.

The correct answer is (c). *(CPA 588 L-36)*

REQUIRED: The basic purpose of the securities laws of the United States.

DISCUSSION: The basic purpose of the federal securities laws is to provide disclosure of adequate information so that investors can evaluate investments. This is accomplished through complex registration and reporting requirements concerning the issuance and subsequent trading of securities.

Answer (a) is incorrect because except to the extent that the disclosure rules and the penalties for violations serve as a deterrent, the securities laws are not designed to prevent unethical conduct. Answer (b) is incorrect because the SEC does not have the means to verify the facts in financial statements. Also, the disclosures required are not limited to financial statement data. The SEC reviews information for completeness and statements fraudulent on their face but not for accuracy. Answer (d) is incorrect because the SEC does not evaluate the merit or value of securities.

2. Under the Securities Act of 1933, the registration of securities offered to the public in interstate commerce is

a. Directed toward preventing the marketing of securities posing serious financial risks to the prospective investor.

b. Not required unless the issuer is a corporation.

c. Mandatory unless the cost to the issuer is "prohibitive" as defined in the SEC regulations.

d. Required unless there is an applicable exemption.

The correct answer is (d). *(CPA 1186 L-31)*

REQUIRED: The true statement about the registration of securities offered to the public.

DISCUSSION: The principal concern of the 1933 Act is to require disclosure of sufficient relevant information when securities are sold by an issuer to the public. The statute essentially mandates a single registration of securities that are to be distributed publicly by the issuer and others such as underwriters who may assist the issuer. There are exceptions, however. Some offerings are exempt (see the next module), and some must be reregistered to comply with the 1933 Act, e.g., treasury stock and stock held by controlling persons.

Answer (a) is incorrect because the securities laws do not require the government to determine the merits of securities. Answer (b) is incorrect because unless an exemption applies, an offering by any issuer, underwriter, or dealer must be registered. Answer (c) is incorrect because the cost to the issuer is irrelevant.

3. The Securities Exchange Act of 1934

   a. Established a voluntary disclosure mechanism for issuers of publicly traded securities.
   b. Primarily relates to initial sales of securities to the public.
   c. Regulates all sales of securities.
   d. Regulates trading of securities subsequent to issuance.

The correct answer is (d). *(Publisher)*

REQUIRED: The general application of the Securities Exchange Act of 1934.

DISCUSSION: The general thrust of the 1934 Act is to regulate public trading of securities subsequent to their initial sale by the issuer. Among its many provisions, the 1934 Act created the Securities and Exchange Commission to administer the various securities laws. It also requires registration of most publicly traded securities, including many exempt under the 1933 Act; regulates exchanges, brokers, and dealers; imposes periodic reporting requirements; and contains stringent anti-fraud and insider trading sections.

Answer (a) is incorrect because the extensive disclosure requirement is mandatory. Answer (b) is incorrect because the Securities Act of 1933 is primarily intended to regulate initial public sales. Answer (c) is incorrect because the 1934 Act essentially regulates subsequent public trading of securities. Moreover, not all companies are covered by the Act.

4. For purposes of federal securities regulation, a security is best defined as

   a. An investment of money in a common enterprise in expectation of earning a profit through the efforts of others.
   b. Any interest or instrument commonly known as a security.
   c. Any interest or instrument specifically mentioned in the Securities Act of 1933 or the Securities Exchange Act of 1934.
   d. Any investment of money or property intended to yield a profit.

The correct answer is (a). *(Publisher)*

REQUIRED: The best definition of a security for securities regulation purposes.

DISCUSSION: Because of the considerable ingenuity of entrepreneurs in devising new forms for the issuance of securities, any definition must necessarily be generalized and capable of encompassing as yet unheard of means of attracting capital. The 1933 Act defines a security as "any note, stock, treasury stock, bond, debenture, evidence of indebtedness, certificate of interest or participation in any profit-sharing agreement, collateral-trust certificate, pre-organization certificate or subscription, transferable share, investment contract, voting trust certificate, certificate of deposit for a security, fractional undivided interest in oil, gas or mineral rights, or, in general, any interest or instrument commonly known as a security." Under the 1934 Act, drafts and notes not maturing more than 9 months from the date of issue are not securities. Answer (a) gives the standard used by the Supreme Court to determine whether an investment contract is a security.

Answer (b) is incorrect because the definition of security is far broader. Also, the economic realities of the transaction may be such that a contract denominated as a security does not satisfy the definition. Answer (c) is incorrect because no listing of securities could be complete since new kinds are constantly being offered. Answer (d) is incorrect because this definition is far too broad. It would apply to almost any business activity not undertaken solely with one's own labor.

5. The sale of which of the following is most likely not a sale of a security?

a. A limited partnership interest.

b. An interest in a compulsory noncontributory pension plan.

c. A plot in an orange grove with a contract for its management.

d. A restaurant franchise.

The correct answer is (b). *(Publisher)*

REQUIRED: The item that is least likely to be considered a security.

DISCUSSION: Under the Securities Act of 1933, an investment contract is a security. The Supreme Court defines an investment contract as an investment of money in a common enterprise in expectation of earning a profit solely through the efforts of others but not the investors themselves (however, the term "solely" is not a strict or literal limitation on the definition). The purchaser must not have merely an intent to consume or to engage in a commercial transaction but must have an investment motive. Other investors must take part in the common venture and be similarly affected by the management activities of third parties. Finally, the investor must reasonably expect to earn a profit through the activities of persons other than the investors. Applying this test, the Supreme Court held that an employee's interest in a pension plan was not a security when participation was required, the employee made no contributions, and the employee did not have the option of receiving the employer's contribution in lieu of pension eligibility.

Answers (a), (c), and (d) are incorrect because each has been held to be a security.

6. In general, which of the following is least likely to be considered a security under the Securities Act of 1933?

a. General partnership interests.

b. Warrants.

c. Limited partnership interests.

d. Treasury stock.

The correct answer is (a). *(CPA 1187 L-6)*

REQUIRED: The item least likely to be considered a security under the Securities Act of 1933.

DISCUSSION: The 1933 Act states that an investment contract is a security. The Supreme Court has stated that an investment contract involves an expectation of profits solely through the efforts of others (see the discussion of the preceding question). A general partner participates in the management of the enterprise, and his/her interest is therefore not regarded as a security.

Answers (b), (c), and (d) are incorrect because each is commonly known as a security.

7. The Securities and Exchange Commission was established in 1934 to help regulate the United States securities market. Which of the following statements is true concerning the SEC?

a. The SEC regulates only securities offered for public sale.

b. Registration with the SEC guarantees the accuracy of the registrant's prospectus.

c. The SEC's initial influence and authority has diminished in recent years as the stock exchanges have become more organized and better able to police themselves.

d. The SEC's powers are broad with respect to enforcement of its reporting requirements as established in the 1933 and 1934 Acts but narrow with respect to new reporting requirements because these require confirmation by the Congress.

The correct answer is (a). *(CMA 1277 3-27)*

REQUIRED: The correct statement concerning the SEC.

DISCUSSION: The SEC only regulates securities offered for public sale. Public sale is a broad term extending beyond trading on a public exchange or in the over-the-counter market. It applies whenever securities are offered for sale to the public.

Answer (b) is incorrect because the SEC does not guarantee the accuracy of a prospectus. The SEC only requires that it be filed, but would take enforcement action if it found inaccuracies or misstatements. Also, investors can sue the issuers, accountants, etc., for damages resulting from inaccuracies or misstatements. Answer (c) is incorrect because the SEC has become more influential and has assumed greater authority through its accounting releases and interpretations. Answer (d) is incorrect because the SEC's powers have broadened rather than narrowed with respect to new requirements, e.g., the Foreign Corrupt Practices Act.

8. The Securities and Exchange Commission is not empowered to

a. Obtain an injunction which will suspend trading in a given security.

b. Sue for treble damages.

c. Institute criminal proceedings against accountants.

d. Suspend a broker-dealer.

The correct answer is (b). *(CPA 577 L-1)*

REQUIRED: The correct statement regarding the SEC's powers.

DISCUSSION: The SEC is not empowered to sue for damages at all. A lawsuit for treble damages is a civil remedy provided for violations of the antitrust laws, and the SEC has no jurisdiction over antitrust violations.

Answer (a) is incorrect because the SEC is entitled to obtain an injunction to suspend trading. Answer (c) is incorrect because the SEC may initiate criminal proceedings against accountants who willfully make an untrue statement or omit a material fact in the registration statement. Answer (d) is incorrect because the SEC has the power to suspend a broker-dealer or to revoke his/her license.

9. Tweed Manufacturing, Inc. plans to issue $5 million of common stock to the public in interstate commerce after its registration statement with the SEC becomes effective. What, if anything, must Tweed do in respect to those states in which the securities are to be sold?

a. Nothing, since approval by the SEC automatically constitutes satisfaction of any state requirements.

b. Make a filing in those states which have laws governing such offerings and obtain their approval.

c. Simultaneously apply to the SEC for permission to market the securities in the various states without further clearance.

d. File in the appropriate state office of the state in which it maintains its principal office of business, obtain clearance, and forward a certified copy of that state's clearance to all other states.

The correct answer is (b). *(CPA 579 L-43)*

REQUIRED: What an issuer of stock registered with the SEC must do in the states in which the securities are to be sold.

DISCUSSION: Although federal securities law must be complied with when applicable, the states also have securities laws, often called "blue-sky laws." Compliance with federal law does not necessarily result in compliance with the state regulations. Tweed will be required to file in those states in which the securities are to be sold to obtain their approval.

Answer (a) is incorrect because federal law is in addition to state law, and SEC registration does not automatically satisfy state requirements. Answer (c) is incorrect because the SEC cannot give permission to market in any state. Answer (d) is incorrect because compliance with the laws of one state does not necessarily result in compliance with laws of another. Registration is necessary in each state.

28.2 Securities Act of 1933

10. Under the Securities Act of 1933, subject to some exceptions and limitations, it is unlawful to use the mails or instruments of interstate commerce to sell or offer to sell a security to the public unless

a. A surety bond sufficient to cover potential liability to investors is obtained and filed with the Securities and Exchange Commission.

b. The offer is made through underwriters qualified to offer the securities on a nationwide basis.

c. A registration statement has been properly filed with the Securities and Exchange Commission, has been found to be acceptable, and is in effect.

d. The Securities and Exchange Commission approves the financial merit of the offering.

The correct answer is (c). *(CPA 577 L-3)*

REQUIRED: When the instruments of interstate commerce may lawfully be used to sell or offer to sell a security to the public.

DISCUSSION: Unless securities are exempt or are involved in an exempt transaction, the Securities Act of 1933 requires a registration statement to be filed with regard to securities offered or sold through the mails or instruments of interstate commerce. The SEC reviews the registration statement for completeness, not necessarily for accuracy. The registration statement will automatically go into effect 20 days after filing unless the SEC requires amendments or issues a stop-order. Until effective (i.e., until after the 20 days), the securities may not be offered for sale in writing or sold.

Answer (a) is incorrect because securities laws do not require the registrant to provide a surety bond. Answer (b) is incorrect because a security is considered sold to the public even when the offer is made through underwriters. It would still be subject to the same registration requirements. Answer (d) is incorrect because the SEC does not judge the financial merit of securities.

11. Global Trucking Corporation has in its corporate treasury a substantial block of its own common stock, which it acquired several years previously. The stock had been publicly offered at $25 a share and had been reacquired at $15. The board is considering using it in the current year for various purposes. For which of the following purposes may it validly use the treasury stock?

a. To pay a stock dividend to its shareholders.

b. To sell it to the public without the necessity of registration under the Securities Act of 1933, since it had been previously registered.

c. To vote it at the annual meeting of shareholders.

d. To acquire the shares of another publicly held company without the necessity of a registration under the Securities Act of 1933.

The correct answer is (a). *(CPA 581 L-26)*

REQUIRED: The purpose for which a corporation may validly use treasury stock.

DISCUSSION: A corporation has the right to reacquire its own shares, and may use such shares to pay stock dividends to shareholders, provide special compensation for employees, sell, cancel, etc. Treasury stock transactions are normally within the discretion of the board of directors.

Answer (b) is incorrect because unless an offering of the treasury stock to the public would constitute an exempt transaction, a new distribution of previously issued shares requires a new registration statement to be filed with the SEC. Answer (c) is incorrect because treasury shares may not be voted. Answer (d) is incorrect because registration with the SEC is required if a sale or offer to sell any security is made unless an exemption is provided. The use of the treasury stock to acquire shares of another company is a disposition of a security for value and meets the definition of a sale under the 1933 Act.

12. Donn & Co. is considering the sale of $11 million of its common stock to the public in interstate commerce. In this connection, Donn has been correctly advised that registration of the securities with the SEC is

a. Not required if the states in which the securities are to be sold have securities acts modeled after the federal act and Donn files in those states.

b. Required in that it is necessary for the SEC to approve the merits of the securities offered.

c. Not required if the securities are to be sold through a registered brokerage firm.

d. Required and must include audited financial statements as an integral part of its registration.

The correct answer is (d). *(CPA 1186 L-32)*

REQUIRED: The true statement about registration statements.

DISCUSSION: Donn's offering does not qualify for an exemption, and a registration statement must be filed. It should contain facts material to sale of the securities, such as 1) the issuer's name and a description of its business; 2) the rights conferred by the securities, their relationship to other securities offered by the firm, and the plan for their distribution; 3) the use to which the proceeds will be put; 4) the names and compensation of directors and officers, names of controlling persons and of those owning 10% or more of the firm's stock, and facts about material transactions with such persons; 5) details of pending legal proceedings; and 6) financial statements audited by an independent accountant, including balance sheets for the 2 most recent fiscal years and statements of income and cash flows for the 3 most recent fiscal years. The purpose of these disclosures is to provide sufficient information to allow an ordinary investor to make an intelligent decision.

Answers (a) and (c) are incorrect because no exemption is provided for compliance with state law or sale by a broker. Answer (b) is incorrect because the SEC determines neither the accuracy of the facts in the statement nor the merits of the securities.

13. The 1933 Securities Act provides for a 20-day waiting period between the filing and the effective date of the registration. During this waiting period the registrant is prohibited from

a. Preparing any amendments to the registration statement or announcing the prospective issue.

b. Accepting offers to purchase the securities being registered from potential investors.

c. Placing an advertisement indicating by whom orders for the securities being registered will be accepted.

d. Issuing a prospectus in preliminary form.

The correct answer is (b). *(CMA 679 3-19)*

REQUIRED: The activity prohibited during the 20-day waiting period.

DISCUSSION: After filing the registration statement (which includes a prospectus) under the 1933 Act, there is a 20-day waiting period before the registration becomes effective. Its effectiveness is automatic unless the SEC requires amendments or issues a stop-order. During this period, the registrant is prohibited from making any written offers or accepting offers to purchase the securities being registered.

Answer (a) is incorrect because amendments may be made (or may be required) during this period. Also, an announcement of the prospective issuance of the securities may be published even though a written offer to sell may not be made. Answer (c) is incorrect because placing an advertisement indicating by whom orders will be accepted is not an actual offer to sell. It is similar to an announcement of prospective issuance. Answer (d) is incorrect because a preliminary ("red herring") prospectus may be issued as long as it is clearly identified and does not constitute an offer to sell.

14. Acme Corp. intends to make a public offering in several states of 250,000 shares of its common stock. Under the Securities Act of 1933,

a. Acme must sell the common stock through licensed securities dealers.

b. Acme must, in all events, file a registration statement with the SEC because the offering will be made in several states.

c. Acme's use of any prospectus delivered to an unsophisticated investor must be accompanied by a simplified explanation of the offering.

d. Acme may make an oral offer to sell the common stock to a prospective investor after a registration statement has been filed but before it becomes effective.

The correct answer is (d). *(CPA 589 L-40)*

REQUIRED: The true statement about a public offering of stock.

DISCUSSION: During the waiting period, Acme may publish a tombstone ad, distribute a preliminary prospectus, and make oral offers. Thus, offers made face-to-face, by telephone, or in sales meetings (if offerees can ask unlimited questions) are permitted.

Answer (a) is incorrect because the 1933 Act imposes no such requirement. Answer (b) is incorrect because various exemptions may be available to Acme. Answer (c) is incorrect because the 1933 Act imposes no such requirement.

15. A prospectus must be delivered to every purchaser of a security registered under the Securities Act of 1933. This document

a. Contains most of the relevant information provided in the registration statement.

b. Cannot be communicated to an investor until the registration statement is effective.

c. Is also known as a tombstone advertisement.

d. May be provided to prospective investors upon request prior to filing but after notice of the prospective offering has been given.

The correct answer is (a). *(Publisher)*

REQUIRED: The true statement about a prospectus.

DISCUSSION: The prospectus is a written document proposing a contract of sale to potential investors in securities. When the securities are required to be registered under the 1933 Act, a preliminary prospectus may be communicated to investors during the waiting period. It must omit the selling price and indicate that the registration statement is not yet effective. The prospectus must contain most of the information in the registration statement, including audited financial statements. A prospectus must be given to each buyer prior to or at the time of delivery of the securities.

Answer (b) is incorrect because a preliminary prospectus meeting statutory requirements may be transmitted only after filing. Answer (c) is incorrect because a tombstone ad is a brief but more extensive version of the pre-filing notice that may appear in financial publications. It is published during or after the waiting period and must state specifically that it is not an offer. Answer (d) is incorrect because a limited notice may be published during the period prior to filing but a prospectus cannot be furnished until after filing.

16. SEC Rule 415 concerns shelf registration of securities. Under Rule 415,

a. An issuer must file a registration statement for each new issue of securities.

b. A registration statement is effective for two years.

c. Shelf registration is available to a first-time issuer.

d. The 20-day waiting period is maintained.

The correct answer is (b). *(Publisher)*

REQUIRED: The true statement about shelf registration.

DISCUSSION: Rule 415 (under the 1933 Act) allows corporations to file registration statements covering a stipulated amount of securities that may be issued over the two-year effective period of the statement. The securities are placed "on the shelf" and issued at an opportune moment without the necessity of filing a new registration statement, observing a 20-day waiting period, or preparing a new prospectus. The issuer is only required to provide updating amendments or to refer investors to quarterly and annual statements filed with the SEC. It is most advantageous to large corporations that frequently offer securities to the public.

Answers (a) and (d) are incorrect because shelf registration is intended to reduce the inflexibility of these requirements. Answer (c) is incorrect because a first-time issuer does not qualify.

17. Which of the following facts will result in an offering of securities being exempt from registration under the Securities Act of 1933?

a. The sale or offer to sell the securities is made by a person other than an issuer, underwriter, or dealer.

b. The securities are non-voting preferred stock.

c. The issuing corporation was closely held prior to the offering.

d. The securities are AAA-rated debentures that are collateralized by first mortgages on property that has a market value of 200% of the offering price.

The correct answer is (a). *(CPA 1188 L-31)*

REQUIRED: The basis for an exemption of an offering of securities from registration.

DISCUSSION: The Securities Act of 1933 requires registration unless the security or transaction is exempt. The Act provides an exemption for transactions by any person other than an issuer, underwriter, or dealer. This applies to the great majority of securities transactions conducted by ordinary investors.

Answers (b), (c), and (d) are incorrect because the basic rule is that all securities transactions must be registered unless a specific exemption applies to the transaction or the securities. None of these transactions qualifies for an exemption.

18. Dee is the owner of 12% of the shares of common stock of D&M Corporation that she acquired in 1983. She is the treasurer and a director of D&M. The corporation registered its securities in 1984 and made a public offering pursuant to the Securities Act of 1933. If Dee decides to sell part of her holdings in 1990, the shares

a. Would be exempt from registration because the corporation previously registered them within 3 years.

b. Must be registered regardless of the amount sold or manner in which they are sold.

c. Would be exempt from registration because she is not an issuer.

d. Must be registered if Dee sells 50% of her shares through her broker to the public.

The correct answer is (d). *(CPA 586 L-24)*

REQUIRED: The true statement as to whether a controlling person's stock sale must be registered.

DISCUSSION: In general, any offer to sell securities in interstate commerce is subject to registration unless the securities or the transaction is exempt. Most transactions are exempt because they involve sales by persons other than issuers, underwriters, or dealers, e.g., transactions by ordinary investors selling on their own account. Dee, however, is considered an issuer because she is a controlling person, that is, one who owns more than 10% of the company's stock and who has the direct or indirect ability to control the company. A sale of 6% of D&M's common stock to the public in the ordinary course of business (e.g., through a broker) would not qualify for an exemption under the Securities Act of 1933 and would be subject to SEC registration.

Answer (a) is incorrect because the previous registration is irrelevant. Answer (b) is incorrect because under Rule 144, an insider who has held restricted securities for at least 2 years may resell without registration in any 3-month period the greater of 1% of the total shares of that class outstanding or the average weekly volume traded. Rule 144 also requires that the sales be in unsolicited brokers' transactions, that notice be given to the SEC, and that adequate information about the issuer be publicly available. Also, the sale might be exempt if no public offer is made or if certain other requirements are met. Answer (c) is incorrect because a controlling person is an issuer.

19. Which of the following is exempt from registration under the Securities Act of 1933?

a. First mortgage bonds.

b. The usual annuity contract issued by an insurer.

c. Convertible preferred stock.

d. Limited partnership interests.

The correct answer is (b). *(CPA 1179 L-28)*

REQUIRED: The security exempt under the Securities Act of 1933.

DISCUSSION: The term "security" is very broadly construed under the Securities Act of 1933. In general, a security is considered to be an investment through which one expects a financial return through the efforts of others. The 1933 Act exempts certain transactions and securities from coverage, including typical annuity contracts issued by an insurer.

Answers (a), (c), and (d) are incorrect because each represents a security that is not exempt from registration.

20. Which of the following securities is exempt from registration under the Securities Act of 1933?

a. A class of shares of stock given in exchange for another class by the issuer to its existing shareholders without payment of a commission.

b. Limited partnership interests sold for the purpose of acquiring funds to invest in bonds issued by the United States.

c. Corporate debentures that were previously subject to an effective registration statement, provided they are convertible into shares of common stock.

d. Shares of common stock, provided their par value is less than $1.00 and they are nonvoting.

The correct answer is (a). *(CPA 589 L-43)*

REQUIRED: The securities exempt from registration under the Securities Act of 1933.

DISCUSSION: If securities are transferred between the issuer and its existing shareholders without payment of commissions or other consideration, the transaction is exempt from registration. Hence, stock dividends and stock splits are exempt. Securities issued in mergers and reorganizations are also exempt if no cash is involved and the securities are given solely for other securities.

Answers (b), (c), and (d) are incorrect because each states no basis for exemption. The purpose for which funds will be used, prior registration, par value, and whether stock has voting rights are irrelevant in the circumstances described.

21. Which of the following is subject to the registration requirements of the Securities Act of 1933?

a. Public sale of its bonds by a municipality.

b. Public sale by a corporation of its negotiable 5-year notes.

c. Public sale of stock issued by a common carrier regulated by the Interstate Commerce Commission.

d. Securities of nonprofit charitable, religious, benevolent, fraternal, or educational institutions.

The correct answer is (b). *(CPA 1184 L-42)*

REQUIRED: The item subject to registration under the Securities Act of 1933.

DISCUSSION: The 1933 Act requires registration of securities to be offered or sold publicly through the mail or any instrumentality of interstate commerce. Drafts, notes, and bankers' acceptances otherwise qualifying as securities required to be registered are exempt if they arise out of current (working capital) transactions, mature in not more than 9 months, and are not advertised for public sale. Five-year notes clearly do not qualify for the exemption.

Answer (a) is incorrect because securities of domestic governments issued for governmental purposes are exempt. Answer (c) is incorrect because an issuance regulated by the ICC is exempt. Answer (d) is incorrect because these securities are specifically exempt.

22. The registration requirements of the Securities Act of 1933 apply to

a. The issuance of a stock dividend without commissions or other consideration paid.

b. The issuance of stock warrants.

c. Securities issued by a federally chartered savings and loan association or by a bank.

d. Securities issued by a common carrier regulated by the Interstate Commerce Commission.

The correct answer is (b). *(CPA 587 L-41)*

REQUIRED: The item to which the registration requirements of the Securities Act of 1933 apply.

DISCUSSION: Stock warrants are securities evidencing the right to purchase shares of stock at a stated price, usually at less than the market value. Hence, warrants have value and are traded independently. They may be issued when bonds or preferred stock are sold, as stock options provided to compensate employees, or as evidence of the preemptive rights of common stockholders. The issuance of stock warrants is not an exempt transaction because it is deemed to be a disposition of securities for value (a sale).

Answer (a) is incorrect because transfers between the issuer and its shareholders without payment of commissions or other consideration are exempt. Answers (c) and (d) are incorrect because these securities are regulated by other federal agencies and are therefore exempt.

23. Which of the following are exempt from the registration requirements of the Securities Act of 1933?

a. All industrial development bonds issued by municipalities.

b. Stock of a corporation offered and sold only to residents of the state in which the issuer was incorporated and doing all of its business.

c. Bankers' acceptances with maturities at the time of issue ranging from 1 to 2 years.

d. Participation interests in a money market fund that consists wholly of short-term commercial paper.

The correct answer is (b). *(CPA 588 L-41)*

REQUIRED: The securities exempt from registration under the 1933 Act.

DISCUSSION: One exemption from registration under the Securities Act of 1933 is an intrastate issue of securities. Under SEC Rule 147, an issue qualifies as intrastate if the issuer is incorporated in the state in which the issue is made, 80% of the proceeds are to be used in that state, 80% of its assets are located in the state of incorporation, the issuer does at least 80% of its business (gross revenues) within that state, all the purchasers and offerees are residents of the state, no resales to nonresidents occur for at least 9 months after the last sale, and steps are taken to prevent interstate distribution.

Answer (a) is incorrect because bonds of a municipality not used for a governmental purpose are exempt. Answer (c) is incorrect because the maturity limit is 9 months. Answer (d) is incorrect because the sale of short-term commercial paper, not interests in a money market fund, is exempt if certain conditions are met.

24. Maco Limited Partnership intends to sell $6,000,000 of its limited partnership interests. The state in which Maco was organized is also the state in which it carries on all of its business activities. If Maco intends to offer the limited partnership interests in reliance on Rule 147, the intrastate registration exception under the Securities Act of 1933, which one of the following statements is correct?

a. Maco may make up to five offers to nonresidents without the offering being ineligible for the Rule 147 Exemption.

b. The offering is not exempt under Rule 147 because it exceeds $5,000,000.

c. Under Rule 147, certain restrictions apply to resales of the limited partnership interests by purchasers.

d. Rule 147 limits to 100 the number of purchasers of the limited partnership interests.

The correct answer is (c). *(CPA 589 L-44)*

REQUIRED: The true statement about the intrastate offering exemption.

DISCUSSION: Rule 147 provides that the securities may not be offered or resold out-of-state for 9 months after the offering (for more, see the discussion of the preceding question).

Answer (a) is incorrect because no nonresident may purchase if the Rule 147 exemption is to apply. Answer (b) is incorrect because Rule 147 states no dollar limit on the amount of the offering. Answer (d) is incorrect because Rule 147 states no limit on the number of intrastate purchasers.

25. Rule 504 of Regulation D of the Securities Act of 1933 provides issuers with an exemption from registration for certain small issues. Which of the following statements is correct?

a. The rule allows sales to an unlimited number of investors.

b. The rule requires certain financial information to be furnished to the investors.

c. The issuer must offer the securities through general public advertising.

d. The issuer is not required to file anything with the SEC.

The correct answer is (a). *(CPA 1189 L-37)*

REQUIRED: The true statement about Rule 504 of Regulation D.

DISCUSSION: A limited offer of securities is exempt from registration if the sale is not advertised generally, the aggregate price is no more than $1,000,000 in a 12-month period, resale is restricted for a 2-year period, no more than $500,000 of the securities is unregistered under state law, and the SEC is notified of the sale. The issuer must 1) note on the certificates that the securities are restricted, 2) provide disclosure in writing to each purchaser prior to sale that the securities are unregistered and thus cannot be resold unless they are registered or an exempt transaction is possible, and 3) inquire whether the purchaser is buying on his/her own account or for others. Rule 504 places no limit on the number or nature of investors, and no disclosure of financial information is required.

Answer (b) is incorrect because no such disclosure is required by federal law. Answer (c) is incorrect because general public advertising is prohibited. Answer (d) is incorrect because the SEC must be notified of the sale.

26. Under the SEC's Regulation D, Rule 505, a small offering of securities is exempt if it meets certain requirements, among them that there are no more than 35 nonaccredited purchasers although there may be any number of accredited purchasers (certain well-to-do persons, insiders of the issuer, and institutional investors). The maximum dollar amount that qualifies for the Rule 505 exemption is

a. $500,000.

b. $1,500,000.

c. $2,000,000.

d. $5,000,000.

The correct answer is (d). *(Publisher)*

REQUIRED: The dollar limit on the Rule 505 exemption.

DISCUSSION: For the Rule 505 exemption, the offering may not exceed $5,000,000 in a 12-month period. Its other main differences from Rule 504 are the limitation on the number of nonaccredited investors and required disclosure of information about the issuer and securities offered.

27. Maco Limited Partnership intends to sell $6,000,000 of its limited partnership interests. If Maco intends to offer the limited partnership interests in reliance on Rule 506 of Regulation D under the Securities Act of 1933 to prospective investors residing in several states, which of the following statements is correct?

a. The offering will be exempt from the antifraud provisions of the Securities Exchange Act of 1934.

b. Any subsequent resale of a limited partnership interest by a purchaser will be exempt from registration.

c. Maco may make an unlimited number of offers to sell the limited partnership interests.

d. No more than 35 purchasers may acquire the limited partnership interests.

The correct answer is (c). *(CPA 589 L-45)*

REQUIRED: The true statement about Rule 506 (the private placement exemption).

DISCUSSION: Like Rules 504 and 505, Rule 506 bars general solicitation and advertising. Rules 505 and 506 also place no limit on accredited investors (certain well-to-do persons, high-level insiders, banks, insurance companies, etc.), restrict sales to 35 nonaccredited investors, and require that certain financial information be supplied if some investors are nonaccredited. Unlike Rule 505, Rule 506 has no dollar limit and requires that the issuer believe that all nonaccredited investors are sophisticated, that is, have sufficient knowledge and experience in business to evaluate the investment.

Answer (a) is incorrect because an exemption under the 1933 Act does not preclude coverage under the 1934 Act. Answer (b) is incorrect because Rules 504, 505, and 506 restrict resale. Answer (d) is incorrect because no more than 35 nonaccredited investors may acquire the securities.

28. Pate Corp. is offering $3 million of its securities solely to accredited investors pursuant to Regulation D of the Securities Act of 1933. Under Regulation D, Pate is

a. Not required to provide any specified information to the accredited investors.

b. Required to provide the accredited investors with audited financial statements for the 2 most recent fiscal years.

c. Permitted to make a general solicitation.

d. Not eligible for an exemption if the securities are debentures.

The correct answer is (a). *(CPA 587 L-44)*

REQUIRED: The true statement about an offering made solely to accredited investors.

DISCUSSION: Rule 504 of Regulation D does not apply to this offering because it exceeds $1,000,000 of which no more than $500,000 is unregistered under the state law. But Rules 505 ($5,000,000 limit) and 506 (no dollar limit) may be relevant. Under Rules 505 and 506 of Regulation D, no financial disclosure is necessary if all investors are accredited. But if some are nonaccredited, all investors must receive certain information. The required disclosures will depend on the amount of the offering and whether the issuer is subject to the reporting provisions of the 1934 Act. Also, Section 4(6) of the 1933 Act governs an offer made solely to accredited investors in an amount not exceeding $5,000,000. Section 4(6) does not require disclosure of information to the investors, restricts resale, and requires the issuer to notify the SEC of the transaction.

Answer (b) is incorrect because this disclosure is not necessary if all investors are accredited. Answer (c) is incorrect because Regulation D prohibits general solicitation. Answer (d) is incorrect because debentures fall within the broad definition of securities stated in the 1933 Act.

29. Securities available under a private placement made pursuant to Regulation D of the Securities Act of 1933

a. Cannot be subject to the payment of commissions.

b. Must be sold to accredited institutional investors.

c. Must be sold to fewer than 20 nonaccredited investors.

d. Cannot be the subject of an immediate unregistered reoffering to the public.

The correct answer is (d). *(CPA 1189 L-38)*

REQUIRED: The requirement for the private placement exemption.

DISCUSSION: A purchaser of securities under a Regulation D exemption may not immediately resell without being considered an underwriter. Thus, the exemption from registration for transactions by a person not an issuer, underwriter, or dealer is inapplicable. Moreover, the issuer must take steps to prevent non-exempt, unregistered resale and must notify the SEC of the sale. After the securities have been held for 2 years, limited resales are allowed without registration. Unlimited resales by a noninsider purchaser are allowed after 3 years. These limits on resale apply to the Rules 504, 505, and 506 exemptions.

Answers (a) and (b) are incorrect because Regulation D imposes no such requirement. Answer (c) is incorrect because these securities may also be sold to a maximum of 35 nonaccredited investors (those who are not insiders of the issuer, well-to-do persons, or institutional investors).

30. Theobold Construction Company, Inc. is considering a public stock offering for the first time. It wishes to raise $1,200,000 by a common stock offering in the least expensive manner. In this connection, it is considering making an offering pursuant to Regulation A of the Securities Act of 1933. Which of the following statements is correct?

a. Such an offering cannot be made to more than 250 people.

b. The maximum amount of securities permitted to be offered under Regulation A is $1 million.

c. Only those corporations that have had an initial registration under the Securities Act of 1933 are eligible.

d. Even if Regulation A applies, Theobold is required to distribute an offering circular.

The correct answer is (d). *(CPA 1180 L-40)*

REQUIRED: The correct statement regarding a public stock offering under Regulation A.

DISCUSSION: Under Regulation A, a small public issue of securities is exempt from full registration with the SEC if certain requirements are met. Regulation A applies to issuances not exceeding $1,500,000 if the issuer files an offering circular with the SEC, provides it to each offeree and purchaser, and observes the 10-day waiting period. Regulation A does not restrict resale, have an investor sophistication requirement, or limit the number of buyers. Also, no disclosure is necessary if the offering is $100,000 or less.

Answer (a) is incorrect because a Regulation A offering is limited by the dollar value of the securities offered, not by the number of offerees. Answer (b) is incorrect because the maximum permitted to be offered is $1,500,000 within a 12-month period. Answer (c) is incorrect because a corporation may be eligible under Regulation A without a prior registration under the 1933 Act. The purpose is to avoid full registration under the 1933 Act.

31. Issuer, Inc., a New York corporation engaged in retail sales within New York City, was interested in raising $2,500,000 in capital. In this connection it approached through personal letters 500 people in New York, New Jersey, and Connecticut, and then followed up with face-to-face negotiations where it seemed promising to do so. After extensive efforts in which Issuer disclosed all the information these people requested, 19 people from these areas purchased Issuer's securities. Issuer did not limit its offers to accredited persons or sophisticated investors. In regard to this securities issuance,

a. The offering is probably exempt from registration under federal securities law as a private placement.

b. The offering is probably exempt from registration under federal securities law as a small offering.

c. The offering is probably exempt from registration under federal securities law as an intrastate offering.

d. The offering is probably not exempt from registration under federal securities law.

The correct answer is (d). *(CPA 575 L-15)*

REQUIRED: The correct statement concerning this issuance of securities.

DISCUSSION: Issuer has offered to sell and has sold securities in interstate commerce and by use of the mails. The offering is subject to registration unless a specific exemption can be found. It does not qualify for the casual sales exemption since the sale is by an issuer. The Rule 504 small offering limit is $500,000. The Rule 506 private placement exemption is not available because some investors or offerees were evidently not "sophisticated." The Rule 505 ($5,000,000 limit) exemption is not applicable if a general solicitation is deemed to have been made (the same limitation is also imposed by Rules 504 and 506). The Regulation A exemption limit is $1,500,000. The $5,000,000 exemption provided by Section 4(6) of the Securities Act of 1933 for offers and sales solely to accredited investors is clearly not applicable.

Answer (a) is incorrect because the offering does not qualify for the private placement exemption. The securities were not offered and sold only to sophisticated investors or to accredited investors (certain insiders, wealthy persons, and institutional investors). Answer (b) is incorrect because the offering does not qualify for the exemption as a small offering under Regulation A, Rule 504, Rule 505, or Section 4(6). Answer (c) is incorrect because an intrastate offering requires that both offers and sales be made to persons of one state.

32. Spiffy Manufacturing plans to offer a new issue of voting stock to the investing public. Assuming that it properly takes advantage of an exemption from registration under the 1933 Act, Spiffy

a. Is also exempt from the antifraud rules of the federal securities laws.

b. Need not supply any offerees and purchasers with any material information about itself or the stock being sold.

c. Need not register with any state securities regulators.

d. Must adhere to both federal antifraud rules and state law.

The correct answer is (d). *(D. Paas)*

REQUIRED: The true statement about legal requirements regarding an exempt offering of stock.

DISCUSSION: An exemption from federal registration will almost never have any effect on the need to register with states where a security is to be sold. Neither will an exemption from registration excuse a seller from obeying any anti-fraud rules.

Answer (a) is incorrect because the Securities Act of 1933 and the Securities Exchange Act of 1934 specifically apply the antifraud rules in the absence of registration. Answer (b) is incorrect because information must be given despite the exemption from registration, Spiffy may still need to make disclosures. The amount of the offering and the nature of the offerees will determine whether disclosure is needed. Also, state law may require disclosure even if federal law does not. Answer (c) is incorrect because the federal securities laws specifically preserve the right of the states to regulate securities transactions concurrently with the federal government.

33. A requirement of a private action to recover damages for violation of the registration requirements of the Securities Act of 1933 is that

a. The plaintiff has acquired the securities in question.

b. The issuer or other defendants commit either negligence or fraud in the sale of the securities.

c. A registration statement has been filed.

d. The securities be purchased from an underwriter.

The correct answer is (a). *(CPA 586 L-20)*

REQUIRED: The requirement of a private action for registration violations.

DISCUSSION: Section 12(1) of the Securities Act of 1933 permits a civil action by an acquirer of securities if the required registration was not made, if a registered security was sold but a prospectus was not delivered, if a security was sold using a prospectus that was not current, or if an offer to sell was made before a required registration. Section 11 allows an acquirer to sue for misstatements or omissions of material facts in the registration statement.

Answer (b) is incorrect because liability for failure to register is absolute, so a defendant will be liable even though neither fraud nor negligence was committed. Answer (c) is incorrect because the failure to file may be the basis for liability. Answer (d) is incorrect because liability is imposed on anyone who violates the rules regarding the time, manner, or content of sales and offers to sell.

34. To be successful in a civil action under Section 11 of the Securities Act of 1933 concerning liability for a misleading registration statement, the plaintiff must prove

	Defendant's intent to deceive	Plaintiff's reliance on the registration statement
a.	Yes	Yes
b.	Yes	No
c.	No	Yes
d.	No	No

The correct answer is (d). *(CPA 1189 L-34)*

REQUIRED: The element(s) of a plaintiff's case under Section 11.

DISCUSSION: Under the 1933 Act, the issuer, its chief executive and directors, its chief finance and accounting officers, other signers, the underwriters, and experts who prepared or attested to the statement are liable for misstatements or omissions of material fact. In a private action, a plaintiff establishes a prima facie case pursuant to Section 11 by proving damages and that (s)he was an acquirer of a security issued under a registration statement that misstated or omitted a material fact. The result is to shift the burden of proof to the defendant, who then must show that (s)he exercised due diligence in regard to determining the accuracy of the statement. An issuer, however, cannot assert the due diligence defense, but any defendant may show that the plaintiff knew of the misstatement or omission at the time of acquisition.

Answer (a) is incorrect because intent to deceive, reliance, and privity need not be shown. Answer (b) is incorrect because intent to deceive need not be shown. Answer (c) is incorrect because reliance need not be shown.

35. One of the elements necessary to recover damages if there has been a material misstatement in a registration statement filed pursuant to the Securities Act of 1933 is that the

a. Plaintiff suffered a loss.

b. Plaintiff gave value for the security.

c. Issuer and plaintiff were in privity of contract with each other.

d. Issuer failed to exercise due care in connection with the sale of the securities.

The correct answer is (a). *(CPA 1189 L-33)*

REQUIRED: The element necessary to recover damages under the 1933 Act.

DISCUSSION: Under Section 11, plaintiff must prove that (s)he was an acquirer of a security covered by a registration statement, (s)he suffered a loss, and the statement misstated or omitted a material fact.

Answer (b) is incorrect because that plaintiff gave value need not be shown. Answer (c) is incorrect because plaintiff may have obtained the security from a party other than defendant. Answer (d) is incorrect because neither negligence nor fraud need be proven by the plaintiff. However, any defendant except an issuer may employ the due diligence defense by proving that (s)he was not negligent, and that (s)he reasonably investigated the statement and reasonably believed it to be free of material falsehoods or omissions.

36. Under Section 12(1) of the Securities Act of 1933, an issuer of an unregistered security required to be registered

a. Will be subject to a civil action for damages or rescission.

b. May assert the defense of due diligence.

c. Incurs criminal liability even though its conduct was not fraudulent.

d. May meet the requirement by delivery of a prospectus.

The correct answer is (a). *(Publisher)*

REQUIRED: The true statement about liability for an unregistered sale.

DISCUSSION: The acquirer of such a security may bring a civil action to rescind the contract of sale and recover the price upon return of the security. If the purchaser no longer owns it, (s)he may sue for damages.

Answer (b) is incorrect because due diligence is a defense to a complaint that the registration statement falsely stated or omitted a material fact. But it would be irrelevant in an action based on failure to register. The liability for an unregistered sale is absolute; i.e., no defense may be pleaded. Answer (c) is incorrect because only civil liability is imposed. Answer (d) is incorrect because both registration and delivery of a prospectus are required.

28.3 Securities Exchange Act of 1934

37. The Securities Exchange Act of 1934

a. Applies exclusively to issuers whose securities are listed on an organized stock exchange.

b. Has no application to issuers who are not required to register.

c. Imposes additional requirements on those issuers who must register and report.

d. Requires registration and reporting by all issuers with $2 million or more of assets or 1,000 or more equity shareholders.

The correct answer is (c). *(CPA 1186 L-35)*

REQUIRED: The true statement about the Securities Exchange Act of 1934.

DISCUSSION: Barring a specific exemption, the following must register: national securities exchanges, brokers and dealers, national securities associations, equity securities traded on national exchanges, and the equity securities traded in interstate commerce of issuers with more than $5,000,000 in assets and 500 or more stockholders of a class of equity securities. Also, annual (10-K), quarterly (10-Q), and material events (8-K) reports must be filed.

Answers (a) and (d) are incorrect because registration of any class of equity securities with 500 or more shareholders is required if the issuer has total assets in excess of $5,000,000. Answer (b) is incorrect because the antifraud provisions apply whether or not securities are registered.

38. Which of the following statements is correct with respect to the registration requirements of the Securities Exchange Act of 1934?

a. They require issuers of non-exempt securities traded on a national securities exchange to register with the SEC.

b. They permit issuers who comply with the Securities Act of 1933 to avoid the registration requirements of the Securities Exchange Act of 1934.

c. They permit issuers who comply with those requirements to avoid state registration requirements.

d. They permit issuers who comply with those requirements to avoid the registration requirements of the Securities Exchange Act of 1933.

The correct answer is (a). *(CPA 587 L-39)*

REQUIRED: The true statement about registration under the 1934 Act.

DISCUSSION: Barring a specific exemption, the following must register: national securities exchanges, brokers and dealers, national securities associations, equity securities traded on national exchanges, and the equity securities traded in interstate commerce of issuers with more than $5,000,000 in assets and 500 or more stockholders of a class of equity securities.

Answers (b), (c), and (d) are incorrect because compliance with one of these Acts does not meet the requirements of the other or of state law.

39. Pace Corp. previously issued 300,000 shares of its common stock. The shares are now actively traded on a national securities exchange. The original offering was exempt from registration under the Securities Act of 1933. Pace has $2,500,000 in assets and 425 shareholders. With regard to the Securities Exchange Act of 1934, Pace is

a. Required to file a registration statement because its assets exceed $2,000,000 in value.

b. Required to file a registration statement even though it has fewer than 500 shareholders.

c. Not required to file a registration statement because the original offering of its stock was exempt from registration.

d. Not required to file a registration statement unless insiders own at least 5% of its outstanding shares of stock.

The correct answer is (b). *(CPA 589 L-41)*

REQUIRED: The effect of the 1934 Act on registration of securities traded on a national exchange but exempt under the 1933 Act.

DISCUSSION: All issuers whose securities are traded on a national exchange must register pursuant to the 1934 Act. Whether the original offering was exempt under the 1933 Act is irrelevant. The number of shareholders is relevant to registration under the 1934 Act only if the securities are not traded on a national exchange.

Answer (a) is incorrect because the amount of the issuer's assets is also not relevant to registration if the securities are traded on a national exchange. Answer (c) is incorrect because the exemption under the 1933 Act does not satisfy the requirements of the 1934 Act. Answer (d) is incorrect because the extent of insider ownership does not determine whether registration is needed.

40. The reporting requirements of the Securities Exchange Act of 1934 and its rules

a. Apply only to issuers, underwriters, and dealers.

b. Apply to a corporation that registered under the Securities Act of 1933 but that did not register under the Securities Exchange Act of 1934.

c. Require all corporations engaged in interstate commerce to file an annual report.

d. Require all corporations engaged in interstate commerce to file quarterly audited financial statements.

The correct answer is (b). *(CPA 1187 L-12)*

REQUIRED: The persons and entities required to report under the 1934 Act.

DISCUSSION: The following must file periodic reports under the 1934 Act: national securities exchanges, an issuer with more than $5,000,000 in assets and 500 or more shareholders of a class of equity securities traded in interstate commerce, an issuer whose securities are traded on a national exchange, and an issuer that has registered under the 1933 Act. These issuers must file annual (10-K), quarterly (10-Q), and material events (8-K) reports, and send similar reports to shareholders. However, an issuer that must report solely on the basis of registration under the 1933 Act need not transmit an annual report to its shareholders.

Answer (a) is incorrect because national exchanges must also report. Answers (c) and (d) are incorrect because doing business in interstate commerce is not a sufficient condition for registering or reporting. Also, statements included in quarterly reports need not be audited.

41. Which of the following is a required disclosure in the annual reports of companies registered with the Securities and Exchange Commission?

a. Audited balance sheets for the last 4 years.

b. Audited summary of earnings for the last 10 years.

c. Identification of registrar and transfer agent.

d. Range of market prices of the common stock of the registrant for each quarter of the last 2 years.

The correct answer is (d). *(CMA 1280 3-27)*

REQUIRED: The disclosure that must appear in the annual reports of companies registered with the SEC.

DISCUSSION: The Securities Exchange Act of 1934 imposes substantial reporting requirements upon those required to register. In addition to other periodic reports, an annual report (Form 10-K) requires disclosure of the market price of the common stock of the registrant, including the high and low sales prices, for each quarter of the last 2 fiscal years and any subsequent interim periods.

Answer (a) is incorrect because audited balance sheets are only required for the current and 2 prior fiscal year-ends. Answer (b) is incorrect because the audited summary of earnings for the current and preceding 2 years must be presented. Answer (c) is incorrect because the registrar and transfer agent are identified only in the initial filing with the SEC; changes are disclosed in Form 8-K.

42. Tulip Corp. is a registered and reporting corporation under the Securities Exchange Act of 1934. As such it

a. Can offer and sell its securities to the public without the necessity of registering its securities pursuant to the Securities Act of 1933.

b. Can not make a tender offer for the equity securities of another registered and reporting corporation without the consent of the SEC.

c. Must file annual reports (Form 10-K) with the SEC.

d. Must distribute a copy of the annual report (Form 10-K) to each of its shareholders.

The correct answer is (c). *(CPA 1186 L-33)*

REQUIRED: The true statement about a registered and reporting corporation under the 1934 Act.

DISCUSSION: If Tulip's securities are traded on a national exchange or if Tulip has more than $5,000,000 in assets and a class of equity securities with 500 or more shareholders, it may file annual (10-K), quarterly (10-Q), and material events (8-K) reports with the SEC. Similar reports are sent to shareholders. An issuer that must report because it has an offering registered under the 1933 Act must meet the same requirements except that it need not send an annual report to its shareholders. The 10-K report contains information about the entity's business activities, securities, management, related parties, disagreements concerning accounting and disclosure, audited financial statements, etc. It is intended to bring the information in the registration statement up to date.

Answer (a) is incorrect because registration under the 1934 Act does not substitute for registration under the 1933 Act. Answer (b) is incorrect because the offeror must make various filings with the SEC but need not obtain its consent. Answer (d) is incorrect because Form 10-K is not distributed to shareholders but the annual report sent to shareholders is comparable.

43. Which of the following statements is correct concerning corporations subject to the reporting requirements of the Securities Exchange Act of 1934?

a. The annual report (form 10-K) need not include audited financial statements.

b. The annual report (form 10-K) must be filed with the SEC within 20 days of the end of the corporation's fiscal year.

c. A quarterly report (form 10-Q) need only be filed with the SEC by those corporations that are also subject to the registration requirements of the Securities Act of 1933.

d. A report (form 8-K) must be filed with the SEC after a material important event occurs.

The correct answer is (d). *(CPA 1188 L-33)*

REQUIRED: The reporting required under the Securities Exchange Act of 1934.

DISCUSSION: Form 8-K is the report that must be filed within 15 calendar days after certain specified material events occur. These events include changes in control of the issuer; a significant revaluation, acquisition, or disposition of assets; default on an issuance of securities; a change in the amount of securities; and "any material important event." However, the resignation of a director or a change of independent accountants must be reported within 5 business days.

Answer (a) is incorrect because Form 10-K must include audited financial statements: balance sheets for the current and 2 prior fiscal year-ends and statements of income, cash flows, and changes in stockholders' equity for the current and preceding 2 years. Answer (b) is incorrect because Form 10-K is due 90 days after the entity's fiscal year-end but some schedules may be filed 120 days after year-end. Answer (c) is incorrect because an entity required to file Form 10-K must also file Form 10-Q for each of the first three quarters.

44. If securities are registered under the Securities Exchange Act of 1934, which of the following disclosure provisions apply?

I. Notice of sales of the registered securities by the corporation's officers must be filed with the SEC.

II. Proxy material for the registered securities must be filed with the SEC.

a. II only.

b. I only.

c. Both I and II.

d. Neither I nor II.

The correct answer is (c). *(CPA 588 L-40)*

REQUIRED: The disclosure provision(s) applicable to securities registered under the 1934 Act.

DISCUSSION: Under Section 16, statutory insiders must disclose their holdings. These insiders include officers, directors, and owners of more than 10% of a class of registered equity securities. They must also promptly report any transactions in those securities. Also, purchases and sales made within 6 months before or after becoming an insider must be reported. A proxy statement must be filed with the SEC 10 days or more prior to being mailed to shareholders.

Answer (a) is incorrect because officers' transactions must be disclosed. Answer (b) is incorrect because proxy material must be filed. Answer (d) is incorrect because both proxy material and officers' transactions must be filed.

45. Rey Corp.'s management intends to solicit proxies relating to its annual meeting at which directors will be elected. Rey is subject to the registration and reporting requirements of the Securities Exchange Act of 1934. As a result, Rey must furnish its shareholders with

a. A copy of its registration statement and bylaws.

b. A preliminary copy of its proxy statement at the same time it is filed with the SEC.

c. An annual report containing its audited statements of income for the 5 most recent years.

d. An annual report containing its audited balance sheets for the 2 most recent years.

The correct answer is (d). *(CPA 1187 L-9)*

REQUIRED: The true statement about proxy solicitation requirements.

DISCUSSION: Financial statements of the company must be provided only for annual meetings at which directors are to be elected (in the annual report) or if a merger or authorization to issue new shares is at issue. Audited statements for the last 2 years should be included. Furthermore, even when no solicitation is made, management must still furnish an information statement similar to a proxy statement to all shareholders who have the right to vote at the meeting.

Answer (a) is incorrect because there is no such requirement. Answer (b) is incorrect because Section 14 seeks to ensure that proxy solicitations are accompanied by adequate disclosure of information about the agenda items for which authority to vote is being sought. One requirement is that the proxy statement be filed with the SEC at least 10 days prior to mailing proxy materials to shareholders. The proxy statement must identify the party making the solicitation and details about the matters to be voted on such as mergers, authorizations to issue new stock, or election of directors. Answer (c) is incorrect because 2 years' audited statements must be included.

46. A proxy is a writing signed by a shareholder that authorizes someone to vote his/her shares at a shareholder meeting. Proxy solicitation is important because most shareholders do not attend shareholders' meetings. Because of the need of investors for information about proxy contests, the SEC has promulgated rules concerning the solicitation of proxies. Which of the following is not required?

a. Management may have to include shareholder proposals in the proxy statement.

b. The shareholders must be provided an opportunity to approve or disapprove each proposal rather than all or none.

c. A shareholder is entitled either to have the management mail the shareholder's proxy material to all the other shareholders (at the shareholder's expense) or to receive a list of all other shareholders.

d. All proxy solicitations must be paid for by the group making the solicitation.

The correct answer is (d). *(Publisher)*

REQUIRED: The statement that is not a requirement of proxy solicitations.

DISCUSSION: Proxy solicitations by the current management of a corporation may be paid for by the corporation under the theory that the shareholders' approval is needed to properly carry out management duties. Shareholders who wish to challenge the current management of a corporation (insurgents) must pay for their own proxy solicitations; however, they are sometimes entitled to reimbursement if they win.

Answer (a) is incorrect because management may have to include shareholder proposals in the proxy statement. A shareholder who meets certain conditions may submit one proposal per meeting to be included in management's proxy statement. In general, the proposal must concern business policy relevant to the company's activities and not be similar to any recently defeated proposal. Answer (b) is incorrect because an opportunity must be given to approve or disapprove each proposal separately. Answer (c) is incorrect because to insure fairness when management itself is soliciting proxies, the SEC has ruled that management must mail the proxy solicitations of insurgents (at the insurgents' expense) or provide a list of all the other shareholders so the insurgents can do their own mailing.

47. James Fisk recently acquired Valiant Corporation by purchasing all of its outstanding stock pursuant to a tender offer. Fisk demanded and obtained the resignation of the existing board of directors and replaced it with his own slate of nominees. Under these circumstances,

a. Fisk had no right to demand the resignation of the existing board members; their resignations are legally ineffective and they remain as directors.

b. If Valiant is listed on a national stock exchange, Fisk would have to file his tender offer with the Securities and Exchange Commission.

c. The former stockholders of Valiant are parties to a tax-free reorganization. Hence, they are not subject to federal income tax on their gain, if any, on transferring their stock to Fisk.

d. If Valiant is engaged in interstate commerce, the acquisition is exempt under the antitrust laws because the Securities and Exchange Commission has jurisdiction.

The correct answer is (b). *(CPA 1174 L-40)*

REQUIRED: The correct statement concerning the acquisition of all a corporation's stock by means of a tender offer.

DISCUSSION: A tender offer is an offer to shareholders to buy their stock in order to gain control of a corporation. Under the Securities Exchange Act of 1934, anyone who makes a tender offer that would result in the purchase of more than 5% of a class of registered equity securities must file his/her tender offer with the SEC. Since Valiant is listed on a national stock exchange, its shares must be registered, and Fisk's tender offer would have to be filed prior to acquisition.

Answer (a) is incorrect because while in some jurisdictions a director of a corporation may be removed only for cause prior to the expiration of his/her term, a director may resign at any time. Answer (c) is incorrect because Fisk's acquisition of Valiant was a purchase, not a tax-free reorganization. The former stockholders of Valiant are subject to tax on their gains. Answer (d) is incorrect because SEC jurisdiction does not exempt the transaction from antitrust laws.

48. On May 1, Apel purchased 7% of Stork Corp.'s preferred stock traded on a national securities exchange. After the purchase, Apel owned 9% of the outstanding preferred stock. Stork is registered under the Securities Exchange Act of 1934. With respect to the purchase, Apel

a. Is not required to file any report or information with the SEC because Apel owns less than 10% of the preferred stock.

b. Is not required to file any report or information with the SEC because the security purchased was preferred stock.

c. Must file with the SEC, the issuer, and the national securities exchange information concerning the purpose of the acquisition.

d. Must file only with the SEC information concerning the source of the funds used to purchase the preferred stock.

The correct answer is (c). *(CPA 587 L-40)*

REQUIRED: The legal implications of purchasing more than 5% of the outstanding preferred shares of a company listed on a national exchange.

DISCUSSION: As part of its regulation of tender offers, the Securities Exchange Act of 1934 requires any person who has acquired more than 5% of any registered equity security to file reports with the issuer, the exchange on which the security is traded, and the SEC. The information reported includes the identity of the purchaser, the source of funding, the purpose of the acquisition, and the number of shares owned.

Answer (a) is incorrect because notification is required if more than 5% (not 10%) of a registered equity security is acquired. Answer (b) is incorrect because the preferred stock was required to be registered, so reports must be filed. Answer (d) is incorrect because reports must also be sent to the issuer and the exchange.

49. Which of the following persons is not an insider of a corporation subject to the Securities Exchange Act of 1934 registration and reporting requirements?

a. The president.

b. A member of the board of directors.

c. A shareholder who owns 8% of the outstanding common stock and whose spouse owns 4% of the outstanding common stock.

d. An owner of 15% of the total face value of the corporation's outstanding debentures.

The correct answer is (d). *(CPA 587 L-42)*

REQUIRED: The individual not deemed an insider liable for short-swing profits.

DISCUSSION: For the purposes of Section 16(b), an insider is an officer, director, or beneficial owner of more than 10% of any class of equity securities registered under the 1934 Act. The holder of debentures would not be considered an insider because a debenture is a debt security, not an equity security.

Answer (a) is incorrect because an officer is an insider. Answer (b) is incorrect because a director is an insider. Answer (c) is incorrect because a 12% owner is considered an insider even though 4% of the ownership is beneficial. A shareholder is a beneficial owner if shares are owned by his/her spouse, minor children, a relative with the same residence, or a trust of which (s)he is a beneficiary.

50. Taylor is the executive vice-president for Marketing of Reflex Corporation and a member of the board of directors. Based on information obtained during the course of his duties, Taylor concluded that Reflex's profits would fall by 50% for the quarter and 30% for the year. He quietly contacted his broker and disposed of 10,000 shares of his Reflex stock at a profit, some of which he had acquired within six months of the sale. In fact, Reflex's profits did not fall, but its stock price declined for unrelated reasons. Taylor had also advised a friend to sell her shares and repurchase the stock later. She followed Taylor's advice, sold for $21, and subsequently repurchased an equal number of shares at $11. A shareholder has commenced a shareholder derivative action against Taylor and the friend for violation of the Securities Exchange Act of 1934. Under these circumstances, which of the following is correct?

a. Taylor is not an insider in relation to Reflex.

b. Taylor must account to the corporation for his short-swing profit.

c. Taylor and the friend must both account to the corporation for their short-swing profits.

d. Neither Taylor nor the friend has incurred any liability under the 1934 Act.

The correct answer is (b). *(CPA 1179 L-27)*

REQUIRED: The correct statement concerning stock transactions by an officer and director.

DISCUSSION: Section 16(b) of the Securities Exchange Act of 1934 requires insiders of firms whose securities must be registered under the 1934 Act to account to their companies for short-swing profits. An insider is an officer, director, or a more than 10% owner. A short-swing profit is one earned on a purchase and sale (or sale and purchase) of a company's equity securities within a 6-month period. Taylor is an insider who has earned a short-swing profit and must therefore account to the corporation for his profit.

Answer (a) is incorrect because any officer, director, or 10% owner of a corporation is an insider. Answer (c) is incorrect because the person who receives such a tip need not account under Section 16(b). However, Taylor and the friend could both be liable under the antifraud provision of Section 10(b). Answer (d) is incorrect because Taylor has incurred liability to the corporation for short-swing profits, and both Taylor and the friend have incurred potential liability under the antifraud provision of Section 10(b).

51. The Securities and Exchange Commission's fraud Rule 10b-5 prohibits trading on the basis of inside information of a business corporation's stock by

a. Officers and directors.

b. All officers, directors and stockholders.

c. Officers, directors and beneficial holders of 10% of the corporation's stock.

d. Anyone who bases his/her trading activities on the inside information.

The correct answer is (d). *(CMA 679 3-22)*

REQUIRED: The person(s) prohibited from trading securities based on inside information.

DISCUSSION: Rule 10b-5 is the SEC rule under the Securities Exchange Act of 1934 that prohibits any person from engaging in manipulative or deceptive acts in the purchase or sale of any security. This prohibits trading on the basis of inside information and applies to anyone who has not made a full disclosure of the inside information. It applies not only to officers, directors, stockholders (and beneficial holders), but also to tippees, i.e., those who receive inside information from insiders.

Answers (a), (b), and (c) are incorrect because each is an incomplete answer.

52. Section 10(b) of the Securities Exchange Act of 1934 and SEC Rule 10b-5 are intended, among other things, to prevent trading of securities using inside information. Which of the following is true?

a. A lawyer for a firm is liable if (s)he learns of its impending merger and trades on that information after making full disclosure to the parties whose purchase or sale might be affected.

b. A secretary for a firm is liable if (s)he acquires inside information while typing papers relevant to a tender offer but takes no action except to tip a friend who trades on the information after it becomes public.

c. An officer of a firm tells a stockbroker about a scandal involving the company. The tippee-broker warns her clients before the news is made public. Although the officer did not receive a personal benefit, the broker is liable if the clients avoided loss because of the tip.

d. A consultant for a firm tells another client in confidence about an unannounced acquisition. Contrary to his promise, the client tells his mother. The consultant expected to gain through enhancement of his reputation with the client. The client and his mother used the information to make profits. The mother is liable.

The correct answer is (d). *(Publisher)*

REQUIRED: The person liable for insider trading under the Securities Exchange Act of 1934.

DISCUSSION: Under Section 10(b) and Rule 10b-5, an insider of a corporation will be liable if (s)he makes a purchase or sale of securities on material, nonpublic corporate information without prior disclosure. Insiders for this purpose include not only officers, directors, and controlling shareholders, but also employees at any level of the company, lawyers, accountants, investment bankers, news reporters, and others entrusted with confidential information for a corporate purpose. Tippees of insiders and their tippees (remote tippees) are also liable if they trade on inside information. A tippee is liable if the tipper breached a fiduciary duty to the company by divulging the information and the tippee knew or should have known of the breach. But no fiduciary duty is breached by the tipper if (s)he derives no personal benefit. Because the tippee's liability under the Act is derived from the tipper's violation, a tippee will escape liability if the tipper committed no breach. Here, since a personal benefit may be a nonmonetary one such as enhancement of professional reputation, the tipper-consultant was in breach. His tippee and the remote tippee are thus also liable.

Answer (a) is incorrect because full disclosure prior to use of the information is one way for an insider to avoid liability. Answer (b) is incorrect because the secretary is an insider, but neither (s)he nor the tippee is liable since both abstained from trading before the information became public. Answer (c) is incorrect because the broker was a tippee of a tipper who did not breach a fiduciary duty because he did not personally benefit. These facts are based on Dirks v. SEC (103 S.Ct. 3255 (1983)). However, the Insider Trading Sanctions Act of 1984 permits the SEC to bring a civil penalty action against anyone purchasing or selling securities while in possession of material nonpublic information.

53. SEC Rule 10b-5 was promulgated pursuant to the Securities Exchange Act of 1934. It is intended to prevent fraud in the trading of securities. Rule 10b-5 applies

a. When brokers with no knowledge of the facts make excessive predictions to customers.

b. Although no means or instrumentality of interstate commerce, the mails, or any facility of a national securities exchange was used by the defendant.

c. Only to the purchase or sale of securities registered under the 1934 Act.

d. Only when the defendant has knowingly misstated a material fact.

The correct answer is (a). *(Publisher)*

REQUIRED: The application of SEC Rule 10b-5.

DISCUSSION: Rule 10b-5 is known as the antifraud provision. It prohibits any device or scheme to defraud in the purchase or sale of securities. This has been used against brokers who make high-pressure sales of securities and wild predictions not based on fact. Rule 10b-5 also makes unlawful an untrue statement of a material fact or omission of a material fact in the sale of securities. This is often used against the issuer and professionals (lawyers and accountants) when there are errors in documents filed with the SEC.

Answer (b) is incorrect because the Rule applies only when interstate commerce, the mails, or a national securities exchange is involved. Answer (c) is incorrect because the Rule applies to the purchase or sale of any security (even if not registered under the 1934 Act). Answer (d) is incorrect because unlike the common law tort of fraud, the Rule creates a duty of affirmative disclosure. The omission of a material fact is also a violation.

54. May-Kit, Inc. is a small, rapidly expanding manufacturing company. May-Kit has just completed a small public offering of its common stock. The offering was exempt from registration under the Securities Act of 1933, as well as the periodic filing requirements of the Securities Exchange Act of 1934. The shares are traded over the counter and are bought and sold in interstate commerce. Do any of the civil liability sections of the 1933 and 1934 Acts apply to this offering and its subsequent trading?

a. None of the civil liability sections applies.

b. The negligence provisions of Section 11 of the 1933 Act apply.

c. The fraud provisions of Section 10-b of the 1934 Act apply.

d. Both the negligence provisions of Section 11 of the 1933 Act and the fraud provisions of Section 10-b of the 1934 Act apply.

The correct answer is (c). *(R. Welton)*

REQUIRED: The applicability of the civil liability sections of the Securities Acts to a small public offering of over-the-counter common stock.

DISCUSSION: The fraud provisions of Section 10-b apply to both registered and unregistered securities that are traded on a national exchange, in interstate commerce, or by use of the instrumentalities of interstate commerce (mail or wire services).

Answers (a), (b), and (d) are incorrect because Section 11 of the 1933 Act applies only to securities required to be registered under the 1933 Act.

55. The concept of materiality is very important under the antifraud provisions. Which of the following is the correct statement with regard to materiality?

a. Material information concerns only current earnings and distributions of a company, not future earnings that cannot be estimated with accuracy.

b. Materiality is a function of whether a reasonable person would attach importance to the information and includes the balancing of both the probability that the event may occur and its potential impact relative to the total company activities.

c. Although the concept of materiality is not specifically defined, the SEC has ruled for administrative convenience that any event involving less than $100,000 is not material.

d. The Supreme Court has ruled that any event or information which a buyer or seller of securities may take into account is material to that person.

The correct answer is (b). *(Publisher)*

REQUIRED: The correct statement concerning materiality under the antifraud provisions.

DISCUSSION: Materiality is not specifically defined under the Securities Acts or the SEC regulations. Several courts have attempted to define materiality in connection with the case before the court. It generally depends on whether a reasonable person would attach importance to the information in deciding on a course of action. It also involves the balancing of the probability that the event may occur and its potential impact relative to total company activities.

Answer (a) is incorrect because those facts that may affect the future of the company are relevant to investors trading in the company's securities. Answer (c) is incorrect because the SEC has not ruled any specific dollar amount to be the limit of materiality. Answer (d) is incorrect because the Supreme Court has not ruled any event or information to be material to a particular person. Rather, the courts generally have provided that materiality depends upon the importance a reasonable person would attach to it.

56. Insofar as the Securities Act of 1933 and the Securities Exchange Act of 1934 are concerned with fraud,

a. The Acts are identical with respect to proscribing fraudulent transactions.

b. The antifraud provisions are contained exclusively in the 1934 Act.

c. The 1933 Act does not require proof of scienter in all circumstances whereas the 1934 Act does.

d. Only the 1933 Act contains criminal sanctions against those found to be guilty of fraud.

The correct answer is (c). *(CPA 1182 L-33)*

REQUIRED: The correct comparison of the antifraud provisions of the 1933 and 1934 Acts.

DISCUSSION: The 1934 Act prohibits the use of any "manipulative or deceptive device or contrivance" in connection with the purchase or sale of any security. The plaintiff must prove scienter (intent to deceive or manipulate). Section 12 of the 1933 Act, however, imposes liability for fraud upon a person who sells or offers to sell a security by means of an oral statement or a prospectus containing an untrue statement of material fact or an omission thereof. Plaintiff need not prove scienter (defendant's knowledge of the falsehood or omission), but defendant may escape liability by proof that (s)he did not know or, in the exercise of reasonable care, could not have known of the falsehood or omission.

Answer (a) is incorrect because the Acts differ. Answer (b) is incorrect because the 1933 Act has two antifraud provisions. The second (Section 17) is incorporated into Rule 10b-5 under the 1934 Act and applied to buyers as well as sellers. Answer (d) is incorrect because both Acts provide for fines and imprisonment for certain willful violations.

57. When there is evidence of a violation of the federal securities laws, the SEC lacks the power to

a. Subpoena witnesses.

b. Compel the production of books and records anywhere in the United States.

c. Order an administrative hearing to determine responsibility for the violation and impose certain sanctions.

d. Prosecute criminal cases.

The correct answer is (d). *(CPA 1184 L-44)*

REQUIRED: The power not exercisable by the SEC.

DISCUSSION: The SEC is a federal administrative agency with both quasi-legislative and quasi-judicial authority. It promulgates rules and regulations under the securities laws, but it is also empowered to enforce these laws. Its powers include the ability to subpoena witnesses, books, and records and to conduct administrative hearings to adjudicate cases involving alleged breaches of the rules and regulations. Since administrative agencies cannot impose criminal sanctions, the Justice Department must prosecute criminal cases involving violations of the securities laws.

58. Which of the following statements is correct with respect to criminal prosecution under the Securities Acts?

a. Reckless disregard for the truth may be a sufficient basis for a criminal conviction.

b. Personal monetary gain from the alleged criminal conduct is required in order to be convicted.

c. The antifraud provisions of the Securities Acts are the only basis upon which a person can be indicted and convicted.

d. Corporations are not subject to criminal prosecution.

The correct answer is (a). *(CPA 584 L-33)*

REQUIRED: The true statement about criminal prosecution under the securities laws.

DISCUSSION: Criminal liability under the federal securities laws is based on their willful violation. A reckless disregard for the truth or falsity of a statement is sometimes deemed to be a willful or intentional act.

Answer (b) is incorrect because personal gain is not an element of the prosecution's case. For example, an intentional falsification of a registration statement need not result in actual personal gain to be subject to a criminal sanction. Answers (c) and (d) are incorrect because uniform criminal penalties may be imposed on any person, including corporations, for willful violation of federal securities statutes, rules, or regulations, or for willful falsification or omission of a material fact needed for an accurate representation in any document required to be filed with the SEC.

59. Cooke, in his capacity as president of Tool Corp., was convicted of willful violations of the Securities Act of 1933 and the Securities Exchange Act of 1934. The sanctions under both acts

a. Permit the imposition of only a fine.

b. Permit the imposition of both a fine and a term of imprisonment.

c. Are different since criminal sanctions are excluded from the Securities Exchange Act of 1934.

d. Are different since criminal sanctions are excluded from the Securities Act of 1933.

The correct answer is (b). *(CPA 1184 L-45)*

REQUIRED: The true statement about criminal sanctions under the securities laws.

DISCUSSION: Uniform criminal penalties may be imposed on any person, including corporations, for willful violation of federal securities statutes, rules, or regulations, or for willful falsification or omission of a material fact needed for an accurate representation in any document required to be filed with the SEC. The maximum penalty may not exceed 5 years in prison and a fine of $10,000 for a violation of the 1933 Act. The 1934 Act provides a maximum of 5 years in prison and a $100,000 fine. A securities exchange that violates these laws may be subject to a fine of up to $500,000.

Answer (a) is incorrect because a prison term may also be imposed. Answers (c) and (d) are incorrect because criminal penalties are imposed under both Acts.

28.4 Foreign Corrupt Practices Act (FCPA)

60. Which of the following corporations are subject to the accounting requirements of the Foreign Corrupt Practices Act (FCPA)?

a. All corporations engaged in interstate commerce.

b. All domestic corporations engaged in international trade.

c. All corporations which have made a public offering under the Securities Act of 1933.

d. All corporations whose securities are registered pursuant to the Securities Exchange Act of 1934.

The correct answer is (d). *(CPA 1183 L-45)*

REQUIRED: The corporations subject to the accounting requirements of the FCPA.

DISCUSSION: The accounting requirements of the FCPA apply to all companies required to register and report under the Securities Exchange Act of 1934. These companies must maintain books, records, and accounts in reasonable detail that accurately and fairly reflect transactions. The FCPA also requires these companies to maintain a system of internal accounting control that provides certain reasonable assurances, including that corporate assets are not used for bribes. If payoffs are made, they must be reflected in the company's records.

Answers (a), (b), and (c) are incorrect because the accounting requirements apply only to publicly held, registered companies under the 1934 Act.

61. A major impact of the Foreign Corrupt Practices Act of 1977 is that registrants subject to the Securities Exchange Act of 1934 are now required to

a. Keep records that reflect the transactions and dispositions of assets and to maintain a system of internal accounting controls.

b. Provide access to records by authorized agencies of the federal government.

c. Prepare financial statements in accord with international accounting standards.

d. Produce full, fair and accurate periodic reports on foreign commerce and/or foreign political party affiliations.

The correct answer is (a). *(CMA 1280 3-26)*

REQUIRED: The major impact of the Foreign Corrupt Practices Act of 1977.

DISCUSSION: The main purpose of the Foreign Corrupt Practices Act of 1977 is to prevent bribery by firms that do business in foreign countries. A major ramification is that it requires all companies which must register with the SEC under the Securities Exchange Act of 1934 to maintain adequate accounting records and a system of internal accounting control.

Answer (b) is incorrect because authorized agents of the federal government already have access to records of SEC registrants. Answer (c) is incorrect because although some international accounting standards have been promulgated, they are incomplete and have not gained widespread acceptance. Answer (d) is incorrect because there are no requirements for providing periodic reports on foreign commerce or foreign political party affiliations.

62. The Foreign Corrupt Practices Act of 1977 prohibits bribery of foreign officials. Which of the following statements correctly describes the Act's application to corporations engaging in such practices?

a. It applies only to multinational corporations.

b. It applies to all domestic corporations engaged in interstate commerce.

c. It applies only to corporations whose securities are registered under the Securities Exchange Act of 1934.

d. It applies only to corporations engaged in foreign commerce.

The correct answer is (b). *(CPA 1180 L-44)*

REQUIRED: The scope of the antibribery provisions of the FCPA.

DISCUSSION: While the requirements of the FCPA relating to the maintenance of accounting records and systems of internal accounting control apply only to companies required to register under the Securities Exchange Act of 1934, the antibribery provisions apply to all domestic business concerns engaged in interstate commerce.

Answers (a), (c), and (d) are incorrect because the FCPA antibribery provisions apply to all corporations engaged in interstate commerce (and also to any form of business organization, not only to corporations). The alternative answers are too limited.

63. Under the Foreign Corrupt Practices Act (FCPA), an action may be brought that seeks

a. Treble damages by a private party.

b. Injunctive relief by a private party.

c. Criminal sanctions against both the corporation and its officers by the Department of Justice.

d. Damages and injunctive relief by the Securities and Exchange Commission.

The correct answer is (c). *(CPA 1182 L-30)*

REQUIRED: The possible result of an action under the FCPA.

DISCUSSION: The SEC may investigate violations of the FCPA, bring civil actions for its enforcement, and recommend that the Justice Department prosecute criminal violations. A director, officer, stockholder, or other agent who acts on behalf of the corporation in willful violation of the FCPA is subject to a fine of up to $10,000 per violation and a prison term of up to five years. A corporation is subject to a fine of up to $1,000,000.

Answers (a) and (b) are incorrect because private parties may not bring an action under the FCPA. Answer (d) is incorrect because although the SEC is empowered to seek injunctions, the Justice Department must seek penalties. Damages are sought by private parties who cannot sue under this statute.

CHAPTER TWENTY-NINE
EMPLOYMENT REGULATION

29.1 Collective Bargaining

1. What are yellow-dog contracts?

a. Agreements that everyone must belong to the union.

b. Agreements between employers to identify union organizers.

c. Agreements with certain employees to spy on co-workers for union activities.

d. Agreements that employees would not join unions.

The correct answer is (d). *(Publisher)*

REQUIRED: The correct definition of yellow-dog contracts.

DISCUSSION: Employers saw unions as a threat to their right to manage and were very much against the organization of unions in the beginning of the century. "Yellow-dog" contracts were commonly used agreements by employers prohibiting employees from joining a union, providing for liquidated damages, and allowing the employee to be fired if the agreement was not kept. These contracts were later outlawed by legislation.

Answer (a) is incorrect because agreements between a union and an employer that all employees must belong to a union are called "closed-shop" or "union shop" agreements. Answers (b) and (c) are incorrect because there is no term associated with either of these agreements.

2. What was the longest lasting result of the employer's ability to hire and fire at will, discriminate against union members, and use the courts to prevent or end strikes?

a. Continual violence between employers and unions.

b. Employee control of businesses.

c. Legislation regulating employers and unions.

d. A change in the court system.

The correct answer is (c). *(Publisher)*

REQUIRED: The longest lasting effect of the superior bargaining position of employers in early union history.

DISCUSSION: In the early 1900s, employers clearly had the superior bargaining position versus unions. There were no restrictions on the power of employers to discriminate against union members. The result was regulating legislation (beginning in the 1930s) to equalize bargaining power and encourage peaceful solution of problems in the collective bargaining process.

Answer (a) is incorrect because violence between employers and unions was substantially eliminated by the enactment of federal legislation dealing with the problem, although some violence continues even today. Answer (b) is incorrect because employees have controlled very few businesses in the United States. Investment of pension funds in corporate stock may change this situation. Answer (d) is incorrect because the court system has not changed, although the attitude of judges has changed from hostility to neutrality or favor. The creation of an administrative agency was also important.

3. The National Labor Relations Act (also known as the Wagner Act) was enacted in 1935 to regulate labor activities in which way?

a. Prohibit unfair labor practices.

b. Outlaw "closed shops."

c. Require all union contracts to be reviewed by the National Labor Relations Board.

d. Exempt child labor from union agreements to discourage its use in the labor market.

The correct answer is (a). *(Publisher)*

REQUIRED: The way in which the National Labor Relations Act regulates labor activities.

DISCUSSION: The essential purpose of the NLRA was to establish the right of labor to organize and to bargain collectively with management. It requires employers to recognize unions and bargain with them in good faith. The Act also created the National Labor Relations Board to settle labor disputes and take action against unfair labor practices. This Act also prohibited unfair labor practices such as discrimination against union members, refusal to bargain with unions, and interference with the rights of employees to organize.

Answer (b) is incorrect because closed shops (required union membership to be hired) were outlawed by the Taft-Hartley Act of 1947. Answer (c) is incorrect because the NLRB has never been required to review all union contracts. Its purpose is to enforce the provisions of the National Labor Relations Act. Answer (d) is incorrect because child labor is not exempted from union contracts, but it is prohibited for most children under age 16 by the Fair Labor Standards Act.

4. The Taft-Hartley Act of 1947 attempted to restore balance between the rights and obligations of employees and those of employers by

a. Permitting strikes in cases of health and safety violations.

b. Outlawing the union shop.

c. Designating a list of unfair labor practices on the part of unions.

d. Providing for compulsory binding arbitration in case of a national emergency.

The correct answer is (c). *(CMA 684 1-33)*

REQUIRED: The provision of the Taft-Hartley Act of 1947.

DISCUSSION: The 1947 Act prohibited certain unfair labor practices by unions: coercion of employees to join unions, discrimination against nonunion employees except when a valid union shop agreement is in place, refusal to bargain in good faith, secondary strikes, featherbedding (payment by employers for work not performed), and charging new members excessive initiation fees.

Answer (a) is incorrect because the Act does not authorize strikes in particular circumstances. Its intent was to equalize the power of unions and management. Answer (b) is incorrect because it outlawed the closed shop (union membership a condition of employment) but allowed the union shop (membership may be required after employment). Answer (d) is incorrect because the Act gives the President power to seek an injunction imposing an 80-day cooling-off period, but not binding arbitration.

5. The Labor-Management Relations Act of 1947 (also known as the Taft-Hartley Act) was enacted after World War II to end several problems in the labor area. Which of the following was not an unfair labor practice prohibited by this act?

a. Featherbedding.

b. Secondary boycotts.

c. The closed shop.

d. Mismanagement of union funds.

The correct answer is (d). *(Publisher)*

REQUIRED: The item not an unfair labor practice prohibited by the Labor-Management Relations Act of 1947.

DISCUSSION: The National Labor Relations Act of 1935 (called Wagner Act) gave labor an advantage that enabled it to call nationwide strikes which crippled the country. The Labor-Management Relations Act of 1947 (Taft-Hartley) was enacted to balance the power between labor and management. It defined certain unfair labor practices prohibited to unions. These did not include the mismanagement of union funds which later became a problem in the labor movement.

Answer (a) is incorrect because feather-bedding required employers to pay for work not actually performed and was outlawed. Answer (b) is incorrect because secondary boycotts (boycotting purchasers to whom the target employer was selling) were also outlawed. Answer (c) is incorrect because the closed shop requiring all employees to be union members before being hired was outlawed as well.

6. Several states in the United States now have "right-to-work laws." In these states,

a. The closed shop is legal.

b. The checkoff, i.e., the deduction of union dues from employee paychecks, is required in all labor contracts.

c. Compulsory union membership is illegal.

d. The nonunion shop is illegal.

The correct answer is (c). *(CMA 1283 1-31)*

REQUIRED: The true statement about right-to-work laws.

DISCUSSION: The Taft-Hartley Act of 1947 outlawed the closed shop, one in which union membership is a condition of employment. It did allow the union shop, in which the employee is required to join the union after employment. But the Act also authorized states to enact right-to-work laws. These prohibit union shops and thus effectively make compulsory union membership illegal.

Answer (a) is incorrect because the closed shop is illegal. Answer (b) is incorrect because a checkoff is not required in right-to-work states. Answer (d) is incorrect because no state makes the nonunion shop illegal.

7. Problems in the labor industry which prompted the Landrum-Griffin Act (also known as the Labor-Management Reporting and Disclosure Act of 1959) included

a. Management superiority in negotiating contracts.

b. Violation of antitrust laws.

c. Corruption, violence, and theft within unions.

d. Inability of unions to enter into contracts with management.

The correct answer is (c). *(Publisher)*

REQUIRED: The problems prompting the enactment of the Landrum-Griffin Act.

DISCUSSION: In the 1950s, the U.S. Senate investigated union activities and found corruption, violence, and theft within the unions. It also discovered that many union officials had criminal records and suspected these criminal activities were continuing. The result was the Landrum-Griffin Act, which provided for regulation of the internal affairs of unions. One important feature established a type of "Bill of Rights" for union members to assure democratic procedures, and required unions to provide periodic financial, internal organization, and other reports disclosing practices possibly detrimental to union members. It also prohibited certain union activities as unfair labor practices.

Answer (a) is incorrect because management did not have superiority in negotiating with the unions; rather, the unions were using illegal methods to obtain contracts. Answer (b) is incorrect because the antitrust laws were not being violated since unions were generally exempt. Answer (d) is incorrect because the unions were able to obtain contracts with management.

8. The National Labor Relations Board (NLRB) was created by the National Labor Relations Act in 1935. Today the NLRB

a. Determines which unions will represent a group of employees.

b. Has become weak and ineffective.

c. Serves in an advisory capacity to the courts.

d. Is responsible for the conduct of representative elections.

The correct answer is (d). *(Publisher)*

REQUIRED: The correct statement concerning the National Labor Relations Board.

DISCUSSION: The NLRB, an administrative agency, has jurisdiction over labor-management relations affecting interstate commerce. It supervises union representation elections, ensures that elections are fairly conducted, and certifies the results. It also has jurisdiction over unfair labor practices by both unions and employers.

Answer (a) is incorrect because the employees of a business largely determine by election which union will represent them. The NLRB, especially the regional director, does have a role in establishing appropriate bargaining units. Answer (b) is incorrect because the NLRB is still very strong, with powers over both employers and unions in the collective bargaining process. Answer (c) is incorrect because the NLRB adjudicates controversies itself, subject to court review. The NLRB does not advise courts. Decisions of the NLRB are final unless properly appealed and overturned by a U.S. Court of Appeals or the Supreme Court.

9. A union for a group of employees is selected by

a. The NLRB.

b. The employer.

c. Statute, depending on the type of industry.

d. The employees by election.

The correct answer is (d). *(Publisher)*

REQUIRED: The basis for choosing a union for a group of employees.

DISCUSSION: Employees elect the union that will represent them, but first a petition for a representation election must be filed with the NLRB. This petition may be filed by an employee, labor organization, or employer. It must claim that the election is desired by a substantial number of employees (currently 30%).

Answer (a) is incorrect because the NLRB supervises elections, but it does not choose the union. The NLRB does select the unit of employees (bargaining unit) appropriate for a union contract and who can vote in the election if the parties disagree. In determining the appropriate bargaining unit, the Board uses a mutuality of interest test, e.g., common employer, plant, craft, etc. Answer (b) is incorrect because the employer can only petition for an election to be held. Answer (c) is incorrect because no statute determines what union will represent the employees of any industry.

10. Atlas, Inc. did not believe that the union representing its employees was supported by the employees any longer. Who can be assured of getting a representation election held?

a. 30% of the employees.

b. Atlas, Inc.

c. Another union.

d. The attorney general of the state.

The correct answer is (a). *(Publisher)*

REQUIRED: The party or group who may demand that a representation election be held.

DISCUSSION: A representation election to decertify a union requires almost the same petition as an original representation election. A substantial number of employees must assert that the current bargaining representative is no longer their choice. To be substantial, 30% of the employees must support such a petition.

Answer (b) is incorrect because although the employer can file a petition for an election if it in good faith believes the union is no longer representative of the employees, the NLRB investigates the petition and decides if an election should be held. Answer (c) is incorrect because another union would have to prove the same facts as an employer, and would also be subject to review by the NLRB. Answer (d) is incorrect because the attorney general of a state has no authority in the collective bargaining process regulated by the federal government.

11. Hanson Tire Company did not want to bargain with the union elected by the majority of its employees. Which of the following does Hanson not have to bargain in good faith with the union?

a. Overtime pay.

b. Cleanliness of the plant.

c. Time that the plant is open.

d. A no-strike clause.

The correct answer is (d). *(Publisher)*

REQUIRED: The item an employer does not have to bargain in good faith with a union.

DISCUSSION: Once a union is selected (certified) as the collective bargaining representative, the employer must bargain in good faith with that union (although it may not result in an agreement). However, the employer need only bargain in good faith over wages, hours, and other conditions of employment. A no-strike clause is not a mandatory (as determined by the NLRB) condition of employment over which an employer is required to bargain in good faith, but most employers are interested in doing so.

Answers (a), (b), and (c) are incorrect because each is an item an employer must bargain in good faith with a union. Overtime pay is an area of wages. Cleanliness of a plant is a condition of employment. The time the plant is open is an issue concerning hours worked.

12. Once a union has been elected and certified as the bargaining agent, it must

a. Represent all employees in the bargaining unit.

b. Represent only the union employees in the bargaining unit.

c. Process grievances only of union employees.

d. Represent all employees only if an agency shop prevails.

The correct answer is (a). *(Publisher)*

REQUIRED: The responsibility of a union to employees in the bargaining unit.

DISCUSSION: Upon election and certification, the union becomes the bargaining agent for all workers in the bargaining unit and has a duty to provide fair and equal representation to nonunion as well as union employees. The union must not only bargain for all employees but also process grievances on an equal basis.

Answers (b) and (c) are incorrect because the union must bargain for and fairly process the grievances of all employees in the unit. Answer (d) is incorrect because the requirement applies regardless of what union security arrangement, if any, is present. An agency shop is one in which union membership is not required but nonunion members must pay the equivalent of union dues and fees. In some states, right-to-work laws prohibit the agency shop.

13. Employer fired Employee who was a member of Union. Union and Employer had a collective bargaining agreement under which a grievance concerning discharge of a worker would be sent to binding arbitration if the parties could not agree to resolve the matter. Employee filed a grievance and Union and Employer could not reach an agreement. The arbitrator found for Employee. Review by

a. A federal court is the usual appeal procedure in arbitration.

b. A court is unlikely.

c. The NLRB is mandatory if the grievance also involved an unfair labor practice.

d. A state court is the usual appeal procedure in arbitration.

The correct answer is (b). *(Publisher)*

REQUIRED: The true statement about a grievance procedure with binding arbitration.

DISCUSSION: The majority of states and the federal government have passed statutes that establish standards for arbitration and make arbitration agreements irrevocable. The parties must therefore abide by the arbitrator's decision and cannot seek judicial review of the result except in very limited circumstances. These include a dispute that is not arbitrable, that is, one outside the scope of the collective bargaining agreement and not involving interpretation or application of the agreement; conduct in bad faith by the arbitrator; a decision or award beyond the power granted to the arbitrator; or a decision that violates the law, such as upholding an illegal provision in the agreement.

Answers (a) and (d) are incorrect because the purpose of arbitration is to avoid the cost and delay of litigation. Answer (c) is incorrect because the policy of both the courts and the NLRB is to defer to the arbitrator.

14. Which of the following is a false statement about the occurrence of representation elections to choose a collective bargaining agent?

a. If the union wins, no election may be held for 12 months.

b. If the union loses, no election may be held for 12 months.

c. In general, if a collective bargaining agreement has been reached, no election may be held for the lesser of three years or the duration of the contract.

d. If a collective bargaining agreement has been reached, an election may be held if 12 months have lapsed, if the union is defunct, or if the employer has greatly changed its operations.

The correct answer is (d). *(Publisher)*

REQUIRED: The false statement about representation elections.

DISCUSSION: Under the contract bar rule, representation elections may not be held for 3 years or the duration of the labor contract, whichever is shorter. The rule has several exceptions. A fundamental disagreement about union policy by its top leaders justifies a new election. Likewise, if the union becomes defunct, the rule is inapplicable. A change in operations may also permit a new election if less than 30% of current employees were working when the agreement went into effect. Moreover, a merger resulting in a new operation with substantial personnel changes and a resumption of business with new workers after closing for an indefinite period are other exceptions.

Answers (a) and (b) are incorrect because a new representation election may not be held for 12 months whether the union won or lost. Answer (c) is incorrect because in general, a new election is barred for the lesser of the life of the contract or 3 years.

15. Workers have the right to strike but certain kinds of strikes are illegal, such as those during a cooling-off period. Which of the following is true?

a. If the collective bargaining agreement is for a definite period, no strike may be called until it expires.

b. If the collective bargaining agreement is for an indefinite period, 30 days' notice must be given to the employer.

c. If the collective bargaining agreement is for a definite period, 60 days' notice must be given if the union wishes to strike to seek modification of the agreement.

d. If the strike concerns an employer's unfair labor practice, 60 days' notice must be given.

The correct answer is (c). *(Publisher)*

REQUIRED: The true statement about strikes by workers.

DISCUSSION: The general principle is that the employer and the Federal Mediation and Conciliation Service must be given 60 days' notice of a strike. This cooling-off period gives the parties an opportunity to negotiate their differences without the necessity of a strike. The 60-day requirement applies whether the collective bargaining agreement is for a fixed or indefinite term and whether the union plans to strike upon the agreement's expiration or while it is still in force.

Answer (a) is incorrect because in the absence of a "no strike" clause, a strike to terminate or modify the agreement is not illegal per se. Answer (b) is incorrect because 60 days' notice must be given. Answer (d) is incorrect because the notice requirement is inapplicable if the strike is to protest an employer's unfair labor practice.

16. If a strike may create a national emergency, the Taft-Hartley Act provides for an 80-day cooling-off period. This provision

a. Is invoked after appointment of a board of inquiry and the Attorney General's petition for a federal court injunction.

b. Results in binding arbitration by the Federal Mediation Service.

c. Does not apply to lockouts.

d. Allows the rank-and-file to vote only on a contract agreed to by the employer and the union bargaining agent.

The correct answer is (a). *(Publisher)*

REQUIRED: The true statement about the cooling-off provision of the Taft-Hartley Act.

DISCUSSION: If a strike or lockout would have a substantial effect on the national economy, impair the national defense, or affect key industries, the President may appoint a board to investigate the consequences. If the board of inquiry finds that a national emergency will result, the President may instruct the Attorney General to petition a federal court for an injunction ordering the cessation of the strike or lockout for 80 days. During this period, Federal Mediation Service works with the parties. If they do not agree, the board conducts new hearings and the company submits the final offer. The members of the union vote on this proposal. If they reject it, the strike or lockout may then resume for an indefinite period.

Answer (b) is incorrect because the mediators have no authority to bind the parties. Answer (c) is incorrect because lockouts are also within the statute. Answer (d) is incorrect because the Taft-Hartley Act allows the membership of the union to vote directly on management's final offer if no agreement is reached.

17. Which of the following is a true statement about hot cargo contracts?

a. The prohibition against such contracts applies to unions but not employers.

b. The prohibition against such contracts applies to unions and employers.

c. The prohibition against such contracts applies to employers but not unions.

d. Such contracts are not prohibited since secondary boycotts are not illegal.

The correct answer is (b). *(Publisher)*

REQUIRED: The true statement about hot cargo contracts.

DISCUSSION: The Taft-Hartley Act as amended by the Landrum-Griffin Act outlawed secondary strikes and boycotts. These in effect are attempts to coerce a second employer with which the union has no dispute to stop dealing with the primary employer with which the union has a conflict. Not working for or refusal to handle or purchase the products of the secondary employer is the secondary boycott. Hot cargo contracts are agreements between the employer and union that the goods of another employer would not be handled (because of a dispute the union has with the other employer or even if another union has a dispute with the other employer). These agreements are illegal as a type of secondary boycott.

18. Which of the following is a true statement about the status of strikers?

a. Even an illegal striker may not be discharged during a strike.

b. An economic striker may not be discharged during a strike and must be rehired at its conclusion.

c. A striker over an unfair labor practice by the employer may not be discharged during a strike and must be rehired but not if a permanent replacement must be discharged as a result.

d. A striker over an unfair labor practice by the employer but not an illegal or economic striker is entitled to reinstatement.

The correct answer is (d). *(Publisher)*

REQUIRED: The true statement about the status of strikers.

DISCUSSION: If workers have engaged in a legal strike to protest their employer's unfair labor practice, they are entitled to reinstatement. This rule applies although permanent replacements hired during the strike must be discharged.

Answer (a) is incorrect because an illegal striker (when the strike is illegal) has no right to reinstatement. Answer (b) is incorrect because an economic striker (when the strike is legal and over economic benefits) has a right to a nondiscriminating review of his/her application for reinstatement but not to displace a permanent employee hired during the strike. Answer (c) is incorrect because an employee who strikes over an employer's unfair labor practice is entitled to his/her job back even if it displaces a permanent replacement.

19. Mourning, Inc. refused to recognize a union that had not been elected by the employees. The union had lost in a representation election eight months previously but now claimed that it had the support of the majority of employees. The union began picketing Mourning, Inc. to try to force recognition.

a. Mourning, Inc. has committed an unfair labor practice by refusing to recognize the union.

b. An election must be held.

c. The employees cannot cross the picket line.

d. The union has committed an unfair labor practice.

The correct answer is (d). *(Publisher)*

REQUIRED: The correct statement concerning picketing by a nonelected union that is not recognized by the employer.

DISCUSSION: Unions, as well as employers, may not commit unfair labor practices. It is often legal for a union to picket an employer for recognition purposes. However, it is an unfair labor practice for a union to picket an employer to try to force recognition when the union has not been certified by the NLRB and a valid representation election has been conducted within the past year.

Answer (a) is incorrect because Mourning, Inc. has no authority to recognize a union which has lost an election and is not certified by the NLRB. It would be an unfair labor practice to do so. Answer (b) is incorrect because an election need only be held if a substantial number of employees (30%) want the election. Answer (c) is incorrect because the employees can cross any picket line. Attempting to prevent employees from crossing a picket line is illegal for the union and the individual picketers.

20. Bango Industries sent a letter to its employees 2 weeks before a representation election was held. This letter announced increased vacation benefits beginning immediately. The union lost the election (resulting in no union representing the employees).

a. The letter was a proper act consistent with the government's interest in providing better benefits for employees.

b. The letter was an unfair labor practice that would be grounds for a new election.

c. The letter was an unfair labor practice resulting in the union's becoming the employees' bargaining representative.

d. The employees cannot reelect another union for 1 year.

The correct answer is (b). *(Publisher)*

REQUIRED: The result when an employer promises benefits just before a representation election.

DISCUSSION: While employers have freedom of speech, those employers who interfere, coerce, or restrain efforts of employees to organize and obtain a bargaining representative are guilty of an unfair labor practice. Notifying employees that they are getting increased vacation benefits immediately before the union election is interference with the election unless the increase was already scheduled. To give the employees and the union a chance to operate without interference, the election would have to be reheld.

Answer (a) is incorrect because the letter was an unfair labor practice. Unions (not the government) have a stated interest in improving workers' benefits under the NLRA. Answer (c) is incorrect because the representation election will have to be reheld. The union cannot become the bargaining representative of the employees without majority approval. Answer (d) is incorrect because a new election must be held. The rule prohibiting a new election within 1 year does not apply until the NLRB certifies the election to be valid.

21. As a result of the Labor-Management Relations Act and the Federal Election Campaign Act, elections for federal offices can be financed by

a. Government funds only.

b. Direct contributions of corporations but not labor unions.

c. Direct contributions of labor unions but not corporations.

d. Direct contributions of neither corporations nor labor unions.

The correct answer is (d). *(CMA 1283 1-33)*

REQUIRED: The true statement about financing of federal elections.

DISCUSSION: Neither corporations nor labor unions may make direct contributions to federal political campaigns, candidates, or parties. However, they can contribute to political action committees which indirectly support candidates, parties, and political issues.

Answer (a) is incorrect because individuals may make contributions; the government only provides matching funds in presidential elections. Answers (b) and (c) are incorrect because neither corporations nor labor unions may make direct contributions for federal political offices.

29.2 Fair Labor Standards Act

22. Stephens is an employee of the Jensen Manufacturing Company, a multi-state manufacturer of rollerskates. The plant in which he works is unionized and Stephens is a dues paying union member. Which statement about the federal Fair Labor Standards Act is true?

a. The Act allows a piece-rate method to be employed in lieu of the hourly-rate method where appropriate.

b. Jensen is permitted to pay less than the minimum wage to employees since they are represented by a bona fide union.

c. The Act sets the maximum number of hours that an employee can work in a given day or week.

d. The Act excludes from its coverage the employees of a labor union.

The correct answer is (a). *(CPA 581 L-58)*

REQUIRED: The correct statement about the federal Fair Labor Standards Act.

DISCUSSION: The federal Fair Labor Standards Act (FLSA) provides for equal pay, minimum wages, and overtime, and prohibits child labor. Under the minimum pay and equal pay provisions, compensation need not be paid on an hourly basis if another method equals the minimum standard. Under the equal pay standard, an employer may differentiate among the employees on the basis of quality or quantity produced. The piece-rate method generally satisfies these requirements.

Answer (b) is incorrect because an employer is not permitted to pay less than the minimum wage even to union employees. Answer (c) is incorrect because the Act does not set the maximum number of hours an employee can work in a given day or week, but provides for an overtime rate for hours worked over 40 per week. Answer (d) is incorrect because the Act does not exempt employees of a labor union. It does exempt executive, administrative, and professional employees.

23. The Fair Labor Standards Act

a. Applies to all employers whether or not engaged in interstate commerce.

b. Requires that double time be paid to any employee working in excess of eight hours in a given day.

c. Prohibits discrimination based upon the sex of the employee.

d. Requires all employees doing the same job to receive an equal rate of pay.

The correct answer is (c). *(CPA 1174 L-30)*

REQUIRED: The correct statement concerning the Fair Labor Standards Act.

DISCUSSION: The Fair Labor Standards Act regulates the relationship between an employer and employees by providing for equal pay, minimum wages, overtime, and prohibition of child labor. The equal pay provision prohibits discrimination on the basis of sex of the employee. It requires equal pay for equal work.

Answer (a) is incorrect because the Fair Labor Standards Act applies only to employers engaged in interstate commerce, since that is the limit on federal jurisdiction over commerce. Answer (b) is incorrect because the only overtime requirement is at least time-and-one-half the regular rate for all hours worked over 40 per week. Answer (d) is incorrect because the Act does not require all employees doing the same job to receive an equal rate of pay, but permits differentials on the basis of seniority, merit, quality, or quantity.

24. The Fair Labor Standards Act

a. Applies to employees of all retail and service enterprises.

b. Applies to hospitals, construction companies, and public but not private schools.

c. Does not apply to most Mom and Pop grocery stores.

d. Applies to business enterprises with annual gross sales of at least $250,000.

The correct answer is (d). *(Publisher)*

REQUIRED: The enterprise coverage of the Fair Labor Standards Act.

DISCUSSION: Originally, the FLSA applied to employees working in interstate commerce or producing goods for interstate commerce. By amendment, the Act now covers all employees (unless specifically exempt) of a firm engaging in interstate commerce. Thus, emphasis has shifted from the employees' activities to those of the enterprise. Under the Act, retail and service businesses with annual gross income of at least $362,500 are covered. Other enterprises with gross sales or business of at least $250,000 are also covered.

Answer (a) is incorrect because retail businesses grossing less than $362,500 are exempt. Answer (b) is incorrect because private schools do not receive an exemption. Answer (c) is incorrect because most small grocery stores have annual gross incomes of at least $362,500. Many of these were previously exempt.

25. Fashion Industries, Inc. manufactures dresses which it sells throughout the United States and South America. Among its 5,000 employees in 1986 were 165 youngsters aged 14 and 15 who worked full-time during the day and were paid at a rate less than the minimum wage. Which statement is correct in accordance with the general rules of the Fair Labor Standards Act?

a. Fashion was exempt from regulation because fewer than 5% of its employees were children.

b. Fashion did not violate the law since both male and female youngsters were paid at the same rate and only worked on Saturdays.

c. Fashion violated the law by employing children under 16 years of age.

d. Fashion was exempt from regulation if more than 10% of its sales were in direct competition with foreign goods.

The correct answer is (c). *(CPA 1177 L-14)*

REQUIRED: The correct statement concerning the general rules of child labor.

DISCUSSION: Under the Fair Labor Standards Act (FLSA), child labor is defined as employment of a child under 16. It is considered oppressive and is prohibited with certain exceptions (14 and 15 year olds may work at sales and clerical type jobs for limited hours and outside of school time). The employment of 165 children aged 14 and 15 to work full time is a violation of the law.

Answer (a) is incorrect because there is no exemption from regulation under the FLSA simply because fewer than 5% of one's employees are children. Answer (b) is incorrect because it is no defense that male and female youngsters were paid at the same rate and only worked on Saturdays. The employment of children is still prohibited. Answer (d) is incorrect because there is no exemption for direct competition with foreign goods. The general rule is that a U.S. employer must comply with the U.S. laws regulating employment.

26. Under the Fair Labor Standards Act, certain employment of children is considered oppressive and is prohibited. Which of the following is not a legal exception to the Act?

a. Employment in agriculture outside of school hours.

b. Employment of children under sixteen by a parent.

c. Newspaper delivery.

d. After school part-time work in the fast-food industry.

The correct answer is (d). *(CPA 582 L-34)*

REQUIRED: The activity not an exception to employment of children.

DISCUSSION: Under the child labor section of the FLSA, most employment of children is considered oppressive and is prohibited. Children ages 14 and 15, in light work occupation, outside school hours, and for a limited number of hours are exempted from the age 16 requirement. However, there is no general exemption for children to work part-time after school in the fast-food industry.

Answers (a), (b), and (c) are incorrect because there are legal exceptions permitting employment of children in agriculture outside of school hours, employment of children under age 16 by their parents, and employment of children for newspaper delivery.

27. Which of the following classes of employees is exempt from both the minimum wage and maximum hours provisions of the federal Fair Labor Standards Act?

a. Members of a labor union.

b. Administrative personnel.

c. Hospital workers.

d. No class of employees is exempt.

The correct answer is (b). *(CPA 577 L-13)*

REQUIRED: The class of employees exempt from the minimum wage and maximum hour provisions.

DISCUSSION: The federal Fair Labor Standards Act (FLSA) regulates the relationship between an employer and its employees by providing for equal pay, minimum wages, overtime, and prohibition of child labor. Certain employees are exempt from coverage under the Act, including administrative personnel (manager types, not general office workers) who usually receive some minimum guaranteed annual wage and are required by conditions of their employment to work as long as necessary to accomplish their task.

Answer (a) is incorrect because employees who belong to a labor union are not exempt at all. Answer (c) is incorrect because although hospital workers are not exempt from minimum wages, they are partially exempt from the overtime provision if they so agree. Hospitals must pay overtime for more than 8 hours daily and for more than 80 hours in 14 days, but not for more than 40 hours in a week. Answer (d) is incorrect because certain classes of employees are exempt, including executives, professionals, administrators, and outside salesmen. Partial exemptions exist for certain others.

28. Which of the following employees are exempt from the overtime provisions of the Fair Labor Standards Act?

a. Independent contractors.

b. Railroad and airline employees.

c. Members of a union recognized as the bargaining agent by the National Labor Relations Board.

d. Office workers.

The correct answer is (b). *(CPA 1182 L-28)*

REQUIRED: The employees exempt from the requirements of the FLSA.

DISCUSSION: Certain workers are exempt from the overtime but not minimum wage provisions. Railroad and air carrier employees, taxi drivers, certain employees of motor carriers, sailors on American vessels, and certain local delivery employees are in this category.

Answer (a) is incorrect because an employer cannot escape coverage under the Act by designating a person as an independent contractor if the circumstances of the employment relation suggest that (s)he is an employee. Answers (c) and (d) are incorrect because neither group is exempted.

29. Which of the following is a false statement about computing wages and hours under the Fair Labor Standards Act?

a. The wages and hours requirements of the FLSA do not apply when an employee is working on a government contract in excess of $10,000.

b. If the employee is on salary, the wages and hours requirements of the FLSA do not apply.

c. If the employee earns more than $20 per month in tips, the minimum wage may be reduced by half.

d. An employer may reduce the minimum wage by an amount equal to the reasonable cost of food and lodging.

The correct answer is (b). *(Publisher)*

REQUIRED: The false statement about wages and hours computations under the FLSA.

DISCUSSION: If a nonexempt employee earns a salary, a regular hourly rate is determined by dividing the salary by the hours normally worked during the period. This amount is then used to compute the statutory overtime rate and to ascertain whether the minimum wage is being paid.

Answer (a) is incorrect because the Walsh-Healy Act applies. It sets minimum wages for contracts to provide goods or services to the federal government. Answer (c) is incorrect because waiters, waitresses, bellhops, parking attendants, and the like are subject to this provision. Answer (d) is incorrect because the reasonable cost of food, lodging, and other facilities provided to employees (for example, hotel and restaurant workers) may be used in computing such employees' pay.

30. Under the Fair Labor Standards Act the Secretary of Labor does not have the power to

a. Issue subpoenas compelling attendance by a witness and the production of records by an employer.

b. Conduct investigations regarding practices subject to the Act.

c. Issue a wage order that requires an employer to pay wages found to be due and owing under the Act.

d. Issue injunctions to restrain obvious violations of the Act.

The correct answer is (d). *(CPA 1182 L-29)*

REQUIRED: The power not given to the Secretary of Labor by the FLSA.

DISCUSSION: The Secretary of Labor has no authority to issue an injunction. (S)he may, however, seek an injunction from a court to prohibit violations of the Act.

Answers (a), (b), and (c) are incorrect because the Department does have power to compel release of information by employers, to conduct investigations, and to order an employer to comply with the Act. With regard to back wages, the Department may supervise payment, the Secretary may file suit on behalf of employees (and obtain an equal amount as liquidated damages), or the employees themselves may sue.

31. The federal Fair Labor Standards Act

a. Prohibits any employment of a person under 16 years of age.

b. Requires payment of time-and-one-half for overtime to actors engaged in making television productions.

c. Contains an exemption from the minimum wage provisions for manufacturing plants located in areas of high unemployment.

d. Prohibits the delivery by a wholesaler to a dealer in another state of any goods if the wholesaler knew that oppressive child labor was used in their manufacture.

The correct answer is (d). *(CPA 574 L-42)*

REQUIRED: The correct statement regarding the federal Fair Labor Standards Act (FLSA).

DISCUSSION: The FLSA makes it illegal for any person knowing goods were produced in violation of the Act to ship or sell them in interstate commerce. One objective of the FLSA is to prohibit child labor, generally defined as employment of children under 16 but subject to some exceptions.

Answer (a) is incorrect because the Act does permit employment of children 14 or 15 in light work outside school hours for a limited number of hours, in agriculture, as actors, by their parents, or for newspaper delivery. Answer (b) is incorrect because actors are professionals exempt from the Act. Answer (c) is incorrect because there are no exemptions from minimum wage provisions for manufacturers located in areas of high unemployment.

32. Ichi Ban Mopeds, Inc., is a Japanese manufacturer which has a manufacturing facility in the United States. United States business comprises 10% of the sales of Ichi Ban, of which 4% is manufactured at its U.S. facility. Under these circumstances,

a. Ichi Ban is exempt from state workers' compensation laws.

b. Ichi Ban is exempt from the Fair Labor Standards Act provided it is governed by comparable Japanese law.

c. Ichi Ban is subject to generally prevailing federal and state laws applicable to American employees with respect to its employees at the United States facility.

d. Ichi Ban could legally institute a policy which limited promotions to Japanese-Americans.

The correct answer is (c). *(CPA 1180 L-58)*

REQUIRED: The correct statement regarding employment by a foreign corporation in the U.S.

DISCUSSION: All employers in the U.S., whether citizens or not, are subject to the same generally prevailing federal and state laws which are applicable to American employees at any facility located in the United States.

Answer (a) is incorrect because a foreign manufacturer with a facility located in the United States is not exempt from state workers' compensation laws, but must fully comply. Answer (b) is incorrect because the foreign manufacturer is not exempt from the U.S. Fair Labor Standards Act for those employees at a U.S. facility, even if a comparable law is provided by the foreign manufacturer's government. Answer (d) is incorrect because no employer in the U.S. may legally institute a promotion policy which discriminates on the basis of race, religion, color, sex, or national origin.

29.3 Discrimination

33. Which federal statute does not apply to discrimination in employment?

a. Section 1981 of the Civil Rights Act (CRA) of 1866.

b. Title VII of the Civil Rights Act (CRA) of 1964.

c. The Occupational Safety and Health Act (OSHA) of 1970.

d. The Rehabilitation Act of 1973.

The correct answer is (c). *(Publisher)*

REQUIRED: The statute not applicable to discrimination in employment.

DISCUSSION: OSHA was enacted to require safe and healthful working conditions in the place of employment. It contains no provisions against discrimination in employment.

Answers (a), (b), and (d) are incorrect because each is concerned with discrimination in employment. Section 1981 of the CRA of 1866 prohibits discrimination based on race. Title VII of the CRA of 1964 prohibits discrimination based on race, color, religion, national origin, or sex. The Rehabilitation Act has sections barring discrimination against the handicapped by those employers who receive federal contracts or assistance.

34. Under Title VII of the Civil Rights Act of 1964, a covered entity is prohibited from engaging in employment discrimination on the basis of race, color, religion, national origin, or sex. The practices subject to the Act include

a. Any term, condition, or privilege of employment.

b. Hiring and discharge by the employer but not classified advertising by an employment agency.

c. Compensation and fringe benefits but not retirement plans.

d. Job taking, classifications, and assignments but not union discrimination.

The correct answer is (a). *(Publisher)*

REQUIRED: The practices subject to the employment discrimination provisions of the CRA of 1964.

DISCUSSION: Covered employers, employment agencies, and unions may not discriminate with regard to the following: classified advertising; receiving, classifying, or referring applicants; job testing and interviewing; hiring or firing; compensation and job classifications or assignments; promotions, transfers, layoffs, or recalls; training; fringe benefits; retirement and disability benefits; and any other term, condition, or privilege of employment.

Answer (b) is incorrect because employment agencies serving an employer with at least 15 employees are covered. Answer (c) is incorrect because retirement plans are covered. Answer (d) is incorrect because unions in industries affecting interstate commerce are covered.

35. A major policy of the Equal Employment Opportunity Commission (EEOC) is

a. To restrict enforcement of the Equal Employment Opportunity Act of 1972 to relatively small companies in order to minimize disruptions.

b. To assume immediate jurisdiction of employment discrimination complaints.

c. To emphasize equality of opportunity over equality of result.

d. To have businesses achieve employment mixes reflecting the local minority and female labor pool.

The correct answer is (d). *(CMA 684 1-31)*

REQUIRED: The true statement of a major policy of the EEOC.

DISCUSSION: The EEOC is a five-member body that is the most important federal agency dealing with employment discrimination. It enforces Title VII of the CRA of 1964, the Equal Pay Act, the Age Discrimination in Employment Act, and certain portions of the Rehabilitation Act of 1973. It issues regulations and guidelines, investigates charges of discrimination, attempts conciliation of disputes, and enforces the statutes by appropriate lawsuits. The EEOC is a significant instrument in the government's attempt to achieve the goal of bringing minority and female work forces up to the appropriate percentages of the relevant local labor pools.

Answer (a) is incorrect because most companies with 15 or more employees are covered. Answer (b) is incorrect because under Title VII of the Civil Rights Act of 1964, a local or state agency will have jurisdiction of an employment discrimination complaint first. The EEOC must wait 60 days before acting. The employer is notified and an investigation is made. If it finds reasonable cause, the EEOC will issue a determination letter to the employer and attempt to resolve the matter through a conciliation conference. If an agreement is not reached, the EEOC or the charging party may file a civil lawsuit in federal court. Answer (c) is incorrect because the law recognizes that mere equal opportunity may not suffice when the effects of past discrimination remain, so equality of result is stressed.

36. Which of the following is a true statement about Title VII of the Civil Rights Act of 1964 as amended in 1972?

a. Bona fide occupational qualification, merit, seniority, but not mere business judgment are defenses to an employment discrimination charge.

b. Covered entities must keep records related to employment opportunities for 6 months and also file annual reports.

c. State and local governments are excluded from coverage.

d. The federal government is excluded from coverage.

The correct answer is (b). *(Publisher)*

REQUIRED: The true statement about Title VII of the CRA of 1964, as amended.

DISCUSSION: Covered entities must maintain records concerning job applications, hiring and firing, promotions and demotions, compensation, etc. of protected groups. These must be retained for 6 months and may not be destroyed while a charge of discrimination is pending. Annual reports about employment of protected classes must also be filed.

Answer (a) is incorrect because a plaintiff must show discrimination to prevail in a suit under Title VII, but an act affecting the plaintiff that is motivated by reasonable business judgment is not discrimination. For instance, firing an employee for incompetence is not unlawful solely because the employee belongs to a protected class. Answers (c) and (d) are incorrect because Title VII essentially covers all employers (e.g., individuals, corporations, partnerships, unions, state and local governments, and the federal government) with 15 or more employees if engaged in an industry affecting interstate commerce.

37. Employment discrimination is prohibited by Title VII of the Civil Rights Act of 1964. Which of the following is least likely to be a violation?

a. Disparate treatment of an individual.

b. A statistical comparison showing a pervasive pattern or practices of discrimination.

c. An express policy of discrimination but supported by business necessity.

d. Disparate impact of a rule neutral on its face.

The correct answer is (c). *(Publisher)*

REQUIRED: The impermissible basis for establishing a Title VII violation.

DISCUSSION: An employer may defend by proving that the challenged practice, rule, or policy was justified by business necessity. The practice, rule, or policy will be upheld if it served a compelling business purpose, effectively carried out this purpose, and no alternative would accomplish the purpose at least as well but with less impact on the protected group. For instance, an Alabama prison system regulation excluding women from employment as guards in male maximum security prisons was justified on the basis that increased assaults on guards, with attendant loss of prison security and thus protection of inmates and guards, would be the likely result of hiring women.

Answer (a) is incorrect because an isolated instance of discrimination is enough to constitute a violation. Answer (b) is incorrect because a statistical comparison may be sufficient to prove a pattern or practice of discrimination, such as when the percentage of a minority group in the defendant's work force is substantially below that in the relevant population. Answer (d) is incorrect because a work rule, regulation, requirement, or practice may be neutral on its face and yet have an impermissibly disparate impact on a protected class, e.g., height, weight, or lifting requirements.

38. Which of the following is a true statement about the treatment of sex discrimination in employment under Title VII of the Civil Rights Act of 1964, as amended?

a. Title VII prohibits discrimination based on an employee's or applicant's sexual preference.

b. Employer health insurance plans need not treat pregnancy in a manner similar to other ailments affecting the ability to work.

c. Title VII's prohibition against sex discrimination applies only to women.

d. Sexual harassment is a basis for suit even though it is not used in exchange for employment opportunities.

The correct answer is (d). *(Publisher)*

REQUIRED: The true statement about employment discrimination based on sex.

DISCUSSION: Sexual harassment will be a basis for a Title VII recovery when sexual advances, requests for sexual favors, and other sexual misconduct occur, and 1) submission thereto is at least implicitly a term or condition of employment, 2) employment decisions affecting the person are based on response to such behavior, or 3) the conduct creates an offensive environment or condition of work.

Answer (a) is incorrect because discrimination based on sexual preference, i.e., homosexuality, is not barred by Title VII. Answer (b) is incorrect because the Pregnancy Discrimination Act of 1978 amended Title VII to bar discrimination based on pregnancy, childbirth, and related conditions. Hiring, firing, sick leave, and health and disability insurance are included. Answer (c) is incorrect because men are also protected.

39. John, an employee of Acme Corp., learned that Acme refused to hire female job applicants solely because of their sex. John filed suit against Acme on the grounds that Acme was engaging in illegal employment discrimination according to the 1964 Civil Rights Act, which outlaws employment discrimination based upon sex. The federal trial court judge dismissed John's suit on a motion from Acme. Which is the most likely reason for this dismissal?

a. The federal court lacked subject-matter jurisdiction over the suit.

b. John lacked standing to sue Acme.

c. Acme was not violating the law.

d. The venue was improper.

The correct answer is (b). *(K.J. Elwell)*

REQUIRED: The reason for dismissal of a sex discrimination suit.

DISCUSSION: To have standing to sue, a plaintiff must have some personal interest in the outcome of the litigation. In this instance, if John wins, he will not benefit because he is already employed by Acme. He is also a male and therefore is not harmed by Acme's discriminatory practices.

Answer (a) is incorrect because federal courts do have subject-matter jurisdiction in cases brought under the Civil Rights Act. Answer (c) is incorrect because from the facts it appears that Acme was violating the law. Answer (d) is incorrect because an improper venue is grounds for transfer, not dismissal, of a lawsuit.

40. Jane Adams applied for a job in a factory, driving a forklift truck. The job requirements included weighing at least 160 pounds to have sufficient strength to pick up the 100-pound boxes the forklift carried and which frequently fell off. Jane only weighs 150 pounds and was refused the job on this basis. Under these facts,

a. The weight requirement is invalid under the Civil Rights Act.

b. The weight requirement can be justified by the work required.

c. The factory must hire Jane.

d. The weight requirement discriminates against women under the Fair Labor Standards Act.

The correct answer is (a). *(Publisher)*

REQUIRED: The correct statement regarding a minimum weight requirement for a job.

DISCUSSION: The Civil Rights Act prohibits discrimination on the basis of race, color, national origin, religion, or sex. Height and weight requirements are discriminatory if they have the effect of screening out employees on the basis of race, sex, national origin, etc. The employer has the burden of proving that the requirement has a valid business purpose and that no alternate method of selection is less discriminatory. In similar cases, courts have held that it is valid to require a certain amount of strength for particular jobs, but a strength test would be less discriminatory than an arbitrary weight or height requirement.

Answer (b) is incorrect because the weight requirement cannot be justified since a strength test would be less discriminatory. Answer (c) is incorrect because the factory need not hire Jane, but it must give her an opportunity to apply for the job in a nondiscriminatory manner. Answer (d) is incorrect because discrimination in wages, not discrimination in hiring, is covered by the Fair Labor Standards Act.

41. The Equal Pay Act of 1963

a. Adopts the comparable worth principle of equal pay for comparable work.

b. Is an amendment of the Fair Labor Standards Act and covers the same employees.

c. Does not apply to pay differentials based on seniority, merit, equality or quantity of production, or any factor other than sex.

d. Applies only to women.

The correct answer is (c). *(Publisher)*

REQUIRED: The true statement about the Equal Pay Act.

DISCUSSION: The Act requires equal pay for equal work. "Equal" means substantially but not identically equal. Equal work means that substantially equal effort, skill, and responsibility are required and that the work is performed under similar but not necessarily equal working conditions. Nevertheless, pay differentials between men and women performing equal work may be lawful based on certain factors. Length of time on the job (seniority); an objective means of merit determination communicated and applied to all employees (merit); and piecework, commission, or quality-control payment methods (quality or quantity of production) are such factors.

Answer (a) is incorrect because the Act did not accept the comparable worth principle. While the Act would apply to male and female flight attendants, it would not operate to equalize pay between, for example, male secretaries and female park rangers. Answer (b) is incorrect because the Equal Pay Act also applies to executives, administrators, professionals, outside salespersons, and employees of state and local governments. Answer (d) is incorrect because the Act applies to men and women.

42. Airline has three cockpit positions: flight officer, co-pilot, and pilot. It has a policy of requiring flight officers to advance to the post of captain or be fired, a progression that takes about 10 to 15 years. The FAA requires retirement at age 60. Applicant is 45 years old and otherwise fully qualified. Airline rejects her application on the basis of its policy of not hiring flight officers over the age of 30. Applicant files suit. At trial, evidence is presented showing that the incidence of aviation accidents decreases as a pilot gains experience and that the best experience for Airline's purposes is acquired by flying in Airline's three cockpit positions. Applicant will most likely

a. Lose because age is a permissible basis for discrimination.

b. Lose because Airline has a bona fide occupational qualification (BFOQ) defense.

c. Win because the BFOQ defense only applies to discrimination based on sex, religion, and national origin.

d. Win because the Age Discrimination in Employment Act applies to persons who are at least 40 but not yet 65.

The correct answer is (b). *(Publisher)*

REQUIRED: The outcome of an age discrimination suit and its legal basis.

DISCUSSION: Under the Age Discrimination Act (ADEA), persons who are at least 40 but not yet 70 are protected from most forms of age discrimination in employment. However, a defendant may prevail by asserting a bona fide occupational qualification (BFOQ) defense. An employment decision based solely on age may be made when age is a BFOQ reasonably necessary to the normal operation of the particular business. Because the experience of captains is related to safety, the company does not permit anyone to follow a career solely as a flight officer or co-pilot. Given that the time required to advance would allow applicant to serve only briefly as a captain, it is reasonable to conclude that Airline's hiring policy is based on a BFOQ.

Answer (a) is incorrect because the ADEA protects persons of Applicant's age. Answer (c) is incorrect because the BFOQ may be asserted to justify limited discrimination based on age, sex, religion, or national origin, but not race or color. Answer (d) is incorrect because the ADEA applies to persons who are at least 40 but not yet 70. Moreover, Airline most likely has a valid BFOQ defense.

43. The Age Discrimination in Employment Act of 1967

a. Applies generally to employers that engage in interstate commerce and have 20 or more employees.

b. Does not apply to governmental entities.

c. Applies to individuals between the ages of 21 and 65.

d. Is limited to discrimination in hiring and discharging employees.

The correct answer is (a). *(Publisher)*

REQUIRED: The true statement about the application of the ADEA.

DISCUSSION: The Act covers most employers (individuals, partnerships, unions, corporations) engaged in interstate commerce that have 20 or more employees. It also applies to referrals by an employment agency to a covered employer regardless of the agency's size.

Answer (b) is incorrect because state and local governmental units are covered. A separate section of the Act sets standards for some parts of the federal government. Answers (c) and (d) are incorrect because the ADEA applies to age discrimination against individuals who are at least 40 but not yet 70. The Act applies to nearly all terms, conditions, and benefits of employment.

44. Affirmative action programs to promote employment of members of minority groups may

a. Establish specific quotas for hiring.

b. Involve reverse discrimination.

c. Not override a bona fide seniority system.

d. Not use race as a criterion.

The correct answer is (c). *(Publisher)*

REQUIRED: The true statement about affirmative action.

DISCUSSION: Title VII of the Civil Rights Act of 1964 is the basis for reverse discrimination suits brought by those who believe themselves to be victimized by affirmative action programs. Clearly, employers can actively recruit women and members of minority groups and provide training programs and other assistance, but the line between such activities and impermissible reverse discrimination is unclear. The Supreme Court has held that a federal court had no power to override a valid seniority system to protect the jobs of recently hired blacks in a layoff ordered in a city's fire department.

Answers (a) and (d) are incorrect because the Supreme Court has held that a university medical school could not reserve a specific number of places in an incoming class for minority applicants but could use race as one criterion in the admissions decision. Answer (b) is incorrect because the language of Title VII is clear: discrimination on the basis of race, color, religion, national origin, or sex is prohibited.

45. Since the passage of the Civil Rights Act of 1964 and the establishment of the Equal Employment Opportunity Commission in 1972, large firms have been required to establish programs to eliminate discrimination. Federal law requires large firms to

a. Give preference in hiring to women and minority groups.

b. Establish quotas for hiring women and minority groups.

c. Set wage scales so that average wages for women equal average wages for men.

d. Set goals to eliminate discrimination and timetables to achieve these goals.

The correct answer is (d). *(CMA 1283 1-35)*

REQUIRED: The true statement about affirmative action.

DISCUSSION: Large employers are required to create and implement a plan of affirmative action to bring female and minority work forces up to the appropriate percentages as they relate to the available labor pool.

Answers (a) and (b) are incorrect because although these goals may involve preferential hiring of women and minorities, such techniques are not required. Answer (c) is incorrect because equality of wages is not based on average wages, but on equal pay for equal work, giving consideration for differing skills and abilities.

29.4 Safety

46. The Occupational Safety and Health Act (OSHA)

a. Is administered by the Occupational Safety and Health Administration of the Department of Commerce.

b. Is administered by the National Institute of Occupational Safety and Health of the Department of Health and Human Services.

c. Applies to all public and private sector employees.

d. Applies to most employees engaged in a business affecting commerce.

The correct answer is (d). *(Publisher)*

REQUIRED: The true statement about OSHA.

DISCUSSION: The primary legislative purpose of OSHA is to require safe and healthful working conditions in the place of employment and to prevent injuries. OSHA has extremely broad coverage because virtually all private employers engaged in a business affecting interstate commerce are covered. However, the federal government and state and local government entities are exempt.

Answer (a) is incorrect because OSHA is administered by the Occupational Safety and Health Administration (which is also called OSHA) in the Department of Labor. Answer (b) is incorrect because the Institute recommends safety standards, conducts research, and formulates training programs to educate workers about work safety. Answer (c) is incorrect because OSHA does not apply to governments (federal, state, or local).

47. Which of the following is a true statement about OSHA inspections?

a. At least 24 hours' notice must be given to the employer.

b. An employee may request an inspection of his/her employer.

c. If an employer refuses to permit an inspection, OSHA may obtain a search warrant upon a showing of probable cause.

d. OSHA gives priority to random inspections of businesses.

The correct answer is (b). *(Publisher)*

REQUIRED: The true statement about OSHA inspections.

DISCUSSION: An employee may file a written request for an inspection when a violation of a standard creates a threat of physical harm or an imminent danger exists. An employee who has no reasonable alternative may in good faith refuse to work and thereby be exposed to the dangerous condition. But the Supreme Court has ruled that an employer need not pay an employee who refuses to work because of a dangerous condition.

Answer (a) is incorrect because an advance notice of no more than 24 hours is permitted in a few situations, but surprise inspections are the rule. Answer (c) is incorrect because the search warrant may be issued under a lesser standard than probable cause, for example, upon a showing that the inspection is at random. OSHA inspectors have a basic right to enter businesses at reasonable times to inspect. The inspector has a right to make a "walk-around" inspection, and the employer has a right to accompany the inspector. Answer (d) is incorrect because OSHA gives highest priority to inspections of imminently dangerous hazards. Next in order are investigations of fatalities and catastrophes, of complaints, and of certain high-risk industries.

48. Which of the following is a true statement about OSHA enforcement procedures?

a. If judicial review is ultimately sought, the employer has a right to a jury trial.

b. Judicial review of an OSHA decision is by a federal District Court.

c. The OSH Review Commission may review the decision of an administrative law judge when a citation is challenged by the employer.

d. An inspector may issue a citation that will become final and unreviewable if not challenged by the employer within 90 days of its receipt.

The correct answer is (c). *(Publisher)*

REQUIRED: The true statement about OSHA enforcement procedures.

DISCUSSION: If a citation, penalty, or abatement period (a reasonable time given to rectify the violation) is challenged, a hearing may be conducted before an administrative law judge. This judge hears witnesses, receives other evidence, and listens to legal arguments. (S)he then makes findings of law and fact and enters an order. An administrative appeal may be taken to the OSH Review Commission. The decision by the Commission is the final agency determination. If the Secretary of Labor or the employer desires further review, the matter may be appealed to a Circuit Court of Appeals.

Answer (a) is incorrect because the 7th Amendment has been held to give no right to a jury trial on OSHA cases. Answer (b) is incorrect because judicial review is by a federal Court of Appeals. Answer (d) is incorrect because an employer has only 15 days to challenge a citation, penalty, or abatement period.

49. Tom and Jerry were employed at Poolywhirl. Their job entailed working at great heights in a factory, protected by a safety net. This net had proven inadequate in the past and when asked to walk on it, they refused for fear of death or great bodily harm. Poolywhirl fired them.

a. They could not be discharged under the Fair Labor Standards Act.

b. They must be reinstated and paid double time for the work missed.

c. They were improperly discharged under the Occupational Safety and Health Act.

d. They have no recourse against Poolywhirl since they refused a directive of their employer.

The correct answer is (c). *(Publisher)*

REQUIRED: The correct statement concerning the discharge of employees for refusing to perform a dangerous task.

DISCUSSION: The Occupational Safety and Health Act (OSHA) prohibits an employer from discharging or discriminating against any employee who exercises a right under the Act. Employees' rights include refusing to work when an employee believes in good faith that (s)he is in risk of death or great bodily harm from the activity. Therefore, the discharge was improper under OSHA.

Answer (a) is incorrect because the Fair Labor Standards Act does not regulate job safety or discharges for refusal to work. Answer (b) is incorrect because although they must be reinstated, there is no provision for double pay for the work missed. Answer (d) is incorrect because OSHA does provide recourse when an employee is forced to work in dangerous conditions and refuses.

50. Which of the following is a correct statement about penalties provided by OSHA?

a. The Act creates a private right of action for workers.

b. No criminal penalties may be sought for OSHA violations.

c. The Secretary of Labor cannot issue an injunction to prevent future violations.

d. Penalties are in lieu of workers' compensation awards.

The correct answer is (c). *(Publisher)*

REQUIRED: The true statement about penalties provided by OSHA.

DISCUSSION: The Secretary of Labor can assess penalties for violations of the Act and of rules and orders issued under it. The extent of the penalties depends upon whether violations are serious, willful, or repeated. Criminal and civil sanctions are available, including jail terms. The Secretary also has the right to seek injunctions against future violations but not to issue them. Only a court can issue an injunction.

Answer (a) is incorrect because OSHA does not create a cause of action for workers against employers, third parties, or against the federal government for violations or not enforcing the Act. Answer (b) is incorrect because the OSHA provides for criminal penalties when serious, willful violations are found. Answer (d) is incorrect because OSHA has no effect on the operation of workers' compensation laws.

51. Which of the following is a true statement about the general duty of an employer to protect employees from cigarette smoke of co-workers?

a. Any duty must rest upon federal law since the federal government has preempted the field of occupational safety.

b. Any right of the employee must be vindicated through workers' compensation proceedings.

c. Any such duty would have to be based upon enactment of a federal or state statute.

d. Employees could reasonably argue that they have a right based upon both common law and federal and state statutes.

The correct answer is (d). *(Publisher)*

REQUIRED: The true statement about the general duty of an employer to protect employees from cigarette smoke of co-workers.

DISCUSSION: Employers have a common law duty to maintain reasonable, safe working conditions. Employers generally are also subject to federal (OSHA) and state legislation regulating occupational hazards. Under OSHA, for example, an employer is liable for failing to render the work place free of hazards that are recognized as likely to cause death or serious physical harm. Because smoking is now almost universally recognized as a major health hazard not only to the smokers but also to those who inhale secondary smoke, cigarette smoke creates an unsafe condition in the work environment that is both foreseeable and preventable by the employer.

Answer (a) is incorrect because OSHA recognizes a concurrent state power to regulate occupational safety. Answer (b) is incorrect because workers' compensation laws relate to monetary recoveries for work-related injuries and do not prohibit administrative action against occupational hazards. Answer (c) is incorrect because the common law duty of employers is also a basis for an action.

29.5 Workers' Compensation and Employer Liability

52. Which of the following regarding workers' compensation is correct?

a. A purpose of workers' compensation is for the employer to assume a definite liability concerning injuries in the workplace in exchange for the employee's surrender of his/her common law rights.

b. It applies to workers engaged in or affecting interstate commerce only.

c. It is optional in most jurisdictions.

d. Once workers' compensation has been adopted by the employer, the amount of damages recoverable is based upon comparative negligence.

The correct answer is (a). *(CPA 1182 L-26)*

REQUIRED: The true statement about workers' compensation.

DISCUSSION: The essence of workers' compensation is that a worker injured on the job is enabled to receive a relatively swift and certain return in exchange for giving up the right to bring an action in tort for negligence against the employer. The employer loses common law defenses (e.g., contributory negligence), and the statutes are broadly interpreted in favor of workers. However, the amount of the recovery is limited by statute, a provision of the law that benefits employers.

Answer (b) is incorrect because each state has workers' compensation laws that are not limited in their effect to workers in interstate commerce. Answer (c) is incorrect because these laws are usually mandatory. Answer (d) is incorrect because workers' compensation awards are made without regard to the negligence of any party for injuries in the course of employment.

53. Harris was engaged as a crane operator by the Wilcox Manufacturing Corporation, a company complying with state workers' compensation laws. Harris suffered injuries during regular working hours as a result of carelessly climbing out on the arm of the crane to make an adjustment. While doing so, he lost his balance, fell off the arm of the crane and fractured his leg. Wilcox's safety manual for the operation of the crane strictly forbids such conduct by an operator. Wilcox denies any liability, based upon Harris's gross negligence, his disobedience and a waiver of all liability signed by Harris shortly after the accident. Wilcox further asserts that Harris is not entitled to workers' compensation because he is a skilled worker and is on a guaranteed biweekly salary. Which of the following is a correct statement insofar as Harris's rights are concerned?

a. Harris cannot elect to sue under common law for negligence.

b. Harris is not entitled to workers' compensation because he is not an "employee."

c. Harris is not entitled to recovery because his conduct was a clear violation of the safety manual.

d. Harris waived his rights by signing a waiver of liability.

The correct answer is (a). *(CPA 1180 L-59)*

REQUIRED: The correct statement of an injured worker's rights.

DISCUSSION: Workers' compensation laws were enacted to provide a sure remedy for injured employees. Under common law, they had to sue the employer, prove negligence, and be subject to various defenses. Today, state workers' compensation is usually the exclusive remedy for an injured employee against the employer. However, certain employees are exempt, such as independent contractors, employees of an employer with fewer than a minimum number of employees, workers for nonprofit and charitable organizations, agricultural workers, domestic workers, and public employees.

Answer (b) is incorrect because a crane operator, no matter if skilled and paid biweekly, is still an employee and not excluded. Answer (c) is incorrect because an injured worker is provided recovery regardless of fault. An employee is entitled to worker's compensation without regard to fault unless the injuries are caused by intentional self-infliction, participation in mutual altercation, or intoxication of the employee. Answer (d) is incorrect because an employee usually cannot waive his/her rights to workers' compensation.

54. In general, which of the following is not an available method of complying with a state's workers' compensation statute for a private employer?

a. Self-insurance by the employer.

b. Participation in the state insurance fund.

c. Participation in a federal insurance fund.

d. Purchase of insurance from a private insurer.

The correct answer is (c). *(CPA 1187 L-15)*

REQUIRED: The method not available for complying with a state's workers' compensation laws.

DISCUSSION: All states have workers' compensation, which may be funded through various methods. Private insurance may be purchased or payments may be made to a state fund. Some states allow self-insurance through establishment of contingency funds that meet state regulations. However, no federal insurance fund is available for this purpose.

Answers (a), (b), and (d) are incorrect because they all represent acceptable methods of complying with a state's workers' compensation statute.

55. Which one of the following statements concerning workers' compensation laws is ordinarily true?

a. Workers' compensation laws are very narrowly construed against employees.

b. The amount of damages recoverable is based on comparative negligence.

c. Employers are strictly liable without regard to whether they are at fault.

d. Workers' compensation benefits are not available if the employee is grossly negligent.

The correct answer is (c). *(CPA 589 L-38)*

REQUIRED: The true statement concerning workers' compensation laws.

DISCUSSION: Workers' compensation is a form of strict liability whereby the employer is liable to an employee for injuries or diseases sustained by the employee that arise out of and in the course of employment. The employee is entitled to workers' compensation benefits without regard to fault unless the injuries are caused by intentional self-infliction, participation in mutual altercation, or intoxication of the employee.

Answer (a) is incorrect because workers' compensation laws are interpreted to benefit employees. They remove common law defenses of employers. Thus, the employee can recover for job-related injuries or diseases with little difficulty. Answer (b) is incorrect because the amount of damages the employee will be allowed is not based on comparative fault but on a scheme prescribed by state statute, usually a percentage of the injured employee's wages. Answer (d) is incorrect because the employee will receive workers' compensation despite his/her gross negligence.

56. Which of the following would be the employer's best defense to a claim for workers' compensation by an injured route salesman?

a. A route salesman is automatically deemed to be an independent contractor, and therefore excluded from workers' compensation coverage.

b. The salesman was grossly negligent in carrying out the employment.

c. The salesman's injury was caused primarily by the negligence of an employee.

d. The salesman's injury did not arise out of and in the course of employment.

The correct answer is (d). *(CPA 1182 L-27)*

REQUIRED: The employer's best workers' compensation defense to a route salesman's claim.

DISCUSSION: The injury must be work-related. It must arise out of the employment in that it must be typical of the kind of employment involved. It must occur in the course of the employment in the sense that the worker must have been actively at work or away from the job location performing employment-related duties. In general, the requirement is liberally construed in favor of workers.

Answer (a) is incorrect because a route salesman is under the control of the employer as to the means of accomplishing the work and is thus not an independent contractor. Independent contractors must furnish their own insurance. Answers (b) and (c) are incorrect because under workers' compensation law, the defenses of contributory negligence, assumption of the risk, and the fellow-servant rule are unavailable.

57. If an employer carried workers' compensation coverage on his/her employees, an injured employee would

a. Probably be covered even if the injury was caused by a co-worker.

b. Not be covered if the injury was caused by grossly negligent maintenance by the employer.

c. Probably not be covered if the injury was due to a violation of plant rules in operating the machine.

d. Be covered if the employee was driving to work from his/her home.

The correct answer is (a). *(CPA 574 L-43)*

REQUIRED: The correct statement concerning the rights of an injured employee.

DISCUSSION: Injuries to employees occurring in the work place are frequently caused by a co-worker. This does not prevent recovery of workers' compensation benefits.

Answers (b) and (c) are incorrect because an injured employee can recover no matter who is negligent and when no one is negligent. Answer (d) is incorrect because an employee is covered under the workers' compensation acts only when in a job-related activity. Normally, driving to work from home is not job-related and is considered to be personal activity. If an employee is also performing a service for the employer while driving to work, however, (s)he would probably be covered.

58. Workers' compensation laws

a. Are uniform throughout the United States with the exception of Louisiana.

b. Have not been adopted by all states except where required by federal law.

c. Do not preclude an action against a third party who has caused an injury.

d. Do not cover employees injured outside the jurisdiction.

The correct answer is (c). *(CPA 575 L-35)*

REQUIRED: The correct statement concerning workers' compensation laws.

DISCUSSION: A worker injured within the course and scope of the employment relationship is limited to workers' compensation benefits and may not pursue a separate action against the employer. However, when an employee's injuries are caused by a third party, the injured employee may, in addition to recovering workers' compensation benefits, pursue a legal action against the third party including, in some jurisdictions, co-workers. An injured employee who recovers against a third person usually must reimburse the employer or its insurance carrier for the workers' compensation benefits received.

Answer (a) is incorrect because workers' compensation laws are not fully uniform, but all states, including Louisiana, have workers' compensation statutes. Answer (b) is incorrect because workers' compensation laws have been adopted by all 50 states but are not subject to federal law. Answer (d) is incorrect because an employee injured outside the state of the place of employment is still covered by workers' compensation law. For example, employees sent from State A to State B by their employer to install machinery would be covered under the workers' compensation laws in State A even though the injury occurred in State B.

59. Nix, an employee of Fern, Inc., was injured in the course of employment while operating a drill press manufactured and sold to Fern by Jet Corp. It has been determined that Fern was negligent in supervising the operation of the drill press and that the drill press was defectively designed by Jet. If Fern has complied with the state's mandatory workers' compensation statute, Nix may

a. Not properly commence a products liability action against Jet.

b. Not obtain workers' compensation benefits.

c. Obtain workers' compensation benefits and properly maintain a products liability action against Jet.

d. Obtain workers' compensation benefits and properly maintain separate causes of action against Jet and Fern for negligence.

The correct answer is (c). *(CPA 587 L-36)*

REQUIRED: The correct statement about the rights of an injured employee.

DISCUSSION: The law of workers' compensation permits recovery for a work-related injury (arising out of and in the course of employment), but a negligence suit against the employer is barred. However, when an employee's injuries are caused by a third party, the injured employee may, in addition to recovering workers' compensation benefits, pursue a legal action against the third party. Thus, a strict liability suit against the manufacturer of defective equipment is not barred.

Answer (a) is incorrect because the law does not bar the employee from suing a third-party manufacturer on a strict liability theory. Answer (b) is incorrect because Nix was injured in the scope of employment, which is all that is required for an employee who is covered by workers' compensation laws to obtain benefits. Answer (d) is incorrect because acceptance of benefits under workers' compensation law precludes an employee from suing the employer for damages in a civil court.

60. Which of the following is a true statement about workers' compensation benefits?

a. Disability benefits are based on a specified percentage of the workers' weekly pay.

b. Death benefits are paid only for burial expenses.

c. Disability payments are based on a specified percentage of actual damages.

d. Medical benefits ordinarily include the cost of a physician's services only if the injured worker does not choose his/her own physician.

The correct answer is (a). *(Publisher)*

REQUIRED: The true statement about workers' compensation benefits.

DISCUSSION: Disability benefits are normally set by statute at between 50% and 66-2/3% of normal pay without regard to overtime. The statute also sets maximum and minimum amounts and limits the number of weeks of benefits. Whether the disability is partial or total and temporary or permanent also affects the amounts paid. A schedule is also usually included in the statute stating the benefits to be paid for loss of a body part. Disfigurement is also compensable in many states, but disability benefits will not be recoverable for up to the first 2 weeks after the injury.

Answer (b) is incorrect because death benefits are also paid to those who were economically dependent upon the decedent. Answer (c) is incorrect because actual damages are irrelevant for disability benefits. Answer (d) is incorrect because medical costs for physicians, nurses, hospitalization, and rehabilitation are usually compensated. A worker may generally choose his/her own physician.

61. Which of the following is a true statement about the workers' compensation claim procedure?

a. No statute of limitations applies to claims.

b. A notice of injury must be given within the statutory period.

c. In the majority of states, courts decide contested claims.

d. Appeals from the decision of the trier of fact are not permitted.

The correct answer is (b). *(Publisher)*

REQUIRED: The true statement about the workers' compensation claim procedure.

DISCUSSION: After the injury occurs, the worker must give notice of the injury within the statutory limit. A statute of limitations also applies to the filing of the claim. In the majority of states, claims are heard by an administrative agency. In some states, courts decide these cases (but most claims are uncontested). When a claim is heard by an agency, the proceeding is judicial but with a more simplified and informal procedure. After hearing testimony and receiving evidence, a decision is made that may be appealed to the court system.

Answer (a) is incorrect because both notice of injury and filing of a claim are subject to time limits. Answer (c) is incorrect because most states have administrative agencies for this purpose. Answer (d) is incorrect because whether the trier of fact is an administrative agency or a court, the decision is appealable.

62. Musgrove Manufacturing Enterprises is subject to compulsory workers' compensation laws in the state in which it does business. It has complied with the state's workers' compensation provisions. State law provides that when there has been compliance, workers' compensation is normally an exclusive remedy. However, the remedy will not be exclusive if

a. The employee has been intentionally injured by the employer personally.

b. The employee dies as a result of his injuries.

c. The accident was entirely the fault of a fellow-servant of the employee.

d. The employer was only slightly negligent and the employee's conduct was grossly negligent.

The correct answer is (a). *(CPA 581 L-60)*

REQUIRED: The circumstance in which workers' compensation is not the exclusive remedy.

DISCUSSION: Normally, when an employee is injured in a work-related activity, the employee's exclusive remedy for such injury is provided for under the state workers' compensation act. Employers and fellow employees are usually exempt from personal liability for such injuries but third parties are not exempt. An additional narrow exception to the exclusive remedy is that an employer is not permitted to use the workers' compensation statutes to insulate him/herself from intentional wrongdoing.

Answer (b) is incorrect because normally the exclusive remedy for an injury (including death) is that the employee or his/her estate must accept the scheduled benefit under state workers' compensation acts. Dependents or other members of the worker's family are allowed in some jurisdictions to recover for direct injuries to themselves as a result of the worker's injury, e.g., loss of marital relations. Answer (c) is incorrect because even though an accident is entirely the fault of a fellow employee, workers' compensation will still be the exclusive remedy. Answer (d) is incorrect because workers' compensation acts are the exclusive remedy for an injured employee without regard to whether the employee or the employer was negligent or grossly negligent.

63. Wilcox works as a welder for Miracle Muffler, Inc. He was specially trained by Miracle in the procedures and safety precautions applicable to installing replacement mufflers on automobiles. One rule of which he was aware involved a prohibition against installing a muffler on any auto which had heavily congealed oil or grease or which had any leaks. Wilcox disregarded this rule, and as a result an auto caught fire causing extensive property damage and injury to Wilcox. Which of the following statements is correct?

a. Miracle has no liability because its rule prohibited Wilcox from installing the muffler in question.

b. Miracle is not liable to Wilcox under the workers' compensation laws.

c. Miracle is liable for damage to the car irrespective of its efforts to prevent such an occurrence and its exercise of reasonable care.

d. Wilcox does not have any personal liability for the damage to the car because he was acting for and on behalf of his employer.

The correct answer is (c). *(CPA 578 L-1)*

REQUIRED: The employer's liability for the negligence of an employee who disregarded a safety rule.

DISCUSSION: The general rule is that the employer is held legally responsible for torts of its employees that occur within the course and scope of employment. Wrongful damage to property is a tort. This rule is not changed by the employee's disregard of safety rules or actions contrary to the employer's instructions. So long as the employee has not abandoned the employment relationship, the employer is liable for job-related torts. The fact that the employer exercises reasonable care does not eliminate its liability.

Answer (a) is incorrect because the employer is liable even though its rule prohibited the employee from taking the action which caused the property damage and injury. Answer (b) is incorrect because the employer is liable to an injured employee under the workers' compensation law even when the worker has disregarded safety instructions and proceeded in a negligent manner. Answer (d) is incorrect because negligent employees are liable to the third persons they injure even if the employer may also be liable.

29.6 Social Security and Unemployment Benefits

64. Eligibility to receive Social Security benefits

a. Is limited to retired and disabled workers.

b. Depends on achieving fully issued status.

c. Depends on having earnings from employment for a specified number of calendar quarters.

d. Is limited to those with fully issued or disability status.

The correct answer is (c). *(Publisher)*

REQUIRED: The true statement about eligibility to receive Social Security benefits.

DISCUSSION: Benefits provided by the Social Security Act as amended are paid to retired workers over a certain age, to the surviving spouse and children of deceased workers, and to disabled workers and certain of their dependents. Also, health and medical insurance are provided for the elderly. Fully insured status is attained by earning nominal amounts (as low as $50) per calendar quarter as an employee or a self-employed person for a certain number of quarters. This number of quarters must be at least 6 and need not exceed 40. A person who falls in between 6 and 40 quarters is eligible if the number is equal to the lesser of the excess of one's age over 21 or the number of years since 1950. This entitles a person to full old age and survivors' benefits. Currently insured (not fully insured) status is based on receipt of credit for at least 6 quarters in the preceding 13. Persons in this status are entitled to only part of the benefits provided to those who have fully insured status. Disability status is based on receipt of credit for 20 of the 40 quarters preceding disablement.

Answer (a) is incorrect because dependents may also receive benefits. Answers (b) and (d) are incorrect because those on currently insured or disability status also qualify but receive lower benefits.

65. Social Security benefits may be obtained by

a. Qualifying individuals who are also receiving benefits from a private pension plan.

b. Qualifying individuals or their families only upon such individual's disability or retirement.

c. Children of a deceased worker who was entitled to benefits until such children reach age 25 or complete their education, whichever occurs first.

d. Only those individuals who have made payments while employed.

The correct answer is (a). *(CPA 1186 L-39)*

REQUIRED: The availability of Social Security benefits.

DISCUSSION: The federal Social Security Act permits qualifying individuals to receive benefits even if they currently receive benefits from a private pension plan as long as the individual has worked for the statutory period of time and/or earned the specified amount of wages.

Answer (b) is incorrect because qualifying individuals or their families are eligible for benefits upon death of the individual in addition to retirement or disability. Answer (c) is incorrect because benefits may be received by dependents of a qualifying deceased worker until the dependents reach age 18 or complete their education, whichever comes first. Answer (d) is incorrect because benefits are not limited to individuals who have made payments while employed. Survivors' benefits are paid to certain members of a deceased worker's family. Also, certain dependents of a disabled worker may receive payments. None of these recipients is required to have made contributions.

66. The federal Social Security Act applies in general to both employers and employees. Hexter Manufacturing is a small business as defined by the Small Business Administration. Regarding Hexter's relationship to requirements of the Social Security Act, which of the following is correct?

a. Since Hexter is a small business, it is exempt from the Social Security Act.

b. Social Security payments made by Hexter's employees are tax deductible for federal income tax purposes.

c. Hexter has the option to be covered or excluded from the provisions of the Social Security Act.

d. The Social Security Act applies to both Hexter and its employees.

The correct answer is (d). *(CPA 1179 L-49)*

REQUIRED: The relationship of a small business to the Social Security Act.

DISCUSSION: The Social Security Act covers most workers or employees in the United States today. Persons employed in industry and commerce, the self-employed, household employees, farm employees, clergy, and members of the armed forces are included. The Act makes no distinction between small and large businesses; all employees are covered.

Answer (a) is incorrect because no employer is exempt from the Social Security Act. Answer (b) is incorrect because payments made by employees to the Social Security system are not deductible for federal income tax purposes. Answer (c) is incorrect because no employee or employer has the option to be excluded from Social Security; coverage is mandatory.

67. Which of the following statements is correct with respect to Social Security taxes and benefits?

a. An individual whose gross income exceeds certain maximum limitations is required to include the entire amount received as disability benefits in the computation of taxable income.

b. Benefits are available to a qualifying individual or that individual's family only upon retirement or disability.

c. An employer that erroneously underwithholds and underpays an employee's share of Social Security taxes will be liable for the unpaid balance of the employee's share.

d. An individual whose private pension benefits exceed certain maximum limitations will have Social Security retirement benefits reduced.

The correct answer is (c). *(CPA 588 L-43)*

REQUIRED: The true statement about Social Security taxes.

DISCUSSION: Under the Federal Insurance Contribution Act (FICA), the employer is required to withhold the employee's share of Social Security taxes from the employee's wages and remit that amount, along with the employer's own equal share, to the government. An employer that underwithholds and underpays is liable for the unpaid balance of the employee's share.

Answer (a) is incorrect because only up to one-half of Social Security benefits are taxable. Answer (b) is incorrect because the family of a qualifying individual is entitled to benefits upon the death of that individual. Answer (d) is incorrect because an individual's income from private pension plans, savings, investments, or insurance does not affect Social Security benefits because those items are not considered earned income.

68. Jane Sabine was doing business as Sabine Fashions, a sole proprietorship. Sabine suffered financial reverses and began to use Social Security and income taxes withheld from her employees to finance the business. Sabine finally filed a voluntary petition in bankruptcy. Which of the following would not apply to her as a result of her actions?

a. She would remain liable for the taxes due.

b. She is personally liable for fines and imprisonment.

c. She could justify her actions by showing that the use of the tax money was vital to continuation of the business.

d. She may be assessed penalties up to the amount of taxes due.

The correct answer is (c). *(CPA 579 L-50)*

REQUIRED: The false statement of liability for misappropriating employment taxes.

DISCUSSION: An employer is required to withhold the employee's share of FICA taxes and income taxes from the employee's wages and remit them to the federal government. Since the funds deducted from employee's wages belong to the government, employers can never justify the action of using such tax funds as operating capital.

Answer (a) is incorrect because a tax due the government is a debt not discharged in bankruptcy. Answer (b) is incorrect because the employer (and the officers, if the employer is a corporation) would be personally liable for certain fines and possibly imprisonment. Answer (d) is incorrect because an employer is subject to a 100% penalty for not turning over employment taxes required to be withheld from employees.

69. Which of the following statements is correct with respect to Social Security taxes and benefits?

a. A self-employed individual with net earnings of $35,000 will pay more tax than an employee with wages of $35,000.

b. Both employees and self-employed individuals are subject to Social Security taxes based on their respective gross wages or gross earnings from self-employment.

c. To the extent the amount received as retirement benefits is less than the amount contributed to the Social Security fund by the individual, it will **never** be included in the individual's adjusted gross income for federal income tax purposes.

d. An individual whose gross income exceeds certain maximum limitations is required to include the entire amount received as disability benefits in the computation of the individual's adjusted gross income for federal income tax purposes.

The correct answer is (a). *(CPA 1188 L-30)*

REQUIRED: The correct statement about Social Security taxes and benefits.

DISCUSSION: For tax years beginning in 1990, an effective tax rate of 15.3% applies to an individual's earnings from self-employment. However, a tax deduction is available for half of the tax. The Social Security tax paid by employers and employees is 7.65% of an employee's wages up to $50,400 in 1990. The employee pays less tax than the self-employed individual because the employer must also pay Social Security taxes on the employee's wages.

Answer (b) is incorrect because net earnings from self-employment, not gross earnings, is the Social Security tax base for a self-employed individual. Answer (c) is incorrect because a portion of Social Security benefits received by an individual may be included in the individual's adjusted gross income. Answer (d) is incorrect because only a portion of an individual's disability benefits is included in his/her gross income if certain limitations on gross income are exceeded. The exact amount is computed on the basis of a formula set forth in the Internal Revenue Code.

70. The Social Security tax does not apply to which of the following?

a. Medical and hospital reimbursements by the employer that are excluded from gross income.

b. Compensation paid in forms other than cash.

c. Self-employment income of $1,000.

d. Bonuses and vacation time pay.

The correct answer is (a). *(CPA 1181 L-30)*

REQUIRED: The payment to which the Social Security tax does not apply.

DISCUSSION: The Social Security tax imposed by the Federal Insurance Contribution Act (FICA) applies to virtually all compensation received for employment, including money or other forms of wages, bonuses, commissions, vacation pay, severance allowances, and tips. Reimbursements by one's employers for medical and hospital expenses which are not included in gross income are not subject to FICA. However, sick pay is subject to FICA.

Answers (b), (c), and (d) are incorrect because each is subject to FICA.

71. What does fully insured mean under the Social Security Act?

a. When an employee is covered by workers' compensation, Social Security, and unemployment insurance.

b. When an employee has worked the required amount of time paying in taxes so as to be entitled to all Social Security benefits.

c. When an employee is entitled to a maximum amount of benefits.

d. When an employee and his/her dependents are all receiving benefits.

The correct answer is (b). *(Publisher)*

REQUIRED: The meaning of "fully insured" under the Social Security Act.

DISCUSSION: "Fully insured" refers to the status of an employee or retired employee who has worked a sufficient amount of time (e.g., 40 quarters) paying in taxes so as to be entitled to all benefits available under Social Security. This does not mean that the employee will receive the maximum dollar amount of benefits, but that (s)he or his/her dependents are entitled to all of these benefits.

Answer (a) is incorrect because although an employee should always be covered by workers' compensation, Social Security, and unemployment insurance, there is no term to describe this. Answer (c) is incorrect because a beneficiary's dollar amount of benefits depends upon average monthly earnings, and the relationship of the beneficiary to the retired, deceased, or disabled worker (if the beneficiary is not the employee). Answer (d) is incorrect because an employee and his/her dependents should not all be receiving benefits concurrently. Many dependents (e.g., survivors) are only entitled to benefits when the retired worker is no longer receiving them.

72. At age 66, Jonstone retired as a general partner of Gordon & Co. He no longer participates in the affairs of the partnership but does receive a distributive share of the partnership profits as a result of becoming a limited partner upon retirement. Jonstone has accepted a part-time consulting position with a corporation near his retirement home. Which of the following is correct regarding Jonstone's Social Security situation?

a. Jonstone's limited partner distributive share will be considered self-employment income for Social Security purposes up to a maximum of $10,000.

b. There is no limitation on the amount Jonstone may earn in the first year of retirement.

c. Jonstone will lose $1 of Social Security benefits for each $1 of earnings in excess of a statutorily permitted amount.

d. Jonstone will be subject to an annual earnings limitation until he attains a stated age which, if exceeded, will reduce the amount of Social Security benefits.

The correct answer is (d). *(CPA 580 L-18)*

REQUIRED: The correct statement regarding the Social Security situation of a retired general partner.

DISCUSSION: Retired employees are subject to an annual earnings limitation (which changes periodically) that reduces the amount of Social Security benefits when exceeded. A limitation is no longer effective when the retiree reaches age 72.

Answer (a) is incorrect because a distributive share from a limited partnership is not considered self-employment income for Social Security purposes at all. Answer (b) is incorrect because a retired person is also subject to the annual earnings limitation in the first year of retirement. Answer (c) is incorrect because an employee will lose $1 in Social Security benefits for each $2 of earnings in excess of the statutorily permitted amount.

73. With respect to federal unemployment taxes and unemployment compensation, which of the following statements is correct?

a. The Federal Unemployment Tax Act requires both the employer and employee to make payments to an approved state unemployment fund.

b. Federal unemployment taxes are offset by a credit equal to the amount the employer contributes to an approved state unemployment fund.

c. Unemployment compensation received in excess of the employer's contributions is, in all cases, fully includible in the recipient's gross income for federal income tax purposes.

d. Payments made by a corporate employer for federal unemployment taxes are deductible as a business expense for federal income tax purposes.

The correct answer is (d). *(CPA 586 L-16)*

REQUIRED: The correct statement concerning federal unemployment taxes and unemployment compensation.

DISCUSSION: Federal law provides general guidelines, standards, and requirements for the program, but the states administer the benefit payments under the program. The federal unemployment tax is calculated as a fixed percentage of each covered employee's salary up to a stated maximum. Federal unemployment tax must be paid by an employer who employs one or more persons covered under the federal Social Security Act, or who pays wages of $1,500 or more during any calendar quarter. A corporate employer is permitted to deduct these payments as a business expense for federal income tax purposes.

Answer (a) is incorrect because federal unemployment taxes are only imposed on the employer, not the employee. Answer (b) is incorrect because an employer is entitled to a credit against its federal unemployment tax equal to 90% of the state unemployment tax rate up to a maximum credit of 2.7%. Answer (c) is incorrect because the taxable amount of a recipient's unemployment compensation is limited to one-half of the recipient's adjusted gross income (excluding taxable unemployment compensation) plus total unemployment compensation.

74. The Federal Unemployment Tax Act

a. Imposes a tax on all employers doing business in the U.S.

b. Requires contributions to be made by the employer and employee equally.

c. Allows an employer to take a credit against the federal unemployment tax if contributions are made to a state unemployment fund.

d. Permits an employee to receive unemployment benefits that are limited to the contributions made to that employee's account.

The correct answer is (c). *(CPA 589 L-36)*

REQUIRED: The true statement about FUTA.

DISCUSSION: The Federal Unemployment Tax Act permits an employer who made contributions to a state unemployment fund to take a credit against the federal unemployment tax.

Answer (a) is incorrect because the tax is imposed on employers having as few as one employee for a portion of a day in each of 20 weeks in any year, or who have a payroll of at least $1,500 in any calendar quarter. Answer (b) is incorrect because employees are not required to pay any tax under FUTA. Answer (d) is incorrect because there are no accounts established for specific employees under FUTA.

75. Tom Marshall was employed by Cool Ice Company. One summer it was very cold so Cool Ice had little business and had to lay Marshall off due to a lack of work. The state unemployment agency found a similar job for Marshall but he did not accept it because he decided to go back to school.

a. Marshall is entitled to unemployment benefits because Cool Ice paid the unemployment insurance tax.

b. Marshall is not entitled to unemployment compensation.

c. Marshall must accept the other job.

d. Cool Ice must pay Marshall's benefits for laying him off without cause.

The correct answer is (b). *(Publisher)*

REQUIRED: The correct statement regarding unemployment compensation for a worker who has been laid off.

DISCUSSION: There are ordianrily three conditions to collect unemployment compensation: 1) the worker was employed and laid off through no fault of the worker; 2) the worker filed a claim for the benefits; 3) the worker is able, available, and willing to work but cannot find employment. Marshall is not entitled to unemployment compensation since he did not accept a suitable job which was available. A worker is disqualified if (s)he refuses other suitable work, was discharged for good cause, or quit voluntarily.

Answer (a) is incorrect because an employer's payment of the tax does not affect the availability of benefits. Answer (c) is incorrect because Marshall is not required to accept the other job, but he is not entitled to the unemployment compensation if he refuses the job. Answer (d) is incorrect because Cool Ice is only required to pay the unemployment tax. The discharged employee is then paid out of the state unemployment compensation fund.

CHAPTER THIRTY
CONSUMER PROTECTION

Consumer law overlaps such topics as bankruptcy, secured transactions, mortgages, credit law, and suretyship. Accordingly, this chapter should be read with the chapters covering these subjects.

30.1 Contract Warranties and Misrepresentations

1. Naive met Slick at a party in Ohio. Slick said she was involved in real estate in Florida where the hot deals were available. Naive had a little extra cash to invest so he invited Slick to come by the next day. Slick showed Naive pictures of beautiful ocean-front property, assured Naive that she had personally visited the property, and told Naive that it was a "steal." Relying on this information, Naive gave Slick money and received a properly executed warranty deed with a legal description of land in Florida. Naive took a trip to Florida a few weeks later to look at the land and discovered that the property described in the deed was located in the middle of a swamp. What is Naive's best remedy?

a. Nothing since the contract was completed and a valid deed cannot be returned.

b. Damages based on the warranties given in the deed.

c. Rescission based on fraud.

d. Nothing since the parol evidence rule will prevent introduction of the oral statements made by Slick.

The correct answer is (c). *(Publisher)*

REQUIRED: The best remedy for a buyer who has received a deed to property that was misrepresented by the seller.

DISCUSSION: Fraud is present when there has been a misstatement of a material fact with the intent to deceive, and on which the plaintiff justifiably relied to his/her detriment. Rescission of a contract is a proper remedy for fraud because there was not a meeting of the minds on the "agreement." The purchaser clearly had different expectations (this would also be true in the case of innocent misrepresentation which is similar to fraud without the intent to deceive).

Naive meets these requirements as a victim of fraud and should attempt to have the contract rescinded with the return of his money. Naive is also entitled to damages under tort law for the fraud.

Answer (a) is incorrect because a deed can be rescinded, reformed, or returned if it was accepted on the basis of fraud. Answer (b) is incorrect because the warranties would only provide that Slick owned and had the right to transfer the land described. As long as Slick did own the swampland, the warranties will not provide Naive any remedies. Answer (d) is incorrect because there are many exceptions to the parol evidence rule, one of which always allows evidence of fraud to be admitted.

2. Judy entered into an agreement with Ralph to buy diamonds from him for $10,000. Which of the following would not prevent Ralph from enforcing the agreement?

a. Ralph said they were worth $10,000, but an appraisal obtained by Judy revealed the fair value to be $5,000.

b. Ralph threatened to break Judy's husband's leg if she did not buy them.

c. Judy knows nothing about financial transactions and Ralph is a trustee and financial adviser for all her assets.

d. The agreement is not in writing.

The correct answer is (a). *(Publisher)*

REQUIRED: The situation that would not prevent a seller from enforcing a contract.

DISCUSSION: Although fraud and even innocent misrepresentation are grounds for preventing a seller from enforcing a contract, there is no indication that either is present in these facts. All fraud and innocent misrepresentation require a misrepresentation of fact. An opinion of value is not considered fact. Also, there is no requirement in contracts that a person must obtain equal economic value.

Answer (b) is incorrect because a threat to break Judy's husband's leg is duress which generally makes a contract voidable. Answer (c) is incorrect because when a trustee and financial adviser sells to his client, there is the possibility of undue influence, which makes the contract voidable by the purchaser. Answer (d) is incorrect because a sale of goods for $500 or more must be in writing and signed by the person against whom enforcement is sought.

3. Collector wanted a certain vase. The vase was too expensive so the clerk at an antique store indicated she could get a replica which would look exactly the same at a much lower price. Collector paid the price and they agreed that the vase would be available within two weeks. When the vase arrived it was of excellent quality, but the artwork on the exterior was not the same as the original antique. It now turns out that an exact duplicate is not available. The antique store refuses to accept the vase back or refund Collector's money.

a. The antique store is liable under an implied warranty.

b. The antique store is liable under an express warranty.

c. Collector has no recourse since she already paid the purchase price and received the vase.

d. The manufacturer of the vase can be held strictly liable.

The correct answer is (b). *(Publisher)*

REQUIRED: A store's liability for a promised product not meeting the specifications.

DISCUSSION: An express warranty can be created by a promise made by the seller relating to the goods and which becomes part of the bargain. Furthermore, a sample or model that is part of the bargain also creates an express warranty that the purchased goods will conform to the sample (UCC 2-313). Since the clerk promised to get an exact replica, Collector can hold the antique store liable on a theory of express warranty when the vase did not meet this criterion.

Answer (a) is incorrect because the warranty in the description was an express warranty, rather than an implied warranty. Answer (c) is incorrect because damages can be obtained for breach of warranty even though the purchase price has been paid and the vase received. Answer (d) is incorrect because the manufacturer did not contract with Collector, and can only be held strictly liable for defects in products which can cause injury.

4. Timely purchased a watch for which the written information contained an explanation that it was a "full" warranty. Shortly thereafter, the watch stopped working. Timely went back to the store where he purchased the watch and requested that it be exchanged for a new one. The store explained it could not be exchanged, but the manufacturer would repair it under the warranty for a $3.00 service charge. What are Timely's rights?

a. Under a "full" warranty, Timely is entitled to have the watch replaced with a new one.

b. Under a "full" warranty, Timely may not be assessed a service charge.

c. If the warranty had stated "limited," the warranty of merchantability could have been disclaimed.

d. Timely can either have the watch repaired or obtain a new one if he can prove that he did not cause the damage.

The correct answer is (b). *(Publisher)*

REQUIRED: A purchaser's rights under a "full" warranty for a defective product.

DISCUSSION: Under the Magnuson-Moss Warranty Act, written warranties must use the words "full" or "limited." Under a "full" warranty, the purchaser is entitled to have a defective product repaired or replaced by the seller (manufacturer) without charge and within a reasonable time. Since Timely received a "full" warranty, the manufacturer must repair or replace the watch and cannot require a $3.00 service charge. There are many other stringent requirements when a "full" warranty is given, and for this reason almost all warranties today are "limited."

Answer (a) is incorrect because the manufacturer may choose to have the watch repaired instead of replaced. Answer (c) is incorrect because the warranty of merchantability is an implied warranty and implied warranties cannot be disclaimed when a written warranty is given. Answer (d) is incorrect because Timely is not required to prove that he did not cause the damage. Unless there is evidence that he did damage the watch, the manufacturer is required to repair or replace it.

5. Nell Novice decided to take up cross-country skiing. She went to Snow Sports, Inc. (SSI) and explained to the clerk that she was a new skier and needed a pair of skis for cross-country skiing. The clerk was new and did not know anything about skis, but showed Novice three pairs of downhill skis and told Novice that they were all very good. Novice purchased one pair and took them home. Several days later, Novice learned from friends that they were downhill skis and not suitable for cross-country skiing. Novice tried to return the skis, but SSI insisted that all sales were final and referred to a prominent sign by the cash register that had been there the day Novice made the purchase. What are Novice's rights?

a. Sue SSI under an implied warranty of fitness for a particular purpose.

b. Sue SSI under an implied warranty of merchantability.

c. None, because Novice made the selection and the sale was final.

d. Rescind the contract on the basis of mistake.

The correct answer is (a). *(Publisher)*

REQUIRED: The rights of a purchaser of inappropriate goods after relying on the seller to choose them.

DISCUSSION: Under UCC 2-315, if a seller has reason to know of a particular purpose for which goods are required and that the buyer is relying on the seller's skill or judgment to select suitable goods, there is an implied warranty that the goods shall be fit for such purpose. Novice did explain to the clerk that she was a new skier and the use to which the skis would be put. SSI is liable under the implied warranty of fitness for a particular purpose even though the clerk was new and had no special skill or knowledge.

Answer (b) is incorrect because the implied warranty of merchantability refers to the quality of the goods, not the use to which they are put. Answer (c) is incorrect because Novice relied on the sales clerk's selection, and the finality of a sale (acceptance) does not prevent recovery of damages for breach of a warranty. Answer (d) is incorrect because Novice did not make a mistake, but relied on the seller's judgment.

30.2 Contract Enforcement and Consumer Liability

6. Alice entered into a contract with Kool-it, Inc. to purchase and have installed central air conditioning in her home. Kool-it required her to sign its standard form contract. Alice is paying for the air conditioner and installation in three monthly payments. Installation is to take place in the month after the second payment. Which of the following will not be upheld by a court?

a. A clause relieving Kool-it from installation until the second payment is made.

b. A clause relieving Kool-it of any liability (in contract or in tort) if a claim is not made within ten days of installation.

c. A clause allowing additional charges for difficult installation even if the contract is determined to be one of adhesion.

d. A clause providing for an additional fee if Alice's payments are late or her checks bounce.

The correct answer is (b). *(Publisher)*

REQUIRED: The clause of a contract that will not be upheld by a court.

DISCUSSION: An exculpatory clause is one that excuses a party from a duty or liability. They can be upheld provided they are reasonable. A clause that tries to limit liability in an unreasonable manner that tends to be unconscionable will not be upheld. A clause relieving Kool-it of any liability in contract or tort is much too broad. It would attempt to eliminate even product liability.

Answer (a) is incorrect because there is no reason a seller of a product cannot limit its installation upon proper payment. Answer (c) is incorrect because a contract of adhesion is a standard form contract required to be used by one of the parties. They are upheld based on the efficiencies of using them. A person can contract to allow additional charges when an installation proves more difficult than expected. Answer (d) is incorrect because late payment charges or return check charges are proper provided they are fully disclosed in advance to the customer.

7. Driver was going on a summer vacation with his family and leased a motor home from Nogo Enterprises. A provision in the form lease disclaimed all liability and warranties for the condition of the motor home, damages resulting from use of the motor home, and any repairs needed on the motor home. Driver was required to initial this provision on the contract in addition to signing the entire agreement. One hundred miles out of town, the transmission broke. A repair shop estimated it would take 1 week to fix and cost $500. Driver left the motor home at the shop and made the trip by airplane. Nogo Enterprises now seeks to hold Driver liable for both the cost of the repairs and the rental of the motor home. Driver is

a. Liable for the rent, but not the repair since repairs are always a responsibility of the lessor.

b. Liable for the repair, but not the rent since he did obtain the use of the motor vehicle.

c. Liable for both the rent and the repair since he initialed the clause in the contract indicating agreement to it.

d. Not liable at all since the contract is unconscionable.

The correct answer is (d). *(Publisher)*

REQUIRED: The extent of Driver's liability for the repairs and rental of the motor home.

DISCUSSION: Courts tend to find consumer contracts (or clauses therein) not enforceable if they are unconscionable (so one-sided or oppressive that it would be against public policy to enforce them). Under UCC 2-302, courts are specifically allowed to refuse to enforce a contract for the sale of goods to avoid an unconscionable result, and courts may refer to this section as an analogy in contracts not for the sale of goods. Furthermore, this rental was a bailment under which the bailor was responsible to provide goods which were reasonably fit for the purpose intended. Obviously, the motor home was not reasonably fit since it broke down after 100 miles.

Answer (a) is incorrect because a court would probably not hold Driver liable for the rent since he only used the motor home for 100 miles and then had to switch modes of transportation. Answer (b) is incorrect because although the parties can shift liability for repairs by contract, this repair was so major that requiring the lessee to pay for it would be unfair and oppressive. Answer (c) is incorrect because the initialing of a clause in a form contract will not bind the party if the court finds that the contract is unconscionable.

8. Johnson bought a television for $450 from Ace Appliances. Johnson signed a promissory note (that stated the holder is subject to all defenses of the maker) and a purchase contract to cover the entire purchase price. The television proved defective so Johnson returned it to Ace. One week later, Easy Finance Company demanded the first payment on the promissory note which it had purchased from Ace without any knowledge that the television was defective.

a. As a holder in due course, Easy Finance is entitled to payment from Johnson because it took free of contractual defenses.

b. Johnson must seek reimbursement from Ace Appliances for the amount he has to pay to Easy Finance.

c. Johnson's liability is not determined by having signed a promissory note instead of a check.

d. Johnson cannot be held liable on the promissory note even if Easy Finance qualifies as a holder in due course under Article 3 of the UCC.

The correct answer is (d). *(Publisher)*

REQUIRED: The correct statement concerning a consumer who buys with a promissory note when the goods are defective.

DISCUSSION: The Federal Trade Commission has issued a regulation protecting consumers who purchase goods in exchange for an installment obligation. Under the regulation, the note is to contain a notice stating that the holder is subject to all claims and defenses of the debtor. This notice prevents a holder of the promissory note from obtaining the rights of a holder in due course. The consumer can thereby assert his/her contractual defenses against such a holder and avoid having to sue the seller separately.

Answer (a) is incorrect because Easy Finance is subject to Johnson's contractual defenses regarding the defective television. Without the FTC regulation, Easy Finance could be a holder in due course who would take free of contractual defenses. Answer (b) is incorrect because Johnson can assert his defense against Easy Finance and avoid having to seek reimbursement from Ace. Answer (c) is incorrect because the FTC regulation does not apply to a check, which can be transferred to a holder in due course.

9. Rubin purchased a set of encyclopedias from a salesperson who called upon her at home. Rubin was a schoolteacher who needed the encyclopedias, which were of good quality and reasonably priced. However, the next day Rubin discovered that she could obtain a competitor's encyclopedia at a lower price. Rubin wishes to rescind the purchase of the encyclopedias from the home salesperson.

a. The Federal Trade Commission allows a purchaser 3 days to cancel a contract or sale entered into with a salesperson who called at home.

b. Although a contract to purchase the encyclopedias could have been rescinded, the completed sale cannot be rescinded.

c. Rubin's purchase cannot be rescinded since the sale was reasonable and Rubin's only reason for rescinding is to obtain a lower price.

d. Rubin cannot rescind the sale because home sales are treated the same as any other sales.

The correct answer is (a). *(Publisher)*

REQUIRED: The correct statement concerning a consumer's ability to rescind a home solicitation sale.

DISCUSSION: The Federal Trade Commission (FTC) has promulgated a regulation allowing a buyer who is a party to a house solicitation sale 3 days to cancel a contract or sale if it was for goods or services costing $25 or more. These 3 days, called a "cooling-off" period, allow in-home buyers to reconsider an agreement which they may have been pressured into entering. Many states have also adopted similar laws.

Answer (b) is incorrect because the right under the FTC regulation to cancel a sale applies whether it is a contract that has been entered into or a completed sale. Answer (c) is incorrect because the 3-day "cooling-off" period is available regardless of the reason for canceling the sale. Answer (d) is incorrect because home sales are specially treated due to the pressure put on by door-to-door salespeople.

10. Gardener ordered an exotic plant by mail from an advertisement in a magazine. Seller received Gardener's check and order, but the plant was out of season. The plant would not be available for shipment for 3 months, but the seller deposited Gardener's check in its bank anyway.

a. Seller can send Gardener a letter explaining that the plant will not be available for delivery for 3 months.

b. Seller must promptly refund Gardener's check.

c. Seller can wait until it has the plants for shipment since Gardener did not pay with a charge card.

d. Gardener's only recourse is to file a suit if Seller refuses to refund the payment.

The correct answer is (b). *(Publisher)*

REQUIRED: The correct statement concerning the requirement imposed on a mail-order seller who cannot ship an order.

DISCUSSION: When a purchaser orders merchandise by mail, the seller must either ship within a reasonable time (not to exceed 30 days) or promptly refund the purchase price. This rule applies if payment was by check or a credit card.

Answer (a) is incorrect because Seller is required to refund the payment if it cannot ship within 30 days. Answer (c) is incorrect because the 30-day shipment rule applies to both checks and credit card purchases. Answer (d) is incorrect because Gardener can file a complaint with the Federal Trade Commission for an unfair trade practice, and also can request the state attorney general where Seller does business to act on the problem.

11. Just before Christmas, Willy received an unordered silk scarf in the mail from a manufacturer. Willy chased the mailman to return the package but could not catch him. Several days later, the scarf was followed by a bill and letter which explained that it was sent for Willy's convenience to use as a Christmas gift. Which of the following statements is correct concerning Willy's liability for payment?

a. Willy has an obligation to pay for the goods or return them.

b. Willy is only obligated for the scarf if he uses it.

c. Willy has 10 days to decide whether to keep the scarf and pay for it, or return it at the manufacturer's expense.

d. Willy may keep and use the scarf without an obligation to pay for it.

The correct answer is (d). *(Publisher)*

REQUIRED: The liability of a person for unordered merchandise received in the mail.

DISCUSSION: Under both federal law and many state laws, unsolicited goods sent by mail may be treated as a gift by the recipient, who may retain, use, or dispose of them as (s)he sees fit. Willy may therefore keep and use the scarf without paying for it.

Answer (a) is incorrect because federal law relieves a mail recipient of unordered merchandise from liability. Answer (b) is incorrect because it is a statement of common law under which use of an unordered good constituted acceptance. Federal and many state laws have exempted mailed merchandise from this rule. Answer (c) is incorrect because Willy may return the scarf at the manufacturer's expense, but is not required to, nor is there a 10-day limit.

12. The Real Estate Settlement Procedures Act (RESPA) is a federal statute enacted to protect buyers of residential property from certain abuses. Which of the following is a correct statement concerning the requirements of the Act?

a. The lender must disclose all costs that the buyer will incur at the closing in addition to the down payment.

b. The Act applies to all sales of residential property to consumers.

c. Violation of the Act can only result in the sale being rescinded.

d. The Act only applies to a real estate closing.

The correct answer is (a). *(Publisher)*

REQUIRED: The correct statement concerning the Real Estate Settlement Procedures Act (RESPA).

DISCUSSION: Under RESPA, a lender must inform the purchaser of a residential home of all costs that will be incurred at closing. These costs include attorney's fees, appraisal fees, credit reports, taxes, and any other items for which a buyer will be responsible.

Answer (b) is incorrect because RESPA only applies to federally related mortgage lenders and would not apply to a sale by an owner who takes back the mortgage him/herself. Answer (c) is incorrect because a violation of the Act can result in the greater of actual damages or $500. Answer (d) is incorrect because in addition to a real estate closing, the Act covers secured loans on a residential home even if the loan was not incurred for the purchase of the home.

30.3 Credit Protection

13. The Consumer Credit Protection Act was enacted due to unfair and predatory practices by creditors in their extension of credit to consumers. Which of the following was not enacted as a part of or as an amendment to the Consumer Credit Protection Act?

a. Truth in lending.

b. Fair credit reporting.

c. Uniform Consumer Credit Code.

d. Credit card liability limitations.

The correct answer is (c). *(Publisher)*

REQUIRED: The statement not enacted as part of the Consumer Credit Protection Act.

DISCUSSION: The Uniform Consumer Credit Code is a model act similar to the Uniform Commercial Code, Model Business Corporation Act, and Uniform Partnership Act. It contains many provisions similar to the Consumer Protection Act; however, it has only been enacted by a few states and is not expected to be a significant uniform statute.

Answers (a), (b), and (d) are incorrect because each is a part of the Consumer Credit Protection Act. They are discussed in further detail in the following questions.

14. Mabel has a long history of using credit. She repaid most debts, but other times she defaulted on loans. With regard to credit information about Mabel which may have been collected by credit reporting agencies, which of the following statements is correct?

a. The credit files on Mabel kept by credit reporting agencies may contain only information about the existence of prior debts and repayment.

b. Mabel is entitled to notification and the right to request information before an investigative report is prepared on her.

c. Businesses, employers, insurers, and government licensing agencies are entitled to receive a credit report on Mabel only with her written approval.

d. Mabel is entitled to see her report file and adjust it.

The correct answer is (b). *(Publisher)*

REQUIRED: The correct statement concerning credit reporting.

DISCUSSION: Under the Fair Credit Reporting Act, an investigative report (concerning character, reputation, etc.) is not to be prepared on a consumer until (s)he is notified and given the right to request information about the investigation. This approval is commonly required by institutions when an individual makes an application for which the report is needed, e.g, employment, insurance, etc.

Answer (a) is incorrect because the information kept in the file will include employment history, judgments, and arrest records. Answer (c) is incorrect because businesses, employers, insurers, and government licensing agencies are entitled to receive consumer credit reports based on the extension of credit to that person. No approval is required. Answer (d) is incorrect because, although Mabel is entitled to see her report file, she has no right to make an adjustment to the file. She is entitled to request that items be changed, but if her request is refused, she may only file an additional memorandum that must be kept in the file.

15. The Equal Credit Opportunity Act was enacted to prevent discrimination in credit extension. Which of the following is not prohibited by the Act?

a. Discrimination based on receipt of welfare.

b. Denial of a married woman from opening a credit account separate from her husband's.

c. Asking if the credit applicant is married.

d. Denial of credit based on lack of assets.

The correct answer is (d). *(Publisher)*

REQUIRED: The item not prohibited by the Equal Credit Opportunity Act.

DISCUSSION: The Act prohibits discrimination based on race, sex, marital status, etc. However, it does not prevent a denial of credit based on a lack of assets. Lack of assets and lack of income are allowable and logical reasons for denying credit.

Answer (a) is incorrect because a lender may not discriminate based on receipt of welfare, since the source of a person's income is generally not to be taken into account. Answer (b) is incorrect because a married woman may not be denied the opening of a credit account separate from her husband's. Answer (c) is incorrect because asking if a credit applicant is married is also prohibited. Marital status is not to be taken into account.

16. Gertrude was recently divorced and received custody of her three children. She was receiving both alimony and child support in substantial amounts, but her former husband had never held a job for a long period of time. Which of the following statements is correct concerning Gertrude's application for credit with Dacy Department Store?

a. Gertrude must disclose her alimony and child support.

b. Dacy may consider the likelihood of Gertrude receiving these payments based on her former husband's work record.

c. Dacy need not take into account former credit extended to Gertrude and her husband in his name only.

d. Dacy may take into account the alimony and child support, but may not consider any public assistance which Gertrude may be receiving.

The correct answer is (b). *(Publisher)*

REQUIRED: The correct statement concerning an application for credit.

DISCUSSION: A credit extender may consider the likelihood of income such as alimony and child support being received. The prior job history of Gertrude's former husband is relevant for Dacy to use as a factor in determining whether Gertrude will be able to pay the charges.

Answer (a) is incorrect because although Dacy must take into account Gertrude's alimony and child support if disclosed, Dacy is also required to tell Gertrude that she does not need to disclose these sources of income unless she relies on them for the credit. Answer (c) is incorrect because a woman is entitled to establish a credit history, which requires credit to be reported in the name of both spouses while married. Answer (d) is incorrect because Dacy must take into account all sources of income which Gertrude receives and discloses, including public assistance.

17. Due to the widespread use of credit cards, federal regulation was needed to control extension and use of this credit. Which of the following statements is not a requirement of those who issue or accept credit cards?

a. A charge cannot be added to the purchase price for the use of a credit card rather than payment with cash or check.

b. Credit cards may not be distributed to persons who have not applied for them.

c. A credit card issuer must place a notice on the consumer contract that any holder is subject to the consumer's defenses against the seller.

d. A credit card holder cannot be liable for more than $50 if the card is stolen or lost.

The correct answer is (a). *(Publisher)*

REQUIRED: The statement not a requirement for the issuance or acceptance of credit cards.

DISCUSSION: There is no longer a prohibition against adding a charge to the purchase price for the use of a credit card. Prior federal law did prohibit this practice but the law no longer exists.

Answer (b) is incorrect because the issuance of credit cards is prohibited except in response to those who apply for them. Answer (c) is incorrect because the credit card issuer must include the anti-holder in due course statement discussed in Question 8 on Page 706. Answer (d) is incorrect because a credit card holder is not liable for more than $50 when the card is stolen or lost.

18. Pico purchased a stereo for $400 with his credit card. At home, Pico discovered the stereo did not work properly. Pico

a. Can refuse to pay the credit card bill if he attempted in good faith to return the stereo or give the store an opportunity to correct the problem.

b. Can refuse to pay the credit card bill if the purchase was made more than 100 miles from home.

c. Cannot refuse to pay the credit card bill because it was for a purchase of more than $50.

d. Must pay the credit card bill, but has a right to damages and attorney's fees against the store under the Uniform Consumer Credit Code.

The correct answer is (a). *(Publisher)*

REQUIRED: The rights of a credit card user when merchandise proves defective.

DISCUSSION: A person who has a problem with property or services purchased with a credit card has the right not to pay the amount due. However, the purchaser must first attempt in good faith to return the goods or give the merchant a chance to correct the problem.

Answer (b) is incorrect because this right to refuse to pay applies if the goods are purchased in Pico's home state or within 100 miles from home. Answer (c) is incorrect because the right to refuse to pay applies if purchase price of goods was for more than $50 (which it was). Answer (d) is incorrect because Pico does have the right to refuse to pay for the goods, and damages and attorney's fees are not available for this problem under the Uniform Consumer Credit Code.

19. The Fair Credit Billing Act places the burden on the creditor to correct billing errors. Under this Act,

a. The creditor has 90 days after sending out a bill to make corrections to it.

b. The creditor must inform the customer of his/her rights with each billing statement.

c. The customer has 90 days in which to make an objection about a bill.

d. The creditor is subject to forfeiting the disputed charge up to $100 for failure to comply with the Act.

The correct answer is (b). *(Publisher)*

REQUIRED: The correct statement concerning the Fair Credit Billing Act.

DISCUSSION: The Fair Credit Billing Act gives the consumer a method of correcting errors on bills and bringing disputed charges to the attention of the creditor. The creditor is required to inform the customer of his/her rights with each billing statement. This need only be a short form disclosure; however, a long form disclosure is required twice a year.

Answer (a) is incorrect because a creditor is not obligated to investigate the records until the customer makes an inquiry about a bill. The correction must be made within 90 days after the consumer's inquiry. Answer (c) is incorrect because a customer has 60 days after receiving a bill to make an inquiry or objection. Answer (d) is incorrect because a creditor will forfeit the charge in dispute only up to $50 if (s)he fails to comply with the Act.

20. Tom Debtor incurred substantial debts. Much of this debt was turned over to a collection agency. Employees of this agency called Debtor repeatedly at home during the middle of the night. They also made collect telephone calls to Debtor from distant places and confronted in the presence of his neighbors and co-workers.

a. Debtor can prevent this harassment with a written note to the collection agency.

b. Debtor can end this harassment only by filing a law suit against the collection agency.

c. Debtor can prevent the disparaging remarks in front of neighbors and co-workers, but telephone calls are not subject to restrictions.

d. In order to have any recourse against the collection agency, Debtor must be able to prove damages.

The correct answer is (a). *(Publisher)*

REQUIRED: The correct statement concerning a debtor who is harassed by a collection agency.

DISCUSSION: A debtor need only notify the collection agency in writing of his/her wish that the agency refrain from contacting him/her or informing the neighbors and co-workers of the debts. The collection agency is then required to stop all further contact, and its sole remedy is to sue Debtor.

Answer (b) is incorrect because Debtor does not have to file a lawsuit since he can write a letter. Answer (c) is incorrect because telephone calls by debt collectors are prohibited before 8 a.m. and after 9 p.m., and collect calls are prohibited. Answer (d) is incorrect because a debt collector can be liable for up to $1,000 without proof of damages for violation of the Act.

21. Which of the following statements is correct concerning usury laws?

a. Usury laws generally apply to businesses or large transactions but not to ordinary consumer transactions.

b. Most usury laws have been held to be a violation of an individual's right to contract.

c. Usury laws are intended to prevent the charging of an excessive interest rate.

d. Usury laws can be avoided by using a lease rather than a bill of sale.

The correct answer is (c). *(Publisher)*

REQUIRED: The correct statement concerning usury laws.

DISCUSSION: Usury laws prevent the charging of interest rates in excess of a legal amount established by state statute. They are intended to prevent the charging of an excessive interest rate to small businesses and consumers.

Answer (a) is incorrect because usury laws generally apply to ordinary consumer transactions. In some states business transactions are exempt, and in most states large transactions are exempt. Answer (b) is incorrect because usury laws have been upheld for a long time and are not considered a violation of an individual's right to contract. Answer (d) is incorrect because usury laws cannot be avoided by use of a lease. The substance of the transaction will control rather than the form.

30.4 Deceptive Trade Practices

22. The Federal Trade Commission (FTC) was given its authority under the Federal Trade Commission Act. A major power of the FTC is to regulate unfair or deceptive acts or practices in trade. Which of the following is not a power held by the FTC?

a. The issuance of a consent order or a cease and desist order.

b. The imposition of criminal sentences.

c. Rule-making in the area of advertising.

d. The investigation of misleading advertising and deceptive practices.

The correct answer is (b). *(Publisher)*

REQUIRED: The statement which is not a power held by the FTC.

DISCUSSION: Although the FTC has the power to enforce many of the antitrust laws, it is engaged mostly in preventing deceptive trade practices. But the FTC is a regulatory agency. As such it has no power to impose criminal sentences. These are pursued by the United States Justice Department and handed down by a court of law.

Answer (a) is incorrect because the FTC does have the power to issue a consent order or a cease and desist order. These are commonly used remedies of the FTC. Answer (c) is incorrect because the FTC does have broad rule-making power in the area of advertising. One of its functions is to prevent unfair or deceptive acts or practices against consumers. Answer (d) is incorrect because the FTC is empowered to and does investigate misleading advertising and deceptive practices.

23. A television commercial depicts a set of false teeth dunked in a glass of bubbly water and then pulled out shining clean and white. In reality, the set of false teeth are not the same stained set which was put into the bubbly water.

a. This is not deceptive advertising if there is simply not enough time during the commercial for the entire cleaning process to occur.

b. This is not deceptive advertising so long as the product really works.

c. This is deceptive advertising unless first cleared with the FTC.

d. This is deceptive advertising since the public is being misled as to the seller's objective proof of a product claim.

The correct answer is (d). *(Publisher)*

REQUIRED: The correct statement concerning the deceptiveness of the television commercial.

DISCUSSION: The Supreme Court has ruled that when an experiment or demonstration is depicted, the advertiser must inform the viewing public if it is not an actual test or demonstration or if there is an undisclosed use of props. In this case, the use of different false teeth is deceptively misleading unless the public is informed.

Answer (a) is incorrect because lack of time is not an excuse for deceptive advertising. According to the Supreme Court, such an argument only indicates that television may not be a suitable medium for that type of commercial. Answer (b) is incorrect because the fact that the product really works does not prevent the advertising from being deceptive or misleading. Answer (c) is incorrect because there is no exception for deceptive advertising cleared with the FTC.

24. The Federal Trade Commission has promulgated a rule called "Guides on Bait Advertising." Which of the following statements is correct concerning this rule?

a. Its purpose is to prevent abuses in the sporting goods industry.

b. It is primarily directed at used car dealers.

c. Its purpose is to prohibit advertisements of an item at a very low price to lure customers into the store.

d. The FTC can only take action if the seller refuses to show the item which was advertised.

The correct answer is (c). *(Publisher)*

REQUIRED: The correct statement concerning bait advertising.

DISCUSSION: Bait (or bait and switch) advertising is advertising a very low price for an item to lure customers into the store. The sales people then try to entice or switch the customer to other and more expensive goods. This practice is prohibited by the FTC.

Answers (a) and (b) are incorrect because the rule against bait advertising is not primarily directed at the sporting goods industry or used car dealers, although it would apply to these also. Answer (d) is incorrect because the FTC can also take action if the seller discourages employees from selling such an item, fails to have adequate stock on hand, or does not deliver the goods within a reasonable period of time.

25. Corrective advertising is sometimes an appropriate remedy after a seller has made false or deceptive advertising statements. Which statement is correct concerning such corrective advertising?

a. The FTC can order such corrective advertising.

b. The FTC must apply to a court for an order for corrective advertising.

c. Corrective advertising must be agreed to by a seller to avoid a lawsuit for damages on behalf of the consumers.

d. The seller must indicate that it is corrective advertising.

The correct answer is (a). *(Publisher)*

REQUIRED: The correct statement concerning corrective advertising.

DISCUSSION: The FTC is empowered to order corrective advertising if companies have previously created false impressions or have been guilty of wrongdoing in their advertising. A recent example of this occurred when the Listerine commercials were required to disclose that Listerine would not help prevent colds or sore throats.

Answer (b) is incorrect because the FTC has the power to issue such an order; this was decided in the Listerine case. Answer (c) is incorrect because corrective advertising may be required by an FTC order and not just as an agreement by the seller. Answer (d) is incorrect because the seller need not always indicate that it is corrective advertising. The courts did not require such a confession in the Listerine case, but also did not specify that it would never be required.

26. ABC Co. manufactures popular skin care products. It has used the term "baby oil" with its products for so long that much of the public associates the term "baby oil" with ABC Co. products. SLZ Co. comes out with a new skin care product and uses the term "baby oil" on it. Which of the following is correct?

a. SLZ can only be stopped if "baby oil" is a trademark of ABC.

b. ABC has a cause of action against SLZ but consumers do not.

c. SLZ must be sued under common law principles of business torts, e.g. palming off.

d. SLZ can be held liable even without intent to deceive and without a showing of damages.

The correct answer is (d). *(Publisher)*

REQUIRED: The rights against a company which uses a deceptive description on its products that is similar to another well-known company's.

DISCUSSION: Under the Lanham Act, any person who uses a false designation or false description in connection with goods or services, including words or symbols falsely describing or representing the original of the product, shall be liable to any person who believes (s)he is likely to be damaged by the false description or representation. This Act can be used to hold a company such as SLZ liable without any intent to deceive and without a showing of actual damages. However, it is primarily designed to provide competitors with a statutory remedy. Consumers might use it if they fit within its terms, but they also have such recourses as the Federal Trade Commission, local attorney general, and the common law of torts.

Answer (a) is incorrect because an injunction can be had against SLZ if a court decides that it has falsely described or represented its product leading buyers to think it is another's. This can be done even without violation of statutory trademark or tradename laws. Answer (b) is incorrect because consumers also have a cause of action against SLZ if they are being misled into believing that the product is actually that of ABC Co. This is deceptive advertising. Answer (c) is incorrect because the Lanham Act is a statutory remedy for this type of problem in addition to the common law principles of business torts.

27. Basil read an advertisement in the newspaper for a sale of "Major" stereos (a very well-known and reputable brand) by Hoodwink Discounters, a large chain distributor of electronics. Basil bought a stereo, but when he got home, he discovered it was a "Magor" brand which looked just like the "Major" brand. Basil returned to Hoodwink but was told that they had no more "Majors" and "Magor" was essentially the same. It turned out "Magor" was manufactured by Hoodwink. Basil could not obtain a refund. Which of the following is not a remedy available to Basil?

a. File a civil lawsuit for damages on the basis of deceptive advertising and possibly fraud.

b. File a civil lawsuit seeking an injunction against Hoodwink on behalf of Basil and all others similarly situated.

c. File a lawsuit seeking criminal penalties against Hoodwink.

d. File a complaint with state authorities and request them to prosecute Hoodwink.

The correct answer is (c). *(Publisher)*

REQUIRED: The remedy not available to a consumer who has been duped by deceptive advertising.

DISCUSSION: An individual has no authority to seek criminal penalties him/herself. Criminal prosecution can only be undertaken by the government (federal, state, or local).

Answers (a), (b), and (d) are incorrect because a consumer who has been duped by deceptive advertising can sue for his/her damages and can seek an injunction against the deceptive advertiser to prohibit the continuation of such conduct. In order to obtain an injunction, the individual must belong to a class harmed by the deceptive advertising. An individual can also seek assistance from governmental authorities. A local district or state attorney, the attorney general of the state, or the Federal Trade Commission are examples of governmental authorities who can act on complaints from consumers and assist in recovering damages and criminally prosecuting the offender.

28. Which of the following types of disclosures are not regulated under the labeling and packaging laws?

a. Standards for partial filling of packages.

b. Distinguishing between label sizes such as regular, giant, medium, large, etc.

c. Ingredients in nonfood products.

d. The number of calories in food products.

The correct answer is (d). *(Publisher)*

REQUIRED: The types of disclosure not regulated under the labeling and packaging laws.

DISCUSSION: Many packaging and labeling laws cover many required disclosures on labels, but at present none of them requires the number of calories in food products to be disclosed.

Answers (a), (b), and (c) are incorrect because each is a disclosure which is regulated under the labeling and packaging laws.

30.5 Products and Safety

Note: See warranties and product liability modules in Chapter 12, "Sales of Goods," for additional questions on these topics.

29. The Surgeon General of the United States has determined that cigarette smoking is dangerous to your health. Which of the following has not been done on behalf of the public in connection with this danger?

a. Cigarette smoking has been banned in various public places.

b. Tobacco growers are no longer subsidized by the U.S. government.

c. Advertising has been banned from the electronic communication medium.

d. Laws have been passed restricting the age of minors who can buy cigarettes.

The correct answer is (b). *(Publisher)*

REQUIRED: The regulatory action which has not been taken to protect the public from the dangers of smoking.

DISCUSSION: Tobacco growers are and have been subsidized by the U.S. government for many years despite considerable public outcry.

Answer (a) is incorrect because cigarette smoking has been banned in numerous public places, including airplanes, elevators, restaurants, and frequently in the workplace. Answer (c) is incorrect because cigarette advertising has been banned from electronic communication media, e.g., television and radio. Answer (d) is incorrect because states typically restrict the purchase of cigarettes by minors.

30. The Consumer Product Safety Commission was established by Congress to gather and disseminate information concerning products sold in the market place. Which of the following is the Commission not authorized to do?

a. Require labels presenting the results of product testing.

b. Compel manufacturers to refund purchase prices or replace dangerous products.

c. Require manufacturers to submit products to it for approval prior to sale.

d. Set product safety standards and require product instruction sheets.

The correct answer is (c). *(Publisher)*

REQUIRED: The action which the Consumer Product Safety Commission is not authorized to do.

DISCUSSION: The Consumer Product Safety Commission is a five-member commission with a major function of gathering and disseminating information relating to product injuries. However, the Commission does not have the authority or power to require manufacturers to submit products to it for approval prior to sale.

Answer (a) is incorrect because manufacturers are required to conduct testing programs concerning safety standards, and the Commission can require labels presenting the results of such testing. Answer (b) is incorrect because the Commission does have the authority to compel manufacturers to refund purchase prices or to replace dangerous products in accordance with their safety rules. Answer (d) is incorrect because the Commission does set product safety standards and requires inclusion of product instruction sheets with numerous goods.

31. The National Traffic and Motor Vehicle Safety Act was enacted to reduce accidents, and also the deaths and injuries occurring in such accidents. In addition to design and construction, the Secretary of Transportation is directed to set safety standards for automobiles and related equipment. What has hindered the Secretary of Transportation from establishing further standards than now exist?

a. The costs to and dissatisfaction of the public.

b. The refusal of the automobile industry to cooperate.

c. The National Motor Vehicle Safety Advisory Council.

d. The lack of authority given to the Secretary of Transportation in the Act.

The correct answer is (a). *(Publisher)*

REQUIRED: The item hindering the Secretary of Transportation from establishing more thorough vehicle safety standards.

DISCUSSION: In setting automotive safety standards, there is a necessary balancing between the cost involved and the desired degree of safety. These costs and public dissatisfaction have hindered the Secretary of Transportation from increasing the safety standards on automobiles.

Answer (b) is incorrect because the automobile industry has generally cooperated with the Secretary of Transportation although it has lobbied hard in Congress and the media against these required standards. Answer (c) is incorrect because the National Motor Vehicle Safety Advisory Council is established by and works with the Secretary of Transportation. Answer (d) is incorrect because the Secretary of Transportation has broad authority under the Act to establish safety standards.

32. Goop Foods, a maker of baby foods, was warned by the FDA through written reprimands after an inspection of unsanitary conditions in its warehouses. The food products in these warehouses were susceptible to numerous rodents and insects. The president of Goop was specifically provided with these letters. One year later the FDA made another inspection of Goop's warehouses and discovered the problems had not been resolved at all. The FDA filed charges against Goop and the president under the Federal Food, Drug, and Cosmetic Act. Who can be held criminally liable under the Act?

a. Only Goop because the president would not have been personally involved in the violations.

b. Only the president because a corporation cannot be criminally liable.

c. Both Goop and the president.

d. Neither Goop nor the president because the FDA does not have the power to charge violators with criminal conduct.

The correct answer is (c). *(Publisher)*

REQUIRED: The parties that can be held liable by the FDA for food product violations.

DISCUSSION: The FDA has the authority to make investigations and issue sanctions for violations of the FDA's sanitary standards. A corporation which violates these standards can be held criminally liable by means of fines. In addition, an officer in a managerial position, such as a president, can also be held criminally liable if (s)he had notice of the violations and was in a position to correct them. Proof of intent to commit the wrongful acts is not required.

Answer (a) is incorrect because the president was provided with notice of the violations and would have the ability to correct them. Answer (b) is incorrect because a corporation can be held criminally liable, although it would be fined rather than imprisoned. Answer (d) is incorrect because the FDA does have the power to charge violators with criminal conduct.

CHAPTER THIRTY-ONE
ENVIRONMENTAL LAW AND REGULATIONS

31.1 Environmental Law: Introduction

1. The most widely used regulatory approach to pollution control in the United States is

a. Pollution charges and fees.

b. Private markets in which pollution rights can be bought and sold.

c. Environmental standards and penalties for noncompliance.

d. Total deregulation of pollution control resulting in state regulation with no federal involvement.

The correct answer is (c). *(CMA 1286 1-27)*

REQUIRED: The most widely used regulatory approach in the United States.

DISCUSSION: The right of landowners to use their property as they wished was a cherished right in the United States for many years. A few decades ago people saw that streams, rivers, and lakes were being polluted. Congress passed the National Environmental Policy Act and created the Environmental Protection Agency to control the pollution in the United States of air, water, and land. Other legislation, such as the Clean Air Act, Water Pollution Control Act, Noise Control Act, and the Solid Waste Disposal Act, has been passed by Congress. Many states have enacted environmental laws that in some instances are more stringent than the federal standards. Violation of federal and state regulations are subject to economic penalties stated in the written legislation.

Answer (a) is incorrect because charges and fees are imposed when environmental regulations are violated. Answer (b) is incorrect because the government regulates how much pollution can be in the environment. Thus, pollution rights cannot be privately purchased. Answer (d) is incorrect because the environment is subject to federal, state, and municipal regulations.

2. A federal regulation sets a quantitative limitation on the amount of a certain pollutant that may be emitted from industrial smoke stacks. Your state also has a standard, but the permissible amount is lower. In determining whether the state's standard is applicable, a court's decision will depend upon

a. The way in which the balance of interests (state versus federal) is best served.

b. Whether the state standard tends to interfere with the purposes of the federal regulations.

c. The way in which the balance of interests (health versus economics) is best served.

d. Whether the state standard tends to be more restrictive or more permissive than the federal standard.

The correct answer is (b). *(S. Sibary)*

REQUIRED: The basis for determining whether state regulation is applicable.

DISCUSSION: Federal regulatory schemes, when legitimate, will preempt state regulations that tend to interfere with the federal purposes. This is true whether the federal regulation is meant to be exclusive (in which case no state regulation will be allowed), or allows parallel state regulation. To decide the case, a court will need to determine whether the effect of the state law is consistent or interferes with the federal goals.

Answers (a) and (c) are incorrect because the courts do not have the authority to favor state interests over federal interests once it has been determined that federal jurisdiction is legitimate. The court must apply the standard for preemption. Answer (d) is incorrect because whether the state standard is more restrictive or more permissive does not answer whether the state standard is consistent with the federal standard.

31.2 National Environmental Policy Act (NEPA)

3. Which of the following statements about the National Environmental Policy Act (NEPA) is most likely to be false?

a. NEPA requires federal agencies to consider certain potential environmental consequences in their decision-making process.

b. NEPA allows the federal government to bring suit against any private person who violates NEPA's provisions.

c. Under NEPA, federal agencies do not have to give environmental considerations priority over other concerns in their decision-making processes.

d. NEPA augments the power of every existing agency with respect to considering the environmental consequences of their proposed actions.

The correct answer is (b). *(Publisher)*

REQUIRED: The false statement about NEPA.

DISCUSSION: The provisions of NEPA focus on federal governmental actions. Federal agencies are specifically directed to incorporate an analysis of environment consequences in their decision-making processes. Actions of private persons are affected by NEPA only when federal involvement (approval, funding, etc.) is necessary before such persons may act (e.g., federal approval before drilling for oil in ocean waters within U.S. jurisdiction). Otherwise, NEPA does not directly concern activities of private persons.

Answers (a), (c), and (d) are incorrect because under NEPA, federal agencies must give environmental considerations a weight equal to but not greater than that afforded nonenvironmental concerns. NEPA augments the existing powers of federal agencies to deal with these environmental matters.

4. The environmental impact statement (EIS) lies at the heart of NEPA. Preparation of an EIS, however, is not automatic. Which of the following states a condition that must be present before a federal agency is required to prepare an EIS?

a. There must be a recommendation or report on a proposal for legislation or certain other "major" federal action.

b. If a "major" federal action is involved, all that is needed is a slight chance that a small amount of irreparable environmental damage may result.

c. Only an embryonic discussion of a legislative proposal is necessary to trigger the preparation of an EIS.

d. Congress must specifically direct a federal agency to begin preparing an EIS.

The correct answer is (a). *(Publisher)*

REQUIRED: The condition necessary for the preparation of an EIS.

DISCUSSION: NEPA directs federal agencies to prepare an EIS for inclusion in every recommendation or report on proposals for legislation and other major federal actions significantly affecting the quality of the human environment.

Answer (b) is incorrect because more than a small amount of environmental damage is needed. The term "significantly affecting" implies more harm (or potential harm) is necessary. Answer (c) is incorrect because the legislation must at least have been prepared, not be in its earliest stage. Answer (d) is incorrect because if a federal agency already is empowered to act in a manner that constitutes "major" federal action, the agency is not allowed to wait until it receives a congressional directive to prepare an EIS.

5. An EIS need not contain

a. The environmental impact of the proposed action.

b. Alternatives to the proposed action.

c. Any adverse environmental effects that cannot be avoided.

d. An independent opinion on the proposed action prepared by the Council on Environmental Quality.

The correct answer is (d). *(Publisher)*

REQUIRED: The item that an EIS need not contain.

DISCUSSION: An EIS must contain, in detail, the environmental impact of the proposed action, any adverse environmental effects that cannot be avoided should the proposal be implemented, alternatives to the proposed action, the effects on maintaining the long-term productivity of the environment affected by the proposal, and the irreparable commitment of resources as a result of the action. The Council on Environmental Quality was created by NEPA in the Executive Office of the President. It has an advisory function but has also promulgated regulations. It does not render opinions.

Answers (a), (b), and (c) are incorrect because an EIS contains each of these items.

6. Before actually preparing an EIS, a federal agency is required under NEPA to

a. Obtain local approval for its proposed actions through an official referendum presented to the people of the locality that will be affected by the agency's actions.

b. Consult with any federal agency that has special expertise with respect to any environmental impact involved.

c. Disregard any comments made by any federal agency with special expertise because, in effect, NEPA requires that each federal agency become its own expert in any environmental area.

d. Obtain approval for its proposed actions from the highest official in each affected locality.

The correct answer is (b). *(Publisher)*

REQUIRED: The requirement before a federal agency prepares an EIS.

DISCUSSION: Prior to preparing an EIS, the federal agency preparing the action must consult with any federal agency that has jurisdiction over the proposal or special expertise with respect to any environmental impact involved. This is consistent with another broad NEPA requirement of a systematic, interdisciplinary approach to decision-making.

Answers (a) and (d) are incorrect because NEPA does not require any formal local approval for an agency's proposed actions. However, the EIS, once prepared, must be open to public comment. Answer (c) is incorrect because agencies with special expertise must be consulted.

7. Under NEPA, if a federal agency determines that an EIS is not necessary, it must nonetheless

a. Telephone the governor of each state that will be affected by its actions and inform them of their decision not to prepare an EIS.

b. Prepare and circulate for public comment a statement of nonassessment of environmental consequences (NEC) within 60 days of its decision.

c. Prepare a finding of no significant impact (FONSI) setting forth the reasons why the proposed action does not require an EIS.

d. Send a letter via certified mail, to the Director of the Environmental Protection Agency stating the reasons why the proposed action does not require an EIS.

The correct answer is (c). *(Publisher)*

REQUIRED: The appropriate course of action when an agency determines that an EIS is unnecessary.

DISCUSSION: An agency must consider environmental issues at the earliest stage of planning. The "threshold decision" is whether to prepare an EIS. If the proposed action is on an agency list of actions that do or do not require an EIS, the appropriate step is taken automatically. Otherwise, an environmental assessment is prepared. If the decision is that an EIS is not needed, regulations promulgated by the Council on Environmental Quality that interpret NEPA require the federal agency to prepare a FONSI setting forth the reasons.

Answers (a), (b), and (d) are incorrect because no other communique is required by either NEPA or its regulations.

31.3 Clean Water Act (CWA)

8. Which of the following statements is true with respect to the Clean Water Act (CWA)?

a. Despite the CWA's prohibitions, it allows persons to discharge pollutants into waters subject to its jurisdiction as long as navigation thereon will not be permanently obstructed.

b. The CWA subjects all bodies of water located in the United States, whether flowing or not, to its protection.

c. The notion of protecting waters within the jurisdiction of the United States began with the CWA.

d. The CWA seeks to restore and maintain the physical and biological integrity of the waters of the United States.

The correct answer is (d). *(Publisher)*

REQUIRED: The true statement about the CWA.

DISCUSSION: The CWA (1972) substantially amended the Federal Water Pollution Control Act of 1948. It seeks to restore and maintain the physical and biological integrity of the waters of the United States. Its objectives are to render water suitable for recreation and propagation of fish and other wildlife and to eliminate discharges of pollutants.

Answer (a) is incorrect because the CWA broadly prohibits any discharges of pollutants into waters subject to the jurisdiction of the United States by any person, except in compliance with the Act. Under the CWA, impairment of navigation is irrelevant. Answer (b) is incorrect because to be subject to federal jurisdiction, and thus the CWA, the waters in which pollutants are discharged must be so-called "navigable waters," which are defined as waters of the United States (including the territorial waters). This broad definition does not encompass all bodies of water located within the bounds of the United States. Answer (c) is incorrect because the Rivers and Harbors Act of the late 1800s was the first major piece of federal legislation promulgated to protect U.S. waterways. Until the passage of the CWA, the Rivers and Harbors Act was also used to combat pollutive discharges, although its original purpose was to keep waterways clear from obstructions to navigation.

9. Which of the following situations is not a "discharge of a pollutant" as defined in the CWA?

a. A construction company's dumping of sand and gravel into the Mississippi River.

b. A utility company's dumping of pure water that is heated to 200°F into Lake Michigan.

c. A landowner's dumping of radioactive waste in a small flooded limestone quarry located on his/her private property and totally self-contained.

d. A state municipality's dumping of garbage into the Ohio River.

The correct answer is (c). *(Publisher)*

REQUIRED: The situation not within the definition of "discharge of a pollutant."

DISCUSSION: The definitions in the statute are quite broad. Thus, the CWA defines the term "discharge of a pollutant," in pertinent part, as any addition of any pollutant to navigable waters from any point source. A "point source" is any discernable, confined, and discrete conveyance. A "pollutant" is an addition to water that alters its chemical, physical, biological, or radiological integrity. But not all waters located in the United States are included in the Act's definition of the term "navigable waters." Having no contact with any other water system, the small flooded limestone quarry is not a body of water of the United States. The CWA has no jurisdiction over such a body of water.

Answers (a), (b), and (d) are incorrect because the Mississippi and Ohio rivers and Lake Michigan are clearly waters of the U.S. Answer (a) is incorrect because sand and gravel might alter the physical integrity of the body of water. Answer (b) is incorrect because thermal discharges may constitute pollution. Answer (d) is incorrect because garbage is an obvious pollutant.

10. Which of the following is most likely not a navigable water of the United States?

a. Boston Harbor.

b. The Mississippi River.

c. A major tributary of the Mississippi River capable of sustaining barge traffic through several states.

d. Sawyer's Ditch, a small creek feeding into a farm pond, both of which are located wholly within the same parcel of land in South Carolina and never achieve a depth of more than 1 ft.

The correct answer is (d). *(Publisher)*

REQUIRED: The alternative not likely to be considered a navigable water of the United States.

DISCUSSION: The concept of a sovereign's ownership of its navigable waterways can be traced to early common law in England. This concept, in much the same form, was carried forward and permeates the CWA's definition of "navigable waters," the jurisdictional basis of the Act.

In its most general sense, waters subject to the federal jurisdiction of the United States must be capable of providing navigation in the aid of interstate commerce and be located within 3 miles of the U.S. shoreline. It is unlikely that Sawyer's Ditch, as described, could support interstate commerce.

Answers (a), (b), and (c) are incorrect because they fall within this very general definition.

11. A person who violates the CWA may be subject to

a. Civil liability, but only for the actual harm caused by the violations.

b. Criminal liability, but only if the person knowingly violated the CWA.

c. Civil and criminal liability.

d. No liability because the CWA, like NEPA, pertains only to the actions of federal governmental agencies.

The correct answer is (c). *(Publisher)*

REQUIRED: The appropriate liability to which violators of the CWA may be subjected.

DISCUSSION: Persons who violate the CWA are subject to civil and criminal liability. Damages, civil penalties, cleanup costs, fines of as much as $25,000 a day, and prison terms of up to 1 year are possible sanctions.

Answer (a) is incorrect because a civil action may be brought for any appropriate relief, including a permanent or temporary injunction. Answer (b) is incorrect because criminal liability may also be imposed on violators who were negligent, a mental state not involving actual knowledge of a violation. Answer (d) is incorrect because the CWA applies to the actions of persons other than federal agencies.

12. Portions of the requirements under the CWA can be viewed as technology forcing, i.e., requirements that force industry to implement or design new or innovative techniques for reducing pollutant discharges. This concept is best reflected in the CWA's requirement that certain point sources use the best

a. Practicable control technology currently available (BPT).

b. Available technology economically achievable (BAT).

c. Conventional pollutant control technology (BCT).

d. Generic technology overall achievable (BGT).

The correct answer is (b). *(Publisher)*

REQUIRED: The most stringent pollution control technology required under the CWA.

DISCUSSION: As the name suggests, BAT is the most stringent of the technology requirements under the CWA. Unlike BPT and BCT, BAT does not require the EPA to take into account prevailing industry practices or cost-benefit analyses when establishing BAT requirements. Thus, BAT best reflects the concept of technology-forcing requirements.

Answers (a) and (c) are incorrect because each is technology based. Answer (d) is incorrect because the acronym BGT does not appear anywhere in the CWA.

31.4 Clean Air Act (CAA)

13. Under the Clean Air Act (CAA), a state must submit a state implementation plan (SIP) after the promulgation of a national ambient air quality standard (NAAQS). The Environmental Protection Agency must approve the SIP if all the statutorily prescribed SIP requirements are contained therein. Which of the following is not a general SIP requirement?

a. The SIP must contain a plan for attaining primary NAAQSs as expeditiously as practicable.

b. The SIP must contain a plan for attaining secondary NAAQSs within a reasonable time.

c. The SIP must include an enforcement program regarding emission limitations for modifying, constructing, or operating any stationary source.

d. The SIP must provide for a so-called pollution tax, which the CAA stipulates must be no less than $500 per stationary source.

The correct answer is (d). *(Publisher)*

REQUIRED: The alternative which is not a general SIP requirement.

DISCUSSION: Nowhere in the CAA is a SIP required to contain a "pollution tax." However, the CAA does provide for civil and criminal sanctions.

Answers (a), (b), and (c) are incorrect because they reflect major SIP requirements, but there are many more. The primary NAAQSs are public health oriented, whereas the secondary standards are directed toward protection of vegetation, climate, economic values, etc. Also, point sources are defined as stationary (e.g., power plants and factories) and moving (automobiles, etc.), and standards have been promulgated for each category.

14. A so-called Part D SIP is required to be submitted by states that have not attained the NAAQS for any listed pollutant in one or more air quality control regions located within their borders. Which of the following is a provision that a Part D SIP must contain?

a. A system for issuing permits to allow new or modified major stationary sources to emit air pollutants.

b. A mechanism for closing highways located in residential areas where the actual levels of pollution exceed primary and secondary NAAQS.

c. Provision for the implementation of all reasonably available control measures (RACM) as expeditiously as possible.

d. In the interim before the full implementation of RACM, the Part D SIP must require the use of the best available control technology (BACT).

The correct answer is (a). *(Publisher)*

REQUIRED: The correct Part D SIP requirement.

DISCUSSION: The CAA prescribes many requirements for Part D SIP. One is the permit requirement for new or modified major stationary sources.

Answer (b) is incorrect because the CAA does not specifically require that heavily traveled highways be closed. Answer (c) is incorrect because a Part D SIP must also provide for the implementation of all reasonably available control measures (RACM) as expeditiously as practicable, not as possible. Answer (d) is incorrect because in the interim, the CAA requires reasonably available control technology to be used.

15. In a state subject to the Part D SIP requirements under the CAA, a person who desires to build a new major stationary source within such state must first obtain a permit. Which of the following will not be a condition of obtaining such a permit?

a. The proposed new source must comply with the lowest achievable emission rate.

b. The owner or operator of the proposed new source must demonstrate that all other major stationary sources owned or operated by such person in the state are actually in compliance (or on schedule for compliance) with all emissions limitations that are applicable to such existing sources by the CAA.

c. The new source will not impede the attainment of reasonable further progress toward NAAQS compliance otherwise required of a state under a Part D SIP.

d. The new source cannot be constructed in a "dirty air area."

The correct answer is (d). *(Publisher)*

REQUIRED: The item not a condition for obtaining a permit to construct a new major stationary source in a state subject to Part D of the CAA.

DISCUSSION: The Part D SIP requirements established by the 1977 Amendments to the CAA departed from the path taken by Congress in the original CAA's SIP requirements. Originally, states were given significant leeway in deciding how to achieve the NAAQSs. Part D of the CAA now imposes specific restrictions on persons who desire to construct new, or modify old, major stationary sources. Under Part D, states are required to impose certain uniform restrictions. One restriction is on construction in "dirty air areas." New sources are permitted if they have the lowest achievable emission rates and if other sources under the operator's control are in compliance with applicable standards.

Answers (a), (b), and (c) are incorrect because each is an important restriction on a person who wishes to build or modify a major stationary source in a state subject to the Part D SIP provisions.

16. Under the CAA, a "major stationary source" is

a. A facility whose emissions will cause an air quality control region of a state to exceed the primary NAAQS.

b. One that directly emits 100 tons per year or more of sulphur dioxide.

c. Any stationary facility or source of air pollutants that emits 20 tons per year or more of any air pollutant.

d. Any source of air pollutants that indirectly emits 20 tons per year or more of an air pollutant for which an NAAQS has been promulgated.

The correct answer is (b). *(Publisher)*

REQUIRED: The definition of a "major stationary source" under the CAA.

DISCUSSION: A major stationary source is any stationary facility or source of air pollutants that directly emits, or has the potential to emit, 100 tons per year or more of any air pollutant. The NAAQSs cover six pollutant categories: hydrocarbons, carbon monoxide, sulphur dioxide, nitrogen oxides, photochemical oxidants, and particulates.

Answer (a) is incorrect because it states an erroneous definition of the term. Answer (c) is incorrect because the statutory threshold amount is 100 tons, not 20 tons. Answer (d) is incorrect because 100 tons of any air pollutant satisfies the definition; the pollutant need not be one for which an NAAQS has been promulgated.

31.5 Comprehensive Environmental Response, Compensation, and Liability Act (CERCLA)

17. The Comprehensive Environmental Response, Compensation, and Liability Act (CERCLA), also generically known as the "Superfund," applies to the release of "hazardous substances." Which of the following is statutorily included in the definition of the term "hazardous substance"?

a. Crude oil.

b. Gasoline.

c. Asbestos.

d. Natural gas.

The correct answer is (c). *(Publisher)*

REQUIRED: The item within the definition of "hazardous substances" as defined in CERCLA.

DISCUSSION: Asbestos is a hazardous substance subject to the provisions of CERCLA.

Answers (a), (b), and (d) are incorrect because the definition of the term "hazardous substance" as used in CERCLA does not include petroleum or any derivatives thereof or natural gas.

18. Dan bought a vacation home in the mountains of North Carolina. One day as he was sitting on the porch of his vacation home, Dan saw a stream of gray liquid bubbling up from an opening in his front yard. Dan immediately notified the EPA, which, after extensive examination, informed him that hazardous substances (within the meaning of CERCLA) had been previously buried deep beneath his house and a shift in the rock formation underlying his house caused a barrel to rupture releasing its contents. Under CERCLA, Dan

a. Will be liable for the actions of the previous owner since CERCLA will not provide him with any defense to CERCLA liability.

b. Is released from all liability under CERCLA simply because he immediately notified the EPA of the release.

c. Will not be liable under CERCLA because he did not own the land at the time when the substances were buried.

d. Will not be liable under CERCLA, despite the Act's broad liability, if he is able to avail himself of the so-called innocent landowner's defense.

The correct answer is (d). *(Publisher)*

REQUIRED: The potential liability of a homeowner under CERCLA.

DISCUSSION: Liability under CERCLA is broadly applied to all owners or operators of "facilities" where releases of hazardous substances occur. Thus, all owners of land where such releases occur are subject to liability under CERCLA.

However, the so-called innocent landowner's defense is available under CERCLA. For the exception to apply, the owner must have purchased the land after the placement of the hazardous substances occurred. Moreover, the owner must prove that (s)he did not know or have any reason to know that such substances were on the land. Finally, the owner must show that someone else caused the release or threat of release of the substances and that (s)he exercised reasonable care and took reasonable precautions in preventing the release of such substances. If Dan proves the foregoing, he will not be subject to CERCLA liability.

Answer (a) is incorrect because CERCLA does provide for defenses, albeit very limited ones. Answer (b) is incorrect because by itself, immediate notification of a release by an owner or operator of an onshore facility will not absolve such person of CERCLA liability. Answer (c) is incorrect because CERCLA liability applies to both past and current owners of property.

19. Under CERCLA, which of the following is not a defense to liability?

a. Proof beyond the preponderance of the evidence that the release of hazardous substances was caused solely by an act of God.

b. Proof beyond the preponderance of the evidence that the release of hazardous substances was caused solely by an act of war.

c. Proof beyond the preponderance of the evidence that the owner or operator's payment of clean-up costs will result in his/her personal or business financial ruin.

d. Proof beyond the preponderance of the evidence that the release of hazardous substances was caused solely by the acts or omission of an unrelated third party, and the owner or operator exercised reasonable care and took reasonable precautions.

The correct answer is (c). *(Publisher)*

REQUIRED: The item not a defense to liability under CERCLA.

DISCUSSION: The inability to pay damages is not an absolute bar to liability under CERCLA.

Answers (a), (b), and (d) are incorrect because they comprise three exceptions to liability under CERCLA. A fourth, the so-called innocent landowner's defense, is indirectly available through the exception in answer (d).

CHAPTER THIRTY-TWO
INTERNATIONAL BUSINESS LAW AND LEGAL ENVIRONMENT

32.1 Nature and Extent of International Business Law

1. The sources of international law do not include

a. Treaties.

b. Common law.

c. Customs.

d. Conventions.

The correct answer is (b). *(Publisher)*

REQUIRED: The sources of international law.

DISCUSSION: International law is a broad area. It is the law that nations recognize when dealing with one another. International law consists of treaties, conventions, and customs. A treaty is a formal agreement between nations, which usually must be ratified by their lawmaking bodies, e.g., the U.S. Congress. A convention is another term for a treaty. It is often used to describe an agreement among many nations, e.g., the Geneva Convention on the treatment of prisoners of war. Customs are long-established practices serving as unwritten law. Common law is not a source of international law because it relates to law made within a country founded upon judicial decisions.

Answers (a), (c), and (d) are incorrect because they are sources of international law.

2. The European Economic Community

a. Provides insurance to American citizens and businesses against certain risks associated with doing business in Europe.

b. Meets 1 month per year to draft uniform international trade laws.

c. Was formed to reduce trade restrictions and tariffs among all nations.

d. Promotes tariff-free trade among its members and has common tariffs for non-members.

The correct answer is (d). *(Publisher)*

REQUIRED: The purpose of the European Economic Community.

DISCUSSION: The European Economic Community (EEC) was created under the treaty of Rome in 1957. The EEC promotes the free movement of workers, goods, and capital, and hopes to establish a single monetary unit to be used by its members. The EEC is governed by a Council of Ministers consisting of a representative from each country. Disputes between members are taken to the Court of Justice, which establishes binding precedents. Nonmembers of the EEC are subject to tariffs. In 1992, the EEC will take another step toward complete economic integration when the last trade among its member nations are eliminated.

Answer (a) is incorrect because providing insurance to businesses with transactions overseas is the purpose of the Overseas Private Investor Corporation, an organization created by the U.S. Congress. Answer (b) is incorrect because the purpose of the United Nations Commission on International Trade Law is to draft uniform trade laws for all countries. An example of a model act is the U.N. Convention on Contracts for the International Sale of Goods. Answer (c) is incorrect because the purpose of the General Agreement on Tariffs and Trades (GATT) is to reduce trade restrictions and tariffs among its many signatories.

3. With regard to activity outside the U.S., U.S. antitrust laws

a. May never be enforced against foreign corporations.

b. May always be enforced against U.S. and foreign corporations.

c. May be enforced against foreign but not U.S. corporations if the activity outside the United States has some substantial effect within the U.S.

d. May be enforced against U.S. and foreign corporations if the activity outside the U.S. has some substantial effect within the United States.

The correct answer is (d). *(Publisher)*

REQUIRED: The applicability of the U.S. antitrust rules.

DISCUSSION: The Sherman Act states that "every contract, combination, or conspiracy in restraint of trade or commerce among the several states or with foreign nations is declared illegal." There has been a considerable amount of litigation in determining how the U.S. can control activities outside its borders. The Foreign Trade Antitrust Improvements Act of 1982 states that the U.S. can control activities that have a direct, substantial, and reasonably foreseeable effect on U.S. commerce or exports. Also, a foreign country's laws will be deferred to if the U.S. interest is outweighed by the foreign country's interest in regulating the activity.

Answers (a), (b), and (c) are incorrect because U.S. antitrust laws can be enforced against U.S. or foreign corporations but only when the activity outside the U.S. has an effect on commerce within the U.S.

4. A government can restrict the sale of goods imported into its country by

a. Arbitration.

b. Tariffs.

c. Expropriation.

d. Repatriation.

The correct answer is (b). *(Publisher)*

REQUIRED: The governmental restriction on the sale of imported goods into its country.

DISCUSSION: A tariff is a tax imposed on imported goods. The governmental purpose of a tariff is to make the product so expensive that its citizens will buy a domestic equivalent of the imported product.

Answer (a) is incorrect because arbitration is a process that permits a dispute to be settled by a third party. Answer (c) is incorrect because expropriation occurs when a government takes a foreign firm's property without adequate compensation. Answer (d) is incorrect because repatriation is conversion of funds held in a foreign country into another currency and remittance of these funds to another nation. A firm must often obtain permission from the currency exchange authorities to repatriate earnings and investments. Regulations in many nations encourage a reinvestment of earnings in the country.

5. The sale of militarily sensitive equipment from a U.S. company to Iran is subject to the restrictions of

a. Sovereign immunity.

b. COCOM.

c. U.S. antitrust laws.

d. Foreign Corrupt Practices Act.

The correct answer is (b). *(Publisher)*

REQUIRED: The restrictions placed on militarily sensitive equipment.

DISCUSSION: The Coordinating Committee for Multilateral Export (COCOM) is a group of western countries that impose export controls on certain goods for political purposes. Agreement must be unanimous, and the restrictions are then enforced through laws passed in each country. A seller's failure to abide by the restrictions will lead to administrative penalties. The sale of militarily sensitive equipment will be restricted by COCOM because Iran currently is an unfriendly government.

Answer (a) is incorrect because sovereign immunity immunizes a government and not persons or corporations. Answer (c) is incorrect because antitrust laws apply when a restraint on trade may occur and the U.S. company could otherwise sell the equipment without being subject to COCOM restrictions. Answer (d) is incorrect because the Foreign Corrupt Practices Act prohibits U.S. companies from giving bribes to foreign officials.

6. The return to the United States of income earned by a U.S. firm in a foreign country is

a. Expropriation.

b. Bankruptcy.

c. Repatriation.

d. Forum non conveniens.

The correct answer is (c). *(Publisher)*

REQUIRED: The return to the U.S. of income earned in a foreign country.

DISCUSSION: Many U.S. firms have business operations abroad. Repatriation is conversion of funds held in a foreign country into another currency and remittance of these funds to another nation. A firm must often obtain permission from the currency exchange authorities to repatriate earnings and investments. Regulations in many nations encourage a reinvestment of earnings in the country.

Answer (a) is incorrect because expropriation is the seizure by a foreign country of assets without adequate compensation. Answer (b) is incorrect because bankruptcy occurs when a person's liabilities exceed assets or (s)he cannot meet obligations when they are due. Answer (d) is incorrect because forum non conveniens is a doctrine that permits a U.S. court the discretion to reject jurisdiction if the case can be heard more conveniently in another forum. This decision turns on such factors as where the events took place, the location of witnesses, and which court is more experienced in deciding the kind of litigation.

32.2 Business Transactions in the International Marketplace

7. Which clause in an international contract states that the laws of a certain country are to apply?

a. Choice of forum.

b. Force majeure.

c. Choice of law.

d. Arbitration.

The correct answer is (c). *(Publisher)*

REQUIRED: The clause in a contract stating that the laws of a certain country are to be applied.

DISCUSSION: An issue arises in international business transactions as to what law to apply in case of a dispute between the parties. When a court must decide which country's law will apply, a conflict of law arises. A choice of law clause will be enforced by the court hearing the case unless it is contrary to the policies of the forum nation.

Answer (a) is incorrect because a choice of forum clause is an agreement as to where a dispute will be litigated. Answer (b) is incorrect because a force majeure ("superior power") clause is inserted in a contract to provide for certain contingencies, e.g., fire, war, or embargo. The clause usually excuses performances when the listed natural disasters or other events occur. Answer (d) is incorrect because an arbitration clause in a contract is an agreement by the parties to be bound by a decision of a third party who will resolve the dispute.

8. Which of the following should not be included in an international contract?

a. A force majeure clause.

b. An open price term clause.

c. A choice of law and forum clause.

d. A commercial arbitration clause.

The correct answer is (b). *(Publisher)*

REQUIRED: The clause that should not be included in an international contract.

DISCUSSION: A contract between foreign parties should be as simple, precise, and complete as possible. The contract should define all essential terms. In a domestic setting, when parties state that the price term is left open, UCC 2-305 provides that the price will be determined at a later time. In an international setting, UCC 2-305 and other gap-filler provisions are not applicable.

Answers (a), (c), and (d) are incorrect because they are all necessary clauses in an international contract.

9. A clause in a contract between a Florida corporation and a Jamaican corporation that states all disputes will be resolved by a Florida court is an example of a(n)

a. Choice of law clause.

b. Choice of forum clause.

c. Arbitration clause.

d. Force majeure clause.

The correct answer is (b). *(Publisher)*

REQUIRED: The contract clause that determines where a dispute is to be resolved.

DISCUSSION: A choice of forum clause is an agreement by parties to a contract as to where a dispute will be resolved. If the effect of the agreement would be unfair or unreasonable, it will not be valid. The question of whether the clause is unreasonable must be decided by ascertaining whether it was negotiated in good faith.

Answer (a) is incorrect because a choice of law clause defines what law will apply to the transaction. Answer (c) is incorrect because an arbitration clause is an agreement among the parties that a neutral third party will resolve their dispute. Answer (d) is incorrect because a force majeure clause in a contract states the parties' responsibilities if a natural disaster or other calamity occurs.

10. XCo is an American company that wants to sell widgets to DCo, a Danish Corporation. XCo is unsure about DCo's ability to pay. XCo should

a. Not transact business with DCo.

b. Transact business with DCo because American law requires DCo to pay.

c. Transact business with DCo because Danish law requires DCo to pay.

d. Require DCo to obtain a letter of credit.

The correct answer is (d). *(Publisher)*

REQUIRED: The method to prevent a foreign corporation from not paying an American corporation for goods purchased.

DISCUSSION: If a U.S. company sells goods to a foreign company based only on a promise to pay, problems of payment may arise. A U.S. company may not know whether the foreign company will pay the contract price, or is solvent, or whether it will reject a delivery of the goods. Requiring a letter of credit will solve such a problem. A letter of credit is an engagement by the issuing bank (DCo's bank in Denmark) to pay on behalf of its customer when the requirements of the letter of credit are complied with. When the beneficiary (XCo) is in another country, the letter of credit is often sent to a confirming bank (in the U.S. in this case), which will pay the beneficiary directly upon presentation of a document of title. The confirming bank will then be paid by the issuing bank.

Answers (a), (b), and (c) are incorrect because XCo may find it profitable to transact business with DCo, but requiring a letter of credit may be preferable to relying on litigation in the event of a breach.

11. Which of the following is incorrect concerning a bill of lading?

a. It is a receipt showing that a seller transferred possession of goods to a shipper.

b. It is a contract under which the shipper agrees to transport goods to the buyer.

c. It is an engagement by a bank or other person made at the customer's request to pay drafts or other demands for its customer.

d. It shows who has ownership of the goods.

The correct answer is (c). *(Publisher)*

REQUIRED: The incorrect statement concerning a bill of lading.

DISCUSSION: A problem in an international sale is whether the seller will be paid. The problem is solved by using a letter of credit and a bill of lading. A bill of lading is a document of title evidencing receipt of goods by the carrier for shipment. A bill of lading is not an agreement with a bank to pay drafts or other demands for its customer. Such an agreement is a letter of credit (UCC 5-103). A seller is paid when (s)he presents the bill of lading to the buyer's bank.

Answers (a), (b), and (d) are incorrect because each is a true statement about a bill of lading.

12. A distribution agreement is

a. An association of two or more persons who as co-owners engage in a limited business transaction.

b. The supplying of manufacturing equipment and other items necessary to operate a foreign business.

c. A contract between a seller and independent contractor in which the independent contractor will sell the goods on his/her own behalf.

d. A contract between a seller and foreign corporation in which the foreign corporation is paid a commission on the goods it sells.

The correct answer is (c). *(Publisher)*

REQUIRED: The definition of a distribution agreement.

DISCUSSION: Many U.S. firms set up distributorships rather than foreign agents in foreign countries. This arrangement avoids the problems associated with direct sale to customers. The distributor purchases the goods, resells them, and retains the profits earned. By setting up a distributorship, the U.S. firm will not have to make a large investment to establish a subsidiary, and it will be able to avoid foreign labor laws applicable to commercial agents in foreign countries. The U.S. firm is not subject to any contracts the distributorship enters into, and rids itself of title to the goods, the need to establish business relationships in the foreign country, and the pressure to resell goods at a profit.

Answer (a) is incorrect because it describes a joint business venture in a foreign country. Answer (b) is incorrect because a turnkey operation is formed when a firm provides the necessaries for starting a foreign business and turns the operation over to a foreign firm. Answer (d) is incorrect because an agency agreement is formed. In contrast with a distributor, an agent does not have title to goods and does not buy the goods.

13. A seller is paid in a bill of lading and letter of credit transaction when the bill of lading is given to the

a. Transport company.

b. Buyer.

c. Seller's bank.

d. Confirming bank.

The correct answer is (d). *(Publisher)*

REQUIRED: The method by which a seller is paid in a bill of lading and letter of credit transaction.

DISCUSSION: The letter of credit and bill of lading transaction assures that the seller will be paid when dealing with a foreign buyer. After the seller and buyer enter into an agreement for the sale of goods, the buyer arranges with a bank to issue a letter of credit. A letter of credit is a promise by a bank to pay a certain amount of money or extend credit to a third party (i.e., the seller). In most of these transactions, the buyer's bank arranges for a bank in the seller's city or country (the confirming bank) to issue the letter of credit to the seller. The seller must meet certain conditions before it can draw on the letter of credit. The seller draws on the letter of credit by writing drafts, which is a process similar to using a checking account. The seller is paid when the bill of lading is presented to the confirming bank.

Answer (a) is incorrect because the bill of lading is issued to the seller when (s)he delivers the purchased goods to the transporting company. Answer (b) is incorrect because the buyer receives the bill of lading after the seller is paid. The buyer does not pay the seller. Answer (c) is incorrect because the buyer's bank, not the seller's, receives the bill of lading.

14. A buyer is entitled to the goods purchased in a bill of lading and letter of credit transaction after the buyer's bank checks the

a. Goods purchased to verify that they conform to the contract of sale.

b. Contract for the purchased goods to verify that it conforms with the bill of lading.

c. Contract for the purchased goods to verify that it conforms with the letter of credit.

d. Bill of lading to verify that it conforms with the terms in the letter of credit.

The correct answer is (d). *(Publisher)*

REQUIRED: The time when the buyer is entitled to the goods purchased in a letter of credit and bill of lading transaction.

DISCUSSION: In a bill of lading and letter of credit transaction, the seller is paid after the bill of lading is turned over to the confirming bank. The confirming bank sends the bill of lading to the buyer's bank that issued the letter of credit. The contract for the sale of goods is independent of the letter of credit and bill of lading. The buyer's bank simply checks the bill of lading to verify that it conforms with the letter of credit. If it conforms, the bank gives the bill of lading to the buyer, and (s)he takes the bill of lading to the transporting company's warehouse to retrieve the purchased goods.

Answer (a) is incorrect because the buyer, not the confirming bank, should examine the goods. Answers (b) and (c) are incorrect because the buyer's bank does not check the contract for the sale of goods because it is independent of the bill of lading.

32.3 Conduct of Foreign Countries in International Business Transactions

15. The Foreign Corrupt Practices Act prohibits

a. Bribes to all foreigners.

b. Small bribes to foreign officials that serve as facilitating or grease payments.

c. Bribery only by corporations and their representatives.

d. Bribes to foreign officials to influence official acts.

The correct answer is (d). *(Publisher)*

REQUIRED: The prohibition of the Foreign Corrupt Practices Act.

DISCUSSION: The Foreign Corrupt Practices Act (FCPA) prohibits any U.S. firm from making bribes to foreign officials to influence official acts. The businesses subject to the FCPA include corporations, partnerships, limited partnerships, business trusts, and unincorporated organizations. Violations of the FCPA are federal felonies. The penalties are 5 years in prison or a $10,000 fine or both for an officer, director, or shareholder who helps make the bribe.

Answers (a) and (b) are incorrect because each is not covered by the provisions in the FCPA. Answer (c) is incorrect because all U.S. firms are subject to the anti-bribery provisions.

16. The government of a foreign country owns all the country's silver mines. No company can mine the silver unless it has government approval. If the foreign country gives Walker Co. a permit to mine, the doctrine that prevents a U.S. court from declaring the permit illegal is

a. Sherman Antitrust Act.

b. Sovereign compulsion.

c. Act of State doctrine.

d. Repatriation.

The correct answer is (c). *(Publisher)*

REQUIRED: The doctrine that prevents a U.S. court from declaring a foreign government's action illegal.

DISCUSSION: The Act of State doctrine prevents U.S. courts from interfering in foreign affairs. Foreign countries are immune from a lawsuit in U.S. courts with regard to their actions in their own territory. Thus, a U.S. court cannot invalidate the permit given to Walker Co. by the foreign government because that government is immune to suit in the U.S. for actions in its own country.

Answer (a) is incorrect because antitrust law is concerned only with restraints on U.S. commerce. Answer (b) is incorrect because the sovereign compulsion doctrine provides a defense to private parties that have been compelled by a non-U.S. government to commit acts within that country's territory that would violate U.S. antitrust laws. Answer (d) is incorrect because repatriation is the conversion of funds held in a foreign country to another currency and their transfer out of that country.

17. If a U.S. company brings an action against a foreign country in a U.S. court, the issue raised is

a. Repatriation.

b. Expropriation.

c. Sovereign immunity.

d. Dumping.

The correct answer is (c). *(Publisher)*

REQUIRED: The problem that arises when an action is brought in an American court against a foreign country.

DISCUSSION: Ordinarily, foreign nations cannot be sued. The Foreign Sovereign Immunities Act (FSIA) was enacted in 1976 to exempt foreign governments and their agents from liability. A foreign government can be sued if it waives the defense of sovereign immunity or carries on a commercial activity within the United States. A commercial activity is defined as one that an individual carries on for profit.

Answer (a) is incorrect because repatriation is the conversion of funds held in a foreign country to another currency and their transfer out of that country. Answer (b) is incorrect because expropriation occurs when a foreign government seizes the assets of a business and gives less than fair market value in return. Answer (d) is incorrect because dumping is the sale by a foreign business of goods at very low prices to gain market share in a domestic market. Dumping is prevented by imposing tariffs on such goods.

18. Articles 85 and 86 of the European Economic Community treaty establish a body of law that

a. Imposes tariffs on goods imported into Europe.

b. Forbids anticompetitive acts within the EEC.

c. Establishes a single monetary unit within Europe.

d. Establishes the proper forum for a dispute to be resolved between two European corporations.

The correct answer is (b). *(Publisher)*

REQUIRED: The content of Articles 85 and 86 of the European Economic Community treaty.

DISCUSSION: Articles 85 and 86 of the European Economic Community (EEC) treaty serve the same purpose as antitrust law. Those laws decide whether prohibited business conduct has occurred and whether a dominant enterprise has exploited its position in a geographic area. Articles 85 and 86 are enforced by the Commission of European Communities. When the Commission receives a complaint of a violation, it investigates and can order the activity to be stopped.

Answers (a), (c), and (d) are incorrect because they are not covered by Articles 85 and 86 of the EEC treaty.

19. Goodman Co., a U.S. corporation, manufactures paper clips in the Philippines. During 1992, a political revolution occurs and all industries in the Philippines are nationalized. The Philippine government pays Goodman 40% of the value of the assets it seized. The seizure of Goodman's assets and payment of less than fair market value is

a. Expropriation.

b. Repatriation.

c. Sovereign immunity.

d. Bribery.

The correct answer is (a). *(Publisher)*

REQUIRED: The term for seizure of assets by a foreign government without just compensation.

DISCUSSION: Many U.S. companies have manufacturing facilities and property in foreign countries. Some of these countries are unstable and subject to political change. Expropriation occurs when a foreign government seizes a U.S. firm's assets and pays less than fair market value for such assets. U.S. firms may insure against expropriation through the Overseas Private Investment Corporation's Foreign Credit Insurance Agency.

Answer (b) is incorrect because repatriation involves transfer of funds out of a foreign country. Answer (c) is incorrect because sovereign immunity is a defense that immunizes a foreign country, unless the country waives the defense or is engaged in a commercial activity with a U.S. business. Answer (d) is incorrect because bribery in an international business environment entails payments to foreign officials to obtain favorable treatment in that country.

BLANK PAGE

CHAPTER THIRTY-THREE
ACCOUNTANTS' LEGAL RESPONSIBILITIES

This chapter is directed specifically toward accountants, especially CPAs, because many students taking more than one business law course are accounting majors. However, many of the concepts apply to other professionals as well. See *Federal Tax Objective Questions and Explanations,* Chapter 24, for the duties of tax return preparers.

33.1 General Standards of Care

1. Which of the following is the best statement of the general standard of performance owed by an accountant in his/her professional work?

a. To do the job correctly and discover all irregularities.

b. To follow generally accepted accounting principles (GAAP) and generally accepted auditing standards (GAAS).

c. To act as a professional and not commit fraud.

d. To exercise the skill and care of the ordinarily prudent accountant in the same circumstances.

The correct answer is (d). *(Publisher)*

REQUIRED: The best statement of an accountant's general standard of performance.

DISCUSSION: An accountant owes a general duty both to clients and other persons affected by the accountant's work to exercise the skill and care of the ordinary prudent accountant in the same circumstances. The accountant is required to exercise reasonable care, i.e., not to be negligent. However, (s)he is not a guarantor or an insurer of the work.

Answer (a) is incorrect because an accountant does not have a duty to discover every irregularity. (S)he is not an insurer or guarantor. Answer (b) is incorrect because although an accountant has a duty to follow GAAP and GAAS, this may not be sufficient in all cases. Answer (c) is incorrect because an accountant should act as a professional, but his/her duty extends to a higher level than merely not committing fraud.

2. The Apex Surety Company wrote a general fidelity bond covering defalcations by the employees of Watson, Inc. Thereafter, Grand, an employee of Watson, embezzled $18,900 of company funds. When his activities were discovered, Apex paid Watson the full amount in accordance with the terms of the fidelity bond, and then sought recovery against Watson's auditors, Kane & Dobbs, CPAs. Which of the following would be the CPAs' best defense?

a. Apex is not in privity of contract.

b. The shortages were the result of clever forgeries and collusive fraud that would not be detected by an audit made in accordance with GAAS.

c. Kane & Dobbs were not guilty of either gross negligence or fraud.

d. Kane & Dobbs were not aware of the Apex-Watson surety relationship.

The correct answer is (b). *(CPA 1178 L-3)*

REQUIRED: The best defense by CPAs who failed to uncover an embezzlement.

DISCUSSION: The best defense would be that the auditors followed the standards of the profession and performed the audit in a prudent manner. Accountants and auditors are not insurers or guarantors. If the embezzlement resulted from clever forgeries and collusive fraud that would not have been detected by an audit made in accordance with GAAS, the auditors would usually not be liable.

Answer (a) is incorrect because auditors can be liable to third parties with whom the auditors did not enter into a contract (privity of contract), but only if the auditors were at least negligent. Answer (c) is incorrect because Kane & Dobbs may be liable to Apex for ordinary negligence if the CPAs knew that Apex was an intended beneficiary of their work. Answer (d) is incorrect because the CPAs should have been aware of the Apex-Watson surety relationship as auditor of Apex. But even if they were unaware of the relationship, they could still be liable for gross negligence and fraud.

3. Magnus Enterprises engaged a CPA firm to perform the annual audit of its financial statements. Which of the following is a correct statement with respect to the CPA firm's liability to Magnus for negligence?

a. Such liability cannot be varied by agreement of the parties.

b. The CPA firm will be liable for any fraudulent scheme it does not detect.

c. The CPA firm will not be liable if it can show that it exercised the ordinary care and skill of a reasonable person in the conduct of his/her own affairs.

d. The CPA firm must not only exercise reasonable care in what it does, but also must possess at least that degree of accounting knowledge and skill expected of a CPA.

The correct answer is (d). *(CPA 1178 L-2)*

REQUIRED: The CPA firm's liability to a client for negligence.

DISCUSSION: A professional is held to a higher standard of care than the ordinary person and must also possess and exercise the knowledge and skill of a member of that profession. Therefore, the CPA firm must exercise both reasonable care and that expected of a CPA.

Answer (a) is incorrect because a CPA may limit liability by agreement with the client. Answer (b) is incorrect because a CPA does not guarantee detection of fraudulent schemes. Answer (c) is incorrect because a CPA firm is held to a higher standard than that of an ordinary reasonable person in the conduct of his/her own affairs.

4. Mary Martinson is a CPA. One of her clients is suing her for negligence alleging that she failed to follow GAAS in the current year's audit, thereby failing to discover large thefts of inventory.

a. Martinson is not bound by GAAS unless she is a member of the AICPA.

b. Martinson's failure to follow GAAS would result in liability.

c. GAAS do not currently cover the procedures that must be used in verifying inventory for balance sheet purposes.

d. If Martinson failed to follow GAAS, she would undoubtedly be found to have committed the tort of fraud.

The correct answer is (b). *(CPA 1175 L-21)*

REQUIRED: The effect of failure of a CPA to follow GAAS.

DISCUSSION: A CPA is a professional who must adhere to professional standards of care in the performance of his/her work. A CPA must perform in accordance with that degree of accounting knowledge and skill expected of a CPA. Whether the CPA has met the required standard is partly determined by whether (s)he has followed GAAS. Failure to follow such standards would result in liability for damages proximately caused by his/her negligence.

Answer (a) is incorrect because a CPA is bound by GAAS regardless of membership in the AICPA. Answer (c) is incorrect because GAAS do cover inventory verification. Answer (d) is incorrect because a failure to follow GAAS might be a negligent or unintentional tort (as opposed to fraud, which is an intentional tort).

5. In an action for negligence against a CPA, "the custom of the profession" standard is used at least to some extent in determining whether the CPA is negligent. Which of the following statements describes how this standard is applied?

a. If the CPA proves (s)he literally followed GAAP and GAAS, it will be conclusively presumed that the CPA was not negligent.

b. The custom of the profession argument may only be raised by the defendant.

c. Despite a CPA's adherence to the custom of the profession, negligence may nevertheless be present.

d. Failure to satisfy the custom of the profession is equivalent to gross negligence.

The correct answer is (c). *(CPA 1183 L-4)*

REQUIRED: The extent of protection provided to a CPA who follows the customs of the profession.

DISCUSSION: In general, courts defer to the accounting profession to determine professional standards. However, courts will not defer to the standards of conduct determined by a profession if that standard is not sufficient to prevent harm to the members of society intended to be protected. In some instances, a CPA will need to do more than the custom or standards require.

Answer (a) is incorrect because in some instances, a CPA will need to do more than follow GAAP or GAAS. Failure to do so may be negligent. Answer (b) is incorrect because the plaintiff can use a CPA's failure to follow the custom of the profession as evidence of the CPA's negligence. Answer (d) is incorrect because failure to follow the custom of the profession might only be ordinary negligence and in some instances not negligence at all depending upon the circumstances.

6. Nast Corp. orally engaged Baker & Co., CPAs to audit its financial statements. The management of Nast informed Baker that it suspected the accounts receivable were materially overstated. Although the financial statements audited by Baker did, in fact, include a materially overstated accounts receivable balance, Baker issued an unqualified opinion. Nast relied on the financial statements in deciding to obtain a loan from Century Bank to expand its operations. Nast has defaulted on the loan and has incurred a substantial loss.

If Nast sues Baker for negligence in failing to discover the overstatement, Baker's best defense would be that

a. Baker did not perform the audit recklessly or with an intent to deceive.

b. Baker was not in privity of contract with Nast.

c. The audit was performed by Baker in accordance with GAAS.

d. No engagement letter had been signed by Baker.

The correct answer is (c). *(CPA 589 L-9)*

REQUIRED: The best defense of auditors who failed to discover an overstated accounts receivable balance.

DISCUSSION: The purpose of an independent external audit of financial statements is the expression of an opinion on whether they are fairly presented in conformity with GAAP. To achieve this objective, the CPA must follow GAAS. At no time during the audit do the auditors assure that all material errors or irregularities will be detected. Thus, their best defense will be to prove that they performed the audit in accordance with GAAS. Although following GAAS does not eliminate the possibility of negligence, it is strong evidence of adherence to the due care standard.

Answer (a) is incorrect because proving that the auditors did not perform the audit recklessly or with an intent to deceive would be a defense to fraud but not negligence. Answer (b) is incorrect because a client is always in privity of contract with the auditors. Answer (d) is incorrect because an engagement letter is not required to form a contract between auditors and their client. The oral agreement therefore required the auditors to perform the audit in a nonnegligent manner.

7. Krim, president and CEO of United Co., engaged Smith, CPA to audit United's financial statements so that United could secure a loan from First Bank. Smith issued an unqualified opinion on May 20, but the loan was delayed. On August 5, on inquiry to Smith by First Bank, Smith, relying on Krim's representation, made assurances that there was no material change in United's financial status. Krim's representation was untrue because of a material change which took place after May 20. First relied on Smith's assurances of no change. Shortly thereafter, United became insolvent. If First sues Smith for negligent misrepresentation, Smith will be found

a. Not liable, because Krim misled Smith, and a CPA is not responsible for a client's untrue representations.

b. Liable, because Smith should have undertaken sufficient auditing procedures to verify the status of United.

c. Not liable, because Smith's opinion only covers the period up to May 20.

d. Liable, because Smith should have contacted the chief financial officer rather than the chief executive officer.

The correct answer is (b). *(CPA 589 L-1)*

REQUIRED: The auditor's liability for assurances given about events subsequent to the report.

DISCUSSION: AU 333, "Client Representations," states that written representations corroborate information received orally from management, but they do not substitute for the procedures necessary to afford a reasonable basis for the assurances given. Moreover, the auditor ordinarily has no responsibility for events after the end of field work or the date of the report, if later. If the auditor decides to assume such responsibility, (s)he must comply with GAAS, including AU 333. Accordingly, the auditor will be liable for failure to exercise due care.

Answer (a) is incorrect because a CPA should make an independent investigation. Answer (c) is incorrect because Smith made assurances to the bank that covered the period subsequent to May 20 and therefore assumed responsibility for the additional period. Answer (d) is incorrect because Smith should have performed additional audit procedures and not have relied solely on management's representations, including those of the chief financial officer.

8. Which one of the following, if present, would support a finding of constructive fraud on the part of a CPA?

a. Privity of contract.

b. Intent to deceive.

c. Reckless disregard.

d. Ordinary negligence.

The correct answer is (c). *(CPA 589 L-7)*

REQUIRED: The action that would support a finding of constructive fraud on the part of a CPA.

DISCUSSION: Whether an accountant is liable for fraud depends on whether (s)he acted with scienter. Scienter means that the person making a representation knew that it was false at the time of making it or acted with a reckless disregard for the truth. The difference between actual and constructive fraud is that the scienter requirement for the latter is met by gross negligence (reckless disregard). Hence, the following four elements are necessary to prove constructive fraud: 1) misrepresentation of a material fact, 2) reckless disregard for the truth, 3) reasonable reliance by the injured party, and 4) injury. Thus, the presence of reckless disregard for the truth would support a finding of constructive fraud on the part of a CPA.

Answer (a) is incorrect because privity of contract is not a necessary element of fraud. Answer (b) is incorrect because intent to deceive is a necessary element of actual fraud. Answer (d) is incorrect because gross, not ordinary, negligence meets the scienter requirement.

33.2 Liability to Clients

9. One of a CPA's major concerns regarding contractual questions arising in the audit of a client's financial statements is

a. The proper court in which to initiate a lawsuit.

b. The question of who has the burden of proof.

c. Whether the parties involved have a clear understanding of the procedures and services to be performed.

d. The admissibility of evidence in court.

The correct answer is (c). *(CPA 1176 L-34)*

REQUIRED: The major concern of CPAs about contractual questions arising from an audit.

DISCUSSION: The basis of an accountant's duty (performance) to a client is their contract. Thus, the parties should have a clear understanding of the procedures and services to be performed. The contract may be oral or written. It is commonly memorialized by an engagement letter sent by the CPA to the client and agreed to by the client.

Answers (a), (b), and (d) are incorrect because each is concerned with the resolution of contract disputes rather than with the formation of the contract.

10. When CPAs fail in their duty to carry out their contracts for services, liability to clients may be based on

	Breach of Contract	Strict Liability
a.	Yes	Yes
b.	Yes	No
c.	No	No
d.	No	Yes

The correct answer is (b). *(CPA 589 L-6)*

REQUIRED: The basis(es) for a CPA's liability to clients.

DISCUSSION: The agreement of the parties to a contract creates legally enforceable duties. The failure to carry out those duties is a breach of contract and is a basis for the liability of the breaching party to the nonbreacher. Strict liability in tort is imposed without regard to the defendant's fault, i.e., even if there is no negligence and no intentional misconduct. The courts and legislatures have decided in certain circumstances that an involved party, although without fault, is better able to bear a loss than the injured party. For example, manufacturers may be held strictly liable for injuries caused by defective products. However, strict liability is not imposed on CPAs.

Answer (a) is incorrect because CPAs cannot be held liable without fault. Answer (c) is incorrect because CPAs are liable for breach of contract. Answer (d) is incorrect because CPAs are liable for breach of contract but cannot be held strictly liable.

11. The firm Meek & Co., CPAs was engaged by Reed, the president of Sulk Corp, to issue by June 15 an opinion on Sulk's financial statements for the fiscal year ended March 31. Meek's engagement and its fee of $20,000 were approved by Sulk's board of directors. Meek did not issue its opinion until June 30 because of Sulk's failure to supply Meek with the necessary information to complete the audit. Sulk refuses to pay Meek. If Meek sues Sulk, Meek will

a. Prevail based on the contract.

b. Prevail based on quasi-contract.

c. Lose, because it breached the contract.

d. Lose, because the June 15 deadline was a condition precedent to Sulk's performance.

The correct answer is (a). *(CPA 1186 L-25)*

REQUIRED: The probable outcome of an action by CPAs to recover fees.

DISCUSSION: Meek's failure to meet the deadline did not result in a breach of contract. Rather, the failure of performance was caused by Sulk's failure to supply Meek with the necessary information to complete the audit. Every contract contains an implied promise each party will not interfere with the other party's performance. Consequently, Meek can enforce the contract because Meek was not in breach.

Answer (b) is incorrect because a quasi-contract is created by a court when one party has been unjustly enriched at the expense of the other. No quasi-contractual remedy is necessary in this case because the parties formed an express contract. Answer (c) is incorrect because as discussed above, Meek did not breach the contract. Answer (d) is incorrect because the condition would have been effective only if Sulk had not interfered with Meek's ability to perform. Sulk's supplying the necessary information was a condition precedent to Meek's duty to perform.

12. Which of the following can a CPA firm legally do?

a. Accept a competing company in the same industry as another of its clients.

b. Establish an association of CPAs for the purpose of determining minimum fee schedules.

c. Effectively disclaim liability to third parties for any and all torts.

d. Effectively establish an absolute dollar limitation on its liability for a given engagement.

The correct answer is (a). *(CPA 1176 L-2)*

REQUIRED: The action of a CPA firm that is legally permissible.

DISCUSSION: Although a CPA contracts with a client to perform services, (s)he is an independent contractor and may also work for others. A CPA firm can legally accept a competing company in the same industry as another client. This practice is advantageous because it permits CPAs to "specialize" and become more knowledgeable and efficient as well as to be of more assistance to clients.

Answer (b) is incorrect because minimum fee schedules are considered a restraint of trade. Answer (c) is incorrect because a CPA may be liable to third parties for negligence or fraud. This liability cannot be disclaimed. Answer (d) is incorrect because a CPA firm cannot establish a dollar limit on its liability for any engagement (partly because the CPA cannot know all the parties who may rely upon his/her work).

13. Which of the following may a CPA do only with permission of the client?

a. Hire other CPAs as employees to help complete the engagement.

b. Hire non-CPAs as employees to help complete the engagement.

c. Delegate the engagement to another CPA.

d. Receive a commission for referring the engagement to another CPA.

The correct answer is (c). *(Publisher)*

REQUIRED: The action a CPA may not take without permission of the client.

DISCUSSION: The engagement to perform professional services is a personal service contract. It may not be delegated without permission of the other contracting party (client).

Answers (a) and (b) are incorrect because a CPA may hire assistants (CPAs or non-CPAs) to assist in performing the engagement as long as the CPA hired by the client supervises the job and is responsible for it. Answer (d) is incorrect because in no event may a CPA receive a commission for referring an engagement.

14. Ritz Corp. wished to acquire the stock of Stale, Inc. In conjunction with its plan of acquisition, Ritz hired Fein, CPA to audit the financial statements of Stale. Based on the audited financial statements and Fein's unqualified opinion, Ritz acquired Stale. Within 6 months, it was discovered that the inventory of Stale had been overstated by $500,000. Ritz commenced an action against Fein. Ritz believes that Fein failed to exercise the knowledge, skill, and judgment commonly possessed by CPAs in the locality, but is not able to prove that Fein either intentionally deceived it or showed a reckless disregard for the truth. Ritz also is unable to prove that Fein had any knowledge that the inventory was overstated. Which of the following two causes of action would provide Ritz with proper bases upon which Ritz would most likely prevail?

a. Negligence and breach of contract.

b. Negligence and gross negligence.

c. Negligence and fraud.

d. Gross negligence and breach of contract.

The correct answer is (a). *(CPA 1186 L-4)*

REQUIRED: The bases upon which a client will most likely prevail when an auditor fails to exercise due care.

DISCUSSION: An accountant's common law liability to a client can be based upon breach of contract, negligence, or fraud. A breach of contract occurs when an accountant fails to perform duties required under a contract. These duties can either be express or implied. All contracts carry the implied duty to perform in a nonnegligent manner. To prevail in an action for negligence, the client must prove that the accountant did not act with the same degree of skill and judgment possessed by accountants in the locality. In an action for fraud, the client must prove scienter (intent to deceive or a reckless disregard for the truth). Ritz would most likely prevail on an action brought for negligence or breach of contract if Fein failed to perform with the knowledge, skill, and judgment commonly possessed by CPAs in the area.

Answers (b), (c), and (d) are incorrect because Ritz is unlikely to prevail in an action based upon gross negligence or fraud given its inability to prove an intent to deceive, a reckless disregard for the truth, or guilty knowledge.

15. One of the elements necessary to hold a CPA liable to a client for conducting an audit negligently is that the CPA

a. Acted with scienter or guilty knowledge.

b. Was a fiduciary of the client.

c. Failed to exercise due care.

d. Executed an engagement letter.

The correct answer is (c). *(CPA 1187 L-28)*

REQUIRED: The element necessary to prove negligence.

DISCUSSION: The elements of a prima facie case of negligence on the part of an auditor are 1) a duty owed to the client by the auditor, 2) a loss incurred by the client, 3) a failure by the auditor to exercise the skill and care of an ordinarily prudent auditor in the same circumstances, and 4) proximate (legal) causation of the loss by the failure to exercise due care.

Answer (a) is incorrect because scienter is an element of fraud, not of negligence. Answer (b) is incorrect because by definition, an auditor and the client have a fiduciary relationship. Answer (d) is incorrect because an engagement letter is a normal part of an audit and does not indicate negligence.

16. Which of the following is a correct statement of the basis of liability of an accountant to a client?

a. Intentionally using data from a prior year rather than developing it currently in financial statements is ordinary negligence.

b. Statutes may be used by third parties to hold an accountant liable, but not by a client.

c. Breach of trust includes disclosing a client's confidential financial data to a third party.

d. Fraud requires an intent to deceive a client.

The correct answer is (c). *(Publisher)*

REQUIRED: The correct statement concerning the liability of an accountant to a client.

DISCUSSION: An accountant has a confidential, fiduciary relationship with a client. The accountant may not use information or assets of a client to benefit anyone other than the client. Disclosing the client's confidential financial data to a third party is thus a breach of trust for which an accountant can be held liable.

Answer (a) is incorrect because intentionally using data from a prior year rather than developing it currently for financial statements is fraud or at least gross negligence. Answer (b) is incorrect because a client can use certain statutes to hold an accountant liable, such as statutes concerning fraud. Answer (d) is incorrect because fraud also may be a reckless disregard for the truth; constructive fraud does not require an actual intent to deceive.

17. You are a CPA retained by the manager of a cooperative retirement village to do "write-up work." You are expected to prepare unaudited financial statements with each page marked "unaudited" and accompanied by a disclaimer of opinion stating no audit was made. In performing the work you discover that there are no invoices to support $25,000 of the manager's claimed disbursements. The manager informs you that all the disbursements are proper. What should you do?

a. Submit the expected statements but omit the $25,000 of unsupported disbursements.

b. Include the unsupported disbursements in the statements because you are not expected to make an audit.

c. Obtain from the manager a written statement that you informed him/her of the missing invoices and his/her assurance that the disbursements are proper.

d. Notify the owners that some of the claimed disbursements are unsupported and withdraw if the situation is not satisfactorily resolved.

The correct answer is (d). *(CPA 575 A-42)*

REQUIRED: The appropriate action by a CPA who discovers a material irregularity while doing compilation work.

DISCUSSION: This situation describes the 1136 Tenants' legal liability case, which imposed liability on a CPA doing compilation work for not pursuing an investigation of a situation that appeared questionable on its face. Although the CPA need not audit the information, (s)he is responsible to take further action concerning information that is incorrect, incomplete, or otherwise unsatisfactory. Such action would include communication with the owners.

Answers (a) and (b) are incorrect because to either include or exclude the unsupported disbursements would subject the CPA to liability for not following up on a questionable item. Answer (c) is incorrect because the owners must be notified and the situation resolved before the CPA continues.

18. Walters & Whitlow, CPAs failed to discover a fraudulent scheme used by Davis Corporation's head cashier to embezzle corporate funds during the past five years. Walters & Whitlow would have discovered the embezzlements promptly if they had not been negligent in their annual audits. Under the circumstances, Walters & Whitlow will normally not be liable for

a. Punitive damages.

b. The fees charged for the years in question.

c. Losses occurring after the time the fraudulent scheme should have been detected.

d. Losses occurring prior to the time the fraudulent scheme should have been detected that could have been recovered had it been so detected.

The correct answer is (a). *(CPA 1175 L-23)*

REQUIRED: The damages not payable by CPAs for negligent failure to discover fraud.

DISCUSSION: If the CPAs have merely been negligent, they will not be liable for punitive damages. Punitive damages are awarded only when the situation presents a case of extreme or aggravated circumstances.

Answer (b) is incorrect because the fees charged would be a proper element of the plaintiff's damages. The defendant violated both its contractual and tort duties to perform in a competent manner. Answer (c) is incorrect because a loss occurring after a scheme should have been discovered is properly recoverable in damages. It flows directly from the defendant's misconduct. Answer (d) is incorrect because although normally an accountant is not liable for losses occurring before a scheme should have been discovered, the accountant is liable when the losses could have been recovered.

33.3 Liability to Third Parties: Common Law

19. What is the basis for an auditor's legal liability to third parties at common law?

a. Fraud only when the third parties were parties to the contract.

b. Gross negligence only if the auditor knew they were intended beneficiaries of the audit.

c. Ordinary negligence even if the auditor did not know they were intended beneficiaries of the audit.

d. Ordinary negligence only if the auditor knew they were intended beneficiaries of the audit.

The correct answer is (d). *(Publisher)*

REQUIRED: The basis for an auditor's legal liability to third parties at common law.

DISCUSSION: An auditor has not contracted with third parties, so the potential liability is not as great as to the client because of lack of privity. Auditors may be liable to third parties for gross negligence and intentional acts of deceit (fraud) without privity. However, auditors are liable at common law for ordinary negligence to third parties whom they should foresee were intended beneficiaries. Intended third-party beneficiaries of a contract have privity.

Answers (a) and (b) are incorrect because the auditor may be liable to third parties for gross negligence or fraud even if they were not in privity. Answer (c) is incorrect because the auditor must know that third parties are intended beneficiaries to be liable to them for ordinary negligence.

20. If a CPA recklessly departs from the standards of due care when conducting an audit, the CPA will be liable to third parties who were unknown to the CPA based on

a. Strict liability.

b. Gross negligence.

c. Negligence.

d. Breach of contract.

The correct answer is (b). *(CPA 1187 L-30)*

REQUIRED: The basis for a CPA's liability to unknown third parties if the CPA recklessly departs from the standards of due care.

DISCUSSION: A CPA's liability to third parties for ordinary negligence is often substantially restricted. But when the CPA has willfully and recklessly disregarded the standards of due care and the consequences of his/her actions, liability will be imposed for constructive fraud (gross negligence). The class of plaintiffs will then include all foreseeable users of the CPA's work product.

Answer (a) is incorrect because CPAs are not subject to strict liability. Answer (c) is incorrect because most states do not yet extend a CPA's liability for negligence to unknown third parties. Answer (d) is incorrect because unknown third parties have no standing to sue for breach of contract. Only parties to the contract and intended beneficiaries may do so.

21. In a common law action against an accountant, the lack of privity may be a defense if the plaintiff

a. Is a creditor of the client who sues the accountant for negligence.

b. Can prove the presence of gross negligence that amounts to a reckless disregard for the truth.

c. Is the accountant's client.

d. Bases his action upon fraud.

The correct answer is (a). *(CPA 1186 L-5)*

REQUIRED: The instance in which lack of privity may be a defense.

DISCUSSION: An accountant is not liable to all persons who are damaged by his/her negligence. Although the majority view is that a broader standard of liability should be applied, lack of privity is still a defense of an accountant in some states, for example, New York. If the accountant has not contracted to perform for the third party, (s)he should not be held liable for damages to that third party. Whether the accountant will be held liable to the third party depends upon the degree of negligence and whether the third party was an intended beneficiary of the accountant's work.

Answers (b) and (d) are incorrect because all foreseeable users of an accountant's work product have standing to sue the accountant for damage based on his/her gross negligence or fraud. Answer (c) is incorrect because an accountant does have privity of contract with the client and intended third-party beneficiaries.

22. One traditional test of whether a third party can recover from an accountant for negligence is the primary benefit test. Which of the following has standing under the primary benefit test?

a. A bank that is considering a loan to the accountant's client and is waiting for the financial statements on which to base its decision.

b. A bank when the accountant was aware financial statements would be sent to many banks as part of loan applications by the client.

c. A shareholder of the client.

d. A general trade creditor of the client.

The correct answer is (a). *(Publisher)*

REQUIRED: The third party who has standing under the primary benefit test.

DISCUSSION: Under the primary benefit test, the accountant must have been aware that (s)he was hired to produce a work product to be used and relied upon by a particular third party. This is the narrowest test, and most courts would allow such a third party to sue the accountant for ordinary negligence.

Answer (b) is incorrect because this bank is only a member of a foreseen class of third parties, not a primary beneficiary. Answers (c) and (d) are incorrect because shareholders and general trade creditors are merely foreseeable users.

23. The traditional common law rules regarding accountant's liability to third parties for negligence

a. Remain substantially unchanged since their inception.

b. Were more stringent than the rules currently applicable.

c. Are of relatively minor importance to the accountant.

d. Have been substantially changed at both the federal and state levels.

The correct answer is (d). *(CPA 1175 L-18)*

REQUIRED: The status of traditional common law rules regarding accountant's liability.

DISCUSSION: The traditional common law rules have been changed with the result that CPAs' liability to third parties for negligence has been greatly increased. Under federal securities regulation, a CPA may be liable to any third party who purchases an initial issue of securities. At the state level, CPAs' potential liability has been increased by extending it to unknown third parties when the CPAs have been grossly negligent (have shown a reckless disregard for the truth).

Answers (a) and (b) are incorrect because the traditional rules have been substantially changed and are now more stringent. Answer (c) is incorrect because the traditional rules still govern the great majority of cases.

24. Which of the following is not within the class of foreseen users of an accountant's work product?

a. A shareholder of the client.

b. A lender bank when the accountant knows only that the client will use the financial statements to obtain a loan from an unspecified source.

c. A bank when the accountant knows the client will rely on the financial statements as the basis for a loan from the bank.

d. An investor if the accountant knows the client is seeking capital from a select group of investors.

The correct answer is (a). *(Publisher)*

REQUIRED: The user of an accountant's work product who is not a foreseen user.

DISCUSSION: Under the foreseen user (or foreseen class of users) test, the third parties who have standing to sue the accountant for ordinary negligence are those who the accountant knows will be given the work product and will rely thereon. This differs from the primary benefit test because the work product need not be produced primarily for the third party's benefit. Shareholders of a client are only foreseeable users; the accountant does not know in fact that they will use the work product.

Answers (b), (c), and (d) are incorrect because the accountant knows that each of these parties will use the work product. The bank in choice (b) and the investor in (d) are each within a foreseen class of users, and the bank in (c) is a specifically foreseen user.

25. Which is the broadest test under which a third party can recover from an accountant for fraud?

a. The intended beneficiary test.

b. The primary benefit test.

c. The foreseen user test.

d. The foreseeable user test.

The correct answer is (d). *(Publisher)*

REQUIRED: The test to determine whether a third party can recover from an accountant for fraud.

DISCUSSION: Because fraud entails moral turpitude, the courts permit all foreseeable users of an accountant's work product to bring suit. The distinctive feature of fraud is scienter, that is, intentional misrepresentation or a reckless disregard for the truth (sometimes found in gross negligence).

Answers (a) and (b) are incorrect because an intended beneficiary is one who acquires rights under the contract between the client and the accountant and can sue the accountant for ordinary negligence. The primary benefit (intended beneficiary) test is the narrowest used by courts to determine the identity of claimants. Answer (c) is incorrect because a foreseen class of users is less broad than the group of all foreseeable users.

Questions 26 and 27 are based on Brown & Co., CPAs which rendered an unqualified opinion on the financial statements of its client, King Corp. Based on the strength of King's financial statements, Safe Bank loaned King $500,000. Brown was unaware that Safe would receive a copy of the financial statements or that they would be used in obtaining a loan by King. King defaulted on the loan.

26. If Safe commences an action for negligence against Brown, and Brown is able to prove that it conducted the audit in conformity with GAAS, Brown will

a. Be liable to Safe because Safe relied on the financial statements.

b. Be liable to Safe because the Statute of Frauds has been satisfied.

c. Not be liable to Safe because there is a conclusive presumption that following GAAS is the equivalent of acting reasonably and with due care.

d. Not be liable to Safe because of a lack of privity of contract.

The correct answer is (d). *(CPA 1187 L-26)*

REQUIRED: The outcome of a negligence suit by a third party not belonging to a foreseen class of users.

DISCUSSION: The auditors could not be held liable for fraud or gross negligence because they followed GAAS. Gross negligence or fraud involves an intentional or reckless failure to exercise due care, but adherence to GAAS indicates at least a good faith effort to apply professional standards. Thus, the auditors are liable at most for ordinary negligence. In most jurisdictions, however, a party who is merely a foreseeable user and not 1) a foreseen user, 2) a member of a class of foreseen users, or 3) in privity of contract will have no standing to bring suit for ordinary negligence.

Answer (a) is incorrect because Safe's reliance is irrelevant. It was not within the class of parties to whom Brown owed a duty. Answer (b) is incorrect because the Statute of Frauds is not germane to this case. Answer (c) is incorrect because depending on the facts, adherence to GAAS may not be a complete defense.

27. If Safe commences an action for common law fraud against Brown, Safe must prove in addition to other elements that it

a. Was in privity of contract with Brown.

b. Was not contributorily negligent.

c. Was in privity of contract with King.

d. Justifiably relied on the financial statements.

The correct answer is (d). *(CPA 1187 L-27)*

REQUIRED: The element of a prima facie case of common law fraud.

DISCUSSION: The tort of intentional misrepresentation (fraud, deceit) consists of a material misrepresentation made with scienter and an intent to induce reliance. The misstatement must also have proximately caused damage to a defendant who reasonably relied upon it. Scienter exists when the defendant makes a false representation with knowledge of its falsity or with reckless disregard as to its truth.

Answers (a) and (c) are incorrect because Safe will have standing to bring an action based on fraud because it was a foreseeable third party. Privity is not required. Answer (b) is incorrect because contributory negligence is a defense to negligence, not fraud.

28. If a stockholder sues a CPA for common law fraud based on false statements contained in the financial statements audited by the CPA, which of the following, if present, would be the CPA's best defense?

a. The stockholder lacks privity to sue.

b. The false statements were immaterial.

c. The CPA did not financially benefit from the alleged fraud.

d. The contributory negligence of the client.

The correct answer is (b). *(CPA 589 L-2)*

REQUIRED: The best defense of a CPA sued for common law fraud by a third party.

DISCUSSION: To recover for the tort of fraud, a plaintiff must prove that the defendant made a misrepresentation, with knowledge that it was false or with a reckless disregard for the truth, with intent that it should be relied upon, and regarding a material fact that was actually relied upon by the third party to his/her detriment. Accordingly, the accountant would prevail by showing that the false statements were immaterial.

Answer (a) is incorrect because privity with the injured party is not an element of fraud. Answer (c) is incorrect because a benefit to the defendant is not an element of common law fraud. Answer (d) is incorrect because the negligence of a client does not exculpate a CPA from liability for intentional misconduct.

33.4 Liability to Third Parties: Securities Law

Questions 29 and 30 are based on West & Co., CPAs, which rendered an unqualified opinion on the financial statements of Pride Corp. These were included in Pride's registration statement filed with the SEC. Subsequently, Hex purchased 500 shares of Pride's preferred stock, which were acquired as part of a public offering subject to the Securities Act of 1933. Hex has commenced an action against West based on the Securities Act of 1933 for losses resulting from misstatements of facts in the financial statements included in the registration statement.

29. Which of the following elements must Hex prove to hold West liable?

a. West rendered its opinion with knowledge of material misstatements.

b. West performed the audit negligently.

c. Hex relied on the financial statements included in the registration statement.

d. The misstatements were material.

The correct answer is (d). *(CPA 1187 L-31)*

REQUIRED: The investor's burden of proof to recover losses from a CPA under the Securities Act of 1933.

DISCUSSION: Section 11 is the most frequently invoked basis for suit under the Securities Act of 1933. Under Section 11, the investor need only prove that (s)he suffered losses in a transaction involving the particular securities covered by the registration statement, and that the registration statement contained a false statement or an omission of a material fact for which the CPAs were responsible, e.g., in the audited financial statements. Unless rebutted, such proof is sufficient to prevail in the lawsuit.

Answer (a) is incorrect because scienter is not an element of a case brought under Section 11. Answer (b) is incorrect because the plaintiff need not show negligence, but the defendant may prevail by proving that it exercised due diligence. Answer (c) is incorrect because the plaintiff need not prove reliance, but the defendant can plead the plaintiff's knowledge of the misstatement or omission as a defense.

30. Which of the following defenses would be least helpful to West in avoiding liability to Hex?

a. West was not in privity of contract with Hex.

b. West conducted the audit in accordance with GAAS.

c. Hex's losses were caused by factors other than the misstatements.

d. Hex knew of the misstatements when Hex acquired the preferred stock.

The correct answer is (a). *(CPA 1187 L-32)*

REQUIRED: The defense least helpful to an accountant sued under the Securities Act of 1933.

DISCUSSION: Under Section 11, the plaintiff-purchaser of securities issued under a registration statement containing a misstatement or omission of a material fact need not prove either reliance or privity. Section 12, however, requires that both elements be proven and that the transaction involve interstate commerce or the mails. Section 12 applies to material misstatements or omissions in any communication made with respect to the offer or sale of a security. Privity under Section 12 has been broadly interpreted to include any act of the accountant that was a substantial factor in the investment decision, such as issuing an opinion on audited financial statements. Thus, even under Section 12, lack of privity of contract may not be a defense.

Answer (b) is incorrect because proof of adherence to GAAS and GAAP is the usual basis for a due diligence defense, i.e., that the accountant was not negligent. Answer (c) is incorrect because another possible defense is that the plaintiff's losses were the result of another's misstatements or omissions or by a widespread stock market decline. Answer (d) is incorrect because the plaintiff's knowledge at the time of purchase of the material misstatement or omission will defeat the claim.

31. One requirement of a private action to recover damages from a CPA for violation of the registration requirements of the Securities Act of 1933 is that

a. The plaintiff has acquired the securities in question.

b. The issuer or other defendants committed either negligence or fraud in the sale of the securities.

c. The plaintiff relied on the registration statement.

d. The securities were purchased from an underwriter.

The correct answer is (a). *(CPA 584 L-29)*

REQUIRED: The requirement for an individual to recover from a CPA under the Securities Act of 1933.

DISCUSSION: Auditors and other experts are liable for misstatements or omissions of material facts provided in registration statements under the Securities Act of 1933. A plaintiff establishes a prima facie case if (s)he proves that (s)he was a purchaser of a security issued under a registration statement that contains either a false statement or an omission of a material fact. Proof of the prima facie case shifts the burden of proof to the accountant who then must ordinarily show that (s)he has exercised due diligence in the preparation of the statements.

Answer (b) is incorrect because the plaintiff need not show negligence or fraud to recover. Answer (c) is incorrect because the plaintiff need not prove reliance. Answer (d) is incorrect because the securities could be purchased from anyone.

32. Gold, CPA rendered an unqualified opinion on the financial statements of Eastern Power Co. Egan purchased Eastern bonds in a public offering subject to the Securities Act of 1933. The registration statement filed with the SEC included the financial statements. Gold is being sued by Egan under Section 11 of the Securities Act of 1933 for the misstatements contained in the financial statements. To prevail, Egan must prove

	Scienter	Reliance
a.	No	No
b.	No	Yes
c.	Yes	No
d.	Yes	Yes

The correct answer is (a). *(CPA 589 L-10)*

REQUIRED: The element(s) of the plaintiff's case under Section 11.

DISCUSSION: The plaintiff's case has the following elements: The plaintiff purchased securities subject to a registration statement, the plaintiff suffered a loss, and a part of the registration statement for which the defendant was responsible contained a misstatement or omission of a material fact. Plaintiff and defendant need not have been in privity of contract, plaintiff need not have relied on the misstatement or omission, and the defendant need not have intended to deceive, manipulate, or defraud anyone.

Answer (b) is incorrect because reliance is not an element of the case. Answer (c) is incorrect because scienter is not an element of the case. Answer (d) is incorrect because neither scienter nor reliance must be shown.

33. Major, Major, & Sharpe, CPAs are the auditors of MacLain Industries. In connection with the public offering of $10 million of MacLain securities, Major expressed an unqualified opinion as to the financial statements. Subsequent to the offering, certain misstatements and omissions were revealed. Major has been sued by the purchasers of the stock offered pursuant to the registration statement that included the financial statements audited by Major. In the ensuing lawsuit by the MacLain investors, Major will be able to avoid liability if

a. The errors and omissions were caused primarily by MacLain.

b. It can be shown that at least some of the investors did not actually read the audited financial statements.

c. It can prove due diligence in the audit of the financial statements of MacLain.

d. MacLain had expressly assumed any liability in connection with the public offering.

The correct answer is (c). *(CPA 581 L-3)*

REQUIRED: The defense available to CPAs who provided audited financial statements that were included in a registration statement.

DISCUSSION: The Securities Act of 1933 imposes liability on CPAs for false statements or omissions of material facts in the portion of registration statements prepared or certified by the CPAs. A right of action exists on behalf of any purchaser of a security subject to such a registration statement who took without knowledge of the falsehood. However, proof of due diligence is sufficient to avoid liability. Auditors who have reasonable grounds for believing that there were no false statements or omissions of material facts would be able to assert the defense of due diligence.

Answer (a) is incorrect because that the errors and omissions were caused primarily by the auditee does not absolve Major of liability. The CPAs must still show that they acted with due diligence. Answer (b) is incorrect because the plaintiff in such actions need not prove reliance on the financial statements. Answer (d) is incorrect because MacLain's express assumption of liability does not absolve Major of liability with respect to third parties.

34. A CPA firm is being sued by a third party purchaser of securities sold in interstate commerce to the public. The third party is relying upon the Securities Act of 1933. The CPA firm had issued an unqualified opinion on incorrect financial statements. Which of the following represents the best defense available to the CPA firm?

a. The securities sold had not been registered with the SEC.

b. The CPA firm had returned the entire fee it charged for the engagement to the corporation.

c. The third party was not in privity of contract with the CPA firm.

d. The action had not been commenced within 1 year after the discovery of the material misrepresentation.

The correct answer is (d). *(CPA 1178 L-11)*

REQUIRED: The best defense available to a CPA firm sued by a purchaser of securities.

DISCUSSION: The statute of limitations on an action by a purchaser of securities relying on the Securities Act of 1933 is 1 year after the false statements or omissions of material fact were discovered or should have been discovered. The latest the suit may be brought is within 3 years after the security was first offered to the public.

Answer (a) is incorrect because unless either the transaction or the securities were exempt, securities sold in interstate commerce to the public are required to be registered; failure to do so is a serious legal violation and not a valid defense. Answer (b) is incorrect because a CPA firm is liable whether paid or not. Answer (c) is incorrect because privity of contract is not required under the Securities Act of 1933.

35. Hugh Gibson is suing Simpson & Sloan, CPAs to recover losses incurred in connection with Gibson's transactions in Zebra Corporation securities. Zebra's annual Form 10-K report contained material false and misleading statements in the financial statements audited by Simpson & Sloan. To recover under the Securities Exchange Act of 1934, Gibson must, among other things, establish that

a. All his past transactions in Zebra securities, both before and after the auditors' report, result in a net loss.

b. The transaction in Zebra securities that resulted in a loss occurred within 90 days of the auditors' report date.

c. He relied upon the financial statements in his decision to purchase or sell Zebra securities.

d. The market price of the stock dropped significantly after corrected financial statements were issued by Zebra.

The correct answer is (c). *(CPA 1183 L-8)*

REQUIRED: The plaintiff's burden of proof to recover for false or misleading information in an annual report filed with the SEC.

DISCUSSION: There are two bases for purchaser or seller of a security to sue an accountant under the 1934 Securities Act: Section 18(a) and Section 10(b). Both require the purchaser or seller of a security to prove reliance on the false or misleading statements. Section 18(a) imposes liability on accountants for misleading or false statements of material fact in reports or documents filed with the SEC, e.g., Form 10-K or the monthly Form 8-K, but the quarterly Form 10-Q, which includes unaudited statements, is excluded. The purchaser or seller must prove reliance, that the misleading or false information caused the damages, and that the security's price was affected. Section 10(b) is a broader provision that applies to purchase or sale of any security if the misleading or false statement of a material fact involves interstate commerce, the mails, or a national securities exchange.

Answer (a) is incorrect because Gibson need merely prove that a transaction resulted in a loss as a result of the audit report. Answer (b) is incorrect because there is no 90-day limit. Answer (d) is incorrect because issuance of corrected financial statements is unnecessary. However, plaintiff must prove that the price was affected.

36. In an action under Section 18(a) of the Securities Exchange Act of 1934 by an investor for misleading or false financial statements prepared by a CPA and included in a report filed with the SEC, a valid defense of the CPA is that

a. (S)he acted without scienter.

b. There is no privity.

c. More than 1 year has elapsed since the report was filed.

d. The investor did not prove negligence.

The correct answer is (a). *(Publisher)*

REQUIRED: The valid defense of a CPA sued under Section 18(a) of the 1934 Securities Act.

DISCUSSION: An accountant may avoid liability under Section 18(a) by proving (s)he acted in good faith and had no knowledge that the information was misleading or false, i.e., that (s)he acted without scienter. Negligence alone is not enough to establish liability under Section 18(a).

Answer (b) is incorrect because privity is not required under the 1934 Act. Answer (c) is incorrect because the applicable statute of limitations prohibits suit more than 1 year after discovery or 3 years after the violation occurred. Hence, the CPA might still be liable if suit is brought more than 1 year after filing. Answer (d) is incorrect because the investor is not required to prove negligence.

37. CPA prepared a Form 10-K for X Corporation. The report made a misleading statement with respect to a material fact. Which of the following statements is false?

a. Unlike the Securities Act of 1933, the 1934 Act placed the burden of proof on the investor to prove that (s)he relied on the statement.

b. The 1934 Act requires proof that the CPA made the misleading statement with the intent to deceive or defraud. Thus, the CPA's good faith is a valid defense under the 1934 Act.

c. The statute of limitations for the 1934 Act is the same as for the 1933 Act.

d. Mere negligence will create liability under both Acts.

The correct answer is (d). *(W. Schuster)*

REQUIRED: The false statement about a CPA's liability under the Securities Acts.

DISCUSSION: Section 18(a) of the 1934 Act is the provision applicable to misleading or false statements in reports to the SEC. It requires scienter on the CPA's part to hold the CPA civilly liable. Scienter is an intent to deceive, manipulate, or defraud. Thus, mere negligence is not sufficient for recovery under Section 18(a) of the 1934 Act. Under the 1933 Act, the plaintiff need not show reliance, privity, negligence, or scienter if a registration statement misstated or omitted a material fact.

Answer (a) is incorrect because the liability provisions of the 1934 Act do place a greater burden of proof on the plaintiff. Answer (b) is incorrect because the 1934 Act does require proof of scienter. Answer (c) is incorrect because each has a 1-year/3-year statute of limitations. Suit must be brought within 1 year of discovery of the violation but no later than 3 years after the violation occurred (Section 18 of the 1934 Act) or the securities were offered to the public (Section 11 of the 1933 Act) or sold (Section 12 of the 1933 Act).

38. Rule 10b-5 under Section 10(b) of the Securities Exchange Act of 1934 imposes liability on an accountant for violation of certain duties. Which of the following is an investor not required to prove to recover from a CPA?

a. The CPA made a misstatement or omission.

b. The CPA's misstatement or omission was material.

c. The investor relied on the CPA's work.

d. The price of the stock was affected.

The correct answer is (d). *(Publisher)*

REQUIRED: The element an investor need not prove under Rule 10b-5 to recover damages from a CPA.

DISCUSSION: A CPA can be held liable for a misstatement or omission of a material fact relied upon by a purchaser or seller of a security, provided the misconduct involves interstate commerce, the mails, or a national securities exchange. The intent to deceive, manipulate, or defraud (called scienter) must be shown in a private action under Rule 10b-5, and the wrongful act must have caused the plaintiff's damages. Unlike Section 18(a), however, Section 10(b) does not require the price of the stock to be affected. It is sufficient that the purchaser or seller would not have invested given correct or additional information and that (s)he was damaged in some way by investing.

Answers (a), (b) and (c) are incorrect because the purchaser or seller must prove each to recover.

39. West & Co., CPAs was engaged by Sand Corp. to audit its financial statements. West issued an unqualified opinion on Sand's financial statements. Sand has been accused of making negligent misrepresentations in the financial statements that Reed relied upon when purchasing Sand stock. West was not aware of the misrepresentations and was not negligent in performing the audit. If Reed sues West for damages based upon Section 10(b) and Rule 10b-5 of the Securities Exchange Act of 1934, West will

a. Lose, because the statements contained negligent misrepresentations.

b. Lose, because Reed relied upon the financial statements.

c. Prevail, because some element of scienter must be proved.

d. Prevail, because Reed was not in privity of contract with West.

The correct answer is (c). *(CPA 588 L-8)*

REQUIRED: The outcome of a suit under Rule 10b-5 against nonnegligent accountants who were unaware of misrepresentations.

DISCUSSION: Rule 10b-5 is an antifraud provision that requires proof of scienter, that is, of an intent to deceive, manipulate, or defraud. In this context, even gross negligence probably does not satisfy the scienter requirement, although some courts have held that it does if the accountants had a fiduciary duty (such as that owed to a client) to the plaintiff. Thus, Reed cannot prove scienter, and West will prevail.

Answer (a) is incorrect because West was not negligent. Moreover, mere negligence is not a basis for recovery under Rule 10b-5. Answer (b) is incorrect because Reed must prove scienter as well as reliance. Answer (d) is incorrect because the class of plaintiffs is much broader than those in privity of contract.

40. Burt, CPA issued an unqualified opinion on the financial statements of Midwest Corp. These financial statements were included in Midwest's annual report and Form 10-K filed with the SEC. As a result of Burt's reckless disregard for GAAS, material misstatements in the financial statements were not detected. Subsequently, Davis purchased stock in Midwest in the secondary market without ever seeing Midwest's annual report or Form 10-K. Shortly thereafter, Midwest became insolvent and the price of the stock declined drastically. Davis sued Burt for damages based on Section 10(b) and Rule 10b-5 of the Securities Exchange Act of 1934. Burt's best defense is that

a. There has been no subsequent sale for which a loss can be computed.

b. Davis did not purchase the stock as part of an initial offering.

c. Davis did not rely on the financial statements or Form 10-K.

d. Davis was not in privity with Burt.

The correct answer is (c). *(CPA 589 L-8)*

REQUIRED: The best defense of a grossly negligent accountant sued under Rule 10b-5.

DISCUSSION: The plaintiff must have relied on the misstatement or omission of a material fact with regard to the purchase or sale of a security if (s)he is to recover under Rule 10b-5. In the case of an omission, reliance is implied by materiality. Davis did not see the relevant annual report or Form 10-K and will therefore have difficulty in proving reliance. Also, Burt's reckless disregard for GAAS may not satisfy the scienter requirement for Rule 10b-5 purposes. An actual intent to deceive, manipulate, or defraud is necessary.

Answer (a) is incorrect because damages may be proven without a subsequent sale. Answer (b) is incorrect because Rule 10b-5 applies to a misstatement or omission of a material fact in connection with any purchase or sale of a security if the wrongful act involved interstate commerce, the mails, or a national securities exchange. Answer (d) is incorrect because privity is not required.

41. Which statement is correct concerning an auditor's statutory legal liability?

a. The Securities Act of 1933 broadened the auditor's common law liability and the Securities Exchange Act of 1934 narrowed it.

b. The auditor has a greater burden of defense under the Securities Act of 1933 than under the Securities Exchange Act of 1934.

c. Criminal liability only arises under state law.

d. Statutory liability usually modifies the auditor's liability to the client.

The correct answer is (b). *(Publisher)*

REQUIRED: The correct statement concerning an auditor's statutory liability.

DISCUSSION: Under the 1933 Act, a purchaser need only prove damages resulting from the purchase of securities covered by a registration statement containing a false statement or omission of a material fact in a section audited or prepared by the auditor. The auditor must then prove that (s)he was not negligent (or fraudulent), usually by showing that (s)he acted with "due diligence." Under the 1934 Act, a purchaser or seller must prove that (s)he did not know of the misstatement or omission, that (s)he relied on it, and that the auditor acted with intent to defraud, manipulate, or defraud.

Answer (a) is incorrect because both statutes impose liability for conduct not previously actionable under the common law, although the 1934 Act places a greater burden of proof on the plaintiff than the 1933 Act. Answer (c) is incorrect because criminal liability can also arise under federal securities law. Answer (d) is incorrect because statutes usually modify the auditor's liability to third parties. The auditor's liability to clients remains contractual.

42. A CPA is subject to criminal liability

a. Under the 1933 Act but not the 1934 Act.

b. For performing an audit in a negligent manner.

c. For willfully omitting a material fact required to be stated in a registration statement.

d. For willfully breaching the contract with the client.

The correct answer is (c). *(CPA 1171 L-1)*

REQUIRED: The basis for a CPA's criminal liability.

DISCUSSION: Under the Securities Act of 1933, any person who willfully makes a false statement or omits a material fact required in a registration statement is subject to criminal liability with a maximum fine of $10,000 and/or up to 5 years of imprisonment.

Answer (a) is incorrect because a CPA can be criminally liable under either the 1933 or the 1934 Act. The 1934 Act is frequently used to impose criminal liability on a CPA. A CPA can be subject to a maximum fine of $100,000 and/or up to 5 years of imprisonment under the 1934 Act. Answers (b) and (d) are incorrect because neither is a criminal act. A tort, such as negligence, is the violation of a civil duty imposed by the law. A breach of contract is a violation of a civil duty created by agreement.

43. Which of the following best describes a trend in litigation involving CPAs?

a. Common law is being used more as a result of the difficulty of suing under the securities laws.

b. There are substantially more lawsuits filed against CPAs and larger judgments against them.

c. They are being held criminally liable less frequently.

d. State laws are rarely used any more because of the existence of the SEC.

The correct answer is (b). *(Publisher)*

REQUIRED: The trend in litigation involving CPAs.

DISCUSSION: The number of lawsuits filed against CPAs has substantially increased, in part because of a general awareness of an auditor's exposure to liability. The judgments against CPAs have also been much larger, making it even more important for a CPA to exercise due diligence in his/her work.

Answer (a) is incorrect because securities laws rather than common law have been used more frequently in recent years. Answer (c) is incorrect because criminal sentences are now being applied more frequently. Answer (d) is incorrect because state laws are also being used more frequently to hold CPAs liable.

33.5 Working Papers and Accountant-Client Privilege

44. Working papers prepared by a CPA in connection with an audit engagement are owned by the CPA, subject to certain limitations. The rationale for this rule is to

a. Protect the working papers from being subpoenaed.

b. Provide the basis for excluding admission of the working papers as evidence because of the privileged communication rule.

c. Provide the CPA with evidence and documentation that may be helpful in the event of a lawsuit.

d. Establish a continuity of relationship with the client whereby indiscriminate replacement of CPAs is discouraged.

The correct answer is (c). *(CPA 1183 L-10)*

REQUIRED: The rationale for the rule that working papers are owned by the CPA.

DISCUSSION: The working papers of an accountant are records made during an audit. They include audit plans, evidence of testing, explanations, reconciliations, and comments about the client's accounting system. In the event of a lawsuit, this information supports a CPA's work and results.

Answers (a) and (b) are incorrect because the working papers are not privileged in most jurisdictions and can be subpoenaed by a court. Answer (d) is incorrect because although the working papers are useful to a CPA in a subsequent year's audit, no policy exists to discourage replacement of CPAs. In any event, the client has a right of access to the working papers.

45. In general, which of the following statements is correct with respect to ownership, possession, or access to working papers prepared by a CPA firm in connection with an audit?

a. The working papers may be obtained by third parties if they appear to be relevant to issues raised in litigation.

b. The working papers are subject to the privileged communication rule, which, in a majority of jurisdictions, prevents third-party access to the working papers.

c. The working papers are the property of the client after the client pays the fee.

d. The working papers must be retained by the CPA firm for a period of 10 years.

The correct answer is (a). *(CPA 1186 L-9)*

REQUIRED: The true statement about a CPA's working papers.

DISCUSSION: The accountant's working papers are owned by the accountant, unless an agreement exists to the contrary. Nevertheless, they can be subpoenaed (compelled to be produced) for use in litigation except in states that recognize a statutory accountant-client testimonial privilege. Even in those states, however, they may be obtained if the client consents. The privilege is not deemed to belong to the accountant but to the client.

Answer (b) is incorrect because the privileged communication rule does not exist at common law and has been created by statute in a minority of states. Also, this rule only applies to communications that were intended to be privileged at the time of communication. Answer (c) is incorrect because the working papers are the property of the CPA unless an agreement exists to the contrary. But the client has a right of access. Answer (d) is incorrect because the working papers should be retained by the accountant to serve as evidence as to the nature and extent of work performed at least for the duration of the statute of limitations in the relevant jurisdiction. Statutes vary, but none would be for as long as 10 years. Moreover, CPAs are not legally required to retain working papers but should do so for obvious reasons.

46. For what minimum period should audit working papers be retained by the independent CPA?

a. For the period during which the entity remains a client of the independent CPA.

b. For the period during which an auditor-client relationship exists but not more than 6 years.

c. For the statutory period within which legal action may be brought against the independent CPA.

d. For as long as the CPA is in public practice.

The correct answer is (c). *(CPA 576 A-13)*

REQUIRED: The minimum period that audit working papers must be retained by a CPA.

DISCUSSION: Audit working papers should be retained by a CPA for the statutory period within which legal action may be brought against the CPA, i.e., the period of the statute of limitations. State and federal statutes specify the period of time within which legal action must be initiated to hold a CPA liable. The auditor may find it beneficial to retain working papers for a longer period, however.

Answers (a) and (b) are incorrect because the continuing client relationship is not determinative. The statute of limitations may be longer, but usually is not as long as 6 years. Answer (d) is incorrect because the life of the CPA's public practice may be extremely long, or it may be shorter than the statute of limitations.

47. The CPA firm of Knox & Knox has been subpoenaed to testify and produce its correspondence and working papers in connection with a lawsuit brought by a third party against one of its clients. Knox considers the subpoenaed documents to be privileged communication and therefore seeks to avoid admission of such evidence in the lawsuit. Which of the following is correct?

a. Federal law recognizes such a privilege if the accountant is a CPA.

b. The privilege is available regarding the working papers because the CPA is deemed to own them.

c. The privileged communication rule as it applies to the CPA-client relationship is the same as that of attorney-client.

d. In the absence of a specific statutory provision, the law does not recognize the existence of the privileged communication rule between CPA and client.

The correct answer is (d). *(CPA 581 L-2)*

REQUIRED: The correct statement concerning the accountant-client privilege.

DISCUSSION: Although communication between lawyers and clients is privileged, no common law concept extends this privilege to the accountant-client. However, some but not the majority of states have enacted statutes recognizing the privilege of communication to be confidential between an accountant and client.

Answer (a) is incorrect because there is no such federal law. Answer (b) is incorrect because although the working papers are the CPA's property, the privilege does not extend to them unless a state statute so provides. Answer (c) is incorrect because even statutes providing for an accountant-client privilege are not usually as extensive as legal principles establishing the lawyer-client privilege. Frequently, for example, an accountant may not refuse to disclose the information if the client consents.

48. With respect to privileged communications of accountants, which of the following is correct?

a. A state statutory privilege will be recognized in a case being tried in a federal court involving a federal question.

b. Most courts recognize a common-law privilege between an accountant and the client.

c. As a result of legislative enactment and court adoption, the client-accountant privilege is recognized in the majority of jurisdictions.

d. The privilege will be lost if the party asserting the privilege voluntarily submits part of the privileged communications into evidence.

The correct answer is (d). *(CPA 1183 L-9)*

REQUIRED: The correct statement concerning privileged accountant-client communications.

DISCUSSION: When the accountant-client privileged communication rule exists (if a state's statutes so provide), it is lost if any part of the privileged communication is voluntarily submitted. The privileged communication rule is technical and must be adhered to strictly.

Answer (a) is incorrect because even if there is a state statutory privilege, the federal courts do not recognize it if the issue involves a federal question, e.g., taxes or federal securities laws. Answer (b) is incorrect because there is no common law privilege of communication between an accountant and a client. Answer (c) is incorrect because only in a minority of jurisdictions have statutes been enacted recognizing the privilege.

49. If a CPA is engaged by an attorney to assist in the defense of a tax fraud case involving the attorney's client, information obtained by the CPA from the client after being engaged

a. Is not privileged because the matter involves a federal issue.

b. Is not privileged in jurisdictions that do not recognize an accountant-client privilege.

c. Will be deemed privileged communications under certain circumstances.

d. Will be deemed privileged communications provided that the CPA prepared the client's tax return.

The correct answer is (c). *(CPA 1187 L-35)*

REQUIRED: The status of information obtained from an attorney's client by a CPA retained to assist in a tax fraud case.

DISCUSSION: The attorney-client privilege would protect the information. The defendant is the client of the attorney, and the CPA is the agent of the attorney. Hence, communications between the CPA and the defendant are, in effect, between the attorney and the defendant. However, if the defendant is the CPA's client, their communications will not be privileged unless the case involves a state tax matter in a jurisdiction that has enacted a statute protecting accountant-client communications.

Answer (a) is incorrect because federal courts recognize the attorney-client privilege even if a federal question is at issue. Answer (b) is incorrect because the attorney-client privilege protects this information. Answer (d) is incorrect because no accountant-client privilege is recognized regarding federal tax returns.

50. A CPA is permitted to disclose confidential client information without the consent of the client to

I. Another CPA who has purchased the CPA's tax practice.
II. A successor CPA firm if the information concerns suspected tax return irregularities.
III. A voluntary quality control review board.

a. I and III only.

b. II and III only.

c. II only.

d. III only.

The correct answer is (d). *(CPA 589 L-5)*

REQUIRED: The accountant's permitted disclosure(s) without the client's consent.

DISCUSSION: The AICPA Code of Professional Conduct (Rule 301) states that a member shall not disclose any confidential client information except with the specific consent of the client. But this rule should not be understood to preclude a CPA from responding to an inquiry made by an investigative body of a state CPA society, the trial board of the AICPA, or an AICPA or state quality review body, or pursuant to a validly issued and enforceable subpoena.

Answer (a) is incorrect because no exception to Rule 301 permits disclosure to a successor CPA. Answers (b) and (c) are incorrect because in the case of tax irregularities, the AICPA has ruled that the predecessor auditor may, if contacted by the successor, suggest that the successor ask the client for consent to discuss all matters freely with the predecessor. The AICPA also recommends that the predecessor seek legal advice. However, this Ethics Ruling stops short of permitting unconsented to disclosure.

CHAPTER THIRTY-FOUR
COMPUTER LAW

34.1 Nature of Computer Law

1. Which of the following is a true statement about the scope and origin of computer law?

a. Computer law is a distinct body of law that has evolved over the last 40 years from court cases involving computers.

b. Invasion of privacy involving computers is a constitutional issue rather than a computer law issue.

c. The introduction of fraudulent data into a computer system but not the copying of micro-computer software is a crime.

d. Computer law uses principles and precedents from other areas of law rather than relying only on court cases involving computers.

The correct answer is (d). *(Publisher)*

REQUIRED: The true statement about computer law.

DISCUSSION: Computer law began to evolve with court cases involving the earliest computers, but the courts have usually relied on principles from other areas of law, such as contracts, warranty, torts, intellectual property, and statutory protection of privacy, in rendering decisions in cases involving computers.

Answer (a) is incorrect because computer law is not a distinct body of law but instead relies on principles and precedents from other areas of law. Answer (b) is incorrect because invasion of privacy using a computer is both a constitutional and computer law issue. Answer (c) is incorrect because introducing fraudulent data into a computer system and unauthorized duplication of copyrighted material could be criminal acts.

Questions 2 and 3 are based on Hacker Corporation, which sold Micro International its Hacker Operating System (HOS) for Micro's new line of personal computers. Hacker's president and several of its key programmers all started their careers at Micro. Unbeknownst to Micro, Hacker developed HOS from proprietary information obtained from Micro while Hacker's founder and programmers were employed there. Micro sold HOS bundled with its new computers to several thousand customers. On Valentine's Day 1991, a Trojan horse program embedded in HOS's code was executed on all computers running HOS. The program rendered all of the programs, data, and files on these computers' hard disks unusable. For these two questions, assume that the transactions between all of the parties were transactions in goods.

---

2. What is Hacker's potential liability to Micro and third parties in regard to these facts?

	Economic Losses	Personal Injury	Punitive Damages
a.	Yes	Yes	Yes
b.	Yes	No	No
c.	No	Yes	No
d.	No	No	No

The correct answer is (a). *(Publisher)*

REQUIRED: The liability by a software developer for damages resulting from the use of the software.

DISCUSSION: Hacker would be liable under the UCC for economic losses for breach of implied warranty of merchantability because the destruction of customers' data implies HOS was not fit for the ordinary purpose for which it was intended. If HOS were the proximate cause of the malfunction of computer operated equipment that injured employees, customers, or innocent bystanders, Hacker would be liable in tort for those personal injuries as well as any economic losses. If the Trojan horse program were intentionally embedded in HOS by Hacker's personnel, Hacker would be liable for punitive damages as well as economic loss and personal injury.

Answers (b), (c), and (d) are incorrect because Hacker could be liable for economic losses, personal injury, and punitive damages.

3. Refer to the data presented on page 749. Micro's proprietary information used by Hacker and its programmers is

a. Micro's intellectual property. Micro is entitled to damages from Hacker for Hacker's unauthorized use of that information.

b. Hacker's intellectual property if Hacker's programmers developed it while at Micro but Micro did not obtain a copyright.

c. The programmers' intellectual property if they created it.

d. Not the property of Micro, Hacker, or the programmers. Courts will not interfere with individual computer users' copying of software.

The correct answer is (a). *(Publisher)*

REQUIRED: The rightful owner(s) of Micro's proprietary information.

DISCUSSION: Although the programmers' employment contracts could state otherwise, Micro probably owns the proprietary information and is entitled to any profits Hacker made with the use of that information. Typically, a programmer's employment contract includes a clause stating that the employer retains ownership of any code, algorithms, and graphic representations the programmer creates during his/her term of employment.

Answers (b) and (c) are incorrect because Micro may have retained ownership rights to any code written by the programmers while employed by Micro. Answer (d) is incorrect because whether courts interfere with illegal copying of software by end-users is irrelevant. Ownership of intellectual property has a long tradition in patent and copyright law. Depending on the programmers' employment contracts with Micro and Hacker, any of the three could own the proprietary information in question.

34.2 Computer Law Under the UCC and Common Law

4. Longhorn Chips, Inc. sold add-on computer graphic boards to several thousand corporate mail-order buyers. Some of the customers found that Longhorn's boards actually degraded the graphics quality of their computer screens. Do buyers have rights under the UCC, or will they have to proceed under contract law in an action against Longhorn?

a. Buyers have rights under the UCC because the courts consider the sale of computer hardware to be the sale of services.

b. Buyers have rights under both the UCC and contract law and may proceed against Longhorn on either basis.

c. Buyers have no rights under the UCC and only limited rights under contract law because of the doctrine of caveat emptor.

d. Buyers have no rights to proceed against Longhorn because of bold disclaimers of liability included with every board.

The correct answer is (b). *(Publisher)*

REQUIRED: The applicability of the UCC and contract law in a transaction involving computer hardware.

DISCUSSION: In cases involving the sale of computer hardware only, the courts have held that the transaction is a sale of goods. As a sale of goods, the transaction falls under Article 2 of the UCC. Under the UCC, the buyer has more protection than under common law. Thus, the buyers may proceed against Longhorn on either basis, but proceeding under the UCC would be more advantageous.

Answer (a) is incorrect because although the buyers have rights under the UCC, hardware items are considered goods, not services. Article 2 of the UCC applies to sales of goods but not services. Answer (c) is incorrect because although the buyers do have only limited rights under contract law under the doctrine of caveat emptor (let the buyer beware), they do have rights under the UCC. Answer (d) is incorrect because the courts may hold that Longhorn's disclaimer is an adhesion contract if the buyers had no opportunity to bargain over the terms of the disclaimer. The disclaimer may therefore not be enforceable if the result is unconscionable.

5. Hightech, Inc. sells several lines of computer-related products. Its product line includes a bundled package of hardware and software, mass-produced application software, and specialized, custom accounting software. With regard to these products, Hightech will be liable under Article 2 of the UCC or common law based on whether the products sold are considered goods or services. If the hardware is relatively more expensive than the software, are Hightech's products goods or services?

	Bundled Package	Mass-produced Application Software	Specialized Custom Software
a.	Goods	Goods	Goods
b.	Both goods and services	Services	Goods
c.	Goods	Services	Goods
d.	Goods	Goods	Services

The correct answer is (d). *(Publisher)*

REQUIRED: The proper classification of computer products as goods or services.

DISCUSSION: When computer products are bundled and sold, courts have held that those transactions involve goods, not services. In making that decision, some courts have considered the relative costs of the hardware and software in determining the parties' intentions. Also, mass-produced software is most likely to be considered goods, but specialized custom software is usually considered a service.

Answer (a) is incorrect because whereas a bundled package and mass-produced software are considered goods, specialized software is considered a service because it is usually the result of services provided by a consultant. Answers (b) and (c) are incorrect because bundled software is not a service. Mass-produced software is usually considered a good and specialized software is considered a service.

6. In 1966, State U. leased a mainframe computer and specialized software for maintaining student records from Monolith, Inc. The lease agreement specifically stated that Monolith would be held blameless for damages caused by the University's negligence. In 1990, an unknown student accessed State U.'s computer system and changed students' records. The student was able to access the system because the old mainframe had been networked to all of the other computers on campus. Several students were denied jobs, loans, and scholarships because of erroneous grade reports. State U. seeks to hold Monolith liable for damages. Who will prevail?

a. State U. will most likely prevail because the transaction with Monolith was a sale.

b. State U. will prevail because Monolith's disclaimer is an exculpatory clause.

c. Monolith will prevail if a third-party vendor connected the mainframe to the network.

d. Monolith will not prevail because the cost of the software far exceeded the cost of the hardware.

The correct answer is (c). *(Publisher)*

REQUIRED: The party that will prevail in an action by the lessee of a bundled computer package against the lessor.

DISCUSSION: Monolith will win if the damages were the result of the negligence of State U. in allowing a third party to network the computers in a way that permitted the security breach. Additionally, if the transaction involved the failure of specialized software rather than Monolith's hardware, State U. will probably have to proceed under common law, not the UCC, and Monolith will most likely prevail.

Answers (a) and (d) are incorrect because State U. will most likely not prevail. If the cost of the software exceeds the cost of the hardware, the transaction will be considered a sale of services, not goods. In that event, State U. must proceed under common law, which favors sellers. Answer (b) is incorrect because Monolith's disclaimer is not an exculpatory clause. In 1966, State U. probably had the power to bargain concerning the clause.

7. Which of the following statements is false regarding the doctrine of unconscionability as applied to computer law?

a. Computer transactions fall under the doctrine of unconscionability because of the equal bargaining power of the parties in forming the agreement.

b. Clauses in contracts for the sale of computer products that disclaim all liability of the seller will probably be found unconscionable if the parties had unequal bargaining power when the contract was formed.

c. Contracts that are found to be unconscionable could be considered adhesion contracts.

d. The doctrine of unconscionability first appeared in the UCC rather than in common law.

The correct answer is (a). *(Publisher)*

REQUIRED: The false statement about the doctrine of unconscionability as applied to computer law.

DISCUSSION: The courts will consider a clause in a contract unconscionable when one of the parties is unjustly injured by the clause, and the parties had unequal bargaining power when the contract was formed. Buyers of computer products typically have little bargaining power relative to sellers of computer products. When this is the case, courts are likely to find a clause that limits sellers' liability to be unconscionable. If the parties have equal bargaining power, the doctrine does not apply.

Answers (b), (c), and (d) are incorrect because they are true statements about the doctrine of unconscionability and computer law.

34.3 Intellectual Property

8. Intellectual property embodied in computer hardware and/or software may be protected via

	Patent Law	Copyright Law	Trade Secret Protection
a.	No	No	No
b.	Yes	No	Yes
c.	Yes	Yes	Yes
d.	No	No	Yes

The correct answer is (c). *(Publisher)*

REQUIRED: The area(s) of law applicable to intellectual property embodied in computer hardware and/or software.

DISCUSSION: To be patentable, the subject matter must be a process, a machine, or a composition of matter. Additionally, the subject matter of the patent must have utility, be a novelty, be nonobvious, and be adequately disclosed. Clearly, computer hardware is patentable. However, the courts have given protection to software under the copyright laws as the expression of an idea, not the idea itself. Finally, hardware or software not patentable or copyrightable may be protected as a trade secret.

Answers (a), (b), and (d) are all incorrect because computer hardware is patentable, computer software is copyrightable, and both may be protected as trade secrets.

9. Has the right of software developers to protect their computer programs against copyright infringement been settled?

a. Yes. Under the Computer Software Copyright Act of 1980, which amended the Copyright Act of 1976, computer programs and databases are copyrightable.

b. Yes. Recent court cases have held that software is copyrightable when it is an integral part of a computer system.

c. Yes. Widespread copying of software has rendered copyright infringement of that software a moot issue.

d. No. Several landmark court cases remain unsettled, thereby casting doubt on the copyrightability of software.

The correct answer is (a). *(Publisher)*

REQUIRED: The applicability of the copyright laws to computer software.

DISCUSSION: The Computer Software Copyright Act of 1980 specifically allows the copyright of computer software for the expression of ideas but not the ideas themselves. The coding of the software, whether or not human-readable, is copyrightable, but distinguishing the idea or concept from its expression may be difficult. Thus, whether the structure or organization of software can be protected is a question still being litigated.

Answer (b) is incorrect because courts have held that a computer system that includes software is patentable, not copyrightable. Answer (c) is incorrect because whether copying of software is widespread is irrelevant. The holder of a copyright for computer software has standing to bring an infringement suit against those who use his/her copyrighted material without permission or payment of royalties. Answer (d) is incorrect because although many computer software cases remain unresolved, the 1980 Act gives specific statutory copyright protection to software meeting its requirements.

10. Orange Computers, Inc. is a supplier of microcomputers to citrus growers in Florida. Orange's system, the Valencia, requires a proprietary operating system developed exclusively by Orange for the Valencia. In 1986, Orange patented its hardware and copyrighted the operating system. In 1987, Washington Computers purchased a Valencia system and used reverse engineering to duplicate it. In 1988, Washington began offering a microcomputer system called the Cherry to northern fruit growers. Washington admits the Cherry is a 100% clone of the Valencia and that the operating system is an exact copy of Orange's proprietary system. In 1989, Orange commenced an action against Washington for copyright and patent infringement. Who will prevail?

a. Washington will prevail because individual computer hardware components are patentable, but complete computers are not.

b. Washington will prevail because the operating system is stored as object code in ROM and is not copyrightable.

c. Orange will prevail because it holds a patent on the hardware and copyright on the operating system.

d. The outcome is indeterminable.

The correct answer is (c). *(Publisher)*

REQUIRED: The status of patent and copyright laws when computer hardware and software are the subject matter.

DISCUSSION: Computer hardware is patentable if the subject matter is a process, machine, or composition of matter. Additionally, it must provide utility, have novelty, and not be obvious. Clearly, Orange's Valencia could meet these conditions. Furthermore, the courts have ruled that the expression of ideas in operating software is copyrightable. If Orange has complied with all statutory filings and disclosures, it will most likely prevail against Washington for patent and copyright infringement.

Answer (a) is incorrect because complete computers are patentable. Answer (b) is incorrect because the courts have ruled that operating systems are copyrightable even if stored as object code in ROM. Also, courts have held that software that is an integral part of a system is patentable. Answer (d) is incorrect because the outcome is clear.

11. Which of the following is a true statement about the merits of the protection offered by these bodies of law? Computer products may be subject to the law of patents, copyrights, or trade secrets.

a. Once granted, the patent is good for the life of the inventor plus 50 years.

b. Copyright law permits ideas to be protected, not expressions of those ideas.

c. Trade secrets must be registered as either a patent or a copyright.

d. Trade secrets have perpetual life until honestly discovered by others, and they require no public filings or disclosure.

The correct answer is (d). *(Publisher)*

REQUIRED: The true statement about the protection of intellectual property.

DISCUSSION: Information is a trade secret if the information gives its owner an advantage, is a protected secret, has value, and is not easily discovered by others. A trade secret has a longer potential life than patents or copyrights, which are limited to 17 years or 50 years plus the author's life, respectively. A trade secret will be protected until honest discovery by another. Moreover, no public filings or disclosures are required for trade secrets.

Answer (a) is incorrect because a patent is good for 17 years. Answer (b) is incorrect because copyrights protect the expression of ideas, not the ideas themselves. Answer (c) is incorrect because trade secrets do not have to be registered.

12. When Steve Zowik was employed at Iron Copiers, he acquired information about a graphical user interface (GUI) that Iron's scientists had invented. Zowik's employment contract did not bind him to secrecy regarding Iron's trade secrets. Furthermore, Iron's top management thought the GUI was of no use to Iron's customers and made no attempt to keep the GUI secret. Zowik left Iron's employ and became partners with Steve Work. Together, they designed, manufactured, and marketed a microcomputer based on Iron's GUI. Iron was aware of Zowik and Work's use of the GUI but again dismissed it as having no business value. Ten years later, revenues of Zowik and Work's microcomputer company exceeded those of Iron. Iron has filed suit against Zowik and Work for unauthorized use of Iron's trade secrets. Who will prevail?

a. Zowik and Work will prevail if Zowik secretly copyrighted the GUI while still employed by Iron.

b. Zowik and Work will prevail because Iron's actions preclude the GUI from being considered a trade secret.

c. Iron will prevail because an invention that is not patented or copyrighted is still protected as a trade secret.

d. Zowik and Work because GUIs are considered ideas, not expressions of ideas, and therefore cannot be trade secrets.

The correct answer is (b). *(Publisher)*

REQUIRED: The outcome and the reason therefor in an action for unauthorized use of trade secrets.

DISCUSSION: The GUI could have been a trade secret for Iron because it was invented by its scientists. Also, Zowik and Work proved that the GUI could provide a competitive advantage. But Iron made no attempt to keep the GUI a secret, Zowik was not bound by his employment contract to keep it a secret, and Iron's top management showed no interest in the GUI. Thus, it was not a trade secret. Because the GUI is not Iron's trade secret and Iron neither patented nor copyrighted it, Iron has no grounds for damages. Zowik and Work will prevail.

Answer (a) is incorrect because if Zowik secretly copyrighted the GUI, he would be liable for breach of duty to his employer. Answer (c) is incorrect because if something is not patented or copyrighted, it is not automatically a trade secret. Answer (d) is incorrect because GUIs are expressions of ideas, not the ideas themselves, and they can be trade secrets.

34.4 Computer Product Liability

13. If a transaction involving computer products is considered a sale of goods, the UCC applies and

a. The seller may be liable for consequential damages even if the contract had an express exclusion of such damages.

b. The agreement of the parties to limit the buyer's remedies will be ineffective.

c. The seller is more likely to prevail because the UCC favors sellers rather than buyers.

d. The implied warranty of fitness for a particular purpose will protect the seller.

The correct answer is (a). *(Publisher)*

REQUIRED: The seller's liability under the UCC for a transaction in computer products.

DISCUSSION: Under the UCC, a seller of goods is liable for economic losses resulting from breach of express and implied warranties. However, an exclusion of the seller's liability for consequential damages may be rendered invalid if it is unconscionable (UCC 2-719). Thus, a seller may be liable for consequential damages despite the terms of the contract.

Answer (b) is incorrect because a contractual modification or limitation of remedies is effective unless the circumstances cause an exclusive or limited remedy to fail of its essential purpose. Answer (c) is incorrect because buyers are favored under the UCC, not sellers. Answer (d) is incorrect because an implied warranty of fitness for a particular purpose protects buyers, not sellers.

14. Mobley Budweiser contracted with International Scientific Machines (ISM) to purchase 100 PS/3 microcomputers and related operating system software for State U. Mobley entered the agreement based on representations made by Skip Jones, ISM's sales representative. Skip claimed the computers would run an advanced operating system that ISM planned to market. The contract between State U. and ISM included a standard integration clause but was silent as to the advanced operating system. Shortly after the computers were delivered and paid for, ISM introduced the new system, which State U. soon learned was incompatible with its PS/3s without substantial additional investment in hardware. Mobley and State U. considered Skip Jones's representations part of the agreement and brought an action against ISM for damages. Is ISM liable?

a. ISM is liable because Jones's representations were included in the contract by the integration clause.

b. ISM is liable because Jones's action was fraudulent.

c. ISM is not liable because a salesperson's representations are excluded from sales contracts unless expressly included.

d. ISM is not liable because the parol evidence rule excludes prior statements if the contract is fully integrated.

The correct answer is (d). *(Publisher)*

REQUIRED: The liability of a seller of computer products for prior representations by its agent if the agreement has an integration clause.

DISCUSSION: The clause indicates that the contract is meant to be complete, that is, to embody the entire understanding of the parties. Thus, the parol evidence rule will apply. It bars evidence of prior agreements or of contemporaneous oral agreements that would vary, alter, or contradict the terms of a written contract intended to be entire. Consequently, ISM will not be liable because evidence of Jones's representations is inadmissible.

Answer (a) is incorrect because an integration clause excludes rather than includes prior agreements. Answer (b) is incorrect because no evidence is given that the elements of fraud are present. Answer (c) is incorrect because in the absence of an integration clause, these representations may be included in sales contracts unless expressly excluded.

15. Bill Galant purchased a car from Smith Motors that was financed by Smith's bank. Galant made monthly payments on time and for the amount specified in the financing agreement. The contract called for 48 monthly payments. Six months later, the bank contacted Galant by mail to give notice of default. Galant replied in writing that he had made the first six payments on time and had the check stubs to prove it. A week later the bank physically repossessed the car. Galant has sued the bank for compensatory and punitive damages. The bank later admitted that the repossession was a computer error made by an outside computer service bureau. The bank relied solely on the representations of the service bureau. The bank is potentially liable for

	Compensatory Damages	Punitive Damages
a.	No	Yes
b.	Yes	Yes
c.	Yes	No
d.	No	No

The correct answer is (b). *(Publisher)*

REQUIRED: The creditor's liability for a computer error made by an outside computer service bureau.

DISCUSSION: The bank is certainly liable for compensatory damages because it was negligent for not ascertaining for itself whether Galant had made his payments according to the financing agreement. Because the bank relied solely on the report of the outside service bureau, it is probably liable for gross negligence, which would subject it to liability for punitive damages as well. Computer errors beyond the control of users do not excuse the users from liability for the damages caused.

Answers (a), (c), and (d) are incorrect because the bank is potentially liable for both compensatory and punitive damages.

16. Leah Laserbones, MD purchased a computer system from Medchips, Inc. The system reduces hospital stays by allowing early release of patients. The patients go home where a Medchips computer continuously monitors their vital signs. This information is transmitted to the doctor's computer for analysis. If a patient's condition requires the attention of a doctor, the computer automatically signals via a pocket pager. Laserbones released Elaine Baxter early under this system. Two days after her release, she ran a high fever that could have been remedied with prompt medical attention. Five days after Baxter's release, her condition deteriorated and she had to be readmitted to the hospital. If the system had operated properly, she would have recovered normally. Is Laserbones or Medchips strictly liable in tort to Baxter?

a. Laserbones is not strictly liable because she purchased the system from Medchips.

b. Both Laserbones and Medchips are strictly liable if the system malfunction was related to the hardware.

c. Both Laserbones and Medchips are more likely to be strictly liable if the system malfunction was related to the software.

d. Medchips is not strictly liable because of a bold disclaimer on all of its equipment.

The correct answer is (b). *(Publisher)*

REQUIRED: The applicability of strict liability in tort principles to the designers and users of computer products.

DISCUSSION: Strict liability is usually imposed for personal injury and property damages from ultrahazardous activities. The early release of a hospital patient to the care of a computer could be considered ultrahazardous given the patient's condition. If the personal injury or damages resulted from hardware failure, both the seller and the manufacturer will likely be held strictly liable.

Answer (a) is incorrect because everyone from the manufacturer to the ultimate seller is strictly liable for ultra-hazardous activities. Answer (c) is incorrect because if the malfunction was software related, Medchips would be more likely to escape strict liability. Standards of care and licensing programs for programmers have not yet been established. Answer (d) is incorrect because a seller's disclaimer does not preclude liability for torts.

34.5 Invasion of Privacy Involving Computers

17. Which federal act gives a student rights with respect to his/her academic records stored on the university's computer?

a. The Family Educational Rights and Privacy Act of 1974.

b. The Freedom of Information Act.

c. The Privacy Act of 1974.

d. The Securities Act of 1933.

The correct answer is (a). *(Publisher)*

REQUIRED: The federal act that protects the privacy of a student's academic records.

DISCUSSION: The Family Educational Rights and Privacy Act of 1974 gives students over 18 and parents of dependent students certain rights of inspection, correction, and disclosure of that information.

Answer (b) is incorrect because the Freedom of Information Act grants citizens access to federal government records. Answer (c) is incorrect because the Privacy Act of 1974 safeguards computerized data in federal agencies and the Federal Reserve Banks. Answer (d) is incorrect because the Securities Act of 1933 concerns the initial registration of publicly traded securities.

18. A legal remedy not available for invasion of privacy regarding information stored in computerized data banks is an action

a. In tort based on the intrusion theory.

b. In tort based on the public disclosure of private facts theory.

c. Based on strict liability in tort.

d. Based on statutory protection from governmental intrusion provided by the Right to Financial Privacy Act of 1978.

The correct answer is (c). *(Publisher)*

REQUIRED: The legal action not available for invasion of privacy of computerized data.

DISCUSSION: Strict liability in tort usually is a valid course of action for personal injury and damages resulting from ultrahazardous activities. Damages in an invasion of privacy case are more likely to be economic losses and are unlikely to involve ultrahazardous activities.

Answers (a), (b), and (d) are incorrect because they are legal remedies for invasion of privacy of computerized data.

19. Herman was an unemployed MBA and computer programmer. One day while experimenting with his modem and personal computer, he breached the security of Ann's computer. Ann was a stockbroker who bought and sold large amounts of securities electronically and maintained a database containing the historical trading records of customers. Without Ann's knowledge, Herman wrote a program that determined which of Ann's customers were the best traders by instantaneously calculating their returns. The program produced a list of securities to buy and sell. Herman did not have any funds to invest so he gave the list to his neighbor, Mike, who used it to make large profits. Mike was bragging at the country club about the fortune he had just made in the market when one of Ann's successful traders overheard him. The trader learned that Mike was buying and selling exactly the same basket of stocks. Who is liable and for what?

a. Mike is liable under the Securities Exchange Act of 1934 for insider trading.

b. Ann cannot be liable for negligence for allowing Herman to breach her computer system.

c. Herman is liable under the Right to Financial Privacy Act of 1978.

d. Herman is liable for the tort of invasion of privacy.

The correct answer is (d). *(Publisher)*

REQUIRED: The extent of liability for unauthorized access to private computerized data.

DISCUSSION: Under the tort theory of intrusion, a person is deemed to suffer damage from an invasion of his/her seclusion or solitude that a reasonable person would regard as offensive. Thus, one has a reasonable expectation of privacy for private records. Trading activities not required to be reported to the SEC are private information. Those who examine another's private records without authorization are liable in tort for invasion of privacy.

Answer (a) is incorrect because Mike is not an insider. Answer (b) is incorrect because Ann could be liable for negligence if her hardware or software did not reasonably control access to confidential customer data. Answer (c) is incorrect because the Right to Financial Privacy Act of 1978 addresses government access to private information held by financial institutions. Such access is permitted only if authorized by the customer or the government follows appropriate procedures.

20. Hal Hutter owned a large portfolio of municipal bonds that paid tax-free interest. When he received the interest payments, he cashed the checks at First National Bank. After receiving the cash, he deposited the money in his account at Second National Bank. The frequent deposits were all greater than $10,000. The teller became suspicious and notified the IRS of Hutter's banking activity. An IRS agent was sent to investigate. Second National Bank allowed the agent to search the bank's computer files for any information on Hutter. Is the IRS liable to Hutter for the tort of invasion of privacy?

a. No, the IRS is not liable because the bank had the obligation to report large unusual cash transactions to the IRS and the IRS has the authority to investigate them.

b. No, the Freedom of Information Act specifically gives the IRS the right to examine banks' computer databases when large cash transactions are involved.

c. Yes, the Right to Financial Privacy Act of 1978 protects Hutter's right to privacy from governmental intrusion.

d. Yes, the Privacy Act of 1974 protects Hutter against governmental intrusion into his private banking records.

The correct answer is (c). *(Publisher)*

REQUIRED: The liability of the IRS for examining a bank depositor's computerized banking records.

DISCUSSION: For the IRS to escape liability, it will have to prove that it followed the specific procedures outlined in the Right to Financial Privacy Act of 1978 when it accessed Hutter's banking records.

Answer (a) is incorrect because although the IRS has authority to investigate taxpayer financial transactions, the bank is required to report large cash deposits to federal banking authorities, not the IRS. Answer (b) is incorrect because the Freedom of Information Act concerns the public's right to access government records. Answer (d) is incorrect because the Privacy Act of 1974 relates to the privacy of government-held computerized databases.

34.6 Computer Crime

21. The Counterfeit Access Device and Computer Fraud and Abuse Act of 1984 as amended in 1986

a. Prohibits the use of a computer to gain unauthorized access to any computer.

b. Prohibits the use of a computer to gain unauthorized access to financial institution computers or to consumer information stored in consumer reporting agency computers.

c. Does not apply to sales of stolen passwords.

d. Is the only federal legislation that imposes criminal penalties for the use of counterfeit bank cards.

The correct answer is (b). *(Publisher)*

REQUIRED: The true statement about the Counterfeit Access Device and Computer Fraud and Abuse Act of 1984 as amended in 1986.

DISCUSSION: The 1986 amendments to the Act prohibit unauthorized access to any computer used by or for the U.S. government; make it a crime to gain unauthorized access to such computers or to those of a financial institution and to alter, damage, or destroy information therein; and also make it a crime to traffic in means (e.g., passwords) for gaining access to computers used by and for the U.S. government. The Act initially protected certain government information, information in financial records of financial institutions, and consumer data in the files of consumer reporting agencies. It also provided penalties for improper use of access devices (codes, cards, account numbers, etc.) or for use of counterfeit access devices. The 1986 amendments broadened the Act's coverage.

Answer (a) is incorrect because the Act does not apply to all computers. Answer (c) is incorrect because the Act prohibits trafficking in the means of gaining unauthorized access to computers used by or for the U.S. government. Answer (d) is incorrect because the Electronic Funds Transfer Act of 1978 also provides criminal penalties for the use of counterfeit bank cards.

22. Criminal liability for the theft of computer time requires

a. A narrow interpretation of state and federal statutes.

b. The intent of the perpetrator to deprive the true owner of computer time.

c. Prosecution under the provisions of federal computer acts.

d. The true owners of the computer time to prove they were deprived by the perpetrator.

The correct answer is (b). *(Publisher)*

REQUIRED: The requirement for criminal liability for theft of computer time.

DISCUSSION: Absent a specific statute, criminal liability for theft of computer time will often require a broad interpretation of traditional state or federal statutes that concern theft or larceny because not all courts regard computer time or data stored in a computer to be property. Also, intent by the perpetrator to deprive, and actual deprivation of, the true owner of his/her rights are necessary elements.

Answer (a) is incorrect because a broad interpretation of statutes is typically required in cases involving criminal liability for the theft of computer time. Answer (c) is incorrect because criminal liability for theft of computer time may be prosecuted under state statutes as well as federal. Answer (d) is incorrect because the burden of proof in criminal cases rests on state or federal prosecutors, not victims.

23. Chuck Choppy was dismissed from his position as a management consultant for SNL, CPAs when he failed to be promoted to partner. Choppy had advised SNL's financial institution clients about computer security of depositor records. After he was dismissed, he used his home computer to breach the security of several of SNL's clients' computers and transfer minuscule amounts from each depositor's account to his own account. Though each individual transfer was immaterial, the aggregate amount transferred was material. Choppy is

a. Not criminally liable under state statutes because the amounts were immaterial.

b. Not criminally liable under the Counterfeit Access Device and Computer Fraud and Abuse Act of 1984 as amended in 1986.

c. Criminally liable under both the Counterfeit Access Device and Computer Fraud and Abuse Act of 1984 as amended in 1986 and the Electronic Funds Act of 1978.

d. Criminally liable under a narrow interpretation of state and federal theft statutes.

The correct answer is (c). *(Publisher)*

REQUIRED: The liability for theft of depositor funds using a computer.

DISCUSSION: The Counterfeit Access Device and Computer Fraud and Abuse Act of 1984 as amended in 1986 prohibits unauthorized access to financial institution computers. The Electronic Funds Transfer Act of 1978 prohibits unauthorized alteration of data in financial institution computers. Hence, Choppy is criminally liable under both acts.

Answers (a) and (b) are incorrect because Choppy is criminally liable regardless of materiality. Answer (d) is incorrect because computer crimes ordinarily require a broad interpretation of state and federal theft statutes to subject an individual to criminal liability.

34.7 Computers and Antitrust Law

24. Government Business Machines (GBM) has greater than an 80% share of the sales of computers to local and state governments. GBM requires all purchasers of its computers to also purchase its proprietary operating system, called GOS. Furthermore, all GBM government contracts require all application software and peripherals to be purchased from GBM. Under which of the following antitrust acts is GBM liable?

	Sherman Act	Clayton Act
a.	Yes	Yes
b.	Yes	No
c.	No	Yes
d.	No	No

The correct answer is (a). *(Publisher)*

REQUIRED: The liability of a computer seller under the federal antitrust law.

DISCUSSION: To be liable for an antitrust violation, a seller must have sufficient economic power to restrain competition and affect a substantial amount of commerce in the market in which it operates. Clearly, GBM's 80% market share is persuasive evidence of economic power and the ability to have a substantial effect on commerce. The Sherman Act makes tying an antitrust violation. Tying occurs when a firm sells two distinct products but purchase of one is conditional on purchase of the other. GBM's requirement that computer buyers purchase GOS is a tying arrangement. The Clayton Act prohibits exclusive dealing, for example, a seller's requiring a buyer to purchase all related products from that seller. GBM's requirement that buyers purchase all application software and peripherals from GBM qualifies as exclusive dealing. Hence, GBM is liable under both the Sherman and Clayton antitrust acts.

Answers (b), (c), and (d) are incorrect because GBM is liable for antitrust violations under both Acts.

CHAPTER THIRTY-FIVE BUSINESS ETHICS

35.1 Nature of Business Ethics

1. The term business ethics refers to the study of

a. Increasing or decreasing a corporation's budget.

b. Good/bad or just/unjust human conduct in a business environment.

c. Whether to expand business facilities.

d. Increasing corporate productivity.

The correct answer is (b). *(Publisher)*

REQUIRED: The definition of business ethics.

DISCUSSION: Many business decisions need to be justified as morally right or wrong. Moral principles are derived from personal beliefs, religion, and culture. Business ethics is the study of whether a business decision is morally right or wrong.

Answers (a), (c), and (d) are incorrect because these are managerial and accounting decisions.

2. Which ethical theory promotes "the greatest happiness for the greatest number of people?"

a. Rationalism.

b. Duty-based theory.

c. Utilitarianism.

d. Egoism.

The correct answer is (c). *(Publisher)*

REQUIRED: The ethical theory promoting the greatest happiness for the greatest number of people.

DISCUSSION: The English philosopher Jeremy Bentham was the foremost proponent of Utilitarianism, which is a result-oriented philosophy. Utilitarians believe that an action should be evaluated as good or just if it produces the greatest balance of happiness over unhappiness. John Stuart Mill was a prominent opponent of this approach. He believed that some types of pleasures are more valuable than others.

Answer (a) is incorrect because rationalism is the belief that man can deduce ethical values and arrive at a moral system through reasoning. Answer (b) is incorrect because duty-based or "deontological" theories focus on a person's intentions and not on the outcome of the situation. Answer (d) is incorrect because egoism refers to a person's selfish desire to be the motive for the outcome.

3. The ethical theory supporting the claim that "the rightness and goodness of an act should be determined by certain rules or duties, not by the act's consequences," is

a. Rationalism.

b. Deontological theory.

c. Utilitarianism.

d. Egoism.

The correct answer is (b). *(Publisher)*

REQUIRED: The ethical theory defining the rightness of an act in terms of certain rules and duties.

DISCUSSION: Deontological or duty-based theory focuses on a person's intentions and not on the outcome of the situation. Proponents of the theory state that people are under a duty to behave in ways that ensure good results. For example, deontological ethical theory argues that a borrower should not promise to repay a loan unless (s)he has a good faith intention to do so.

Answer (a) is incorrect because rationalism is the belief that man can deduce ethical values and arrive at a moral system through reasoning. Answer (c) is incorrect because utilitarianism defines an action as good if it results in the greatest amount of happiness for the greatest number of people. Answer (d) is incorrect because egoism is a person's selfish desire to be the motive for the outcome.

4. The ethical theory most likely to support the continued publication of a sensational magazine that writes defamatory stories and has high sales is

a. Rationalism.

b. Affirmative action.

c. Utilitarianism.

d. Duty-based theory.

The correct answer is (c). *(Publisher)*

REQUIRED: The ethical theory supporting a continued publication of a sensational magazine that writes defamatory stories.

DISCUSSION: Utilitarianism approves actions that result in the greatest amount of happiness for the greatest number of people. If a sensational magazine has a large readership, the good feelings of the readers arguably outweigh the bad feelings of the subjects of the magazine articles. Such a position, however, has obvious drawbacks. For example, how can happiness and unhappiness be quantified? Also, are we prepared to say that the end justifies the means?

Answer (a) is incorrect because the rationalists would reason that publishing defamatory stories is immoral. Answer (b) is incorrect because affirmative action pertains to hiring members of minorities and is not an ethical theory. Answer (d) is incorrect because deontologists believe an act is just if the person has intended to behave in accord with an objective duty to assure a good outcome.

5. The golden rule states, "Do unto others as you would have them do unto you." It is reflected in

a. Duty-based theory.

b. Rationalism.

c. Utilitarianism.

d. Egoism.

The correct answer is (a). *(Publisher)*

REQUIRED: The ethical theory that supports the golden rule.

DISCUSSION: Duty-based or deontological theory focuses on a person's intentions and not on the outcome of the situation. The golden rule is derived from the deontological belief that treating a person fairly is a prerequisite for reciprocal fair treatment.

Answer (b) is incorrect because rationalism is the belief that man can deduce ethical values and arrive at a moral system through reasoning. Answer (c) is incorrect because utilitarianism focuses on the outcome of a situation and not intentions. Answer (d) is incorrect because egoism is concerned with a person's selfish desires and not his/her actions toward other people.

6. Which of the following is not a criticism of utilitarianism?

a. No single scale can measure the greatest benefit for the greatest number of people.

b. It is subjective in defining what is good and what is bad.

c. One worthy principle may conflict with others.

d. Businesses focus their records more on computing costs than benefits.

The correct answer is (c). *(Publisher)*

REQUIRED: The item that is not a criticism of utilitarianism.

DISCUSSION: The need to choose among conflicting ethical principles has been a basis of criticism of deontological or duty-based theories. Deontological theories emphasize the need to act in accordance with one's duty, but a decision may be difficult when moral duties conflict. Utilitarianism, however, expressly compares the outcomes of different actions without regard to conflicting duties.

Answer (a) is incorrect because a major criticism of utilitarianism is that no method exists to quantify benefits. Answer (b) is incorrect because a criticism of utilitarianism is that what is a good or bad outcome may be purely subjective. Answer (d) is incorrect because a criticism of utilitarianism is that businesses can compute the costs of an action more readily than the benefits.

7. Thievery is a violation of

a. The ethics of excellence.

b. Community ethics.

c. Individualist ethics.

d. The ethics of duty.

The correct answer is (d). *(Publisher)*

REQUIRED: The ethical system that prohibits crimes.

DISCUSSION: Ethical systems may be considered to establish either ethics of duty or ethics of excellence. Ethics of duty emphasize obeying the law. If the law is violated, punishment will occur. Thievery is a violation of the ethics of duty because the law prohibits such conduct.

Answer (a) is incorrect because the ethics of excellence consist of the goals, aspirations, and standards of perfection a person sets out for him/herself. A violation of the ethics of excellence is not a violation of law. Answer (b) is incorrect because community ethics place the emphasis on the good of society, with individual rights being sacrificed for the benefit of society. Answer (c) is incorrect because individualist ethics hold the individual interest to be superior to society's.

8. Which ethical system is concerned with the ideals of perfection and achieving the good life?

a. Ethics of duty.

b. Ethics of excellence.

c. Individualist ethics.

d. Societal ethics.

The correct answer is (b). *(Publisher)*

REQUIRED: The ethical system that is based upon the ideals of perfection and achieving the good life.

DISCUSSION: The ethics of excellence are goals, aspirations, and standards of perfection a person sets for him/herself. The ethics of excellence consist of a person's ideals of total honesty, perfect justice, and complete loyalty. A person will not be blamed for violating ethics of excellence, but in comparison will be blamed for violating ethics of duty.

Answer (a) is incorrect because ethics of duty are a person's moral obligations to uphold the law. Answer (c) is incorrect because individualist ethics state that the individual's interest is superior to society's. Answer (d) is incorrect because societal ethics are beliefs of good and bad, including all political and religious theories.

9. Ethical standards that apply to family, friends, and neighbors are described as

a. Community ethics.

b. Marketplace ethics.

c. Intimate ethics.

d. Personal ethics.

The correct answer is (c). *(Publisher)*

REQUIRED: The proper ethical standard that applies to family, friends, and neighbors.

DISCUSSION: The intimate ethics standard is applicable when an individual has business dealings with family, friends, and neighbors. An individual holds him/herself to a higher standard of loyalty and honesty when dealing with family, friends, and neighbors. An individual has a different set of ethical standards when dealing with people in a business setting. Standards of loyalty and honesty tend to be lowered in a business relationship.

Answer (a) is incorrect because community ethics sacrifice the individual right for the benefit of society. Answer (b) is incorrect because marketplace ethics are the principles a person observes in business transactions. Answer (d) is incorrect because personal ethics refer to the broad notion of defining what is right or wrong in reference to one's own moral code.

10. Ethical standards that apply when dealing with people in a business relationship are described as

a. Intimate ethics.

b. Marketplace ethics.

c. Community ethics.

d. Individualist ethics.

The correct answer is (b). *(Publisher)*

REQUIRED: The ethical standard applicable when dealing with a person in a business relationship.

DISCUSSION: "Marketplace ethics" concern ethical standards in a business relationship. A person's ethical standards of honesty and loyalty are usually lower in these circumstances than in interactions with friends and family.

Answer (a) is incorrect because a person holds him/herself to an intimate ethics standard when dealing with a close relative, family friend, or neighbor. Answer (c) is incorrect because community ethics emphasize the sacrifice of the individual's rights for the benefit of society. Answer (d) is incorrect because individualist ethics emphasize that the individual's rights are superior to society's interests.

11. Joe and Bill have been good friends for over 15 years. Bill was developing a campground and asked Joe one night while playing cards, "Do you want to purchase the campground when it is completed?" Joe agreed to purchase the campground for $10,000 down and $20,000 payable in installments in years 2 and 3. The camp netted $250 the first summer. Joe complained that he had been overcharged by $8,000 and that Bill misrepresented the camp's earning potential. Which ethical consideration would a court hold that Bill violated?

a. Marketplace ethics.

b. Intimate ethics.

c. Community ethics.

d. None of the above.

The correct answer is (d). *(Publisher)*

REQUIRED: The ethical standard violated in a sale of property between friends.

DISCUSSION: In Eaton v. Santag, the parties were friends for over 15 years and entered into a business relationship. The Santags argued that because they were friends for over 15 years with the Eatons, the Eatons had a higher duty than that implied by the customary arm's-length business relationship. The court refused to hold the Santags to a higher ethical standard in this situation.

Answer (a) is incorrect because the marketplace imposes a lower standard than that customary in most other situations. Answer (b) is incorrect because although Bill may have breached intimate ethics, a court does not enforce such standards. Answer (c) is incorrect because the community's interest is not directly involved.

35.2 Ethics In the Professions and Corporations

12. The legal and medical profession's ethics are governed by

a. Congress.

b. Federal administrative agencies.

c. State bar and medical associations.

d. State legislatures.

The correct answer is (c). *(Publisher)*

REQUIRED: The governing bodies of the legal and medical professions.

DISCUSSION: Business associations have codes of ethics that are voluntary and not binding or enforceable. The legal and medical profession's codes of ethics are different from those of business groups because they are enforceable by state bar and medical associations. A person must be licensed to practice law or medicine, but does not have to have a license to participate in a trade or business.

Answers (a), (b) and (d) are incorrect because these groups have no authority to regulate the legal or medical professions.

13. F. Walton Book Company's $3 million contribution to launch a drive against functional illiteracy is an example of corporate

a. Social responsiveness.

b. Mismanagement of funds.

c. Liquidation.

d. Reorganization.

The correct answer is (a). *(Publisher)*

REQUIRED: The ethical principle that allows corporations to donate money to charity.

DISCUSSION: Corporations were absolutely prohibited from giving to charity by early common law. In today's society, private corporations donate money to charity because much of the nation's wealth is in corporate hands. Corporate social responsiveness may be reflected when corporations help out society by donating money to charity and engaging in other philanthropic activities.

Answer (b) is incorrect because corporate mismanagement of funds occurs when corporate management spends corporate funds for ventures not in the best interest of the corporation. Answer (c) is incorrect because a corporate liquidation occurs when a corporation goes out of business and distributes assets to shareholders. Answer (d) is incorrect because a corporate reorganization occurs through certain transactions (recapitalizations, divisions, mergers) that take place without recognition of gain or loss if the transactions comply with the tax law.

14. What duty does a corporation owe to its employees?

a. A corporation owes no duty to its employees.

b. A corporation owes a duty to pay a higher than competitive wage.

c. A corporation owes a duty to pay a competitive wage.

d. A corporation owes a duty to give its employees a 2-hour lunch break every day.

The correct answer is (c). *(Publisher)*

REQUIRED: The duty a corporation owes to its employees.

DISCUSSION: A corporation owes a duty to its employees to pay a competitive wage. The wage paid should be equivalent to what the market bears.

Answer (a) is incorrect because a corporation does owe a duty to its employees to pay a competitive wage and establish reasonable working conditions. Answer (b) is incorrect because if a corporation pays a higher than competitive wage, production costs and prices will be higher as a result. Thus, the corporation will have a conflict of the duties owed to its employees and consumers. Answer (d) is incorrect because a corporation owes no duty to give employees a 2-hour lunch break every day. A 1-hour lunch break would be considered a reasonable working condition fringe benefit, but a 2-hour break would be unreasonable for the employer.

15. Landon Motor Company sells minibikes for off-the-road use. The owner's manual and a sticker on each bike sold states in bold print that the bike should not be used on public roads. A child riding a Landon minibike was injured on a public road after being told by her parents not to ride in the street. Did Landon breach an ethical duty to the consumer?

a. Yes. A manufacturer is strictly liable for the harm caused by its products.

b. Yes. A manufacturer is absolutely liable for the harm caused by its products.

c. No. A manufacturer is not strictly liable for the products it put in the stream of commerce.

d. No. The bold print in the owner's manual was sufficient to satisfy the duty to warn.

The correct answer is (d). *(Publisher)*

REQUIRED: The ethical duty a manufacturer owes to the consumer.

DISCUSSION: When a product is not defectively manufactured, and warnings concerning its appropriate use are adequate, a manufacturer is not liable for an accident and resulting injuries. In Baughn v. Honda Motor Co., a case from the state of Washington, Honda designed a minibike for use on dirt roads. A sticker on the bike stated that it was only for off-the-road use. A similar statement appeared in the owner's manual. The court held that the warnings were adequate to protect Honda from liability.

Answer (a) is incorrect because a manufacturer is held strictly liable for products that are unreasonably dangerous when the product is placed in the consumer's hands without giving adequate warnings to the consumer regarding safe use. Landon gave adequate notice by placing a sticker on the minibike and by boldly printing instructions in the owner's manual. Answer (b) is incorrect because the law imposes strict, not absolute, liability. Answer (c) is incorrect because a manufacturer is strictly liable when the product sold to the consumer is not accompanied by adequate instructions as to how to use the product safely.

16. Ethical issues arise when U.S. companies build plants in third world countries because

a. U.S. citizens are being deprived of employment.

b. U.S. corporations are avoiding paying income taxes.

c. U.S. companies are escaping many U.S. safety and environmental regulations.

d. U.S. companies are not acting in the best interests of their shareholders.

The correct answer is (c). *(Publisher)*

REQUIRED: The ethical considerations that arise when a corporation builds plants in third world countries.

DISCUSSION: U.S. companies build factories in foreign countries for economic reasons, such as a lower cost of labor. Ethical issues are involved if the reason is to take advantage of lax safety regulations. An example is the Union Carbide factory that leaked 25 tons of methyl isocyanate that caused 2,000 deaths and 100,000 injuries in Bhopal, India. The plant in India did not have a computerized safety system, a requirement in the United States.

Answer (a) is incorrect because a U.S. company is not under an ethical duty to give U.S. citizens employment. Answer (b) is incorrect because U.S. companies operating outside the United States are still subject to income tax. Answer (d) is incorrect because increasing business productivity overseas may be in the best interests of the corporation.

17. A discretionary expenditure by a corporation for conservation of natural resources raises a direct ethical conflict between which parties?

a. Corporation and employee.

b. Corporation and shareholder.

c. Employee and shareholder.

d. Both (a) and (b).

The correct answer is (d). *(Publisher)*

REQUIRED: The ethical conflict that arises when a corporation makes an expenditure for conserving the environment.

DISCUSSION: If the corporation makes discretionary expenditures for environmental conservation, the cost of products and services will increase, and some of the increased price will be passed on to the consumer. Moreover, increased costs may reduce profits and the ability to give pay increases to employees or to hire new workers. Indeed, employment may diminish. Lower profits will also decrease dividends paid to the shareholders. Consequently, the corporation's duty to pay a reasonable wage to its employees will conflict with the duty to stockholders to be profitable.

Answer (a) is incorrect because the corporation is also in an ethical conflict with the shareholder. Answer (b) is incorrect because the corporation is in conflict with its employees. Answer (c) is incorrect because the shareholder and employee are not in direct conflict, but the corporation is in direct conflict with the employee as well as the shareholder.

18. According to Milton Friedman's model of corporate social responsibility, the corporation

a. Is to be managed solely for the stockholders' benefit.

b. Has a responsibility to its stockholders, employees, customers, and the public.

c. Has four kinds of responsibilities: economic, legal, ethical, and discretionary.

d. Should adhere to law and ethical custom, but otherwise use all its resources to increase its profits.

The correct answer is (d). *(Publisher)*

REQUIRED: The view of corporate social responsibility developed by the economist Milton Friedman.

DISCUSSION: There are many models of corporate social responsibility. Adam Smith's free-market view was that the public interest was best served by permitting individuals to pursue their interests without interference. Adolph Berle modified Smith's model of corporate social responsibility in the early 1930s to emphasize that corporate executives are above all trustees for the stockholders and thus should promote their interests, not the public good. Friedman's model is different from Berle's. Friedman believes a corporation needs to make the highest profit possible for the benefit of the shareholders, but must conform to the basic rules of society embodied in laws and in ethical customs. Friedman does not define the term "ethical custom," but he does state examples of what it is not. For instance, environmental protection is a governmental, not a corporate, concern, and "ethical custom" does not require spending more to control pollution than is mandated by law or a company's interests. By spending more money than is necessary for the environment, corporate managers are taking "someone else's money," e.g., the shareholder's dividend.

Answer (a) is incorrect because it describes Adolph Berle's model of social responsibility. Answer (b) is incorrect because it states the trusteeship model of E.M. Dodd. The corporation's responsibility to its shareholders is to use the corporate assets safely with a fair rate of return. Also, the employees have a right to a fair wage, the customers have a right to a good product, and the public has a right to expect the corporation to perform its duties as a good citizen. Answer (c) is incorrect because A.B. Carroll's social responsibility model divides a business's social responsibilities into these four categories. For example, Carroll argues that society expects corporations to do more than meet their economic and legal responsibilities. A corporation has ethical duties, however poorly defined, and additional discretionary social responsibilities about which society has not given a "clear-cut message."

19. A corporation's refusal to buy stock in a corporation that has interests in South Africa is an example of

a. The business judgment rule.

b. Whistleblowing

c. Reverse discrimination.

d. Social investing.

The correct answer is (d). *(Publisher)*

REQUIRED: The characterization of a corporation's refusal to invest in another corporation that has interests in South Africa.

DISCUSSION: A new ethical trend in business is to make decisions on whether to invest in corporations based on the moral beliefs of the investor. The decision may hinge on certain social responsibility issues, such as whether the corporation manufactures safe products, hires minorities, or sells products to South Africa. Such considerations are examples of social investing.

Answer (a) is incorrect because the business judgment rule immunizes corporate management from liability for actions undertaken in good faith. Answer (b) is incorrect because whistleblowing occurs when an employee chooses not to ignore unsafe, illegal, or unethical activities and complains to an authority about the employer. Answer (c) is incorrect because reverse discrimination entails discrimination against a majority group in favor of minority groups by affirmative action programs.

35.3 Ethics in Other Areas of Business

20. An add-on clause for a new installment purchase of goods is

a. Unethical because prior goods purchased from a vendor are subject to repossession.

b. Unethical because add-on clauses have been outlawed in many states.

c. Valid because it gives vendors in low-income areas additional security and thereby increases the availability of credit.

d. Valid because it allows finance companies to increase finance costs to poor credit risks.

The correct answer is (c). *(Publisher)*

REQUIRED: The ethical issue that arises when an add-on clause is used in a sale of goods.

DISCUSSION: An add-on clause is often imposed on a sale of consumer goods in low-income areas. It is an agreement that failure to make payment on the goods purchased permits not only the items purchased under the current contract to be repossessed, but also any prior items purchased from the same seller. Courts have sometimes invalidated such clauses because they offend notions of public policy. On the other hand, add-on clauses are used to give vendors additional security for a purchaser's failure to repay. If add-on clauses are invalidated, vendors will be less likely to sell goods on credit to low-income families.

Answer (a) is incorrect because one effect of an add-on clause is to give low-income families an opportunity to purchase goods on credit. The right to repossess prior goods is not unethical. It gives a vendor additional security in the case of nonperformance by the purchaser. Answer (b) is incorrect because states do not have an absolute prohibition on add-on clauses. Answer (d) is incorrect because add-on clauses should be used to give vendors additional, reasonable security on goods sold to low-income families, not as a means to charge usurious rates.

21. That an individual who takes out a large insurance policy on a building has less motivation to protect the building from potential fire than a person without insurance is an example of

a. Moral hazard.

b. Fraud.

c. Innocent misrepresentation.

d. Defamation.

The correct answer is (a). *(Publisher)*

REQUIRED: The situation that occurs in the insurance industry when individuals or entities have little disincentive to be negligent.

DISCUSSION: Moral hazard is a term used in the insurance industry when people take out large insurance policies with low deductibles. The person with the low deductible has little disincentive to be negligent. (S)he will be less likely to take precautions against fire because (s)he may be indifferent to the consequences. The issue is whether the owner of the building has an ethical responsibility to prevent the building from being burned to the ground.

Answer (b) is incorrect because fraud is a false representation of a material fact made with scienter (knowledge of the falsehood or reckless disregard of its possible falsity). Obtaining fire insurance for a building is not fraud if no false representation is made to the insurance company. Answer (c) is incorrect because innocent misrepresentation is a false representation made to another party without scienter. Answer (d) is incorrect because defamation occurs when material is published or spoken publicly that causes injury to a person's good name, reputation, or character.

22. Which of the following has been a consequence of recent changes in the bankruptcy code?

a. Corporations are not able to avoid collective bargaining agreements negotiated in good faith.

b. Corporations are able to avoid collective bargaining agreements negotiated in good faith.

c. Creditors are requiring less security in making loans.

d. Creditors are charging less interest to everyone.

The correct answer is (b). *(Publisher)*

REQUIRED: The consequence of the recent changes in the bankruptcy code.

DISCUSSION: A debtor is provided a chance to start over when relief is granted under the bankruptcy law. When a debtor is provided relief under the bankruptcy law, the creditor is not allowed to force the debtor to repay the obligation. The question of moral hazard arises in bankruptcy because debtors have an incentive to use the law to avoid meeting obligations. Thus, the 1984 bankruptcy amendments attempted to address some abuses. For example, they limited, but did not eliminate, the power of a debtor to avoid collective bargaining agreements. Hence, a debtor may avoid a collective bargaining agreement only if the debtor proposed "necessary" contract modifications to the union "in good faith" and the union rejected the modifications without good cause.

Answer (a) is incorrect because bankrupt corporations are able to avoid collective bargaining agreements negotiated in good faith. Answer (c) is incorrect because creditors are requiring more security for debtors as a result of the relaxed bankruptcy law. Answer (d) is incorrect because interest rates charged to debtors have increased as the bankruptcy code has become more lenient.

23. Which of the following is not an ethical issue in the workplace?

a. Affirmative action.

b. Whistleblowing.

c. Reverse discrimination.

d. Social investing.

The correct answer is (d). *(Publisher)*

REQUIRED: The ethical issue that does not arise in the workplace.

DISCUSSION: Social investing entails making investment decisions based on ethical or social considerations. For example, some investors have liquidated their holdings in companies that do business in South Africa or that fail to meet other social-responsibility standards.

Answer (a) is incorrect because a major ethical concern that has arisen from employment law has been the hiring of employees unfairly on the basis of race, sex, age, and nationality. Such discrimination has been reduced through the use of employer affirmative action programs that give special consideration to minorities. Answer (b) is incorrect because whistleblowing is another ethical issue in the workplace. An employee may be faced with the choice of ignoring unethical activities in the workplace or complaining to the employer and risking dismissal. Answer (c) is incorrect because a problem with affirmative action programs is that majority groups are perceived as being discriminated against in favor of minority groups (reverse discrimination).

BLANK PAGE

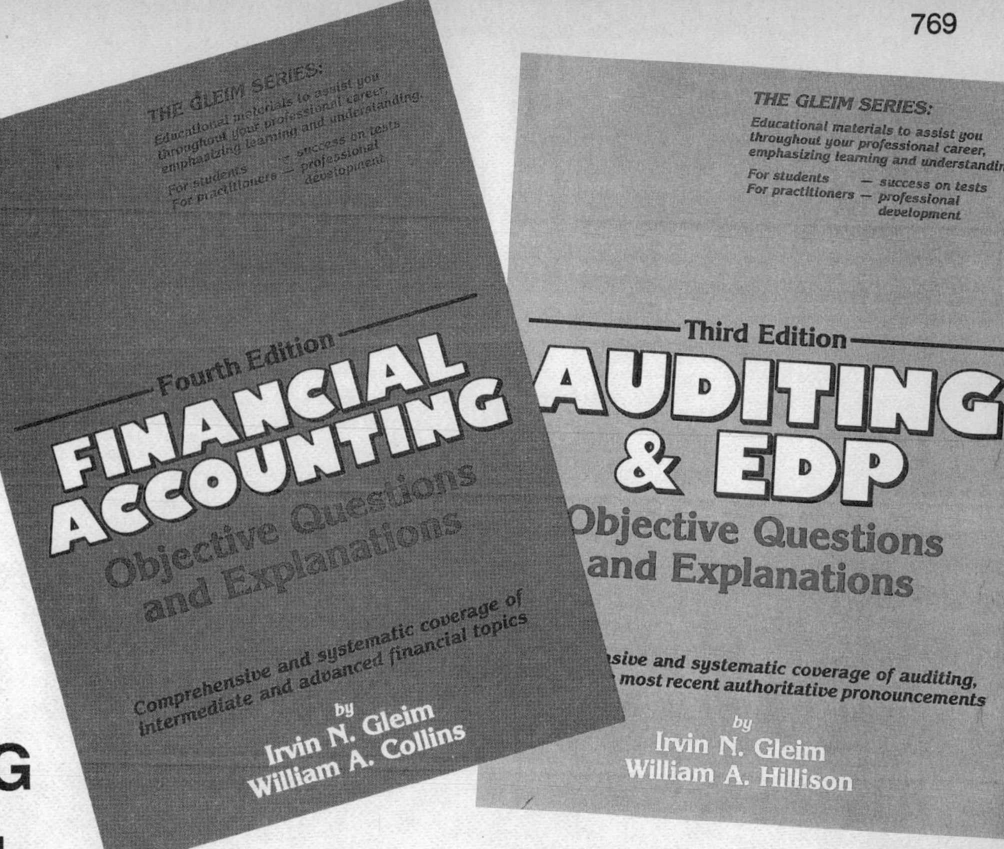

THE GLEIM SERIES:
Educational materials to assist you throughout your professional career, emphasizing learning and understanding.
For students — success on tests
For practitioners — professional development
Fourth Edition
FINANCIAL ACCOUNTING
Objective Questions and Explanations
Comprehensive and systematic coverage of intermediate and advanced financial topics
by
Irvin N. Gleim
William A. Collins
THE GLEIM SERIES:
Educational materials to assist you throughout your professional career, emphasizing learning and understanding.
For students — success on tests
For practitioners — professional development
Third Edition
AUDITING & EDP
Objective Questions and Explanations
most recent authoritative pronouncements
by
Irvin N. Gleim
William A. Hillison

SUCCESSFUL CAREERS IN ACCOUNTING BEGIN WITH THE GLEIM SERIES OF OBJECTIVE QUESTIONS AND EXPLANATIONS . . .

THE GLEIM SERIES:
Educational materials to assist you throughout your professional career,
For students — success on tests
For practitioners — professional development
Third Edition
Third Edition
MANAGERIA
Objective Questions and Explanations
Comprehensive and systematic coverage of cost and managerial accounting topics
by
Irvin N. Gleim
Terry L. Campbell
THE GLEIM SERIES:
Educational materials to assist you throughout your professional career, emphasizing learning and understanding.
For students — success on tests
For practitioners — professional development
Fourth Edition
FEDERAL TAX
Objective Questions and Explanations
Comprehensive and systematic coverage of basic through advanced topics including the 1988 TAMRA
by
Irvin N. Gleim
Sandra S. Kramer
Holger D. Gleim

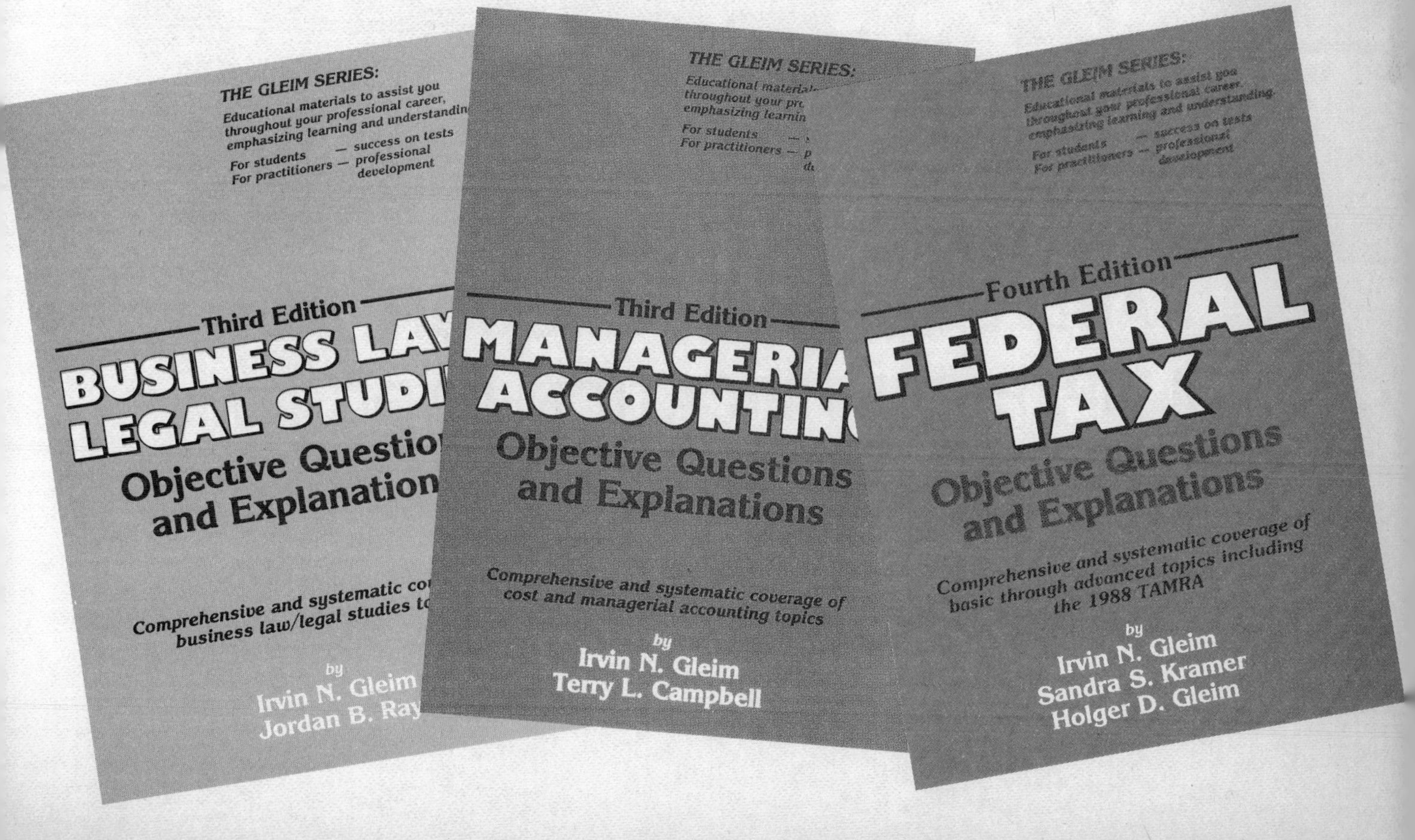

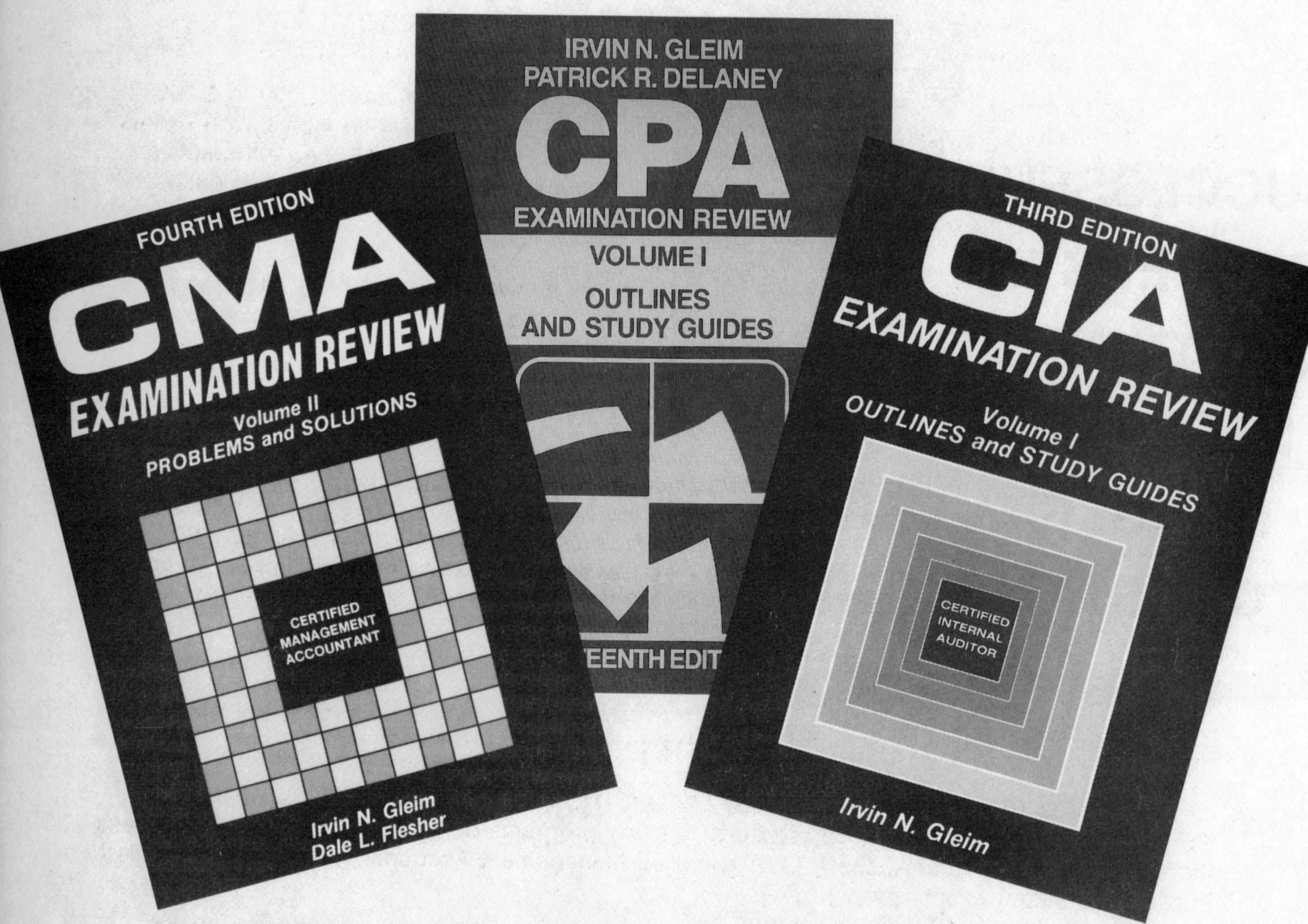

. . . AND CONTINUE THROUGH MULTIPLE CERTIFICATION PROGRAMS

ACCOUNTING PUBLICATIONS, INC. • *P.O. Box 12848* • *Gainesville, FL 32604* • *(904) 375-0772*

"THE GLEIM SERIES" OBJECTIVE QUESTION AND EXPLANATION BOOKS

Title	Details	Price	Amount
AUDITING & EDP	*(720 pages • 1,847 questions)*	$14.95	$______
BUSINESS LAW/LEGAL STUDIES	*(800 pages • 1,928 questions)*	$14.95	$______
FEDERAL TAX	*(768 pages • 2,380 questions)*	$14.95	$______
FINANCIAL ACCOUNTING	*(720 pages • 1,835 questions)*	$14.95	$______
MANAGERIAL ACCOUNTING	*(672 pages • 1,967 questions)*	$14.95	$______

CIA EXAMINATION REVIEW *(3rd Edition, published February 1989)*

Title	Details	Price	Amount
VOLUME I: Outlines & Study Guides	*(784 pages)*	$21.95	$______
VOLUME II: Problems & Solutions	*(776 pages)*	$21.95	$______
1990 CIA UPDATING EDITION	*(304 pages)*	$15.95	$______
All three of the above CIA books . . . (save $9.95)		$49.90	$______

CMA EXAMINATION REVIEW *(4th Edition, available July 1990)*

Title	Details	Price	Amount
VOLUME I: Outlines & Study Guides	*(768 pages)*	$23.95	$______
VOLUME II: Problems & Solutions	*(800 pages)*	$23.95	$______

CPA EXAMINATION REVIEW (published by John Wiley & Sons, Inc.)

TWO-VOLUME SET *(16th Edition, published June 1989)*

Title	Details	Price	Amount
Volume I: Outlines & Study Guides	*(1,398 pages)*	$35.95	$______
Volume II: Problems & Solutions	*(1,154 pages)*	$35.95	$______

THREE-VOLUME SET *(published January 1990)*

Title	Details	Price	Amount
Auditing	*(622 pages)*	$24.95	$______
Business Law	*(570 pages)*	$24.95	$______
Theory and Practice	*(1,472 pages)*	$34.95	$______

Florida Residents must add 6% sales tax . . . . . $______

Foreign Surcharge (call or write for charges) . . . . . $______

Payment must be in U.S. dollars and payable on a U.S. bank . . . . . **TOTAL** $______

1. We process and ship orders daily, generally 1 day after receipt of your order.
2. Please PHOTOCOPY this order form as necessary.
3. No CODs. All mail orders from individuals must be prepaid and are protected by our unequivocal refund policy.

   Library and company orders may be purchased on account.

   Shipping charges will be added to telephone orders and to orders not prepaid.
4. Accounting Publications, Inc. guarantees immediate, complete refund on all mail orders if resalable texts are returned in 30 days.

NAME (please print) ______________________

ADDRESS ______________________

____

CITY ______________________ STATE ____ ZIP ______

__ MasterCard __ VISA __ Check/Money Order

MC/VISA No ____-____-____-____

Exp. Date ___/___ Mo. / Yr.

Signature ______________________

081

FIVE CPE PROGRAMS USING OBJECTIVE QUESTION FORMAT

These CPE programs constitute a totally new approach to CPE. The courses are based on self-diagnosing objective questions. They are designed to meet the needs of practitioners by providing low-cost, easy-to-use, effective CPE.

All of these programs provide you with an opportunity to review and study a wide range of topics.

- First, they provide a self-diagnosis of your knowledge.
- Second, they constitute a review and study of the professional and technical standards that have come to be the basic proficiency package expected of CPAs. As such, each individual course is a formal program of learning that contributes directly to your professional competence.
- Third, they are interactive in the sense that you must continually respond to multiple-choice or true-false questions. Thus, you challenge yourself to do well. When you have difficulty, a thorough, easy-to-understand explanation is provided.
- Fourth, these courses are organized in a programmed learning format through a careful ordering of questions, i.e., from general to specific, easy to difficult, etc.

EASY TO USE

With each program, you receive:

1. Objective Question and Explanation Study Book
2. CPE Book of final exam questions
3. Machine-readable final exam answer sheet *
4. Complete, easy-to-follow instructions

- You study the questions and explanations in the Objective Question and Explanation Study Book when and where you want.
- Then, you take a final exam (open book) using our machine-readable answer sheet.
- Lastly, you return the answer sheet to use for grading, and if you score 70% or above, we will send you a certificate of completion.

* In each program, you have the option of taking all of the courses, just one course, or any combination of courses. All of the courses in a single program can be completed at no additional charge by using the one answer sheet provided with each program. If you want to obtain CPE credit for a few courses at a time, there is a $15 grading fee (additional answer sheet) for each subsequent submission.

*FEDERAL TAX CPE $95

16 separate courses with up to 57 CPE hours

Course	Hours
1. Gross Income and Exclusions	4
2. Business Expenses and Losses	3
3. Investment and Personal Deductions	4
4. Individual Loss Limits, Tax Calculations, and Credits	4
5. Property I	4
6. Property II	4
7. Partnerships	4
8. Corporate Formations and Operations	5
9. Advanced Corporate Topics	4
10. Accounting Methods and Employment Taxes	4
11. Estates, Trusts, and Wealth Transfer Taxes	4
12. Tax Preparer Rules, Process, and Procedure	3
1988 Tax Law Changes	
13. TAMRA: Individuals	3
14. TAMRA: Losses, Depreciation, Credits, Accounting Changes	3
15. TAMRA: Trusts and Estates	2
16. TAMRA: Corporations	2

*AUDITING & EDP CPE $75

8 separate courses 46 CPE hours

Course	Hours
1. Audit Environment, Standards, and Ethics	7
2. Internal Control	5
3. Audit Evidence and Procedures	8
4. Electronic Data Processing	8
5. Statistical Sampling	3
6. Audit Reports	7
7. Special Reports and Other Reporting Issues	3
8. Internal Auditing	5

BUSINESS LAW CPE $50

16 separate courses with up to 43 CPE hours

Course	Hours	Course	Hours
1. Our Legal System	3	9. Suretyship and Bankruptcy	3
2. Torts and Crimes	2	10. Property	5
3. Contracts	5	11. Insurance, Estates, and Trusts	4
4. Sales of Goods	3	12. Antitrust	1
5. Agency and Partnerships	4	13. Federal Regulation	1
6. Corporations	3	14. Employment Regulation	2
7. Commercial Paper	3	15. Consumer Protection	1
8. Secured Transactions	2	16. Accountants' Liability	1

*FINANCIAL ACCOUNTING CPE $75

13 separate courses with up to 46 CPE hours

Course	Hours
1. Basic Concepts and the Accounting Process	4
2. Current Assets	4
3. Noncurrent Assets	4
4. Current and Noncurrent Liabilities	3
5. Present Value, Pensions, and Leases	4
6. Shareholders' Equity and EPS	4
7. Income Tax Allocation, Accounting Changes, Error Corrections	2
8. Financial Statements and Disclosures	3
9. Statement Analysis, Interim Statements, and Segment Reporting	4
10. Equity Method and Business Combinations	5
11. Price-Level Changes and Foreign Exchange	2
12. Government and Nonprofit Accounting	4
13. Specialized Industry and Partnership Accounting	3

*MANAGERIAL ACCOUNTING CPE $60

11 separate courses with up to 43 CPE hours

Course	Hours
1. Cost Accounting Overview and Job Order Costing	4
2. Process Costing; Spoilage, Waste, & Scrap	4
3. Joint Products and By-Products	2
4. Service Cost Allocations and Direct Costing	3
5. Cost-Volume-Profit Analysis	5
6. Budgeting and Responsibility Accounting	4
7. Standard Costs	6
8. Nonroutine Decisions and Inventory Models	4
9. Capital Budgeting	4
10. Probability and Statistics; Regression Analysis	4
11. Linear Programming and Other Quantitative Approaches	3

*** NEW, 1989 REVISIONS**

FIVE CPE PROGRAMS USING OUTLINES, EXAMPLES, AND TRUE/FALSE STUDY QUESTIONS FORMAT

PASSIVE LOSS RULES CPE $50

4 separate courses with up to 8 CPE hours

- Course 1 - Passive Activities, Taxpayers, Material Participation

  Course 2 - Passive Activity Income and Loss

  Course 3 - Loss Limitations, Carryovers, and Credits

  Course 4 - Rental Activities
- Limitations on the deduction of losses from passive activities are a result of the Tax Reform Act of 1986. The IRS has issued some 70 pages of regulations which go beyond and contain far more detail than discussed in the Code, Committee Reports, or even the explanation prepared by Staff of the Joint Committee on Taxation.
- Now you can master the requirements of this complex labyrinth of law and regulation with easy-to-read outlines and hundreds of clear and concise examples. These outlines do NOT follow the confusing format of the regulations. They are organized to take you from beginning concepts right through to ultimate use of disallowed losses in an easy-to-follow modular breakdown.
- DO NOT be fooled. The passive loss rules apply to much more than tax shelters. You need to know how they apply and how to use them for any taxpayer who rents property, is a sole proprietor of a business, is a partner, or is a shareholder of an S corporation, personal service corporation, or closely held corporation.
- A detailed index is provided.

1987 REVENUE ACT CPE $35

1 complete course with 4 CPE hours

- **COMPREHENSIVE:** A complete CPE program covering all tax changes in one book. This was written exclusively for continuing education. It does not require you to study the Committee Reports, Internal Revenue Code, or other books.
- **EASY TO COMPLETE:** Study outlines, examples, and true/false study questions. Take an open-book final exam.
- **EASY TO UNDERSTAND:** Our outlines and large number of examples have been very carefully written to help you UNDERSTAND the 1987 Revenue Act. You should be able to remember and explain it to others after taking this course.
- **A VALUABLE REFERENCE BOOK:** As you encounter unfamiliar issues in practice, you will be able to research them easily. A detailed index is provided.

1988 TAX LAW (TAMRA) CHANGES

These are courses 13-16 in FEDERAL TAX CPE (see opposite page)

The Technical and Miscellaneous Revenue Act of 1988 (TAMRA) is presented in outline format for ease of understanding this new tax law. Also included are the relevant areas of the Family Support Act of 1988 and the Medicare Catastrophic Coverage Act of 1988.

SAS 52-61 UPDATE CPE $50

2 separate courses each with 4 CPE hours

- Course 1: SASs 52, 53, 54, 55, 56
- Course 2: SASs 57, 58, 59, 60, 61
- These are the new "expectation gap" standards issued in the Spring of 1988 with effective dates of January 1989, except SAS 55, which becomes effective January 1990.

CMA CPE $95

35 separate courses with up to 88 CPE hours

- **BROADEN YOUR BACKGROUND:** Comparable to a mini-MBA program, this will assist you both in your own business endeavors and with your clients. It is more user-oriented with respect to financial statements instead of preparer-oriented.
- **BECOME A CMA:** CMA stands for Certified Management Accountant. This CMA CPE program will thoroughly prepare you for the CMA exam as you earn CPE credits.

35. *The CMA Examination: Exam Grading and Self-Study (2 hrs.)

PART 1: ECONOMICS AND BUSINESS FINANCE (20 hrs.)

1. Microeconomics
2. Macroeconomics
3. Working Capital Finance
4. Capital Structure Finance
5. International Economics
6. Governmental Regulation of Business

PART 2: ORGANIZATION AND BEHAVIOR, INCLUDING ETHICAL CONSIDERATIONS (9 hrs.)

7. Organization Theory and Decision Making
8. Motivation and the Directing Process
9. Communication
10. Planning and Budgeting
11. The Controlling Process
12. Ethics and the Management Accountant

PART 3: PUBLIC REPORTING STANDARDS, AUDITING, AND TAXES (25 hrs.)

13. Financial Accounting: Development of Theory and Practice
14. Financial Statement Presentation
15. Special Reporting Problems
16. The SEC and Other Government Agencies
17. External Auditing
18. Internal and Operational Auditing
19. Internal Control
20. Audit Sampling
21. Income Taxation of Corporations

PART 4: INTERNAL REPORTING AND ANALYSIS (15 hrs.)

22. Financial Statements
23. Ratio Analysis
24. Process and Job Order Costing
25. Budgeting and Responsibility Accounting
26. Standard Costs and Variance Analysis
27. Cost-Volume-Profit Analysis
28. Direct (Variable) Costing

PART 5: DECISION ANALYSIS, INCLUDING MODELING AND INFORMATION SYSTEMS (17 hrs.)

29. Incremental Costing
30. Capital Budgeting
31. Decision Making Under Uncertainty
32. Inventory Models
33. Quantitative Methods
34. Information Systems

*Course 35 covers Chapters 1 through 4 of Volume I of CMA EXAMINATION REVIEW. It should be completed before any of the other courses are taken.

BLANK PAGE

INDEX

BLANK PAGE

Please forward your suggestions, corrections, and comments concerning typographical errors, etc. to **Irvin N. Gleim • c/o Accounting Publications, Inc. • P.O. Box 12848 • University Station • Gainesville, Florida • 32604**. Please include your name and address so we can properly thank you for your interest.

1. ______________________________

2. ______________________________

3. ______________________________

4. ______________________________

5. ______________________________

6. ______________________________

7. ______________________________

8. ______________________________

9. ______________________________

10. ______________________________

11. ______________________________

12. ______________________________

13. ______

14. ______

15. ______

16. ______

17. ______

18. ______

19. ______

20. ______

21. ______

22. ______

23. ______

24. ______

Name: ______

Company: ______

Address: ______

City/State/Zip: ______